Marketing · Essentials

Third Edition

Teacher Wraparound Edition

Lois Schneider Farese
Marketing Education Teacher-Coordinator
Northern Highlands Regional High School
Allendale, New Jersey

Grady Kimbrell
Educational Consultant
Santa Barbara, California

Carl A. Woloszyk
Professor
Consumer Resources and Technology
Western Michigan University
Kalamazoo, Michigan

 Glencoe
McGraw-Hill

New York, New York   Columbus, Ohio   Woodland Hills, California   Peoria, Illinois

REVIEWERS

Anne Cocroft Agyemang
Randolph Vocational Technical Center
Detroit, MI

Elizabeth Battle
Wake Forest Rolesville High School
Wake Forest, NC

Miranda Nixon Blocker
Heyward Career and Technology
Center
Columbia, SC

Allen Buntin
Cactus High School
Glendale, AZ

Jennifer Clock
Indian River High School
Chesapeake, VA

Barb Crum
Vidalia High School
Vidalia, LA

Holly DeMarco
Amherst High School
Amherst, NY

Anna Diekman
Clay High School
Oregon, OH

Todd Farr
Palmdale High School
Palmdale, CA

Matt Kuffel
Hartford High School
Hartford, WI

Dennis C. Lane
Parkway North High School
St. Louis, MO

Lucinda Mason
Demopolis High School
Demopolis, AL

Kay Masonbrink
Rancho Bernardo High School
San Diego, CA

LouGene McKinney
Laramie High School
Laramie, WY

Patrick J. O'Reilly
Woodland Hills High School
Pittsburgh, PA

Laurie Jean Orszulak
Covenant Academy
Town of Tonawanda, NY

Elizabeth S. Pitts
Cass High School
Cartersville, GA

Mark Rael
Cooper City High School
Cooper City, FL

Stephen Rappaport
Beverly Hills High School
Beverly Hills, CA

Kathy Rudinsky
Lake Wales High School
Lake Wales, FL

Michael Stanzione
Beach Channel High School
Rockaway Park, NY

Bradley Tichenor
Amherst High School
Snyder, NY

CONTRIBUTING WRITER

Priscilla McCalla
Professional and Program
Development Director
DECA
Reston, Virginia

Glencoe/McGraw-Hill
A Division of The McGraw-Hill Companies

Send all inquiries to:
Glencoe/McGraw-Hill
21600 Oxnard Street, Suite 500
Woodland Hills, CA 91367

ISBN 0-02-644191-8 (Student Edition)
ISBN 0-07-824951-1 (Teacher's Wraparound Edition)

2 3 4 5 6 7 8 9   027   05 04 03 02 01

ABOUT THE AUTHORS

Lois Schneider Farese, a nationally recognized secondary marketing educator, has been the marketing teacher and DECA advisor at Northern Highlands Regional High School in Allendale, New Jersey, for more than 30 years. She has been involved in organizing and running New Jersey regional and state DECA conferences and has also participated as series director and event manager at state and national DECA conferences. The State Officer Action Team presented Farese with the Outstanding Service Award for her dedication, professionalism, and commitment to New Jersey DECA in 1993, 1996, and 1999, as well as with the Honorary Life Membership Award in 1990 for setting a new level of professionalism for local advisors. She was inducted into the DECA Hall of Fame in 1996.

As a result of her outstanding teaching methods and involvement in numerous marketing-related activities, Farese was named "Teacher of the Year" in 1981 by the Marketing Education Association of New Jersey. In 1982 she was recognized by the New Jersey Division of the American Vocational Education Association. In 1986 she became the first recipient from her school of the prestigious New Jersey Governor's Teacher Recognition Program. In 1993 and 1999, the University of Richmond recognized Farese for her contributions to the intellectual growth and achievement of students who graduated from her marketing program. In 2000, Farese was the nominee from Northern Highlands Regional High School for the Princeton Prize for Distinguished Secondary School Teaching.

Farese holds a bachelor's degree in business and distributive education and two master's degrees (one in business and one in psychology) from Montclair State University in New Jersey. She has numerous additional credits in education, administration, and supervision.

Grady Kimbrell, a nationally recognized author and consultant on career education, began his career in education teaching high school business in Kansas. After relocating to Southern California, Kimbrell taught business courses and coordinated students' in-class activities with their on-the-job experience. He later directed the work experience program for the high schools of Santa Barbara, California.

A pioneer in the use of computers as a tool for educational research, Kimbrell has assisted school districts with a wide variety of research and evaluation activities. His research into on-the-job work activities led to the development of a new type of career interest inventory used in career guidance. In addition, Kimbrell has served on numerous state instructional program committees and writing teams, designed educational computer programs, and produced educational films.

Kimbrell holds degrees in business administration, educational psychology, and business education.

Carl A. Woloszyk is a university professor with an extensive background in marketing education. He teaches undergraduate and graduate courses in career and technical education (CTE) at Western Michigan University in Kalamazoo. He has served as a state department of education consultant for marketing and cooperative education, DECA and Delta Epsilon Chi state advisor, CTE administrator for a regional education service agency, and a secondary marketing teacher-coordinator. As a secondary marketing teacher-coordinator, he taught beginning and advanced marketing courses, supervised a school store, placed cooperative education students in work-based learning situations, and served as a local DECA chapter advisor. His students have received numerous awards at district, state, and national DECA conferences. Woloszyk has served on the board of directors for National DECA and the Marketing Education Association Foundation, and as a state representative to MarkED, a national marketing research and curriculum development center in Columbus, Ohio. He is a charter and board member of the Michigan Marketing Educators' Association.

Woloszyk received his undergraduate degree in business administration and his doctorate in business and distributive education from Michigan State University. He also holds a master's degree in business education from Eastern Michigan University and an educational specialist degree in occupational education from the University of Michigan.

Contents
Marketing Essentials Teacher Wraparound Edition

CONTENTS

CONTENTS

CONTENTS

CONTENTS

UNIT 6 LAB

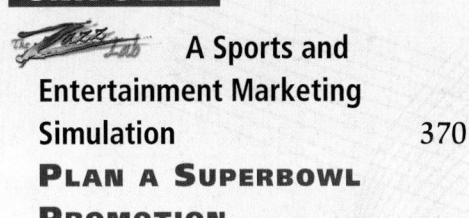

A Sports and
Entertainment Marketing
Simulation 370
PLAN A SUPERBOWL
PROMOTION

UNIT ▪ 7 Distribution 372

CONTENTS

CONTENTS

CONTENTS

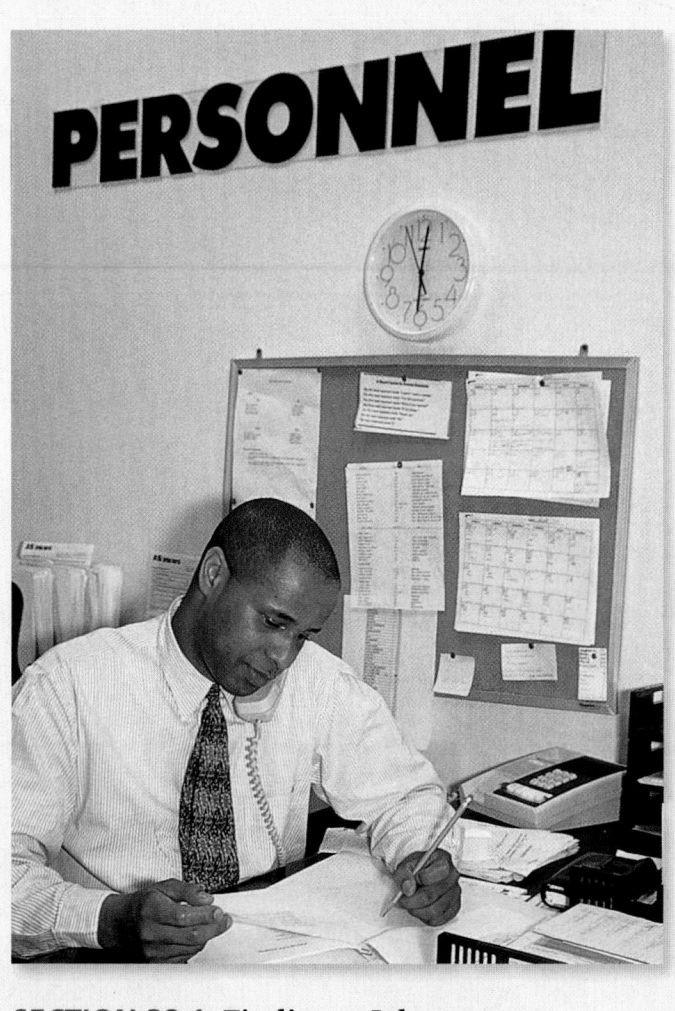

GLENCOE
Marketing Essentials

It's everything a marketing program should be!

Correlated to the National Marketing Education Standards!

A Truly Readable Marketing Text!

No other program brings so many rich resources to every class you teach.

One look will prove it! Glencoe *Marketing Essentials* offers you more than any other marketing program. You can see the difference throughout the text, from the 12 new Sports and Entertainment Marketing Unit Labs, to the new DECA preparation activities in every chapter, to the integrated coverage of current issues in marketing like e-commerce and the globalization of business. New program resources include a Marketing Research Project Workbook with Teacher Manual to help your students prepare for DECA research events, an Interactive Lesson Planner CD-ROM with a built-in calendar and links to thousands of pdf program resources, *BusinessWeek* Case Studies that employ active reading models to reinforce contemporary marketing topics, and Internet Resources activities for every chapter.

Focus on the Features

Each chapter contains six features, which vary in length and focus. These features help students understand the practical application of the concepts that they master throughout this book. While they vary in content, they all show a realistic and creative approach to marketing. Each feature ends with a question, or a series of questions, that ask students to expand on what they have learned with critical or creative thinking.

Careers in Marketing Careers in Marketing places the spotlight on different careers involved in marketing. Each feature contains an interview with a successful marketing professional. In addition to sharing some of their keys to success, these professionals also tell about their likes and dislikes on the job. Practical information is also included, such as necessary experience and skills, as well as the career outlook for those ready to enter the job market.

Case Study This feature gives an in-depth look at the realistic applications of marketing concepts. Each case study offers a real-world story about a marketing decision or situation facing a company. At the conclusion of the case study, there are three questions to help students understand how the chapter's principles apply to the real-life situation. The final question ask students to evaluate an issue of ethics.

Careers in Marketing

PRODUCT MANAGEMENT

Lori Tauber Marcus
Director of Brand Management
Pepsico Fountain Beverage Division

What does your job entail?

"I supervise the development, production, and sale of Pepsi brands for Pepsi's fountain beverage division, the part of the company that sells beverages to restaurants and theaters. I conduct research to determine the profitability of products being developed, then I oversee the marketing of the product. I also help with advertising and training the sales force. After the product has been marketed, I conduct follow-up research to determine how well it is doing and what changes may need to be made to increase profitability."

What kind of training did you have?

"A few years after earning a bachelor's degree in marketing in college, I went to work for Pepsi, first in the food service marketing division and then as an associate product manager for Pepsi's Mountain Dew brand. I was promoted to customer marketing manager for retail marketing, customizing Pepsi promotions for mass retailers like Target and Kmart. I became area marketing manager for the eastern seaboard, then senior product manager for new cola concepts."

What skills are most important?

"Leadership skills are essential—as a brand manager you lead teams of many people, each performing different functions who are pivotal in bringing your product to market. It is important to have the ability to think creatively and strategically. It is also important to have an aptitude for gathering and analyzing data and making decisions based on the data."

What is your key to success?

"I really love doing what I do. Also, I have been fortunate to have always worked with very smart and highly motivated people from whom I'm constantly learning."

Thinking Critically
What types of experience would you emphasize when applying for a job as a brand manager?

Career Facts

Education and Training: A bachelor's or master's degree in marketing or business and coursework in communication, economics, and math is recommended. College coursework should be accompanied by several years of sales experience.

Aptitudes, Abilities, and Skills: Analytical skills, organizational skills, leadership skills, communication skills, interpersonal skills, and math skills are necessary.

Career Outlook: Many new jobs are opening in the computer and Internet industry, as well as in the electronics industry in general.

Career Path: A typical path to brand manager is through a management trainee job. A staff position in the marketing department can sharpen analytical skills.

Case Study

Got Milk?

To get the message to teens to drink milk, MilkPEP and Dairy Management Inc. are using popular athletes as their models in "got milk?" ads. Teenagers' zeal for collecting milk mustache ads of their favorite sports stars is what marketers are counting on to get across a serious message.

Milk consumption drops in the teenage years, just when teens may need it most. It appears that seven out of ten teen boys and nine out of ten teen girls do not get their daily calcium requirements.

To target teens, the message for the promotion must be viewed as "cool" and the media must reach teens. Using popular athletes in the "got milk?" ads helps to get the message across. Print ads in *TV Guide*, which is read by 5.4 million teens, was one effective vehicle used to communicate the message.

9 essential nutrients.

Want game?
Milk is packed with vitamins and minerals that active bodies need.

got milk?

Case Study Review

1. Why were "got milk?" ads popular with teens?
2. How can "got milk?" ads target different market segments by age, gender, generation, and ethnic background?

A Matter of Ethics

3. Is it ethical to use popular athletes to persuade teens to take a specific action? Would it change your opinion if the action were other than "drink milk"?

Creative Marketing

This feature focuses on how individuals in history or in modern society have applied creative thinking, knowledge, and problem solving skills to achieve success in marketing. These people were either faced with a business problem, or were able to identify a customer need that was not currently being met. This feature ends with a "Thinking Creatively" question, which allows students to tackle a marketing problem using their own unique creativity.

Thinking Creatively

This Creativity Challenge asks students to solve a problem using creative thinking skills.

Cross-Cultural Communication

As boundaries become less important and nations move toward a global marketplace, it is important to understand the nuances of global cultures and traditions. Every country is unique and has different ways of handling everything from a proper greeting to a business meeting. This feature will increase students' awareness of those global differences that are important to know when moving across boundaries.

Thinking Critically

The Thinking Critically question asks students to analyze, interpret, and apply a concept in the feature.

Technology Revolution

Electronic Frontiers focuses on the pervasive impact that technology is having on marketing, and gives perspective on the virtual marketing revolution. Students will evaluate the Internet marketing efforts of famous and not-so-famous companies. This feature shows how marketers use the Internet in their marketing strategies, customer relationships, and day-to-day work. It also discusses the legal and ethical issues often involved with e-commerce.

Thinking Critically:

The Thinking Critically question asks students to analyze, interpret, and apply a concept in the feature.

The Real World

This feature is filled with fun facts and stories about important developments in marketing. Some features focus on issues such as product and brand development, advertising, and successful entrepreneurs of the past and present. Other features focus on recent developments in marketing and speculate about what the future holds for this exciting and ever-changing field.

Thinking Critically

The Thinking Critically question asks students to analyze, interpret, and apply a concept in the feature.

The DECA Connection

No other marketing program gives you as many competitive events preparation activities and resources than *Marketing Essentials*! The preparation for all competitive events begins in the marketing education classroom, and *Marketing Essentials* has been designed to be one of your primary preparation resources. Several parts of the text as well as end-of-chapter activities in *Marketing Essentials* are devoted to preparing students for DECA competition. For example, studying Unit 6, Promotion, will help prepare students for the Advertising and Visual Merchandising Services Series event. Studying Unit 11, Entrepreneurship, will help students prepare for the Entrepreneurship event. In fact, Chapters 35 and 36 give students step-by-step instructions on how to prepare for DECA's entrepreneurship written event which requires students to write a business proposal for a new business.

DECA Role Play Activities Each chapter assessment in Marketing Essentials contains a DECA-approved role-play activity. These activities provide opportunities for students to practice for DECA's participating events and are based upon the same premise of a DECA role-play situation. Students are given a marketing situation to contemplate and are asked to come up with a plan or solution and present it to the teacher/judge who, in the role-play situation, represents a manager, a staff member, or other marketing personnel. Each role-play activity provides the teacher with a list of performance indicators to use as criteria in evaluating students' abilities.

For more role play practice, go to the Student Activity Workbook, which has an additional role play activity for each chapter!

Role Play: Toy Company Intern

Situation You are to assume the role of an intern in the marketing department of a consumer product manufacturing company that specializes in toys and electronic games. A new electronic game is being developed and the Research and Development (R&D) Director (judge) has asked for your input. You are to meet with the R&D Director (judge) in fifteen minutes.

Activity You must decide what you will tell the R&D Director (judge) about the strategies to use for product, place, price, and promotion decisions (the four Ps) of the marketing mix. In your presentation include consideration of the product's consumers and customers, as well as concepts such as target marketing and market segmentation.

Evaluation You will be evaluated on how well you meet the following performance indicators:
- Define target marketing
- Explain the difference between consumers and customers
- Explain the role of market segmentation
- Explain marketing mix strategies
- Demonstrate appropriate creativity

Zazz Lab Competitive Events Correlations
Each Zazz Sports and Entertainment Marketing Unit Lab includes correlations to several DECA competitive events. This explains to students how the concepts they have learned and activities they have performed correlate to real DECA competitive events. This will help your students make the connection between what they have learned and how they can apply that knowledge in DECA competition.

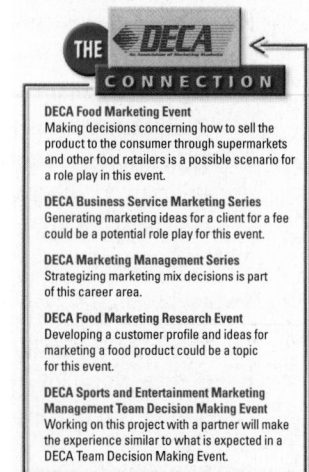

DECA Food Marketing Event
Making decisions concerning how to sell the product to the consumer through supermarkets and other food retailers is a possible scenario for a role play in this event.

DECA Business Service Marketing Series
Generating marketing ideas for a client for a fee could be a potential role play for this event.

DECA Marketing Management Series
Strategizing marketing mix decisions is part of this career area.

DECA Food Marketing Research Event
Developing a customer profile and ideas for marketing a food product could be a topic for this event.

DECA Sports and Entertainment Marketing Management Team Decision Making Event
Working on this project with a partner will make the experience similar to what is expected in a DECA Team Decision Making Event.

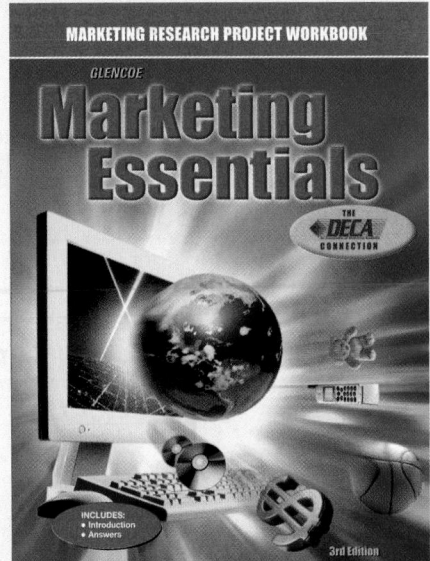

MARKETING RESEARCH PROJECT WORKBOOK

GLENCOE

Marketing Essentials

THE DECA CONNECTION

INCLUDES:
• Introduction
• Answers

3rd Edition

Marketing Research Project Workbook The Marketing Research Project Workbook was designed for the purpose of preparing students for DECA marketing research events. It offers a detailed, step-by-step procedure for students to follow in conducting a marketing research project. It provides clear explanations of the research process and includes hands-on activities that will help students improve their research skills and prepare them for DECA competition. Each chapter is devoted to key elements in the research process and is followed by a workbook-style Vocabulary Review, Fact and Idea Review, and Marketing Research Application Problems. The final workbook section of each chapter, called Your Marketing Research project, gives students the required steps to apply what they learned in the chapter to their own marketing research study. Any student participating in a DECA Research project would benefit from this workbook because it provides all the details for reporting, analyzing, and presenting the findings of a marketing research study, all of which are required in DECA competition.

THE DECA CONNECTION — ADVISOR CORNER

Mentor a New DECA Chapter Check with your state advisor to find the name of a DECA chapter that is inactive and/or a potential new chapter in your area. Brainstorm with your chapter members to plan activities that will demonstrate the value and benefits of DECA membership—including programs, recognition, leadership skills, networking, scholarships, and fun. This is a great time to allow your chapter officers to assume a leadership role in making contacts, arranging visits, etc. Serving as a mentor will educate others about the value of DECA. Chapter members can also apply basic marketing concepts to this activity—using the inactive/new chapter as the target market and DECA membership as the product.

DECA ADVISOR CORNER DECA Advisor corner offers tips and tricks for running a successful DECA chapter. Written by DECA advisors for DECA advisors, this feature's topics include how to better plan and organize, increase business and student involvement, and promote community awareness and recognition.

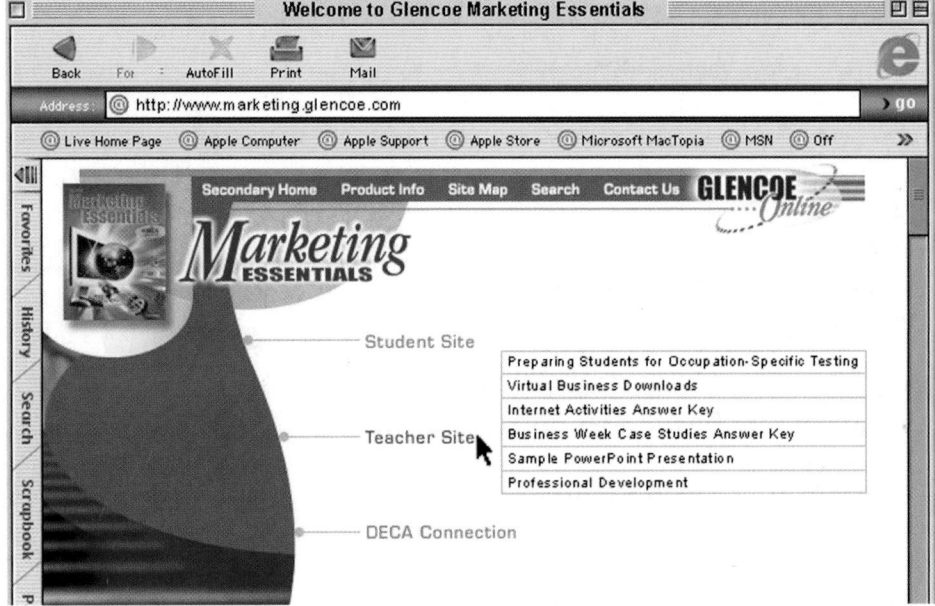

Marketing Essentials Web Site Due to popular demand, Glencoe is now offering resources for the teaching and assessment of occupation-specific vocabulary on the new *Marketing Essentials* Web site (www.marketing.glencoe.com). Free features include occupation-specific glossaries, occupation-specific test banks, and links to associations and journals in each occupational area. There has never been a better free resource for preparing your students for DECA's occupation-specific testing!

THE DECA CONNECTION — COMPETITIVE EVENTS AND MARKETING ESSENTIALS

Series and Written Events DECA's Competitive Events Program is grouped into two categories: series events and written events. The Individual Series events allow students to demonstrate competencies in nine occupational areas. Students take a comprehensive exam that tests general marketing and occupationally specific knowledge. The role-play situations allow students to combine knowledge gleaned from the classroom and on-the-job and DECA activities into a spontaneous presentation. The 16 Written Events participants to complete an activity, such as community service, then write a report they present to a judge during a fifteen-minute presentation.

DECA Competitive Events and Marketing Essentials This feature, in every TWE chapter, correlates DECA competitive events to the chapter's content. DECA Competitive Events and *Marketing Essentials* explains how you can use each chapter's lessons to better prepare your students for DECA competition.

Introducing the Marketing Essentials

Online resources for teachers, students, and parents

The *Marketing Essentials* Web site provides teachers, students, and parents with a wide range of materials. On the student site, chapter links bring a world of relevant marketing resources to enrich and extend classroom learning. The student site provides students with self-check, self-scoring quizzes for each chapter in fun formats such as crossword puzzles, concentration, or drag and drop learning games. The teacher site contains professional development resources, file downloads of additional *BusinessWeek* Case Studies and Internet activities, and DECA preparation resources that will help you prepare your students for occupation-specific testing.

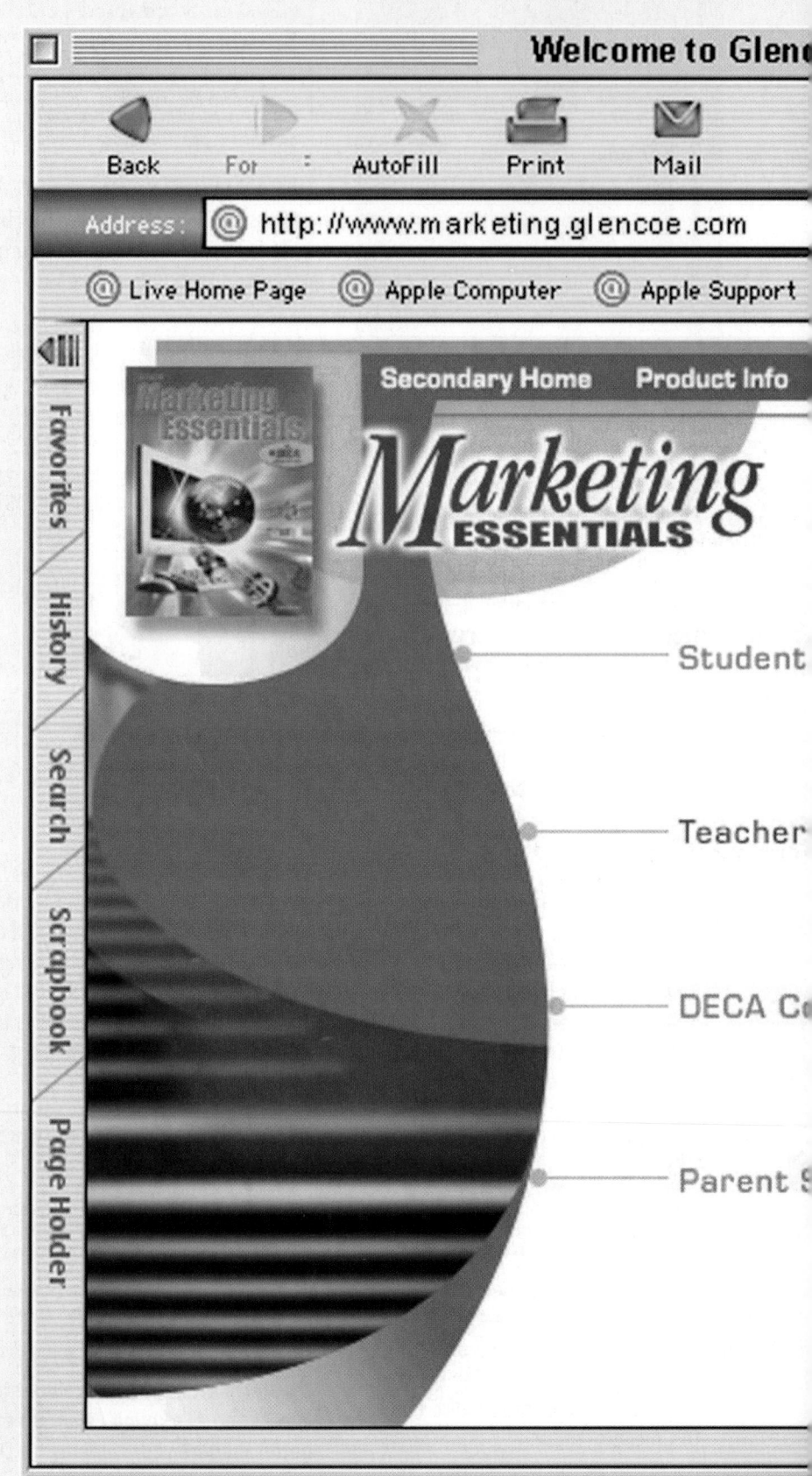

Web Site www.marketing.glencoe.com

keting Essentials

> go

Store @ Microsoft MacTopia @ MSN @ Off »

Search   Contact Us   **GLENCOE** *Online*

Preparing Students for Occupation-Specific Testing

Virtual Business Downloads

Internet Activities Answer Key

Business Week Case Studies Answer Key

Sample PowerPoint Presentation

Professional Development

Glencoe McGraw-Hill

FEATURES INCLUDE:

- DECA preparation activities and resources
- Virtual Business activities custom-designed for the *Marketing Essentials* program
- Downloads of *BusinessWeek* Case Studies
- Resources to teach and assess occupation-specific vocabulary
- Interactive Internet activities for every chapter
- An Interactive Tutor with game and puzzle tests for every chapter
- Links to local, state, and national marketing organizations
- Teacher-to-teacher exchange
- Professional articles

AND MUCH MORE!

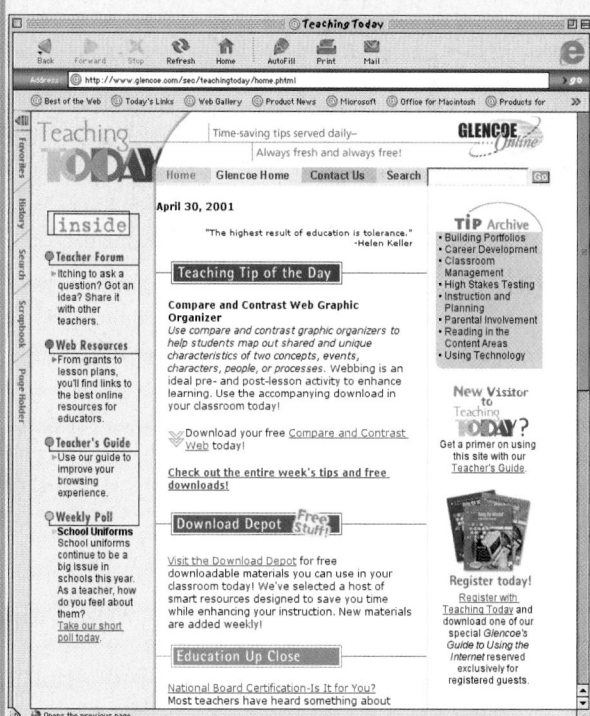

Glencoe's Teaching Today Web site features daily teaching tips, free downloadable materials, annotated Web resources, educational news, and more! The site contains a wealth of information on topics from high stakes testing to classroom management.

A Sports and Entertainment Marketing Simulation

Your students will take an exciting journey through the world of sports and entertainment marketing in each Zazz Sports and Entertainment Marketing Unit Lab! Sports and entertainment are two of the hottest industries in the world—businesses spend hundreds of millions of dollars each year capitalizing on the huge popularity and high visibility of these industries in the United States and worldwide. High school students have a universal interest in sports and entertainment—and the *Marketing Essentials* Zazz Labs will reinforce marketing concepts while they explore this exciting marketing occupational area.

In the Zazz Labs, students will relate the foundations and functions of marketing to sports and entertainment situations. Each lab is built around the Unit's objectives. Students learn marketing principles by studying the Unit; then they apply these principles to a sports and entertainment scenario just as they would in the real world of marketing. The real-life situations contained within each Zazz Lab require students to demonstrate an understanding of the text's fundamental marketing theories as well as exhibit critical thinking and decision-making skills.

By completing the Zazz labs, your students will learn about:

- sponsorships
- endorsements
- licensing agreements
- sports merchandising
- concert tour planning and promotion
- sports event planning and promotion
- sports and entertainment product planning
- sports camp marketing
- athlete management
- entertainment distribution
- event ticket and concessions pricing
- sports resort and theme park planning and pricing
- recreation marketing
- sports and entertainment marketing research
- team naming
- sports stadium design and amenities
- sports product branding, packaging, and positioning
- team franchising
- amusement park business planning
- legal issues in sports and entertainment
- sports and entertainment marketing career research

The Zazz Lab

A Sports and Entertainment Marketing Simulation

WELCOME

Welcome to Zazz Sports and Entertainment Marketing Company. Zazz is devoted to serving the needs of its clients who include college, university, and professional sports teams, professional athletes, sporting events, and sports arenas plus major consumer product corporations, as well as television networks and movie studios. As an intern, you will have the opportunity to work on different clients' projects. All of your work will be assigned and reviewed by your department supervisor.

MARKET A SPORTS DRINK

SITUATION

Your client is RJF Beverage Company, the creator of a new sports drink. The company is entering the "active thirst" market—beverages consumed by people when they're hot and sweaty. The market has been dominated by Gatorade, the sports drink made by Quaker Oats. Other competing brands are Powerade (Coca-Cola) and AllSport (Pepsi). Your client thinks it has a formula for a new sports drink that's even better than Gatorade's. Your client believes that affiliation with a popular sport would help get this new product off the ground.

ASSIGNMENT

Your supervisor wants you to conduct an analysis of the current sports drink market for the new client. You have also been asked to generate creative ideas with regard to the marketing mix for the new product. *Product* ideas should include designing the container and naming the product. *Place* suggestions involve deciding how to get the product into the hands of the consumer. *Price* recommendations should be based on the competitor's pricing strategies. *Promotion* ideas should be creative. Consider sponsorship of a sports team or an endorsement by a professional athlete as part of the promotional mix.

Tools and Resources

To complete this assignment, you will need to conduct research at a library or on the Internet. You will also need a word processing program, a spreadsheet program, and presentation software. Trade publications that may be helpful include *BrandWeek, Advertising Age, Sports Business Journal,* and *Sports Business Daily.*

Research

Research the sports drink market and the major competitors. Find out how much is sold and who buys it. For your customer profile, research geographics, demographics, and psychographics. Determine the market share (percentage of total market) each competitor enjoys. Study each major competitor's product, pricing, promotion, and place decisions. Find out which sports drinks are being endorsed by sports personalities, teams, or leagues, and whether they have special agreements. See if any of the main competitors have Web sites; if they do, find out what is included. Secure samples of competitors' advertising and promotions if possible. You want to see what the RJF company needs to do to break into the sports drink market.

Report

Prepare both a written report and a computer presentation for the client. Use a word processing program to prepare a double-spaced report. Use a spreadsheet program to create a pie chart to illustrate the current market share of the major competitors in the sports drink market. Include the pie chart in your written report. Also include samples of competitors' advertising. Arrange your written report around the following headings:

- Background on the sports drink market
  - The market
  - Market trends
  - Customer analysis (demographics, geographics, psychographics)
- Analysis of major competitors
  - Product, place, price, and promotion decisions
- Proposed target market for RJF
- Marketing mix decisions for RJF
  - Product (name, container), place, price, and promotion (main theme, slogan, publicity, special promotions, advertising) decisions

Using computer presentation software, prepare a presentation of your ideas for the client that includes:
- Key topics covered in your written report
- Graphic illustrations that are relevant to each slide's topic
- Very little text
- Minimum of 10 slides

Presentation and Evaluation

In addition to your written report, your supervisor wants you to present your ideas orally and show him your presentation. The presentation will later be shown to the client. You will be evaluated on your oral presentation skills, including:
- Knowledge of the sports drink market and marketing mix strategies
- Continuity of presentation
- Voice quality
- Eye contact

Portfolio

Print out a copy of your completed report and presentation for your Portfolio.

THE DECA CONNECTION

DECA Food Marketing Event
Making decisions concerning how to sell the product to the consumer through supermarkets and other food retailers is a possible scenario for a role play in this event.

DECA Business Service Marketing Series
Generating marketing ideas for a client for a fee could be a potential role play for this event.

DECA Marketing Management Series
Strategizing marketing mix decisions is part of this career area.

DECA Food Marketing Research Event
Developing a customer profile and ideas for marketing a food product could be a topic for this event.

DECA Sports and Entertainment Marketing Management Team Decision Making Event
Working on this project with a partner will make the experience similar to what is expected in a DECA Team Decision Making Event.

T27 Unit 1 ■ *The World of Marketing*   *The Zazz Lab* **T27**

Unit 1 The World of Marketing
Market a Sports Drink

Unit 2 Economics
License a Sports-Theme Video Game

Unit 3 Business and International Marketing
Plan a Rock Group World Tour

Unit 4 Academic Concepts and Skills
Establish a Children's Soccer Camp

Unit 5 Selling
Sponsor a NASCAR Driver

Unit 6 Promotion
Plan a Superbowl Promotion

Unit 7 Distribution
Establish Distribution for a Teen Sports Magazine

Unit 8 Pricing
Market a Golf Resort

Unit 9 Marketing Information Management
Conduct Marketing Research for a New Minor League Baseball Franchise

Unit 10 Product and Service Management
Create a Sports Product

Unit 11 Entrepreneurship and Finance
Prepare a Business Proposal for a New Amusement Park

Unit 12 Career and Professional Development
Apply for a Job or an Internship Program

Exploring the Unit

Marketing Essentials is divided into 12 units, each beginning with a unit opener. The unit opener utilizes exercises and graphics to prepare the student for the information covered in the following chapters.

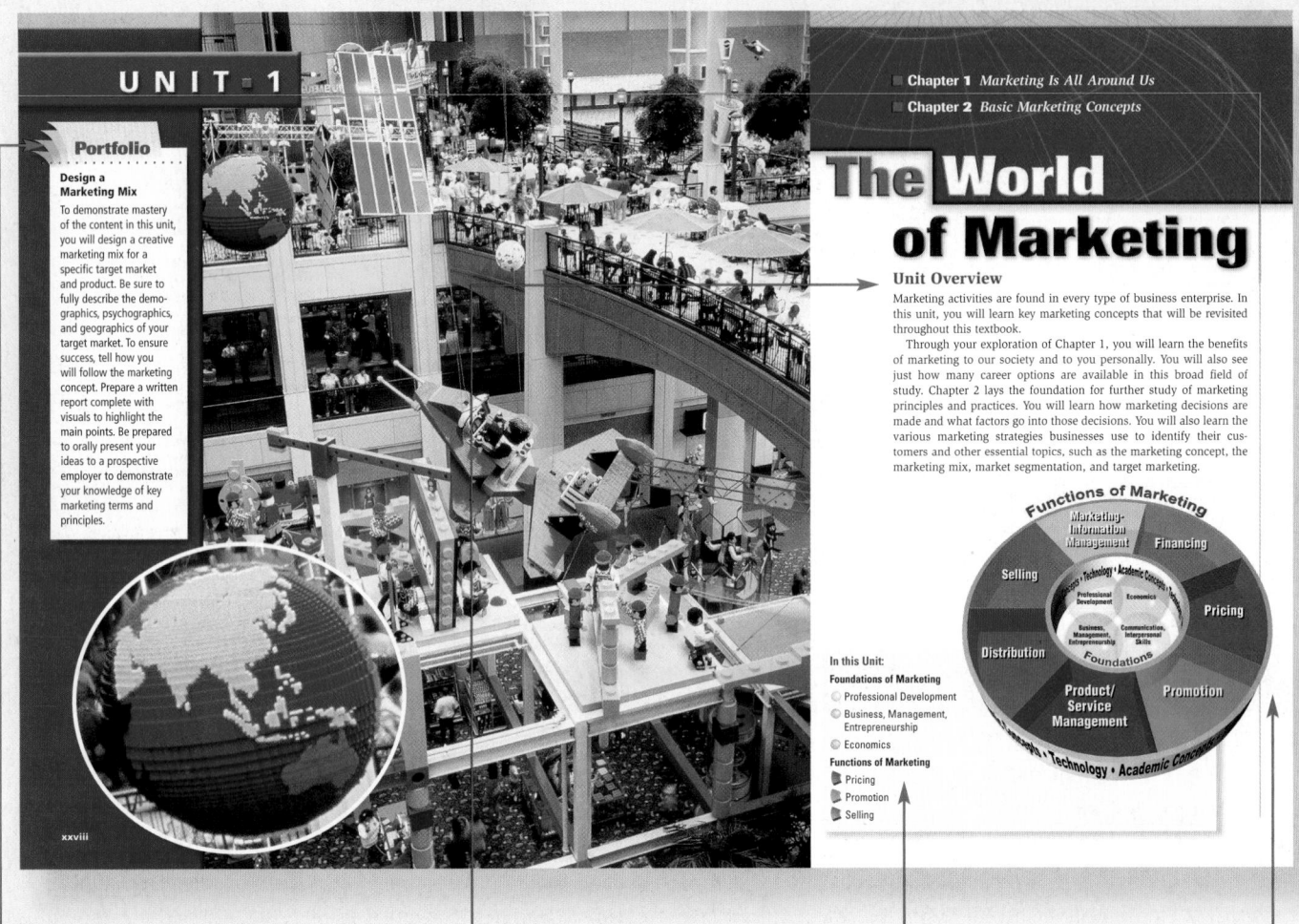

Portfolio offers students the opportunity to demonstrate the skills mastered in each unit. After completing portfolio projects, a student can select his or her best work to highlight in a portfolio that can be used during a career search. A portfolio contains elements of successful projects and samples of outstanding work.

Unit Overview offers a brief summary of materials covered in the unit. It introduces the concepts that will be explored, acting as a preview for what is to follow in the unit.

Foundations and Functions Studied in this Unit shows the functions and foundations of marketing that will be the focus of the unit's chapters.

The Marketing Wheel is a visual representation of the National Marketing Standards. The wheel highlights the two main parts of marketing—the foundations and the functions. The foundations of marketing are broad areas that are essential to understanding the concepts of marketing: Business, Management, and Entrepreneurship; Communication and Interpersonal Skills; Economics; and Professional Development. The functions of marketing are more specific and relate to how marketing is practically applied in the business world. The seven functions are Distribution, Financing, Marketing-Information Management, Pricing, Product/Service Management, Promotion, and Selling. In the unit opener, the marketing wheel will highlight the functions and foundations that you will study in the unit.

Exploring the Chapter and Section

EXPLORING THE CHAPTER AND SECTION *Marketing Essentials* provides a consistent chapter/section structure that is easy for students to comprehend. Sections are self-contained lessons on specific topics. New material is based on previous knowledge and the text follows an organized flow of concept development.

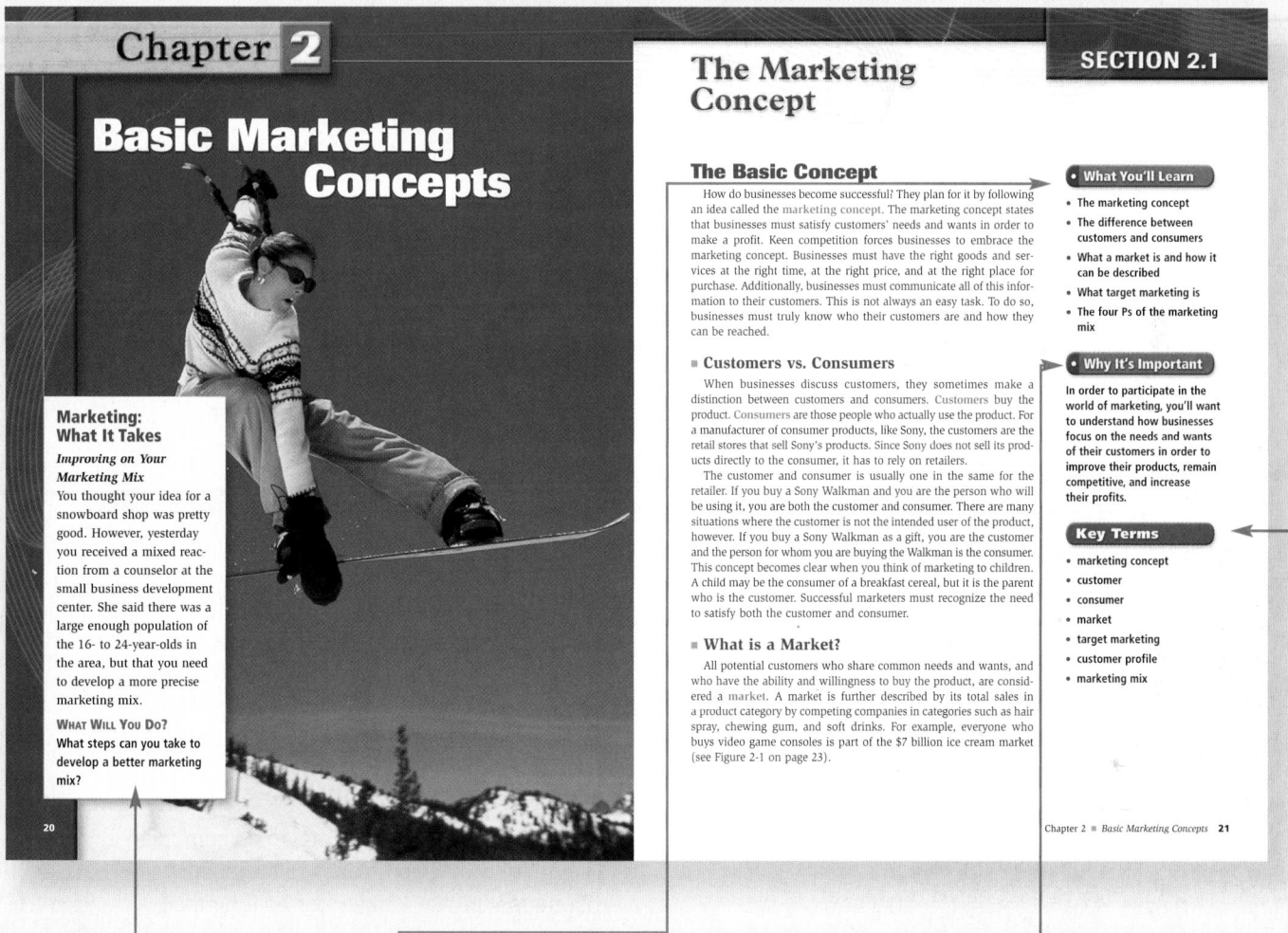

Marketing: What It Takes presents students with a marketing situation that requires a business decision. Students will be called on to apply common sense and marketing knowledge. Each scenario is followed by a "What Will You Do?" question to encourage class discussion.

What You'll Learn lists the chapter's most important concepts and tells students the skills and knowledge they can expect to master once the chapter is completed. This helps students read with a goal in mind.

Why It's Important explains the relevance of the lesson. It helps students make a connection between the specific concepts being discussed and how they fit into the larger "business picture."

Key Terms is a list of the vocabulary terms that are introduced throughout the section. Key terms are printed in blue boldface the first time that they are introduced in the text and are accompanied by clear, in-context definitions.

Exploring Assessment

REINFORCING CHAPTER CONCEPTS Each section and chapter ends with assessment questions to evaluate students' understanding of the chapter. The section assessment is a brief version of the chapter assessment, which goes into more detail and offers students more opportunities to demonstrate a more complex understanding of the chapter's concepts. Chapter Assessment activities are designed to be flexible and to address the varying levels of students' abilities.

Thinking Critically This question offers students the chance to demonstrate an in-depth understanding of the concepts in the chapter. Students are asked to interpret, analyze, compare, or make judgments based on ideas from the chapter.

2.2 ASSESSMENT

Reviewing Key Terms and Concepts

1. What do demographics, psychographics, geographics, and product benefits have in common?

2. How can a market be segmented using demographics?

3. What does the study of psychographics involve?

4. Provide one example of how a marketer can segment a market based on product benefits.

5. Of what significance are the combined African-American, Hispanic, and Asian-American populations to marketers?

Thinking Critically

6. How can Procter and Gamble market household products to a male market segment? What problems might P&G encounter in that endeavor?

Integrating Academic Skills

7. **COMMUNICATION** Write an ad campaign theme for Sunsweet Prunes to target baby boomers who are looking for healthy foods. Develop a second campaign theme to target a younger generation with Sunsweet Prunes.

Reviewing Key Terms and Concepts This exercise requires recall of important section material and terms introduced in the text.

Integrating Academic Skills This question focuses on math or communication skills that are related to concepts mastered in the section.

Vocabulary Review This activity will call on students' recollection of the vocabulary words introduced throughout the chapter. Students may be asked to write sentences, a dialogue, or even play a game that tests their understanding of the application of these words.

Thinking Critically This question offers students the chance to demonstrate an in-depth understanding of the concepts in the chapter. Students are asked to interpret, analyze, compare, or make judgments based on ideas from the chapter.

Applying Marketing Concepts This section is intended for students to work on outside of class. All questions incorporate technology with concepts that are studied in the chapter.

The DECA Connection Here is your opportunity to help your students polish their role playing skills for DECA competition. Each of these features is modeled after real DECA events. Students are presented with a situation and perform an activity based on the setting. Each Role Play lists the performance indicators upon which students will be evaluated.

Chapter 2 ASSESSMENT

VOCABULARY REVIEW

Write one paragraph to show your understanding of how the following concepts are related to one another.

- marketing concept
- consumer
- customer
- market
- target marketing
- customer profile
- marketing mix
- market segmentation
- demographics
- psychographics
- geographics

FACT AND IDEA REVIEW

1. What is the marketing concept? (2.1)
2. Provide an example of when a consumer is not the customer of a product purchased in a retail store. (2.1)
3. Define the concept of a market and give an example of one. (2.1)
4. Name the four Ps of the marketing mix and explain how they should be used in target marketing. (2.1)
5. Explain market segmentation and the four main ways a market can be segmented. (2.2)
6. Why do generations make good markets to segment? Name the three recent generations that marketers use to segment the market. (2.2)
7. What is the difference between disposable income and discretionary income? (2.2)

8. How have cosmetic companies targeted African-American women? (2.2)
9. Which ethnic group is the most affluent? (2.2)
10. How might a shampoo manufacturer segment the market according to product benefits? (2.2)

THINKING CRITICALLY

1. The United States is becoming more affluent. Because of this, change a regular food product to create an upscale image for that product—a premium brand.
2. How can a marketer of consumer products use the data from the U.S. Census 2000?
3. How would you position BenGay to young adults? How would you position the same product to senior citizens? Would you use the same appeal? Why or why not?
4. Using market segmentation based on income, explain Wal-Mart's success.

BUILDING WORKPLACE SKILLS

1. **Human Relations** A shabbily dressed couple enters a luxury automobile showroom, but the sales associates are not eager to approach them. A younger associate finally does and eventually sells them a $50,000 car. The couple puts down $20,000 cash as a down payment. What is the point of this story? What does it say about how lifestyle characteristics can be misleading?
2. **Technology** You have been hired by a stockbroker to research the geographic areas in the country that include high-income households. What technology is available to help you in this endeavor?

APPLYING MARKETING CONCEPTS

1. **Summarizing Key Concepts** Summarize an article that demonstrates any of the key concepts in this chapter. In the summary, identify the specific concepts in parentheses. Use business publications, such as *Brandweek, Adweek, Business Week, Fortune, Forbes, Marketing News,* and *Nation's Business,* to find an applicable article.
2. **Analyzing Marketing Strategies** Using the Internet, find research that describes characteristics of the teenage market. Then visit the Web sites of five companies (manufacturers or retailers) that target teens. Use a word processing program to write a short report analyzing each company's marketing mix strategies and citing your sources of information. Do all four Ps target teenagers effectively? Select one company to provide recommendations on how it could improve its marketing mix strategies when trying to target teens.
3. **Recognizing Target Marketing** Using the Internet, research the holidays of Kwanzaa (African-American celebration of racial pride and unity), Diwali (Hindu festival of lights), and Hanukkah (traditional Jewish celebration). Report how American marketers use knowledge of such holidays.
4. **Researching Psychographic Trends** Research one of the trends noted in the text. Make an oral presentation to the class using presentation software. Be sure to include current examples of how the trend is being used by different companies in their marketing mix strategies. Lastly, evaluate their effectiveness with your classmates.

LINKING SCHOOL TO WORK

Thinking Skills Develop a profile of a local company's customers based on their geographic, demographic, and psychographic characteristics.

THE DECA CONNECTION

Role Play: Toy Company Intern

Situation You are to assume the role of an intern in the marketing department of a consumer product manufacturing company that specializes in toys and electronic games. A new electronic game is being developed and the Research and Development (R&D) Director (judge) has asked for your input. You are to meet with the R&D Director (judge) in fifteen minutes.

Activity You must decide what you will tell the R&D Director (judge) about the strategies to use for product, place, price, and promotion decisions (the four Ps) of the marketing mix. In your presentation include consideration of the product's consumers and customers, as well as concepts such as target marketing and market segmentation.

Evaluation You will be evaluated on how well you meet the following performance indicators:
- Define target marketing
- Explain the difference between consumers and customers
- Explain the role of market segmentation
- Explain marketing mix strategies
- Demonstrate appropriate creativity

interNET CONNECTION

Head Count
The Census Bureau undertakes a count of the population every 10 years to track changes in population size and demographics.

Connect
- Locate the U.S. Census Web site. Find the current figures and percentages of age and income by ethnic groups (Caucasian, African-American, Hispanic, and Asian-American).

Fact and Idea Review This exercise requires recall of information found in the text. The numbers after each question identify the section in which the material is located in the chapter.

Building Workplace Skills This section challenges students to make realistic applications of chapter concepts. The topics may include human relations, technology, writing, language arts, social studies, or science.

Linking School to Work These activities are designed to relate marketing principles to students' work experiences or to the specific work experiences of friends, family members, or people in the community. Students will be asked to apply practical and analytical skills as they would on the job, or they may interview someone who is employed to gain perspective. Each question is linked to SCANS competencies.

Internet Connection This element consists of a two-part activity, which is designed to enhance students' Internet skills. The first part states a scenario or other fact that is valuable to students' learning. The "Connect" heading contains a Web-based activity for students to complete.

The National Marketing Education Standards

In this era of accountability for education, there has been a groundswell of interest in the development of standards. Due to the request of many of its members, the Marketing Education Resource Center (Mark-Ed), a consortium of 41 state education departments and other organizations, updated its standards in 2000 through a national project involving hundreds of marketing educators and professionals throughout the nation.

Marketing Essentials Correlation to the Standards

If you are using, or plan to use, the National Marketing Education Standards to guide changes in your marketing curriculum, you can be assured that *Marketing Essentials* aligns with the standards. *Marketing Essentials* is a program that provides numerous opportunities for students, teachers, and school districts to meet the National Marketing Education Standards.

Correlations on each unit interleaf show the close alignment between *Marketing Essentials* and the National Marketing Education Standards. In the unit correlation tables, relevant performance indicators and associated assessment activities are listed by chapter and section. *Marketing Essentials* explores many of the concepts within the National Marketing Education Standards, and hands-on enrichment and assessment activities reinforce the marketing concepts emphasized in the standards.

About the Curriculum

The marketing curriculum can be viewed as a continuum that begins in the primary grades with career awareness and exploration and continues through secondary and postsecondary education with the emphasis becoming more specialized to the learner's individual interest in marketing.

Mission of Marketing Education

The mission of Marketing Education is to enable students to understand and apply marketing, management, and entrepreneurial principles; to make rational economic decisions; and to exhibit social responsibility in a global economy.

Premises of the Curriculum

The Marketing Education curriculum should:
- Encourage students to think critically.
- Stress the integration of and articulation with academics.
- Be sequenced so that broad-based understandings and skills provide a foundation to support advanced study of marketing.
- Enable students to acquire broad understandings of and skills in marketing so that they can transfer their skills and knowledge between and among industries.
- Enable students to understand and use technology to perform marketing activities.
- Stress the importance of interpersonal skills in diverse societies.
- Foster a realistic understanding of work.
- Foster an understanding and appreciation of business ethics.
- Utilize a variety of types of interactions with the business community.

The Marketing Education Curriculum

The marketing education curriculum is divided into two primary parts: Foundations and Functions. The **Foundations** are fundamental to an understanding of marketing and can be viewed as co-requisites and as prerequisites for marketing. The content of the Marketing Foundations must be mastered in order for marketing-specific content to have relevance to student learning. There are four broad-based foundational areas: Business, Management, and Entrepreneurship; Communication and Interpersonal Skills; Economics; and Professional Development.

The **Functions** define the discipline of marketing as applied in business operations. They address marketing from the perspective of how it is practiced. Each function is viewed from its relationship to the marketing of a good, service or idea. The seven functions are Distribution, Financing, Marketing-Information Management, Pricing, Product/Service Management, Promotion, and Selling.

Understanding the Standards

Since students can demonstrate their understanding in a variety of ways, the National Marketing Education Standards are supported by a series of performance indicators: learner expectations for each standard. They require students to demonstrate both their knowledge and skill.

The development approach to learning is exemplified through these performance expectations. For each standard, there are performance expectations for five curriculum planning levels: entry level, career-sustaining, marketing specialist, marketing supervisor, and manager/entrepreneur. The levels serve as building blocks for curriculum development and indicate the complexity of course/program content, ranging from development of employability skills to development of skills needed to manage/own a small business. At a minimum, a high school marketing curriculum would address performance indicators at the first two levels. Depending on time available and ability level of students, high school instructors could incorporate performance indicators from the specialist level. Post-secondary instructors would be responsible for the performance indicators at the specialist and higher levels.

The complete list of performance indicators for the Foundations can be found in the **National Curriculum Planning Guide**. To order the guide, contact Mark-Ed at **www.mark-ed.com.**

FOUNDATIONS

Business, Management, and Entrepreneurship Understands fundamental business, management, and entrepreneurial concepts that affect business decision making

Communications and Interpersonal Skills Understands concepts, strategies, and systems needed to interact effectively with others

Economics Understands the economic principles and concepts fundamental to marketing

Professional Development Understand concepts and strategies needed for career exploration, development, and growth

FUNCTIONS

Distribution Understands the concepts and processes needed to move, store, locate, and/or transfer ownership of goods and services

Financing Understands the financial concepts used in making business decisions

Marketing-Information Management Understands the concepts, systems, and tools needed to gather, access, synthesize, evaluate, and disseminate information for use in making business decisions

Pricing Understands concepts and strategies utilized in determining and adjusting prices to maximize return and meet customers' perceptions of value

Product/Service Management Understands the concepts and processes needed to obtain, develop, maintain, and improve a product or service mix in response to market opportunities

Promotion Understands the concepts and strategies needed to communicate information about products, services, images, and/or ideas to achieve a desired outcome

Selling Understands the concepts and actions needed to determine client needs and wants and respond through planned, personalized communications that influences purchase decisions and enhances future business opportunities

National Marketing Education Standards Scope and Sequence

MARKETING FOUNDATION TOPICS	PERFORMANCE INDICATOR	LOCATION
Marketing Foundation: Economics		
Basic Concepts	Determine forms of economic utility created by marketing activities.	Section 1.2
	Explain the principles of supply and demand.	Section 3.2, Section 26.1
	Explain the concept of economic resources.	Section 4.1
	Distinguish between economic goods and services.	Section 4.1
	Describe the nature of economics and economic activities.	Section 4.1
Economic Systems	Explain the types of economic systems.	Section 3.1, Section 4.1
	Explain the concept of private enterprise.	Section 3.1
	Explain the concept of competition.	Section 3.1
	Determine factors affecting business risk.	Section 3.1
	Identify factors affecting a business's profit.	Section 3.1
	Explain the relationship between government and business.	Section 3.2, 4.1, 6.1
	Explain the concept of private enterprise.	Section 33.1
Cost-Profit Relationships	Explain the concept of productivity.	Section 4.2
Economic Indicators/Trends	Explain the concept of Gross Domestic Product.	Section 4.2
	Explain measures used to analyze economic conditions.	Section 4.2
	Explain the nature of the Consumer Price Index.	Section 4.2
	Determine the impact of business cycles on business activities.	Section 4.2
International Concepts	Explain the nature of international trade.	Section 6.1
	Evaluate influences on a nation's ability to trade.	Section 6.1
	Identify the impact of cultural and social environments on world trade.	Section 6.2
Marketing Foundation: Communication, Interpersonal Skills		
Fundamentals of Communication	Explain the nature of effective communications.	Section 8.1
	Apply effective listening skills.	Section 8.1
	Make oral presentations.	Section 8.2
	Handle telephone calls in a businesslike manner.	Section 8.2
	Explain the nature of written communications.	Section 8.2
	Use communications technology/systems.	Section 8.2
Staff Communications	Explain the nature of staff communications.	Section 10.2
Group Working Relationships	Treat others fairly at work.	Section 5.2
	Foster positive working relationships.	Section 10.1, Section 11.2
Customer Relationships	Handle customer inquiries.	Section 14.2
Participate as a Team Member	Participate as a team member.	Section 10.2
Marketing Foundation: Professional Development		
Self-Understanding	Demonstrate ethical work habits.	Section 5.2
	Identify personality traits important to business.	Section 10.1
	Adjust to change.	Section 10.1
	Demonstrate appropriate creativity.	Section 20.2
	Identify desirable personality traits important to business.	Section 33.1, Section 37.2
Self-Development	Assess personal interests and skills needed for success in business.	Section 37.1
Career Planning	Explain employment opportunities in marketing.	Section 1.3
	Explain employment opportunities in business.	Section 33.2, Section 37.3
	Identify tentative occupational interest.	Section 37.1
	Analyze employer expectations in the business environment.	Section 37.2
	Identify sources of career information.	Section 37.2, Section 38.1

Job-Seeking Skills	Utilize job-search strategies.	Section 38.
	Complete a job application.	Section 38.2
	Write a letter of application.	Section 38.2
	Prepare a résumé.	Section 38.2
	Interview for a job.	Section 38.3
	Write a follow-up letter after job interviews.	Section 38.3
Continuing Development	Identify skills needed to enhance career progression.	Section 1.3, Section 37.3

Marketing Foundation: Business, Management and Entrepreneurship

Business Fundamentals	Describe marketing functions and related activities.	Section 1.1
	Explain marketing and its importance in a global economy.	Section 1.1, Section 1.3, Section 5.1, Section 22.2
	Explain the role of business in society.	Section 2.2, Section 5.1, Section 5.2
	Explain the concept of management.	Section 11.1
	Describe the role of management in the achievement of quality.	Section 11.2
	Explain the nature and scope of purchasing.	Section 23.1
	Explain the nature of the buying process.	Section 23.2
	Conduct vendor search.	Section 23.2
	Describe the nature of profit-and-loss statements.	Section 27.1
	Explain the types of business ownership.	Section 33.2
	Explain the concept of accounting.	Section 36.2
	Explain the nature of balance sheets.	Section 36.2
	Explain the nature of environmental regulations.	Section 5.2
	Explain the nature of trade regulations.	Section 6.2
	Describe legal issues affecting businesses.	Section 32.2, Section 33.2
Technological Tools	Identify ways that technology impacts business.	Section 9.1
	Demonstrate basic word-processing skills.	Section 9.2
	Demonstrate basic database skills.	Section 9.2
	Demonstrate basic spreadsheet skills.	Section 9.2
	Demonstrate basic presentation software skills.	Section 9.3
	Demonstrate basic search skills on the Web.	Section 9.3
Business Risks	Identify speculative business risks.	Section 33.1
	Explain the types of business risk.	Section 33.1, Section 34.1
	Explain the nature of risk management.	Section 34.1
	Explain routine security precautions.	Section 34.2
	Describe the concept of insurance.	Section 34.2
Organizing	Plan and organize the work efforts of others.	Section 35.2
Leading	Explain the nature of leadership in organizations.	Section 10.2, Section 11.2
	Explain the nature of management/supervisory training.	Section 11.1
	Encourage team building.	Section 11.2
	Explain the concept of staff motivation.	Section 11.2
Controlling	Interpret financial statements.	Section 36.
	Describe the nature of cash-flow statements.	Section 36.2
Planning	Explain the nature of a business plan.	Section 35.1, Section 36.1
	Explain external planning considerations.	Section 35.1
	Develop business plan.	Section 35.2

Marketing Function: Distribution

Nature and Scope	Explain the nature of channels of distribution.	Section 21.1
	Explain the nature of channel members relationships.	Section 21.1
	Explain the nature and scope of distribution.	Section 21.2, Section 22.1

Order Fulfillment	Use information system for order fulfillment.	Section 16.3
Warehousing/Stock Handling	Explain the shipping process.	Section 22.1
	Explain storing considerations.	Section 22.2
	Explain the nature of warehousing.	Section 22.2
	Explain the receiving process.	Section 24.1
	Explain stock handling techniques used in receiving deliveries.	Section 24.1
Management of Distribution	Explain the nature of channel strategies.	Section 21.2
	Select channels of distribution.	Section 21.2
Inventory Control	Explain the nature of inventory control systems.	Section 24.2
	Explain the types of inventory control systems.	Section 24.2

Marketing Function: Financing

Nature and Scope	Explain the nature and scope of financing.	Section 35.3, Section 36.1
Extending Credit	Explain the purpose and importance of credit.	Section 16.2, Section 32.2
Obtaining Business Credit	Explain the purposes and importance of obtaining credit (business).	Section 32.2
	Determine financing needed to start a business.	Section 35.3
	Describe sources of financing for businesses.	Section 35.3

Marketing Function: Marketing Information Management

Nature and Scope	Describe the need for marketing information.	Section 28.1
	Explain the nature of marketing research in a marketing-information function.	Section 28.1, Section 29.1
	Describe the use of technology in the marketing-information management function.	Section 29.2
Information Gathering	Identify information monitored for marketing decision making.	Section 28.2
	Describe sources of secondary data.	Section 29.1
	Collect marketing information from others.	Section 29.2
Information Processing	Use data for information analysis.	Section 29.1
Marketing Planning	Explain the nature of sales forecasts.	Section 28.2
	Explain the nature of marketing plans.	Section 35.2

Marketing Function: Pricing

Nature and Scope	Explain legal considerations for pricing.	Section 25.2
	Explain the nature and scope of the pricing function.	Section 25.1, Section 26.1, Section 27.1
Determining Prices	Determine discounts and allowances that can be used to adjust base prices.	Section 16.3, Section 27.2
	Select approach for setting a base price.	Section 25.1, Section 26.2
	Determine cost of product (break-even, ROI, markup, price).	Section 25.1, Section 26.2
	Explain factors affecting pricing decisions.	Section 25.2, Section 26.2
	Calculate break-even point.	Section 25.2
	Identify strategies for pricing new products.	Section 26.1
	Set prices.	Section 26.2, Section 27.1

Marketing Function: Product Service Management

Nature and Scope	Explain the nature and scope of the product/service management function.	Section 30.1
	Identify the impact of product life cycles on marketing decisions.	Section 30.2
Quality Assurances	Explain warranties and guarantees.	Section 32.1
	Identify consumer protection provisions of appropriate agencies.	Section 32.1
Product Mix	Explain the concept of product mix.	Section 30.1
	Plan product mix.	Section 30.1
Positioning	Describe factors used by marketers to position products/businesses.	Section 30.2
	Explain the nature of branding.	Section 31.1

Retail Product Considerations	Plan purchases.	Section 23.1
Marketing Function: Promotion		
Nature and Scope	Explain the role of promotion as a marketing function.	Section 17.1
	Identify the elements of the promotional mix.	Section 17.1
	Describe the use of technology in the promotion function.	Section 20.2
Advertising	Explain the types of advertising media.	Section 19.1
	Evaluate the effectiveness of advertising.	Section 19.1
	Calculate media costs.	Section 19.2
	Select advertising media.	Section 19.2
	Explain the components of advertisements.	Section 20.1
Publicity/Public Relations	Develop public relations plan.	Section 17.3
	Analyze costs/benefits of participation in community activities.	Section 17.3
	Obtain publicity.	Section 17.3
Sales Promotion	Develop sales promotion plans.	Section 17.2
	Analyze the use of specialty promotion.	Section 17.2
	Explain the use of visual merchandising to create a image.	Section 18.1
	Explain the types of display arrangements.	Section 18.1
	Explain the relationship of merchandising and visual merchandising (display).	Section 18.2
	Prepare merchandise for display.	Section 18.2
	Maintain displays.	Section 18.2
Management of Promotion	Explain the use of advertising agencies.	Section 20.1
Marketing Function: Selling		
Nature and Scope	Explain the nature and scope of the selling function.	Section 12.1
	Explain key factors in building a clientele.	Section 12.2
Product Knowledge	Analyze product information to identify product features and benefits.	Section 2.2
	Analyze product information for use in selling.	Section 12.1
Process and Techniques	Address the needs of individual personalities.	Section 2.1
	Identify customer's buying motives for use in selling.	Section 12.1
	Facilitate customer buying decision.	Section 12.1
	Determine customer/client needs.	Section 12.2, Section 13.2
	Differentiate between consumer and organizational buying behavior.	Section 12.2
	Explain the selling process.	Section 13.1
	Prepare for the sales presentation.	Section 13.1
	Establish relationship with client/customer.	Section 13.1
	Assess customer/client needs.	Section 13.2
	Demonstrate product.	Section 14.1
	Recommend specific product.	Section 14.1
	Convert customer/client objections into selling points.	Section 14.2
	Close the sale.	Section 15.1
	Sell good/service/idea to individuals.	Section 15.1
	Facilitate customer buying decisions.	Section 15.1
	Demonstrate suggestion selling.	Section 15.2
	Plan follow-up strategies for use in selling.	Section 15.2
	Address the needs of individual personalities.	Section 16.2
Support Activities	Process sales documentation.	Section 15.2, Section 16.1
	Calculate miscellaneous charges.	Section 16.2
Management of Selling Activities	Analyze technology for use in the sales function.	Section 16.1

Unit Planning Guide

The information in the Unit Planning Guide gives you a comprehensive overview of the unit content along with the background information what will help you provide the best possible learning situation for your class. On the first two pages of each unit planning guide, you can easily identify unit objectives and unit enrichment resources. You will also find program resources available to you for each chapter in the unit. Refer to these pages as you plan each lesson in order to make the most of the numerous instructional material included with *Marketing Essentials*.

Enrichment Resources This is a list of resources related to the unit content.

Unit Objectives A bulleted list presents the performance-based objectives each student should be able to achieve once the unit is completed.

Teacher Classroom Resources A comprehensive list of chapter resources provides a quick reference for planning your instruction.

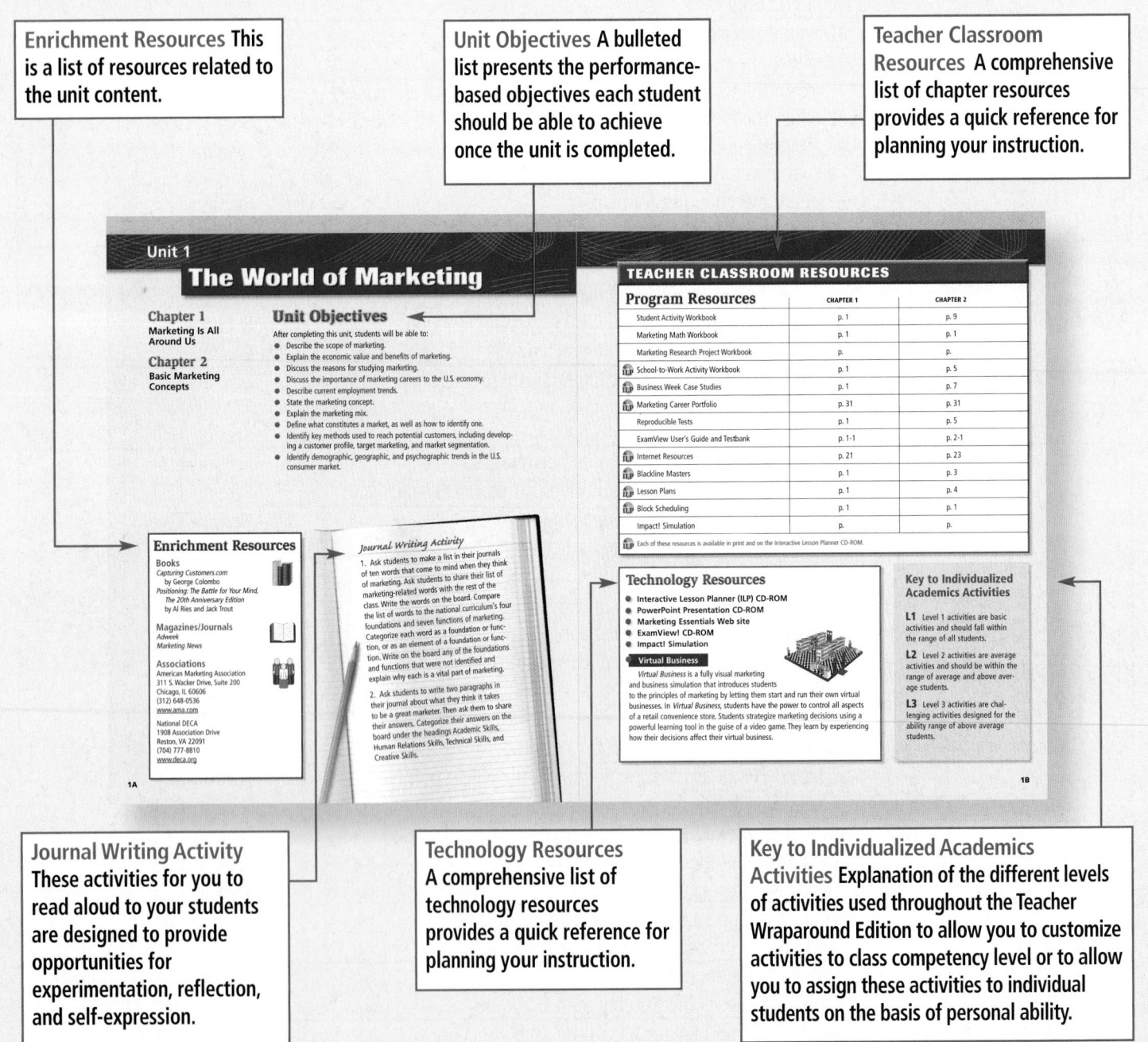

Journal Writing Activity These activities for you to read aloud to your students are designed to provide opportunities for experimentation, reflection, and self-expression.

Technology Resources A comprehensive list of technology resources provides a quick reference for planning your instruction.

Key to Individualized Academics Activities Explanation of the different levels of activities used throughout the Teacher Wraparound Edition to allow you to customize activities to class competency level or to allow you to assign these activities to individual students on the basis of personal ability.

National Marketing Education Standards Assessment Correlation

If you are using, or plan to use, the National Marketing Education Standards to guide changes in your marketing curriculum, you can be assured that *Marketing Essentials* aligns with the standards. On the second two pages of each unit planning guide, you will find a table presenting correlations between *Marketing Essentials* content and the National Marketing Education Standards. Relevant performance indicators and associated assessment activities are listed by chapter and section.

Performance Indicators
Performance indicators from the National Marketing Education Standards are detailed for each section of every chapter in the unit.

Assessment Correlations In-text assessment activities related to each performance indicator are detailed by section and chapter assessment.

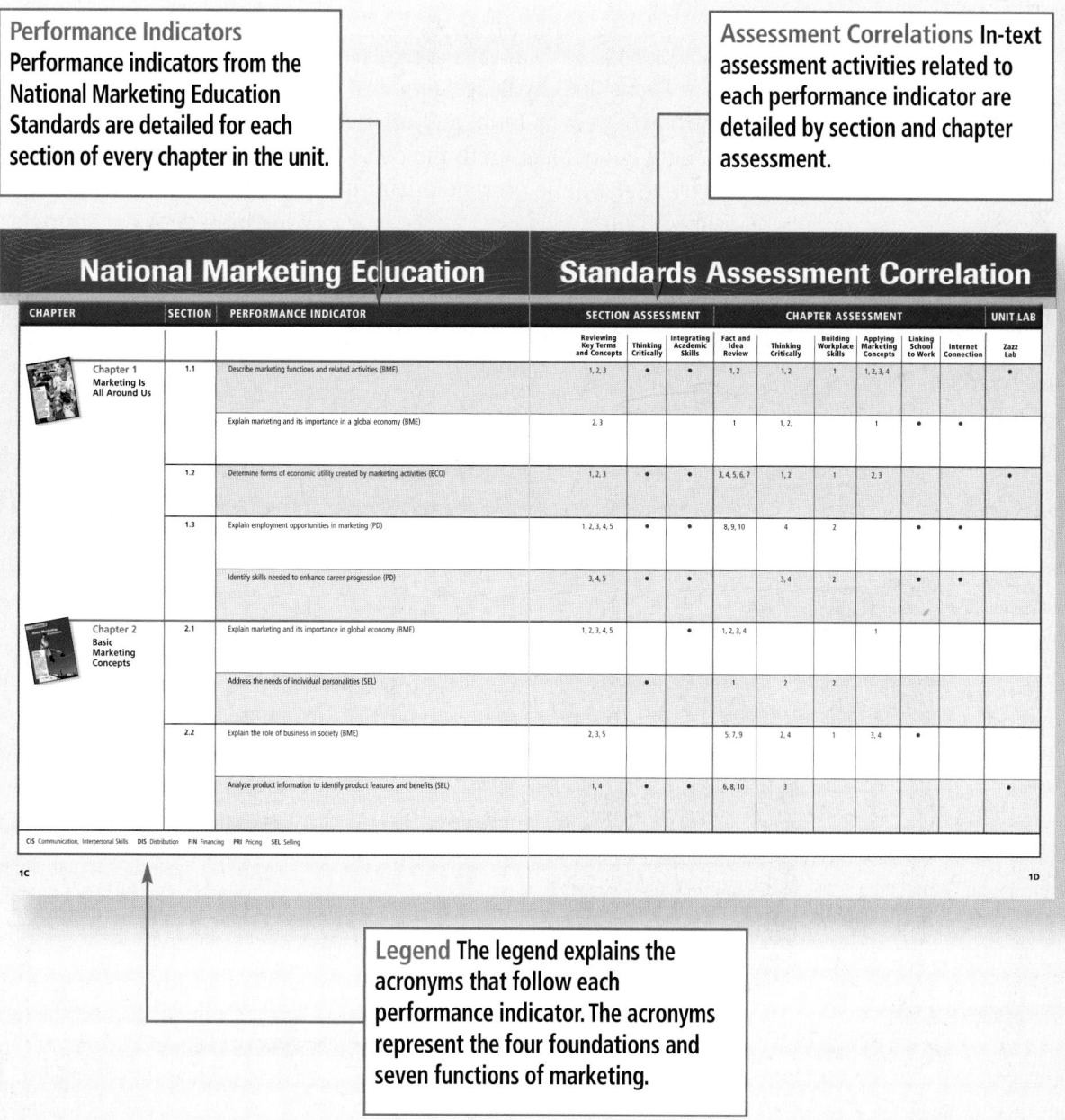

National Marketing Education / Standards Assessment Correlation

CHAPTER	SECTION	PERFORMANCE INDICATOR	SECTION ASSESSMENT			CHAPTER ASSESSMENT							UNIT LAB
			Reviewing Key Terms and Concepts	Thinking Critically	Integrating Academic Skills	Fact and Idea Review	Thinking Critically	Building Workplace Skills	Applying Marketing Concepts	Linking School to Work	Internet Connection	Zazz Lab
Chapter 1 Marketing Is All Around Us	1.1	Describe marketing functions and related activities (BME)	1, 2, 3	•	•	1, 2	1, 2	1	1, 2, 3, 4			•
		Explain marketing and its importance in a global economy (BME)	2, 3			1	1, 2,		1	•	•	
	1.2	Determine forms of economic utility created by marketing activities (ECO)	1, 2, 3	•	•	3, 4, 5, 6, 7	1, 2	1	2, 3			•
	1.3	Explain employment opportunities in marketing (PD)	1, 2, 3, 4, 5	•	•	8, 9, 10	4	2		•	•	
		Identify skills needed to enhance career progression (PD)	3, 4, 5	•	•		3, 4	2		•	•	
Chapter 2 Basic Marketing Concepts	2.1	Explain marketing and its importance in global economy (BME)	1, 2, 3, 4, 5		•	1, 2, 3, 4			1			
		Address the needs of individual personalities (SEL)		•		1	2	2				
	2.2	Explain the role of business in society (BME)	2, 3, 5			5, 7, 9	2, 4	1	3, 4	•		
		Analyze product information to identify product features and benefits (SEL)	1, 4	•	•	6, 8, 10	3					•

CIS Communication, Interpersonal Skills   DIS Distribution   FIN Financing   PRI Pricing   SEL Selling

1C   1D

Legend The legend explains the acronyms that follow each performance indicator. The acronyms represent the four foundations and seven functions of marketing.

Inside the Teacher Wraparound Edition

Introduction

Today marketing students bring to the classroom a variety of learning styles and needs. The *Teacher Wraparound Edition* of *Marketing Essentials* provides you and your students with a wide range of activities to fit your classroom needs. Designed to assist both new and experienced teacher by providing a wealth of teaching suggestions, resources, and professional notes, the *Teacher Wraparound Edition* has been designed as a convenience for you and to allow you to maximize the program's effectiveness.

The Four-Step Teaching Plan

Each section of each chapter in the *Teacher Wraparound Edition* is divided into four instructional sections according to a master approach designed to help you develop the chapter concepts and materials in an organized, consistent manner. This widely accepted instructional method develops students' understanding of subject matter while providing a consistent framework that makes it easy for you to teach the material. The four steps in the plan are **Focus**, **Teach**, **Assess**, and **Close**.

Chapter Overview previews chapter content.

1 **Springboard** presents the content through an activity that helps spark student interest.

2 **Prereading** briefly previews chapter content.

3 **Preteaching Marketing Vocabulary** introduces students to the chapter vocabulary.

FOCUS

The **Focus** activity is designed to introduce new material and provide a motivational lead-in to the concepts that will be presented later in the section.

4 **Bell Ringer Activity** helps students "switch gears" from their previous class and focus on the task at hand.

5 **Introducing the Section** gives you a way to dive into section material.

TEACH

The **Teach** section contains the central core of the lesson, encompassing a teaching plan designed to give you maximum flexibility to meet the learning needs of your class.

6 **Technology Resources** directs you to the section's PowerPoint presentation.

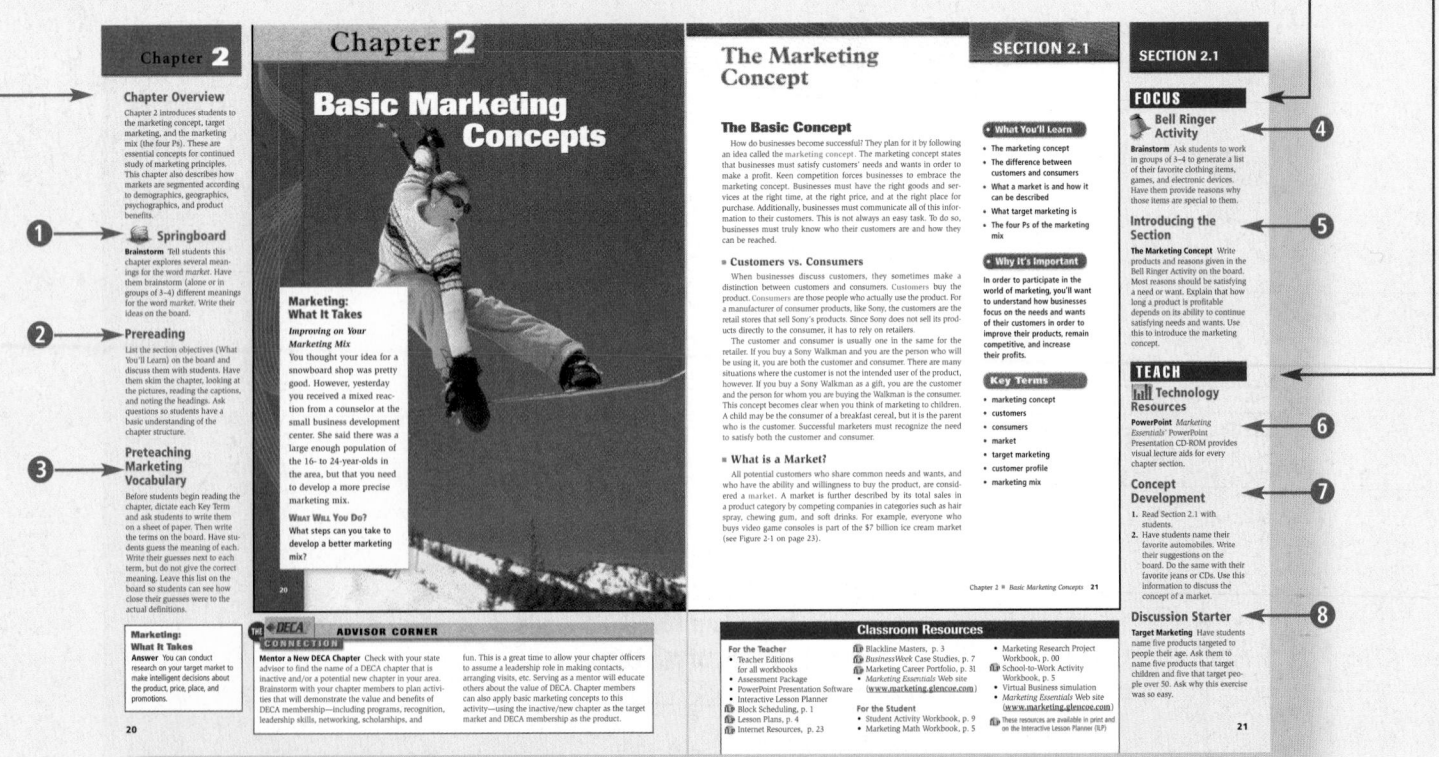

❼ Concept Development includes strategies for teaching concepts inductively through the use of examples and non-examples. This approach actively involves students in constructing a personal understanding of a new concept.

❽ Discussion Starter helps you involve students in section material. This encourages students to use dialogue as a tool to enhance thinking and understanding.

❾ Thinking Critically activities offer students the chance to demonstrate a more in-depth understanding of the section's concepts.

❿ Cooperative Learning activities add the element of social interaction to marketing education and engage students in an interactive approach to processing information. This results in greater retention of subject matter, improved attitudes toward learning, and enhanced interpersonal relations among group members.

⓫ Independent Practice includes activities in which students work by themselves to demonstrate and rehearse new knowledge.

ASSESS

Because students have different learning styles and learn at differing rates, the **Assess** section provides a variety of evaluation and reteaching activities designed to accommodate a wide range of learning abilities.

⓬ Reteaching activities help reinforce section concepts by presenting the same concepts in different manners.

⓭ Enrichment activities extend students' understanding of the section and enhance the learning experience for those who have mastered the section content and are ready for more in-depth, experiential learning.

⓮ Evaluation refers you to relevant assessment resources.

⓯ Technology Resources directs you to the Marketing Essentials Web site, where you can access resources to teach and assess occupation-specific vocabulary.

⓰ Virtual Business explains how section concepts can be taught and reinforced using Knowledge Matters' Virtual Business visual simulation.

CLOSE

The final step in the teaching plan provides you with an activity to summarize the section's contents and be sure students have retained the key point of each section.

T41

GREAT IDEAS

Chapter 1
Lucinda Mason
Demopolis High School
Demopolis, AL

Chapter 2
Rahnda Jaquays
Mecosta Osceola Career Center
Big Rapids, MI

Chapter 3
Allen L. Gancarz
East Syracuse-Minoa High School
East Syracuse, NY

Chapter 4
Paula Smith Mendoza
Bryan Adams High School
Dallas, TX

Chapter 5
Jennifer Prout
River Ridge High School
Lacey, WA

Chapter 6
David Haar
Eaglecrest High School
Aurora, CO

Chapter 7
Cecil Lara
Brackenridge High School
San Antonio, TX

Chapter 8
Tammie Carlson
Tri-County Technology Center
Bartlesville, OK

Chapter 9
Mary Valigura
Sandia High School
Albuquerque, NM

Chapter 10
Laresa Slater
Paseo Academy of Fine and
Performing Arts
Kansas City, MO

Chapter 11
John Bucci
Arvada High School
Arvada, CO

Chapter 12
Maggie Rathert
Verona Area High School
Verona, WI

Chapter 13
Richard L. Schwasinger
Goodland High School
Goodland, KS

Chapter 14
Michelle Walker, Ph.D.
University of North Texas
Applied Technology,
Training and Development
Denton, TX

Chapter 15
Karen Brettingen
Eden Prairie High School
Eden Prairie, MN

Chapter 16
Sandra Hinesly
Newman Smith High School
Carrollton, TX

Chapter 17
Jay Walker
James W. Robinson Secondary School
Fairfax, VA

Chapter 18
Patricia D. King
Windham High School
Willimantic, CT

Chapter 19
Jim Konrad
Cherry Creek High School
Englewood, CO

from the Marketing Classroom

Chapter 21
Lois Farese
Northern Highlands Regional High School
Allendale, NJ

Chapter 22
Lanette Duncan
Daniel Webster High School
Tulsa, OK

Chapter 23
Miranda Nixon Blocker
Heyward Career and Technology Center
Columbia, SC

Chapter 24
Roberta Pennington
Shawnee Mission West High School
Overland Park, KS

Chapter 25
Priscilla McCalla
National DECA
Reston, VA

Chapter 26
Grady Kimbrell
Educational Consultant
Santa Barbara, CA

Chapter 27
Carl Woloszyk
Western Michigan University
Kalamazoo, MI

Chapter 28
Greg Gregoriou
Parkside High School
Dundas, Ontario
Canada

Chapter 29
Dennis Sweetapple
Spanish River Community High School
Boca Raton, FL

Chapter 31
Lisa Jones
Centennial High School
Franklin, TN

Chapter 32
George Lee
Kamiakin High School
Kennewick, WA

Chapter 33
Pam Naylor
Shades Valley High School
Birmingham, AL

Chapter 34
Mark Rael
Cooper City High School
Cooper City, FL

Chapter 35
Elizabeth S. Pitts
Cass High School
Cartersville, GA

Chapter 36
Roger Cartee
North Country Career Center
Newport, VT

Chapter 37
Kevin Reisenauer
Minot High School
Minot, ND

Chapter 38
Barb Crum
Vidalia High School
Vidalia, LA

Chapter 20
Keith Smith
Pendleton Memorial High School
Falmouth, KY

Chapter 30
Rhonda Cmerek
Taylor High School
Taylor, TX

TEACHER CLASSROOM RESOURCES

The Student Activity Workbook with Teacher Annotated Edition provides Vocabulary Review, Fact and Idea Review, Marketing Applications, Role Plays for DECA preparation, and Computer Activities for spreadsheet, database, and word processing programs.

New!

The Marketing Research Project Workbook with Teacher Manual is a new addition to the *Marketing Essentials* program. This text-workbook offers a detailed, step-by-step procedure for students to follow in conducting a marketing research project. It provides clear explanations of the research process and includes hands-on activities that will help students improve their research skills and prepare for DECA competition. After completing the workbook, students will have executed their own in-depth marketing research study, complete with rationale for all decisions, a report of the findings and conclusions, recommendations based on the original research problem and study objectives, and an annotated bibliography.

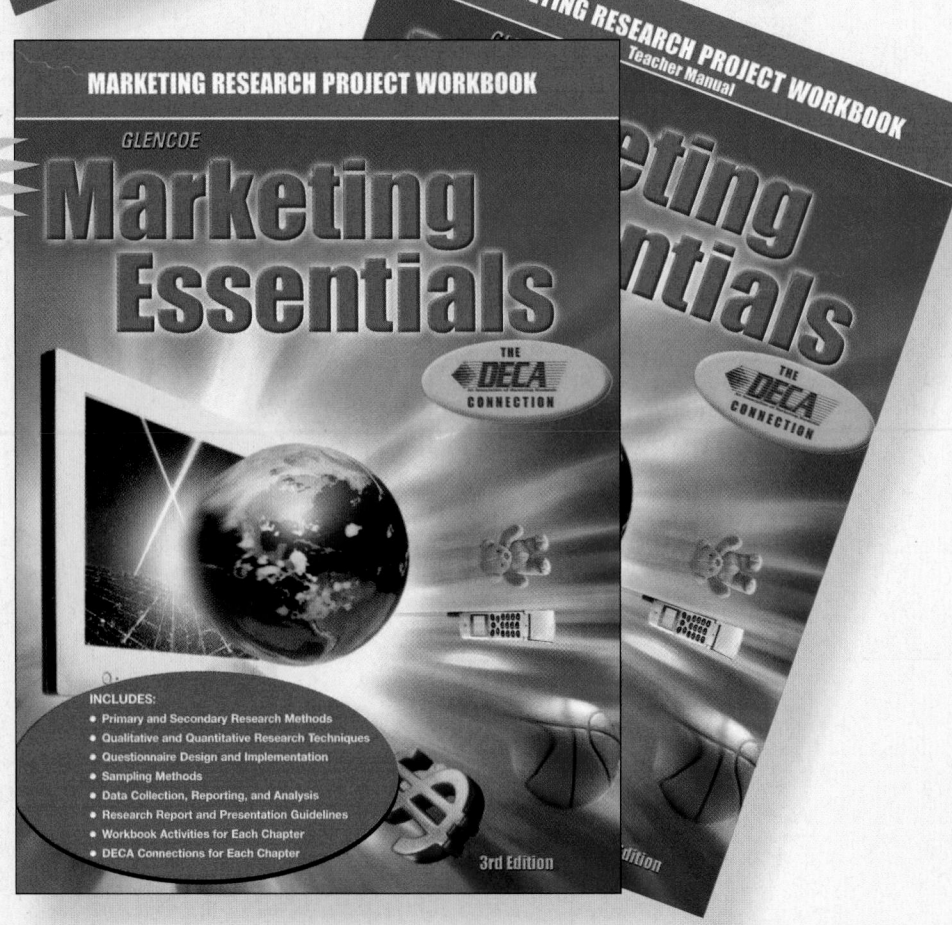

T44

The Marketing Math Workbook with Teacher Annotated Edition offers supplementary math activities for every unit in the student text. The workbook offers marketing math pretests; table, graph, and spreadsheet activities; sales transaction practice; promotional budgeting activities; buying, distribution, and pricing activities; marketing research computations; financial statement calculations; and numeric keypad drills.

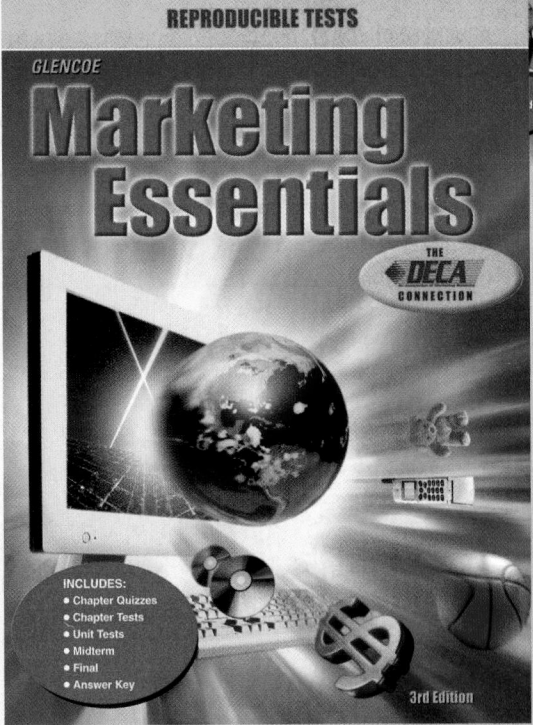

The ExamView Pro User's Guide and Testbank is the manual and testbank for the ExamView CD-ROM. With ExamView, you can design and create your own test instruments.

The Reproducible Tests book includes quizzes, tests, and answer keys for all 38 chapters and 12 units.

TEACHER CLASSROOM RESOURCES

The Block Scheduling Implementation Guide assists teachers in organizing class periods within 90 minutes. The guide is divided by unit and chapter, estimating the number of days to teach each chapter, and offering an estimation of the time required to include additional activities. The guide is designed to help you use the *Marketing Essentials* program to meet your particular classroom needs and to accommodate your style of teaching.

Lesson Plans provides a checklist of components for each chapter and cross-references all of the *Marketing Essentials* resource materials. Using Lesson Plans will allow you to organize and customize each lesson to your needs, allowing you to focus on the important task of teaching instead of planning.

Internet Resources will help you and your students understand the basics of the Internet and how it can be used as a source of information. Internet Resources includes 38 chapter-related activities that will help your students connect the Internet to their marketing education.

Blackline Masters includes figures, charts, and graphs from *Marketing Essentials* in a simple to use and reproduce format.

INTERACTIVE LESSON PLANNER

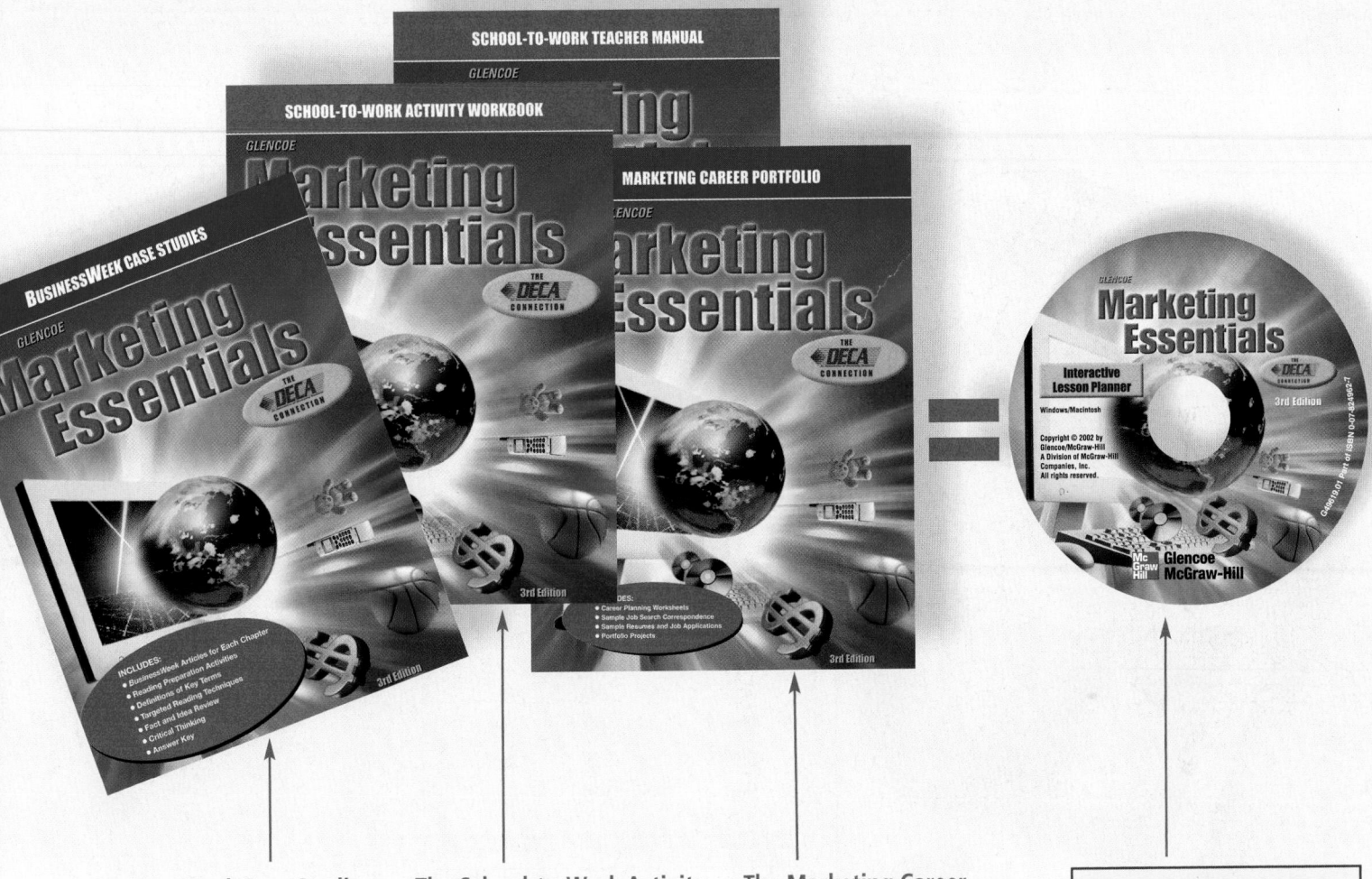

BusinessWeek Case Studies contains *BusinessWeek* articles related to each chapter's content. These activities employ active reading strategies, modeling for students the kind of thinking and questioning processes that skillful readers use. Each *BusinessWeek* Case Study includes activities for vocabulary, prereading, critical thinking, discussion, and performance assessment.

The School-to-Work Activity Workbook helps students relate their class work to their on-the-job experience. It provides activities for every chapter and involves your students in work-site analysis and working with mentors. Students are also provided with the scoring rubrics on which their performance will be evaluated. An extensive Teacher Manual provides guidelines for integrating marketing and school-to-work programs, as well as suggested student responses.

The Marketing Career Portfolio features 12 sample portfolio projects and a teacher's resource booklet with suggestions for managing the portfolio development process, descriptions of each part of the suggested student portfolio, model documents, and suggestions for documents that students should include in their portfolios.

The Interactive Lesson Planner (ILP) gives you instant access to all these print resources in one easy-to-use CD-ROM. The ILP allows instructors to plan lessons in a calendar format. It includes customizable built-in lesson plans and lists of and links to thousands of pdf files of print program resources.

TEACHER CLASSROOM RESOURCES

The *Marketing Essentials* PowerPoint Presentation provides over 1,000 high interest, visually-motivating slides. Each chapter presentation includes text highlights, charts, graphs, and figures, as well as a graphic organizer that helps students conceptually structure a major marketing concept.

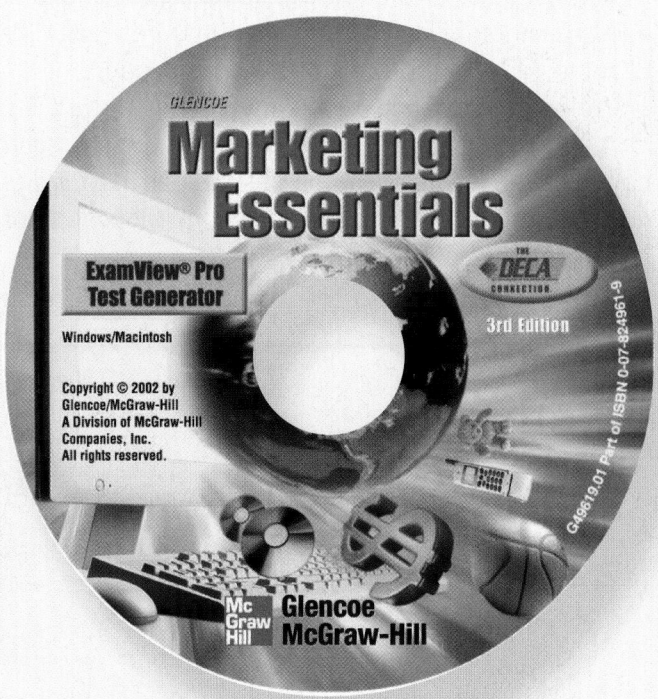

Impact! Sports and Entertainment Marketing Mini-Simulations will expose your students to the excitement of this growing marketing occupational area. The text's seven mini-simulations teach the four Ps of marketing (product, price, place, and promotion), the marketing mix as a whole, selling, and entrepreneurship.

The ExamView® CD-ROM is one of the most comprehensive test packages on the market. It provides an accurate and exhaustive source of text items for a wide variety of examination styles. It contains thousands of questions, organized around learning objectives and categorized by chapter and unit.

Virtual Business and Marketing Essentials

What is Virtual Business?

Virtual Business is a fully visual marketing and business simulation that introduces students to the principles of marketing by letting them start and run their own businesses. Clearly relevant and truly exciting, *Virtual Business* will attract students to your class. *Virtual Business* is designed to complement, not replace, the current teaching model. *Virtual Business* is designed and developed based on research conducted by Knowledge Matters, Inc. for the U.S. Department of Education.

Unlike previous business simulations, *Virtual Business* is highly visual. Students learn by literally seeing how their decisions affect the business. In *Virtual Business* students have the power to control all aspects of a retail convenience store.

What You Get

The *Virtual Business* classroom package contains everything you need to get your students excited, motivated, and eager to learn about marketing. It also makes prep time a breeze.

The CD-ROM contains the *Virtual Business* software, an interactive tutorial, 21 pre-saved modular activities with lesson plans, and the *Virtual Business* Analyzer companion software for post-activity classroom analysis and discussion. Now you can have your students actually making marketing decisions including merchandising, pricing, promotion, and market research. It doesn't get any closer to the real thing. Your students can even utilize an exciting set of online tools located at www.knowledgematters.com.

The "Multiplayer" Add-On

Students love competitions. With the multiplayer add-on you can have head-to-head competitions over a network. Students compete in the same virtual economy LIVE against other students in your school via your local area network or against other students anywhere in the world using the Internet.

DECA and Virtual Business

Virtual Business has a special partnership with DECA. Via DECA's website, there are special Virtual Business activities and competitions that are available to every DECA chapter. *Virtual Business* will not only provide your chapter a great team building activity, but also better prepare your members for competition.

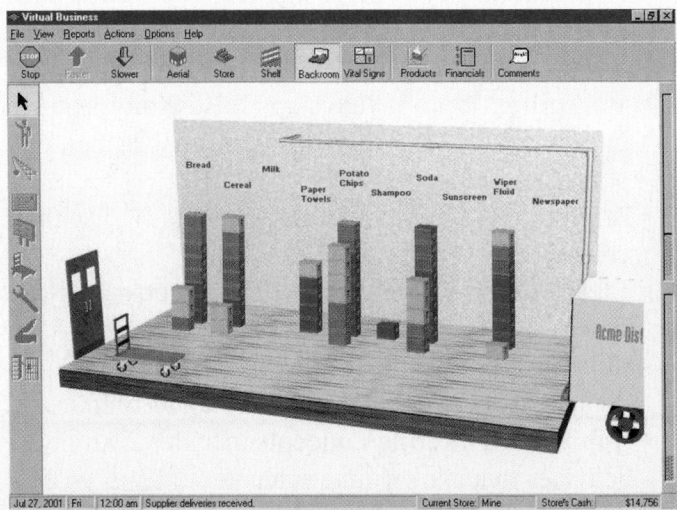

The Virtual Business CyberConsultant

The Virtual Business CyberConsultant is your tireless helper in succeeding with *Virtual Business*. She is, in fact, an expert system packed with artificial (and real) intelligence on how to run a business. She will review eight aspects of your business and give you critical advice to increase market share and profits. As a teaching tool she will individually grade the eight aspects of the business and assign an overall grade. Have students upload their virtual business simulations for review by the CyberConsultant. She even assigns grades!

User's Manual

Instructor's Manual

Virtual Business™

Virtual Business School Edition Quick Facts	
Product Type:	Highly visual computerized business simulation
Objective:	To supplement existing curriculum
Grade-Level:	Middle school through College
Curriculum:	25 prepared prepared lesson plans complete with detailed Instructor's and User's Manuals.
Assessment:	Online and offline grading tools
Student Use:	Individual or in teams up to five
Support:	Phone & Internet

Using Assessment

As a marketing educator, you will need a variety of ways to assess what your students have learned. One traditional method of measuring student progress is the written test that evaluates recall of subject content. This program contains an **Assessment Package** with **Exam-View** software and **Reproducible Tests** as traditional methods of assessment. However, it is also necessary to assess more than students' rote learning skills. Current curriculum objectives focus on the acquisition of knowledge and skills that will help students analyze situations and create plans to address those situations. The acquisition of these skills is not so easily assessed using the traditional paper-and-pencil test.

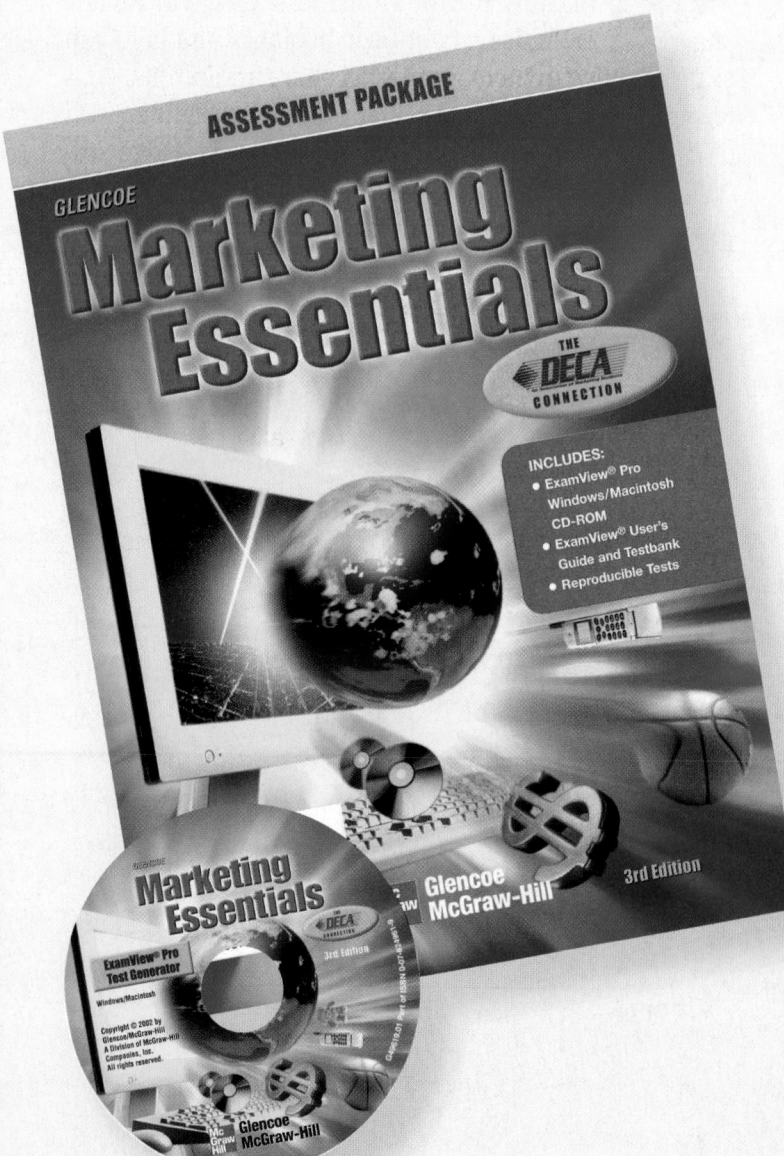

Using Alternative Assessment

The *Marketing Essentials* textbook provides a multitude of activities, projects, and situations that will help you to create opportunities for alternative assessment.

- **Role Play** activities in each chapter assessment ask students to act out various marketing scenarios, such as responding to a customer's complaint or handling a work-related conflict.
- **Marketing: What it Takes** and **Case Study** features in each chapter require students to analyze contemporary marketing situation.
- **Bright Ideas** features challenge students to use their creativity in developing ideas.
- **Electronic Frontiers**, **Life in the Diverse Marketplace**, and **Real World Marketing** include critical thinking activities that can give you insight into students reasoning and problem-solving techniques.
- **Applying Marketing Concepts** includes a variety of activities that allow you to evaluate students' writing and oral communication skills. These projects also allow you to assess students' abilities in collecting information, organizing it in a logical flow, analyzing its meaning, and applying it to the solution of a particular marketing situation.
- **Portfolio** activities are included in the unit opener sections of the student textbook. The **Marketing Career Portfolio** provides 12 portfolio projects as well as suggestions to help you implement student portfolio activities.
- **Integrating Academic Skills** provides opportunities for students to analyze situations and use information to solve problems.
- **Thinking Critically** questions can give you insight into students reasoning and problem-solving techniques.

Determining Assessment Strategies

The chart shown on the opposite page can help you determine which assessment strategies will work best for you and your students.

ASSESSMENT STRATEGIES	ADVANTAGES	DISADVANTAGES
Objective measures Multiple choice Matching Item sets True/False	Reliable, easy to validate Objective, if designed effectively Low cost, efficient Automated administration Lends to equating	Measures cognitive knowledge effectively Limited on other measures Not a good measure of overall performance
Written measures Essays Restricted response Written simulations Case analysis Problem-solving exercises	Face validity (real life) In-depth assessment Measures writing skills and higher level skills Reasonable developmental costs and time	Subjective scoring Time consuming and expensive to score Limited breadth Difficult to equate Moderate reliability
Oral measures Oral examinations Interviews	Measures communications and interpersonal skills In-depth assessment with varied stimulus materials Learner involvement	Costly and time consuming Limited reliability Narrow sample of content Scoring difficult, need multiple raters
Simulated activities In-basket Computer simulations	Moderate reliability Performance-based measure	Costly and time consuming Difficult to score, administer, and develop
Portfolio and product analysis Work samples Projects Work diaries and logs Achievement records	Provides information not normally available Learner involvement Face validity (real life) Easy to collect information	Costly to administer Labor and paper intensive Difficult to validate or equate Biased toward best samples or outstanding qualities
Performance measures Demonstrations Presentations Performances Production work Observation	Job-related Relatively easy to administer In-depth assessment Face validity	Rater training required Hard to equate Subjective scoring Time consuming if breadth is needed
Performance records References Performance rating forms Parental rating	Efficient Low cost Easy to administer	Low reliability Subjective Hard to equate Rater judgment
Self-evaluation	Learner involvement and empowerment Learner responsibility Measures dimensions not available otherwise	May be biased or unrealistic

Building Academic Skills

To succeed as marketing professionals, students need a range of specific skills and training. Among the skills your students will need in order to compete in the workforce are general strengths in communications, human relations, technology, and math. For example, all marketing professionals need to know how to write letters, scripts for presentations, work orders, and proposals; how to read memos, letters, and reports; how to speak coherently with a purpose or goal in mind; how to interact effectively with coworkers; and how to perform simple mathematics functions. Basic academic skills will support your students in completing tasks and roles, such as these, that their jobs will demand.

Academics in the Marketing Curriculum

It is as important to foster your students' learning in academic areas as it is to make sure they have a firm foundation in marketing. Integrating academic skills into the marketing classroom can easily be done by making academics a regular part of your classroom activities. For example, by having students read class assignments and texts, write letters and reports, give presentations, and perform mathematics exercises you are helping them improve their academic skills. These activities include the academic skills that we want to foster in our students.

Class assignments should include a component of these skills as part of your on-going evaluation of students' progress. For example, if you ask your students to prepare a report with a requirement that there are no typographical errors, you have built accuracy and attention to detail in the technical area of word processing or data entry into your assessment requirements.

The following are some specific ways in which you can effectively emphasize the academic skills your students need for the challenges of their careers.

IDENTIFY STUDENTS WHO NEED EXTRA HELP IN ACADEMIC AREAS. Early identification of students who need help in academic areas increases their chances of success in your course. You can gain insight into your students' levels of experience by taking a writing sample the first day of class, giving a preliminary reading comprehension exercise, or asking students to tell about themselves. Writing clinics, developmental courses, tutoring, and peer counseling are all formal ways to assist your students in areas of weakness.

EXAMPLE: On the first day of class, have students write about their previous and current job experiences and how they might relate to marketing. In these samples you will collect information about individual students that will help you relate to them better and help them relate course content to their prior learning. You will also determine who has difficulties with writing.

INCORPORATE ACADEMIC SKILLS IN YOUR CLASS ASSIGNMENTS AND ACTIVITIES. Emphasizing the importance of academic skills in your classroom will impress upon your students that these skills are necessary. As you talk about assignments, identify for students which academic areas they will be using. In this way they can identify the tasks required and the strategies they will need to complete the assignment satisfactorily.

Example: To help students learn how to market themselves, have them prepare a written description of their abilities that they would use as a basis for an interview. Tell them the description will also be part of a written application, and they will be evaluated on 1) a mock interview and 2) the written statement. Discuss the qualities of an effective written statement and positive interview skills before they begin the assignment, and evaluate them on how well they meet the standards.

USE ASSESSMENTS THAT REQUIRE AND INCORPORATE ACADEMIC SKILLS. For example, when you require that students comprehend what they're reading, write coherently, or adhere to principles of public speaking when they give a presentation, you are again reinforcing the skills needed to be successful in these academic areas.

Example: Have students prepare a presentation, with a written summary and visuals, that explains a training process for implementing a new sales strategy or system. Give students a checklist prior to the presentation that defines the criteria for assessment of their speech with categories such as: clear statement of purpose, effective speaking, organized presentation, appropriate use of visuals, etc. Also give them the requirements for the written summary—clearly organized, structured appropriately for the purpose, grammatically correct, accurate physical presentation (no typos) and correct format. By building these assessments into the assignment, you emphasize the importance of the skills, and also make the students aware of the necessity for competence in these areas.

Classroom Resources

To help you enhance your students' academic skills and integrate academic skills into your classroom, we have provided numerous academic activities and teaching strategies in this text.

- The end-of-section activities include **Integrating Academic Skills** activities. These activities provide realistic, creative applications of chapter concepts to communications and math.
- The chapter assessment activities include **Building Workplace Skills** activities. These activities provide applications of chapter concepts to technology, human relations, and various other topics.
- The side margins of the *Teacher Wraparound Edition* include a variety of **Individualized Practice** activities on applied academics that give students additional opportunities to strengthen their skills. These activities are written at three skill levels so that they may be adapted to the competency levels of your students.

Building Critical Thinking Skills

The process of teaching students critical thinking skills is a goal of education in all disciplines. Today's business environment—be it a corporate setting, self-employment, or a small business—is highly competitive and demands skilled employees. Your students will be a part of this business environment, competing for positions. One of the differentiating factors in achieving success in the workforce is an individual's ability to deal with the varied demands of the fast-paced world of business that requires insightful decision making, creative problem solving, and interactions with diverse groups—be it employees, management, investors, customers, or clients. By teaching your students critical thinking, you are equipping them with essential skills necessary for achieving success in today's workforce.

Critical thinking is the process of reasonably, or logically deciding what to do or believe. Critical thinking involves the ability to:

- compare and contrast,
- solve problems,
- make decisions,
- analyze and evaluate,
- synthesize and transfer knowledge, and
- conduct metacognitive exercises.

Critical thinking skills are important for the following reasons:

- Critical thinking skills help students investigate their own ways of solving problems and finding creative resolutions.
- Critical thinking skills lead students to investigations that compare and contrast what they know with unknowns.
- Critical thinking skills allow students to make decisions about their own learning and also make them aware of the processes they use.

How to Teach Critical Thinking

How, then, do we teach critical thinking? Doesn't all learning require thinking? What is meant by higher-level thinking? These questions and questions like them require teachers to reflect on the instructional strategies used in daily lessons and include opportunities for students to reason and think about what is being learned.

All learning does require thinking. Benjamin Bloom's Taxonomy of the Cognitive Domain is probably the most widely recognized schema for levels of thinking.

Each of Bloom's cognitive categories includes a list of a variety of thinking skills and indicates the kind of behavior students are to perform at the objectives or goals of specific learning tasks. Here are some examples:

Knowledge: define, recognize, recall, identify, label, understand, examine, show, collect

Comprehension: translate, interpret, explain, describe, summarize, extrapolate

Application: apply, solve, experiment, show, predict

Analysis: connect, relate, differentiate, classify, arrange, check, group, distinguish, organize, categorize, detect, compare, infer

Synthesis: produce, propose, design, plan, combine, formulate, compose, hypothesize, construct

Evaluation: appraise, judge, criticize, decide

The wealth of activities and guidance provided both in the student text and this *Teacher Wraparound Edition* will help you integrate critical thinking skills into your daily plans. Below are some guidelines for integrating and teaching these skills.

LET STUDENTS KNOW THEY ARE ENGAGING IN ASPECTS OF CRITICAL THINKING, be it comparison/contrast analysis, evaluation, synthesis, or determining relationships, such as cause-effect.

Example: If you have groups of students analyze a business letter for its purpose (to inform, entertain, or persuade), tell the students that they are analyzing. You should also broaden the application of this skill to other areas of the students lives—tell them that they constantly analyze music, conversations with their friends, articles they read in magazines, television programs. This will help demonstrate to students that they have had experience in using the skill.

USE ACTIVITIES THAT FOCUS ON OPEN-ENDED PROBLEMS. Activities with no "right answers" foster greater growth and a safe environment for using creative approaches to problem solving.

Example: Have students in groups compare and contrast two reports written by an employee to a supervisor, offering suggestions for improving the time it takes to respond to customer orders in a mail-order business. Then have the groups draft their own report which could be a presentation, a cause-effect study, or a report in a different format. This introduces several major skills: comparison/contrast, evaluation of a product, creation of a better product (creative problem solving).

ORGANIZE YOUR STUDENTS IN COOPERATIVE LEARNING GROUPS so that they can see how others solve problems, give each other feedback, and try out new ideas in a safe environment.

Example: Have students in groups prepare a statement that will accompany a presentation to a client. Assign different organization patterns to each group (enumeration, generalization with examples, cause and effect, comparison/contrast). After each group completes its statement, have the entire class analyze the effectiveness of the statements and discuss ways that presentations can be hampered or helped by their organizational structures.

PROVIDE FEEDBACK AND USE ASSESSMENTS THAT MEASURE STUDENTS' GROWTH AND PERFORMANCE IN THEIR NEWLY ACQUIRED SKILLS. Your feedback is important in encouraging students to feel comfortable experimenting with new ideas and new ways to look at problem solving and critical thinking.

Example: Using the above example, each student could write his or her own written statement. In this way you allow an individual response that will better measure each student's growth and understanding of the skills.

PROMOTE CRITICAL THINKING Examples of questions that promote thinking at various levels are shown below. Questions such as those listed can be used to promote and stimulate critical thinking.

Knowledge
   The identification and recall of information:
      Who, what, when, where, how...?
      Describe...
Comprehension
   The organization and selection of facts and ideas:
      Retell in your own words...
      What is the main idea of...?

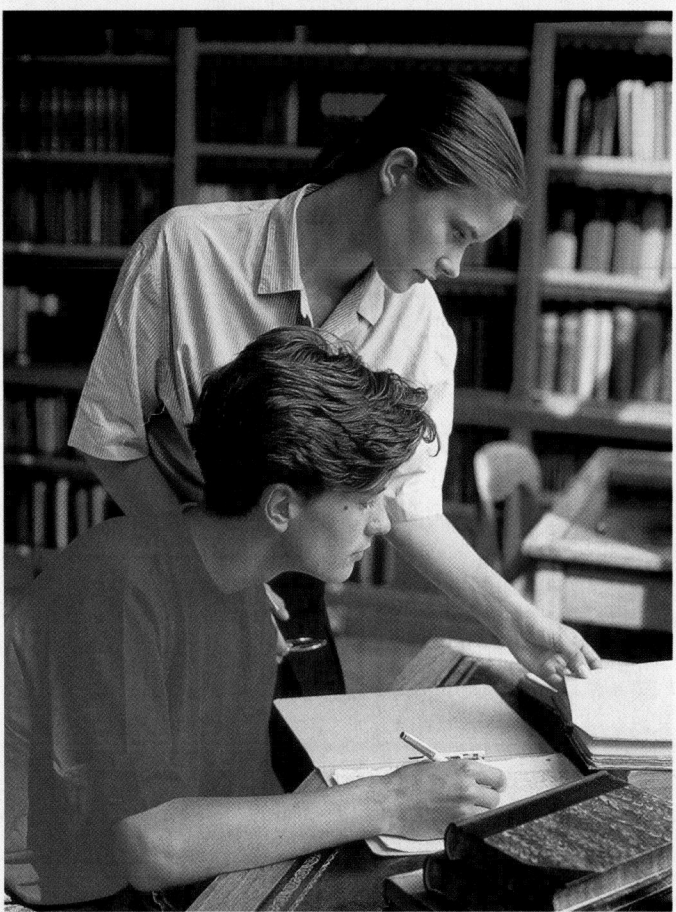

By teaching students critical thinking, you are equipping them with essential skills necessary for achieving success in today's workforce.

Application
   The use of facts, rules, principles:
      How is...an example of...?
      How is...related to...?
Analysis
   The separation of a whole into component parts:
      What are the parts or features...?
      Classify...according to...
      How does...compare/contrast with...?
Synthesis
   The combination of ideas to form a new whole:
      What would you predict/infer from...?
      What might happen if you combined...with...?
Evaluation
   The development of opinions, judgments, or decisions:
      What do you think about...?
      Prioritize...

BUILDING WORKPLACE SKILLS

SCANS and *Marketing Essentials*

In 1991, the U.S. Department of Labor released a report entitled What Work Requires of Schools: A SCANS Report for 2000. The SCANS report identified five competencies, which in conjunction with a three-part foundation of skills and personal qualities, lie at the heart of job performance and are needed by all workers in order to prosper in the emerging workplace. These skills and competencies have been integrated into the *Marketing Essentials* program.

THE FOUNDATION	MARKETING ESSENTIALS
Basic Skills—reading, writing, mathematics, speaking and listening.	The following chapters deal specifically with mathematics. Chapters 7, 16, 27, and 29 The following chapter deals specifically with reading, writing, speaking, and listening. Chapter 8
Thinking Skills—creative thinking, decision making, problem solving, knowing how to learn, and reasoning.	The following chapters deal specifically with thinking skills. Chapters 1-38
Personal Qualities—individual responsibility, self-esteem, self-management, sociability, and integrity.	The following chapters deal specifically with personal qualities. Chapters 10, 11, 37, and 38
Resources—allocated time, money materials, space and staff.	The following chapters deal specifically with resources. Chapters 11, 16, 19, 22, 25, 33, 35, and 36
Interpersonal skills—work in teams, teach others, serve customers, lead, negotiate, and work with people from culturally diverse backgrounds.	The following chapters deal specifically with interpersonal skills. Chapters 10, 11, 12, 13, 14, 15, 33
Information—acquire and evaluate data, organize and maintain files, interpret and communicate information, use computers to process information.	The following chapters deal specifically with information. Chapters 2, 4, 7, 9, 16, 25, 28, 29
Systems—understand social, organizational, and technological systems; monitor and correct performance; design and improve systems.	The following chapters deal specifically with systems. Chapters 11, 21, 22, 24, 28, and 29
Technology—select equipment and tools, apply technology to specific tasks, and maintain and troubleshoot technologies.	The following chapters deal specifically with technology. Chapters 9, 16, 23, 24, and 29

Using Cooperative Learning

Introduction

Studies show that students learn faster and retain more information when they are actively involved in the learning process. Cooperative learning is one method that gets students actively involved in learning and at the same time allows for peer teaching.

Using Cooperative Learning

Your marketing course provides many opportunities for students to learn and apply the skills necessary for positive interpersonal relationships. Through the use of cooperative learning, the teacher can offer a structured method of teaching team-building, collaborative social skills, and team decision making while teaching basic concepts—essential skills for the workplace. This learning structure is especially effective for more difficult learning tasks, such as problem solving, critical thinking, and conceptual learning.

Cooperative Learning in this Text

In *Marketing Essentials*, students and teachers have a variety of materials to assist with cooperative learning activities. Many of the features and section and chapter assessment activities can be completed in a cooperative learning environment. These activities include the **Case Study, Building Academic Skills, Building Workplace Skills, Integrating Academic Skills, The DECA Connection, Internet Connection**, and the **Zazz Lab.**

The Benefits of Cooperative Learning

- Cooperative learning emphasizes working toward group goals as opposed to the traditional emphasis on individual competition and achievement.
- Students discover that not only must they learn the material themselves, but also they are responsible for helping everyone in the group learn the material.
- Cooperative learning increases academic achievement and develops essential social skills.
- Students discover how to work with people of all types.
- Students learn valuable problem-solving, team-building, and creativity skills that transfer to real-world occupations and work environments.
- People who help each other and work together toward a common goal generally begin to feel more positive about each other and interact constructively when performing collective tasks.
- Students do not feel as isolated, and they gain self-esteem.
- Students have the opportunity to perceive other students as colleagues rather than competitors. As a result, they recognize the value of helping others rather than working competitively.

Meeting Individual Needs and Learning Styles

One of your greatest challenges as a teacher is to provide a positive learning environment for all students in your classroom. Because each student has his or her own unique set of abilities, perceptions, and needs, the learning styles and the physical abilities of your students may vary widely.

Assisting Students with Individual Needs

In order to help you provide all your students with a positive learning experience, this text provides a variety of activities. This diversity will stimulate student interest, motivate learning, and facilitate understanding. The *Teacher Wraparound Edition* also provides **Individualized Practice** activities that reinforce chapter learning while allowing students to progress at their own pace.

Teaching Students with Special Needs

Students in your classroom may have orthopedic impairments. They may have hearing or vision impairments, learning disabilities, or behavior disorders—all of which may interfere with their ability to learn. The learning styles of your students may also vary. Some students may be visual learners; others may learn more effectively through hands-on activities.

Some students may work well independently, while others need the interaction of others. Students may come from a variety of cultural backgrounds, and some may be second language learners.

Once you determine the special needs of your students, you can identify the areas in the curriculum that may present barriers to them. In order to remove those barriers, you may need to modify your teaching methods.

On the following pages are two charts. The first chart, **Meeting Special Needs**, describes some of the special needs you may encounter with students in your classroom and identifies sources of information. Also provided are tips for modifying your teaching style to accommodate the special needs of your students.

The second chart, **Eight Ways of Learning**, will help you identify your students' learning styles. The chart gives a description of each type of learner; describes the likes of each type, what each type is good at, and how each type learns best; and names some famous learners. Once you have identified each student's learning style, you can modify your teaching strategies to best suit his or her needs.

MEETING SPECIAL NEEDS

Subject	Description	Sources of Information
Second Language Learners	Certain students often speak English as a second language, or not at all. Customs and behavior of people in the majority culture may be confusing for some of these students. Cultural values may inhibit some of these students from full participation in the classroom.	• *Teaching English as a Second Language* • *Mainstreaming and the Minority Child*
Behavior Disorders	Children with behavior disorders deviate from standards or expectations of behavior and impair the functioning of others and themselves. These children may also be gifted or have learning disabilities.	• *Exceptional Children* • *Journal of Special Education*
Visual Impairments	Children with visual impairments have partial or total loss of sight. Individuals with visual impairments are not significantly different from their sighted peers in ability range or personality. However, blindness may affect cognitive, motor, and social development.	• *Journal of Visual Impairment and Blindness* • *Education of Visually Handicapped* • *American Foundation for the Blind*
Hearing Impairments	Children with hearing impairments have partial or total loss of hearing. Individuals with hearing impairments are not significantly different from their peers in ability range or personality. However, the chronic condition of deafness may affect cognitive, motor, social, and speech development.	• *American Annals of the Deaf* • *Journal of Speech and Hearing Research* • *Sign Language Studies*
Physical Impairments	Children with physical impairments fall into two categories—those with orthopedic impairments (use of one or more limbs severely restricted) and those with other health impairments.	• *The Source Book for the Disabled* • *Teaching Exceptional Children*
Gifted	Although no formal definition exists, these students can be described as having above average ability, task commitment, and creativity. They rank in the top 5 percent of their classes. They usually finish work more quickly than other students and are capable of divergent thinking.	• *Journal for the Education of the Gifted* • *Gifted Child Quarterly*
Learning Disabilities	All students with learning disabilities have a problem in one or more areas, such as academic learning, language, perception, social-emotional adjustment, memory, or ability to pay attention.	• *Journal of Learning Disabilities* • *Learning Disability Quarterly*

Tips for Instruction

- Remember that students' ability to speak English does not reflect their academic ability.
- Try to incorporate students' cultural experiences into your instruction. The help of a bilingual aide may be effective.
- Include information about different cultures in your curriculum to help build students' self-image.
- Avoid cultural stereotypes.
- Encourage students to share their cultures in the classroom.

- Work for long-term improvement; do not expect immediate success.
- Talk with students about their strengths and weaknesses, and clearly outline objectives.
- Structure schedules, rules, room arrangement, and safety for a conducive learning environment.
- Model appropriate behavior for students and reinforce proper behavior.

- Modify assignments as needed to help students become independent.
- Teach classmates how to serve as guides for the visually impaired.
- Tape lectures and reading assignments for the visually impaired.
- Encourage students to use their sense of touch; provide tactile models whenever possible.
- Verbally describe people and events as they occur in the classroom for students with visual impairments.

- Limit unnecessary noise in the classroom.
- Provide favorable seating arrangements so students with hearing impairments can see speakers and read their lips (or interpreters can assist); avoid visual distractions.
- Write out all instructions on paper or on the board; overhead projectors enable you to maintain eye contact while writing.
- Avoid standing with your back to the window or light source.

- With the student, determine when you should offer aid.
- Help other students and adults understand students with physical impairments
- Learn about special devices or procedures and if any special safety precautions are needed.
- Allow students to participate in all activities including field trips, special events, and projects.

- Emphasize concepts, theories, relationships, ideas, and generalizations.
- Let students express themselves in a variety of ways including drawing, creative writing, or acting.
- Make arrangements for students to work on independent projects.
- Make arrangements for students to take selected subjects early.

- Provide assistance and direction; clearly define rules, assignments, and duties.
- Allow for pair interaction during class time; utilize peer helpers.
- Practice skills frequently. Distribute outlines of material presented to class.
- Allow extra time to complete tests and assignments.

EIGHT WAYS OF LEARNING

Type	Description	Likes to…
Verbal/Linguistic Learner	Intelligence is related to words and language, written and spoken.	read, write, tell stories, play word games, and tell jokes and riddles.
Logical/Mathematical Learner	Intelligence deals with inductive and deductive thinking and reasoning, numbers, and abstractions.	perform experiments, solve puzzles, work with numbers, ask questions, and explore patterns and relationships.
Visual/Spatial Learner	Intelligence relies on the sense of sight and being able to visualize an object, including the ability to create mental images.	draw, build, design, and create things, daydream, do jigsaw puzzles and mazes, watch videos, look at photos, and draw maps and charts.
Naturalistic Learner	Intelligence has to do with observing, understanding, and organizing patterns in the natural environment.	spend time outdoors and work with plants, animals, and other parts of the natural environment; good at identifying plants and animals and at hearing and seeing connections to nature.
Musical/Rhythmic Learner	Intelligence is based on recognition of tonal patterns, including various environmental sounds, and on sensitivity to rhythm and beats.	sing and hum, listen to music, play an instrument, move body when music is playing, and make up songs.
Bodily/Kinesthetic Learner	Intelligence is related to physical movement and the brain's motor cortex, which controls bodily motion.	learn by hands-on methods, demonstrate skill in crafts, tinker, perform, display physical endurance, and challenge self-physically.
Interpersonal Learner	Intelligence operates primarily through person-to-person relationships and communication.	have lots of friends, talk to people, join groups, play cooperative games, solve problems as part of a group, and volunteer help when others need it.
Intrapersonal Learner	Intelligence is related to inner states of being, self-reflection, metacognition, and awareness of spiritual realities.	work alone, pursue own interests, daydream, keep a personal diary or journal, and think about starting own business.

Is good at...	Learns best by...	Famous Learners
memorizing names, dates, places, and trivia; spelling; using descriptive language; and creating imaginary worlds.	saying, hearing, and seeing words.	Maya Angelou—poet Abraham Lincoln—U.S. President and statesman Jerry Seinfeld—comedian Mary Hatwood Futrell—international teacher, leader, orator
math, reasoning, logic, problem solving, computing numbers, moving from concrete to abstract, thinking conceptually.	categorizing, classifying, and working with abstract patterns and relationships.	Stephen Hawking—physicist Albert Einstein—theoretical physicist Marilyn Burns—math educator Alexa Canady—neurosurgeon
understanding the use of space and how to get around in it, thinking in three-dimensional terms, and imagining things in clear	visual images. visualizing, dreaming, using the mind's eye, and working with colors and pictures.	Pablo Picasso—artist Maria Martinez—Pueblo Indian famous for black pottery Faith Ringgold—painter, quilter, and writer I.M. Pei—architect
measuring, charting, mapping, observing plants and animals, keeping journals, collecting, classifying, participating in outdoor activities.	visualizing, hands-on activities, bringing outdoors into the classroom, relating home/classroom to the	natural world. George Washington Carver—agricultural chemist Rachel Carson—scientific writer Charles Darwin—evolutionist John James Audubon—conservationist
remembering melodies; keeping time; mimicking beat and rhythm; noticing pitches, rhythms, and background and environmental sounds.	rhythm, melody, and music.	Henry Mancini—composer Marian Anderson—contralto Midori—violinist Paul McCartney—singer, songwriter, musician
physical activities such as sports, dancing, acting, and crafts.	touching, moving, interacting with space, and processing knowledge through bodily sensations.	Marcel Marceau—mime Jackie Joyner-Kersey—Olympic gold medalist in track and field Katherine Dunham—modern dancer Dr. Christian Bernard—cardiac surgeon
understanding people and their feelings, leading others, organizing, communicating, manipulating, mediating conflicts.	sharing, comparing, relating, cooperating, and interviewing.	Jimmy Carter—U.S. President and statesman Eleanor Roosevelt—former first lady Lee Iococca—president of Chrysler Corporation Mother Teresa—winner of Nobel Peace Prize
understanding self, focusing inward on feelings/dreams, following instincts, pursuing interests, and being original.	working alone, doing individualized projects, engaging in self-paced instruction.	Marva Collins—educator Mara Montessori—educator and physician Sigmund Freud—psychotherapist Anne Sexton—poet

Integrating Ethics

During their marketing careers, your students will encounter many situations that will require them to make decisions about their own actions. Helping students learn about ethical behavior and how to consider the effects of a decision before it is made are important topics for your marketing course.

The goal of introducing ethics into your course is not to teach values, but rather to help students clarify their own ethical beliefs and to learn how to evaluate ethical situations in light of their personal beliefs. Students need to learn how to evaluate their own actions and to ask themselves questions such as, "Will I think well of myself if I take this action?" "Would I want others to know about my actions?"

The Ethical Decision Model

Your students will learn to analyze ethical situations better if they have a model to use in deliberating the issues and the people affected by a decision. Several decision models exist, but the basic steps for an ethical decision model are as follows:

1. Determine the ethical issue.
2. Identify the actions for handling the situation.
3. Identify the people affected by the situation.
4. Analyze how the situation affects the people involved.
5. Decide which of the actions to take.

Classroom Strategies

Several methods may be used to integrate discussions of ethical issues into your marketing course. You may use the chapter Case Study or collect current articles that portray ethical dilemmas. Have students analyze the situations in class or write short reports of their analyses and conclusions.

Case Study Approach Using case studies from the textbook, have the entire class use the ethical decision model to analyze the issues and the possible actions to take. Make sure your students feel free to voice their opinions. If a full-class discussion becomes unwieldy, you may want to use small groups in a cooperative learning activity.

Cooperative Learning Groups Small groups of students are especially well suited to discussing cases and sharing their ideas about ethical issues. Divide students into groups of four to five. Observe groups to be sure that all students are participating. Allow each group to reach its conclusions, then ask a member of each to share that group's ideas with the class.

Role Plays and Debates Have your students role play ethical situations, using their own ideas about how to respond to a given situation. Discuss class responses to the role play, guiding students in using the ethical decision model. Set up debate teams to present different sides of an ethical issue.

Case Study Review

1. Why is computerized data collection becoming a part of baseball?
2. How can baseball owners use bar coded ticket information to improve customer service?

A MATTER OF ETHICS

3. Is it ethical to ask for background information before issuing a fan loyalty card? Why or why not?

Each chapter in the textbook contains a Case Study, which asks students to answer A MATTER OF ETHICS question. You may want to use these cases for class discussion or have your students develop their writing skills by requiring short reports analyzing the ethical aspects of a case.

Integrating Cultural Diversity

As future marketers, your students will be faced with a diverse marketplace in which people of many different cultures are both workers and consumers. Cultural knowledge may be the difference between success and failure in marketing products in the global economy. For students to become productive workers and responsible citizens, they must be open to cultural differences.

As students learn about skills needed to be successful in a marketing career, they should keep in mind the wide diversity of the people they are likely to encounter in every aspect of their working and personal lives. In the classroom and in one-on-one conferences, you can help your students consider the diversity of the U.S. population, not only in terms of ethnicity, but also in terms of customs, attitudes, religious beliefs, language backgrounds, and physical capabilities. High school students need to understand that ability and success are not related to skin color or gender.

Life In The Diverse MARKETPLACE

What Does Yes Really Mean?

In many Asian societies, it is impolite to say "no," so "yes" has multiple meanings. "Yes" can mean that listeners recognize that they are being spoken to, although they don't understand what is being said, or that the speaker's words are understood, but not agreed with. It can also mean that something is understood, but other people must be told of it before any final decisions are made. "Yes" can also mean that an offer is comprehended, but if the situation were to change, their "yes" would also be subject to change.

Thinking Critically
Why is having a keen cultural ear important in cross-cultural marketing?

Multicultural Education

Multicultural education incorporates the idea that all students—regardless of their gender and social class, and their ethnic, racial, or cultural characteristics—should have an equal opportunity to learn in school. Learning about other cultures concurrently with their own culture helps children recognize similarities and appreciate differences, without perceiving inferiority or superiority of one or the other. To foster cultural awareness:

• Recognize that all students are unique, having special talents, abilities etc.
• Promote uniqueness and diversity as positive
• Know, appreciate and respect cultural backgrounds of your students.
• Use authentic situations to provide for cultural learning and understanding
• Make sure people of all cultures are represented fairly and accurately
• Make sure that historical information is accurate and nondiscriminatory
• Make sure that materials do not include stereotypical roles
• Make sure there is gender equity
• Welcome parent and community involvement
• Use current news stories or advertisements to call students' attention to cultural differences that influence the marketing of products

Textbook Resources Every chapter in *Marketing Essentials* includes a feature entitled Life in the Diverse Marketplace that highlights different aspects of ethnic culture. This feature addresses the global marketplace and gives specific insights about other cultures. You can use this feature as the basis of class discussion on cultural diversity.

Integrating Global Marketing

The environment that American businesses of every size are operating in is rapidly becoming more international. The collapse of communism has brought hundreds of millions of new consumers and producers into the world economy. Major trade regions are being formed, breaking down long-standing barriers between countries and regions. Thus, it is vital that we integrate a global perspective into all of our marketing courses. We can't treat the topic of international marketing as a separate entity any more.

Just as businesses are operating more and more globally, students preparing to enter business must be ready to operate in an international arena in the future. As the world gets smaller and communication gets faster, we can't remain comfortable in doing what has been done in the past. Faster communication and distribution makes competition possible from farther and farther distances. A few years ago, a business needed only to be concerned with local competitors; in a global economy, a serious competitive threat may now be ten time zones away.

Marketing Essentials is designed to provide your students with the international perspective that is so important to success in marketing. The third edition of *Marketing Essentials* not only integrates global topics throughout the text but also includes a unit devoted to business and international marketing.

Integrating E-Commerce

The advent of the e-commerce is closely related to the increasing importance of the international marketplace. Today's marketers are facing an international marketplace that is rapidly becoming more competitive, specialized, and reliant on the Internet. The Internet has brought global opportunities not only for big business, but also for small and startup companies taking advantage of technological changes. International business is no longer the sole domain of multinational corporations. Many small, flexible, and innovative companies from all corners of the globe are now major players in international trade.

Coverage of technology has been integrated throughout the third edition of *Marketing Essentials*. Many of the Case Studies and features deal with firms that are technology based or have made electronic commerce a key component of their operations. Technology has become so important to marketing that *Electronic Frontiers* features have been included in every chapter. *Electronic Frontiers* illustrates the pervasive impact that technology is having on marketing. Topics covered in this feature include:

- The introduction of electronic books
- The challenges of branding on the Internet
- The Internet's impact on society
- Shopping robots that perform price comparisons on the Internet
- Internet cookies
- Internet ethics
- Linked technologies
- Viral marketing
- Digital distribution
- Wireless commerce
- Real-time pricing

Integrating Computer Technology into Your Marketing Program

Our economic society is rapidly changing from an industrial to an information-based society. As a result, your students' future marketing careers will be touched by computer technology. Technology is changing the way people work, play, and live. Access to the Internet allows people to do research and exchange ideas with others from all over the world. Telecommuting often allows people to work from home and spend more time with their families. Teaching students about technology is important when teaching about marketing, because technology helps business market in new and more precise ways.

Integrated Technology Activities

The *Marketing Essentials* program helps you integrate technology into your classroom through computer-based activities. The *Applying Marketing Concepts* activities in the Chapter Assessment allow students to practice various computer applications. These activities ask students to apply their marketing knowledge using various types of technology. The *Internet Resources* supplement presents an overview of the Internet as well as 38 Internet activities correlated to each chapter of the textbook.

The *Student Activity Workbook* supplement of *Marketing Essentials* includes a computer activity for each chapter in the textbook. These computer activities require students to use commercial software programs for word processing, database, or spreadsheet applications. In addition, activity questions require students to interpret their calculations or activity results and to extrapolate the information to broader marketing situations.

Using the Internet in the Classroom

The Internet is a remarkable tool that allows people from all over the world to communicate instantly. Students can use it to gather data; business owners can use it to advertise and sell; consumers can use it to research and purchase.

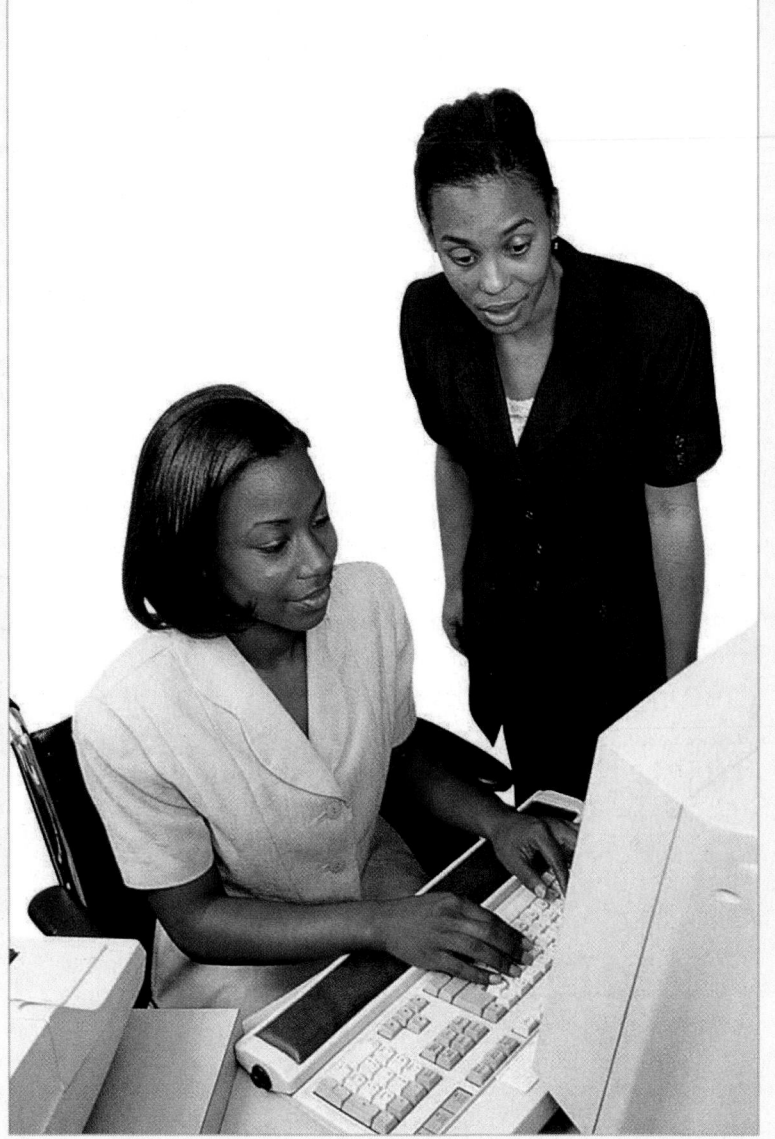

To use the Internet effectively in the classroom, look for sites that are created by the government or by universities (their URLs end in *.gov* or *.edu*). These are reliable sites with factual integrity and stability. Find out who created the site and why it was created. If the purpose of the Web site is unclear, its content may be unreliable. Use multiple search engines and Web directories when you are looking for information on a topic. This will help you find as many of the pertinent sites as possible. Combine Internet research with traditional research methods. Visit your school or local public library and ask the librarians and experts for sources and information. Use books and magazines.

DECA is an association of marketing students. It is a cocurricular club with chapters in more than 6,000 high schools. DECA's membership includes representation from all 50 states, four U.S. territories, the District of Columbia, two Canadian provinces, Mexico, and Europe. All DECA activities further student development in one or more of the following areas: leadership development, social intelligence, vocational understanding, and civic consciousness. Through the integration of individual and group DECA activities with the marketing education instructional program, students' skills are cultivated to ensure they have great potential to become future leaders in the areas of marketing and management.

Leadership Skills

The structure of a DECA chapter encourages leadership development. Each chapter elects officers who, with the membership, identify an annual program of work. The identified program of work often includes committee chairpeople to organize and execute the activities. Chapter activities encourage all members to act responsibly as a leader or member of a group and typically focus on the advantages of participation in a free enterprise system, marketing research, an individual's civic responsibility within the community.

National DECA provides opportunities for local chapter officers and members to receive additional leadership and chapter development training. Annual Regional Conferences are held in the fall. In the spring, students may attend the Leadership Development Academy at the Career Development Conference (CDC). During the summer, a State Officer Leadership Institute is available.

Competitive Events

One part of the DECA program of student activities is the competitive events program. The events are both competency and curriculum based and assist students in the refinement of workplace skills required for entry and/or advancement in the field of marketing. All events are centered around those skills expected by employers in all marketing fields—effective communication skills, ability to solve problems, ability to make decisions, and ability to function responsibly as either a leader or member or a team. Some events are for individuals and others require students to function as members of a group. The competitive events program provides recognition for student excellence at the local, state, and national level of competition. The recognition received by both individuals and teams within a DECA chapter serve as a showcase of the marketing education program to the local school and community.

DECA Team Events — *Marketing Essentials*

DECA Written Events

Business and Financial Services Marketing	All chapters
Entrepreneurship	Chapters 37-40
Food Marketing Research	Chapters 32-36, 39, 40
General Marketing Research	Chapters 32-36, 39, 40
Hospitality and Recreation Marketing Research	Chapters 5-7, 32-36, 39, 40
Retail Marketing Research	Chapters 19-23, 32, 33, 39, 40

DECA Participating Events

Entrepreneurship	Chapters 37-40
Fashion Merchandising Promotion Plan	Chapters 19-23, 39, 40

DECA Project Events

Civic Consciousness	Chapters 3-7
Creative Marketing Research	Chapters 32, 33
Learn and Earn	Chapters 37-40
Public Relations	Chapters 19-23
DECA Quiz Bowl	All chapters
Free Enterprise	Chapters 3-7
International Marketing	Chapters 5-7

DECA Preparation *Marketing Essentials* is designed to be one of your primary DECA preparation resources. The table above lists DECA's team events and the corresponding chapters in *Marketing Essentials* that will help students prepare for the events.

Team Events

Team projects and events may be completed by teams composed of one to three DECA members. All team events require completion of a written manual. Each year, DECA identifies a specific topic for each team event category. All events must include research related to the topic and follow the identified format. Excellence in the written events is evaluated on both the quality of the written report and performance during an interview conducted by a judge from the business community. When completed, the written manuals could be included in a students' portfolios and would be of significant interest to both educators and businesspeople reviewing the portfolio.

Through their research and writing, team event participants are expected to:
- function as leaders or members of a group.
- prepare complex reports.
- demonstrate initiative and creativity.
- communicate recommendations based on their research to business executives.

DECA COMPETITIVE EVENT OCCUPATIONAL AREAS

- Advertising and Visual Merchandising Services
- Apparel and Accessories Marketing
- Finance and Credit Services
- Food Marketing
- General Marketing
- Hospitality and Tourism Marketing
- Retail Merchandising
- Quick Serve Restaurant Management
- Full Service Restaurant Management
- Vehicles and Petroleum Marketing

Occupational Areas These are DECA's competitive event occupational areas. Students participate in the event categories in their areas of occupational interest within the field of marketing.

Individual Series Events

As participants in the individual series event program, students are evaluated on their proficiency in handling simulated business situations. Each event is directly related to competencies mastered through classroom instruction and/or related job experience. The following are the instructional areas included in DECA's competitive events program:

Economic Concepts and Principles—economics, marketing, and business

Basic and Social Skills—mathematics, communications, human relations, and career development

Marketing Functions—financing, pricing, promotion, product/service management, distribution, selling, marketing-information management)

A typical individual series event includes a comprehensive written exam and two role-play events. In each series students are presented with a business situation. Students must then use the skills acquired through participation in their marketing class to make decisions and spontaneously react to the situation. A business executive judges students' performance while playing the role of the second party in the role play.

THE DECA CONNECTION

Using *Marketing Essentials* to prepare for DECA

Marketing Essentials is designed to be one of your primary DECA preparation resources. The text and end-of-chapter activities are devoted to preparing students for DECA. For example, Unit 11, Entrepreneurship and Finance, gives students step-by-step instructions on how to prepare for DECA's entrepreneurship written event, which requires students to write a business proposal for a new business.

In addition, each Chapter Assessment includes a DECA Connection Role Play in which students practice for DECA's participating events. Students are given a marketing situation to contemplate. For example, students may have to create a promotion plan for a product or make a distribution decision. They are asked to come up with a plan or solution and present it to the teacher who, in the role-play situation, represents a manager, a staff member, or other marketing personnel. Role-play activities provide the teacher with a list of performance indicators to use as criteria in evaluating students' performances. The Student Activity Workbook includes an additional DECA Role Play activity for every chapter.

If your students are competing in one of DECA's marketing research events, you will find the *Marketing Essentials* Marketing Research Project Workbook and invaluable preparation resource.

In addition to *Marketing Essentials*, there are several resources available that provide added training for students preparing for competition. Two of these resources are the Career Competency in Marketing Series published by Glencoe/McGraw-Hill and the event-specific Student Training Guides available through DECA Images (www.deca.org).

COURSE PLANNNING GUIDE

ONE SEMESTER COURSE		
WEEK	**CHAPTER**	
1	Chapter 1	Marketing Is All Around Us
2	Chapter 2	Basic Marketing Concepts
3	Chapter 3	The Free Enterprise System
	Chapter 4	Global Economies
4	Chapter 5	Business and Social Responsibility
	Chapter 6	International Trade
5	Chapter 8	Communication Skills
	Chapter 10	Interpersonal Skills
6	Chapter 12	Preparing For The Sale
	Chapter 13	Initiating The Sale
7	Chapter 14	Presenting The Product
	Chapter 15	Closing The Sale
8	Chapter 16	Using Math In Sales
	Chapter 17	Promotional Concepts And Strategies
9	Chapter 18	Visual Merchandising And Display
	Chapter 19	Advertising
10	Chapter 21	Channels Of Distribution
	Chapter 22	Physical Distribution
11	Chapter 23	Purchasing
	Chapter 24	Stock Handling and Inventory Control
12	Chapter 25	Price Planning
	Chapter 26	Pricing Strategies
13	Chapter 28	Marketing Research
	Chapter 30	Product Planning
14	Chapter 31	Branding, Packaging, and Labeling
	Chapter 33	Entrepreneurial Concepts
15	Chapter 35	Developing A Business Plan
	Chapter 36	Financing The Business
16	Chapter 37	Identifying Career Opportunities
	Chapter 38	Finding and Applying for a Job

COURSE PLANNNING GUIDE

FULL-YEAR COURSE—SIX-WEEK GRADING SYSTEM

GRADING PERIOD	CHAPTER
First	Chapter 1 Marketing is All Around Us
	Chapter 2 Basic Marketing Concepts
	Chapter 3 The Free Enterprise System
	Chapter 4 Global Economies
	Chapter 5 Business and Social Responsibility
	Chapter 6 International Trade
Second	Chapter 7 Basic Math Skills
	Chapter 8 Communication Skills
	Chapter 9 Computer Applications and Skills
	Chapter 10 Interpersonal Skills
	Chapter 11 Management Skills
	Chapter 12 Preparing For The Sale
Third	Chapter 13 Initiating The Sale
	Chapter 14 Presenting The Product
	Chapter 15 Closing The Sale
	Chapter 16 Using Math In Sales
	Chapter 17 Promotional Concepts And Strategies
	Chapter 18 Visual Merchandising And Display
Fourth	Chapter 19 Advertising
	Chapter 20 Preparing Print Advertisements
	Chapter 21 Channels Of Distribution
	Chapter 22 Physical Distribution
	Chapter 23 Purchasing
	Chapter 24 Stock Handling and Inventory Control
	Chapter 25 Price Planning
Fifth	Chapter 26 Pricing Strategies
	Chapter 27 Pricing Math
	Chapter 28 Marketing Research
	Chapter 29 Conducting Marketing Research
	Chapter 30 Product Planning
	Chapter 31 Branding, Packaging, and Labeling
	Chapter 32 Extended Product Features
Sixth	Chapter 33 Entrepreneurial Concepts
	Chapter 34 Risk Management
	Chapter 35 Developing A Business Plan
	Chapter 36 Financing The Business
	Chapter 37 Identifying Career Opportunities
	Chapter 38 Finding and Applying for a Job

COURSE PLANNNING GUIDE

FULL-YEAR COURSE—NINE-WEEK GRADING SYSTEM

GRADING PERIOD	CHAPTER
First	Chapter 1 Marketing is All Around Us
	Chapter 2 Basic Marketing Concepts
	Chapter 3 The Free Enterprise System
	Chapter 4 Global Economies
	Chapter 5 Business and Social Responsibility
	Chapter 6 International Trade
	Chapter 7 Basic Math Skills
	Chapter 8 Communication Skills
	Chapter 9 Computer Applications and Skills
	Chapter 10 Interpersonal Skills
Second	Chapter 11 Management Skills
	Chapter 12 Preparing For The Sale
	Chapter 13 Initiating The Sale
	Chapter 14 Presenting The Product
	Chapter 15 Closing The Sale
	Chapter 16 Using Math In Sales
	Chapter 17 Promotional Concepts And Strategies
	Chapter 18 Visual Merchandising And Display
	Chapter 19 Advertising
	Chapter 20 Preparing Print Advertisements
Third	Chapter 21 Channels Of Distribution
	Chapter 22 Physical Distribution
	Chapter 23 Purchasing
	Chapter 24 Stock Handling and Inventory Control
	Chapter 25 Price Planning
	Chapter 26 Pricing Strategies
	Chapter 27 Pricing Math
	Chapter 28 Marketing Research
	Chapter 29 Conducting Marketing Research
Fourth	Chapter 30 Product Planning
	Chapter 31 Branding, Packaging, and Labeling
	Chapter 32 Extended Product Features
	Chapter 33 Entrepreneurial Concepts
	Chapter 34 Risk Management
	Chapter 35 Developing A Business Plan
	Chapter 36 Financing The Business
	Chapter 37 Identifying Career Opportunities
	Chapter 38 Finding and Applying for a Job

Unit 1

The World of Marketing

Chapter 1
Marketing Is All Around Us

Chapter 2
Basic Marketing Concepts

Unit Objectives

After completing this unit, students will be able to:

- Describe the scope of marketing.
- Explain the economic value and benefits of marketing.
- Discuss the reasons for studying marketing.
- Discuss the importance of marketing careers to the U.S. economy.
- Describe current employment trends.
- State the marketing concept.
- Explain the marketing mix.
- Define what constitutes a market, as well as how to identify one.
- Identify key methods used to reach potential customers, including developing a customer profile, target marketing, and market segmentation.
- Identify demographic, geographic, and psychographic trends in the U.S. consumer market.

Enrichment Resources

Books
Capturing Customers.com
  by George Colombo
Positioning: The Battle for Your Mind, The 20th Anniversary Edition
  by Al Ries and Jack Trout

Magazines/Journals
AdWeek
Marketing News

Associations
American Marketing Association
311 S. Wacker Drive, Suite 200
Chicago, IL 60606
(312) 648-0536
www.ama.com

National DECA
1908 Association Drive
Reston, VA 22091
(704) 777-8810
www.deca.org

Journal Writing Activity

1. Ask students to make a list in their journals of ten words that come to mind when they think of marketing. Ask students to share their list of marketing-related words with the rest of the class. Write the words on the board. Compare the list of words to the national curriculum's four foundations and seven functions of marketing. Categorize each word as a foundation or function, or as an element of a foundation or function. Write on the board any of the foundations and functions that were not identified and explain why each is a vital part of marketing.

2. Ask students to write two paragraphs in their journals about what they think it takes to be a great marketer. Then ask them to share their answers. Categorize their answers on the board under the headings Academic Skills, Human Relations Skills, Technical Skills, and Creative Skills.

TEACHER CLASSROOM RESOURCES

Program Resources	CHAPTER 1	CHAPTER 2
Student Activity Workbook	p. 1	p. 9
Marketing Math Workbook	p. 1	p. 1
Marketing Research Project Workbook	p. 1	p. 1
ILP School-to-Work Activity Workbook	p. 1	p. 5
ILP *BusinessWeek* Case Studies	p. 1	p. 7
ILP Marketing Career Portfolio	p. 31	p. 31
Reproducible Tests	p. 1	p. 5
ExamView User's Guide and Testbank	p. 1-1	p. 2-1
ILP Internet Resources	p. 21	p. 23
ILP Blackline Masters	p. 1	p. 3
ILP Lesson Plans	p. 1	p. 4
ILP Block Scheduling	p. 1	p. 1
Impact! Simulation	p. 1	p. 1

ILP Each of these resources is available in print and on the Interactive Lesson Planner CD-ROM.

Technology Resources

- Interactive Lesson Planner (ILP) CD-ROM
- PowerPoint Presentation CD-ROM
- Marketing Essentials Web site
- ExamView! CD-ROM
- Impact! Simulation

Virtual Business

Virtual Business is a fully visual marketing and business simulation that introduces students to the principles of marketing by letting them start and run their own virtual businesses. In *Virtual Business*, students have the power to control all aspects of a retail convenience store. Students strategize marketing decisions using a powerful learning tool in the guise of a video game. They learn by experiencing how their decisions affect their virtual business.

Key to Individualized Academics Activities

L1 Level 1 activities are basic activities and should fall within the range of all students.

L2 Level 2 activities are average activities and should be within the range of average and above average students.

L3 Level 3 activities are challenging activities designed for the ability range of above average students.

National Marketing Education

CHAPTER	SECTION	PERFORMANCE INDICATOR
Chapter 1 **Marketing Is All Around Us**	1.1	Describe marketing functions and related activities (BME)
		Explain marketing and its importance in a global economy (BME)
	1.2	Determine forms of economic utility created by marketing activities (ECO)
	1.3	Explain employment opportunities in marketing (PD)
		Identify skills needed to enhance career progression (PD)
Chapter 2 **Basic Marketing Concepts**	2.1	Explain marketing and its importance in global economy (BME)
		Address the needs of individual personalities (SEL)
	2.2	Explain the role of business in society (BME)
		Analyze product information to identify product features and benefits (SEL)

CIS Communication, Interpersonal Skills   **DIS** Distribution   **FIN** Financing   **PRI** Pricing   **SEL** Selling

Standards Assessment Correlation

SECTION ASSESSMENT			CHAPTER ASSESSMENT						UNIT LAB
Reviewing Key Terms and Concepts	Thinking Critically	Integrating Academic Skills	Fact and Idea Review	Thinking Critically	Building Workplace Skills	Applying Marketing Concepts	Linking School to Work	Internet Connection	Zazz Lab
1, 2, 3	●	●	1, 2	1, 2	1	1, 2, 3, 4			●
2, 3			1	1, 2,		1	●	●	
1, 2, 3	●	●	3, 4, 5, 6, 7	1, 2	1	2, 3			●
1, 2, 3, 4, 5	●	●	8, 9, 10	4	2		●	●	
3, 4, 5	●	●		3, 4	2		●	●	
1, 2, 3, 4, 5		●	1, 2, 3, 4			1			
	●		1	2	2				
2, 3, 5			5, 7, 9	2, 4	1	3, 4	●		
1, 4	●	●	6, 8, 10	3					●

Unit Overview

Unit 1 provides a base of knowledge that will be built upon throughout the text. Chapter 1 defines marketing, explains the benefits of marketing, and provides an overview of careers in marketing. Chapter 2 lays the foundation for marketing principles and practices. It focuses on the marketing concept and the 4 Ps of the marketing mix, target marketing, and market segmentation.

Introducing the Unit

Ask students to generate a list of products that come in different models, styles, varieties, etc. *(Possibilities may include athletic shoes, jeans, cars, computers, and ice cream.)* After students generate their lists, ask why there are so many versions of one type of product. Then have students speculate about the people a product is targeted to, and how a manufacturer discerns their needs and determines how to reach a target audience. Tell students that answering these questions begins their journey into the world of marketing.

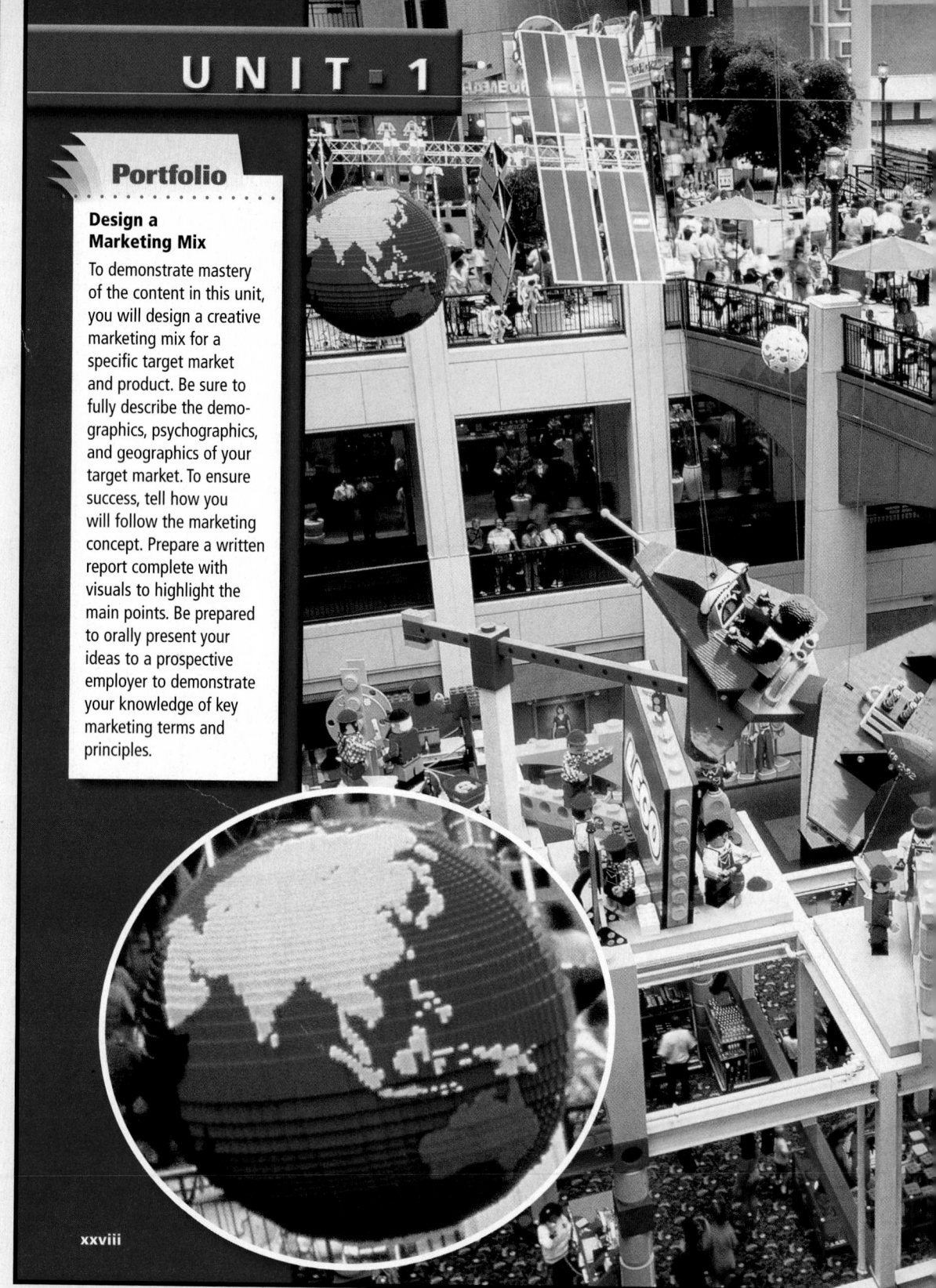

U N I T · 1

Portfolio

Design a Marketing Mix

To demonstrate mastery of the content in this unit, you will design a creative marketing mix for a specific target market and product. Be sure to fully describe the demographics, psychographics, and geographics of your target market. To ensure success, tell how you will follow the marketing concept. Prepare a written report complete with visuals to highlight the main points. Be prepared to orally present your ideas to a prospective employer to demonstrate your knowledge of key marketing terms and principles.

xxviii

Field Trip Suggestions

Plan a Trip to a Local Mall Have your students work in teams and look for examples of the nine marketing functions and five economic utilities. On the next day of class, have each team report their findings. Follow with a general discussion of marketing functions and economic utilities.

- Chapter 1 *Marketing Is All Around Us*
- Chapter 2 *Basic Marketing Concepts*

The World of Marketing

Unit Overview

Marketing activities are found in every type of business enterprise. In this unit, you will learn key marketing concepts that will be revisited throughout this textbook.

Through your exploration of Chapter 1, you will learn the benefits of marketing to our society and to you personally. You will also see just how many career options are available in this broad field of study. Chapter 2 lays the foundation for further study of marketing principles and practices. You will learn how marketing decisions are made and what factors go into those decisions. You will also learn the various marketing strategies businesses use to identify their customers and other essential topics, such as the marketing concept, the marketing mix, market segmentation, and target marketing.

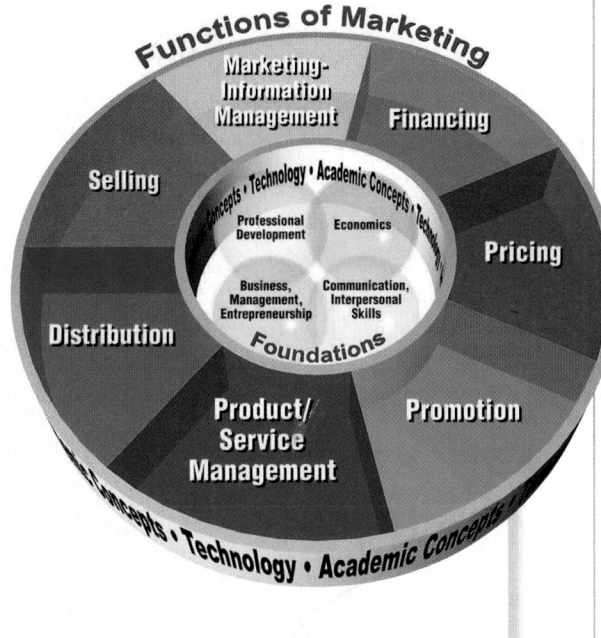

In this Unit:

Foundations of Marketing

- Professional Development
- Business, Management, Entrepreneurship
- Economics

Functions of Marketing

- Pricing
- Promotion
- Selling

Unit Project

After completing the unit, have students select the DECA competitive area in which they want to compete. Have them interview a person employed in that area. Students should draft questions relating to the information in Chapters 1 and 2. After they have conducted their interviews, ask students to share their research.

www Go to the *Marketing Essentials* Web site (**www.marketing.glencoe. com**) for resources to teach and assess occupation-specific vocabulary.

Unit Closure

Have each student select a consumer item that can be demonstrated in class, such as a book, pen, grooming aid, or hat. Ask students to conduct library or Internet research to determine to whom their item was marketed when it first appeared (original customer profile) and to whom it is marketed today (current customer profile). Have students determine how the product has changed over the years. Ask: What features have been added to the product and/or packaging that increase the product's usefulness? How have these changes added value to the product?

Guest Speaker Suggestions

Local Business Owners Invite a panel of local business owners to discuss marketing and its functions as they relate to their businesses. To be most effective, you should include owners or managers of a wide variety of businesses.

Chapter Overview ✓

Chapter 1 sets the stage for the study of marketing and the exploration of marketing as a career. It presents an overview of the marketing process in daily life, identifies the four foundations and seven functions of marketing, and discusses the economic benefits of marketing. The chapter concludes with reasons for studying marketing and career information.

 ## Springboard ✓

Brainstorm Ask students why they are taking the course. Write all answers on the board. Then tell students that no matter what careers they choose, this course will help them develop the basic skills, thinking skills, and personal qualities needed to succeed in school and the workplace. A secondary benefit is that they will be informed, proactive consumers and voters.

Prereading ✓

List the section objectives to discuss with students. Have students skim the chapter, looking at the pictures, reading the captions, and noting the headings. Ask questions to ensure that students have a minimal understanding of the chapter structure.

Preteaching ✓
Marketing Vocabulary

List the vocabulary words on the board. Tell students to draw a picture that represents each concept. Have students share their pictures and concepts.

Marketing:
What It Takes
Answer It entails developing, promoting, and distributing products to satisfy customers' needs and wants. The seven functions should be considered: distribution, financing, marketing-information management, pricing, product/service management, promotion, and selling.

Marketing Is All Around Us

Marketing: What It Takes

Toy Story
Each holiday season, a toy emerges from obscurity to become the holiday item that everybody wants. Poo-chi, Furby, Tickle Me Elmo, Pokemon, Beanie Babies, and Cabbage Patch dolls are just a few examples of this phenomenon. You think you have an idea for a unique toy that could be the next big thing. You know marketing is essential to your toy's success.

WHAT WILL YOU DO?
What does marketing entail? What functions of marketing must you consider to make your toy the next holiday phenomenon?

2

THE DECA CONNECTION
ADVISOR CORNER

Induction Ceremonies Conduct an induction and installation ceremony for your new chapter officers and members. Make the ceremony as nice as possible, including a guest speaker, handing out impressive certificates, presenting members with DECA membership pins and cards, and possibly serving refreshments. Require your chapter members to dress professionally for the event. Invite the principal and other key players to attend the ceremony. For guidance with conducting these types of ceremonies and other chapter events, DECA Images has a *Chapter Management System* that provides valuable tools for managing your chapter. To order, contact DECA at **www.deca.org**. *Cyndee Richards, Chesapeake H. S., Pasadena, MD.*

Defining Marketing

What Is Marketing?

Marketing is the process of developing, promoting, and distributing products to satisfy customers' needs and wants. **Products** include goods and services, both of which have monetary value and satisfy customers' needs and wants. **Goods** are the kinds of things you can touch or hold in your hand. Hammers, automobiles, soft drinks, clothing, and computers are goods. **Services** are the kinds of things you can't physically touch. Services are tasks performed for a customer. Dry cleaners, amusement parks, income tax preparers, and movie theaters provide services.

Marketing helps connect businesses to their customers. After goods are created, they are sent to the marketplace where they are made available to consumers. The marketplace is the commercial environment where exchanges are made. An **exchange** takes place every time something is sold in the marketplace.

■ Marketing and You

When you carefully consider the definition of marketing, you'll realize that you experience marketing principles and techniques daily. Let's look at an average day to discover all the ways that marketing touches you.

When you wake up in the morning, you go to the kitchen for breakfast. Perhaps you look at cereals, all with different ingredients and packaging. Think ahead to the products you will use this morning—shampoo, soap, toothpaste—they are all created to meet your needs. *Product planning* and *packaging* are part of marketing.

You check the newspaper for last night's sports news. It's filled with national and local retail advertising. One ad in particular might catch your attention, so you ask a few friends to go with you to the mall after school. *Advertising* is part of marketing.

You go to the mall, where all of the retail stores that help to distribute manufacturer's products are part of marketing. At the mall, enticing window displays encourage you to enter certain stores. Some of the stores have sales featuring price reductions of 20 to 50 percent. *Displays* and *promotional techniques* are part of marketing.

You are greeted in the store by a sales associate who is ready to assist you with your purchase decisions. *Personal selling* is part of marketing.

Did you see trucks on your way to the mall? Those trucks were moving goods from producers of products to consumers. Those products were sold to other businesses for resale or use. During the buying-selling process, prices and delivery as well as credit terms were decided. All those *selling* and *distribution* functions are part of marketing.

What You'll Learn

- The meaning of marketing
- The foundations of marketing
- The functions of marketing

Why It's Important

To be successful in business requires being marketing oriented. Learning how businesses and people operate from a marketing point of view will help you in all your future endeavors. You will also get a good idea of whether marketing is a potential career for you.

Key Terms

- marketing
- products
- goods
- services
- exchange

Chapter 1 ■ *Marketing Is All Around Us* **3**

FOCUS

🔔 Bell Ringer Activity ✓

Analyze Ask students to tell you what the foundation of a building is. (*It is the underlying groundwork or base of support.*) Then ask students how you would create a building without first creating a foundation. (*It is not possible if you want the structure to be solid and enduring.*) Explain that in this chapter they will begin to lay the groundwork (or foundation) for their knowledge of marketing.

Introducing the Section ✓

Defining Marketing Tell students that they will build their knowledge of marketing on not one but four foundations: economics, communication and interpersonal skills, business management and entrepreneurship, and professional development. Draw each foundation in a separate circle (see the marketing wheel for a model) while students do the same on a sheet of paper. Tell students they will study further these foundations in Units 2, 3, and 4, but that the concepts are woven throughout the course.

Now draw the outer rim of the wheel and divide it into seven sections. Have students do the same on their papers. Explain that all marketing activities are classified into seven functions that connect the people who make products (business) with those who buy them (customers). In this section, they will look at each function and fill them in on their papers as the lesson progresses.

TEACH

📊 Technology Resources ✓

PowerPoint The *Marketing Essentials* PowerPoint Presentation CD-ROM provides visual lecture aids for every chapter section.

Classroom Resources

For the Teacher
- Teacher Editions for all workbooks ✓
- Assessment Package ✓
- PowerPoint Presentation Software
- Interactive Lesson Planner ✓
- ILP Block Scheduling, p. 1
- ILP Lesson Plans, p. 1 ✓
- ILP Internet Resources, p. 21 ✓

- ILP *BusinessWeek* Case Studies, p. 1
- ILP Marketing Career Portfolio, p. 31
- *Marketing Essentials* Web site (**www.marketing.glencoe.com**)

For the Student
- Student Activity Workbook, p. 1
- Marketing Math Workbook, p. 1

- Marketing Research Project Workbook, p. 1
- ILP School-to-Work Activity Workbook, p. 1
- Virtual Business simulation
- *Marketing Essentials* Web site (**www.marketing.glencoe.com**)

ILP These resources are available in print and on the Interactive Lesson Planner (ILP)

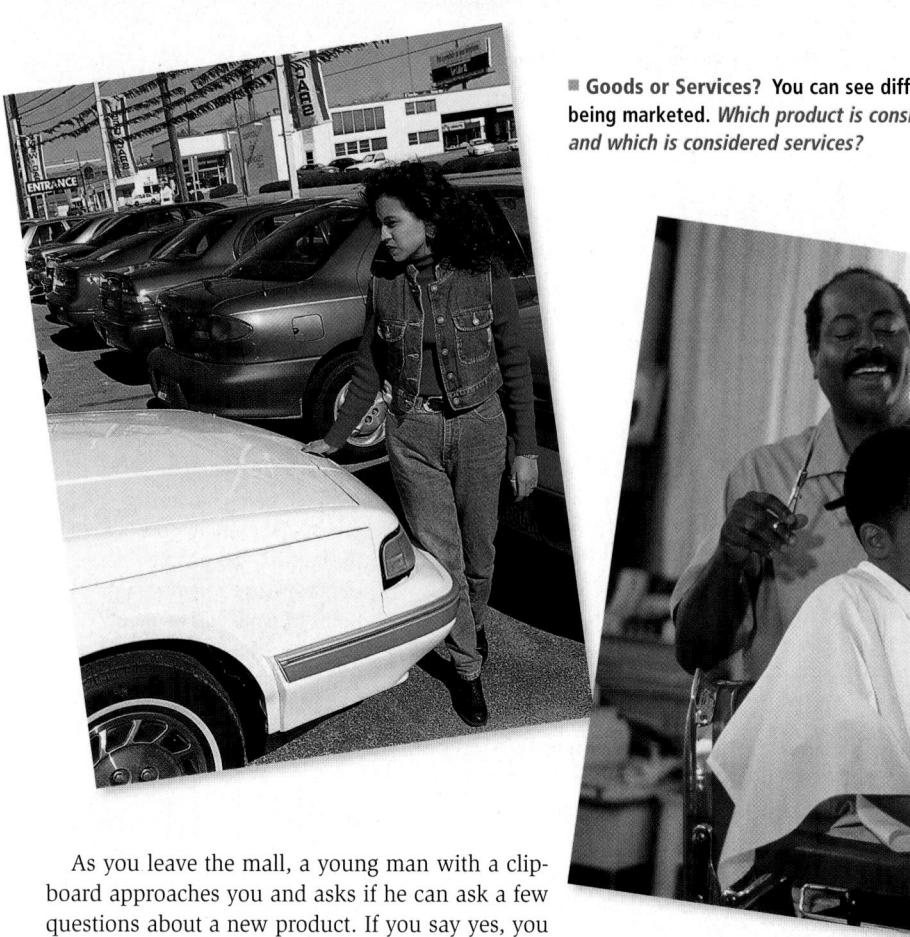

■ **Goods or Services?** You can see different products being marketed. *Which product is considered goods and which is considered services?*

As you leave the mall, a young man with a clipboard approaches you and asks if he can ask a few questions about a new product. If you say yes, you are participating in a *marketing research* study. Why does the company doing the research want your viewpoint? You are part of a *target audience* and you might consider buying its product. *Marketing research* is part of marketing.

As you can see, marketing is truly all around us. If you look for it, you will realize that you observe marketing every day.

■ Foundations of Marketing

As you begin to study marketing, you will learn the four basic *foundations* of marketing. You will see how building on these foundations helps you to acquire marketing skills that are relevant to your own career development.

The topics you will study in *Marketing Essentials* are based on these foundations of marketing:

- *Business, Management, Entrepreneurship*— Understanding the basics of business, management, and entrepreneurial concepts that affect business decision making.
- *Communication and Interpersonal Skills*— Understanding concepts, strategies, and systems needed to interact effectively with others.
- *Economics*—Understanding the economic principles and concepts that are basic to marketing.
- *Professional Development*—Understanding concepts and strategies needed for career exploration, development, and growth.

4 Unit 1 ■ *The World of Marketing*

GREAT IDEAS **from the Marketing Classroom**

Lucinda Mason
Demopolis High School
Demopolis, AL

After studying the marketplace functions, I use this exercise as reinforcement. Put students into groups of three or four and give each half of a poster board. Assign each group one of the marketing functions. A member of the group will write the name of the function on the poster board and the group will then define the function. After two or three minutes, the poster board will be passed to the next group who will add a simple example. The next group will draw an illustration of the function. Finally, the next group will write a short role-play that illustrates the function.

■ **Marketing Functions** Many marketing functions are evident in grocery stores. *What marketing functions are illustrated here?*

■ Functions of Marketing

All of the marketing activities that you encounter daily can be classified into the seven *functions* of marketing. These can be seen on the marketing wheel that is featured in the unit overview of each unit of *Marketing Essentials*. The seven functions are the categories that make up the wheel's outer wedges. They include distribution, financing, marketing information management, pricing, product/service management, promotion, and selling. These functions define marketing as it is applied in business operations. Functions address marketing from the perspective of how it is practiced. Each function is viewed from its relationship to the marketing of a good, service, or idea.

Distribution involves deciding where and to whom products need to be sold in order to reach the final users. The logistics of physically moving and storing goods are also part of distribution planning. Primary methods of transportation are by truck, rail, ship, or air. Some large retail chains store products in central warehouses for later distribution. Distribution also involves the systems that track products so that they can be located at any time.

Financing is getting the money that is necessary to pay for the operation of a business. Business owners often obtain bank loans to start a new business. Some also form corporations and sell shares of the business, or stock. Financing also involves decisions about whether to offer credit to customers. Most retailers offer customers payment options such as MasterCard or Visa, while some other stores offer their own credit services.

Getting the necessary information to make sound business decisions is known as *Marketing Information Management*. Most of this information is obtained through marketing research. Have you ever been asked to complete a questionnaire about the service at a restaurant or other type of business? If so, you have participated in marketing research. Companies conduct marketing research to learn more about their customers' preferences and how to better market products.

Pricing decisions dictate how much to charge for goods and services in order to maximize profits. Most pricing decisions are based on competitive pricing and determining how much customers are willing to pay. Other pricing goals include gaining

---

CAPTION ANSWER
Marketing Functions Selling, packaging, pricing, displays, and promotional techniques are illustrated in this picture.

Independent Practice ✓

Research and Review Have students take a mental walk through the local business district and list 20 products sold there. Then have them label each product as a good or a service. Review these lists in class.

Individualized Practice

Communication Skills

Students should know the seven functions of marketing without referring to their texts. To help them reach this point, have them list the functions on a sheet of paper and create a mnemonic device, a word or image that will help them remember each function. (For example, the image of a cash register might evoke selling.)

L1 Divide students into pairs. Have each student explain his or her mnemonic devices to the other student. After hearing the whole list, the listener should try to recite it back without having taken any notes. How many tries did it take for each listener to get the whole list correct?

L2 Ask students to answer these questions either orally or on paper:

- Did you find this exercise difficult or easy? Why?

- Tell some practical ways you could increase your memory skills. *(For example, you could read an article in the newspaper and then try to recall as much of the content as possible.)*

L3 Have students think of reasons why good memory skills are important on the job. Discuss their reasons in class. *(Answers will vary but could include the importance of remembering employer policies, safety and security procedures, how to operate equipment, instructions from upper management and supervisors, and customer requests for goods or services that your business should carry or provide.)*

ASSESS

Reteaching ✓

Fact and Idea Assign and review Fact and Idea Review questions 1 and 2 from the Chapter Assessment.

Enrichment ✓

1. **Extend** Assign and review the corresponding activities from *BusinessWeek Case Studies* and *Internet Resources.* **ILP**
2. **Review** Assign and review the appropriate Thinking Critically questions from the Chapter Assessment.

Evaluation ✓

Assign and review the Section 1.1 Assessment.

Technology Resources ✓

> **GO TO** **Assessment Resources**
> Go to the *Marketing Essentials* Web site (**www.marketing.glencoe. com**) for resources to teach and assess occupation-specific vocabulary.

CLOSE

Section Wrap-Up ✓

Have students complete this statement: Marketing is . . . *(the process of developing, promoting, and distributing products in order to satisfy customers' needs and wants.)*

When in Germany
Answer Germans may be wrongfully stereotyped as unfriendly because they typically do not display affection in public.

market share and achieving a certain return on an investment. Pricing concepts and strategies are utilized in determining and adjusting prices to maximize return and meet customers' perceptions of value.

Product/Service Management is obtaining, developing, maintaining, and improving a product or a *product mix* in response to market opportunities. Product/Service Management decisions are most often made on the basis of marketing research, which highlights consumer needs and wants.

Communicating with potential customers to inform, persuade, or remind them about a business's products makes up *promotion*. Television and radio commercials are forms of promotion known as advertising. Promotion is carried out in other media, including print and online. Promotion is used to improve a company's public image—such as showing that the company is socially responsible, perhaps by recycling materials or cleaning up the environment. This is known as public relations. Promotion concepts and strategies are used to communicate information about products, services, images, and/or ideas to achieve a desired outcome.

Selling provides customers with goods and services they want. This includes selling in the retail market to you, the customer, and selling in the business-to-business market to industrial users. Selling concepts and activities are used to determine client needs and wants and respond through

Life In The Diverse MARKETPLACE

When In Germany

When you see a friend walking down the street, do you wave to say hello? If you were in Germany, that would be considered rude! To get someone's attention in Germany, you should raise your hand, palm facing out, with only the index finger extended. While Germans are very open and friendly with close friends, they frown upon grand shows of affection in public. Only the rude and impolite would shout or wave. This does not mean that Germans are cold or unfriendly, it is just a different manner of greeting.

Thinking Critically
Why might someone stereotype Germans as cold or unfriendly? Would this be a correct judgment?

planned, personalized communication that influences purchasing decisions and enhances future business opportunities. It also includes selling in the business-to-business (industrial) market where products are purchased for use in business operations.

1.1 ASSESSMENT

Reviewing Key Terms and Concepts

1. What is an exchange?
2. Which of the seven functions of marketing were illustrated in the average day described in this section?
3. Which of the seven functions of marketing were not illustrated in that same discussion?

Thinking Critically

4. How is a presidential political campaign an example of marketing?

Integrating Academic Skills

5. **COMMUNICATION** Write three questions that could be used to survey students' satisfaction with the prices, selection, and quality of food served in your school cafeteria.

1.1 ASSESSMENT ANSWERS

Reviewing Key Terms and Concepts
1. An exchange is the sale of something in the marketplace.
2. The marketing functions described were distribution, marketing-information management, pricing, product/service management, promotion, and selling.
3. Financing was not illustrated in the discussion.

Thinking Critically
4. Answers will vary. A presidential political campaign involves the process of planning and executing ideas (campaign promises). The exchange process involves votes instead of money.

Integrating Academic Skills
5. **COMMUNICATION** Questions will vary.

Economic Utilities

Economic Benefits of Marketing

Have you ever thought about the benefits of marketing to businesses and to you personally? Marketing bridges the gap between you and the maker or seller of an item. Marketing makes buying easy for customers. It also creates new and improved products at lower prices.

■ Added Value

The functions of marketing add value to a product. That added value in economic terms is called utility. Utilities are the attributes of a product or service that make it capable of satisfying consumers' wants and needs.

There are five economic utilities involved with all products—form, place, time, possession, and information. Form utility is the only one that is not directly related to marketing; the remaining four are marketing utilities.

FORM UTILITY Form utility involves changing raw materials or putting parts together to make them more useful. In other words, it deals with making, or producing, things.

Let's look at a tree to determine its utility. In its original state, a tree has value as an object of beauty. A tree prevents soil erosion, provides homes for animals, and produces oxygen for us to breathe. When the tree is cut down to use in making other products, however, its usefulness changes. Lumber from the tree might be used to make pencils, paper, furniture, and buildings. The raw material (wood) becomes part of finished items that have a different value to us than the raw material itself.

The same would be true if a manufacturer were assembling parts into a product. The parts of a lounge chair—the wood frame, the fabric used for the upholstery, the glue and nails used to hold the parts together, and the reclining mechanism—are less useful by themselves. Putting them together adds form utility.

PLACE UTILITY Place utility involves having a product where customers can buy it. Businesses study consumer shopping habits to determine the most convenient and efficient locations to sell products. Some businesses use a direct approach by selling their products through catalogs, and other businesses rely on retailers to sell their products.

TIME UTILITY Time utility is having a product available at a certain time of year or a convenient time of day. Marketers increase the value of products by having them available when consumers want them. In order to achieve that goal, marketers must plan their operations in advance.

● What You'll Learn

- The benefits of marketing
- The meaning of economic utility
- The five economic utilities and how to distinguish the four that are related to marketing

● Why It's Important

By understanding the benefits of marketing, you will see how the functions of marketing add value to products. You will also see how marketing activities lead to lower prices and new and improved products.

● Key Terms

- utility
- form utility
- place utility
- time utility
- possession utility
- information utility

FOCUS

Bell Ringer Activity ✓

Brainstorm Have students help you generate a list on the board of at least five products that students and/or faculty in your school would want to buy at your school site and use daily or weekly. Have students choose one product for this activity.

Introducing the Section ✓✓

Economic Utilities Using the product chosen for the Bell Ringer Activity, ask students to answer the following questions. Write their answers on the board, dividing them into columns by economic utility.

1. What raw materials went into the making of this product? (*Form utility*)
2. Where would you place (distribute) this product so your customers would have access to purchasing it? (*Place utility*)
3. When would be the best time of day to sell this product? The best time of year? (*Time utility*)
4. How would students and/or faculty pay for this product? (*Possession utility*)
5. How would you get information about this product to your potential customers? (*Information utility*)

Tell students that by answering the questions above, they have told how they would add economic value—or economic utility—to a product so that it can be sold.

TEACH

📊 Technology Resources ✓

PowerPoint The *Marketing Essentials* PowerPoint Presentation CD-ROM provides visual lecture aids for every chapter section.

Classroom Resources

For the Teacher
- Teacher Editions for all workbooks
- Assessment Package
- PowerPoint Presentation Software
- Interactive Lesson Planner
- ILP Block Scheduling, p. 1
- ILP Lesson Plans, p. 2
- ILP Internet Resources, p. 21

- ILP Blackline Masters, p. 1
- ILP *BusinessWeek* Case Studies, p. 1
- ILP Marketing Career Portfolio, p. 31
- *Marketing Essentials* Web site (**www.marketing.glencoe.com**)

For the Student
- Student Activity Workbook, p. 1
- Marketing Math Workbook, p. 1

- Marketing Research Project Workbook, p. 1
- ILP School-to-Work Activity Workbook, p. 1
- Virtual Business simulation
- *Marketing Essentials* Web site (**www.marketing.glencoe.com**)

ILP These resources are available in print and on the Interactive Lesson Planner (ILP)

Concept Development ✓

1. Read Section 1.2 with students.
2. Have students read aloud the Case Study and review the answers in class.

Discussion Starter ✓

Utilities Have students describe which of the four utilities are created by the work they do in their co-op jobs. *(Answers will vary. One possibility is: "In my job, I arrange products in displays at the ends of aisles and by the cash registers. This adds information utility because the displays inform consumers of the products and their features or special prices.")*

Consider toy manufacturers and retailers. Toy manufacturers introduce their new products to retailers each February at a toy fair held in New York City. That is when retailers decide which products they will sell during the holiday season nine months later.

Retailers also offer convenient shopping hours to accommodate their customers. Mall stores are generally open 10 a.m. to 9 p.m., and some convenience stores are open 24 hours a day.

POSSESSION UTILITY How do you come into possession of the items you want? Unless they are given to you as a gift, you generally buy them for a price. The exchange of a product for some monetary value is possession utility.

Retailers may accept alternatives to cash, like personal checks or credit cards, in exchange for their merchandise. They may even offer installment or layaway plans (delayed possession in return for gradual payment). Every one of these options adds value to the product being purchased. In fact, without these options, some customers would not be able to buy the items they want.

In business-to-business situations, companies also grant their customers credit. They may give them a certain period (for example, 30 days) to pay a bill. This adds value to the products they sell.

Possession utility is involved every time legal ownership of a product changes hands. Possession utility increases as purchase options increase.

INFORMATION UTILITY Information utility involves communication with the consumer. Salespeople provide information to customers by explaining the features and benefits of products. Displays communicate information, too. Packaging and labeling inform consumers about qualities and uses of a product. The label on a frozen food entree will tell you the ingredients, nutritional information, directions for preparation, and any safety precautions needed. Advertising informs consumers about products, tells where to buy products, and sometimes tells how much products cost. Many manufacturers provide owners' manuals that explain how to use their products.

Businesses must transform materials into products that have value and use in order to experience successful sales. They do this by employing the five economic utilities. Figure 1-1 on page 9 presents an overview of this process using a single product as an example.

■ Lower Prices

Marketing activities add value to products and increase demand. When demand is high,

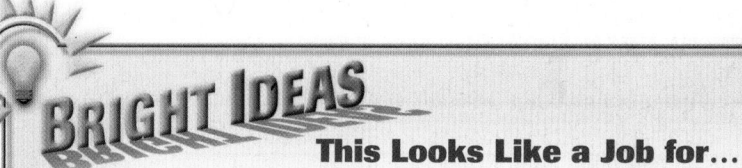

This Looks Like a Job for...

It's a bird! It's a plane! It's Superman! Created by then-teenagers Jerry Siegel and Joe Shuster, the legend of Superman has endured for over 60 years, although the character of Superman has had many incarnations. The first Superman was a bald villain with mental powers who appeared in a fanzine called "Reign of the Superman." Later that year, he was molded into a rugged world-traveler, but he didn't catch on with readers. In 1934, Siegel and Shuster created the definitive version of Superman. They tried to sell their creation as a syndicated comic strip, but it was rejected by newspaper editors who thought that a man in a bright red and blue outfit looked ridiculous. In 1938, an editor looking for something new featured Superman in *Action Comics #1*. The superhero became an instant success! Superman has gone on to star in radio, television, cartoons, and major motion pictures.

Thinking Creatively

Create a new superhero. Think about Siegel and Shuster's trials and errors. How would you market your new hero?

 BRIGHT IDEAS **This Looks Like a Job for . . .**
Answer Ideas will vary.

FIGURE 1-1
ECONOMIC UTILITIES

Economic utilities reflect the value that producers and marketers add to raw materials when they make them into products and offer them for sale to the public. Consider a backpack like the one you use to carry books.

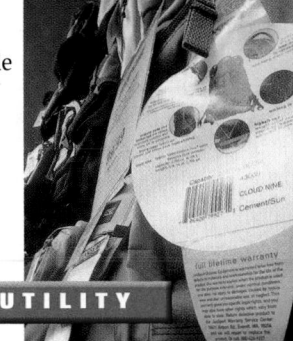

FORM UTILITY

Fabric, leather, thread, zippers, and dye are useless to a student in their raw forms. However, once processed and put together, they have increased value (or utility) as a backpack.

INFORMATION UTILITY

To encourage sales, retailers may feature information about products and special offers and inform potential customers through ads, signs, or displays.

PLACE UTILITY

The manufacturers ship their backpacks to retail businesses—sporting goods stores, drugstores, school bookstores, and mass merchandisers that make them available to consumers.

TIME UTILITY

Retailers selling backpacks stock them regularly but may offer larger supplies in late summer, near the beginning of the school year.

POSSESSION UTILITY

As part of the actual sales transaction, the customer pays for the backpack (with cash, check, credit card, or debit card) and takes possession of it.

Chapter 1 ■ *Marketing Is All Around Us* **9**

SECTION 1.2

Thinking Critically ✓

Lower Prices Have students name some products whose prices have dropped significantly over the years as a result of their increasing popularity and increasing competition in the marketplace. *(Answers will vary but could include CD players, telephone answering machines, cellular telephones, pagers, stereo equipment, FAX machines, software, and home exercise equipment.)*

Independent Practice ✓

Analyze Choose a local business and describe how it provides the marketing utilities discussed in this chapter for three products.

ASSESS

Reteaching ✓

1. **Vocabulary** Assign and review the vocabulary terms for this section.
2. **Fact and Idea** Assign and review Fact and Idea Review questions 3–7 from the Chapter Assessment.
3. **Utilities** Have students name two products to which marketers add time utility, place utility, possession utility, and information utility. *(Answers will vary but could include holiday merchandise [time utility]; soft drinks and workout clothing in a health club, batteries in a toy store [place utility]; layaway plans for clothing purchases, 90 days/same as cash deals on major appliances [possession utility]; written labels and warnings on over-the-counter medications, owner manuals from product manufacturers [information utility].)*

Did You Know?

Very few manufacturers do anything in real time. Fashion retailers buy at least six months to one year ahead of a season. Magazines are produced six months prior to publication, requiring editors to celebrate the Fourth of July in December. Textbooks are traditionally published to be available the spring before the fall of their intended use.

SECTION 1.2

Enrichment

1. **Extend** Assign and review the corresponding activity from the *School-to-Work Activity Workbook.* **ILP**
2. **Review** Assign and review the appropriate Thinking Critically questions from the Chapter Assessment.
3. **Research and Summarize** Many stores add possession utility by offering payment plans. Have students research three stores to determine what payment plans each offers. Then have them write a 100-word summary of the plans.

Evaluation

Assign and review the Section 1.2 Assessment.

Technology Resources

 Assessment Resources
Go to the *Marketing Essentials* Web site (**www.marketing.glencoe. com**) for resources to teach and assess occupation-specific vocabulary.

CLOSE

Section Wrap-Up

Have students complete the following statement: The functions of marketing add value to a product by making it more useful. This added value is also called . . . (*utility.*)

Pick a Card—Any Card!

Answer Answers will vary. Because the Talking Online Business Card is not tangible, the customer may delete the e-mail or forget about the business. The CD-ROM card could malfunction.

10

manufacturers can make products in larger quantities, which reduces the unit cost of each product. This is because the fixed costs—such as the rent on a building—remain the same whether the company produces 10 units or 10,000 units. When a company produces a larger quantity of a product, it spends less per unit on fixed costs. The company can charge a lower price per unit, sell more units, and make more money.

Here is an example using a fixed cost of $20,000.

Quantity Produced	Fixed Cost Per Unit
10,000	$2.00
200,000	.10

As you can see, the increased quantity significantly reduces the fixed cost per unit.

In addition, when products become popular, more competitors enter the marketplace. To remain competitive, marketers find ways to lower their prices. For example, when they were first introduced, videocassette recorders were priced at more than $600. Now you can purchase a VCR for as little as $100. That's one-sixth of the original price!

■ New and Improved Products

New and improved products are another result of increased competition generated by marketing. As businesses continue to look for opportunities to better satisfy customers' wants and needs, the result is a larger variety of goods and services. For example, personal computers have gotten smaller, more powerful, and less expensive. More people use computers, and this market continues to grow.

A review of detergents demonstrates the change in consumer preference and competition in that market. For years, only powder detergents were available; now, consumers can choose between

Pick a Card—Any Card!

Some people think business is a matter of playing your cards right—and a new generation of business cards is making business a whole lot more interesting. The wallet-size CD-ROM card, which looks like a thick credit card, plays in a CD-ROM tray for either PCs or Macs. It holds enough information for several minutes of text, animation, and graphics. Water Design in New York uses a CD-ROM card in its campus-recruiting program. Maryland-based Ideal-Link uses CD-ROM technology as a calling card for its Networking Mobile Web and IT Reference Library. The Talking Online Business Card combines e-mail technology and sounds files, eliminating the need for a card altogether! CD-ROM technology has upped the ante in business—but who knows how the rules may change in the future.

Thinking Critically
Compare and contrast the advantages and disadvantages of the CD-ROM card to the Talking Online Business Card. Which would work better for a large business? A small business?

powder and liquid detergents. They can also choose other options like detergent with bleach and unscented detergent. Easy-to-use containers with measuring caps demonstrate how marketers have responded to changing consumer trends.

1.2 ASSESSMENT

Reviewing Key Terms and Concepts

1. What is meant by the economic concept of utility?
2. Which economic utility is not classified as a marketing utility? Why?
3. Besides added value, what are two other benefits of marketing?

Thinking Critically

4. Explain the following statement: Marketing is more than just promotion.

Integrating Academic Skills

5. **MATH** Fixed costs for manufacturing widgets are $25,000. Determine the fixed cost per unit when the quantity produced is (a) 5,000 and (b) 75,000.

10 Unit 1 ■ *The World of Marketing*

1.2 ASSESSMENT ANSWERS

Reviewing Key Terms and Concepts
1. Utility means value added usefulness.
2. Form utility is not classified as a marketing utility because it is concerned with production of a product.
3. Lower prices and the creation of new and improved products are two other benefits or marketing.

Thinking Critically
4. Marketing includes all activities from the conception of a product to its final consumption.

Integrating Academic Skills
5. **MATH** $25,000 ÷ 5,000 = $5
$25,000 ÷ 75,000 = $.33

Careers in Marketing

Why Study Marketing?

By studying marketing, you will have the opportunity to evaluate marketing as a potential career. Even if you don't think marketing is for you, you will learn how important it is for personal success. The skills and knowledge you gain from studying marketing will help you in school and on the job.

Marketing skills are useful in any career because they involve understanding business, as well as relating and communicating effectively with others. These are basic skills that employers expect from all levels of employees.

Through the study of marketing, you will learn how businesses function on a day-to-day basis. In order to apply marketing practices in our free enterprise system, you must understand how businesses operate.

Marketing is communicating. A businessperson's ability to present ideas to employees, customers, and others has a direct impact on a business's success or failure.

Interpersonal skills are another important element of studying marketing. Understanding the techniques and principles of human relations will improve your ability to get along with others. This will help you in your dealings with supervisors, coworkers, customers, and friends.

Is Marketing a Career for You?

Throughout this text, you will have opportunities to investigate marketing careers through the *Careers in Marketing* feature. By the time you have finished studying this text, you will have a good idea of the vast array of marketing careers and some that may be the right career choice for you.

■ An Overview of Marketing Careers

About 33 million Americans earn a living in marketing. Marketing provides a great diversity of opportunities in any career field—from buying merchandise to being the president of a company, from selling clothes to designing ads.

Careers in marketing include all the activities required to plan, develop, promote, and distribute goods and services to consumers. When considered in this broad sense, marketing activities account for about one in every three jobs in the United States.

• What You'll Learn

- The importance of marketing careers to the U.S. economy
- The benefits of working in marketing
- Employment opportunities for people trained in marketing
- Examples of jobs within marketing occupational areas and at different skill levels

• Why It's Important

You'll want to learn about the requirements, opportunities, rewards, and trends of marketing if you are considering a career in this exciting field.

Key Terms

- benefits
- occupational area

FOCUS

Bell Ringer Activity

Write Have students write one marketplace trend that they have observed through reading news publications, watching television, or observing the local economy. *(Examples may include proliferation of computers of all sizes and vehicles for communication, such as modems, laptop computers, cellular phones, use of the Internet for business, shopping, and entertainment, computer games.)*

Introducing the Section

Careers in Marketing This section looks at the varied employment opportunities in marketing and the benefits of a marketing career.

Make a board list of the trends that students generate. Then have students generate ways employment trends follow marketing trends. *(Answers will vary. One example may be increased need for computer technicians, programmers, as well as general computer competency required in all jobs.)*

Chapter 1 ■ *Marketing Is All Around Us* **11**

Classroom Resources

For the Teacher
- Teacher Editions for all workbooks
- Assessment Package
- PowerPoint Presentation Software
- Interactive Lesson Planner
- **ILP** Block Scheduling, p. 1
- **ILP** Lesson Plans, p. 3
- **ILP** Internet Resources, p. 21

- **ILP** Blackline Masters, p. 1
- **ILP** *BusinessWeek* Case Studies, p. 1
- **ILP** Marketing Career Portfolio, p. 31
- *Marketing Essentials* Web site (**www.marketing.glencoe.com**)

For the Student
- Student Activity Workbook, p. 1
- Marketing Math Workbook, p. 1

- Marketing Research Project Workbook, p. 1
- **ILP** School-to-Work Activity Workbook, p. 1
- Virtual Business simulation
- *Marketing Essentials* Web site (**www.marketing.glencoe.com**)

ILP These resources are available in print and on the Interactive Lesson Planner (ILP)

Concept Development

1. Read Section 1.3 with students.
2. Your students will benefit from taking an occupational interest survey. California Testing Bureau/McGraw-Hill (CTB), (800) 538-9547, offers the Kuder Occupational Interest Survey, which is especially useful for high school students who are identifying potential careers, setting career goals, and making choices about advanced education. CTB also offers the Kuder Preference Record that measures students' preferences in ten broad career areas.
3. Have your school guidance counselor discuss with your students the advantages of having a career goal. He or she should also discuss how to set short-term and long-range goals in anticipation of reaching a career goal. Finally, this person should discuss how the guidance department in your school can facilitate career exploration.

Case Study

"Fad to Stay" or "Fade Away"?

Bell bottoms, cargo pants, acid washed jeans, virtual pets—these are just some fads that have passed in and out of popular culture. *Fads* are briefly popular fashions or crazes that benefit producers, wholesalers, and retailers. The challenge is to market these products so that their appeal lasts.

Push scooters from Taiwan illustrate this kind of marketing opportunity. Lightweight, foldable, and fun, these scooters became wildly popular among American kids in 2000. They appeal to the market of bicycle owners, skaters, and skateboard enthusiasts.

Smart marketing, however, is aimed at broadening the consumer base. One company is designing push scooters with larger platforms to accommodate larger feet. Larger wheels on these new models address safety issues. Another company is marketing a scooter with three wheels to increase stability. These changes appeal to adult consumers. Advertising campaigns address adult consumers by stressing the ease of transportation and fewer parking problems when commuting by push scooter. Upscale models with more features are planned to appeal to an even broader market.

Although marketing campaigns stress safety features such as handlebars and low platforms, experts do not seem to agree about scooter safety. Despite that, production companies and thousands of retailers hope that this fad will not fizzle.

Case Study Review

1. How does the evolution of push scooters support the theory that marketing helps to create new and improved products?
2. Two appeals of scooters are that they are inexpensive and maintenance free. Is it wise for manufacturers to add "upscale" features that increase price and maintenance? Why or why not?

A MATTER OF ETHICS

3. If safety experts do not agree that push scooters are safe, is it ethical to promote their safety in ad campaigns? How might advertisers improve safety in the use of these products?

■ Employment Trends

According to the Bureau of Labor Statistics (BLS), employment in marketing and sales is projected to increase 20.6 percent in the period 1992–2005 (2,671,000 new jobs). During that same time period, employment in service-related industries is expected to increase 33.4 percent (6,462,000 new jobs).

The occupational structure of employment opportunity in marketing is based on the type of employment, regardless of the industry. This measure indicates that there has been an increase in managerial, sales, and service positions in all industries. Department of Labor projections indicate that managerial jobs in marketing-related fields will continue to be plentiful.

Case Study Review Answers

"Fad to Stay" or "Fade Away"?

1. Safety and comfort were improved because of marketing.
2. Answers will vary.

A MATTER OF ETHICS

3. Answers will vary. Marketers can contribute to the safe use of the product by suggesting that riders wear protective gear and obey traffic laws.

Job opportunities in marketing are growing, while those in production are decreasing. This is because production jobs lend themselves to automation and mechanization. In recent years, the number of production workers in many companies has been reduced. Marketing, on the other hand, has not been mechanized as much because it requires personal contact.

As an example, consider the use of computers. A single computer and a series of industrial robots can replace a whole production line of workers. A computer system installed in a marketing department, however, is far more likely to enhance the capabilities of its employees than it is to replace them.

Indeed, changes in the marketplace have created the need for more, rather than fewer, marketing professionals. Factors such as changing gender roles, the rise in the number of single-parent households, changing preferences in recreational activities, and the increase in foreign competition must be monitored through market research and marketing information systems. To track these and other quickly developing trends, companies need to expand their marketing programs and staffs.

■ Benefits of a Marketing Career

Perhaps the most obvious benefit of a career in marketing is the opportunity to make an above-average income. Even in an entry-level job, however, it's nice to know that potential earnings in marketing are excellent.

Besides providing a good salary, a position in marketing may entitle you to some helpful and valuable extras. Benefits are privileges, or monetary payments beyond salary or wages, that go with a job. Examples include the use of a company car, an expense account, and bonuses for outstanding work.

In addition, most jobs in marketing, especially those beyond entry-level positions, are interesting and varied. Many involve a great deal of contact with people.

You will usually have more opportunities to advance in a marketing career than in almost any other area of business. This is because of the high visibility that many marketing positions have.

Consider a few examples. People who work in marketing frequently present and shape their ideas in meetings with company managers and executives. People who work in sales get constant feedback on their efforts in the form of sales figures that are

REAL WORLD MARKETING

Harry Potter's Secret to Promotion

Mystery and magic draw fans to Harry Potter, the fictional British schoolboy/magician. To promote the fourth book in the series and propel sales, the book's publishers, Bloomsbury and Scholastic, tried a little wizardry themselves. They cast a spell of secrecy, distributing no advance copies of the book to critics and reviewers. The plot, cover design, and even the title were all kept secret to increase anticipation and to spark the imaginations of their readers. Author J.K. Rowling had a different reason for the secrecy: Her intention was to not spoil children's enjoyment of the book with advance word about the plot.

Thinking Critically
Can you name an advertising campaign that has used secrecy to launch a product?

regularly reviewed by upper-level management. People who work in advertising may develop ad campaigns that win critical acclaim from professional associations. What all these situations make clear is that people who work in marketing do the kinds of things that command attention, especially from management. They are far more likely to be credited and rewarded for successes. In terms of a job, this means that individuals typically win promotions faster in marketing than they do in other careers.

In fact, because of their high visibility, marketing and sales careers offer the fastest route to middle and top management. A recent survey showed that more chief executive officers (CEOs) reach the top of their organizations through marketing and sales than through any other career area. Figure 1-2 on page 14 lists just a few of the companies whose CEOs fit this description. All of these CEOs earn several hundred thousand dollars per year plus bonuses—some earn millions.

Chapter 1 ■ *Marketing Is All Around Us* **13**

SECTION 1.3

4. If you have not already done so, introduce students to such classic career resources as the *Occupational Outlook Handbook.* Take them to your school library or to a public library for an introduction to the career section and to online career information services.
5. When discussing the 21 marketing occupational areas (see p. 14), introduce the five levels of employment in marketing: entry level, career sustaining, specialist, supervisor, and manager/entrepreneur.

Discussion Starter

Benefits of Work Have students identify some of the rewards and benefits of work. *(Answers may include income, perks, such as a company car and bonuses or awards for a job well done, high visibility, job satisfaction from doing what you like to do.)*

REAL WORLD MARKETING

Harry Potter's Secret to Promotion
Answer Answers will vary but can include a huge number of consumer products from autos to computers.

Marketing Occupational Areas

Dividing occupations into areas makes it easier to see the thousands of jobs available in marketing. An **occupational area** is a category of jobs that involves similar skills and aptitudes. It's much easier to find information about the career area that interests you if you can focus on one or two areas. There are 21 generally accepted areas, or career applications, within the field of marketing. Job titles within the following career applications are featured throughout this text in the *Careers in Marketing* feature. These areas include:

- Advertising
- Customer Service
- E-Commerce
- Entrepreneur
- Fashion Merchandising
- Financial Services
- Food Marketing
- Hospitality Marketing
- Importing/Exporting
- International Marketing
- Marketing Research
- Product Management
- Professional Sales
- Public Relations
- Real Estate
- Restaurant Management
- Retail Management
- Sales Management
- Service Marketing
- Sports Marketing
- Travel/Tourism Marketing

Job Levels in Marketing

Many jobs exist within each of the occupational areas, or career applications, of marketing. In apparel marketing, you could work as a cashier in a small shoe store or as a women's sportswear buyer for a large department store chain. These two jobs would have different educational, skill level, and experience requirements. Jobs in each marketing area can be categorized according to five skill levels: entry level, career sustaining, marketing specialist, marketing supervisor, and manager/owner. Figure 1-3 on page 15 shows possible job titles at each of the skill levels.

14   Unit 1 ■ *The World of Marketing*

FIGURE 1-2

Corporate CEOs with Marketing Backgrounds

Avon	Andrea Jung (1999–)
WalMart.com	Jeanne Jackson (2000–)
Campbell Soup	David W. Johnson (1990–)
Colgate-Palmolive	Reuben Mark (1984–)
E-bay	Meg Whitman (1998–)
General Mills	Stephen W. Sanger (1995–)
Hewlett-Packard	Carly Fiorina (1999–)
IBM	Louis V. Gerstner (1993–)
Kmart	Charles Conaway (2000–)
Kraft Foods	Betsy D. Holden (2000–)
McDonald's	Jack M. Greenberg (1999–)
Nordstrom	John J. Whitacre (1996–)
Ogilvy & Mather	Shelly Lazarus (1997–)
Oxygen Media	Geraldine Laybourne (1998–)
Pearson	Marjorie Scardino (1997–)
J.C. Penney	J.E. Oesterreicher (1998–)
Quaker Oats	Robert S. Morrison (1997–)
Ralston-Purina	W.P. McGinnis (1992–)
Sears Roebuck	Arthur C. Martinez (1995–)
Xerox	Paul A. Allaire (1990–)

■ **Marketing Education** Corporate CEOs are frequently drawn from the ranks of marketing professionals. *Why do you think that marketing professionals make good candidates for CEOs?*

Entry-level jobs usually require no prior experience and involve limited decision-making skills. Entry-level jobs are usually characterized by routine activities, such as working as a cashier at a fast food restaurant or clothing store. These acquired skills increase general employability and job readiness. They also help an individual to develop good business skills and learn appropriate behavior in the workplace.

FIGURE 1-3

Job Titles at the Five Skill Levels in Marketing Occupation Areas

Career Applications	Entry Level	Career Sustaining	Marketing Specialist	Marketing Supervisor	Manager/ Owner
Advertising	Proofreader, Assistant display specialist	Copywriter, Display specialist	Ad campaign manager	Account executive	President
Customer Service	Customer service clerk	Sales clerk	Customer service representative	Customer service manager	Sales manager
E-Commerce	Web site tester	Web designer	E-Commerce marketing specialist	E-Commerce marketing manager	Interactive marketing agency owner
Entrepreneur	Business owner's assistant	Small business manager	Small business marketing manager	Marketing supervisor	Sole proprietor of retail or wholesale business
Fashion Merchandising	Buyer's assistant	Salesperson, Model, Display specialist	Buyer, Manufacturer's showroom salesperson	District sales manager	Store manager
Financial Services	Bank teller	Bookkeeper	Loan officer, Accountant	Accounting department manager	Vice president
Food Marketing	Grocery bagger, Stock clerk	Cashier	Food buyer, Food broker	Bakery manager	Store manager
Hospitality Marketing	Maid, Bellhop	Desk clerk	Cruise ship or resort social director	Hotel manager	Chain manager
Importing/ Exporting	Shipping/receiving clerk	Warehouse manager	Transportation specialist	Inventory manager	Broker
International Marketing	Marketing assistant	International marketing associate	International trade economist	Agency manager	Agency owner
Marketing Research	Research assistant	Interviewer, Report writer	Statistician, Analyst	Field work director	Director, Consultant
Product Management	Quality control clerk	Sales representative	Finance/research specialist	Associate manager, Brand manager	Category manager
Professional Sales	Cashier	Appliance sales, Auto sales, Insurance sales	Manufacturer's sales representative	Department manager	Owner of retail or wholesale business
Public Relations	Office assistant	Copywriter	Account manager	Public relations representative	Owner of public relations firm
Real Estate	Office staff	Real estate agent	Real estate broker	Sales manager	Owner of real estate office
Restaurant Management	Waiter, Hostess, Cook	Head waiter, Shift manager	Restaurant manager	Chef	Owner, Executive chef
Retail Management	Cashier, Stock clerk	Assistant buyer/manager	Buyer, Department manager	District manager	V.P. of Operations
Sales Management	Telemarketing	Sales representative	Regional sales manager	National sales manager	V.P. of Sales
Service Marketing	Customer relations clerk	Assistant manager of customer relations	Manager of customer relations	V.P. of customer relations	Owner of service marketing company
Sports Marketing	Ticket agent	Airline clerk, Car rental agent	Booking agent	Venue manager	Team owner, Agency owner
Travel/Tourism Marketing	Receptionist, Car rental service attendant	Travel agent	Specialized tour guide	Agency manager	Travel agency owner

■ **Pick a Job** This table shows examples of the types of jobs in each career application, at each of the five skill levels. *What skills are required at the Import/Export Broker level?*

FIGURE 1-3 ANSWER
Pick a Job In the Importing/Exporting occupational area, a broker would be at the manager/owner skill level. Manager/ owners must be highly skilled in a number of areas. Brokers must have good management skills, excellent communication skills, and a good understanding of other cultures, as well as the ability to interpret regulations.

ASSESS

Reteaching

1. **Vocabulary** Assign and review the vocabulary terms for this section.
2. **Fact and Idea** Assign and review Fact and Idea Review questions 8–10 from the Chapter Assessment.
3. **Marketing Careers** Ask students why they think marketing provides such a diversity of career opportunities. *(Answers should include the fact that most businesses need product development, distribution, selling, and promotion, which are key activities in marketing.)*
4. **Occupational Areas** Review with students the 21 occupational areas within marketing.

Enrichment

1. **Review** Assign and review the Chapter 1 activities in the *Student Activity Workbook.*
2. **Review** Assign and review the appropriate Thinking Critically questions from the Chapter Assessment.
3. **Review** Assign and review the following Chapter Assessment activities: Building Workplace Skills, Applying Marketing Concepts, Linking School to Work Activities, The DECA Connection Role Play, and Internet Connection.
4. **Guest Speakers** Have graduates of your school's marketing education program who are now working successfully in marketing talk to your class about how they started, where they are now, and where they would like to be in five years. Speakers should discuss the advantages and disadvantages of their jobs, duties, and how their marketing education classes helped them.

Career sustaining jobs require a higher level of skills and more decision making than entry-level jobs. It is often the second step for someone considering a career in marketing. These jobs allow the employee some control over the work environment as well as more responsibility.

Marketing specialist employees must show leadership ability and make many decisions on a daily basis. Being a marketing specialist is a long-term career goal for many people in marketing. This type of job requires not only strong job-related skills, but also good leadership skills.

Marketing supervisors must have good management skills, the ability to make many decisions on a daily basis, and excellent marketing skills. This is a career level many people aspire to reach. The prestige and income are generally quite high, and there is less risk involved than at the top management level.

Manager/owner is the top level. People at this level are competent to run a small business or a significant part of a large business. They must be highly skilled in a number of areas. They are responsible for the final success of the enterprise. They are also responsible for any failures or problems that occur along the way. People at this level must be ready to accept responsibility for both the successes and failures of the business.

■ **Business Class** Travel to interesting places may be one benefit to a career in marketing. *What are some other possible benefits?*

1.3 ASSESSMENT

Reviewing Key Terms and Concepts

1. What proportion of the U.S. work force is involved in marketing activities?
2. Name one employment trend.
3. List two major benefits of working in marketing.
4. What basic skills are needed for success in a marketing career?
5. According to the Bureau of Labor Statistics, approximately how many new marketing and sales jobs will be created between 1992 and 2005?

Thinking Critically

6. Discuss how the marketing skills you would learn in a fast-food restaurant could be transferred to an industrial sales position.

Integrating Academic Skills

7. **MATH** In your entry-level job as a sales-clerk, you made $15,000 a year. After many years of hard work and a long series of promotions, you became director of marketing at $150,000 a year. This is what percent of your original salary?

16 Unit 1 ■ *The World of Marketing*

16

Careers in Marketing

HOSPITALITY MARKETING

Mark Bingle
Hotel Manager, Four Seasons Hotels,
The Regent Beverly Wilshire Hotel

What do you like most about your work?

"There are never two days alike in the hotel business. Daily activities are dictated by which guests are arriving and what needs to be done before their arrival. Let's say that the First Lady is arriving today—I am most likely meeting with Secret Service to discuss the arrival plans. Imagine instead that it is the CEO of Coca-Cola checking in—I could be ensuring that any non-Coke products have been removed from the private bar in the room prior to arrival. There is no monotony in my business—it changes every moment."

How did you get into hotel management?

"The hiring philosophy for Four Seasons hotels is that we can train anyone to do anything. The only condition, however, is a friendly disposition and positive attitude. Our industry is service, and we can teach anyone to serve, but the smile has to be there ahead of time. I had no experience when I joined, but I wanted to work in a beautiful environment where quality was a top priority. The hotel took me under its proverbial wing, based on my educational background and commitment to service, and gave me a chance."

What training do you recommend?

"Go to a five-star hotel and watch the interaction of the guests and staff. The enthusiasm has to be there all day long, almost as if one is on stage; if you can keep that up, you've won half the battle. A college education is important for management candidates who want to move up, but not required. Being multilingual is a huge incentive for any employer to hire a candidate, especially in this business."

What is your key to success?

"The key to success in the hotel industry is understanding people's needs and wants. My number one success tool is my education at Georgetown University. Attending an internationally integrated university allowed me to travel and live abroad, which broadened my perspective."

Thinking Critically

What aspect of this job do you find most appealing?

Career Facts

Education and Training: High school classes in marketing, speech, food, accounting, and computer science are helpful, as well as part-time work in hotels or restaurants. Post-secondary training is recommended in business administration, accounting, and food service management.

Aptitudes, Abilities, and Skills: Good people and communication skills (especially in stressful situations), strong problem-solving abilities, good organizational skills, and experience with numerical and clerical data are helpful.

Career Outlook: Positions are expected to grow as fast as the average for all occupations through the year 2006. Manager jobs will not grow as rapidly as the hotel industry in general due to the increase in economy-class accommodations.

Career Path: Many managers are promoted from within the ranks. Geographical mobility is essential for advancement in chain-operated hotels.

Careers in Marketing

Ask a student to read the Careers in Marketing feature aloud to the class. Discuss the skills and aptitudes required for a career in hospitality marketing. Ask students whether they think they would like or dislike a career in hospitality marketing. Discuss the pros and cons of such a career.

Thinking Critically Answer
Answers will vary.

Guest Speaker
Invite a hotel/motel manager to class to discuss his/her job and factors he/she considers when making marketing decisions.

Exploring Careers

Why Work?
1. Read to students the following reasons that people work:
   - People work for money.
   - People work for recognition.
   - People work to feel good about themselves.
   - People work to be useful.
   - People work to be with others.
2. Call on students to complete the following statements as you read each one aloud:
   - I will work to earn money because _____.
   - I want recognition for the following things: _____.
   - At work I want to feel good about _____.
   - At my work I want to feel useful by doing the following things: _____.
   - At work I want to be with other people because _____.
3. Finally, ask students to discuss what they think is the main reason they will be (are) working.

Lifelong Learning

The Job Search
The job search process can be ongoing throughout a career. Even employed individuals should be aware that when companies are bought and sold, some people will need to find new positions. It is up to the individual to keep informed and to update skills and redefine goals.

Meeting Individual Needs

Students With Learning Disabilities
Students with learning disabilities may need study aids to get the most out of textbook material. You can make chapter audio tapes so they can listen and read simultaneously. Tapes can be made with the help of other students whose speech is articulate. While recording, use a bell or clicker to signal when to turn pages. Getting all students involved can make this a real class project.

Vocabulary Review

Paragraphs will vary. See Glossary for definitions.

Fact and Idea Review

1. Marketing is the process of developing, promoting, and distributing products to satisfy customers' needs and wants.
2. The seven functions of marketing are distribution, financing, marketing information management, pricing, product/service management, promotion, and selling.
3. No, all marketing functions are important for business success. Each contributes to making the product more useful to the customer.
4. Place, time, possession, and information are related to marketing.
5. The raw materials that go into a pen are less useful by themselves. Once they are processed into parts and assembled in the production process, they have increased value, or utility.
6. Marketing can lower prices by increasing demand for a product, which reduces the unit cost.
7. New and improved products are another result of increased competition.
8. The study of marketing is helpful in any career because it involves understanding business, as well as effectively relating and communicating with others.
9. The number of marketing jobs will continue to increase, according to the Department of Labor.
10. Job opportunities in marketing are growing while those in production are shrinking. Production jobs lend themselves to automation and mechanization, but marketing requires personal contact.

Thinking Critically

1. Answers will vary. Students should use the marketing utilities to justify marketing costs.
2. Some possible answers are computers, big-screen TVs, DVD players, and CD players.
3. Answers will vary.
4. Answers will vary. One possibility is that employers want employees who understand both their roles in the total operation of a business and the importance of customers. Employees who realize that profit is necessary for businesses to survive will develop the type of

---

VOCABULARY REVIEW

In a paragraph, define marketing and then explain the relationship of the following terms to it.

- products
- goods
- services
- exchange
- utility
- form utility
- place utility
- time utility
- possession utility
- information utility
- benefits
- occupational area

FACT AND IDEA REVIEW

1. What is marketing? (1.1)
2. Identify the seven functions of marketing. (1.1)
3. Of the four marketing utilities, is one the most important for business success? (1.2)
4. Which of the five economic utilities are related to marketing? (1.2)
5. Using a ballpoint pen as an example, explain the concept of form utility. (1.2)
6. How can marketing help lower prices? (1.2)
7. Explain marketing's role in developing new and improved products. (1.2)
8. Why is the study of marketing helpful in any career? (1.3)
9. What do Department of Labor projections predict for marketing jobs? (1.3)
10. How do the trends in marketing and production compare? What accounts for the differences in the trends? (1.3)

THINKING CRITICALLY

1. It is often said that marketing costs represent approximately 50 percent of the selling price of an item. Select a product of your choice to justify the need for marketing and its related costs in the sale of that product.
2. When handheld calculators were introduced, they sold for $100. As they became popular, more companies introduced better and less expensive ones. Now you can purchase a handheld, solar-powered calculator for as little as $5. Provide examples of other products that were more costly when they were first put on the market than they are now.
3. Explain the meaning of the following statement: Marketing is more than just promotion.
4. Why do you think employers want employees who have an understanding of business as well as good interpersonal and communication skills?
5. You have decided to be a marketing entrepreneur. What kinds of character traits and interpersonal skills will you need?

BUILDING WORKPLACE SKILLS

1. **Human Relations** Assume you are a salesperson in a computer store. A customer is hesitant about buying the mid-priced laptop computer you've been showing her. Her objection is that it will sell for much less in a year. Do you think she's correct? What would you say to her?
2. **Technology** You're interested in marketing as a possible career, but you're not sure about the availability of jobs in marketing. Using career Web sites on the Internet, research the current availability of marketing jobs. Prepare a brief written report on your findings.

---

attitude and skills needed for successful employment. Also, employees must be able to get along with co-workers and supervisors as well as customers. Good communication skills are helpful in maintaining these relationships.

5. Answers will include positive attitude, initiative, and cooperative, competitive, and ethical traits, as well as leadership, team player, decision-making, and above average communication skills.

Building Workplace Skills

1. Students should be willing to concede that the customer is probably right. The increased demand and competition created by marketing will likely bring prices down. In the interim, however, he or she will be doing without the convenience of a laptop. Making one available to her now, in a neighborhood store, with informative displays and sales support (time, place, and information utilities) makes the purchase worth the slightly higher price (possession utility).
2. Reports will vary.

APPLYING MARKETING CONCEPTS

1. **Understanding Marketing Functions** With 2–3 classmates, use a word processing program to write a short report about a new fruit beverage that you believe will be popular with teenagers. Assume your team develops this new product and wants to start selling it. Cover all of the seven marketing functions in your report. When you introduce each function, note this in parentheses.

2. **Applying Economic Utilities** Using the short report written in the first project, identify examples of the five economic utilities. What did your group do to create form, time, place, possession, and information utility? What challenges did you face addressing these?

3. **Summarizing Key Concepts** Using a word processing program, summarize an article related to one of the seven functions of marketing or the five economic utilities. Use business publications such as *BrandWeek*, *Adweek*, *BusinessWeek*, *Fortune*, *Forbes*, *Nation's Business*, *Sales & Marketing Management*, or *Marketing News*. Share your article summary with classmates.

4. **Preparing Presentations** Use a computer and a presentation program to prepare a graphic representation of the seven functions of marketing.

LINKING SCHOOL TO WORK

Basic and Information Skills Ask an employer to identify five-to-ten characteristics of an effective employee. Categorize those characteristics as a *business understanding,* an *interpersonal skill,* or a *communication skill.* Were there any characteristics that did not fit into one of those three categories? Which characteristic was regarded as most important to your employer? Why?

THE DECA CONNECTION

Role Play: Store Manager

Situation You are to assume the role of manager of a local supermarket. A disgruntled customer (judge) complains to you about how manufacturers and retailers waste money on marketing. The customer (judge) thinks retail prices could be significantly reduced if manufacturers spent less money on marketing their products.

Activity Take this opportunity to respond to the customer (judge).

Evaluation You will be evaluated on how well you meet the following performance indicators:

• Describe marketing functions and related activities
• Explain the concept of marketing and market identification
• Explain marketing and its importance in a global economy
• Handle customer inquiries
• Determine forms of economic utility created by marketing activities

inter NET CONNECTION

Marketing Degrees
You have decided that you would like to learn more about earning a marketing degree.

Connect
• Locate the Web sites of two colleges that offer bachelor's degrees in marketing and two community colleges that offer associate's degrees in marketing.
• Locate information about distance learning and marketing institute programs.
• Contact schools for further information and share the information with your class as part of an information bulletin board.

Students should be evaluated on the performance indicators noted in the Role Play.
• For another DECA Role Play, go to the *Student Activity Workbook*, p. 5.
• For more in-depth Role Play practice, refer to DECA's *Essential Competitive Events Handbook.* To order, contact DECA at **www.deca.org**.

*inter*NET CONNECTION
Information will vary.

Mini Quiz
Administer the Mini Quiz orally. For an expanded chapter quiz, go to page 1 of the *Reproducible Tests* book.

1. <u>Marketing</u> is the process of developing, promoting, and distributing products to satisfy customers' needs and wants.

2. Business, management and entrepreneurship, communication and interpersonal skills, economics, and professional development are the four marketing <u>foundations</u>.

3. The five economic utilities are <u>form, place, possession, time, and information</u>.

4. Besides added value, the two other consumer benefits of marketing are <u>lower prices and new and improved products</u>.

5. Job opportunities in marketing are <u>growing</u>, while those in production are <u>shrinking</u>.

Applying Marketing Concepts

1. Reports will vary.
2. Responses will depend on reports written for first project.
3. Summaries will depend on articles selected.
4. Presentations will vary.

Linking School to Work

Answers depend on the work situation.

1. **Assessment** Have students complete the Reproducible Test for Chapter 1 or construct your own test using the ExamView software.
2. **Enrichment** Have students complete the corresponding activities in the following workbooks:
   • *Marketing Math Workbook*, p. 1
   • *Marketing Research Project Workbook,* p. 1

Chapter 2

Basic Marketing Concepts

Chapter Overview

Chapter 2 introduces students to the marketing concept, target marketing, and the marketing mix (the four Ps). These are essential concepts for continued study of marketing principles. This chapter also describes how markets are segmented according to demographics, geographics, psychographics, and product benefits.

 Springboard

Brainstorm Tell students this chapter explores several meanings for the word *market*. Have them brainstorm (alone or in groups of 3–4) different meanings for the word *market*. Write their ideas on the board.

Prereading

List the section objectives *(What You'll Learn)* on the board and discuss them with students. Have them skim the chapter, looking at the pictures, reading the captions, and noting the headings. Ask questions so students have a basic understanding of the chapter structure.

Preteaching Marketing Vocabulary

Before students begin reading the chapter, dictate each Key Term and ask students to write them on a sheet of paper. Then write the terms on the board. Have students guess the meaning of each. Write their guesses next to each term, but do not give the correct meaning. Leave this list on the board so students can see how close their guesses were to the actual definitions.

Marketing: What It Takes
Answer You can conduct research on your target market to make intelligent product, price, place, and promotion decisions.

Marketing: What It Takes

Improving on Your Marketing Mix
You thought your idea for a snowboard shop was pretty good. However, yesterday you received a mixed reaction from a counselor at the small business development center. She said there was a large enough population of the 16- to 24-year-olds in the area, but that you need to develop a more precise marketing mix.

WHAT WILL YOU DO?
What steps can you take to develop a better marketing mix?

20

THE DECA CONNECTION — ADVISOR CORNER

Mentor a New DECA Chapter Check with your state advisor to find the name of a DECA chapter that is inactive and/or a potential new chapter in your area. Brainstorm with your chapter members to plan activities that will demonstrate the value and benefits of DECA membership—including programs, recognition, leadership skills, networking, scholarships, and fun. This is a great time to allow your chapter officers to assume a leadership role in making contacts, arranging visits, etc. Serving as a mentor will educate others about the value of DECA. Chapter members can also apply basic marketing concepts to this activity—using the inactive/new chapter as the target market and DECA membership as the product.

The Marketing Concept

The Basic Concept

How do businesses become successful? They plan for it by following an idea called the marketing concept. The marketing concept states that businesses must satisfy customers' needs and wants in order to make a profit. Keen competition forces businesses to embrace the marketing concept. Businesses must have the right goods and services at the right time, at the right price, and at the right place for purchase. Additionally, businesses must communicate all of this information to their customers. This is not always an easy task. To do so, businesses must truly know who their customers are and how they can be reached.

■ Customers vs. Consumers

When businesses discuss customers, they sometimes make a distinction between customers and consumers. Customers buy the product. Consumers are those people who actually use the product. For a manufacturer of consumer products, like Sony, the customers are the retail stores that sell Sony's products. Since Sony does not sell its products directly to the consumer, it has to rely on retailers.

The customer and consumer is usually one in the same for the retailer. If you buy a Sony Walkman and you are the person who will be using it, you are both the customer and consumer. There are many situations where the customer is not the intended user of the product, however. If you buy a Sony Walkman as a gift, you are the customer and the person for whom you are buying the Walkman is the consumer. This concept becomes clear when you think of marketing to children. A child may be the consumer of a breakfast cereal, but it is the parent who is the customer. Successful marketers must recognize the need to satisfy both the customer and consumer.

■ What is a Market?

All potential customers who share common needs and wants, and who have the ability and willingness to buy the product, are considered a market. A market is further described by its total sales in a product category by competing companies in categories such as hair spray, chewing gum, and soft drinks. For example, everyone who buys video game consoles is part of the $7 billion game console market (see Figure 2-1 on page 23).

- **What You'll Learn**
  - The marketing concept
  - The difference between customers and consumers
  - What a market is and how it can be described
  - What target marketing is
  - The four Ps of the marketing mix

- **Why It's Important**

In order to participate in the world of marketing, you'll want to understand how businesses focus on the needs and wants of their customers in order to improve their products, remain competitive, and increase their profits.

- **Key Terms**
  - marketing concept
  - customers
  - consumers
  - market
  - target marketing
  - customer profile
  - marketing mix

FOCUS

Bell Ringer Activity

Brainstorm Ask students to work in groups of 3–4 to generate a list of their favorite clothing items, games, and electronic devices. Have them provide reasons why those items are special to them.

Introducing the Section

The Marketing Concept Write products and reasons given in the Bell Ringer Activity on the board. Most reasons should be satisfying a need or want. Explain that how long a product is profitable depends on its ability to continue satisfying needs and wants. Use this to introduce the marketing concept.

TEACH

📊 Technology Resources

PowerPoint *Marketing Essentials'* PowerPoint Presentation CD-ROM provides visual lecture aids for every chapter section.

Concept Development

1. Read Section 2.1 with students.
2. Have students name their favorite automobiles. Write their suggestions on the board. Do the same with their favorite jeans or CDs. Use this information to discuss the concept of a market.

Discussion Starter

Target Marketing Have students name five products targeted to people their age. Ask them to name five products that target children and five that target people over 50. Ask why this exercise was so easy.

Classroom Resources

For the Teacher
- Teacher Editions for all workbooks
- Assessment Package
- PowerPoint Presentation Software
- Interactive Lesson Planner
- ILP Block Scheduling, p. 1
- ILP Lesson Plans, p. 4
- ILP Internet Resources, p. 23

- ILP Blackline Masters, p. 3
- ILP *BusinessWeek* Case Studies, p. 7
- ILP Marketing Career Portfolio, p. 31
- *Marketing Essentials* Web site (**www.marketing.glencoe.com**)

For the Student
- Student Activity Workbook, p. 9
- Marketing Math Workbook, p. 1

- Marketing Research Project Workbook, p. 1
- ILP School-to-Work Activity Workbook, p. 5
- Virtual Business simulation
- *Marketing Essentials* Web site (**www.marketing.glencoe.com**)

ILP These resources are available in print and on the Interactive Lesson Planner (ILP)

Thinking Critically

Target Marketing Ask students to select a product created for a target market that changed its design or promotion to target a different market. Can a company address the needs of low income, middle income, and high-income customers with the same product by only changing its brand name? *(They also must change promotion, place, and price strategies for different target markets.)*

Independent Practice

Research and Identify Have students study the pharmaceutical industry to see how companies that sell prescription drugs (i.e., Claritin, Rogaine) advertise to consumers, even though they cannot purchase those drugs without a prescription. Have them identify the consumers.

ASSESS

Reteaching

1. **Review** Assign and review Fact and Idea Review questions 1–4 from the Chapter Assessment.
2. **The Marketing Mix** To reteach the concept of the marketing mix, select a product and review its characteristics. Consider name, packaging, ingredients, etc., and the other Ps of the marketing mix. Each time you cover an element of the marketing mix, write it on the board with an arrow pointing to a profile of the target market for the product.

FIGURE 2-2
MARKETING MIX

The strength of a particular marketing mix depends on two things—how well the target market is defined and how well all marketing decisions are directed toward that market. The target market for Polaroid's I-Zone camera is males and females, 12 to 18 years old. *How does the marketing mix for this product measure up to these two standards?*

1 PRODUCT STRATEGIES

Product strategies include what product to make, how to package it, what brand name to use, and what image to project. Polaroid's choice is a pocket-size instant camera with an indoor flash that produces self-developing miniature photos or photo stickers. Polaroid Pocket Film is designed for use with the I-Zone camera. The cameras come in fashionable colors and carry the Polaroid I-Zone brand name.

2 PLACE STRATEGIES

Place strategies determine how and where a product will be distributed. Polaroid's choice is to reach customers through mass market and specialty stores in the United States.

3 PRICE STRATEGIES

Price strategies should reflect what customers are willing and able to pay. Polaroid's choice of suggested retail price for the I-Zone camera is $24.99, which includes a trial pack of six-exposure sticker film and two AA batteries; Polaroid Pocket Film has a suggested retail price of $5.99 (non-sticker) and $6.99 (sticker) film.

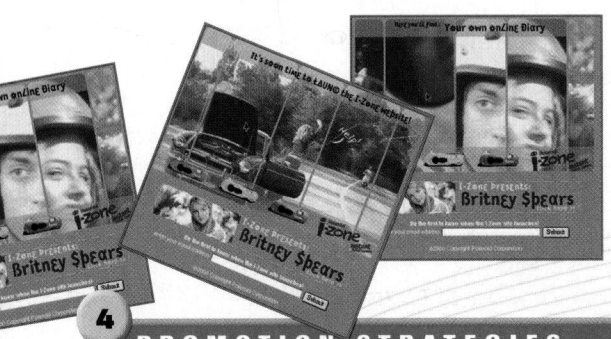

4 PROMOTION STRATEGIES

Promotion strategies deal with how potential customers will be told about the new product, what the message will be, when and where it will be delivered, and with what inducements to buy. Polaroid's choices include television commercials, a public relations effort, and a Web site offering users a variety of interactive activities. The image Polaroid wants to create is "self expression" and "creativity."

22 Unit 1 ■ *The World of Marketing*

GREAT IDEAS **from the Marketing Classroom**

Rahnda Jaquays
Mecosta Osceola Career Center
Big Rapids, MI

When teaching the four Ps of the marketing mix, let your students take part in a hands-on project. Once finished with the instruction, have your students create the four Ps using either Legos or Play Dough. Instruct them to develop an original and unique product, giving it a name and explaining its use. Then have them go through place, price, and promotion. Have your students create the actual promotion—the newspaper advertisement, tape-recorded radio spot, and/or video-taped television commercial. Display the projects for open house or parent night. Show/play their promotional tapes for the class. I guarantee your students will enjoy this activity!

Satisfying the needs and wants of all customers in a product category would be difficult without further defining and analyzing the current and potential customers of a given commodity. That is where target marketing comes in. Target marketing is focusing all marketing decisions on a very specific group of people who you want to reach. The more information you have on your target market, the easier it is to make the marketing decisions.

To develop a clear picture of that target market, businesses create a customer profile. A customer profile can include information about the target market with regard to the age, income level, ethnic background, occupation, attitudes, lifestyle, or geographic residence of the targeted customer. Marketers spend a lot of money on research to clearly identify the most important characteristics of the target market's customer profile to help them make intelligent marketing decisions.

▪ Marketing Mix

The marketing mix comprises four basic marketing strategies, collectively known as the four Ps—product, place, price, and promotion. These strategies involve the decisions that a business must make. The marketing mix is dependent on how well the target market is defined and how well all strategies are directed toward that target audience. Once a target market is clearly identified, it is easier to make decisions regarding strategies that hit the mark.

The four elements of the marketing mix are interconnected. Actions in one area affect decisions in

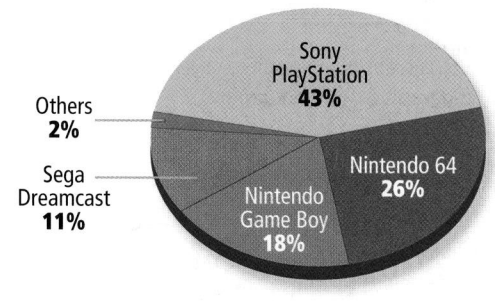

FIGURE 2-1

1999 U.S. Game Console Market

Sales $7 billion

▪ **Fun and Games** A market can be described as the people who are potential customers of a product, as well as by the classification of a product in a category. *Would you be considered part of the market for game consoles? Why or why not?*

- Sony PlayStation 43%
- Nintendo 64 26%
- Nintendo Game Boy 18%
- Sega Dreamcast 11%
- Others 2%

another. Each part of the marketing mix contains countless alternatives. From all of the alternatives, management must select a combination of marketing mix decisions that will satisfy target markets and achieve organizational goals.

Let's use a specific product in the instant camera category, Polaroid's I-Zone camera, as an example. (See Figure 2-2 on page 22.)

2.1 ASSESSMENT

Reviewing Key Terms and Concepts

1. What does the marketing concept state?
2. Who are the customers of Sony Electronics and Hershey Chocolates? Who are their consumers?
3. What is a market?
4. What is target marketing?
5. What are the four Ps of the marketing mix?

Thinking Critically

6. Many women's magazines like *Glamour* and *Elle* publish advertisements for men's cologne. Explain the rationale for this practice.

Integrating Academic Skills

7. **MATH** Baking soda toothpastes presently represent 25 percent of the $1.4 billion toothpaste market. What does that percentage represent in dollar sales?

Enrichment

Extend Assign and review the corresponding activities from *BusinessWeek Case Studies*, *Internet Resources*, and the *School-to-Work Activity Workbook.* **ILP**

Evaluation

Assign and review the Section 2.1 Assessment.

Technology Resources

GO TO **Assessment Resources**
Go to the *Marketing Essentials* Web site (**www.marketing.glencoe.com**) for resources to teach and assess occupation-specific vocabulary.

◀ VIRTUAL BUSINESS ◀

GO TO **The Marketing Mix**
Introduce the marketing mix to students using Knowledge Matters' Virtual Business visual simulation. Go to the *Marketing Essentials* Web site (**www.glencoe.marketing.com**) to download the Virtual Business Marketing Mix activity specially designed for the *Marketing Essentials* program. Students will see the relationship between the four Ps of the marketing mix. Have students run the Virtual Business tutorial before beginning this activity.

CLOSE

Section Wrap-Up

Ask students to explain the significance of the four Ps. *(For product success, all four Ps must be directed at the target market.)*

FIGURE 2–1 ANSWER
Fun and Games If you do not purchase, you are not part of the market and vice-versa.

2.1 ASSESSMENT ANSWERS

Reviewing Key Terms and Concepts

1. It states that businesses must satisfy customers' needs and wants to make a profit.
2. The customers for Sony are retail stores and for Hershey Chocolates are the general shopping public. Consumers are the users of the product.
3. A market is all of the potential customers who share common needs and wants and who have the ability and willingness to buy the product.
4. It focuses all marketing decisions on a very specific group of people you want to reach.
5. product, price, place, and promotion

Thinking Critically

6. Men's cologne can be advertised to women as gifts to buy for men.

Integrating Academic Skills

7. **MATH** $350 million

23

SECTION 2.2

Market Segmentation

FOCUS

Bell Ringer Activity

List and Identify Ask students to make a list of all extended family members (aunts, uncles, cousins, grandparents) and where they live, as well as their genders, ages, occupations (if applicable), and interests or hobbies.

Introducing the Section

Market Segmentation Use the list generated in the Bell Ringer Activity to introduce the concept of market segmentation. Have students sit in groups of 3–4 to share their lists. Ask students to group family members who share common characteristics, such as age, gender, hobbies/interests, and ethnic background.

TEACH

Technology Resources

PowerPoint *Marketing Essentials'* PowerPoint Presentation CD-ROM provides visual lecture aids for every chapter section.

[handwritten: Section 2.2 has to do with]

◆ What You'll Learn

[handwritten: "]
- What market segmentation is and the four methods used to segment a market. *[handwritten: "]*

[handwritten: As well as]

[handwritten: "]
- The current demographic, psychographic, and geographic trends. *[handwritten: "]*

[handwritten: This section is important because]

◆ Why It's Important

[handwritten: "] Businesses must know who their customers are to achieve success. In other words, they must know their markets. This section will introduce you to the U.S. marketplace and the different ways businesses classify and characterize its segments. *[handwritten: "]*

◆ Key Terms

- market segmentation
- demographics
- Baby Boom Generation
- Generation X
- Generation Y
- disposable income
- discretionary income
- psychographics
- geographics

[handwritten: Please read P.2 under age]

[handwritten: Please read]

[handwritten: The first generation mentioned is the Baby Boom Generation]

[handwritten: War]

[handwritten: Born: 1946-1964 (76 million)]
[handwritten: Political: JFK assassination]
[handwritten: Social: @ Home   RFK   MLK]
[handwritten: Products: Vacations, Summer Homes, Prescription Drugs, Paying College Tuitions, Weddings, Grandchildren]
[handwritten: Economical: Lots of $]

Analyzing Markets

Market segmentation is a way of analyzing a market by specific characteristics in order to create a target market. Once that target market is clearly identified, a business can customize its product offerings and marketing strategies to that specific group of potential customers. To accomplish that goal, businesses may segment a market by demographics, psychographics, geographics, and product benefits. With the vast technological resources now available to marketers, all four methods might be used to identify a very specific group of people—a target market. Let's look at each one separately for now.

[handwritten: Can anyone tell me the four ways the four methods that marketers use to identify a target market?]

■ Demographics

Demographics refers to statistics that describe a population in terms of personal characteristics. These include age, gender, income, ethnic background, education, and occupation. Once marketers know the demographics of a particular market, they can categorize and develop their products to appeal to its members.

[handwritten: Who can tell me what demographics are and why they are important.]

AGE Marketers can easily use age to segment the market in product categories such as toys, clothing, and food products. For example, toy manufacturers often identify on the packaging the recommended age group for each toy or game. Jeans manufacturers create jeans for toddlers, children, teens, and adults. Cap'n Crunch cereal is targeted to kids, while Kellogg's All Bran cereal is marketed to adults.

When marketers study age, they classify everyone according to certain generations. The reason for this practice is that each generation tends to have common bonds because of their collectively shared experiences. This makes them good market segments to target. The last three generations were the Baby Boom Generation, Generation X, and Generation Y.

[handwritten: Remember that "each generation tends to have common bonds because of ...]

The 76 million babies born in the United States between 1946 and 1964 are called the **Baby Boom Generation**. Tracking this group's life pays off for marketers because of its large size. Also, as baby boomers get older, their income and spending power increases. In fact, they control $2.6 trillion and have about 51 percent of the wealth in the country. Thus, they are prime targets for all types of luxuries and recreational items. Marketers are watching the baby boomers' age—the oldest baby boomers will turn 65 in 2011 and the number of Americans over 65 will nearly double by 2030. The graying baby boomers will certainly remain a strong market for all kinds of products related to an aging population.

Classroom Resources

For the Teacher
- Teacher Editions for all workbooks
- Assessment Package
- PowerPoint Presentation Software
- Interactive Lesson Planner
- ILP Block Scheduling, p. 1
- ILP Lesson Plans, p. 5
- ILP Internet Resources, p. 23

- ILP Blackline Masters, p. 4
- ILP *BusinessWeek* Case Studies, p. 7
- ILP Marketing Career Portfolio, p. 31
- *Marketing Essentials* Web site (**www.marketing.glencoe.com**)

For the Student
- Student Activity Workbook, p. 9
- Marketing Math Workbook, p. 1

- Marketing Research Project Workbook, p. 1
- ILP School-to-Work Activity Workbook, p. 5
- Virtual Business simulation
- *Marketing Essentials* Web site (**www.marketing.glencoe.com**)

ILP These resources are available in print and on the Interactive Lesson Planner (ILP)

Case Study

Got Milk?

To get the message to teens to drink milk, MilkPEP and Dairy Management Inc. are using popular athletes as their models in "got milk?" ads. Teenagers' zeal for collecting milk mustache ads of their favorite sports stars is what marketers are counting on to get across a serious message.

Milk consumption drops in the teenage years, just when teens may need it most. It appears that seven out of ten teen boys and nine out of ten teen girls do not get their daily calcium requirements.

To target teens, the message for the promotion must be viewed as "cool" and the media must reach teens. Using popular athletes in the "got milk?" print and TV ads helps to get the message across. Print ads in *TV Guide*, which is read by 5.4 million teens, was one effective vehicle used to communicate the message.

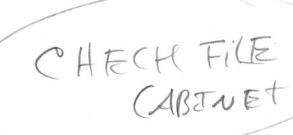

Case Study Review

1. Why were "got milk?" ads popular with teens?
2. How can "got milk?" ads target different market segments by age, gender, generation, and ethnic background?

A MATTER OF ETHICS

3. Is it ethical to use popular athletes to persuade teens to take a specific action? Would it change your opinion if the action were other than "drink milk"?

(handwritten: CHECK FILE CABINET)

(handwritten: Please read)

The more than 40 million Americans born between 1965 and 1976 are called **Generation X**. Many members of Generation X are products of dual-career households or divorced parents. They have been bombarded with media from an early age, therefore the members of Generation X tend to be savvy and skeptical consumers. Generation Xers are better educated than any previous generation, and they are more financially cautious and conservative. They are prime consumers of cosmetics, fashionable clothing, movies, and electronic items. To reach this group, marketers must use sharp images, music, a sense of humor, and a little irreverence.

(handwritten: Booklet   Please read)

The 77 million Americans born between 1977 and 1997 are referred to as **Generation Y**. This generation is growing up during a computer revolution. They are accustomed to interactivity and used to doing more than one thing at a time. They strive to be different from their parents, and they are very comfortable using computers and "surfing the net." This group has $130 million in spending power and influences $250 billion in purchases. It is easy to see why marketers are interested in Generation Y. They want to build brand loyalty by attracting consumers when they are teens. Marketers have learned that teens buy many of their own personal

Chapter 2 ■ Basic Marketing Concepts **25**

(handwritten margin notes: Generation X / Born: 1965–1976 (40 million) / Political: Vietnam War, Watergate / Social: Both Parents work, increasing divorce rate / Economical: financially cautious, conservative / Products: Cosmetics, Clothing)

Case Study Review Answers

Got Milk?

1. The ads feature popular celebrities.
2. The "got milk?" ads target different segments by using different celebrities that are popular to different ages, generations, genders, or ethnicities.

A MATTER OF ETHICS

3. Answers will vary based on students' opinions.

More About . . .

Market Segmentation

Market segmentation is easier for companies today—thanks to computers. Kraft General Foods has an 800 number that receives roughly a half million calls a year. As each call is logged into a computer, so is data about the caller (age group, income level, geographic area, buying preferences).

Discussion Starter

1. **Gender Segmentation** Ask students to name some gender neutral products that are promoted to both sexes with the same main theme but with slightly different approaches. *(Answers will vary. One product is Tropicana orange juice, which uses different models to appeal to each gender.)*

2. **Age Demographics** Ask students whether they think senior citizen or children's discounts are fair. Have students support their positions. *(Answers will vary. Some students will point out that retirees and older people often have lowered income levels, making them logical discount recipients. Other students might feel that today's elderly are very well off as a group compared to former generations. Some students might believe that a children's discount would be more fair, since today children are the fastest-growing group among the nation's poor.)*

3. **Ethnicity Segmentation** To introduce the concept of segmenting the market by ethnicity, ask the students what ethnic foods they like to eat. This will help to make students aware of the variety of ethnic groups in the United States.

4. **Psychographics** To introduce the concept of psychographics, ask students how they and their family members spend their leisure time, as well as what family values they share.

Pixels or Paper?

E-book readers, electronic devices that can store and display the text of books, were introduced with great fanfare in 1998. However, the infant industry faces many obstacles. E-book manufacturers are caught up in a classic chicken-and-egg quandary. To attract readers, they must offer cheap e-book devices and a wide variety of titles, but to persuade publishers to sell titles, they have to show that there is a market and that the technology is secure from piracy. Although not everyone agrees about how and when e-books will take hold, Microsoft has predicted that e-titles will outsell their paper counterparts by 2010.

Thinking Critically:

Do you agree with Microsoft's prediction? Why or why not?

■ **The Generation Gap** Generations share common bonds because they experienced their lives during the same era—politically, socially, and economically. Thus, they tend to have the same values and attitudes about life in general. Marketers who want to reach a specific generation must understand that generation's thinking. *Which generation do you think marketers are trying to reach in this advertisement? Why?*

26 Unit 1 ■ *The World of Marketing*

care products, including deodorant, shampoo, and toothpaste. According to Sony, 60 percent of 12– to 17-year-olds have their own CD players. Teens also do the family shopping and influence big-ticket family purchases, like autos and computers. Therefore, smart marketers target teens. MCI Communications Corp has targeted teens with a collect phone call service 1-800-COLLECT.

GENDER Gender helps to create market segments as well. Jockey, a men's underwear company doubled its sales when it entered the women's market with Jockey underwear for women.

Sensor razors for men and new Sensor razors for women, as well as Mennen Speed Stick and Lady Speed Stick demonstrate how companies that traditionally marketed men's products can extend their product lines to enter the women's market. Gender-neutral products may use different advertising media and messages when trying to reach men and women. For example, ads for the Palm Pilot have featured famous professional women when trying to attract the female segment and famous professional men when trying to reach the male market.

Pixels or Paper?

Answer Answers will vary. Students who agree may say this process will take place because more people have computers. Also, the music industry is setting a precedent by making music available over the Internet. Regarding the price, the cost of producing and storing printed books will not be required, making the price lower for the customer but profitable for the publisher. Those who disagree may be skeptical about reading a book on a computer screen. They may also note that some people prefer tradition.

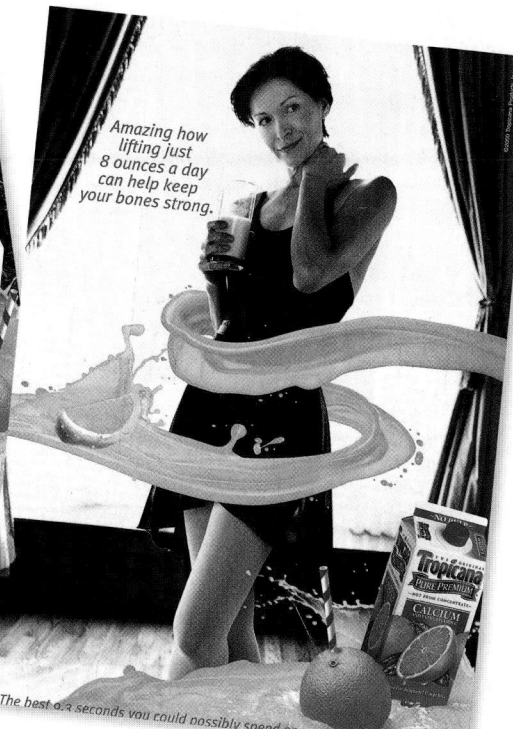

■ **Orange Juice—A Gender-Neutral Product** Gender-neutral products can still segment the market by appealing to males and females with a different ad message. *How did Tropicana Orange Juice, a gender-neutral product, target men and women in these two ads?*

It takes longer to read the list of vitamins than it does to drink it.

Tropicana Pure Premium Orange Juice. Pure, delicious, and thoroughly nutritious. Amazing how something this easy can be so good for you.

The best 9.3 seconds you could possibly spend on yourself. Everyday.

Amazing how lifting just 8 ounces a day can help keep your bones strong.

The best 9.3 seconds you could possibly spend on yourself. Everyday.

[handwritten: Next, the book talks about disposable + discretionary income. Who can tell me the difference?]

INCOME Marketers want to know how much money is available for spending on different products. For this reason, they look at two types of income measurement: disposable income and discretionary income.

Disposable income is the money left after taking out taxes. Marketers who produce and distribute products that are necessities are interested in changes in consumers' disposable income. **Discretionary income** is the money left after paying for basic living necessities such as food, shelter, and clothing. Marketers who sell luxury products are interested in changes in consumers' discretionary income. *[handwritten: What do you spend your discretionary income on?]*

Marketers also study the different income levels in the United States. In many cases, income levels help to distinguish different socioeconomic groups from one another. The affluent are a small percentage of the population. In 2000, approximately eight million households reported household income of $100,000 or more. Even though these affluent households are small in number, they account for upwards of half of all discretionary spending in the United States.

ETHNIC BACKGROUND The U.S. population is becoming more diverse, mainly as a result of increased immigration. The Caucasian population is declining, while the other ethnic populations are increasing. Combined African-American, Hispanic, and Asian-American populations make up 28 percent of the U.S. population. By 2025 these ethnic groups will represent 37.2 percent of all Americans (see Figure 2-3 on page 28). Let's take a look at these growing markets.

African-Americans number approximately 35 million, represent 12.2 percent of the total population, and spend roughly $400 billion annually.

To reach the African-American market, businesses may use ethnically targeted magazines, such as

[handwritten bottom: Lower Class — lower lower, upper lower | Middle Class — lower middle, upper middle - Readin | Upper Class — lower upper (NEW $) Gates, Winfrey, Martha Stewart; upper upper (OLD $) Vanderbilt, Rockefeller, Kennedy]

Thinking Critically

1. **Cultural Demographics** Have students brainstorm a list of cultures that have significantly different orientations from U.S. demographic or psychographic characteristics. As a starting point, use the U.S. preoccupation with youth as an example. Have students suggest some cultures that value old age and summarize the possible effect of such a cultural attitude on product marketing. *(Cultures that value age might include various Asian and African cultures. The consequences for marketing would include more older people in ads for all products; a slower, calmer, more reflective pace in advertisements; and an emphasis on respect for older people and the life experiences they have accumulated. Other cultural attitudes that students might consider include value placed on material wealth, extended families, and preservation of natural resources.)*

2. **Trends** Have students suggest current trends that have made an impact on what they eat, buy, and how they spend free time. What products have addressed those new trends? *(Cell phones address the trend of being connected at all times.)*

CAPTION ANSWER
Orange Juice—a Gender Neutral Product This ad targets women and men by using the same layout design and tagline, but different models and text appropriate for each gender.

THE DECA CONNECTION

COMPETITIVE EVENTS AND MARKETING ESSENTIALS

Series and Written Events DECA's Competitive Events Program is grouped into two categories: series events and written events. The Individual Series events allow students to demonstrate competencies in nine occupational areas. Students take a comprehensive exam that tests general marketing and occupation-specific knowledge. (For resources to teach and assess occupation-specific vocabulary, go to the *Marketing Essentials* Web site: **www.marketing.glencoe.com**.) Students also test their marketing knowledge in spontaneous role-play situations. The 16 Written Events require participants to complete an activity, such as community service, then orally present a written report to a judge during a fifteen-minute presentation.

Cooperative Learning

Market Segmentation In order to extend students' understanding of market segmentation, break the class into small groups. Give each group a product such as a bottle of vitamins, a hair-care product, a pair of sneakers, or a box of facial tissues. Have the groups develop the key benefit of their products to target a specific market that has been segmented by geographics, demographics, or psychographics. Then have the groups identify a different market segment that could be targeted with only minor changes to the product or packaging.

Independent Practice

1. **Prepare** Using more than one variable to segment a market, have students prepare a customer profile for a new soft drink, breakfast food, automobile, or video game.

2. **Research and Compare** Have students research the current population reports on consumer income published by the U.S. Census Bureau and U.S. Department of Commerce. Suggest that students compare their information to the information in the book and describe any trends that seem to be developing. In particular, suggest that they look for changes in population and income distribution.

REAL WORLD MARKETING

¡Yo Quiero Taco Bell!

Taco Bell's creative advertising helped it to become the nation's leading Mexican fast-food restaurant. Its sales now exceed $5 billion. In addition to its popular advertising campaign featuring a talking Chihuahua, the company integrated many other promotional activities. They include offering talking Chihuahua dolls as in-store premiums and entering into licensing agreements with major retailers to sell keychains, hats, backpacks, T-shirts, and full-size versions of the Chihuahua. Taco Bell's integrated marketing campaign has proven to be a huge success.

Thinking Critically
Do you think Taco Bell's advertising targets only one ethnic group? Why or why not?

census.gov

Essence and *Black Enterprise*. Businesses have learned that to effectively reach this market they must back up promotional activities with community support. An example is Maybelline, who formulated the Shades of You line of cosmetics for African-American women. The company also runs Black History Month promotions and has worked with The Coalition of 100 Black Women, a national organization dedicated to improving the lives of women.

Understanding the culture and religion of an ethnic group is important. For example, J.C. Penney utilized the African-American tradition of wearing white to church on the fifth Sunday of a month to promote white suits in African-American women's magazines. That promotion helped to sell out white suits in the chain's urban locations.

Hispanics number approximately 32 million, representing over 11 percent of the U.S. population. Hispanics will surpass African-Americans as the largest U.S. ethnic group by 2010.

Marketers would be wise to understand that the Hispanic culture is diverse and comprises 21 nationalities, including Mexican, Spanish, Puerto Rican, Cuban, Dominican, Caribbean, and others of Central and South American ancestry. Approximately 70 percent of Hispanics are Roman Catholics. Hispanic

FIGURE 2-3

Population Projection

| | Year 2000 | Year 2025 |

SOURCE: U.S. CENSUS

- **Caucasian** 71.4% / 62.0%
- **African-American** 12.2% / 12.8%
- **Hispanic** 11.8% / 18.2%
- **Native American** .7% / .8%
- **Asian-American** 3.9% / 6.2%

■ **Census 2000** The United States conducts a census every ten years to determine the characteristics of the population. Marketers use that information to segment the market for their products. *Which ethnic group is declining? Which ethnic groups are increasing?*

REAL WORLD MARKETING

¡Yo Quiero Taco Bell!
Answer Answers will vary. Most students will say "no" because the humor used in Taco Bell's advertising is geared for the general population, not just the Hispanic audience.

FIGURE 2–3 ANSWER
Census 2000 The U.S. population is becoming more diverse. The Caucasian population is declining, while the other ethnic populations are increasing.

3. **Research** Have students conduct demographic research on their own neighborhoods. Suggest that they obtain information from the U.S. Census Bureau, county or regional planning board, local real estate agencies, or even the local newspaper.
4. **Prepare a Table** Have students present their findings in table form. Possible entries include but are not limited to the following: population; number of males/females; number or percentage of people in different age groups; number of households; average number of people per household; median household income; educational background of residents; occupations of residents; and percentage of area zoned for residential, commercial, and rural uses.
5. **Write and Discuss** Once the tables have been presented, have students organize their thoughts by writing composite descriptions of their community (the area served by their school). Then discuss these community profiles by asking students which findings they anticipated and which came as a surprise to them.

■ **Who's Watching TV?** Marketers of products for the Hispanic population look for Spanish-speaking media to get their message out. Univision has become America's number one growth network by catering to a Spanish-speaking audience. *Why is television a good medium to use when targeting the U.S. Hispanic population?*

culture centers around the family, and these families tend to be larger than the U.S. average (3.4 people vs. 2.6 for all U.S. families). Food marketers know that when they sell products in Hispanic neighborhoods, the package sizes must be big.

To reach Hispanics, marketers should consider using Spanish-language television. Statistics show Hispanics watch television approximately four hours on weekdays, and most of that time is spent watching Spanish-language programming. Two magazines that can be used to target Hispanics are *People en Espanol* and *Latina*. Radio advertising is also a good medium to reach Hispanics because music is a major part of the Latino culture.

The Asian-American population numbers a little more than 11 million, representing almost 4 percent of the total U.S. population. Americans of Asian descent are the fastest-growing and most affluent population group. Like Hispanics, Asian-Americans are a diverse ethnic group. This group includes

16 different nationalities, including Chinese, Filipino, Japanese, Asian-Indian, Korean, and Vietnamese.

To reach the Asian-American market, it is important to understand its culture and priorities. More Asian-Americans are college graduates than any other ethnic group, and a higher percentage hold professional jobs. Marketers of financial services, computers, telecommunications, and new vehicles may target this segment because Asian-Americans are big consumers of such commodities.

Because there is no national broadcast media for Asian-Americans, marketers can use less costly local media to reach them. Asian-Americans prefer to communicate in their native languages, so it is very important for marketers to understand their languages. When advertising a banking institution, the major theme, such as financial security, can be the same for Chinese and Koreans, but the copy and models must be different to reflect the two groups.

Chapter 2 ■ *Basic Marketing Concepts* **29**

CAPTION ANSWER
Who's Watching TV? Statistics reveal that Hispanics watch approximately four hours of television each weekday, and most of that time is spent watching Spanish-language programming.

Did You Know? Marketers outside the United States have a more difficult time collecting data on their customers than marketers inside the United States. In the United Kingdom, for example, the Data Protection Act outlaws gathering data on an individual that includes the individual's address without written consent of the individual.

■ Psychographics

Psychographics involves studies of consumers based on social and psychological characteristics. People's attitudes and what they value are of importance to marketers, as are their lifestyles. Consumer lifestyles, which include how people spend their time and money, are closely related to people's attitudes and values. If you made a list of all of your present activities, you would come to realize just how many market segments can be identified by psychographics. It is amazing how similar the attitudes are of people who share common interests. You simply need to begin by looking at people involved in certain sports, such as tennis, golf, skiing, and boating, to see similarities in the participants. Magazine publishers recognize psychographic similarities and publish magazines geared to specific consumer interests. *Golf Digest*, *Photography*, *Ski*, and *Sports Illustrated* are just a few examples.

TRENDS In addition to segmenting people by their leisure time interests and membership in a given generation, marketers observe changes in households, the economy, politics, and the workplace. These factors contribute to changes in personal attitudes about health, time, fun, and living in general.

Health, eating properly, and exercising are trend-setting issues for marketers in the twenty-first century. A promotional campaign for Kellogg's Special K cereal tells women to "Reshape Your Attitude" by eating sensibly and encourages them to establish a healthier lifestyle. A walk through the supermarket will also tell the story, as more and more foods come with claims that they are organically grown, low-fat, fat-free, low-sodium, vitamin-enriched, calcium-fortified, and even cholesterol-lowering.

Work, fun, and indulgence are also key lifestyle issues. A current workplace trend is dressing down. Businesses call it business casual attire. Wisk with Wrinkle Reducer is a product that addresses that trend, as casual clothing generally requires more ironing.

Many Americans are being encouraged to take a break and indulge themselves. Ben & Jerry's tells consumers to "Stop and taste the ice cream." The ice cream company is suggesting "work stoppages,"

Life In The Diverse MARKETPLACE

What Does Yes Really Mean?

In many Asian societies, it is impolite to say "no," so "yes" has multiple meanings. "Yes" can mean that listeners recognize that they are being spoken to, although they don't understand what is being said, or that the speaker's words are understood, but not agreed with. It can also mean that something is understood, but other people must be told of it before any final decisions are made. "Yes" can also mean that an offer is comprehended, but if the situation were to change, their "yes" would also be subject to change.

Thinking Critically

Why is having a keen cultural ear important in cross-cultural marketing?

so workers can take an indulgence break during the workday. Häagen Dazs ice cream ran a similar promotion called "Passport to Indulge."

Time has become a commodity to market. With the stresses of work, time has become a luxury and vacations have become the number one luxury enjoyed by Americans. Enjoying one's leisure time has become paramount. Proof of this trend can be seen in the increase in spending on entertainment, including concerts, museums, theater, theme parks, sports, toys, and electronics.

Upscaling is another trend that has become apparent due to the strong economy. It seems more and more people (upper and middle classes alike) desire the better things in life. In 1975 only 38 percent of Americans said a lot of money was part of a good life; now 63 percent do. Name brand products and premium versions of everyday products are being sold in discount stores. Architect and designer Michael Graves has designed hundreds of everyday items that are sold at Target stores. The luxury market is definitely a consumer trend, as individuals define themselves through the products and brands they buy.

Life In The Diverse MARKETPLACE

What Does Yes Really Mean?

Answer Understanding subtle cultural differences is important in interpreting what is spoken and perceiving it as intended. Business deals may be lost due to misunderstanding the true intentions of the parties concerned.

Cultural differences are apparent in advertising. For example, American advertising is often ineffective in Japan because of subtle differences in U.S. and Japanese cultures. Western ads are often direct and focus on the individual; Japanese ads offer subtle messages and emphasize the person as part of a community or family. Japanese ads take a soft-sell approach.

■ Geographics

The term **geographics** refers to segmentation of the market based on where people live. To segment a market geographically, you can refer to local, regional, national, or even global markets. Some businesses, by their very nature, segment their market locally. For example, a small independent restaurant generally caters to people who live in its vicinity. There are products that are marketed nationally and internationally, such as Coca Cola and Pepsi. Marketers study where their customers live in order to decide which media to use and where to market their products.

Marketers also study geographics in relation to ethnic concentrations. For example, when selecting advertising media to reach the Hispanic market, businesses look at the four states with the highest Hispanic population: New York, Texas, California, and Florida. When segmenting the market for the Hispanic population, the Ford Motor Company created a Spanish language vehicle catalog in 2000 for dealerships in those states.

Where people live is often studied in relation to age, ethnic background, and income. To assist in such study, the U.S. government created Metropolitan Statistical Areas (MSAs). These are specifically defined geographic areas used by the

■ **Need a Vacation?** Two current psychographic trends involve time and indulgence. With the stresses of work, enjoying one's limited free time has become an important commodity. *How did this candy company utilize that trend in this ad?*

Wear Your Office

Clothing designers are responding to customers' desire for style in the new digital age by creating clothing with functional pockets for the portable electronic gadgets we carry. Savvy consumers are now sporting cleverly designed clothing with extra pockets to keep their beepers, pagers, cell phones, and palmtops in handy reach. The gizmo-oriented pocket is even starting to be offered in clothing appropriate for the office. Brooks Brothers has responded to the new portability craze by adding cell phone pockets in all outerwear and an extra inner pocket to its suit jackets.

Thinking Creatively
With the technology revolution all around us, what other products could be redesigned to capitalize on the psychographic trend of being connected wherever you go?

Chapter 2 ■ *Basic Marketing Concepts* **31**

BRIGHT IDEAS   Wear Your Office

Answer Cellular phone manufacturers make phones that allow automobile drivers to speak hands-free. Some phones have the technology to respond to voice commands. Voice recognition technology is so advanced that no one except the owner can activate the phone. Other new products that capitalize on being connected are hand-held computers and watches that send messages or make telephone calls.

SECTION 2.2

Enrichment

1. **Review** Assign and review the Chapter 2 activities in the *Student Activity Workbook.*
2. **Review** Assign and review the appropriate Thinking Critically questions from the Chapter Assessment.
3. **Review** Assign and review the following Chapter Assessment activities: Building Workplace Skills, Applying Marketing Concepts, Linking School to Work Activities, The DECA Connection Role Play, and Internet Connection.
4. **Identify** Ask students to identify a psychographic trend that is relevant to teenagers and the impact that trend is having on the sales of certain products. *(Trends will vary. Possibilities include eating healthier foods, which has led to the development of a wide range of natural beverages, like bottled teas and waters; staying fit which has manifested itself through interest in new forms of exercise like in-line skating and the marketing of fashionable workout attire.)*
5. **Write** Have students review the special advertising section on the Hispanic Market in the July 26, 1999 edition of *BrandWeek.* Ask them to provide a written summary of the main theme of the advertising section. *(The Hispanic market is growing and more marketers should learn more about that population and how to effectively reach them.)*

government in the distribution of federal aid, such as Medicare payments and grants for urban development. Marketers use MSAs to target consumers and launch promotional campaigns. *Sales and Marketing Management* magazine reports on where people are moving and how much spending power residents have in the various MSAs.

In general, the geographic trend in the United States has been for people to move to the South, the West, and the Southwest. Certain states are growing faster than others. Nevada was the fastest growing state in 2000. Other states that have been experiencing fast growth include Arizona, Colorado, Georgia, and Idaho.

The propensity to use and buy products in a given region is also an important issue to marketers, especially when introducing a new product. Marketers determine which geographic areas would be most receptive to a new product using sales data coupled with psychographic data. For example, a new energy drink, Torq, was first introduced in California and the Pacific Northwest, where research indicated consumers were more receptive to "energy" drinks with special ingredients, like ginseng. Psychographic data shows that trendsetters tend to be located in these regions of the country.

■ Product Benefits

Segmenting a market by product benefits involves studying consumers' needs and wants. Companies market benefits, not simply the physical characteristics of a product. For example, sports shoe manufacturers identify separate market segments for people who jog, walk, play tennis, or do aerobics. Each activity requires a shoe with a particular design. Thus, manufacturers market different shoes for each segment. A shampoo manufacturer may segment the market according to people with different types of hair (oily, dry, or normal), people who have dandruff, or people who wash their hair frequently. Soda manufacturers cater to specific segments by developing diet and caffeine-free soft drinks.

2.2 ASSESSMENT

Reviewing Key Terms and Concepts
1. What do demographics, psychographics, geographics, and product benefits have in common?
2. How can a market be segmented using demographics?
3. What does the study of psychographics involve?
4. Provide one example of how a marketer can segment a market based on product benefits.
5. Of what significance are the combined African-American, Hispanic, and Asian-American populations to marketers?

Thinking Critically
6. How can Procter and Gamble market household products to a male market segment? What problems might P&G encounter in that endeavor?

Integrating Academic Skills
7. **COMMUNICATION** Write an ad campaign theme for Sunsweet Prunes to target baby boomers who are looking for healthy foods. Develop a second campaign theme to target a younger generation with Sunsweet Prunes.

Careers in Marketing

PRODUCT MANAGEMENT

Lori Tauber Marcus
Director of Brand Management
Pepsico Fountain Beverage Division

What does your job entail?

"I supervise the development, production, and sale of Pepsi brands for Pepsi's fountain beverage division, the part of the company that sells beverages to restaurants and theaters. I conduct research to determine the profitability of products being developed, then I oversee the marketing of the product. I also help with advertising and training the sales force. After the product has been marketed, I conduct follow-up research to determine how well it is doing and what changes may need to be made to increase profitability."

What kind of training did you have?

"A few years after earning a bachelor's degree in marketing in college, I went to work for Pepsi, first in the food service marketing division and then as an associate product manager for Pepsi's Mountain Dew brand. I was promoted to customer marketing manager for retail marketing, customizing Pepsi promotions for mass retailers like Target and Kmart. I became area marketing manager for the eastern seaboard, then senior product manager for new cola concepts."

What skills are most important?

"Leadership skills are essential—as a brand manager you lead teams of many people, each performing different functions who are pivotal in bringing your product to market. It is important to have the ability to think creatively and strategically. It is also important to have an aptitude for gathering and analyzing data and making decisions based on the data."

What is your key to success?

"I really love doing what I do. Also, I have been fortunate to have always worked with very smart and highly motivated people from whom I'm constantly learning."

Thinking Critically
What types of experience would you emphasize when applying for a job as a brand manager?

Career Facts

Education and Training: A bachelor's or master's degree in marketing or business and coursework in communication, economics, and math is recommended. College coursework should be accompanied by several years of sales experience.

Aptitudes, Abilities, and Skills: Analytical skills, organizational skills, leadership skills, communication skills, interpersonal skills, and math skills are necessary.

Career Outlook: Many new jobs are opening in the computer and Internet industry, as well as in the electronics industry in general.

Career Path: A typical path to brand manager is through a management trainee job. A staff position in the marketing department can sharpen analytical skills.

Chapter 2 • *Basic Marketing Concepts* • **33**

Careers in Marketing

Ask a student to read the Careers in Marketing feature aloud to the class. Discuss the skills and aptitudes required for a career in product management. Ask students whether they think they would like or dislike a career in product management. Discuss the pros and cons of such a career.

Thinking Critically Answer
Experience managing and working as part of a team should be emphasized as well as leadership and communication skills.

 Guest Speaker
Invite a brand manager from a local company to come to class to discuss his/her job.

Exploring Careers

Matching Careers to Learning Styles
1. Read to students the eight different ways that people learn:

Linguistic: You like to talk, write, read, and listen. You learn best through listening and interacting verbally and in writing.

Logical/Mathematical: You like to work with numbers and do experiments. You learn best in mathematical terms and working with patterns.

Bodily/Kinesthetic: You are athletic and like to move your body.

Spatial: You are creative and like to draw, build, and design things.

Musical: You like to play and listen to music. You learn well through music.

Interpersonal: You like to interact with people.

Interpersonal: You like to learn alone at your own pace.

Naturalistic: You learn best in a natural environment.

2. Ask students to list their top three ways of learning.

Lifelong Learning

Basic Marketing Concepts
Learning a second (or third) language is a lifelong process. High school and college are good places to learn languages. The language must be practiced regularly outside the classroom for the speaker to gain and maintain fluency. For those interested in a marketing career, Spanish and/or an Asian language could be valuable.

Meeting Individual Needs

Students With Hearing Impairments
If you have students with hearing impairments, face the class while you speak. Avoid talking as you write on the board or when you are not facing the students. Many students with hearing impairments depend on lipreading to facilitate comprehension. Remember to enunciate clearly and speak in a natural tone of voice.

Vocabulary Review

Paragraphs will vary. See Glossary for definitions.

Fact and Idea Review

1. The marketing concept ensures profit by focusing on the needs and wants of customers.
2. A parent buying cereal for a child is an example.
3. A market is all of the potential customers who share common needs and wants, and have the ability and willingness to buy a particular product. People who buy ice cream are one part of the ice cream market.
4. The four Ps are product, price, place, and promotion. Decisions made about the four Ps should be focused on the target market.
5. It is categorizing the market into smaller groups who share characteristics. A market can be segmented by demographics, psychographics, geographics, and product benefits.
6. Each generation shares certain common bonds because they live in the same era. Three are the Baby Boom Generation, Generation X, and Generation Y.
7. Disposable income is the money left after taxes. Discretionary income is the money left after paying basic living necessities.
8. They have formulated lines of cosmetics for ethnic skin and marketed those products through ethnically targeted magazines.
9. Asian-Americans
10. They can segment by product benefits for people with different hair types (oily, dry, or normal), with dandruff, with color-treated hair, or by people who shampoo often.

Thinking Critically

1. Answers will vary.
2. Census data can be used because it shows what products, promotions, prices, and places to sell products to reach specific groups.
3. Answers will vary. BENGAY can be marketed to young adults for muscle aches due to strenuous exercise, and to seniors for arthritis symptoms. Different markets require different appeals.
4. The income level of Wal-Mart's target market (value-oriented consumers) is lower than that of an affluent target market.

34

Chapter **2** ASSESSMENT

VOCABULARY REVIEW

Write one paragraph to show your understanding of how the following concepts are related to one another.

- marketing concept
- customers
- consumers
- market
- target marketing
- customer profile
- marketing mix
- market segmentation
- demographics
- psychographics
- geographics

FACT AND IDEA REVIEW

1. What is the marketing concept? (2.1)
2. Provide an example of when a consumer is not the customer of a product purchased in a retail store. (2.1)
3. Define the concept of a market and give an example of one. (2.1)
4. Name the four Ps of the marketing mix and explain how they should be used in target marketing. (2.1)
5. Explain market segmentation and the four main ways a market can be segmented. (2.2)
6. Why do generations make good markets to segment? Name the three recent generations that marketers use to segment the market. (2.2)
7. What is the difference between disposable income and discretionary income? (2.2)

8. How have cosmetic companies targeted African-American women? (2.2)
9. Which ethnic group is the most affluent? (2.2)
10. How might a shampoo manufacturer segment the market according to product benefits? (2.2)

THINKING CRITICALLY

1. The United States is becoming more affluent. Because of this, make a plan to change a regular food product to create an upscale image for that product—a premium brand.
2. How can a marketer of consumer products use the data from the U.S. Census 2000?
3. How would you position BENGAY to young adults? How would you position the same product to senior citizens? Would you use the same appeal? Why or why not?
4. Using market segmentation based on income, explain Wal-Mart's success.

BUILDING WORKPLACE SKILLS

1. **Human Relations** A shabbily dressed couple enters a luxury automobile showroom, but the sales associates are not eager to approach them. A younger associate finally does and eventually sells them a $50,000 car. The couple puts down $20,000 cash as a down payment. What is the point of this story? What does it say about how lifestyle characteristics can be misleading?
2. **Technology** You have been hired by a stockbroker to research the geographic areas in the country that include high-income households. What technology is available to help you in this endeavor?

Building Workplace Skills

1. Lifestyle variables are not always the same for different socio-economic groups.
2. You can find high-income households by conducting research using CD-ROMs that include this information, or you can research Internet databases.

Applying Marketing Concepts

1. Summaries will depend on articles selected.
2. Research and recommendations will vary based on the companies researched. Students should cite their resources and provide rationale for their recommendations.
3. Reports will vary, but examples include: for Kwanzaa, retail stores carry cards, candles, gifts, and unity cups; for Diwali, American Hindus call family abroad, so U.S. phone companies offer discounted rates on calls to India at that

APPLYING MARKETING CONCEPTS

1. **Summarizing Key Concepts** Summarize an article that demonstrates any of the key concepts in this chapter. In the summary, identify the specific concepts in parentheses. Use business publications, such as *BrandWeek, Adweek, BusinessWeek, Fortune, Forbes, Marketing News,* and *Nation's Business,* to find an applicable article.

2. **Analyzing Marketing Strategies** Using the Internet, find research that describes characteristics of the teenage market. Then visit the Web sites of five companies (manufacturers or retailers) that target teens. Use a word processing program to write a short report analyzing each company's marketing mix strategies and citing your sources of information. Do all four Ps target teenagers effectively? Select one company to provide recommendations on how it could improve its marketing mix strategies when trying to target teens.

3. **Recognizing Target Marketing** Using the Internet, research the holidays of Kwanzaa (African-American celebration of racial pride and unity), Diwali (Hindu festival of lights), and Hanukkah (traditional Jewish celebration). Report how American marketers use knowledge of such holidays.

4. **Researching Psychographic Trends** Research one of the trends noted in the text. Make an oral presentation to the class using presentation software. Be sure to include current examples of how the trend is being used by different companies in their marketing mix strategies. Lastly, evaluate their effectiveness with your classmates.

LINKING SCHOOL TO WORK

Thinking Skills Develop a profile of a local company's customers based on their geographic, demographic, and psychographic characteristics.

THE DECA CONNECTION

Role Play: Toy Company Intern

Situation You are to assume the role of an intern in the marketing department of a consumer product manufacturing company that specializes in toys and electronic games. A new electronic game is being developed and the Research and Development (R&D) Director (judge) has asked for your input. You are to meet with the R&D Director (judge) in fifteen minutes.

Activity You must decide what you will tell the R&D Director (judge) about the strategies to use for product, place, price, and promotion decisions (the four Ps) of the marketing mix. In your presentation include consideration of the product's consumers and customers, as well as concepts such as target marketing and market segmentation.

Evaluation You will be evaluated on how well you meet the following performance indicators:

- Define target marketing
- Explain the difference between consumers and customers
- Explain the role of market segmentation
- Explain marketing mix strategies
- Demonstrate appropriate creativity

*inter*NET CONNECTION

Head Count
The Census Bureau undertakes a count of the population every 10 years to track changes in population size and demographics.

Connect
- Locate the U.S. Census Web site. Find the current figures and percentages of age and income by ethnic groups (Caucasian, African-American, Hispanic, and Asian-American).

Chapter 2 ■ *Basic Marketing Concepts* **35**

THE DECA CONNECTION

Students should be evaluated on the performance indicators noted in the Role Play.
- For another DECA Role Play, go to the *Student Activity Workbook,* p. 15.
- For more in-depth Role Play practice, refer to DECA's *Essential Competitive Events Handbook.* To order, contact DECA at **www.deca.org**.

*inter*NET CONNECTION

Search the U.S. Census Bureau's Web site to get the current figures.

Mini Quiz

Administer the Mini Quiz orally. For an expanded quiz, go to page 5 of the *Reproducible Tests* book.

1. The marketing concept states that businesses must satisfy customers' needs and wants to make a profit.

2. Target marketing focuses marketing decisions on a specific group of people.

3. The four Ps of the marketing mix are: product, place, price, and promotion.

4. Analyzing a market by specific characteristics in order to create a target market is called market segmentation.

5. Four ways a marketer can segment a market are: demographics, psychographics, geographics, and product benefits.

---

time; for Hanukkah, retailers sell gifts, specialty food items, and menorahs.
4. Presentations will vary but should focus on a trend that is covered in the text.

Linking School to Work

Students' profiles will depend on the selected company. Evaluate for thoroughness of the company profile.

GO TO
1. **Assessment** Have students complete the Reproducible Test for Chapter 2 and Unit 1 or construct your own tests using the ExamView software.
2. **Enrichment** Have students complete the corresponding activities in the following workbooks:
   - *Marketing Math Workbook,* p. 1
   - *Marketing Research Project Workbook,* p. 1

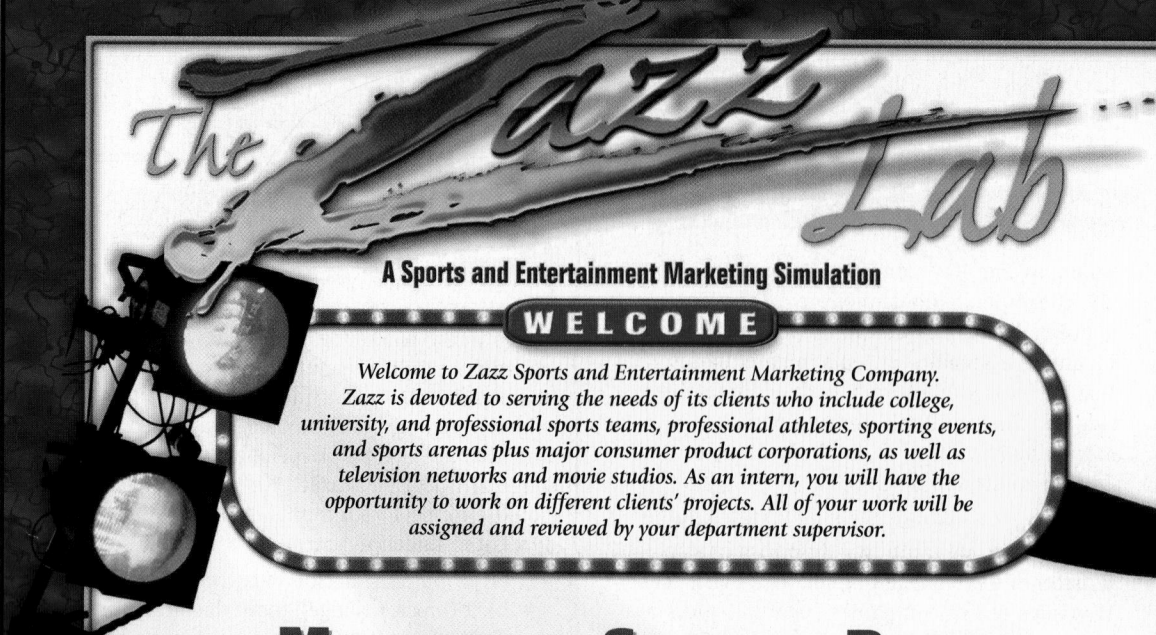

The Zazz Lab...

A Sports and Entertainment Marketing Simulation

WELCOME

Welcome to Zazz Sports and Entertainment Marketing Company. Zazz is devoted to serving the needs of its clients who include college, university, and professional sports teams, professional athletes, sporting events, and sports arenas plus major consumer product corporations, as well as television networks and movie studios. As an intern, you will have the opportunity to work on different clients' projects. All of your work will be assigned and reviewed by your department supervisor.

MARKET A SPORTS DRINK

SITUATION

Your client is RJF Beverage Company, the creator of a new sports drink. The company is entering the "active thirst" market—beverages consumed by people when they're hot and sweaty. The market has been dominated by Gatorade, the sports drink made by Quaker Oats. Other competing brands are Powerade (Coca-Cola) and AllSport (Pepsi). Your client thinks it has a formula for a new sports drink that's even better than Gatorade's. Your client believes that affiliation with a popular sport would help get this new product off the ground.

ASSIGNMENT

Your supervisor wants you to conduct an analysis of the current sports drink market for the new client. You have also been asked to generate creative ideas with regard to the marketing mix for the new product. *Product* ideas should include designing the container and naming the product. *Place* suggestions involve deciding how to get the product into the hands of the consumer. *Price* recommendations should be based on the competitor's pricing strategies. *Promotion* ideas should be creative. Consider sponsorship of a sports team or an endorsement by a professional athlete as part of the promotional mix.

Tools and Resources

To complete this assignment, you will need to conduct research at a library or on the Internet. You will also need a word processing program, a spreadsheet program, and presentation software. Trade publications that may be helpful include *BrandWeek, Advertising Age, Sports Business Journal,* and *Sports Business Daily.*

Research

Research the sports drink market and the major competitors. Find out how much is sold and who buys it. For your customer profile, research geographics, demographics, and psychographics. Determine the market share (percentage of total market) each competitor enjoys. Study each major competitor's product, pricing, promotion, and place decisions. Find out which sports drinks are being endorsed by sports personalities, teams, or leagues, and whether they have special agreements. See if any of the main competitors have Web sites; if they do, find out what is included. Secure samples of competitors' advertising and promotions if possible. You want to see what the RJF company needs to do to break into the sports drink market.

CRUSHING THE COMPETITION

With a huge head start in the sports drink market, Gatorade crushes the competition at the finish line and the checkout line. The popular drink is loaded with electrolytes—mineral salt solutions that are needed for cells to work normally. In 1999 Gatorade commanded 82 percent of the U.S. sports drink market and had global sales of $1.83 billion. Profits topped $250 million in 1999, Gatorade's fastest growth year ever with a 12 percent rise in U.S. sales.

Presentation and Evaluation

In addition to your written report, your supervisor wants you to present your ideas orally and show him your presentation. The presentation will later be shown to the client. You will be evaluated on your oral presentation skills, including:

- Knowledge of the sports drink market and marketing mix strategies
- Continuity of presentation
- Voice quality
- Eye contact

Portfolio

Print out a copy of your completed report and presentation for your Portfolio.

Report

Prepare both a written report and a computer presentation for the client. Use a word processing program to prepare a double-spaced report. Use a spreadsheet program to create a pie chart to illustrate the current market share of the major competitors in the sports drink market. Include the pie chart in your written report. Also include samples of competitors' advertising. Arrange your written report around the following headings:

- Background on the sports drink market
  - The market
  - Market trends
  - Customer analysis (demographics, geographics, psychographics)
- Analysis of major competitors
  - Product, place, price, and promotion decisions
- Proposed target market for RJF
- Marketing mix decisions for RJF
  - Product (name, container), place, price, and promotion (main theme, slogan, publicity, special promotions, advertising) decisions

Using computer presentation software, prepare a presentation of your ideas for the client that includes:

- Key topics covered in your written report
- Graphic illustrations that are relevant to each slide's topic
- Very little text
- Minimum of 10 slides

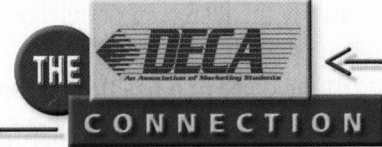

THE DECA CONNECTION

DECA Food Marketing Event
Making decisions concerning how to sell the product to the consumer through supermarkets and other food retailers is a possible scenario for a role play in this event.

DECA Business Service Marketing Series
Generating marketing ideas for a client for a fee could be a potential role play for this event.

DECA Marketing Management Series
Strategizing marketing mix decisions is part of this career area.

DECA Food Marketing Research Event
Developing a customer profile and ideas for marketing a food product could be a topic for this event.

DECA Sports and Entertainment Marketing Management Team Decision-Making Event
Working on this project with a partner will make the experience similar to what is expected in a DECA Team Decision-Making Event.

COOPERATIVE LEARNING

Teamwork This unit lab lends itself to working in teams of two to four students. The teams could compete with one another to come up with the best marketing strategies.

ASSESS

Enrichment

Investigate Have students investigate the pros and cons of having a professional athlete endorse a product. Have them include problems that have occurred in the past. Ask them to cite their sources in a written report. *(Problems could occur if the athlete is accused or found guilty of a crime; sustains injuries and is no longer in the limelight; or no longer uses the product because it hurts their performance, e.g., Vince Carter and Nike shoes.)*

Evaluation

The rubrics for evaluation of the written, oral, and computer presentation are included in the student text. (See the outline and guidelines for the written report, the computer presentation, and the skills' assessment for oral presentations.) It might be best to replicate those rubrics to evaluate the students' work. A separate rubric could be created to evaluate the work of a team.

CLOSE

Lab Wrap-Up

Ask students: How are the marketing concept, marketing mix strategies, and target marketing demonstrated in the marketing of sports drinks? *(marketing concept—drink to satisfy the needs of athletes; marketing mix—product includes ingredients to help improve endurance, and containers are designed with athletes in mind; promotion—advertising and promotion targets young athletes; place—product may be purchased in food stores and other places where athletes go; price—competitively priced. Target marketing—customer profile suggests that the primary target market is young male athletes with secondary markets for young women and children athletes.)*

Economics

Chapter 3
The Free Enterprise System

Chapter 4
Global Economies

Unit Objectives

After completing this unit, students will be able to:

- Summarize the key principles on which a modified free enterprise system is based.
- Explain how supply and demand interact to set prices.
- Identify various types of economies.
- Identify various economic measurements.
- Discuss the role of the government and the consumer in a market economy.
- Identify the factors of production and relate them to the three basic questions that all economies must answer.
- List the goals of a healthy economy and explain how they are measured.
- Describe the four phases of the business cycle.

Enrichment Resources

Books
Economics of Our Free Enterprise System by K.W. Brown and A. R. Warner
The Statesman's Yearbook 2001: The Politics, Cultures, and Economies of the World by Barry Turner, Editor

Magazines/Journals
BusinessWeek
Economist

Associations
American Economic Association
2014 Broadway, Suite 305
Nashville, TN 37203
(615) 343-7590
www.vanderbilt.edu/AEA/org.htm

National Association for Business Economics
1233 20th Street NW, Suite 505
Washington, DC 20036
(202) 463-6223
www.nabe.com

Journal Writing Activity

1. Ask students to freewrite in their journals for five minutes about their own concepts of economics in the United States. Let their work sit for part of the class time. Then have students share their journal entries by reading them to the class. Explain to students that a free enterprise system is characterized by private ownership, competition, profit, and risk.

2. Ask students to freewrite in their journals for 5–10 minutes about their concepts of economics in other countries, compared to the United States. Have students identify some advantages and disadvantages of some different world economies. Ask some volunteers to share their journal entries by reading them to the class. Write on the board different types of foreign economies. Ask the class to name some countries that have each type of economy. Then lead students in a discussion about the free enterprise system versus other types of world economies.

TEACHER CLASSROOM RESOURCES

Program Resources	Chapter 3	Chapter 4
Student Activity Workbook	p. 19	p. 27
Marketing Math Workbook	p. 5	p. 5
Marketing Research Project Workbook	p. 15	p. 15
ILP School-to-Work Activity Workbook	p. 9	p. 13
ILP *BusinessWeek* Case Studies	p. 13	p. 19
ILP Marketing Career Portfolio	p. 32	p. 32
Reproducible Tests	p. 13	p. 19
ExamView User's Guide and Testbank	p. 3-1	p. 4-1
ILP Internet Resources	p. 25	p. 27
ILP Blackline Masters	p. 5	p. 6
ILP Lesson Plans	p. 6	p. 8
ILP Block Scheduling	p. 2	p. 2
Impact! Simulation	p. 11	p. 11

ILP Each of these resources is available in print and on the Interactive Lesson Planner CD-ROM.

Technology Resources

- **Interactive Lesson Planner (ILP) CD-ROM**
- **PowerPoint Presentation CD-ROM**
- **Marketing Essentials Web site**
- **ExamView! CD-ROM**
- **Impact! Simulation**
  - **Virtual Business**

Virtual Business is a fully visual marketing and business simulation that introduces students to the principles of marketing by letting them start and run their own virtual businesses. In *Virtual Business*, students have the power to control all aspects of a retail convenience store. Students strategize marketing decisions using a powerful learning tool in the guise of a video game. They learn by experiencing how their decisions affect their virtual business.

Key to Individualized Academics Activities

L1 Level 1 activities are basic activities and should fall within the range of all students.

L2 Level 2 activities are average activities and should be within the range of average and above average students.

L3 Level 3 activities are challenging activities designed for the ability range of above average students.

National Marketing Education

CHAPTER	SECTION	PERFORMANCE INDICATOR
Chapter 3 **The Free Enterprise System**	3.1	Explain the types of economic systems (ECO)
		Explain the concept of private enterprise (ECO)
		Explain the concept of competition (ECO)
		Determine factors affecting business risk (ECO)
		Identify factors affecting a business's profit (ECO)
	3.2	Explain the relationship between government and business (ECO)
		Explain the principles of supply and demand (ECO)
Chapter 4 **Global Economies**	4.1	Explain the types of economic systems (ECO)
		Explain the concept of economic resources (ECO)
		Distinguish between economic goods and services (ECO)
		Describe the nature of economics and economic activities (ECO)
		Determine the relationship between government and business (ECO)
	4.2	Explain the concept of productivity (ECO)
		Explain the concept of Gross Domestic Product (ECO)
		Explain measures used to analyze economic conditions (ECO)
		Explain the nature of the Consumer Price Index (ECO)
		Determine the impact of business cycles on business activities (ECO)

CIS Communication, Interpersonal Skills **DIS** Distribution **FIN** Financing **PRI** Pricing **SEL** Selling

Standards Assessment Correlation

SECTION ASSESSMENT			CHAPTER ASSESSMENT						UNIT LAB
Reviewing Key Terms and Concepts	Thinking Critically	Integrating Academic Skills	Fact and Idea Review	Thinking Critically	Building Workplace Skills	Applying Marketing Concepts	Linking School to Work	Internet Connection	Zazz Lab
				1		1			
1, 3			1	1, 2, 3, 4, 5		2			●
2	●		2	1, 2, 3, 4, 5	1	1, 3			●
4		●		2		1, 3	●		
5	●	●	3, 4	2		1, 3			
1, 3	●		5, 6, 7, 8, 9	1, 3, 4	2	1, 2			
2, 4, 5		●	10	2, 4, 5	1				
1, 3, 4, 5		●	3, 4, 5	1		1, 2			
		●	1						
2			5			1			●
	●			2		2, 4			
	●	●	2	2		1		●	
1			6	3		1			
3		●	7			2, 3	●		
2, 3, 5	●	●	7, 8, 9		1	2, 3, 4		●	
3	●		8			1, 2		●	
4, 5	●		10	4		2, 3, 4			

Unit Overview

Unit 2 discusses some of the most basic principles of economic and political systems. Chapter 3 deals with the economic system the students are most familiar with—our own free enterprise system, characterized by private ownership, competition, profit, and risk. Chapter 4 launches students on a comparison of that system with other economic systems and the various political systems that go with them. The principles and practices explored in this unit will be used throughout the text to help students understand and appreciate why marketing is necessary in a market economy.

Introducing the Unit

Ask students why so many immigrants see the United States as the land of opportunity. *(U.S. citizens enjoy so many freedoms. These include but are not limited to economic freedoms like opening one's own business, making a profit, competing, and owning private property.)*

UNIT · 2

Portfolio

Controlling Interest Rates

Once you have completed this unit, you will research the economy of the United States or another country of your choice for the past year. Assume you are the government agency that controls the interest rates in that country. Analyze the economic indicators and decide what to do to improve the economy. You can decide to keep interest rates where they are, increase them, or decrease them based on your analysis of the economy and what you see as trends in the economy. Using computer software, prepare a written report and a presentation. Begin your report with a review of the recent history of the economy and indicate the trends you see. Then provide your recommendations for interest rates and your rationale for your decision. Prepare charts and graphs of the key economic indicators in your report. Print copies of your report and presentation for your Portfolio.

38

Field Trip Suggestions

Visit a Community Service Organization

Arrange for your students to visit the office of a local community service organization or local charity to observe its operation in your community and the support and resources made available to them by local and national businesses.

Economics

Unit Overview

Before you can study marketing, it is essential that you understand the economic principles that govern the way marketing functions in different economic systems. Chapter 3 covers the free enterprise system, characterized by private ownership, competition, profit, and risk. Chapter 4 addresses other types of economic systems found around the world and the operating philosophies that govern them. The second section of Chapter 4 provides the information on how an economy is measured and different stages that an economy can experience.

All these economic concepts will give you a better understanding of how governments, businesses, and consumers function during various economic phases and under different economic philosophies. As future marketers, those economic foundations become essential to knowing where, when, and how to market goods.

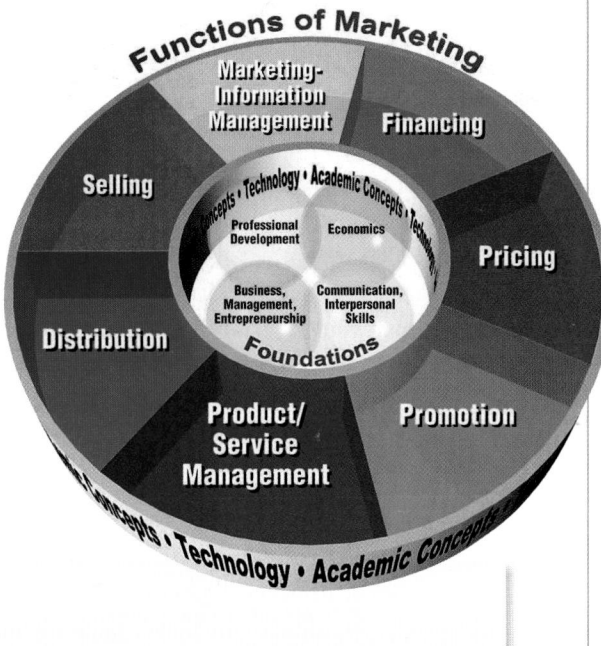

In this Unit:

Foundations of Marketing

◯ Economics

UNIT 2

◀ *DECA* **Unit Project**

Have chapter members prepare the National DECA Free Enterprise Project. Project guidelines may be obtained from National DECA, 1908 Association Drive, Reston, Virginia 22091.

As an alternative, have students conduct a survey of local business owners. The survey should focus on why they opened their own businesses and how the current economy and government are helping or hindering their success at the present time.

www Go to the *Marketing Essentials* Web site (**www.marketing.glencoe.com**) for resources to teach and assess occupation-specific vocabulary.

Unit Closure

Have students research and prepare a written report that compares the U.S. economy with that of another country, such as Japan, Germany, China, Brazil, Cuba, or North Korea. Require that students submit for your approval a detailed outline with references before giving them the go-ahead to write the final research paper.

Guest Speaker Suggestions

Business Owner Have a business owner who has immigrated to this country speak to your class about how the free enterprise marketplace in this country differs from the economic system in his or her native country. Ask the business owner to also discuss how state and federal government regulations affect his or her business.

Stockbroker Have your students select a company that interests them, then have them follow and record the company's stock price every trading day for a month. At the end of that period have a stockbroker explain market fluctuations to the class and how outside influences can affect stock prices.

Chapter 3

The Free Enterprise System

Chapter Overview

Chapter 3 describes the operation of the U.S. free enterprise system. The chapter identifies the basic principles of such a system. It also elaborates on government's role in our economy and the power of consumers.

Springboard

Brainstorm and Write Have students pretend they are would-be restaurateurs. Tell them to consider their options (type of restaurant, location, hours, menu prices), then write down their choices and share them. Note for later reference when the concepts of competition, profit, monopoly, and supply and demand are mentioned in any form.

Prereading

List the section objectives to discuss with students. Have students skim the chapter, looking at the pictures, reading the captions, and noting the heads. Ask questions to ensure that students have a minimal understanding of the chapter structure.

Preteaching Marketing Vocabulary

Dictate each of the vocabulary terms and ask students to write them on a sheet of paper. Then write the terms on the board and have students guess at the meanings. Write their guesses next to each term, but do not give the correct meaning. Leave this list on the board so that as students work through the chapter, they can see if their guesses were correct.

Marketing: What It Takes

Answer Answers will vary. You could invest the $25,000 in the stock market and be a part owner of a corporation (stockholder), start a new business enterprise, or invest in someone else's business.

Marketing: What It Takes

Exploring the Free Enterprise System

Imagine that you just inherited $25,000 with a restriction that you must invest it to prove you understand the United States free enterprise system. You cannot spend it on yourself.

WHAT WILL YOU DO? How will you go about investigating possibilities for investment?

40

Monopoly is a trademark for its real estate trading board game equipment. ©1990, 1995 Hasbro, Inc. All Rights R

YELLOW LINE RAILROAD

CHANCE

ROLL AGAIN

$2 $2

THE DECA CONNECTION — ADVISOR CORNER

Preparing for Competition Challenge your students to participate in one of DECA's competency-based Series Events. Help them to better understand what will be expected of them during the competition. Why not create a game show with competency-based questions? Divide the students into teams and have a competition. Offer a DECA novelty item (i.e., T-shirt, key chain, or hat) to members of the winning team. To prepare your students for occupation-specific questions, use the occupation-specific resources available on the *Marketing Essentials* Web site: **www.marketing.glencoe.com**. Another preparation resource is the event-specific *Student Training Guides* available through DECA Images. To order, contact DECA at **www.deca.org.**

Capitalism

Basic Principles

In the United States, we have the freedom to make decisions about where we work and how we spend our money. We also have the freedom to elect the people who represent us in our government. Our nation's founders believed that individuals should have freedom of choice and created the philosophy of the free enterprise system.

In theory, a free enterprise system encourages individuals to start and operate their own businesses without government involvement. The free enterprise system we have today is modified because the government does intervene on a limited basis. It does this to protect citizens and still support the basic principles of free enterprise. Let's look at the basic principles upon which free enterprise is established.

■ Freedom of Ownership

Individuals in our free enterprise system are free to own personal property, such as cars, computers, and homes, as well as natural resources such as oil and land. You can buy anything you want as long as it is not prohibited by law. You can also do what you want with your property in a free enterprise system. You can give it away, lease it, sell it, or use it yourself.

The free enterprise system encourages individuals to own businesses. There are, however, some restrictions on how and where those businesses may operate. Businesses that make things may be forced to comply with certain environmental measures. They may also be restricted in where they can locate. Most kinds of businesses are zoned out of areas intended for private housing.

Intellectual property rights are included in this freedom. Let's say that you get a patent on an invention—you alone own the property rights to that item or idea. To ensure that protection, you would apply for a patent in the U.S. Patent and Trademark Office. Anyone who wanted to manufacture your product would have to pay you for its use through a licensing agreement.

When a company wants to use another's name, symbol, or product, it must get permission to do so and pay a fee for the use. A licensing agreement protects the originator's name and products. A T-shirt manufacturer might be granted a licensing agreement with the National Football League (NFL) so that it can produce T-shirts with NFL logos on them. The company will have to pay NFL Properties a fee for this privilege. It will also have to agree to certain standards of operation imposed to protect the NFL's reputation.

• What You'll Learn

- Basic principles of a free enterprise system
- The role of competition
- The importance of risk and profit

• Why It's Important

In this chapter, you will develop an understanding of how our economic system operates. You will learn how prices are determined, as well as what roles the government and consumers play in that system.

• Key Terms

- free enterprise system
- competition
- price competition
- nonprice competition
- monopoly
- risk
- profit

Chapter 3 ■ The Free Enterprise System **41**

SECTION 3.1

FOCUS

Bell Ringer Activity

Discuss Ask students if they have earned money by baby-sitting, cutting lawns, making decorations or holiday gifts, or selling lemonade. If so, tell them that they were taking advantage of our free enterprise system.

Introducing the Section

Capitalism Ask students if any one of them could start their own business. Ask why that is possible. *(Because of the economic system we have in the United States.)* This will help you introduce the freedoms of our free enterprise system.

TEACH

Technology Resources

PowerPoint The *Marketing Essentials* PowerPoint Presentation CD-ROM provides visual lecture aids for every chapter section.

Concept Development

1. Read Section 3.1 with students.
2. Ask students: Do you have the freedom to decide:
   - if you want to work for someone or work for yourself?
   - to go to college or directly to work after high school?
   - which goods and services you are going to buy?
   - if you want to invest in a friend's new business or save your money in a bank?
   Answers to these questions will help introduce the freedoms of ownership, competition, profit, and risk.
3. Have students read aloud the Case Study on page 44. Review answers in class.

Classroom Resources

For the Teacher
- Teacher Editions for all workbooks
- Assessment Package
- PowerPoint Presentation Software
- Interactive Lesson Planner
- ILP Block Scheduling, p. 2
- ILP Lesson Plans, p. 6
- ILP Internet Resources, p. 25

- ILP *BusinessWeek* Case Studies, p. 13
- ILP Marketing Career Portfolio, p. 32
- *Marketing Essentials* Web site (**www.marketing.glencoe.com**)

For the Student
- Student Activity Workbook, p. 19
- Marketing Math Workbook, p. 5

- Marketing Research Project Workbook, p. 15
- ILP School-to-Work Activity Workbook, p. 9
- Virtual Business simulation
- *Marketing Essentials* Web site (**www.marketing.glencoe.com**)

ILP These resources are available in print and on the Interactive Lesson Planner (ILP)

Discussion Starter

Profit and Risk To emphasize the concepts of profit and risk, tell students that their class is going to start a new business selling T-shirts to students in your school. Go to several individual students and ask them how much of their own money they are willing to invest in that new business. Start off by asking if they are willing to invest $100. If there are few "investors," reduce the amount (and consequent risk) and keep reducing it until it is very low—possibly as little as $5 or even $1.

You will probably find that some students will not be willing to invest even $1, while others might be willing to invest more. After all students called on have committed themselves to a given amount, ask them why they decided on that figure. Then ask the class what they observed in their classmates' responses to the investment opportunity. *(The main point is that with potential for profit comes risk. Most people don't fully appreciate what that means until it is personalized by having them put their own money on the line. More astute students may bring up other important issues, such as competition; the proportionality of investment and risk— the greater the risk, the greater the chance for higher profits if successful; and the fact that not all businesses succeed.)*

CAPTION ANSWER
Protecting Tiger Tiger Woods is being paid by Titleist to promote its products through a licensing agreement.

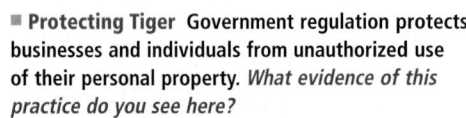
■ **Protecting Tiger** Government regulation protects businesses and individuals from unauthorized use of their personal property. *What evidence of this practice do you see here?*

Even professional athletes make use of licensing agreements to protect their names and images. The professional golfer Tiger Woods has several licensing agreements with a variety of businesses. Some of those businesses include Nike, American Express, Rolex, Titleist, and Wheaties. All of those businesses pay Tiger Woods a fee for the use of his name in their advertising and promotion.

■ Competition

Businesses that operate in a free enterprise system try to attract new customers and keep old ones. Other businesses try to take those same customers away. This struggle between companies for customers is called competition.

Competition is an essential part of a free enterprise system. It is one of the means by which the free enterprise system functions to benefit consumers. Competition forces businesses to produce better-quality goods and services at reasonable prices.

Businesses constantly look for ways to develop new products and improve old ones to attract new customers. Competition results in a wider selection of products to choose from. The results of these efforts increase the nation's output of goods and services, as well as its standard of living.

Marketing strategies determine how businesses will compete with one another. Marketing helps by determining what customers want and the best way to make those products available. There are two basic ways businesses compete—through price competition and nonprice competition.

PRICE AND NONPRICE COMPETITION Price competition focuses on the sale price of a product. The assumption is that, all other things being equal, consumers will buy the products that are lowest in price.

The marketing strategies used by the Wiz, a discount electronics store, and Ross, the national discount store chain, are examples of price competition. The first insists, "Nobody beats the Wiz,"

GREAT IDEAS from the Marketing Classroom

Allen L. Gancarz
East Syracuse-Minoa High School
East Syracuse, NY
One DECA project that works well on an annual basis is the Free Enterprise Project, which encourages students to study our free enterprise system. I require students to complete an educational segment with the Junior Achievement organization,

which has a prepared curriculum about free enterprise geared for elementary students. A representative from Junior Achievement comes to school and works with DECA members. The teacher-advisor can make arrangements with elementary school principals and teachers. Once a week for five weeks, the DECA members travel to elementary schools and teach students about free enterprise.

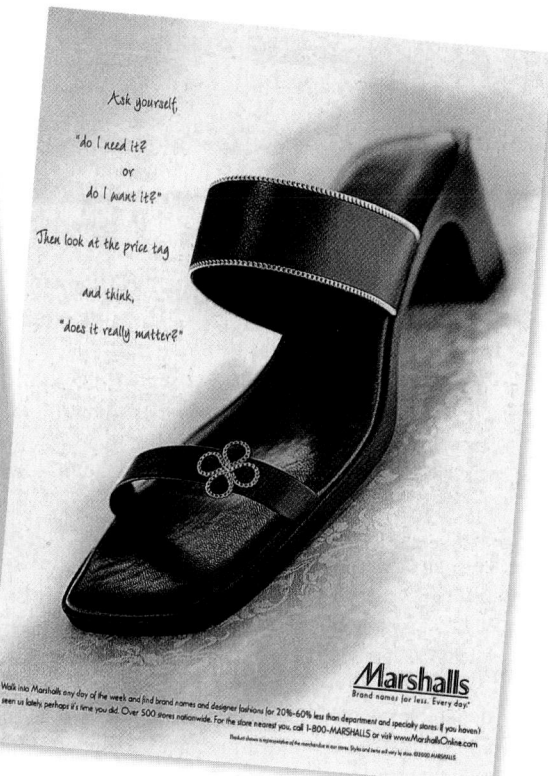

■ **Price vs. Nonprice Competition** Keen competition is the key to success for most businesses, especially in retail. *Which advertisement demonstrates price competition? Nonprice competition? Why?*

while the second promises to help you "Dress for Less." Both stress price as the primary focus of their competitive advantage.

In **nonprice competition**, businesses choose to compete on the basis of factors that are not related to price. These factors include the quality of the products, service and financing, business location, and reputation. Some nonprice competitors also stress the qualifications or expertise of their personnel. Businesses that use nonprice competition may charge more for products than their competitors do.

Nordstrom is a fine clothing specialty retailer that prides itself on providing complete customer satisfaction. Nordstrom's personnel do whatever it takes to please their customers. The store provides a unique shopping environment in addition to the high-quality goods and customer service. One way the store does this is by providing live piano music that echoes through the store.

The examples for price and nonprice competition seem to suggest that businesses adopt one strategy or the other. It is not uncommon, however, in our value-oriented society for businesses to try to do both. As competition increases, you may see more price-oriented competitors offering services they never offered in the past. Wal-Mart, the national discount chain store, offers customers the chance to meet friends, eat at the food service area, shop, and listen to Garth Brooks concerts broadcast throughout the store. Add their huge product selection, and you can see why Wal-Mart is the essence of one-stop shopping and customer convenience. Wal-Mart's Web site also offers customers the ability to check out what's happening in each local community and store.

SECTION 3.1

Thinking Critically

1. **Competition** Ask students why competition is such an essential element in our free enterprise system. *(Without it, there would be monopolies that would control the prices, quality, and variety of goods and services available in our country. With competition, companies are forced to improve those things because otherwise they would go out of business.)*
2. **Competition** Suggest a type of business (fast-food restaurant, supermarket, cinema, or music/video store). Have students identify 3–5 establishments in the community that compete directly with each other for customers. *(Answers will vary. McDonald's, Burger King, and similar businesses are likely examples of competitors.)*

CAPTION ANSWER
Price vs. Nonprice Competition Bloomingdale's is nonprice competition because the image is upscale. Marshalls is price competition—note the copy mentions price and the tagline reads, "Brand names for less. Everyday."

Independent Practice

List Tell students to select a local business and list the ways that the owner competes using price and/or nonprice competition.

Case Study

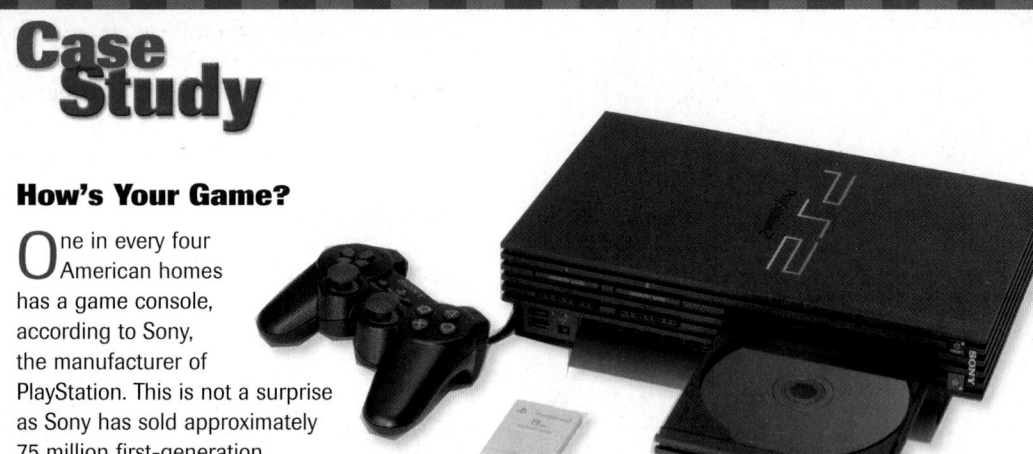

How's Your Game?

One in every four American homes has a game console, according to Sony, the manufacturer of PlayStation. This is not a surprise as Sony has sold approximately 75 million first-generation PlayStations. Sony is just one of the players in the game console market, which reached $20 billion in 2000, according to *Time* magazine.

This market is so hot that *Newsweek* devoted its front cover and a feature article to the fall release of Sony's PlayStation2 in March 2000. Hype surrounding the release of the new Sony product culminated in Web-based auction sites selling the game console at over 10 times the retail price. PlayStation2 has excellent resolution graphics and sound, generating remarkably lifelike images that can be mistaken for a film of the real thing. Games such as *Madden NFL 2001* and *SSX*, which is an extreme snowboarding game, are already getting attention. A great cost-saving feature is that the PlayStation2 is compatible with all 800 games from the original PlayStation. It features Internet access for online games, Web browsing, e-mail, and capacity for downloading software, music, and video. It also functions as a DVD player as well as a CD player, serving as a home theater and stereo system. Sony is referring to its latest creation as more of a "computer entertainment system" than just a console.

As with any successful product category, there is competition. Nintendo is releasing its next-generation game console, and Microsoft will enter the market with its X-Box game console. Sega's Dreamcast also introduced its online multiplayer game called "ChuChu Rocket" before the other competitors. Sega's Dreamcast also comes Internet-ready.

Sony took risks in developing PlayStation2 with over $2 billion invested in product development. The revenue to cover these costs and expenses will hopefully be covered by selling software, which is the real money maker in the game console business. In the past, seven to eight games have been purchased for every game console sold.

Case Study Review
1. How do consumers benefit from the competition in this game console market?
2. Why is Sony willing to lose money on PlayStation2?

A MATTER OF ETHICS
3. Is it ethical for a company to sell a product at a low price, knowing that it will make more money on the necessary accessories or supplies (i.e. video games and printer cartridges)?

Camera, cell phone

Case Study Review Answers

How's Your Game?
1. Consumers benefit from new and improved products, lower prices, and a larger selection of goods.
2. Sony will make up the loss through the sale of software that is sold by Sony for the new product. That software has a large profit margin.

A MATTER OF ETHICS
3. Answers will vary. Most students will see nothing wrong with this marketing decision since the company needs to make up for the loss to stay profitable. Others might complain about getting locked into a product that costs so much to operate (i.e., color printer cartridges).

MONOPOLIES When there is no competition and one firm controls the market for a given product, a monopoly exists. A **monopoly** is exclusive control over a product or the means of producing it.

Monopolies are not permitted under a free enterprise system because they prevent competition. A company can charge whatever it wants without competition. It can also control the quality of a product and who gets it. Without competition, there is nothing stopping a company from acting without regard to customer wants and needs.

One of the most publicized monopoly cases in recent history involved Microsoft, the computer software company. A federal judge declared Microsoft a monopoly. Its technology dominance was said to have "stifled innovation" and "hurt consumers."

The U.S. government has allowed a few monopolies to exist, mainly in industries where it would be wasteful to have more than one firm. These regulated monopolies, however, are on the decline. Telephone service was a government-regulated monopoly until the breakup of American Telephone and Telegraph (AT&T) in 1982. The government decided that deregulating long-distance telephone service would increase competition and benefit consumers. Now many different communication companies, like MCI and Sprint, compete for long-distance telephone business.

Currently, utility companies are being deregulated. This will allow customers to choose their own electric and gas suppliers. In order for the deregulation to work, the government will still control gas and electric companies by imposing price restrictions, forcing the former regulated monopolies to not exceed certain prices. The restrictions will provide an opportunity for unregulated suppliers to compete with the existing utility companies.

■ Risk

Along with the benefits that come from private ownership of property and competition, businesses also face risk. **Risk** is the potential for loss or failure in relation to the potential for improved earnings. As the potential for earnings gets greater, so does the risk. Putting money in the bank with guaranteed interest rates is less risky than investing in the stock market.

Businesses take risks all the time. Simply starting up is a risk. If you wanted to open your own business, you would probably put your savings into the enterprise. You make money if the business is successful; if the business fails, you lose all your savings and more.

One out of every three businesses in the United States fails after one year of operation. This risk

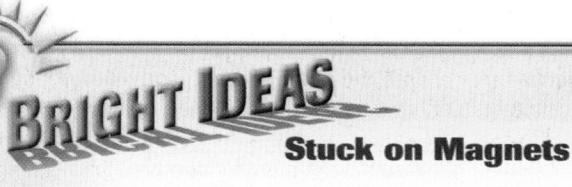

BRIGHT IDEAS

Stuck on Magnets

"It all started five years ago as a tool I made for myself to help my songwriting," says Dave Kappell, the 36-year-old founder of Magnetic Poetry, Inc. "I suffered from writer's block. At first, I'd photocopy my journal entries or a letter from a girlfriend. I'd cut out the words and move them around until it looked more interesting. It worked great until I sneezed." Kappell later applied the words to magnets and used his refrigerator as a composition board. When friends expressed interest, Kapell interviewed local retailers and gathered sales and marketing information. These retailers sold his first Magnetic Poetry Kits successfully, and Kapell hired sales representatives to sell the kits. Magnetic Poetry, Inc. now offers 50 different products in five languages and has annual sales near $6.5 million.

Thinking Creatively
Give an example of how you could turn your hobby into a business opportunity.

Individualized Practice

Math Skills

Ask students to determine if the following businesses made a profit, suffered a loss, or broke even. In the case of profit/loss responses, have students give a dollar amount.

L1 Business A had revenues of $100,000 and expenses of $95,000. *(profit of $5,000).* Business B had revenues of $2,000,000 and expenses of $2,025,000. *(loss of $25,000)*

L2 Business had sales revenue of $50,000 and sales returns of $3,000; a cost of goods sold of $22,000; and expenses of $20,000. *(profit of $5,000: $50,000 - $3,000 = $47,000 net sales; $47,000 - [$22,000 + $20,000] = $47,000 - $42,000 = $5,000.)*

L3 Business had sales revenue of $1,500,000 and sales returns of $50,000; a cost of goods sold that was 60 percent of net sales; and expenses of $580,000. (broke even: $1,500,000 - $50,000 = $1,450,000; $1,450,000 x .60 = $870,000; $1,450,000 - [$870,000 + $580,000] = $1,450,000 - $1,450,000 = 0)*

BRIGHT IDEAS **Stuck on Magnets**
Answer A hobby is an outlet for your personal interest. If you love to cook you might open a restaurant or sell baked goods at a fair. A sports enthusiast might open a store to sell sports memorabilia or equipment. A photography hobbyist might open a camera or film processing store.

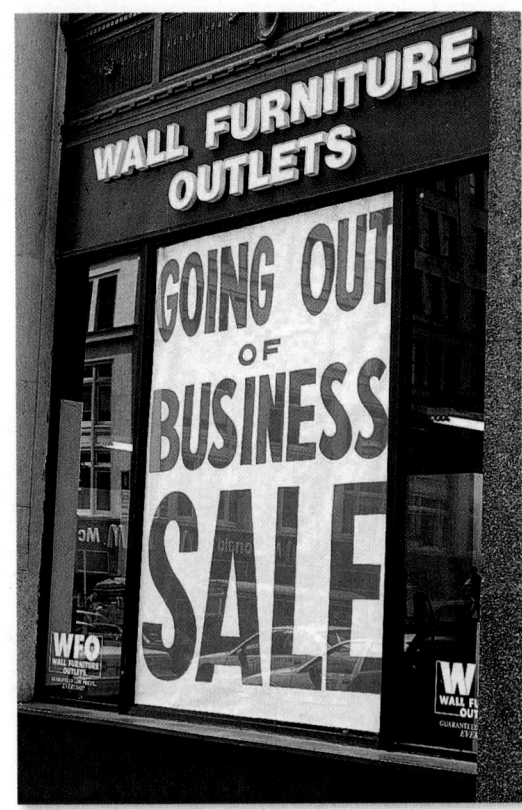

■ **Closing Shop** Going out of business usually means that a business wasn't successful. One in three U.S. businesses fail after one year of operation. *What component of the free enterprise system does this photo demonstrate?*

continues even if a business survives the first few years. When an industry develops and profits are great, more people enter that industry. This increases competition and the risk of failure for individual firms.

Risk is also involved in the development of new products. Product introductions are costly and risky; up to 85 percent of new products fail in the first year. Procter and Gamble (P&G), manufacturer of consumer products such as Tide detergent, Crest toothpaste, and Cover Girl cosmetics, is constantly developing new products. Noxzema Skin Fitness was one product that did not experience much success. Wal-Mart and other dissatisfied retailers discontinued the line of skin care products after only seven months.

■ Profit

Profit is the money earned from conducting business after all costs and expenses have been paid. Profit is often misunderstood. Some people think the money a business earns from sales is its profit. That is not true. The range of profit for most businesses is 1–5 percent of sales; the remaining 95–99 percent goes to pay costs, expenses, and business taxes.

Profit is the motivation for taking the risk of starting a business. It is the reward for taking that risk. It is also the reward for satisfying the needs and wants of customers and consumers.

Profits are good for our economy in many ways. The concept of profit is the driving force in our free enterprise system. It encourages people to develop new products and services in the hope of making a profit. Without profit, few new products would be introduced.

Profit remains high when sales are high, and costs are kept low. This encourages companies to work in an efficient way that helps to conserve precious natural resources. Profits provide money for a company to keep its facilities and machinery up to date. Then the business can produce goods more efficiently.

ECONOMIC COST OF UNPROFITABLE FIRMS An unprofitable business faces many problems. One of the first things businesses do when their profits decline is to lay off employees. When businesses are not profitable, they can lose money. Investors in public companies can lose money if the stock value falls below what they paid for it. As more investors sell their stock in the poorly performing company, the company has fewer resources with which to conduct business. It is forced to cut back on research and development for new products, as well as on the purchase of goods and services needed for operation. This, in turn, affects the profitability of the suppliers and transportation companies that depend on those business transactions.

Government also suffers when business profits decline. Poorly performing businesses pay less money to the government in taxes. When businesses lay off workers, there is a rise in unemployment. This causes an increase in the cost of social services and puts more stress on such agencies. Everyone loses when businesses are not profitable.

CAPTION ANSWER
Closing Shop The photo demonstrates risk.

ECONOMIC BENEFITS OF SUCCESSFUL FIRMS

Profitable businesses hire more people and pay them well. Employees generally not only have higher incomes, but also have better benefits and higher morale. Investors earn money from their investments, which they spend or reinvest. Vendors and suppliers make more money, too. As employment and profits climb, the government makes more money from taxation of individuals and businesses. Companies and individuals are also more likely to donate to charities when they are doing well.

Remember that profitable companies attract competition, which is beneficial to the consumer. Businesses compete with one another to sell their products to you and other consumers. To satisfy consumer wants and needs, they try to offer new products, the lowest prices, the highest quality, and the best service. For consumers, competition means choice. Companies learn to operate more efficiently in order to lower prices.

As people earn higher incomes they have more money to spend freely. There is an increase in a need not only for expensive products such as cars and homes, but also for services such as vacations.

Ever heard the sound a stoplight makes?

A Greener Car The Toyota Prius is a "hybrid" electric/gas car that doesn't need to be plugged in. *How does this ad suggest that consumers and the economy can benefit from profitable companies, like Toyota?*

3.1 ASSESSMENT

Reviewing Key Terms and Concepts

1. Provide an example of how freedom of ownership may be limited by government.
2. Provide an example of a business that uses price competition and one that uses nonprice competition.
3. What principle of free enterprise provides the incentive for people to risk their money on business ventures?
4. What is risk, and why is it relevant to a free enterprise system?
5. How do profitable businesses benefit the economy?

Thinking Critically

6. Applications for patents for new technology-related business processes are increasing. Patents for a one-click system for online orders are pending. What are some consequences of such patents being granted?

Integrating Academic Skills

7. **COMMUNICATION** Assume a friend has a great idea for a new computer software product. Write a letter to your friend to give advice about how to make money with that idea in our free enterprise system.

SECTION 3.1

VIRTUAL BUSINESS

GO TO **Start-Up Basics** Introduce entrepreneurship basics to students using Knowledge Matters' Virtual Business visual simulation, "Entrepreneurship—Start-up Basics." In this simulation, students get a first person view of free enterprise, capitalism, and entrepreneurship. They directly experience the concepts of ownership, promotion, risk, and profit. If needed, have students run the Virtual Business tutorial before beginning the activity. For additional instructions and teaching tips for this simulation, go to the *Marketing Essentials* Web site (www.marketing.glencoe.com).

CLOSE

Section Wrap-Up

Have students name the four key principles of our free enterprise system. *(ownership, competition, risk, and profit)*

CAPTION ANSWER
A Greener Car There are many benefits of new products from profitable companies. New products are developed to better satisfy customers' needs and wants. Profitable businesses are able to spend more money on research and development which helps create competition, increased tax money for the government, and new jobs. This ad suggests that new goods and services may evolve as a result of the new electric car.

3.1 ASSESSMENT ANSWERS

Reviewing Key Terms and Concepts

1. limit where businesses can locate
2. Businesses that use price competition are Wal-Mart or Target; nonprice competition are Nordstrom or Macy's.
3. the incentive to make a profit
4. Risk is the potential for loss in relation to potential for improved earnings. Greater profit potential translates into greater risk.
5. They provide more employment, investment in stocks, support suppliers, pay taxes, contribute to charities, and attract competition.

Thinking Critically

6. The patent may block other sites from using this innovation.

Integrating Academic Skills

7. **COMMUNICATION** Answers will vary.

SECTION 3.2

Government and Consumer Functions

Bell Ringer Activity

Discuss Ask students: How do you personally benefit from the government's role in our *free* enterprise system? Emphasize the qualifying word *free* to lead students to the correct answer. (Note: For private school students, reword the question to focus on how "most young people ages 5 to 18" benefit from the government's role in our free enterprise system.)

Introducing the Section

Government and Consumer Functions Students should recognize that they are receiving an education at public expense. Next ask what other services local, state, and federal governments provide. *(police and fire protection, military protection, Medicare, Medicaid, welfare, etc.)* Ask students: How is the government able to provide these services? *(through taxation)* Then ask how all of us can have a say in how our tax dollars are spent. *(through voting for government representatives who have views similar to our own)*

What You'll Learn

- The roles government plays in our free enterprise system
- The supply and demand theory

Why It's Important

As a consumer, you need to know your power to affect the prices you pay for products. As a voter, you have a responsibility to understand how decisions made by the government affect you, your investments, and your life in general.

Key Terms

- supply
- demand
- surpluses
- shortages
- equilibrium

The Role of Government

Government plays four roles in our free enterprise system. It provides general services, supports businesses, regulates industry, and acts as a competitor in a few instances.

This government involvement in the economy classifies the United States as a modified free enterprise system. To understand what that means, we have to take a closer look at the government's various roles.

■ Provider of Services

To ensure the safety and general welfare of people in the United States, our government provides military, police, and fire protection, as well as free public education. Government expands its educational role to provide retraining for some people who have lost their jobs as a result of changes in the marketplace and/or foreign competition. The Joint Training Partnership Act (JTPA) is one example of this sort of activity.

To improve transportation in the United States, our government supports the building of roads and bridges. Public libraries are paid for with government funds, as is our social welfare system. Medicare and Medicaid are two programs that are part of that system. Both provide medical care—Medicare for the elderly and Medicaid for the poor.

■ Supporter of Business

Our government also serves businesses. Throughout the years, floods and earthquakes have devastated communities nationwide. Government provided disaster assistance to help both businesses and home owners rebuild in the affected areas.

To support and encourage our free enterprise system, our government runs the Small Business Administration (SBA). The SBA provides counseling and educational materials to prospective business owners to help ensure their success. Additional support comes in the form of loan guarantees for some business owners who cannot get conventional loans.

The government is the single largest consumer of goods and services in the United States. All government projects require purchases of goods and services produced by U.S. companies. Those products range from uniforms for military personnel to defense equipment and systems.

Classroom Resources

For the Teacher
- Teacher Editions for all workbooks
- Assessment Package
- PowerPoint Presentation Software
- Interactive Lesson Planner

ILP Block Scheduling, p. 2
ILP Lesson Plans, p. 7
ILP Internet Resources, p. 25

ILP Blackline Masters, p. 5
ILP *BusinessWeek* Case Studies, p. 13
ILP Marketing Career Portfolio, p. 32
- *Marketing Essentials* Web site (**www.marketing.glencoe.com**)

For the Student
- Student Activity Workbook, p. 19
- Marketing Math Workbook, p. 5

- Marketing Research Project Workbook, p. 15
ILP School-to-Work Activity Workbook, p. 9
- Virtual Business simulation
- *Marketing Essentials* Web site (**www.marketing.glencoe.com**)

ILP These resources are available in print and on the Interactive Lesson Planner (ILP)

Finally, to encourage more global business activity, our government establishes trade alliances and agreements with other countries. Those agreements often make it easier for U.S. companies to do business in foreign markets.

■ Regulator

Making laws is one of the principal functions of government. In the United States, most laws are designed to protect the safety, health, and welfare of individuals and the freedom of businesses to operate in our free enterprise economic system.

CONSUMER AND WORKER PROTECTION At the federal level, laws are carried out by regulatory agencies. Several of these agencies have been set up specifically to protect workers and consumers. They include the Food and Drug Administration (FDA), the Equal Employment Opportunity Commission (EEOC), the Occupational Safety and Health Administration (OSHA), and the Consumer Product Safety Commission (CPSC).

At the state and local levels, government agencies require licensing of people who perform certain services, such as hairstylists and manicurists. Health departments inspect restaurants and other food-handling businesses to protect consumers. Finally, to ensure that workers can maintain a certain standard of living, both state and federal governments mandate a minimum wage.

The government seeks not only to protect both employees and workers, but also beyond that to control how our natural resources are used. To protect our environment, the Environmental Protection Agency (EPA) was established in 1970. Local zoning ordinances help to maintain the value of residential real estate and provide for uses that are consistent with the public good.

The Securities and Exchange Commission (SEC) regulates the sale of securities (stocks and bonds). It is responsible for licensing brokerage firms and financial advisers. It also investigates any dealings among corporations, such as mergers, that affect the value of stocks. This type of regulation helps protect investors from deceptive practices. The SEC also protects corporations, whose stock is traded, by requiring that all information about the corporation that is given to investors be truthful.

BUSINESS PROTECTION To protect our private property rights, government provides laws and regulations regarding patents, copyrights, and trademarks. These laws protect businesses for a period of time from having others copy their creative ideas and identifying symbols.

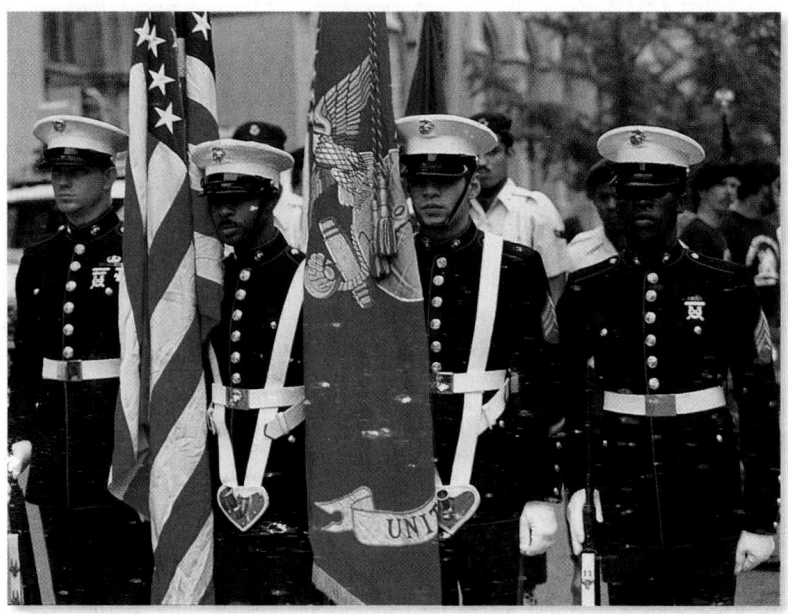

■ **Paid for by the U.S. Government** Local, state, and federal governments spend so much money that they are considered the largest single consumer in the United States. *How does that spending benefit business?*

CAPTION ANSWER
Paid for by the U.S. Government Government spending generates business for all kinds of industry; the government purchases stationery supplies for all offices as well as printing services, computers, office furniture, and food, clothing, and linens for military personnel.

TEACH

▥ Technology Resources

PowerPoint The *Marketing Essentials* PowerPoint Presentation CD-ROM provides visual lecture aids for every chapter section.

Concept Development

1. Read Section 3.2 with students.
2. Tell students that the name of the government agency in charge of workers' safety is the Occupational Safety and Health Administration (OSHA). Ask them to supply examples of how businesses must provide a safe working environment for employees under the law. *(Answers will vary. Two possibilities include: By providing hard hats for people who work in construction, and proper ventilation for people who work in industries where there are toxic fumes.)*

Discussion Starter

Supply and Demand Ask students how much they would pay for a concert ticket for their favorite musical artist or group. After coming to a consensus on the amount, raise the price of the ticket and ask how many would pay the higher amount. Keep probing until you reach a peak amount and only a few students have their hands raised. Ask them what this line of questioning says about consumer demand. *(As prices go up, fewer people are willing to pay them. This is the law of demand in supply and demand theory.)*

Thinking Critically

Competition Ask students if they would consider the U.S. government a competitor because it charges fees for people to visit or camp in national parks, such as Glacier National Park. *(Answers will vary, but many may agree that national parks are in competition with private tourist attractions and campgrounds.)*

Cooperative Learning

Put students into groups and assign each group one product with which they are familiar, such as a CD player, compact disc, pair of jeans, a soft drink, etc. Have them develop the following: a demand schedule, a supply schedule, and a graph that depicts the equilibrium point for that product. Have each group orally present and defend its supply and demand graph to classmates.

Independent Practice

1. **Research and Report** Tell students to investigate local ordinances dealing with the following subjects:
   - Type and size of signs allowed businesses in your community
   - Zoning laws in your immediate area
   - Blue laws (laws that stipulate businesses must be closed on Sundays)
   Have them present their findings in both oral and written reports.
2. **List** Have students list products that have experienced changes in supply and demand and corresponding changes in price, supporting supply and demand theory.
3. **Prepare Charts** Have students develop their own supply and demand curves with the equilibrium point identified for a hypothetical or real good or service.

Businesses must try to protect their products from theft by foreign and domestic companies in this new wave of global competition. It is becoming more common to find companies stealing ideas and patents from other companies.

The government regulates trade with other countries. U.S. companies are not permitted to sell certain products abroad if such sales might jeopardize the national defense. To protect domestic industries, the U.S. government sometimes imposes trade restrictions on foreign-made products.

The government also passes laws to regulate how businesses operate (see Figure 3-1 on page 51). One of these laws that prevents monopolies is the Sherman Antitrust Act (1890). It outlawed all contracts and agreements that would limit trade or competition in interstate commerce. It also prevents one company from under-charging for an item or service in order to put the competition out of business. This practice is known as *predatory pricing*.

A second law, called the Clayton Antitrust Act, was passed in 1914 to reduce loopholes in the Sherman Antitrust Act. In that same year, the Federal Trade Commission (FTC) was established to enforce both acts. The FTC's powers have since been expanded to include investigations of deceptive and misleading business practices, like false advertising.

To ensure economic stability for businesses, the government monitors our economy and controls our monetary supply through the Federal Reserve System. This is our nation's banking system. When the Federal Reserve Board of Governors thinks that the economy is moving too fast or too slowly, it reacts to correct the problem. When prices are going up too fast, the board may increase interest rates to slow economic activity. Higher interest rates generally make it more difficult to borrow money and therefore discourage expansion by businesses.

■ Competitor

There are three business operations that our government runs. They are the Tennessee Valley Authority (TVA), the U.S. Postal Service, and Amtrak. The TVA provides electricity to parts of the rural South. It was established during the Great Depression when private companies were unwilling to invest in dams and power plants for the area. The U.S. Postal Service provides mail delivery nationwide. There are several specialized delivery

■ Fly Like an Eagle The U.S. Postal Service is a competitor in the free enterprise system. *What competition does it face?*

companies that now compete with the Postal Service—DHL, United Parcel Service (UPS), and Federal Express. Amtrak is a passenger rail service that was established under the Rail Passenger Act of 1970. The act was necessary because rail line owners no longer wanted to offer passenger service.

The U.S. government also runs national parks and campgrounds. These tourist attractions are sometimes in competition with privately owned tourist attractions.

The Role of the Consumer

Most of the goods and services produced in the United States are bought by consumers for personal use. Therefore, the role of the consumer must be part of any discussion of our free enterprise system.

Consumers do two major things in the marketplace. First, they pick the winners—the products and businesses that will be in the marketplace tomorrow. They also determine the demand for any given product, and therefore help determine prices.

CAPTION ANSWER
Fly Like an Eagle Direct competition for the U.S. Postal Service comes from DHL, United Parcel Service (UPS), and FedEx, as well as e-mail.

FIGURE 3-1

Summary of Legislation that Involves Marketing

Competition Regulating Legislation

LEGISLATION	PURPOSE
Sherman Antitrust Act (1890)	Prohibits monopolies
Clayton Antitrust Act (1914)	Prohibits price discrimination
Federal Trade Commission (FTC) Act (1914)	Establishes FTC and prohibits unfair competition
Robinson-Patman Act (1936)	Strengthens Clayton Antitrust Act; regulates price discounts and allowances
Wheeler-Lea Act (1938)	Extends FTC Act to include unfair competition
Consumer Goods Pricing Act (1975)	Eliminates federal and state laws permitting manufacturers to set retail prices

Deregulation Legislation

Airline Deregulation Act (1978)	To allow competition among airlines
Telecom Act (1996)	To allow for competition in local phone service

Consumer Protection Legislation

Pure Food and Drug Act (1906)	Regulated food & drug labeling and safety
Food, Drug, and Cosmetic Act (1938)	Amended Pure Food and Drug Act of 1906
Automobile Information Disclosure Act (1958)	Post suggested retail price on new vehicles
Fair Packaging and Labeling Act (1966)	Regulates packaging and labeling
Cigarette Labeling and Advertising Acts (1966 & 1969)	Label cigarettes as "hazardous to your health" and prohibits TV advertising of cigarettes
Consumer Product Safety Act (1972)	Established Consumer Product Safety Commission; rules on products that are unsafe
Children's Television Act (1990)	Limits advertising time on children's programs

Worker Protection Legislation

Occupational Safety and Health Act (1970)	Established Occupational Safety and Health Administration for workplace safety and health

■ **Marketing Legislation** The U.S. is considered a modified free enterprise system partially due to the legislation featured in this table. *Why are these laws needed?*

Individualized Practice

Human Relations Skills

Tell students to assume they work as cashiers in a retail store and have been approached by a customer who wants to buy a scarf. The item is clearly marked $25, but the customer demands that it be sold to her for $5 because she found it on a table designated for sale merchandise at that price; a sign on the table indicates that all scarves there are only $5.

L1 Ask students what they would do in this situation.

L2 Ask students what they would say to the customer.

L3 Have students role-play the situation. Tell the student who plays the customer to act very upset and demand that he or she be allowed to purchase the scarf for $5. Tell the student who plays the cashier that he or she cannot sell the scarf for less than the ticketed price of $25 but must nonetheless maintain the customer's goodwill.

FIGURE 3-1 ANSWER
Marketing Legislation These laws are needed to regulate competition—an essential component of a free enterprise system—and to protect consumers and workers.

THE DECA CONNECTION

COMPETITIVE EVENTS AND MARKETING ESSENTIALS

Study the Free Enterprise System The use of DECA's Free Enterprise Event will allow your students to expand their knowledge and understanding of the concepts presented in this chapter. The purpose of the Free Enterprise Event is to encourage students to study our free enterprise system, and then by using the knowledge they have obtained, to make presentations about the free enterprise to organized groups and/or the general public. The students then record their experiences in a 30-page written manual. The appendix portion of the manual allows the use of photographs so your students can document their activities. This event is one of DECA's chapter projects, which encourages participation by your entire class.

Decision-Making Skills

Have students suggest prices for T-shirts that their school marketing club might sell to other students, and what the demand for those shirts would be at those prices.

L1 Ask how many students they think would buy the T-shirts at each price.

L2 Ask students to prepare a supply and demand curve for T-shirts that their marketing club plans to sell. Tell them to identify the equilibrium price and provide a rationale for their curve.

L3 Ask students to defend their supply and demand curve for T-shirts that their marketing club plans to sell, and to tie their T-shirt pricing decisions to the following principles: competition, risk, and profit.

■ Deciding Which Businesses Survive

The United States is known as a consumer-oriented society. Consumers have the power to decide which products will be produced and which companies will stay in business. They do this by shopping. Every time they make a purchase, they are "voting" with their dollars. The more votes (or sales) a product gets, the more likely that product and the company that produces it will succeed.

■ Determining Prices

In a market economy, supply and demand determine the prices and quantities of goods and services produced. Consumers play a major role in supply and demand theory. In this role, consumers are responsible for setting the prices for their goods and services. Figure 3-2 on page 53 illustrates how this theory works.

To understand how prices are determined, you have to look at both demand and supply—the willingness and ability of producers to provide goods and services at different prices in the marketplace.

Supply is the amount of goods producers are willing to make and sell. The law of supply is an

Trade Across Boundaries

Producing a trade show takes a lot of planning. Organizing travel, meeting space, seminars, and exhibits can be overwhelming; but imagine doing this all in a country under a U.S. trade embargo. Trade show organizer Peter Nathan did this when he produced a medical equipment and pharmaceutical industry trade show in Cuba. He pursued the idea because of the important humanitarian aspect. It took three years to get Washington's approval; however, Havana approved it in just 10 days.

Thinking Critically
Does the government have a right to determine whether a company can organize a trade show in other countries?

Pleased to Meet You!

A handshake is a handshake. Correct? Not in the global marketplace. A handshake is the traditional greeting in North America and Europe, but not in other regions. The Japanese greet each other with a bow, while in Southeast Asia, people press together their palms (as if praying) to welcome another person. Those people who do opt for the handshake should be careful though, as the firm grip characteristic of Americans is looked upon as aggressive by others around the world.

Thinking Critically
You are entertaining Japanese clients for business. What is the appropriate way to greet each other when you meet?

economic rule that price and quantity supplied move in the same direction. This means that as prices rise for a good, the quantity supplied generally rises, and as the price falls, the quantity supplied by sellers also falls. Thus, suppliers want to supply a larger quantity of goods at higher prices so their businesses can be more profitable.

Demand refers to consumer willingness and ability to buy products. The law of demand is an economic theory that states that as the price of a good increases, the quantity of the good demanded falls.

When supply and demand interact in the marketplace, conditions of surplus, shortage, or equilibrium are created. These conditions often determine whether prices will go down, up, or stay the same.

Surpluses of goods occur when supply exceeds demand. If prices are too high or seem unreasonable to the customers their decision will affect the market. When this happens, businesses respond by lowering their prices in order to encourage people to buy more of the product. There may be a promotion or a sale to encourage people to purchase the product.

One of the best examples of surpluses can be found in the produce section of a supermarket. A large supply of peaches, apples, broccoli, or other produce

Trade Across Boundaries
Answer The U.S. government regulates trade with other countries if such sales could jeopardize the national defense. To protect domestic industries, the government imposes trade restrictions.

Pleased to Meet You!
Answer Answers will vary, but students should show respect for the other culture by bowing and then following the lead of the client. The visitor may extend his or her hand, in which case you should shake it, but not too firmly.

FIGURE 3-2
SUPPLY AND DEMAND THEORY

Supply and demand interact to determine the price customers are willing to pay for the number of products producers are willing to make.

DEMAND

Demand refers to consumer willingness and ability to buy products. According to the law of demand, if the price is low enough, demand for a product usually increases. This is reflected in the demand schedule. It provides the points to plot a demand curve.

SUPPLY

Supply is the amount of goods producers are willing to make and sell. The law of supply states that at a higher price, producers will offer a larger quantity of products for sale. At a lower price, they will offer fewer products. This is reflected in the supply schedule. It provides the points to plot a supply curve.

Demand Schedule for Athletic Shoes Sold at Retail	
Price per Shoe	Number Demanded
$155	600
140	800
125	1,100
110	1,500
95	2,000
80	3,000
65	3,400
50	4,600
35	6,200

Supply Schedule for Athletic Shoes Sold at Retail	
Price per Shoe	Number Supplied
$155	6,000
140	5,800
125	5,600
110	5,400
95	5,000
80	4,400
65	3,400
50	2,000
35	1,000

EQUILIBRIUM

Equilibrium exists when the amount of product supplied is equal to the amount of product demanded. On the graph, this is the point where the supply and demand curves meet. It is also the point where both producer and consumer are satisfied with the price. The equilibrium price, therefore, is the price at which customers are willing to buy and producers are willing to sell.

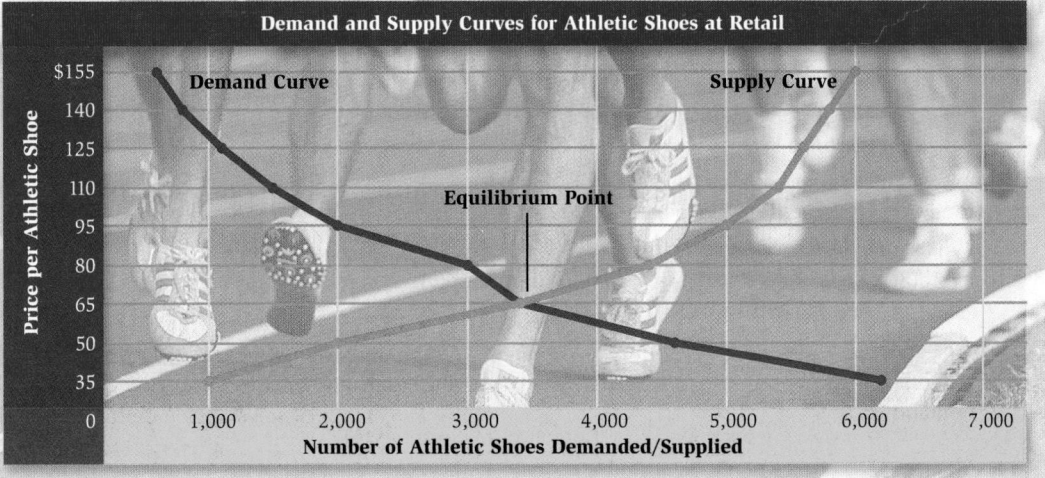

Demand and Supply Curves for Athletic Shoes at Retail

SECTION 3.2

ASSESS
Reteaching

1. **Vocabulary** Assign and review the vocabulary terms for this section.
2. **Fact and Idea** Assign and review Fact and Idea Review questions 5–10 from the Chapter Assessment.
3. **Role of the Consumer** To reteach the concept of the role of the consumer, ask students to name products that they buy on a regular basis. Then ask them to explain how their buying actions decide the fate of those businesses.

Enrichment

1. **Review** Assign and review the Chapter 3 activities in the *Student Activity Workbook*.
2. **Review** Assign and review the appropriate Thinking Critically questions from the Chapter Assessment.
3. **Review** Assign and review the following Chapter Assessment activities: Building Workplace Skills, Applying Marketing Concepts, Linking School to Work Activities, The DECA Connection Role Play, and Internet Connection.

Did You Know?

OSHA has reorganized and increased its fines for companies that fail to comply with its restrictions. In cases of willful noncompliance, fines can rise as high as $50,000 per occurrence. OSHA has also added a free consultation service to help small businesses cope with its regulations and develop safety standards and safe work environments.

SECTION 3.2

Evaluation

Assign and review the Section 3.2 Assessment.

 Assessment Resources
Go to the *Marketing Essentials* Web site (**www.marketing.glencoe. com**) for resources to teach and assess occupation-specific vocabulary.

CLOSE

Section Wrap-Up

Have students explain why the United States is considered a modified free enterprise system and why consumers are still the rulers in such a system. *(The U.S. economic system is modified because of government involvement in it. Consumers rule because they decide both what products are going to be produced and which businesses will succeed and which will fail.)*

Tale or Trail: Cookies

Answer Answers will vary. Some companies are trying to end data spillage by regulating the use of information they gather.

---

may be priced very low one week due to supply. When there is an excess of a given crop when it is in season, farmers lower their prices to sell large quantities. Supermarkets that buy large quantities of the crop at the low price do the same. The surplus affects the price all the way down the line. Think again of the example of the produce section of a grocery store. You can see how a produce shortage affects produce prices. When there is a poor season for oranges, you will find that the price of oranges is higher. When the product in question is a necessity, customers will pay the price determined by the market.

When demand exceeds supply, shortages of products occur. When shortages occur, businesses can raise prices and still sell their merchandise. An oil shortage increases the price of gasoline, so consumers who want to drive their vehicles pay the higher price.

When the amount of a product being supplied is equal to the amount being demanded, equilibrium exists. When supply and demand are balanced, everyone wins. Customers are able to purchase goods and services at a fair price, and retailers experience a steady flow of business. Customers buy the entire stock of the product that is available. Retailers clear their shelves of merchandise. Everyone's needs and wants are satisfied in the most efficient manner possible.

Tale or Trail: Cookies

Small text files—called cookies—can be stored and read on a user's computer hard drive. Cookies allow Web sites and advertising companies to see where customers travel on the Internet and which advertisements they view; this information is used by companies to improve their target marketing. To many users, cookies are perceived as an invasion of privacy. Congress is looking into the legality of this issue, sometimes referred to as "data spillage." Data spillage is the distribution of data collected from Web sites that is automatically sent to outside parties, mostly Internet advertising agencies, which track the information.

Thinking Critically
Many advertising agencies claim to use only basic geographic information taken from a user's Internet address to target its ads. Are these practices fair, or an invasion of privacy?

3.2 ASSESSMENT

Reviewing Key Terms and Concepts

1. Name four ways government is involved in our free enterprise system.
2. Why is the United States said to have a modified free enterprise system?
3. What is the FTC, and what does it do?
4. In the U.S. free enterprise system, who decides which businesses will survive and what prices will be charged for the goods sold?
5. What is the equilibrium point in supply and demand theory?

Thinking Critically

6. A new airline starts up with low fares and many new routes. At the same time, established airlines drop their fares and add new flights to match the routes of the new airline. Is this against the law? Explain your position.

Integrating Academic Skills

7. **MATH** Determine the profit a company makes with sales of $2,456,700, costs of $1,246,100, and expenses of $1,112,332. What percentage of sales does the profit represent?

3.2 ASSESSMENT ANSWERS

Reviewing Key Terms and Concepts
1. provider of services, supporter of business, regulator, and competitor
2. It is involved in the economy.
3. The FTC (Federal Trade Commission) was established to enforce the Clayton and Sherman Antitrust Acts. It investigates deceptive and misleading business practices.
4. consumers
5. It is the place at which the amount of the product being supplied is equal to the amount of product being demanded.

Thinking Critically
6. Those actions would be considered predatory practices and should be stopped.

Integrating Academic Skills
7. **MATH** Profit is $98,268; 4%.

Careers in Marketing

E-COMMERCE

Amber Nevens
Prefer Network
Internet Marketing Specialist

What does an Internet Marketing Specialist do?

"Internet marketing specialists serve as consultants to clients who want to develop or enhance online business Web sites. They develop Internet marketing strategies that include promotional plans and campaigns for product launches. Internet marketing specialists work with technical departments, sales teams, advertising departments, and financial analysts of the companies they represent."

What skills are most important to you?

"Research skills are vital to learn about industry trends. It is important to know what shoppers value in their online experience and what motivates their purchases. This information helps me present my product in a way that drives new customers, ensures a positive shopping experience, and builds a lasting relationship."

What do you like most about your work?

"The small number of employees makes it vital for everyone to work together. This environment is conducive to learning, and being surrounded by bright individuals is inspiring."

How does your workload vary?

"I am constantly juggling many projects at a time. It is important to be aware that things can change unexpectedly—budgets can be cut or technological difficulties can affect your ability to carry out promotions as planned. It is necessary to be able to adapt to these changes quickly."

What is your key to success?

"My key to success is being well informed on breaking industry developments. The Internet industry is always ripe for new ideas; therefore, learning about other's successes and misses is vital to marketing your product or service. I sign up for every relevant newsletter (ClickZ Network and Ebiz) and read industry publications (*The Industry Standard* and *IMarketing News*)."

Thinking Critically
Why is it so important to keep up with changes in the industry of e-commerce?

Career Facts

Education and Training: Most firms require an MBA for management positions, or a bachelor's degree in marketing, journalism, or communications. Candidates should have experience with Web site development.

Aptitudes, Abilities, and Skills: Ability to work independently and with a team, above average communication skills, ability to manage numerous projects at once, and creativity are necessary.

Career Outlook: Opportunities for Internet marketing managers are expected to grow faster than other management-level marketing opportunities as e-commerce expands.

Career Path: Experience in both marketing and Web site design may lead to careers in Internet marketing management. Product management and online advertising production also provide entry into this career.

Careers in Marketing

Ask a student to read the Careers in Marketing feature aloud to the class. Discuss the skills and aptitudes required for a career as an Internet Marketing Specialist. Ask students whether they think they would like or dislike a career as an Internet Marketing Specialist. Discuss the pros and cons of such a career.

Thinking Critically Answer
The industry changes at an alarming rate in e-commerce, so it is necessary to stay informed.

Guest Speakers
Invite an Internet Marketing Specialist to class to discuss his/her job and factors he/she considers when making marketing decisions.

Exploring Careers

Hobbies and Careers
1. Write the following list of hobby categories on the board and read them to the students.
   - Collecting
   - Sports
   - Music
   - Reading
   - Animals/pets
   - Sewing/fashion
   - Art/drawing
   - Cooking
   - Other
2. Ask students to name several specific hobbies in each category, and write their answers on the board.
3. Then have students choose which hobbies they enjoy the most and explain why.
4. Discuss with students what jobs might correspond or be related to the various hobbies they enjoy. For example, if students choose hobbies in the Animal/pets category, they might be interested in pursuing an occupation involved with veterinary medicine.

Lifelong Learning

The Free Enterprise System
Studying consumer issues is an ongoing process. New issues arise and new products are introduced every day. Staying on top of developments can help students become involved consumers. By studying marketing and reading magazines, such as *Consumer Reports,* students will be better able to make informed purchasing decisions.

Meeting Individual Needs

Students with Behavior Disorders
Students with behavior disorders struggle to maintain the level of attention needed to deal with challenging material. To assist these students and encourage them to persist, you might speak to them on an individual basis about their strengths and weaknesses. It might also be helpful to outline chapter objectives with an eye toward helping them feel successful.

Chapter **3** ASSESSMENT

Vocabulary Review

Presentations will vary. See Glossary for definitions.

Fact and Idea Review

1. The four principles of the free enterprise system are: freedom of ownership, competition, risk, and profit.
2. Competition forces businesses to produce better quality goods and services at reasonable prices.
3. Profit provides the incentive for people to risk their money on business ventures.
4. Unprofitable businesses lay off employees, lose investors, and cut back on operations, which adversely affects their suppliers and distributors. All parties involved pay less in taxes, lowering government revenues.
5. The SBA provides counseling and educational materials to prospective business owners as well as loan guarantees to help some business owners who cannot get conventional loans.
6. Some government regulatory agencies include the FDA, EEOC, OSHA, Consumer Product Safety Commission, EPA, and SEC.
7. These are two laws that were passed to prevent monopolies.
8. The Federal Reserve may increase interest rates to curb economic activity if prices are going up too fast.
9. The government controls the TVA, Amtrak, and the U.S. Postal Service.
10. When supply exceeds demand, there is a surplus, and prices go down. When demand exceeds supply, shortages of products occur, which allows businesses to raise prices. The price at which buyers will buy and sellers will sell is called the equilibrium price.

Thinking Critically

1. Answers will vary. Those who oppose government action might suggest that smaller stores use a variety of non-price techniques to compete. Those who support government action might advocate using zoning laws to keep retail giants outside of the city limits.
2. New businesses are not guaranteed success. Competition, consumers choice, and economic

VOCABULARY REVIEW

Use presentation software on the computer to design a presentation based on this chapter's content. Write captions and select graphics to illustrate ten of the following terms:

- free enterprise system
- competition
- price competition
- nonprice competition
- monopoly
- risk
- profit
- supply
- demand
- surpluses
- shortages
- equilibrium

FACT AND IDEA REVIEW

1. What are the four basic principles of a free enterprise system? (3.1)
2. Why is competition essential to the free enterprise system? (3.1)
3. What role does profit play in our free enterprise system? (3.1)
4. What happens when businesses are not profitable? (3.1)
5. How does the Small Business Administration support and encourage our free enterprise system? (3.2)
6. Name three government regulatory agencies that protect consumers and workers. (3.2)
7. What do the Sherman Antitrust Act of 1890 and the Clayton Antitrust Act of 1914 have in common? (3.2)
8. What might the Federal Reserve do if prices are going up too fast? (3.2)

9. What three major businesses make our government a competitor in the marketplace? (3.2)
10. How do supply and demand interact to determine price in our free enterprise system? (3.2)

THINKING CRITICALLY

1. What, if anything, should the government do to help "mom-and-pop" retailers compete with retail giants like Wal-Mart, Home Depot, and Staples?
2. Are new businesses guaranteed success in our free enterprise system? Explain your answer, and give examples to support your viewpoint.
3. Why are patents and copyrights allowed in a free enterprise system? Aren't they in direct conflict with the concept of competition? Explain.
4. If three of the large automobile manufacturers wanted to merge into one large corporation, do you think the U.S. government would allow them to do so? Why or why not?
5. Provide examples from your own experience of supply and demand theory at work. Then, try to think of one example each to illustrate surplus, shortage, and equilibrium.

BUILDING WORKPLACE SKILLS

1. **Human Relations** A customer questions why your video store's rental fees are 50 cents higher than those of the video store in the next town. You know the competing store does not carry the selection you do, and its late charges are double yours. Given these facts, prepare a response for the customer.
2. **Writing** Write a story about a country that did away with competition as part of its economic system. Tell what life would be like there.

conditions can change in ways that reduce business, force price cuts, and trim profits—even to the point of failure.
3. Patents and copyrights do interfere with competition to a degree; however, they help encourage development of new products. The inventors and creative people (owners) get the benefits (profits) of the time and money (risk) they spent in their work.
4. No, because it would violate antitrust laws.
5. Examples will vary.

Building Workplace Skills

1. Responses will vary. Students should explain that the additional cost affords a better selection and lower late fees.
2. Stories should depict monopoly control and its consequences—poor quality products, stagnant product development, high prices, and lack of response to consumer or social responsibility concerns.

Applying Marketing Concepts

1. Summaries will depend on the selected articles.

APPLYING MARKETING CONCEPTS

1. **Summarizing Key Concepts** Using current business publications like *Fortune, Forbes, BusinessWeek, Inc., Nation's Business,* or the business section of your local newspaper, find an article related to the content of this chapter. Use a word processing program to summarize the article and explain how it illustrates, reinforces, or extends one or more of the chapter's concepts.

2. **Understanding Regulatory Agencies** Research three federal regulatory agencies on the Internet. Use a computer database program to create a database of your findings. It should include basic information, including headquarter office locations, when the agency was established, its responsibilities, and a current issue that is facing the agency.

3. **Evaluating Licensing** Use the Internet to research professional athletes who have licensed their names on specific products. What are the potential problems for manufacturers that use those celebrities to promote their products? Use presentation software to prepare an oral presentation that you will give to your class.

4. **Understanding Government Regulation** Interview a local business owner about governmental policies that have cost the business owner any money or caused any problems. Using a word processor, write a letter to the governmental or federal regulatory agency addressing the problems that are addressed in your interview.

LINKING SCHOOL TO WORK

Thinking and Information Skills Ask your employer to share the OSHA and EEOC rules that must be followed where you work or in a local business. Share your findings with the class.

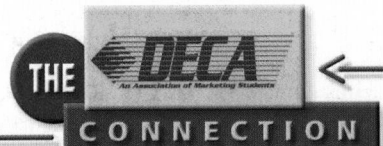

THE DECA CONNECTION

Role Play: Salesclerk

Situation You are to assume the role of salesclerk at the Lakeview Drugstore. This local establishment has been serving the residents of your town (which has a population of 30,000) for more than 25 years. In one month, however, a new discount drugstore is scheduled to open just two miles away. The owner of the Lakeview Drugstore (judge) has asked her employees for help.

Activity What would you suggest the owner (judge) do to meet the new competition?

Evaluation You will be evaluated on how well you meet the following performance indicators:

- Explain the concept of competition
- Determine factors affecting business risk
- Identify factors affecting a business's profit
- Make oral presentations

inter**NET** CONNECTION

My Aching Back!
Your employees work on a computer for long hours. What safety precautions and responsibilities do you have as an employer?

Connect
- Use the Internet to research ergonomics.
- Research ergonomic rules established by OSHA with regard to preventing on-the-job injuries to the neck, back, and wrist.

THE DECA CONNECTION

Students should be evaluated on the performance indicators noted in the Role Play.
- For another DECA Role Play, go to the *Student Activity Workbook,* p. 19.
- For more in-depth Role Play practice, refer to DECA's *Essential Competitive Events Handbook.* To order, contact DECA at **www.deca.org**.

inter**NET** CONNECTION

Ergonomics is the science of adapting the work environment to suit the worker. OSHA is working on ergonomic standards and rules that require employers to reduce the risk of injury on the job. Employers could be responsible for altering workstations or changing tools to reduce risks.

Mini Quiz

Administer the Mini Quiz orally. For an expanded chapter quiz, go to page 13 of the *Reproducible Tests* book.

1. The struggle between companies for customers is called <u>competition</u>.

2. <u>Profit</u> provides the incentive for people to risk their money on business ventures.

3. The government agencies that help protect consumers and workers are examples of how the government is considered a(n) <u>regulator</u>.

4. In a free enterprise system, <u>consumers</u> decide which products will be produced and which companies will stay in business.

5. <u>Supply</u> and <u>demand</u> interact to determine the price customers are willing to pay for the number of products producers are willing to make.

---

2. Databases will vary based on chosen agencies.
3. Presentations will vary. A celebrity could represent too many other companies, thus being over-exposed. A celebrity's behavior could negatively affect the good name of the manufacturer. The celebrity could die or no longer be active in their business; an athlete could get injured.
4. Letters will vary depending on interviewee responses.

Linking School to Work
Answers depend on the work situation.

1. **Assessment** Have students complete the Reproducible Test for Chapter 3 or construct your own test using the ExamView software.
2. **Enrichment** Have students complete the corresponding activities in the following workbooks:
   - *Marketing Math Workbook,* p. 5
   - *Marketing Research Project Workbook,* p. 15

Global Economies

Chapter Overview

Chapter 4 introduces students to different economic systems. In the course of comparing market, command, and mixed economies, it develops key economic concepts like resources, scarcity, and basic economic questions. The chapter also presents an overview of economic measurements countries use to assess their economies.

 Springboard

Imagine To introduce the concepts of economic resources and scarcity, ask students to imagine life in an underdeveloped area, such as a small village in Africa, India, or South America.

Prereading

List the section objectives to discuss with students. Have students skim the chapter, looking at the pictures, reading the captions, and noting the headers. Ask questions to ensure that students have a minimal understanding of the chapter structure.

Preteaching Marketing Vocabulary

Dictate each of the vocabulary terms and ask students to write them on a sheet of paper. Then write the terms on the board. Have students guess at the meaning of each. Write their guesses next to each term. Leave this list on the board so students can see how close their guesses were to the actual definitions as they work through the chapter.

Marketing: What It Takes

Answer Research should be done on the political system and economic differences in infrastructure, factors of production, and economy. Economic measurements, such as inflation, GDP, productivity, and unemployment, indicate the state of the current economy.

Marketing: What It Takes

Judging an Economy
Your marketing professor suggests that you study abroad for a semester. You need to select a country that differs from the United States politically and economically. The deadline is approaching for submitting your country request, and you're still not sure where you want to go.

WHAT WILL YOU DO?
What factors will you research in selecting the country?

58

THE **DECA CONNECTION**

ADVISOR CORNER

Playing the Stock Market After discussing the stock market and the risks of investments, have your chapter members participate in a stock market simulation or the Stock Market Game. Start by giving each chapter member the same amount of play money to invest. Have each chapter member choose and research a particular stock and then invest in it. Then have members follow their stock throughout the month or even the school year. Offer a prize for the DECA member who earns the most money, as an incentive for other members to get involved in this game. When you are finished with this activity, invite a stockbroker to come speak to your class about the risks and rewards of investing in the stock market.

What Is an Economy?

What Is an Economy?

An economy, or economic system, is the way a nation makes economic choices. The choices that must be made involve how the nation will use its resources to produce and distribute goods and services. Let's take a closer look at the resources common to all nations.

■ Resources

Resources are all the things used in producing goods and services. The technical term economists use for resources is factors of production. Economists also attach special meanings to the four categories that comprise the factors of production: land, labor, capital, and entrepreneurship.

Land refers to everything on the earth that is in its natural state, or the Earth's natural resources. This includes everything contained in the earth or found in the seas. Coal and crude oil are natural resources, and so is a lake and all of the living things in the lake.

Labor refers to all the people who work in the economy. Labor includes full- and part-time workers in both the private and public sectors.

Capital includes money needed to start and operate a business. It also includes the goods used in the production process. Factories, office buildings, computers, and tools are all considered capital resources. Raw materials that have been processed into a more useful form (such as lumber or steel) are also considered capital.

Entrepreneurship refers to the skills of people who are willing to risk their time and money to run a business. Entrepreneurs organize the other factors of production to create the goods and services desired in an economy.

Each of the four factors of production presents its own set of problems and opportunities within an economy. The easiest way to appreciate this is to consider the plight of developing nations. Such nations may want to attract certain kinds of industries; however, they may be limited by the educational level of their workers. The value that an economic system places on education can profoundly impact one of its most important economic resources—its labor pool.

Capital is often an equally difficult problem for developing nations. Capital includes infrastructure, or the physical development of a country, including its roads, ports, sanitation facilities, and utilities, especially telecommunications. These things are necessary for production and distribution of goods and services in an economy. Imagine trying to operate a modern factory without electricity. Think of the challenges of trying to run an international business without dependable phone service.

What You'll Learn

- What is meant by the term *economy*
- The factors of production
- The three basic economic questions
- The difference between a market economy, command economy, and mixed economy
- Different types of economic philosophies

Why It's Important

Before you can study international trade, you need to understand how a country's economy is related to its resources and political system. This will help you understand how a country is viewed in terms of its ability to function in our global marketplace.

Key Terms

- economy
- resources
- factors of production
- land
- labor
- capital
- entrepreneurship
- infrastructure
- scarcity
- market economy
- command economy
- capitalism
- socialist
- communist
- privatization

Chapter 4 ■ *Global Economies* **59**

FOCUS

Bell Ringer Activity

Identify Ask students to name some of the things they or their families have bought in the last two weeks.

Introducing the Section

What is an Economy? Note the variety of items named in the Bell Ringer Activity. Tell students that all of them as consumers benefit from our economy because they are able to buy goods and services like these produced by our economic system.

Classroom Resources

For the Teacher
- Teacher Editions for all workbooks
- Assessment Package
- PowerPoint Presentation Software
- Interactive Lesson Planner
- ILP Block Scheduling, p. 2
- ILP Lesson Plans, p. 8
- ILP Internet Resources, p. 27

- ILP Blackline Masters, p. 6
- ILP *BusinessWeek* Case Studies, p. 19
- ILP Marketing Career Portfolio, p. 32
- *Marketing Essentials* Web site (**www.marketing.glencoe.com**)

For the Student
- Student Activity Workbook, p. 27
- Marketing Math Workbook, p. 5

- Marketing Research Project Workbook, p. 15
- ILP School-to-Work Activity Workbook, p. 13
- Virtual Business simulation
- *Marketing Essentials* Web site (**www.marketing.glencoe.com**)

ILP These resources are available in print and on the Interactive Lesson Planner (ILP)

Concept Development

1. Assign a fourth of Section 4.1 to each of four groups so that all topics are covered. Give students time to read and take notes on their assigned topic(s)—economy and resources, scarcity and three economic questions, market economies, and command and mixed economies. Then have one student from each of the "expert" groups establish a new group. Have students teach each other the information in Section 4.1.

2. To introduce the concept of infrastructure, ask students to cite differences in the roads, telephone service, and living conditions found in a poor country vs. an industrialized country like the United States. Ask students how a manufacturing business could function in a country without a strong infrastructure.

CAPTION ANSWER

Shop 'til You Drop This shopping scene addresses what should be produced and for whom. Consumer purchases dictate what should be produced. A consumer's earning power decides who will get what is produced.

▪ Scarcity

All economies have different proportions of resources. The United States has an educated labor force, a great deal of capital, an abundance of entrepreneurs, and many natural resources. Most underdeveloped nations are not that fortunate. They have natural resources to spare but not the capital or skilled labor to develop them.

Even the United States, with a plethora of resources, cannot meet the needs and wants of all its citizens. It has homeless and other people living below the poverty level. Businesses go bankrupt on a regular basis. It is apparent that nations have unlimited wants and needs for growth and development but limited resources to meet them. This difference between wants and needs and available resources is called scarcity. Scarcity forces nations to make economic choices.

How Does an Economy Work?

Nations must answer three basic questions when deciding how to use their limited resources. The way nations answer these questions defines their economic system.

1. *What goods and services should be produced?*
2. *How should the goods and services be produced?*
3. *For whom should the goods and services be produced?*

Economists have studied the way nations answer the three basic economic questions and have classified their economic systems into two broad categories. They are market (or capitalist) systems and command (or planned) systems.

No economy can be called purely market or purely command. Elements of both systems are found in all economies, making all economies mixed. To establish this, let's consider the two basic types of economic systems in their purest form. Then we can demonstrate how all economies are mixed.

▪ Market Economies

The United States is a market economy, so you already know much about how a market economy operates. In a pure market economy, there is no government involvement in economic decisions. The government lets the market answer the three basic economic questions.

▪ **Shop 'til You Drop!** Consumers play an active role in a market system. *What two basic economic questions are being addressed in this scene?*

1. *What?* Consumers decide what should be produced in a market economy through the purchases that they make in the marketplace. Those items that satisfy consumers' needs and wants are purchased, and those are the ones that succeed. Products that do not satisfy consumers' needs are not purchased and therefore will not achieve success.

2. *How?* How products will be produced is left up to businesses in a market economy. Businesses must be competitive in such an economy and produce quality products at lower prices than their competitors. It is necessary for them to find the most efficient way to produce their goods and services and the best way to encourage customers to buy these products.

3. *For whom?* In a market economy, the people who have more money are able to buy more goods and services. To obtain money, people are motivated to work and invest the money they make.

GREAT IDEAS from the Marketing Classroom

Paula Smith Mendoza
Bryan Adams High School
Dallas, TX

This activity requires several regular decks of cards (different styles). Divide the class into teams of four or five people. Mix up as many decks of cards as you have teams and give each team 52 cards. The students move around to negotiate "trades" with other teams to get a complete set of cards. The first team to get a complete deck (52 cards) wins the game. Students will find that some teams are very easy to trade with while some are more difficult. One team member can stay with the team's cards, and others can go out to trade. Discuss supply and demand, economic systems, trade negotiations, and other topics that may come up.

Command Economies

A command economy is a system in which the government controls the factors of production and makes all decisions about their use. In a command economy, the government is responsible for answering the three basic economic questions.

1. *What?* One person (a dictator) or a group of government officials (a central planning committee) decides what products are needed based on what they believe is important. The former Soviet Union, for example, was more interested in creating products for military use than in producing consumer goods for its people. As a result, they had frequent shortages of consumer goods.

2. *How?* Since the government owns all means of production in a command economy, the government runs all businesses. It decides how goods and services will be produced. It employs all workers and controls all employment opportunities and workers' benefits. In the most extreme command economy, the government tells people where they will work and how much they will get paid.

3. *For whom?* The government decides who will receive what is produced in a command economy. Wealth is shared equally among all people, in principle, to ensure that everyone's basic needs are met. The idea is that all people are equal and are offered the same opportunity. The government provides subsidies for housing and food for everyone, as well as medical care, education, and jobs for everyone who wants to work. There is much security for people in such a system—but at the cost of individual freedom and choice.

Mixed Economies

As you learned in Chapter 3, our free enterprise system is not a pure market system. There is some government involvement in the economy through mandatory laws and regulations that businesses follow. These include labor laws that limit how much people can work, at what age they can start working, and the minimum wage they can be paid. Our government provides social programs for those who need help, such as welfare and Medicaid for the poor and Medicare for the elderly. Based on these mixed influences, the U.S. economy is technically a mixed economy.

All economies in the world today are mixed. The most meaningful economic classification is based on how much government interferes with the free market. Looking at the difference between the two economic philosophies on a continuum, it is easier to see the degree of economic freedom permitted. Figure 4-1 shows a continuum of economic systems. Left of center would be more closely related to a command economy, and right of center would indicate a market-driven economy. Economic freedom to the right of center encourages competition and lets the market decide where the resources should flow.

Where a country fits on that continuum is most often determined by its philosophy of government. The philosophy of a government reflects not only the laws and rules, but how individuals are treated. The three political philosophies that have shaped world economies are capitalism, socialism, and communism.

Discussion Starter

Economic Choices Give students five minutes to develop lists of things they would most like to buy for themselves or their families. Tell students to pretend that you have given each of them $50 on the condition that they buy something on their "wish lists." Ask them what that would be. Then ask them if the $50 was enough to get everything on their wish lists. Most will say they need more money. Tell them that they have just made an economic choice because of scarcity.

Thinking Critically

Government and Economies Ask students if it is possible to have economic freedom without a democratic form of government. Let them start with a specific example—perhaps a communist nation like China or Cuba—and review what they know about life there.

Once they have discussed a number of examples like these, have them formulate a response to the first question. *(Answers should acknowledge that in this era of mixed economies, there are some repressive governments that do preside over successful market-oriented economies in such countries as Singapore and South Korea.)*

FIGURE 4-1

Continuum of Economic Systems

| Command Economy Communism on far left | Socialism left of center but right of Communism | Market Economy Capitalism on far right |

■ **Continuum of Economic Systems** When studying different economic systems, it is best to view them on a continuum, as depicted here. *Where on the continuum would you place the United States? Canada? North Korea?*

FIGURE 4-1 ANSWER
Continuum of Economic Systems The United States is closer to the right side but not at the far right; Canada is closer to the middle; and North Korea is at the far left.

Cooperative Learning

Economic Systems Divide students into groups of three or four. Assign each group one of the three economic systems: capitalism (free enterprise), socialism, communism. Tell each group to imagine that they are the government leaders of a developing nation. The nation has natural resources of fresh water and oil and its major agricultural products are wheat, corn, and citrus fruits. About one-third of the population lives comfortably, while half barely make ends meet and the remaining 20 percent live in poverty. Using their assigned economic systems, the groups should make decisions regarding what to produce, how to produce, and how to distribute what is produced. Have the groups share their ideas with the class. Discuss which economic system(s) brought about the most effective plans.

Independent Practice

1. **Research and Report** Have students research the resources of different developing countries by referring to the World Almanac and locating recent articles from business publications. Have them report their findings to the class in oral and written report forms.
2. **Research and Report** Have students research socialism and communism, focusing on the theories, history, problems, and benefits of each system. Require students to prepare written reports with references.

CAPITALISM Capitalism is an economic system characterized by private ownership of businesses and marketplace competition. It is the same as free enterprise. Government in a capitalist society is also concerned about its people and cares for those who cannot care for themselves. The number of social services, however, does not match that of a socialist country.

The political system most frequently associated with capitalism is democracy. Nations that practice democracy believe that political power should be in the hands of the people. There is usually more than one political party from which to choose representatives to run the government in a democratic country. People in a democracy are free to elect those candidates who agree with their philosophy on how the government and the economy should be run. The United States and Japan are two examples of countries that are classified as capitalistic and have a democratic form of government.

SOCIALISM In a socialist political system, there is increased government involvement in people's lives and the economy. The main goal is to keep prices low for all people and to provide employment for many. The government runs key industries and makes economic decisions. Those state-controlled, noncompetitive companies are generally found in industries such as telecommunications, mining, transportation, and banking.

Socialist countries tend to have more social services to ensure a certain standard of living for everyone. Medical care is free or low cost in most socialist countries, as is education from elementary school through college. These countries have systems for pensions and elderly care. Businesses and individuals pay much higher taxes than in capitalist countries to pay for all these "free" government services.

Today most countries that are characterized as socialistic also have democratic political institutions. The difference from capitalist nations is the increased amount of government involvement in people's lives and the economy. Canada, Germany, Great Britain, Sweden, and Australia are countries that are generally characterized as socialist.

COMMUNISM Communist countries have a totalitarian form of government, which means that the government runs everything. One political party—the Communist party—runs the government. This is done to ensure that all people share common economic and political goals.

In a communist country all people who are able to work are assigned jobs. Theoretically, there is no unemployment. Employees who don't go to work continue to get paid under this system. The government decides the type of schooling people will receive and also tells them where to live. Housing accommodations are assigned according to need. Food and housing subsidies keep prices low, so everyone has a place to live and food to eat. Medical care is free. As you can see, there is a little or no economic freedom associated with communism.

■ **Work for Food** In a command economy with a communistic philosophy, many people do not work and their standard of living is poor. *Why are these two conditions so prevalent in a command economy?*

CAPTION ANSWER
Work for Food There is no incentive in such a system for people to increase their productivity.

Did You Know?
In September 1994 the *Moscow Times* introduced its own daily stock market index as a way to regulate Russia's new stock exchange. Prior to this, the country had no centralized stock exchange report, such as the U.S. Dow Jones Industrial Average. Information about stock prices was inconsistent and inadequate, making people hesitant to invest.

Case Study

The Chaebol Economy

In 1961, Park Chung Hee, the autocratic leader of South Korea, passed the Law for Dealing with Illicit Wealth Accumulation. He then arrested leading businessmen and gave them a choice—go to prison or invest in a government-identified industry. The government funneled funds from foreign loans to these companies under the guise of "special capitalistic projects," in addition to loans from domestic banks. The government and business leaders worked together to build up specific industries, starting with textiles and light manufacturing, later moving on to steel and chemicals, and finally electronics and automobiles. This gave the government a degree of control in each of these industries. This created a concentration of capital and profits in the hands of a few key companies called chaebol. What was Park Chung Hee's motive? The South Korean economy needed a strong boost to rise above its poor agrarian state to compete with industrializing nations. Much of South Korea's economic growth has been due to the export-led growth of chaebol, the politically connected, family-owned conglomerates that include such companies as Hyundai, Samsung, LG, and Daewoo.

Chaebol are business conglomerates with a holding company that acts as the controlling arm of the firm. Today, chaebol are no longer dependent on the now democratic government for credit or assistance. In the late 1990s, the chaebol were blamed for plunging South Korea into financial crisis by recklessly and rapidly expanding into a variety of unrelated businesses on borrowed money. This prompted the government to force chaebol to restructure by merging overlapping subsidiaries. This restructuring led to mass layoffs and labor unrest.

Chaebol are also suffering with the Internet explosion as key employees leave to start their own companies. Samsung, one of Korea's top four chaebol, lost 6,000 employees to start-up firms in one year. It now allows employees to set up their own businesses during company time. Samsung lets these in-house ventures spin off if they are successful, taking half of the shares in the new company. Both employer and employee benefit from this arrangement. If the venture does not work, the employees still have a job with Samsung.

Case Study Review

1. Why is it difficult to classify South Korea's economic philosophy in the 1960s when Park Chung Hee first established the "chaebol"?
2. How would you classify today's South Korean economic philosophy, taking chaebol into consideration?

A MATTER OF ETHICS

3. Is it ethical for a company to take half of the shares of a new enterprise that was created by a company employee?

Case Study Review Answers

The Chaebol Economy
1. The government orchestrated the chaebols. It did not own them but dictated the operations of those businesses.
2. Since there is no more government assistance for the chaebols today, the economic philosophy would be more market-driven.

A MATTER OF ETHICS
3. Answers will vary. Some will acknowledge the company's right to do so because they gave the employee resources and time.

ASSESS

Reteaching

1. **Vocabulary** Assign and review the vocabulary terms for this section.
2. **Fact and Idea** Assign and review Fact and Idea Review questions 1–5 from the Chapter Assessment.
3. **Economic Resources** To reteach the concept of economic resources, ask students to identify everything that would be used to make and sell a pair of jeans. Keep probing until all four economic resources have been identified.

Enrichment

1. **Review** Assign and review the appropriate Thinking Critically questions from the Chapter Assessment.
2. **Extend** Assign and review the corresponding activities from *BusinessWeek Case Studies, Internet Resources,* and the *School-to-Work Activity Workbook.* **ILP**
3. **Brainstorm** Have students think of reasons why communist countries have had problems with low productivity. *(One reason may be lack of incentive among workers.)*

Evaluation

Assign and review the Section 4.1 Assessment.

Technology Resources

 Assessment Resources
Go to the *Marketing Essentials* Web site (**www.marketing.glencoe. com**) for resources to teach and assess occupation-specific vocabulary.

SECTION 4.1

VIRTUAL BUSINESS

Supply and Demand

Introduce the concept of supply and demand to students using Knowledge Matters' Virtual Business visual simulation, "Economics—Supply and Demand." Students compute the capacity of a town to support stores. They then predict how many stores will survive a shake-out. If needed, have students run the Virtual Business tutorial before beginning this activity. For additional instructions and teaching tips for this activity, go to the *Marketing Essentials* Web site (**www.marketing.glencoe.com**).

CLOSE

Section Wrap-Up

Ask students to name and provide examples of the four resources of all economies and to tell which, if any, they are part of at the present time. *(Those with part-time jobs are labor; those who run their own summer enterprises are entrepreneurs.)*

Too Close for Comfort

Answer North Americans may not be comfortable with touching in a conversation (hand on the arm, etc.), based on their need for personal space; people from other cultures may be more comfortable with this.

64

There are very few totally communist countries left in the world today. The economies of such countries have tended to collapse in recent years. In such a system there is no incentive for people to increase their productivity.

The few countries that can still be classified as communist include Cuba and North Korea. Even China, which is politically still dominated by a communist party, is liberalizing its economic practices.

ECONOMIES IN TRANSITION The breakup of the former Soviet Union probably provides the best examples of societies making the difficult change from command to market economies. Most Eastern European countries that were once communist satellites have embraced capitalism. They have also moved to more democratic forms of government.

The state-owned industries have been privatized in many of these nations. Privatization refers to the process of selling government-owned businesses to private individuals. This process generates much-needed revenue for the governments involved. It also demonstrates a high level of commitment to making the transition to a market system.

Today even socialist countries are selling some of their state-run businesses to help balance their budgets as the costs for national health care, unemployment, and retirement programs soar. Great Britain has sold its national phone company, national steel company, and national sugar company, as well as Heathrow Airport, a hotel business, water suppliers, and an automobile company it owned. These sales generated approximately $63 billion for Great Britain.

Too Close for Comfort

Arm's length—or 30 inches—is the average amount of personal space that a North American expects while in conversation. Upon leaving the United States, however, one might notice a shift in this space. Asians usually stand farther apart, while Middle Easterners and South Americans might get a little too close for the North American's comfort. It is important not only to respect personal space, but also to respect the person who might seem a little too close. Backing away or shifting uncomfortably may give off an unfriendly vibe!

Thinking Critically
Based on this information, what do you think about the cultural differences regarding touching during a conversation?

4.1 ASSESSMENT

Reviewing Key Terms and Concepts

1. What is an economy?
2. Name the factors of production necessary to create goods and services in an economy.
3. Explain how command and market economies answer the three basic economic questions.
4. Why are all economies mixed?
5. How do capitalist, socialist, and communist economies differ from each other?

Thinking Critically

6. How can developing countries improve their economies with regard to the factors of production?

Integrating Academic Skills

7. **COMMUNICATION** Assume your pen pal from a communist or socialist country has asked how people in the United States afford vacations, medical care, and retirement. In your letter of response, compare the U.S. mixed economy with the economic system under which your pen pal lives.

64 Unit 2 ■ *Economics*

4.1 ASSESSMENT ANSWERS

Reviewing Key Terms and Concepts
1. It is the way a nation uses resources to produce and distribute goods and services.
2. labor, capital, and entrepreneurship
3. In a command economy, the government answers all three questions; in a market economy, *what* and *for whom* are answered by the consumer, and *how* is answered by businesses.
4. Elements of both systems are in all economies.

5. Capitalist economies are far right of economic freedom; socialist economies closer to command economy; communist economies far left.

Thinking Critically
6. Encourage foreign investment; put money into education; encourage capital investment.

Integrating Academic Skills
7. **COMMUNICATION** Comparisons will vary.

Understanding the Economy

When Is an Economy Successful?

Soon you will be voting on issues and candidates who will represent your interests in government. You may also decide to invest in the stock market. All of these decisions can have an impact on your financial well being. Therefore, you must be able to recognize the signs of a healthy economy. This may affect your choices as you cast your ballot and invest your money. It is the goal of all economies to increase productivity, decrease unemployment, and maintain stable prices. All nations analyze their economies to see how well they are doing. Their analysis helps them determine which phase of the business cycle their economies are in. This determination, in turn, allows businesses, consumers, and governments to make appropriate economic decisions.

■ Economic Measurements

Accurate information about an economy is essential to the whole process. Let's look at key economic measurements that nations routinely use to determine their economic strength. These measurements include employee productivity, Gross Domestic Product (GDP), inflation, and unemployment.

EMPLOYEE PRODUCTIVITY Productivity is output per worker hour that is measured over a defined period of time, such as a week, month, or year.

Businesses can increase their productivity in a number of ways (see Figure 4-2 on page 66). They can invest in new equipment or facilities that allow their employees to work more efficiently. Providing additional training or financial incentives can also increase staff productivity. Finally, businesses can reduce their workforces and increase the responsibilities of the workers who remain. This makes an organization not only more financially efficient, but more effective as well.

Moves such as these have in recent years helped to increase the productivity of American workers. Suppose a steel manufacturer with an aging plant could produce 1.25 million tons of steel a year with a work force of 550. That manufacturer retooled to double its output and reduced its work force by 150. What would the result be? The calculations would look something like this:

$$\text{Productivity} = \text{output per year (in tons)}$$
$$\text{workers} \times \text{hours} \times \text{weeks} = 2{,}500{,}000 \text{ tons}$$
$$400 \times 40 \times 52 = 2{,}500{,}000 \text{ tons}$$
$$832{,}000 \text{ worker hours} = 3 \text{ tons of steel per worker hour}$$

The resulting figure is nearly triple the old productivity rate (1.09 tons per worker hour).

Chapter 4 ■ *Global Economies* **65**

● What You'll Learn

- The goals of an economy
- The various measurements used to analyze an economy
- The four phases of the business cycle

● Why It's Important

It is essential that you understand how an economy is measured and what factors contribute to a strong or weak economy. It is important to know how you, businesses, and the government influence the economy.

Key Terms

- productivity
- Gross Domestic Product (GDP)
- inflation
- Consumer Price Index (CPI)
- Producer Price Index (PPI)
- business cycle
- prosperity (expansion)
- recession
- depression
- recovery

TEACH

Technology Resources

PowerPoint The *Marketing Essentials* PowerPoint Presentation CD-ROM provides visual lecture aids for every chapter section.

Concept Development

1. Read Section 4.2 with students.
2. Have students read aloud the Case Study and review the answers in class.
3. To illustrate the term economic measurement, ask students how they would measure their own performance if they were asked to make pizzas for three hours. *(Their answers should help define the meaning of worker productivity, or output per worker hour—in this case, the number of pizzas made per hour.)*
4. To introduce the concept of GDP, tell students that all nations measure their productivity, too. Ask students if they know what the letters GDP stand for. *(Gross Domestic Product)* Then have them speculate about what would be included in the measurement of GDP. *(amount of consumer spending [two-thirds of GDP], business investment, net exports [exports–imports], and government spending—federal, state, and local)*

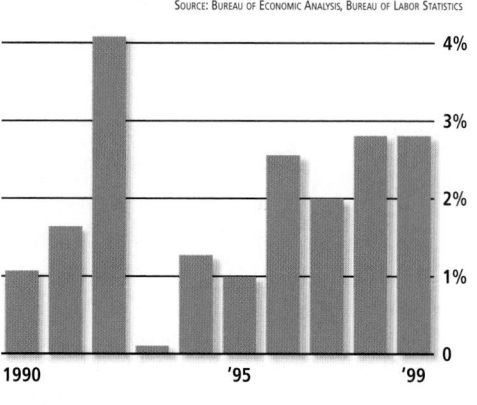

FIGURE 4-2
Productivity

SOURCE: BUREAU OF ECONOMIC ANALYSIS, BUREAU OF LABOR STATISTICS

■ **Productivity and Standard of Living** Productivity is a crucial factor in a country's standard of living. *What would you surmise about the United States' standard of living for the last five years depicted on this chart?*

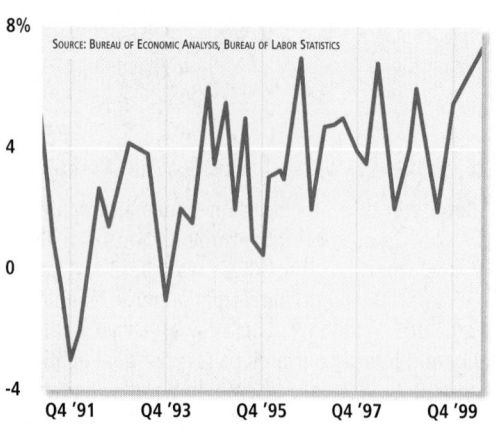

FIGURE 4-3
Gross Domestic Product

SOURCE: BUREAU OF ECONOMIC ANALYSIS, BUREAU OF LABOR STATISTICS

■ **Gross Domestic Product** GDP is the total output of goods and services produced in a country. *What does this chart tell you about the United States' GDP and its economy in general?*

GROSS DOMESTIC PRODUCT (GDP) Most governments study productivity by keeping track of an entire nation's production output. Today the principal way of measuring that output in the United States is gross domestic product, or GDP. Gross Domestic Product is a measure of the goods and services produced using labor and property located in this country (see Figure 4-3).

INFLATION RATE Inflation refers to rising prices. A low inflation rate (1–5 percent) is good because it shows that an economy is stable. Double-digit inflation (10 percent or higher), on the other hand, devastates an economy. When inflation gets that high, money does not have the same value as it did with lower inflation. The period from the mid-1960s to the early 1980s was a highly inflationary period. Prices went up threefold in the United States during that time. People who live on a fixed income are especially hurt by high inflation.

Controlling inflation is one of a government's major goals. When inflation starts to go up, many governments raise interest rates to reduce everyone's ability to borrow money. The result is a slowdown in economic growth, which helps to bring inflation down.

Two measures of inflation used in the United States are the Consumer Price Index (CPI) and the Producer Price Index (PPI). The CPI measures the change in price over a time of some 400 specific retail goods and services used by the average urban household. It is also called the cost-of-living index. Food, housing, utilities, transportation, and medical care are a few of its components. The core CPI excludes food and energy prices, which tend to be unpredictable. The PPI measures wholesale price levels in the economy. It is often a trendsetter, as producer prices generally get passed along to the consumer. When there is a drop in the PPI, it is generally followed by a drop in the CPI (see Figure 4-4 on page 67).

UNEMPLOYMENT RATE All nations chart unemployment, or jobless, rates (see Figure 4-5 on page 67). The higher the unemployment rate, the greater the chances of an economic slowdown. The lower the unemployment rate, the greater the chances of an economic expansion. This is true because when more people work, there are more people spending money and paying taxes. Businesses and government both take in more money, and the government doesn't have to provide as many social services.

66 Unit 2 ■ *Economics*

FIGURE 4-2 ANSWER
Productivity and Standard of Living The U.S. standard of living has been improving because productivity has been up.

FIGURE 4-3 ANSWER
Gross Domestic Product Since 1991, when the U.S. experienced its last recession, the GDP has been growing. This shows that the economy is strong.

Other Indicators

The Conference Board provides additional indicators to help economists evaluate the performance of the U.S. economy. The Conference Board is a private business research organization that is made up of businesses and individuals who work together to assess the state of the economy. One Conference Board indicator is the Consumer Confidence index (see Figure 4-6 on page 68). Consumers are polled to see how they feel about personal finance, economic conditions, and buying conditions. The survey reviews not only how customers feel about the current economic environment, but also how they feel about the future. Retail sales are studied to see if Consumer Confidence polls match consumer actions in the marketplace. Along those same lines, the rate of housing starts are reviewed, as are sales of trucks and autos. These are big expenditures that tend to be affected by the economy and interest rates.

Wages and new payroll jobs provide additional information about the strength of the economy at any given point in time. When everyone is employed, supply and demand theory would suggest that wages would increase due to the shortage of workers. Economists study these factors, as they may effect inflation and other economic indicators.

(see Figure 4-6 on page 68)

Discussion Starter

Standard of Living Do a simple exercise to demonstrate the high standard of living we enjoy in the United States because of employee productivity and the country's GDP. Have students stand if they have at least one working TV in their home. Everyone in the class will most likely be standing. Tell students to remain standing if they have two? three? four? five? Ask students if they think households in other parts of the world have that many TV sets? Then have them suggest other indices of country's productivity and standard of living.

Thinking Critically

Inflation Ask students which they would prefer—high or low inflation rates, and why. (*Answers will vary. Those concerned with purchasing power and borrowing will likely favor low inflation. Those more concerned with savings and investments that earn interest, might accept at least moderate inflation.*)

FIGURE 4-4

Inflation Barometers

Year-over-year change
SOURCE: LABOR DEPARTMENT

Year-over-year change excluding food and energy
SOURCE: LABOR DEPARTMENT

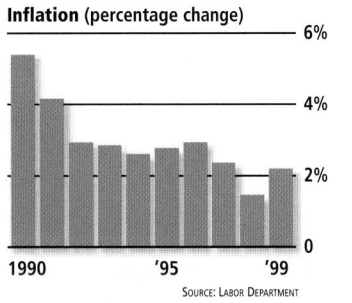
Inflation (percentage change)
SOURCE: LABOR DEPARTMENT

■ **CPI and PPI** CPI and PPI are barometers for inflation. The CPI Core and PPI Core take out the volatile food and energy prices from the indexes. *Based on these three charts, how would you describe inflation in the United States for the latter part of the 1990s?*

FIGURE 4-5

Jobless Rate

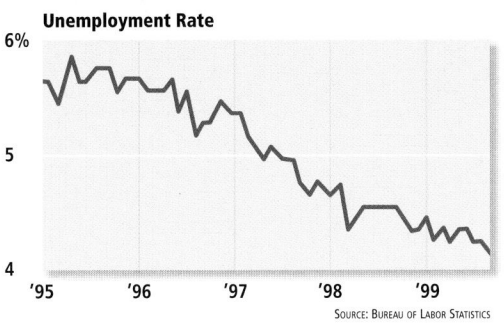
Unemployment Rate
SOURCE: BUREAU OF LABOR STATISTICS

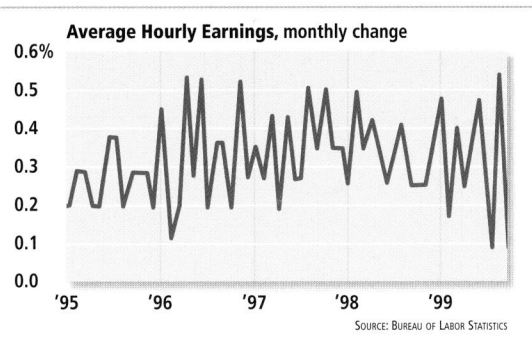
Average Hourly Earnings, monthly change
SOURCE: BUREAU OF LABOR STATISTICS

■ **Jobless Rate** One of the goals of an economy is low unemployment. *After viewing this chart on the jobless rate, what can be said about the United States' attempt to reach that goal?*

Chapter 4 ■ *Global Economies* **67**

FIGURE 4-4 ANSWER
CPI and PPI According to the charts, inflation in the United States has been very low, between two and three percent in the latter part of the 1990s.

FIGURE 4-5 ANSWER
Jobless Rate The chart shows that the United States is moving in the right direction to reach its goal, because unemployment has shown a continual decline since 1995.

Independent Practice

1. **Research and Report** Have students use newspaper and magazine articles to research and report on the current economic climate in the United States and other countries. Suggest that they check economic indicators like GDP, unemployment, inflation, and productivity.

2. **Research and Analyze** Have students research the interest rates for home mortgages for the past five years to determine trends and to study the effect those rates have had on the real estate market.

3. **Research and Compare** Have students research inflation, its causes, and the methods used to control it. Suggest that they compare how the government intervened to control inflation during the Carter administration (1976–1980) with how the government tries to control inflation now.

4. **Chart** Have students chart U.S. business cycles from 1920 to the present.

5. **Research and Compare** Have students research how the 1990 recession and subsequent recovery were different from all others.

■ The Business Cycle

Governments keep statistics in order to determine the stage their economies are in at any given time. History shows that sometimes an economy grows, and at other times it slows down. These recurring changes are called the **business cycle** (see Figure 4-7 on page 69).

The four main phases of a business cycle are prosperity, recession, depression, and recovery. **Prosperity**, which is also known as expansion, is the time when the economy is flourishing. This is a good time for new businesses to start up.

As business activity slows down, there is always the danger that the economy will move into a recession. A **recession** is a period of economic slowdown that lasts for two quarters, or six months. Companies reduce their workforces and consumers have less money to spend.

A **depression** is a period of prolonged recession. During a depression, it becomes nearly impossible to find a job and many businesses are forced to shut down.

The time comes when the economy cannot reach lower depths, often referred to as the *trough*. Eventually, the GDP will slowly begin to increase. This shift in the economic cycle leads to a period of recovery. **Recovery** is the increase in the overall economic activity. During this stage business picks up, people find jobs, and the demand for goods increases.

Electronic Frontiers

Eliminating Bugs

Buggy software is a global headache, so engineers around the world are coordinating their efforts to find a solution. Some of these results show promise. An international movement called "Open Source" draws programmers from around the globe to constantly debug major programs. The Internet provides a platform for discussion and instant feedback. With thousands of programmers pooling their skills to build and test software programs, bugs can be discovered early, saving time and money. Programmers like Linus Torvalds, the creator of Linux, has addressed this problem by including the source code written in comprehensible computer language in his commercial software. This simple code can be read and understood by any computer programmer; therefore problems can be solved easily. Now the industry waits for others to follow Torvalds's lead.

Thinking Critically

Why is the Open Source movement a benefit to the global economy?

FIGURE 4-6

Consumer Confidence

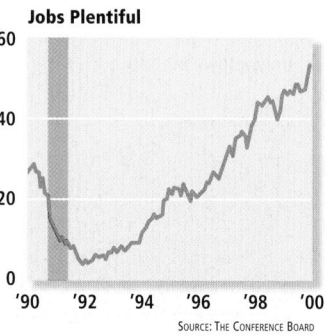

| Consumer Confidence | Expectations | Jobs Plentiful |

SOURCE: THE CONFERENCE BOARD   SOURCE: THE CONFERENCE BOARD   SOURCE: THE CONFERENCE BOARD

■ **Consumer Confidence** Consumer confidence is another economic indicator, which provides a view of how consumers feel about their economic prospects (employment, spending). *What information can be drawn from a review of these three charts? What trend is apparent?*

Electronic Frontiers

Eliminating Bugs

Answer When accurate software can be developed, or if bugs can be worked out quickly, the speed of doing business and processing transactions will increase, time and money can be saved.

FIGURE 4-6 ANSWER
Consumer Confidence There appears to be a correlation among the three charts with consumer confidence rising along with expectations and plentiful jobs; all three show an upward trend.

FIGURE 4-7

THE BUSINESS CYCLE

Economists have identified four phases that comprise the business cycle. The phases are prosperity, recession, depression, and recovery.

PROSPERITY

Prosperity is a period of economic growth and expansion. Nationwide there is low unemployment, an increase in the output of goods and services, and high consumer spending. Sometimes this period is called peak prosperity.

RECESSION

Recession is a period of economic slowdown. Unemployment begins to rise, fewer goods and services are produced, and consumer spending decreases. Recessions can end relatively quickly or last for a long period of time.

DEPRESSION

Depression is a period of prolonged and deep recession. During a depression, consumer spending is very low, unemployment is very high, and production of goods and services is down significantly. Poverty results because so many people are out of work and cannot afford to buy food, clothing, or shelter. The Great Depression of the early 1930s best illustrates this phase of the business cycle.

RECOVERY

Recovery is a period of renewed economic growth following a recession or depression. Recovery is characterized by reduced unemployment, increased consumer spending, and moderate expansion by businesses. Periods of recovery differ in length and strength.

Individualized Practice

Communication Skills

Tell students that they have been asked to suggest ways to increase productivity in the mailroom of a medium-sized company. Each day the mailroom handles approximately 500 pieces of mail. These are sorted and delivered to approximately 50 different people within the organization.

L1 Ask students to suggest ways to improve the process and to communicate those ideas to you in memorandum form. *(Possible suggestions include improved sorting methods [by floor or department first] and robotic delivery of mail to eliminate kibitzing.)*

L2 Tell students to present ideas for improving the process to you in a role-play situation. Tell them that they should be prepared to talk from their notes rather than read them. They should also be prepared to answer any questions you may have about their suggestions.

L3 Tell students they must make a formal presentation of their ideas to the class, who will be sitting in session as a board of directors of the company. Tell the speakers that they must be prepared to speak persuasively, field questions from multiple sources at any point in the presentation, and defend their proposals.

THE DECA CONNECTION — COMPETITIVE EVENTS AND MARKETING ESSENTIALS

International Marketing You can use DECA's International Marketing Event to heighten your students' interest in world economics. The International Marketing Event provides students with the opportunity to apply marketing skills in an international setting and prepare a written proposal for a new business venture. Begin with Part III A of the event guidelines.

This part is a description of a country's economic system. Allow each student to select a country. Then assign the study and have students research that country's economic system. By completing this assignment, your students will have made a start on the International Marketing Event, and be better able to place their knowledge in a geographic context.

Individualized Practice

Decision-Making Skills

Tell students they work for a small company that makes a component needed in the manufacture of automobile air bags. The company is thinking of borrowing $1 million to expand. However, the federal government just increased interest rates by 3/4 percent to control inflation.

L1 Ask students what effect that increase in interest rates might have on the economy. *(They might slow it down.)*

L2 Tell students that the economy appears to be in recovery, but that the recent increase in interest rates may slow down economic activity. Ask them to decide whether they would recommend that the owners continue their plans for expansion. Have them write up their recommendation and rationale in memorandum form. *(Recommendations will vary. Some will indicate that the owners should borrow the money now, before interest rates go any higher. Others may suggest pulling back just in case the increase in interest rates causes a recession and less demand for cars.)*

L3 Have students orally present and defend their written recommendations and rationales for the owners' plan for expansion. Tell students to be prepared to answer questions and defend their proposal.

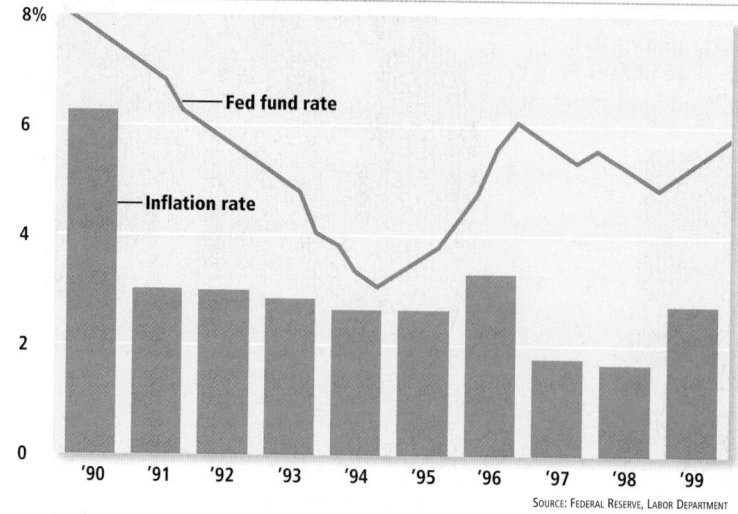

FIGURE 4-8

Managing the Economy

■ **Manipulating Rates** The federal funds rate (rate banks charge each other for overnight loans) and the discount rate (rate the U.S. Federal Reserve charges banks that borrow money from it) are used to speed up or slow down an economy. *From this chart, what do you think the motivation of the Federal Reserve Board was in 1991? In 1999?*

SOURCE: FEDERAL RESERVE, LABOR DEPARTMENT

FACTORS THAT AFFECT BUSINESS CYCLES
Business cycles are affected by the actions of businesses, consumers, and the government. In turn, businesses, consumers, and the government are affected by business cycles.

Businesses tend to react to business cycles by expanding their operations during periods of recovery or prosperity and curtailing their operations during periods of recession. Expansion may involve investments in new properties, equipment, and inventories, as well as hiring more employees. When the economy moves into a recession, one of the first things a business does is lay off workers. Businesses also cut back on inventories to match lowered demand for goods and services in a recession or depression. This has a ripple effect in the economy as business suppliers feel the effects of lost revenues.

During a period of recession, consumers' biggest fear is losing their jobs; the other big fear is a decrease in wages. These fears result in a loss of consumer confidence in the economy, which reduces consumer spending. Reduced consumer spending causes businesses to reduce their operations in response to lower demand. The opposite is true during periods of prosperity and recovery.

During those periods, consumers are more optimistic. They spend more money on material goods and luxury items. Businesses will also respond by producing more goods. This cycle shows how important consumers are to an economy—consumer spending makes up two-thirds of the U.S. GDP.

A government influences business cycles through its policies and programs. Taxation has a strong bearing on what happens in an economy. As the government requires more money to run programs, higher taxes are needed. When taxes are raised, businesses and consumers have less money with which to fuel the economy. When the economy needs a boost, the government may reduce interest rates, cut taxes, or institute federally funded programs to spark a depressed economy. Figure 4-8 illustrates ways the Federal Reserve can control the economy. One example of an action a government can take to spur economic growth involves Japan's decision to hand out free shopping coupons to its citizens. In 1999, Japan slashed income tax rates and distributed nearly $6 billion in shopping coupons to encourage people to spend. The government took the dramatic actions to spur consumption and revive an economy in its worst recession in 50 years.

FIGURE 4-8 ANSWER
Manipulating Rates In 1991 the Fed wanted to speed up the economy, so it lowered rates. In 1999 it wanted to slow down the economy, so it increased rates.

THE GLOBAL ECONOMY Early in the 1990s there was a *global recession*. This means that many countries all around the world were in recession at the same time. Some countries rebounded more quickly and soundly than others.

The recovery phase for the United States began in March 1991, but this recovery was different from others. Job growth did not increase as quickly. Instead of hiring new employees as conditions improved, businesses asked existing employees to work longer hours. U.S. manufacturing workers who escaped layoff during the recession were working an average of 41 hours a week in 1993. This increased worker productivity.

Increased investment in equipment, which displaced workers but increased output, also contributed to the recovery trend. U.S. workers were rated the most productive in the world by 1994. The U.S. economy continued to grow and expand into the new millennium. The jobless rate fell to the lowest point in 30 years, inflation was low, and economic output continued to increase.

The same was not true for Southeast Asia. Southeast Asian economies appeared to be improving as businesses and governments began big projects for expansion. Most of those projects were supported by large amounts of international capital, much of which was short-term loans in foreign currency. When it was time to pay back those loans, businesses and governments did not have the money. Bank debts reached $1 trillion in the region. The financial fragility caused by these outstanding debts forced devaluation of several countries' currency and led to an increase in interest rates, causing further economic turmoil. Thailand is generally regarded as the domino that set off the devastating Asian economic crisis with the devaluation of its currency—the Baht—in July 1997. The economies in Thailand, Indonesia, the Philippines, Malaysia, Singapore, Hong Kong, and South Korea collapsed in late 1997. Their over ambitious plans were compounded by scandal-ridden banking systems and government interference in the private sector. There was a rippling effect on the stock market, causing stock markets to decline throughout Asia and around the world. On October 27, 1997, the U.S. stock market plunged 554 points in one day after the news about Asia's troubled stock markets. Stock prices also plummeted in Latin American countries, such as Brazil, Mexico, Venezuela, and Argentina.

The economic recession that occurred following this financial crisis created higher import prices and lower wages for workers, which caused a decline in domestic demand. In a global economy, this discouraged foreign investors from investing in a country

ASSESS

Reteaching

1. **Vocabulary** Assign and review the vocabulary terms for this section.
2. **Fact and Idea** Assign and review Fact and Idea Review questions 6–10 from the Chapter Assessment.
3. **Productivity** To reteach productivity, ask students how they could increase their productivity when preparing typed reports that may need several revisions over a period of time. *(They could use a word processor to increase their productivity.)*

Enrichment

1. **Review** Assign and review the Chapter 4 activities in the *Student Activity Workbook*.
2. **Review** Assign and review the appropriate Thinking Critically Activities from the Chapter Assessment.
3. **Review** Assign and review the following Chapter Assessment activities: Building Workplace Skills, Applying Marketing Concepts, Linking School to Work Activities, The DECA Connection Role Play, and Internet Connection.

Evaluation

Assign and review the Section 4.2 Assessment.

BRIGHT IDEAS

Sticking with It

It saves us from tying our shoes, zipping our jackets, and strapping on our watches. What would we do without the miracle of VELCRO? VELCRO—created by Swiss mountaineer George de Mestral—was invented by accident. De Mestral returned from walking his dog to find that both he and his dog were covered with burrs. Intrigued by the small plant seed sac's ability to cling to fur, de Mestral examined a burr under a microscope. The stiff hooks on the seed inspired de Mestral to develop a fastener based on the design of the burr. Initially the idea was met with laughter; after some trial and error in design, de Mestral finally patented the VELCRO product in 1955. Today VELCRO is a multimillion dollar industry.

Thinking Creatively

Inventing requires imagination. Suppose that you were de Mestral and you were stung by a bee while walking that day. What product might you have invented instead?

Chapter 4 ■ *Global Economies* **71**

BRIGHT IDEAS Sticking with It

Answer Students' answers will vary but should reflect creative problem solving.

More About . . .

Economies in the 1990s
Improvement in the U.S. economy following the global recession came gradually and was not felt by all parts of the country at the same time. The East Coast felt the recovery first. However, parts of the West Coast—especially Los Angeles and its environs, damaged further by earthquakes and floods—had not pulled all the way out of recession as of 1995.

Technology Resources

Assessment Resources
Go to the *Marketing Essentials* Web site (**www.marketing.glencoe. com**) for resources to teach and assess occupation-specific vocabulary.

VIRTUAL BUSINESS

Business Cycles
Introduce the concept of business cycles to students using Knowledge Matters' Virtual Business visual simulation, "Economics—Business Cycles." In this simulation, students manage a store through a wild economic downturn, then upturn driven by changes in the town's population. Students learn when to be cautious and frugal vs. when to invest and build. If needed, have students run the Virtual Business tutorial before beginning this activity. For additional instructions and teaching tips for this activity, go to the *Marketing Essentials* Web site (**www.marketing.glencoe.com**).

CLOSE

Section Wrap-Up

Have students complete this statement: An economy is most healthy when . . . *(prices are stable, unemployment is low, and worker productivity is high.)*

REAL WORLD MARKETING
Hold the Anchovies, but Add Two Videos, Please!
Answer TelePizza provides a new distribution channel for Terra, and Terra's products may encourage customers to choose TelePizza.

72

---

where they would have a difficult time selling their goods due to low consumer demand. Asian businesses that wanted to succeed had to cut prices in order to boost sales at home and more importantly through exports to pay back their foreign debts. Those lower prices from Asian countries contributed to lower inflation, having a positive influence on European countries and the United States.

There were other reasons why the United States remained stable after the stock market scare of October 1997. Most companies in the United States were financially strong and had lower interest rates on their loans, making the loans easy to repay. Corporate earnings were up, as was productivity. Due to downsizing, which is the reduction of staff to cut costs and increase efficiency, and investment in technology, the U.S. economy continued to grow despite the Asian economic crisis.

Asian countries, like South Korea, rebounded in the new millennium. Many of them were able to "export" their way out of trouble by increasing sales to foreign customers, especially the United States. The economic boom in the United States helped to fuel Asia's recovery by maintaining huge demand for Asian exports like computers, electronics, machinery, toys, and textiles. The International Monetary Fund was also a big influence as it helped countries regulate their currencies by loaning them money and forcing them to restructure their financial sectors. Many countries confronted government corruption to reassure foreign investors of their stability and desirability as a business partner.

REAL WORLD MARKETING

Hold the Anchovies, but Add Two Videos, Please!

TelePizza is Spain's leading fast food company, operating 767 outlets. In 2000, TelePizza had to come up with creative solutions in an effort to expand its business and remain a leader. Rather than offer different menu items, TelePizza joined with Terra, the leading Internet Service Provider in Spanish- and Portuguese-speaking countries. The e-commerce network offers TelePizza customers a wide range of products including videos, compact discs, books, and other entertainment goods along with their pizza orders.

Thinking Critically
What is the benefit for each company of this joint venture?

4.2 ASSESSMENT

Reviewing Key Terms and Concepts

1. What are the goals of any economy?
2. Name four measurements used to gauge the success of an economy.
3. Describe in the briefest terms what each of the following stands for: GDP, CPI, PPI, and Core CPI.
4. Describe the four phases of the business cycle.
5. What stage of the business cycle was the United States in during the year 2000?

Thinking Critically

6. Assume the economy was growing rapidly and there were increases in the CPI, PPI, as well as in employee wages and spending. What might the government do to reduce the risk of inflation?

Integrating Academic Skills

7. **MATH** If inflation is up 2.5 percent from last year and last year the price of a loaf of bread was $1.59, how much would it be selling for now?

4.2 ASSESSMENT ANSWERS

Reviewing Key Terms and Concepts
1. increase productivity, decrease unemployment, and maintain stable prices
2. employee productivity, GDP, inflation, and unemployment
3. GDP is Gross Domestic Product; CPI is Consumer Price Index; PPI is Producer Price Index; and Core CPI is CPI without the volatile food and energy prices included.

4. prosperity—economic growth and expansion; recession—economic slowdown; depression—prolonged recession; recovery—renewed economic growth following a recession or depression
5. economic prosperity/expansion

Thinking Critically
6. increase interest rates and or raise taxes

Integrating Academic Skills
7. **MATH** $1.63 because $1.59 x 1.025 = $1.62975

Careers in Marketing

IMPORTING / EXPORTING

Kara Schick
Epicurean Enterprises
Importer/Exporter

What does your job entail?

"I work in both importing and exporting. I arrange for the purchase and transportation of foreign food delicacies to sell domestically, as well as the purchase and transportation of domestic goods in foreign countries. Dealing with domestic and foreign shipping companies is part of the job. I oversee the staff who handle the necessary documentation for importing and exporting. I am responsible for keeping abreast of shipping and receiving regulations, and training staff in tariff laws as well as import and export quotas."

What do you like most about your job?

"My favorite aspect of my job is the extensive travel. I spend a good deal of time in European cities developing relationships with clients and arranging for the most effective and efficient shipping methods for the products that I buy and sell."

What kind of training do you recommend for students?

"Fluency in a foreign language and knowledge of other cultures are excellent preparation for students interested in the import/export business. This can be attained through travel or study abroad. It is also helpful to take business courses in high school and college."

What is your key to success?

"My key to success lies in my commitment to stay well-informed of changes or trends in the industry. It is important to be aware of any changes in tariff laws or trade embargoes that may affect my business."

Thinking Critically

How could work as a customs entry clerk be effective training for a career in importing/exporting?

Career Facts

Education and Training: Travel abroad is important. Courses in English, business, economics, marketing, accounting, consumer education, and data processing are recommended. Familiarity with currency exchange rate is necessary.

Aptitudes, Abilities, and Skills: An interest in locating and coordinating resources is important in this field. An eye for quality and value is also required. Importers/exporters should have good clerical and numerical skills. They should enjoy meeting people and must have strong communication skills.

Career Outlook: Opportunities will vary with the economy. The impact of e-commerce on the import/export business is unknown.

Career Path: Work as an import/export clerk or a customs-entry clerk provides good background. Experience working as an import/export agent in an import/export agency may also lead to management or buying positions. Experience in shipping and receiving for a retail store, or as a shipping agent for a transportation company is also valuable.

Careers in Marketing

Ask a student to read the Careers in Marketing feature aloud to the class. Discuss the skills and aptitudes required for a career in importing and exporting. Ask students whether they think they would like or dislike a career in importing and exporting. Discuss the pros and cons of such a career.

Thinking Critically Answer
Answers will vary but may include that such work could provide a good background for the business.

 Guest Speakers
Invite an importer/exporter to class to discuss his/her job and factors he/she considers when making marketing decisions.

Exploring Careers

Flexible Hours Around the World
1. Explain that the customs regarding punctuality differ around the world.
2. Describe these global practices to the class:
- In Latin America it is normal to have meetings 15 minutes to 2 hours late. Being on time is considered rude.
- In the Middle East, business people are punctual but often leave long after the planned meeting end time.
- Being on time is expected in the United States, the Far East, and Australia.

3. Discuss with students the advantages and disadvantages of these customs.

Lifelong Learning

World Economies
Studying international economies can be useful for identifying information about the U.S. job market. Years ago, General Motors had its property privatized by Argentina's government. However, GM continued to reinvest in that country, encouraged by a more stable economy. That decision will affect employment for the rest of GM.

Meeting Individual Needs

Students with Learning Disabilities
Students with learning disabilities can have difficulty processing information in written and/or verbal form. It is important that they receive and give information in a way that works best for them. These students find it helpful to have the text tape-recorded. Getting information from visual representations, such as charts and tables, also helps.

Vocabulary Review

Stories will vary. See Glossary for definitions.

Fact and Idea Review

1. Infrastructure is necessary for the production and distribution of goods and services in a nation's economy because without good roads or telephone systems communication is difficult.
2. All economic systems are market or command systems.
3. The government lets the market answer all three questions in a market system.
4. The former Soviet Union's central planning committee decided that the country should spend more of its resources on creating military products.
5. Possibilities for increasing productivity include investing in plant and equipment or providing employee training and/or incentives.
6. The Gross Domestic Product reports the nation's production output.
7. When inflation gets into double digits, the money people have does not buy as much as it did a short time before.
8. When more people work, there are more people spending and being taxed. Businesses and government pull in more money, and government does not have to provide as many social services.
9. Business, consumers, and government all affect business cycles.

Thinking Critically

1. Most countries will acknowledge that the market system seems to work the best, mainly because it provides an incentive for people to work and open businesses.
2. Many will recognize that all those government guarantees cost money (taxes) and mean a loss of individual freedom. However, some may be willing to pay higher taxes and sacrifice some freedom to ensure social fairness.
3. Such a policy would force businesses to keep employees who might not be productive. That situation would be costly both to the businesses and to other employees who might have to take up the slack.

Chapter 4 ASSESSMENT

VOCABULARY REVIEW

Work in groups to develop a story about a new country that incorporates fifteen of the terms below. Assume the country is trying to answer the three basic questions about its economy.

- economy
- resources
- capital
- land
- labor
- entrepreneurship
- factors of production
- infrastructure
- scarcity
- command economy
- market economy
- capitalism
- socialist
- communist
- privatization
- productivity
- Gross Domestic Product (GDP)
- inflation
- Consumer Price Index (CPI)
- business cycle
- prosperity
- recession
- depression
- recovery

FACT AND IDEA REVIEW

1. Explain how the infrastructure of a country is related to the factors of production. (4.1)
2. Into what two broad categories have economists classified all economic systems? (4.1)
3. In which economic system does the government let the market answer the three basic economic questions? (4.1)

4. Why were there always shortages of consumer goods in the former Soviet Union? (4.1)
5. How can businesses increase productivity? (4.2)
6. What economic measurement does the U.S. government use to report the nation's production output? (4.2)
7. Why is double-digit inflation bad for an economy? (4.2)
8. Why is low unemployment good for a nation? (4.2)
9. What three factors affect business cycles? (4.2)

THINKING CRITICALLY

1. Why are most world economies moving to a market system?
2. Would you enjoy living in a country where the government guaranteed employment, housing, food, and medical care for all people? Why or why not?
3. Until the 1990 global recession, Japanese companies offered workers lifetime employment. Do you think U.S. companies should consider offering their workers such an arrangement? Why or why not?

BUILDING WORKPLACE SKILLS

1. **Technology** Look up information on the Asian economic crisis of the late 1990s on the Internet. Prepare an outline of your findings and cite your sources.
2. **Human Relations** Your company hired an efficiency expert to streamline the operations of the business during an economic recession. He would like you to prepare a memo that will warn employees that they may lose their jobs within the next six months due to downsizing.

Building Workplace Skills

1. Outlines and sources will vary.
2. Answers may vary. Students may suggest that the memo be informative, yet sensitive. The company should offer employee assistance in the form of résumé preparation and help finding a new job.

Applying Marketing Concepts

1. Summaries will vary depending upon chosen articles but should include identified concepts.

2. BEA.gov and BLS.gov are two government Web sites that students may use. They can back up that research with articles from *BusinessWeek, Investor's Business Daily, Wall Street Journal, Newsweek*. Reports and presentations will vary.
3. Reports will vary, but two possible theories are wage/price theory spiral and cost-push theory.
4. Reports will vary but should include the strong economic indicators, as well as touch on the influence of the Internet and e-commerce.

APPLYING MARKETING CONCEPTS

1. **Summarizing Key Concepts** Summarize an article that demonstrates any of the key concepts in this chapter. In the summary, identify the specific concepts in parenthesis. Use publications, such as *BusinessWeek, Fortune, Forbes,* and *Nation's Business,* to find an applicable article.

2. **Analyzing Economic Phases** Using the government Internet sites and other sources, research the current U.S. GDP and inflation, interest, and unemployment rates. Use the figures you gather to determine the business cycle phase of the U.S. economy at the present time. Using presentation software, create an oral report based on your findings.

3. **Studying Economic Theory** Research the cost-push different theory of inflation and the wage-price spiral associated with that theory. Study how the presidential administration of Richard Nixon handled problems with inflation in the 1970s. Using design software, prepare a report that highlights your findings and utilizes graphics and charts.

4. **Researching Economic Expansion** Using the Internet and other sources, study the economic expansion of the 1990s into the new millennium. Research the factors that contributed to that prosperous period in U.S. history. Write your conclusions in a two-page report using a word processing program.

LINKING SCHOOL TO WORK

Thinking and Information Skills Interview an employer about the cost of government taxes and employee benefits for the employer's company. Ask the employer what can be done to cut down on labor costs. Share your findings with the class.

THE DECA CONNECTION

Role Play: Public Relations Intern

Situation You are to assume the role of intern in a public relations firm. A client has requested that your firm prepare a learning packet on the business cycle to teach children (ages 10–12) about the economy. This project is part of your client's school-business partnership with an elementary school.

Activity Since you are the youngest person in the PR firm, your supervisor (judge) asked you to develop a rough draft of what you think should be included in the learning packet. You have only 15 minutes to organize your ideas.

Evaluation You will be evaluated on how well you meet the following performance indicators:
* Determine the impact of business cycles on business activities
* Explain measures used to analyze economic conditions
* Prepare simple written reports
* Demonstrate appropriate creativity
* Follow directions

*inter*NET CONNECTION

Ups and Downs
Since everyone is talking about the ups and downs of the stock market, you decide to see what it is all about. Conduct research on the Internet to find more information.

Connect
* Find recent (within the past month) articles that reported current economic measurements.
* Find reports on the stock market on the day of and the day after these announcements.
* Write two paragraphs explaining how the announcements of economic measurements affected the stock market.

Chapter 4 Assessment

THE DECA CONNECTION

Students should be evaluated on the performance indicators noted in the Role Play.
* For another DECA Role Play, go to the *Student Activity Workbook,* p. 27.
* For more in-depth Role Play practice, refer to DECA's *Essential Competitive Events Handbook.* To order, contact DECA at **www.deca.org**.

*inter*NET CONNECTION

Answers will vary depending on current events. Economic measurements are reported regularly by the United States Bureau of Labor Statistics and the Bureau of Economic Activity.

Mini Quiz

Administer the Mini Quiz orally. For an expanded chapter quiz, go to page 19 of the *Reproducible Tests* book.

1. Name the four factors of production. <u>land, labor, capital, and entrepreneurship</u>

2. List the three economic questions all countries must answer. <u>What will be produced? How will it be produced? Who will get what is produced?</u>

3. Name the three goals of any economy. <u>stable prices, low unemployment, and high productivity</u>

4. Why is a country's GDP an important economic measurement? <u>It reflects the productivity of a country, because it is all goods and services produced using labor and property in a country.</u>

5. Name the four stages of the business cycle. <u>prosperity or expansion, recession, depression, and recovery</u>

Linking School to Work

Answers depend on the work situation.

GO TO

1. **Assessment** Have students complete the Reproducible Test for Chapter 4 and Unit 2 or construct your own tests using the ExamView software.
2. **Enrichment** Have students complete the corresponding activities in the following workbooks:
   * *Marketing Math Workbook,* p. 5
   * *Marketing Research Project Workbook,* p. 15

Unit Lab Overview

In this Zazz Lab, students will use their knowledge of the free enterprise system, competition, profit, and licensing to license a sports-theme video game.

Bell Ringer Activity

Identify and Compare Ask students: What is your favorite video game? Why is that game better than others?

Discussion Starter

Ask students how a video game designer can capitalize on someone's favorite sport. *(Design a video game with that sport as the focus.)* Ask students: What is your favorite sport? Have you ever played a video game that is based on a favorite sport or sports figure? Could you make a better one?

Thinking Critically

1. **Licensing Agreements** Ask students: If your name was placed on products, what criteria would you use to decide whether or not to approve licensing? *(product quality, projected image, reliability of the company, financial stability and reputation of the company, where it would be sold, how it would be promoted, and other license agreements)*
2. **Product Endorsements** Ask students why professional athletes, teams, and leagues offer licensing agreements to businesses. *(Licensing agreements provide revenue. Professional athletes may make more money from product endorsements than from salary.)*

The Zazz Lab

A Sports and Entertainment Marketing Simulation

WELCOME

Welcome to Zazz Sports and Entertainment Marketing Company. Zazz is devoted to serving the needs of its clients who include college, university, and professional sports teams, professional athletes, sporting events, and sports arenas plus major consumer product corporations, as well as television networks and movie studios. As an intern, you will have the opportunity to work on different clients' projects. All of your work will be assigned and reviewed by your department supervisor.

LICENSE A SPORTS-THEME VIDEO GAME

SITUATION

Prima Sports Videos Company, a designer of sports-related video games, is looking to license sports teams or sports celebrities through Zazz. Prima has developed new video game technology that allows users to "play" alongside professionals. For example, a user could play a simulated golf tournament against Tiger Woods. The games will be available for all game console platforms. Prima Sports Videos expects to pay for the licensing rights of one or more of Zazz's properties. There is also some debate about when to market the product because a majority of video games are launched and sold in the fourth quarter of the year for holiday shoppers. Prima Sports Videos wants Zazz's help to determine if it is best to go with sports that are in season at that time or the most popular sports year-round.

ASSIGNMENT

Your supervisor wants you to select and provide rationale for a sports organization or a specific sports celebrity to license for Zazz's new client. You may assume that Zazz represents or will negotiate a deal with the professional athlete or sports organization of your choice. You must convince Zazz's management that the sports organization or celebrity you have

chosen is a perfect match for Prima Sports Videos. Prepare a brief description of your suggested video game, as well as ideas on how and when the video may be merchandised and promoted.

Tools and Resources

To complete this assignment, you will need to conduct research at a library or on the Internet. You will also need a sample Product Licensing Proposal to use as a guide, and presentation software. *BusinessWeek* and *BrandWeek* may provide you with the business perspective for this assignment, while *Sports Trend* and *NFL Retail Buzz* provide sports related information. Other helpful trade publications include *The Licensing Book, TLB—Team Licensing Business, Street & Smiths Sports Business,* and *Playthings,* a monthly list of best-selling toys and videos.

Research

Research the demographics of sports-theme video game players. Research sports organizations and sports celebrities. Study the demographics of the fans to see which would best fit the sports-theme video game market. Choose three sports organizations or sports celebrities and research current licensing agreements. Determine the popularity and current

LICENSING AND CORPORATE SPONSORSHIPS

When a company's name appears on any promotional material, this is a type of licensing and corporate sponsorship. That name costs money—in the form of license fees. When someone (the licensee) wants to use the licensor's name, there are two kinds of licensing agreements. One is based on the sale of goods to the consumer (retail licensing), and one is based on product promotions (premium licensing). Both require agreements and fees. The licensee compensates with fees, royalty guarantees, and royalties at a rate of 5 to 7 percent of net sales of whatever is being promoted. That sounds good for simply "renting" your name or likeness on product packaging and promotional materials!

sales of those licensed products, as well as how they are being merchandised, marketed, and distributed. Research your client's competition. Research the distribution outlets in which these sports video games are sold.

Report

Prepare a written report and a computer presentation. Use a word processing program to prepare a double-spaced report. Include a table showing the correlation between the demographics of video game players and the fans for the sports organization or sports celebrity you selected to license the video game. Be sure to provide a heading for the table and introduce it in the text prior to its inclusion on that page. Arrange your report around the following headings:

- Review of licensed sports-theme video games
  - Popularity of licensed sports-theme video games
  - Video games currently licensing sports teams or figures
  - Method of distribution (sales outlets)
- Review of sports organizations and sports celebrities
  - Criteria used for review
  - Selection of top three
- Correlation of demographic profiles
  - Sports video game players
  - Fans for top three selections
- Current product license agreements for top three selections
  - Products
  - Popularity of products
  - Methods of merchandising, marketing, and distribution
  - Potential conflicts
- Sports organization or sports celebrity selected
  - Rationale
  - Suggested video content
  - Suggested method(s) of merchandising and marketing
  - Suggested distribution method(s)

Presentation and Evaluation

Present your ideas in a written report and an oral presentation. You will be evaluated on your oral presentation skills, including:

- Knowledge of sports-theme video game market
- Knowledge of sports licensing agreements
- Selection of a viable sports organization or celebrity for the new client
- Rationale for licensee (why that Zazz property) and rationale for the licensor (why a video game)
- Ability to persuade others
- Continuity of presentation
- Voice quality
- Eye contact

Portfolio

Print out a copy of your completed report and presentation for your Portfolio.

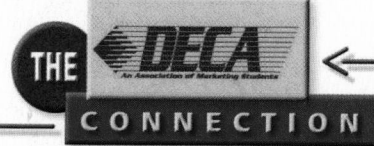

THE DECA CONNECTION

DECA Business Services Marketing Series
Negotiating product licensing agreements for a client could be a role play in this event.

DECA Marketing Management Series
Developing a plan to market a new sports-theme licensed product could be the basis of a role play in this event.

DECA Retail Merchandising Series, Management Level
A possible role play might involve evaluating the purchase of licensed sports video games, given current marketplace trends.

DECA Sports and Entertainment Marketing Management Team Decision-Making Event
Working in teams on this project ties together all aspects of team decision making, as well as the fields of sports and entertainment marketing.

COOPERATIVE LEARNING

Teamwork This unit lab lends itself to working in teams of two to four students. Have teams compete with one another to come up with the best plan for the new client.

Independent Practice

Research and Report Have students research other licensed products to identify market trends. Ask them if sales are flat for licensed apparel and accessories. Why or why not? *(Some answers may be yes, because, for example, the teen market might find brand name clothing like Tommy Hilfiger more fashionable than clothing licensed by athletes and sports teams; or no, because fans find little difference between an expensive authentic jersey and an inexpensive replica.)* Have students prepare a written and oral report.

ASSESS

Enrichment

Research and Analyze Have students research other factors that could affect the sale of licensed sports products, including video games. Ask them: Why would sports teams offer exclusives to certain companies? *(They can be profitable.)* What effect has e-commerce had on the sale of licensed sports products? *(Web sales are booming.)*

Evaluation

The rubrics for evaluation of the written, oral, and presentation software are included in the student text. (See the outline and guidelines for the written report, the computer presentation, and the skills' assessment for oral presentations.) It might be best to replicate those rubrics to evaluate the students' work. A separate rubric could be created to evaluate the work of a team.

CLOSE

Lab Wrap-Up

Ask students how sports product licensing is part of our free enterprise system. *(The system allows freedom to own property. Property rights are protected under copyrights and trademark laws. Sports property is the name of a sports figure, team, or league.)*

Business and International Marketing

Chapter 5
Business and Social Responsibility

Chapter 6
International Trade

Unit Objectives

After completing this unit, students will be able to:

● Tell what a business is and explain its basic functions.

● Identify and classify different types of businesses.

● Discuss business ethics and areas in which businesses are thought to have social responsibility.

● Discuss the importance of international trade and government methods to encourage or discourage it.

● Explain how businesses can get involved in international trade and what factors they should consider before doing so.

Enrichment Resources

Books
Do's and Taboos Around the World by Roger Axtell
Global Marketing by Warren J. Keegan and Mark C. Green
7 Secrets of Marketing in a Multi-Cultural World by G. Clotaire Rapaille and Clotaire Rapaille

Magazines/Journals
Culturegram
International Business

Associations
Business Marketing Association
400 N. Michigan Avenue
15th Floor
Chicago, IL 60611
(800) 664-4262
www.marketing.org

World Marketing Association
Local addresses can be found at:
www.worldmarketing.org

Journal Writing Activity

1. Have students find an article about international business in the international or business section of a newspaper. Ask students to jot down the headline or title in their journals and summarize the article's main idea or thesis. Then have students create an outline of the article's main ideas and subtopics.

2. Ask students to find and read a newspaper article on international business and summarize the main ideas in one paragraph. Have students share their summaries in class. After students have read aloud, have the class identify topics in their articles that are related to the three major functions of business—production, marketing, and management—as well as topics, such as the environment, consumer rights, ethics, and trade issues. Explain to students that the topics covered in this unit on doing business internationally are applicable in today's global marketplace.

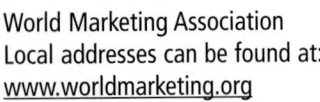

TEACHER CLASSROOM RESOURCES

Program Resources

Program Resources	Chapter 5	Chapter 6
Student Activity Workbook	p. 37	p. 45
Marketing Math Workbook	p. 13	p. 13
Marketing Research Project Workbook	p. 29	p. 29
ILP School-to-Work Activity Workbook	p. 17	p. 21
ILP *BusinessWeek* Case Studies	p. 27	p. 33
ILP Marketing Career Portfolio	p. 33	p. 33
Reproducible Tests	p. 27	p. 33
ExamView User's Guide and Testbank	p. 5-1	p. 6-1
ILP Internet Resources	p. 29	p. 31
ILP Blackline Masters		p. 13
ILP Lesson Plans	p. 10	p. 12
ILP Block Scheduling	p. 3	p. 3
Impact! Simulation	p. 19	p. 19

ILP Each of these resources is available in print and on the Interactive Lesson Planner CD-ROM.

Technology Resources

- Interactive Lesson Planner (ILP) CD-ROM
- PowerPoint Presentation CD-ROM
- Marketing Essentials Web site
- ExamView! CD-ROM
- Impact! Simulation

Virtual Business

Virtual Business is a fully visual marketing and business simulation that introduces students to the principles of marketing by letting them start and run their own virtual businesses. In *Virtual Business*, students have the power to control all aspects of a retail convenience store. Students strategize marketing decisions using a powerful learning tool in the guise of a video game. They learn by experiencing how their decisions affect their virtual business.

Key to Individualized Academics Activities

L1 Level 1 activities are basic activities and should fall within the range of all students.

L2 Level 2 activities are average activities and should be within the range of average and above average students.

L3 Level 3 activities are challenging activities designed for the ability range of above average students.

National Marketing Education

CHAPTER	SECTION	PERFORMANCE INDICATOR
Chapter 5 **Business and Social Responsibility**	5.1	Explain the role of business in society (BME)
		Explain marketing and its importance in a global economy (BME)
	5.2	Explain the role of business in society (BME)
		Treat others fairly at work (CIS)
		Demonstrate ethical work habits (PD)
		Explain the nature of environmental regulations (BME)
Chapter 6 **International Trade**	6.1	Explain the nature of international trade (ECO)
		Evaluate influences on a nation's ability to trade (ECO)
		Determine the relationship between government and business (ECO)
	6.2	Identify the impact of cultural and social environments on world trade (ECO)
		Explain the nature of trade regulations (BME)

CIS Communication, Interpersonal Skills   **DIS** Distribution   **FIN** Financing   **PRI** Pricing   **SEL** Selling

Standards Assessment Correlation

SECTION ASSESSMENT			CHAPTER ASSESSMENT						UNIT LAB
Reviewing Key Terms and Concepts	Thinking Critically	Integrating Academic Skills	Fact and Idea Review	Thinking Critically	Building Workplace Skills	Applying Marketing Concepts	Linking School to Work	Internet Connection	Zazz Lab
1, 2, 3	●	●	1, 2, 3, 4, 5	2, 3		1, 3			
4						1			●
1, 4		●	6, 8, 9, 10		1	1	●	●	
5				4					
3	●		7						
2				1	2	1, 2, 4			●
1, 3		●	1, 2	1, 5	1	1, 3	●		
2, 4	●		3			1			
5			4, 5	2		1			
1, 4, 5	●		6, 7, 8, 9, 10	3, 4, 5	2	1, 4			●
2, 3		●				1, 2			●

Unit Overview

This unit introduces students to what businesses are all about and then explores doing business abroad. Chapter 5 spells out the three major functions of business: production, marketing, and management. Then it provides a thorough presentation of types of businesses and the social responsibilities of business to society at large with regard to the environment, consumers, and ethics. Chapter 6 takes the student into the global marketplace with a discussion of international trade principles and practices. Chapter 6 also covers standard business practices involved in doing business abroad.

Introducing the Unit

Tell students to imagine that they have $10,000 to invest in one corporation listed on the New York Stock Exchange, American Stock Exchange, or NASDAQ (over-the-counter) stock exchange. Have them prepare a list of factors that they would consider when making their decision about where to invest this money. *(Possibilities include the type of business, trends in that industry, competitors, price of the stock, current economy, and market[s] served, especially if it does business here and abroad.)* Query students about what factors are on their lists and write their responses on the board. After a list is compiled on the board, tell students that all of the included factors are ones they will study in this unit.

UNIT·3

Portfolio

Develop a Marketing Plan

To demonstrate mastery of the content in this unit, you will develop a marketing plan for a business that wants to get involved in international trade. You are free to select a country and a product to market in that country. You may change the product to successfully gear it toward the target market in the selected country. Research several countries' economic, political, and social characteristics until you find one that is suitable for your product. Research the company to see if it has any international operations in that country. Prepare an outline with the following topics: rationale for the country selected, rationale for the product selected, target market and rationale, and proposed marketing plan (product, place, price, promotion). Provide a description and rationale for each of the four Ps, including samples when appropriate. Use presentation software to prepare your maketing plan for an oral presentation to the company's marketing team.

78

Field Trip Suggestions

Plan Trips to Stores Arrange for your students to visit a store or stores that cater to specific ethnic groups to observe the types of products they carry as well as the merchandising techniques they employ. A second part of this trip would be to visit a mainstream store that carries ethnic products and compare the merchandising of those products.

Business and International Marketing

Unit Overview

In this unit you will have the opportunity to see what business is all about, in the United States and abroad. Chapter 5 discusses different types of business, as well as social responsibility in the marketplace and workplace. Chapter 6 introduces you to the global marketplace as you review international trade. You will learn why international trade is important, as well as how businesses operate in foreign countries.

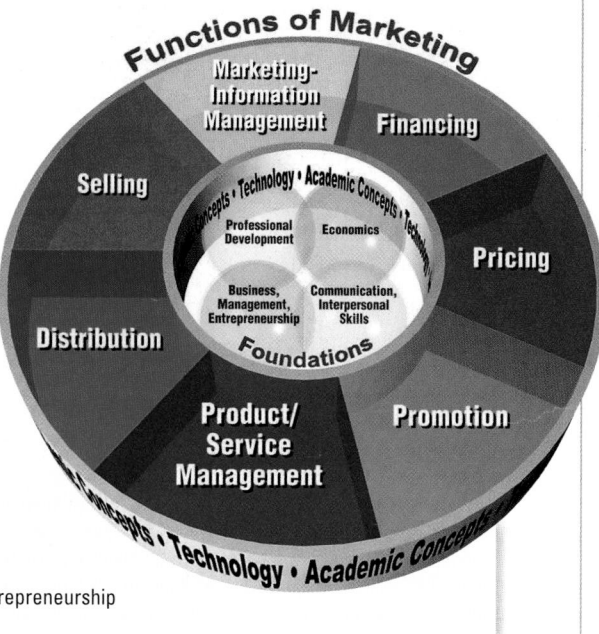

In this Unit:

Foundations of Marketing

● Economics

● Business, Management, Entrepreneurship

○ Professional Development

○ Communication, Interpersonal Skills

Unit Closure

Have students prepare a bulletin-board display of products, ads, and articles related to doing business in the domestic and global marketplaces. Ask students to supply materials and captions that present a complete picture of the following key concepts: types of businesses, current business practices (including ethical and social issues), and doing business in the global marketplace.

Guest Speaker Suggestions

Small Business Owners Have owners/managers of small and mid-size businesses explain how they use demographics and psychographics in the operation of their businesses.

Import/Export Marketing Manager Have the marketing manager of an import/export business explain to the class the types of research the company uses when making decisions about products to import or export.

Chapter Overview

Chapter 5 discusses the classification of businesses and the function or purpose of each. It also looks at workplace trends and concerns, as well as the key issues of ethics and social responsibility that businesses face in marketing their goods and services.

 Springboard

Research and Identify Ask each student to bring to class a list of three local businesses that provide a good or service to the community. The next day generate a master list of these businesses. Have students characterize each entry as large or small, domestic or global, profit or nonprofit, public or private, provider of goods or services, catering to consumer or industrial markets. Leave the list on the board.

Prereading

List the section objectives to discuss with students. Have students skim the chapter, looking at the pictures, reading the captions, and noting the heads. Ask questions to ensure that students have a minimal understanding of the chapter structure.

Preteaching Marketing Vocabulary

Dictate each of the vocabulary terms and ask students to write them on a sheet of paper. When they finish, write their guesses next to each term. Leave this list on the board as students work through the chapter.

Marketing: What It Takes
Answer Answers will vary but may include health food stores, nature-oriented stores like The Nature Company, or online markets.

Business and Social Responsibility

Marketing: What It Takes

Responsible Recycling

You are the sales manager at a new company that produces stationery, greeting cards, and journals made from recycled paper products. You are finding that the sales figures for the first three months are not as strong as anticipated. You are currently marketing the products in drug stores and mall card stores.

WHAT WILL YOU DO?
What are some nontraditional avenues that you could explore to market the cards to an audience that values recycled products?

80

THE DECA CONNECTION **ADVISOR CORNER**

Community Volunteering Have students prepare a short report on how they personally benefit from the volunteer activities of others every day. Then have students come up with at least five volunteering activities that they can do individually or as a chapter to make their community a better place. List on the board all chapter activities that students have suggested.

Then have the group select at least one activity to participate in per month that addresses a community need. Your chapter members will begin to realize how many needs there are in your community and will find it difficult to limit their activities. Your DECA chapter will also receive positive recognition in the community for members' volunteer activities.

Defining Business

What Is Business?

Business is all of the activities involved in producing and marketing goods and services. Organizations involved in such activities are called companies, or businesses. Every business seeks to satisfy economic needs by planning, organizing, and controlling resources in order to produce and market goods or services.

■ The Functions of Business

Business has two primary functions—the production and the marketing of goods and services. These primary functions depend on the important support activity of management. Management is used to plan, organize, and control all available resources to reach company goals.

PRODUCTION The process of creating, growing, manufacturing, or improving on goods and services is called production. A songwriter *creates* a song. A farmer *grows* wheat. Ford Motor Company *manufactures* cars. Van conversion companies *improve* newly manufactured vans to make them more suitable for camping and travel.

Now consider an extended example. Weyerhauser Lumber Company produces lumber by cutting down tall trees and slicing them up into pieces of wood. The raw goods—freshly cut trees—are processed to make usable lumber and shipped all over the world. Mobile home manufacturing companies buy the processed lumber, which serves as one of the main materials in their product. Harvesting the trees, cutting them into lumber, and making the lumber into buildings are all production activities.

MARKETING When goods or services are created, grown, or manufactured, they must be sold in the marketplace. The marketplace exists wherever a product is sold to a customer. It may be in a store, an outdoor market, or simply wherever two or more people agree to buy and sell a product.

Recall that the selling of something in the marketplace is the essence of the exchange process. The exchange process occurs when customers *exchange* their money (or their promise to pay) for the goods and services offered. The lumber processed by Weyerhauser in the example above earns no profit for the company and cannot be used for building anything until the exchange process has taken place. The exchange process is the focus of the broad range of activities that we call marketing.

● What You'll Learn

- What a business is
- The basic functions of a business
- How to distinguish businesses from each other based on general characteristics
- The importance of e-commerce
- The concept of derived demand
- The major types of businesses that comprise the industrial market

● Why It's Important

Marketing is part of doing business. In order to understand the world of marketing, you will want to understand what's involved in doing business and some of the different types of businesses.

● Key Terms

- business
- management
- production
- marketplace
- finance
- nonprofit organizations
- public sector
- private sector
- industrial market
- derived demand
- wholesalers
- retailers
- e-commerce

Chapter 5 ■ *Business and Social Responsibility* **81**

SECTION 5.1

FOCUS

Bell Ringer Activity

Draw and Identify Draw two large circles on the board. Above the circles, write *Functions of Business*. Have students draw the circles on a sheet of paper, and write in each circle what they consider to be one function of business.

Introducing the Section

Defining Business Solicit students' answers from the Bell Ringer Activity until you get the correct ones *(production and marketing of goods and services)*. Then ask how students think a company's resources are planned, controlled, and organized to produce and market goods and services. *(You will probably have to coach them on this function, which is management.)* Write the word *management* between the two circles. Tell students that this diagram will help them remember the functions of business.

TEACH

📊 Technology Resources

PowerPoint The *Marketing Essentials* PowerPoint Presentation CD-ROM provides visual lecture aids for every chapter section.

Classroom Resources

For the Teacher
- Teacher Editions for all workbooks
- Assessment Package
- PowerPoint Presentation Software
- Interactive Lesson Planner
- ILP Block Scheduling, p. 3
- ILP Lesson Plans, p. 10
- ILP Internet Resources, p. 29

- ILP *BusinessWeek* Case Studies, p. 27
- ILP Marketing Career Portfolio, p. 32
- *Marketing Essentials* Web site (**www.marketing.glencoe.com**)

For the Student
- Student Activity Workbook, p. 37
- Marketing Math Workbook, p. 13

- Marketing Research Project Workbook, p. 29
- ILP School-to-Work Activity Workbook, p. 17
- Virtual Business simulation
- *Marketing Essentials* Web site (**www.marketing.glencoe.com**)

ILP These resources are available in print and on the Interactive Lesson Planner (ILP)

Concept Development

1. Read Section 5.1 with students.
2. Ask students to add their co-op jobs to the list on the board. Next to each new entry, indicate whether the business is large or small, profit or non-profit, and what type of good or service it provides.
3. Ask students how many different ways they can think of to classify businesses. Generate a list on the board. Use the list when covering the various types of businesses. You may need to prompt the students with simple questions about businesses with which they are familiar to get the response you are looking for.

Discussion Starter

Types of Businesses Draw a Venn diagram of two overlapping circles on the board. Use the Venn diagram to compare and contrast two types of businesses (i.e., Microsoft Corporation and the Metropolitan Opera). Read the various business classifications aloud (large, small, domestic, global, profit, nonprofit, public, private, goods, services, consumer, industrial). As you read the classifications, record areas of commonality in the intersecting segment of the circles and record differences in the appropriate nonintersecting segments of the circles. This exercise will illustrate that businesses can be categorized in many ways.

CAPTION ANSWER
Different Marketplaces Both marketplaces are places where products are sold to consumers.

MANAGEMENT Businesses use natural resources, labor, and capital to produce and market goods or services. These resources must be brought together through good management. Management is the process of achieving company goals by effective use of resources through planning, organizing, and controlling. You will learn more about management in Chapter 11.

The word finance has several meanings in business. It can mean money or anything that can be sold very quickly to get money. It can also mean borrowing money. You may have heard someone talk about financing a car. This means borrowing money to buy the car. As a supporting function for management, finance means money management. You will learn more about finance in Unit 11.

■ Types of Businesses

Businesses come in a variety of shapes and sizes and are classified using various terms. In order to understand their differences, it is important to understand the terminology associated with business classifications. Keep in mind that a business may be classified in more than one category. Businesses can be categorized in the following ways:

- *By size* Is the business large or small?
- *By profit orientation* Is the business a profit or nonprofit concern?
- *By market served* Does the business serve the consumer or industrial market?
- *By kind of product provided* Does the business provide goods, services, or something else?

LARGE VS. SMALL Businesses can be categorized by their size. A small business is one that is operated by only one or a few individuals, and generally has less than 100 employees. A larger business is generally considered one that employs over 1000 people. These organizations are usually national or global and contain many different departments.

Nationwide, there are thousands of small businesses, or "mom-and-pop" operations. They include neighborhood grocery stores, florists, gift shops, photocopy and print shops, and secretarial services. This category also contains many Internet start-up companies and "dot com" businesses that often start off with small budgets and staffs. About 95 percent of all U.S. businesses are classified as small businesses. They employ over half of the private-sector (nongovernment) work force.

DOMESTIC VS. GLOBAL A domestic market comprises buyers in a single country. The global market is the exchange of goods and services among nations.

The advent of the Internet, along with faster transportation and financial flows, makes it easier to do business globally. Products produced in one country are now finding greater acceptance around the world. The trend is moving from domestic markets to a larger global market.

Established companies that have achieved domestic success for many years are now facing international competitors in their own back yards. A company that does not establish a foothold in the global market will forgo profits internationally—and also risk losing business at home.

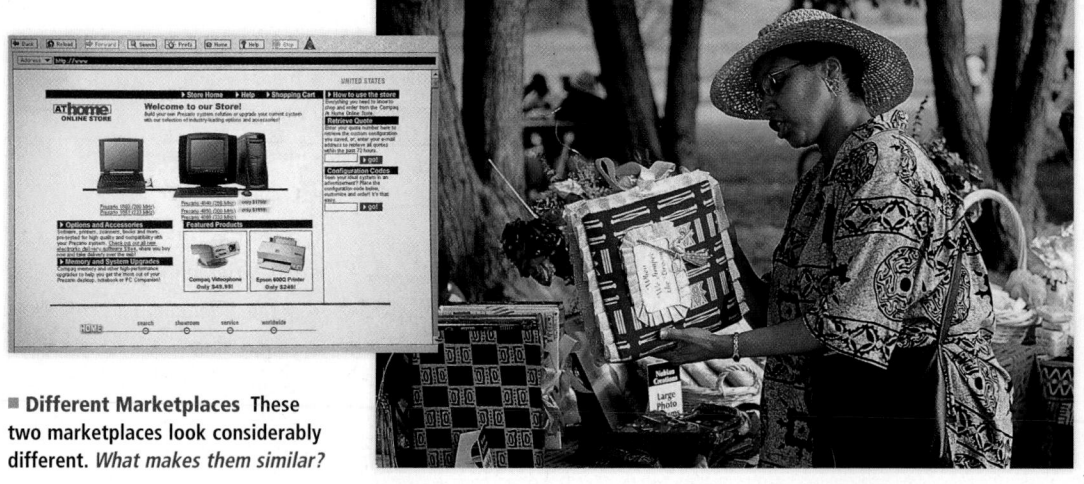

■ **Different Marketplaces** These two marketplaces look considerably different. *What makes them similar?*

GREAT IDEAS from the Marketing Classroom

Jennifer Prout
River Ridge High School
Lacey, WA

Have students own their own apple orchard. Bring in all different varieties of apples to have them taste and determine what type of apples they want their orchard to produce. Have them develop a background on their company, logo, brochure, and a profile of their target industrial consumer. Then have them create their marketing strategies as to how they would sell to an industrial market (bakery, sauce company, candy company, etc.). Have them make an industrial sales presentation. Then invite an actual apple farmer (or someone similar) to speak to your students about industrial sales.

The free enterprise system of the United States has nourished some of the world's most successful global businesses. One of the most dramatic success stories in modern American business is that of McDonald's Corporation—the fast-food giant.

Founder Ray Kroc, who sold restaurant equipment for a living, borrowed money to start the company. The first McDonald's opened in 1955, and by 1962, the company had domestic sales of $76 million. By 2000, McDonald's was a global leader, with 25,000 restaurants in 119 countries and annual sales of $17 billion in the United States, $10 billion in Europe, $8 billion in Asia/Pacific, and another $2 billion in Latin America. McDonald's is now the largest and best-known food service retailer in the world.

PROFIT VS. NONPROFIT Businesspeople in a free market economy, like that of the United States, may earn a profit for satisfying the needs and wants of consumers. People who want to work for themselves and make a profit establish thousands of businesses each year in the United States. Many of these businesses achieve great success.

Microsoft, the computer software company, was started by Bill Gates in 1975 when he was 18 years old. The company earned more than $12 billion in 2000 and was the worldwide leader in software for personal computers.

While profit is the motivating factor in starting most businesses, this is not always the case. Service organizations, called nonprofit organizations, are not operated for the purpose of making a profit.

Examples include the Boys/Girls Clubs of America, and the YMCA and YWCA.

Like any business, nonprofit organizations must hire employees and pay the costs and expenses of running the organization. All the income remaining after expenses are paid goes for the charitable cause outlined in the organization's charter. That means it does not earn a profit.

PUBLIC VS. PRIVATE In addition to charitable institutions, there are other organizations that operate as businesses do but are not intended to earn a profit. Most local, state, and federal government agencies and services, such as public schools and public libraries, fall into this category. These organizations are said to be part of the public sector.

Public sector organizations purchase one-third of all goods and services sold in the United States each year. Government agencies are usually required to buy the least expensive product that meets written minimum specifications. To be considered by the government, a business usually must submit a bid quoting its prices. Businesses not associated with government agencies are part of the private sector.

GOODS OR SERVICES Another way to classify businesses is by looking at the type of products they provide. Some businesses provide goods, like the bread sold in the supermarket or the flour used to make it. Other businesses provide services, like dry cleaning for your clothes or security for the mall where you work.

■ **Not for Profit** Although most large universities are nonprofit, they are still managed much like a for-profit business. *What do you think they do with their excess income?*

Chapter 5 ■ *Business and Social Responsibility* **83**

SECTION 5.1

Thinking Critically

Nonprofit Businesses Give some examples of nonprofit businesses that are not mentioned in the text. *(churches, homeless shelters and missions, meals-on-wheels projects, student vocational organizations such as DECA, Special Olympics.)* Then ask students: Why would anyone want to work for a business that does not have profit as a motive for operation? *(emotional satisfaction; different type of work environment, i.e., one that stresses services rather than production and sales; enjoyment of people attracted to such work)*

Independent Practice

1. **Research and List** Have students use the local phone book to compile a list of three nonprofit businesses. The next day in class, add these businesses to the board list.
2. **Read and Discuss** Have students find one article on an e-commerce company to share with classmates. Suggest that they focus on their successes and failures.

More About . . .

Small Businesses
What qualifies as a "small" business varies from industry to industry. Usually, size is determined by annual revenue or gross receipts. For example, service businesses with receipts under $2 million dollars generally qualify for Small Business Administration (SBA) loans.

CAPTION ANSWER
Not for Profit Excess income may help pay for improving buildings, hiring new instructors, and granting scholarships.

Reteaching

1. **Vocabulary** Assign and review the vocabulary terms for this section.
2. **Fact and Idea** Assign and review Fact and Idea Review questions 1–5 from the Chapter Assessment.
3. **Profit and Nonprofit Businesses** By now you should have a sizable list of local profit and nonprofit businesses on the board. Divide the class into two or three teams and have them face away from the board list. Assign a scorekeeper. Call out the names of local businesses from the list, and ask if each one is small or large, profit or nonprofit, and what major product it provides. (Give one point for each correct answer.) The team with the most points at the end of the questioning wins.

Enrichment

1. **Review** Assign and review the appropriate Thinking Critically questions from the Chapter Assessment.
2. **Extend** Assign and review the corresponding activities from *BusinessWeek Case Studies, Internet Resources,* and the *School-to-Work Activity Workbook.* **ILP**
3. **Brainstorm** Have students create a mnemonic device to help them remember the many ways that businesses can be categorized.

Evaluation

Assign and review the Section 5.1 Assessment.

Risky Business

How do you keep readers coming back? Online magazines—especially ones focusing on computer hardware and software—face this challenge. In 2000, the Macintosh News Network (MNN) got in trouble for soliciting and posting a "sneak peak" story with inside information about a new version of the popular software program Adobe Photoshop. Adobe claimed that the unauthorized "exclusive inside look" provided trade secrets to competitors. The online news publisher said the information came from a public Web site and claimed it didn't know that the original source was confidential. Although the story was removed from the site, the damage to Adobe could equal tens of millions of dollars in lost sales.

Thinking Critically

Should "anything go" on the Internet? Is it ethical for MNN to post "sneak peaks"?

There are finer distinctions among types of services. *Business* services include financial planning, insurance, real estate, transportation, shipping, communications, utilities, data processing, and advertising. The services of doctors, dentists, lawyers, and other professionals are called *professional* services. Newspapers and magazines provide *information* services. There are also categories for businesses that promote people, like political candidates, or places, such as tourism destinations.

Beginning in the 1990s, a whole new area of services arose with the rise of the Internet. Such services include Internet service providers, Web page designers, and an explosion of telecommunications providers.

American business will continue to grow during the early years of the 21st century. The direction, though, will be different. More of the growth will be concentrated in service industries than in manufacturing, and the Internet will continue to expand and shape business.

■ Consumer vs. Industrial

The type of market served is another way of classifying businesses. When we think of goods and services, most of us think of the consumer products that satisfy our own needs and wants. There is another side of marketing that is even larger than the consumer market—the industrial or business-to-business market. Business-to-business marketing involves all the customers who make purchases for business purposes.

The **industrial market** is based on, or derived from, the demand for consumer goods and services. For this reason, the demand for industrial goods is called **derived demand**.

Marketers of industrial goods need to be aware of how their markets will change as a result of changes in the consumer market. When consumers decide to buy more automobiles, the derived demand for auto components (tires, radios, batteries, electronic parts, etc.) increases. Businesses that are involved in the industrial market are extractors, construction and manufacturing businesses, and wholesalers and retailers.

Extractors are businesses that take something from the earth or sea. They include agriculture, forestry, fishing, and mining. The products are primarily sold to other businesses.

Construction companies build structures like houses, office buildings, and manufacturing plants. *Manufacturing* involves producing goods to sell to other manufacturers or to wholesalers and retailers, which is often referred to as business-to-business marketing.

Wholesalers obtain goods from manufacturers and resell them to industrial users, other wholesalers, and retailers. Wholesalers are also called distributors. **Retailers** buy goods from wholesalers or directly from manufacturers and resell them to the consumer. For the most part, retailers cater to the consumer market.

E-COMMERCE E-commerce has become a whole new category of business. Short for electronic commerce, e-commerce is the buying and selling of goods through the use of electronic networks, usually the Internet. Electronic commerce can also be classified as any activity that uses electronic communication in the exchange of goods and services.

Electronic commerce has really existed for many years before the World Wide Web came to be in 1996.

Risky Business

Answer Answers will vary but should discuss the ethical issues involved with leaking information. The Adobe case involves ethical issues and follows Microsoft's effort to remove content from the open-source news site, slashdot.org. Microsoft charged the news site was posting Microsoft trade secrets. In that case, the information in question was available for download to anyone willing to treat the data as confidential.

Going Online! It seems like most businesses are entering the world of e-tailing; traditional brick and mortar companies like Sears began marketing washers and dryers online in 2000. *What are some of the benefits of selling products online?*

Consider the familiar task of shopping for groceries. When the supermarket cashier scans your grocery items, data is transmitted through a computer network to the store's suppliers, who track and replenish the store's stock. When you pay for your purchase using an ATM terminal, funds are electronically transferred from your bank account to the store's bank account. This transaction was made possible through the use of electronic networks.

After only the first five years of the World Wide Web, e-commerce rivaled the size of century-old business sectors, such as automotive, energy, and telecommunications. Sector growth that took a hundred or more years to build during the Industrial Age is being matched by e-commerce at a rate about 20 times faster in the "new economy" of the 21st century.

The market research firm, Socratic Technologies, Inc., found that over half of the businesses it surveyed said the Internet is central to their daily business activities. All types of businesses use the Internet. Even traditional retailers are adapting their marketing to e-commerce—producing the term *e-tailing*.

Use of the Internet for e-commerce will be discussed in greater depth in Chapter 9.

5.1 ASSESSMENT

Reviewing Key Terms and Concepts

1. What is a business?
2. What are the two primary functions of business?
3. List four ways that businesses can be categorized.
4. Discuss the significance of e-commerce.

Thinking Critically

5. Why would someone want to start a small business? Describe the success of a small business with which you are familiar.

Integrating Academic Skills

6. **COMMUNICATION** Conduct a telephone interview with a representative of your local chamber of commerce. Ask what new businesses have joined the organization in the past year. Also, find an evaluation of the economic, political, and other conditions facing businesses in your community. Write about your findings in a one-page report.

5.1 ASSESSMENT ANSWERS

Reviewing Key Terms and Concepts

1. A business is all of the activities involved in producing and marketing goods and services.
2. The two primary functions are the production and the marketing of goods and services.
3. by size, by profit orientation, by market served or by the kind of product provided
4. E-commerce provides a new powerful way to deliver the marketer's message.

Thinking Critically

5. Answers may include: to be one's own boss; opportunity to make more money; belief that he or she has creative and marketable idea; sense of adventure; willingness to take risks and work hard.

Integrating Academic Skills

6. **COMMUNICATION** Reports will vary.

SECTION 5.2

Ethics and Social Responsibility

Bell Ringer Activity

Brainstorm Write the terms *social* and *responsibility* on the board. Ask students to help you brainstorm some meanings for both terms. They should come to the conclusion that *social* means *"of society"* and *responsibility* means *"moral or legal liability or accountability."* Now ask students to brainstorm a general definition for the term *social responsibility.* They should arrive at a general definition of *"a moral and/or legal liability or accountability to society."*

Introducing the Section

Ethics and Social Responsibility
Generate a board list as students brainstorm answers to this question: What responsibilities, if any, do businesses have to society? Accept all answers, trying to classify them as they're given into these categories: Ethics, Environment, Consumers, and Employees.

What You'll Learn

- The areas in which businesses are thought to have social responsibilities
- The ways that business activities have impacted our environment
- The definition of ethics and how marketers can make ethical choices
- The meaning of consumerism and a brief history of the movement
- The current trends and concerns in the workplace for employees

Why It's Important

You know the importance of being considerate of others in your daily life. As you move toward a career in adult life, you will want to understand the importance of ethics and social responsibility in business.

Key Terms

- green marketing
- ethics
- consumerism

Marketing and Social Responsibility

Anyone can choose to go into business in a free enterprise system, but everyone must abide by state and federal laws that apply to businesses. Some of those laws encourage fair business practices, while others protect consumers, workers, investors, and the environment.

Apart from following the law, should businesses have any further social responsibility? Some businesses feel they should. Society's expectations of businesses in regard to social and environmental responsibility have changed dramatically in recent years. Most consumers feel that businesses should act in a socially responsible manner. Because so many consumers have taken an interest in the issue, organizations have been increasingly encouraged to consider the social and environmental consequences of their actions. Social responsibility means that businesses are part of a larger society and should be held accountable to that society for their actions. Companies that have instituted socially responsible programs and policies include Ben & Jerry's Homemade, Inc., and McDonald's.

Ben & Jerry's, the ice cream manufacturer, donates 7.5 percent of its pretax earnings to the disadvantaged and the needy. The company also contributes to groups that strive for social change and environmental protection.

McDonald's Corporation funds Ronald McDonald Houses near children's hospitals. The parents of young cancer patients stay at these residences while their children are receiving medical treatment. There are more than 150 Ronald McDonald Houses across the United States. McDonald's founder, Ray Kroc, also endowed a charitable foundation that has funded millions of dollars in medical research and programs to combat alcoholism.

Let's look at some of the issues that concern socially responsible companies like these. Those issues include protection of the environment, ethical conduct in the marketplace, and the treatment of both consumers and employees.

▪ Environmental Issues

Laws govern many environmental issues that affect us. They prohibit improper disposal of medical, chemical, and other hazardous wastes. Socially responsible businesses follow the laws and understand their roles in helping to preserve our natural resources.

Classroom Resources

For the Teacher
- Teacher Editions for all workbooks
- Assessment Package
- PowerPoint Presentation Software
- Interactive Lesson Planner
- ᴵᴸᴾ Block Scheduling, p. 3
- ᴵᴸᴾ Lesson Plans, p. 11
- ᴵᴸᴾ Internet Resources, p. 29

- ᴵᴸᴾ *BusinessWeek* Case Studies, p. 27
- ᴵᴸᴾ Marketing Career Portfolio, p. 32
- *Marketing Essentials* Web site (**www.marketing.glencoe.com**)

For the Student
- Student Activity Workbook, p. 37
- Marketing Math Workbook, p. 13

- Marketing Research Project Workbook, p. 29
- ᴵᴸᴾ School-to-Work Activity Workbook, p. 17
- Virtual Business simulation
- *Marketing Essentials* Web site (**www.marketing.glencoe.com**)

ᴵᴸᴾ These resources are available in print and on the Interactive Lesson Planner (ILP)

AIR AND WATER POLLUTION The federal government established the Environmental Protection Agency (EPA) to protect the environment from pollution. The EPA is probably best known for the Clean Air Act, which was revised in 1990 to intensify actions to protect our environment. All automobile manufacturers have had to modify their engines to meet EPA emission standards. It is also mandatory that cars use unleaded gasoline to protect people and nature from the harmful effects of lead. Manufacturers are still working to perfect EVs, or Electronic Vehicles, that run on battery energy as opposed to gasoline and oil.

Chlorofluorocarbons (CFCs) were once used as propellants in spray products such as hairspray, insecticide, and paint cans until research proved that they contributed to the depletion of the ozone layer. Less ozone is a health hazard and increases exposure to the Sun's harmful rays. An international agreement was reached to phase out the use of CFCs before 2000, but they are still being used in some countries. Socially responsible companies have substituted different propellants or switched to pump sprays.

One popular CFC, freon, was widely used in automobile and building air-conditioning systems. Federal law now requires manufacturers to use safer chemicals. As of 1996, no freon is produced in the United States. Garages and repair shops are required to recycle freon products under a law passed in 1997.

Although agricultural pesticides and chemical fertilizers are frequently used to grow bigger crops and more attractive fruits and vegetables, the EPA tightened laws regarding food exposure to pesticides with the Food Quality Act of 1996.

Many pesticides have had harmful effects on animals and people. The EPA is constantly checking pesticides to determine possible harmful effects. Some have already polluted our land, streams, lakes, and underground water supplies. This is true for household products that are used as pest control, too. The EPA required S.C. Johnson & Son, Inc. to remove AllerCare Dust Mite Powder and Allergen Spray from store shelves in January 2000 when it was found to cause some customers to have asthma attacks, breathing problems, and skin rashes.

Chlorine gas is the most heavily used pesticide in the United States, acting as a disinfectant for swimming pools, drinking water, and sewage systems. The EPA issued the Chlorine Gas Reregistration Eligibility Decision (RED) to limit the use of chlorine only to trained professionals who understand the hazards of handling this potentially dangerous substance. Chlorine products were to be re-labeled for "restricted use only" beginning in 2000.

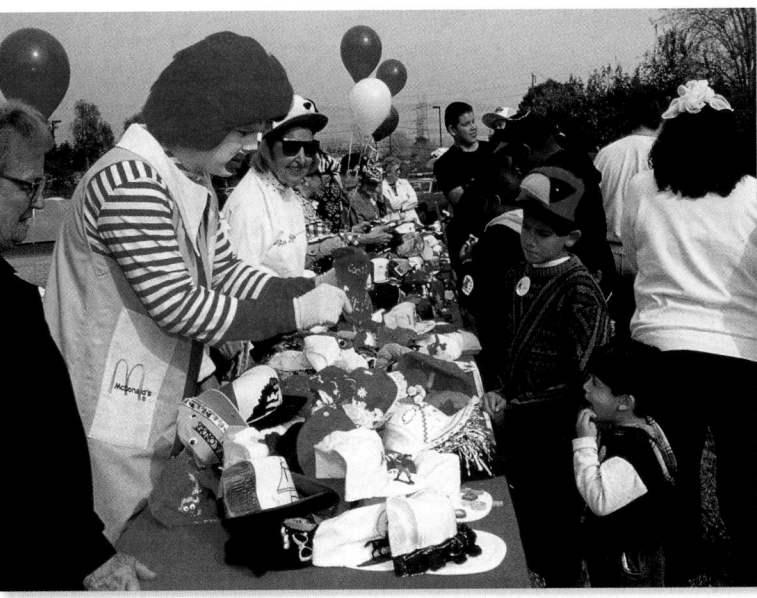

■ **Reaching Out** McDonald's is one of many organizations that promotes charitable programs and practices social responsibility. *Why would an organization become involved in activities such as these?*

Chapter 5 ■ *Business and Social Responsibility* **87**

TEACH

⎍⎍⎍ Technology Resources

PowerPoint The *Marketing Essentials* PowerPoint Presentation CD-ROM provides visual lecture aids for every chapter section.

Concept Development

1. Read Section 5.2 with students.
2. Have students read aloud the Case Study and review the answers in class.
3. Have students consider the social concerns facing the businesses on the list generated in the chapter Springboard activity. Again, categorize these as matters of ethics, environment, etc.

Discussion Starter

Ethics Most large concert tours of major rock groups have enormous corporate sponsorship—often from beer companies. Is such sponsorship ethical when (a) many people in the audience may be below the legal drinking age, and (b) when the advertising might encourage over-indulgence of those legally old enough to drink? *(Some may feel that the First Amendment right of free speech includes the freedom to advertise, no matter the product or the consequences. Others may feel that any company has a moral and ethical obligation to monitor advertising to special populations or in special situations.)*

CAPTION ANSWER
Reaching Out There are many possible answers, but most students will say to give something back to the community and to create good public relations.

Cooperative Learning

Employee Policies Divide your class into four groups. Have each group select one type of business, assume the roles of managers in that business, and formulate an employee policy based on the workplace trends listed in **Figure 5-1** on pages 92–93. For example, if students choose a restaurant business, how would they accommodate male and female employees who have newborn babies or young children? Would they offer parents first preference on early shifts or on-site child care? Have students present their policy statements to the class for comment and questions. Be sure the discussion includes a look at the downside of some of these workplace trends. *(Flextime, for example, makes meetings difficult to schedule.)*

■ **Recycle, Please** 3M's Scotch-Brite Never Rust Wool Soap Pads appeal to customers because they are made of recycled soda bottles. This makes them more expensive than competing brands. *Do you think that this will affect the environmentally-conscious customer's decision to buy?*

Industrial waste poses another problem for the environment. Industrial waste often finds its way through porous soil into the underground water supplies used by cities. The EPA found that in 1996, 208 million tons of municipal solid waste were generated by the United States. The EPA has increased its efforts to enforce proper waste disposal to protect our water and resources. The executives of some manufacturing companies have even been sentenced to prison for violation of safe disposal standards.

CONSERVATION AND RECYCLING Oil consumption became a concern during the oil crisis of the 1970s, and it still is today. According to the *International Energy Outlook 2000*, worldwide oil demand will reach 113 million barrels a day by 2020. The price and availability of oil is greatly affected by political and economic disruptions; therefore it can often be unpredictable. In 2000, Arab nations restricted oil output, and gas prices rose abruptly. Exploration of other fuels has become necessary. Car manufacturers have responded by producing smaller, more fuel-efficient automobiles.

BRIGHT IDEAS

Be Kind—Rewind and Recycle

A handful of entrepreneurs are making money by erasing, cleaning, and repackaging videotapes. Once recycled, they are sold to a variety of users looking to work within tight budgets. The lower price of a recycled tape versus a new tape appeals to young film students, independent movie studios, and public broadcasting networks. This $30 million dollar industry has continued to grow in the past 30 years as these modern day recyclers find treasure in the unwanted discards from TV networks, corporations, and security-camera outfits. Recyclers also earn revenue by reconditioning used tapes and returning them to the original owners for use. Other customers pay to have their videotapes destroyed, in order to keep their video footage from reappearing elsewhere.

Thinking Creatively
On what other products could these specialized recycling businesses concentrate?

CAPTION ANSWER
Recycle, Please Answers will vary. Students' personal opinions will vary depending on their commitment to recycling at any cost.

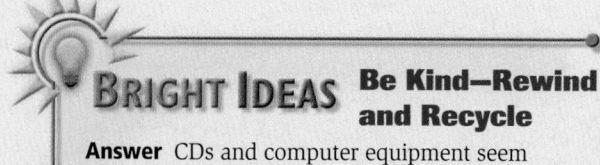

BRIGHT IDEAS
Be Kind—Rewind and Recycle

Answer CDs and computer equipment seem to be an extension of a videotape recyclers' product line.

Alternatives to the traditional transportation fuels of gasoline and diesel fuel are currently being developed. Some vehicle fuels, because of physical or chemical properties, create less pollution than do today's gasolines. These are called "clean fuels." These include certain types of alcohol, electricity, natural gas, and propane. Researchers say that a "fuel cell" vehicle will be available to the public before too long.

Gasoline is toxic and emits complex mixtures of compounds that lead to the formation of ground-level ozone. While steps have been taken to reduce the risk of pollution, many large cities still have not seen a reduction of their ozone problem. The use of clean fuel slows the atmospheric buildup of the "greenhouse gas," carbon dioxide, which contributes to the potential for global warming. While combustion of any carbon-based fuel produces carbon dioxide, fuels produced from biomass (crops, trees, etc.) and from natural gas result in less carbon dioxide accumulation than fuels made from petroleum or coal.

While electric or battery-powered vehicles give off virtually no pollution, the driving range of today's electric cars is limited by the amount of power the battery can provide. Currently, the cost of electric vehicles is high and batteries take hours to recharge. Recent developments in electric vehicle technology show much promise for the future—and offer one of the best options for reducing motor vehicle pollution.

Conservation of our natural resources depends heavily on cooperation of business, government, and consumers. Most local governments require mandatory recycling of glass, plastic, and aluminum through local trash collection, and many companies are making similar efforts.

GREEN MARKETING Consumer concern over the environment is increasing, and marketers are paying attention. The growing importance of ecological issues has brought about green marketing. In green marketing, companies make an effort to produce and promote environmentally safe products. Such products are often labeled as ozone-safe, recyclable, environmentally friendly, or biodegradable. Green marketing strategies have become an increasingly important way for companies to build consumer loyalty. A significant number of consumers are willing to pay more for products that are environmentally friendly and ecologically sound.

Life In The Diverse MARKETPLACE

Finding a Balance

Sustainable development is a strategy by which communities seek economic development approaches that also benefit the local environment and quality of life. It provides a framework for communities to use resources efficiently, create efficient infrastructures, protect and enhance quality of life, and create new businesses to strengthen their economies. Efforts to achieve sustainable development have been difficult for developing countries dealing with concerns such as poverty. Organizations work together to develop sustainable development strategies that can help rich and poor countries alike.

Thinking Critically

Why are sustainable development issues important to all nations, not just developing countries?

■ Business Ethics

Ethics are guidelines for good behavior. Ethical behavior is based on knowing the difference between right and wrong—and doing what is right. Ethical behavior is truthful and fair and takes into account the well-being of everyone.

Laws are made to address ethical concerns involving products or marketing. Unethical practices such as bait-and-switch advertising, price fixing, and selling unsafe products are prohibited. Ethical questions that involve debate between our guaranteed freedom of speech and our guaranteed freedom to compete are not as easily answered, however. The ethics of marketing products such as tobacco and liquor as glamorous or romantic is often questioned. To make the right ethical choices, marketers must answer these three basic questions:

1. Is the practice right, fair, and honest?

2. What would happen if the product were marketed differently?

3. What practice will result in the greatest good for the greatest number of people?

Life In The Diverse MARKETPLACE

Finding a Balance

Answer These issues are important to all nations because economic situations affect all countries in a global economy.

Problem-Solving Skills

L1 Present students with this problem: Your supervisor has asked you to keep track of the number of times one of your coworkers comes in late during the week. Would you agree to do this? Is it ethical of the supervisor to ask you to do this? Why or why not? *(Answers will vary. Some students may agree to it, feeling that it is ethical since their coworker is breaking company rules and the supervisor should know about it. Other students may refuse to do it, feeling that it is unethical of the supervisor to put one employee in a position of spying on another.)*

L2 Tell students that unfortunately people in business sometimes do get caught in situations that will probably have undesirable consequences, no matter what they do. Ask: What are the undesirable consequences if you agree to keep track of the number of times your coworker is late? What are the undesirable consequences if you do not agree to do it? *(Answers will vary. If you agree to do it, your coworker may find out about it and your relationship will probably never be positive again. If you refuse your supervisor's request, however, you may damage your relationship with him or her, which will probably affect your work.)*

L3 Ask: If a supervisor or coworker requests that you do something at work that you feel is morally or legally wrong, what recourse do you have? *(Answers will vary. One possibility: Tell the person that the request goes against your personal code of ethics. If he/she persists, document the incident and speak to your personnel director. If your company is small and there is no personnel department, speak to the owner.)*

Case Study

The Wired Hotel

Hotels depend on business travelers for large profits and therefore compete for their business by offering innovative services. Many chains offer lower room rates for business customers, and some make agreements with airlines to credit customers' accounts with mileage redeemable for airline tickets.

Most big brand hotels have started offering comprehensive business services. Many chains offer high-speed Internet connections, conference rooms, and work areas with speakerphones, fax machines, and printers. Even less expensive hotel chains are getting in the act to meet customers' needs.

The Starwood Hotel company has tapped into this lucrative market with its W hotel chain, which concentrates exclusively on the business travel market. Every W hotel room is a fully wired virtual office with a high-speed Internet connection, Web browser television, fax port, two-line cordless telephone, and multimedia support. The high-speed Internet access connects at speeds up to 50 times faster than conventional dial-up access. W offers meeting spaces called "creative think tanks" that are designed to inspire creative thought. W's guest rooms are luxuriously stocked with Aveda bath products and goose down comforters. Guests even have the option of arriving to a prestocked refrigerator, with their advance order delivered via WebGrocer. At the end of the day, guests can unwind at the spa or state-of-the-art gym, complete with personal trainers.

Examining the needs of business travelers and providing the services that make it easier for them to conduct their business on the road is smart marketing. If business customers have a positive experience, it is likely that they will pass their recommendations on to their business associates.

Case Study Review

1. How are hotels catering to businesspeople who travel as part of their jobs?
2. What are some risks involved in making changes in a hotel to better serve business travelers?

A MATTER OF ETHICS

3. What ethical concerns can you see when a hotel offers lower room rates to a specific type of customer—such as a business traveler?

Case Study Review Answers

The Wired Hotel
1. By providing hotel rooms fully equipped with Internet connections, fax ports, two-line cordless telephones, and multimedia support, as well as meeting spaces called "creative think tanks."

2. Some risks may be: overestimating demand for the services; the possibility of an economic downturn affecting business travel; and technology becoming obsolete before investment is recaptured.

A MATTER OF ETHICS
3. Answers will vary.

PRODUCT RECALLS Businesses sometimes look at the legal issues involved in addition to their perceived social responsibility when making choices involving ethics. To reduce losses that could arise from future lawsuits, a socially responsible business will recall an unsafe product before the government forces it to do so. Irresponsible businesses that do not recall a product on their own may be forced to do so by a government agency like the Consumer Product Safety Commission.

Businesses may recall products even if they are not responsible for design flaws or other problems. A historically important example is when McNeil Consumer Products pulled Tylenol products off store shelves nationwide in 1982 after someone was fatally poisoned by a capsule that had been tampered with. The company immediately alerted all Tylenol users to return their capsules to the stores where they had purchased them. The manufacture of Tylenol capsules was temporarily discontinued while McNeil worked with other drug companies to develop tamper-resistant packaging. Thanks to their efforts, today most over-the-counter drugs are packaged with a seal around the bottle top or around the entire package.

CODE OF ETHICS The American Marketing Association has developed a code of ethics for marketers. The code includes detailed provisions about the truthfulness and fairness of marketing activities such as advertising, selling, pricing, marketing research, and product development and use.

■ Consumerism

Social responsibility involves the relationship of marketing with all of society. Consumerism, however, involves the relationship of marketing only with those who buy a company's goods or services. Consumerism is the societal effort to protect consumer rights by putting legal, moral, and economic pressure on business. Individual consumers, consumer groups, government, and socially responsible business leaders share this effort.

Consumerism had its beginning in the early 1900s, when it focused on product purity, product shortages, antitrust concerns, postal rates, and banking. From the 1930s to the 1950s, consumerism concentrated on product safety, labeling, misrepresentation, deceptive advertising, consumer refunds, and bank failures.

CONSUMER RIGHTS The greatest growth in consumerism took place from the early 1960s until about 1980. It involved all areas of marketing. President John F. Kennedy's Consumer Bill of Rights dominated the beginning of this consumer period. It stated that consumers have four basic rights:

- To be informed and protected against fraud, deceit, and misleading statements, and to be educated in the wise use of financial resources
- To be protected from unsafe products
- To have a choice of goods and services
- To have a voice in product and marketing decisions made by government and business

Several widely read books gave impetus to consumerism during the 1960s and 1970s. Ralph Nader's *Unsafe at Any Speed* focused public attention on what the automobile industry could do to make cars safer. Rachel Carson's *Silent Spring* detailed how marketing contributed to a decaying environment. Vance Packard's *Hidden Persuaders* revealed marketing's influence on society.

Consumers were increasingly dissatisfied with poor-quality products, deceptive business practices, and the lack of concern for consumer complaints. They got angry and demanded action. The Federal Trade Commission responded by expanding its role in consumer issues.

Companies are more responsive to customer complaints and environmental concerns than they have been in the past. Many companies now consider consumer concerns when developing their marketing plans. Product containers that can be recycled, for example, are a direct response to consumers' environmental concerns. For example, McDonald's changed their packaging from a difficult-to-recycle polystyrene plastic to a more environmentally friendly kind of packaging in response to pressure from customers.

■ Workplace Trends and Concerns

As interest in traditional social responsibility concerns has receded, other concerns have replaced them. Employee issues have been in the center of public interest since the 1990s.

Figure 5-1 on pages 92 and 93 presents an overview of other trends and concerns in the workplace, including telecommuting, flextime, family leave, on-site child care, help for the physically challenged, and health care reform.

Thinking Critically

1. **Consumer Advocates**
Some consumer advocates have become recognized for their work, as have some journalists who investigate consumer issues. Ask students whether we should accept the reports of consumer advocates and investigative journalists without question. *(Answers will vary. Consumer advocates have their place but they, like people who run businesses, are human and have biases. Before making decisions about any product, read several reports about it, both pro and con.*

2. **Social Responsibility**
Corporations such as Kmart are now including the physically challenged in their television commercials. Ask students what this says about the sense of social responsibility of these companies. *(This shows a sensitivity to the physically challenged as well as an awareness that they are a part of the consumer population.)*

THE **DECA** CONNECTION

COMPETITIVE EVENTS AND MARKETING ESSENTIALS

Civic Consciousness DECA's Civic Consciousness Project provides your students with the opportunity to develop a better understanding of the role civic activities have in society. By participating in this project, your students will plan and conduct a project to benefit a community service or charity. The Civic Consciousness Project is designed to make use of the basic marketing principles your students are learning in class. Upon completion of the project your students should follow the event guidelines to complete the written manual they will enter in competition. One to three members participating in the project can represent your chapter and give an oral presentation about the project in competition.

Reteaching

1. **Vocabulary** Assign and review the vocabulary terms for this section.
2. **Fact and Idea** Assign and review Fact and Idea Review questions 6–10 from the Chapter Assessment.
3. **Social Responsibility** Draw a large circle on the board and write in it the term *social responsibility*. Draw four "spokes" from the circle, and ask students to name the four areas in which businesses have social responsibility *(business ethics, environment, consumers, and employees)*. Then have students brainstorm anything they can recall from the text dealing with these areas. Add these to the diagram.

FIGURE 5-1

WORKPLACE TRENDS AND ISSUES

Today's socially responsible businesses are offering their employees a more user-friendly workplace and even redefining the term workplace.

TELECOMMUTING

Telecommuting involves working at home, usually on a computer. Completed jobs are transmitted either by mail-in disk or manuscript form, or by phone, using a fax machine or a modem.

FLEXTIME

Flextime allows workers to choose their work hours. Possible arrangements include early start/early finish (7 A.M.–3 P.M.), late start/late finish (10 A.M.–6 P.M.), and even four-day workweeks (four 9- or 10-hour days followed by three-day weekends).

FAMILY LEAVE

Family leave is now legally required by federal law for large employers. Workers are entitled to up to 12 weeks of nonpaid family leave every two years. This allows people to cope with births, deaths, and family illnesses without fear of job loss.

HELP FOR THE PHYSICALLY CHALLENGED

Help for the physically challenged is mandated by the Americans with Disabilities Act (1990). Employers must provide physically challenged people with the same job opportunities and work site access that others have. To make this possible, employers may have to alter their workplaces physically, change the way a job is done, or provide individual assistance.

HEALTH CARE REFORM

Health care reform at the national level is an employee issue because so many Americans receive health insurance benefits through their jobs. Of the 37 million Americans who do work, many are employed by small businesses or hold minimum-wage jobs. How to cover these people and how to hold the line on costs for those who have coverage are key issues in the national health care debate.

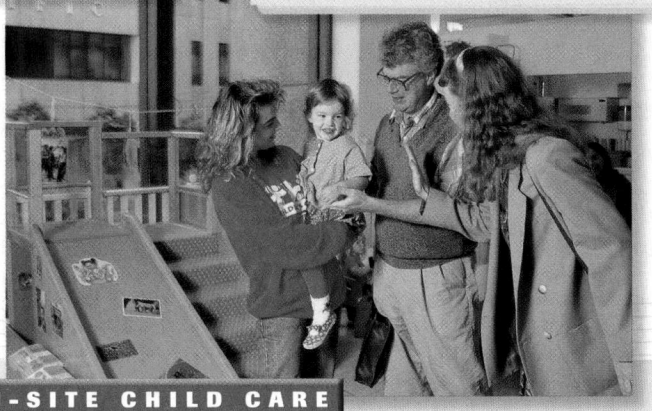

ON-SITE CHILD CARE

On-site child care is a benefit that has grown in popularity with the increase in two-income families. Some employers have expanded it to include on-site schools and on-site clinics for children who are ill. Where the benefit is provided in any form, it tends to reduce employee turnover.

SECTION 5.2

Enrichment

1. **Review** Assign and review the Chapter 5 activities in the *Student Activity Workbook*.
2. **Review** Assign and review the appropriate Thinking Critically questions from the Chapter Assessment.
3. **Review** Assign and review the following Chapter Assessment activities: Building Workplace Skills, Applying Marketing Concepts, Linking School to Work Activities, The DECA Connection Role Play, and Internet Connection.
4. **Brainstorm and Present** Divide the class into at least four groups. Have each group generate an ethical problem that can occur at work, perhaps one that they have encountered on their co-op jobs. Problems could include such things as employee theft or having someone else punch your time card after you leave work. Have each group prepare a dramatization of the problem and present it or, depending on the level of the group, role-play it to the class. Once each group has finished, lead a discussion on the ethical considerations of the situation and how the problem could be solved.

Evaluation

Assign and review the Section 5.2 Assessment.

CLOSE

Section Wrap-Up

On the board, draw the circle with four spokes that you drew for the Reteaching exercise. Have students fill in the term that belongs in the circle *(social responsibility)* and the terms that belong on each spoke *(business ethics, environment, consumers, and employees)*. Then have students write one or two things next to each spoke that they can recall about chapter content.

Pepsi: Back to School
Answer Pepsi's motivation in targeting this market is that the students will drink Pepsi outside of school as well.

Other workplace concerns include sexual harassment, computer privacy and security, and employee computer use. The increase in the number of lawsuits alleging sexual harassment has become one of the most challenging issues businesses face today. The Equal Employment Opportunity Commission (EEOC) defines sexual harassment as unwelcome sexual attention or the creation of "an intimidating, hostile, or offensive working environment." As a response to sexual harassment concerns, many companies have policies defining harassment and procedures for handling complaints.

Computer privacy and security are also emerging as important workplace issues. As more and more companies' computer networks are connected to the Internet, the need for computer security has become increasingly important. To achieve a level of security, computer engineers have developed firewalls. Firewalls are hardware or software that restrict access from a business's internal network to the Internet and vice versa. Think of a firewall as a checkpoint at which all data, incoming and outgoing, is stopped to make sure that it is acceptable.

Many companies also track employee computer use to ensure that computers are being used appropriately and for work-related business only. Employee monitoring is more widespread than ever today, as managers need to ensure appropriate business behavior and high performance levels.

REAL WORLD MARKETING

Pepsi: Back to School

In England's Thames Valley, Pepsi has gained exclusive rights to sell its products in high school vending machines. People who felt schools were becoming overly commercialized opposed the deal. Nutritional concerns were also an issue. In an effort to help fund school activities, the school board decided to accept Pepsi's proposal. The schools will receive 60 percent of the revenue from bottled drinks and 40 percent from cans. Pepsi would probably not have been allowed to sell on school grounds without this marketing idea to raise funds from the proceeds of soda sales.

Thinking Critically
What is Pepsi's motivation in targeting this market?

5.2 ASSESSMENT

Reviewing Key Terms and Concepts

1. What are some areas in which businesses are thought to have social responsibility?

2. In what ways have business activities impacted our environment?

3. Define the term ethics and explain how marketers can make ethical choices.

4. Define consumerism and give a brief history of the movement.

5. What current trends are likely to improve the workplace for employees?

Thinking Critically

6. How are business ethics related to personal ethics?

Integrating Academic Skills

7. **MATH** If the local recycling plant pays $.06 per pound for aluminum cans, how many pounds of cans would it take to get $10?

5.2 ASSESSMENT ANSWERS

Reviewing Key Terms and Concepts

1. environmental issues; business ethics; consumerism; and employee issues
2. pollution of air and water
3. Ethics are guidelines for good behavior. Marketers must ask: Is the practice right, fair, and honest? What would happen if the product were marketed differently? What practice will result in the greatest good for the greatest number of people?

4. Consumerism is the societal effort to protect consumer rights by putting legal, moral, and economic pressure on business. It began in the 1900s with growth from the 60s–80s.
5. sexual harassment legislation, flextime, telecommuting, etc.

Thinking Critically
6. Personal ethics affect business ethics.

Integrating Academic Skills
7. **MATH** 167 pounds; $10.00 ÷ .06 = 167.

Careers in Marketing

TRAVEL AND TOURISM MARKETING

Natasha Lawe
Travel Consultant
Liberty Travel

What does your job entail?

"The main focus of my job is making people happy—I sell dream vacations. Travel consultants make travel arrangements for clients, planning travel routes and schedules, determining fares, and reserving seating. They also book accommodations, arrange tours, and reserve rental cars. Travel is a required part of the job—you need to know a destination in order to sell it."

What training do you recommend for students?

"Students should study geography and be familiar with travel destinations. *Travel Weekly* is one magazine that keeps you updated on all of the popular destinations and selling tools."

What skills are most important?

"Patience—it takes time and patience when dealing with customers. It is important to know documentation criteria for international travel. Some customers may never have left their towns, and they count on you for thorough and accurate information. You also need excellent communication skills and computer skills."

How does your workload vary?

"The busy season is normally from October to April, when people are planning their summer vacations; this makes work slower in the summer. On an average day, I confirm about 10–15 reservations and receive approximately 20–30 phone inquiries on sales promotions."

What is your key to success?

"My key to success is knowing my priorities and what I want out of life. To be successful, travel consultants need to know their products and develop personal relationships with their customers. People have to trust you 100% to make their vacations pleasurable."

Thinking Critically

Why would vacationers choose to use a professional travel consultant instead of using a travel Web site to make their plans?

Career Facts

Education and Training: A high school diploma is required. Courses in travel consulting can be taken at vocational schools, community colleges, and some four-year colleges. Recommended courses include business classes, geography, world history, foreign languages, and word processing.

Aptitudes, Abilities, and Skills: Patience, people skills, organizational skills, ability to work under stress and keep up with industry changes are necessary.

Career Outlook: Money spent on travel is expected to increase through 2010 so employment should grow faster than average.

Career Path: Experience as a tour guide, hotel reservation clerk, or receptionist in a travel agency may provide entry into this career. Travel agents may advance to other managerial positions.

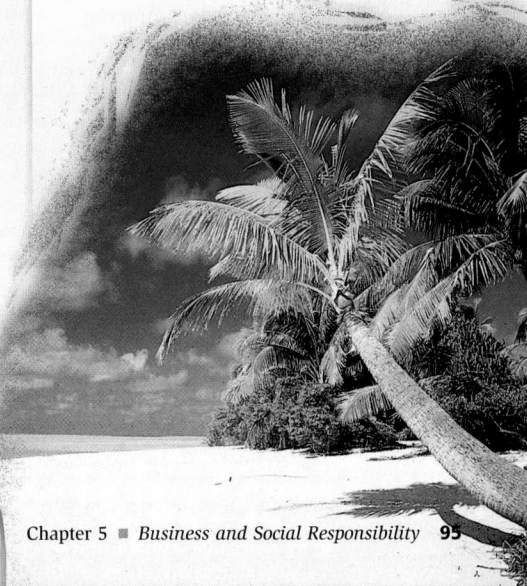

Chapter 5 ■ *Business and Social Responsibility* **95**

Lifelong Learning

Business and Social Responsibility
Learning about marketing and social responsibility is the first step in a lifelong commitment to make choices based on information. Which products to use and how to dispose of them affect the student's environment as well as the global environment. By reading a variety of publications and joining in community and school activities, students can make a difference.

Meeting Individual Needs

Second Language Learners
Imagine you were a student in another country using a language unfamiliar to you. Your native language wouldn't help you. You would require extra assistance to comprehend discussions. If your class includes second language learners, provide outlines of lectures or discussion topics in advance. Students can review materials at a slower pace.

Vocabulary Review

Sentences will vary. See Glossary for definitions.

Fact and Idea Review

1. The primary functions of business are the production of goods and services and the marketing of goods and services.
2. The three functions of management are planning, organizing, and controlling.
3. About 95% of U.S. businesses are classified as small businesses.
4. Nonprofit organizations provide a service; all income remaining after paying the expenses of employees and running the organization goes for the charitable cause of the organization. Profit businesses are motivated by the desire to earn as much profit as possible for the owner through business efforts.
5. Answers will vary. McDonald's, Microsoft, and Weyerhauser are examples of private sector businesses. Public-sector organizations include public school systems and government agencies.
6. Businesses should have some social responsibility in the environment (pollution, conservation, recycling); business ethics; consumerism; and employee issues.
7. Marketers must ask: Is the practice right, fair, and honest? What would happen if the product were marketed differently? What practice will result in the greatest good for the greatest number of people?
8. Consumerism has put legal, moral, and economic pressure on businesses to protect consumer rights.
9. Consumers have the right to be informed and protected against fraud, deceit, and misleading statements, and to be educated in the wise use of financial resources.
10. Flextime allows workers to choose their own hours, while telecommuting allows them to choose where they work, which is usually at home.

Thinking Critically

1. Answers will vary but might include fines and cleanup costs. Encourage students to come up with imaginative answers.
2. Answers may include increased sales and committed employees.

Chapter 5 ASSESSMENT

VOCABULARY REVIEW

Use each of the following words in a sentence that demonstrates you know its meaning:

- business
- production
- marketplace
- management
- finance
- nonprofit organizations
- public sector
- private sector
- industrial market
- derived demand
- wholesalers
- retailers
- e-commerce
- green marketing
- ethics
- consumerism

FACT AND IDEA REVIEW

1. Name the two primary functions of business. (5.1)
2. What are the three major functions of management in business? (5.1)
3. What percentage of U.S. businesses are small businesses? (5.1)
4. Explain how the operation of a nonprofit organization differs from a profit-making enterprise. (5.1)
5. Provide an example of both a private-sector and a public-sector organization. (5.1)
6. In what areas are businesses thought to have some degree of social responsibility? (5.2)

7. What are the questions that marketers must ask themselves to make ethical business choices? (5.2)
8. How has consumerism affected the way that businesses conduct themselves? (5.2)
9. What rights do consumers have according to the Consumer Bill of Rights? (5.2)
10. How does flextime differ from telecommuting? (5.2)

THINKING CRITICALLY

1. How should local, state, or federal governments handle industries that pollute the environment?
2. What unexpected benefits might a company receive if it believes in and practices social responsibility?
3. Do consumers have a duty to be socially responsible in their purchasing? What might be some examples of this sort of conduct?
4. Employee benefits, such as on-site childcare, tend to stabilize a company's workforce. Given this fact, why do you think more companies don't offer such benefits?

BUILDING WORKPLACE SKILLS

1. **Writing** Write a letter to a local government official describing the importance and benefits of recycling.
2. **Human Relations** You work for a company that produces textiles, and you have just discovered that the company has been disposing of its wastes in a manner that is unsafe for the environment. What will you do?

---

3. Most students will probably say yes. Consumers can show social responsibility by buying recycled products; buying from socially responsible companies; buying in bulk to save excess packaging; and buying brands manufactured by companies that observe fair labor practices.
4. The high cost of running an on-site childcare facility prevents many companies from offering this benefit.

Building Workplace Skills

1. Letters will vary.
2. Students may suggest first going to their supervisor to complain and then going higher up in the company if no satisfactory action is taken. Notifying government authorities is another possibility.

APPLYING MARKETING CONCEPTS

1. **Summarizing Key Concepts** Summarize an article that demonstrates any of the key concepts in this chapter. In the summary, identify the specific key concepts in parenthesis. Use business publications, such as *BusinessWeek, Fortune, Forbes,* and *Nation's Business,* to find an applicable article.

2. **Recycling in Your Community** With a group of other students, research the recycling centers in your community. Use a presentation software program to make a presentation with charts, graphs, and other information about the centers. Include their locations, their hours of operation, the materials they accept, and the rates they pay for those materials.

3. **Understanding Small Businesses** Find a local mom-and-pop business and interview the owners. Ask them to give you a brief history of the business. Find out what they like and dislike about having their own business. Use a word processing program to write a two-page report summarizing the interview.

4. **Conserving Resources** Think of a project that would help your school conserve resources and protect the environment. Then use a word processing program to write an editorial for the school newspaper. In the editorial, explain your idea and try to persuade other students to participate in your project.

LINKING SCHOOL TO WORK

Thinking and Personal Skills Ask an employer whether he or she believes business has social responsibilities, and why or why not. Report back to the class and discuss the answers you and your classmates received. Some good interview questions might be:
- In what ways does your business show awareness of social responsibility?
- How do you think it might improve?

THE DECA CONNECTION

Role Play: Plant Employee

Situation You are to assume the role of employee at a plant experiencing a serious problem with productivity. Much of the problem can be traced to days lost by employees with young children. When their day-care arrangements don't work out or when their children get sick, these employees must leave early or take time off. As a result, production and quality drop. The workers have a solution and they've chosen you as their spokesperson.

Activity Make the case to your employer (judge) for an on-site child-care facility. What will you say in your presentation?

Evaluation You will be evaluated on how well you meet the following performance indicators:
- Explain the concept of productivity
- Explain the role of business in society
- Foster positive working relationships
- Convince others of point of view
- Make oral presentations

inter NET CONNECTION

New Century Social Responsibilities
You are a management trainee in a large corporation that has a poor record for social responsibility. The new management is interested in working toward a more socially responsible image and has asked for your input on what is expected in the 21st century.

Connect
- Use the Internet to research what specific social responsibilities are expected of businesses in the 21st century.
- In your search, use key words and phrases, such as "business responsibility," "environment," "ozone layer," and "pollution."
- Use a word processing program to write a two-page summary of your findings.

Chapter 5 ■ *Business and Social Responsibility* **97**

Students should be evaluated on the performance indicators noted in the Role Play.
- For another DECA Role Play, go to the *Student Activity Workbook*, p. 37.
- For more in-depth Role Play practice, refer to DECA's *Essential Competitive Events Handbook*. To order, contact DECA at **www.deca.org**.

inter NET CONNECTION
Summaries will vary.

Mini Quiz
Administer the Mini Quiz orally. For an expanded chapter quiz, go to page 27 of the *Reproducible Tests* book.

1. What are the two functions of business? production and marketing
2. What process is used to plan, organize, and control all available resources to reach company goals? management
3. Most local, state, and federal agencies and services, like your library, are said to be part of the public sector.
4. The industrial market is based on the demand for consumer goods and services, so the demand for industrial goods is called derived demand.
5. Ethics are guidelines for good behavior.

Applying Marketing Concepts
1. Summaries will vary depending on chosen articles.
2. Presentations will vary.
3. Reports will depend on the businesses selected.
4. Editorials will vary.

Linking School to Work
Answers will depend on the work situation.

1. **Assessment** Have students complete the Reproducible Test for Chapter 5 or construct your own tests using the ExamView software.
2. **Enrichment** Have students complete the corresponding activities in the following workbooks:
   - *Marketing Math Workbook*, p. 13
   - *Marketing Research Project Workbook*, p. 29

Chapter Overview

Chapter 6 explains the need for international trade, its benefits, and how governments are involved in it. It also explains balance of trade, trade barriers, and trade alliances, and introduces the practical side of doing business abroad.

Springboard

Brainstorm Write this question on the board: Is trading with foreign countries good or bad for the U.S. economy? Have each student write a list of points supporting his or her opinion. Then discuss and formulate a class position to compare with the chapter content.

Prereading

List the section objectives to discuss with students. Have students skim the chapter, looking at the pictures, reading the captions, and noting the heads. Ask questions to ensure that students have a minimal understanding of the chapter structure.

Preteaching Marketing Vocabulary

Dictate each of the vocabulary terms and ask students to write them on a sheet of paper. Then write the terms on the board. Have students guess at the meaning of each term. Write their guesses next to each term. Leave this list on the board so students can see how close their guesses were to the actual definitions as they work through the chapter.

Marketing:
What It Takes
Answer Information about the economy (GDP, inflation, employment, income/wages infrastructure), culture (mores, religion, etiquette), and politics (trade agreements, government stability) would improve your business proposal.

International Trade

Marketing: What It Takes

Doing Business Abroad
You have a great idea for a product that you believe could be marketed in China. A potential investor likes your product idea but is not convinced it will sell in China.

WHAT WILL YOU DO?
What information about the country, trade agreements, and trade practices will help you improve your business proposal?

THE DECA CONNECTION — ADVISOR CORNER

International Chapter Partnerships Thinking of planning a DECA adventure? There are a number of excellent and reputable sources for student exchange and travel programs. Participating in an international marketing exchange program with an international partner school offers your chapter members the opportunity to experience firsthand the exciting, practical challenges in the career areas of international marketing and management. Even if international travel to visit your partner school is not possible, by utilizing technology, your students can gain a wealth of knowledge through communicating with your international partner. This activity will help chapter members learn more about the global marketplace.

The Global Marketplace

Defining International Trade

International trade involves the exchange of goods and services between nations. Imports are goods and services purchased from other countries. Conversely, exports are goods and services sold to other countries. These exchanges occur between businesses but are controlled by the governments of the countries involved.

■ Interdependence of Nations

Most countries need to get some of their goods and services from other nations. This is called economic interdependence, and it happens because different countries possess unique resources and capabilities.

Resources may include a country's weather, raw materials, labor force, capital sources, and location. Some countries, such as the United States and Canada, have good climates for agriculture. The Middle East, Africa, and Mexico have crude oil, while Russia has coal. Countries such as those in Eastern Europe and Asia, have inexpensive labor forces. Others, like the United States and Japan, have the capital and technology necessary for manufacturing.

Since nations need different things, they find it helpful to trade with each other. There are two types of advantages in international trade—absolute and comparative.

Absolute advantage occurs when a country has special natural resources or talents that allow it to produce an item at the lowest cost possible. China produces close to 80 percent of all the silk in the world, which gives them absolute advantage.

Trade is still valuable even when absolute advantage does not exist. This is because of comparative advantage. Comparative advantage is the value that a nation gains by selling the goods that it produces most efficiently. When countries specialize in products well suited to their capabilities, they may gain a comparative advantage in international trade.

U.S. businesses are well suited to producing high-tech goods and services in the 21st century. Their specialties include products such as airplanes, computers, high-tech machinery, entertainment, and telecommunications. These products give the United States a comparative advantage over less developed nations.

Some emerging nations have large, unskilled labor forces available at low costs. Labor-intensive industries, which rely on labor as opposed to machinery, do well in such an environment. Emerging nations can produce labor-intensive toys, clothing, and shoes at a lower

• What You'll Learn

- The interdependence of nations
- The benefits of international trade
- Government involvement in international trade
- Balance of trade
- Trade barriers
- Trade agreements and alliances

• Why It's Important

The global marketplace makes all people and businesses in the world potential customers, as well as potential employees or employers. In this chapter you will explore the key concepts that govern international trade and help create the global marketplace.

• Key Terms

- international trade
- imports
- exports
- absolute advantage
- comparative advantage
- balance of trade
- tariff
- quota
- embargo
- World Trade Organization (WTO)
- North American Free Trade Agreement (NAFTA)
- European Union (EU)

Chapter 6 ■ *International Trade* **99**

FOCUS

Bell Ringer Activity

List Ask students to list products that they are able to enjoy because the United States allows international trade with other countries.

Introducing the Section

The Global Marketplace On the board, write the products (with brand names) that students listed in the Bell Ringer Activity. This activity will help students develop an appreciation of the variety of goods U.S. citizens have available to them because of international trade.

TEACH

Technology Resources

PowerPoint The *Marketing Essentials* PowerPoint Presentation CD-ROM provides visual lecture aids for every chapter section.

Concept Development

1. Read Section 6.1 with students.
2. Ask students why most of the tea and coffee we buy comes from outside of the United States. Their answers will help introduce the concept of interdependence of nations.
3. Ask students which is better and why—when a country imports more than it exports or when it exports more than it imports. *(It's better when a country exports more than it imports, because it means the country's businesses are selling more abroad than its consumers and businesses are buying from foreign producers.)*

Classroom Resources

For the Teacher
- Teacher Editions for all workbooks
- Assessment Package
- PowerPoint Presentation Software
- Interactive Lesson Planner
- **ILP** Block Scheduling, p. 3
- **ILP** Lesson Plans, p. 13
- **ILP** Internet Resources, p. 31

ILP Blackline Masters, p. 13
ILP *BusinessWeek* Case Studies, p. 33
ILP Marketing Career Portfolio, p. 33
- *Marketing Essentials* Web site (**www.marketing.glencoe.com**)

For the Student
- Student Activity Workbook, p. 45
- Marketing Math Workbook, p. 13

- Marketing Research Project Workbook, p. 29
ILP School-to-Work Activity Workbook, p. 21
- Virtual Business simulation
- *Marketing Essentials* Web site (**www.marketing.glencoe.com**)

ILP These resources are available in print and on the Interactive Lesson Planner (ILP)

cost than most industrialized nations. They have a comparative advantage when making these goods. It is more cost-effective for high-wage countries, like the United States, to buy those items from emerging nations rather than to make them themselves.

■ Benefits of International Trade

Consumers, producers, workers, and nations benefit from international trade in different ways. Consumers benefit from the competition that the foreign companies offer. This competition encourages the production of high-quality goods with lower prices. The variety of goods increases as more producers market their goods in other countries.

Producers can expand their business by conducting operations in other countries. Much of business for many producers now takes place abroad. Almost one-third of the profits of U.S. businesses comes from international trade and foreign investment.

Workers are another group that benefits from trade. Increased trade leads to higher employment rates both at home and abroad. Exports sustained about six percent of U.S. jobs in the year 2000.

■ **Sold in the U.S.A.** Many foreign-made products are sold in the United States. *What are some consumer benefits of international trade?*

■ **The Flower Market** Holland is known for its beautiful flowers, in part due to its research in flower cultivation, packaging, and shipping know-how. Approximately 59 percent of the world's cut flowers come from Holland. *Would you consider that an absolute advantage?*

You can see how nations as a whole benefit from international trade. Increased foreign investment in a country often improves the standard of living for that country's people. Individuals have more options to choose from when making purchasing decisions. These economic alliances often turn into political alliances. Think of the results of ending relations with a country that is a large market for U.S. exports or one that has many business investments here.

Government Involvement in International Trade

All nations control and monitor their trade with foreign businesses. The U.S. government monitors imports through the customs division of the U.S. Treasury Department. All people and goods that enter the United States from a foreign country are subject to search and review by U.S. customs officials. Other countries also check incoming goods. All U.S. citizens and firms must meet the customs requirements of foreign countries when visiting or exporting goods.

GREAT IDEAS from the Marketing Classroom

David Haar
Eaglecrest High School
Aurora, CO

Students can understand international trade through the following activity. Purchase small items, such as candy bars, toys, and pencils. Distribute them in paper bags and close the bags. Make some bags attractive and others unattractive.

Have each student pick a bag. Play several "rounds" where students can trade part or all of their items with classmates. Conclude by asking: Were you satisfied with your bag? Did you trade? Why or why not? Why were those who had much able to trade some of their goods, while others never traded? What is the "law of diminishing returns"? How does this relate to resource distribution in our world?

Balance of Trade

Nations must keep track of their trade to be aware of their economic status. The difference in value between exports and imports of a nation is called its balance of trade. A positive balance of trade, or trade surplus, occurs when a nation exports more than it imports. A negative balance of trade, or trade deficit, occurs when a nation imports more than it exports.

Figure 6-1 illustrates the large trade deficit in the United States. This trade gap may seem surprising because the United States is the world's largest exporter. Some analysts believe this situation exists because Americans purchase more goods and services than do people of other nations. Others believe that the United States has started to focus more on providing services than on manufacturing and farming, making it more economical to import goods that were once domestically manufactured.

An unfavorable balance reduces a nation's revenue. When more money leaves a country than comes in, that country becomes a debtor nation. Another effect of a negative balance of trade can be increased unemployment. People may lose their jobs as foreign competitors take business away from domestic firms. Domestic businesses must become competitive or they will fail.

Trade Barriers

A nation's government may impose trade barriers or restrictions when it wants to limit trade. These controls restrict the flow of goods and services among nations. The three main types of trade barriers are tariffs, quotas, and embargoes.

TARIFFS A tariff (sometimes called a duty) is a tax on imports. Tariffs may be used to produce revenue for a country. Revenue-producing tariffs were used in the United States as a primary source of income before income taxes were established in 1913. These tariffs exist today, but they are as low as 25 cents or less per item or pound.

Another type of tariff is protective. A protective tariff is generally high. Its purpose is to increase the price of imported goods so that domestic products can compete with them. This kind of tariff can prevent foreign businesses from trading with the United States. This would protect new domestic industries from foreign competition and domestic jobs.

QUOTAS An import quota limits either the quantity or the monetary value of a product that may be imported. The U.S. government might place a quota on foreign automobiles, limiting the number that may be imported. This controls the amount of a good that enters the economy.

Individualized Practice

Math Skills

Have students study **Figure 6-1**.

L1 Call students' attention to the first graph. Ask: By how many percentage points did U.S. imports grow from 1991 to 1992? *(approximately 10%)* During this same period, while U.S. imports were trending sharply upward, what was happening to other nations' imports? *(They were continuing a gradual but steady decline.)*

L2 Call students' attention to the second graph and the caption. Ask: From 1992 to 1993, what effect did excess imports have on the U.S. gross domestic product? How do you know? *(More imports than exports created a trade deficit that pulled the U.S. GDP down. Graph shows trade deficit's "contribution" to be in negative numbers—bars extending below the zero level.)*

L3 Have students analyze the relationship of the first graph to the second graph. Tell them to concentrate on the entire period from 1988 to 1993, comparing the trend in imports with its effect on the nation's GDP. *(The relationship is inverse: When the import line moves up, the GDP bars tend to fall into negative numbers; when the import line goes down, the GDP bars surge into positive numbers. Clearest correspondences are for the years 1990 and 1991.)*

FIGURE 6-1
Trade Deficit

U.S. Trade

U.S. Trade Deficit By Region
August 2000

Pacific Rim 46%
Eastern Europe 2%
Western Europe 14%
North America 16%
Other 8%
OPEC Countries 11%
South and Central America 3%

■ **U.S. Trade Deficit** The U.S. trade gap in August 2000 was $29 billion. One effect of a trade deficit is a weaker dollar. *Should that help or hurt U.S. exporters? Why?*

FIGURE 6-1 ANSWER
U.S. Trade Deficit The trade deficit should help exporters because it would make it easier for them to sell their products, which would be cheaper for foreign customers.

Did You Know?

When President Clinton signed the order ending the 19-year trade embargo with Vietnam in 1995, Pepsi released a photo of a giant Pepsi can placed in a main square of Ho Chi Minh City. Coca-Cola flew a 30-foot-tall inflatable Coke bottle to a Vietnamese celebration. Both companies are vying for dollars in a country where per capita income is $200 a year.

Thinking Critically

Trading Partners Ask students what country they think is the United States' number one trading partner, and ask them why they think so. *(It is Canada, our neighbor to the North and fellow member of NAFTA, a trade agreement between the U.S., Canada, and Mexico. NAFTA helped to reduce trade barriers to make it easier and less expensive to trade.)*

Independent Practice

Research Have students use the *World Almanac* or the Internet to research a country of their choice, focusing on its major industries and natural resources, as well as on what the country normally imports and exports.

Sometimes one trading partner might voluntarily put quotas on exports to improve relations. Japan placed quotas on its auto exports to the United States to improve trade relations between the two countries.

EMBARGOES An embargo is a total ban on specific goods coming into and leaving a country. A government can impose an embargo for health reasons. The U.S. government embargoed Chilean grapes in 1989 as a precaution after inspectors found poisoned fruit in a shipment. That embargo was lifted within a week.

Embargoes are more often used for political reasons. The United Nations imposed an embargo on Iraq during the Persian Gulf War. The goal of this sanction was to end the war through economic, rather than military, means. The United States still observed that embargo in the early 21st century.

Embargoes based on political differences can continue for a very long time. The United States lifted its 20-year embargo on Vietnam in 1994 so that trade relations could be cultivated between the two nations. The U.S. embargo against Cuba—imposed in 1960 when Fidel Castro created a communist state—still remains in effect. Certain aspects of this embargo were under consideration in 2000; however, there are no plans to completely repeal the embargo.

■ Trade Agreements and Alliances

Governments make agreements with each other to establish guidelines for international trade and to set up trade alliances. Some milestones in the progress toward worldwide free trade are the World Trade Organization, the North American Free Trade Agreement, and the European Union.

THE WORLD TRADE ORGANIZATION The World Trade Organization (WTO) is a global coalition of 135 governments that makes the rules governing international trade. The creation of those rules requires a unanimous vote. This means that agreeing on new rules may take years of negotiating.

The WTO was formed in 1995 as the successor to the General Agreement on Tariffs and Trade (GATT). GATT was an international trade agreement designed to open markets and promote global free trade among agreeing nations. It reduced tariffs and created a common set of trading rules. GATT had no enforcement power, so it created the WTO to police the agreement and resolve disputes among nations.

Life In The Diverse MARKETPLACE

Promoting World Trade

You have probably heard of the World Trade Center in New York, but there are many such centers, perhaps even in your city. World Trade Centers are symbols for international commerce and serve as meeting points for those involved in foreign trade. The first World Trade Center in North America was built in 1927 in Houston, Texas. There are now trade centers operating in 97 countries across 5 different continents, including cities like New York, Paris, Cairo, and Beijing.

Thinking Critically

What types of services could be marketed to tenants of a World Trade Center?

The WTO also manages world trade by studying important trade issues and evaluating the health of the world economy. It addresses the activities that GATT was not able to, including intellectual property rights, investment, and services.

Supporters of the WTO and free trade stress that globalization and the expansion of trade have created enormous wealth in both rich and previously poor countries. Free trade supporters believe global prosperity can be maintained and expanded only through a borderless economy. This requires a set of rules that are universally accepted. Advocates argue that such a system is the only way to ensure fairness and avoid damaging trade wars.

Critics of the WTO raise concerns about democracy, labor rights, and the environment. They charge that the WTO makes decisions affecting all of society on a commercial basis. They do not like the idea of having a non-elected body that has the power to overrule the government on issues of environmental protection and labor rights. Some of the more radical critics want the organization disbanded. Others want to transform it to include social and environmental concerns.

Life In The Diverse MARKETPLACE

Promoting World Trade

Answer Language training and interpretation services, meeting and business services, and information services.

Case Study

The European Union

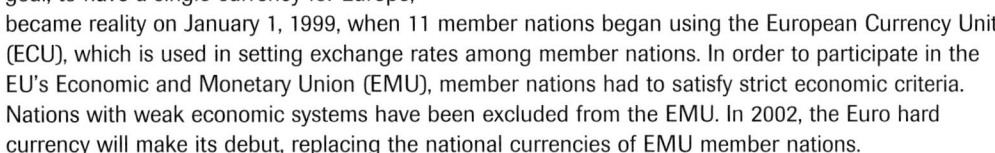

The European Union (EU) may be the most important regional trade agreement in the world today. Originally called the European Economic Community (EEC), the EU was formed in 1957 in an effort to speed western Europe's economic recovery after World War II. It has grown from six countries in 1957 to 15 countries in 2000, and many more nations have requested membership.

The primary goal of the EU was to create a free trade zone in Europe. The EU's other goal, to have a single currency for Europe, became reality on January 1, 1999, when 11 member nations began using the European Currency Unit (ECU), which is used in setting exchange rates among member nations. In order to participate in the EU's Economic and Monetary Union (EMU), member nations had to satisfy strict economic criteria. Nations with weak economic systems have been excluded from the EMU. In 2002, the Euro hard currency will make its debut, replacing the national currencies of EMU member nations.

Eventually, the EU will have a common currency for over 350 million European consumers. It will rival the United States in market size.

Case Study Review

1. Why was the EU created?
2. What is the Economic and Monetary Union?

A MATTER OF ETHICS

3. Is it ethical for the EU to exclude some member nations from its Economic and Monetary Union?

NORTH AMERICAN FREE TRADE AGREEMENT (NAFTA) The North American Free Trade Agreement (NAFTA) is an international trade agreement among the United States, Canada, and Mexico. It went into effect on January 1, 1994. The principal benefit of NAFTA was increased trade with Mexico.

The goal of NAFTA was to get rid of all trade barriers and investment restrictions among the three countries by 2009. Tariffs were eliminated immediately on more than half of the 9,000 goods traded between Mexico and the United States.

EUROPEAN UNION (EU) The European Union (EU) is the term for Europe's trading bloc. The goal of the EU is to encourage economic integration as a single market. Established by the Maastricht Treaty, the intent of the EU was for free trade among the member nations, as well as for a single European currency and a central bank. Other treaty provisions related to fair competitive practices, environmental and safety standards, and security matters.

Figure 6-2 on page 104 points out those countries that are involved in the EU and NAFTA.

Chapter 6 ■ International Trade **103**

ASSESS

Reteaching

1. **Vocabulary** Assign and review the vocabulary terms for this section.
2. **Fact and Idea** Assign and review Fact and Idea Review questions 1–5 from the Chapter Assessment.
3. **Interdependence** To reteach the concept of interdependence of nations, divide the word *interdependence* into its two component parts and ask students to define them. *(inter: "between"; dependence: "relying on someone else.")*
4. **Protective Tariffs** To reteach the concept of protective tariffs, ask students what a tax is. Then ask them to consider how a tax such as a sales tax might dissuade people from buying. Finally, have them compare this effect if the tax is only 5 percent of the item's price versus 50 percent.
5. **Quotas** To reteach the concept of quotas, ask students what this statement means: The quota for fund-raising projects per club this year is two. Explain how nations set up quotas in the same manner to restrict trade.

Enrichment

1. **Review** Assign and review the appropriate Thinking Critically questions from the Chapter Assessment.
2. **Extend** Assign and review the corresponding activities from *BusinessWeek Case Studies, Internet Resources,* and the *School-to-Work Activity Workbook.* **ILP**
3. **Research** Have students research the concept of protectionism—protecting domestic products by restricting imports or making them too expensive for consumers to buy.
4. **Research and Write** Ask students to research the current U.S. balance of trade with its top trading partners. Have students present their findings in written report.

Evaluation

Assign and review the Section 6.1 Assessment.

Technology Resources

 Assessment Resources
Go to the *Marketing Essentials* Web site (**www.marketing.glencoe. com**) for resources to teach and assess occupation-specific vocabulary.

CLOSE

Section Wrap-Up

Have students complete this statement: Countries need to trade with each other because . . . *(most are not completely self-sufficient—they need to obtain goods and services from other nations.)*

**FIGURE 6-2 ANSWER
International Trade Agreements & Alliances**
They reduce tariffs and quotas so countries can let the market decide on prices for goods and services.

FIGURE 6-2

NAFTA and EU

■ **International Trade Agreements & Alliances** Depicted on this map are two major trading blocks or markets—NAFTA and the EU. *How do these trade alliances foster free trade?*

6.1 ASSESSMENT

Reviewing Key Terms and Concepts

1. Explain the concept of economic interdependence of nations.

2. Provide an example of comparative advantage and absolute advantage for two different countries.

3. What benefits do consumers and nations derive from international trade?

4. Name three types of trade barriers.

5. What is the common goal or purpose of WTO, NAFTA, and the EU trade agreements?

Thinking Critically

6. What problems occur when trade between nations is not equal? What measures could the United States take in order to reduce its trade deficit with Japan?

Integrating Academic Skills

7. **COMMUNICATION** Translate a magazine ad into a foreign language for international use. Make any changes necessary to promote the product. Present your new ad in class, and report any problems.

6.1 ASSESSMENT ANSWERS

Reviewing Key Terms and Concepts

1. Most countries need to obtain some goods and services from other nations.

2. The U.S. has comparative advantage with airplanes, computers, and high-tech machinery. China has absolute advantage with silk.

3. Consumers benefit from competition, nations from foreign investment and alliances.

4. tariffs, quotas, and embargoes

5. to promote free trade through reduction of tariffs and common rules.

Thinking Critically

6. A negative balance can occur. The U.S. could negotiate a new trade agreement or impose trade barriers.

Integrating Academic Skills

7. **COMMUNICATION** Magazine ads will vary.

International Business

Business Involvement in International Trade

While governments make trade agreements, it is businesses that actually trade with one another. It is important to understand how those businesses operate across international boundaries. There are three basic means of getting involved in international trade—importing, exporting, and setting up shop abroad.

■ Importing

Imports to the United States are subject to more than just the requirements of the U.S. Customs tariff. They must also meet the same standards as domestic products, such as those imposed by the Food and Drug Administration. If these standards are met, most products can be imported without prior government approval. Only special items, such as alcoholic beverages and prescription drugs, require such approval. A quota can also limit entry of certain goods into the country.

Certain imported products may be subject to reduced duties under international trade agreements. Knowing the details of importing is difficult. U.S. businesses usually hire customs brokers, specialists who are licensed by the U.S. Treasury Department. Customs brokers know the different laws, procedures, and tariffs. Customs brokers handle over 90 percent of all imports because of the necessary complex procedures.

■ Exporting

Other nations have similar means of controlling and documenting imports that U.S. businesses must follow when exporting their goods. Most businesses hire international freight forwarders licensed by the U.S. Maritime Commission to handle export details.

You can imagine the risks involved in transporting goods from one country to another. The costs of transportation and insurance needed for these shipments vary greatly. Shipping mink coats would require different handling than shipping steel. It is wise for businesses to purchase special insurance when dealing with international shipments.

■ Setting Up Shop in a Foreign Country

Multinationals are large corporations that have operations in several countries. According to *International Business*, about one-third of the world's private-sector assets are controlled by some 37,000 transnational corporations with over 170,000 foreign affiliates (see Figure 6-3 on page 106).

• What You'll Learn

- How businesses can get involved in international trade
- The standard business practices involved in importing and exporting
- The cultural, economic, and political factors that should be considered when deciding whether to do business abroad

• Why It's Important

Doing business in a foreign country can be very different than doing business in the United States. Besides language barriers, there are many other factors that must be considered in international business. Costly problems may arise without this understanding.

Key Terms

- customs brokers
- freight forwarders
- multinationals
- mini-nationals
- joint ventures
- nationalize

FOCUS

Bell Ringer Activity

Brainstorm Ask students how U.S. businesses can get involved in international trade. To guide their thinking, tell them to consider a U.S. automobile manufacturer and what it could do to trade internationally. Most students will be able to come up with the correct answers to the Bell Ringer Activity. *(importing, exporting, setting up shop abroad)*

Introducing the Section

International Business Write these terms on the board: importing, exporting, setting up shop in a foreign country. Lead the class briefly in explaining these three basic means of getting involved in international trade.

Classroom Resources

For the Teacher
- Teacher Editions for all workbooks
- Assessment Package
- PowerPoint Presentation Software
- Interactive Lesson Planner
- ILP Block Scheduling, p. 3
- ILP Lesson Plans, p. 12
- ILP Internet Resources, p. 31

- ILP Blackline Masters, p. 15
- ILP *BusinessWeek* Case Studies, p. 33
- ILP Marketing Career Portfolio, p. 33
- *Marketing Essentials* Web site (**www.marketing.glencoe.com**)

For the Student
- Student Activity Workbook, p. 45
- Marketing Math Workbook, p. 13

- Marketing Research Project Workbook, p. 29
- ILP School-to-Work Activity Workbook, p. 21
- Virtual Business simulation
- *Marketing Essentials* Web site (**www.marketing.glencoe.com**)

ILP These resources are available in print and on the Interactive Lesson Planner (ILP)

Technology Resources

PowerPoint The *Marketing Essentials* PowerPoint Presentation CD-ROM provides visual lecture aids for every chapter section.

Concept Development

1. Read Section 6.2 with students.
2. Ask students if they ever traveled to another country and/or crossed a U.S. border. Ask them what their experience involved. *(Answers will vary.)*
3. Ask students why there is such concern over comings and goings between countries. *(Keeping track of the people and products that enter and leave a country can involve public welfare, national security, or economics. Some items, like agricultural products, require special inspections or handling. Other items, like purchases made abroad, require payment of a duty.)*

Discussion Starter

Cultural Differences Ask students the following multicultural quiz questions: In which country would you not sell items in quantities of four? *(Japan. The number four in Japan is equivalent to the U.S. number 13, and it is considered unlucky.)* In which of the following countries would you not give a clock as a gift: China, Brazil, or Mexico? *(China. Clocks are associated with funerals in China.)* In which country would you not give knives as a gift: China, Brazil, or Mexico? *(Brazil. Knives symbolize severing a relationship in Brazil.)*

FIGURE 6-3

World's Top 25 Companies, as of April 2000

Company	Country	Sector
General Electric	US	Electrical Equipment
Cisco Systems	US	Telecommunications Equipment
Intel	US	Semiconductors
Microsoft	US	Software
NTT Docomo	Japan	Wireless Telecommunication Services
Vodafone Airtouch	UK	Telecommunication Services
Exxon Mobil	US	Oil
Wal-Mart Stores	US	Discount Stores
Nokia	Finland	Telecommunications Equipment
Citigroup	US	Banks
NTT	Japan	Fixed-line Telecommunications Services
Oracle	US	Software
Deutsche Telekom	Germany	Fixed-line Telecommunications Services
Toyota Motor	Japan	Automobiles
Royal Dutch/Shell	Netherlands/UK	Oil
Lucent Technologies	US	Telecommunications Equipment
BP Amoco	UK	Oil
Intl Business Machines	US	Computer Hardware
AIG Group	US	Insurance
Pfizer	US	Pharmaceuticals
Merck	US	Pharmaceuticals
Ericsson	Sweden	Telecommunications Equipment
France Telecom	France	Fixed-line Telecommunications Services
AT & T	US	Fixed-line Telecommunications Services
Sun Microsystems	US	Computer Hardware

■ **International Business** All the companies listed in this table have subsidiaries or operations in many countries. *How many of these companies do you recognize?*

Mini-nationals are midsize and smaller companies that have operations in foreign countries. The key characteristic that sets multinationals and mini-nationals apart from domestic businesses is foreign investments in factories, offices, and other facilities abroad that are used for operations. These investments are referred to as foreign direct investments (FDI). Some countries attract more FDI than others.

Direct investment is only possible if you have a domestic partner in some countries. Foreign investors are not permitted to own 100 percent of a business in these countries. Such partnerships, called joint ventures, allow companies to participate in a country's economy with a partner. This is often a good idea even when not mandated by law. Domestic business partners know the market and procedures for conducting business in their own country. This is how many U.S. fast-food chains have granted franchises to companies in foreign countries.

Often joint ventures are formed on a country-by-country basis. Royal Crown Cola is one example of a company that forms many relationships with companies in different countries. In one year, they entered the markets in Mexico, Argentina, Syria, Portugal, Australia, and Indonesia.

106 Unit 3 ■ *Business and International Marketing*

Globetrotters: UPS

United Parcel Service, the U.S. parcel delivery company with the trademark brown uniforms and trucks, now covers the globe. It already has 17,000 trucks in Europe and lands 300 intercontinental flights daily. UPS has purchased a French postal operation and is thinking about buying a partner in Asia to continue its expansion plans. Despite overseas growth at double-digit rates, UPS still has some cultural obstacles to overcome. Driving a truck was once considered a demeaning job in Germany; and in France, UPS acquired a tombstone delivery company.

Thinking Critically

Why do you think UPS is concentrating on overseas advancement?

FIGURE 6-3 ANSWER
International Business Answers will vary depending on students' exposure to the company's products and/or services.

Globetrotters: UPS

Answer UPS may be concentrating on overseas advancement to create a larger market as competition increases in the U.S. market. Also, the increase in international business necessitates increased global shipping.

Special Considerations in International Business

When doing business internationally, companies must be aware of many special considerations, such as differences in language and customs as well as political and legal considerations.

■ Cultural Factors

Differences in language and culture make international trade more challenging than doing business at home. When General Motors tried to sell its Chevrolet Nova in South America sales did not meet expectations. The reason? The words *no va* in Spanish mean "No go!"

Social and business etiquette is important when doing business abroad. A common practice in one country may take on a different meaning elsewhere. You would not want to cross your legs in Japan because showing the bottom of your feet is considered rude. Gift giving is another area of concern. A gift may be considered part of business etiquette in the Far East; however, it might seem to be an illegal bribe in the United States or Canada.

Building a relationship before doing business is important in Japan and other Asian countries. It is best to plan a night of dinner and entertainment without any mention of business when conducting business in those countries. Once a personal relationship has been established, then business may be discussed. It is important for you to be aware of these cultural differences before a big business meeting.

■ Economic Factors

You should consider the key factors of economic cost when considering starting up a business in another country. These include infrastructure, cost of labor, taxes, and currency exchange rates. You should also consider the population's standard of living if you want to sell goods in another country.

Infrastructure can be a deciding factor. Things like undependable telephone service or inadequate roads would rule out a location for some businesses. These same factors would be an opportunity for other companies involved in building roads, energy plants, and telecommunications systems.

The quality and cost of the labor force also should be reviewed. You would want to know the educational and skill levels of the workers, as well as the customary wages and employment laws. Employers are responsible for paying a fair amount for mandated employee benefits above and beyond wages in some countries.

Other costs include taxes. Taxes on property and profits are common. Countries that want to attract foreign investment may offer reduced taxes for a period of time as an incentive.

Standard of living can be a consideration if a business is eyeing a country as a market rather than a manufacturing site. When Honda entered China's consumer market, it recognized that most Chinese people could not afford cars. The company targeted the motorcycle market instead and was very successful.

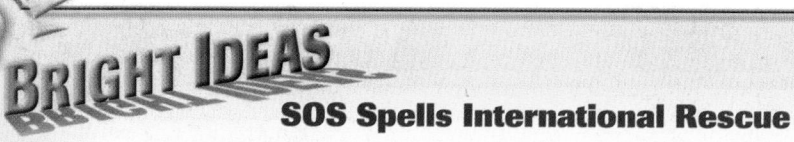

BRIGHT IDEAS

SOS Spells International Rescue

Imagine being in China on business and suddenly facing a medical emergency, or being caught in Rome during a terrorist attack. What would you do? International SOS to the rescue! International SOS began in 1974 as a provider of emergency services to business travelers. The company now operates offices in more than 30 cities around the globe. The need for emergency assistance is greater than ever with the increasing amount of necessary business travel; many companies pay International SOS a fee to have emergency assistance available worldwide. SOS will go into an emergency situation and provide immediate medical care and assistance including transportation and exit clearances if needed.

Thinking Creatively

How might handling international emergencies differ from handling emergencies in the United States?

Chapter 6 ■ *International Trade* **107**

Cooperative Learning

Researching Countries Have students break into 3–4 teams in order to research a country of their choice. Based on their research, students should identify at least three U.S. products that would sell well in the particular country, and provide a rationale for their choices. As a group, have students decide on one of those products. Then have them brainstorm ideas for packaging, promoting, and selling that product in the country.

Independent Practice

1. **Research and Compare** Have students look through issues of *International Business* to find ads for customs brokers, freight forwarding companies, or other firms serving businesses involved in international trade. Tell them to list all the services these companies offer, and compare those services to the activities involved in exporting and importing described in the chapter. Have them note any services not mentioned in the text.

2. **Research and Explain** Tell students to research the current exchange rate for the U.S. dollar and another currency. Have them explain in class discussion why that rate would or would not be good for U.S. companies doing business in the country issuing the selected currency.

3. **Write and Report** Have students write to various multinational corporations and ask for copies of their annual reports. Have them review their plans for expansion in other countries. Have students orally present their findings to the class.

BRIGHT IDEAS   SOS Spells International Rescue

Answer International emergencies may involve overcoming language barriers, differences in medical standards, knowledge of foreign medical facilities, and visa and passport issues.

FIGURE 6-4

CUSTOMIZATION VS. GLOBALIZATION

When marketing products in foreign countries, companies must make product and promotion decisions. Some companies create completely new products for specific countries (customization), while others do not change anything about their product or their promotions (globalization). Between the two are companies that keep their products' brand names while varying their products and/or promotions enough to meet local tastes. Here are some examples of each.

Fuerza Ford para tu vida.

PROMOTION ADAPTATION

Many companies do not change their products, only their promotions to better meet the foreign customers' way of thinking. Ford adapted its advertising message because the one it used in the United States would not be interpreted the same way by Spanish speakers.

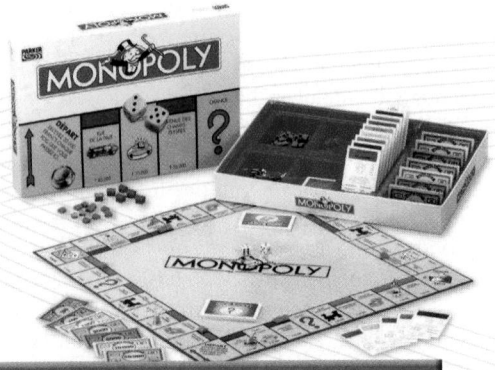

PRODUCT ADAPTATION

Changing a product in some way to make it more appropriate for a country's preferences is a product adaptation strategy. Monopoly is the world's favorite board game. It is available in 25 languages.

CUSTOMIZATION

Customization is inventing a totally new product for a different country's market. Swanson creates soups for different palates around the world. Watercress and Duck Gizzard Soup is a favorite in China.

GLOBALIZATION

Globalization is keeping the product and advertising message the same around the world. Its benefit is global brand recognition. Coca-Cola does not change its products or its ad message for the global market.

108 Unit 3

THE DECA CONNECTION

COMPETITIVE EVENTS AND MARKETING ESSENTIALS

International Trade Return to DECA's International Marketing Event to reinforce the concepts of international trade. Assign Section III A-2 and A-3. These sections will require your students to research their selected country's form of government and trading laws. If you want to pursue this chapter in greater depth, assign Section III B-1, B-2 and B-3. This section requires research on the trading area and a cultural analysis. Completion of these two sections will also complete approximately half of the research required for this competitive event. For the complete guidelines of the International Marketing Event, go to **www.deca.org**.

The number of middle income workers is increasing in poorer nations in the 21st century. This increases the demand for all types of ordinary consumer goods. U.S. consumer products like soaps, detergents, breakfast cereals, snack foods, and soft drinks are gaining popularity among consumers in emerging nations.

Finally, the exchange rate for a nation's currency based on the U.S. dollar is an important factor to consider. Changes in a nation's currency exchange affect businesses that sell abroad. If a product has a high price in U.S. dollars and is converted into an even higher price on the international market, it may be difficult to attract customers.

■ Political and Legal Factors

A government's stability is an important factor when considering international business operations. There is always the possibility that new rulers might nationalize private property in countries where military takeovers or popular revolutions are common. When a country nationalizes property, the government takes ownership, and the owners generally get nothing in return. Bolivia, for example, nationalized all of its businesses in the early 1950s. You can imagine how costly this would be today when businesses routinely invest millions of dollars in buildings and equipment.

An unstable government can create problems for a business's employees as well. Business executives may be used as political pawns in countries where political corruption is common. There may be unspoken rules or practices that must be learned. Payoffs to government officials are the only means of getting necessary licenses or approval to conduct business in some countries. The political climate of a county may change very quickly. This can be difficult for businesses to keep up with. There are companies that monitor political situations on a country-by-country basis. Such companies maintain databases that contain information about each country including new laws, the political climate, and potential risk.

Countries that want to be part of the global marketplace, however, may encourage foreign investment. These governments offer stability and support to businesses. They may be moving toward a market economy by privatizing state-run industries. They may reduce tariffs, develop laws to protect intellectual property, and increase the percentage of business ownership allowed by foreign investors (see Figure 6-5).

FIGURE 6-5

U.S. Contracts with China

■ **U.S. Investments in China** This graph shows that U.S. companies have been cutting down on their investments in China. *With China being one of the largest potential markets in the world, why do you think companies are reluctant to invest?*

FIGURE 6-6

Household Technology

Households in China

Television — 89%

Radio — 57%

Telephone — 25%

■ **Household Technology** As you can see by this graph, not many homes in China have standard telephones. One reason is because China doesn't have adequate infrastructure, which makes the cost of telephone service very high. *What type of phone is selling like hotcakes in China because of this?*

Chapter 6 ■ *International Trade* **109**

SECTION 6.2

ASSESS

Reteaching

1. **Vocabulary** Assign and review the vocabulary terms for this section.
2. **Fact and Idea** Assign and review Fact and Idea Review questions 6–10 from the Chapter Assessment.
3. **Cultural Factors** To reteach the concept of cultural factors that should be considered if one plans to do business abroad, ask students how they would greet someone in the United States. Follow up by asking them what they would do differently if they were in China or Japan. *(bow instead of shake hands)*

Enrichment

1. **Review** Assign and review the Chapter 6 activities in the *Student Activity Workbook*.
2. **Review** Assign and review the appropriate Thinking Critically questions from the Chapter Assessment.
3. **Review** Assign and review the following Chapter Assessment activities: Building Workplace Skills, Applying Marketing Concepts, Linking School to Work Activities, The DECA Connection Role Play and Internet Connection.
4. **Research and Report** Have students write to the embassy of a country of their own choice and request information regarding the following:
   • Economic data
   • Political data
   • Cultural data
   Have students report their findings to the class in both written and oral form.

FIGURE 6-5 ANSWER
U.S. Investments in China China's consumer spending is weak. Although China has 1.2 billion people, about 850 million live in poor, rural areas. U.S. exports to China in 1999 were only 1.8 percent of total U.S. exports. Companies are reluctant to invest in China because of the ruling communist party, bureaucratic barriers, as well as corruption.

FIGURE 6-6 ANSWER
Household Technology Wireless and cellular phones are selling in China, because the cost of telephone service is high due to inadequate infrastructure.

Technology Resources

Assessment Resources
Go to the *Marketing Essentials* Web site (www.marketing.glencoe.com) for resources to teach and assess occupation-specific vocabulary.

Evaluation

Assign and review the Section 6.2 Assessment.

CLOSE

Section Wrap-Up

Have students recall one cultural, one economic, and one political/legal factor that a business should consider when deciding to get involved in international business. *(Answers will vary. Cultural factors: differences in language, greeting practices. Economic factors: infrastructure, cost and educational level of labor, taxes. Political/legal factors: stability of government, receptiveness to foreign investment.)*

Business to Business: Cutting Costs through Online Ordering

Answer One advantage is that key personnel can access order status instantly, which simplifies correspondence, cuts down on time, and lessens the chance of human error.

110

▪ Technological Factors

Technology is changing the ways that businesses can get involved in international trade. When studying a country's technology, you need to look at the use of computers, faxes, voice mail, cellular phones, and the Internet. Some countries, like Finland and the United States, are already well connected, while emerging countries are just beginning to adapt to technological advances (see Figure 6-6 on page 109).

Underlying any economic environment is its technological base—the technical equipment and technical skills and knowledge of the people. The technological base of a country has a great affect on the availability of opportunities.

In general, complex and sophisticated industries are found in countries with advanced levels of technology, while more basic industries are found in countries with lower levels of technology. People in technologically advanced nations have higher incomes than people in less technologically developed markets.

When researching the level of technology in a country, even the most basic technologies should be taken into consideration. Factors such as measurement systems and electric voltage standards can be important. A business cannot assume that the same technology that is available in its home country is available or used in other countries.

Business to Business: Cutting Costs through Online Ordering

While many of us think of consumer sites like Amazon and CDNOW when it comes to the Internet, business-to-business Internet purchases are 10 or more times larger than consumer purchases. Businesses have found that conducting business on the Internet can streamline operations and cut costs. Consider the example of BOC Company in New Jersey. It places its product orders online and within seconds, its Japanese supplier receives the million-dollar orders. No phone calls or faxes are required, nor are any invoices or shipping orders necessary. Key personnel can access order status instantly, which trims correspondence, processing time, and the chance for human error.

Thinking Critically
What are the advantages to conducting business over the Internet?

6.2 ASSESSMENT

Reviewing Key Terms and Concepts

1. How can a business get involved in international trade?
2. Why do importers use customs brokers?
3. What type of business helps exporters?
4. What difficulty did Chevrolet have in South America with its Nova model automobile?
5. How can a country's poor infrastructure create opportunities for foreign businesses?

Thinking Critically

6. Do you see anything wrong with countries that offer incentives, such as reduced taxes, to foreign investors but not to local businesses?

Integrating Academic Skills

7. **MATH** Assume the currency exchange rate between the United States and Canada is 1.25, which means one U.S. dollar is equal to $1.25 in Canadian currency. How much would a $20 T-shirt cost a U.S. citizen shopping in Montreal?

6.2 ASSESSMENT ANSWERS

Reviewing Key Terms and Concepts

1. by importing, exporting, and/or setting up shop in a foreign country
2. Customs brokers know the different import laws, procedures, and tariffs.
3. freight forwarding companies
4. "No va" means "no go" in Spanish.
5. It can provide opportunities for building roads, energy plants, and telecommunications systems.

Thinking Critically

6. Those with reservations may say domestic businesses are not being given the same opportunity. Others may see the opportunity to build a country's economy with the influx of foreign investors.

Integrating Academic Skills

7. **MATH** It would cost $16. $20 ÷ 1.25 = $16

Careers in Marketing

INTERNATIONAL MARKETING

Sigrid Ann Davison
International Sales
Marketing Director

What does your job entail?

"I am responsible for the sales, marketing, and distribution of motion pictures and television products in the international marketplace. This involves licensing all individual media rights in foreign countries. Most transactions occur at international film markets, including the American Film Market in Los Angeles, the Cannes Film Festival in France, the London Premiere Screening in England, and MIFED in Milan, Italy. Once media rights have been licensed and sold to distributors, the filmmaking begins. I then put together the marketing strategy, including advertising (posters, artwork, trailers, and TV spots), publicity, and promotion, on a territory-by-territory basis. When the film is completed, I oversee the release in each country."

What training do you recommend for students?

"I recommend a bachelor's degree, or preferably a master's degree specializing in international marketing. A knowledge of foreign languages is helpful. Try to start out in a company that handles the type of product or service in which you want to specialize."

What do you like most about your job?

"My favorite aspect of my job is the international travel, which enables me to have business dealings with people all over the world. Not all cultures conduct business in the same manner as the United States, and it is fascinating to figure out the best way to achieve a positive outcome in both sales and marketing."

What is your key to success?

"My key to success—hard work, hard work, and hard work! A willingness to roll up my sleeves and tackle everything that needs to be done, from mundane tasks to challenging international marketing problems, is necessary. I try to learn as much as I can about all aspects of the entertainment industry. Finally, I make a conscious effort to treat everyone I work with and for with respect—in a way that I would want to be treated."

Thinking Critically
How might a strong sense of humor be useful in any job?

Career Facts

Education and Training: A degree in international business, or an MBA, and marketing experience is good preparation.

Aptitudes, Abilities, and Skills: Excellent communication skills and an appreciation of other cultures, as well as an ability to travel, flexibility, good decision-making skills, organizational skills, and leadership skills are required.

Career Outlook: Opportunities are expected to increase faster than average with the increased use of Internet technology.

Career Path: Product management, team management, marketing positions, and extensive travel can lead to a career in international marketing. International marketing specialists can advance to VP of international sales.

Careers in Marketing

Ask a student to read the Careers in Marketing feature aloud to the class. Discuss the skills and aptitudes required for a career in international marketing. Ask students whether they think they would like or dislike a career in international marketing. Discuss the pros and cons of such a career.

Thinking Critically Answer
Answers will vary, but some of the bonuses of business travel might be the opportunity to see new places and develop good communication skills. The drawbacks might include the changing schedule, the details of traveling, and being away from home frequently.

Guest Speakers
Invite a marketing director to class to discuss his/her job and factors he/she considers when making marketing decisions.

Exploring Careers

Working with Others
1. Have your students find an adult friend or family member who has worked with someone from a different country.
2. Give the students these questions to ask the adult regarding their experience:
   - What did you have in common?
   - How did you differ?
   - What did you each contribute to the job you were doing?
   - What did you learn about yourself by working with the other person? About the other person?
3. Then ask the students to write a brief report based on the answers they received from their interviews.

Lifelong Learning

International Trade
Keeping up with international trade is a challenge. The rules of the game are complex, and they can change overnight—so can the players. Think of the fall of the Berlin Wall in 1990 and its aftermath. Encourage your students to read at least one business periodical on a regular basis. Also, suggest watching international news on television.

Meeting Individual Needs

Students with Orthopaedic Impairments
Make sure your students with orthopaedic impairments have access to the classroom. A barrier can be a stair, a curb, a narrow walkway, a heavy door, or an elevator door that does not allow time for a wheelchair exit. Remember that some students in wheelchairs have full use of their hands and others do not.

Vocabulary Review

Paragraphs will vary. See Glossary for definitions.

Fact and Idea Review

1. Nations trade with each other because they are not self-sufficient, and they must obtain certain products from other nations.
2. A benefit for producers is opportunity to grow their businesses in other countries. A benefit for workers is more job opportunities.
3. The U.S. negative balance of trade is surprising because the United States is the world's largest exporter.
4. Trade barriers improve balance of trade, protect domestic jobs or new industries, or safeguard national security.
5. The World Trade Organization (WTO) was formed to police the GATT treaty.
6. Multinationals are large corporations; mini-nationals are smaller, midsize companies. A similarity between the two is that both engage in FDI.
7. Companies create completely new products for specific countries by customization. Companies keep the product and advertising message the same around the world during globalization.
8. Some difficulties with international business may be: product names can have embarrassing connotations in another language (Chevy's Nova); eye contact can be misread; social gestures, like gift giving, may be governed by different rules as to when, where, what, and how.
9. Economic factors that can discourage international trade are labor costs, infrastructure, and taxes. Some political factors are political corruption, government instability, and failure to protect a business's intellectual property.
10. Companies of all sizes can create Web sites and begin doing business abroad. You need to consider the use of computers, faxes, voice mail, cellular phones, and the Internet when studying a country's technology.

Thinking Critically

1. Answers will vary. Most students will note foreign-made products they enjoy.
2. U.S. auto franchisees would have to raise prices to cover the tariffs;

112

Chapter 6 ASSESSMENT

VOCABULARY REVIEW

For each group of terms, write a paragraph explaining the relation of each term to the heading.

- **International Trade:** balance of trade, imports, exports, absolute advantage, comparative advantage, multinationals, mini-nationals, customization, globalization
- **Trade Concerns:** tariff, quota, embargo, joint ventures, customs, brokers, freight forwarders, nationalize
- **Trade Alliances:** World Trade Organization (WTO), North American Free Trade Agreement (NAFTA), European Union (EU)

FACT AND IDEA REVIEW

1. Why do nations trade globally? (6.1)
2. How do producers and workers benefit from international trade? (6.1)
3. Why is it surprising that the United States has a negative balance of trade? (6.1)
4. What are trade barriers? (6.1)
5. What organization was established to police the GATT treaty? (6.1)
6. Compare multinationals to mini-nationals. (6.2)
7. How do the marketing strategies of customization and globalization differ? (6.2)
8. Cite three examples of cultural factors that can make doing business abroad more difficult. (6.2)
9. Cite an economic factor and a political factor that could discourage a business from engaging in international trade. (6.2)
10. What impact can technology have on doing business abroad? (6.2)

THINKING CRITICALLY

1. How have you personally benefited from international trade?
2. Assume a South Korean company sold hair dryers in the United States below market prices. To retaliate, the United States increased tariffs on South Korean automobiles. How would that hurt U.S. consumers and U.S. auto franchisees who carry South Korean autos?
3. When a Japanese investor bought New York City's Rockefeller Center in the 1980s, it brought out xenophobia in many U.S. citizens. Xenophobia is a distrust of foreigners. Since foreign investment is supposed to be good for a country, why do you think these people reacted this way?
4. What measures could a business take to avoid cultural blunders if it wants to get involved in international trade?
5. React to the following statement: International trade benefits everyone and harms no one. Do you agree or disagree?

BUILDING WORKPLACE SKILLS

1. **Human Relations** A customer in your store wants to buy a silk blouse that matches her outfit perfectly. However, the blouse is made in China and she has told you that she only buys American-made products. What would you do?
2. **Public Speaking** You have been asked to make a presentation to the foreign language club on the need for bilingual employees in business. In your presentation, discuss the need to understand different cultures when marketing products in foreign countries.

---

if quotas were instituted, reduced inventories could hurt the business's ability to make a profit. The price of the autos would go up for the U.S. consumer.
3. Possible reasons for xenophobia include fear of the unknown and concern about the nation's losing its economic independence.
4. Answers will vary. Possibilities include hiring executives with international trade experience, diversifying the firm's workforce, and providing language and cross-cultural training for employees.
5. Answers will vary.

Building Workplace Skills

1. Answers will vary. Some students might try to convince the customer that such trade makes goods more affordable for consumers. Others will simply look for another blouse to match the outfit.
2. Speeches will vary. Students should include some facts about multi and mini-nationals, as well as provide examples of mistakes that occur when a business employee doesn't know a foreign culture and/or language.

APPLYING MARKETING CONCEPTS

1. **Summarizing Marketing Concepts** Using a word processing program, summarize an article related to one topic in this chapter. Review publications such as *International Business, The Economist, BusinessWeek, Forbes,* and *Fortune.*

2. **Understanding NAFTA** The NAFTA agreement had many supporters, but there were many people who debated the effects that it would have on Americans. Using the Internet and business magazines, research both sides of this debate. Write a report using a word processing program discussing the viewpoints of those who supported NAFTA and those who were against it. Then give your own opinion based on your research.

3. **Researching Exporting Patterns** International trade provides people access to goods from all over the world. Research the top exports for the following countries: Japan, China, Mexico, India, the United States, France, and Switzerland. Using presentation software, prepare an oral report of your findings. Present your report to your class.

4. **Analyzing Foreign Trade Alliances** Using a word processing program, write a report that explains the trend among multinationals to forge strategic alliances with foreign companies. What are the reasons for these alliances, and what have been the outcomes?

LINKING SCHOOL TO WORK

Thinking and Information Skills Ask an employer if his or her company is involved in international trade. Find out the particulars of its involvement. You can ask companies that are not involved with foreign trade if there are any products manufactured by foreign companies sold by the business. Write a short report of your findings, and share it with your classmates.

THE DECA CONNECTION

Role Play: Marketing Intern

Situation You are to assume the role of an intern in a marketing firm that specializes in international trade. You have been asked to be part of an extensive training program for firm employees doing business in Japan.

Activity Your task is to instruct your fellow employees in the proper way to exchange business cards. Your supervisor (judge) wants to see your presentation before you begin this training program with others.

Evaluation You will be evaluated on how well you meet the following performance indicators:
- Identify the impact of cultural and social environments on world trade
- Develop cultural sensitivity
- Make oral presentations
- Give directions for completing job tasks
- Foster positive working relationships

The Emerald Isle
You are a travel agent and your client wants to go on a vacation to Ireland.

Connect
- Use the Internet to plan a written itinerary for your client, who wants information on major cities, castles, the Blarney Stone, and golf.

Mini Quiz
Administer the Mini Quiz orally. For an expanded chapter quiz, go to page 33 of the *Reproducible Tests* book.

1. Goods coming into a country are called <u>imports</u>; going out of a country, they are called <u>exports</u>.

2. Economic <u>interdependence</u> occurs because different nations possess unique resources and capabilities.

3. China has a(n) <u>absolute</u> economic advantage in the production of silk.

4. The difference between exports and imports of a nation is called its <u>balance of trade</u>.

5. Three common trade barriers are <u>tariffs</u>, <u>quotas</u>, and <u>embargoes</u>.

FOCUS

Unit Lab Overview

In this Zazz Lab, students will use their knowledge of marketing, management, and standard business practices involved in doing business internationally to plan a rock group world tour.

Bell Ringer Activity

Identify Ask students to name their favorite rock groups. (Note: For more information about rock groups and the music industry in general, refer the students to **www.ubl.com**, The Ultimate Band List lists rock groups, vocalists, and venues. Additional resources are *Rolling Stone, Q,* and *Spin* magazines.)

Discussion Starter

Ask students if any of their favorite groups have performed in concert outside the United States. Their answers will lead to a discussion of various countries around the world.

TEACH

Thinking Critically

1. **Economic Factors** Ask students: What makes determining ticket prices and projecting revenue for rock group tours more difficult in foreign countries than in the United States? *(Currency exchange rates change daily; and popularity of the groups may be different in different parts of the world.)*
2. **Weather Factors** Ask students: Why would a promoter of rock groups suggest that all performances on a world tour take place in warm weather? *(Answers will vary but may recognize that holding concerts outside in warm weather provides more flexibility in venue selection.)*

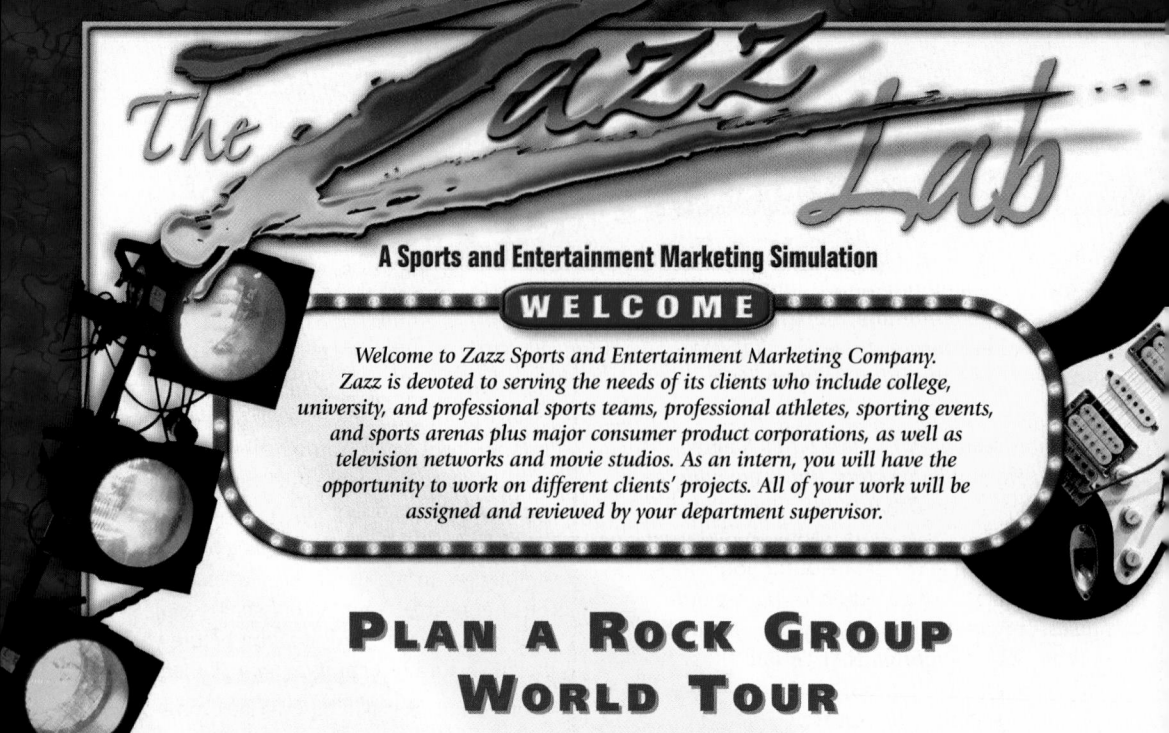

The Zazz Lab

A Sports and Entertainment Marketing Simulation

WELCOME

Welcome to Zazz Sports and Entertainment Marketing Company. Zazz is devoted to serving the needs of its clients who include college, university, and professional sports teams, professional athletes, sporting events, and sports arenas plus major consumer product corporations, as well as television networks and movie studios. As an intern, you will have the opportunity to work on different clients' projects. All of your work will be assigned and reviewed by your department supervisor.

PLAN A ROCK GROUP WORLD TOUR

SITUATION

Zazz would like to arrange a world tour for a popular rock group to make money and support a worthy cause. Zazz is willing to guarantee $25 million to the rock group if they play 25 shows outside the United States with at least two shows performed in developing countries. The net proceeds from ticket sales will have the following breakdown: 80 percent to the rock group, 10 percent to Zazz, and 10 percent to the chosen cause. The breakdown for merchandising (sale of programs, T-shirts, etc.) will be 80 percent for the rock group and 20 percent for Zazz.

ASSIGNMENT

Your supervisor wants you to suggest the rock group that will have the highest potential for success, as well as the best cause to benefit from the tour. Careful selection of the countries to tour is crucial to ensure that the $25 million guarantee is covered and that Zazz makes a profit.

Tools and Resources

To complete this assignment, you will need to conduct research at a library or on the Internet. You will also need a word processing program, a map of the world, and presentation software. Magazines that report on rock groups and their tours, such as *Rolling Stone* or *Spin*, may be helpful.

Research

Research popular rock groups and worthy causes that have universal appeal, such as AIDS or cancer research, or hunger. Review past record and concert sales as well as new album releases. Review the itinerary and ticket prices of current rock group tours to see how they are organized and what venues are used (stadiums, open fields, arenas). To select the best cities and to determine appropriate ticket prices, you must research economic factors such as the unemployment rate, inflation rate, productivity level, and currency exchange rate. Review the demographics of each tour city, including population by age and average household income. To determine the itinerary, research travel distances between cities and the proximity of countries you want to include in the tour. Research normal weather patterns, which will impact venue selection and travel considerations.

114 Unit 3 ■ *Business and International Marketing*

TRUCKING ALONG IN SWITZERLAND

When planning the transportation for rock concert personnel and equipment, it is important for tour managers to be aware that Switzerland does not allow any trucks on its roadways during weekends. Switzerland also has very strict rules about truck weights. In many cases, additional trucks must be rented in order to move a band's equipment through this Alpine country.

Report

Prepare a written report and a computer presentation. Use a word-processing program to prepare a double-spaced report. Prepare a table with a heading and introduction in the text, showing the current rock group tours you researched. Prepare a map that identifies the tour destinations and dates of your proposed itinerary. Arrange your report around the following headings:

- Current rock group tours
  - Name and description of three current tours
    - Popularity of group
    - Targeted audience
    - Album being promoted (if any)
    - Cities, countries, venues, and ticket prices
- Proposed rock group
  - Popularity of group
  - Targeted audience
  - Album being promoted (if any)
- Proposed cause or charity to benefit from tour
  - Description of cause or charity
  - Rationale for selection
  - Relationship or fit with suggested rock group
- Proposed tour itinerary
  - Countries selected
    - Industrialized nations
    - Developing countries (two)
    - Map showing the location of all concert sites
- Rationale for cities and countries selected
  - Economic factors
  - Demographic factors
  - Proximity to other countries in tour
  - Weather patterns
  - Conflict with other rock group tours
  - Cultural and religious considerations
- Itinerary—(table)
  - Dates
  - Cities, countries, venues, and ticket prices
  - Travel distance between cities (time and mileage)
- Conclusion
  - Potential ease in marketing this tour
    - Tour theme
    - Media selection (i.e. television, radio, magazine, Web site)
    - Tour promotion
  - Potential revenue generated from the tour

Using computer presentation software, prepare a presentation of your ideas for your supervisor that includes:
- Key topics covered in your written report
- Graphic illustrations that are relevant to each slide's topic
- Very little text
- A minimum of 10 slides

Presentation and Evaluation

Your supervisor wants you to present your ideas in a written report and an oral presentation. Your oral evaluation will be based on the following:
- Knowledge of rock group tours
- Selection of a worthy cause/charity
- Knowledge of other countries' economics, demographics, and cultural differences
- Realistic planning of the itinerary
- Ability to persuade others
- Continuity of presentation
- Voice quality
- Eye contact

Portfolio

Print out a copy of your completed report and presentation for your Portfolio.

THE DECA CONNECTION

DECA Business Services Marketing Series
Recommending prices and marketing ideas for a rock concert tour could be a role play in this event.

DECA Marketing Management Series
Developing business proposals is part of this career area.

DECA Business and Financial Marketing Research Event
Conducting research for a proposed rock concert tour could be a topic for this written research event.

DECA Sports and Entertainment Marketing Management Team Decision-Making Event
Planning a rock concert tour could be a potential topic for this event.

COOPERATIVE LEARNING

Teamwork This unit lab lends itself to working in teams of two to four students. Have teams compete with one another to come up with the best proposal for the rock group charity tour. Assign different sections of the proposal (report) to different groups. One team can research various charities and causes; one team can research selected countries and travel distances; and another team can research rock groups and current tours, including venues and prices. The information can then be disseminated to all teams for completion of the proposal, which should include the itinerary, theme, and marketing ideas.

UNIT 3
Zazz Lab

Independent Practice

Research, Write, and Present
Have students research charity events conducted by rock groups, actors, and athletes to see how well the events are received by the public. Have students write a report, citing sources, and give an oral presentation on their research.

ASSESS

Enrichment

Research and Report Have students research businesses that sponsor rock concert tours that target teens. Ask them to report on how each party benefits from such an alliance. *(For example, Sears and Levi's sponsored the Backstreet Boys' 1999 tour and the Christina Aguilera 2000 tour. The Backstreet Boys' 2000 tour was sponsored by Burger King. Both the businesses and artists benefited from maximum exposure to the teen market through sales and publicity.)*

Evaluation

The rubrics for evaluation of the written, oral, and computer presentation are included in the student text. (See the outline and guidelines for the written report, the computer presentation, and the skills' assessment for oral presentations.) It might be best to replicate those rubrics to evaluate the students' work. A separate rubric could be created to evaluate the work of a team.

CLOSE

Lab Wrap-Up

Ask students what concerns musical groups would have with regard to conducting tours in foreign countries. *(They have the same concerns as other businesses would have, such as a country's economy, demographics of the residents, political stability, safety, language and cultural differences, holidays, etc.)*

115

Unit Objectives

After completing this unit, students will be able to:

● Perform essential math functions with whole numbers, fractions, and decimal numbers.
● Effectively communicate by speaking, listening, writing, and reading.
● Discuss the uses of computers in business and in marketing.
● Facilitate understanding of others through personal attitude and interpersonal skills.
● Explain the basic functions of management and discuss effective management techniques.

Enrichment Resources

Books

Be Your Own Executive Coach: Master High Impact Communications Skills for Dealing with Difficult People, Improving Your Personal Image, Learning by Peter Delisser
Peter Drucker on the Profession of Management by Nan Stone, Editor

Magazines/Journals

BusinessWeek
Fast Company
PC Magazine

Associations

Marketing Research Association
1344 Silas Deane Highway, Suite 306
P.O. Box 230
Rocky Hill, CT 06067-0230
(860) 257-4008
www.mra-net.org

National DECA
1908 Association Drive
Reston, VA 22091
(704) 777-8810
www.deca.org

Journal Writing Activity

1. Ask students to write a paragraph in their journals about why understanding academic concepts and developing academic skills would be vital for success in marketing. Then write the following skills on the board: basic math, communication, computer applications, interpersonal, and management. Ask students to identify which skill areas are mentioned in their own journal entries.

2. Ask students to pick a skill area from a board list that includes basic math, communication, computer applications, interpersonal, and management skills. Then have students think of a marketing-related occupation that might require that particular skill area. Ask several students to share their journal entries with the class. Remind students that academic concepts and skills apply in the real world of work.

TEACHER CLASSROOM RESOURCES

Program Resources	Chapter 7	Chapter 8	Chapter 9	Chapter 10	Chapter 11
Student Activity Workbook	p. 55	p. 63	p. 73	p. 81	p. 89
Marketing Math Workbook	p. 19	p. 19	p. 19	p. 19	p. 19
Marketing Research Project Workbook	p. 47	p. 47	p. 47	p. 47	p. 47
ILP School-to-Work Activity Workbook	p. 25	p. 29	p. 33	p. 37	p. 41
ILP *BusinessWeek* Case Studies	p. 41	p. 49	p. 55	p. 63	p. 69
ILP Marketing Career Portfolio	p. 34	p. 34	p. 34	p. 34	p. 34
Reproducible Tests	p. 41	p. 47	p. 51	p. 55	p. 59
ExamView User's Guide and Testbank	p. 7-1	p. 8-1	p. 9-1	p. 10-1	p. 11-1
ILP Internet Resources	p. 33	p. 35	p. 37	p. 39	p. 41
ILP Blackline Masters	p. 18	p. 21			p. 23
ILP Lesson Plans	p. 14	p. 16	p. 18	p. 21	p. 23
ILP Block Scheduling	p. 4	p. 4	p. 4	p. 4	p. 4
ILP Impact! Simulation	p. 29	p. 29	p. 29	p. 29	p. 29

ILP Each of these resources is available in print and on the Interactive Lesson Planner CD-ROM.

Technology Resources

- **Interactive Lesson Planner (ILP) CD-ROM**
- **PowerPoint Presentation CD-ROM**
- **Marketing Essentials Web site**
- **ExamView! CD-ROM**
- **Impact! Simulation**

Virtual Business

Virtual Business is a fully visual marketing and business simulation that introduces students to the principles of marketing by letting them start and run their own virtual businesses. In *Virtual Business*, students have the power to control all aspects of a retail convenience store. Students strategize marketing decisions using a powerful learning tool in the guise of a video game. They learn by experiencing how their decisions affect their virtual business.

Key to Individualized Academics Activities

L1 Level 1 activities are basic activities and should fall within the range of all students.

L2 Level 2 activities are average activities and should be within the range of average and above average students.

L3 Level 3 activities are challenging activities designed for the ability range of above average students.

National Marketing Education

CHAPTER	SECTION	PERFORMANCE INDICATOR
Chapter 7 **Basic Math Skills**	7.1	Solve basic math problems (Math)
		Solve math problems involving fractions (Math)
	7.2	Operate a calculator (Math)
		Solve mathematical problems involving percentages (Math)
		Read charts and graphs (Math)
Chapter 8 **Communication Skills**	8.1	Explain the nature of effective communications (CIS)
		Apply effective listening skills (CIS)
	8.2	Make oral presentations (CIS)
		Handle telephone calls in a businesslike manner (CIS)
		Explain the nature of written communications (CIS)
		Use communications technology/systems (CIS)
Chapter 9 **Computer Applications and Skills**	9.1	Identify ways that technology impacts business (BME)
	9.2	Demonstrate basic word-processing skills (BME)
		Demonstrate basic database skills (BME)
		Demonstrate basic spreadsheet skills (BME)
	9.3	Demonstrate basic presentation software skills (BME)
		Demonstrate basic search skills on the Web (BME)
Chapter 10 **Interpersonal Skills**	10.1	Foster positive working relationships (CIS)
		Identify personality traits important to business (PD)
		Adjust to change (PD)
	10.2	Participate as a team member (CIS)
		Explain the nature of leadership in organizations (BME)
		Explain the nature of staff communications (CIS)
Chapter 11 **Management Skills**	11.1	Explain the concept of management (BME)
		Explain the nature of management/supervisory training (BME)
	11.2	Foster positive working relationships (CIS)
		Describe the role of management in the achievement of quality (BME)
		Encourage team building (BME)
		Explain the concept of staff motivation (BME)
		Explain the nature of leadership in organizations (BME)

CIS Communication, Interpersonal Skills   **DIS** Distribution   **FIN** Financing   **PRI** Pricing   **SEL** Selling

Standards Assessment Correlation

SECTION ASSESSMENT			CHAPTER ASSESSMENT						UNIT LAB
Reviewing Key Terms and Concepts	Thinking Critically	Integrating Academic Skills	Fact and Idea Review	Thinking Critically	Building Workplace Skills	Applying Marketing Concepts	Linking School to Work	Internet Connection	Zazz Lab
1, 3, 4	•		1, 3	3					
2, 5		•	2, 4						
1		•	5	1, 2		3	•		
2, 3			6, 7	4		1, 2		•	
	•		8		1	4			
1, 2, 5	•		1, 2, 3, 4			4			
3, 4		•	5, 6	1, 2					
1, 2, 3			7, 8	4, 5					•
4			9						
5	•		10	3	1	2, 3	•	•	
		•			2	1, 2, 3, 4		•	•
1, 2, 4, 5	•	•	1, 2, 3, 8	1	1				
1		•	4			2			•
2, 5	•		5, 6, 7	2		3	•		
2						4			
4			7			3			•
1, 2	•	•	9	3	2	1, 4		•	•
1, 2, 3, 4, 10		•	1, 3	1, 3	1, 2	3		•	•
2, 3, 4, 10	•	•	2, 3, 4, 5	1, 2, 3, 5	1	1, 2, 3		•	•
3, 4			2, 3	4	2				
1, 2, 3, 4, 10	•	•	6, 7, 8, 9	2, 3, 4		4	•		•
2, 3, 4	•		7, 9	2, 4	2	1, 4	•		•
2, 3, 10		•	7, 8	5	2	1			•
1, 2, 3, 4	•	•	1, 2, 4, 5	1, 3		1	•	•	•
4		•	3, 5		1, 2	1, 4			•
2, 3, 4	•		8, 9	2, 3		2, 4	•		•
2			6, 7	2		3			•
3	•		9	2	2	1, 2, 3	•		•
1, 2, 3, 4	•		7, 8	2, 3	2	3, 4			•
3	•	•	6, 7	1, 3		3, 4		•	•

Unit Overview

This unit introduces students to the concepts of business, marketing, and economics, and the basic skills necessary for success in the real world of work. Chapter 7 provides a review of basic mathematical skills, and Chapter 8 includes information on important communication skills. Chapter 9 discusses current computer technology. Chapter 10 familiarizes students with teamwork and interpersonal skills, while Chapter 11 introduces management functions and techniques.

Introducing the Unit

Explain to students that they are in charge of hiring personnel for Widget, Inc., a leading wireless technology company. The company will be hiring qualified individuals for the following jobs: circuit design engineer, trade show and industry event planner, production supervisor, senior technical writer, and financial analyst. (Briefly describe each job to students.) Divide the class into groups for each job title. Have students brainstorm a list of skills and knowledge job candidates would require. Have each group report and post the written lists. Compare the skills the jobs have in common. *(Skills could be math, communication, computer, interpersonal, and managerial.)* Discuss the importance of these skills that will be reviewed in this unit.

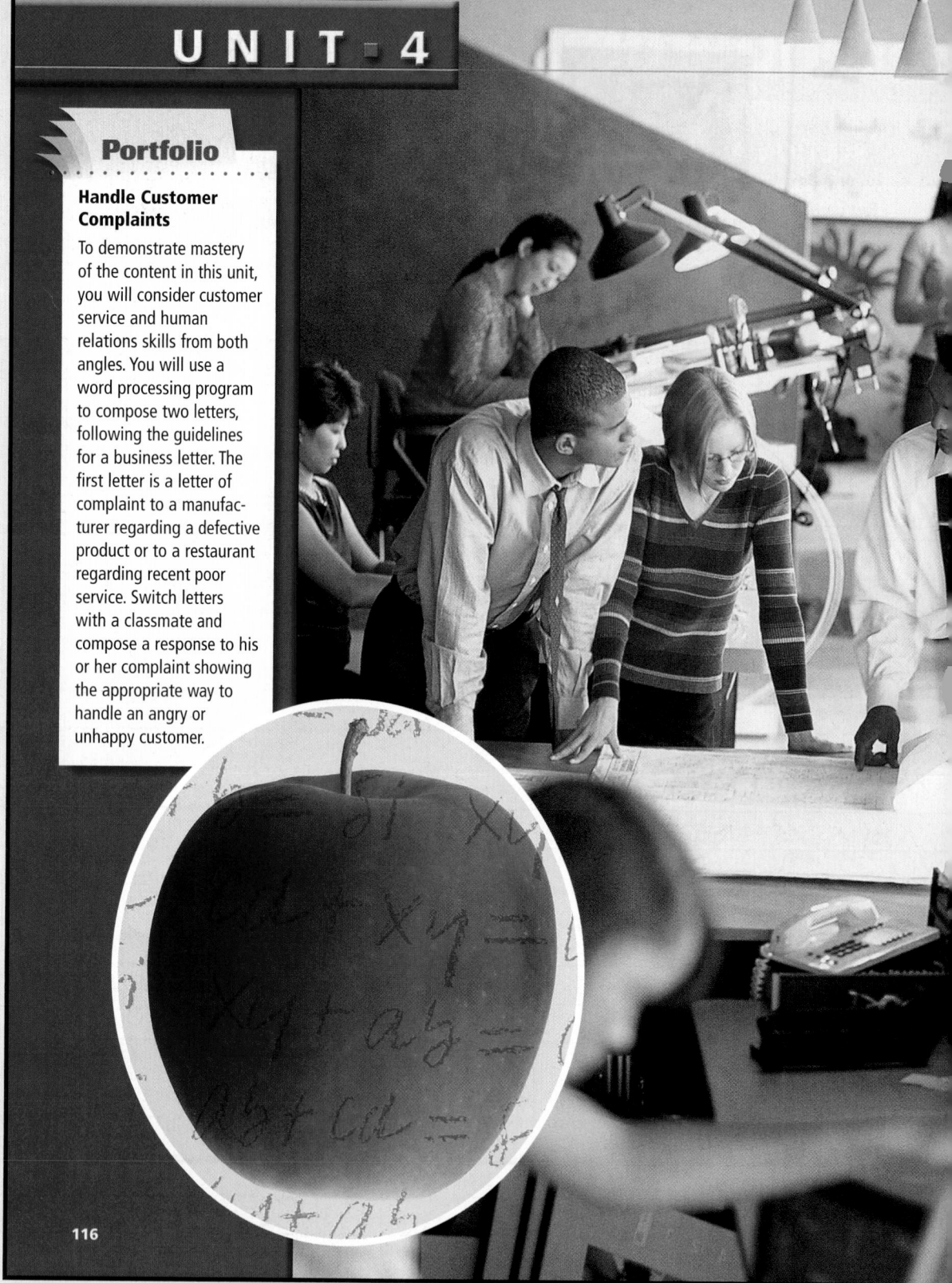

UNIT·4

Portfolio

Handle Customer Complaints

To demonstrate mastery of the content in this unit, you will consider customer service and human relations skills from both angles. You will use a word processing program to compose two letters, following the guidelines for a business letter. The first letter is a letter of complaint to a manufacturer regarding a defective product or to a restaurant regarding recent poor service. Switch letters with a classmate and compose a response to his or her complaint showing the appropriate way to handle an angry or unhappy customer.

116

Field Trip Suggestions

Plan a Virtual Field Trip Arrange for your students to take a virtual field trip. Visit either your school library or another place where there are computers available with Internet access. Have your students explore several Web sites that offer online classes in basic academic skills. Pre-select the Web sites and assign individual students or groups of students to check two or three and then report back to the class.

Academic Concepts and Skills

Unit Overview

The first three units introduced you to economics, business, and marketing. In this unit, you will learn some of the real world skills that you will need to succeed in a career in marketing.

In Chapter 7, you will review basic skills in math that you may not have used for a while, but will be needed in a marketing career. In Chapter 8, you will see that there is much more to listening than just hearing, and you will learn how to listen to understand the message. In Chapter 9, you will learn new things about computer technology—the fastest-growing field the world has ever known. Chapter 10 will help you in your interpersonal relationships on the job, and Chapter 11 will provide a background in management skills.

In this Unit:

Foundations of Marketing

● Communication, Interpersonal Skills

● Professional Development

● Business, Management, Entrepreneurship

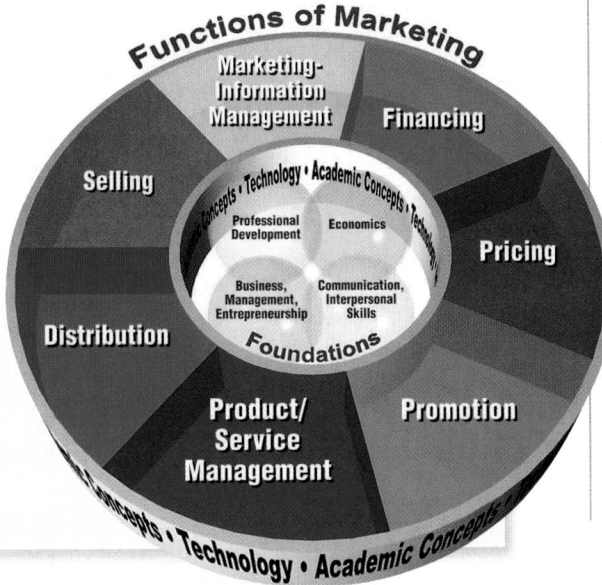

Functions of Marketing

Marketing-Information Management · Financing · Pricing · Promotion · Product/Service Management · Distribution · Selling

Foundations: Professional Development · Economics · Business, Management, Entrepreneurship · Communication, Interpersonal Skills

Academic Concepts · Technology

DECA Unit Project

Put chapter members into teams to develop a training and policy manual to be used in running a business. This could be for a local business or the school store. The manual should be set up like those issued by a human resources department to new employees. After studying this unit, have students decide which concepts apply to the manual.

Go to the *Marketing Essentials* Web site (**www.marketing.glencoe.com**) for resources to teach and assess occupation-specific vocabulary.

Unit Closure

Discuss with students the management structure of your school. Compare its organization to that of local small businesses. Ask students: Which communication, interpersonal, and management skills are used to make the school run smoothly? Through this discussion, students should understand that management as a process is not limited only to the business setting. Explain to students that they can develop and practice their management skills in team sports, classes, clubs, and jobs.

Guest Speaker Suggestions

Human Resources Manager Ask the human resources manager for a business or department store to speak to your class about the personality traits and qualities they look for when interviewing and hiring new personnel. You should ask that they specifically explain the types of pre-employment testing required of job applicants and how those test scores are evaluated. The speaker should explain that those tests include tests to assess math, grammar, and computer skills.

Chapter Overview

Chapter 7 reviews the basic math skills that students will use in their marketing careers, as well as in daily life. In addition to discussions of number concepts and basic operations, the chapter includes instructions on how to use a calculator and an introduction to charts and graphs.

 Springboard

Brainstorm Successful business people love numbers. Ask the students if they agree with this statement, and why or why not. Then have students brainstorm ways that math is used in people's work and everyday lives, and write the responses on the board. Explain that successful business people love numbers because math is used to make, save, and spend money.

Prereading

List the section objectives to discuss with students. Have students skim the chapter, looking at the pictures, reading the captions, and noting the heads. Ask questions to ensure that students have a minimal understanding of the chapter structure.

Preteaching Marketing Vocabulary

Dictate the vocabulary terms and ask students to write them on a sheet of paper. Write the terms on the board and have students guess the meaning of each. Write their guesses next to each term and leave this list on the board so students can see how close their guesses were to the actual definitions as they work through the chapter.

Marketing:
What It Takes
Answer Answers will vary, but the local Chamber of Commerce would be a good place to begin researching answers.

Chapter **7**

Basic Math Skills

Marketing: What It Takes

Room for One More?

You are considering opening your own bookkeeping and accounting business. You have a good understanding of basic math and you like working with numbers. You enjoyed your high school bookkeeping class so much that you've taken some accounting courses at the local city college. You feel confident that you could do a good job for your clients, but you're wondering if there is a large enough market for your new business. You are also concerned about the competition you would have to face.

WHAT WILL YOU DO?

How can you determine whether there is a market for your new business venture? How and what can you learn about your competition?

118

Five Fiscal Year
Compounded Annual
Growth of Net Income—
26%

THE DECA CONNECTION
ADVISOR CORNER

Showcase Your DECA Chapter If your chapter has access to a display case at your school, utilize that space throughout the year to display awards, trophies, pictures from trips, and other exciting memorabilia to showcase your DECA chapter activities. This is an excellent way to improve the image of your marketing program and DECA chapter by recognizing student achievement and showing others at your school the many exciting opportunities available through DECA membership. If no display case is available, use a counter in the school's office, or post a display on a bulletin board in the hall or classroom to create interest in and enthusiasm about DECA.

Math Fundamentals

Writing Whole Numbers

The numbering system we use is composed of ten basic symbols: 0, 1, 2, 3, 4, 5, 6, 7, 8, and 9. These symbols are called **digits**. Each digit represents a number and can be combined to represent larger numbers, such as 14; 215; 7,901; and 36,852.

The numbers above are all whole numbers because they can be written without fractions or decimals. Each digit in a whole number represents *how many* of something. The digit on the right represents the number of *ones*. The next digit represents the number of *tens*. So, in the number 25, there are five *ones* and two *tens*.

Knowing the placement name for each digit and for groups of digits is necessary for reading numbers and writing them in words. You use this skill, for example, when you write a check. The check format requires that amounts be written in both figures and words. Follow these five steps when you read whole numbers or write them in words.

1. Separate the number into groups of three digits: units, thousands, and millions. Very large numbers may include groups of digits for billions, trillions, and so on.

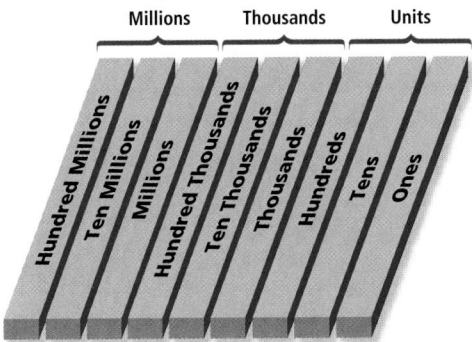

2. Separate the groups with commas.

• What You'll Learn

- How to write numbers in words using commas and hyphens correctly
- How to understand and know the meaning of fractional amounts
- How to perform basic math operations with decimal numbers
- How to round answers, especially amounts of money
- How to convert fractions to decimal equivalents

• Why It's Important

Virtually every job in marketing and business requires a good understanding of math fundamentals. Many young people have skipped over some of the basic skills. Others need a review to provide a good foundation in math. In this section, you will have an opportunity to sharpen your math skills.

Key Terms

- digits
- fractions
- numerator
- denominator
- mixed number
- decimal number

FOCUS

 ### Bell Ringer Activity

Write and Calculate Write the following numbers on the board. Have students respond to the questions:

1. 25 (What digit represents the number of tens? the number of ones?)
2. 11456789 (Insert commas in correct places.)
3. 580; 31; 5,000,675 (Write these numbers in words.)
4. 7/8 (What number is numerator? denominator?)
5. 5/5 (Convert this fraction to a whole number.)
6. 8/5 (Convert this fraction to a mixed number.)
7. 16.07 (Write this decimal number in words.)
8. 16.891 and 67.63 (Add these decimal numbers.)
9. 1.578 from 896.57 (Subtract these decimal numbers.)
10. 10.3 and 5.6 (Multiply these decimal numbers.)
11. 17.889; 14.842 (Round these numbers to the nearest tenth.)
12. 1.80 by 1.60 (Divide these decimal numbers.)
13. 1/8 (Convert this fraction to a decimal.)

Introducing the Section

Math Fundamentals Review the answers to the Bell Ringer Activity:

1. The 2 represents the number of tens; the 5, the number of ones.
2. With commas: 11,456,789.
3. Five hundred eighty; thirty-one; five million, six hundred seventy-five.
4. Numerator is 7, denominator 8.
5. 1
6. 1 3/5
7. Sixteen and seven-hundredths, or sixteen point zero seven.
8. 84.521
9. 894.992
10. 57.68
11. 17.9; 14.8
12. 1.125
13. 0.125

Classroom Resources

For the Teacher
- Teacher Editions for all workbooks
- Assessment Package
- PowerPoint Presentation Software
- Interactive Lesson Planner
- ILP Block Scheduling, p. 4
- ILP Lesson Plans, p. 14
- ILP Internet Resources, p. 33

- ILP *BusinessWeek* Case Studies, p. 41
- ILP Marketing Career Portfolio, p. 33
- *Marketing Essentials* Web site (**www.marketing.glencoe.com**)

For the Student
- Student Activity Workbook, p. 55
- Marketing Math Workbook, p. 19

- Marketing Research Project Workbook, p. 47
- ILP School-to-Work Activity Workbook, p. 25
- Virtual Business simulation
- *Marketing Essentials* Web site (**www.marketing.glencoe.com**)

ILP These resources are available in print and on the Interactive Lesson Planner (ILP)

3. When writing whole numbers, never use the word *and*.

360 ——→ three hundred sixty

> No *and*

4. Use hyphens in numbers less than 100 that are written as two words.

29 ——→ twenty-nine

> Use a hyphen.

5. When a three-digit group is made up of only zeros, do not write the name of the group.

3,000,375 ——→ three million, three hundred seventy-five

> No words are written for the thousands group.

■ **Everyday Math** Despite the rising popularity of ATM and debit card machines as a form of payment, there are still times when you will write out a check the old-fashioned way. This is an example of when everyday math skills are necessary. *Can you think of other daily activities that require an understanding of mathematical foundations?*

120 Unit 4 ■ *Academic Concepts and Skills*

Fractions

You learned about fractions when you were in grade school, but you may not have had much practice using them. Many jobs in business, especially in marketing, require a good understanding of fractions.

Fractions are numbers used to describe a part of some standard amount. The top number, the **numerator**, represents the number of parts being considered. The bottom number, the **denominator**, represents how many parts in a whole or how many *total* parts are being considered. For example, the shaded area in the rectangle below is $3/5$ (three-fifths) of the total rectangle.

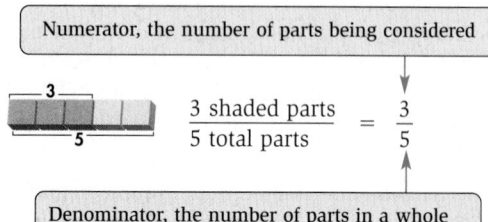

> Numerator, the number of parts being considered

$$\frac{3 \text{ shaded parts}}{5 \text{ total parts}} = \frac{3}{5}$$

> Denominator, the number of parts in a whole

In the example below, the number of circles is $2/7$ (two-sevenths) of the total number of shapes.

$$\frac{2 \text{ circles}}{7 \text{ shapes}} = \frac{2}{7}$$

Here are more examples illustrating the same principle. The answers represent the number of *shaded* parts.

$$\frac{\text{Number of shaded parts}}{\text{Total number of parts}} = \frac{3}{8}$$

$$\frac{3 \text{ shaded parts}}{\text{Total number of parts}} = \frac{3}{3} = 1$$

> One whole circle is shaded.

$$\frac{5 \text{ shaded triangles}}{4 \text{ triangles in a square}} = \frac{5}{4} \text{ of a square}$$

A fraction can describe a number greater than 1.

When the numerator is greater than the denominator, the fraction describes a number greater than 1. It can be written as a **mixed number**, a whole number and fraction together.

$$\frac{6}{5} = 1\frac{1}{5}$$ ← Mixed number

Numerator is greater than denominator.

PRACTICE 1

What fraction of the total number of shapes are triangles?

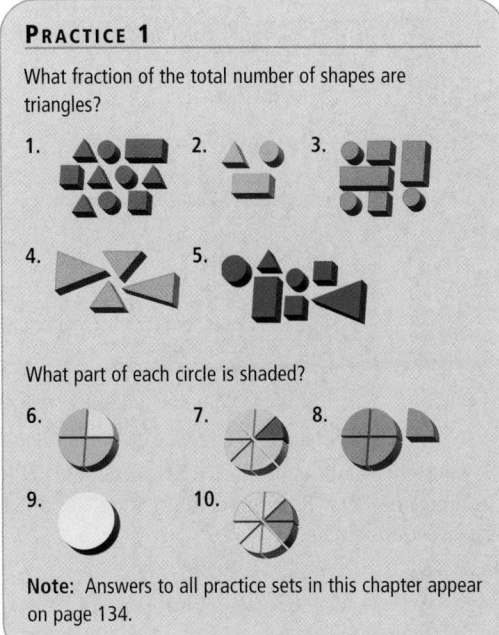

1.
2.
3.
4.
5.

What part of each circle is shaded?

6.
7.
8.
9.
10.

Note: Answers to all practice sets in this chapter appear on page 134.

Decimal Numbers

A **decimal number** is a fraction or mixed number whose denominator is a multiple of 10. The decimal number 5.3 means $5 + 0.3$ or $5 + \frac{3}{10}$ or $5\frac{3}{10}$. The decimal number 935.47 can be broken down as $900 + 30 + 5 + \frac{4}{10} + \frac{7}{100}$.

Knowing placement names is necessary for reading decimals and writing them in words. Decimal placement names apply to digits to the right of the decimal point.

Hundreds Tens Ones Tenths Hundredths Thousandths Ten Thousandths

Decimal point   Decimal placement names

To read a decimal number or write it in words, follow the steps below. Use 15.083 as an example.

1. Begin with the whole number to the left of the decimal point *(fifteen)*.

2. Read or write *and* for the decimal point.

3. Read or write the number to the right of the decimal point as a whole number *(eighty-three)*.

4. Use the name of the decimal place of the final digit *(thousandths)*.

The result is *fifteen and eighty-three thousandths.*

There is another way to read numbers with decimal points. You may also hear decimal numbers read using the whole number and only the names of the digits in the decimal places, with *point* for the decimal point. For example, 9.7 could also be read as *nine point seven*; 15.083 might be read as *fifteen point zero eight three.*

Why is it important for you not only to know how to write decimals and fractions, but to understand the relationship between the two as well? Understanding the relationship between decimal numbers and fractions is important when you are writing a check. After writing the amount in decimal form, you must write it again, using words for the dollars and a fraction for the cents.

Decimal form

Pay to the order of XYZ Company $324.57

Three hundred twenty-four and $^{57}/_{100}$ Dollars

Dollars written in words   Cents written as a fraction

SECTION 7.1

Thinking Critically

Cumulative Process Ask: What do we mean when we say that acquiring math skills is a cumulative process? *(Cumulative means "increased by successive additions." Explain to students that they will increase their knowledge of how to perform math functions by starting with the basics, as this chapter does, and building on that basic knowledge to learn more advanced functions.)*

Independent Practice

Research There are hundreds of challenging and fun, free math activities available on the Internet that students can use independently. Activities such as "Math Journey", "Math Baseball", and "Dream Car Math" provide students with an entertaining and competitive format to practice the math fundamentals covered in this chapter. These skills are usually found in the 7th to 8th grade math curriculum. To locate these activities, use a search engine, such as *about.com,* and key in *math activities.*

GREAT IDEAS from the Marketing Classroom

Cecil Lara
George W. Brackenridge High School
San Antonio, TX

As a result of the 1983 report on "A Nation at Risk" and the "SCANS Report" of 1992, the American business community and political leaders made "work" the centerpiece of education.

My assessment strategy makes 40 percent of a student's grade dependent on professionalism. A dramatic revelation occurs with a modified professionalism grade component. Strategies designed to measure professionalism differ from those designed to measure cognitive or performance skills. By using a variety of assessment strategies and techniques, students can attain the desired learning goals.

Individualized Practice

Communication Skills

A journal is a written account that students keep to record what they have learned.

L1 Encourage your students to write a short (50-word) paragraph in their journals for each period you spend on this chapter. Have them explain in their own words what they learned in each lesson and give one example.

L2 In their journals, have students answer one open-ended question about the day's class work in addition to their paragraphs. Examples:

- What relationship do you see between the things you learned today and the things you learned yesterday?

- Where else in your life or on your job have you used the information that you learned today?

L3 When students have finished studying this section, have them write a 100-word paragraph in their journals that summarizes the concepts and skills they learned.

PRACTICE 2

Write the decimal numbers in words. Write the amounts of money (as indicated by $) as you would on a check.

1. 5.6   5. 3.12   8. 25.48
2. 0.7   6. 9.05   9. $155.87
3. 14.5   7. 10.33   10. $545.67
4. 0.09

■ Adding and Subtracting Decimal Numbers

To add or subtract decimal numbers, first list the numbers vertically, keeping the decimal points in line with each other. Then add or subtract as you would with whole numbers. Sometimes you may need to write zeros to fill a column.

$$1.45 + 3.4 = ?$$

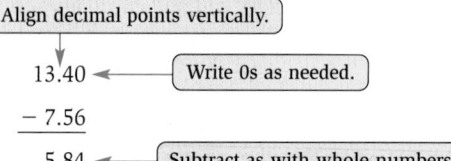

Align decimal points vertically.

```
  1.45
+ 3.40   ◄── Write 0s as needed.
  ----
  4.85   ◄── Add as with whole numbers.
```

$$13.4 - 7.56 = ?$$

Align decimal points vertically.

```
  13.40   ◄── Write 0s as needed.
-  7.56
  -----
   5.84   ◄── Subtract as with whole numbers.
```

■ Multiplying Decimal Numbers

To multiply decimal numbers, use the following two-step process.

1. Multiply the two numbers as if they were whole numbers. Pay no attention to the decimal points yet.

2. Add the number of decimal places in the two numbers being multiplied. Then, *working from the right,* count off the same number of decimal places in the product and insert the decimal point. *Note:* When counting off places from the right, you may have to add a zero in order to place the decimal point.

$$9.05 \times 4.31 = ?$$

```
   9.05   ◄── 9.05 has two decimal places.
 ×4.31   ◄── 4.31 has two decimal places.
 -----
   905
  2715
  3620
 ------
 390055 ──► 39.0055
```

The answer must have four decimal places.

$$0.25 \times 0.3 = ?$$

```
  0.25   ◄── 0.25 has two decimal places.
× 0.3   ◄── 0.3 has one decimal place.
 -----
 0.075
```

Write a 0 in the product in order to have three decimal places.

Multiply amounts of money as you would other decimal numbers. Remember to include the dollar sign in your answer.

```
 $4.98
 ×   2
 -----
 $9.96
```

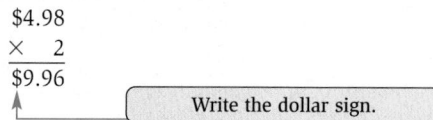

Write the dollar sign.

PRACTICE 3

Complete the following addition and subtraction problems with decimal numbers.

1. 5.4 + 8.6 =
2. 7.5 + 9.6 =
3. 9.8 + 7.5 =
4. 18 + 7.7 =
5. 17.5 + 4.75 =
6. 7.04 + 71.5 =
7. 6.7 + 0.6 + 2.67 + 7 =
8. 4.6 − 3.3 =
9. 45.9 − 7.76 =
10. $8 − $3.76 =
11. 5.7 − 1.11 + 14.078 =
12. 23.6 − 8.431 =

13. Bob's Bicycle Shop paid the following bills in September: $86.45 for gas, $114.86 for electricity, $187.58 for telephone, $98.36 for insurance, and $875 for rent. What is the total?

14. From a 40-yard bolt of fabric, Carol sold the following pieces: 3.33 yards, 4.5 yards, 2.25 yards, 2.125 yards, and 3.875 yards. How many yards are left?

Rounding Decimal Numbers

Sometimes you may have to round a decimal number. This is especially common when multiplying with amounts of money, as when figuring tax amounts, discounts, and so on.

Use the following steps to round decimal amounts. Round 16.842, 16.852, and 16.892 to the nearest tenth.

1. Find the decimal place you are rounding to.

16.842   16.852   16.892

Tenths place

2. Look at the digit to the right of that place.

16.842   16.852   16.892

Digit to the right

3. If the digit to the right is less than 5, leave the first digit as is. If the digit is 5 or greater, round up.

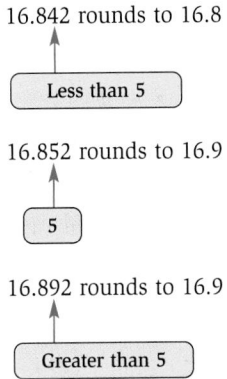

16.842 rounds to 16.8

Less than 5

16.852 rounds to 16.9

5

16.892 rounds to 16.9

Greater than 5

When you are working with amounts of money, use the same steps to round your answer to the nearest cent (the nearest hundredth).

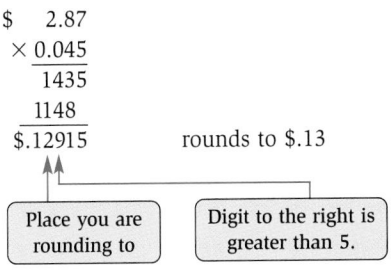

$ 2.87
× 0.045
─────
1435
1148
─────
$.12915   rounds to $.13

Place you are rounding to

Digit to the right is greater than 5.

Dividing Decimal Numbers

Division of decimal numbers is similar to division of whole numbers. Follow the steps below to divide decimal numbers.

1. Set up the division problem as you would with whole numbers.

   69.7 divided by 1.7 = $1.7\overline{)69.7}$

   69.7 divided by 1.724 = $1.724\overline{)69.7}$

2. Shift the decimal point in the divisor so that the divisor becomes a whole number. Then shift the decimal point in the dividend the same number of decimal places. Write zeros in the dividend, if necessary, in order to place the decimal point.

$1.7\overline{)69.7}$ ⟶ $17.\overline{)697.}$

Shift the decimal point one place to the right.

More About . . .

Rounding Decimal Numbers
What seems like an insignificant detail can end up being a very expensive mistake. For example, even a small mistake in rounding off a purchase order can cause a computer to kick it out for hand processing. This can cause further delays. Always double-check rounded amounts.

ASSESS

Reteaching

1. **Vocabulary** Assign and review the vocabulary terms for this section.
2. **Fact and Idea** Assign and review Fact and Idea Review questions 1–5 from the Chapter Assessment.
3. **Practices** Do an oral review of Practices 1–5. By now, students should have a good grasp of all of the concepts. If they do not, however, reviewing the practices will help you determine where you need to give additional instruction.

Enrichment

1. **Review** Assign and review the appropriate Thinking Critically questions from the Chapter Assessment.
2. **Extend** Assign and review the corresponding activities from *BusinessWeek Case Studies*, *Internet Resources*, and the *School-to-Work Activity Workbook.* **ILP**
3. **Calculate** Have students keep track of all the purchases made in your school store for one week, or make these figures available to students. For each type of item sold, have them calculate the total cost of the items, the total sales, and the difference between the two.

Write 0s.

$$1.724\overline{)69.700} \longrightarrow 1724.\overline{)69700.}$$

Shift the decimal point three places to the right.

3. Place a decimal point in the answer space directly above its new position in the dividend. Then divide as with whole numbers.

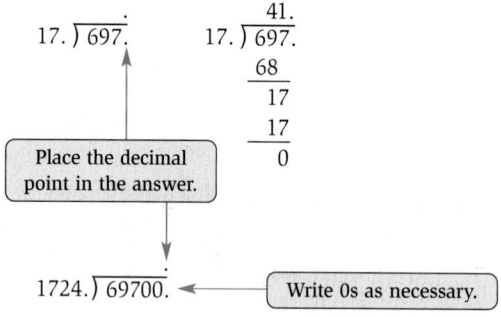

$$17.\overline{)697.}$$

Place the decimal point in the answer.

$$17.\overline{)697.} \quad \begin{array}{r} 41. \\ \underline{68} \\ 17 \\ \underline{17} \\ 0 \end{array}$$

$$1724.\overline{)69700.}$$ Write 0s as necessary.

Sometimes you may need to write extra zeros after the decimal point in order to have a remainder of zero.

$$16.38 \div 6.5 = ?$$

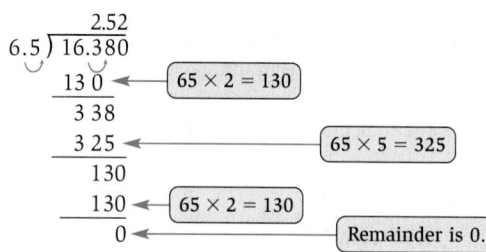

$$6.5\overline{)16.380} \quad \begin{array}{r} 2.52 \\ \end{array}$$

13 0 ← $65 \times 2 = 130$
3 38
3 25 ← $65 \times 5 = 325$
130
130 ← $65 \times 2 = 130$
0 ← Remainder is 0.

Divide and Conquer

The way a computer looks at and sorts data takes more than just a speedy processor. A set of instructions is required to solve complex problems, so an algorithm is created to make sense of the masses of data. An algorithm is a new way of looking at an old problem. Online marketing departments collect huge amounts of data from their customers by tracking information such as customer purchases from frequently visited Web pages. Companies use this information to personalize their Web sites or adjust their pricing. An analyst would not be able to look at every bit of information accurately; instead, algorithms are created to regroup, divide, and merge information into more easily classifiable units. This method of dividing tasks and then regrouping them saves time for individuals and the company as a whole. Algorithms to the rescue!

Thinking Critically
What use do algorithms have in marketing?

Some decimal answers will continue infinitely as you write zeros to the right of the decimal point. *Repeating decimals* will repeat a number or pattern of numbers.

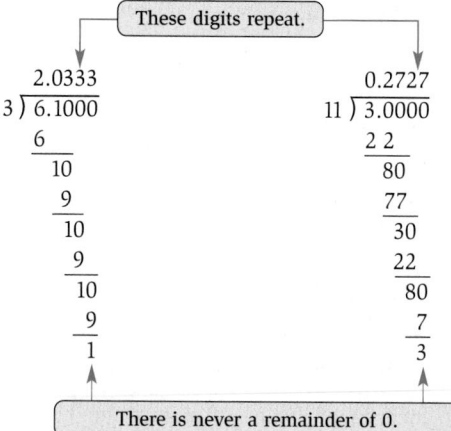

These digits repeat.

$$3\overline{)6.1000} \quad \begin{array}{r} 2.0333 \\ \end{array} \qquad 11\overline{)3.0000} \quad \begin{array}{r} 0.2727 \\ \end{array}$$

6
10
9
10
9
10
9
1

2 2
80
77
30
22
80
7
3

There is never a remainder of 0.

Divide and Conquer

Answer Algorithms can assist in the management of marketing information. Because an analyst may not be able to review all the data from customers, algorithms save time.

PRACTICE 5

Do the following division problems. Round answers to the nearest hundredth.

1. $0.75 \div 1.8 =$ 4. $8.4 \div 0.015 =$

2. $4.76 \div 3.8 =$ 5. $0.063 \div 2.1 =$

3. $1.758 \div 4.64 =$ 6. $6.002 \div 0.3 =$

7. Software Corporation paid $2,366.05 for computer paper. If the paper costs $29.95 per box, how many boxes did the corporation buy?

8. Edward averages 80 questions per hour when typing test questions into a computer testbank. How long will it take him to enter 1,800 questions?

■ Converting Fractions to Decimals

As you read in the section on fractions, decimal equivalents of fractions are important in many jobs in marketing. To convert any fraction to a decimal, simply divide the numerator by the denominator.

Numerator → Denominator →
$$\frac{1}{4} = 1 \div 4 = 4\overline{)1.00}$$
$$\begin{array}{r} 0.25 \\ 4\overline{)1.00} \\ \underline{8} \\ 20 \\ \underline{20} \\ 0 \end{array}$$

$$\frac{2}{3} = 2 \div 3 = 3\overline{)2.000}$$
$$\begin{array}{r} 0.666 \\ 3\overline{)2.000} \\ \underline{1\,8} \\ 20 \\ \underline{18} \\ 20 \\ \underline{18} \\ 2 \end{array}$$

There is never a remainder of 0.

In its decimal form, $^2/_3$ is a repeating decimal. When working with repeating decimals, you may round to the nearest hundredth for most applications.

Thus, $^2/_3 = 0.67$.

7.1 ASSESSMENT

Reviewing Key Terms and Concepts

1. Write the whole number 2,000,265 in words, using commas and hyphens correctly.

2. Explain the meaning of $^3/_5$.

3. Multiply: $\$4.99 \times 5$.

4. Round the answer from question 3 to the nearest dollar.

5. Convert the fraction $^3/_4$ to its decimal equivalent.

Thinking Critically

6. Sometimes rounding decimal numbers to whole numbers makes a complicated math problem easy to do "in your head." Name at least one example when rounding is helpful.

Integrating Academic Skills

7. **COMMUNICATION** Each of the following numbers can be expressed in three ways. Fill in the blanks.

Fraction		Decimal	Percentage
$\frac{3}{5}$	=	_____	_____
$\frac{2}{70}$	=	_____	_____
$\frac{1}{1,000}$	=	_____	_____

7.1 ASSESSMENT ANSWERS

Reviewing Key Terms and Concepts

1. two million, two hundred sixty-five

2. The fraction 3/5 describes three out of five parts.

3. $24.95

4. $25.00

5. 0.75

Thinking Critically

6. Answers will vary but may include estimating travel mileage, number of yards gained in a football play, or the cost of some purchases.

Integrating Academic Skills

7. **COMMUNICATION** $3 \div 5 = 0.6 = 60\%$, $2 \div 70 = 0.029 = 2.9\%$, $1 \div 1000 = 0.001 = 0.1\%$

SECTION 7.1

Evaluation

Assign and review the Section 7.1 Assessment.

Technology Resources

 GO TO

Assessment Resources
Go to the *Marketing Essentials* Web site (www.marketing.glencoe.com) for resources to teach and assess occupation-specific vocabulary.

CLOSE

Section Wrap-Up

Have students complete these statements:

• A whole number is written without _____. *(fractions and decimals)*

• In a fraction, the numerator expresses _____. and the denominator expresses _____. *(number of parts being considered/ number of parts in a whole)*

• A decimal number is _____. *(a fraction or mixed number whose denominator is a multiple of ten)*

Interpreting Numbers

FOCUS

Bell Ringer Activity

Explain Write the following on the board:

Gross Monthly Sales for 2000
Metro Pet Emporium

January	$8,670
February	7,955
March	8,995
April	11,690
May	13,200
June	13,567
July	14,688
August	16,780
September	16,555
October	14,500
November	15,600
December	17,800

Tell students to present a comparison of the above sales figures for 2000. How would they do it? On the board, write a list of students' answers.

Introducing the Section

Interpreting Numbers Ask students to assist you by drawing two sets of axes on the board—one for a bar graph and one for a line graph. Then have the students label each vertical axis with the words *Sales* (in thousands) and the numbers 1–20. Have them label each horizontal axis with the word *Months* and abbreviations for the 12 months of the year. (See **Figure 7-2** on page 131 for an example.)

Once the graph structures have been laid out, explain the concepts of bar and line graphs. Then ask students to help you plot the figures from the Bell Ringer Activity.

Draw a circle on the board, and ask students how they would plot the same information on a circle graph. (The circle represents the total for the year of $160,000, divided into 12 slices for each month's figure.)

• What You'll Learn

- How to use a calculator to solve math problems
- The procedure used to convert percentages to decimals and decimals to percentages
- The ways to read different types of graphs used to present mathematical data

• Why It's Important

Most jobs in marketing require the use of a calculator. Many require using a computer to generate graphic presentations. You will improve your skill level on the calculator as you study this section. You will also gain a greater understanding of graphs and charts.

Key Terms

- percent
- bar graph
- line graph
- circle graph
- pie chart

Using a Calculator

Calculators simplify the math that is common in both the business world and in people's personal lives. Many people find calculators vital when paying bills, creating a budget, and balancing their checkbook. Nearly everyone in marketing and business uses calculators. There are two basic types. The most widely used type employs the *algebraic entry system*. This is the type of calculator used in the problems that follow. The other type uses the *reverse-entry system*.

The basic difference is that with the reverse-entry system, you enter the first amount, then the second amount, and then the operation (added to, subtracted from, multiplied by, or divided into the first amount). If you have a calculator that uses the reverse-entry system, read the instruction book that accompanies your calculator very carefully. You will get a very different answer if you enter numbers as if using an algebraic entry system when working with a reverse-entry calculator.

If you expect to be hired in sales or any other marketing job, you will almost certainly use a calculator. Besides simply knowing which buttons to press, you will be expected to work with accuracy, know how to work with fractions and amounts of money, and have an understanding of how the calculator computes with multiple operations.

■ Estimate, then Operate

When using a calculator, many people follow the *guess-and-check method*. They estimate first, then enter the problem in the calculator. Finally, they check the displayed answer against the estimate.

$$388 + 995 = ?$$

Estimate: $400 + 1{,}000 = 1{,}400$

Enter the problem:

③ ⑧ ⑧ ⊞ ⑨ ⑨ ⑤ ⌸
1383

Displayed answer

Check: 1,388 is reasonably close to the estimate of 1,400.

$$480 \times 112 = ?$$

Estimate: $500 \times 100 = 50{,}000$

Enter the problem:

④ ⑧ ⓪ ⊠ ① ① ② ⌸
53760

Displayed answer

Check: 53,760 is reasonably close to the estimate of 50,000.

Classroom Resources

For the Teacher
- Teacher Editions for all workbooks
- Assessment Package
- PowerPoint Presentation Software
- Interactive Lesson Planner
- ⒾⓁⓅ Block Scheduling, p. 4
- ⒾⓁⓅ Lesson Plans, p. 15
- ⒾⓁⓅ Internet Resources, p. 33

- ⒾⓁⓅ Blackline Masters, p. 18
- ⒾⓁⓅ *BusinessWeek* Case Studies, p. 41
- ⒾⓁⓅ Marketing Career Portfolio, p. 33
- *Marketing Essentials* Web site (**www.marketing.glencoe.com**)

For the Student
- Student Activity Workbook, p. 55
- Marketing Math Workbook, p. 19

- Marketing Research Project Workbook, p. 47
- ⒾⓁⓅ School-to-Work Activity Workbook, p. 25
- Virtual Business simulation
- *Marketing Essentials* Web site (**www.marketing.glencoe.com**)

ⒾⓁⓅ These resources are available in print and on the Interactive Lesson Planner (ILP)

You may wonder why it is important to estimate your answers when you use a calculator. Surely the calculator is more accurate than your estimate. Sometimes, though, you may make errors when entering numbers or even press the wrong operation key. It's important to have an estimate of the answer in mind. For example, if you're expecting an answer of about 300, you'll know something is wrong if the displayed answer on your calculator is 3,300.

Another way to ensure accuracy when using a calculator is to check the display after you enter each number and before you press the operation key. If you have made an error, press the Clear Entry key $\boxed{CE}$ to remove the last entry. Suppose you want to multiply 5.8×7.2, but you enter $\boxed{5}$ $\boxed{.}$ $\boxed{8}$ $\boxed{\times}$ $\boxed{7}$ $\boxed{2}$. Press $\boxed{CE}$ to delete the last two keystrokes. Then you can reenter the second number correctly. The first number will remain in the calculator. Press the Equals key $\boxed{=}$, and the answer will be displayed: 41.76.

■ How to Make Entries

Keep in mind as you enter digits that you can disregard leading zeros to the left of the decimal point (as in 0.6 or 0.375) and final zeros after the decimal point (as in 9.250 or 41.500). You don't need to enter these zeros. The calculator will display all the digits needed.

Number	Keystrokes Entered	Display
0.785	$\boxed{.}$ $\boxed{7}$ $\boxed{8}$ $\boxed{5}$	0.785
5.10	$\boxed{5}$ $\boxed{.}$ $\boxed{1}$	5.1

When dealing with mixed numbers or fractions, you must first convert the fractions to decimal form. Do this by dividing the numerator by the denominator. For example, to enter $5\frac{1}{4}$, first enter $\boxed{1}$ $\boxed{\div}$ $\boxed{4}$. Then add the whole number by entering $\boxed{+}$ $\boxed{5}$.

When solving problems dealing with money, remember to write the dollar sign in the answer. You may also have to round the displayed answer to the nearest cent.

Display	Answer Written as Money Amount
5.25	$5.25
25.368216	$25.37 (Round to nearest cent.)
46.0194	$46.02 (Round to nearest cent.)
76514.1	$76,514.10 (No commas shown in large numbers on most calculators.)

A calculator can operate on only two numbers at a time. However, you can perform a string of involved calculations on more than two numbers if you are very careful. When only addition and subtraction are involved, the calculator will perform these operations as they are entered.

$\boxed{8}$ $\boxed{.}$ $\boxed{6}$ $\boxed{+}$ $\boxed{.}$ $\boxed{2}$ $\boxed{5}$ $\boxed{+}$ $\boxed{1}$ $\boxed{1}$ $\boxed{.}$ $\boxed{9}$
$\boxed{-}$ $\boxed{3}$ $\boxed{.}$ $\boxed{6}$ $\boxed{2}$ $\boxed{=}$ 17.13

When only multiplication and division are involved, the calculator will also perform these operations as they are entered.

$\boxed{7}$ $\boxed{7}$ $\boxed{5}$ $\boxed{\times}$ $\boxed{.}$ $\boxed{9}$ $\boxed{6}$ $\boxed{\div}$ $\boxed{5}$ $\boxed{\times}$
$\boxed{1}$ $\boxed{.}$ $\boxed{9}$ $\boxed{6}$ $\boxed{=}$ 291.648

However, when a calculation involves a combination of addition or subtraction with multiplication or division, not all calculators work the same way. You will need to check how your calculator performs the operations in this type of problem. Most calculators will do the operations as they are entered.

$6 + 4 \ \times 6$ will be calculated as

$6 + 4 \ \times 6 =$

$10 \quad \times 6 = 60.$

$6 \times 4 \ + 6$ will be calculated as

$6 \times 4 \ + 6 =$

$24 \quad + 6 = 30.$

$9 - 5 \ \times 2 + 6 \div 7 =$ will be calculated as

$9 - 5 \ \times 2 + 6 \div 7 =$

$4 \quad \times 2$

$8 + 6$

$14 \div 7 = 2.$

Did You Know? The most common error made when using a calculator or adding machine is transposing, inputting the reverse of a given pair of numbers. For example, 798 would be entered as 789. If you are entering a long string of numbers, enter the calculations twice to see if the totals agree. If the difference of the two sums is devisable by nine, you may have transposed numbers.

Discussion Starters

1. **Most Used Concepts** Ask students: Which concepts discussed in this section do you use most often and thus feel that you understand the best? *(Answers will vary.)*
2. **Least Used Concepts** Ask students: Which concepts discussed in this section do you use the least and thus feel that you need to understand better? What course of action would best help you become more familiar with those concepts? *(Answers will vary.)*

Thinking Critically

1. **Estimating Numbers** Ask students to list occasions when they routinely estimate numbers. *(Answers will vary but may include estimating travel mileage, gross pay for a pay period, number of yards gained in a football play, number of cookies that a recipe will produce, and how much a date with dinner and a movie will cost.)*
2. **Using Calculators** Have students speculate about why they are taught to estimate and do math computations by hand when they could use a calculator instead. *(Answers will vary but should include the following: A calculator may not always be available for a computation. Also, knowing how to perform a math operation without a calculator helps you understand the logic of the process and thus apply it better.)*

Percentages

Percent means parts per hundred. Thus, a number expressed as a percent represents the number of parts per hundred.

To write a whole number or a decimal number as a percent, multiply it by 100. A simple way to do this is to move the decimal point two places *to the right*.

$$0.70 = 0.7 \times 100 = 70\% \quad \text{or} \quad 0.70 = 70\%$$
$$0.05 = 0.05 \times 100 = 5\% \quad \text{or} \quad 0.05 = 5\%$$
$$2.5 = 2.5 \times 100 = 250\% \quad \text{or} \quad 2.50 = 250\%$$

Move the decimal point two places to the right.

Write 0s as needed.

You can use a calculator to do this operation.

$\boxed{.}\boxed{7}\boxed{\times}\boxed{1}\boxed{0}\boxed{0}\boxed{=}$ 70 = 70%

$\boxed{2}\boxed{.}\boxed{5}\boxed{\times}\boxed{1}\boxed{0}\boxed{0}\boxed{=}$ 250 = 250%

■ Converting Fractions to Percentages

To write a fraction or mixed number as a percent, first convert the fraction to decimal form. Do this by dividing the numerator by the denominator. If there is a whole number, add it to the converted fraction. Then multiply by 100. You can use a calculator to do this operation.

$\frac{1}{2}$ = $\boxed{1}\boxed{\div}\boxed{2}\boxed{\times}\boxed{1}\boxed{0}\boxed{0}\boxed{=}$ 50 = 50%

$\frac{3}{8}$ = $\boxed{3}\boxed{\div}\boxed{8}\boxed{\times}\boxed{1}\boxed{0}\boxed{0}\boxed{=}$ 37.5 = 37.5%

$4\frac{2}{5}$ = $\boxed{2}\boxed{\div}\boxed{5}\boxed{+}\boxed{4}\boxed{\times}\boxed{1}\boxed{0}\boxed{0}\boxed{=}$ 440 = 440%

■ Converting Percentages to Decimals

Sometimes it may be easier to complete a math problem by changing a percentage to a decimal. There is a simple method that can be followed when you are asked to do this. You can change a percent to a decimal number by dividing by 100. A simple way to do this is to move the decimal point two places *to the left*.

Move the decimal point two places to the left.

$$24.8\% = 24.8 \div 100 = .248 \quad \text{or} \quad 24.8\% = 0.248$$
$$0.5\% = 0.5 \div 100 = 0.005 \quad \text{or} \quad 0.5\% = 0.005$$

Write 0s as needed.

You can use a calculator to do this operation.

12.6% = $\boxed{1}\boxed{2}\boxed{.}\boxed{6}\boxed{\div}\boxed{1}\boxed{0}\boxed{0}\boxed{=}$ 0.126

1.4% = $\boxed{1}\boxed{.}\boxed{4}\boxed{\div}\boxed{1}\boxed{0}\boxed{0}\boxed{=}$ 0.014

You can also convert a percent with a fraction or mixed number to a decimal by using a calculator.

$7\frac{1}{4}\%$ = $\boxed{1}\boxed{\div}\boxed{4}\boxed{+}\boxed{7}\boxed{\div}\boxed{1}\boxed{0}\boxed{0}\boxed{=}$ 0.0725

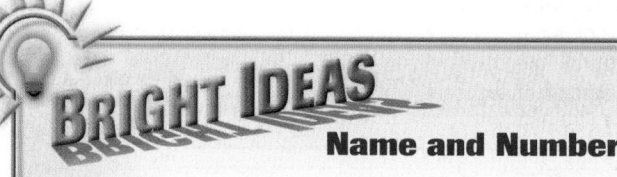

BRIGHT IDEAS

Name and Number

The first Datsun sports car that arrived in the United States from Japan in 1970 was named *Fair Lady*—a tribute to the popular play. The car was never marketed because the executives in the United States feared that the name would turn people off. This name would work in Japan, where cars are named for things like flowers; however, Americans favor cars with huge engines and tough images. There was little time to brainstorm for a new name, so they went with the company's internal designation for the car. The car made its debut in the United States as the 240Z. The name stuck, and the company (now Nissan) still names their sports car with numbers.

Thinking Creatively

What are some other products that are well-suited to number names? What are some products for which a number might not be a suitable name?

BRIGHT IDEAS   Name and Number

Answer Answers may vary, but some other ideas for products with number names are computers and cellular phones. Items like clothing and food might be confusing with a number name.

Inches or Centimeters?

The rest of the world is hooked on the metric system; however, Americans still favor the standard English system of measurements. NASA learned this lesson in September 1999 when the Mars Orbiter went off track. Why? One team of engineers was working with English units and the other with the metric system. Some countries in the European Union have demanded that they will only import U.S. goods that are metrically labeled. Whether it is inches or centimeters or miles or kilometers, the global marketplace calls for a common unit of measurement.

Thinking Critically
What challenges does the United States face in switching to the metric system?

■ **Calculating Price** It is helpful to understand how to properly use a calculator both in business and when dealing with personal finances. *Why would it be important to have a calculator at your disposal when making an investment like financing or leasing a car?*

■ Percent Problems

Percent problems are often encountered on a job. For example, you may be asked to figure a discount amount or the amount of sales tax. You may have to figure the total selling price, including the tax. Maybe you will be asked to figure the percent commission on your total sales.

Most percent problems will involve finding a percent of a number. To do that, multiply the decimal equivalent of the percent by the number.

> Decimal equivalent of 5½%

$5½\%$ of $\$35 = 0.055 \times \$35$

> *Of* tells you to multiply.

Use these steps to help you solve percent problems.

1. Estimate the answer.
2. Translate the problem into a math statement.
3. Do the calculations.

4. If necessary, round money amounts to the nearest cent.

5. Check your answer.

Many calculators have a Percent key ⊞ that can simplify percent calculations. Read the instructions for your calculator to find out how to use this key.

Two types of percent problems are explained below. The problems can be solved with a calculator without the use of a Percent key.

1. Suppose you have sold a set of skis listed at $395.99 to someone eligible for a 15 percent discount. How much in dollars and cents will you allow as a discount on the skis?

- *First: Estimate the answer.* Round the list price to $400. Figure that 10 percent of $400 is $40. Since 15 percent is 1½ times 10 percent, estimate the discount at about $60 (1½ times $40).

- *Second: Translate the problem into a math statement.*

    15% of $395.99 = 0.15 × 395.99

Cooperative Learning

Concepts and Calculations Pair each student who is having difficulty with a student who has mastered the concepts presented in this section. Give the following problems to each pair.

1. Make these entries on your calculator by converting the fractions to decimals (divide the numerator by the denominator to convert to decimal form and add the whole number):
   a. 6 1/8 *(6.125)*
   b. 7 2/5 *(7.4)*
   c. 9 1/4 *(9.25)*
   d. 10 5/12 *(10.42)*
   e. 4 5/18 *(4.28)*
2. Write these amounts as money (round to the nearest cent):
   a. 7.622 *($7.62)*
   b. 788.99876 *($789)*
   c. 7.35 *($7.35)*
   d. 366563.333 *($366,563.33)*
   e. 8916.98 *($8,916.98)*
3. Use your calculator to write these decimal numbers as percentages (multiply by 100):
   a. .89 *(89%)*
   b. 3.6 *(360%)*
   c. .005 *(0.5%)*
   d. 8.15 *(815%)*
   e. .0009 *(0.09%)*

While students are doing these problems, walk around the classroom, helping students as necessary and making sure that the less skilled students are participating fully.

CAPTION ANSWER
Calculating Price A calculator could help you figure out your total cost with additional features and calculate your interest rates and payments.

Life In The Diverse
MARKETPLACE

Inches or Centimeters?
Answer Some challenges of switching to the metric system include teaching people a new system, changing labels, signs, and other commonplace items that are labeled with the standard English system, and people resisting change.

Independent Practice

1. **Review and Calculate** Review with students the sales tax rate in your area. Then using a magazine or local newspaper, locate an ad for specified computer hardware and have them figure the total cost of the items, such as a computer, monitor, and printer, including sales tax. Discuss the amount of tax because students are frequently surprised at the amount of sales tax on large ticket goods. Relate why some businesses and individuals buy products online where sales tax is sometimes exempted.

2. **Research, Write, and Report** Have students use a readily available career resource, such as the *Encyclopedia of Careers and Vocational Guidance*, the *Occupational Outlook Handbook*, or the *Dictionary of Occupational Titles*, to research one career in marketing that interests them. Working from the written profile that they find in their research, have them take notes on the basic duties of the job and try to determine if and how math is used as part of the job. Have students share their findings.

REAL WORLD MARKETING

Creative in Numbers

As calculators grow more sophisticated, so do the opportunities for marketing them to today's students. Graphing calculators, which run graph equation programs, are being credited for changing the way students think about solving math problems. Unfortunately, they are also turning into the next generation of classroom distractions. Programs can now be downloaded to morph the devices into TV and VCR remote controls and even Game Boys.

Thinking Critically
What might marketers of graphing calculators do to resolve the negative criticism they receive?

- *Third: Do the calculations.*
  $0.15 \times \$395.99 = \$59.3985$
- *Fourth: Round the answer to the nearest cent, if necessary.*
  $\$59.3985$ rounds to $\$59.40$
- *Finally: Check the answer against your estimate.* The amount $59.40 is reasonably close to the estimate of $60. The discount is $59.40.

  2. If sales tax is $6\frac{1}{2}$ percent, how much tax should you collect on the sale of the skis? Before you can figure the tax, you have to find out the net selling price.

  List price − discount = net price
  $\$395.99 - \$59.40 = \$336.59$

  Now you can proceed, following the guidelines given above.

- *Estimate:* Round $6\frac{1}{2}$ percent to 7 percent and $336.59 to $300. A 7 percent sales tax means that $7 tax is collected on every $100 in sales. So, you can estimate the tax to be $21 ($3 \times \$7$).

- *Translate:*
  $6\frac{1}{2}$ percent of $336.59 = $0.065 \times \$336.59$
- *Calculate:*
  $0.065 \times \$336.59 = \$21.8784$
- *Round:*
  $\$21.8784$ rounds to $\$21.88$
- *Check:* $21.88 is reasonably close to the estimate of $21. The sales tax to be collected is $21.88.

Reading Charts and Graphs

Often in marketing, people need to use numbers to describe market trends, growth of sales, and other data. Graphs are a way of presenting such information in a way that is easier to understand than a long series of numbers. Because graphs are drawings, they make it possible for people to *see* information and grasp it more readily. It's easier to tell that one bar is longer than another, or that a line is going up or down, than it is to try to understand data by reading. Usually a graph shows the relationship between two kinds of data, or statistical information.

■ Bar Graphs

A **bar graph** is a drawing made up of parallel bars whose lengths are proportional to the qualities being measured. The bar graph in Figure 7-1 on page 131 was used by Morning Glory Music in its market research. It shows the relationship between the number of compact disks people bought and the age of the buyers. The bottom of the graph lists the age groups that purchased compact disks. Each group is represented by a bar of a certain height. There is a vertical line along the left side of the graph indicating the number of disks sold.

To discover how many disks 19- to 24-year-olds bought, simply draw an imaginary line across the top of the bar that represents that age group. Then note where that line intersects the left side of the graph. As you can see, 19- to 24-year-olds bought 800 disks that month, more than any other group.

Look at the bar representing 25- to 34-year-olds. The top of this bar is halfway between the 600 and 700 sales level. You can estimate that this group bought 650 CDs that month. You can also easily see that the younger group bought about 150 more CDs

REAL WORLD MARKETING

Creative in Numbers

Answer Marketers may consider enhancing the calculators with systems that prevent them from being re-engineered or provide support material that explains how the calculators can be used to enhance rather than decrease student performance.

than the 25- to 34-year-olds and about 600 more than people over 60. The relative heights of the bars give the store an instant picture of the age distribution of its customers.

■ Line Graphs

Another kind of graph you have probably seen often in magazines and newspapers is a line graph. A line graph uses a line that joins points representing changes in a variable quantity, usually over a specific period of time. It is very useful for charting sales, prices, profits, output—things that people expect to change over time. The information is useful in predicting future trends so that businesses can make plans to prepare for them.

The line graph shown in Figure 7–2 charts the ups and downs in compact disk sales at Morning Glory Music over a 12-month period. Along the bottom of the graph are the months of the year. Along the left side are the number of units sold. As you can see by following the line, by far the most sales (10,000) occurred in December. There was also a big jump in sales at the beginning of the summer and smaller increases in April and September. These were all followed by declines. This kind of information can help the store decide how much merchandise to order the following year.

Individualized Practice

Math Skills

For this activity, students will need a watch with a second hand or a stopwatch. Have each student select a 30-minute evening entertainment or news program.

L1 As they watch the program, they should record the following:

- Total number of minutes devoted to commercials during the program

- Total number of minutes devoted to news updates

- Total number of minutes given over to public service announcements

- Total number of minutes the program itself actually aired

L2 Students should calculate what fraction of the half-hour program was made up of commercials, news updates, public service announcements, and the actual program itself. (*Answers will vary.*)

L3 Students should calculate what fraction of the half-hour program was made up of commercials, news updates, public service announcements, and the actual program itself. Have students convert the fractions they developed and convert the percentages to decimals. (*Answers will vary.*)

FIGURE 7-1

Morning Glory Music—Compact Disk Sales by Age Group

■ **Bar Graphs** Bar graphs help you to see quickly how one piece of data is related to another. *According to this bar graph, how did Morning Glory Music's oldest customers compare with its youngest in terms of purchases?*

FIGURE 7-2

Morning Glory Music Compact Disk Sales

■ **Line Graphs** Line graphs chart change over time—in this case, the change is sales figures over a period of 12 months. *How would you summarize the progression of Morning Glory Music's sales over the course of a year?*

Chapter 7 ■ *Basic Math Skills* **131**

FIGURE 7-1 ANSWER
Bar Graphs The youngest customers (13–18 years old) purchased 400 CDs, which is twice the amount purchased by the oldest customers (60+ years old), who purchased 200 CDs.

FIGURE 7-2 ANSWER
Line Graphs June and December show the highest sales, most likely because of summer vacation and the holiday season.

Circle Graphs

A **circle graph** is a geometric representation of the relative sizes of the parts of a whole. Businesses often choose such a graph to compare things like the costs of different aspects of manufacturing the expenditures of one specific department, or the ways income from sales is used by a company.

Circle graphs offer a visual that is easy to understand when considering how a large figure is broken down into several parts. A circle graph is better known as a **pie chart**, because it looks like a pie cut into slices of different sizes. The proportions of the different "slices" are sometimes expressed as percentages of the whole circle and sometimes as dollar amounts.

The pie chart in Figure 7-3 shows a percentage breakdown of where the money from the retail sale of a compact disk went. Even without reading the numbers, you can easily see who received the largest portion of the money and who received the least amount. You can see from the chart that twice as much of the sale price went to retail profit as to the artists who made the recording. The biggest portion of the "pie" went to the record company. Look at the area representing manufacturing costs. You can see that it accounted for the smallest portion of the retail price.

This kind of chart enables companies to see at a glance which costs take the largest bite out of their revenues. The companies can then determine whether this breakdown accurately reflects their priorities. If not, they can institute cost-cutting measures as they see fit to restructure the breakdown of the pie.

FIGURE 7-3

Morning Glory Music Retail Price Distribution—Compact Disks

■ **Circle Graphs** A circle graph shows a whole—here, the price of a compact disk—divided into parts. *Which two price components account for more than half of what Morning Glory Music charges for a CD?*

Case Study

The Best Deal

More customers are beginning to shop at discount chain stores, attracted by the lower prices and convenience. Discount chains have gained popularity over small local stores as more people shop at them. Does this mean that they offer the best deal? Many customers seem to think so. On the surface, the price is what draws customers in. A lower price, however, does not always guarantee the same quality offered at a specialized store.

Consider the example of a seemingly similar bike sold at two stores—a discount chain store, "Mega-Mart," and a more expensive local bicycle shop. The discount chain store Mega-Mart sells a children's bike for $70. A bike with the same features costs $120 at the small bike shop. The bike from Mega-Mart seems like a better deal; however, research shows that the two bikes are not the same.

The more expensive bike is built from stronger materials and has replaceable parts. It is adjustable for different sized riders. When the rider outgrows the bike after two years, it can probably be resold for $60. This price is a reasonable estimation based on the "wear and tear" that the bike will receive in the two years.

The cheaper bike is not adjustable to account for growth and has a life span of one year. The cheaper materials are more likely to dent, rust, and chip, which makes reselling the bike difficult.

The lesson for the consumer is that the bike that costs more was truly a better buy. There are many factors that must be considered when making such a purchase—and price should not always be the deciding factor.

Case Study Review

1. How much does it cost per year to ride the more expensive bike? The cheaper bike?
2. Express the ratio of the cost of riding the more expensive bike to the cost of riding the Mega-Mart bike as a percentage.

A MATTER OF ETHICS

3. The manufacturer and seller of the Mega-Mart bike make $37 profit on the sale, while the profit on the sale of the expensive bike is $32. Is it ethical to make more profit on a less costly product than an expensive product? Why or why not?

Case Study Review Answers

The Best Deal

1. It costs approximately $60 per year to ride the more expensive bike, as compared to $75 per year for the cheaper bike.
2. 40:65 = 62%

A MATTER OF ETHICS

3. Answers will vary based on students' opinions.

ASSESS

Reteaching

1. **Vocabulary** Assign and review the vocabulary terms for this section.
2. **Fact and Idea** Assign and review Fact and Idea Review questions 6–10 from the Chapter Assessment.
3. **Graphs** Bring several packages of M & M candies (both peanut and plain). Have the students count the different colors in each kind of package and then summarize the information in a table format on the board. Then have the students help you create bar, line, and circle graphs summarizing the data.

Enrichment

1. **Review** Assign and review the Chapter 7 activities in the *Student Activity Workbook*.
2. **Review** Assign and review the appropriate Thinking Critically questions from the Chapter Assessment.
3. **Review** Assign and review the following Chapter Assessment activities: Building Workplace Skills, Applying Marketing Concepts, Linking School to Work Activities, The DECA Connection Role Play, and Internet Connection.
4. **Calculate** Return to Metro Pet Emporium's gross sales listed in the Bell Ringer Activity for this section. Ask students to determine the percentage of the store's gross annual sales ($160,000) that each month's sales figure represents.

   Jan—.054 or 5%; Feb—.050 or 5%; Mar—.056 or 6%; Apr—.073 or 7%; May—.083 or 8%; Jun—.085 or 9%; Jul—.092 or 9%; Aug—.105 or 11%; Sep—.103 or 10%; Oct—.091 or 9%; Nov—.098 or 10%; Dec—.111 or 11%

   Have students prepare a pie chart presenting the data.

Evaluation

Assign and review the Section 7.2 Assessment.

Technology Resources

 Assessment Resources
Go to the *Marketing Essentials* Web site (**www.marketing.glencoe.com**) for resources to teach and assess occupation-specific vocabulary.

VIRTUAL BUSINESS

 Math Skills
Introduce interpreting numbers to students using Knowledge Matters' Virtual Business visual simulation. Go to the *Marketing Essentials* Web site (**www.marketing.glencoe.com**) to download the Virtual Business "Math Skills" classroom activity specially designed just for the *Marketing Essentials* program. In this simulation, students will interpret market share data, financial data, and interpret and compare financial data. If needed, have students run the Virtual Business tutorial before beginning this activity.

CLOSE

Section Wrap-Up

Have students complete this statement: Charts and graphs make it possible to . . . *(see information and thus grasp it more readily.)*

Answers to Practice Sets

PRACTICE 1 (PAGE 121)
1. $4/10$ (or $2/5$) 6. $3/4$
2. $1/3$ 7. $1/8$
3. 0 8. $5/4$ (or $1\,1/4$)
4. $4/4$ (or 1) 9. No parts shaded.
5. $2/7$ 10. $2/8$ (or $1/4$)

PRACTICE 2 (PAGE 122)
1. Five and six-tenths
2. Seven-tenths
3. Fourteen and five-tenths
4. Nine-hundredths
5. Three and twelve-hundredths
6. Nine and five-hundredths
7. Ten and thirty-three hundredths
8. Twenty-five and forty-eight hundredths
9. One hundred fifty-five and $87/100$
10. Five hundred forty-five and $67/100$

PRACTICE 3 (PAGE 122)
1. 14 8. 1.3
2. 17.1 9. 38.14
3. 17.3 10. $4.24
4. 25.7 11. 18.668
5. 22.25 12. 15.169
6. 78.54 13. $1,362.25
7. 16.97 14. 23.92 yards

PRACTICE 4 (PAGE 123)
1. 36.4 7. 5.50974
2. 28.06 8. 61.2
3. 244.92 9. 0.0332
4. 199.08 10. $345.63
5. 3.4544 11. $188.07
6. 24.8

PRACTICE 5 (PAGE 125)
1. 0.42 5. 0.03
2. 1.25 6. 20.01
3. 0.38 7. 79 boxes
4. 560 8. 22.5 hours

7.2 ASSESSMENT

Reviewing Key Terms and Concepts
1. Use a calculator to find the decimal equivalent of $1/7$.
2. What is the decimal equivalent of 60 percent?
3. What are three forms of graphic representation?

Thinking Critically
4. A market researcher plans to present data about purchases of colas by age group. She can't decide whether to use a bar graph or to list her groups on a chalkboard in order of size. What should she do, and why?

Integrating Academic Skills
5. **MATH** Use a calculator to solve the following problem: You want to start a word processing business. The equipment you want to purchase costs $9,000. How many hours of work will it take to pay for the equipment if you charge your customers an average $25 per hour?

7.2 ASSESSMENT ANSWERS

Reviewing Key Terms and Concepts
1. $1 \div 7 = 0.14$
2. $60\% = 0.6$
3. Three forms of graphic representation are bar graphs, line graphs, and circle graphs.

Thinking Critically
4. Answers will vary. A bar graph has the advantage of being easier to understand than a list of data because it includes a visual representation of the data.

Integrating Academic Skills
5. **MATH** 360 hours. $9,000 \div 25 = 360$ hours.

Careers in Marketing

RESTAURANT MANAGEMENT

Bill Duffy
Restaurant Manager
Spike & Charlie's

Career Facts

What does your job entail?

"The main function of my job is to coordinate staff and control the operation of the restaurant. I organize the work of approximately 120 individuals to prepare and serve meals. Some restaurant managers plan the menu and order food and supplies; however, I try to delegate much of that work to the kitchen staff. Restaurant managers are routinely responsible for hiring, training, maintaining schedules, and overall troubleshooting at the restaurant."

What skills are most important to you?

"A restaurant manager must have very good organizational skills. Efficiency is necessary when coordinating activities, resources, and staff. I also believe that it is necessary to have excellent communication skills that enable you to let servers know what is expected of them. This must be communicated clearly and quickly because of the fast-paced environment."

What do you like most about your work?

"The best part about my job is the social experience of meeting many different people who come in to dine. Going out to dinner is like a mini-vacation and I get to be a part of that. I generally get to deal with people on very good terms in a nice environment."

How does your workload vary?

"My duties include keeping track of inventory, maintaining budgets, developing promotional marketing programs or events, coordinating staff, scheduling, and general maintenance of the restaurant."

What is your key to success?

"My motto is 'think big, concentrate small.' If you focus on your objectives (establishing menu prices, planning restaurant decor, etc.) you can work efficiently and effectively."

Thinking Critically

What are the four Ps of marketing in restaurant management?

Education and Training: Many community colleges and four-year colleges offer certificates and degrees in restaurant management and food service management. Employers are increasingly hiring candidates with four-year degrees who have strong backgrounds in business administration, marketing, sales, or hotel management. Experience as a food service worker provides valuable training.

Aptitudes, Abilities, and Skills: The ability to work under stress, good organization skills, good communication skills, good management skills, basic clerical skills, and the desire to serve people are necessary.

Career Outlook: Faster than average growth is expected to occur in restaurant management positions through the year 2006.

Career Path: Restaurant managers are often promoted from within a company. Large restaurant chains offer management-training programs allowing employees to advance to assistant management and then manager positions.

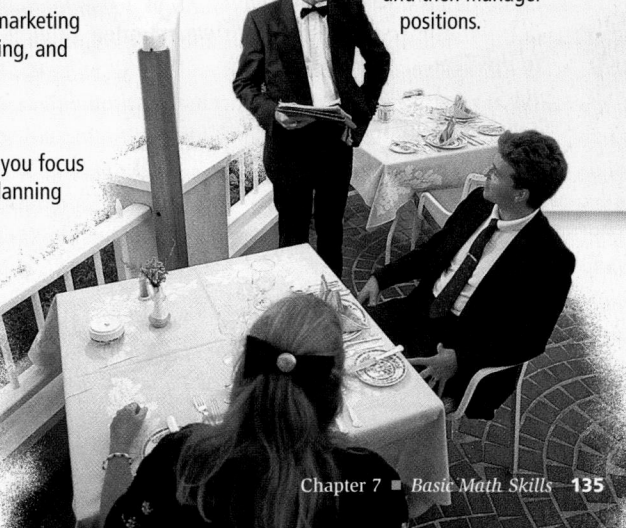

Chapter 7 ■ *Basic Math Skills* **135**

Vocabulary Review

Puzzles will vary. See Glossary for definitions.

Fact and Idea Review

1. millions, thousands, and units (ones)
2. It is a number that describes a part of some standard unit.
3. When the digit to the right of the place that you are rounding to is five or more, you round up; if it is less than five, you leave it as is.
4. You would divide 5 by 9, which yields that repeating decimal of 0.555, which can be rounded to 0.56.
5. Estimate before doing the calculation and check the display after entering each number and before pressing an operation key.
6. First convert the fraction to a decimal form, and then move the decimal point two places to the right.
7. Estimate the answer; translate the problem into a math statement; do the calculations; round monetary amounts to the nearest cent; and check your answer.
8. A bar graph uses bars of different heights to represent differences in variables. A line graph uses points connected by a line to show growth or decline in one variable over time.

Thinking Critically

1. They are the same as when using a calculator—to be sure the final answer is consistent with common sense and to catch simple arithmetic errors.
2. Answers will vary depending on students' opinions.
3. Multiply the number of sales times $15.
4. It results from dividing the foreign currency cost by the converted exchange rate. Answers will vary, depending on the current exchange rates. However, as a guide, these year 2000 rates would yield the following answers:
   1) If $1 equals 104.87 Japanese yen, the answer is $1,250.
   2) If $1 equals .63 GB pounds, the answer is $1,350.
   3) If $1 equals 7.8 Hong Kong dollars, the answer is $1,450.
   4) If $1 equals 6.8 French francs, the answer is $1,550.

Building Workplace Skills

1. Students who are motivated by competition will probably support posting the percentages, while those who are pressured by competition will likely oppose it.
2. 304.55 hours

Chapter 7 ASSESSMENT

VOCABULARY REVIEW

Build a crossword puzzle using the terms below. Use graph paper to arrange your entries. Then write short definitions for them.

- digits
- fractions
- numerator
- denominator
- mixed number
- decimal number
- percent
- bar graph
- line graph
- circle graph
- pie chart

FACT AND IDEA REVIEW

1. You should separate whole numbers into groups when you write them in words. What are these groups? (7.1)
2. What is a fraction? (7.1)
3. How do you decide whether to round a decimal number up or down? (7.1)
4. Describe how you would convert $5/9$ to a decimal number. Give your answer rounded to the nearest hundredth. (7.1)
5. What can you do to increase accuracy when using a calculator? (7.2)
6. Describe how you would convert a fraction to a percentage. (7.2)
7. What are the five steps in solving a percent problem? (7.2)
8. How is a bar graph different from a line graph? (7.2)

THINKING CRITICALLY

1. Estimating an answer before doing the math on a calculator is a good idea. What are some reasons for estimating before doing the same problem on paper?
2. Should students be allowed to use calculators when taking math exams? Defend your answer.
3. If the price of the compact disks in Figure 7-2 is $15, how would you find out how much money each point on the line represents?
4. You are purchasing computer parts for assembly in your company's plant in California. Locate current world currency exchange rates on the Internet or in a newspaper. Then compute the cost in U.S. dollars for the following orders:

   Order #1 from Japan: 131,087.5 yen

   Order #2 from Great Britain: 850.5 pounds

   Order #3 from Hong Kong: 11,310 Hong Kong dollars

   Order #4 from France: 10,540 francs

BUILDING WORKPLACE SKILLS

1. **Human Relations** You are the supervisor of a telemarketing team. Your records show that the success rate of your workers varies from 10 percent to 70 percent. Do you think it would be helpful to display these percentages in a chart for everyone to see? Why or why not?
2. **Math** Use a calculator to solve the following problem: You want to start a lawn mowing business. The equipment you will need will cost you $6,700. If you charge your customers $22 per hour, how many hours of work will it take to pay for the equipment?

APPLYING MARKETING CONCEPTS

1. **Analyzing Sales Patterns** Imagine that you sell computer parts. In January, you had $15,000 in sales. In February, your sales increased by 15 percent. From March through June, your sales continued to increase 15 percent a month. Use a spreadsheet program to prepare a line graph to show your sales by month.

2. **Researching the Computer** Research the history of the computer at the library or on the Internet. Find out when and where the first computers were built. Compare the uses, memory capacity, and cost of computers in the 1960s with those of today. Use a word processing program to write a 300-word report on your findings.

3. **Comparing Graphing Calculators** Research graphing calculators at the library or on the Internet. Why are they important, and what are some situations in which they are helpful? Use presentation software to prepare an oral report on your research, answering those questions and showcasing the best models you found.

4. **Using Circle Graphs** Keep track of how much money you spend in one week. Include money that you spend on food, transportation, and entertainment (buying CDs, clothing, going to the movies). Using a computer program, create a circle graph based on these amounts. You can divide your graph into as many parts as you would like. Then turn this graph into a bar graph. Which do you find easier to interpret?

LINKING SCHOOL TO WORK

Technology Skills Prepare a demonstration illustrating the way calculators are used at a local business. Include electronic cash registers if you work with one on the job.

THE DECA CONNECTION

Role Play: Motorcycle Dealership Employee

Situation You are to assume the role of employee at a local motorcycle dealership. You will be required to explain the company's two compensation plans to new employees. Employees can choose to work for a salary of $250 a week plus a commission of 8% of the price of the motorcycles they sell. Under that plan, if they don't sell any motorcycles, they get the salary but no commissions. The other choice is to work for commissions only. Under this plan employees will receive a 15% commission on the price of the motorcycles they sell, and no other salary. Prospective employees have average weekly living expenses of $475, so the base salary of $250 is tempting.

Activity You must demonstrate to the dealership manager (judge) that you are capable of presenting these options to new employees.

Evaluation You will be evaluated on how well you meet the following performance indicators:
- Explain the compensation plans
- Calculate financial ratios
- Make oral presentations
- Orient new employees

---

inter NET CONNECTION

Tax Break
You are figuring out your income taxes and know that the tax rate increases as your income goes up.

Connect
- Locate the Internal Revenue Service Web site and find the tax tables you need.
- Determine where the income break points are for the different tax rates.
- Calculate the tax on a taxable income of $49,700.

THE DECA CONNECTION

Students should be evaluated on the performance indicators noted in the Role Play.
- For another DECA Role Play, go to the *Student Activity Workbook,* p. 55.
- For more in-depth Role Play practice, refer to DECA's *Essential Competitive Events Handbook.* To order, contact DECA at www.deca.org.

*inter*NET CONNECTION
Answers will vary depending on the current tax rate.

Mini Quiz
Administer the Mini Quiz orally. For an expanded chapter quiz, go to page 41 of the *Reproducible Tests* book.

1. Write the amount $3,028.49 in words as you would on a check. <u>Three thousand, twenty-eight and 49/100</u>

2. In the number 6,035,274, which digit represents the thousands? <u>5</u>

3. Round 376,023 to the nearest ten thousandth. <u>380,000</u>

4. What kind of graph best shows changes over time? <u>line</u>

5. What kind of graph best shows a whole divided into parts? <u>circle or pie</u>

Applying Marketing Concepts

1. Points defining graph's line: Jan. $15,000; Feb. $17,250; Mar. $19,838; Apr. $22,813; May $26,235; June $30,170.
2. Reports will vary but should reflect accurate research.
3. Presentations will vary based on highlighted calculators.
4. Graphs will vary depending on individual budgets.

Linking School to Work

Answers will depend on the work situation.

GO TO
1. **Assessment** Have students complete the Reproducible Test for Chapter 7 or construct your own tests using the ExamView software.
2. **Enrichment** Have students complete the corresponding activities in the following workbooks:
   - *Marketing Math Workbook,* p. 19
   - *Marketing Research Project Workbook,* p. 47

Chapter Overview

Chapter 8 covers the basic communication skills essential to clear expression of thought in the business world and in daily life.

Springboard

Brainstorm Ask students to help you list the various types of communication *(listening, reading, speaking, and writing)*. Ask how they use these types of communication in their jobs, in school, and at home. Accept answers including listening to music, assisting customers, reading textbooks, sending e-mail, talking on the telephone. Tell students that this chapter will help them develop skills to communicate better on and off the job.

Prereading

List the section objectives and discuss them with students. Have students skim the chapter, looking at the pictures, reading the captions, and noting the heads. Ask questions to ensure that the students have a minimal understanding of the chapter structure.

Preteaching Marketing Vocabulary

List vocabulary terms on the board. Divide students into groups and have each group generate meanings for the terms. Limit this exercise to 15 minutes. When time is up, have each group give their definitions. If the groups disagree in their definitions, clarify information.

Marketing: What It Takes

Answer Encourage your employees to listen carefully and repeat or summarize customers' requests. Prepare price lists and signs to inform customers about costs and services; and prepare advertisements and brochures to promote your business.

Chapter 8

Communication Skills

Marketing: What It Takes

Copy House Communications

Imagine yourself as the owner of a copy center. Your services include providing copy machines, fax transmittals, and computers with e-mail and Internet connections. You pride your business on friendly, personal, and quick service. Your marketing advisor suggests you explore training employees on communication skills to enhance your venture.

WHAT WILL YOU DO?
What techniques can you employ to enhance effective communication between your employees and customers?

THE DECA CONNECTION — ADVISOR CORNER

Constructive Criticism Discuss with students methods of giving positive, constructive criticism, and include in the discussion the value of such feedback to organizations, to businesses, and for personal development. Develop an evaluation form and have your students evaluate your next chapter meeting, giving extra credit to those who help to improve the quality of your meetings. Discuss the evaluation results with chapter members and make plans for incorporating appropriate suggestions for improving future DECA meetings. This exercise gives students an opportunity to practice giving constructive criticism; as chapter meetings improve, students will realize the value of constructive criticism.

Defining Communication

The Communication Process

Communication is the process of exchanging information, ideas, and feelings. Good communication is an essential factor when developing interpersonal relations. They are also an important element of conducting successful business activities.

■ Senders and Receivers

The simple act of sending a message is just one facet of communicating—every message must be sent, received, and understood. Both verbal and nonverbal means are used to send and receive messages. Speaking and writing are verbal means. Nonverbal means include facial expressions and *body language,* your gestures, movements, and mannerisms that communicate your thoughts, which will be discussed more in Chapter 10.

You are often a sender and a receiver at the same time in face-to-face conversations. Suppose that you have asked your employer, Mr. Sanchez, how he wants you to arrange a window display. He sends a message by speaking as he explains the arrangement. You receive the message by listening. As you listen, though, you may be sending a message at the same time—even if you don't say a word. The expression on your face may be saying, "I don't understand." Mr. Sanchez may receive this message and start over, or he may rephrase the message.

■ Messages

The substance of any form of communication is the message—the information, ideas, or feelings the sender wants to share. All communication is made up of verbal and nonverbal symbols. Messages are represented by symbols, which can be anything that stands for something else.

Every word is a verbal symbol with a meaning that can be understood by others who know the same language. Avoiding nonstandard language, such as slang expressions and highly technical terms, will increase the chances that your message will be understood.

■ Channels

Channels are the avenues by which the message is delivered. In face-to-face conversations, the channels are sound and sight. The participants listen to and look at one another. The channel in telephone conversations is the sound that is transmitted and received over telephone lines. The participants speak to and listen to one another.

● What You'll Learn

- The six primary elements of communication
- How to arrange the setting for a business meeting
- How to use listening skills to improve your understanding of messages
- Three blocks to listening with understanding
- Three skills that will help you read with understanding

● Why It's Important

Studies have shown that 70 percent of our waking hours are spent communicating. Most jobs in business, especially in marketing, require good communication skills. You need to understand the communication process to become a more effective communicator.

● Key Terms

- communication
- channels
- feedback
- blocks
- setting
- distractions
- emotional blocks
- jargon

Chapter 8 ■ *Communication Skills* **139**

🔔 Bell Ringer Activity

Explain Pair students in the class and explain that they are to learn what their partner plans to do during the upcoming weekend. However, the students may not use oral or written communication. Allow 3–5 minutes for students to "communicate" in this manner. Then allow them 1–2 minutes to verbally clarify what each student was trying to explain.

Introducing the Section

What is Communication? After the students have found out what their partner plans to do this weekend, critique the activity by calling on students and asking these questions: 1) How did you feel when trying to explain your weekend plans? 2) Were any of your gestures misunderstood? (Ask for examples.) Should you have done anything differently? 3) What was difficult about trying to interpret your partner's gestures? Could you have done anything differently?

Explain that without being able to use oral and written expression, it is difficult to convey accurate and complete information. For communication to exist, it must not only be sent, but also received and understood. Several students probably experienced the concept of not understanding the messages in the exercise; therefore, communication did not take place for them.

TEACH

📊 Technology Resources

PowerPoint The *Marketing Essentials* PowerPoint Presentation CD-ROM provides visual lecture aids for every chapter section.

Classroom Resources

For the Teacher
- Teacher Editions for all workbooks
- Assessment Package
- PowerPoint Presentation Software
- Interactive Lesson Planner
- ⒾⓁⓅ Block Scheduling, p. 4
- ⒾⓁⓅ Lesson Plans, p. 16
- ⒾⓁⓅ Internet Resources, p. 35

ⒾⓁⓅ *BusinessWeek* Case Studies, p. 49
ⒾⓁⓅ Marketing Career Portfolio, p. 34
- *Marketing Essentials* Web site (**www.marketing.glencoe.com**)

For the Student
- Student Activity Workbook, p. 63
- Marketing Math Workbook, p. 19

- Marketing Research Project Workbook, p. 47
ⒾⓁⓅ School-to-Work Activity Workbook, p. 29
- Virtual Business simulation
- *Marketing Essentials* Web site (**www.marketing.glencoe.com**)

 ⒾⓁⓅ These resources are available in print and on the Interactive Lesson Planner (ILP)

139

Concept Development

1. Read Section 8.1 with students.
2. This chapter deals with basic communication skills. As you work through it, you may discover some students who need remedial help in reading and writing. Encourage those experiencing difficulties to speak with you privately so you can refer them to resources, such as the school's guidance counselors or reading teachers, for additional information and materials. Having good communication skills is more critical than ever for those entering the workforce.

Discussion Starter

Hearing and Listening Have the students follow your instructions. Say: "Extend your left arm straight in front of you." You should demonstrate. Then say: "Make a circle with your thumb and index finger," and demonstrate. Then say "Now bring your hand to your *chin*." But you should put your hand on your *cheek* (not your *chin*). Many students will have followed your lead and put their hand on the cheek, so it may take a few seconds for all to realize what happened and change their hand position. Ask students: Did everyone *hear* the direction? Did everyone *listen* to the direction? This is an example of *hearing but not listening*. This chapter will help increase students' understanding of communication.

Look Into My Eyes
Answer Answers will vary but may include speaking with a loud voice.

Another channel of communication is the written word. On the job, many messages are delivered in the form of e-mail, letters, memoranda, and reports. The participants write messages and read each other's messages.

■ Feedback

Feedback is the receiver's response to the message. When your employer explains your part in a new advertising program, you will probably ask some questions. This is feedback. You may restate some of your employer's words to assure that you understand the message. Feedback is important in communication because it allows participants to clarify the message and know that both (or all) parties gave the same meaning to the message.

When reading reports, you have little opportunity for feedback. You can respond to a letter or memorandum, but it takes more time than it would to give feedback in a conversation. E-mail is fast, but it doesn't allow for reading body language. The greatest opportunity for feedback is in a face-to-face conversation with another person.

■ Blocks

Blocks interfere with understanding the message. The three primary blocks to understanding are *distractions, emotional blocks,* and *planning a response*. These will be discussed later in the chapter.

■ Setting

The setting is where communication takes place. Outdoor settings are varied and often hard to control. Indoor settings in a job situation may vary from a large hall to a small office. You may have control over choosing the room and arranging the furniture.

When you choose the setting for a group meeting, make sure that it is large enough to accommodate everyone who will attend. Arrange the chairs so that everyone can see the main speaker. Check to make sure there is adequate lighting. Make sure that you have the appropriate equipment, an electrical outlet, and an extension cord if you are giving a visual presentation. You may want to bring in coffee, water, and snacks.

When you are discussing something with one other person in a face-to-face conversation, a small room is more comfortable than a large one. You will also be more comfortable in your own workplace

Look Into My Eyes

Stand tall with your head up and look at someone straight in the eye! This could be the typical advice given to a young person in North America before the first day of school or a job interview. Eye contact is expected—and respected—in the United States, where it is a sign of confidence and ease. In countries like Japan and Korea, however, young people are trained to avert their eyes during a conversation. It is believed that direct eye contact is intimidating and overbearing.

Thinking Critically

What are some other communication norms in the United States that could be misinterpreted by people from another culture?

than in someone else's. If you want to make a person feel comfortable in a conversation, go to his or her workplace.

Listening

You have learned that about 70 percent of your waking hours are spent communicating. Studies show that approximately 45 percent of that time is spent listening. Unfortunately, some people never learn the difference between hearing and listening. Hearing is primarily a physical process that takes place in the ears. Listening is a mental process that requires using the brain to assimilate information gathered.

■ Listening Skills

Learning to use listening skills is a vital part of being an effective communicator. Listening skills help you understand the messages you receive. These skills involve knowing what to listen for and what to think about as you listen. These same skills can be applied to understanding written messages.

GREAT IDEAS **from the Marketing Classroom**

Tammie Carlson
Tri-County Technology Center
Bartlesville, OK

Trade places with your students and let them be the teacher. Cooperative learning is utilized as students work together to achieve chapter objectives. I have my students work in small groups of two or three to plan, produce, and deliver an assigned chapter per team. I allow the team to use the Teacher Wraparound Edition, technology resources, and guest speakers to assist them. Each member of the team must participate in the presentation. The "teachers" and the students take exams to ensure the objectives have been achieved. Allowing your students to teach each other enhances communication skills and self-esteem.

IDENTIFYING THE PURPOSE You should always know the purpose of a meeting that has been scheduled to discuss a particular topic before the speaker begins to talk. When meeting with customers, you may not have advance notice of the purpose of the message. Then you have to identify the purpose from the content of the message. The sooner you can do this, the easier it will be for you to understand the whole message.

LOOKING FOR A PLAN When you listen to a structured speech, try to identify a plan of presentation. This makes it easier to see the different parts of the message fit together to convey the whole message. Sometimes a speaker makes generalizations and then supports them with specific evidence. The speaker may use contrasts and comparisons or show cause-and-effect relationships. When you know the plan, you can often anticipate what the speaker will say next. You will also be able to sort out the relevant and irrelevant information.

Face-to-face conversations between two (or even several) people are usually not as well planned as a formal speech. In these informal conversations, as long as you know the purpose of the message, it is not important to know the plan.

GIVING FEEDBACK If you are conversing with another person or even in a small group, give feedback to show whether you understand the message. Without interrupting, you can nod your head, raise an eyebrow, or frown. You may have an opportunity to ask questions when the speaker pauses. When the speaker has completed the message, summarize your understanding of it in your mind. Ask the speaker for clarification if you think that it is possible that your understanding of the message is different from that intended by the sender.

SEARCHING FOR AN INTEREST On the job, many of the messages you receive from your employer or from co-workers will relate to your job performance. Since you want to succeed at your job, show an interest in anything that will improve your performance.

You may attend meetings or conferences where the messages seem uninteresting and you want to tune them out. This can become a habit that will cause you to miss important information. Remember, you can learn valuable information from even the most uninteresting message. Listen carefully to find something that applies to you or interests you.

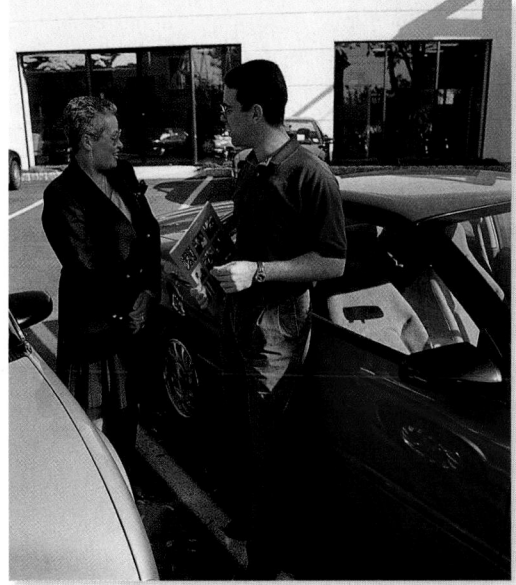

■ **All Ears!** Good salespeople are good listeners. *How can this salesman show that he understands what the customer is telling him?*

EVALUATING THE MESSAGE There are times for listening with empathy and times for listening and making judgments. You must be able to distinguish which type of listening is appropriate in every situation.

A friend may express the need to share his or her innermost feelings with you; this is a time to listen with empathy and understanding. Making judgments would be inappropriate.

In most other conversations and when listening to messages, making judgments can help you listen with understanding. Your mind becomes more actively involved in the listening process when you make logical judgments. You will not understand messages you do not like if you let your emotions get in the way. Always keep an open mind.

As you listen, evaluate the validity of the message. Try to distinguish between fact and opinion and evaluate whether the information presented is relevant to the purpose of the message.

LISTENING FOR MORE THAN VERBAL CONTENT There is usually more to the speaker's message than the meaning of the words. The manner in which the speech is delivered affects the meaning of the message. The rate of speech, pitch, volume, and

CAPTION ANSWER
All Ears! He can tell the customer what he understood her to say and ask if his understanding is correct. Giving feedback also shows if he understands the message.

Cooperative Learning

Written and Verbal Communication Create a paragraph of 3–4 sentences that is somewhat complex. Ask for three volunteers (A, B, and C) to leave the room. Distribute a copy of the paragraph to all remaining students in the class so each can read it carefully. Ask for a volunteer to summarize this paragraph and pass on the information to one of the students who will come in the room. Bring in Student A, and have the student that read the paragraph now relate the information in his/her own words to Student A. Then bring in Student B and have Student A relate the information. Then bring in Student C and have Student B relate the information. By this time, the oral message barely resembles the original written message. Now re-read aloud the original paragraph. Ask students: What could have been done to keep the message intact? How might this affect communication in the workplace?

Independent Practice

Write and Discuss Have students write examples of body language in which physical actions and positions of the body communicate thoughts and tell what they mean. *(Some examples are smile, frown, hands on hips, clapping hands, raised index finger, furrowed brow, eyes closed, etc.)* Remind students that such nonverbal cues can be positive or negative, depending on the person and the situation. Allow students time to record these on paper, and then begin a list on the board drawing from the students' examples. Have students provide examples of how body language can positively and negatively affect one's actions. Discuss the importance for a marketer to not only read and interpret these situational examples, but also to use body language with customers, vendors, and coworkers.

Communication Skills

L1 Have students photocopy and read a 200-word, business-related or marketing-related article from a newspaper or magazine. Then, have them complete the following:

• The purpose of this article is _____.

• Another title for this article could be _____.

• List the vocabulary words and the jargon that you could not figure out by the way terms are used. List the meaning you found in the dictionary for each term.

• Did you know anything about the subject of this article before you read it? Did it help you understand the article better?

L2 Have students outline a 200-word business- or marketing-related article.

L3 Have students find two articles on the same business- or marketing-related subject and compare and contrast the two pieces. Ask students: How did understanding the first article help them evaluate the second article?

ASSESS

Reteaching

1. **Vocabulary** Assign and review the vocabulary terms for this section.
2. **Fact and Idea** Assign and review Fact and Idea Review questions 1–6 from the Chapter Assessment.
3. **Communication Process** Using the vocabulary words and the chapter content for Section 8.1, have students draw a simple diagram of the communication process and label each part. Allow them to draw a diagram of the process using any types of symbols.

REAL WORLD MARKETING

Hello Kitty!

Hello Kitty, the tiny Japanese ambassador of friendship, is only one of the popular Sanrio characters that draws huge annual sales. Sanrio has been developing a social communication business since 1960 that ranges from novelty items and greeting cards to apparel and accessories. "In order to get along with one another, we need to respect and love," said Shintaro Tsuji, Sanrio's President and CEO. "Whether one is sad, down, happy or whatever . . . We want people to share these important feelings with one another," adds Tsuji. Mr. Tsuji shouldn't be feeling sad or down based on his company's record annual revenue of over $1 billion!

Thinking Critically
What businesses might be a logical extension of Sanrio's social communication business?

voice quality can add and change meaning. Some experts estimate that 40 percent of the meaning of oral communication is due to vocal cues—not the actual words spoken but the way they are said.

LISTENING FOR A CONCLUSION Listen for the speaker's conclusion. You may want or need to take action based on it. You can summarize the main points and then draw your own conclusion if you don't let your emotions get in the way. Don't jump to a conclusion before the speaker has presented the facts or opinions to support it.

TAKING NOTES Always take notes on the main points presented in a business meeting. Employers appreciate employees who care enough to write down what is being discussed. It may be necessary to refer back to these notes at a later time.

FOLLOWING DIRECTIONS It is important to listen carefully when someone gives you directions. Be sure you understand each step if there is more than one. Give frequent feedback to the person instructing you so that he or she knows you have understood each step.

REAL WORLD MARKETING

Hello Kitty!
Answer Answers will vary but could include anything from flower and food delivery to long distance telecommunication services using its animal brands.

■ Blocks to Listening with Understanding

Some things interfere with or *block* effective listening. Avoid these blocks, and you will be able to concentrate on the message.

Distractions are blocks to effective listening that include noises, environmental factors, interruptions by other people, and competing thoughts that creep into your mind. To avoid a distraction, you may decide to move to a different area or even postpone a meeting. Most messages that you receive on the job will be important. Exercise the discipline necessary to keep your mind on the message despite distractions.

Emotional blocks are biases against the opinions expressed by the sender that prevent you from understanding. It is especially important to listen and understand, even when you don't agree with the sender's ideas. Otherwise, you will not be able to give a meaningful response.

Planning a response blocks understanding because you can't concentrate on the message and your response at the same time. When the speaker says something that you want to respond to, it's tempting to think about your response and tune out the speaker. You may miss some key points in the message if you do this and respond inappropriately. Listen to the entire message before you plan your response.

Reading

Reading, like listening, is a process of trying to understand a message. Reading with understanding is a necessity in every career. Even when applying for a job you have to read Help-Wanted ads, whether online or in print.

■ Knowing the Purpose of Your Reading

You will be a more efficient reader if you know why you are reading before you begin. When you read a novel or magazine, you are reading for pleasure. You can read as fast or as slowly as you want. When you read a job application form or a company memo, you have to read every word for complete understanding.

Reading for Meaning

One of the many things required to succeed on the job is reading and understanding written messages. These three skills can help you: focusing your mind, forming pictures, and improving your vocabulary.

No one's mind focuses on a subject automatically. Your mind will *focus* only through constant concentration. When you don't concentrate, the message will be unclear. Monitor your thoughts when you read, and if your mind wanders, refocus on the subject.

It can be difficult sometimes to comprehend the written word without other visual aids. A message may be easier to understand when you see elements of the message in your mind. Try to *form pictures* of the people, places, things, and situations described when you read.

You may come across words that are unfamiliar when reading. Skipping over these unfamiliar words may cause you to miss key points in the message. Try to figure out the meaning by the way the word is used in the sentence or paragraph and then look up the word in a dictionary. This will *improve your vocabulary* and broaden your understanding of written communication.

You will come across some technical terms called jargon in your job-related reading. Jargon is technical or specialized vocabulary used by members of a particular profession or industry. Many of these words aren't even listed in most dictionaries. Most marketing jobs have their own jargon, which you will learn as you study this book.

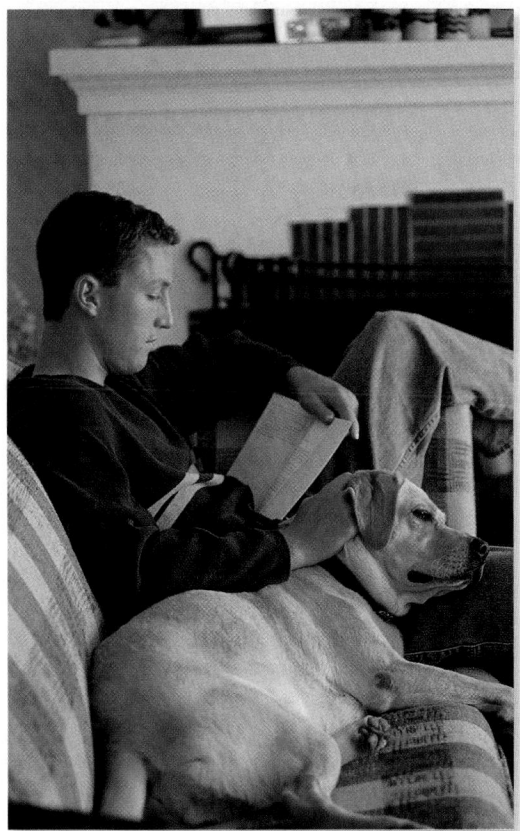

■ **A Novel Experience** Good reading skills are necessary in almost all careers. *How is this young man developing good job skills?*

8.1 ASSESSMENT

Reviewing Key Terms and Concepts

1. What are the six primary elements of communication?
2. How would you arrange the setting for a business meeting?
3. What listening skills can help you better understand messages you receive?
4. What are three blocks to listening with understanding?
5. What are three skills you need to read better?

Thinking Critically

6. Describe an appropriate setting for an in-home cosmetics presentation and for a stockbroker's meeting. How and why should the two settings be different?

Integrating Academic Skills

7. **COMMUNICATION** Watch the television or a video with the sound turned off. Make a list of the nonverbal messages you observe. What can you interpret from them?

Chapter 8 ■ *Communication Skills* **143**

SECTION 8.1

Enrichment

Extend Assign and review the appropriate activities from *BusinessWeek Case Studies, Internet Resources,* and the *School-to-Work Activity Workbook.* **ILP**

Evaluation

Assign and review the Section 8.1 Assessment.

Technology Resources

 Assessment Resources
Go to the *Marketing Essentials* Web site (**www.marketing.glencoe. com**) for resources to teach and assess occupation-specific vocabulary.

VIRTUAL BUSINESS

 Talking Business
Introduce business communications to students using Knowledge Matters' Virtual Business visual simulation, "Entrepreneurship—Talking Business." Students learn to communicate verbally about business by managing a store in relay-race fashion. If needed, have students run the Virtual Business tutorial before beginning the activity. For additional instructions and teaching tips for this simulation, go to the *Marketing Essentials* Web site (**www.marketing.glencoe.com**).

CLOSE

Section Wrap-Up

Ask students to give you definitions for this section's vocabulary words without looking at their books.

CAPTION ANSWER
A Novel Experience Reading for pleasure and enjoyment helps to develop the skills necessary to understand written messages.

143

8.1 ASSESSMENT ANSWERS

Reviewing Key Terms and Concepts

1. senders and receivers, messages, channels, feedback, blocks, and setting
2. Choose a room. Arrange chairs; check for lighting; arrange for/check equipment.
3. identify purpose and plan, give feedback; search for interest; evaluate message; listen for more than verbal content; take notes; follow directions

4. distractions, emotional blocks, and planning a response
5. focus mind, form pictures, improve vocabulary

Thinking Critically

6. Answers will vary.

Integrating Academic Skills

7. **COMMUNICATION** Lists and answers will vary.

Elements of Speech and Writing

FOCUS

Bell Ringer Activity

Brainstorm Tell students to imagine that a friendly space alien is here to visit the class. The space alien can understand English. However, she has no understanding of the concept of shoes. No one on her planet wears them because all of the soil there is sandy and soft; there are no hard floors or cement streets. Obviously, she must wear shoes while here on earth to protect her tender feet. The students are to decide what type of shoes she would be most comfortable wearing. Then have the students help you generate the following: (a) a succinct definition for shoes so the alien understands the concept; (b) a list of instructions that tell her how to put on her shoes; and (c) tips for taking good care of her shoes.

Introducing the Section

Elements of Speech and Writing Marketing jobs often require supervisors to train employees in tasks in which the employees have little prior on-the-job experience. It takes clear communication and empathy to not only train employees but also to deal with customers from other cultures who may not understand English well. The Bell Ringer Activity may have taken students longer than they expected and might have prompted some disagreement, as well as a good discussion.

Have students answer the following questions: What was the purpose of this communication? *(to inform)* How could you use your voice and body language to let the alien know you are friendly and sincerely want to help? *(Use a pleasant, relaxed voice and non-defensive body language.)*

144

• What You'll Learn

- The three most common purposes for speaking
- The four basic patterns for organizing a formal speech
- The four-step method for training
- Parliamentary procedure and its purposes
- Proper telephone skills
- The three basic considerations in writing

• Why It's Important

You will use spoken and written communication on every job throughout your life. In large part, the success you attain in your career will depend on how well you speak and write.

Key Terms

- parliamentary procedure
- quorum

Speaking

Many jobs in marketing require above-average speaking skills. Whatever your job, you will need to express yourself clearly so your employer, customers, and co-workers can understand the messages you want to send.

■ Knowing the Purpose

Before you decide what you will say, know the purpose of the message you want to send. In most cases, you will speak to inform, persuade, or entertain.

In most casual conversations and business meetings, the main purpose of speaking is to *inform*. Participants exchange information, frequently changing roles from sender to receiver and back again. When speaking to inform, get to the point clearly and concisely.

In any job, there will be times when you will need to *persuade* others to see or do things a certain way. Perhaps the most important skill in persuading others is determining the listeners' needs and showing how you can satisfy at least some of those needs. This is a salesperson's most important skill. You will look at this more closely in Unit 5.

Sometimes the purpose of speaking is to *entertain* others. Salespeople frequently need to entertain clients. It is not necessary to be a comedian to enjoy joking and telling stories. This kind of informal speaking helps create a friendly and comfortable atmosphere.

■ Using Your Voice

You will need to use your voice effectively to be a good communicator. With practice, you can develop a pleasant voice that is neither too high nor too low. Your voice will sound relaxed if you speak in a medium, even tone.

Speak loudly enough to be heard without blasting your listeners. Vary your inflections by stressing certain words and syllables. Variations of speed and loudness will help you communicate your message in an interesting way.

■ Speaking Formally

Many jobs in marketing will require you to inform or persuade others with structured messages, or *oral presentations*. The use of good body language (gestures, movements, and mannerisms) and eye contact with your listeners are necessary skills for an effective presentation.

A formal speech begins with an opening statement and concludes with a closing statement. In between, there are four basic patterns you may use to organize a structured message.

Classroom Resources

For the Teacher
- Teacher Editions for all workbooks
- Assessment Package
- PowerPoint Presentation Software
- Interactive Lesson Planner
- ILP Block Scheduling, p. 4
- ILP Lesson Plans, p. 17
- ILP Internet Resources, p. 35

- ILP Blackline Masters, p. 21
- ILP *BusinessWeek* Case Studies, p. 49
- ILP Marketing Career Portfolio, p. 34
- *Marketing Essentials* Web site (**www.marketing.glencoe.com**)

For the Student
- Student Activity Workbook, p. 63
- Marketing Math Workbook, p. 19

- Marketing Research Project Workbook, p. 47
- ILP School-to-Work Activity Workbook, p. 29
- Virtual Business simulation
- *Marketing Essentials* Web site (**www.marketing.glencoe.com**)

ILP These resources are available in print and on the Interactive Lesson Planner (ILP)

■ **Key Words in the Sale**
Enumerating the features of a package ski vacation to these customers gives them many reasons to want to buy. *What signal words can the travel agent use to make clear the number of reasons to buy a vacation?*

ENUMERATION *Enumeration* is listing several items in order. When instructing a new worker on how to perform a certain task, you may begin by saying, "There are four steps in performing this task." The new worker will listen for four separate but related things to do. The steps will be easier to understand because the listener is expecting them. Use *signal words,* such as *first, second, third,* or *next,* to help the listener. These signal words show the relationship between what you have already said and what you will say next.

GENERALIZATION WITH EXAMPLE Many speakers use *generalizations*—statements that are accepted as true by most people—to make a point. They support the generalizations with examples and evidence to show that the statement is true. When you make a general statement such as, "Everybody agrees that high definition television has the best picture quality and will soon take over the market," you should back it up with "A Sony survey reported 80 percent of owners say the picture clarity is worth the higher price." Using evidence to support your generalization clarifies your message and helps your listeners remember the main points. Signal words, such as *for instance* and *for example,* can help get your point across.

CAUSE AND EFFECT When you discuss an issue in terms of cause and effect, you lead the listener from the cause of something to the effect. This is an effective way to explain many topics. You can reverse this method by first presenting the effect and then considering possible causes. Use signal words, such as *therefore, consequently,* and *as a result.*

COMPARE AND CONTRAST It may be most efficient to explain something using the compare and contrast method. You can explain new concepts by showing how they are similar to or unlike those your listeners already know. Use signal words, such as *similarly, however, nevertheless,* and *on the other hand.*

■ Training

Training involves a specialized form of speaking and is usually combined with showing one or more other people how to perform a particular task.

When you are responsible for training others, you will find that the following four-step training plan is effective in almost all training situations. First, explain the task that is to be performed. Second, demonstrate how to perform the task—by actually doing it yourself. Third, let the other person or persons try doing the task. Finally, provide a critique that explains what was done correctly and discusses the strong points so the trainee will feel accomplished. After this encouragement, discuss the changes that should be made to perform the task properly and completely. Make the trainee feel as though it is a cooperative effort. This will motivate him or her to improve and minimize any feelings of inadequacy.

Chapter 8 ■ *Communication Skills* **145**

CAPTION ANSWER
Key Words in the Sale Agent can list features numerically, using signal words like *first, second, third* to offer clear reasons why this vacation spot is the best choice.

Thinking Critically

1. Purpose of Communication

Ask students whether the purpose of each message that follows is to inform, entertain, or persuade. (Each message may have more than one purpose.)

- a sales presentation to a customer *(to inform and to persuade)*
- a report to your supervisor on ways to improve your department's customer service *(to inform and possibly to persuade if you want your supervisor to take your recommendations)*
- beginning a speech with a funny anecdote *(to entertain and catch people's attention, which will thus persuade them to listen more closely)*

2. Basic Statement Patterns

Ask students to identify which of the basic patterns for organizing a structured statement (enumeration, generalization with example, cause and effect, and comparison and contrast) each of the following statements illustrates:

- Sales for the year are down due to international economic problems. As a result, employee layoffs will occur. *(cause and effect)*
- There are four steps in tying your shoes. First, take one lace in each hand. Second, place the right lace under the left. Third, loop the left lace under the right. Fourth, tie the ends of the right and left lace into a knot. *(enumeration)*
- In the past, if guests at the Ocean Point Hotel lost their room key, they had to pay a $10 charge to have the room re-keyed. Now, however, the new keyless entry system eliminates that inconvenience for guests. *(comparison and contrast)*

■ Parliamentary Procedure

If you have ever been a member of a student organization like the student council, you are probably familiar with parliamentary procedure. **Parliamentary procedure** is a structure for holding group meetings and making decisions. It is meant to make meetings democratic and decision-making orderly. Parliamentary procedure favors the opinion of the majority of a group. However, this does not mean that the viewpoint of the minority is overlooked. Every issue that comes up is discussed freely and thoroughly before a final decision is reached. Parliamentary procedure is used in government, business, and social clubs. The rules that govern it vary depending on the contexts. Certain elements, however, are almost always present. Learning about them will help prepare you for formal business meetings.

A QUORUM In order for business to be conducted at a meeting, there must be a quorum. A **quorum** is a proportion of the membership needed to conduct official business. The organization's constitution usually covers what a quorum must be. It may be a set number, like 20, or a percentage of members, like 51 percent.

ORDER OF BUSINESS The meeting follows a standard *order of business*, which is called an agenda. The standard format for a meeting is as follows:

1. *Call to order* The president or chairperson opens the meeting by saying, for example "I now call this meeting to order." This statement alerts all members that the meeting is beginning and that they should be quiet. The chairperson's job is to make sure the meeting runs according to the rules.

2. *Minutes of the meeting* The secretary reads the minutes, which are a written record that outlines the decisions made at the last meeting. The minutes also cover such information as the date and time of the previous meeting and the members who were in attendance. The president or chairperson asks all members if there are any additions or corrections to the minutes. The minutes are accepted as a permanent record of the organization if there are no corrections.

3. *Treasurer's report* The treasurer reports the money that the organization received since the last meeting and the money it spent, as well as the current balance.

4. *Committee reports* Committees are set up in organizations to do research or plan events. Each committee presents a report at a meeting to let the entire membership know what they have done and what they plan to do. Committees that exist year after year are called *standing committees*. Other committees may be established as the need arises. Some standing committees for a local DECA chapter may oversee fund raising or civic-minded projects.

BRIGHT IDEAS
Mouse Potatoes

You've all heard the term couch potatoes, but have you ever heard of a "mouse potato"? Well La-Z-Boy recliner chair manufacturers certainly have. Their latest product—the La-Z-Boy Explorer "e-cliner"—was created with the mouse potato in mind. This comfy recliner lets customers kick back their legs to relax with their computer at their fingertips on the special keyboard tray. The chair also includes a power outlet, a storage tray in the right arm, as well as a WebTV hookup with a two-month free subscription. Mouse potatoes can kick back as they surf the Web, check their stocks, and watch television all from the comfort of their recliner.

Thinking Creatively

The Internet has already made life more convenient for many people. What are other ways that using the Internet can be simplified even more?

BRIGHT IDEAS Mouse Potatoes

Answer Answers will vary but should include high technology possibilities related to the wireless Web.

Did You Know?

The term *quorum* comes from the Latin "of whom." In modern legal language, a quorum is defined as the specific number of persons needed to act on behalf of a committee, board of directors, shareholders, or legislative bodies. For example, in order for a law to pass in Congress, a specific number of representatives must vote or the vote is not valid.

■ **Parliamentary Procedure** Parliamentary procedure allows formal meetings to run smoothly, making sure there is a time for all that needs to be discussed. *Why would it be important to read the minutes of the last meeting before moving on to important topics?*

Communication Skills

Robert's Rules of Order by Henry M. Robert is the classic guide to parliamentary procedure. Bring three or four copies to class.

L1 Divide students into three or four groups. Give each group a copy of *Robert's Rules*, and have students find definitions for the following terms:

- acclamation
- aye
- ballot
- call to question
- Chair
- Convene
- have the floor
- motion
- nay
- point of order
- second table

L2 Using *Robert's Rules*, have groups of students find definitions for the following types of motions:

- motion to reconsider
- motion to postpone
- motion to limit/extend debate
- motion to table
- motion to appeal
- motion to withdraw

L3 Have students hold a meeting on a relevant group project. Take notes on the things students do well and on the areas in which they need to improve. Ask these questions:

- If one of you decided to abstain from voting on an issue, would that vote go with the minority or the majority? *(the majority)*

- What happens to a motion if no one seconds it? *(It dies.)*

National DECA (www.deca.org) offers a concise booklet called *Guide for DECA Chapter Officers.* It provides a good synopsis of parliamentary procedures, motions, and orders of business.

5. *Old business* Any issues that were discussed at the previous meeting but were not decided on become old business. Old business is reported at this point in the meeting.

6. *New business* New ideas that members would like to have considered are brought up at the end of the meeting. It is important to discuss only one new issue at a time.

7. *Adjournment* The president or chairperson entertains a motion to adjourn the meeting. If accepted, this is the official end of the meeting. The secretary records the time of adjournment in the minutes.

THE MOTION After being recognized, or allowed to speak by the chairperson, one member makes a *motion*, or a proposal. Then, another member must *second* the motion. A period of discussion follows when a motion has been made and seconded. If no one seconds the motion, it is not discussed. The procedure of making and accepting motions is one

that can be formal or informal. The formal method calls for much discussion and must repeat the motion, call for a discussion, establish the voting time, and announce the result. In other cases, when a move motion is used, the chair may adopt the policy of *general consent*. In this case, the chair will introduce an issue and propose the logical action that could be taken. He or she would then ask if there were any objections; if not, this would be the decision of the group. This is most often used when discussing issues that are not controversial or sensitive. Once a member is recognized by the chairperson, he or she has the right to speak for a certain length of time without being interrupted. Only one member is permitted to speak at a time to assure that each person is heard. When the time for discussion is up, the chairperson asks for a vote. This is known as *calling the question*. A majority vote is usually enough to *win adoption*, otherwise known as *carrying the motion*.

Chapter 8 ■ *Communication Skills* **147**

Cooperative Learning

Telephone Skills Have students review the section on Telephone Skills while you write these situations on the board:

- An irate customer calls to complain that the new car you sold her two months ago has been in the repair shop four different times.
- A non-English speaking customer, who lives about ten miles away, calls to ask for directions to your store.

Divide students into pairs. Have each pair choose one of the above situations and generate a five-minute phone conversation between the caller and the receiver. Then have each pair role play the script for the class. Let the class be the judge of how effectively each situation was handled and give suggestions on alternative ways of handling the situation.

A Prescription for Success

Is there a doctor in the house? If you have Internet access the answer is "yes." An increasing number of doctors today are making house calls: E-mail house calls, that is. Patients can log onto Web sites like AmericasDoctor.com and ask questions and chat with physicians. With long lines in doctors' offices, restrictive HMO plans, and overbooked doctors, the patient/doctor relationship has suffered. The Internet has helped to bridge the communication gap between patients and doctors. Physicians with their own Web sites believe that this new mode of communication helps inform and educate patients and improves upon the health-care experience.

Thinking Critically

Why are reading and writing skills crucial to Internet physician communication?

Telephone Skills

If you take a job in marketing, you will probably speak to many people on the telephone. A pleasant voice is even more important on the telephone than in face-to-face conversations. Your listener can't see you, so you can't rely on facial expressions and body language to help get your message across.

Answer the telephone with a cheerful but formal greeting. Your greeting should also confirm with the caller that he or she has reached the right number. Working in customer relations, you might say, "Customer relations, this is Maria, how may I help you?"

Use a pleasant tone, enunciate clearly, and speak directly into the mouthpiece. Speak loudly enough for the other person to hear, but don't shout. Listen as well on the telephone as you do in a face-to-face conversation. Develop the habit of being courteous and never interrupt when the other person is speaking.

Be prepared to take a message. Have a pencil and paper ready to write down the time of the call, the

caller's name and message, and the return phone number. Repeat the telephone number to the caller to make sure it is correct. Some businesses have phone logs in which to record every incoming call.

Writing

Writing a message takes more time and thought than simply having a conversation, but there are times when it is more appropriate. Writing a message helps you organize your thoughts.

Many people forget most of the message in a conversation within 24 hours, but a written message is a permanent record. It's hard to ignore a written message. The person receiving it is more likely to take appropriate action than if the same message were delivered in a conversation.

■ Basic Considerations in Writing

In every type of writing, it is important to know the precise reason for which you are writing a message. Three basic considerations when writing are to know your reader, know your purpose, and know your subject.

Before you begin writing even your first draft, think about how well you *know your reader*. Who are the people who will receive your message? Why will they read your message? What do they know about the subject? These answers will help you to write a more meaningful message.

The second consideration before you begin writing your message is that you *know your purpose*. Most of your writing will be done to inform, request, confirm, persuade, inquire, or complain. Some messages, of course, combine two or more of these purposes.

You will need to *know your subject* well to write a clear message about it. You may be well-educated on particular subjects for your job, but sometimes further research will be necessary.

■ Developing a Writing Style

The executives of a company generally establish the writing style. You can read company letters, e-mail, memos, and reports before writing any yourself to help you determine your company's style.

The trend in business writing is toward a direct, conversational style. Remember, you are writing to

A Prescription for Success

Answer Reading and writing skills are crucial because medical information is critical to patient's health. Doctors must be able to interpret written communication and respond to patients with direct written communication.

More About . . .

Using Your Voice
The phone presents special challenges to those who work in a multicultural environment. Native speakers of English need to think about how some idiomatic expressions sound to those who are not native speakers of English, and practice refraining from gum chewing and speaking idiomatically when they answer phones in a business setting.

Case Study

"Soft Skills" Work!

When the U. S. and global economies are doing well, there is considerable competition for good employees. Companies must develop strategies to hold on to them. Making sure managers and employees are proficient at "soft skills" gives a real boost.

The term "soft skills" refers to interpersonal skills that managers use when problem solving and supervising employees. Employees are more loyal when their managers have good interpersonal skills. Effective communication and teamwork skills are also essential in today's team-based organizations. Schools or private training companies that provide training in these soft skills are enjoying a boom in the 21st century.

Many companies are training their lower-level employees in soft skills as well. Companies have discovered that teams that are low in technical skills but work well together are more productive than teams with good technical skills but poor teamwork.

Companies still save money despite training expenses. One study showed that training current employees saved $12,000 per worker over hiring new employees. Training managers to be more sensitive to employees' needs gives companies an edge in holding on to their best employees—those who could find work anywhere.

Case Study Review

1. How are personal skills important in raising productivity?
2. Is it more important for workers or managers to take soft skills training? Defend your position.

A MATTER OF ETHICS

3. If someone has great technical skills and works harder than his co-workers but has a terrible temper and can't get along with anyone, do you think it is ethical to fire him? Why or why not?

---

communicate a message to one or more receivers. Use a crisp, clear style that is easy to read. Don't use extensive vocabulary to impress others. Use a word processing program with spelling and grammar checkers to eliminate common errors. You should always review the letter one final time to ensure that no mistakes were overlooked.

Personalize your message by using the name of the person who will receive it. The receiver will have a warmer feeling toward you if you do.

You may need to use some jargon in your messages to people in your career field. However, avoid jargon when you can or explain any jargon you must use when writing to those outside your field.

Independent Practice

1. **Research and Write** Have students look through the local want ads for jobs that interest them, preferably in marketing and sales. Each student should choose one for which they might like to apply, then write a formal letter of application that incorporates the eight standard parts of a business letter pictured in Figure 8-1. Instruct the students to write the letters as though they have the relevant experience, discussing the reasons why they are suitable for the job.

2. **Research and Report** Have students research the Internet and prepare a written report for rules of e-mail etiquette, often referred to as *Netiquette*. Students should include suggestions for how best to insure the effectiveness of e-mail.

Case Study Review Answers

"Soft Skills" Work!

1. Answers will vary. People who work together well don't waste time, find solutions to problems more quickly, are more cooperative with management requests.
2. Answers will vary.

A MATTER OF ETHICS

3. Answers will vary.

FIGURE 8-1

BUSINESS LETTERS

 ost business letters include eight standard parts.

1

The return address is the address of the letter writer. Most companies have their addresses printed on stationery called letterhead. When you type a business letter on blank paper, type the return address at the top of the page.

3

The inside address is the name and address of the person who will receive the letter. The same address is typed on the envelope.

11061 West Olympic Boulevard Los Angeles, California 90064

2

The date line shows the reader when the letter was written. In business, it is important to document when you write a letter.

August 30, 2002

Mr. Dan Provost
Super Sports Magazine
3119 South Barrington Avenue
Suite G
Los Angeles, CA 90066

Dear Mr. Provost:

4

The salutation is the greeting. The most commonly used salutation is, "Dear (Mr., Mrs., Miss, Ms.)." If you usually call the person by his or her first name, you can use it in the salutation: "Dear Adam." If you are not sending the letter to a specific person, make the salutation to the department to which you are sending the letter: "Dear Customer Service Department." A colon always follows the salutation in a business letter.

5

The body is the message of the letter.

Today we received your written request for four (4) reams of Pale Yellow 24-pound writing bond. We are ordering it for you from our supplier, who promises to have it to us in five (5) days. I will call you as soon as it comes in.

Thank you for thinking of Southland for your office supply needs. We look forward to filling this order and to doing business with you in the future.

Sincerely yours,

Jessica H. Johnston

Jessica H. Johnston, Manager

jhj/ktb

6

The closing is a respectful goodbye. Formal closings for business letters are, "Yours very truly" and "Yours truly." Less formal, more friendly closings are, "Sincerely" and "Cordially." A comma should follow the closing.

7

The signature block includes the handwritten and typed name of the writer. Sign your name in ink above your typed name. Write both your first and last name, unless you are on a first-name basis with the reader.

8

The reference initials are the initials of the writer and sometimes the initials of the typist. They are typed two spaces below your typed signature, beginning at the left margin. The writer's initials are always typed first.

THE DECA CONNECTION

COMPETITIVE EVENTS AND MARKETING ESSENTIALS

Public Relations and Communication Skills DECA's Public Relations Project is an excellent competitive event to allow your students to demonstrate both their written and oral communication skills. This project is a chapter project that involves the planning, organizing, implementation, and evaluation of a public relations campaign conducted by your students.

The students' written communication skills are expanded by the completion of a 30-page report evaluating the public relations campaign's planning, organization, and implementation. Oral communication skills are put to use in preparing for a 15-minute presentation made to a businessperson/judge explaining their public relations campaign.

Letters, E-mail, Memos, and Reports

There are many types of written communications. In business, most written messages are in the form of letters, e-mail, memos, or reports.

The main form of written communication with people outside your own company will be business letters. Business letters are always typed or word processed and printed on a laser printer (see Figure 8-1 on page 150).

In recent years, e-mail has become the method of choice for fast communication with both those inside and outside of your own company. In many companies, it has almost replaced memos for in-house communication (see Figure 8-2).

E-mail has advantages over other means of written communication because messages are sent immediately. This ensures that urgent messages will be received in a timely manner. It is also cost-effective and environmentally friendly, as no paper is used.

An interoffice e-mail typically contains:

- An informative subject title
- A traditional (not personal) greeting
- A concise, clearly stated body of text
- A statement regarding the type of response needed
- A formal closing and signature (for the signature, type your name, company, address, phone and fax number, and e-mail address)

Although e-mail has a reputation for speed and informality, it is important to compose your e-mail messages carefully. E-mails should have a style appropriate to the situation and conventional business language. Any information that pertains to issues other than those stated in the subject field should be sent in different e-mails.

One of the greatest dangers of business e-mail is that it is often treated informally. E-mail should not be considered private. In fact, it should be considered more permanent than traditional letters, memos, and reports because it will continue to exist in digital form long after it has been deleted or erased from a hard drive. This is because companies store many backups of every computer's hard drive in many places.

When the U.S. Justice Department pursued antitrust charges against Microsoft in 1998 and 1999, the evidence against Microsoft was in the form of millions of pages of internal e-mails. Because of this, more and more companies are developing strict e-mail policies. The following are some general rules found in most e-mail policies:

- Only save essential e-mail
- Don't forward e-mail without the sender's express permission
- Use extreme care when forwarding privileged e-mails
- Delete any copyrighted materials that you don't have permission to use

FIGURE 8-2

Business E-mail

From: Jessica H. Johnston <j.h.johnston@southlandoffice.net>
To: Dan Provost <danprovost@supersportsmagazine.org>
Date: Wednesday, August 30, 2002, 4:26 PM
Subject: Your request

Dear Mr. Provost,

Today we received your written request for four (4) reams of Pale Yellow 24-pound writing bond. We are ordering it for you from our supplier, who promises to have it in five (5) days. I will call you as soon as it comes in.

Thank you for thinking of Southland for your office supply needs. We look forward to filling this order and to doing business with you in the future.

Jessica H. Johnston

Jessica H. Johnston
Senior Manager
j.h.johnston@southlandoffice.net
Phone: (800) 867-5309
Fax: (888) 867-5309

■ **Business E-mail** E-mail is commonly used for communication within an office or company. Although e-mail has a reputation for speed and informality, it is important to compose your e-mail messages carefully. *Why do you think this is so?*

FIGURE 8-2 ANSWER
Business E-mail E-mail should not be considered private. It is more permanent than letters, memos, and reports because it exists in digital form on backup copies even after deletion from a hard drive.

ASSESS

Reteaching

1. **Vocabulary** Assign and review the vocabulary terms for this section.
2. **Fact and Idea** Assign and review Fact and Idea Review questions 7–10 from the Chapter Assessment.
3. **Communication Formats** Have students tell whether they would write a letter, memo, e-mail, or report in each of these situations:
   - an apology to a customer for poor customer service he or she received *(letter)*
   - a warning to all employees that company supplies and copying are not to be for personal use *(memo)* and
   - a request for product information from another company *(letter or e-mail)*

Enrichment

1. **Review** Assign and review the Chapter 8 activities in the *Student Activity Workbook.*
2. **Review** Assign and review the appropriate Thinking Critically questions from the Chapter Assessment.
3. **Review** Assign and review the following Chapter Assessment activities: Building Workplace Skills, Applying Marketing Concepts, Linking School to Work Activities, The DECA Connection Role Play, and Internet Connection.
4. **Write and Present** Assign students to write and deliver five-minute demonstration/training speeches. Students are to demonstrate or train the class on how to do something. Examples might be how to prepare a favorite food, fix a bicycle flat tire, leave a voice mail, etc. Require students to use a prop in the presentation.

Technology Resources

Assessment Resources
Go to the *Marketing Essentials* Web site (**www.marketing.glencoe. com**) for resources to teach and assess occupation-specific vocabulary.

VIRTUAL BUSINESS

Business Writing
Introduce business writing to students using Knowledge Matters' Virtual Business visual simulation, "Office Applications—Business Writing." Students start a store but then must pass it to another team to manage. They must give instructions using a written memo. If needed, have students run the Virtual Business tutorial before beginning the activity. For additional instructions and teaching tips for this simulation, go to the *Marketing Essentials* Web site (**www.marketing.glencoe.com**).

CLOSE

Section Wrap-Up

Have pairs of students write and deliver a four-line rhyming "ditty" about one of the topics in this section, such as speaking, training, telephone skills, and writing. *(An example for telephone skills is:*

> *For your business to grow*
> *It's important that you know*
> *To always keep a pleasant tone*
> *When speaking on the telephone)*

FIGURE 8-3 ANSWER
Memorandum Memos are usually within the company, therefore you know the person you are writing to, and informality is acceptable.

A memo, the abbreviation for memorandum, is a written message to someone in your company. It is usually brief and covers only one subject. Most memos are written in a simple format that has a standard set of headings. The standard headings include the sender's and receiver's names, the date, the subject, and then write your message in paragraph form. Look at the sample memo in Figure 8-3.

Business reports cover such topics as yearly sales, survey results, or problems that need attention. Some are called *in-house reports* because they are to be read only by company employees. Others, such as reports to stockholders, are written for a wider audience. An in-house report can be written by a company department to let management know the results of a project, or a report might move from one department to another. The sales department may produce a report to tell the design department how customers like a product. Several people may give input to produce the report, but one person is usually responsible for the final writing.

■ Company Publications

Many marketing companies produce internal publications for their employees. These might include employee handbooks that outline policies and procedures or newsletters. Companies also produce external publications, such as promotional brochures about the company or individual products. Internal publications are usually written by the corporate communications department, while external publications are often written by the marketing department.

FIGURE 8-3
Memorandum

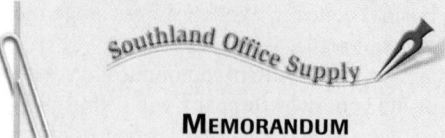

MEMORANDUM

To: All Office Employees
From: Jessica Johnston
Subject: Filling Special Stationery Requests
Date: August 30, 20--

Over the last three weeks, we have received three (3) customer requests for 24-pound writing bond in unusual colors that *we do not regularly stock.* Please fill any such orders from South Bay Suppliers in Santa Monica at 391-4300.

Let me know if you have any questions.

JHJ

■ **Memorandum** Memos are used for communication within an office or company. Their format is more informal than a business letter. *Why do you think this is so?*

8.2 ASSESSMENT

Reviewing Key Terms and Concepts

1. What are the three most common purposes for speaking?
2. What are the four basic patterns used to organize a spoken message?
3. What is parliamentary procedure? Why is it used?
4. What types of information should you write down when taking a telephone message?
5. What are the three basic things you should consider when writing?

Thinking Critically

6. Your co-worker has asked you to review a letter he has written to a customer. What elements will you look for in his business letter?

Integrating Academic Skills

7. **MATH** To send a fax anywhere in the United States, a local business charges $4 for the first page and $1 for subsequent pages. If a fax machine costs $600 to purchase, how many single-page documents could you send commercially for the same price?

8.2 ASSESSMENT ANSWERS

Reviewing Key Terms and Concepts
1. to inform, persuade, and entertain
2. enumeration, generalization with example, cause and effect, and compare and contrast
3. It is a structure for holding group meetings and making decisions, used to make meetings democratic and decision making orderly.
4. time of call, caller's name and message, and return phone number

5. your reader, purpose, and subject

Thinking Critically
6. return address, date, inside address, salutation, well-written body, closing, signature, and reference initials

Integrating Academic Skills
7. **MATH** 150 documents. $600 \div 4 = 150$

Careers in Marketing

REAL ESTATE

William Cusick
Vice President/Real Estate Broker
Birmingham Real Estate Inc.

What does your job entail?

"Real estate brokers are independent real estate agents who sell residential and business property owned by others. Some brokers manage properties for a fee. My primary responsibility is asking people what they need and searching the marketplace to find a match. Brokers may be involved in arranging for title searches, financing, and closing details. Real estate brokers spend time listing properties for sale, as well as hiring and supervising real estate agents, advertising properties, and handling the business matters of their office."

What skills are most important to you?

"Interpersonal skills—especially listening—are important in my field. Real estate brokers and agents must be honest, customer oriented, work well with the public, and have good memories for names and details. Networking with other professionals in the communities where they work and cultivating personal contacts are also important."

What kind of training did you have?

"For most people, real estate is learned from experience. I would recommend that students take Real Estate courses in college in addition to classes dealing with finance, marketing, business, business law, and economics."

What do you like most about your work?

"My job offers a lot of variety. The workload varies tremendously, especially since I work on a client's schedule. A broker could turn down an assignment because he or she is too busy, but one never knows what the "pipeline" of work will be in two weeks once current assignments are completed. I enjoy the sense of being my own boss, and the satisfaction of completing a project where the customer finds what he or she wants and is happy with it."

What is your key to success?

"Timing—I was in the right place at the right time!"

Thinking Critically
How can a real estate broker get feedback to improve his or her marketing skills?

Career Facts

Education and Training: A state license is necessary in order to practice as a broker. Experience as a real estate agent is needed as well as a bachelor's degree, in some cases.

Aptitudes, Abilities, and Skills: Honesty, good decision-making skills, customer oriented, good memory for details and names, and strong knowledge of business conditions and property values are essential.

Career Outlook: Employment of real estate brokers and real estate agents is expected to continue to grow through 2008. The ability of customers to conduct their own property searches through Web sites, however, may decrease the need for brokers and agents.

Career Path: Experienced real estate agents can advance to sales managers or may obtain their broker's license. Experienced agents may also become real estate appraisers. Brokers may move on to the fields of mortgage financing, real estate investment counseling, or property management.

153

Chapter 8 ASSESSMENT

Vocabulary Review

Papers will vary. See Glossary for definitions.

Fact and Idea Review

1. Communication is the process of exchanging information, ideas, and feelings.
2. A message must be sent, received, and understood to make communication complete.
3. Feedback allows participants to clarify the message and know that all parties understand it.
4. A small room makes people feel more comfortable.
5. Making judgments is important when listening to messages and when listening to most conversations.
6. It helps you remember the main ideas and indicates you think what is being said is important.
7. explanation, demonstration, trial, and critique
8. The standard parts of a meeting agenda are the call to order, minutes of the last meeting, treasurer's report, committee reports, old business, new business, and adjournment.
9. Answer a business telephone with a cheerful but formal greeting, giving the company name and/or your name and department.
10. There is more opportunity to organize thoughts, review, and revise your message before it is sent. A written message provides a permanent record that is more apt to be remembered.

Thinking Critically

1. We spend nearly as much time listening as we do speaking, reading, and writing combined. In school, you will most likely know the speaker's purpose—to inform. If you are given an opportunity to ask questions, providing feedback to clarify the message is one of the most important of the listening skills. Taking notes will also improve your learning.
2. Answers will vary but should take into account when it is appropriate to offer advice and when it is best to just be a good listener. Generally speaking, it is best to listen when it is a personal or emotional matter.
3. Answers will vary based on the chosen career, but good reading skills can help people on all jobs.
4. Answers will vary but should follow the training procedures discussed in this chapter.

154

VOCABULARY REVIEW

Use each of the following in a 250-word paper on communication.

- communication
- channels
- feedback
- blocks
- setting
- distractions
- emotional blocks
- jargon
- parliamentary procedure
- quorum

FACT AND IDEA REVIEW

1. What is communication? (8.1)
2. Describe how the communication of a message is a two-way process. (8.1)
3. Why is it important to give feedback when someone is giving you directions? (8.1)
4. Why is a small room a good setting for a meeting with one other person? (8.1)
5. Discuss when and how making judgments as a listener can be helpful. (8.1)
6. Discuss why taking notes is part of being an effective listener. (8.1)
7. Name the four steps used in training. (8.2)
8. Name the seven parts of a meeting agenda. (8.2)
9. How should you answer a business call? (8.2)
10. What are some of the advantages of a written rather than a verbal message? (8.2)

THINKING CRITICALLY

1. Why is it important to be a good listener? Which listening skills could help you most in school? How?
2. Describe a situation in which it would be appropriate and helpful to make judgments as a listener. Describe another situation in which it would not be helpful.
3. Choose a career that interests you. Describe how being a good reader could help you in that job.
4. Which of the four patterns in this chapter would you discuss when instructing a fellow employee on how to complete a task? Explain.
5. In parliamentary procedure, when is a formal procedure of motions used? When would an informal procedure be appropriate? Why?

BUILDING WORKPLACE SKILLS

1. **Writing** Using a word processing program, write a business letter to the principal of your school, describing a plan to raise funds for new football uniforms. Include all the standard parts of a business letter, and use the spelling and grammar check feature of your program.
2. **Human Relations** You are a manager of a home electronics store. You observe a new salesperson who is trying to impress a customer with his technical expertise and terminology. You can see that his overuse of jargon is offensive to the customer. What should you do?

Building Workplace Skills

1. Letters will vary. They should include all key parts of a business letter.
2. Students should provide well thought out solutions that address the use of jargon and when it is and is not appropriate.

APPLYING MARKETING CONCEPTS

1. **Defining E-mail Policies** You are the manager at a telecommunications software company that relies on e-mail for internal and external communication. Lately it seems that employees are spending more time using their computers for personal e-mail. Prepare an oral report using presentation software that outlines appropriate e-mail standards and behavior to be discussed at a future meeting.

2. **Preparing a Business Letter** Use a word processing program to write a formal business letter from your company, Jack's Construction, to Acme Hardware. The hardware store has delivered faulty pipe to you, and you are writing to correct the situation.

3. **Researching Marketing Fields** Choose a marketing field you are interested in. Use a word processing program to write a business letter to an executive of a company in this marketing field. (Your librarian can help you find the correct address.) Request information about preparing for the career that interests you.

4. **Creating Marketing Materials** You have just started a new job as the marketing director at a nonprofit organization that provides professional clothing and uniforms to economically-challenged men and women who are looking for employment. The organization's brochures are outdated, and your first duty is to create an up-to-date one. Using design software, create a brochure including information on your organization and how people can help support it.

LINKING SCHOOL TO WORK

Information Skills Interview an employer to find out how often written communication is necessary at the workplace. How often does he or she need to write a business letter, report, or memo? What other types of writing does he or she need to do? Share your findings with the class.

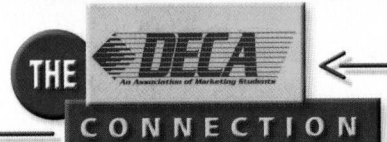

THE DECA CONNECTION

Role Play: Clerk Trainer

Situation Assume the role of a newly promoted assistant manager of the parts department at a local auto dealership. You will be responsible for training new parts clerks.

Activity Before you begin training others, the manager (judge) has asked that you demonstrate to him that you can complete the following tasks: orient new employees; reinforce service orientation through communication; use proper grammar and vocabulary; handle customer/client complaints; and give directions for completing job tasks.

Evaluation You will be evaluated on how well you meet the following performance indicators:
- Explain the four-step plan for training employees
- Understand essential topics that should be covered with new employees
- Use formal speech
- Display effective listening skills

inter NET CONNECTION

Meeting Notes
You have been asked to prepare the minutes from the student government meeting, and you don't know what format to use.

Connect
- Find the Web sites of local government agencies, such as the water board and planning commission, and look for links to their meeting records.
- Compare the meeting minutes of two or three different agencies.
- Develop your own format for student government minutes based on your research.

Chapter 8 ■ *Communication Skills* **155**

THE DECA CONNECTION

Students should be evaluated on the performance indicators noted in the Role Play.
- For another DECA Role Play, go to the *Student Activity Workbook*, p. 163.
- For more in-depth Role Play practice, refer to DECA's *Essential Competitive Events Handbook*. To order, contact DECA at www.deca.org.

interNET CONNECTION
Meeting notes will vary.

Mini Quiz

Administer the Mini Quiz orally. For an expanded chapter quiz, go to page 47 of the *Reproducible Tests* book.

Indicate if the following statements are *true* or *false*. For statements that are false, explain why.

1. Simply sending a message is communicating. False: The message must be sent, received, and understood.

2. In the process of listening, it is important to provide feedback to the speaker. True

3. Communication is only done to inform or entertain. False: It is also done to persuade.

4. Training is a specialized form of speaking which uses demonstration of a task. True

5. Because it is seldom used today, it is not important to know the standard business letter format. False: It is still the main form of communication outside of the company.

Applying Marketing Concepts

1. Presentations will vary, but should discuss the ethical use of e-mail at work.
2. Letters should follow the format outlined in the chapter.
3. Letters will vary based on the chosen career.
4. Brochures will vary but should target the audience.

Linking School to Work

Answers will depend on the work situation.

GO TO
1. **Assessment** Have students complete the Reproducible Test for Chapter 8 or construct your own tests using the ExamView software.
2. **Enrichment** Have students complete the corresponding activities in the following workbooks:
   - *Marketing Math Workbook*, p. 19
   - *Marketing Research Project Workbook*, p. 47

Chapter Overview

Chapter 9 familiarizes students with the world of computers and popular software applications. It also discusses both current and anticipated uses of specialized computer technology in marketing.

Springboard

Brainstorm Ask students to brainstorm a list of examples of how computers are used in marketing jobs. The list may include creating letters, brochures, Web pages, financial statements and customer lists; inventory control; pricing; processing customers at checkout; invoicing; doing marketing research; shopping the competition; tracking shipments, etc. Explain that computers continue to dominate all aspects of business today and that this chapter should broaden their understanding of computer usage.

Prereading

List the section objectives to discuss with students. Have students skim the chapter, looking at the pictures, reading the captions, and noting the heads. Ask questions to ensure that the students have a minimal understanding of the chapter structure.

Preteaching Marketing Vocabulary

Bring a personal computer to your classroom. Point to each part of the computer and ask the class to help you name each part as one student writes the terms on the board. This activity will serve as a pretest to see how much students already know.

Marketing: What It Takes

Answer By asking customers for their zip codes, mailings can be directed to customers who come into the store and to other homes in those zip code areas since they may have similar interests.

Computer Applications and Skills

Marketing: What It Takes

Rewarding Regular Customers

You are the assistant manager of a large retail computer store. Because you have more background and experience in advertising than the manager, you are responsible for planning and carrying out the advertising program. Your manager likes the advertisements you have written for the local newspaper, but wonders how you might get more repeat business from those who make purchases at your store.

WHAT WILL YOU DO?
How will you plan to entice more repeat business from current customers?

156

THE DECA CONNECTION   **ADVISOR CORNER**

Putting Technology to Use Have students list two ways that your chapter can use computers and/or technology for each of the following: 1) to create newsletters and flyers, 2) to increase membership, 3) to improve your school store (if applicable), 4) to build community and business support, and 5) to save time and money.

After giving students an appropriate amount of time to complete the task, discuss their findings. Then develop a master list for each category, making sure to eliminate any duplication of ideas. Develop this into a final plan for utilizing technology for the benefit of your chapter.

Computers in Marketing

Computers

Businesses use computers to generate correspondence, maintain lists of customers or clients, and control inventory. They also use computers to create advertising materials, calculate and produce financial reports, and communicate electronically with other computer users. Most businesses today could not compete successfully in the world market without the use of computer technology.

Computers make it possible for businesses to process a large quantity of information with enhanced speed, ease, and accuracy—and at a reduced cost! They also allow businesses to reduce the number of staff members they require, improve their profit margins, enhance inventory control, and effectively track customer sales patterns. Most businesses find that their investment in computer technology is money well spent.

Computers and related technology have been credited for the immense increase in productivity seen in the late 1990s and into the 2000s. The tiny microprocessor—the silicon chip—has expanded the use of computer technology and moved the world into the Age of Technology. Throughout the 1990s and early 2000s, U.S. industry spent more money on computers and communications equipment than on all other types of capital equipment combined. This included all machinery needed for manufacturing, mining, agriculture, construction, and all other fields of production.

It is usually a matter of time before the technological strides that advance one industry are adopted by other industries. This is illustrated by the example of robotics, or the technology of computer controlled machines. In the 1940s, the first simple robots handled dangerous radioactive materials. In the 1950s, scientists at MIT learned how to control robots using computer technology. In the early 1960s, the company Unimation built and promoted the first robots used for manufacturing.

Aided by computer technology, scientists are able to manipulate a robot's "hands" closely. This advancement moved robotics into medicine. Surgeons are beginning to use robots to perform delicate open-heart surgery. The surgeon sits at a computer screen and uses a device similar to a video game's joystick to control the robot. The robot's "hands" are tiny and much steadier than any human hand, making it possible to perform surgery with smaller incisions and less injury to the body.

This technology that was invented for the military was adapted for use in both business and health fields. Shared technology such as this will continue to improve efficiency of work and quality of life.

What You'll Learn

- The major ways computers are used to save businesses money
- The characteristics of different types of computers
- The functions of basic pieces of computer hardware

Why It's Important

Computers have changed our personal lives in many ways, including the way that we engage in marketing. Success in the business world increasingly depends on an understanding of and proficiency in the use of computer technology.

Key Terms

- supercomputer
- mainframe
- minicomputer
- microcomputer
- laptop
- PDAs
- hardware
- disk drive
- CD-ROM
- DVD
- scanner
- software

Chapter 9 ■ *Computer Applications and Skills* **157**

FOCUS

Bell Ringer Activity

Name a Computer Ask students if they have pets at home and what their names are. Ask if any students have named their computer and what the names are. Then depending on what is in your classroom, have students think of a name for their own computer or reach a consensus on names for the computers in the classroom. Students should explain why they chose a particular name.

Introducing the Section

Computers in Marketing Tell students that naming a computer might transform it from a nameless hunk of metal and plastic to a "friend" with whom you feel a connection. Tell them that the computer will be among their nearest and dearest friends in whatever their future career may be. The more they learn now, the more comfortable they will be with advancing computer technology.

Ask students if they can describe the following items as you write them on the board: supercomputer, mainframe, minicomputer, microcomputer, laptop, PDA, hardware, software, disk drive, scanner, CD-ROM, DVD, and software.

As computer technology revolutionizes the work place, computers are replacing people. Statistics show that effective organizations are decreasing in size. Increased efficiency through computer technology has allowed many businesses to reduce their clerical and managerial staff. People can connect to a server from their home computer and complete the same work previously done in an office. The types of jobs are changing, too. There is an overall shift away from manufacturing toward services. In 2000, white collar jobs had increased to 60 percent of the workforce.

Types of Computers

Computers range widely in size, cost, speed, and power. The largest and most powerful type of computer is called a supercomputer. Supercomputers are used for the most sophisticated work, such as directing space missions or tracking hurricanes.

Mainframe computers are large, sometimes filling a whole room. Mainframe computers are used where many people in a large organization need frequent access to the same information. Large corporations, universities, and government organizations generally use mainframe computers.

Minicomputers are next in size and power, and are used by many businesses. The capabilities of a minicomputer lie somewhere between those of mainframes and those of personal computers. Minicomputers are ideal for organizations and companies that cannot afford or do not need a mainframe system. They enable smaller organizations to deal with large amounts of information and complex processes, and give access to multiple users.

Most medium and smaller businesses use the microcomputer, which is also referred to as the personal computer, or PC. It is the computer most people use at home. Since its introduction in the early 1980s, this machine has thrived as a business tool. Many businesses connect a powerful microcomputer as a *server* to a number of work stations. The server provides computing power and large amounts of storage.

A laptop is a smaller, portable personal computer. Laptops are fully functional microcomputers. Also called notebooks, they can operate on plug-in current or with special batteries. Laptops are rapidly acquiring all capabilities of the nonportable PC.

Life In The Diverse MARKETPLACE

Celtic Tiger

Green fields, sheep farmers, and Riverdance—these images may be what people associate with Ireland. This is changing as technological and economic growth in Ireland is on the upswing. Ireland surpassed the GDP and standard of living of Great Britain in 1997, overcoming their stereotypes. This showed the world that the "Celtic Tiger" was a force to watch. In addition to the plants operated by Dell and Intel, many Internet start-up companies are being established in Ireland. This makes it clear that the Irish plan to stay a contender.

Thinking Critically
Why would developing countries that are lagging in the technological race look to Ireland for inspiration?

Laptops, in recent years, have become not only smaller and lighter but also more affordable to travelers and students alike.

Personal digit assistants (PDAs) are the smallest of portable computers. Often, they are no larger than the palm of your hand. PDAs, also called palmtops, are much less powerful than notebook or desktop computers. Many PDAs can be connected to larger computers. You can use a palm-size computer for a variety of functions, including sending and receiving e-mail and communicating via the Internet. PDAs are often used as personal organizers, incorporating an address book, memo pad, date book, and calculator. Advanced models have high resolution graphics and can function as entertainment devices capable of playing movie trailers, digital photography, and arcade games!

The wireless cell phone, too, is utilizing more computer technology. Cell phones can now be used to send and receive e-mail messages. Despite their increasingly sophisticated components, cell phones are often affected by factors as simple as the location where they are used.

Life In The Diverse MARKETPLACE

Celtic Tiger
Answer Developing countries that are lagging behind technologically can look to Ireland as an example because the Irish overcame stereotypes and gained success by staying on the cutting edge of Internet technology.

Computer System Components

The components of a computer system are hardware and software. Hardware and software work together to enable a computer to function. Let's take a closer look at these components.

■ Hardware

Hardware is the equipment—the physical components that make up a computer system. Hardware comprises all of the interconnected electronic devices that you can use to control the computer's operation, input, and output.

The system unit is the main part of the computer, with the central processing unit (CPU) at the heart. Most system units contain one or more disk drives—the device that holds a disk. A disk drive is used to read data from and write data to a disk. Some disks are built into the drive and are not meant to be removed. Other kinds of disk drives enable you to remove and replace disks. The storage capacity of disks varies, but rapid developments in technology continually make it possible to buy more storage capacity for less money.

Other types of data storage devices include CD-ROM and digital versatile disk (DVD) drives. Compact disks (CDs) are used in CD-ROM drives and are a type of optical storage device identical to audio music CDs. A DVD disk is a high-density optical storage device capable of storing a full-length movie on a single disk the size of a CD.

The keyboard is used to type information and commands into the computer and to control its action. It looks like the keys on a typewriter with a numeric keypad and function keys added. People often use a mouse as an input device. You can give a computer commands by moving a mouse on a flat surface and pushing its buttons.

A monitor displays computer output, such as a business letter or computer graphics. A monitor is either a cathode ray tube (CRT) similar to a TV set or liquid crystal display (LCD) similar to digital display clocks or watches. Most monitors today display your work in millions of colors.

A printer reproduces an image from the computer onto paper. Laser and ink jet printers are very popular and have excellent print quality. Color ink jet printers produce outstanding photographic prints and other graphic images.

Computer hardware may also include other options. Scanners have become very popular. A scanner reads and transforms images into digital data. Scanners are also used to convert photographs into digital files for editing and manipulation in a photo editing program (See Figure 9-1 on page 160).

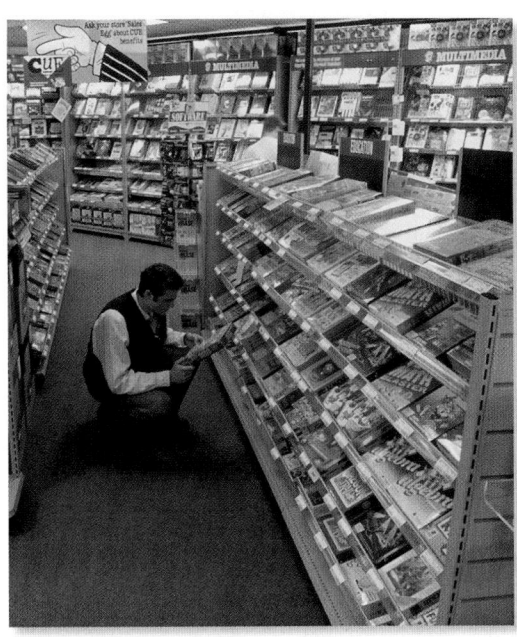

■ **Updated Version** Application software for personal computers is continually being improved. *What types of upgrades do you envision for the next generation of software?*

GREAT IDEAS from the Marketing Classroom

Mary Valigura
Sandia High School
Albuquerque, NM

A fun teaching strategy is to have individual students teach unit segments to the class. I recommend student teams of no more than three per team. Divide a unit into topics and let the team members create the instruction. Have them wear business attire on their presentation day and introduce and conduct themselves in a professional manner. Give each student in the class some Post-it notes and have each one evaluate their peers for eye contact, voice tone, and enthusiasm. Collect the Post-it notes, assemble them, and review them with the student teacher of the day, so they have immediate feedback on their presentation skills.

Reteaching

1. **Vocabulary** Assign and review the vocabulary terms for this section.
2. **Fact and Idea** Assign and review Fact and Idea Review questions 1–4 from the Chapter Assessment.
3. **Computer Parts** Using one of your classroom computers, point to each part of the computer and have students name it.

Enrichment

1. **Review** Assign and review the appropriate Thinking Critically questions from the Chapter Assessment.
2. **Extend** Assign and review the corresponding activities from *BusinessWeek Case Studies* and *Internet Resources.***ILP**
3. **Research and Present** Have students use the Internet or a newspaper to locate a computer-related cartoon. Students should print or make a copy of the cartoon, then present the cartoon to the class, and display it in the classroom.

FIGURE 9-1
COMPUTER PERIPHERALS

Computer Peripherals connect to your computer and make it more versatile and powerful. *Which of these devices have you used? What other peripherals have you used?*

CD-ROM OR DVD DRIVE

A CD-ROM drive is a specialized type of disk drive that enables a computer to read data from a compact disk. DVDs provide high-resolution graphics, animation, video, and digital sound. DVDs can store large amounts of information, including text, pictures, and sound.

MOUSE, TRACKBALL, OR TRACKPAD

A mouse, trackball, or trackpad is a small hand-operated device with a button, ball, or just a pad that is sensitive to movement. These are used to move a cursor or arrow to different locations on the screen, and then "clicked" to perform functions.

MODEM

A modem connects your computer to the phone, cable, DSL, or ISDN connection lines. It allows your computer to connect with others in a local network, and to connect to the Internet. Most computers have built-in modems.

PRINTER

A printer is used to print out copies of text, graphics, numerical data, or whatever you have created on your computer.

SCANNER

A scanner allows you to input text or a graphic image into your computer. The scanner translates the visual image into digital data. The scanner software then displays the text or graphic image on your computer screen.

■ Software

Software is a set of electronic instructions that directs the CPU to carry out a specific task. These sets of instructions are also known as programs or applications and each one has a specific purpose.

Most software falls into two major categories: system software and application software. One major type of system software, called *operating software*, tells the computer how to use its own components. The operating system basically determines what programs you can run on your computer. Applications must be compatible with the operating system of the computer platform you use. Two widely used platforms are the IBM-compatible—called PC—and the Apple Macintosh. Most Apples use the Macintosh operating system, while most PCs use the Windows operating system.

Application software is used for many different functions, such as word processing or production of graphics. These functions will be described in Section 9.2.

Some companies create specific software to meet their needs. Most common applications, though, are available commercially. Software publishing has become America's fastest growing industry. Major software publishing companies, such as Microsoft, Novell, Borland, and Oracle, continually compete to produce the newest, most technologically advanced products in this booming market.

Linking Technologies

Microsoft has something new up its sleeve with its plans to link all technological devices together. Imagine visiting a zoo to collect information for a report through your handheld computer/phone, then sending digital photos to friends. Your friends could view the images on their televisions and immediately transfer them to a digital picture frame. How about using a mobile phone to find a doctor in a new city, choose which insurance company policy to use for billing, schedule an appointment, and send medical records to the new doctor. While this software is basically developed, Microsoft is waiting for computer hardware to develop accordingly before releasing this technology on the market.

Thinking Critically
What other ideas may become realities utilizing linked technologies?

9.1 ASSESSMENT

Reviewing Key Terms and Concepts

1. What are three ways that computers can save businesses money?
2. What are the functions of four basic pieces of computer hardware?
3. What is the function of a scanner?
4. What is operating system software?

Thinking Critically

5. What are some advantages and disadvantages of the use of robots in the medical field?

Integrating Academic Skills

6. **COMMUNICATION** Your employer wants to upgrade the computer hardware in your marketing firm. The supervisor of information management is an expert on computers. She has been asked to explain the capabilities of the latest equipment and to assess employees' needs. However, she speaks in *computerese* (using technical computer terms). What could you say to this supervisor to help solve the problem?

SECTION 9.1

Evaluation

Assign and review the Section 9.1 Assessment.

Technology Resources

GO TO **Assessment Resources**
Go to the *Marketing Essentials* Web site (www.marketing.glencoe.com) for resources to teach and assess occupation-specific vocabulary.

CLOSE

Section Wrap-Up

Several years ago IBM Corporation ran an ad with the following copy: "A computer isn't smart enough to make a mistake. Computers are dumb—fast and efficient and dumb. No computer ever had an idea." Have students comment on what they think this comment means, whether or not they agree with the statement and why. *(Answers may include the concept of human intelligence and logic, and how computers do the rote work quickly.)*

Linking Technologies

Answer Answers will vary but may include online purchasing or information downloads.

9.1 ASSESSMENT ANSWERS

Reviewing Key Terms and Concepts
1. reduce staff, improve profit, enhance inventory control
2. CPU, keyboard, monitor, printer
3. It transforms images from documents and photos into digital data.
4. It is the computer's master control program.

Thinking Critically
5. Advantages are that they are highly accurate and have consistent precise movements. Disadvantage is patients may feel uncomfortable due to lack of contact between patient and doctor.

Integrating Academic Skills
6. **COMMUNICATION** Answers will vary.

SECTION 9.2

Computer Applications

FOCUS

Bell Ringer Activity

Explain Call on students and ask what is directing their physical actions at this very moment. For example, what makes them able to turn their heads, raise their hands, stand up, sit down, etc. *(They are directing their own actions by their thoughts.)*

Introducing the Section

Computer Applications Software programs direct computers to perform specific tasks just as your thoughts direct your body. Without software, the computer is unable to function. Software programs, such as word processing or desktop publishing programs, are the "directors" that tell a computer what to do. In this section students will look at seven popular software programs used in business—programs that they may use and even decide to purchase for home or office use in the future.

• What You'll Learn

- Eight types of popular computer application programs
- How these programs are used in business

• Why It's Important

Computer technology is the driving force behind the most productive economy the world has ever known. It is likely that you will use computer hardware and software on the job; in fact, your career success may be measured by your understanding and skillful use of these applications.

Key Terms

- word processing programs
- database programs
- spreadsheet programs
- desktop publishing programs
- graphics and design programs
- presentation software
- home page
- Web page editors
- Web page
- hypertext markup language (HTML)
- communications programs
- e-mail

Software

Software application programs have been developed to help us manage just about every facet of our lives. People use software applications to manage their time and money. Medical practices use programs to schedule patients and manage billing. Hotels use software applications to manage room assignments and generate bills. Universities use application software to keep track of thousands of students and their class schedules. Farmers use software to manage their livestock and crops. Architects use computer aided design (CAD) programs to design buildings. There is even software available to help programmers write more software!

There are endless types of software available to meet our needs. In this section, we will discuss eight popular types of software applications commonly used in marketing. These types include word processing, database management, spreadsheets, desktop publishing, graphics and design, presentation, Web page editors, and communications programs.

■ Word Processing Programs

Word processing programs are software applications used to create documents that are primarily text but may also contain some graphics.

Many businesses use word processing programs to
- Write letters and memos
- Produce research papers and reports
- Write business plans
- Create contracts
- Record meeting minutes
- Create announcements

It is likely that you've used a word processing program for writing a letter or preparing a research paper for school; if so, you are aware of how these programs simplify your work. Word processing allows you to make changes in your documents while viewing the changes on screen. Word processing programs help you to produce sophisticated, polished documents in a fraction of the time it would take on a typewriter.

Most word processing programs contain a thesaurus, dictionary, spelling checker, and grammar checker. These features help users produce more accurate documents.

Many word processing programs are available in the commercial market. Among the more popular word processing programs are Microsoft Word and WordPerfect.

Classroom Resources

For the Teacher
- Teacher Editions for all workbooks
- Assessment Package
- PowerPoint Presentation Software
- Interactive Lesson Planner
- **ILP** Block Scheduling, p. 4
- **ILP** Lesson Plans, p. 19
- **ILP** Internet Resources, p. 37

- **ILP** *BusinessWeek* Case Studies, p. 55
- **ILP** Marketing Career Portfolio, p. 34
- *Marketing Essentials* Web site (**www.marketing.glencoe.com**)

For the Student
- Student Activity Workbook, p. 73
- Marketing Math Workbook, p. 19

- Marketing Research Project Workbook, p. 47
- **ILP** School-to-Work Activity Workbook, p. 33
- Virtual Business simulation
- *Marketing Essentials* Web site (**www.marketing.glencoe.com**)

ILP These resources are available in print and on the Interactive Lesson Planner (ILP)

Database Programs

Database programs are software applications used to collect related data, which can be sorted, searched through, and printed as needed. Much like a warehouse, a database is a storage area for collections of related data. Database software enables businesses to track products, orders, shipments, customers, and more. Once your information is entered in the computer, the database program allows you to organize and analyze the information quickly and easily.

Database programs can be used to complete many business functions. Businesses use database programs to

- Maintain customer lists for automated mass mailings
- Keep information about guests and vendors for parties and events
- Catalog furniture and assets for insurance records
- Manage time and track billable hours
- Catalog personnel records

Suppose you have entered into the computer your company's mailing list, which contains the names and addresses of 3,000 of your customers. You could alphabetize all the names or group the addresses by zip code or display only those customers who live in a certain location with just one keystroke. Including your customers' birthdays in the database would make it possible to pull up all the customers with birthdays and send them birthday cards each month. Customer purchase history in your database would allow you to quickly pull up all those customers who made purchases during a certain month or who purchased a certain dollar amount of merchandise. Consider the following example of how one business uses database software.

Tim Hilton, owner of Top Dog, a small business that breeds pedigreed Labrador dogs, uses a database to keep information about each of his dogs. The database information includes size of litter, gender, name of the mother and father, the color, weight, date born, and feeding record. It also includes the selling price and information about the owner who purchased the dog. Hilton can use his database to quickly analyze his sales records and use the data for future planning.

There are numerous types of database application programs. Some popular commercial database programs are Filemaker Pro, Lotus Approach, and Microsoft Access.

Spreadsheet Programs

Spreadsheet programs are software applications used to organize, calculate, and analyze numerical data. Spreadsheets enable you to perform financial and scientific calculations, organize numeric information, illustrate data with charts and graphs, and create professional-looking reports. Spreadsheets are used in business to

- Develop a budget
- Analyze financial performance
- Track loans or mortgages
- Track stock and bond performance
- Schedule projects
- Manage business assets
- Produce profit-and-loss statements
- Calculate and produce a payroll

■ **A Penny Saved** Programs that automate bookkeeping tasks save money for small businesses. *How could you use bookkeeping software?*

Chapter 9 ■ *Computer Applications and Skills* **163**

SECTION 9.2

TEACH

📊 Technology Resources

PowerPoint The *Marketing Essentials* PowerPoint Presentation CD-ROM provides visual lecture aids for every chapter section.

Concept Development

1. Have students brainstorm a list of software titles they have used at home, school, or work. Have them name the programs and what they use them for. (*Some examples include desktop publishing to create newsletters, database for bibliography, etc.*)
2. Read Section 9.2 with students.
3. Have students read aloud the Case Study and review the answers in class.

Discussion Starter

Software Programs There are literally thousands of software programs available on the market. Ask students: How do people identify what software they want to buy? (*They must first decide what they want to accomplish because that will determine the category of software. Then they must decide which particular program will best suit their needs and budget.*)

CAPTION ANSWER
A Penny Saved Bookkeeping software could be used for budgeting, financial analysis, asset management, profit and loss statements, payroll, loan mortgage amortization, investment tracking, and project scheduling.

Thinking Critically

Intellectual Property Ask students: What is "Intellectual Property"? *(This refers to the copyright, trademark, or patent held by an individual or corporation.)* Ask students: Have you ever made a copy of a program and given it to someone else? It is estimated that pirated software is equal to the amount of legitimate software. Have students discuss the ethics and possible consequences of software piracy. If possible, bring in a copy of a software license agreement and read the main points.

Cooperative Learning

Software Categories Divide students into seven groups and assign each group one of the software categories discussed in this section. Using magazines, newspapers, retail stores, or Internet sites that sell software, have each group locate within that category four to six popular software programs currently on the market. Students should identify the titles and publishers and include the cost, features, benefits, and availability location of each program. Students should produce the data in either a spreadsheet or database to get practice using the software.

REAL WORLD MARKETING

Pen Man Ships Pens

The Fountain Pen Hospital may only have 12 employees, but $5 million in annual revenues in the sales and service of new and antique fountain pens is nothing to shake your pen at. The Fountain Pen Hospital has managed to succeed by tracking individual customer preferences and matching them to inventory. To do this, the company hired a computer programmer to design a customer database and inventory management system that can display each customer's contact information, as well as prior sales by date, pen type, and amount spent.

Thinking Critically

How do customer databases assist businesses?

Data are entered into squares, or cells, on a grid. A spreadsheet program calculates the data mathematically with amazing speed and accuracy not possible by hand or with a calculator. Working with a grid like this, you can easily change any one number and all related numbers will be adjusted automatically.

One common use of a spreadsheet is to produce a financial statement. Many businesses and organizations use spreadsheet programs to analyze their annual income and spending. The data can be used to produce a graphic picture, such as a line graph or a pie chart. The chart might depict what percent of the total outlay went toward salaries, building maintenance, research and development, or even phone bills. This pie chart illustration might be included in the annual report or in a presentation to potential investors.

Spreadsheet programs are available to suit a variety of different needs. Some popular commercial spreadsheet programs are Lotus 1-2-3 and Microsoft Excel.

■ Desktop Publishing Programs

Desktop publishing programs are software applications used to design and produce professional printed materials. These programs allow you to combine word processing and graphics. Businesses may use desktop publishing to

- Create layouts for newsletters, books, brochures, advertisements
- Create professional-looking forms, such as invoices and project planning sheets

Many businesses have learned to save large amounts of money by using desktop publishing programs. In the past, they paid a graphic design or printing firm to work for them. Now they can produce the work themselves. Take the following business for example.

Mass Potential is a business that promotes and produces training seminars nationwide. It offers one-day seminars, such as "How to Deal with Difficult Employees," "Time Management," and "Stress Reduction." Using desktop publishing software, it produces elaborate course catalogs that are distributed in mass mailings. At the seminars, each participant receives a nametag and an area map. Both items are produced with desktop publishing. During the seminars, instructors often use overlays on an overhead projector and distribute handouts. Both, of course, are produced with desktop publishing software!

Desktop publishing has become a valuable tool for professionals in all fields. It helps a company put its best foot forward and make a good impression. Desktop publishing software can produce documents that are creative, eye-catching, attractive, professional, and easy to read. Some popular commercial desktop publishing programs are Adobe Pagemaker, Corel-Ventura, and QuarkXPress.

■ Graphics and Design Programs

Graphics and design programs are software applications used to produce drawings and designs. Graphics programs can be used by businesses to

- Create professional-looking illustrations
- Design a logo or letterhead
- Illustrate floor plans and furniture arrangements
- Make flowcharts or seating and organizational charts

REAL WORLD MARKETING

Pen Man Ships Pens

Answer Customer databases can provide businesses with accurate information on their sales and customers. In turn, businesses can process the information to change marketing efforts, such as adding or deleting products, changing inventory volume, or reworking pricing.

Independent Practice

Assess You may wish to assess your students' computer competency level by assigning a word-processing exercise in which students must successfully complete several tasks, such as using boldface and italics, changing margins, creating numbered and bulleted lists, and creating superscript and subscript. For those students who are unable to complete these basic tasks, schedule a tutorial or assign a peer tutor to teach these skills.

Graphics and design programs can be used to produce simple drawings or elaborate designs. They can be used to create a simple flowchart of the structure of an organization. They can also be used to create stunning artwork, 3D images, technical drawings, engineering graphics, and elaborate diagramming. Sound and animation can be added for multimedia presentations.

Most graphics and design programs come with professionally created art—called *clip art*. The images are usually grouped together in categories like business, food, sports, people, places, animals, cartoons, or holidays. Some popular graphics and design programs include Adobe Illustrator, and CorelDRAW.

■ Presentation Software

Presentation software is used to create slide shows or multimedia presentations all in one program. It is helpful with organizing, illustrating, and presenting ideas during a meeting or on the Internet. Presentation software can be used by businesses to

- Prepare verbal and visual copy for meetings
- Present ideas interactively with clients that are located in other cities or countries via the Internet
- Create slide shows using pictures or Web pages

Presentation software is used to produce a series of slides. Slides are single screen images that usually contain a combination of text and graphics, such as pictures or charts. Colorful graphics and concise text can be used in sales presentations to persuade clients and close sales.

Presentation software handles both graphics and text with equal ease to create well-crafted presentations. It is possible to add voice narration so that it seems as if you are truly at a conference, though you may be thousands of miles away.

Gone are the days of presentation boards propped up on stands in the front of a conference room. Now large screens can showcase presentations that are put in action with the click of a mouse. Programs like this are useful for large companies like Coca-Cola or McDonald's, who have shareholders and manufacturers located all over the world. The head of a department can create a presentation using text, bulleted lists, graphs, photos, and even screen shots from the company Web page. This can be broadcast to conference rooms in numerous different countries. As global interaction in the business world increases, programs like this simplify communication and cut down on travel time. Some examples of presentation software programs are Microsoft PowerPoint and Metacreations Office Advantage.

■ Web Page Editors

Most businesses either have a Web site or are preparing one. Businesses use their Web sites to promote their company and its products. Most also revise and improve their Web sites regularly. Many Web sites contain a top level home page that has links to other pages throughout the site.

Web page editors are applications used to create Web pages. A Web page usually contains text, photos, graphics, and hyperlinks. Also called HTML editors, Web editing software makes the work of coding a Web page with HTML easier. Web pages are written

Chapter 9 ■ *Computer Applications and Skills* **165**

CAPTION ANSWER
Desktop Publishing Magazines, books, brochures, reports, ads, posters, business forms, signs—just about anything that is printed can be created with desktop publishing software.

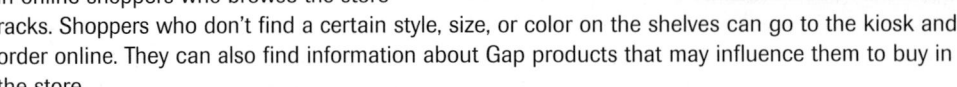

Case Study

Buying Online at the Mall

You might think online marketing is limited to people surfing the Web from home. Retail stores are installing Web kiosks so customers can shop online right inside the store.

Executives at Gap, the clothing retailer, don't believe that online shopping causes in-store sales to decrease; rather, they complement each other. Web kiosks bring in online shoppers who browse the store racks. Shoppers who don't find a certain style, size, or color on the shelves can go to the kiosk and order online. They can also find information about Gap products that may influence them to buy in the store.

Some online marketers are opening stores so shoppers can see and test their products before buying. One marketing analyst says that marketers need a physical outlet, in addition to a Web site, to attract a mass market.

Some retailers offer interactive kiosks that don't connect to the Internet but to an in-store intranet. These provide information about products or related activities. A camping equipment store may offer information about camping, fishing, hiking, and canoeing.

Web and information kiosks are creative ways to combine computer and online technology with in-store shopping. Future marketers will use this development to come up with even more ways to market their goods and services.

Case Study Review

1. Why would a store choose to have in-store network kiosks rather than connect to the Internet?
2. How could it help a camping store to provide information to customers about local campgrounds?

A MATTER OF ETHICS

3. What ethical issues are involved when an e-tailer sells your address to another marketer?

---

in a language called **hypertext markup language (HTML)**. Before a Web page can be viewed in a Web browser, it must be formatted in HTML. The HTML coding tells the browser how to display the text, whether as a heading, a table, or a link. The coding also tells the browser when and how to display images and when to link to another page. Viewing the code "behind" an HTML page reveals a complicated jumble of words and numbers. Basic HTML is relatively simple, and more and more HTML editing programs are automating coding so that Web page authoring can be as simple as using a standard word processor.

To understand and troubleshoot Web pages that are not working properly, it is important to have a basic understanding of HTML. Fortunately, there are many excellent resources available on the Web that would-be Webmasters can refer to. Among the more popular Web page design programs are Microsoft FrontPage and Adobe PageMill.

166 Unit 4 ■ *Academic Concepts and Skills*

Case Study Review Answers

Buying Online at the Mall

1. A possible answer may be that a store might not have a Web site.
2. Many answers are possible, including more interest could increase sales; kiosk may draw more people into the store; and kiosk may alert shoppers to previously overlooked items that might be needed when planning a camping trip.

A MATTER OF ETHICS

3. Answers will vary but students' answers should discuss privacy issues. The discussion should also include the need to check e-tailer's privacy policies.

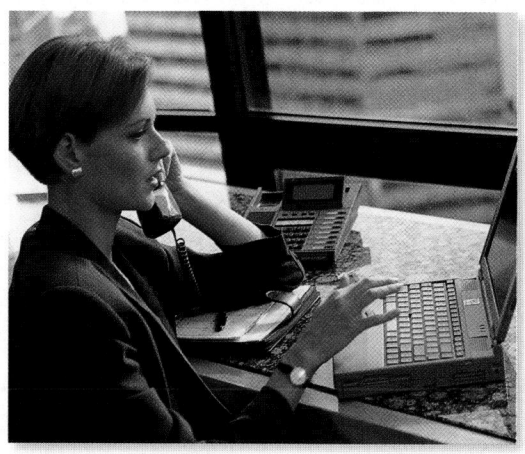

Visual Communication This woman is in her office in New York, yet she is able to see and speak to clients in Hong Kong using technology. *What is this process of meeting with someone using the computer called?*

■ Communications Programs

Communications programs are software applications used to establish communication between your computer and other computers. Many communications programs require a modem to allow the computer to send information—usually through a telephone line or cable. Wireless communication technology allows you to communicate via radio waves. One of the most far-reaching applications of data communications is electronic mail (e-mail). E-mail is a system of exchanging written messages as well as voice and video messages and electronic files through a computer network. Many communications programs allow you to attach data files— such as spreadsheet files or word processed documents—to your e-mail message. This means that people can share files even when they don't have access to the same storage devices. A few of the popular commercial communications programs are Lotus Notes, Microsoft Outlook, and Netscape Messenger.

In addition to e-mail, communications software can also facilitate teleconferencing and videoconferencing. A teleconference is a virtual meeting in which people in different locations conduct discussions by typing messages to each other. Each message can be seen by all of the other people in the teleconference. Users can actually see and speak to each other as they conduct their meeting if they have the necessary hardware and software. This process is known as videoconferencing.

Videoconferencing has many practical advantages. Perhaps the greatest professional advantage to videoconferencing is that it can lessen a business's travel expenses. Travel expenses can be dramatically reduced by holding meetings by videoconference rather than in person.

9.2 ASSESSMENT

Reviewing Key Terms and Concepts

1. What are eight types of software applications commonly used by businesses?
2. What are three tasks that a database program simplifies for businesses?
3. What did businesses have to do to create marketing materials before the creation of desktop publishing programs?
4. What is presentation software used for? What are some examples of presentation software?
5. What is the process of videoconferencing?

Thinking Critically

6. What type of software would you use to track the financial performance of your company?

Integrating Academic Skills

7. **MATH** At your computer shop, orders are placed by e-mail messages. Each e-mail message costs four cents. If the cost of a telephone order was 72 cents, and the shop places eight orders a day, what are the savings per business week?

167

Technology Resources

Assessment Resources
Go to the *Marketing Essentials* Web site (**www.marketing.glencoe. com**) for resources to teach and assess occupation-specific vocabulary.

VIRTUAL BUSINESS

Annual Report
Introduce the process of writing an annual report to students using Knowledge Matters' Virtual Business visual simulation, "Office Applications—Annual Report." Students build a chain of stores in a highly competitive environment and finish by writing a mock annual report for their corporation. If needed, have students run the Virtual Business tutorial before beginning the activity. For additional instructions and teaching tips for this simulation, go to the *Marketing Essentials* Web site (**www.marketing.glencoe.com**).

CLOSE

Section Wrap-Up

Have students complete this statement: The seven categories of software programs discussed in this section include . . . *(word processing, database management, presentation, spreadsheets, desktop publishing, graphics and design, and communications.)*

CAPTION ANSWER
Visual Communication This process is known as videoconferencing.

9.2 ASSESSMENT ANSWERS

Reviewing Key Terms and Concepts

1. word processing, database management, spreadsheet, desktop publishing, graphics and design, presentation software, Web page editors, and communications programs
2. maintain customer lists; keep information about guests and vendors; catalog assets; and catalog personnel records.
3. They sent promotional work to graphics companies.
4. It is used to create slide shows or multimedia presentations. Examples are Microsoft PowerPoint and Metacreations Office Advantage.
5. Meetings held using computer hardware and audio and video software.

Thinking Critically

6. Spreadsheet programs are best.

Integrating Academic Skills

7. **MATH** (.72 x 8 x 7) − (0.04 x 8 x 7) = $38.08

SECTION 9.3

Computer Technology

Imagine Tell students to imagine that it is a regular workday in the year 2025. They have just arrived at their marketing job. How will they use computers in this marketing office of tomorrow?

Introducing the Section

Computer Technology Review students' answers from the Bell Ringer Activity and encourage them to really stretch their imaginations. The ideas they generate now may be in limited use, in product development, or will be in development within the next few years. *(Answers will vary but may include computers being smaller, thousands of times faster, and able to calculate much more complex data; receiving and sending voice and video messages on a computer; wearing the computer on our body as a watch or glasses; speaking into the computer and not having to key; teleconferencing via computer; sending 3-dimensional objects through the computer; having the computer read your thoughts and write your correspondence.)*

• What You'll Learn

- The types of computer systems that are affecting the world of marketing
- How the Internet increases productivity
- Insight into the future of computer technology

• Why It's Important

As in all other fields, technological advances are changing the scope of marketing every day. With innovations that speed up the transfer of information and development of the Internet, new markets are constantly being introduced. This section will help you understand the value of this specialized technology.

Key Terms

- point-of-sale (POS) system
- Internet
- World Wide Web
- browser
- http
- URL

Specialized Computer Technology for Marketing

The uses for computer technology in marketing appear to be endless. In addition to the software applications discussed in Section 9.2, some computer technology that is helping to shape the way we conduct business today includes point-of-sale systems, interactive touch-screen computers, interactive TV, and the Internet.

■ Point-of-Sale Systems

A common use of computers in retailing is the point-of-sale (POS) system. This system uses light pens, handheld laser guns, stationary lasers, or slot scanners to feed information directly from merchandise tags or product labels into a computer. This information is used to update inventory and monitor purchasing patterns. POS systems will be discussed further in Chapters 16 and 24.

■ Interactive Touch-Screen Computers— The Computerized Salesperson

In retail marketing, there is a strong move toward the greater use of interactive technology. This technology allows consumers to interact with the computer. Interactive computers are frequently placed on shelves in retail stores and in stand-alone kiosks in malls and airports. The customer reads and responds to questions on the touch-sensitive screen. In this way, the "computerized salesperson" directs the customer to the correct product.

Cosmetic companies, such as Clairol and Cover Girl, use on-shelf computers to help consumers choose the right shade of hair color or eye shadow. Office supply stores provide an on-shelf computer to help customers select the correct replacement cartridge for their computer printers. Wedding registries in department stores are often computerized using this type of technology. By typing in either of the couple's names and touching the appropriate boxes on the screen, you can find the perfect wedding gift.

Warner-Lambert's Canadian division, a maker of health care and consumer products, has installed on-shelf computers in the cough-cold sections of more than 600 drugstores. The computers help consumers choose the appropriate product for their symptoms. The computer asks a series of questions about symptoms before recommending one of 26 products, 10 of which are competing brands. It then describes the packaging so consumers can find the product.

Classroom Resources

For the Teacher
- Teacher Editions for all workbooks
- Assessment Package
- PowerPoint Presentation Software
- Interactive Lesson Planner

ILP Block Scheduling, p. 4
ILP Lesson Plans, p. 20
ILP Internet Resources, p. 37

ILP *BusinessWeek* Case Studies, p. 55
ILP Marketing Career Portfolio, p. 34
- *Marketing Essentials* Web site (**www.marketing.glencoe.com**)

For the Student
- Student Activity Workbook, p. 73
- Marketing Math Workbook, p. 19

- Marketing Research Project Workbook, p. 47
ILP School-to-Work Activity Workbook, p. 33
- Virtual Business simulation
- *Marketing Essentials* Web site (**www.marketing.glencoe.com**)

ILP These resources are available in print and on the Interactive Lesson Planner (ILP)

■ **Point-of-Sale Systems** Point of Sale computer systems are able to provide management with more information than just the amount of sales. *What other functions do they provide?*

■ Interactive TV

Interactive TV is the marriage of television with Internet-style selectivity and interactivity. It uses a new generation of satellite receiving dishes, DVD players, and television set-top units that have modems, microprocessors, hard drives, operating systems, and software, including browsers.

Though the interactive TV market is still in its infancy, it is garnering a lot of attention because it allows businesses and advertisers to provide various kinds of information and hyperlinks within the same frame as a television program or commercial. These allow the viewer to interact with the programming as it progresses. The marketing possibilities for this technology are endless and include interactive television-facilitated e-commerce, product demonstrations, direct-response targeted advertising, and marketing research.

Today, companies are developing and testing ways in which interactive television can be used for advertising and promotion. Businesses are trying to determine what types of interactive TV work best and what consumers consider to be intrusive. Most agree, however, that this technology will revolutionize the way companies advertise.

■ The Internet

You're probably already a user of the Internet, the world's biggest computer network. Actually, it's not one network but a network of networks, all exchanging information. It began in 1969 as ARPANET, a small U.S. Department of Defense (DOD) network, that linked together the DOD and military research contractors. Soon after ARPANET was established, the scientists who had access to the system were given permission to exchange unofficial information through the system. ARPANET originally connected just three computers in California and one in Utah, but it grew quickly to cover the continent then the world. In the mid-1980s, the National Science Foundation used this technology to create NSFNET, a network connecting educational and research sites. After the establishment of NSFNET, ARPANET and NSFNET "internetworked" by linking their networks. This is where the Internet got its name. In 1990, ARPANET and NSFNET bowed out in favor of commercially run networks that allow transfer of much more information—and it became the Internet.

Internet use in the early 2000s is increasing at a pace similar to that of television fifty years ago. In 2000, about 100 million computers were connected to the Internet, and there were about 300 million users. The number continues to grow about 40 to 50 percent each year. As it exists today, the Internet has become a business tool, an advertising medium, a distribution channel, a source of entertainment, and a "virtual" meeting place for people with similar interests.

You can see that the Internet is equally valuable at home and at work. We'll discuss five common uses of the Internet as used in the workplace. Another common use, locating sources of jobs on the Internet, will be discussed in Chapter 38.

CAPTION ANSWER
Point-of-Sale Systems Some other functions of POS systems are inventory, purchasing patterns, and banking.

TEACH

ᴵᴵᴵᴵ Technology Resources

PowerPoint The *Marketing Essentials* PowerPoint Presentation CD-ROM provides visual lecture aids for every chapter section.

Concept Development

1. Read Section 9.3 with students.
2. Set up a demonstration of the Internet for your class. Visit the Web sites of some large marketing firms and discuss the future of e-marketing.

Discussion Starter

Computer Security A major issue for the business world today is computer security, not only from outside the company but also from within. Businesses are increasingly monitoring employee electronic communications, including e-mail, voice mail, and computer files. In 2000 it was estimated that more than 50 percent of all businesses regularly monitor these communications with the percentage expected to rise to 75 percent within a few years. Companies are resorting to these measures to ensure employee productivity while trying to restrict personal activities done on company time, as well as to protect themselves from lawsuits arising from e-mail viruses, chain letters, hoaxes, leaks of trade secrets, and sexual harassment. Of course, this monitoring has prompted a loud outcry of "invasion of privacy" from employees. So far the courts have sided with the employers, as long as employees have received notification of the monitoring. This topic should invoke lively discussion with your students but try to have them see it from both sides.

Cooperative Learning

Computer Care Provide students with markers and construction or butcher paper and have them work in teams to create posters of "The Top Ten Computer Care Tips," a list of guidelines for proper computer, printer, and disk care. *(Answers will vary but could include the following: Use a dust cover on PCs and printers. Don't touch the shiny parts of floppy disks and always return disks to a dust-free box. Never allow anyone to smoke, eat, or drink near your computer. Never leave floppy disks near your computer or printer because the magnetic waves in the motor of each can destroy information on your disk. Never remove or disconnect cables while the computer is turned on. Never turn off a computer or remove a disk from a disk drive while the drive is still turning. Never try to fix a computer yourself.)* The posters can be displayed in your classroom to serve as a reminder about proper computer equipment care.

Independent Practice

Research and Summarize Have students research the Internet or current publications for the "latest and greatest" advances in technology. These may be from fields such as medical, sports, business, software, etc. Students should prepare a 50-word summary of their findings and share the information with the class. *(Answers will vary. Some possibilities include wireless products, chips that are more powerful and faster, life-saving medical equipment, etc.)*

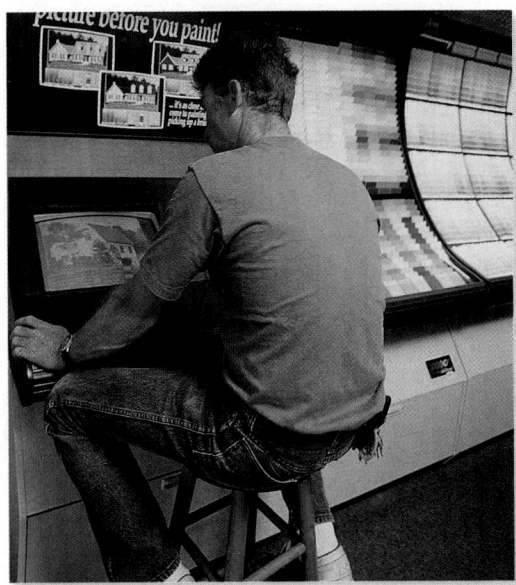

■ **Paint by Numbers** Have you ever wanted to buy paint but couldn't remember the color? Kiosks, like this one, can help you select the right house paint. *Can you think of other reasons stores would install interactive computers?*

THE WORLD WIDE WEB Although the terms World Wide Web (Web) and Internet are often used synonymously, they are actually two different things. The Web resides on the Internet as a collection of interlinked documents. You can view these pages with your browser, the software program that lets you see Web pages. They contain *hyperlinks*, or *links*, which direct you to other sites. When you click on a link, your browser brings up the connected page.

The British researcher Tim Berners-Lee invented the technology that created the Web. In addition to creating HTML, Tim developed the hypertext transport protocol (http) that links documents together. Finally, Tim developed the Uniform Resource Locator (URL)—the code used to identify and locate Web pages on the Internet.

Today there are tens of millions of pages on the Web. Thousands of new Web pages are added every week. Because the World Wide Web does not have a system for locating or categorizing content, an assortment of Web directories and search engines are available. One of the most comprehensive is Yahoo! It is an extensive directory with a menu that lists thousands of Web sites, organized by topic. Yahoo! also offers a search engine that looks for specified words in titles and addresses of the Web sites within the Yahoo! directory.

ELECTRONIC MAIL The single most common use of the Internet is for the exchange of e-mail. E-mail can be sent within a computer network or using the Internet. There are many Web-based e-mail services for which you don't need any special software other than a Web browser.

The greatest advantages of e-mail is that it is very efficient and inexpensive. An appliance store employee can e-mail an order for new merchandise to the shipper. The shipper can acknowledge the order within minutes, and the merchandise can be prepared for shipment almost immediately. E-mail users also find it convenient, economical, and ecological—no envelopes, stamps, or long-distance phone calls are needed!

INFORMATION RETRIEVAL If you are involved in business or do any type of research, the Internet has already changed your world view. Useful information can be accessed on computers at any time. If you are considering starting up a new business, you can research the competition on the Internet. You are also able to locate people you have lost track of in directories that search phone books and other sources throughout the entire United States. You can plan vacations and business trips, and make airline, hotel, and car rental reservations all on a single Web site. You can buy and sell stocks on the New York Stock Exchange. The possibilities truly are endless!

INTRANETS AND EXTRANETS Many businesses use e-mail and Web technologies within their companies on their own internal networks, called *intranets*. An intranet is a private, secure network usually within a company or organization, that contains proprietary company data and restricts access to designated personnel. They work like a private World Wide Web, but only internal users are allowed to access information or resources on an intranet system. Some businesses have developed networks for their customers, employees, partners, and suppliers. These networks, called *extranets*, enable external users to access a portion of an organization's internal network. By setting up an extranet, a company can enable customers to access data stored on an internal server. The security of such sensitive information is maintained through a firewall. A

170 Unit 4 ■ *Academic Concepts and Skills*

CAPTION ANSWER
Paint by Numbers Stores may install interactive computers to do market research and to provide other information that would persuade a customer to buy or encourage people to come into the store.

Did You Know? Add "getting a degree" to the list of things you can do online. The University of Phoenix allows students the option of attending classes online to receive both undergraduate and graduate degrees. Classes are online by modem. Such programs require good work habits and self-motivation but can be a boon to people who have full-time jobs.

firewall is hardware and software checkpoint at which all data, incoming and outgoing, are stopped to make sure that the data are acceptable.

ELECTRONIC COMMERCE Electronic commerce, usually called e-commerce, means the process of conducting business transactions on the Internet. The Internet makes possible new ways of doing business that are simpler, faster, and cheaper. E-commerce is redefining the relationship between the seller and the buyer. Web markets differ from traditional markets in that they are open for business 24 hours a day, seven days a week. They are also unencumbered by costly middlemen and distribution channels.

Retail businesses that sell directly to the consumer through the Web are known as *e-tailers*. Another common term for e-tailing is *B2C*, shorthand for business to consumer. You may have purchased products on the Internet, perhaps from a company like Amazon, the book and music superstore. Major companies are adapting to this trend as they promote and sell their products through Web pages.

Many companies request personal information, like your e-mail address and credit card number, when you make online purchases. E-tailers often store at least some of the personal information you provide, along with your preferences regarding their products. Later, they will use this information to promote their products on their Web sites and even in messages sent directly to your e-mail address.

E-commerce is much more than companies selling directly to consumers via the Internet. Business-to-business (*B2B*) sales are expected to be ten times as big as B2C by 2002. B2B allows manufacturing companies using the Internet to be in quick and constant communication with suppliers of parts and materials needed for production. Business analysts agree that B2B transactions will total more than $1 trillion a year before 2005.

The Future of Computer Technology

As more powerful and smaller technology is developed, one can't help but wonder what the future holds. One example that shows how quickly technology is changing the face of the market is the automobile industry. Jaguar used voice-activated technology in its 2000 models that enables the driver to control features such as temperature and the radio. Jaguar's "Global Positioning System" uses satellites to monitor position on the road and then offers the driver voice and visual guidance to reach the desired location. This technology, which seemed advanced at its introduction, will be further developed with sensors placed on cars and highways that

BRIGHT IDEAS
Radical Marketing of Storage Devices

Radical marketers focus on listening to their customers and making these concerns a top priority. This style of marketing is usually employed to counteract hefty advertising budgets of large competitors. EMC, a mainframe data storage company, employed this technique when going up against IBM. EMC convinced customers that their systems were a technological weapon and customers listened. As a result, EMC owns 32 percent of the market for large external storage systems, compared to IBM's 22 percent. L.L. Bean discovered that they could process transactions so fast that they added a full day to their holiday shopping season and still promised on-time delivery of goods. It is radical tactics such as these that keep customers coming back for more.

Thinking Creatively

How could you use radical marketing when starting a new online company that sells art posters and prints?

BRIGHT IDEAS Radical Marketing of Storage Devices

Answer Answers will vary but may include offering free shipping, discounts on framing, and providing customers with framing and matting services online.

Individualized Practice

Communication Skills

Although software programs contain spell checkers and grammar checkers, nothing takes the place of proofreading when it comes to correcting your letters, memos, reports, and manuscripts.

L1 Tell students to look in a dictionary or editorial style book for the common proofreader's marks and copy them on a sheet of paper to keep permanently in their notebooks. Review each of the marks with your students and tell them that this "shorthand" is a common "language" that proofreaders have used for decades.

L2 Give students an editing test with many errors in it to check their understanding of proofreaders' marks and their current level of editorial skill. When they have finished, review the test with the class and have students assess their own level of editorial skill. Ask students: What common errors did you always seem to miss? Where do you need to improve?

L3 Have each student make up an editing test based on common proofreaders' marks. Have each student exchange his or her test with another student. Then have each student review the other's test.

ASSESS

Reteaching

1. **Fact and Idea** Assign and review Fact and Idea Review questions 9–10 from the Chapter Assessment.
2. **Section Concepts** Have students write one or two sentences about each major section in this lesson to briefly summarize the concepts.

1. **Review** Assign and review the Chapter 9 activities in the *Student Activity Workbook*.
2. **Review** Assign and review the appropriate Thinking Critically questions from the Chapter Assessment.
3. **Review** Assign and review the following Chapter Assessment activities: Building Workplace Skills, Applying Marketing Concepts, Linking School to Work Activities, The DECA Connection Role Play, and Internet Connection.

Evaluation

Assign and review the Section 9.3 Assessment.

Technology Resources

Assessment Resources
Go to the *Marketing Essentials* Web site (**www.marketing.glencoe. com**) for resources to teach and assess occupation-specific vocabulary.

CLOSE

Section Wrap-Up

Reinforce the fact that the Internet is dramatically changing the world of business. Ask students to complete the following statement: My advice to any business is to . . . *(learn to use technology to your advantage or you may be left behind.)*

CAPTION ANSWER
Global Positioning Computers can diagnose problems, regulate temperature and humidity, calculate mileage and fuel needs, lock and unlock doors, as well as sense intrusion and sound alarms in automobiles.

172

can judge a car's location, maintain a safe speed, and control traffic. The ability to verbally tell your car to change the radio station is just the beginning.

Technology is reducing everything from books to the human voice to small bits that can be read, translated, and manipulated by computers. In addition, the plug is becoming less necessary as the wireless technology that produced remote controls and cellular phones expands. Wireless Internet access will become the standard, as messages and news updates will be obtained on watch-size devices that can be worn on the wrist.

In the future, bits of electronic data will primarily be read by machines instead of people. In time, machines will communicate between each other and cut out the need for the human middleman. The days of grocery shopping lists and spoiled milk will end as your appliances will keep track of this information for you. Your refrigerator will keep track of its food inventory, using wireless scanners to read bar codes on your food packages.

This technology explosion will not be limited to the Western world. In the early 2000s, use of the Web all over the world will skyrocket. Most of these new Web users will be from other countries, especially China. This change may lead to a marked decrease in the U.S. dominance of the Internet. The changing face of Internet use will open the global market to more countries and may level the playing field between technology-rich countries and the developing world.

■ **Global Positioning** The computer in this car is constantly calculating the car's location. It communicates with a global positioning satellite in space. In case of an accident, the computer can notify emergency personnel exactly where the car is. *What other functions can computers have in automobiles?*

9.3 ASSESSMENT

Reviewing Key Terms and Concepts

1. What are five types of computer systems?
2. What are two advantages that the Internet provides businesses?
3. What is the difference between the Internet and the Web?
4. What is a URL?
5. What is one change in computer technology that is expected in the future?

Thinking Critically

6. What are some ways in which using the Internet will increase your productivity, both in your personal life and on the job?

Integrating Academic Skills

7. **MATH** If there are 500 million users of the Internet now, and the number of users is expected to rise 40 percent each year over the next five years, how many Internet users will there be in five years?

9.3 ASSESSMENT ANSWERS

Reviewing Key Terms and Concepts
1. point-of-sale systems, interactive videodiscs, interactive TV, online services, and electronic mail
2. speed of communication and elimination of middlemen
3. The Internet is a global computer network; the Web resides on Internet as a collection of interlinked documents.
4. A URL, or Uniform Resource Locator, is the code used to locate and identify a Web page.

5. One answer is computerized bar codes on food items read by a refrigerator.

Thinking Critically
6. Answers will vary.

Integrating Academic Skills
7. **MATH** 500,000,000 x (5 x 1.4) = 2,689,120,000

Careers in Marketing

E-COMMERCE

Dan Linfield
Web Designer
Discovery.com

What does a job in Web design entail?

"Web designers design, develop, and maintain home pages for use on the Internet, working closely with advertisers, staff, and customers. Web designers are responsible for overseeing Web site usage and security policies. When working with online shoppers, Web designers provide technical assistance, validate credit card information, and supply information."

What kind of training did you have?

"I have a BS degree in Visual Communications and I worked in print design for seven years before getting into Web design. I learned most of the software that I use on the job."

What training do you recommend for students?

"I would suggest finding a college program that starts out with a solid foundation in design principles, such as color theory and typography. They should have software training in Adobe Photoshop, Adobe Illustrator, and Macromedia Flash, which is getting bigger on the Web. Basic knowledge of html and javascript is helpful."

What skills are most important to you?

"Good design skills are a must no matter what the medium. There are a lot of people doing Web design who know the software very well, but do not have strong skills in color, typography, and layout."

What is your key to success?

"The key to success in the Web world is keeping up with technology and your competition. The capabilities of the Web expand every day, and you need to keep up with these changes to stay successful. The easiest way to do this is to look at the Web every day and look for new innovations."

Thinking Critically

Why is flexibility so important in the field of Web design?

Career Facts

Education and Training: High school students should take college preparatory classes in computer science, science, mathematics, and accounting. A bachelor's degree in computer science with course work in operating systems and database language is recommended.

Aptitudes, Abilities, and Skills: Design skills, creativity, ability to learn new technologies quickly, good logic skills, and attention to detail are all helpful.

Career Outlook: The rapid expansion of the Internet should increase the demand for Web designers through 2006.

Career Path: A typical path to Web designer is employment as a computer programmer or experience with database languages and the Internet.

Chapter 9 ■ *Computer Applications and Skills* **173**

Vocabulary Review

Paragraphs will vary. See Glossary for definitions.

Fact and Idea Review

1. Mainframe computers are large computers that can be used by hundreds of people at the same time. Microcomputers are the types of computers that most people use at home.
2. A modem allows a computer to connect to other computers or to the Internet through phone, cable, DSL, or ISDN connection lines.
3. The software controls the functioning of the hardware and directs its operation.
4. Word processing is faster than typing, easier to edit as it checks grammar and spelling, and produces a more professional looking document.
5. A database program is a software program used to collect related data, which can be sorted, searched through, and printed as needed.
6. You would use a desktop publishing program when you want to combine word-processed text with graphic design elements.
7. A graphic and design program is used to produce drawings and designs.
8. A POS system feeds information directly from merchandise tags or product labels into a computer.
9. E-mail is faster, cheaper, more reliable, more economical, and more convenient than posted mail.

Thinking Critically

1. Answers will vary. Privacy would be an issue. Errors in information would be more serious if many people had access. People might be discriminated against because of the information.
2. Answers will vary. Desktop publishing software should make the process cheaper, allowing publishers to take more chances. This will most likely increase the number of self-published magazines and books.
3. Since e-mail saves time and money, companies' profits should increase. Because order turn-around time is shorter, businesses can stay more responsive to customers' needs. However, employees may use personal e-mail on company time.

Chapter 9 ASSESSMENT

VOCABULARY REVIEW

Choose at least eight of the words below and write a 250-word paragraph explaining how you would use a computer in business.

- supercomputer
- mainframe
- minicomputer
- microcomputer
- laptop
- PDA
- hardware
- disk drive
- scanner
- software
- word processing programs
- database programs
- spreadsheet programs
- desktop publishing programs
- graphics and design programs
- presentation software
- Web page editors
- Web page
- hypertext markup language (HTML)
- communications programs
- point-of-sale (POS) system
- e-mail
- browser

FACT AND IDEA REVIEW

1. What is the difference between a mainframe and a microcomputer? (9.1)
2. What does a modem do? (9.1)
3. Why is computer software necessary? (9.1)
4. Why would you use a word processing program rather than a typewriter when producing a business document? (9.2)
5. What is a database program? (9.2)
6. When would you use desktop publishing? (9.2)
7. What is a graphic and design program used for? (9.2)
8. How is a point-of-sale system used? (9.3)
9. What advantages does e-mail have over traditional mail? (9.3)

THINKING CRITICALLY

1. Some people have discussed the possibility of everyone in the country being in one database with credit and income information and personal histories included. What kinds of concerns might this kind of database raise?
2. What do you think has been the effect of desktop publishing software on the book and magazine publishing industry?
3. Explain the possible effects of the widespread use of e-mail.

BUILDING WORKPLACE SKILLS

1. **Human Relations** You are the manager at an exclusive make up and beauty supply chain store. Your district manager has decided to install an interactive touch-screen computer in each store to assist shoppers in making choices. Prepare a brief presentation to explain the benefits of the new computer and to explain that the role of the salesperson will be in conjunction with the computer device.
2. **Technology** Your company's computer system provides access to the Internet, and you've noticed several employees writing e-mail messages and doing personal research not related to their work assignments. What can you do to prevent or minimize employees' personal use of company computers?

Building Workplace Skills

1. Presentations will vary but should discuss how salespeople still play an important role in the store because they offer human interaction, can answer questions, and can assist customers with finding and trying products.
2. Answers will vary. You could recommend the installation of a program that tracks the work done by employees or a program that blocks personal work.

APPLYING MARKETING CONCEPTS

1. **Analyzing Computer Use in Marketing Careers** Choose a possible marketing career and use the Internet to research how computers are used in it. Speculate on what new uses computers might have in the future in that career. Use a word processing program to write a two-page report and present your report orally to the class.

2. **Interacting With Your Television** Research interactive television programs and participate in the program of your choice. Using a word processing program, write a summary of your experience.

3. **Understanding Publishing Software** Visit a local book publisher or newspaper publisher with your class or on your own to learn how these businesses use desktop publishing software. Ask for a demonstration, and then use graphics design software to produce a newsletter about class activities.

4. **Using Everyday Computer Skills** You are searching for the book of your choice for summer reading. Using the Internet, check the price of the book (with shipping and handling) at three e-tailers. Then, check the price of the book at three local retailers. Create a spreadsheet comparing the prices. Which offers the best value?

LINKING SCHOOL TO WORK

Technology Skills Find out from an employer how many different computer applications are in use at the workplace. List their names and what they are used for. Share your findings with the class. Tally which seem to be most popular.

Role Play: Software Salesperson

Situation You are to assume the role of a salesperson selling computer software to a record store owner (judge). As a salesperson, you will be expected to help the record store owner choose the software needed to keep track of the store's expanding customer base.

Activity Give a general explanation of the benefits of each part of the computer system.

Evaluation You will be evaluated on how well you meet the following performance indicators:

- Demonstrate basic database skills
- Explain the use of databases in organizing marketing data
- Design a database for retrieval of information
- Use database information analysis

inter NET CONNECTION

The Choice Is Yours
You are interested in doing graphic design as a career, and you want to choose the best computer platform and software for the job.

Connect
- Find the Web sites of graphics software manufacturers.
- Read about the various features of different graphics software programs and how they run on different platforms.
- Choose software and hardware that most suit your needs.
- Write a one-page report explaining and providing rationale for your choice.

THE DECA CONNECTION

Students should be evaluated on the performance indicators noted in the Role Play.
- For another DECA Role Play, go to the *Student Activity Workbook*, p. 73.
- For more in-depth Role Play practice, refer to DECA's *Essential Competitive Events Handbook*. To order, contact DECA at www.deca.org.

inter NET CONNECTION
Research results will vary.

Mini Quiz

Administer the Mini Quiz orally. For an expanded chapter quiz, go to page 51 of the *Reproducible Tests* book.

1. The U.S. Weather Bureau uses the largest and most powerful computer known as a supercomputer.
2. A computer does not know what to do without software.
3. The world's biggest computer network is known as the Internet.
4. Buying and selling products on the Internet is called e-commerce.
5. The fastest growing component of Internet commerce is business to business or B2B.

Applying Marketing Concepts

1. Reports will vary depending on careers chosen.
2. Summaries will vary depending on the students' interactive television experience.
3. Newsletters will vary depending on programs used and information presented.
4. Spreadsheets will vary based on students' findings.

Linking School to Work

Answers will depend on the work situation.

1. **Assessment** Have students complete the Reproducible Test for Chapter 9 or construct your own tests using the ExamView software.
2. **Enrichment** Have students complete the corresponding activities in the following workbooks:
   - *Marketing Math Workbook*, p. 19
   - *Marketing Research Project Workbook*, p. 47

Chapter Overview

Chapter 10 provides an overview of the key personal traits, interpersonal skills, and elements of teamwork, all of which are critical for job success.

 Springboard

Brainstorm and Compare Write the following scenario on the board: Assume you are the marketing manager for a startup Internet-based company. What are the desired characteristics you would like to see in your boss? What are the desired characteristics you expect in employees who report to you? Using the students' answers, write two lists. Ask what the differences and the similarities were between the groups. Have students justify their responses. Explain that they will learn and discuss those personal qualities necessary for success in their marketing careers.

Prereading

List the section objectives to discuss with students. Have students skim the chapter, looking at the pictures, reading the captions, and noting the heads. Ask questions to ensure that the students have a minimal understanding of the chapter structure.

Preteaching Marketing Vocabulary

Review the vocabulary list and have students brainstorm definitions for each vocabulary word and provide examples from their personal experiences.

Marketing: What It Takes

Answer It is important to recognize that your job is not just limited to the duties discussed when you were hired. Responsibilities can change depending on the needs of your employer, so try to be flexible. Doing the tasks your employer assigns is part of your job—and you need to do them if you want a promotion.

Chapter 10

Interpersonal Skills

Marketing: What It Takes

The Importance of Being Flexible

You are a salesperson in a sporting goods store. Most of your time is spent helping customers select items to purchase and answering their questions. Sometimes you help set up displays of new merchandise. Recently, your supervisor asked you to help with the repackaging of products to be returned to manufacturers. You were not told that this was one of your job responsibilities when you were hired, and you don't like doing it. Yesterday, you nearly snapped at your supervisor, telling her that repackaging is not part of your job.

WHAT WILL YOU DO?
Should you point out to your supervisor what duties were discussed when you were hired? Should you try looking differently at your job and the duties you are asked to do?

176

THE DECA CONNECTION

ADVISOR CORNER

Planning Chapter Activities Develop a Program of Work for your DECA chapter for the year. Include in the POW chapter goals proposed chapter activities to achieve the goals as well as fund raising plans to finance these activities. Include some chapter activities that focus on each point of the DECA Diamond (social intelligence, vocational understanding, civic consciousness, leadership development) so your members will gain a better understanding of what DECA stands for. It is a good idea to include at least one activity for each month of the school year so your chapter stays actively involved and enthusiastic about DECA.

Human Relations

Understanding Others

The first step in getting along with others is getting to know them. Finding out others' interests helps you understand them better. Interests often reflect values, and an understanding of a person's values is helpful in a relationship.

Trying to understand the reasons for others' behavior also facilitates good relationships both on and off the job. You can learn to be sensitive to certain aspects of everyone's behavior. Observe the way a person deals with others. Does the person relate differently to different people in the same situations? Can you figure out why? Which of the person's personality traits might affect your relationship with him or her?

Observing body language is another key way to learn about a person. Body language is the gestures, posture, mannerisms, and eye contact through which a person communicates thoughts with others. A person who leans slightly forward and nods in agreement with you is obviously paying attention. A person with an expressionless stare is looking but not listening.

Facial expressions are often good indicators of emotions and feelings. A pleasant, smiling expression, for instance, usually indicates a positive outlook. Your eyes tell a lot about you, too. When you are happy, for example, your pupils get larger; when you are unhappy, your pupils constrict. Suppose you are interviewing a candidate to help you with an advertising campaign. As you explain the job responsibilities, look into the person's eyes for an indication of his or her feelings.

One study of body language found that people sometimes say one thing verbally and another through body language. Body language is often the more accurate indicator of the person's thoughts and feelings. By observing people in many different situations, you can learn to read body language with considerable accuracy.

Personal Traits

Understanding others is only the first step in getting along with them. The way you interact with others will determine how successful and satisfied you are in the marketing world. The traits described here will help improve your interpersonal relations, on the job and with your friends and family.

■ Friendliness, Courtesy, and Tact

Getting along well with others is a lot easier when you display a friendly, outgoing personality. It's not always easy to do, especially if you're naturally quiet or shy. Show sincerity and you will be treated the same way.

What You'll Learn

- The importance of understanding others
- The personal traits that can help you be more effective in relations with other people
- The personal skills you should master for successful interpersonal relations
- How interpersonal skills may be used in marketing

Why It's Important

You use interpersonal skills in your personal life every day. Getting along well with others will serve you well on any job. In fact, studies show that between 80 and 85 percent of a person's success in the world of work is due to good interpersonal skills.

Key Terms

- body language
- initiative
- empathize
- assertive

Chapter 10 ■ *Interpersonal Skills* **177**

FOCUS

Bell Ringer Activity

Define Ask students: What is the difference between the words *subjective* and *objective*? Generate a list of student definitions and arrive at a consensus. *(Subjective means arising from conditions within the self that are not directly caused by external stimuli. Objective means dealing with facts or conditions as perceived without distortion by personal feelings, prejudices, or interpretations.)*

Introducing the Section

Human Relations Ask students: What do you find most difficult in working and dealing with a variety of people? Students might cite such issues as prejudice or personal dislike of a person's actions or beliefs. List these issues. Ask students what can make it easier to deal with difficult people. List these answers on the board.

Most everyone in the world of work has heavy contact with people who can sometimes be the source of daily conflict. None of us like everything everyone else does, says, or believes. However, tell students that their negative feelings about others can be minimized if they remain objective *(focused only on the facts)* instead of being subjective *(allowing their personal feelings to affect and/or impair their judgment of people and situations).*

Classroom Resources

For the Teacher
- Teacher Editions for all workbooks
- Assessment Package
- PowerPoint Presentation Software
- Interactive Lesson Planner
- **ILP** Block Scheduling, p. 4
- **ILP** Lesson Plans, p. 21
- **ILP** Internet Resources, p. 39

ILP *BusinessWeek* Case Studies, p. 63
ILP Marketing Career Portfolio, p. 34
- *Marketing Essentials* Web site (**www.marketing.glencoe.com**)

For the Student
- Student Activity Workbook, p. 81
- Marketing Math Workbook, p. 19

- Marketing Research Project Workbook, p. 47
ILP School-to-Work Activity Workbook, p. 37
- Virtual Business simulation
- *Marketing Essentials* Web site (**www.marketing.glencoe.com**)

ILP These resources are available in print and on the Interactive Lesson Planner (ILP)

TEACH

📊 Technology Resources

PowerPoint The *Marketing Essentials* PowerPoint Presentation CD-ROM provides visual lecture aids for every chapter section.

Concept Development

1. Read Section 10.1 with students.
2. Have students read aloud the Case Study on page 181 and review the answers in class.
3. Ask students to think of times when they made snap judgments about people and their judgments were wrong. Throughout the lesson stress the importance of remaining objective about others, including customers and co-workers, where judging others not only affects your interaction with them but may impede your job performance.
4. As you teach the components of this chapter, it is important to have students contribute examples of positive and negative experiences as you discuss the traits and skills. Students need to hear that each element discussed is equally important. In those negative examples, elicit responses from students about what could have been done differently or how individuals handled the situation. If you need additional resources, there are many training materials, such as books, articles, and videos, available on the Internet, in your local library, or from MarkEd on dealing with difficult personalities in the workplace.

■ **Body Talk** A person's body language sometimes speaks louder than words. *What message is the listener in this conversation conveying?*

Baby's First Cell Phone

Interested in a flip phone that features a picture of Queen Amidala of *Star Wars: Episode One* legacy? You might not be, but you might know an eight-year-old who would love one. Tiger Electronics is now empowering kids with the same electronic tools that adults have. Along the lines of cellular phones, Tiger's Power Talk sends and receives short voice messages up to 90 feet. The toy runs about $25 and replaces the toy push-button phone of the past. Another Tiger device, Lightning Mail, is capable of wireless sending and receiving of text messages at up to 50 feet. When the same device is plugged into a standard telephone jack, it can communicate via e-mail to anywhere in the world.

Thinking Critically

What other toys might you create that imitate an adult tool or product?

Courtesy is closely related to friendliness. Good manners and a polite demeanor should come naturally, even in awkward situations. It is not always easy to be courteous and pleasant, but tactfulness is always necessary. When you act with tact, you show respect in handling a situation and all the people involved. There is always a way to provide constructive criticism without offending or hurting someone unnecessarily.

■ Personal Ethics

Demonstrating personal ethics is essential in every aspect of life, especially on the job. Ethical behavior includes honesty, integrity, and a sense of fair play—things that all people desire and deserve. When you behave ethically, people trust you. This is particularly important on the job. You may be giving people information to help them decide whether to buy something. Being untruthful or withholding negative information leads to customer dissatisfaction.

It's also important to demonstrate good personal ethics toward your employer and coworkers. Honesty is a job requirement that cannot be overlooked.

■ Creativity, Initiative, and Responsibility

Creativity is the act of using your imagination to be inventive. It allows you not only to come up with new products but also to find new ways of doing your job. Incorporating creative thinking into daily tasks at work will make your job even more enjoyable.

Creativity is a form of self-expression that lets personality traits, which often go unnoticed at work, shine through. Creativity also helps you analyze situations and problems from a new and fresh perspective.

Initiative means doing what needs to be done without being urged. Once you have used your creativity to come up with a new idea, it will go nowhere unless you use your initiative to act on it.

Responsibility is being accountable for your actions and doing your duty. After taking the initiative to begin a job, you must accept responsibility for completing it. Employers value responsible employees because they can be counted on to work without much supervision.

CAPTION ANSWER
Body Talk By leaning toward the person speaking, she is conveying that she is interested in what the other person is saying. She may nod affirmatively occasionally if she agrees with what is being said.

 Baby's First Cell Phone

Answer Answers will vary but could include meeting schedulers, laptop computers, and handheld organizers.

Attitude

Your attitude refers to the mental outlook you have toward people and situations. Try to see the good in the people you deal with. People with a positive attitude welcome a difficult assignment as a challenge. People with a negative attitude complain.

Specific traits that foster a positive outlook are interest and enthusiasm. You can develop interest in a particular subject by learning more about it. Finding out why inventory is necessary makes the process more interesting. It will help you do the job with more enthusiasm.

Self-Control and Orderliness

People who exercise self-control are tactful and slow to anger. They don't indulge their impulses, but behave in a disciplined way. This is important in marketing where you will be in contact with the public. Self-control and orderly behavior inspire confidence in customers and in coworkers. People who can't control themselves and do things in a sloppy, inattentive way are not likely to be given much responsibility.

Self-Awareness and Willingness to Change

Knowing yourself is the first step in making personal changes. You can begin by making a list of all your personal strengths and weaknesses. Then decide which weaknesses you would like to work on improving. Practice the traits that will help you improve your weaknesses.

■ **Service with a Smile** Good customer service is one key to success. Cashiers at Safeway grocery stores show courtesy by thanking all customers by name (which they learn from the ATM card or by asking). *What are other ways that employees in retail can be courteous?*

It's also important to be willing to listen to the feedback of others and act on it. Sometimes we aren't aware of the effect we are having on other people. We can move ahead in our own personal growth if we are willing to change attitudes and

---

BRIGHT IDEAS

Girl Tech

Dr. Janese Swanson, a founder of Girl Tech, does more than come up with bright ideas—she brings them to market. Dr. Swanson has created a line of affordable electronic gadgets for girls. One item, the Password Journal, is a book-size voice-activated plastic box that holds a diary. Using voice recognition technology, this diary is accessible only when its owner speaks the password. Girl Tech's Door Pass sets off an alarm when someone tries to sneak into the owner's bedroom. Dr. Swanson's inspiration comes from her ten-year-old daughter, who is always searching for "cool" toys for girls. Girl Tech most certainly fills this niche with its very cool gadgets.

Thinking Creatively

Think of a cool toy that you would have loved when you were ten years old. Invent this product now with the help of modern technology.

BRIGHT IDEAS **Girl Tech**

Answer Answers will vary based on students' interests, creative ideas, and knowledge of modern technology.

CAPTION ANSWER
Service with a Smile Courtesy is closely related to friendliness. It can be shown by smiles, handshakes, or wishes for a good afternoon or evening.

Discussion Starter

Time Management Provide this scenario to students: "The school principal has just advised us that our school has been awarded $86,400 for school improvement but it must be spent within the next 24 hours. Our class has been asked to determine how this money should be spent." Ask students for suggestions and estimated prices. Be specific on brands and quantities while keeping a running total. This should be a fairly involved process and perhaps difficult for the class to reach agreement. When you have determined how to spend the $86,400, ask if there is a reasonable consensus on this. If so, begin a discussion of time management. Then ask what does time management have to do with spending the $86,400? Each of us each day gets exactly 86,400 seconds (no more, no less), and how we spend that time is what time management is all about. It is not always easy to decide how to spend it.

Thinking Critically

Customer Service Ask students what this phrase means: "Good customer service is no longer enough." Is this true? Why or why not? *(It means that in this highly competitive global marketplace, you have to distinguish yourself. You have to provide superior service; you have to do what you say you will, how you say you will, when you say you will, at the price promised, plus you must tell every customer "I appreciate your business." If you don't, your competitor will.)*

Cooperative Learning

Interpersonal Skills Divide the class into four groups. Have each group role-play one situation in which a person has used inter-personal skills in the following situations:

- An employer accuses an employee of using company materials for personal use.
- A new manager explains to an employee that an entirely new system is being implemented for handling customer returns.
- A friend wants to give you the money for you to buy an expensive leather jacket from the store where you work so you can get the 20% employee discount.

Independent Practice

Negotiating Negotiating is an important skill that students will need in their personal and work lives. Students may think that it involves sitting around a table and hammering out agreements. However, marketers negotiate daily for such things as salary, the price at which to buy or sell, terms of contracts, delivery times, work hours, etc. Have students write one or two paragraphs about a time in their lives when they successfully used negotiation. *(Examples may be trying to get a favorite toy or an extended curfew time, buying a car, or settling a disagreement between two people.)* They should describe the situation and identify what skills they used to successfully negotiate. Several excellent articles on negotiating are available at **www.negotiationskills.com**.

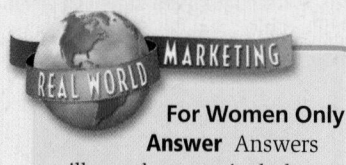

For Women Only Answer Answers will vary but may include changing the packaging to appeal to men or advertising in men's magazine or in primarily male gyms.

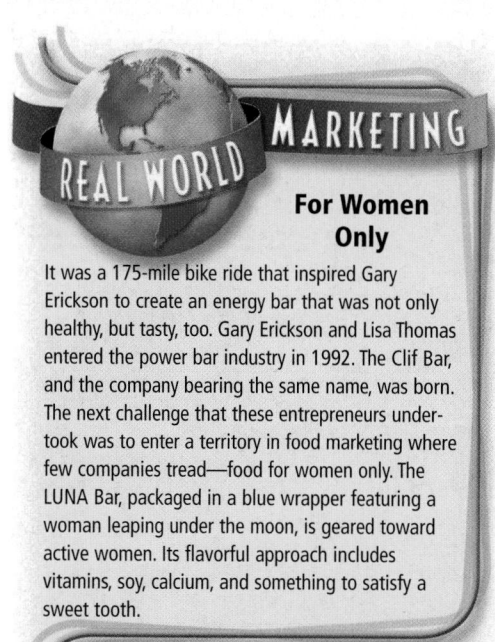

REAL WORLD MARKETING

For Women Only

It was a 175-mile bike ride that inspired Gary Erickson to create an energy bar that was not only healthy, but tasty, too. Gary Erickson and Lisa Thomas entered the power bar industry in 1992. The Clif Bar, and the company bearing the same name, was born. The next challenge that these entrepreneurs under-took was to enter a territory in food marketing where few companies tread—food for women only. The LUNA Bar, packaged in a blue wrapper featuring a woman leaping under the moon, is geared toward active women. Its flavorful approach includes vitamins, soy, calcium, and something to satisfy a sweet tooth.

Thinking Critically
What approaches might Clif Bar Inc. take if it was marketing a new energy bar to men only?

behaviors that are negative. Being willing to change also means being willing to adapt to changes around you. Sometimes you may be asked to perform a task that isn't part of your job. Flexibility is essential.

■ Self-Esteem

Self-esteem is your perceived worth or value. Good self-esteem helps you see yourself as being able to do your job. It helps you get along with others.

To help others gain self-esteem, treat them with the respect and kindness that you would like to be treated with yourself. A cashier who looks a customer in the eye, smiles at him, and gives a friendly hello is fostering that person's self-esteem. So is an employee who praises a coworker's effort. Raising someone's self-esteem may be as simple as remembering his or her name.

■ Empathy

You can earn a person's trust and respect faster by empathizing. To **empathize** means to understand a person's situation or frame of mind. Learn to

respect the other person's point of view, even when you don't agree with it. This technique is especially important in dealing with customers who are upset or angry. There may be other factors contributing to their moods.

Personal Skills

There are some personal skills that can help you get along with people on the job, in addition to the personal traits discussed earlier. Using the following skills can help you succeed in your career.

■ Assertiveness

Being **assertive** means standing up for your rights, beliefs, and ideas. People will respect you if you can be assertive without being pushy or aggressive. Show confidence and speak with authority. This does not mean you should sound like a know-it-all, but you do have to know what you are talking about.

Assertiveness is a skill that takes a while to learn. You will gain confidence as you gain more experi-ence. This will put you in a better position to influence others.

■ Solving Someone's Problem

People are far more willing to listen to a new idea when they can see how it will benefit them. Look for ways your idea will solve a problem for others. It may save them time or make it unnecessary for them to perform some unpleasant tasks. Always keep those benefits foremost in your mind—and in their minds—when presenting your idea. Phrase your idea in terms of their needs.

■ Time Management

Learning to budget your time and to record impor-tant deadlines or appointments are part of time management. It's not possible to be effective in your work unless you are able to use time wisely. A salesperson who misses an appointment with a client is not likely to make the sale—or any other sale—to that client.

■ Goal Setting

Setting goals for your career and personal devel-opment is essential. How can you get anywhere if you don't know where you are headed? Procedures for setting goals are outlined in Chapter 37.

GREAT IDEAS from the Marketing Classroom

Laresa Slater
Paseo Academy of Fine and
Performing Arts
Kansas City, MO

I use a novel strategy to teach marketing to fine and performing arts students to make it interesting, fun, and relevant. Students produce and market an in-school musical production for a public audience.

The first semester utilizes entertainment and perform-ing arts case studies to teach the fundamental market-ing knowledge and skills that students will need to effectively execute the musical production. The sec-ond semester utilizes an application model. Students plan, organize, and execute a musical production, which takes students through every marketing foun-dation and function.

Case Study

Schmoozing

The word "schmooze" has a bad reputation! For many, it implies being nice to others just to get something from them—a job contact or a sales opportunity. To some, schmoozing involves using someone or unfairly taking advantage of a situation. There is more to schmoozing than that. It's a way of using your interpersonal skills to turn strangers into friends and friends into customers. Learning the elements of schmoozing can also help you get along with people in your workplace.

Schmoozing is about being generous with sincere compliments. It requires people to move out of their comfort zones and strike up conversations with people they don't know. To perfect the art of schmoozing, it is important to get over any fears of being rejected. Be confident, be yourself, and be prepared by "knowing your audience." To know your audience you must understand what the people you want to schmooze with will want to talk about. It is also important to find ways to help people. If you've just met a person who has a need you can solve, be sure to give the person your business card and assure him or her that you will follow up. A handy way to remember such promises is to get the person's business card and write what you promised on the back of the card. This will help you remember to write down the task on your to-do list. Be sure to end the conversation by thanking the person and reiterating your promise to follow up on anything you may have offered. If they've talked to you about something that they're involved in and you're interested in, ask them to keep you informed on their progress.

The key to schmoozing is sincerity. If you have an ulterior motive, people will not feel comfortable with you. Good schmoozers are able to find interests and attitudes they share with others. They ask questions and are sincerely interested in the responses. They are good listeners. They smile when they meet people and maintain eye contact. Most importantly, they truly enjoy people. They value what they can offer to a person just as much as they value any potential benefits from the relationship.

Many people at the top of their fields are great schmoozers. They've learned that making others feel valued and appreciated is great for business. It's time to downplay the negative connotations of the word schmooze and develop your own schmoozing skills!

Case Study Review

1. What interpersonal skills do good schmoozers show?
2. How do you think learning to be a good schmoozer could help you in working in a team environment?

A MATTER OF ETHICS

3. Do you see a connection between schmoozing's bad reputation and ethical concerns? What are those concerns?

ASSESS

Reteaching

1. **Vocabulary** Assign and review the vocabulary terms for this section.
2. **Fact and Idea** Assign and review Fact and Idea Review questions 1–5 from the Chapter Assessment.
3. **Customer Relations** Have students relate instances that they have observed where people in a working situation acted poorly or negatively, such as a salesperson who was not helpful or rude. What did they do? What are instances of individuals whom they think went "above and beyond"? If you have trouble getting responses, ask students why more employees are not willing to go above and beyond?

Enrichment

1. **Review** Assign and review the appropriate Thinking Critically questions from the Chapter Assessment.
2. **Extend** Assign and review the corresponding activities from *BusinessWeek Case Studies*, *Internet Resources*, and the *School-to-Work Activity Workbook.* **ILP**
3. **Research and Report** Have students research topics in business etiquette. This is a huge area but some suggested topics include "the how-to's" of introductions, handshakes, conversation, telephoning, dining, office meetings, dress, and traveling. Students should report their findings to the class.

Case Study Review Answers

Schmoozing

1. Good schmoozers display empathy, positive attitude, enthusiasm, interest in others, and the desire to raise others' self-esteem when interacting with other people.
2. Students' answers will vary. People tend to work better together if they feel appreciated and valued; therefore, they will share leadership more willingly.

A MATTER OF ETHICS

3. Answers will vary. Insincere schmoozing can be used to deceive people or to mislead them. Schmoozing that is used only to reach a personal goal is termed *empty schmoozing* and is often detected and frowned upon by others.

Technology Resources

Assessment Resources
Go to the *Marketing Essentials* Web site (**www.marketing.glencoe. com**) for resources to teach and assess occupation-specific vocabulary.

CLOSE

Section Wrap-Up

Students should provide an ending for the following story: Two sisters are arguing because each wants the one single orange that is remaining and each tries different tactics to secure the orange. Finally, the mother intercedes and . . . *(Students may say that she cuts the orange in half, giving one half to each girl or that she eats it so neither one gets it. Some may say the mother asks the girls why each wants the orange and discovers that one girl wants the juice from the orange to drink, and the other girl wants the pulp and rind for making marmalade. The wise mother then squeezes the orange giving one girl the juice and the remainder to the other girl.)*

CAPTION ANSWER
Customer Assistance This employee can observe body language, show interest and enthusiasm, and practice empathy.

Interpersonal Skills in Marketing

Certain interpersonal skills are needed to deal with the special relationship between marketing employees and their customers. The following is a list of some basic procedures you may be asked to handle that will require the use of your interpersonal skills.

1. *Handle customer requests and questions.* You will need to learn the proper procedures for handling customer requests and questions. You will also need to know what you should say to customers if you cannot answer their questions yourself.

2. *Provide customers with directions to your store location.* You will need to be able to give clear and concise directions.

3. *Understand management's role in customer relations.* You will need to know under what circumstances a manager should be called to talk to a customer. Policies differ from business to business.

4. *Understand procedures for handling difficult customers.* Having clear procedures helps to prevent you from becoming upset when dealing with customers who may be angry.

5. *Explain business policies to customers.* This includes return or exchange policies and whether the business accepts checks or credit cards.

6. *Handle customer complaints.* You will be better able to provide a customer with an acceptable response, whether positive or negative, if you have a specific procedure to follow.

■ **Customer Assistance** Having good interpersonal skills can help you avoid problems in working with customers. *What skills can this employee use to try to ensure the customer's satisfaction?*

10.1 ASSESSMENT

Reviewing Key Terms and Concepts

1. Why is it important to understand others?
2. What are the personal traits that can help you be more effective with other people?
3. What are four personal skills that you should master for successful interpersonal relations in the marketing world?
4. How can interpersonal skills be used in marketing?

Thinking Critically

5. Describe the body language you would expect to see in a shy person, a defensive person, and a self-confident person.

Integrating Academic Skills

6. **COMMUNICATION** As an insurance agent, you have just met with a prospective buyer and discussed a particular health insurance plan. Write a brief, effective follow-up note.

10.1 ASSESSMENT ANSWERS

Reviewing Key Terms and Concepts
1. It facilitates good relationships.
2. friendliness, courtesy, tact, personal ethics, creativity, initiative, responsibility, positive attitude, self-control, orderliness, self-awareness, willingness to change, self-esteem, and empathy
3. assertiveness, solving someone's problem, time management, and goal setting
4. to handle customer requests, questions, and complaints, etc.

Thinking Critically
5. A shy person may avert their eyes. A defensive person may speak with a loud voice. A self-confident person may keep direct eye contact.

Integrating Academic Skills
6. **COMMUNICATION** Notes will vary.

Working Together

Teamwork

Have you ever been on a team? While you were growing up, did you play baseball, basketball, or other sports on the playground? Have you ever participated in a school or club car wash or decorated the gym for a dance? All of these activities were performed by teams. A team is a group of people who work together to achieve a goal. Teamwork is the skill they use to achieve that goal.

Teamwork is important in the business world. You will learn in Chapter 11 about new models of management where entire companies are organized into teams. A manager at Sun Life Insurance Company said, "People rise and fall according to how they work with their peers."

■ Training

To be an effective team member, you must have training for all the tasks you will perform. You have probably heard of cross-training in sports. That's a way of staying in shape that includes doing many different activities—swimming, running, and weight training, for example. Each one of the sports uses a different set of muscles and leads to a different kind of strength.

On the job, people are cross-trained for many tasks on a team. This gives the team flexibility and several strengths. Work becomes more enjoyable when you know you will not be doing the same thing every day.

At Hallmark Cards, teams of editors, writers, artists, and production specialists oversee the entire process of making greeting cards. Twenty percent of the team's time during the first year is spent in training.

■ Team Planning

Imagine that you and your friends have decided to throw a surprise birthday party. If each friend goes ahead and does what he or she thinks should be done, the result may be chaos. If, however, you plan who will send invitations, set up decorations, be in charge of music, and buy the food, the result will probably be a great party. The same goes for running a successful team project at work. Before you start, make a plan. Since you will be working as a team, plan as a team. Team planning involves setting goals, assigning roles, making agreements, sharing responsibility, and communicating regularly.

• What You'll Learn

- The importance of teamwork in the business world
- Six aspects of successful teamwork

• Why It's Important

Teamwork in business is like teamwork in the sports arena. You may not wear a uniform in the work world, but you will be a member of a team dedicated to achieving a specific goal. Develop the habit of being a good team member by always fulfilling your responsibilities, and you won't let your team down on your job.

Key Terms

- consensus
- agreement

Chapter 10 ■ *Interpersonal Skills* **183**

FOCUS

Bell Ringer Activity

Solve For this activity you will need a small collection of puzzles or brainteasers. Divide the class into a variety of group sizes. Then have groups solve their puzzles. Provide a small reward for the group that solves the most problems in the assigned time.

Introducing the Section

Working Together Ask students the following questions about the above activity:
1. Was teamwork an important component of this activity?
2. Was anyone unhappy with the outcome? Why?
3. Do you think you will be in teamwork situations in your careers?

Explain to students that teamwork is essential in the workplace and school. In this section of the chapter, students will look at what it takes for effective teamwork.

Concept Development

1. Read Section 10.2 with students.
2. Ask students: Have you ever been a member of a team? Discuss their responses and the many kinds of teams people work in every day.

TEACH

Technology Resources

PowerPoint The *Marketing Essentials* PowerPoint Presentation CD-ROM provides visual lecture aids for every chapter section.

Classroom Resources

For the Teacher
- Teacher Editions for all workbooks
- Assessment Package
- PowerPoint Presentation Software
- Interactive Lesson Planner
- ILP Block Scheduling, p. 4
- ILP Lesson Plans, p. 22
- ILP Internet Resources, p. 39

- ILP *BusinessWeek* Case Studies, p. 63
- ILP Marketing Career Portfolio, p. 34
- *Marketing Essentials* Web site (**www.marketing.glencoe.com**)

For the Student
- Student Activity Workbook, p. 81
- Marketing Math Workbook, p. 19

- Marketing Research Project Workbook, p. 47
- ILP School-to-Work Activity Workbook, p. 37
- Virtual Business simulation
- *Marketing Essentials* Web site (**www.marketing.glencoe.com**)

ILP These resources are available in print and on the Interactive Lesson Planner (ILP)

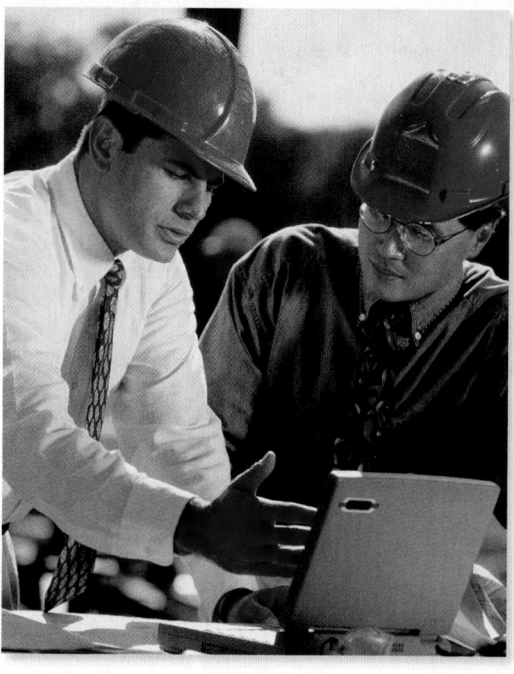

■ **Working Together** Effective teamwork requires respect for each other. *What other qualities help you get along with others in the workplace?*

■ Team Goals

Before a team can begin to act, the team has to have clearly defined goals. Team members must feel involved in defining a goal in order to feel committed to it. At Subway sandwich shops, for example, production teams set goals for the time required to make each sandwich and for the quality of the product. Companies that involve employees in setting goals show that they respect and value employee opinions. This results in greater company loyalty and stronger team spirit.

Team members set specific goals for their teams, in addition to setting company goals. Usually, members must reach a consensus about goals. A **consensus** is a decision that each member agrees to. In order for this to happen, it is important that all team members be allowed to state their opinions. Other members must respect this right and not interrupt. Respectful discussion continues until the group reaches an agreement. The final agreement may require team members to make a compromise. This means that some members may need to adjust their original positions. It is important that all members be comfortable with the final decision of a compromise. This prevents employees from saying later that their opinions were not acknowledged.

■ Assigning Roles

Remember the party you planned? You could have chosen one friend to oversee the process. Then the tasks might have been done more efficiently. Likewise, team projects often work more smoothly if the team appoints a team leader. This is especially true for self-directed teams. The facilitator coordinates the tasks so that the team works efficiently. It is also important to assign roles to each member of the team.

Each person on the team needs to know which part of the process he or she is responsible for each day. Members are usually assigned tasks based on their skills and experience. Sometimes a less experienced member will be paired up with someone more skilled, so he or she can receive training while completing the task.

■ Agreements

An **agreement** is a specific commitment that each member makes with the group. It is similar to a contract or a promise to perform a certain task within a certain period of time. When team members make agreements, the team becomes more cohesive and stronger. A team's agreements must be consistent with its goals.

At some franchises of Pizza Hut, the agreement is that dine-in customers receive their pizza in 20 minutes or the pizza is free. Each affected team member must complete his or her part of the process. Sometimes this can be accomplished by cutting out unnecessary steps, or it may be that people have to work at top speed. In another situation, all employees at a retail store might agree to greet customers with the same greeting.

Each person is motivated to keep his or her agreement when everyone has agreed on the goal. The whole team's performance suffers if one person doesn't keep his or her agreement. It is important that each team member feels connected to company goals as well as the team as a whole. Team loyalty and positive peer pressure help to encourage people to keep their agreements.

■ Shared Responsibility and Shared Leadership

Each member must feel responsible for the whole team's efforts in order for a team to work. That is shared responsibility. If a team is to function effectively and efficiently, then a standard must be set by the whole team. It's not enough to do your own job well and then complain if others don't seem to be doing theirs. That's where shared leadership comes in.

Team members take action to bring the whole team's performance up to the standards the team has agreed on in shared leadership. Teams do this by having meetings at which they give feedback about individual performance and about specific parts of the team's work. Feedback about someone's performance must be given with respect. If it is done in a way that is overly critical or harsh, it will not serve its purpose and it will alienate the team member in question.

If the feedback is about some aspect of the team process, it needs to be specific so team members can provide specific responses. For example, rather than saying, "We seem to be wasting a lot of time walking around," more specific feedback would be, "It takes two minutes to walk from my work station to the pizza oven." A team member might then suggest, "Could we move the work station closer to the oven to save time?"

Shared leadership allows all team members to perform some management functions. As employees get a glimpse of other roles and responsibilities in an organization, it gives them a greater appreciation for management. It makes employees feel more powerful because it actually gives them more power. Shared responsibility and shared leadership are essential elements of teamwork.

In your marketing career, you will certainly be a member of many teams. Any group that works together to achieve something—reach a sales goal, perform an inventory—is a team. A department can act as a team. You may serve on different teams for various projects that you work on or clients that you represent. You may also serve on interdepartmental or cross-functional teams. Teamwork skills will always be valuable interpersonal skills.

■ **Team Players** Teamwork can improve productivity, creativity, and customer satisfaction. *How does working in teams prevent the process from being dominated by one person?*

CAPTION ANSWER
Team Players Teams prevent one person from dominating the process because members make arrangements with each other, share leadership, and stress individual roles.

Did You Know?

The famous sales training leader Dale Carnegie coined the phrase, "Act enthusiastic and you'll be enthusiastic!" to point out that enthusiasm is like spontaneous combustion in that it feeds on itself and can grow into a regular behavior if practiced regularly. Similarly, research has shown that smiling promotes relaxation and a feeling of well being.

Individualized Practice

Human Relations Skills

Have pairs of students role-play the following scenarios:

L1 An employee has asked to take a week's vacation. She has earned the vacation days, but you are in a busy season and need all employees. How would you handle this situation?

L2 One of your trusted employees tells you that John, an employee, is having someone else punch his time card at 7:00 p.m. each night, even though he leaves the stockroom at 6:45. How would you handle this situation?

L3 You see one of your employees dealing with a customer in a rude manner. How would you handle this situation?

ASSESS

Reteaching

1. **Vocabulary** Assign and review the vocabulary terms for this section.
2. **Fact and Idea** Assign and review Fact and Idea Review questions 6–9 from the Chapter Assessment.

Enrichment

1. **Review** Assign and review the Chapter 10 activities in the *Student Activity Workbook*.
2. **Review** Assign and review the appropriate Thinking Critically questions from the Chapter Assessment.
3. **Review** Assign and review the following Chapter Assessment: Building Workplace Skills, Applying Marketing Concepts, Linking School to Work Activities, The DECA Connection Role Play, and Internet Connection.

Evaluation

Assign and review the Section 10.2 Assessment.

Technology Resources

 Assessment Resources
Go to the *Marketing Essentials* Web site (**www.marketing.glencoe. com**) for resources to teach and assess occupation-specific vocabulary.

VIRTUAL BUSINESS

 Down to Business
Students are challenged to use the talents of their team members to maximize their store's profits in Knowledge Matters' Virtual Business visual simulation, "Competitions—Down to Business." If needed, have students run the Virtual Business tutorial before beginning this simulation. For additional instructions and teaching tips for this activity, go to the *Marketing Essentials* Web site (**www.marketing.glencoe.com**).

CLOSE

Section Wrap-Up

Put students in teams of two or three to create a one-line slogan on teamwork. *(Examples are: "There is no I in Teamwork" and "Together Everyone Achieves More.")*

There's No "I" in Team
Answer Some may believe that workplace harmony could help companies prosper; others may believe Japan could become more prosperous by adopting more cutthroat business practices.

186

■ Being a Valuable Team Member

A team can only be as successful as its members. For a team to be successful, it is important that each member is willing and able to work to achieve the team's goals.

What makes a person a good team member? The following list describes valuable attitudes and actions. As you read the list, consider how following these conventions can help teams overcome obstacles.

- Make the team's goals your top priority
- In meetings, listen actively and offer suggestions
- Build positive group dynamics with team members
- Continue to communicate with team members outside meetings
- Follow up on what you've been assigned to do
- Work to resolve conflicts among team members
- Respect the other members of your team
- Try to inspire other employees to get involved

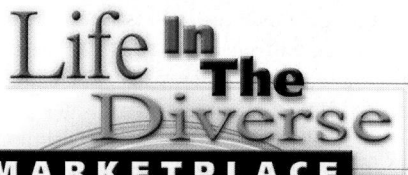

There's No "I" in Team
People in the United States put an emphasis on individual excellence and winning, which in turn encourages competition and entrepreneurship. In Japan, the emphasis is placed on teamwork and consideration of others. Taxi drivers wear white gloves, and sick individuals wear surgical masks to prevent infecting others. High school baseball teams bow to each other at the beginning of each game. The point is to enjoy harmony, or common experience, in all aspects of life. Perhaps this emphasis is a result of population size and square footage—125 million Japanese live in an area the size of California.

Thinking Critically
Can Japan succeed as an economic superpower with its view toward harmony in the workplace?

10.2 ASSESSMENT

Reviewing Key Terms and Concepts
1. What is teamwork? Why is it important in the business world?
2. List six aspects of successful teamwork.
3. What is a consensus?
4. What is the idea behind shared leadership?

Thinking Critically
5. Why would employees be more motivated to perform well on a team than in an individual effort?

Integrating Academic Skills
6. **MATH** You have calculated that your idea to use plastic instead of metal when manufacturing your company's paper towel holders would save $.13 per item. If your company can produce 600 paper towel holders per day, and there are 250 production days in the year, how much will your idea save the company in a year?

10.2 ASSESSMENT ANSWERS

Reviewing Key Terms and Concepts
1. Teamwork is a skill used to achieve goals.
2. training, team goals, assigning roles, agreements, shared responsibility, and shared leadership
3. A consensus is a decision with which each team member agrees.
4. Shared leadership lets all members of a team take responsibility for getting the job done right.

Thinking Critically
5. Answers may vary. Team spirit is a motivator because you have the opportunity to work with those who share ideals and goals. The team bond can encourage members to work to their highest potential.

Integrating Academic Skills
6. **MATH** $0.13 x 600 x 250 = $19,500 per year

Careers in Marketing

HOSPITALITY MARKETING

Krista Brennecke White
Flight Attendant
USAirways

What does your job entail?
"My job as a flight attendant is ultimately to ensure the safety and comfort of the passengers on board the aircraft. I serve as the main link between USAirways and its customers, which draws on the public relations and customer service aspects of my job. Flight attendants not only serve the customers during the flight, but are also responsible for preparing the aircraft and galleys for each trip. This entails ensuring that necessary supplies and food are on board and that all equipment is working. Aside from greeting and assisting passengers, other duties include answering questions, enforcing regulations, and assisting during emergencies."

What kind of training did you have?
"My training consisted of an eight-week rigorous schedule of classes and drills that covered customer service, first aid, federal air regulation safety procedures, and emergency evacuations. We also learned about the history of USAirways and the airline industry as a whole. High school students who are interested in this career should take courses in English, geography, health, and foreign language."

How does your workload vary?
"My workload varies constantly. One flight may be completely full and the next may be very light. Some of the flights are as short as thirty minutes, while others are more than eight hours. Passengers' demands also fluctuate depending on various times of the year and different regions of the country."

What is your key to success?
"I'm always flexible, patient, and open to different personalities."

Thinking Critically
How is the flight attendant a key to the marketing success of an airline company?

Career Facts

Education and Training: Most employers require that applicants have a high school diploma or equivalent. Most companies have their own mandatory training programs that prepare you for this career. Knowledge of passport and customs regulations is required. Training as a nurse is helpful, but not required.

Aptitudes, Abilities, and Skills: Good health, keen hearing, corrected eyesight of at least 20/50, stamina to endure long shifts and irregular hours, adequate strength and dexterity to operate safety and emergency equipment, and knowledge of first aid procedures are necessary. You must also have good people skills, good communication (especially verbal) skills, and an outgoing personality.

Career Outlook: The market for flight attendants is expected to grow much faster than the general employment market through the year 2006.

Career Path: Employment as a travel agent in a private company or as a ticket or reservation agent for an airline can lead to a flight attendant position. Flight attendants may advance to positions of in-flight supervisors, flight attendant instructors, or sales representatives.

187

Vocabulary Review

Paragraphs will vary. See Glossary for definitions.

Fact and Idea Review

1. It can further help you understand their motivations and values.
2. creativity, initiative, and responsibility
3. Developing an interesting and enthusiastic attitude can foster a positive outlook.
4. When you understand yourself, you can begin to change your negative traits or habits.
5. You stand up for your rights, values, and beliefs without being aggressive.
6. It is the practice of learning many different skills so that you can fulfill many team functions.
7. Each member is allowed to speak with no interruptions, and respectful discussion continues until the group agrees.
8. Team members must have training; the team must have a goal; and members must know their responsibilities.
9. They help each member feel responsible for the whole team's effort. Team members bring the whole team's performance up to the standards the team has agreed on.
10. Answers may include three of the following conventions: make the teams goals your top priority; listen actively in meetings and offer suggestions; continue to communicate with team members outside meetings; follow up on what you've been assigned to do; work to resolve conflicts among team members; respect the other members of your team; and try to inspire other employees to get involved.

Thinking Critically

1. Marketing depends on customers trusting the marketer; if marketers are not ethical, they will lose customer trust.
2. It is important that all members of a team carry equal weight when making decisions and performing tasks. Members must have the initiative to share opinions and new ideas and the responsibility to carry them out.
3. Treat them with respect and kindness and be sure to give positive feedback when appropriate.
4. Answers will vary but may include homework assignments, contracts

188

Chapter 10 ASSESSMENT

VOCABULARY REVIEW

Write a paragraph that includes all the following words. Use them in ways that demonstrate that you know their meanings.

- body language
- initiative
- empathize
- assertive
- consensus
- agreement

FACT AND IDEA REVIEW

1. Why does finding out other people's interests help you understand them better? (10.1)
2. What three personal traits allow you to come up with and follow through on new ideas? (10.1)
3. What attitudes can you cultivate that will foster a positive outlook? (10.1)
4. How can self-awareness help you to change weaknesses to strengths? (10.1)
5. What does it mean to be assertive? (10.1)
6. In a teamwork context, what is cross-training? (10.2)
7. How does a team arrive at a consensus? Why is consensus important? (10.2)
8. What must a team do before it can act? (10.2)
9. Why does shared responsibility and shared leadership help a team to work well? (10.2)
10. Name three conventions that can help teams overcome obstacles. (10.2)

THINKING CRITICALLY

1. Why is it necessary for people in the marketing world to behave ethically?
2. How do the personal traits of initiative and responsibility aid in building teamwork?
3. Describe some ways in which you can increase other people's self-esteem.
4. In teamwork, team members make agreements with the group. Describe some agreements you have made in your own life.
5. Would you prefer to work on a team where you do different tasks requiring different skills from day to day or to work alone on the same sort of work each day? Explain your choice.

BUILDING WORKPLACE SKILLS

1. **Human Relations** Go to a store and ask a salesclerk for assistance in finding a type of product. Do not smile at the salesclerk. Go to another store. This time, make eye contact with the clerk and smile. Describe the two experiences.
2. **Public Speaking** You have just been hired as the manager at a sandwich shop. Some employees don't respect your authority. They come in late and avoid eye contact with you. You think that they are trying to see how far they can push the limits with a new boss. You need to set team standards; however, you do not want to come off only as a stern disciplinarian. Prepare a speech to present at the next staff meeting to discuss these issues and to tactfully establish yourself as the boss. What kind of body language will you use when speaking?

---

with your parents, or commitment to a sports team or activity.
5. Answers will vary based on students' preferences.

Building Workplace Skills

1. Students' experiences will vary. When smiling, students should receive a better response.
2. The results of this project will vary.

Applying Marketing Concepts

1. Descriptions will vary. Students should describe feelings from both points of view and explore the results from both perspectives.
2. In this project, students' presentations will depend on the time management system that they selected.
3. Fliers will vary based on software used and the class that each student picks. Encourage students to take self-esteem and assertiveness classes.
4. Students should include all six aspects presented in the chapter.

APPLYING MARKETING CONCEPTS

1. **Understanding Empathy** Imagine that you work for a company that is suffering financially and needs to terminate jobs. Put yourself in the position of both the manager who needs to carry out the job terminations and the assistant who will lose his or her job. Describe your feelings, concerns, and needs. Write your descriptions using your word processing program.

2. **Comparing Computer Software** Using the library or the Internet, research different systems for time management. Use presentation software to create a presentation comparing at least two of them. Point out similarities and differences; then decide which one you like best.

3. **Researching Training Opportunities** Use the Internet to research training in assertiveness or self-esteem. Find out what kinds of classes are available and how they relate to success in business. Pick one and use design software to create a flyer advertising it.

4. **Analyzing Teamwork Skills** Use a word processing program to write a report comparing and contrasting the teamwork skills involved in playing a team sport with the teamwork skills used on the job. Describe how each type of team uses the six aspects of teamwork discussed in the chapter.

LINKING SCHOOL TO WORK

Interpersonal Skills Are the employees at your workplace organized into teams? If they are, report to the class on how the teams work. If they aren't, write a 250-word description of how you would organize your coworkers into a team.

THE DECA CONNECTION

Role Play: Fast Food Manager

Situation You are to assume the role of new day assistant manager at a local fast-food restaurant. You believe production would improve if the restaurant used a team approach to cooking and serving the food.

Activity It's your job to convince the restaurant manager (judge) that the team approach is worth a try.

Evaluation You will be evaluated on how well you meet the following performance indicators:
• Participate as a team member
• Foster positive working relationships
• Treat others fairly at work
• Explain the nature of staff communication
• Persuade others

*inter*NET CONNECTION

Skills Training
Your company wants to hire a career-training company to train employees in how to deal effectively with customer complaints.

Connect
• Find Web sites of career-training companies.
• Narrow your search to training related to customer relations.
• Compare offerings of different companies and choose the one that you feel addresses the complaint issue best.
• Write a one-page report explaining and providing rationale for your choice.

Chapter 10 ■ *Interpersonal Skills* **189**

THE DECA CONNECTION

Students should be evaluated on the performance indicators noted in the Role Play.
• For another DECA Role Play, go to the *Student Activity Workbook,* p. 81.
• For more in-depth Role Play practice, refer to DECA's *Essential Competitive Events Handbook.* To order, contact DECA at **www.deca.org**.

*inter*NET CONNECTION
Summaries presented by the students will vary accordingly.

Mini Quiz
Administer the Mini Quiz orally. For an expanded chapter quiz, go to page 55 of the *Reproducible Tests* book.

1. An indicator of a person's thoughts and feelings is known as <u>body language</u>.
2. To point out the correct way to do something without offending the individual requires <u>tact</u>.
3. An employee who did what was needed to be done without being told demonstrated <u>initiative</u>.
4. Being able to understand your customer's frame of mind indicates you have <u>empathy</u>.
5. Before a team can begin to work together, it must first establish its <u>goals</u>.

Linking School to Work
The students' answers will depend on the work situation.

 GO TO

1. **Assessment** Have students complete the Reproducible Test for Chapter 10 or construct your own tests using the ExamView software.
2. **Enrichment** Have students complete the corresponding activities in the following workbooks:
   • *Marketing Math Workbook,* p. 19
   • *Marketing Research Project Workbook,* p. 47

Chapter **11**

Chapter Overview

This chapter explores types of management structures including horizontal and vertical organization and self-managed work teams. The chapter also looks at the basic management functions of planning, organizing, and controlling with a discussion of effective management techniques.

 ## Springboard

Define and Discuss Ask students to define *management* and write their answers on the board. Then write the following definition: "Management is the process of achieving goals by effective use of resources; it involves planning, organizing, and controlling." Then ask what are the management responsibilities for a large movie theater complex, writing these on the board. Have students categorize the duties as planning, organizing, or controlling.

Prereading

List the section objectives to discuss with students. Have students skim the chapter, looking at the pictures, reading the captions, and noting the heads. Ask questions to ensure that students have a minimal understanding of the chapter structure.

Preteaching Marketing Vocabulary

Dictate each of the vocabulary terms and ask students to provide a brief definition of each. Ask students where they have heard or seen these words before and ask them to note their meanings as they work through this chapter.

Management Skills

Marketing: What It Takes

Promoting Initiative
Imagine that you are a management trainee for a full-service restaurant with about 20 employees. You notice that many of the employees don't do any work until told directly by the manager exactly what to do.

WHAT WILL YOU DO?
Suppose that you are made the manager of this location. What changes would you consider making?

190

Marketing: What It Takes

Answer Answers will vary but may include meeting with employees, either individually or as a group, and explaining the importance of initiative.

THE DECA CONNECTION — ADVISOR CORNER

Operation Holiday Help Your DECA Chapter can be of service to your school and your retail business community by conducting an Operation Holiday Help project in the fall. Operation Holiday Help is a real-life management experience for DECA members. This project provides training and employment for all students in your school who want to work during the holiday season. Chapter members are assigned to committees and tasks. Contact members of your local retail business community and/or your local Chamber of Commerce to get them involved in the project. This is an excellent way to be of service to your school and your business community. The free training materials can be ordered from DECA (www.deca.org).

Management Structures

Types of Management Structure

Management is the process of reaching goals through the use of human resources, technology, and material resources. To facilitate effective management, businesses are organized in two ways—vertically and horizontally.

▪ Vertical Organization

Managers look up to higher levels of management or down to employees within a single department in large, traditional companies. The managers' goal is to perform a particular department function well. The up-and-down structure of this kind of organization is called vertical organization.

There are three basic levels of management in the traditionally organized company: top management, middle management, and supervisory-level management. Figure 11-1 on page 192 distinguishes these three levels.

▪ Horizontal Organization

Today, purely vertical organization is being displaced by new ways of structuring management. While vertical management will continue to exist in many companies, it will no longer be the only option. Many corporations downsized in the late 1980s and early 1990s to increase their efficiency and productivity. The thought was that if fewer workers could produce the same amount or an increased amount of a product, profits would rise. Unfortunately, this was not the result for more than half of the companies that downsized. Employee morale suffered, customer dissatisfaction rose, and profits fell as a result.

Clearly, more than staff cuts were needed to make companies more efficient. The answer was a new kind of management structure—horizontal organization. Horizontal organization involves self-managing teams that set their own goals and make their own decisions. It is organized by process instead of function and is customer-oriented.

The movement toward horizontal organization in business is definitely a trend. For some companies, it has been extremely successful. Ford, for example, reduced the time it takes to develop and produce a new model from five years to three. That's a 40-percent reduction!

Not all companies, however, have been quick to restructure their workforces. Shifting from the familiar vertical model, with its levels of management, requires reorganization that can take years. For many companies, there will probably always be a mix of the two types.

• What You'll Learn

- How horizontally organized companies differ from traditionally organized companies
- The three levels of management
- How a self-managing team functions

• Why It's Important

You will probably have an opportunity to work in management at some point in your career. Management involves the communication and interpersonal skills discussed in the last two chapters. A job in management is a challenge for anyone, and a basic understanding of management structure and functions, presented in this section, will give you an advantage.

• Key Terms

- vertical organization
- top management
- middle management
- supervisory-level management
- horizontal organization
- empowerment

Chapter 11 ▪ *Management Skills* **191**

FOCUS

Bell Ringer Activity

Describe Explain to students that the management structure of every company is slightly different. Some have strong leadership from the top and only allow mid-level and supervisory-level managers to execute orders from top executives. In other companies, self-managed work teams make many of the daily decisions. Have students describe the management structure of a business with which they are familiar and note what factors determine the structure.

Introducing the Section

Horizontal and Vertical Management Structures Make a T-bar on the board and label one side *horizontal* and the other side *vertical*. Call on students to describe their management structure from above and categorize whether the businesses are horizontally or vertically structured.

TEACH

📊 Technology Resources

PowerPoint The *Marketing Essentials* PowerPoint Presentation CD-ROM provides visual lecture aids for every chapter section.

Concept Development

1. Read Section 11.1 with students.
2. Pose this situation to students: A new quick-serve restaurant, the Potato Palace, will serve potato dishes with limited additional menu items from 6 A.M. to 10 P.M., seven days a week. Identify the best management structure for this restaurant.

Classroom Resources

For the Teacher
- Teacher Editions for all workbooks
- Assessment Package
- PowerPoint Presentation Software
- Interactive Lesson Planner
- ILP Block Scheduling, p. 4
- ILP Lesson Plans, p. 23
- ILP Internet Resources, p. 41

- ILP Blackline Masters, p. 23
- ILP *BusinessWeek* Case Studies, p. 69
- ILP Marketing Career Portfolio, p. 34
- *Marketing Essentials* Web site (**www.marketing.glencoe.com**)

For the Student
- Student Activity Workbook, p. 89
- Marketing Math Workbook, p. 19

- Marketing Research Project Workbook, p. 47
- ILP School-to-Work Activity Workbook, p. 41
- Virtual Business simulation
- *Marketing Essentials* Web site (**www.marketing.glencoe.com**)

ILP These resources are available in print and on the Interactive Lesson Planner (ILP)

191

Discussion Starter
Management Structures
Explain that managers face challenging situations in their duties every day, such as drugs in the workplace, sexual harassment, industrial espionage, material shortages, union issues, etc. Ask students: How might each style of management structure make the manager's job easier or more difficult?

Thinking Critically
Self-Managed Work Teams Ask students to identify the advantages and disadvantages of working on a self-managed work team. *(Advantages are shared responsibility and greater adaptability due to the different viewpoints. Disadvantages are difficulty getting along and keeping everyone on goal.)*

Cooperative Learning
Theories of Motivation Have students research theories of motivation, e.g., Maslow's Hierarchy, McClelland's Achievement Motivation, Herzberg's factors, etc. Ask students: How do these theories assist managers in the performance of their duties?

Independent Practice
Research and Explain To provide students with practice in organizational charts, have them:
1) interview a manager or owner of a local business to determine its management structure and prepare an organization chart based on the information learned; or
2) locate an organizational chart for a business on the Internet and print out a copy. Students should include an explanation of the chart. *(Answers will vary.)*

FIGURE 11-1
LEVELS OF MANAGEMENT

All managers perform the same basic functions, but their responsibilities differ according to their management level.

TOP MANAGEMENT
Those who make the planning decisions that affect the whole company are top management. CEO (Chief Executive Officer), President, COO (Chief Operating Officer), and Vice President are some top management titles. Their decisions have the broadest effect on the company.

MIDDLE MANAGEMENT
It's the job of middle management to implement the decisions of top management. They plan ways that departments under them can work to reach top management's goals. They communicate with and support supervisory level managers.

SUPERVISORY-LEVEL MANAGEMENT
These front-line managers supervise the activities of employees who carry out the tasks determined by the plans of middle and top management. They assign duties and evaluate the work of production or service employees.

GREAT IDEAS from the Marketing Classroom

John Bucci
Arvada High School
Arvada, CO
Improve classroom attendance by rewarding students for perfect attendance. Hold "perfect attendance" contests and watch daily attendance improve with increasing enthusiasm! First, obtain various prizes (i.e., gift certificates and merchandise) from local businesses. Announce a perfect attendance period in class. For example, all students who maintain perfect attendance in Marketing Education class for the next month will be eligible to win. Names of students with perfect attendance at the end of the specified time go into a drawing; the winner's name is announced. Vary the length of your perfect attendance periods and be sure to thank prize donors.

SELF-MANAGING TEAMS At the heart of horizontal organization is a restructuring of the traditional management hierarchy. Levels of management have been eliminated and the number of supervisors reduced. This is known as "flattening" the organization. Instead of reporting up a chain of command, employees are organized into teams that manage themselves.

Here's the way it works. Each team has someone called an "owner." This person is the nearest to an overall manager. He or she has ultimate responsibility for making sure the team meets its goals. The owner doesn't do this by issuing orders, however. He or she acts more like a coach than a boss. The owner works together with the whole team to define all the individual steps necessary to meet its goals.

This is based on the idea that the people actually doing the work are the best source of information about how the work should be done. The team manages itself by sharing opinions and brainstorming. It also shares responsibility for the consequences of its decisions.

Encouraging team members to contribute to and take responsibility for the management process is known as empowerment. Empowerment reinforces team spirit and contributes to company loyalty. It ultimately increases profits and productivity.

ORGANIZATION BY PROCESS A second characteristic of horizontal companies is organization by process. Self-managing teams are organized around particular processes, such as developing new products or providing customer support. Teams made up of people with different specializations replace functional divisions, like the finance department or engineering department. The product development team, for example, might include people from marketing research, design, engineering, and finance. These team members share opinions, decisions, and responsibility for the success or failure of the products they develop. One challenge of organization by process is that it may require many levels of organization. A company that produces sophisticated technical equipment, for example, will require more levels of management than a company that produces golf balls.

CUSTOMER ORIENTATION The third characteristic of horizontal organization has to do with where teams get their direction. The source of direction is management in vertical organizations; in horizontal companies, it's the customer. This type of organization supports the principle of customer satisfaction. Customer orientation can be based on a type of industry or the channel of distribution used. A firm may have one department that deals specifically with wholesalers and another that deals with retailers. By focusing on customers instead of product or process, managers have direct access to customer feedback. The ideal results of customer satisfaction for a company are large profits, high productivity, and satisfied investors.

11.1 ASSESSMENT

Reviewing Key Terms and Concepts

1. What is the principal difference between the structure of a vertical company and the structure of a horizontal company?

2. What are the three levels of management?

3. Why did many companies choose to downsize in the 1980s and 1990s?

4. What is the role of the "owner" in a self-managing team?

Thinking Critically

5. Would you feel more comfortable in a traditional company, where you answer to only one supervisor, or in a horizontal company, where you have many people giving you feedback about your efforts? Compare the advantages of each organizational model, as you see them.

Integrating Academic Skills

6. **COMMUNICATION** Imagine that you are the manager of a large bookstore. One of your salesclerks makes a suggestion about rearranging the children's section to include a few small tables and chairs. You like the idea and intend to carry it out. Write a note to the salesclerk praising the suggested improvement.

11.1 ASSESSMENT ANSWERS

Reviewing Key Terms and Concepts

1. Vertical companies are organized in departments; orders come from management. Horizontal companies are organized into self-managing teams that set their goals and make decisions.

2. top management, middle management, and supervisory-level management

3. They downsized in order to increase efficiency.

4. "Owner" coaches team to meet goals.

Thinking Critically

5. Managers are subject to more criticism in a traditional company and endure more stress because they share less responsibility. Horizontal company managers must be open to suggestions and have less power.

Integrating Academic Skills

6. **COMMUNICATION** Thank-you notes will vary.

ASSESS

Reteaching

1. **Vocabulary** Assign and review the vocabulary terms for this section.

2. **Fact and Idea** Assign and review Fact and Idea Review questions 1–5 from the Chapter Assessment.

3. **Vertical and Horizontal Organizations** Have students write a 50-word report on how vertically organized companies differ from horizontally organized companies.

Enrichment

1. **Review** Assign and review the appropriate Thinking Critically questions from the Chapter Assessment.

2. **Extend** Assign and review the corresponding activities from *BusinessWeek Case Studies, Internet Resources,* and the *School-to-Work Activity Workbook.* **ILP**

3. **Research and Write** Have students research and write a report about Total Quality Management (TQM) management principles written by the late W. Edwards Deming.

Evaluation

Assign and review the Section 11.1 Assessment.

Technology Resources

 Assessment Resources
Go to the *Marketing Essentials* Web site (**www.marketing.glencoe. com**) for resources to teach and assess occupation-specific vocabulary.

CLOSE

Section Wrap-Up

Have students explain these words by Ken Blanchard: "Empowerment is all about letting go so that others can get going."

193

Management Functions

FOCUS

Bell Ringer Activity

Organize Place students into teams of four and tell them they have been asked to organize a fund raising activity to buy additional technology equipment for the school. In their teams, they should decide on an effective fundraising activity. Allow students time to complete the activity. Then have each group list the steps they followed to make their decisions.

Introducing the Section

Management Functions Have students share their answers (the steps followed) to the Bell Ringer Activity by writing their responses on the board. Review and discuss the students' answers. Introduce the six-step decision-making process in the textbook (see Figure 11-2 on page 195). Then compare the students' descriptions of their processes to the textbook process, noting similarities.

What You'll Learn

- The three functions of management
- The management techniques used by effective managers
- How to motivate employees through a system of rewards

Why It's Important

The concept of management is changing. It is allowing more employees to fulfill management functions, whatever their job titles. Understanding the functions of management will help you to excel in any career you choose.

Key Terms

- planning
- organizing
- controlling
- mission statement

What Managers Do

All managers perform certain basic functions of planning, organizing, and controlling during their career. The decisions that a manager makes in these areas affect all employees. This means that communicating and motivating people are especially important management skills.

■ Basic Management Functions

All managers must plan when they set goals and determine how to reach them. They organize when they decide who will do what and how each task will be done. They control when they set standards and evaluate performance.

All three of these management functions involve making decisions. Some decisions will be fairly simple or routine, while others may be difficult and complicated. Following the formal, six-step procedure shown in Figure 11-2 (page 195) can be helpful when making complicated decisions.

PLANNING The first step in the management process is planning. Planning involves deciding what will be done and how it will be accomplished. A CEO who sets a sales goal to increase profits by 10 percent by expanding the company's product line is engaged in planning.

Good management planning at any level is realistic, comprehensive, and flexible. It includes plans for the short- and long-range uses of people, technology, and material resources.

To be an effective management tool, a management plan should be reduced to written form. When writing their plans, managers or management teams should not try to anticipate every possibility. An overly long and detailed document offers too many opportunities for misinterpretation.

Once the written plan is complete, it should be distributed to and discussed with everyone who is involved. Managers should keep their plans flexible so that they can be easily revised in response to comment or change. Plans should be reviewed and revised often to reflect changes in the organization.

ORGANIZING Organizing is a coordinated effort to reach a company's planning goals. It involves assigning responsibility, establishing working relationships, staffing, and directing the work of employees.

Assigning responsibility and establishing working relationships (see Figure 11-3 on page 195) are functions usually carried out by top and middle management, even in horizontal companies. Staffing, which includes selecting and training new employees, is often shared by middle management and supervisors. Because supervisors usually direct an employee's work, it is important that they be part of the hiring process.

The organizing function in large companies is complex. There may be hundreds of middle-level managers, thousands of supervisors, and tens of thousands of employees. Since the work is divided among so many people, middle managers and supervisors in traditional companies are usually given a narrow range of responsibilities.

In horizontal companies, middle management responsibilities are much wider. Because employees are empowered to do much of the organizing themselves, managers are able to advise and troubleshoot rather than give orders. Managers in smaller vertically organized companies usually have a wide range of organizing responsibilities as well.

CONTROLLING Controlling is the process of comparing what you planned with actual performance. It involves three basic activities—setting standards, evaluating performance according to those standards, and solving any problems revealed by the evaluation. A manager must analyze the financial records for the year to monitor progress toward financial goals. Controlling helps identify problems and ways to avoid or solve them.

FIGURE 11-2

Decision-Making Process

■ **Investigate All Options** In order to reach a wise decision on complex questions, it's important to consider all the options. A process like this can help assure that decision-makers do not leave out important considerations. *What could happen if the problem is not well defined at first?*

 1. Define the problem.

 2. Identify the options available.

 3. Gather information and determine the consequences of each option.

 4. Choose the best option.

 5. Take action.

 6. Evaluate results.

FIGURE 11-3

■ **Vertical or Horizontal** This chart shows a company organized along traditional vertical lines. *How would the chart differ if the company were organized horizontally?*

Chapter 11 ■ *Management Skills* **195**

FIGURE 11-2 ANSWER
Investigate All Options When a problem is not identified up front, time may be wasted on work that might not be relevant to the problem, and there may be difficulty doing any of the follow-up steps.

FIGURE 11-3 ANSWER
Vertical or Horizontal A company that is horizontally organized would replace third management level with teams organized around a specific goal, including the production employees who are part of the team.

SECTION 11.2

TEACH

Technology Resources

PowerPoint The *Marketing Essentials* PowerPoint Presentation CD-ROM provides visual lecture aids for every chapter section.

Concept Development

1. Read Section 11.2 with students.
2. Have students read aloud the Case Study on page 199 and review the answers in class.
3. Invite a local manager to speak to the class about his/her job. Ask the individual to include a discussion of his/her job responsibilities, required skills and training, management techniques and style, challenges, positive aspects, as well as a description of the management structure.

Discussion Starters

1. **Good Managers** Have students brainstorm the qualities of what makes a good manager. Write their answers on the board and ask them to provide an example of when they have witnessed this skill being utilized. Compare their answers to the effective management techniques described in the textbook.
2. **Job Orientation and Training** Ask students who have or have had a job to describe the orientation and training they received when they were first hired. What did they like and dislike about the training? On what subjects or issues did they feel they needed more information? How would they convey their needs to their manager?

FIGURE 11-4

Federal Express Mission Statement

MISSION STATEMENT

Federal Express is committed to our PEOPLE-SERVICE-PROFIT PHILOSOPHY. We will produce outstanding financial returns by providing totally reliable, competitively superior global air-ground transportation of high-priority goods and documents that require rapid, time-certain delivery. Equally important, positive control of each package will be maintained utilizing real-time electronic tracking and tracing systems. A complete record of each shipment and delivery will be presented without request for payment. We will be helpful, courteous, and professional to each other and the public. We will strive to have a satisfied customer at the end of each transaction.

David Bronczek,
Chairman and CEO

■ **United with the Company** A mission statement is designed to outline the goals and values of a company. *What are some ways that employees at Federal Express can uphold their mission statement?*

Before setting standards, many companies compose a mission statement. A mission statement describes the ultimate goals of a company in a brief paragraph or two. A mission statement summarizes why a company exists. It identifies products or services offered and the target market. While mission statements may vary in length and detail, the goal is the same for all—to support the company's mission. An example of a longer mission statement, for Federal Express, is shown in Figure 11-4.

Once a company establishes goals in a mission statement, it will adopt standards that are consistent with them. These standards will apply to all aspects of the firm's operation. Here are some possibilities:

- Financial standards—profit, cash flow, sales
- Employee standards—productivity, professional conduct, dress
- Customer satisfaction standards—sales returns, customer complaints, repeat business, referrals
- Quality control standards—production line checks for defects in materials or workmanship, repair requests, recalls

Once standards have been established, managers can then use them to evaluate both company and individual performance. When performance does not meet established standards, managers must identify and solve the problem. The defect rate in company products may be up sharply because of malfunctioning equipment. A solution to this case might involve replacement of the equipment.

■ Effective Management Techniques

Whether you find yourself a supervisor in a traditionally organized company or a member of a self-managing team, you will need to develop management skills. While this may sound intimidating, the most effective management techniques are usually a matter of common sense. You can judge for yourself as you read the suggestions below for effective management.

GIVE CLEAR DIRECTIONS Directing others requires good communication skills. Good communication is necessary at every level of management. Even the best employees will not be productive if they don't know what they are expected to do.

As a supervisor, give all the direction required for each job. Remember that you may need to repeat some of your directions, perhaps using a different approach. Encourage employees to ask questions about your directions. Communication will improve dramatically when they feel comfortable doing this.

THE DECA CONNECTION **COMPETITIVE EVENTS AND MARKETING ESSENTIALS**

Management Team Decision-Making Events This chapter presents an opportunity for you to introduce your students to DECA's Management Team Decision-Making Events. These events are designed for a team of two students to analyze elements essential to the effective operation of a business in one of the four occupational areas. The business management problem to be studied is presented as a case study. The students are given 30 minutes to analyze the business situation using a management decision-making format. Then, they present their analysis to a judge. The occupational areas offered include Financial Services, Hospitality Services, Sports and Entertainment Marketing, and Travel and Tourism Marketing.

TRAIN NEW EMPLOYEES WELL All new employees need some on-the-job training and orientation. As a supervisor, you may train new employees yourself or delegate this task. You may choose to delegate the task of training to someone else. Choose a person who knows the job well and is a good teacher, and supervise the training. Make sure that all job duties are explained and that the new employees understand how to complete them.

Orienting new employees includes more than simply training them for their positions. New employees may be frightened at the prospect of a new workplace, new coworkers, and new skills to learn. It is important to make new employees feel valued and welcome and to familiarize them with the working environment. Studies have shown that properly oriented employees are more satisfied with their work, more productive, and more likely to stay in the job.

Orientation may take as little as a couple of hours or as long as a few days. It commonly includes the following:

- Tour of the company and introduction to coworkers
- Discussion of the company's history, mission and values
- Description of what the company does
- Training on equipment, such as cash registers and computers
- Information on where key facilities are located
- Information about payroll, benefits, and company policies

REAL WORLD MARKETING

Downsizing

As a result of corporate downsizing and the Internet boom in the 90s, many companies have removed layers of management between top executives and people in the field to create a flatter organization structure. A recent study conducted by the University of Southern California found that 78 percent of companies had removed at least one layer of management in the last decade. This flatter structure allows companies to react quickly to changing market conditions, consumers' needs, and technology. With fewer people to communicate with, companies are able to speed up processes and transfer information more efficiently. Advocates of the flatter structure include successful companies such as Cisco and Wal-Mart.

Thinking Critically

How might a flatter structure help management work more efficiently?

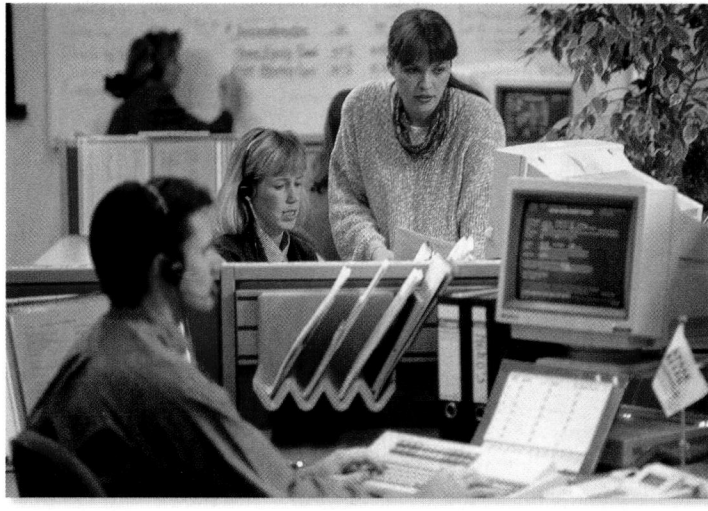

■ **Management Roles** Managers are planners, organizers, and controllers. *Which function of management is the standing woman performing?*

Cooperative Learning

Management Skills To provide students with an opportunity to practice their management skills, divide them into groups and have each group select a small business that they would like to run for one day. Students will discuss the planning, organizing, and controlling phases of management for that business.

The groups are to assume that their businesses have at least five employees. These are the decisions the groups must make:

- First, they are to write a mission statement.
- With regard to planning, students should decide on business location, equipment, products/services to be sold, pricing, hours of business operation, and company policies such as merchandise returns.
- With regard to organizing, students should decide on a management structure, number of employees needed (at least five) and their required skill set, work shifts, and employee schedules.
- With regard to controlling, students should decide on procedures and time expectations for delivery of goods or services, standards for interacting with customers, handling money, and maintaining the workplace. They will also have to decide how they will evaluate employees to maintain the standards they set, and how they will deal with problems that come up in the course of a day, such as employee absences, etc.

Have each group share its decisions in an oral presentation to the class. Class members may be able to suggest additional considerations in planning, organizing, and controlling.

REAL WORLD MARKETING

Downsizing

Answer A flatter structure allows managers to react more quickly to situations.

CAPTION ANSWER

Management Roles She is directing an employee's work, which is part of the organizing function of management.

Independent Practice

Write and Discuss A common occurrence in business involves an individual being promoted from among a group of peers with whom he/she must now supervise. Tell students to imagine that they have just been promoted and now must manage three friends with whom they were originally hired. Considering this situation, have students write answers to these questions:

- How might your friends initially react to your promotion? Will they be jealous or happy that your hard work was rewarded?
- How would you deal with any negative reactions?
- What are some issues that you yourself might have to deal with and overcome? *(One possibility might be insecurity at supervising people who were formerly your peers.)*
- Will your relationship with these friends likely change? Why/why not?
- How do you keep your relationship with your friends professional?

Some students may already have had relevant experiences at their co-op jobs. For this reason, it will be beneficial to discuss their answers and their experiences in class.

BE CONSISTENT If you have decided that a job must be done in a certain way, make sure that all employees follow this standard. Don't make exceptions unless there is a good reason to do so.

Always follow through on what you say. If you announce that you intend to deduct part of an employee's salary for being late to work, do it. It will be hard to gain employee respect if you don't follow through on your decisions.

TREAT EMPLOYEES FAIRLY Whenever possible, do what is best for your employees. You do not need to say yes to every employee request; however, you should always consider the employees' point of view when making decisions. Listen to suggestions from your employees and consider acting on them. Take time to explain your reasoning if you believe an employee is wrong.

Take any necessary actions that can help them without sacrificing the amount or quality of work that is done. Talk with your immediate supervisor about changes that will benefit your employees. Employees will be more productive when treated fairly. Set reasonable standards of performance and apply those standards to everyone. Don't give special privileges to a few favorites.

BE FIRM WHEN NECESSARY Sometimes supervising others requires a firm hand. This can be done without losing your temper.

Each situation requiring disciplinary action is different. A friendly suggestion may be all that is necessary to get most employees on the right track. Others may not respond to the friendly approach, and you may have to be direct and firm. Give whatever directions are appropriate, and be certain the employee understands what you expect.

Employee problems that are caused by the inappropriate behavior of one employee toward another may be difficult to handle. A discussion may be the only way to clear up anger and solve the problem. Listen to what both parties have to say, and be reasonable but firm.

SET A GOOD EXAMPLE Set a good example in everything you do on the job. Doing this one simple thing will make your supervisory job much easier.

Let's consider the example of Frank, a department manager in a large retail store. He wrote computer programs at night to earn extra money and seldom went to sleep before 2 a.m. He found it very difficult to arrive at the store on time. Other employees in his department noticed that Frank was usually a half hour late. They decided they could sleep 20 minutes longer and still arrive at the store ahead of him. By following Frank's example, the whole department began arriving late for work. After several weeks of this, Frank was replaced.

Maria, the new department manager, always arrived at the store a few minutes early. When the other employees realized this, they reset their alarm clocks and began arriving early, too. Maria didn't have to say a word to anyone. She simply set a good example.

■ **Delegation** Managers who fail to delegate suffer the consequences—stress and lack of time for family and other interests. Sometimes it's necessary to bring work home, but if it happens too often, it could be a sign you have too much responsibility. *How could doing less of the work yourself be good for the company?*

CAPTION ANSWER
Delegation Overstressed and overworked people don't perform as effectively. Delegating responsibility will allow you more time to concentrate on the most important tasks.

More About . . .

Part-Time Employees
Along with horizontal management and other recent innovations, another feature of modern management is the use of part-time employees. These employees can either work less than full time or be self-employed individuals who work for more than one employer. They make up a quarter of the work force.

Case Study

Long Distance Management

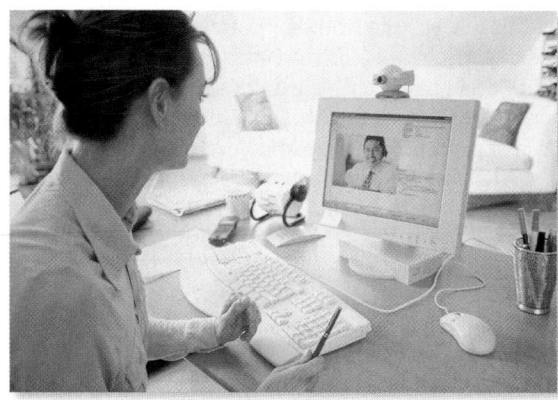

Many managers offer the option of telecommuting to attract top prospects to their companies. Some perks for the telecommuter are the ability to work from home, set your own hours, and avoid a commute to the office.

Managing telecommuters requires new approaches because managers are used to dealing with people they can see throughout the day. Managers must clearly state what they expect from telecommuting employees. E-mail and online chats can help keep communication clear.

How do managers know the employee is working on the job and not on his or her vegetable garden? In reality, they can't know. They need to focus on results and meeting schedules.

Managers find that it is important to have face-to-face contact—once or twice a week if possible, and less often if travel time is long. This helps telecommuters stay connected with the rest of the team and keeps relations fresh and friendly. It is important that full-time telecommuters understand that telecommuting is a privilege, not an entitlement. Clear lines of communication and contact with coworkers is crucial in maintaining a productive work environment. Coworkers who work on-site must feel comfortable calling telecommuters at home. There are also internal benefits for employers who allow employees to telecommute. This invests a certain amount of trust in the individual, who, in turn, should want to prove to his or her employer that this was not a poor decision. Another benefit of employee telecommuting is cost-avoidance. Employees who work from home may use their own computer, which will defray the costs of an employer providing them with one. Recruiting costs and training replacements can be expensive, costing upwards of $12,000 for some employees. It is more cost-efficient to make allowances for employees who have already proven responsible and reliable.

As information technology continues to grow, there will be more people who spend their workdays at home rather than in office cubicles. Learning how to manage these workers benefits both the company and the employee.

Case Study Review

1. What can managers do to encourage team spirit in people working away from the office?
2. Which management structure, horizontal or traditional, do you think is more compatible with using telecommuters? Defend your position.

A MATTER OF ETHICS

3. Some workers are allowed to telecommute, while others must come to the office each day. Do you think that is unfair? Why or why not?

Individualized Practice

Decision-Making Skills

L1 Based on what they have learned about management in this section, ask students if they would make the decision to explore it further as a career option. Why or why not?

L2 Pose this problem to students: You have just been offered a promotion to supervisory-level management in the store where you've worked for two years. You will receive about $25 more per week, be responsible for supervising five people, and work longer hours without getting paid for overtime. (At present, you work a straight 40-hour week and don't have to supervise anyone.) You plan to stay at the store another year, while you finish your education. Would you take the promotion? Why or why not?

L3 Pose this problem to students: Having been promoted, you have been in a management position at a store for six months. While you like the company and had planned to stay in the field for several years, you are definitely not enjoying the additional burdens of your new position. You find yourself thinking a great deal about how much you enjoyed your old position before the promotion. What would you do?

Case Study Review Answers

Long Distance Management

1. Managers can ask telecommuters for their opinions and listen to their feedback.
2. Most students will say that traditional management structure is more compatible with managing telecommuters because horizontal organization is dependent on effective teamwork, and teamwork is easier if people are in the same location.

A MATTER OF ETHICS

3. Answers will vary.

DELEGATE RESPONSIBILITY Some supervisors and many middle managers simply do too much work themselves. Some take work home almost every night. This may be necessary at times, but it usually means resources are not being managed well. Those who take work home are probably not delegating many tasks and responsibilities to others. Yet they often have capable employees with lighter workloads who would be willing to do more.

As a supervisor, don't try to do everything yourself. Organize your work responsibilities, and then decide which ones you can delegate to others. Decide which employee can best handle each task. Take time to teach some employees how to do new tasks. Follow up by monitoring and evaluating the tasks that have been delegated. This will allow you more time to concentrate on the most important tasks.

Empowering employees is company policy in horizontal organizations. You will be expected to delegate. That way, you will do a better job with your remaining responsibilities. Your employees, in turn, will appreciate the chance to show that they can handle more responsibility. They will become more productive.

FOSTER TEAMWORK As mentioned earlier in the chapter, teamwork is especially important in horizontally organized companies. As a manager or group "owner," you can foster teamwork in a number of ways. Encourage team members to step outside their areas of specialization and learn about other aspects of the process for which they are responsible. Try to promote honest and frank discussion before decisions are made. Listen respectfully to the comments and opinions of other team members, and encourage others in the group to do likewise. Respond to the comments and concerns of team members to develop a feeling of trust. You must ensure that all team members feel they are treated equally and fairly. A team will not succeed if members believe that some individuals are treated differently.

■ Employee Motivation

The more people feel that they are appreciated, the harder they will work. Keep this in mind when you become a manager. Provide frequent feedback to employees and formally evaluate them each year. Identify goals to be achieved over a period of years. Then reward employees who contribute to these goals.

It is important to reward smart work, not busy work. A person who looks busy may not necessarily be getting the work done; if you reward results, however, you will get results in return.

It is also important to reward those individuals who simplify work as opposed to creating more complexities on the job. Ordering a $2.79 pen from the supplies department at Intel Corporation, for example, used to take 95 steps and 12 pieces of

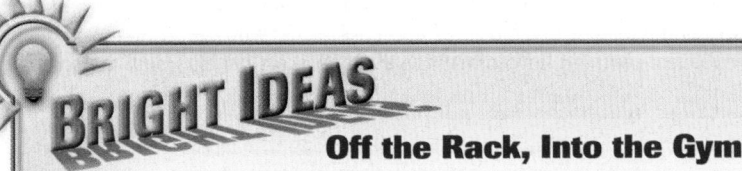

BRIGHT IDEAS

Off the Rack, Into the Gym

Step aerobics, the Nordic Track, WalkFit treadmill, the MotorBall—all of these revolutionary exercise techniques are attributed to one man. Inventor William Wilkinson is back in shape with another fitness idea—a workout suit made of spandex. Designed to help people burn off extra calories while exercising, the sleek black outfit looks like it came straight from the wardrobe of Cat Woman or Batman. Weighing less than a pound, Spandex panels are sewn into the suit and lie parallel to muscle groups, adding resistance to the body's natural movements. Result: You expend 50 to 75 percent more energy depending on how much you move.

Thinking Creatively

If you were helping Wilkinson develop his product, what types of individuals might you interview when conducting product research?

Did You Know? The Bureau of Labor Statistics predicts that by 2005, professional, managerial, and technical positions will rise 12.4 percent, 3 percent, and 8.3 percent, respectively. Deficits show up in crafts fields, for operators of machinery, and laborers. This means more opportunities for those with education and ability to solve complex problems.

paper. Intel recognized the problem and simplified the procedure. Now it takes 8 steps and 1 piece of paper.

Doing the job right the first time lowers costs and increases productivity and worker pride. Identify those workers who value quality, not speed. Ask them to suggest ways to improve job performance. Seek out those employees who quietly do a good job. Take a sincere interest in them, and they will perform even better.

A reasonable amount of conformity is necessary in every company, but do not let conformity stifle creativity. Encourage employees to be creative and remind them that they won't be penalized for mistakes. Sometimes it is necessary to take risks when avoiding conformity, but these risks may produce positive results and should be rewarded.

A young engineer named Steve Wozniak was bored with his job working on computer chips. He asked on three occasions if he could work on designing a personal computer. His manager said no each time. So he built the first Apple computer in his garage and became one of the most successful entrepreneurs in history.

Enthusiastic long-term employees are the key to success in most companies. Reward loyalty by investing in continuing education for employees and promoting from within.

Life In The Diverse MARKETPLACE

Trading Cards

The exchange of business cards cannot be taken merely at face value—in many countries it is more of an art. While in the United States it may be quite casual to give someone your card, in other parts of the world there is more ritual. Japanese people always offer their *meishi*, or business cards, with two hands. The person who is receiving the card must accept it with two hands, study the card, and bow slightly to it. The card is then placed in a special case and placed in a jacket or shirt pocket, never in the pants pocket or the wallet.

Thinking Critically

Why do you think that giving someone your card has the potential to become a ritual?

■ **Employee Rewards** Companies often give gifts or awards to employees who excel. Continental Airlines gives employees a monetary bonus every month that the airline is in the top five of on-time flight arrivals. *Why is it important to reward effective work?*

Enrichment

1. **Review** Assign and review the Chapter 11 activities in the *Student Activity Workbook*.
2. **Calculate** Assign the Unit 4 Activity in the *Marketing Math Workbook*.
3. **Review** Assign and review the appropriate Thinking Critically questions from the Chapter Assessment.
4. **Review** Assign and review the following Chapter Assessment activities: Building Workplace Skills, Applying Marketing Concepts, Linking School to Work Activities, The DECA Connection Role Play, and Internet Connection.
5. **Research and Report** One of the toughest jobs a manager has to face is terminating an employee. Have students research just causes for termination as well as the legal risks involved with this duty. Students may research on the Internet for appropriate articles or speak with company supervisors or personnel directors to find the information. Have students write a report and share with the class.

Evaluation

Assign and review the Section 11.2 Assessment.

Technology Resources

 Assessment Resources Go to the *Marketing Essentials* Web site (**www.marketing.glencoe. com**) for resources to teach and assess occupation-specific vocabulary.

Life In The Diverse MARKETPLACE

Trading Cards

Answer Answers will vary, but some may say that your card represents your identity and label at work. Therefore, exchanging cards cannot be taken at face value. Because of its importance in many countries, rituals develop.

CAPTION ANSWER

Employee Rewards It is important to reward effective work because work that gets rewarded gets done, and rewards offer an incentive to work productively.

VIRTUAL BUSINESS

Management Report

GO TO Introduce the major functional areas of management to students using Knowledge Matters' Virtual Business visual simulation, "Office Applications— Management Report." Students operate a store then receive a report on eight specific areas of their business from a Cyber-Consultant. If needed, have students run the Virtual Business tutorial before beginning this simulation. For additional instructions and teaching tips for this activity, go to the *Marketing Essentials* Web site (**www.marketing.glencoe.com**).

CLOSE

Section Wrap-Up

Have students stand up and form a circle. Toss a soft sponge ball or bean bag to a student and have him/her say what they thought was an important concept learned in the chapter. The student should throw to someone else, naming a concept, and continue until each student has had a turn.

Big Brother

Answer Some students may feel that monitoring will improve performance. Others may find it creates a negative work environment.

■ Leadership in the 21st Century

The business world should expect to face many changes in the 21st century. As corporations dominated by controlling executives become obsolete, global competition increases. The expanding vision of international business and technology will affect organizations, people, production, and the fundamentals of management.

In light of these changes, many product life cycles may be counted in months, not decades. There will be fewer projects led by one executive. Management is turning to teams of cooperative leaders to create a vision and rally the organization around that vision to achieve exceptional results. This prevents one single person from being responsible for a product failure.

A recent study shows that marketing and sales is the fast track to top management. Considering the global economy, international experience follows marketing as the quickest way to advance in business.

Effective managers are making increased use of new technology, and customer satisfaction is a top priority as competition heats up. New leaders are diverse, even in jobs at the very top level. There are more women in positions such as CEO or Senior Vice President for large corporations. Global competition is creating companies and managers who are united by common goals and ideals.

Big Brother

Nearly three-fourths of major U.S. companies monitor their employees at the workplace. Common practices consist of reviewing e-mail, monitoring Internet usage or computer files, or listening in on telephone conversations. Special software, which costs companies between $25,000 to $65,000, is available to analyze online communication patterns without the knowledge of those being monitored. These software programs help companies cut down on this problem of "cyberslacking." Reasons cited for the extra eye included legal protection, productivity measures, and performance reviews.

Thinking Critically

If you were a manager in a large corporation, would you employ the practice of monitoring employees in the workplace? Explain your reasoning.

11.2 ASSESSMENT

Reviewing Key Terms and Concepts

1. What are the basic functions of management?
2. What is the value of employee orientation?
3. What does it mean to delegate responsibility?
4. What are two ways to reward employee loyalty?

Thinking Critically

5. How could a manager's openness to suggestions from employees influence employee loyalty to a company?

Integrating Academic Skills

6. **MATH** The vice president of a company makes an annual salary of $65,000 and works an average of 40 hours per week. The president of the company makes an annual salary of $100,000 and works an average of 60 hours per week. Assume both work 50 weeks a year. What does each person earn per hour? On a per-hour basis, who earns more money?

11.2 ASSESSMENT ANSWERS

Reviewing Key Terms and Concepts
1. planning, organizing, and controlling
2. Employee orientation ensures that all new employees learn the same thing, easing the difficulty of beginning a new job.
3. Delegating means giving jobs or duties to other people, rather than trying to do it all yourself.
4. Two ways are to invest in continuing education for employees and promote from within.

Thinking Critically
5. If employees feel that their ideas are taken seriously and are important, they may feel like a part of the team and be more loyal.

Integrating Academic Skills
6. **MATH** The vice president earns $32.50 per hour. The president earns $33.33 per hour, which is $.83 per hour more.

Careers in Marketing

FASHION MERCHANDISING

Carole Friedman
Fashion Merchandiser
Basically Kids

What does your job entail?

"It is my job to develop products, which sometimes requires working with the design department and/or sales department. In design, you have to determine what designs are fashionable and what sells, while in sales, you have to work with how to sell your designs to satisfy customer needs. It is nice to be involved with everything from product planning to product placement, and it keeps you traveling frequently. It is often necessary to visit retailers and buyers and find out what they need—and how best to help them move product."

What skills are most important?

"Typically, one needs to be good with numbers and math—especially when working on the sales end. You also really need to know your product. This is a two-sided occupation, and you need to have solid skills in design and sales while keeping your ear on the pulse of the industry."

What training would you recommend to students?

"Students should develop a strong marketing background. Most fashion merchandisers come up through either the sales or design departments. Getting training at a reputable fashion school, like the Fashion Institute of Technology or the Parsons School of Design, is important because the school will train you in the knowledge of fashion. Combining knowledge of design and fabric textures with creativity will take you far in this business."

What is your key to success?

"The secret to success in this field is to be able to go into the market and have a feeling for the trends. The buyers won't know what they want, so you have to look at what is selling and make judgments from there. It's like going shopping: you need to know what you want before you can buy it."

Thinking Critically
Think of another career that requires knowledge of both sales and design. Why are those skills important to the career you chose?

Career Facts

Education and Training: High school courses in marketing, business administration, consumer education, foreign language (especially French), and economics are valuable preparation for this career, as well as college preparatory courses. A college degree is not essential, but many universities and trade schools offer programs in merchandising and retailing.

Aptitudes, Abilities, and Skills: A highly developed sense of personal fashion and knowledge of trends is essential, in addition to communication skills, a strong ability to coordinate data and resources, and a good sense of color, design, and textiles.

Career Outlook: Competition is very keen; however, other management positions in the fashion industry may be more plentiful and may lead to fashion merchandising positions.

Career Path: Assistant to fashion coordinator positions or department management positions prepare employees for this position. Advancement often means moving to a larger company.

Chapter 11 ■ *Management Skills* **203**

Careers in Marketing

Ask a student to read the Careers in Marketing feature aloud to the class. Discuss the skills and aptitudes required for a career in fashion merchandising. Ask students whether they think they would like or dislike a career in fashion merchandising. Discuss the pros and cons of such a career.

Thinking Critically Answer
Answers will vary but discussion may include careers such as interior designer and advertising illustrator.

 Guest Speakers
Invite a fashion merchandiser to class to discuss his/her job and factors he/she considers when making marketing decisions.

Exploring Careers

Qualities Leading to Promotion

1. On the board list the following qualities of people who get promoted:
   - Seniority (length of time on job)
   - Knowledge and ability to perform basic skills
   - Willingness to learn
   - Initiative (taking the first step)
   - Perseverance
   - Cooperativeness
   - Thinking Skills
   - Adaptability
   - Education and training
   - Attitude

2. Ask students to prioritize the list, writing it on a separate sheet of paper, numbering the qualities from 1–10 in order of importance, with number 1 being most important.
3. Discuss with students which qualities they chose to be most important and least important, and have them explain why.

Lifelong Learning

Management Skills
Given the central role of computer technology in many of the best-paying jobs today, general education must be supplemented with actual hands-on computer knowledge. Encourage students to commit to developing and maintaining their computer skills by taking classes, learning new programs, and familiarizing themselves with the many computer applications.

Meeting Individual Needs

Gifted
This chapter offers a look at real-world organizational behavior. Encourage gifted students to take on a variety of enrichment and independent practice activities that put them in contact with people in the business world to observe practices leading to success. Have students present written reports of their experiences and share with the class.

Chapter 11 ASSESSMENT

Vocabulary Review

Explanations will vary. See Glossary for definitions.

Fact and Idea Review

1. Managers look up to higher levels of management or down to employees within a department structure.
2. top management level
3. A supervisor assigns duties to and supervises workers on the job while carrying out the plans of middle management.
4. It means eliminating levels of management and reducing the number of supervisors.
5. Departments are organized by function; self-managing teams are organized by process.
6. A good management plan is realistic, comprehensive, and flexible. It is in written form that is neither overly long nor overly detailed, and it is distributed to employees for comment and revision.
7. Organizing includes assigning responsibility, establishing working relationships, staffing, and directing the work of employees.
8. Feedback helps to determine if the directions were understood or not.
9. A manager can have team members learn all aspects of the process for which they are responsible; promote honest and frank discussion; listen to the comments and opinions of group members and encourage others to do so; and work towards a consensus.

Thinking Critically

1. In a large company, top management would consist of the chief executive officer (CEO) or president and other key executives, such as the vice president(s). Most small, locally owned businesses have only one manager.
2. Employees will be more productive, effective, and loyal under your supervision if you treat them fairly. Experiences will vary.
3. Answers will vary. Students may conclude that rewards encourage creativity and contribution, while fear causes people to spend most of their time conforming and protecting themselves.
4. Students will likely agree that businesses should commit themselves to ethical practices. However, they may differ as to whether this commitment "goes without saying" or needs to be in writing.

VOCABULARY REVIEW

Write a paragraph that includes all the following words. Use them in ways that demonstate that you know their meanings.

- vertical organization
- horizontal organization
- top management
- middle management
- supervisory-level management
- planning
- organizing
- mission statement
- controlling
- empowerment

FACT AND IDEA REVIEW

1. Describe traditional management structure. (11.1)
2. A vice president in a vertically organized company would be part of which management level? (11.1)
3. What does a supervisor do? (11.1)
4. What does it mean to "flatten" an organization? (11.1)
5. What is the main difference between a department and a self-managing team? (11.1)
6. What are the characteristics of a good management plan? (11.2)
7. What is usually involved in the organizing function of management? (11.2)
8. Why is it important to ask for feedback after giving directions to an employee? (11.2)
9. How can the owner of a management team foster teamwork in the group? (11.2)

THINKING CRITICALLY

1. Compare top-level management in a large company to what you think it would be in a small company.
2. Discuss why being fair is an effective and important management skill. Describe experiences you have had or heard about in which managers were not fair. What were the results of the unfair treatment?
3. Why do you think rewards get better results than punishments?
4. Do you think a company's mission statement should include a commitment to doing business ethically? Should ethics be as important as profits? Defend your answer.

BUILDING WORKPLACE SKILLS

1. **Technology** Use the Internet to find information about management opportunities in the marketing field. Then use a word processing program to write a brief summary of your findings.
2. **Human Relations** Ramesh works as a travel agent for a small firm. The manager of the travel agency has just hired a new agent who happens to be a close personal friend. The manager is showing her friend obvious favoritism. Ramesh likes his job, but he feels increasingly uncomfortable with the manager's unfair and inconsistent behavior. What should he do?

Building Workplace Skills

1. Information gathered will vary.
2. Answers will vary. Given the size of the company, Abe probably has three choices: take his problem to a higher-level (the agency owner perhaps), talk to the manager in private, or look for another job.

APPLYING MARKETING CONCEPTS

1. **Planning an Event** Use your word processing program to describe what would go into the planning, organizing, and controlling of a school club car wash.

2. **Building a Cohesive Team** You are the manager of a bookstore that recently merged with a neighboring coffee shop. While all employees will remain under their former manager, it is necessary to create a united group of workers. Brainstorm ideas for team-building activities. Pick your favorite activity and, using design software, make a flyer describing your event.

3. **Creating a Mission Statement** Use the Internet to research a company's mission statement of your choice. Then imagine that you are starting a similar company in the same field. Using the mission statement as a model, write your own mission statement. Use presentation software to prepare a presentation of your mission statement and of how you created it.

4. **Developing a Training Program** You are a manager at a phone card telemarketing company. You have just hired three new employees who need training. You have received feedback in the past that the training process is ineffective and could be more intensive. Using a computer program, develop a schedule for a two-day orientation.

LINKING SCHOOL TO WORK

Resource and Systems Skills Ask a supervisor or employer what he or she thinks about the newer management structures that emphasize teamwork and organization by process. Report your findings to the class. After everyone has shared the various responses he or she obtained, discuss any trends that are apparent and speculate about the reasons for them.

Role Play: Management Trainee

Situation You are to assume the role of management trainee at a local outlet of a traditionally organized national sporting goods company.

Activity As part of your training, you have been asked by the store manager (judge) to draw up a chart showing the different management levels in your local branch of the company. Once you have completed the chart, you must explain it to the store manager (judge).

Evaluation You will be evaluated on how well you meet the following performance indicators:
- Explain the concept of management
- Demonstrate orderly and systematic behavior
- Follow directions
- Prepare simple written reports

Which Is Better?
Your company is considering changing from a traditional to a horizontal organization. You are concerned and decide to find out which is more effective.

Connect
- Use the Web to research and compare the corporate culture and financial performance of several traditional and horizontal companies.
- Write a report making comparisons between the two types of organization.

Chapter 11 ■ *Management Skills* **205**

Students should be evaluated on the performance indicators noted in the Role Play.
- For another DECA Role Play, go to the *Student Activity Workbook*, p. 89.
- For more in-depth Role Play practice, refer to DECA's *Essential Competitive Events Handbook*. To order, contact DECA at **www.deca.org**.

*inter*NET CONNECTION
Comparisons will vary.

Mini Quiz
Administer the Mini Quiz orally. For an expanded chapter quiz, go to page 59 of the *Reproducible Tests* book.

Indicate if the following statements are *true* or *false*. For statements that are false, explain why.

1. The older traditional form of management structure is the horizontal organization. <u>False: It is vertical.</u>
2. When an organization has experienced "flattening," it means additional layers of management have been added. <u>False: Layers have been reduced.</u>
3. Employees who have been encouraged to assume additional responsibility are said to be empowered. <u>True</u>
4. The three basic levels of management are top, middle, and supervisory level. <u>True</u>
5. A manager who takes work home regularly may not be delegating responsibility and should examine other's workloads. <u>True</u>

Applying Marketing Concepts
1. Planning techniques for the school car wash will vary.
2. Fliers will vary depending on how students decide to encourage group cohesiveness and positive work morale.
3. Ideas for mission statements will vary.
4. Orientation schedules will vary based on what students view as important aspects of necessary training.

Linking School to Work
Answers depend on the work situation.

 1. **Assessment** Have students complete the Reproducible Test for Chapter 11 and Unit 4 or construct your own tests using the ExamView software.
2. **Enrichment** Have students complete the corresponding activities in the following workbooks:
- *Marketing Math Workbook*, p. 19
- *Marketing Research Project Workbook*, p. 47

205

Unit Lab Overview

In this Zazz Lab, students will use their knowledge of the concepts of business, marketing, economics, management, and human relations, as well as teamwork and interpersonal skills to establish a children's soccer camp franchise.

 Bell Ringer Activity

Identify Ask students what country won the 1999 Women's World Cup in Soccer. *(The United States won.)*

Discussion Starter

Ask students what effect a winning team might have on that sport. *(It would bring the sport into the limelight, thus creating more interest in the sport.)*

Thinking Critically

1. **Social Skills** Ask students: If you were hiring employees for a soccer camp, what basic and social skills would you expect them to possess? *(Answers will vary. Possible responses might include good communication skills, organizational skills, human relations skills, soccer proficiency, and liking children.)*

2. **Promotional Features** Ask students: What unique features of the camps would you stress in the promotional materials designed for potential franchise owners? *(Answers will vary. Responses may include having a well-known name of the professional soccer player sponsor, experience of the camp owners, quality of the instructors, and comprehensiveness of the program.)*

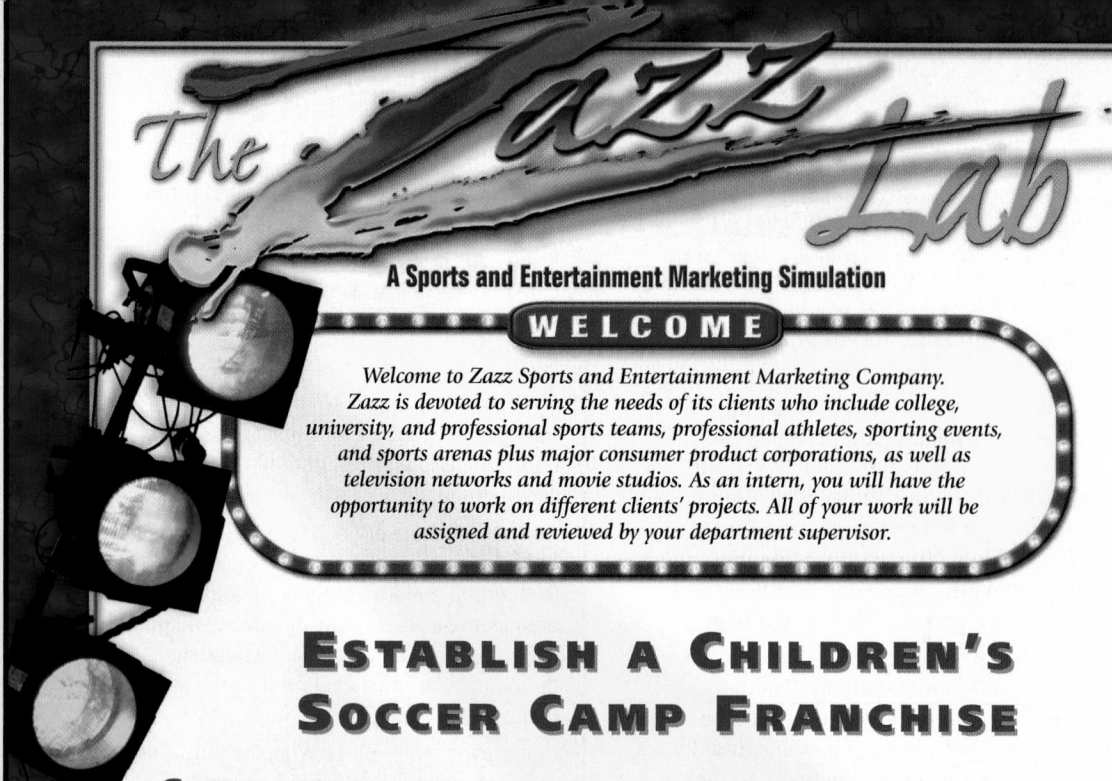

The Zazz Lab

A Sports and Entertainment Marketing Simulation

WELCOME

Welcome to Zazz Sports and Entertainment Marketing Company. Zazz is devoted to serving the needs of its clients who include college, university, and professional sports teams, professional athletes, sporting events, and sports arenas plus major consumer product corporations, as well as television networks and movie studios. As an intern, you will have the opportunity to work on different clients' projects. All of your work will be assigned and reviewed by your department supervisor.

ESTABLISH A CHILDREN'S SOCCER CAMP FRANCHISE

SITUATION

One of Zazz's long-standing properties—a professional soccer player—is preparing to retire. To stay involved in soccer and to generate retirement income, he wants to run children's soccer camps around the United States. The camps would cater to three age groups—6–9, 10–13, and 14 and older. He has asked Zazz to establish the format and prospectus so his name and concept for the camps can be franchised. The new camps will be in competition with established camps that have been catering to soccer players for many years.

ASSIGNMENT

You must determine the four *P*s of the marketing mix, as well as guidelines for consistent management of the camps. *Place* strategies should discuss minimum requirements for location sites. *Product* suggestions involve camp format and a sample daily schedule for each age group. Besides soccer drills, include team-building activities and social skills for the first two age groups and game strategies for the older age group. Also include leisure activities. *Promotion* efforts include a letter and brochure. Determine a realistic pricing structure for the camps. Write a mission statement discussing the philosophy and goals of the camps. Compile an employee handbook discussing the client's philosophy, job responsibilities, behavior guidelines, and management's expectations. Provide two human relations scenarios for employees to analyze and respond to—one situation involving coworkers and the other involving children. These can be used for employee training.

Tools and Resources

To complete this assignment you will need to conduct research at a library or on the Internet. You will need a word processing program and computer presentation software. Required reading would include *Soccer America*, a national soccer magazine.

Research

Research soccer to get an appreciation for the sport and its popularity. Research soccer camps for children, including where and when they are held, average length, who runs them, cost, typical activities, and promotional activities. Research team-building activities and human relations skill development for inclusion in the camp's schedule and employee handbook. Study management strategies for training employees and keeping them motivated.

206 Unit 4 ■ *Academic Concepts and Skills*

SOCCER OR FOOTBALL—WHICH IS IT?

During the 19th century, it was the fashion among English schoolboys to shorten words and assign nicknames. In England *Association Football* was the formal name for what we know as soccer. The name changed when boys shortened the word association and added the suffix *er*, which was a common practice at that time. Thus, the word *assoccer* was created. The name was again shortened to simply *soccer*—much easier to say. However, *football* is still the standard name for soccer in every country except the United States. The word "football" also appears in formal designations, for example the Federation Internationale de Football Association (FIFA).

Report

Prepare a written report and a computer presentation for the client. Use a word processing program to prepare a double-spaced report. Within the report, prepare a table that shows a comparison of four existing camps. Also create a table for the daily schedule for each age group, listing the times and activities in an easy-to-follow format. Be sure each table has a title and is introduced in the text prior to its inclusion on the page. Arrange your written report around the following headings:

- Background on soccer
  - Worldwide and United States
  - Current trends
- Analysis of existing soccer camps—(table)
  - Formats, locations, pricing structure, and promotion
- Proposed soccer camps
  - Mission statement
  - Location requirements (place)
  - Suggested format (product)
    - Duration (weekly, overnight)
    - Classifications (age, gender)
    - Activities
      - Sample daily schedule (table)
      - Sample team-building activity
      - Sample social skills activity
  - Promotion of camps
    - Sample letter and brochure
- Pricing structure
- Employee handbook
  - Role plays
  - Camp philosophy
  - Job responsibilities
  - Guidelines for behavior

Using computer presentation software, prepare a presentation of your ideas for the client that includes:

- Key topics covered in your written report
- Graphic illustrations that are relevant to each slide's topic
- Very little text
- A minimum of 10 slides

Presentation and Evaluation

Your supervisor wants you to present your ideas in a written report and an oral presentation. The oral presentation will later be shown to the client. You will be evaluated on your oral presentation skills, which include:

- Knowledge of soccer and soccer camps
- Proposed ideas for soccer camp franchise
- Comprehensiveness of report
- Continuity of presentation
- Enthusiasm
- Voice quality
- Eye contact

 Portfolio

Print out a copy of your completed report and presentation for your Portfolio.

THE CONNECTION

DECA Business Service Marketing Series
Creating the format and promotional ideas for a business franchise could be a potential role play for this event.

DECA Marketing Management Series
Preparing an employee handbook and training plan is part of this career area.

DECA Hospitality and Recreation Marketing Research Event
Conducting research and planning a soccer camp for children is a possible topic for this written event.

DECA Entrepreneurship Participating Event
Developing a business proposal for a soccer camp for children is a possible topic for this event, as long as financial information is included.

DECA Sports and Entertainment Marketing Management Team Decision-Making Event
Working on this project with a partner will make the experience similar to what is expected in a DECA Team Decision-Making Event.

COOPERATIVE LEARNING

Teamwork This unit lab lends itself to working in teams of four to eight students. Assign students to research soccer and soccer camps, so all students gain a background on the topic. Then assign three different teams to the various facets of the project (proposed soccer camps, promotion and pricing, and employee handbook). Finally, have the class put together the complete project. In larger classes, the main topics could be further delineated to create additional teams.

Independent Practice

Design and Write Ask students to develop a Web site for the franchised children's soccer camps. Tell them to create a home page and include links to each camp's philosophy and mission statement, location, format, and registration information. If some students don't have the technical knowledge to create a Web site, have them write a Web site plan on paper.

ASSESS

Enrichment

Research and Calculate Have students research the cost of the equipment and supplies required to begin a soccer camp, as well as the estimated number of employees needed and their salaries. Have students use a spreadsheet program to determine how much money is needed from investors.

Evaluation

The rubrics for evaluation of the written, oral, and presentation software are included in the student text. (See the outline and guidelines for the written report, the computer presentation, and the skills' assessment for oral presentations.) It might be best to replicate those rubrics to evaluate the students' work. A separate rubric could be created to evaluate the work of a team.

CLOSE

Lab Wrap-Up

Ask students why management and basic and social skills are so vital in the operation of a soccer camp for children. *(They are important to profitability and smooth operations. Basic and social skills are especially important because of the constant interaction with co-workers, coaches, and the children attending the camp, as well as with parents.)*

Unit 5

Selling

Unit Objectives

After completing this unit, students will be able to:

- Use the seven steps of the sales process on the job.
- Explain the process and techniques of both retail and business-to-business selling.
- Identify ways to prepare for selling.
- Demonstrate appropriate techniques to initiate a sale and determine customer needs.
- Demonstrate proper product presentation techniques.
- Handle customer objections during the selling process.
- Demonstrate effective suggestion selling and sale closing techniques.
- Perform the cashiering and math procedures of retail and business-to-business sales transactions.
- Evaluate sales as a profession for career-planning purposes.

Enrichment Resources

Books

Endless Referrals by Bob Burg
The 25 Sales Strategies That Will Boost Your Sales Today by Stephan Schiffman
Upside-Down Marketing by George R. Walther

Magazines/Journals

Personal Selling Power
Sales & Marketing Management

Associations

American Marketing Association
250 S. Wacker Drive, Suite 200
Chicago, IL 60606
(312) 648-0536
www.ama.com

National Association of Sales Professionals
8300 North Hayden Road, Suite 207
Scottsdale, AZ 85258
(480) 951-4311
www.nasp.com

Journal Writing Activity

1. Ask students to make a list in their journals of ten words that come to mind when they think of selling. Ask students to share their selling-related words with the rest of the class. Write the words on the board. Categorize their words into skills, aptitudes, and processes. Write on the board any aspects of selling that were not identified and explain why each is a vital part of selling.

2. Ask students to write two paragraphs in their journals about what they think it takes to be a great salesperson. Then ask them to share their answers. Categorize their answers on the board under the headings Academic Skills, Human Relations Skills, Technical Skills, and Creative Skills. Lead students in a discussion on the definitions of the various skills, the importance of each skill, and how each skill relates specifically to selling. Explain to students that success at selling, like any career, is the result of training, apprenticeship, and experience.

TEACHER CLASSROOM RESOURCES

Program Resources	CHAPTER 12	CHAPTER 13	CHAPTER 14	CHAPTER 15	CHAPTER 16
Student Activity Workbook	p. 97	p. 107	p. 117	p. 125	p. 133
Marketing Math Workbook	p. 31	p. 31	p. 31	p. 31	p. 31
Marketing Research Project Workbook	p. 65	p. 65	p. 65	p. 65	p. 65
ILP School-to-Work Activity Workbook	p. 45	p. 49	p. 53	p. 61	p. 65
ILP *BusinessWeek* Case Studies	p. 77	p. 85	p. 91	p. 97	p. 103
ILP Marketing Career Portfolio	p. 35	p. 35	p. 35	p. 35	p. 35
Reproducible Tests	p. 69	p. 73	p. 77	p. 81	p. 85
ExamView User's Guide and Testbank	p. 12-1	p. 13-1	p. 14-1	p. 15-1	p. 16-1
ILP Internet Resources	p. 43	p. 45	p. 47	p. 49	p. 51
ILP Blackline Masters	p. 26	p. 27			p. 28
ILP Lesson Plans	p. 25	p. 27	p. 29	p. 31	p. 33
ILP Block Scheduling	p. 5	p. 5	p. 5	p. 5	p. 5
Impact! Simulation	p. 41	p. 41	p. 41	p. 41	p. 41

ILP Each of these resources is available in print and on the Interactive Lesson Planner CD-ROM.

Technology Resources

- **Interactive Lesson Planner (ILP) CD-ROM**
- **PowerPoint Presentation CD-ROM**
- **Marketing Essentials Web site**
- **ExamView! CD-ROM**
- **Impact! Simulation**
- **Virtual Business**

Virtual Business is a fully visual marketing and business simulation that introduces students to the principles of marketing by letting them start and run their own virtual businesses. In *Virtual Business*, students have the power to control all aspects of a retail convenience store. Students strategize marketing decisions using a powerful learning tool in the guise of a video game. They learn by experiencing how their decisions affect their virtual business.

Key to Individualized Academics Activities

L1 Level 1 activities are basic activities and should fall within the range of all students.

L2 Level 2 activities are average activities and should be within the range of average and above average students.

L3 Level 3 activities are challenging activities designed for the ability range of above average students.

National Marketing Education

CHAPTER	SECTION	PERFORMANCE INDICATOR
Chapter 12 **Preparing for the Sale**	12.1	Explain the nature and scope of the selling function (SEL)
		Analyze product information for use in selling (SEL)
		Identify customer's buying motives for use in selling (SEL)
		Facilitate customer buying decisions (SEL)
	12.2	Determine customer/client needs (SEL)
		Explain key factors in building a clientele (SEL)
		Differentiate between consumer and organizational buying behavior (SEL)
Chapter 13 **Initiating the Sale**	13.1	Explain the selling process (SEL)
		Prepare for the sales presentation (SEL)
		Establish relationship with client/customer (SEL)
	13.2	Determine customer/client needs (SEL)
		Assess customer/client needs (SEL)
Chapter 14 **Presenting the Product**	14.1	Demonstrate product (SEL)
		Recommend specific product (SEL)
	14.2	Convert customer/client objections into selling points (SEL)
		Handle customer inquiries (CIS)
Chapter 15 **Closing the Sale**	15.1	Close the sale (SEL)
		Sell good/service/idea to individuals (SEL)
		Facilitate customer buying decisions (SEL)
	15.2	Demonstrate suggestion selling (SEL)
		Process sales documentation (SEL)
		Plan follow-up strategies for use in selling (SEL)
Chapter 16 **Using Math in Sales**	16.1	Analyze technology for use in the sales function (SEL)
		Process sales documentation (SEL)
	16.2	Calculate miscellaneous charges (SEL)
		Explain the purpose and importance of credit (FIN)
		Address the needs of individual personalities (SEL)
	16.3	Determine discounts and allowances that can be used to adjust base prices (PRI)
		Use information system for order fulfillment (DIS)

CIS Communication, Interpersonal Skills   **DIS** Distribution   **FIN** Financing   **PRI** Pricing   **SEL** Selling

Standards Assessment Correlation

SECTION ASSESSMENT			CHAPTER ASSESSMENT						UNIT LAB
Reviewing Key Terms and Concepts	Thinking Critically	Integrating Academic Skills	Fact and Idea Review	Thinking Critically	Building Workplace Skills	Applying Marketing Concepts	Linking School to Work	Internet Connection	Zazz Lab
1, 2, 3		●	1		2	1			●
4	●		2, 3, 4	1, 2	1	2, 4	●		●
4	●		1, 3, 4, 5	1, 2, 3, 4		3, 4		●	●
5	●					2, 4			●
1, 4, 5		●	6, 7, 8	2, 4					●
2, 3, 4	●		7		2	3			●
4		●	9						
1, 2, 5	●		1, 3	1, 5		1, 2, 3	●		●
2, 3, 4	●	●	4	1, 3, 4, 5	2	1, 2, 3		●	●
2, 4		●	1, 2, 3	2, 3, 4, 5			●		
1, 2, 3, 4	●	●	5, 7, 9	2, 4, 5	1, 2	2	●	●	●
3, 4, 5	●		6, 8, 9	2, 5	1, 2	1, 2	●	●	●
1, 2, 3, 4	●	●	1, 3, 4	1, 2, 3a, 3c, 3e	2	1	●		
2, 3, 4			1, 2, 3, 4		1				
1, 2, 3, 4, 5			5, 6, 7, 8, 9	3a, 3b, 3c, 3d, 3e, 4		2, 3		●	●
4, 5		●	6, 8	2, 3d, 3e, 4		2, 3	●	●	●
2, 3, 4		●	1, 3, 4, 5	1a, 1b, 1c, 1d		1	●	●	
1			1, 2	3	2	2, 4		●	●
1, 2	●	●	1, 2, 4	3, 5				●	●
1, 2, 3, 4			6, 7	2	1	1, 2		●	
		●							
5	●		8, 9		2	3, 4	●	●	●
1, 4, 5	●		1, 2, 3	1, 2, 4	2, 7	1, 2, 3, 4		●	
1, 2, 3, 5	●		2, 4	2, 5	1, 2, 7	5	●		
3	●		8	2		5			
1	●		5, 6, 7			3			
1, 2	●			1, 3, 4	1		●		
2, 3			9, 10	2					
1	●	●	9	1, 5		1, 4		●	

208D

Unit Overview

Selling is the first of the functions of marketing to be explored in *Marketing Essentials*. Chapter 12 helps students prepare for the sale by introducing the concept of feature-benefit selling and the importance of product and customer knowledge. It also covers how to find customers through prospecting. Chapter 13 introduces the students to all the steps of the sale, but concentrates on the first two—approaching customers and determining their needs. In Chapter 14 students learn the principles and practices of presenting the product and handling customers' objections. Closing the sale, suggestion selling, and the concept of relationship marketing are covered in Chapter 15. Chapter 16 reviews the mathematics involved in retail and business-to-business selling.

Introducing the Unit

To introduce this unit, ask students to share their perceptions of salespeople with the class. *(In many cases, perceptions will be negative because their only exposure to selling has been through minimally trained salespeople in mainstream retail selling situations.)*

To get students to revise their perspectives, ask questions like this one: Do you think Xerox or IBM salespeople would misrepresent their products' capabilities in order to make a sale to a Fortune 500 company? Why or why not? A key follow-up question is: What happens when the salesperson shows up for the next sale call?

UNIT·5

Portfolio

The Sales Presentation

Upon completion of this unit, you will be expected to conduct an actual sales presentation, demonstrating mastery of each step of the sales process. Have your teacher select a classmate to play the role of your customer, and if possible, videotape the presentation. To prepare for this activity, you will need to research a product of your choice, prepare a written feature-benefit chart for it, and decide on your sales situation (retail or business-to-business). Prepare an evaluation sheet for your teacher and classmates to use in judging your sales demonstration. Include spaces to rate all the steps of the sale (approach, determining needs, product presentation, handling objections, closing the sale, and suggestion selling), as well as relationship marketing and ability to communicate. Under each step of the sale, indicate items to be evaluated and points assigned to each. The evaluation sheet should total 100 points.

208

🚌 Field Trip Suggestions

Observe Selling Situations Arrange for your students to visit a variety of different types of stores. Include a department store, an upscale clothing store, a computer store, a hardware store, and any other stores you wish to add. Have your students observe the types of sales approaches used by the salespeople in the stores and compare them, adding the reasons why they feel those approaches are used.

Selling

Unit Overview

This unit is designed to prepare you for employment in a sales position. The practical aspect of this unit will be beneficial to you even if you don't pursue a specific career in sales—selling an idea, being elected to a political position, and even getting hired for a job often requires these skills.

Chapter 12 helps you prepare for the sale by performing product and customer research. Chapter 13 introduces you to the steps of a sale in retail and business-to-business sales, focusing on approaching customers and determining their needs. Chapter 14 discusses product presentation and how to handle any customer questions or objections. Chapter 15 explains how to close the sale, conduct suggestion selling, and begin a long-standing relationship with your customers. The final chapter in this unit addresses the mathematical aspect of selling, including operating a sales register and filling out necessary forms.

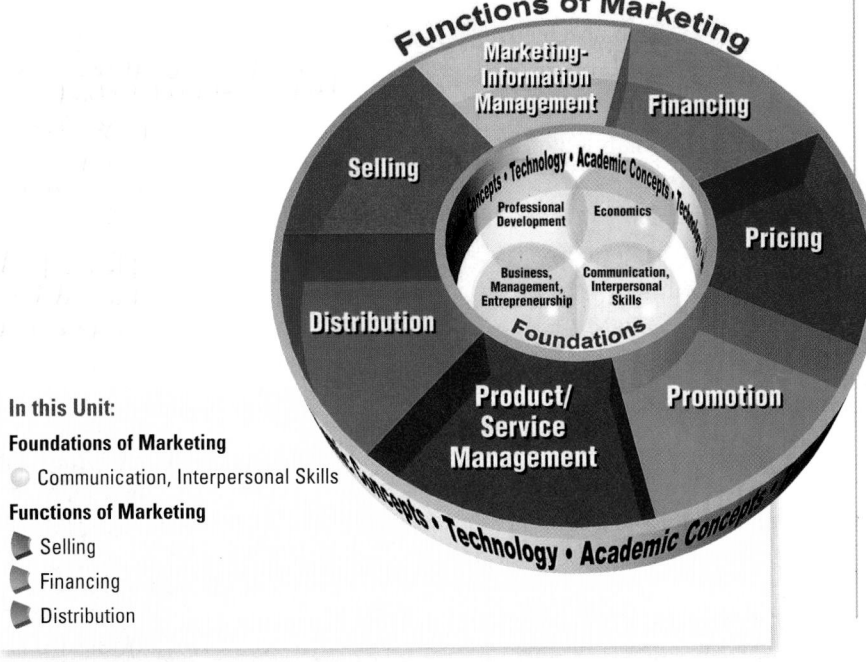

In this Unit:

Foundations of Marketing

◯ Communication, Interpersonal Skills

Functions of Marketing

◥ Selling

◥ Financing

◥ Distribution

◀DECA Unit Project

The culmination of the unit should be an actual sales presentation based on the sales training manuals that students write as an ongoing project while working on the unit. To make the presentations more instructive, videotape them, if possible, and play back the tapes for class or DECA chapter evaluation.

www Go to the *Marketing Essentials* Web site (**www.marketing.glencoe. com**) for resources to teach and assess occupation-specific vocabulary.

Unit Closure

Have students brainstorm ways of evaluating salespeople based on the key principles learned for each step of the selling process. Tell students that the standards they compile will be used in observation research.

Arrange with the managers of several local retail stores to have your students evaluate the salespeople's performance. Have the managers ask for volunteers for the project. Suggest to the managers that they tell the volunteers when they will be evaluated (within a week) but not who will be doing the evaluating. Students should work in pairs so that they can help each other remember exactly what was said during their sales encounter. Students should analyze their findings carefully and report them in written form. Finished reports should then be passed along to the store managers.

🎙 Guest Speaker Suggestions

Sales Professional Ask a local representative of the Sales and Marketing Executives International to speak to your class about selling as a career and the career potential in sales. Ask him or her to discuss the many types of jobs in sales as well as the various types of companies with sales departments. Have him or her explain to students that success in selling, like success at any career, is the result of training, apprenticeship, and experience.

Chapter Overview

Chapter 12 covers how a salesperson prepares for a sale. Personal selling is defined, and three basic sales situations are reviewed—retail, business-to-business, and telemarketing. The twin goals of selling are discussed. Section 12.2 covers how to find information about the product and industry.

 ## Springboard

Writing Have students write summaries of the best and worst experiences they have had with salespeople. This can open discussion about the twin goals of selling and types of salespeople.

Prereading

List the section objectives to discuss with students. Have students skim the chapter, looking at the pictures, reading the captions, and noting the heads. Ask questions to ensure that students have a minimal understanding of the chapter structure.

Preteaching Marketing Vocabulary

Dictate each of the vocabulary terms and ask students to write them on a sheet of paper. When they finish, write the terms on the board. Then have students guess at the meaning of each. Write their guesses next to each term. Leave this list on the board so students can see how close their guesses were to the actual definitions as they work through the chapter.

Marketing: What It Takes

Answer Helpful information would be how and where the company's products are produced, fabrics and styles, features and benefits, garment care, policies on ordering, and fashion trends. You can find this information in the company's catalog, by asking employees, and reading labels.

210

Preparing for the Sale

Marketing: What It Takes

Fashion, Fabrics, and Styles

You have just been accepted as an intern for a clothing manufacturer. You will be working in the manufacturer's showroom in New York City as a sales consultant for the summer. Prior to starting your internship, you decide that it would be a good idea to learn about the company's products and customers.

WHAT WILL YOU DO?

What information will you need? How will you find it?

210

THE DECA CONNECTION

ADVISOR CORNER

Presenting DECA to Businesses Present information on DECA to local business people. Group students in twos or threes and have them develop presentations based on the core principles of DECA—the four points of the DECA Diamond (social intelligence, vocational understanding, civic consciousness, leadership development). Designate a day or two for the teams to visit business people in your community. Have students invite them to become business members of your local DECA chapter. Provide a photo, books, and/or DECA brochures for students to take along. Expanding chapter membership to include members of the business community is a great way to gain valuable insight and support for your chapter.

Knowing Your Product and Your Customer

Selling

Does anybody recall what personal selling is?

The act of personal selling occurs in a retail setting, a business-to-business setting, or even over the telephone. **Personal selling** is any form of direct contact occurring between a salesperson and a customer. The key factor that sets it apart from other forms of promotion is that there is two-way communication between the seller and the buyer.

Retail selling is unique because customers come to the store. Non-personal selling techniques, such as advertising and displays, help to create store traffic. The salesperson's job in the store is to help the customer. The salesperson is available to answer any questions about the product or its features.

Mike said... Does anyone have anything to add?

Business-to-business selling may take place in a manufacturer's or wholesaler's showroom (inside sales) or a customer's place of business (outside sales). In the latter case, it is up to the salesperson to make contact with the customer. Sales representatives, in most cases, will call to make an appointment prior to their visit. In other cases, a sales representative may make a "cold call," which means he or she will appear without an appointment.

The next one that we look at is business to business selling. Can anyone tell me what that is?

This is an important chapter because we deal with salespeople on a regular basis and some of you might become salespeople in the future.

The last type of personal selling situation is **telemarketing**, which is the process of selling over the telephone. Consumer products and services that are commonly sold over the telephone include magazine or newspaper subscriptions; service contracts for newly purchased appliances, televisions, and computers; and long distance telephone services. Products that may be telemarketed to businesses are items that are purchased on a regular basis, such as stationery, cleaning supplies, or office supplies like computer paper.

Next, who can tell me what telemarketing is? The telephone. The telephone is where you get the term tele.

On page 211, it says "The goals of selling are the same regardless of the sales situation."

The goals of selling are the same regardless of the sales situations. They are to help customers make satisfying buying decisions, which create ongoing, profitable relationships between buyer and seller. Repeat business is crucial to the success of any company. It is easier and less expensive to keep current customers happy than it is to generate new customers. If a business is successful at keeping customers happy, it is likely that the customers will pass along positive recommendations to friends and family.

you really need to know the goals of selling. Can anyone tell me what the goals of selling are?

Salespeople accomplish those goals by solving customers' problems and by understanding their needs and wants. A customer may say that she is having a problem with her feet because she stands all day in her new job. An alert salesperson will suggest shoes designed for people who stay on their feet all day. This analysis of the customer's needs combined with product knowledge should please the customer and make the sale.

This is something I expect everyone to be able to tell me. How do salespeople accomplish those goals. Miho, please explain.

What You'll Learn

There is a lot of information here in Section 12.1 such as ("What you'll learn")

- The definition and goals of selling
- The various sales situations encountered in the business world
- The definition of feature-benefit selling
- How customers make decisions and the difference between rational and emotional buying decisions

Why It's Important

Learning how to research products and customers is helpful when selling any type of product or idea. Learning how to find customers is also essential. In this chapter you will learn key selling concepts that link products to customers.

Key Terms

- personal selling
- business-to-business selling
- telemarketing
- feature-benefit selling
- product features
- customer benefits
- rational motive
- emotional motive
- extensive decision making
- limited decision making
- routine decision making

Chapter 12 ■ *Preparing for the Sale* **211**

FOCUS

Bell Ringer Activity

Discuss Ask students how seeing an advertisement that is selling something is different from personal selling or going to a store and having a salesperson help you. *(In advertising there is only one-way communication; in selling there is two-way communication.)*

Introducing the Section

Selling Use the students' answers to the Bell Ringer Activity to develop the definition of personal selling. *(It is direct contact between a salesperson and a customer, involving an oral presentation to one or more potential customers.)*

TEACH

Technology Resources

PowerPoint The *Marketing Essentials* PowerPoint Presentation CD-ROM provides visual lecture aids for every chapter section.

Concept Development

1. Read Section 12.1 with students.
2. Ask students: Why is it so important for a salesperson to help customers make satisfying buying decisions? *(Students should recognize the need for repeat business as one of the primary reasons.)*
3. Ask students: How does a company like IBM sells its products to other companies? How does a manufacturer of small engines sells its products to other manufacturers? *(They use salespeople from their companies to sell their products, which is what we call business-to-business selling.)*

211

Classroom Resources

For the Teacher
- Teacher Editions for all workbooks
- Assessment Package
- PowerPoint Presentation Software
- Interactive Lesson Planner
- **ILP** Block Scheduling, p. 5
- **ILP** Lesson Plans, p. 25
- **ILP** Internet Resources, p. 43

- **ILP** Blackline Masters, p. 26
- **ILP** *BusinessWeek* Case Studies, p. 77
- **ILP** Marketing Career Portfolio, p. 35
- *Marketing Essentials* Web site (**www.marketing.glencoe.com**)

For the Student
- Student Activity Workbook, p. 97
- Marketing Math Workbook, p. 31

- Marketing Research Project Workbook, p. 65
- **ILP** School-to-Work Activity Workbook, p. 45
- Virtual Business simulation
- *Marketing Essentials* Web site (**www.marketing.glencoe.com**)

ILP These resources are available in print and on the Interactive Lesson Planner (ILP)

Discussion Starter

Customer Buying Motives Ask students to share their last product purchase with the class and tell why they bought the item. This will allow you to introduce customer buying motives and the distinction between rational and emotional motives. Have students categorize their motives as one or the other.

Thinking Critically

Customer Benefits Ask students what customers are really looking for (which benefits) when buying the following products: jewelry, apparel, winter coat, running shoes. *(Answers will vary. Some possibilities include: jewelry—makes purchaser and recipient, if a gift, feel good; apparel—improves buyer's appearance; winter coat—keeps buyer warm; running shoes—makes running easier on the feet and legs.)*

Independent Practice

1. **Create a Display** Have students create a bulletin-board display of selected advertisements arranged according to buying motives. The ads on one side should depict rational motives; those on the other, emotional motives.
2. **Research and Compare** Have students select three competing products that require limited decision making. Ask students to research product and company information for each product. Tell them to determine how the products compare and which one has the most customer benefits. Have students present their findings in a table that displays the comparison.

Feature-Benefit Selling

[handwritten: What is feature-benefit selling?]

Matching the characteristics of a product to a customer's needs and wants is a concept called **feature-benefit selling**. Many people believe that customers do not buy products; rather, they buy what the products will do for them. Leather shoes are purchased for their appearance, easy care, comfort, and longevity. A computer is purchased for increased productivity. Insurance is purchased for emotional and financial security.

[handwritten: What are product features? Very good.]

PRODUCT FEATURES A salesperson needs to learn how a product's features will benefit the customer. **Product features** may be basic, physical, or extended attributes of the product or purchase. The most basic feature of a product is its intended use. A person buys an automobile for transportation or a watch to tell time.

[handwritten: On page 212 it says, "Consumers look for certain physical..."]

Consumers look for certain physical qualities in products that differentiate competing brands and models. In a vehicle a consumer might consider price, color, automatic transmission, car stereo system, tires, air bag, and antilock brakes.

Additional features add more value to a product and provide the reasons for price differences among product models. An iron that turns itself off after sitting unused will cost more than the basic model. Then there are extended product features. Extended features for a vehicle might include the warranty, service policy, and available financing. Customers might even consider the reputation of a company to be an extended feature because there is reduced risk doing business with a secure, well-established company. Customers are faithful to a reputable company that stands behind its products.

[handwritten: Next is customer benefits. What is customer benefits all about?]

CUSTOMER BENEFITS When the features of a product are developed into customer benefits, they become selling points. **Customer benefits** are the advantages or personal satisfaction a customer will get from a good or service. It is a salesperson's job to analyze the product features from the customer's point of view to determine the benefits.

[handwritten: I think a lot of people don't understand this, so listen up. When the features of a product are developed into customer selling points.]

You, as a salesperson, will need to answer two questions about each product feature:

1. *How does the feature help the product's performance?* The answer to this question represents the first step in developing a customer benefit. For example, air pockets in the heel of a running shoe cushion the impact on pavement.

2. *How does the performance information give the customer a personal reason to buy the product?* What value is the product to the customer? In the case of the running shoe, the air pockets give the wearer more comfort when running or walking and help to protect the foot from injury.

After identifying the features of a product and their benefits, you should put together a feature-benefit chart. This is a chart in which each product feature is listed with its corresponding customer benefits. In preparing such a chart, remember that the more useful a feature, the more valuable the product is to the customer. Figure 12-1 on page 213 shows a feature-benefit chart for a digital video camera.

[handwritten: What you will see sometimes is a feature-benefit chart. Please look at page 213. Why is this chart a good thing to have if you are a salesperson?]

[handwritten: Please look at page 212, down at the bottom. It says, "Telemarketing may be..."]

■ **A Phone Call Away** Telemarketing may be used to sell all types of goods and services for personal and business use. In some cases, businesses are using computer-generated voices to conduct telemarketing instead of human beings. *Why do you think some businesses use computer-generated voices for sales?*

[handwritten: You have probably got a call like this before.]

CAPTION ANSWER
A Phone Call Away Answers will vary. Most will note that it is difficult to train and keep telemarketers because of the rejection factor involved in that type of selling. Others might address the cost factor; it is less expensive to have a computer making the calls.

FIGURE 12-1

Feature-Benefit Chart for Sharp VL-SD2OU Digital Video Camera

FEATURE	BENEFIT
3" High Resolution Color LCD View Screen (fingerprint reduced) and Low Reflectivity	Viewing area is 4.27 square inches with 89,856 pixels, which means you will be able to see a very clear image of what you are recording. It allows you to make adjustments while you are recording, so you don't waste any footage. Screen is coated with a special resin that reduces fingerprints (cleaning is simple with a clean, soft cloth). The low reflectivity (one percent) feature absorbs 99 percent of all reflective light, making it easy to perform well in all lighting conditions, indoors and outside.
100x Digital Zoom	The 100x digital zoom is in addition to the 10x optical zoom (regular analog recording). It kicks in as soon as you zoom in past 10x and allows you to magnify that image 100 times. Great for those times when you cannot get close to the subject you want to record, like in a zoo or during a sporting event, where you are restricted in distance from the subject.
Digital Gamma Brightness Correction	This feature has a new backlight compensation which adjusts only the dark spots of a shot to optimal brightness levels and leaves the bright sections untouched, so they don't become glaringly washed out. No more worry about the degree of lightness in the area in which you are recording—you are guaranteed clear recordings all the time.
i.LINK™ Digital Interface In/Out (IEEE 1394)	the iLINK cable capability allows for incredibly high-speed (up to 400 Mbps) transfer of full motion video from digital camcorders to computers or other i.LINK capable camcorders. Since there is no need to convert digital data into analog, there is no loss of image quality. It is the ideal vehicle for transmitting digital camcorder data. (iLINK is a trademark of Sony Electronics, Inc.)
Digital Image Stabilization (D.I.S.)	The D.I.S. circuit senses movement of the user holding the camera and helps to reduce image shake and jitter, delivering a more stable picture.
270 degree Variable Angle Recording	You can hold the Viewcam in a variety of angles to record over people and objects or close to the ground. You can even record yourself by rotating the view screen 180 degrees.
Dimensions (W × H × D Inches) 16.2 × 3.8 × 2.9 and Approximate Weight: 1.2 lbs. (without tape or battery)	Compact and lightweight Viewcam makes it easy to handle and transport.
Suggested retail price is $999.99, which includes the following accessories: AC Adaptor/Charger (for the house), Battery Pack, Two Lithium Ion Batteries, DC Cable (for the car), Shoulder Strap, A/V Cable (for television), and Lens Cap	Good value for all the features and benefits of this new technology, as well as all the included accessories.
Sharp Electronics	A reputable electronics company that stands behind its products.
90-day limited warranty	The warranty is reassurance of the good quality of the product. Worry-free because anything that goes wrong with the Viewcam will be fixed during the warranty period free of charge.

SOURCE: SHARP ELECTRONICS WEB SITE.

■ **Feature-Benefit Chart** Combining a product or extended feature with its corresponding customer benefit creates selling points. *In this feature-benefit chart, which features are product features and which ones are extended features?*

Decision-Making Skills

Have students list three or four different kinds of products.

L1 Ask students to write as many rational and emotive motives as they can think of for buying each of these products.

L2 Have students write as many rational and emotive motives as they can think of for buying each of these products. Then have students write selling sentences that connect product features with those motives for buying the products.

L3 Have students select one of the products to use as the basis for a magazine ad, complete with headline (main buying motive) and ideas for illustrations (photos or artwork) that would help demonstrate the most important buying motives and their connection to specific product features. Have students defend their ads in an oral presentation to the class.

FIGURE 12-1 ANSWER
Feature-Benefit Chart Sharp Electronics' reputation as the manufacturer and the 90-day limited warranty are both extended features.

GREAT IDEAS from the Marketing Classroom

Maggie Rathert
Verona Area High School
Verona, WI

This activity is designed to help students understand the importance of product knowledge and how to identify the difference between features and benefits. Have students bring in five or six products, both hard-line and soft-line products. Fun products are products they use, such as personal stereos, cameras, and sweatshirts. Have blank copies of a feature-benefit analysis sheet. Put students into teams of four or five. Give each team a product and an analysis sheet. Have them examine the product and fill out the sheet in ten minutes. Have groups share their analyses with the class. Ask students to listen for the correct identification of features.

Does anybody recall from the reading what a rational motive is? Very good.

There is alot of information here. I have a question to ask. Do you recall what factors affect how a person makes a purchase decision? Very good.

SECTION 12.1

ASSESS

Reteaching

1. **Vocabulary** Assign and review the vocabulary terms for this section.
2. **Fact and Idea** Assign and review Fact and Idea Review questions 1–5 from the Chapter Assessment.
3. **Product Information and Feature-Benefit Selling** Bring in a newly purchased item that has its hangtags attached, a catalog or ad listing the item, and an owner's manual. Read aloud the information on the previous items. Then read the ad, catalog, and/or owner's manual copy. Have students identify product features. Once students have compiled their own feature lists, have them suggest one or more customer benefits for each feature. Then students should complete a feature-benefit chart.

Enrichment

1. **Review** Assign and review the appropriate Thinking Critically questions from the Chapter Assessment.
2. **Extend** Assign and review the corresponding activities from *BusinessWeek Case Studies, Internet Resources,* and the *School-to-Work Activity Workbook.* **ILP**
3. **Chart and Present** Have students take a common product that they bring to school daily (like a knapsack) and prepare a feature-benefit chart for it. Allow time for students to present their finished charts to the class.

■ Customer Buying Motives

To understand relevant consumer benefits for certain product features, salespeople must develop knowledge of customers. They must know what motivates customers to buy and what decisions customers make before the final purchase.

Customers may have rational or emotional motives for making purchases. A **rational motive** is a conscious, logical reason for a purchase. Rational motives include product dependability, time or monetary savings, health or safety considerations, service, and quality. An **emotional motive** is a feeling experienced by a customer through association with a product. Emotional motives are feelings such as social approval, recognition, power, love, or prestige. Many buying decisions involve a combination of both buying motives. *The next that the book talks about is emotional motive.*

Successful salespeople determine customers' rational and emotional motives in a potential buying situation. Then they suggest the features and benefits of the product that best matches those motives. People buy automobile tires for safety reasons (rational motive) because they care about loved ones that will share the vehicle with them (emotional motive). *(On eisel)*

*rational motive versus emotional motive
dependability   love*

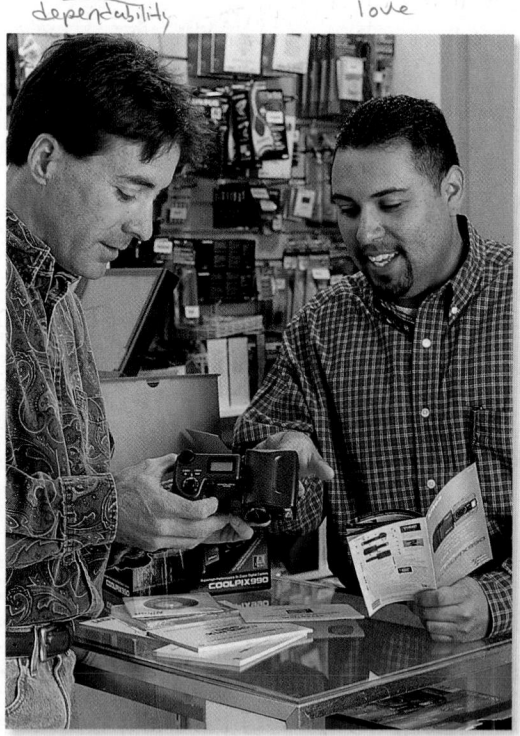

■ Customer Decision Making

Some customers need no help from salespeople, and others require significant time and effort. This difference has its roots in three distinct types of decision making—extensive, limited, and routine. How a person makes a decision is affected by the following factors:

- Previous experience with the product and company
- How often the product is purchased *frequency of*
- The amount of information necessary to make a wise buying decision
- The importance of the purchase to the customer
- The perceived risk involved in the purchase (fear that the product will cause financial loss or will not function properly) *financial*
- The time available to make the decision

Who can tell me what extensive decision making is

EXTENSIVE DECISION MAKING **Extensive decision making** is used when there has been little or no previous experience with an item. This category includes those goods and services that have a high degree of perceived risk, are very expensive, or have high value to the customer. Products in this category include expensive manufacturing machinery, land for a new building site, or an individual's first home.

Who can tell me what limited decision making

LIMITED DECISION MAKING **Limited decision making** is used when a person buys goods and services that he or she has purchased before but not regularly. There is a moderate degree of perceived risk involved, and the person often needs some information before buying the product.

Consumer goods and services in this category might include a second car, certain types of clothing, furniture, a vacation, and household appliances. Goods and services that a firm might buy using limited decision making include accounting services, ad agency services, computer programs, office equipment, and certain products used in manufacturing.

*Extensive   Limited   Routine
Home   Vacation   Newspaper*

Please look at page 214, down at the bottom. It says, "there are three...

■ **Making the Sale** There are three degrees of decision making for most sales situations. They are routine, limited, and extensive. *Which decision-making process do you think this customer is using?*

CAPTION ANSWER

Making the Sale Answers will vary. Most will say limited decision making because digital video cameras are somewhat expensive, and people don't buy them very frequently. Thus there is a moderate degree of risk involved in this purchase.

214

Handwritten at top: Lastly, what is routine decision making? Does anybody have anything to add to that?

ROUTINE DECISION MAKING Routine decision making is used when a person needs little information about a product that he or she is buying. This is generally attributed to a high degree of prior experience with it or a low perceived risk. The perceived risk may be low because the item is inexpensive, the product is bought frequently, or satisfaction with the product is high. Some consumer goods and services in this category are grocery items, newspapers, dry-cleaning services, hair-dressing services, and certain brand name clothing and cosmetics. Customers who have developed brand loyalty for a product will use routine decision making. Expensive items, such as automobiles, may be purchased routinely if the customer has strong brand loyalty to one car manufacturer. This is the same for electronic or computer products. A customer may be more likely to routinely purchase, for example, Sony electronics because of Sony's good reputation and overall popularity.

Handwritten: I think people figure, "Oh!, buying an automobile is not routine decision making. That is incorrect.

Businesses that simply reorder goods and services without much thought are using routine decision making. Products that businesses often buy routinely include raw materials, office supplies, maintenance services, and other staple goods. Many offices may have a standing order with an office supply company for computer paper, pens, and stationary. They know how much they use each month and assume that those quantities will remain constant. These items will continue to be routine purchases until there is a problem with the product or with the supplier. When this happens, limited decision making would be required to change suppliers or products.

Electronic Frontiers

Viral Marketing: It's Spreading

Getting your customers to become a part of your salesforce is a great way to conduct business. Instead of relying on banner advertisements or expensive marketing campaigns, companies look to their customers as a source of publicity. Many companies include "e-mail this information to a friend" buttons on their Web sites. On the Internet, word of mouth via e-mail can propel product recognition into purchases, especially if your happy customer is able to recommend a great experience to others. A customer who discussed the benefits of a particular make-up brush in an online discussion group provided a link to a beauty retailer. Over the next five days, that beauty retailer sold 3,000 brush sets. Companies hope that once the message is e-mailed, it spreads from person to person.

Thinking Critically

Customers are becoming aware that their endorsement is valuable to a company. Would it make sense for a company to reward them? If so, how?

SECTION 12.1

Evaluation

Assign and review the Section 12.1 Assessment.

Technology Resources

GO TO **Assessment Resources**
Go to the *Marketing Essentials* Web site (www.marketing.glencoe.com) for resources to teach and assess occupation-specific vocabulary.

CLOSE

Section Wrap-Up

Ask students: How is feature-benefit selling related to the two goals of selling? (*A salesperson must discover a customer's needs and wants. Once a salesperson knows these, he or she must communicate how the product's features match those needs and wants by changing the features into customer benefits.*)

Viral Marketing: It's Spreading

Answer Some online companies are providing products, services, or even cash rewards for friends or associates passing on an advertising message.

12.1 ASSESSMENT

Reviewing Key Terms and Concepts

1. What is personal selling?
2. Name three settings where personal selling may occur.
3. What are the goals of selling?
4. Explain the concept of feature-benefit selling.
5. What are the three levels of decision making that customers may use when purchasing goods or services?

Thinking Critically

6. Explain this statement: Customers do not buy products, they buy what the products will do for them.

Integrating Academic Skills

7. **COMMUNICATION** Write a classified advertisement for a sales position in a school store. Include job responsibilities and required skills.

12.1 ASSESSMENT ANSWERS

Reviewing Key Terms and Concepts

1. It is direct contact between a salesperson and a customer, involving an oral presentation.
2. retail, business-to-business, and telemarketing settings
3. The goals are to help customers make satisfying buying decisions and to create an on-going profitable relationship.
4. It matches the features of a product to a customer's needs and wants.
5. extensive, limited, and routine

Thinking Critically

6. Answers should note satisfaction from item—how product's features satisfy consumer needs and wants.

Integrating Academic Skills

7. **COMMUNICATION** Ads will vary.

SECTION 12.2

Preparation

FOCUS

Bell Ringer Activity

Product Information Have students recall the concept of feature-benefit selling from Section 12.1. Ask them if there was no feature-benefit chart for the Sharp Digital Viewcam, where would they get the information they needed to prepare one. List all the students' responses on the board.

Introducing the Section

Preparing for the Sale Using the list prepared in the Bell Ringer Activity, introduce the four main sources of product information by classifying everything the students noted into one of the four categories: direct experience, written materials, other people, and formal training.

[Handwritten: Recap / There is a lot of information in this section such as "what you'll learn"]

• What You'll Learn

- Sources for developing product information
- Prospecting sources and methods
- How leads are developed
- Preparation for the sale in business-to-business selling and retail selling

[Handwritten: On page 216, it says this section is important because,"]

• Why It's Important

As a salesperson, you will need to prepare for the sale by learning about the industry and the products you will be selling. In specific sales situations, you may also need to find customers. The tools and techniques for accomplishing these tasks are covered in this section.

Key Terms

- preapproach
- prospect
- referrals
- endless chain method
- cold canvassing

*[Handwritten notes:
Does anybody recall what direct experience is?
(on eisel before)
Sources of Product Information
Direct Experience — Use merchandise, visit manufacturing facility
Publications — catalogs, brochures, warranties, labels, website
People — Friends, Relatives, Co-workers
Training — attend training session, observation time with experienced sales reps.]*

[Handwritten: Section 12.2 had a lot to do with how salespeople prepare themselves for the sale]

The Preapproach

[Handwritten: Can anyone tell me what the preapproach is?]

There are some steps that a salesperson follows when preparing to assist customers. The **preapproach** is getting ready for the face-to-face encounter in a selling situation. *[Handwritten: Recall that the prefix pre means before. It's what the salesperson does before the sale.]*

Salespeople prepare for the sale by studying their products, keeping abreast of industry trends, researching potential customers, and developing familiarity with their company's policies and procedures.

■ Product Information

[Handwritten: Who can tell me how a salesperson can obtain product information]

Product knowledge is essential for success in selling. Knowing how to use and care for a product is essential when educating consumers and demonstrating a product. *[Handwritten: On page 216, it says "salespeople can generally]*

Developing product knowledge is easy—if you know where to look for the information. Salespeople can generally find all the product information they need through four main sources—direct experience, written publications, other people, and formal training.

Using a product is probably the best source of direct experience. Some businesses offer discounts to their salespeople to encourage employees to buy and use the company's merchandise. You can also get direct experience with a product by studying display models or visiting the manufacturing facility to see how the product is made.

Printed materials can offer facts and background necessary to develop familiarity with a product. These include user manuals, manufacturer warranties and guarantees, catalogs, and promotional materials. Labels provide important information for clothing items or prepackaged goods. Manufacturers, retailers, and wholesalers often have Web sites where products may be explained and purchased.

A personal opinion is valuable because it offers a human touch when sharing a product with a customer. Friends, relatives, and customers can tell you what they liked about the product as well as how they used it. Coworkers, supervisors, and manufacturers' representatives who have extensive product knowledge can also share their expertise.

Formal training may be the best way to educate salespeople on certain products. Most industrial sales representatives receive much of their product knowledge through formal training sessions. Some sales representatives spend several months attending classes and observing experienced sales representatives before going out on their own. In retail settings, training is likely to be less structured. Information might be funneled informally to the sales staff as new merchandise is received or selected for promotion.

[Handwritten: → On page 217, right hand side, it says "A manufacturer's catalog provides]

Classroom Resources

For the Teacher
- Teacher Editions for all workbooks
- Assessment Package
- PowerPoint Presentation Software
- Interactive Lesson Planner
- ILP Block Scheduling, p. 5
- ILP Lesson Plans, p. 26
- ILP Internet Resources, p. 43

- ILP *BusinessWeek* Case Studies, p. 77
- ILP Marketing Career Portfolio, p. 35
- *Marketing Essentials* Web site (**www.marketing.glencoe.com**)

For the Student
- Student Activity Workbook, p. 97
- Marketing Math Workbook, p. 31

- Marketing Research Project Workbook, p. 65
- ILP School-to-Work Activity Workbook, p. 45
- Virtual Business simulation
- *Marketing Essentials* Web site (**www.marketing.glencoe.com**)

ILP These resources are available in print and on the Interactive Lesson Planner (ILP)

[handwritten: Next, we will look at industry trends. What is industry trends all about?]

Industry Trends

[handwritten: On page 217, at the top it says, "All industries have trade publications related to that industry." Please look at page 217 down to the bottom it says "S & P..."]

Sales representatives read periodicals related to their trade to gain insight into the industry. As a sales representative for an apparel manufacturer, you might read *Women's Wear Daily*. At the retail level of selling, a sales representative may read consumer fashion magazines, such as *Vogue*, to stay current with up-to-date colors and trends. All industries have trade publications related to their industry.

Standard & Poor's is another publication that is a must for researching industry trends. This publication offers a trade report by industry. It is available in most college libraries, in some public libraries, and online.

Sources and Methods of Prospecting

[handwritten: Next, your book mentions Sources and Methods of Prospecting. This section has a lot to do with how salespeople find new customers.]

Looking for new customers is called prospecting. A **prospect**, or a lead, is a potential customer. Many types of businesses require salespeople to find new prospects, while others do not. Most retail selling situations are not involved with prospecting because salespeople do not need to go out and find customers—customers come to the store.

Prospecting is especially important in business-to-business selling situations. Salespeople are evaluated on how many new accounts they open through prospecting efforts. A rich supply of prospect sources is available to enterprising salespeople, including various kinds of directories, periodicals, lists, and suggested leads.

[handwritten: Prospecting is important to salespeople because it says on page 217 that "Salespeople are evaluated on how many new accounts they open through prospecting efforts."]

[handwritten: Does anybody recall from the reading where a salesperson can find potential customers? (List on easel before)]

Comfort-Rated to -20°F

STORM TRAC
For freezers and cold environments.

- Constructed of 430 denier urethane coated Caprolan® nylon.
- Insulated with 10 oz. DuPont Hollofil® polyester fiberfill.
- Two needle stitching & bound seams throughout.
- Rivet reinforced stress points and heavy-duty brass zippers.
- Covered storm flaps protect leg zippers.

High Bib Trousers
High-rise design protects chest, back and kidneys.

Coverall
Complete protection from the elements. Sewn-on orlon pile lined hood and deep insulated front pockets.

Quilted Hood
(Not shown)

Jacket
Hip length jacket features two insulated pockets, elastic back, orlon pile collar and knit wristlets.

High Bib Trousers
High bib trousers protect chest, back and kidney areas.

Lightweight Coverall
200 denier urethane coated oxford nylon outershell. Insulated with 7.5 oz. polyester fiberfill. Orlon pile collar.

■ **Customer Catalogs** A manufacturer's catalog provides details of products as well as important information regarding their purchase by other businesses. *How could the information on this catalog page be helpful to a sales representative for RefrigiWear?*

Refrigerated & Frozen Foods
RFF
SERVING FOOD PROCESSORS

MEAT & POULTRY®

BAKING BUYER

Food Logistics®

■ **Getting the Word Out There** Standard & Poor's provides data on industry trends, as do trade journals. *How could all these trade journals be useful to a company like RefrigiWear, an insulated clothing manufacturer?*

Chapter 12 ■ *Preparing for the Sale* **217**

TEACH

📊 Technology Resources

PowerPoint The *Marketing Essentials* PowerPoint Presentation CD-ROM provides visual lecture aids for every chapter section.

Concept Development

1. Read Section 12.2 with students.
2. Have students read aloud the Case Study on page 220 and review the answers in class.
3. To introduce the preapproach, ask students what the prefix *pre* means. *(before)* Then have students brainstorm to develop things that would be involved in the retail preapproach and the business-to-business pre-approach.

Discussion Starter

Prospecting Remind students that gold miners in the Old West were said to be *prospecting*. Ask students what the term meant in that context. Use the students' answers to introduce the concept of prospecting for customers as practiced by salespeople who must generate their own potential customer lists.

CAPTION ANSWER
Customer Catalogs Answers will vary. Most students will mention that knowing the garment's features and comfort rating for the garments would be helpful to a sales representative.

CAPTION ANSWER
Getting the Word Out There All these trade journals cover industries that have cold environments in which their employees must work. Articles in these publications may provide RefrigiWear and its sales representatives with ideas to solve potential customers' problems. RefrigiWear may also elect to advertise in these publications in order to solicit business.

Thinking Critically

1. **Product information** Tell students to assume they are selling ready-to-wear clothing. Ask where they could find information on how to care for a particular garment. For example, how would they know whether to wash or dry-clean it? *(Look at care labels inside the garment. Also, read hangtags.)*

2. **Prospecting** Ask students which type of prospecting they would prefer using, cold canvassing or the endless chain method, and why. *(Most students would agree that the endless chain method is easier because it allows you to use the name of a mutual acquaintance to get a foot in the door.)*

3. **Preapproach** Tell students to imagine that they sell stationary bicycles and that they have an appointment with the buyer of a new sporting goods store. Ask how they might get acquainted with the store before their sales call. *(Visit unannounced and note the location, merchandise mix, size, and amount of customer traffic.)*

Small Talk in Sales

Answer Answers may include that many consumers are rushed and want to make purchases with as little conversation as possible; this trend towards convenience and fast service has led many people to use the Internet.

I think people figure "Ohh, salespeople are on their own when finding new customers. That is incorrect.

EMPLOYER LEADS Some firms employ entire telemarketing teams to generate leads for their sales staffs. Telemarketers in such firms often perform preliminary research on these leads so that salespeople have information about the prospects before meeting them. Other firms rely entirely on their salespeople to find new customers.

Most businesses probably fall somewhere between those two extremes. Many employers do what they can to help locate potential customers for their salespeople. Figure 12-2 on page 219 provides some insight into how leads are created and pursued.

The next one they talk about in the book is telephone directories.

TELEPHONE DIRECTORIES The White Pages telephone directory provides names, addresses, and telephone numbers of potential customers in given geographic areas. The Yellow Pages lists businesses that may be potential customers for certain industrial goods and services.

I think we all understand what the telephone directory is.

The next one mentioned is trade + professional directories.

TRADE AND PROFESSIONAL DIRECTORIES Business-to-business sales representatives can use trade and professional directories to locate potential customers by type of business. One well-known directory frequently used by sales representatives is *Thomas' Register of American Manufacturers*.

You have to be smart. You have to realize that this is what salespeople do. I know I had something like this happen to me.

NEWSPAPERS Newspapers provide good leads for some salespeople. Birth announcements are good leads for insurance salespeople. Engagement announcements provide bridal shops, caterers, florists, and printers with prospects. Reports of business mergers and announcements of new personnel in business firms provide leads for business-to-business salespeople.

The next one mentioned in the book is commercial lists.

COMMERCIAL LISTS Salespeople may buy lists of potential customers from companies that specialize in categorizing people by such criteria as education, age, income, credit card purchases, and location. Lists of businesses categorized according to net sales, profits, products, and geographic locations are also available.

Can anyone tell me what commercial lists are?

I think a lot of people don't understand this so listen up. On page 218, it says companies specialize...

E-mail lists of people interested in the same subject or employed in the same industry are also available. Most e-mail list services are free, making them an economical way to identify potential customers.

(or used before) Demographics Geographics Behavior Psychographics

218 Unit 5 ■ Selling

Small Talk in Sales

In today's fast-paced society, American salespeople have been trained to make the sale with as little small talk as possible. This is not the case in Europe, where sales presentations take a different pace. Small talk and conversation about current events, sports, art, and other unrelated topics are part of the sales process. This practice of "friendly" selling is so common, in fact, that most Europeans are suspicious of a hard sale, where there is little talk and complete focus on making the deal.

Thinking Critically

Why are many Americans turned off by overly chatty salespeople and sales presentations that involve more talking than selling?

Does anybody recall from the reading what referrals are?

CUSTOMER REFERRALS Satisfied customers often give salespeople **referrals**—the names of other people who might buy the product. Referrals open the market to those potential customers you might not have reached without a recommendation. When salespeople ask previous customers for names of potential customers, they are said to be using the **endless chain method**. Some companies offer discounts or gifts to customers who give referrals.

This is where you get to learn endless chain method.

COLD CANVASSING In **cold canvassing**, a salesperson tries to locate as many potential customers as possible without checking out leads beforehand. In cold canvassing, potential customers are selected at random, such as by going door-to-door or selecting names from a telephone directory. This is also sometimes called blind prospecting. One example is a real estate agent going door-to-door in a neighborhood, asking people if they would like to sell their homes. Another example of cold canvassing is a stockbroker selecting names from a telephone book at random and calling them.

Lastly, cold canvassing is mentioned. Who can tell me what that is? Does anybody have anything to add?

Making a Sales Presentation DECA's Technical Marketing Representative Event provides an excellent opportunity for your students to experience first-hand the importance of proper preparation for making a sales presentation. This competitive event evaluates an individual student's ability to organize and deliver a sales presentation for one or more technical

products and/or services. The sales presentation is delivered in 15 minutes to a businessperson/judge role-playing a potential buyer for the technical product/service. Students acquire their product knowledge by researching the product and target market. In addition to making the sales presentation, student participants take a 100-question comprehensive exam.

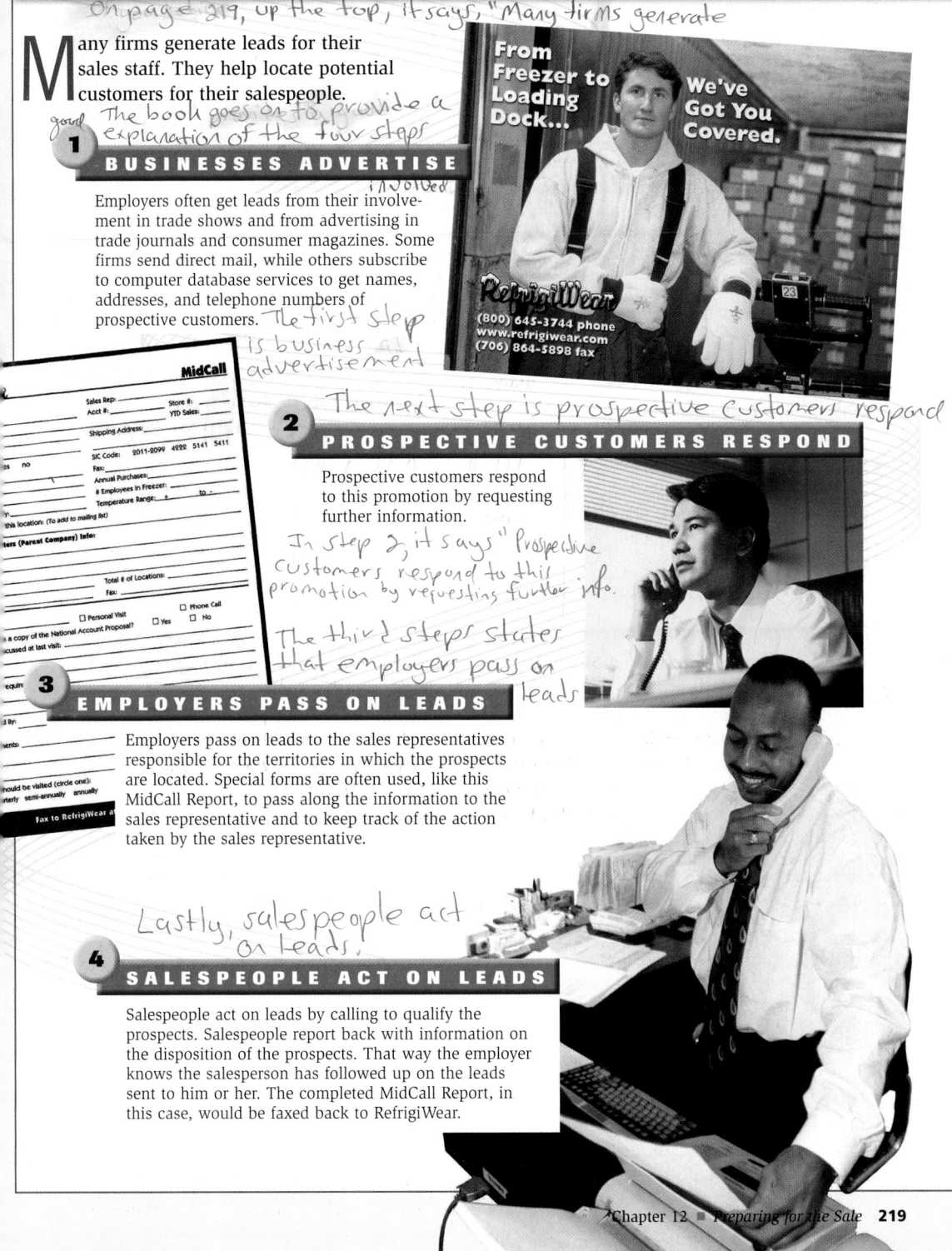

FIGURE 12-2

HOW EMPLOYER LEADS ARE DEVELOPED

On page 219, up the top, it says, "Many firms generate

Many firms generate leads for their sales staff. They help locate potential customers for their salespeople.

good *The book goes on to provide a explanation of the four steps involved*

1 BUSINESSES ADVERTISE

Employers often get leads from their involvement in trade shows and from advertising in trade journals and consumer magazines. Some firms send direct mail, while others subscribe to computer database services to get names, addresses, and telephone numbers of prospective customers. *The first step is business advertisement*

From Freezer to Loading Dock... We've Got You Covered.

RefrigiWear
(800) 645-3744 phone
www.refrigiwear.com
(706) 864-5898 fax

The next step is prospective customers respond

2 PROSPECTIVE CUSTOMERS RESPOND

Prospective customers respond to this promotion by requesting further information.

In step 2, it says "Prospective customers respond to this promotion by requesting further info."

The third step states that employers pass on leads

3 EMPLOYERS PASS ON LEADS

Employers pass on leads to the sales representatives responsible for the territories in which the prospects are located. Special forms are often used, like this MidCall Report, to pass along the information to the sales representative and to keep track of the action taken by the sales representative.

Lastly, salespeople act on leads.

4 SALESPEOPLE ACT ON LEADS

Salespeople act on leads by calling to qualify the prospects. Salespeople report back with information on the disposition of the prospects. That way the employer knows the salesperson has followed up on the leads sent to him or her. The completed MidCall Report, in this case, would be faxed back to RefrigiWear.

MidCall

Sales Rep:
Acct #:   Store #:
                 YTD Sales:
Shipping Address:

SIC Code: 2011-2099 4222 5141 5411
Fax:
Annual Purchases:
Employees in Freezer:
Temperature Range: ±   to -

this location: (To add to mailing list)

ers (Parent Company) Info:

Total # of Locations:
Fax:

□ Personal Visit   □ Phone Call
a copy of the National Account Proposal? □ Yes   □ No
cussed at last visit:

equire

d By:
ents:

hould be visited (circle one):
terly semi-annually annually

Fax to RefrigiWear a

More About . . .

Telemarketing

Telemarketers have had such negative reaction that even Miss Manners, the etiquette expert, advised people to hang up on them. Technology like caller ID and call-blocking can also work against telemarketers. Customers who have telephones with these features may not pick up the phone if they see a phone number displayed that they don't recognize.

(oreisel)

SECTION 12.2

Cooperative Learning

Product Labels Bring to class owner's manuals, product labels, and some actual products. Have students break into groups, and give each group one or more items to study as a source(s) of product information. At the end of 15 minutes, have each group report what kind of information the item provided. Then ask students what other information they would need to sell that product and where they could get it.

Can anybody tell me happen

Independent Practice *in*

1. **Prospecting** Have students *step 1, 3, 4?* interview a business-to-business salesperson or any businessperson who must generate his or her own sales leads. Have them ask the salesperson to describe the prospecting methods used and evaluate which were the most effective and why. Also, suggest they ask what the salesperson does with the leads once they are generated.

2. **Prospecting** Have students research ways a new photographer can find customers. Tell students that this photographer's services include wedding photography, portraits, and commercial photography. (The latter classification includes photos for ads, brochures, annual reports, and the like.) Remind students to use all the possible prospecting methods discussed in this section. Have them find examples of each method or write what they would do to utilize a given method. Tell them they will be expected to share their ideas with classmates in an oral presentation to the class.

What I would like to have you do right now is get into groups of two. Pretend you and your partner have just become photographers and need to find customers. You can do weddings, portraits, etc. How would you go about prospecting?

219

Human Relations Skills

Present students with this scenario: A shoe salesperson is waiting on a mother and her three little boys. When one child starts crying uncontrollably, the mother is exasperated and wants to leave. But the salesperson has already found the shoes for the children and is ready to have them tried on.

L1 Ask students: If you were the salesperson, what would you do to salvage the sale?

L2 Ask students to identify the traits that an effective salesperson would demonstrate. *(Answers will vary. Most will suggest empathy, patience, problem-solving ability, good communication skills, and a positive attitude.)*

L3 Have students role-play the previous scenario, demonstrating the personal characteristics and skills of an effective salesperson.

Try to remember your last encounter with a salesperson. What I would like to have you do right now with a partner is identify the traits that made that particular salesperson effective or ineffective (or else).

What does the book say to do when dealing with previous customers?

Who remembers what the book says to do when dealing with new customers?

Case Study

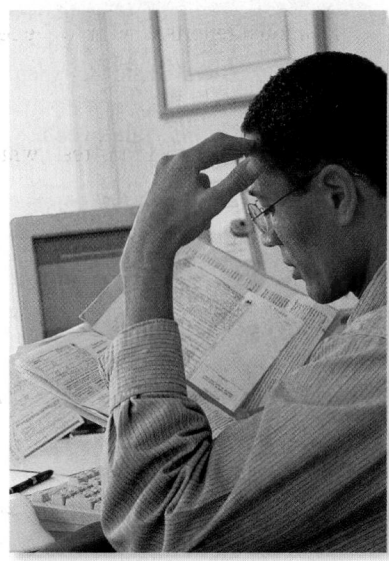

Customer Management Software

Customer management software is changing how companies keep track of their customers. The software company Siebel Systems Inc. has created a program that helps sales representatives track their customers and analyze markets. The program publishes monthly analyses that detail customer problems and needs. Honeywell, a company that makes jet engines and avionics, uses Siebel's software. In Honeywell's first report, they found that airlines were frustrated with managing parts inventories. Honeywell executives responded with new services that will spare airlines that headache. "Our focus used to be from the inside out. Now it's the reverse," says division General Manager Lynn Brubaker.

Clarify, another software company, has a program that combines multiple databases into one huge database so companies can view all customer information in one place. H&R Block, for example, uses Clarify software to combine and coordinate the customer records at its tax offices, discount brokerage, Web site, and customer-service center. With easy access to this central warehouse of information, salespeople in the company's stock trading division can look at detailed descriptions of tax customers and size up who would be good prospects.

Case Study Review

1. How did Honeywell's use of customer management software provide the company with an opportunity to increase its business with the airline companies?
2. How did H&R Block's salespeople in the stock trading business benefit from the company's adoption of Clarify's software?

A MATTER OF ETHICS

3. Do you think it is ethical for H&R Block to use its database from one operation to sell products in another division of the company? Why or why not?

If you recall from the reading, preapproach activities vary depending on whether the sales call is with a previous customer or a new prospect.

▪ Preparing for the Sale in Business-to-Business Selling

In business-to-business (B-to-B) sales, preapproach activities vary depending on whether the sales call is with a previous customer or a new prospect. When dealing with previous customers, salespeople analyze past sales records and review their notes about the buyer's personality, family, interests, and hobbies.

When dealing with a new customer, the salesperson must do some homework before jumping into the selling process. Questions that the salesperson should research include the following:

- Does the prospect need this product or service?
- Does the prospect have the financial resources to pay?
- Does the prospect have the authority to buy?

Does anybody know where a salesperson would look for this information?

Case Study Review Answers

Customer Management Software
1. Honeywell increased its business with airline companies by solving a problem the companies had. Honeywell created a new service that helps them manage their parts inventories.
2. Salespeople in H&R Block's stock trading business were able to look at detailed descriptions of tax customers and decide who would be good prospects.

A MATTER OF ETHICS
3. Answers will vary. Some may see H&R Block's actions as an invasion of customers' privacy.

To find answers to these questions, you may make inquiries by calling other sales representatives who sell noncompeting lines. You may read the company's annual reports. A visit to the retail store or the manufacturing facility can answer some questions. To determine if the prospect has the appropriate financial resources, you may subscribe to a company like Dun & Bradstreet, which offers credit services.

Some of the above concerns can be addressed during your telephone conversation with the prospect. By asking tactful questions such as what competing products the prospect carries, you can determine satisfaction with the present supplier. You may find that your product could better satisfy your prospect's needs. Other questions might help to determine how your product could help improve the prospect's business.

All of this research brings you to the final step—the appointment to see the prospect. This is necessary in most business-to-business selling situations whether or not the client is a regular customer or a new prospect. Your research will have saved you time and money, especially if a prospect is not a likely customer for your product. If the prospect is a good lead, your research can be the basis of a strong sales presentation when you finally meet face-to-face.

REAL WORLD MARKETING

Zing It to Me

Tired of lugging around folders of photos and computer software to every presentation? Making a long distance presentation can be easier and more colorful, thanks to online photo sharing and storage Web sites. The online photo sharing company Zing allows you to store and organize your photos or PowerPoint slides for free and update presentations when necessary. You create a ZingAlbum with a personalized title that is available to clients or coworkers from any location. Companies such as Adobe, Intel, and Kodak are catching on and offering similar services.

Thinking Critically
Why would online companies offer free services such as photo sharing?

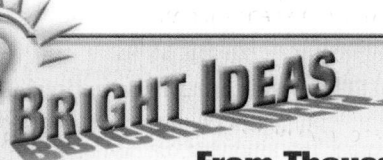

BRIGHT IDEAS

From Thousands of Users to Millions—Yahoo!

Yet Another Hierarchical Officious Oracle. Sound familiar? Those are the words that are abbreviated in the acronym Yahoo!, the online Web directory guide. In 1994, David Filo and Jerry Yang, Ph.D. candidates in Electrical Engineering at Stanford University, started keeping track of their personal interests on the Internet. They soon found their lists to be too cumbersome, and they converted their hobby into Yahoo!. "What we did took 20 hours a day, but we were one of the first to [try and organize the Web], and we did it better than anyone," says Yang. Today, Yahoo's income is mainly generated from advertisers. Yahoo! generates over 95 million daily page views and now serves more than 30 million users monthly.

Thinking Creatively
What are some challenges in having a business like Yahoo! grow from thousands to millions of users in just a few years?

Chapter 12 ■ *Preparing for the Sale* **221**

Reteaching

1. **Vocabulary** Assign and review the vocabulary terms for this section.
2. **Fact and Idea** Assign and review Fact and Idea Review questions 6–10 from the Chapter Assessment.
3. **Salesperson's Duties** Ask students if the following activities should be part of a salesperson's job:
   - Checking in stock received from the manufacturer
   - Rearranging stock
   - Returning goods to stock from dressing rooms
   - Putting price tickets on goods

   Have students defend their answers.

Enrichment

1. **Review** Assign and review the Chapter 12 activities in the *Student Activity Workbook*.
2. **Review** Assign and review the appropriate Thinking Critically questions from the Chapter Assessment.
3. **Review** Assign and review the following Chapter Assessment activities: Building Workplace Skills, Applying Marketing Concepts, Linking School to Work Activities, The DECA Connection Role Play, and Internet Connection.
4. **Read, Write, and Present** Have students read issues of *Personal Selling Power* and *Sales & Marketing Management* magazines to find articles that pertain to prospecting and the preapproach. Ask students to summarize the articles they read in a written report and then share the key points orally with the class.

REAL WORLD MARKETING

Zing It to Me
Answer Online companies are looking for you to return to their sites. By offering free online image storing or cataloging, you might purchase processing and reprints.

BRIGHT IDEAS From Thousands of Users to Millions—Yahoo!

Answer Challenges associated with quick growth include remaining true to your original concept, providing quality products and service, and managing your resources effectively.

Technology Resources

 Assessment Resources Go to the *Marketing Essentials* Web site (www.marketing.glencoe.com) for resources to teach and assess occupation-specific vocabulary.

CLOSE

Section Wrap-Up

Ask students why it is necessary for most business-to-business salespeople to do prospecting, but most retail salespeople do not have to do so. *(The retailers generate store traffic through advertising and displays, so customers come to the salespeople. In b-to-b selling, the salespeople must find new customers on their own.)*

CAPTION ANSWER
House-Keeping While doing those tasks, an astute salesperson is learning about the products and their features, prices, and stock location.

[handwritten: the next topic that they talk about in the book is "Preparing for the Sale in Retail Selling"]

■ Preparing for the Sale in Retail Selling

[handwritten: Who can tell me what happens here?]

Since the customer comes to you in retail selling situations, the preparation centers around the merchandise and work area. It involves stockkeeping and housekeeping activities. Those activities include:

- Straightening, rearranging, and replenishing the stock
- Adjusting price tickets before and after special sales
- Learning where stock is located and how much is available
- Taking inventory
- Arranging displays
- Vacuuming the floor, dusting the shelves, and keeping the selling area neat and clean

[handwritten: Do you think it is a smart thing for salespeople to be involved in stocking shelves and other activities?]

The above activities are important because they give you an opportunity to learn about the merchandise. You can learn what goods go well together, as well as the prices of the merchandise. Keeping all the merchandise in an orderly fashion is beneficial—especially when you have to look for a specific item requested by a customer.

■ **House-Keeping** Much of the preapproach in retail selling involves stockkeeping and housekeeping. *How does folding and arranging stock in a retail store help a salesperson prepare for the actual face-to-face sales situation?*

12.2 ASSESSMENT

Reviewing Key Terms and Concepts

1. What are four categories for sources of product information?
2. Why don't all businesses require salespeople to find prospects?
3. Name five sources of prospecting.
4. What is the difference between the endless chain method and cold canvassing as methods for prospecting?
5. What is the focus of the preapproach in retail sales?

Thinking Critically

6. You have been asked to research a new prospect for your boss. Your research of this lead found that the company's owner is a 90-year-old sole proprietor. The company is financially sound and pays its bills on time. The only concern is that there is no heir-apparent (someone to take over if the owner is no longer capable of running the business). Would you qualify this prospect as a worthy customer? Why or why not?

Integrating Academic Skills

7. **MATH** In preparing a sales presentation for your company's all-purpose cleaner, you gather the following data on your products and a competitor's products:

Cleaner	Fluid Ounces	Price
A	22	$3.79
B	28	$4.29
C	40	$6.99
Yours	44	$7.19

Calculate the price per ounce for each cleaner. Then identify which, if any, competing product beats your own.

12.2 ASSESSMENT ANSWERS

Reviewing Key Terms and Concepts

1. direct experience, written publications, other people, and formal training
2. Because customers come to some businesses.
3. employer leads, telephone directories, trade and professional directories, newspapers, and commercial lists
4. Endless chain method: You ask previous customers for names of potential customers or referrals. Cold canvassing: A salesperson locates potential customers usually with a telephone directory.
5. stockkeeping and housekeeping.

Thinking Critically

6. Answers will vary.

Integrating Academic Skills

7. **MATH** B beats your price. A: $.17, B: $.15, C: $.17, Yours: $.16.

Careers in Marketing

SALES MANAGEMENT

Michael Dougherty
Vice President of Sales
Unilever

What does your job entail?

"It involves working with teams and knowing how to motivate people. Unilever is a British-Dutch consumer products company. Its brands include Lipton, Ragu, Skippy, Slim-Fast, and Dove and Ponds skin care products. I manage a concept and a team of professionals who have the responsibility of acting as entrepreneurs within our company. It is my responsibility to select people for the team from areas within our organization who represent marketing, sales, distribution, and finance. This is far different from the way we operated ten years ago, when each department acted on its own. Today, every new product has a team behind it. The team brainstorms the idea for the new product and develops a business plan for it. After input from all the areas (marketing, sales, distribution, and finance), the team decides if the product is worth a go or not. It is my job to see that these teams are functioning well. "

What skills are most important?

"Flexibility and working well with people are the two most important skills I need for my job. With the emphasis on teamwork, it is important to leave your ego at the door. That means you need to be able to win through a group instead of being a solo player. That is why flexibility and getting along with others are so important. Integrity, honesty, and being goal oriented are essential, in addition to being a good listener."

What is your key to success?

"Never giving up. Believing in your idea and staying with it is essential to success. You can't let yourself get frustrated when you encounter obstacles. Although you must base your decisions on facts, you still must go with "gut" instincts in the decision-making process. The last guiding principle is "follow the consumer." You want to make products the consumer will need in the future; so you never want to forget that the consumer is your end game."

Thinking Critically

What skills do you have that would make you a good Vice President of Sales?

Career Facts

Education and Training: An MBA, or at least minimum courses in marketing, accounting, finance, economics, international business, and data processing systems. As many as ten years sales and supervisory experience may be necessary for promotion to such a top-level job.

Aptitudes, Abilities, and Skills: Excellent problem-solving and decision-making skills, sound business judgment, outstanding verbal and written communication skills, and diplomacy in working with customers and employees are needed for this job. Leadership and administrative skills that foster organizational growth are also required for top-level executives.

Career Path: Participation in management development programs is a typical point of entry for aspiring executives.

Career Outlook: Average growth is predicted for executive positions through the year 2008.

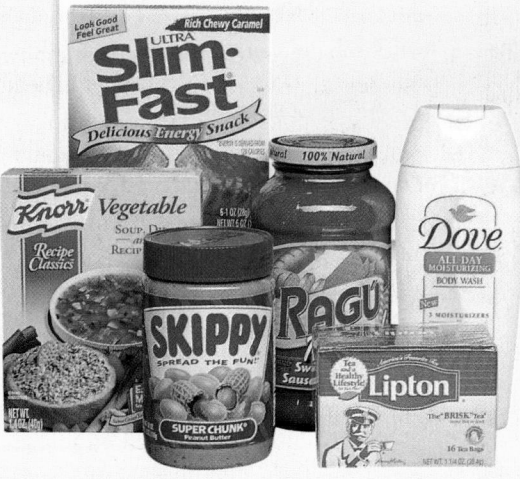

Chapter 12 ■ *Preparing for the Sale* **223**

Careers in Marketing

Ask a student to read the Careers in Marketing feature aloud to the class. Discuss the skills and aptitudes required for a career in sales management. Ask students whether they think they would like or dislike a career in sales management. Discuss the pros and cons of such a career.

Thinking Critically Answer
Answers will vary.

 Guest Speakers
Invite a sales manager to class to discuss his/her job and factors he/she considers when making marketing decisions.

Exploring Careers

Career Interest Areas
1. Read the following six career interest areas to students and ask them to rate themselves for each area from 1–5 (5 is the strongest fit) on a separate sheet of paper.

Creator: I am a creative thinker and am independent, and artistic. I like to use materials or machines.

Investigator: I am a logical thinker; I like experiments, research, science, math, and history.

Influencer: I am a leader and good at convincing others. I am a risk-taker.

Organizer: I like to be neat, organized, and follow rules. I work well as part of a team.

Doer: I'm always busy and full of energy. I like to use tools and machinery. I love to be outdoors.

Helper: I am friendly, fun, patient. I am always ready to help. I'm a good communicator.

2. Discuss with students which description of the career interest areas fits them the best. Ask what jobs could match the type of person in the career interest areas.

Lifelong Learning

Preparing for the Sale
Not everyone sells products, but everyone buys them on a regular basis. Knowing the steps a salesperson goes through can help a person avoid being pressured into unwanted purchases. It can also allow individuals to understand that a salesperson is simply doing a job.

Meeting Individual Needs

Second Language Learners
If you have students with differing levels of English fluency, sales material can present challenges—especially in the area of role-playing. Pair nonnative with native speakers for verbal exercises when appropriate. In class, allow sufficient time for nonnative speakers to answer verbal questions. This will help them gain confidence in their communication skills.

Vocabulary Review

The outlines for the training plans will vary. See Glossary for definitions.

Fact and Idea Review

1. They will become repeat customers.
2. A basic feature of the camera is that it takes photos. Answers may vary for physical and extended features, but automatic focus is a physical feature, and a warranty is an extended feature.
3. Features are selling points when combined with customer benefits.
4. The salesperson asks how the feature helps the product's performance and how the performance information gives the customer a personal reason to buy the product.
5. A rational motive is a conscious, factual reason for a purchase. An emotional motive is a feeling of satisfaction a derived from a product.
6. Salespeople can study their products and keep abreast of industry trends.
7. Prospecting is looking for new customers.
8. It is selecting a new potential customer at random, as by going from door-to-door.
9. The final step is to make an appointment to see the prospect.

Thinking Critically

1. Customer benefits include the ability to get messages when away from home; making the camera easy to use and assuring focused shots; and no need to change CDs frequently.
2. Answers will vary but might include that you can have salespeople visit the factory to see how the garment is made, give them a jacket to wear, and conduct formal sales training.
3. Answers will vary. Students may point out the resale value of the diamond and its quality. Emotional motives involve love and affection, and possibly prestige.
4. Answers may include that customers don't like high-pressure sales tactics and/or salespeople who put their commissions before the needs and wants of customers.

VOCABULARY REVIEW

Work in groups to create an outline for a sales training session that defines and organizes the following topics:

- feature-benefit selling
- product features and customer benefits
- rational and emotional motives
- extensive, limited, and routine decision making
- retail and business-to-business sales preparation
- preapproach
- prospect
- referral
- endless chain method
- cold canvassing

FACT AND IDEA REVIEW

1. Why is it important for customers to be pleased with their purchases? (12.1)
2. What is a basic, a physical, and an extended product feature for a camera? (12.1)
3. When do product features become selling points? (12.1)
4. What two aspects of a product feature help a salesperson determine a customer benefit? (12.1)
5. Explain the difference between a rational motive and an emotional motive. (12.1)
6. In all selling situations, what can salespeople do to prepare for the sale? (12.2)
7. What is prospecting? (12.2)
8. What is cold canvassing? (12.2)
9. What is the final step of the preapproach in a business-to-business selling situation? (12.2)

[handwritten: pg-219 #4]

THINKING CRITICALLY

[handwritten: For this section, just do #'s 2-4]

1. Determine a customer benefit for each of the following product features: remote access on a telephone message machine; automatic focus on a camera; and ten-CD capacity on a CD player. *[handwritten: Please forget about #1]*
2. You are the manufacturer of a unique jacket designed so that parts of it can be added or removed for various weather conditions. What would you do to train your sales force? What would you do to help retailers train their salespeople to sell the jacket?
3. Assume you are selling a diamond engagement ring. What rational and emotional motives might the customer have in this situation?
4. Explain your reasons for agreeing or disagreeing with the following statement: Customers love to buy but hate to be sold.

BUILDING WORKPLACE SKILLS

1. **Writing** To prepare for a sales demonstration with a product of your choice, write a letter to the product's manufacturer. Introduce yourself and tell the reason for writing the letter. Explain why you selected that company's product for your research. Identify the specific information you are requesting. Request the information in a way that makes it easy for the reader to comply.
2. **Human Relations** Assume you work for a local ski shop and receive a 20-percent employee discount, which can only be used by you and your immediate family members. Your friend is in the market for a new pair of skis and asks you to buy them for him so he can benefit from your discount. What would you do? Why?

Building Workplace Skills

1. Letters will vary.
2. Answers will vary. The ethical choice would be to refuse to purchase the item at discount.

Applying Marketing Concepts

1. Student spreadsheets will vary based on their want ads.
2. Charts will vary. Suggest that students select products with which they are familiar.

3. Lists and scripts will vary but should show an understanding of how to reach a target audience. Some ways to pinpoint the audience are to get customer lists from sports stores, or mailing lists from magazines, or get information on college campuses.
4. Presentations will vary. To appeal to the buyer's rational side, the student might highlight the lightweight appeal. To appeal to the emotional side, the student might stress the safety factors.

APPLYING MARKETING CONCEPTS

1. **Categorizing Sales Jobs** Using a spreadsheet program, prepare a table on the various requirements for sales positions found in newspaper or Internet "Help Wanted" ads. Organize the table in these categories: retail, business-to-business, and telemarketing; previous experience required; educational requirements; and salary.

2. **Preparing Feature-Benefit Charts** Select a product and prepare a feature-benefit chart for it, using a spreadsheet program. The product should be one that would require limited decision making. You will use this project to develop a sales training manual in later chapters.

3. **Researching Potential Customers** Your publishing company is launching a new extreme sports magazine. Your first step is to research potential customers. Using a word processing program, list three ways that you could pinpoint your target audience. Write a script to be used by your staff of telemarketers to encourage subscriptions.

4. **Understanding Consumer Motives** Your company has launched a marketing campaign for a new children's car seat. Research your competition on the Internet. Using presentation software, create a presentation to appeal to the rational and emotional motive of the typical car seat buyer.

LINKING SCHOOL TO WORK

Thinking Skills and Information Prepare a background report on a company, including its history and how it sells its products. Discuss what types of salespeople are employed and what company policies related to sales are important for a new salesperson to know.

THE DECA CONNECTION

Role Play: Sales Associate

Situation You are to assume the role of employee at a clothing store. Every day when you arrive, your assistant manager (judge) tells you to check the incoming stock, return clothes left in the dressing rooms, and rearrange stock. You were hired as a sales associate, but you have not yet met your weekly sales quotas.

Activity At this point you are discouraged and decide you must discuss the situation with your manager (judge).

Evaluation You will be evaluated on how well you meet the following performance indicators:
- Prepare for the sales presentation
- Acquire product information for use in selling
- Facilitate customer buying decisions
- Use appropriate assertiveness

interNET CONNECTION

Features, Features, Features!
It is important to learn all you can about the product featured in this chapter, as it will be revisited in other chapters.

Connect
- Use the Internet to obtain all the features of the digital video camera featured in Figure 12-1 (page 213).
- Add those features to the feature-benefit chart provided in Figure 12-1.

THE DECA CONNECTION

Students should be evaluated on the performance indicators noted in the Role Play.
- For another DECA Role Play, go to the *Student Activity Workbook*, p. 97.
- For more in-depth Role Play practice, refer to DECA's *Essential Competitive Events Handbook*. To order, contact DECA at **www.deca.org**.

interNET CONNECTION

You may want the students to use the additional features found from this activity to create an extension to the feature-benefit chart provided in the text. Students can practice creating selling points or features combined with consumer benefits.

Mini Quiz
Administer the Mini Quiz orally. For an expanded chapter quiz, go to page 69 of the *Reproducible Tests* book.

1. Matching the characteristics of a product to customers' needs and wants is called <u>feature-benefit</u> selling.
2. Product features may be <u>basic</u>, <u>physical</u>, or <u>extended</u> attributes of the product or purchase.
3. A customer may have <u>rational</u> and <u>emotional</u> motives for buying a new car.
4. Getting ready for the sale is called the <u>preapproach</u> in selling.
5. Looking for new customers is called <u>prospecting</u>.

Linking School to Work
Answers will depend on the work situation.

GO TO

1. **Assessment** Have students complete the Reproducible Test for Chapter 12 or construct your own tests using the ExamView software.
2. **Enrichment** Have students complete the corresponding activities in the following workbooks:
   - *Marketing Math Workbook*, p. 31
   - *Marketing Research Project Workbook*, p. 65

*Chapter 13 has to do with
Initiating to sale*

Chapter Overview

Chapter 13 introduces students to all the steps in the sales process. It then explores in detail the first two steps—approaching the customer and determining needs.

 Springboard

Discuss To introduce the steps of a sale, have students think of the last sales situation in which they used limited decision making. Take them through the stages of a sale by asking questions. For example, to illustrate approaching the customer, ask what happened when they walked into the store. You should be able to elicit all the steps in this fashion.

Prereading

List the section objectives to discuss with students. Have students skim the chapter, looking at the pictures, reading the captions, and noting the heads. Ask questions to ensure that students have a minimal understanding of the chapter structure.

Preteaching Marketing Vocabulary

Before students begin reading the chapter, dictate each of the vocabulary terms and ask students to write them on a sheet of paper. When they finish, write the terms on the board. Then have students guess at the meaning of each. Write their guesses next to each term. Leave this list on the board so students can see how close their guesses were to the actual definitions as they work through the chapter.

Marketing: What It Takes

Answer In business-to-business selling, needs should be determined through preapproach research and the approach occurs in a scheduled meeting. In a retail setting, the style of approach depends on the situation and needs should be determined through observing, listening, and questioning.

226

Initiating the Sale

Marketing: What It Takes

One-on-One
You have completed your research on fabrics and industry trends during training for your new position as a sales associate at a retail furniture store. You feel you are ready to meet with customers, but your sales instructor is not so sure. She wants to know exactly what you will say and do when you are face-to-face with your first retail customers and your first business-to-business customers.

WHAT WILL YOU DO?
How will your sales approach and method of determining needs be different in the two selling situations?

226

THE **DECA** CONNECTION

ADVISOR CORNER

Customer Service for Your Chapter Develop a customer service plan for your chapter. How can your chapter officers keep members involved and committed? Have chapter leaders discuss a plan for giving back to your members, community, and school. National DECA Week provides the perfect opportunity for your DECA chapter to demonstrate customer appreciation to chapter members, to your school, and to your community. If you run a school-based enterprise, ask your store employees to develop a customer service campaign for it.

The Sales Process

Steps of a Sale

[handwritten: what I would like to do first is read the seven steps]

Professional salespeople go through seven steps when helping a customer make a purchase (see Figure 13-1 on page 228). *[handwritten: professional salespeople go through]*

1. *Approaching the customer*—greeting the customer face-to-face

2. *Determining needs*—learning what the customer is looking for in a good or service in order to decide what products to show and which product features to present first in the next step of the sale

3. *Presenting the product*—educating the customer about the product's features and benefits *[handwritten: (on eisel)]*

4. *Overcoming objections*—learning why the customer is reluctant to buy, providing information to remove that uncertainty, and helping the customer to make a satisfying buying decision

5. *Closing the sale*—getting the customer's positive agreement to buy

6. *Suggestion selling*—suggesting additional merchandise or services that will save your customer money or help your customer better enjoy the original purchase

7. *Relationship building*—creating a means of maintaining contact with the customer after the sale is completed

In this chapter, we will concentrate on the first two steps—the approach and determining needs. The other five steps will be examined in later chapters.

[handwritten: Can anyone tell me what the purpose of step 1 is?]

Approaching the Customer

The approach is the first face-to-face contact with the customer. Although different selling situations require the use of different methods in the approach, the importance and general purposes of the approach are the same in all selling situations.

Salespeople can make or break a sale during their first few minutes with a customer; therefore, the initial approach is critical. Customers who are turned off by the approach will be difficult to win over later on.

The approach sets the mood or atmosphere for the other steps of the sale. It has three purposes: to begin conversation, to establish a relationship with the customer, and to focus on the merchandise. Let's look at how these purposes are accomplished.

To begin conversation, you need to be alert to customers' interests. This may be easier in business-to-business selling because you can conduct research prior to the initial meeting. In retail selling, you must observe the customer from the moment he or she enters the store.

[handwritten: How would you explain the first purpose? (begin conversation)]

[handwritten: You have to make sure that, ...]

Chapter 13 ■ *Initiating the Sale* **227**

[handwritten top: There is a lot of information in Chapter 13 such as,]

What You'll Learn

- The seven steps of a sale
- The importance and purposes of the approach in the sales process
- How business-to-business sales representatives conduct the initial approach
- The three initial approach methods used by retail salespeople

[handwritten: It is an important Chapter because,]

Why It's Important

Knowing the seven steps of a sale gives you an overview of how a sale is conducted from beginning to end. Learning the various methods of approaching a customer is the first step in that process.

Key Terms

- service approach method
- greeting approach method
- merchandise approach method

FOCUS

Bell Ringer Activity

Describe Ask students what most retail salespeople say to them when they initially approach them in a store.

Introducing the Section

The Sales Process Most students will answer the Bell Ringer Activity by saying that "Can I help you?" is the most common approach used by retail salespeople. Ask students what their normal reaction is to that approach. (*Most will say, "No, I'm just looking."*)

This line of questioning will help introduce the importance of the initial approach and its main purposes. You also can use this information later in the chapter to show why the other two retail approaches are often more effective than the service approach.

Classroom Resources

For the Teacher
- Teacher Editions for all workbooks
- Assessment Package
- PowerPoint Presentation Software
- Interactive Lesson Planner
- ILP Block Scheduling, p. 5
- ILP Lesson Plans, p. 27
- ILP Internet Resources, p. 45

- ILP Blackline Masters, p. 27
- ILP *BusinessWeek* Case Studies, p. 85
- ILP Marketing Career Portfolio, p. 35
- *Marketing Essentials* Web site (**www.marketing.glencoe.com**)

For the Student
- Student Activity Workbook, p. 107
- Marketing Math Workbook, p. 31

- Marketing Research Project Workbook, p. 65
- ILP School-to-Work Activity Workbook, p. 49
- Virtual Business simulation
- *Marketing Essentials* Web site (**www.marketing.glencoe.com**)

ILP These resources are available in print and on the Interactive Lesson Planner (ILP)

Concept Development

1. Read Section 13.1 with students.
2. Ask students what a salesperson's goal should be during the initial approach to a customer. **(establish rapport with customer, focus on the merchandise, and begin conversation)**
3. To help students understand the business-to-business approach, have them introduce themselves as a sales representative from XYZ company and shake your hand, as though you were the customer. Walk around the room and conduct this exercise with several students. After each encounter, evaluate the student's handshake as good, too weak, or too strong. This will help emphasize the importance of making a good first impression.

FIGURE 13-1 ANSWER

Steps of a Sale Each letter stands for the steps of a sale: approach, needs determined, product presentation, objections, closing the sale, and suggestion selling. Customer relationship building is the goal of a sale. You want to develop a relationship with customers so they become repeat customers.

FIGURE 13-1
Steps of a Sale

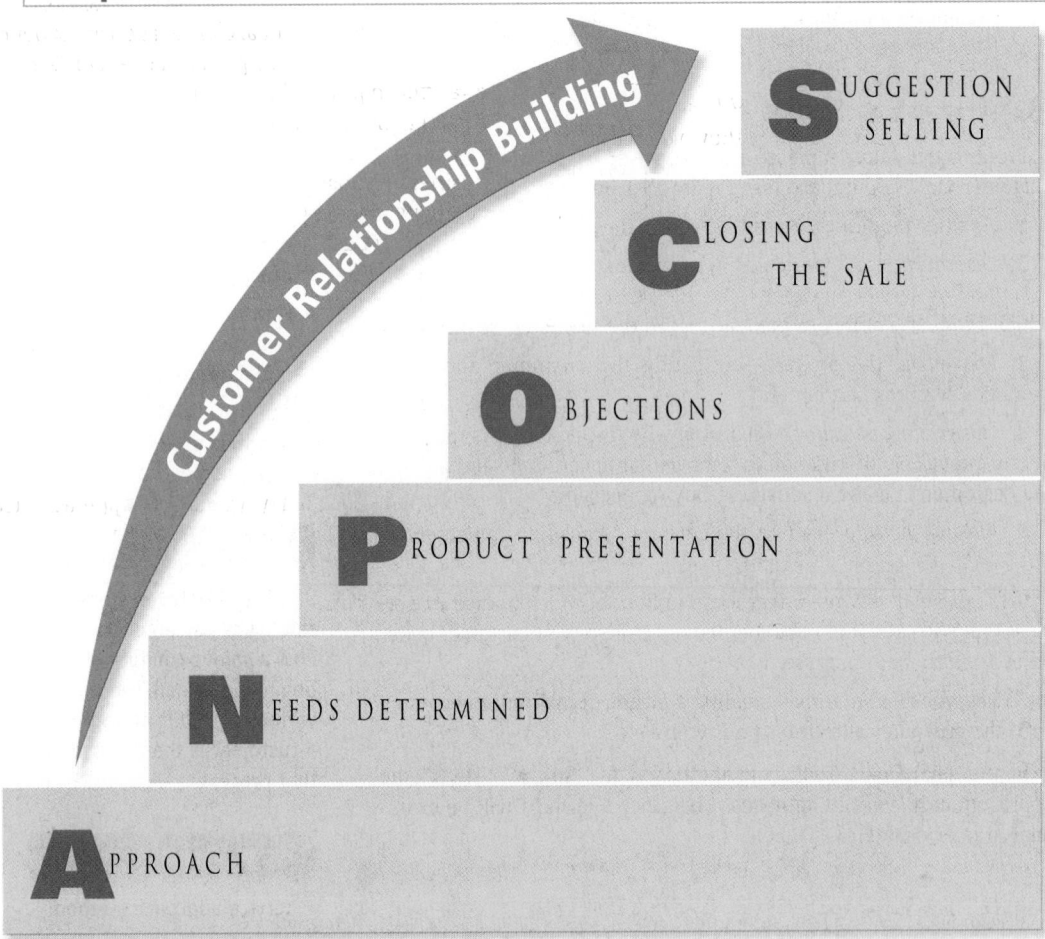

■ **Steps of a Sale** Sometimes is it easy to remember many steps by creating a mnemonic device, such as ANPOCS for the steps of a sale. *What is the significance of each letter in this mnemonic device? How is "Customer Relationship Building" part of the sales process?*

[handwritten: How would you explain the second purpose? (establish a relationship)]

To establish a relationship, treat the customer as an individual. There should be no stereotyping of a person because of age, sex, race, religion, or appearance or any other reason.

You must be perceptive about the customer's buying style. Some customers like to do business quickly. Others prefer a more methodical, slower pace. In any case, a customer likes to feel important.

To put a customer at ease and establish a positive atmosphere you should be enthusiastic,

courteous, and respectful. Show sincere interest by maintaining good eye contact and showing genuine friendliness. It may be useful to learn the customer's name to personalize the sale. Time the approach appropriately in a retail situation; this could mean giving the customer time to browse before initiating communication. Always ask business-to-business customers if it is a good time to see them. This courtesy is appreciated by busy business people.

228 Unit 5 ■ Selling

[handwritten: On page 228, it says "To establish a relationship...]

GREAT IDEAS from the Marketing Classroom

Richard L. Schwasinger
Goodland High School
Goodland, KS

I teach marketing, using on-the-job instruction as a teaching technique for my senior marketing students. To get my students interested in local businesses and to emphasize our "Support Your Local

Business" free enterprise campaign, I conduct community projects that provide students the opportunity to work with local retailers and provide Goodland's business the opportunity to work with marketing students. Have students create a Monopoly board or computer game, using local retailer's businesses or a historical sketch of a local retail business, using PowerPoint presentation software.

The Approach in Business-to-Business Selling

[handwritten: Does anybody recall what the approach in Business-to-Business Selling should be like]

In business-to-business selling, the salesperson will set up an appointment in the preapproach stage of the sale. Then the salesperson calls on the customer at his or her place of business. Arriving early for the appointment will show your customer that you are interested, and give you time to organize your thoughts. Introduce yourself and your company with a firm handshake and a smile. Use the customer's name. Some salespeople may give the customer a business card. It is sometimes appropriate to give your customer a gift. See Figure 13-2 for some hints for approaching customers in a cross-cultural business-to-business selling situation. *[handwritten: You might...]*

The initial approach depends on your prior dealings with the customer or the work you did in the preapproach. When meeting with customers you visit frequently, you can be more personal. Comments on recent happenings in the customer's industry or personal recollections about the customer's family, interests, or hobbies can create a smooth initial meeting. When used correctly, this technique puts the customer at ease and helps open lines of communication. Learning what is appropriate to say regarding personal matters is critical. When personal conversation is not appropriate, you can still engage in small talk to establish a relationship with the customer.

When meeting a new customer, choose your words carefully. Some good opening statements in business-to-business settings discuss how your company can help the customer reduce costs, increase productivity, improve profits, and generate more business. Prior research on the prospect conducted in the preapproach will suggest other possible opening comments.

[handwritten: Can anyone tell me how the approach differs depending on whether or not you have had prior dealings with the customer?]

The Approach in Retail Selling

[handwritten: Next is "the Approach in Retail Selling" who can tell me what happens in this situation?]

Good technique must be learned when approaching customers in a retail setting. When customers are in an obvious hurry, you should approach them quickly. When customers seem undecided, it is best to let them look around before making the approach. Encourage customers who are comparison-shopping to look around and ask questions.

[handwritten: Does anybody have a question yet?]

[handwritten: Does anybody have anything to add?]

◼ Equal Attention Salespeople often take turns greeting and waiting on customers based on a rotating system. *In this photo, assume that both customers arrived at the same time when only one salesperson is available. How could the salesperson tactfully handle this situation?*

Chapter 13 ◼ *Initiating the Sale* **229**

CAPTION ANSWER
Equal Attention One way to tactfully handle this situation is for the salesperson to ask who arrived first and wait on that customer first, while telling the other customer that someone will be with them momentarily.

Independent Practice

Initial Sales Approach Have students read issues of *Personal Selling Power* and *Sales & Marketing Management* magazines to find articles that pertain to the initial approach in retail and industrial sales settings. Have students research both types of selling situations and prepare a written report comparing the similarities and differences between them.

Individualized Practice

Math Skills

Tell students to assume that they work for a major department store and they are working during a special one-day sale.

L1 During this sale, an additional 25 percent will be taken off the prices of items with red price tickets. Have students calculate the net purchase price for the following: three items priced at $99.99, $19.99, and $57.99 (only the first item has a red ticket). *([$99.99 x .75] + $19.99 + $57.99 = $74.99 + $19.99 + $57.99 = $152.97)*

L2 Management is also offering a special coupon for 10 percent off one item of merchandise that has not been marked down. The customer wants to apply the additional 25 percent discount to a $57.99 item. Have students determine the total price the customer must pay, including 6 percent sales tax. *(merchandise: $74.99 + $19.99 + [$57.99 x .90] = $74.99 + $19.99 + $52.19 = $147.17; sales tax: $147.17 x 1.06 = $156)*

L3 Tell students that the customer who purchased a $19.99 item returned and wants to exchange it for a $23.99 item. Have them calculate how much the customer owes the store. *(merchandise difference: $23.99 - $19.99 = $4; sales tax difference: $4 x .06 sales tax = $.24. Total owed: $4 + $.24 = $4.24)*

230

FIGURE 13-2

DOs AND DON'Ts OF THE SALES APPROACH IN FOREIGN COUNTRIES

Saying and doing the appropriate thing is important when selling your products in a foreign country. Simply scheduling the right time for an appointment can be a challenge if you don't know the appropriate time for meetings! Knowing what to do and say when you first meet your prospective customer is equally challenging. Let's look at the some of the basics of that first face-to-face encounter when dealing with customers from other countries.

GIFT GIVING

Do not give a French person wine as a gift, but do give a gift of French origin. The Japanese prefer a gift from the United States, especially one with a well-known brand name. Also, take the time to wrap the gift nicely, even elaborately if the person receiving it has a high position in the company. Do not send red or yellow flowers as a gift in Mexico because those colors represent evil and death. In Belgium it is not a good idea to send white chrysanthemums, because they are used in funerals.

THE GREETING AND HANDSHAKE

In Arab and South American countries, the handshake is light and lasts for a long time. In the United States, Poland, and Hungary the handshake is firm and short in duration. In Japan, one firm handshake coupled with a slight bow is appropriate. In Singapore your greeting (salaam) involves sliding palms together and bowing.

More About . . .

Prospecting

Certain industries—copier sales, temporary personnel sales, and local advertising sales—rely heavily on the cold canvassing technique. Salespeople in these areas often walk into a prospective client's office with no appointment in order to gain information, such as number of employees, decor, style of doing business, and level of professionalism.

APPOINTMENTS

In France, do not schedule a sales appointment before 10:00 A.M. Do not schedule a sales meeting during siesta time in Spain. In Germany, do not schedule a breakfast meeting and always be on time. Punctuality is very important not only in Germany, but in Japan as well. Power breakfasts are appropriate in the United States, but not in very many other countries.

REAL WORLD MARKETING

Ad Campaign Brews Results

In an effort to raise coffee drinkers' understanding of the importance of freshness in quality coffee, Peet's coffee created Coffee Freshness Week. Freshness is actually determined by how long ago the beans were roasted. Peet's contracted an interactive advertising company to custom-blend their advertising approach. An online sweepstakes giveaway of 25,000 one-pound gift packs attracted Peet's online visitors to the coffee maker's promotional Web page. Banner advertising generated 78 percent of the traffic while targeted e-mail campaigns pulled more than 14 percent of the online visitors. Results: Peet's online sales increased 16 percent during the promotional period.

Thinking Critically
In what ways do you think online advertising helped Peet's to initiate sales?

Many customers prefer to shop around before buying and appreciate salespeople who show interest while giving them the space to make their own decisions.

There are three methods you can use in the initial approach to retail customers—the service approach, the greeting approach, and the merchandise approach. You must evaluate the selling situation and the type of customer to determine which method is best.

SERVICE APPROACH METHOD In the **service approach method**, the salesperson asks the customer if he or she needs assistance. This is often best stated as "How may I help you?" Open-ended questions such as this one offer the customer a greater opportunity to respond with more than "yes" or "no." This method is acceptable when the customer is obviously in a hurry or if you are an order-taker for routine purchases. In most other sales situations, this method is ineffective because it usually elicits a negative response, such as "No,

Handwritten margin notes:
Next, who can tell me what the three methods used in the initial approach to retail customers are?
Can anybody explain which is the best method to use?

Does anybody remember what the service approach method is all about?

Who can tell me when it is acceptable to use this method and not acceptable to use it?

Chapter 13 ■ *Initiating the Sale* **231**

REAL WORLD MARKETING

Ad Campaign Brews Results
Answer The advertising campaign served as an online salesperson by greeting customers and giving attention to the product.

ASSESS

Reteaching

1. **Vocabulary** Assign and review the vocabulary terms for this section.
2. **Fact and Idea** Assign and review Fact and Idea Review questions 1–5 from the Chapter Assessment.
3. **Retail Approaches** To reteach the best retail approach, have students develop merchandise approaches for several different products sold in the school store. Possible products include sweatshirts, notebooks, and book covers. *(Possible responses include: "All our sweatshirts have the school logo imprinted on them." "I see you are looking at the science lab notebooks required by your teacher." "Those bookcovers you are looking at are made of a stretch material that fits all different book sizes.")*

Enrichment

1. **Review** Assign and review the appropriate Thinking Critically questions from the Chapter Assessment.
2. **Extend** Assign and review the corresponding activities from *BusinessWeek Case Studies, Internet Resources,* and the *School-to-Work Activity Workbook.* ILP
3. **Research and Analyze** Have students go to an online retail Web site and a business-to-business Web site to see how the customer is greeted. Have students analyze the similarities and differences between the Web site greetings and the approach step of the sale in face-to-face selling situations.

■ **Service Approach Method** Counter salespeople generally fill the role of an order-taker. *In this selling situation, is it okay to use the service approach method? Why or why not?*

■ **Merchandise Approach** The merchandise approach is the most effective when a customer fixates on a specific item. *What might you say to this customer to demonstrate the merchandise approach?*

I'm just looking." In this case, you lose control of the sales situation. In addition, the customer may feel awkward asking for help later after initially rejecting it. If such a situation occurs, take a moment to remind the customer to ask any questions that he or she may have later on. You might say, "Please feel free to ask any questions after you have had some time to look around. My name is Janice and I'll be on the floor if you need anything."

GREETING APPROACH METHOD In the greeting approach method, the salesperson simply welcomes the customer to the store. This lets the customer know that the salesperson is available for any questions or assistance. The greeting can be formal, such as "Good morning." When you know the customer, an informal greeting is appropriate with a personal comment specifically related to the customer. When using the greeting approach, it is important to use a rising tone in your voice. A falling tone sounds unfriendly and would start the sale off on the wrong note. Regardless of whether the customer responds in a friendly or unfriendly manner, it is extremely important that the sales person smiles and continues to act friendly.

After greeting the customer, pause for a few seconds. Out of courtesy, most customers will respond. If they need help, they will tell you how you can assist them. If they are just looking, they will let you know. While this approach method does not highlight the merchandise, it does establish a positive atmosphere and opens the lines of communication.

MERCHANDISE APPROACH METHOD In the merchandise approach method, the salesperson makes a comment or asks questions about a product in which the customer shows interest. This method can only be used if a customer stops to look at a specific item. You may open with a statement about the product's features and benefits.

In the merchandise approach, the salesperson walks up to the customer and starts talking about the merchandise without asking the customer whether he or she wants to be waited on. The opening comment that is used in the merchandise approach should be the most appropriate to the situation. Ideally, it should give the customer some information that is not immediately apparent to the eye.

CAPTION ANSWER
Service Approach Method Yes. The customers often know what they want prior to entering into that type of business.

CAPTION ANSWER
Merchandise Approach Answers will vary. A possible response might be: "Did you know that garment is made of a new high-tech fabric that stays wrinkle-free?"

Notice what interests the customer and make that the focus of your conversation. If a customer is looking at a label, you might say, "That shirt is made of a cotton and polyester blend, so it's machine washable." If a customer is simply looking at an item and you have no indication of the exact interest, you can talk about the item's popularity, its unusual features, or its special values. You can also ask a question about the item, such as "Is that the size you need?" or "Are you interested in a specific color?"

The merchandise approach method is usually the most effective initial approach in retail sales because it immediately focuses attention on the merchandise. It also gives you an opportunity to tell the customer something about the features and benefits of the merchandise. This helps arouse customer interest and could encourage a purchase.

It is possible that customers might not see their desired style, size, or color on the selling floor. The merchandise approach can easily clear up this confusion and opens lines of communication.

[handwritten: Can anyone give me examples of merchandise approach?]

[handwritten: On page 233, it say "the merchandise approach method..."]

Customer Service Online

Have you ever browsed through a virtual mall, then made your purchase at a brick-and-mortar shop because you have unanswered questions? Liveperson.com is here to serve you. Liveperson.com makes it possible for Web sites to have customers consult with customer service representatives in real time. It is one of a growing number of businesses that provides e-commerce companies with a solution to customer service issues. One satisfied client is iQVC.com, a virtual shopping mall, which has live salespeople available 24 hours a day. Customers can ask questions about sizes and colors, or get advice on the best products available to meet their needs. This approach works—many new customers are returning for the quality products and the quality service. This is proof that personalized service increases sales.

Thinking Critically

Why is personalized service important to consumers?

13.1 ASSESSMENT

Reviewing Key Terms and Concepts

1. List the seven steps of a sale.
2. What are the purposes of the approach in selling?
3. What three general things would a business-to-business sales representative say and do during the initial approach?
4. Name the three approach methods retail salespeople use, and suggest when it is appropriate to use each method.
5. Of the approach methods used in retail sales, which is generally the most effective? Why?

Thinking Critically

6. You are given the opportunity to train new retail sales associates in the art of approaching customers. What three key concepts would you make sure you covered first? Why?

Building Workplace Skills

7. **COMMUNICATION** You are approaching a new customer for the first time in a business-to-business selling situation. Introduce yourself and your company to a classmate. Be sure to use the prospect's name and offer an opening statement that will get your customer's attention. Was this easy or difficult for you? Why?

Chapter 13 ■ *Initiating the Sale* **233**

SECTION 13.1

Evaluation

Assign and review the Section 13.1 Assessment.

Technology Resources

GO TO **Assessment Resources**
Go to the *Marketing Essentials* Web site (**www.marketing.glencoe.com**) for resources to teach and assess occupation-specific vocabulary.

CLOSE

Section Wrap-Up

Have students complete the following statement: The initial contact with a customer can . . . *(make or break a sale depending on the impression the salesperson makes.)*

Customer Service Online

Answer By providing personalized customer service, a company can establish a relationship between itself and the customer. Trust is established and purchases are made in a welcome environment.

13.1 ASSESSMENT ANSWERS

Reviewing Key Terms and Concepts

1. approach customer, determine needs, present product, overcome objections, close sale, suggestion selling, relationship building
2. begin conversation, establish a relationship, focus on merchandise
3. introduce himself or herself with a firm handshake and smile; use customer's name; give customer a business card
4. *service* for hurried customers; *greeting* when you know customer; *merchandise* when customer is looking at item
5. merchandise approach method

Thinking Critically

6. importance of first impressions, purposes of approach; three methods to conduct approach

Integrating Academic Skills

7. **COMMUNICATION** Introductions and answers will vary.

SECTION 13.2

Determining Needs in Sales

Bell Ringer Activity

Listening Have students think about the various parts of their heads. Then tell them to complete the following statement: Nature gave us two _____, two _____, and one _____. *(ears/eyes/mouth)*

Introducing the Section

Determining Needs in Sales

Once students get the answers to the Bell Ringer Activity, connect those sense organs to the three ways we determine needs—by listening (ears), observing (eyes), and asking questions (mouth). You can also suggest that nature gave us two eyes and two ears (vs. one mouth) to help us remember to do more listening and observing than talking when determining the customers' needs.

Technology Resources

PowerPoint The *Marketing Essentials* PowerPoint Presentation CD-ROM provides visual lecture aids for every chapter section.

- **What You'll Learn**

- Why determining needs is an essential step in the sales process
- Three methods used for determining needs

- **Why It's Important**

A thorough analysis of customers' needs and wants is necessary when planning and executing effective sales presentations. Customers vary greatly in their perceptions and requirements, so salespeople must learn how to uncover those differences. This section will help you to accomplish that goal.

- **Key Terms**

- nonverbal communication
- open-ended questions

Handwritten note (left margin near Key Terms): The book mentions that a salesperson should determine the customer's needs as early as possible in the sales process. why is that?

Handwritten note (top): There is a lot of important information in section 13.2. You will learn, why... three... It is an important section because...

Determining Needs

Customer needs are directly related to buying motives. As you may recall from Chapter 12, these motives can be rational, emotional, or a combination of both. These buying motives will greatly affect the outcome of the sales process. *The book states that your job is to uncover the customer's reasons for wanting to buy.* In this step of the sale, your job is to uncover the customer's reasons for wanting to buy. In some instances, these motives or needs may be quite obvious, but that is not always the case. *Recall from Chapter 12 that motives can be rational, emotional, or both.*

Whether the customer's needs are obvious or not, taking a sincere interest in the customer is essential. Everyone benefits when the customer's needs are satisfied. Not only does the business profit, but the satisfied customer may become a repeat customer as well. When customer needs are met, the salesperson experiences a feeling of success. *Remember that customer satisfaction is important. Why is that?*

■ When to Determine Needs

The salesperson's focus should be to determine the customer's needs as early in the sales process as possible. Here is an example of what can happen when a salesperson does not determine needs early on.

Salesperson: "This is one of our most popular tennis racquets. It's perfect for you—the grip is the correct size and the large sweet spot can improve your game."

Customer: "That's very interesting, however I'm not buying the racquet for myself. It's actually a gift for my nine-year-old daughter."

In this example, the salesperson went right into the product presentation before determining the customer's needs. After the initial approach, the salesperson could have asked, "Are you interested in a racquet for yourself?"

The answer to that simple question could have guided the salesperson into additional questions about the person for whom the racquet was being purchased. It also could have helped the salesperson decide which racquet to show the customer and which features to emphasize. In the situation above, the racquet recommended for a child would be quite different than the one the salesperson chose to introduce.

In retail selling, the salesperson should begin to determine needs immediately after the approach. In business-to-business selling, needs can be determined in the preapproach. In both situations, the salesperson should continue determining needs throughout the sales process.

Classroom Resources

■ **Reading Body Language** Body language is often very telling with regard to a customer's feeling about a product. *In this photo, what does this customer's body language tell you?*

■ How to Determine Needs

There are three methods that will help you determine customer needs. They are observing, listening, and questioning. *[handwritten: Can anyone tell me the three way of determining need]*

OBSERVING When you observe a customer, you look for buying motives that are communicated nonverbally. **Nonverbal communication** is expressing *[handwritten: on cise]* yourself through body language. Facial expressions, hand motions, eye movement, and other forms of nonverbal communication can give you clues about a customer's mood and interest in a product and mood. *[handwritten: It's important that sales people are tuned in to observation of the customer]*

There are other details you can observe in retail and business-to-business selling situations that may provide more clues about customers. Observing how long a customer in a retail store looks at a product can give you an initial idea about the level of interest. How long the customer holds the product during a sales presentation (if he or she holds it at all) can indicate the level of feelings for it.

In a business-to-business selling situation, you can generally get ideas about a buyer's interests by looking around his or her office. For example, you may observe trophies from company-sponsored tennis tournaments, paintings of horses, or educational certificates and diplomas. All of these are likely to indicate personal interests.

When calling on a retail buyer, walk through the store first. This will give you information about the types of customers the retailer serves, the price levels of lines carried, complementary and competing products offered, and opportunities for additional sales.

The key to observing is the proper selection of facts. You want only those that are important to the sales process. Avoid stereotyping people or drawing conclusions from your observations before getting additional facts. *[handwritten: It is important to point out that you want to "avoid stereotyping people]*

LISTENING Listening helps you pick up clues to the customer's needs. You can use this information for the product presentation. Here's an example.

Customer: "I want a copier for my home business that is simple to use and reliable. My last copier broke down often, which was a problem. I usually make one or two copies at a time. However, I occasionally may make up to 50 copies at once."

Chapter 13 ■ *Initiating the Sale* **235**

Concept Development

1. Read Section 13.2 with students.
2. Have students read aloud the Case Study on page 237 and review the answers in class.
3. Ask students to write ten questions that could be used to determine what type of athletic shoe (or camcorder or video game) a person might want to buy. Tell them to begin with general questions about past experience with such a product, intended use, and special functions they would like.

Discussion Starter

Determining Customer Needs
Ask students if they think it is a good practice to begin determining customers' needs by asking how much they want to spend. *(Students may answer probably not because it puts customer on the spot.)* Then ask students how they could avoid asking this question. *(Students may say ask about intended use, past experience, etc., and derive price from the answers.)*

CAPTION ANSWER
Reading Body Language
Answers will vary, but most will say that the customer appears to like the suit.

Cooperative Learning

Determining Customer Needs

Put students into groups of three or four and give each group a different item (i.e., jacket, golf putter, CD player, calculator, electronic organizer, etc.). Charge each group with the responsibility of developing questions that may be used to determine the needs of a potential customer. Then have them role-play the determining needs step of the sale to demonstrate how effective those questions are with two different customers. Each customer must respond differently to the questions to show that not all customers have the same motives for buying a product. This exercise will also help students see that their original questions may need to be modified, depending on customer responses. This may lead the groups to write different questions for different types of customers.

Independent Practice

1. **Research** Have students research the use of computer technology for determining customer needs.

2. **Research and Report** Have students visit e-tailing Web sites and business-to-business Web sites to see if the Web sites help customers determine their own needs. For example, does the Web site ask the customer questions? If so, what were those questions? Does the Web site allow the customer to generate questions that are answered by the online business before searching the catalog for goods? Have students report their findings in writing and have them share their findings with classmates in an oral presentation for the entire class or in smaller groups.

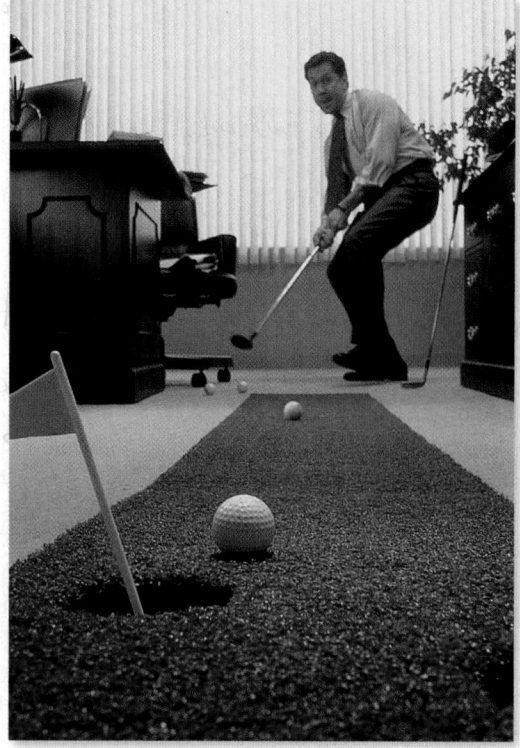

■ **Analyzing Free Time** Knowing what interests the customer sometimes creates a common bond if the salesperson shares those interests. *In this photo, what can you tell about the prospective customer's interest? How could that knowledge be helpful in the sales process?*

From these statements, you've learned that the customer is not looking for a top-of-the-line copier. Since the copier is for a home business, size is a factor.

In Chapter 8 we explored listening skills as well as the potential blocks to listening with understanding. To develop good listening skills, you must learn how to listen to and understand others. Remember these five important listening skills when you are talking to your customers:

- Maintain good eye contact
- Provide verbal and nonverbal feedback
- Give customers your undivided attention
- Listen with empathy and an open mind
- Do not interrupt

QUESTIONING In order to listen to customers, you must get them talking. One way of engaging a customer in conversation is to ask questions. Not all customers can clearly express their needs and motives when making a purchase. In such a situation, well-chosen questions can help you uncover needs and buying motives while putting the customer at ease.

When you begin determining needs, first ask general questions about intended use of the product and any previous experience with it. Build your questions around words like who, what, when, where, how, and why. You might ask the following questions of someone who wants to purchase a copier:

BRIGHT IDEAS

Freebord—On a Roll

Freebord Manufacturing has brought snowboarding to suburbia. Half snowboard, half skateboard—this six-wheeled contraption can spin 360 degrees and is sure to impress anyone in the concrete jungle. The goal is to imitate the slippery slide of a downhill ski slope on city streets. Now you can work on your boarding technique in your board shorts before hitting the slopes in winter. Freebord Manufacturing co-owner Steen Strand developed the product at Stanford University to merge his two loves—skateboarding and snowboarding. Strand designed two dozen models before he hit on just the right product. In business and in debt since 1997, the company recently sold 4,000 boards through 225 independent retail outlets. In a time when board sports are hot, Strand is finally looking to turn a profit.

Thinking Creatively

What type of sales approach would you suggest Freebord take to initiate future sales with independent retail outlets?

CAPTION ANSWER

Analyzing Free Time It is obvious that the prospective customer likes to golf. If the salesperson is a golfer, he may invite the prospective customer to play golf in the near future to solidify their business relationship.

BRIGHT IDEAS Freebord— On a Roll

Answer The salespeople should be prepared to speak about what is important to the customer such as profits and business generation.

Case Study

The Personal Touch

Approximately 25 to 30 percent of all customers are not satisfied with the service they receive from online businesses. Online retailers are striving to provide better service by adding a human touch.

HomeTownStores.com and Cameraworld.com have human beings personally greet each visitor with a typed offer of help. Other businesses have humans available to answer typed questions, while still others provide Internet-telephone capability for customers to talk with sales reps at the same time they view their computer screen.

Software needed for this extra service may cost upwards of $500,000, and that does not include installation, maintenance, or people expense.

Is it worth the expense? Some online retailers think it is. At HomeTownStores.com, sales rose 30 percent within a month after a new personal-greeter service was started. Cameraworld.com reported that after it added the human sales reps via Internet phone calls, 25 percent of the customers bought something, as compared with 3 percent for all visitors to the site.

Case Study Review

1. Why did the e-tailers noted in this article add live support to their Web sites?
2. Of what significance are the first two steps of a sale (approach and determining needs) to online selling?

A MATTER OF ETHICS

3. Is it ethical for online retailers to use the "personal touch" in the electronic age because most people can manage their purchases without such help (especially since the cost of doing so will most likely be passed on to consumers in the form of higher prices)?

- *Who* will be using the digital copier?
- *What* type of copier is the person presently using?
- *How* much experience has the person had with copiers?
- *How* many copies will the person be making every week or month?

Once you have an idea of the customer's general needs, then you can ask more specific questions relating to the product. These might include inquiries about size, color, and any special features desired.

In the case of the copier, questions could be asked about the need to enlarge or reduce the size of copy, as well as the need to collate and staple copies.

Questioning is an important skill that must be done carefully. Always bear in mind that some customers will be protective of their privacy; they may resent even general, nonpersonal questions. When selling skis it is often necessary to determine the customer's weight. In such a situation, you might have the various weight classes listed on a sheet of paper that you hand the customer. Then you

---

ASSESS

Reteaching

1. **Vocabulary** Assign and review the vocabulary terms for this section.
2. **Fact and Idea** Assign and review Fact and Idea Review questions 6–10 from the Chapter Assessment.
3. **Determining Needs** To reteach the concept of determining needs, have students recall a visit to the doctor. Ask them what questions were asked and how their answers helped in diagnosing the problem and prescribing a remedy. Then ask: How is that procedure similar to what salespeople do when working with customers during a sale? *(Both procedures use questions to define problems/needs, and knowledge of products to solve problems/meet needs.)*

Enrichment

1. **Review** Assign and review the Chapter 13 activities in the *Student Activity Workbook*.
2. **Review** Assign and review the appropriate Thinking Critically questions from the Chapter Assessment.
3. **Review** Assign and review the following Chapter Assessment activities: Building Workplace Skills, Applying Marketing Concepts, Linking School to Work, The DECA Connection Role Play, and Internet Connection.

Case Study Review Answers

The Personal Touch

1. Some e-tailers have added human service to their Web sites to reduce customer dissatisfaction with online purchasing.
2. Answers will vary but may include that most online retailers felt it was important to have human beings handle those two steps in the sales process.

A MATTER OF ETHICS

3. Most students will say it is ethical because the additional expense is necessary to provide the service.

Evaluation

Assign and review the Section 13.2 Assessment.

Technology Resources

Assessment Resources
Go to the *Marketing Essentials* Web site (**www.marketing.glencoe.com**) for resources to teach and assess occupation-specific vocabulary.

CLOSE

Section Wrap-Up

Have students complete the following statement: You should begin determining needs . . .
(as soon as possible in the sales process.)

Beware 13!
Answer It is necessary to research superstitions because they may prevent potential customers from doing business at a company or using a service (for example, staying on the 13th floor of a hotel).

238

can simply ask which category the customer falls into. In this way, you avoid asking the person, "How much do you weigh?"

Here are some other dos and don'ts guidelines for questioning. *Notice that open-ended question is highlighted who can tell me a lot that!*

1. *Do ask open-ended questions that encourage customers to do the talking.* **Open-ended questions** require more than a yes or no answer, such as "What do you dislike about the copier you're presently using?" The answer to such a question will provide valuable information about a customer's needs.

2. *Do ask clarifying questions to make sure you understand customers' needs.* To do this, use opening lines such as "Let me see if I understand you" or "Am I correct in assuming you're looking for a product that can...?"

3. *Don't ask too many questions in a row.* This will make customers feel as if they are being cross-examined.

4. *Don't ask questions that might embarrass customers or put them on the defensive.* Never ask, "How much do you want to spend?" Instead, ask about intended use of the product and any past experience. That should give you enough information to determine the correct price range on your own.

Beware 13!

Have you ever suffered a bout of triskaideka-phobia? You might have and not realized it as triskaidekaphobia is the fear of the number 13. Many people in the United States are so superstitious about the number 13 that most hotels have banished this floor number from their buildings. In many Mexican cultures, however, the number 13 has more positive connotations of the sun and positive energy. Is it silly to market based on superstitions like these? Apparently Tiffany & Company doesn't think so. They sell their glassware only in sets of five in Japan, where the number four, "shi," also means death.

Thinking Critically
Do you think that it is important for companies to know the traditions and superstitions of other cultures?

13.2 ASSESSMENT

Reviewing Key Terms and Concepts

1. Why is determining needs an essential step in the sales process?

2. When should you begin determining needs in the sales process?

3. At what point in the sales process do you stop determining the customer's needs?

4. Name three methods used to determine customers' needs.

5. Without asking a direct question, how could you find out how much a customer weighs in order to properly outfit him or her with the proper size skis?

Thinking Critically

6. You are a salesperson in a rug store that carries inexpensive area rugs, medium-priced area rugs, and very expensive handmade rugs. How would you determine your customer's price range so you know which category of rugs to show?

Integrating Academic Skills

7. **MATH** Your customer is located 100 miles from your office. You can travel an average of 45 miles in one hour. If you have a 10:30 a.m. appointment and you want to arrive 15 minutes early, what time do you have to leave your office?

13.2 ASSESSMENT ANSWERS

Reviewing Key Terms and Concepts
1. When a customer's needs are satisfied, everyone benefits.
2. as soon as possible
3. You continue determining needs throughout the sales process.
4. observing, listening, and asking questions
5. You might use a chart with various weight-class categories identified on the chart and ask the customer which is his or her category.

Thinking Critically
6. Answers will vary. You do not want to ask them their price range. Instead ask questions about the intended use, which will provide the information needed for the next step.

Integrating Academic Skills
7. **MATH** 8 A.M. $100 \div 45 = 2.22$ hours, or 21 1/4 hours travel time, plus 15 minutes for early arrival = 21 1/2 hours before appointment

Careers in Marketing

PROFESSIONAL SALES

Al Watson
Vice President of Pharmaceutical Sales
Pfizer, Inc.

What does your job entail?

"My job is to oversee the sales of our product. Our clients include physicians, hospital personnel, pharmacists, nursing home personnel, and other health care organizations. We sell through one-on-one sales contacts, as well as in group situations to multiple physicians. My staff conducts educational programs on Pfizer products to educate physicians on guidelines and recommendations for product use. It is important to sell the benefits of products—it must be clear to the client how the product will help them. The most important aspect of my job is to continually strive to increase my technical knowledge."

What skills are necessary?

"The most essential skill is technical knowledge—pharmaceutical detailers must be able to answer all questions on their products. All Pfizer representatives need to have a good understanding of the diseases that our products treat, and a thorough knowledge of the competition. In all careers it is necessary to be self-motivated, responsible, determined, and persistent, but these traits are particularly important in sales. Once the sale is made, consistency and follow-up with customers help ensure repeat business."

What kind of training do you recommend?

"Pfizer offers three types of ongoing training—technical, comprehensive sales, and professional development. The technical training focuses on disease facts and product awareness; if you are selling antibiotics, you need to know what diseases these medicines would be used for. Comprehensive sales training focuses on how to sell in one-on-one situations and large group settings. Professional development courses increase professional and personal development."

What is your key to success?

"I find that the key to my success has been a strong work ethic. A solid academic background is necessary. A strong liberal arts background exposes students to many different ideas."

Thinking Critically

Why must salespeople learn to make their points in a short period of time?

Career Facts

Education and Training: Students interested in a career in pharmaceutical sales should take high school and college courses in biology, chemistry, marketing, business, accounting, speech, and data processing.

Aptitudes, Abilities, and Skills: Ability to read and understand technical material, good record keeping skills, self-motivation, good telephone skills, and a willingness to travel and work long hours are necessary.

Career Outlook: Average growth is expected through the year 2008.

Career Path: Previous work for a physician or pharmacy can lead to a pharmaceutical detailer position. Sales representatives can advance to sales management positions.

Chapter 13 ■ *Initiating the Sale* **239**

Careers in Marketing

Ask a student to read the Careers in Marketing feature aloud to the class. Discuss the skills and aptitudes required for a career in sales. Ask students whether they think they would like or dislike a career in sales. Discuss the pros and cons of such a career.

Thinking Critically Answer
Answers will vary but may note that salespeople can make or break a sale during the first few minutes with a customer, so that short period of time is critical.

 Guest Speakers
Invite a sales manager or sales executive to class to discuss his/her job and factors he/she considers when making marketing decisions.

Exploring Careers

Talking to People About Their Work

1. Have students talk to a friend or relative about his or her job. Have students choose someone working in a career area that interests them.

2. On the board, write these questions students should ask:
- What is your job title?
- What do you do?
- Do you work alone or with other people?
- What is your work schedule?
- What are the chances for advancement in your job?
- What education or training do you need for your job?
- What do you like and/or dislike about your work?

3. Have students compile the answers and write a short report, including answers to the following questions:
- What did you learn about the job?
- Would you consider working at this job? Why or why not?

Lifelong Learning

Initiating the Sale

The chapter's techniques are useful for all circumstances involving persuasion, not just sales. Have students try the techniques in these situations: convincing your family to vacation in the mountains instead of at the beach; asking for a raise after six months when company gives raises annually; and asking a professor for an extension on a paper.

Meeting Individual Needs

Students with Visual Impairments

Students with visual impairments may not be able to maintain good eye contact or may have no control over eye movement. This may be a disadvantage in the sales process. However, they may excel at giving undivided attention because they are not distracted by visual images. Often listening skills are enhanced with visual impairment.

Chapter 13 ASSESSMENT

Vocabulary Review

Stories will vary. See Glossary for definitions.

Fact and Idea Review

1. First impressions are formed during the first few minutes of the sales call.
2. The customer may reply by saying, "No, I'm just looking."
3. The salesperson should pause and wait for response.
4. The most effective retail approach is the merchandise approach.
5. The best time is after the approach; in business-to-business selling, during the preapproach.
6. Look for facial expressions, how a customer looks at or holds product, and other forms of nonverbal communication. In industrial situations, look for buyer's personal interests through contents of office and the store's customers, prices, and competing merchandise offered.
7. Ask about intended use and previous experience with the product.
8. Ask open-ended questions.
9. Avoid asking too many questions in a row and questions that put the customer on the defensive or make him or her feel embarrassed.

Thinking Critically

1. Answers will vary, but most will realize that not all steps must be followed in every sale.
2. Answers will vary. Some may say retailers are on their way out, while others will stress the need to see the actual product and speak with a human being.
3. Pull off the road and call the client to advise that you are running late. This will give you more credibility. In the future, take a practice run, listen to traffic reports, and allow more time for travel delays or emergencies.
4. service approach method, greeting approach method, and merchandise approach
5. They can keep personal records of their customers' purchases—Nordstrom's salespeople are encouraged to do so.

VOCABULARY REVIEW

Work in groups to develop a story about two salespeople using the following terms:

- service approach method
- greeting approach method
- merchandise approach method
- nonverbal communication
- open-ended questions

FACT AND IDEA REVIEW

1. Why is the approach a critical part of the sales process? (13.1)
2. What is wrong with saying, "May I help you?" as a retail approach? (13.1)
3. What should a salesperson do after using the greeting approach method with a retail customer? (13.1)
4. Which retail approach is most effective? (13.1)
5. When should you begin determining needs in retail selling and in business-to-business selling? (13.2)
6. What can you look for when you observe customers in retail situations? In business-to-business selling situations? (13.2)
7. What questions should be asked first when determining customer needs? (13.2)
8. What is the best way to encourage customers to do the talking? (13.2)
9. What two things should you avoid doing when questioning a customer? (13.2)

THINKING CRITICALLY

1. Do you think all seven steps of a sale are followed in every sale? Why or why not?
2. With the rise in e-tailing, hypothesize about the need for retail salespeople in ten years and in fifty years.
3. You are stuck in traffic and are going to be late for your first meeting with a potential customer. What should you do? How could you prevent this situation from happening again?
4. You are responsible for training new retail sales associates in the art of approaching customers. What three concepts would you make sure you covered first?
5. How can retail salespeople know the needs and wants of their customers prior to these customers entering the store? Explain.

BUILDING WORKPLACE SKILLS

1. **Human Relations** Role-play the determining needs steps of a sale with a classmate by using a personal product, such as a jacket, calculator, or purse. Make a list of guidelines for listening, observing, and asking questions. At the conclusion of the role play, provide the salesperson with constructive criticism. Change the product and switch roles with your partner to repeat the assignment.
2. **Writing** Write merchandise approaches that can be used in a retail selling situation for a cellular phone, a pair of jeans, and a pair of work boots.

Building Workplace Skills

1. Students' role plays will vary based on the product selected.
2. Answers will vary. Some possibilities include:
   - "That camera is very easy to use—it's completely automatic."
   - "Those jeans are the ones shown in *Seventeen* magazine."

APPLYING MARKETING CONCEPTS

1. **Training Sales Associates** Create a sales training manual using the product for which you prepared a feature-benefit chart in Chapter 12. Write the approach section, using a word processing program. Explain how to approach a customer properly and provide a few suggested sample approaches in dialogue form.

2. **Determining Needs** Using presentation software, prepare a presentation about determining needs. Begin with a brief description of the importance of determining needs. Present ten questions that could be used to determine a customer's needs. Begin with general questions regarding intended use and previous experience. End with specific questions about the particular features of the product. Base your questions on the product for which you prepared a feature-benefit chart. Print out your presentation and include it in your sales training manual.

3. **Comparing Retail Approach Methods** Pretending to be a customer, conduct your own informal survey of the professionalism of three retail salespeople. After your encounter with each, note what he or she did (or failed to do) to put you at ease and establish a positive atmosphere in the initial approach. Identify which retail approach method each salesperson used. Using a word processing program, write a two-paragraph summary of your findings.

LINKING SCHOOL TO WORK

Thinking and Interpersonal Skills, Personal Qualities Interview two sales representatives of a firm to determine how well prepared they are to approach customers and determine customers' needs.

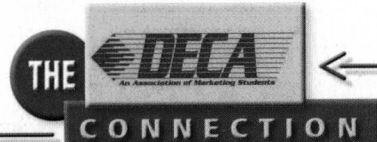

THE DECA CONNECTION

Role Play: Sales Trainer

Situation You are to assume the role of assistant manager of a shoe store. You are responsible for training and evaluating the sales staff. Omar (judge), a new employee, is having difficulty making sales. Each time you observe him with a customer, you see several pairs of shoes in front of the customer. The sad part is that nine times out of ten, Omar's (judge's) customers don't make a purchase.

Activity You must have a talk with Omar (judge) and help him with his sales technique.

Evaluation You will be evaluated on how well you meet the following performance indicators:
- Determine customer/client needs
- Address the needs of individual personalities
- Identify customers' buying motives
- Assess customer/client needs
- Give directions for completing job tasks

inter NET CONNECTION

Online Sales
As a wholesaler of electronics, you want to try selling your products online. You will need to create questions to help a customer decide on a purchase.

Connect
- Investigate the Web site of a computer e-tailer.
- See how customers' needs are determined through questions.
- Adapt those questions to your company's needs by writing five questions that may be used when selling a digital camera for business or personal use.

THE DECA CONNECTION

Students should be evaluated on the performance indicators noted in the Role Play.
- For another DECA Role Play, go to the *Student Activity Workbook*, p. 107.
- For more in-depth Role Play practice, refer to DECA's *Essential Competitive Events Handbook*. To order, contact DECA at **www.deca.org**.

inter NET CONNECTION
Research and questions will vary but some possible questions might be:
- Have you ever used a digital camera?
- What type of camera are you presently using?
- For what purpose will you be using the digital camera?

Mini Quiz

Administer the Mini Quiz orally. For an expanded chapter quiz, go to page 73 of the *Reproducible Tests* book.

1. The first two steps of a sale are approaching the customer and determining needs.

2. The three purposes of the approach are to begin conversation, establish rapport with the customer, and focus on the merchandise.

3. The most effective retail sales approach is the merchandise approach.

4. The purpose of the determining the needs step is to discover the customer's motives, needs, and wants.

5. Three methods to determine needs are listening, observing, and asking questions.

Applying Marketing Concepts

1. The approach section will vary depending on the product but should include sample dialogues.
2. Presentations will vary depending on the product.
3. Summaries will vary based on the research conducted.

Linking School to Work
Answers will depend on the work situation.

1. **Assessment** Have students complete the Reproducible Test for Chapter 13 or construct your own tests using the ExamView software.

2. **Enrichment** Have students complete the corresponding activities in the following workbooks:
   - *Marketing Math Workbook*, p. 31
   - *Marketing Research Project Workbook*, p. 65

Chapter Overview

Chapter 14 covers two essential steps in the sales process: presenting the product and overcoming objections. Section 14.1 provides examples of what to do and say during the product presentation. Section 14.2 involves handling customer questions and objections. It also suggests how to plan for them and ways to cope with them.

 Springboard

Write Have students recall their last major purchase and have them write down anything that the salesperson did to impress them with the product's features.

Prereading

List the section objectives to discuss with students. Have students skim the chapter, looking at the pictures, reading the captions, and noting the heads. Ask questions to ensure that students have a minimal understanding of the chapter structure.

Preteaching Marketing Vocabulary

Dictate each of the vocabulary terms and ask students to write them on a sheet of paper. When they finish write the terms on the board. Then have students guess at the meaning of each. Write their guesses next to each term. Leave this list on the board so students can see how close their guesses were to the actual definitions as they work through the chapter.

Marketing: What It Takes

Answer Explain the ability to upload the photo from the camera into a computer and send it by e-mail. Speed and convenience are the major advantages. Objections may be the high price and skepticism about the quality of photo.

Chapter 14

Presenting the Product

Marketing: What It Takes

What's Next
Your customers—parents of an active high school athlete—are in the market for a new camera. Currently, they scan photos of their child's activities into their computer and e-mail them to friends and grandparents. The only problem is that they have to get the photos developed first. You think a digital camera is the best option for this couple.

WHAT WILL YOU DO?
How will you effectively present the digital camera's selling points? What objections or obstacles do you anticipate?

242

THE DECA CONNECTION — ADVISOR CORNER

Develop a Sales Project Adopt a new education approach to the nagging problem of money for chapter activities. Incorporate a real sales project into your regular marketing curriculum as a lab project. Advisors suggest selecting a useful product, i.e., holiday and all-occasion cards, and to do this in conjunction with your classroom studies. Relate the students' sales effort to marketing concepts. Parents and students alike will understand the connection between the actual sales project and the classroom material. By incorporating a real sales project into classroom instruction, your students will gain hands-on experience in real-life marketing applications.
(John Bucci, Arvada H.S., Arvada, CO)

Presenting the Product

Handwritten note: This is important because it tells you what to do and say during the product presentation.

Product Presentation

During the product presentation phase of a sale, you show the product and tell about it. As you determine the customer's buying motives, you should display products that match the needs you have discovered. The goal of the product presentation is to match the customer's needs with appropriate product features and benefits. You can achieve this goal by following certain guidelines that can make your product presentation smooth.

Handwritten note: If you recall, there are certain guidelines to follow to make sure your product presentation flows smoothly.

■ Show and Tell

Your first decision in the product presentation step of the sale is what product or products to show your customer. Then you must think about what you are going to say and how you are going to say it. This is the step of the sale where you have the opportunity to share your expertise with the customer. The preparation that you have put into learning about the product or products you sell and how to communicate their selling points will assist you now.

Handwritten note: You really need to know your product

WHICH PRODUCTS TO SHOW After you have learned the intended use of the product, you should be able to select a few items that match those needs. You may select a technically advanced camera for a customer who wants a camera for professional use. Novice customers might want to select a fully automatic camera.

Handwritten note: On pg 243, it says "The product prop..." Does anybody remember which products to show?

WHAT PRICE RANGE TO OFFER When you don't know the customer's price range and your knowledge of the intended use is insufficient to determine a price range, begin by showing a medium-priced product. You can move up or down in price once you begin to get the customer's feedback.

Handwritten note: Do anybody remember what price range to show the customer? Why?

HOW MANY PRODUCTS TO SHOW To avoid overwhelming your customer, show no more than three products at a time. It is difficult for most people to remember all the features of more than three items during a presentation. When a customer wants to see more than three, put away the displayed products in which the customer shows no interest.

Handwritten note: Does anybody recall how many products to show to customer? Why?

WHAT TO SAY In this step of the sales process, talk about the product's features and benefits. This is a good time to use your feature-benefit chart. Tell your customer the product features that match his or her buying motives and needs.

Use highly descriptive adjectives and active verbs when describing product features. Avoid unclear words, such as nice, pretty, and fine.

Handwritten note: The next topic that is mentioned in the book is "What to say" Who can tell me about that?

Handwritten note: The book says "use highly descriptive adjectives

---

• What You'll Learn

- The goal of the product presentation
- How products are selected for the presentation
- What to say during the product presentation
- Four techniques that will make a lively and effective product presentation

• Why It's Important

Selling is, in many ways, like putting together a jigsaw puzzle. When you do a puzzle, you analyze the various parts by shape and size. You select the straight-edged pieces to use for the frame. When you sell, you analyze your customer's needs and buying motives. Then you use that information to begin framing your product presentation.

• Key Terms

- layman's terms

FOCUS

Bell Ringer Activity

Discuss Ask students how the determining needs step is related to the next step of the sales process, the product presentation.

Introducing the Section

Product Presentation In response to the Bell-Ringer Activity, most students will say that once you have some information regarding what a customer is looking for, you would immediately begin to show products that include those features.

TEACH

Concept Development

1. Read Section 14.1 with students.
2. Have students read aloud the Case Study on page 245 and review the answers in class.
3. Ask students if they would always show the same product feature to all customers during the product presentation. Have them explain their answers. (Note: If there is no response, ask how they would know which feature to present first in the product presentation.) *(The one feature most important to that particular customer would be the one that would be shown first. Thus, the first feature shown will vary with the customer.)*
4. Have students brainstorm creative ideas for presenting and demonstrating product features for the following items: non-stick cookware and jet skis. *(Possible ideas include: non-stick cookware: Set up a table with a portable burner and have a person prepare foods with the cookware; vacuum with an old vacuum cleaner and then use a new one to show its superiority.)*

Classroom Resources

For the Teacher
- Teacher Editions for all workbooks
- Assessment Package
- PowerPoint Presentation Software
- Interactive Lesson Planner
- **ILP** Block Scheduling, p. 5
- **ILP** Lesson Plans, p. 29
- **ILP** Internet Resources, p. 47

- **ILP** *BusinessWeek* Case Studies, p. 91
- **ILP** Marketing Career Portfolio, p. 35
- *Marketing Essentials* Web site (**www.marketing.glencoe.com**)

For the Student
- Student Activity Workbook, p. 117
- Marketing Math Workbook, p. 31

- Marketing Research Project Workbook, p. 65
- **ILP** School-to-Work Activity Workbook, p. 53
- Virtual Business simulation
- *Marketing Essentials* Web site (**www.marketing.glencoe.com**)

ILP These resources are available in print and on the Interactive Lesson Planner (ILP)

■ **Displaying the Product** How you display the product has a bearing on the customer's image of it. *Do you think this product is properly displayed? Why or why not?*

REAL WORLD MARKETING

Demo or Doom

In the world of computer software and hardware manufacturing, the marketplace leaders are those who are able to stand before a crowd and demonstrate how products work in real time. Successful demonstrations strike the imagination and hearts of customers. Hand Technologies uses a team of sales consultants to demonstrate computer products in homes and at local seminars to win customers. Every sale begins with a handshake and continues with hand-holding to get a customer started and supported down the line. Hand's product line includes well-respected brands, and its prices are comparable to those of electronic superstores.

Thinking Critically
Have you ever seen any product demonstrations? Explain.

244 Unit 5 ■ *Selling*

You might say, "This full-cut sleeve allows complete rotation of the arm, making it extremely comfortable for skiing."

Choose your words carefully. Avoid slang and double meanings. For example, when selling an expensive suit to an executive, you would not say, "You look cool in that suit."

When selling industrial products, use the appropriate jargon to communicate with industrial buyers at their level of expertise. As mentioned in Chapter 8, *jargon* is technical or specialized vocabulary used by members of a particular profession or industry. When selling products to retail customers, use layman's terms. **Layman's terms** are words the average customer can understand.

■ Make the Presentation Come Alive

Planning is necessary for an effective product presentation. Consider how you will display and handle the merchandise. What will you do to demonstrate the product's selling points? What sales aids will add to your presentation? Finally, how will you involve the customer?

DISPLAYING AND HANDLING THE PRODUCT Creatively displaying the product is the first step in an eye-catching presentation. Some products, of course, lend themselves more naturally to visual display. Others will challenge your creativity. Diamond rings, for example, look best on a black velvet display pad. An attractive display of vacuum cleaners, on the other hand, takes more creative planning.

The way you physically handle a product presents an image of its quality. Handle it with respect and use hand gestures to show the significance of certain features. Expensive crystal goblets, for instance, should be held up to the light to show the quality of the glass.

DEMONSTRATING Demonstrating the product in use helps to build customer confidence. This is especially true if you are showing an item that requires manipulation or operation, such as a television, camera, CD player, food processor, or computer. To demonstrate the features of a copier, you may show how it can enlarge or reduce a document, as well as collate and staple multiple copies.

To prove selling points or claims made by the manufacturer, you may need to demonstrate a

Case Study

Sales Techniques Using E-Commerce

Customer involvement is important in the product presentation step of a sale. To make use of that concept when selling online, businesses customize their Web sites and make them interactive. Fannie May Candies online sales tripled when they let customers select their favorite candies and bypass the ones they did not like to create their box of candy.

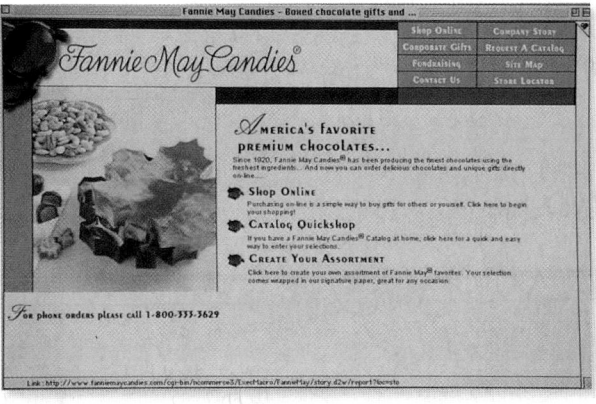

Getting customers involved helps increase "stickiness," which means a site is so attractive that customers "stick" to it for a long time. Fannie May customers stay at the site for an average of 19 minutes, which is longer than most of the popular sites. Ebay.com is among the most "sticky" sites with visitors staying for 15 minutes. For Fannie May, not only do customers stay longer, they buy more, too.

Stickiness can also be helped by virtual tours. Customers use a computer mouse to navigate up, down and around and to zoom in within photos. This on-screen mobility may be used to show off aircraft, automobiles, or building interiors. Gulf Stream, the jet manufacturer, sold a used jet online for $22.9 million. Other businesses that use virtual tours include real estate, automotive, travel, and hospitality companies, such as Century 21 Real Estate, Princess Cruises, and Hilton Hotels.

Case Study Review

1. How did Fannie May utilize the concept of customer involvement in its online sales process?
2. What types of companies are making use of virtual tours to sell their products on the Internet?

A MATTER OF ETHICS

3. Is it ethical for a business to replace its salespeople by selling its products over the Internet?

Independent Practice

Research, Identify, and Write
Ask students to record all the techniques used to present a product the next time they go shopping for an item that requires sales assistance. Have them write about the techniques used and how effective they were. Also ask them to share their findings with classmates in an oral presentation.

Individualized Practice

Decision-Making Skills

L1 Ask students how many items they think a salesperson should display in front of a customer at one time. Ask them why. *(No more than three items at one time is recommended.)*

L2 Ask students to suggest ways to avoid showing more than three items at one time, even when a customer keeps asking to see additional ones.

L3 Have students role-play the following situation: A customer asks a salesperson to show him/her six different cameras. Tell the student-customers to keep asking to see additional merchandise beyond what was originally requested.

ASSESS

Reteaching

1. **Vocabulary** Assign and review the vocabulary terms for this section.
2. **Fact and Idea** Assign and review Fact and Idea Review questions 1–4 from the Chapter Assessment.
3. **Product Presentations** Have students recall the last time they were customers in a sales situation. Ask what the salesperson did during the product presentation.

---

product in a more dramatic way. To prove that a fabric is water resistant, you can pour water on the garment to show how the fabric repels water. At Saturn car dealerships, salespeople jump up and down on a car door that has been removed to show high durability and dent-proof construction.

USING SALES AIDS When it is impractical to demonstrate the actual product or when you want to emphasize certain selling points, you can use sales aids in your presentations. Sales aids include samples, reprints of magazine and newspaper articles, audiovisual aids, models, photographs, drawings, graphs, charts, specification sheets, customer testimonials, and warranty information.

Computers play an increasingly important role in product presentations as many business-to-business sales representatives make use of computer presentation software.

Be creative when determining which sales aids will help you in your particular product presentation. A manufacturer of industrial machinery might show a videotape of how quickly a machine performs. An insurance salesperson might use graphs and charts to show how dividends will accumulate or to compare the benefits of one policy to another. He or she might even use a computer to personalize the presentation of that information for each customer and show different policy plans for that person.

Chapter 14 ■ *Presenting the Product* **245**

Case Study Review Answers

Sales Techniques Using E-Commerce

1. Fanny May lets customers select their favorite candies and bypass the ones they do not like to create a customized box of candy.
2. Some types of companies that are utilizing virtual tours in selling are jet manufacturers (Gulf Stream), real estate (Century 21), automotive, travel (Princess Cruises), and hospitality (Hilton Hotels) companies.

A MATTER OF ETHICS

3. Answers will vary. Some will say yes, because it works well and it is less costly. Others might suggest that the livelihood of their salespeople should be a concern.

Enrichment

1. **Review** Assign and review the appropriate Thinking Critically questions from the Chapter Assessment.
2. **Extend** Assign and review the corresponding activities from *BusinessWeek Case Studies, Internet Resources,* and the *School-to-Work Activity Workbook.* ⒾⓁⓅ

Evaluation

Assign and review the Section 14.1 Assessment.

Technology Resources

 Assessment Resources
Go to the *Marketing Essentials* Web site (**www.marketing.glencoe.com**) for resources to teach and assess occupation-specific vocabulary.

CLOSE

Section Wrap-Up

Have students complete the following statement: In order to make a sales presentation come alive, salespeople should . . . *(creatively display the product, handle the item with care, demonstrate product features, have customers hold and manipulate the product and/or verbally confirm selling points, and use appropriate sales aids.)*

CAPTION ANSWER

Free Demonstrations Some responses might be a catalog, photos of the oven installed in a home, letters from satisfied customers, and a copy of the warranty.

Next, you should mention involving the customer

INVOLVING THE CUSTOMER It is best to get the customer *physically & verbally* involved with the product as soon as possible in the sales presentation. You could have your customers hold and swing golf clubs, try on and walk around in a pair of shoes, use a computer keyboard or mouse, test-drive an automobile, or taste and smell food products. *How can you get the customer physically involved?*

You can also involve your customer verbally during the sales presentation by confirming selling points. You might say, "This camera is extremely versatile with its power zoom and panorama feature. Did you ever feel torn between wanting a camera that could take great close-ups of the kids and one that could take wide-angle shots of a gorgeous view?" (Pause for customer's answer.) "Now you can have both of those cameras in one." Getting the customer's agreement on several selling points helps to ensure that you are on the right track with the selected product.

When you involve a customer in the sale, you help the person make intelligent buying decisions. You also help yourself because a customer is generally more attentive when doing more than just listening to what you say. *You have to realize that customers want to do more than just listen*

When you are losing your customer's attention, ask a simple question. You might say, "Now that you've seen the features of this camera, what do you think about it?" Regaining your customer's attention is essential if you are to continue with the sales presentation. The key is keeping the customer involved.

Remember it is important to always keep your customer's attention.

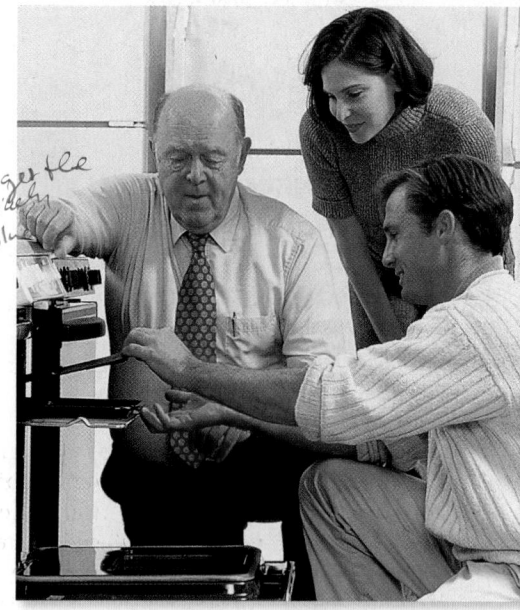

■ **Free Demonstrations** This salesperson is demonstrating how easy it is to take apart the oven for cleaning purposes. *What other sales aids might be appropriate to use in this sales situation?*

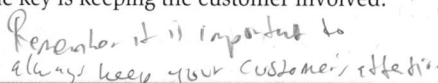
14.1 ASSESSMENT

Reviewing Key Terms and Concepts

1. What is the goal of the product presentation?
2. Which products and how many of them should be selected for the presentation?
3. Give some guidelines for what to say during the product presentation.
4. Describe four techniques that will make the product presentation lively and effective.

Thinking Critically

5. Tell what is wrong with these selling statements: "You look great in that suit," and "This fabric is made of 420/420 denier nylon."

Integrating Academic Skills

6. **COMMUNICATION** Select an item you have in your backpack or purse to sell to a classmate. Assume you have already approached your customer (classmate) and determined his or her needs. Demonstrate your ability to effectively present the item's features and benefits. Role-play with your partner and then switch roles. When you play the role of the customer, evaluate your partner's knowledge of the product presentation step of the sale and his or her sales ability.

14.1 ASSESSMENT ANSWERS

Reviewing Key Terms and Concepts

1. match the customer's needs with appropriate product features and benefits
2. Select a few items to match customer's needs and wants for product presentation.
3. Talk about product's features benefits that match customer's buying motives needs. Use descriptive adjectives active verbs. Avoid slang.

4. display product creatively, handle with respect; demonstrate product selling points; use sales aids; involve customer in presentation

Thinking Critically

5. not descriptive enough; uses technical language

Integrating Academic Skills

6. **COMMUNICATION** Role plays will vary.

Objections and Rejections

Understanding Objections

Objections are concerns, hesitations, doubts, or other honest reasons a customer has for not making a purchase. Objections should be viewed as positive because they give you an opportunity to present more information to the customer. *[handwritten: You have to realize that objections are good. why?]*

[handwritten: Can anyone tell me the difference between objections + excuses?]

Objections can be presented as either questions or statements. An example of a question would be: "Do you carry any other brands?" and a statement would be: "These shoes don't fit right."

Excuses are insincere reasons for not buying or not seeing the salesperson. Customers often use excuses when they are not in the mood to buy or when concealing real objections. Here are some general excuses:

"I'm too busy to see you today."
"We don't need any more . . . ."
"I'm just shopping around."
"I didn't plan to buy anything today."

[handwritten: Please look in the book in the middle of page 247 for some examples of excuses]

It is often hard to distinguish between objections and excuses. A statement or question that seems to be an objection may really just be an excuse. When you are faced with this in a retail selling situation, be polite and courteous. Encourage the customer to look around and ask you any questions he or she may have. *[handwritten: Does anybody recall how to deal with excuses in retail situation + business to business situation?]*

In a business-to-business selling situation, the procedure is different. Leave a business card if a potential customer refuses to see you when you make a call, and ask if it is possible to see the person at a more convenient time.

There are cases when excuses are actually attempts to hide real objections. "I didn't plan to buy today" may really mean, "I don't like the styles you have available." When you suspect that may be the case, ask additional questions to get to the real reason for the disinterest in your product or products. *[handwritten: The book says "There are cases when excuses are actually..."]*

■ Welcome and Plan for Objections

Objections can occur at any time during the sales process and should be answered promptly. A customer who must wait to hear responses to questions or concerns tends to become preoccupied with the objection. When that happens, you may lose the customer's attention and confidence. *[handwritten: Who can tell me why it is a good idea to answer objections promptly.]*

Objections can guide you in the sales process by helping you redefine the customer's needs and determine when the customer wants more information. A customer may say, "This item is very expensive." What the person may really mean is "Tell me why this product costs

[handwritten: Remember that objections are a good thing. This is something I expect everyone to be able to see]

Chapter 14 ■ *Presenting the Product* **247**

[handwritten top: Notice on page 247, What You'll learn...]

● What You'll Learn

- The difference between objections and excuses
- The five buying decisions upon which common objections are based
- The general four-step method for handling customer objections
- The six specific methods of handling objections and when each should be used

[handwritten: This section is important because coc]

● Why It's Important

Anticipating and planning potential answers to objections will help you feel more confident in your responses to customers. Selecting the most appropriate method for handling those objections will make you a superior salesperson.

● Key Terms

- objections
- excuses
- objection analysis sheet
- paraphrase
- boomerang method
- superior point method
- third party method

FOCUS

🔔 Bell Ringer Activity

Identify Ask students if they have ever gone shopping without the intention of buying anything. Ask them to identify the statements they used in those circumstances when salespeople tried to help them.

Introducing the Section

Handling Customer Objections
The responses to the Bell Ringer Activity will help you introduce the difference between sincere objections and excuses for not buying. Note that some of the very same lines used for excuses can be used as sincere objections by other people wishing to buy. Have students identify some of those lines. Then ask students how they will be able to tell the difference between objections and excuses in those cases. *(It's an ability that will come with experience.)*

[handwritten: It's important to point out that sales ability comes with experience.]

[handwritten: ① Redefine needs ② Lets you know why reluctant ③ Opportunity to bring out additional merchandise, etc.]

Classroom Resources

For the Teacher
- Teacher Editions for all workbooks
- Assessment Package
- PowerPoint Presentation Software
- Interactive Lesson Planner
- ILP Block Scheduling, p. 5
- ILP Lesson Plans, p. 30
- ILP Internet Resources, p. 47

- ILP *BusinessWeek* Case Studies, p. 91
- ILP Marketing Career Portfolio, p. 35
- *Marketing Essentials* Web site (**www.marketing.glencoe.com**)

For the Student
- Student Activity Workbook, p. 117
- Marketing Math Workbook, p. 31

- Marketing Research Project Workbook, p. 65
- ILP School-to-Work Activity Workbook, p. 53
- Virtual Business simulation
- *Marketing Essentials* Web site (**www.marketing.glencoe.com**)

ILP These resources are available in print and on the Interactive Lesson Planner (ILP)

Concept Development

1. Read Section 14.2 with students.

2. Ask students when they think a salesperson should answer an objection—immediately, after some time has elapsed in the sale process, or after they have covered all selling points. *(Answers will vary but should have appropriate rationales. However, as a general rule, it is best to answer objections promptly in order to avoid having a customer become preoccupied with them.)*

3. Have students brainstorm objections a customer may have to any product with which they are familiar. (Product options include jeans, winter coats, snow skis, computers, etc.) List the objections on the board. Use the board list to help students identify the five types of objections: those based on need, product, source, price, and time. *(Most will be examples of product objections, although price objections may be represented well.)* Have students generate examples of the other three common objections (need, source, and time).

4. Have students acknowledge and then paraphrase the following objection in writing: "I worry about the radiation leaking from the door of a microwave oven. That can be dangerous." *(I appreciate your concern and want you to know that other customers have noted the same fear about the safety of microwave ovens.)*

5. To introduce the boomerang method of handling objections, ask students what a boomerang does. *(It comes back at you.)* Tell students how an objection can come back to the customer as a selling point.

so much." This objection not only lets you know why the customer is reluctant to buy but also gives you an opportunity to bring out additional selling points.

You should therefore welcome objections—they are not necessarily the sign of a lost sales process. Research shows that there is a positive relationship between customer objections and a successful sales outcome.

You can prepare yourself for most objections that might occur in a sales situation by completing an objection analysis sheet, which lists common objections and possible responses to them. Although the actual objections may be slightly different from those you anticipated, thinking of the responses gives you an idea of how to handle other objections.

You can incorporate anticipated objections into your product presentation so they do not become objections. You must be cautious about this, however. You don't want to include so many objections in your product presentation that you introduce doubt —especially if none existed before. Saying "I guess you're worried about the safety of this snowmobile," may introduce a fear that was not a previous concern.

A better way to handle the same situation would be to emphasize the safety features of the vehicle. You might say, "The suspension on this snowmobile is specially designed to keep it stable. It's very safe to operate."

■ Common Objections

When you list general customer objections, you will see that they fall into certain categories. Most objections are based on key decisions the customer must make before buying—decisions about need, product, source, price, and time. This is true for both retail and business-to-business sales situations. The actual objections will vary due to the difference in purchase motivation. Retail customers generally are making a purchase for personal use, while business-to-business customers are buying for a company's operation.

The following are examples of customer objections in a retail situation. Both provide a starting point for the creation of an objection analysis sheet.

NEED Objections related to need usually occur when the customer does not have an immediate need for the item or wants the item but does not truly need it. A comment such as "I really like this sweater, but it doesn't match anything I have," is an objection based on a conflict between a need and a want.

PRODUCT Objections based on the product itself are more common. They include concerns about such things as construction, ease of use, quality, color, size, or style. "I don't like the way this jacket fits me," is such an objection.

BRIGHT IDEAS

Direct From Dell

Mom and Dad will be in town—better hide that computer in my bathtub. This is what Michael Dell did with his IBM PCs back in 1984 when his family came to visit at the University of Texas-Austin. He didn't want them to think his dorm-room business would distract him from his education. Dell Computer Corporation has since grown into the world's leading "direct" computer systems company, selling and shipping directly to the consumer without using resellers or retailers. "Buying a computer from Dell is more than just a purchase—it's the beginning of a relationship in which we do our best to ensure that the total customer experience reflects the highest possible standards of quality and service every step of the way," says Michael Dell. You can bet his family is not upset with his business anymore, as revenues for last year totaled over $13 billion!

Thinking Creatively

What other business ventures can a college student become involved with while living on campus?

BRIGHT IDEAS Direct From Dell

Answer A college student can get involved with businesses that offer services for cleaning dorm rooms, cooking, typing papers, doing laundry, or offering rides to the local airport or bus station on weekends.

Shopping for Knowledge

Imagine replacing your traditional classroom experience with an online teacher and interactive classroom. It's already happening. You can read course materials on your monitor and submit homework by e-mail. Now, a group of Internet entrepreneurs is trying to capitalize on this new trend by offering online students a variety of products while they study. Students enrolled in photography courses may be offered cameras and film. Someone learning French may be offered a travel guide or airline tickets. Some educators, however, view the combination of sales and classrooms as purely advertising and not instructional.

Thinking Critically

Do you think that marketing to students interferes with learning?

[handwritten: Next is source objection]

SOURCE Objections based on source often occur because of negative past experiences with the firm or brand. A retail customer might say, "The last time I put an outfit on layaway, you couldn't find it for a week. I'm not so sure I want to take that chance again."

[handwritten: Who can explain price objection?]

PRICE Objections based on price are more common with high-quality, expensive merchandise. You might hear statements like "That's more than I wanted to spend."

[handwritten: Last is Time objection. Why can explain this?]

TIME Objections based on time reveal a hesitation to buy immediately. These objections are sometimes excuses. Customers usually have a real reason for not wanting to make a purchase on the spot. A customer might say, "I think I'll wait until July when you have your summer sale to buy those sandals."

You will probably hear many different kinds of objections once you begin selling. You should note them for future reference.

[handwritten: Recall that salespeople use four basic steps when handling objection! they are listen, acknowledge, restate, and answer.]

■ Four-Step Process for Handling Objections

Successful salespeople have learned to use a very basic strategy when answering all objections. It consists of four basic steps for handling objections—listen, acknowledge, restate, and answer.

LISTEN CAREFULLY To demonstrate sincere concern for your customer's objections, follow the key rules you learned in Chapter 8. Remember to be attentive, maintain eye contact, and let the customer talk.

[handwritten: Remember that you want to show sincere concern for your customer's objection like book says. remember to be attentive]

ACKNOWLEDGE THE CUSTOMER'S OBJECTIONS Acknowledging objections demonstrates that you understand and care about the customer's concerns. Some common statements used to acknowledge objections are "I can see your point" or "Other customers have asked us the same question."

These acknowledgments make a customer feel that his or her objections are understandable, valid, and worthy of further discussion. It does not mean that you agree with the customer, but it acknowledges the objection. Disagreeing with the customer, or saying "You're wrong," will put the customer on the defensive, and you might lose the sale. Always try to acknowledge a customer's objections in a positive way.

[handwritten: Why is it important to acknowledge customer's objection? The book says these acknowledgments]

RESTATE THE OBJECTIONS To be sure you understand the customer, you can restate his or her objections in a number of ways:

"I can understand your concerns. You feel that . . . . Am I correct?"

[handwritten: Next the book mention restate the objection. Who can tell me what salespeople do here.]

"In other words, you feel that . . . ."

"Let me see if I understand. You want to know more about . . . ."

Don't repeat the customer's concerns word for word. Instead, **paraphrase** the objections, or restate them in a different way. A customer might say, "The style is nice, but I don't like the color." You could paraphrase the objection by asking, "Would you be interested in the jacket if we could find your size in another color?"

[handwritten: It's important that when paraphrasing "don't change the meaning"]

When paraphrasing, don't change the meaning or content of what your customer says. Accurate paraphrasing shows the customer you are listening and understand the objections. It also helps you open the lines of effective communication when a customer has difficulty expressing concerns.

Chapter 14 ■ *Presenting the Product* **249**

Individualized Practice

Communication Skills

Have students generate three product objections for the telephone answering machine. Ask students to select one objection to answer.

L1 Ask students to use the four-step method of handling objections. Have them prepare responses to their chosen objection in written form.

L2 Pair students according to which objection they generate and have the pairs try their hands at answering the objections. After both members of each pair have had a chance to answer orally, have them read the written versions of the same responses prepared by their partners and evaluate how well their answers matched up.

L3 Have pairs of students work together to create a response to the objection. Have students submit these joint responses for your evaluation.

CAPTION ANSWER

A Perfect Fit Listen carefully, acknowledge the customer's objection by saying, "I see your point." Restate the objection by saying, "You like the garment, but not the color." Answer the objection by saying, "I have two additional colors of that garment in your size, hopefully one will appeal to you."

ANSWER THE OBJECTIONS Answer each objection tactfully. Never answer with an air of superiority or suggest that the person's concern is unimportant.

Think of yourself as a consultant, using the objections to further define or redefine the customer's needs. When price is the objection, go back to determining the customer's needs. Offer a higher-priced item to a customer if it is warranted. Explain the features and benefits of the more expensive model and why that item is better suited to the customer.

■ Specialized Methods of Handling Objections

There are six specialized methods for handling objections: boomerang, question, superior point, denial, demonstration, and third party. Some of these techniques are effective only in specific situations, while others are used more commonly. Any one of these methods may be used as the last step in the four-step process for handling objections.

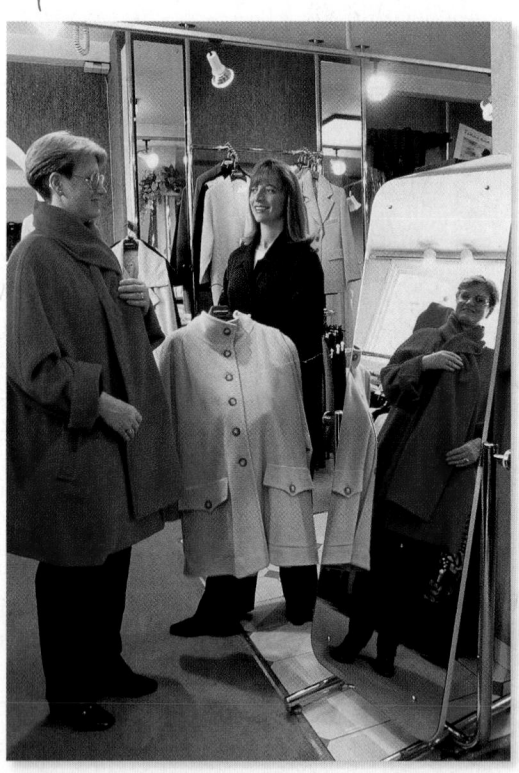

BOOMERANG An objection can be returned to the customer in the same way that a boomerang returns to the thrower. The boomerang method brings the objection back to the customer as a selling point. Here is an example:

Customer: "This ski jacket is so lightweight. It can't possibly keep me warm."

Salesperson: "The jacket is so light because of an insulation material called Thinsulate. The manufacturer guarantees that Thinsulate will keep you warmer than fiberfill insulation, without the bulk and extra weight."

When using the boomerang method, you must be careful not to sound as if you are trying to outwit the customer. Use a friendly, helpful tone to explain how the objection is really a selling point.

QUESTION The question method is a technique in which you question the customer to learn more about the objections. Your questions may reveal hidden objections and may help you learn more about the customer's needs and wants. While answering your inquiries, the shopper may even come to realize that an objection may not be valid. Here is an example:

Customer: "I don't see the point of having two sinks in our master bathroom, as featured in your suggested layout."

Salesperson: "Do you and your husband ever need to get ready to go out at the same time?"

Customer: "Yes."

Salesperson: "Do either one of you have to wait for the other to finish using the sink on those occasions?"

Customer: "Yes. I see your point."

Never ask questions in an abrupt manner—this may seem rude and create a defensive atmosphere. Suppose a customer comments, "I don't think my sister will like this purse." Never respond with a simple "Why not?" Show courtesy and respect instead by asking a more complete question, such as "Why don't you think she'll like it?"

■ **A Perfect Fit** Successful salespeople use a four-step method to answer objections. *If the customer does not like the color or fit of a garment, how would you use the four-step method to handle this objection?*

GREAT IDEAS from the Marketing Classroom

Michelle Walker, Ph.D.
University of North Texas
Denton, TX

As a capstone activity that reinforces knowledge and skills learned in a marketing course, have students plan and implement one activity that promotes teamwork and demonstrates effective human relations and marketing activities for your program audience (training station employers, Marketing Education students, DECA members, parents, and school personnel). Students can decide upon date, time, location, and components. They will then organize into subcommittees with specific tasks and estimate the cost for their portion of the activity. Have subcommittees present and exchange ideas as well as promote the activity.

Next is the superior point method. Who can tell me what that is?

SUPERIOR POINT The **superior point method** is a technique that permits the salesperson to acknowledge objections as valid yet still offset them with other features and benefits. The superior point method allows you to admit disadvantages in certain products but then present superior points to offset or compensate for them. This technique puts the customer in a position to decide between the different features and thus see additional reasons for buying. Here is an example:

Customer: "Your prices are higher than the prices of your competitors."

Salesperson: "That's true. Our prices are slightly higher, but with good reason. We use better quality nylon in our garments that will last five to ten years longer than our competitors'. Plus, we guarantee the quality for life. You can return the product if you ever have a problem with it and we'll repair it free of charge."

Next is the denial method. Who can tell me when to use this method?

DENIAL The denial method is when the customer's objection is based on misinformation. It is best to provide proof and accurate information in answer to objections. This method is also used when the objection is in the form of a question. When using the denial method, you must back up the negative reply with proof and accurate facts. Consider an example:

Customer: "Will this shirt shrink?"

Salesperson: "No, it won't shrink because the fabric is made of 50 percent cotton and 50 percent polyester. The polyester will prevent shrinkage."

DEMONSTRATION The demonstration exemplifies the adage "Seeing is believing." Here is an example:

Customer: "I can't believe that food won't stick to the bottom of the pan if you don't use oil or butter."

What should a salesperson remember when conducting a demonstration?

■ **Counteracting Objections** Columbia Sportswear brand jackets have unique features that set them apart from the competition. *Which specialized method would you use to handle an objection based on price for Columbia Sportswear jackets? Why?*

CAPTION ANSWER
Counteracting Objections Answers will vary. Most will utilize the superior point method, which allows you to agree with the customer's price objection but then point out the superior points (all the features and benefits) of the Columbia jacket which are used to offset the objection.

Life In The Diverse
MARKETPLACE

Thumbs Up!
Answer Some other hand symbols are a wave, the "OK" sign, a salute, or hand signals when driving or riding a bike.

ASSESS
Reteaching

1. **Vocabulary** Assign and review the vocabulary terms for this section.
2. **Fact and Idea** Assign and review Fact and Idea Review questions 5–10 from the Chapter Assessment.
3. **Types of Objections** To reteach the five common types of objections, ask students to recall some of the objections they voiced regarding products that they or their families purchased in the last year. List the students' objections on the board. Then have students classify them according to buying decision.
4. **Common Objections** Recite the following objections and have the students identify the buying decision on which the concern is based:
   1) "I'm really not sure I want to spend that amount of money on an automobile." (*price*)
   2) "I just love the shoes, but I'm not sure I'll have much use for them after the wedding." (*need*)
   3) "I don't like the assortment of rakes I received." (*product*)
   4) "I really don't know if I want to spend my money in this store. The last time I charged something and returned it, you refused to credit my charge account. All I got was store credit." (*source*)
   5) "I want to think about it. I don't buy the first thing I see that I like. I like to shop around." (*time*)

1. **Review** Assign and review the Chapter 14 activities in the *Student Activity Workbook.*
2. **Review** Assign and review the appropriate Thinking Critically questions from the Chapter Assessment.
3. **Review** Assign and review the following Chapter Assessment activities: Building Workplace Skills, Applying Marketing Concepts, Linking School to Work, The DECA Connection Role Play, and Internet Connection.

Evaluation

Assign and review the Section 14.2 Assessment.

Technology Resources

Assessment Resources
Go to the *Marketing Essentials* Web site (**www.marketing.glencoe. com**) for resources to teach and assess occupation-specific vocabulary.

CLOSE

Section Wrap-Up

Have students complete the following sentence: An objection analysis sheet is . . . *(a means of anticipating objections and planning responses to those objections in preparation for a sale.)*

CAPTION ANSWER
On Recommendation
Answers may suggest the third party method because satisfied customers would be able to address those concerns most effectively.

252

Salesperson: "I'm glad you brought that up. Let me demonstrate how the Teflon coating lets you cook without fats of any kind."

The demonstration method can be quite convincing and should be used when appropriate. Only conduct demonstrations you have tested, and make sure they work before using them on a customer in a sales situation. *Theylast method for handling objection, is the third party method. who can tell what thed is?*

THIRD PARTY The third party method involves using a previous customer or another neutral person who can give a testimonial about the product. Some salespeople keep letters from satisfied customers to use as testimonials when handling objections. Others get permission from previous customers to allow prospective customers to call and verify the salesperson's claims. Here's how the method works:

Customer: "I can't see how this machine can save me $1,000 in operating costs the first year."

Salesperson: "Frank Smith, one of my customers, questioned the same point when he bought his machine a year ago. He now praises its efficiency and says that his costs have gone down by $1,200. Here's a letter I recently received from him."

In any given sales situation, it is unlikely that you will use all six methods of handling objections. You will create effective combinations over time that work best for you.

■ **On Recommendation** Customers may sometimes have concerns about the quality or capabilities of a product or the need and cost of repairs. *Which specialized method for handling objections might be best to use in those cases? Why?*

14.2 ASSESSMENT

Reviewing Key Terms and Concepts

1. Distinguish between objections and excuses.
2. Why should you welcome objections in the sales process?
3. Name the five buying decisions upon which common objections are based.
4. List the four steps involved in the process for handling customer objections.
5. Name six specific methods of handling objections.

Thinking Critically

6. Why is restating the objective often a successful method in turning around objections?

Integrating Academic Skills

7. **MATH** Your customer wants to buy 6¾ yards of fabric and the price per yard is $12.50. How much would you charge?

14.2 ASSESSMENT ANSWERS

Reviewing Key Terms and Concepts

1. Objections are concerns, hesitations, doubts, or other honest reasons. Excuses are insincere reasons.
2. Objections can guide you by helping to redefine the customer's needs.
3. need, product, source, price, and time
4. listen carefully, acknowledge the objection, restate the objection, and answer the objection
5. boomerang, question, superior point, denial, demonstration, and third party

Thinking Critically

6. Objection may be the price. Customer may not realize value of features and benefits.

Integrating Academic Skills

7. **MATH** $84.38 per yard of fabric

Careers in Marketing

SALES MANAGEMENT

Ken Montgomery
District Sales Manager
L'Oreal

What does your job entail?

"I manage four regional managers and one national account manager who are responsible for the eastern United States. We sell and merchandise our products to drug chain stores, mass merchandisers, and food chain stores. My job is to attain my quarterly and yearly sales quota and to keep within budget. I work with the marketing and sales planning departments to develop strategies for selling new items and supporting existing brands. I set goals with key regional and account managers. My goal is to keep people focused on our marketing plans."

How does your workload vary?

"When I am not in internal planning meetings or making account calls, I work with the regional or district managers visiting stores to check on the display conditions and to measure stock. I travel weekly and am away from home one to three nights a week and two to three weekends per year."

What skills are most important?

"Superior verbal and written communication is important. The demands of time and speed have made communication skills even more important—people want answers quickly so that they can move on to the next issue. Other helpful skills are computer literacy, organization, and good time management."

What is your key to success?

"You have to be flexible and open as your career progresses. Companies expect you to adapt and be willing to do many different jobs while developing your career. Finding a mentor is also important, as that person can support your efforts and help you move up in a company. Treat everyone with respect—remember names and say good morning. It is good to have a friendly working relationship with people across all levels in an organization."

Thinking Critically

Why is it especially important to develop good relationships with all employees as a district sales manager?

Career Facts

Education and Training: In addition to having sales experience, a college degree and a background in business administration are helpful, with courses in marketing, accounting, economics, psychology, and communications.

Aptitudes, Abilities, and Skills: Understanding of the industry, excellent supervisory experience, strong people skills, and good decision-making skills are needed for this job.

Career Outlook: Opportunities for sales management positions should remain stable through 2008.

Career Path: Promotion from within a company is the most common entry into district sales management. Successful managers may advance into regional, national, or international sales management positions.

Chapter 14 ASSESSMENT

Chapter 14 ASSESSMENT

Vocabulary Review

Paragraphs will vary. See Glossary for definitions.

Fact and Idea Review

1. Begin with the middle price range because you can go up or down from there.
2. Jargon is appropriate when selling to industry professionals who understand the jargon. Use layman's terms when the customer is not well versed in the technical vocabulary associated with the product.
3. Sales aids include samples, reprints of magazine and newspaper articles, audio-visual aids, models, photographs, drawings, graphs, charts, specification sheets, customer testimonials, and warranty information.
4. To involve a customer physically, have the customer hold the product, try it on, taste it, or test it. Involve the customer verbally by having the customer answer questions to confirm selling points.
5. Objections can occur at any time during the sales process.
6. Customers who must wait to hear responses to questions or objections tend to become preoccupied with them.
7. Create an objection analysis sheet.
8. The objection comes back to the customer as a selling point.
9. superior point method

Thinking Critically

1. Show the china on a dining room table, complete with tablecloth, napkins, and other pieces in the place setting.
2. For a copy machine, you may have the customer make copies using special features, like enlargement, reduction, collator, and stapler. For a universal gym, you may have customer try out the equipment and various functions of the gym.
3. a. Demonstration method: Allow customer to see the TV screen image and determine if it is clear enough.
   b. Superior point method: Acknowledge that automatic focus cameras do cost more, but point out all the additional benefits they provide.
   c. Question method: Suggest some common situations in which reductions or enlargements are needed and ask if customer has ever encountered such situations.

VOCABULARY REVIEW

Write a paragraph incorporating the following terms:

- layman's terms
- objections
- excuses
- objection analysis sheet
- paraphrase
- boomerang method
- superior point method
- third party method

FACT AND IDEA REVIEW

1. When you cannot determine a customer's intended price range, what priced product should you show? Why? (14.1)
2. When is it appropriate to use jargon? When should you use layman's terms? (14.1)
3. Name five sales aids you can use in the product presentation. (14.1)
4. How could you involve a customer in the product presentation physically and verbally? (14.1)
5. When can objections occur? (14.2)
6. Why should objections be answered promptly? (14.2)
7. How can you prepare for objections? (14.2)
8. What happens to a customer's objection when you use the boomerang method? (14.2)
9. Which specialized method of handling objections allows you to offset an objection with other features and benefits? (14.2)

THINKING CRITICALLY

1. How would you effectively display a set of china during a sales presentation?
2. What would you do to involve your customer if you were selling a copying machine for a business? A universal gym for home use?
3. Identify the best method for handling these objections:
   a. "This is the smallest TV I've ever seen. How can it have a clear picture?"
   b. "I didn't think automatic focus cameras cost so much."
   c. "I'm not sure I need a copier that enlarges and reduces, especially at $300 more than the basic model."
   d. "Will this nylon and polyester fiberfill vest need to be dry-cleaned?"
   e. "These running shoes are so lightweight. Are they definitely for avid runners?"
4. Why should you welcome objections in the sales process?

BUILDING WORKPLACE SKILLS

1. **Human Relations** A woman looking at the size 8 dresses says, "I used to wear size 8, but I've gained a few pounds." In reality, the customer is probably a size 12. How would you direct her to the correct size?
2. **Technology** Choose one product to sell (investment services, an automobile, or makeup and hair coloring) and identify the hardware, software, and audiovisual capabilities that can help you effectively present that product to a prospective customer.

---

d. Denial method: Point out the care label and indicate that both fabrics are washable under normal circumstances.
e. Boomerang method: Explain that lightweight is a feature deliberately designed into the shoe to ease strain and fatigue over the long haul.
4. They can help you redefine the customer's needs and determine when the customer wants more information. There is a positive relationship between customer objections and a successful sales outcome.

Building Workplace Skills

1. A possible response is: All manufacturers cut their sizes differently, so it might be a good idea to take a few sizes in the dressing room so we can see which size fits you best.
2. Answers will vary depending on products selected.

Applying Marketing Concepts

1. Projects will vary depending on products selected. Provide students with a rubric that covers the topics that must be included.

APPLYING MARKETING CONCEPTS

1. **Communicating Product Features** Using the product for which you prepared a feature-benefit chart in Chapter 12, prepare a detailed plan for the product presentation step in the sales training manual. For each product feature, include what you will say, how you will demonstrate that feature, what sales aids you will use, how you will use them, and how you will involve your customer with each feature. When appropriate, incorporate sample dialogue. Prepare this report using a word processing program.

2. **Handling Objections** Use a word processing program to write the section of your sales training manual that deals with handling objections. Include an objection analysis sheet for the product for which you prepared a feature-benefit chart. Present one objection for each of the specialized methods you learned in this chapter (total of six).

3. **Analyzing Objection Approaches** Interview a salesperson in retail and one in business-to-business sales. Ask both salespeople what the most common objection is that they hear and how they handle it. Ask what the most unusual objection is that a customer ever raised, and how they responded. Finally, ask how they prepare for objections that occur during a sales presentation. What similarities did you find in their responses? What differences? Use a word processing program to report your findings.

LINKING SCHOOL TO WORK

Basic Skills and Information Ask an employer how the company's computer system provides the sales force with information needed to make effective product presentations.

Role Play: Product Presentation Trainer

Situation You are to assume the role of sales associate for a home electronics store. Because you have one of your store's best sales records, your supervisor (judge) has asked you to take part in a company training program. The portion of the program for which you will be responsible is titled, "Making Product Presentations Come Alive."

Activity You must make a presentation for your company training program in which you share your secrets for success.

Evaluation You will be evaluated on how well you meet the following performance indicators:
- Recommend specific products
- Demonstrate products
- Explain the nature of sales training
- Make oral presentations
- Demonstrate interest and enthusiasm

inter NET CONNECTION

Internet "Show & Tell"
You are creating a new Web site for your company and must decide on the design for product presentation and overcoming objections.

Connect
- Find Web sites of three manufacturers and three retailers that sell products to the consumer.
- Evaluate their Web site design for effectiveness of product display and addressing questions.

Chapter 14 ■ *Presenting the Product* **255**

THE DECA CONNECTION

Students should be evaluated on the performance indicators noted in the Role Play.
- For another DECA Role Play, go to the *Student Activity Workbook,* p. 117.
- For more in-depth Role Play practice, refer to DECA's *Essential Competitive Events Handbook.* To order, contact DECA at **www.deca.org**.

inter NET CONNECTION
Answers and designs will vary based on the research conducted and the Web sites chosen.

Mini Quiz
Administer the Mini Quiz orally. For an expanded chapter quiz, go to page 77 of the *Reproducible Tests* book.

1. The goal of the product presentation is to match customers' needs and wants with product features.
2. When you don't know your customer's price range, and knowledge of the intended use is insufficient to determine a price range, it is best to begin showing a medium-priced product.
3. Objections are concerns, hesitations, doubts, or other honest reasons a customer has for not making a purchase.
4. You should welcome and plan for objections because they can help you redefine the customer's needs and determine when the customer wants more information.
5. The five buying decisions upon which most objections are based include need, product, source, price, and time.

---

2. Projects will vary depending on products selected. Provide students with a rubric that covers the topics that must be included.
3. Answers will vary depending on salespeople's responses. Evaluate students' work based on completeness.

Linking School to Work
Answers will depend on the work situation.

 GO TO

1. **Assessment** Have students complete the Reproducible Test for Chapter 14 or construct your own tests using the ExamView software.
2. **Enrichment** Have students complete the corresponding activities in the following workbooks:
   - *Marketing Math Workbook,* p. 31
   - *Marketing Research Project Workbook,* p. 65

255

Chapter Overview

Chapter 15 covers the last three phases of the sales process: closing the sale, suggestion selling, and relationship marketing. These steps should come naturally if the salesperson has determined the customer's needs and communicated the product's features.

Springboard

Brainstorm Have the class think about the nature of buying signals, those actions that make it obvious a customer is ready to buy. Tell them to use their own behavior when making a difficult purchase decision as a guide. Compile a list of the suggestions.

Prereading

List the section objectives to discuss with students. Have students skim the chapter, looking at the pictures, reading the captions, and noting the heads. Ask questions to ensure that students have a minimal understanding of the chapter structure.

Preteaching Marketing Vocabulary

Dictate each of the vocabulary terms and ask students to write them on a sheet of paper. When they finish write the terms on the board. Then have students guess at the meaning of each. Write their guesses next to each term, but do not give the correct meaning. Leave this list on the board so students can see how close their guesses were to the actual definitions as they work through the chapter.

Marketing: What It Takes

Answer Review the features and benefits of the product(s) in relation to their needs. Look for minor agreements on selling points. Call customers in a few days, add them to the mailing list, or send newsletters.

Closing the Sale

Marketing: What It Takes

Making Customers Happy
This growing family has just bought their first new car from you. You explained and demonstrated the features and benefits of this car, and you just made the sale.

WHAT WILL YOU DO?
How will you make sure these customers are satisfied with their buying decision? How can you keep them as customers?

256

THE DECA CONNECTION — ADVISOR CORNER

Organize a Blood Drive Emphasize the importance of civic consciousness and practice sales and marketing skills by having your DECA chapter organize a blood drive at school. Work with your local Red Cross and give each chapter member a responsibility. Since many students may not be eager to participate in a blood drive, chapter members will have to use their selling skills when closing the deal with their fellow students. Other members will apply marketing strategies and promotion techniques to plan and promote the event. Include incentives for students who participate in the blood drive, such as prizes donated by local businesses. Your chapter's efforts will help many people in your community.

Customer Buying Signals

Closing the Sale

Recall that "closing the sale is obtaining positive agreement"

Closing the sale is obtaining positive agreement from the customer to buy. All your efforts up to this step of the sale (preapproach, approach, product presentation, and handling objections) have involved helping your customer make buying decisions. Closing the sale should be a natural part of the sales process; sometimes, it is so natural that your customer closes the sale for you by saying, "I'll take it." In many sales situations, however, the customer waits for you to initiate the close. That is why it is important for you to learn when and how to close a sale.

The book mentions that "Sometimes, it is so natural"

■ Timing the Close

Can anyone tell me when it is an appropriate time to close the sale.

Close the sale when your customer is ready to buy. Some customers are ready to buy sooner than others; therefore, you must be flexible. You may show a customer a product and almost immediately detect an opportunity to close the sale. Other times, you may spend an hour with a customer and still find that he or she is having difficulty making a decision.

It is important to realize that all customers are different.

You should never feel obligated to complete an entire sales presentation just because you have planned it that way. Remember, the key to closing the sale is customer readiness.

Remember that you have to be flexible and able to adapt to different customers.

Next, the book mentions buying signals.

BUYING SIGNALS When trying to close a sale, look for **buying signals**, the things customers do or say to indicate a readiness to buy. Buying signals include facial expressions, body language actions, and comments. A customer who is holding merchandise and smiling is usually sending you buying signals. A customer who has removed a jacket from its hanger and draped the garment over his or her arm is also sending buying signals. Comments that imply ownership are buying signals. You know a customer is ready to buy when he or she says "This is exactly what I was looking for."

Can anyone tell me what buying signals are?

Can anyone give me some examples of buying signals?

TRIAL CLOSE You may attempt a trial close to test the readiness of a customer and your interpretation of a positive buying signal. A **trial close** is an initial effort to close a sale.

The next topic that they talk about in the book is the trial close. It says that you may attempt a trial close. Why is a trial close a good thing?

Trial closes are beneficial for two reasons. First, even if the close does not work, you will learn from the attempt. The customer will most likely tell you why he or she is not ready to buy. Second, if the trial close does work, you will reach your goal of closing the sale. You have control of the sale in both situations and are in an excellent position to continue with the sales process.

What you will learn in Section 15.1 is, "The buying signals..."

● What You'll Learn

- The buying signals that a customer sends
- The rules for closing a sale
- The specialized methods of closing a sale

On page 259, it says, "At a certain point in the sales..."

● Why It's Important

At a certain point in the sales process, your customer will be ready to make a purchase. Sometimes the decision to buy is quick and easy. At other times, it's more difficult. In this section, you will learn how to recognize customer buying signals and how to close a sale.

Key Terms

- closing the sale
- buying signals
- trial close
- which close
- standing-room-only close
- direct close
- service close

FOCUS

Bell Ringer Activity

Analyze Ask students when they think they should attempt to close the sale. Should they wait until they have covered all selling points before closing? Could they close immediately after the approach? What is the rule of thumb? *(They should close as soon as possible. No, don't wait. Yes, they could close after the approach. Rule of thumb is always be closing.)*

Introducing the Section

Customer Buying Signals In response to the Bell Ringer questions, get students to realize that the time to close the sale is as soon as the customer is ready. This will help you introduce buying signals, timing the close, and rules for closing.

TEACH

Technology Resources

PowerPoint The *Marketing Essentials* PowerPoint Presentation CD-ROM provides visual lecture aids for every chapter section.

Classroom Resources

For the Teacher
- Teacher Editions for all workbooks
- Assessment Package
- PowerPoint Presentation Software
- Interactive Lesson Planner
- ILP Block Scheduling, p. 5
- ILP Lesson Plans, p. 31
- ILP Internet Resources, p. 49

- ILP *BusinessWeek* Case Studies, p. 97
- ILP Marketing Career Portfolio, p. 35
- *Marketing Essentials* Web site (**www.marketing.glencoe.com**)

For the Student
- Student Activity Workbook, p. 125
- Marketing Math Workbook, p. 31

- Marketing Research Project Workbook, p. 65
- ILP School-to-Work Activity Workbook, p. 61
- Virtual Business simulation
- *Marketing Essentials* Web site (**www.marketing.glencoe.com**)

ILP These resources are available in print and on the Interactive Lesson Planner (ILP)

Concept Development

1. Read Section 15.1 with students.
2. Ask students: What are the benefits of a trial close? *(If you fail to close, you have learned something; if you succeed, you reach your goal of making a sale.)*
3. Tell students to imagine themselves in the following situations:
   - You have just finished an exceptionally effective product presentation.
   - You have just responded effectively to a key customer objection.

   Then ask students why these two situations present perfect opportunities to close the sale. *(Customer is in a positive frame of mind.)*

Discussion Starter

Closing the Sale Have students react to the following statement: After closing the sale, it is best not to continue talking about the product. Ask students if they agree or disagree, and have them cite examples to support their positions. *(Answers will vary. To keep the discussion on track, be sure to distinguish instances of suggestion selling, or talking about other merchandise, from further talk about the product itself. Have the group carefully analyze instances in which further talk lost a sale. Be sure students understand the kind of talk that leads to problems and the nature of the problems caused. For example, praising the minimal shrinkage of a garment or noting how beautifully it dry cleans could give the customer who hadn't considered shrinkage or dry-cleaning costs cause to rethink his/her purchase decision.)*

CAPTION ANSWER
Judging Buying Signals From the smile on this customer's face, it appears that he is ready to buy.

■ Judging Buying Signals Buying signals may be verbal or nonverbal. *How would you interpret this customer's body language—ready to buy or not?*

■ General Rules for Closing the Sale

Professional salespeople start closing the sale the first moment they begin talking to the customer. They rely on proven and tested techniques, and they often have the following behavioral traits in common:

(handwritten: The book states that professional salespeople often have the following behavioral traits in common)

- They radiate enthusiasm throughout the sales process
- They are sincere and confident
- They truly want to help solve their customers' problems
- They enjoy their profession
- They watch for early buying signals and close as soon as possible
- They constantly practice sale-closing techniques

You will find it easier to attempt trial closes and to close more sales if you follow a few simple guidelines. Professional salespeople use guidelines, including recognizing opportunities, helping customers make a decision, and creating an ownership mentality for the customer. There are also a few things that you want to avoid saying or doing when closing a sale.

RECOGNIZE CLOSING OPPORTUNITIES You should always use major objections that have been resolved to close the sale. The effect of having a major obstacle removed usually makes a customer receptive to buying the product or service. You can also use effective product presentations to close the sale. Dramatic product presentations often prove important selling points and get a customer excited about owning the product. Take advantage of high customer interest at these times and attempt to close.

(handwritten: The book says to "take advantage of high customer interest")

(handwritten: Can anyone remember when a customer will be most receptive to buy?)

258 Unit 5 ■ Selling

HELP CUSTOMERS MAKE A DECISION When a customer is having difficulty making a buying decision, stop showing additional merchandise. You should also narrow the selection of items by removing those things that are no longer of interest to the customer. You can do this by asking, "Which of these items do you like the least?" Once you get the selection down to two, you can help a customer decide by summarizing the major features and benefits of a product. You can also explain any advantages or disadvantages of the item being considered. Both methods help you to focus the decision making on important considerations.

(handwritten: Can anyone tell me what you should do to help a customer make a decision)

CREATE AN OWNERSHIP MENTALITY Use words that indicate ownership, such as you and your. When presenting selling points, say things such as, "You'll enjoy using this camera on your vacation." Look for minor agreements from the customer on selling points that lead up to the close. Ask questions such as, "Those walking shoes are comfortable, aren't they?" In general, if you get positive reactions from your customer throughout the sales process, that same positive frame of mind will help create a natural closing.

(handwritten: You have probably heard salespeople use lines like)

DON'T TALK TOO MUCH AND DON'T RUSH A CUSTOMER If you think the customer is ready to make a buying decision, stop talking about the product. Continuing to sell to a ready customer may have a negative effect or even cause you to lose the sale.

(handwritten: Lastly the book says "Don't talk too much")

Don't rush a customer into making a buying decision. Be patient, courteous, polite, and helpful, and always remember that your primary interest is customer satisfaction.

GREAT IDEAS from the Marketing Classroom

Karen Brettingen
Eden Prairie High School
Eden Prairie, MN

Looking for an alternative to the traditional reading of a chapter? Partner students, split assigned reading, and have each student read their section. As they read, students complete one section of a corresponding worksheet. Students teach each other the material they read and complete the remaining portion of their worksheet. Then the instructor checks for two complete worksheets, and students complete an assessment using their worksheets to reinforce their learning: a partner quiz, partner role play, or a "story" incorporating all the key terms/concepts. This strategy provides excellent reinforcement of key points.

■ Specialized Methods for Closing the Sale

Attempt to close the sale as soon as you recognize a buying signal. How you go about this depends on the selling situation. Certain selling situations warrant the use of specialized methods, such as the *which, standing-room-only, direct,* and *service closes.*

WHICH CLOSE The which close encourages a customer to make a decision between two items. If you follow the general rules for closing a sale, you will remove unwanted items to bring the selection down to two. Review the benefits of each item and then ask the customer, "Which one do you prefer?" This method makes it easy for a customer because only one simple decision must be made.

STANDING-ROOM-ONLY CLOSE The standing-room-only close is used when a product is in short supply or when the price will be going up in the near future. This close should be used only when the situation honestly calls for it because it may be perceived as a high-pressure tactic. In many situations, a salesperson can honestly say, "I'm sorry, but I can't promise that I'll be able to make you this same offer later." This approach is often used in selling high-demand real estate. Customers must often be prompted to act on a hot property that will be off the market quickly.

[handwritten margin notes:] Recall from the reading that there are four specialized methods for closing the sale

First, the book mentions the which close method who how win one work

Next, the book tells about the standing room only close. What does this one state. When should it be used? Why?

Life In The Diverse

MARKETPLACE

The Universal Sign

The smile, a universal sign, generally needs no translation across boundaries. A smile in the wrong place, however, might cause some confusion. In Thailand, Singapore, and the Philippines, a smile or nervous laughter is often used to cover up embarrassment or an awkward situation. Japanese people smile not only when they are happy or amused but also when they are confused or angry. How can you interpret a smile? Look at the eyes. A genuine smile will cause other changes in the facial expression, such as the crinkled skin in the corner of the eyes.

Thinking Critically

How might a misinterpreted smile cause a problem?

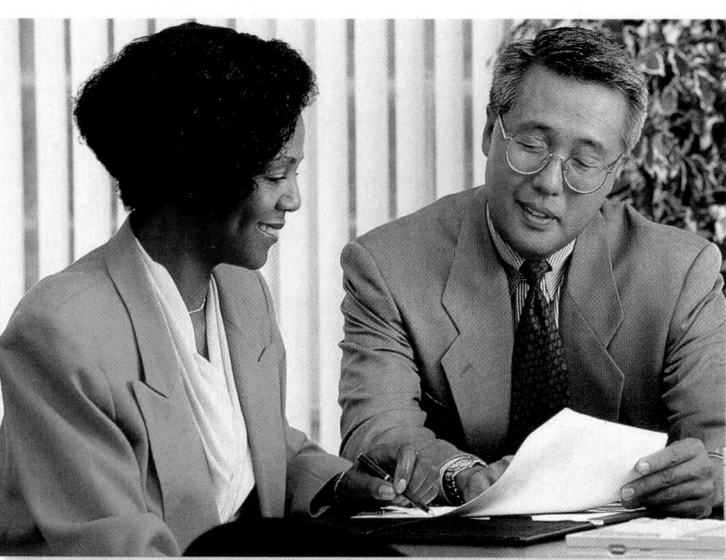

■ **Asking the Right Questions** In business-to-business sales situations, closing the sale often requires signing a contract. *What preliminary questions or statements could the salesperson have used in this situation to access the customer's readiness to sign on the dotted line?*

SECTION 15.1

Cooperative Learning

Brainstorm and Perform Put students into groups to generate examples of the specialized closing techniques. Create an equal number of groups that will create scenarios for retail sales situations and business-to-business sales situations. Give each group a different product. At the end of the time period allotted, have each team perform the scenario (one person acting as the customer and the other being the salesperson). Have other students guess what specialized method was demonstrated in each scenario.

Independent Practice

1. **Read and Summarize** Have students read issues of *Personal Selling Power* and *Sales and Marketing Management* magazines to find articles related to closing the sale. Have students orally summarize the articles in a written report and share their key points with the class.

2. **Research and Identify** The next time students go shopping have them record the responses salespeople used to close the sale. Have them identify the selling situation and note any differences due to the product or type of business.

CAPTION ANSWER
Asking the Right Questions A salesperson may say, "Based on what I have shown you, how do you feel about the program I have developed for your firm?" or "It appears that you are pleased with what you have seen. Am I correct?" or "That should wrap it up."

SECTION 15.1

Individualized Practice

Problem Solving

Set this scene for students: You are a sales associate for an electronics store where you earn $7 per hour plus a 5 percent commission on all sales. It's the last day of the work week, and you are $300 short of your weekly sales quota. You have just spent 30 minutes with a couple buying a portable TV for their daughter. They're having difficulty choosing between one model that's on sale for $349 and another model for $399. At this point your supervisor tells you to take your lunch break because she expects the store to get very busy around noon. It's 11:30 a.m. when you attempt your first close, which is unsuccessful.

L1 Ask students: What are your options in this situation? List each on a separate sheet of paper. *(Answers will vary. Possibilities include: Ask to take the next lunch break or to forgo lunch until after the noontime rush. Explain the situation to the couple and ask again for a decision. Hand off the couple to a co-worker and either ask to share the commission or decide to lose it.)*

L2 Have students evaluate the alternatives available and choose one. Then have them explain their choices in written form. *(Answers will vary. However, asking to take a later lunch is probably the most satisfactory solution. It would give students the opportunity to close, earn full commission, and make their weekly sales quota.)*

L3 Have students role-play exactly what they would say to their (a) supervisor, (b) co-worker, and/or (c) customers. *(Answers will vary.)*

REAL WORLD MARKETING

Ladies and Gentlemen, Start Your Computer Engines

One-third of all car buyers use the Internet for auto product and pricing information. General Motors just made this process easier with their Web site, Gmbuypower.com. Consumers can choose the vehicle options they want, find a dealer in their area that has the make and model in stock, and even schedule a test drive. Dealers get hot leads at a lower cost than through traditional television, print, and radio advertising. Customers can shop from the comfort of their homes and then purchase from 500,000 cars at 6,000 dealers without ever having to leave their living rooms.

Thinking Critically

What are some challenges of shopping for a car online?

260 Unit 5 ■ Selling

[Handwritten note: Next, we will look at direct close. Who remembers when to use the direct close?]

DIRECT CLOSE The **direct close** is a method in which you ask for the sale. You would use the direct close method when the buying signal is very strong. Here are a few direct close approaches:

- "Based on what I've shown you, how do you feel about this product?"
- "Can I assume that we're ready to talk about the details of your order?"

Positive statements by the customer to direct close approaches lets you know that the customer is ready to buy. You can continue the closing by addressing the specifics of the order. In a retail situation, you might simply ask a question regarding payment, such as "How would you like to pay for this purchase—cash, check, or credit card?"

[Handwritten note: The last one mentioned is the service close. If you recall, you use this method when...]

SERVICE CLOSE Sometimes you may run into obstacles or instances that require special services in order to close the sale. The **service close** explains services that overcome obstacles or problems. Such services include gift-wrapping, a return policy, special sales arrangements, warranties and guarantees, and bonuses or premiums. You might want to explain the store's return policy when a customer hesitates but seems to be willing to make the purchase anyway. This is an especially good idea when the item is being purchased as a gift for someone else.

Special sales arrangements are used to close the sale when the customer needs help in paying for the item or order. In an industrial selling situation, the sales representative would talk about the terms of the sale, discussing such points as when payment is expected. For example, payment could be due 30 or 60 days after the date of the invoice. A customer may also need information about credit terms to help him or her decide to buy. In a retail selling situation, the use of credit and checks, as well as special buying plans such as layaway, can be suggested. When a customer questions the quality of the merchandise, perhaps you can explain that a warranty, or guarantee, is offered on the product. When your business offers the same quality merchandise at the same price as your competitors, your service may be the only factor that affects the buying decision.

[Handwritten note: At the bottom of page 260, it says "when your business offers the same quality"]

■ **Special Circumstances** In some sales situations, the salespeople need to solve customers' problems by providing special services. *In this case, what do you think helped to close this sale?*

REAL WORLD MARKETING

Ladies and Gentlemen, Start Your Computer Engines

Answer Some challenges of shopping for cars online are that you cannot investigate first for any damage, and you have to rely on photographs.

CAPTION ANSWER

Special Circumstances The fact that the business offers clothing alterations helped close the sale.

260

Failure to Close the Sale

Don't despair if your initial attempts to close a sale are unsuccessful. It should not be inferred that every sales presentation should result in a sale. Even the best salespeople can sell only a fraction of the prospects called upon. You will have many more opportunities for success, particularly if you treat your customers with courtesy and respect. Research suggests that perseverance is the way to succeed.

In a retail setting, invite the customer to shop in your store again. In business-to-business selling, the sale is rarely closed on the first call. Business-to-business salespeople may negotiate with large accounts for over a year before closing the sale.

Experienced salespeople are able to capitalize on defeat and come away from an unsuccessful selling experience with something to show for it. It is important to keep in mind that even a customer who does not make a purchase is still a prospect for future business. Be alert to what purchases today's nonbuyer might make in the future.

In a business-to-business selling situation, ask if you may call again. Remember that every sales contact has the potential to become a successful sale in the future. In some business-to-business selling situations, the buyer has some feelings of guilt for rejecting your sales proposition in favor of a competitor's. This is especially true when you and the buyer have established a good relationship. In such a case, the buyer may respond to an appeal for consideration on the next order.

If you have established excellent rapport with the buyer, you may be able to ask him or her what factors led to the decision to buy from another source. An appeal for constructive criticism may work for you if you have earned the buyer's respect.

The attitude of the salesperson who has not made the sale should be no different than that of the successful salesperson. It is very important for the salesperson to smile and act friendly after trying in vain to make a sale. In business-to-business selling situations, it is not uncommon for a buyer to be convinced by a sales presentation, but not yet ready to buy. In such a situation, it is extremely important that the salesperson leave an opening for a return sales call. If you clearly sense an impending turn-down, it is better to make a graceful exit, leaving the door open for a future sales call. You should carefully consider the situation before bowing out, as it will greatly increase selling costs.

One popular misconception about selling is that salespeople are born, not made. Success at selling, like success at any career, is the result of training, apprenticeship, and experience.

[handwritten note:] You have to be smart. You have to realize that "even a customer who does not make a purchase is still a prospect for future business. You might ask the buyer why they decided to buy from another source.*

15.1 ASSESSMENT

Reviewing Key Terms and Concepts

1. What are customer buying signals?
2. When is the right time to close a sale?
3. Provide an example of each of the following closing methods: which close, standing-room-only close, direct close, and service close.
4. Why is the failure to close not a true failure?

Thinking Critically

[handwritten note:] Self-evaluation is so important. Id says that, "The attitude of the salesperson. How many know people who work in sales? Do you think they were born to sell or they learned it?

5. A customer seems to be frustrated because she likes three of the items you have shown her. How can you make her buying decision easier?

Integrating Academic Skills

6. **COMMUNICATION** As a salesperson, how do you close the sale when a customer says, "Your presentation was terrific, and I like those skis. But I think I'll wait until they go on sale."

15.1 ASSESSMENT ANSWERS

Reviewing Key Terms and Concepts

1. Buying signals are things a customer does or says to indicate a readiness to buy.
2. as soon as a customer is ready to buy
3. A which close is: "Of the two remaining, which do you prefer?" A standing room-only close is: "That is the last one I have in your size." "That should wrap it up. How many would you like?"

is a direct close. A service close is: "We accept credit cards if you don't want to pay cash."
4. Every sales contact could become a future sale.

Thinking Critically

5. Get three items down to two items by asking customer which she likes least.

Integrating Academic Skills

6. **COMMUNICATION** Answers will vary.

ASSESS

Reteaching

1. **Vocabulary** Assign and review the vocabulary terms for this section.
2. **Fact and Idea** Assign and review Fact and Idea Review questions 1–6 from the Chapter Assessment.
3. **Closing a Sale** To reteach the specialized methods of closing a sale, write the four methods on the board. Provide scenarios illustrating each method, and have students identify the method used to close in each situation.

Enrichment

1. **Review** Assign and review the appropriate Thinking Critically questions from the Chapter Assessment.
2. **Extend** Assign and review the corresponding activities from *BusinessWeek Case Studies*, *Internet Resources*, and the *School-to-Work Activity Workbook*. **ILP**

Evaluation

Assign and review the Section 15.1 Assessment.

Technology Resources

 Assessment Resources Go to the *Marketing Essentials* Web site (**www.marketing.glencoe.com**) for tools to teach and assess occupation-specific performance indicators.

CLOSE

Section Wrap-Up

Ask students what they would do if a customer had four items in front of him/her and was confused about a purchase decision. *(Get the selection down to two items by asking the customer which one he/she likes least, and then close.)*

261

SECTION 15.2

Effective Selling

FOCUS

Bell Ringer Activity

Tell Ask students what the counter person at McDonald's or Burger King routinely asks after a customer orders a hamburger. (*Would you like fries, a soft drink, etc., with that?*)

Introducing the Section

Suggestion Selling Use answers to the Bell Ringer Activity to introduce the concept of suggestion selling. The example should make it easy for students to understand and appreciate the technique.

What you will learn in Section 15.2 is "why suggestive

• What You'll Learn

- Why suggestion selling is important
- The rules for effective suggestion selling
- Specialized suggestion selling methods
- The concept of relationship marketing and how it is related to the sales process

• Why It's Important

The goal of selling is to help customers make satisfying buying decisions so they buy from you again. In this section you will learn how to create a relationship with your customers so they will continue to do business with you in the future.

This section is important because you will learn how to

Key Terms

- suggestion selling
- relationship marketing

The book states that companies make more $ when the spend the extra time on suggestion selling.

Suggestion Selling

Who can recall what suggestion selling is?

Suggestion selling is selling additional goods or services to the customer. It does not mean loading customers with unneeded or unwanted goods and services. Instead, it involves selling customers other items that will ultimately save time and money or make the original purchase more enjoyable. *It's important to point out that it doesn't mean "loading"*

Consider the customer who buys a camera, takes it home, and only then realizes that he or she has no film for it. That means another trip to the store before the camera can be used. The salesperson would have had a sure sale by suggesting that the customer buy film.

■ Benefits of Suggestion Selling

Who can remember why suggestion selling benefits the salesperson, the customer, and the company?

Suggestion selling benefits the salesperson, the customer, and the company. You benefit because customers will want to do business with you again. Your customer benefits because he or she is more pleased with the original purchase. The firm benefits because the time and cost involved in suggestion selling is less than the cost of making the original sale.

Selling is a process of persuasion, and the principles of persuasion apply to it. When a counter clerk at McDonald's asks you whether you would like a drink, French fries, or a hot apple pie with your meal, the clerk is using a suggestion selling approach.

Consider the two purchases below. The second includes an extra item, a suggestion from the salesperson.

Purchase		Purchase	
pants	$75	pants	$ 75
		shirt	35
Total	$75	Total	$110
Cost of goods	−37	Cost of goods	−55
Gross Profit	$38	Gross Profit	$ 55
Expenses	−12	Expenses	−15
Net profit	$26	Net profit	$ 40

Note that the extra time spent on suggestion selling significantly increased the firm's net profits. Expenses rose—but not in proportion to the sales volume. There are two reasons for this. First, less time and effort are needed for suggestion selling compared to the initial sale. Second, certain business expenses (such as utilities and rent) remain the same despite the extra sales activity.

Classroom Resources

For the Teacher
- Teacher Editions for all workbooks
- Assessment Package
- PowerPoint Presentation Software
- Interactive Lesson Planner
- ILP Block Scheduling, p. 5
- ILP Lesson Plans, p. 32
- ILP Internet Resources, p. 49

- ILP *BusinessWeek* Case Studies, p. 97
- ILP Marketing Career Portfolio, p. 35
- *Marketing Essentials* Web site (**www.marketing.glencoe.com**)

For the Student
- Student Activity Workbook, p. 125
- Marketing Math Workbook, p. 31

- Marketing Research Project Workbook, p. 65
- ILP School-to-Work Activity Workbook, p. 61
- Virtual Business simulation
- *Marketing Essentials* Web site (**www.marketing.glencoe.com**)

ILP These resources are available in print and on the Interactive Lesson Planner (ILP)

■ **A Perfect Match** Evaluate this salesperson's suggestion selling technique. *What is the salesperson doing right?*

[handwritten: Suggestion Selling Approach / Pair of jeans / sneakers / camera / suit / bicycle / Salon / on eisel]

■ Rules for Suggestion Selling

[handwritten: Next, Let's read the basic rules for suggestion selling mentioned in the book.]

There are five basic rules for suggestion selling.

- *Do suggestion selling after the customer has made a commitment to buy, but before payment is made or the order written.* Introducing additional merchandise before the sale has been closed can create pressure on the customer. The only exception to this rule involves products whose accessories are a major benefit, like film for a camera or clothes for a doll. Salespeople who sell such products often introduce the additional items during the sales process to help close the sale. *[handwritten: Please read the 1st one. Who might say, "Why not?"]*

- *Make your recommendation from the customer's point of view and give at least one reason for your suggestion.* You might say, "If you want to use your camera immediately, you might want to buy film for it." A customer is usually willing to listen to your suggestion when it seems that you seem to have his or her best interests at heart. *[handwritten: you should be able to explain to the customer why your suggestion is valid.]*

[handwritten: In the book, it says "If you want to use your camera..."]

- *Make the suggestion definite.* Don't ask, "Will that be all?" Instead say, "This oil is recommended by the manufacturer for this engine." In most cases, general questions invite a negative response. *[handwritten: You have all probably heard statements like this before. Why do you think this is a good idea?]*

- *Show the item you are suggesting.* Merely talking about it is not enough. In many cases, the item will sell itself if you let the customer see and handle it. You may put a matching purse next to the shoes a customer just decided to buy, particularly with some commentary. You might say, "This purse matches your shoes perfectly, doesn't it?"

- *Make the suggestion positive.* You could say, "This scarf will complement your coat beautifully. Look how perfectly it matches the color and how fashionable it looks." You certainly would never say, "You wouldn't want to look at scarves for your new coat, would you?" Such a negative statement shows a lack of enthusiasm or a lack of confidence on the part of the salesperson. *[handwritten: You might say things like... You would never say things like...]*

Chapter 15 ■ *Closing the Sale* **263**

CAPTION ANSWER

A Perfect Match The salesperson is following some of the key rules for suggestion selling, such as showing the item being suggested, making the suggestion definite and positive, and making the suggestion from the customer's point of view.

TEACH

Technology Resources

PowerPoint The *Marketing Essentials* PowerPoint Presentation CD-ROM provides visual lecture aids for every chapter section.

Concept Development

1. Read Section 15.2 with students.
2. Have students read aloud the Case Study on page 264 and review the answers in class.
3. To introduce the benefits of suggestion selling, ask students if they think the technique is beneficial to the customer and/or the business. Have them explain their answers. *(It's beneficial to both. Customers save time and money, and tend to be more pleased with their original purchases. Businesses make more money and have more satisfied customers.)*
4. To introduce the rules for suggestion selling, invite students to recall their own experiences. Ask: As a buyer, when did you least appreciate suggestion selling efforts? Why didn't the technique work in that particular case? *(Answers will vary.)*

Discussion Starter

Ethics Ask students if they think it is ethical under all circumstances to encourage customers to buy larger quantities of an item. Have them describe clearly any circumstances under which they would limit use of the technique.

Case Study

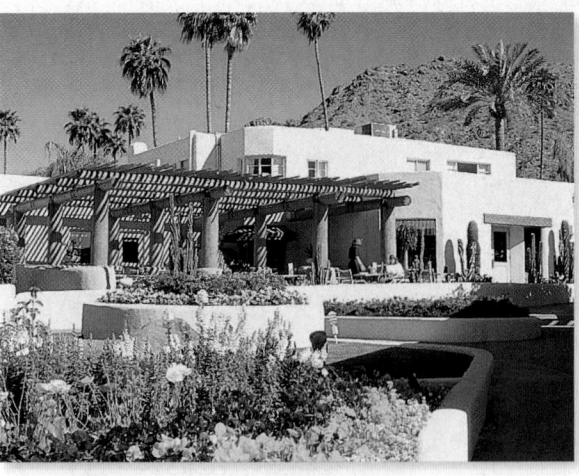

How to Pamper Customers? Get to Know Them!

Knowing your customers gives you an edge. With today's computer technology, Marriott tracks customers' needs and preferences from their previous stays at the hotel chain. Personal planners from the chain's resorts are able to access the central Marriott database so they can anticipate the amenities repeat customers want. The spa at Marriott's Camelback Inn in Scottsdale, Arizona, is so popular that guests must book their spa services well in advance of their stay there. Personal planners, who know that a guest had spa services in the past, are in a good position to suggest those services again. They even take care of making the required reservations.

Marriott's personal planners also are prepared to plan an entire itinerary for a guest. This may include restaurant reservations, golf tee times, shopping sprees, and sightseeing tours. These personal planners can also arrange for child care and activities while parents enjoy an evening at the theater. Flowers for a spouse upon arrival also can be arranged. Personal planners may suggest fee-generating activities, such as hot-air balloon rides. All these services make guests' vacations hassle-free, which makes them want to repeat their positive experience in the future.

Case Study Review

1. **How is the Marriott hotel chain following the concept of relationship marketing?**
2. **How are Marriott's personal planners making use of suggestion selling?**

A MATTER OF ETHICS

3. **Is it ethical for the Marriott to keep such detailed records of guests? How could such a practice cause problems with regard to privacy issues?**

The book says that there are three methods used in suggestion selling. Who can remember what they are? Very good!

■ Suggestion Selling Methods

There are three methods used in suggestion selling. They are offering related merchandise, recommending larger quantities, and calling attention to special sales opportunities (see Figure 15-1 on page 265).

The first one mentioned in the book is

OFFERING RELATED MERCHANDISE Related *who can sell one what is* merchandise can be a good or service that would increase the use or enjoyment of the customer's original purchase. Introducing related merchandise is probably the easiest and most effective suggestion selling method. There are usually accessory items

that can be sold with the original purchase—a tie to match a new suit or a special service contract for a new appliance.

Next is recommending larger quantities. Who can explain that?

RECOMMENDING LARGER QUANTITIES Suggesting a larger quantity usually works in retail settings when selling inexpensive items or when savings in money or time and convenience are involved. You may tell a customer who wants to buy one pair of pantyhose, "One pair costs $4, but you can buy three pairs for $10. Buying three pairs will save you a trip to the store next time you need a pair and will also save you $2."

I think a lot of people figure, Yes, Oh, why not?

264 Unit 5 ■ Selling

FIGURE 15-1

SUGGESTION SELLING METHODS

After customers have made a commitment to buy, it is a good practice to suggest something specific that will help them better enjoy their original purchase. There are three methods of accomplishing that goal. Let's examine how they may be used in a business-to-business sales situation that involves the sale of cameras to an electronics retailer.

LARGER QUANTITIES

In business-to-business sales situations, a sales representative may suggest larger quantities of goods to make a customer eligible for special discounts, payment terms, or delivery charges. Sometimes qualifying retailers may be given free merchandise when they buy a larger quantity of goods.

RELATED MERCHANDISE

The sales representative should suggest these related items of merchandise to the retail store buyer. The rationale for the suggestion would be that these accessories may be needed or wanted by the retailer's customers.

SPECIAL SALES OPPORTUNITIES

When a company runs a special promotion on products unrelated to the original purchase, or wants to introduce a new product, it is up to the sales representative to share that information with the customer. That information is often disseminated after the commitment to buy the original item has been made.

[handwritten: Notice that you are encouraged to buy more to get special service]

Individualized Practice

Decision-Making Skills

Have students consider a situation in which a salesperson uses a voice-activated tape recorder to record their sales calls for evaluation purposes.

L1 Ask students if they think it would be ethical to use a voice-activated tape recorder to record their sales calls. *(Answers will vary. Some will find the procedure ethical because the tape is being made for purely educational purposes. Others will find it unacceptable because the customers are apparently being given no choice about participation in the procedure.)*

L2 Ask students what problems could occur if a salesperson used a voice-activated cassette and a customer found out. *(Possibilities include: anger, distrust of not just the salesperson but the company as well, loss of pending and future sales, and even legal action.)*

L3 Have pairs of students role-play this situation. Tell them to pretend that an irate customer—one who has just learned that all of his sales calls have been taped—is on the phone. Allow students some time to get in character. Tell them that "customers" will be evaluated on how well they articulate the reasons for their anger; "salespeople" on how well they mollify their callers.

In business-to-business sales situations, the salesperson may suggest a larger quantity so the customer can take advantage of lower prices or special considerations. Some manufacturers also include special services in addition to a better price per item. Buying a certain quantity, for instance, may allow a retailer to take advantage of an opportunity for free freight or free advertising.

CALLING ATTENTION TO SPECIAL SALES OPPORTUNITIES Salespeople are obligated to communicate special sales opportunities to their customers. This is true even if those opportunities are not related to the original purchase. Often they involve new merchandise, special sales, and holiday items. *[handwritten: the book say they often involve]*

In retail sales, routinely inform your customer of the arrival of new merchandise. Regular customers appreciate this special service because they like having the opportunity to see new merchandise before others do.

Most shoppers appreciate the opportunity to take advantage of a bargain. Salespeople are obligated to both the store and the customer to pass along such information. You could comment on a special sale by explaining, "We're having a one-day sale on all items in this department. You might want to look around before I write up your purchase."

Special occasions and holidays present an opportunity to sell more merchandise. You can suggest gift items to customers around occasions such as Christmas, Kwanzaa, Hanukkah, Valentine's Day, Father's Day, and Mother's Day. Here's an example of what you can say: "If you haven't finished your holiday shopping for the men in your life, you may want to look at the special display of gift ideas we have in the men's department. You'll be amazed at the variety and creativity of some of the items. If you would like to follow me, I'll show you what I mean."

In business-to-business sales situations, sales representatives often show new items to their customers after they have completed the sale of merchandise requested. Thus, the salesperson has an opportunity to establish a rapport with the customer before introducing new merchandise.

[handwritten: Read, the book mention]

Relationship Marketing

[handwritten: What does the term relationship marketing come from]

A popular trend among companies today is relationship marketing. **Relationship marketing** involves the strategies businesses use to stay close to their customers. In today's competitive marketplace, after-sale activities are an important part of this trend. They are used to develop and nurture customer relationships.

The value of a good relationship is not a new idea. Marketers have long recognized that identifying the needs of customers and satisfying them can be profitable. However, it is only recently that firms have made a dedicated effort to use relationship marketing. By examining successful partnerships in

[handwritten: Recall that today's competitive business environment requires relationship marketing!]

[handwritten: I'm sure that some of you have probably heard statements like this before. Do you think it is smart to call attention to special sales opportunities? Why?]

BRIGHT IDEAS

Wired and Admired

Treat your own employees lavishly? Sure. How about the salespeople who have the power to sell your product? Noel Lee of Monster Cable says why not treat salespeople well, especially because he depends on suggestion selling to make a profit. When selling a new home entertainment system, salespeople may promote Monster's gold-tipped electromagnetically shielded cable. The high cost ($3 to $125 per foot) encourages salespeople to have a good sales push, because the average cable is 25 cents per foot. To spur sales, Monster Cable's Noel Lee flies top producers from electronics stores to all-expenses-paid weekends in Napa Valley, Hawaii, and Germany. He also lets them drive one of his sports cars. Sometimes, salespeople need motivation to move the product.

Thinking Creatively

What other incentives could be offered to motivate a salesforce?

[handwritten: Paid Vacation   Bonus   Extra Vacation   Stock Option   Company Car]

[handwritten: Company Vacation   Perks]

BRIGHT IDEAS   Wired and Admired

Answer Besides offering all-expense-paid vacations and use of sports cars, cash, discounts, free product, automobiles, free rent, etc., could also be offered to motivate salespeople.

business and elsewhere, marketers have discovered that enduring relationships are built on trust and commitment and require a lot of time and effort to maintain.

Relationship marketing is alive and well in both traditional and e-commerce marketing. Consider the example set by Harley Davidson, the motorcycle manufacturer. The company established a club for its members, and it markets services such as motorcycle insurance and travel assistance to those members. An e-commerce example of relationship marketing is Amazon.com's practice of collecting information about customers' book purchases and then e-mailing personalized information about promotions and merchandise within the customer's established range of interest. *The book says*

Customer loyalty cannot be taken for granted, especially with the high levels of competition in today's market. A company can stay close to its customers and keep them happy by having the sale be the first step in developing a relationship, not the final one. Think of after-sale activities as part of an ongoing dialog with customers in preparation for future sales. This is simplified with the use of e-mail, which can be used to keep customers informed about sales, new products, and important company news. *Relationship marketing is very interesting. What you will*

■ Taking Payment/Taking the Order *see* *Sometimes is a birthday card, reminder et. reminder of service dates. Valvoline*

Take payment or the order with courtesy. Work quickly to complete the paperwork. Avoid saying or doing anything to irritate your customer at this stage of the sale. You have probably heard an annoyed customer say, "Forget the order. I don't want it anymore." If you are courteous and efficient, you can usually avoid this type of negative response from an unhappy or disappointed customer. *Can anyone tell me the rules for taking the order?*

■ Departure

Before the customer departs, or before you leave your client's office, reassure the person of his or her wise buying choices. If an item needs special care or specific instructions, take the time to educate your customer about it. You may want to remind the

Does anybody recall what a salesperson should do during the departure?
o Reassure
o Special instruction
o Thank them
o Invite them back
o Permission to call, etc.

customer, for example, that to get the best results from a Teflon-coated frying pan, it is best to preheat the pan. If you are selling a customer a new automobile, this would be a good time to remind him or her when the oil should be changed and when tune-ups are necessary. Helpful comments like this will make your customer feel you are interested and concerned. They also help ensure customer satisfaction.

Always thank your customers. Even when a customer does not buy, express your gratitude for the time and attention given to you. Invite him or her back to the store, or ask for permission to call again in the near future.

Chapter 15 ■ *Closing the Sale* **267**

Electronic Frontiers — E-mail as a Sales Tool

Answer After asking customers if they want to receive e-mails, a company can send out e-mail with order status, sales, special discounts, and even a personalized newsletter to encourage sales.

ASSESS
Reteaching

1. **Vocabulary** Assign and review the vocabulary terms for this section.
2. **Fact and Idea** Assign and review Fact and Idea Review questions 7–10 from the Chapter Assessment.
3. **Suggestion Selling** To reteach suggestion selling, describe sales situations that break one or more of the key rules for that type of selling (offering related merchandise; recommending larger quantities; and calling attention to special sales opportunities). After each description, ask students what went wrong, and have them tell you what the salesperson could have done to achieve a favorable outcome.

Enrichment

1. **Review** Assign and review the Chapter 15 activities in the *Student Activity Workbook*.
2. **Review** Assign and review the appropriate Thinking Critically questions from the Chapter Assessment.
3. **Review** Assign and review the following Chapter Assessment activities: Building Workplace Skills, Applying Marketing Concepts, Linking School to Work Activities, The DECA Connection Role Play, and Internet Connection.
4. **Invite a Guest Speaker** Invite both a retail salesperson and a business-to-business salesperson to speak to the class about the kinds of suggestion selling and after-sale activities they perform in the course of their respective jobs to reinforce their relationships with customers. After the visits, have students compare and contrast the closing and relationship marketing techniques used in the two situations.

Evaluation

Assign and review the Section 15.2 Assessment.

Technology Resources

 Assessment Resources Go to the *Marketing Essentials* Web site (**www.marketing.glencoe. com**) for tools to teach and assess occupation-specific performance indicators.

CLOSE

Section Wrap-Up

Have students complete this statement: When properly used, suggestion selling saves the customer . . . *(time and money.)*

268

■ Follow-Up

[handwritten: Do you thk this is a good thing to do, why?]

The follow-up includes making arrangements to follow through on all promises made during the sales process. It also includes checking on your customer's satisfaction with his or her purchase. Some follow up ideas:

- Call the shipping department to confirm a special delivery date.
- Check to make sure that delivery occurs as promised.
- Call the customer and explain any delay.
- Phone the customer a week or two after the purchase to see if he or she is happy with his or her selection. *[handwritten: I'm sure some of you have experienced this before]*
- Send a thank-you note with your business card attached. *[handwritten: I think a lot of salespeople forget to do this. It's very important]*

[handwritten: Please read"] You can use the time immediately after the sale to plan for your next encounter with the customer. Take notes on your conversation with the customer. Keep this in a file for future reference. In retail sales, note a customer's preference in color, style, and size, as well as the person's address and telephone number. In business-to-business selling, record personal information on the buyer's marital status, children, and hobbies to assist with future sales visits. Record changes in buying patterns that may lead to future sales. You also want to note any future service dates for appliances or cars so that you can send a reminder when the time comes.

■ Evaluation

[handwritten: Does anybody remember what type of businesses send survey questionnaires]

Some businesses send questionnaires or call customers to check on how well they were treated by the sales and service staff. The results of such surveys are passed on to salespeople so they can improve their technique.

Even if your company has a formal method of reviewing your efforts, you should conduct your own evaluation. In your evaluation, consider the following: *[handwritten: Please read.]*

- What were the strong points of your sales presentation?
- What did you do wrong?
- How could you have improved your performance?
- What would you do differently next time?
- What can you do now to solidify your relationship with your customer if you made the sale?

Objective self-evaluation is a helpful tool in any career. Asking yourself these questions can help you improve your selling skills as well as your business skills in general. They will enable you to look forward to your next sales opportunity. That kind of attitude will help you become more effective with each sales contact. It will also help you become more successful in building a strong relationship with your customers.

15.2 ASSESSMENT

Reviewing Key Terms and Concepts

1. What is suggestion selling, and why is it important?
2. Suggest two rules for suggestion selling.
3. Identify three methods used for suggestion selling.
4. What is relationship marketing and how is it related to the sales process?
5. Why are after-sale activities (such as departure, follow-up, and evaluation) important?

Thinking Critically

6. Assume you work for a bank and are in charge of selling commercial loans. You just sold a real estate developer a $3.5 million loan for a new shopping center. What could you do now to solidify your relationship with this customer?

Integrating Academic Skills

7. **MATH** What is the total amount due from a customer who purchases three shirts at $25 each, two pairs of pants at $40 each, and four ties at $14 each? The sales tax on the clothing is 5 percent.

15.2 ASSESSMENT ANSWERS

Reviewing Key Terms and Concepts

1. It is selling additional goods or services; creates customer satisfaction and profit.
2. Do it after the close but before payment; make the recommendation from the customer's point of view; make the suggestion definite.
3. suggest related merchandise, larger quantity, and special sales opportunities
4. It includes strategies businesses use to stay close to customers. Sale is the first step in developing a relationship with customers.
5. future sales and repeat customers

Thinking Critically

6. You could take the developer out for dinner; offer additional services.

Integrating Academic Skills

7. **MATH** $221.55.

Careers in Marketing

SALES MANAGEMENT

Martin Swinehart
Sales Promotion Manager
Revolution Marketing

What does your job entail?

"I am in the business of sampling and promotion. My job is to assist clients with selling their product or service. When you are at an event and are given a free can of soda or box of cereal, that is sampling and promotion. My company does direct hand-to-hand promotions, as opposed to mail order; this allows consumer interaction, which creates greater logo recognition. Direct promotion offers higher quality sampling and a better sampling of the demographic. It saves money over mailing, costing only 15 to 20 cents per impression, while a mailing can cost more than 33 cents per impression."

What skills are most important?

"Communication on all levels is the most important skill to have in this business. You need to keep a straight head and be able to transition from the high-pressure business meetings to a casual climate in a second."

How does your job vary?

"It changes every day—there is a huge amount of variety in my job. I am the captain of my own fate because I pick my own clients and run my business my own way. I have quite a bit of variety and freedom, which really allows for a lot of creativity."

What kind of training would you suggest for students?

"It's important to get out into the real world. You have to understand trends, demographics, how people work, how they think, and how they communicate. You need to gain insight about how people really are, as opposed to reading about something in a book. For this job, you need to be out in the field."

What is your key to success?

"Innovative thinking and presenting solutions to clients. I am in the business of problem solving, and must base my actions on that."

Thinking Critically

Why is it important to understand human behavior in the sales promotion field?

Career Facts

Education and Training: A bachelor's degree in marketing is the ideal preparation. Experience in negotiating complex contracts and facilitating market research is necessary.

Aptitudes, Abilities, and Skills: The ability to coordinate information, make decisions based on numerical and statistical information, and promote the cooperative work of various groups of employees. Analytical skills and above average communication and presentation skills are helpful.

Career Outlook: Average growth in opportunities is projected through the year 2006. Growth in e-commerce sales promotion is likely to be stronger.

Career Path: Sales promotion directors must have several years of increasingly responsible sales and marketing experience. They may advance from regional to national sales promotion directors, and finally to global sales promotion directors.

Chapter 15 ■ *Closing the Sale* **269**

Careers in Marketing

Ask a student to read the Careers in Marketing feature aloud to the class. Discuss the skills and aptitudes required for a career in sales management. Ask students whether they think they would like or dislike a career in sales management. Discuss the pros and cons of such a career.

Thinking Critically Answer
It is important to understand human behavior in sales promotion because you can understand buying patterns and how customers make decisions.

Guest Speakers
Invite a sales promotion manager to class to discuss his/her job and factors he/she considers when making marketing decisions.

Exploring Careers

Signs of a Good Listener
1. Explain to students the importance of good listening skills on the job. Then discuss with them how to analyze the way one person listens to another.
2. Read aloud the following sentences to students, and ask them whether each sentence is true or false.
- The listener should focus on the main ideas presented by the speaker. *(True)*
- The listener should not react with positive body language and facial expressions. *(False)*
- The listener should react by making comments and asking questions. *(True)*
3. Then read aloud the correct answers and discuss with students why these characteristics of active listeners might facilitate good communication on and off the job.

Lifelong Learning

Closing the Sale
It is important that students recognize that they can apply their school work in sales to other areas of their lives. Activities such as making a major consumer purchase, choosing a college, buying or renting a home, or joining a health club all involve dealing with sales or service representatives. Knowing sales psychology can be extremely helpful.

Meeting Individual Needs

Students With Hearing Impairments
Many students with hearing impairments communicate mainly by sign language. Written English is like a second language. Many factors affect the comfort level of students with hearing impairments, including personality, intelligence, degree of deafness, residual hearing, age of onset of deafness, and family environment.

Vocabulary Review

Stories will vary. See Glossary for definitions.

Fact and Idea Review

1. Even if trial closes fail, you've still learned valuable information about why the customer is not ready to buy.
2. Continuing to sell after the customer has made a decision could have a negative effect on the customer and prevent the sale from happening.
3. Remove unwanted items to bring the selection to two; review benefits; and ask customer which item he or she prefers.
4. It should be used when a product is in short supply or when the price will be going up in the near future.
5. In a retail situation, you should invite customer to shop in your store again. In a business-to-business situation, you can ask if you may call again.
6. The salesperson benefits by future business. The customer is generally more pleased with the original purchase. The company sees an increase in net profits.
7. You should try after the customer has made a commitment to buy but before payment is made or the order is written.
8. A salesperson can plan by taking notes on conversation with the customer and keeping them for future reference.
9. It is important to help improve your selling skills and make you look forward to your next sales opportunity.

Thinking Critically

1. a) Service close—to suggest other means of payment.
   b) Which close—to get selection down to two and help customer make decision.
   c) Service close—return policy will solidify sale.
   d) Service close—to reassure with firm's willingness to stand behind product with warranty or extended service contract.
2. Items for a suit include: a shirt/blouse, tie/scarf, hose; for a camera: film, carrying case, special lenses, tripod, photo album; for a bicycle: water bottle, specially designed seat, cycling attire, helmet.
3. Answers will vary.

270

Chapter 15 ASSESSMENT

VOCABULARY REVIEW

Write a story, using the terms below, about a sales situation in which you are asked to close the sale for a colleague.

- closing the sale
- buying signals
- trial close
- which close
- standing-room-only close
- direct close
- service close
- suggestion selling
- relationship marketing

FACT AND IDEA REVIEW

1. Why are trial closes important? (15.1)
2. Why should a salesperson stop talking about a product once strong buying signals are detected from a customer? (15.1)
3. What are the three steps of the which close method? (15.1)
4. When should the standing-room-only close be used? (15.1)
5. What should you do if you did not close the sale in a retail situation? In a business-to-business situation? (15.1)
6. How does suggestion selling benefit the salesperson, the customer, and the company? (15.2)
7. When should you try suggestion selling? (15.2)
8. How can a salesperson use the time immediately after the sale to plan for his or her next encounter with that customer? (15.2)
9. Why should you evaluate yourself when the sales process is over? (15.2)

THINKING CRITICALLY

1. Select the most appropriate closing method and provide your rationale.
   a. "I like this TV, but I don't have the money with me to buy it today."
   b. "You've shown me so many pairs of gloves I like that I can't make up my mind."
   c. "My parents are fussy. What if I buy them this clock and they don't like it?"
   d. "I had a bad experience with my last computer and am concerned about this one's reliability."
2. List three related items that could be used for suggestion selling after a customer's decision to buy a suit, a camera, and a bicycle.
3. What are five criteria that you think should be used when evaluating a salesperson's technique?

BUILDING WORKPLACE SKILLS

1. **Writing** Prepare a memo explaining the importance of suggesting related merchandise to customers to all new sales employees. Include examples, recommendations, and guidelines to encourage suggestion selling.
2. **Human Relations** A customer wants to return a clock radio because he was not able to set the time or the alarm. The customer is probably not aware of a memory key that must be depressed while such settings are being made. How would you handle the return? How could the whole situation have been avoided?

Building Workplace Skills

1. Memos will vary but should be done in correct format (with To/From/Subject/Date heading).
2. Answers will vary but should include demonstrating proper use of the memory key. The situation could have been avoided by doing this.

Applying Marketing Concepts

1. Students' work will vary depending on product.
2. Written conclusions will vary but should be consistent with the rest of the manual.
3. Presentations will vary depending on the business. For example, a computer business may install software for customers, offer free classes on computer use, and offer a service contract.
4. Flyers will vary but should integrate skills from the chapter to encourage shoppers to come into the store. Marketing should be geared towards Generation X.

APPLYING MARKETING CONCEPTS

1. **Developing Sales Strategies** Write about closing the sale and suggestion selling for your continuing sales training manual project. Explain each step's importance and timing, then write four different dialogues to demonstrate each of the different closing methods. List all the related merchandise that can be sold with your product. Select one related item and write a dialogue of exactly what you would say to demonstrate the rules of suggestion selling. Use a word processing program to prepare this report.

2. **Recognizing Relationship Marketing** Use a word processing program to write the conclusion for your sales training manual. Stress the concept of relationship marketing.

3. **Developing Customer Relationships** Using presentation software, show ways a computer business and a car dealership can ensure customer satisfaction and develop ongoing relationships with their customers.

4. **Reaching Out to Customers** You manage a funky clothing store that caters to Generation Xers. You are inviting valued customers to a special preseason sale. Using design software, create a flyer to be mailed to your regular customers encouraging them to come back to your store.

LINKING SCHOOL TO WORK

Thinking, Interpersonal, and Information Skills Interview a salesperson from a company to find out what closing techniques he or she uses, as well as what is done to develop an ongoing relationship with customers. Prepare a written report on your findings.

THE DECA CONNECTION

Role Play: Sales Associate

Situation You are to assume the role of sales associate in a sporting goods store. A new store manager (judge) has asked all employees to share with him or her the sales practices they have found most successful.

Activity Develop a master plan that can be used storewide to ensure customer satisfaction through effective closing techniques, suggestion selling, and relationship marketing. Even though you work in several departments, you need select only one to comply with the store manager's (judge's) request.

Evaluation You will be evaluated on how well you fulfill the following performance indicators:

- Close the sale
- Demonstrate suggestion selling
- Explain the selling process
- Plan follow-up strategies for use in selling
- Explain the nature of effective verbal communications

interNET CONNECTION

Who Closes the Sale?

You have been asked to design a Web site for a sporting goods business. Before beginning, research the sales-closing strategies and relationship marketing techniques of other e-tailers.

Connect

- Report on how various e-tailers close the sale.
- Report on how these businesses develop a relationship with customers.
- Create a flowchart from the home page for the sporting goods dealer, including closing the sale and relationship marketing links.

Chapter 15 ■ *Closing the Sale* **271**

Chapter 15 Assessment

THE DECA CONNECTION

Students should be evaluated on the performance indicators noted in the Role Play.

- For another DECA Role Play, go to the *Student Activity Workbook,* p. 125.
- For more in-depth Role Play practice, refer to DECA's *Essential Competitive Events Handbook.* To order, contact DECA at www.deca.org.

interNET CONNECTION

Reports and home pages will vary but should include closing the sale and relationship marketing links.

Mini Quiz

Administer the Mini Quiz orally. For an expanded chapter quiz, go to page 81 of the *Reproducible Tests* book.

1. You close the sale when your customer is ready to buy.

2. To detect an opportunity to close the sale, look for buying signals.

3. When a customer is having difficulty making a buying decision, stop showing additional merchandise and narrow the selection to two items.

4. Suggestion selling involves selling customers items that will save them time and money or make the original purchase more enjoyable.

5. One of the five rules for suggestion selling is (any of the following:) do suggestion selling after the customer has made a commitment to buy; make the recommendation from the customer's point of view; make the suggestion definite; show the item you are suggesting; or make the suggestion positive.

Linking School to Work

Answers depend on the work situation.

GO TO

1. **Assessment** Have students complete the Reproducible Test for Chapter 15 or construct your own tests using the ExamView software.
2. **Enrichment** Have students complete the corresponding activities in the following workbooks:
   - *Marketing Math Workbook,* p. 31
   - *Marketing Research Project Workbook,* p. 65

Chapter Overview

This chapter looks at the conclusion to the sales process—recording the transaction, presenting the customer with a sales receipt in retail sales, and the forms for a sale in business-to-business sales. It also covers the functions of cash registers, types of sales transactions, and the steps of filling out sales checks, purchase orders, and invoices.

 Springboard

Analyze Begin the chapter by asking students what they find challenging about making change, transacting credit card sales, or processing returns. Tell students that with this chapter they will get a chance to improve their ability to do sales transactions.

Prereading

List the section objectives to discuss with students. Have students skim the chapter, looking at the pictures, reading the captions, and noting the heads. Ask questions to ensure that students have a minimal understanding of the chapter structure.

Preteaching Marketing Vocabulary

Dictate each of the vocabulary terms and ask students to write them on a sheet of paper. When they finish, write the terms on the board. Then have students guess at the meaning of each. Write their guesses next to each term. Leave this list on the board so students can see how close their guesses were to the actual definitions as they work through the chapter.

Marketing:
What It Takes
Answer Contacting other merchants in the area and searching the Internet are possible sources. An advantage of accepting credit cards is increased sales and a disadvantage is the cost.

Chapter **16**

Using Math In Sales

Marketing: What It Takes

Ski Lodge Inn— A Mountain High or a High-Risk Idea?
You and three friends are giving serious thought to opening a restaurant in a ski resort area. The four of you have been meeting regularly to study the feasibility of opening the restaurant. Your discussions have included the potential market, start-up costs, sources of financing, food and equipment suppliers, and many other issues. Now it's time to begin your research. Your first responsibility is to learn about the advantages and disadvantages of accepting various credit cards for payment.

WHAT WILL YOU DO?
How will you research the advantages and disadvantages of accepting credit cards for payment?

272

THE DECA CONNECTION · ADVISOR CORNER

Rewarding DECA Members To make your fundraising projects more meaningful to your students, give them a personal incentive for their efforts. Establish and keep an individual DECA account for each chapter member. Funds earned by each student go into that student's account to be used for chapter activities. Having funds available creates a powerful incentive for members to get involved, because at least part of the cost of a conference or field trip is already covered. This is a great way to get 100 percent participation in sales projects and to have more members take advantage of DECA events beyond the classroom.
(John Bucci, Arvada H.S., Arvada, CO)

Cash Registers

Cash Register Operations

The sales transaction is the process of recording a sale and presenting the customer with proof of payment. Most retailers today use cash registers to record sales and provide customers with receipts. Cash registers fill three important functions of sales transactions:

- *Recording sales* Cash registers provide a convenient way to enter information about a sale. This usually includes the department, the type of transaction, the salesperson, and the amount of the sale. The salesperson also enters the amount of money given by the customer. The register responds with the amount of change due.
- *Storing cash and sales documents* Cash registers provide a convenient, organized way to keep cash, personal checks, credit sales checks, and refund slips. Coupons and other sales-related documents may also be kept in the cash register drawer.
- *Providing receipts* Cash registers automatically provide a receipt for the customer. This is the customer's record of the sale and proof of payment.

Most salespeople operate a cash register. In some retail stores, including many department stores and all supermarkets, cash register operations are the responsibility of a cashier or checkout clerk. Before you assume the responsibility of using a cash register and handling money, you will need to become familiar with all aspects of cash register operations.

■ Electronic Cash Registers

Electronic cash registers automatically perform many functions of a sales transaction, including totaling quantity purchases, figuring sales tax, subtracting refunds and returns, and calculating the change due to a customer.

Information on sales transactions can be entered into an electronic cash register in a number of ways:

- *Manual key entry* Even with electronic cash registers, some businesses have their salespeople enter sales transactions manually, using the register keys. All registers provide a numeric keyboard for entry in case other input devices don't function properly.
- *Electronic wand entry* More and more retailers (especially department and clothing stores) are using electronic wands to enter sales transactions. The salesperson moves the point of the wand across the data printed on a tag attached to the article sold.

● What You'll Learn

- The three general functions of all cash registers
- The arrangement of currency and coins in a cash register drawer
- The two methods of making change
- The two most important rules for safeguarding money at the cash register
- The general content of sales checks and the basic ways of generating them

● Why It's Important

Your customer's decision to buy does not conclude the sales process. You must record the transaction and present the customer with proof of payment —or secure a promise to pay in the future. In this section, you will explore cash register operations. You will learn the basics of operating both manual and electronic registers.

● Key Terms

- sales transaction
- Universal Product Code (UPC)
- Universal Vendor Marketing (UVM)
- till
- opening cash fund

Chapter 16 ■ *Using Math in Sales* **273**

FOCUS

Bell Ringer Activity

Read and Calculate Have students read this section before you discuss it in class. The day you begin the lesson, bring an empty cash drawer to class. Have on hand "play" coins and currency, enough to constitute an opening cash fund and enough additional money for students to use for simulated purchases. Call on volunteers to help you, and have students do the following:

- Count the opening cash fund. (Suggest appropriate amounts, e.g., $75 or $100 in coins and currency.)
- Place coins and currency in the drawer in the appropriate compartments. (Do not allow students to study the text diagram beforehand.)
- Identify where such things as checks, food stamps, and coupons would go.
- Handle various small and large cash payments.

Introducing the Section

Cash Registers The Bell Ringer Activity will show you where students still need help in conducting cash transactions. As you work through this section, use the cash drawer and "play" money for demonstration purposes and role-playing exercises.

TEACH

▌▍▎ Technology Resources

PowerPoint The *Marketing Essentials* PowerPoint Presentation CD-ROM provides visual lecture aids for every chapter section.

Concept Development

1. Read Section 16.1 with students.
2. For additional chapter resource material, you may wish to use Glencoe's program entitled *The Cashier*, which includes a text workbook, a teacher's manual/key, and six sound filmstrips.
3. Invite a representative from your local police department or a security company to talk to students about safety precautions one must take when dealing with money in a public venue, such as a store.

Discussion Starter

Accepting Currency Have students speculate about why some stores and other businesses will not accept currency larger than $20 bills. *(Answers will vary but could include the following: The risk of getting a counterfeit bill increases with larger bills, such as 50s and 100s. Accepting larger bills forces you to keep higher levels of change in the cash drawer, which is a security risk. Mandating that only smaller bills can be accepted is an employee theft deterrent, because it's easier for management to keep track of a smaller amount of money in the till.)*

CAPTION ANSWER

UPC It is a UPC code. Each item has a distinctive UPC and can be scanned by passing the item over an optical scanner, enabling many items to be scanned quickly.

■ **UPC** There are two types of product codes. *Which is shown in this photo? Why might it be more effective?*

- *Optical scanning* Supermarkets have improved their efficiency in recording sales transactions by installing optical scanners at checkout counters. Salesclerks drag items across the scanner so it can read the bar codes on the product packaging. If the scanner cannot read the code, the salesclerk keys the information manually.

Two types of codes are widely used for electronic entry. The Universal Product Code (UPC) is the bar code referred to in the photograph above. Bar codes are composed of a series of vertical parallel black and white lines and a row of numbers. Each item has its own distinctive UPC. The Universal Vendor Marketing (UVM) code is another code that appears as a series of numbers across the top of a price tag. A UVM code is designed to be read by an electronic wand.

Once read and entered into a register, coded information can be transferred to a mainframe computer for further processing. Many electronic cash registers are linked to such computers as part of a POS system (see Figure 16-1 on page 275). Using the data, the computer can update inventory records with each sale and automatically reorder items in short supply. It can also store customer information and make it available for marketing or credit-check purposes. It can also print out financial statements, sales trends, and sales personnel productivity reports.

■ The Cash Drawer

Checks and currency collected in sales transactions are generally deposited in the till. The till is the cash drawer of a cash register.

CASH DRAWER ARRANGEMENT The till normally has ten compartments—five in the back and five in the front. Although some companies vary the arrangement, bills are usually kept in the back of the drawer and coins in the front.

In the section for bills, the first compartment on the left often remains empty. It is reserved for checks or other special items. The second compartment contains $20 bills, the third $10 bills, and the fourth $5 bills. The last compartment on the right is used for $1 bills. When a customer tenders a $2 bill, it is placed under the $1 bills.

In the section for coins, the first compartment on the left is used for silver dollars and half-dollars. The next compartment is for quarters, the following one for dimes, and the one after that for nickels. The last compartment on the right is for pennies.

This arrangement facilitates making change because the bill and coin compartments are related and in descending order of value. Each pair has at least one digit in common. The $20 bills are behind the quarters ($.25). The $10 bills are behind the dimes ($.10). The $5 bills are behind the nickels ($.05), and the $1 bills are behind the pennies ($.01).

OPENING CASH FUND The manager or other designated person will provide a limited amount of money for the cash register at the beginning of each business day. This opening cash fund consists of the coins and currency designated for the register for a given day's business. To verify the fund, the assigned person first counts the coins and places them, one denomination at a time, in the correct compartment; then he or she does the same with the currency.

As the coins and currency are counted, the amount is written down to make sure the total matches the amount planned for the register. The change fund is even when it matches exactly. When there is more than planned, the fund is over; if there is less than planned, the fund is short. An opening cash fund that is short or over should be reported immediately to the person who supplied the money.

■ *GREAT IDEAS* **from the Marketing Classroom**

Sandra Hinesly
Newman Smith High School
Carrollton, TX

Tape a one-dollar bill on the board. Ask for a volunteer to identify the portraits on $1, $2, $5, $10, $20, $50, and $100 bills. The first student who gets them all correct wins the dollar. Begin a discussion of setting up the till with the bills, portrait side up. Explain that understanding the design and security features of currency can help you detect altered bills or counterfeit currency and may stop con artists. Invite a Secret Service agent or local bank representative to visit the classroom and bring samples of altered bills and counterfeit currency. This basic currency knowledge can be a fun way to learn about cash handling.

FIGURE 16-1

POS TERMINAL FUNCTIONS

Point of sale (POS) computer terminals are connected to an in-store network that keeps track of sales, inventory, and often the ordering of new merchandise.

SCANNING PRODUCTS

The checker passes each item over the scanner so that it can read the code printed on the package. The checker will key in the sale amount if the code label is torn or missing.

TRANSFERRING INFORMATION

The price and name of each item are displayed on the screen. The terminal also shows the total amount of the sale after it computes any special discounts. Customers can pay by cash, check, or credit or debit card. This terminal also sends the information to the central store computer, where store inventory is updated and new merchandise can be ordered if stocks are low.

RECORDING SALES

The terminal calculates the amount of change that the customer is due and prints a tape receipt listing each item sold along with prices, the date and time of sale. If the sale was by credit or debit card, usually the customer's name and some account information are also printed on the tape. The checker gives the customer any change due and the receipt. This completes the sale.

Chapter 16 ▪ *Using Math in Sales* **275**

Thinking Critically

1. **Cashiering** Ask: Why is good cashiering good customer service? *(Answers will vary. Customers usually grow impatient if their sales transactions are not conducted in a timely fashion. They may feel they are being kept waiting in return for the privilege of giving their money to the store. If they are served rapidly and accurately, their satisfaction increases with both the purchase and the store.)*

2. **Cash Register Features** Because many employees are math phobic, have poor math skills, or are less familiar with U.S. currency, businesses today are resorting to cash registers that minimize computation. Ask students to think of some features that these registers have. *(keyboards with words and pictures instead of numbers and programs that compute cash back for the customer)*

Independent Practice

1. **Brainstorm and Calculate** Have students generate a list of five purchase amounts and corresponding amounts tendered. For example, if the purchase amount is $14.49, the customer might tender $20.50. (Each purchase amount and amount tendered should be under $100.)

2. **Role Play** Have students work in pairs to role play making change from the amounts generated in #1.

3. **Role Play** Have students role play to convince a customer to open a store credit account.

Individualized Practice

Math Skills

Give students this hypothetical situation: Assume you work as a salesclerk in an art supply store. Shortly before the store opens, you are given a cash bag containing one roll each of pennies, nickels, dimes, and quarters (50 coins to a roll) plus ten $1 bills, two $5 bills, and two $10 bills. This is your opening cash fund. You should start the day with $70.50 in your register.

L1 Ask students: Do you have the correct amount? Verify your fund. *(Bills: [10 x $1] + [2 x $5] + [2 x $10] = $10 + $10 + $20 = $40. Coins: [50 x $.01] + [50 x $.05] + [50 x $.10] + [50 x $.25] = $.50 + $2.50 + $5 + $12.50 = $20.50. Total: $40 + $20.50 = $60.50. Fund is $10 short.)*

L2 The art supply store has just closed, and you must balance the cash drawer. This procedure involves totaling all the cash, checks, and credit slips in the drawer and then subtracting the opening cash fund and any refunds given to customers. The result is the day's receipts. If this figure matches the total on the register tape, the drawer is balanced.

You have $157.84 in cash, $212 in checks, and $325.50 in credit slips. There was one refund for $22.16. The register tape puts the day's receipts at $602.68. Does your drawer balance? *(Yes: [$157.84 + $212 + $325.50] - [$22.16 + $70.50] = $695.34 - $92.66 = $602.68)*

L3 Suppose the register tape for the day's receipts reads $607.45. What does that mean, and what could account for it? *(The drawer is $4.77 short, possibly because a customer was given too much change, a transaction was input incorrectly, or petty cash was removed without a petty cash slip being placed in the register.)*

■ **Cash Flow** The money in a cash drawer is laid out in order of value from right to left. *Why do you think this arrangement is always the same?*

MAKING CHANGE A salesperson who handles a large number of cash transactions during a business day may run short of certain denominations at some time. Check your cash drawer during any slack time you have to see if you need any bills or coins, and request the change then. This procedure can prevent delays when customers are waiting for service.

A customer who has made a decision to buy usually wants to pay quickly and move on. That is why accuracy and speed are of primary concern in recording sales. You should take special care with cash transactions. Be thorough and accurate when making change, and follow these five steps:

1. Once the transaction has been entered in the cash register, announce to the customer the total amount of the sale. You might say, "That will be $17.65."

2. Announce the amount tendered when the customer offers payment in cash, saying, for example, "Out of $20."

3. Place the money on the cash drawer ledge and leave it there until you have given change to the customer. This eliminates most disputes over amount tendered.

4. Count silently while removing change from the cash drawer. The most common method is to count up from the purchase price, taking out smaller denominations of coins and currency first. Use as few coins as possible in making change.

5. Count aloud when handing the change to the customer. Say, "That's $17.65 out of $20—$17.75 (giving the customer a dime), $18 (giving a quarter), $19, and $20," (giving two $1 bills, one at a time).

Many customers try to avoid accumulating small change by tendering an odd amount of change to pay for their purchases. A customer might give you $20.39 for a sales total of $18.39. You would use the 39 cents to cancel the "odd cents" of the sale and give change for the $20 bill. The same customer might also tender $20.50, in which case you would count the odd cents first, starting at $18.39.

Most newer cash registers calculate and display the amount of change. You may find it easier to begin with the largest denomination when using this type of machine. When the register displays $2.35 due the customer for a $17.65 purchase, you may select the change from the cash drawer by taking out two $1 bills, a quarter, and a dime. The customer knows from the display what change is due; therefore, you can count it out the same way.

> #### PRACTICE 1
>
> How would you make or arrange for change in the following situations using the smallest number of bills and coins possible?
>
> **1.** A customer gives you a $50 bill to pay for a $22.61 purchase. What change would you give her?
>
> **2.** A customer is buying two audio cassettes that total $15.09, including tax. The smallest bill he has is $20, and he doesn't want too much change back. What is your response?
>
> **3.** A customer gives you $40.15 for a $27.15 purchase. How would you count back the change?
>
> **4.** You are a cashier at Long's Drugstore, and a customer gives you $20.75 to pay for a purchase of $13.63. Count the customer's change back to him. Why did he give you the change along with the $20 bill?
>
> **Note:** Answers to all practice sets in this chapter appear on page 287.

SALES TALLY Salespeople and cashiers who use a cash register must account for the day's sales and money at closing. This process goes by a number of names, including balancing the cash or balancing the till.

CAPTION ANSWER
Cash Flow The layout of a cash drawer is always the same so that once it is learned, making change can be done very quickly.

More About . . .

Handling Cash Payments
The most common trick played by con artists on unsuspecting cashiers is the "Can I have change for a $5 bill?" trick. Once change is given, another request is made and another. By the time the requests are finished, the con artist is richer, and the clerk may not even realize there's a problem until the cash drawer is reconciled at the end of the day.

FIGURE 16-2

Sales Check—Single Purchase

masons
15154 RYLAND AVENUE
ABINGTON, PA 19001

LUGGAGE & FINE LEATHER GOODS

Date ___5-11___ 20 --

Sold to ___CASH___

Address ___—___

Emp. # ___11335___

Dept	Qty	Article	Price	Amount	
511	1	WALLET	24.99	24	99
		Mdse Subtotal		24	99
		Sales Tax		1	50
		Total		26	49

■ **Single Purchase Sales Check** A sales check like this provides more information than a simple cash register receipt. *Why would a customer prefer to have a record like this one?*

Most cash registers automatically keep a sales tally, or summary of the day's sales. This makes the job of balancing the cash much simpler. The person responsible for each register counts the money and fills out a brief closing balance report. Then he or she removes the tape from the cash register and sends the money, report, and tape to management.

Some older cash registers do not keep an automatic sales tally. Sales checks may be written for each sale and the information recorded on a tally sheet after each transaction. At the end of the day, sales must be reviewed to balance the cash.

SAFEGUARDS AGAINST THEFT Every employee who uses a cash register should be familiar with some safeguards against the theft of money. The first rule is always to close the cash drawer between transactions. While you are counting change to a customer, you should partially close the drawer.

Remove the money tendered by the customer from the register ledge after giving change. You should always lock the register if you leave it.

You may occasionally encounter a customer who interrupts you while you are counting change. It is best to ignore the interruption while you are making change. Don't allow yourself to get distracted, because this could cause you to make incorrect change. You can respond politely once the transaction has been completed.

Counterfeit bills show up in almost every city at some time. Every company has, or should have, printed information on how to identify counterfeit money. Recently, changes were made to the design of U.S. currency to thwart counterfeiters. To make the currency more secure from reproduction techniques, the U.S. Department of the Treasury redesigned most denominations with new security features. The redesigned bills include a polymer thread embedded vertically in the bill, concentric fine-line printing, a watermark, color-shifting ink, and an enlarged, off-center portrait.

The best way to guard against counterfeit money is to become very familiar with U.S. currency. Examine suspect notes and look for difference in the quality of printing and paper characteristics.

Genuine currency has tiny red and blue fibers embedded throughout. The portrait on a genuine bill appears lifelike and stands out distinctly from the background. Counterfeit portraits are usually lifeless and flat, with details merged into the background. Also, the fine-line printing on the border of a genuine bill is clear and unbroken. On a counterfeit, the lines on the border scrollwork may be blurred and indistinct.

■ Sales Checks

Since small firms account for such a large percentage of U.S. businesses, you may find yourself working for a company that does not use automated cash registers. That means you will have to prepare a handwritten sales check like the one shown in Figure 16-2 for every sale. Take the time to familiarize yourself with its basic entries.

A sales check is a written record of a sales transaction. That includes such information as the date of the transaction, the items purchased, and the purchase price. It is valuable to a customer as an itemized receipt in this form. In its most complete form, a sales check can contain customer

---

FIGURE 16-2 ANSWER
Single Purchase Sales Check A single-purchase sales check shows more details about what was purchased so the customer can keep better records.

ASSESS
Reteaching

1. **Vocabulary** Assign and review the vocabulary terms for this section.
2. **Fact and Idea** Assign and review Fact and Idea Review questions 1–4 from the Chapter Assessment.
3. **Making Change** Have students make change, using "play" money, as you give them different purchase totals and amounts tendered. Complete enough exercises to cover the rules of giving back change when the register does not give the correct amount of change. (lowest possible denominations; state the amount of purchase and amount tendered; keep amount tendered outside the register until transaction is complete; use addition, starting with the lowest denomination to count back the change).

Enrichment

1. **Review** Assign and review the appropriate Thinking Critically questions from the Chapter Assessment.
2. **Extend** Assign and review the corresponding activities from *BusinessWeek Case Studies and Internet Resources.* **ILP**
3. **Discuss** Have students think of special security procedures taken by stores to guard against theft. How is money transported from cash register to store safe? *(For example, in some stores, money is transported to a manager's office via a pneumatic tube or a one-way drop box.)*
4. **Research and Discuss** Have students bring in sales slips produced by cash registers that use different sorts of entry systems. Discuss which sales slips provide the most information.
5. **Research** Have students use the Internet to see what information is requested when making a purchase online. How are sales slips produced?

Evaluation

Assign and review the Section 16.1 Assessment.

Technology Resources

 Assessment Resources
Go to the *Marketing Essentials* Web site (**www.marketing.glencoe. com**) for resources to teach and assess occupation-specific vocabulary.

CLOSE

Section Wrap-Up

Have students complete this statement: Cash registers fill three important functions of sales transactions: . . . *(recording sales, storing cash and sales documents, and providing receipts.)*

Thumbs Up?

Answer When traveling abroad, it is important to know these differences in hand gestures used with counting, because there may already be a language barrier creating miscommunication.

278

---

information (name, address, and phone number) and details such as the time of the sale and the identity of the salesperson. This is additional information that a business would find valuable.

Most businesses use electronic cash registers and POS systems, which result in fewer handwritten sales checks. The electronic registers provide customers with a portion of the cash register tape as a receipt. The POS systems provide computer-generated sales checks. (Sales and customer information are input by keyboard. The computer then prints out a sales check for the customer and a duplicate for the store.)

With technological advances like these, why would you concern yourself with written sales checks? Many small businesses do not have access to electronic registers and POS systems. Their salespeople record transactions by hand in sales check books that contain two or three copies of each form. They also use sales check registers, metal or plastic devices that contain a supply of continuous sales checks in duplicate or triplicate form. (When a slip is completed, you simply pull a handle and eject one or two copies. A second or third copy is kept inside the sales register, and a new sales check moves into place for the next transaction.) In these instances, the written sales checks provide both customer and company with the details that the cash register tape does not.

MARKETPLACE

Thumbs Up?

Standing at a crowded fast food restaurant, you may hold up your index finger to say "just one soda." This seems simple enough; however, it is not if you are abroad. In Germany, the upright thumb represents the number one and the forefinger shows the number two. While most Westerners begin counting with the thumb, the Japanese start with the index finger. This means that number five is reached at the thumb, not the pinky finger. Holding up your thumb may result in five sodas! Count on the wrong finger and you just might find yourself with one, two, or five hamburgers, depending on how your signal is interpreted!

Thinking Critically

Why is it helpful to know the differences in hand gestures for counting when travelling abroad?

16.1 ASSESSMENT

Reviewing Key Terms and Concepts

1. What are three functions that all cash registers perform?

2. From left to right, how are the coins arranged in a typical cash register drawer? The bills?

3. A customer gives you a $50 bill for a purchase of $37.73. How will you count the change back to her?

4. What can you do to help prevent theft from a cash register?

5. What sort of information does a sales check use to detail a sales transaction?

Thinking Critically

6. What advantages do you think using an electronic wand would have over manually entering prices?

Integrating Academic Skills

7. **COMMUNICATION** Write a memo to all cashiers at Francisco's grocery explaining the reasons you are switching from manual to electronic cash registers.

16.1 ASSESSMENT ANSWERS

Reviewing Key Terms and Concepts

1. record sales, store cash and sales documents, and provide receipts
2. coins: 50, 25, 10, 5, 1; bills: $20, $10, $5, $1
3. Say: "That's $37.73 out of $50: $.74, $.75, $38, $39, $40, and $50."
4. Close the cash drawer between transactions. Keep the drawer partially closed while making change. Lock the register any time you leave.

5. date, items and quantity purchased, purchase price, tax, and amount due; sometimes name, address, and phone number of customer

Thinking Critically

6. It offers the benefits of speed, elimination of keying errors, reduction in training costs, and compiling of inventory data.

Integrating Academic Skills

7. **COMMUNICATION** Memos will vary.

Sales Transactions

Retail Sales

As a salesperson or cashier, you will handle several types of sales transactions. Most will be cash and debit or credit card sales, in addition to layaway (or will-call) sales, on-approval sales, and cash on delivery (COD) sales. You will also be dealing with returns, exchanges, allowances, sales tax, and shipping charges.

■ Cash Sales

A cash sale is a transaction in which the customer pays for the purchase with cash or a check. The simplest sale occurs when the customer pays in cash. The cashier records the transaction on the register, gives the customer change and a receipt, and wraps the purchase.

Each business has rules about accepting checks, and you will have to learn the policy of your company or store. When a customer writes a check, you may need to verify his or her identity by requesting a driver's license and another form of identification.

Some math is necessary when preparing handwritten sales checks. The five steps of this process are shown in Figure 16-3 on page 280. Occasionally, you will not be given a unit price, and it is necessary to calculate it on your own. This occurs when items are sold in multiple quantities, such as three pairs of stockings for $12. To find the selling price of one item in an instance like this, you divide the price instead of multiplying it. One pair of stockings in this example would be $4 ($12 ÷ 3).

When the division is uneven, any fractional amount is charged to the customer. The price of one pair of stockings when three pairs are $10.99 is calculated as follows: $10.99 ÷ 3 = $3.663 or $3.67.

PRACTICE 2

Do the sales calculations indicated below.

1. Calculate the amount for each item by multiplying the unit price times the quantity purchased.

Dept.	Quantity	Item	Unit Price
12	10	Vests	$85.00
16	5	Footballs	$15.95
18	11	Clocks	$26.50
21	20	Irons	$39.95

2. If all of the above items were part of a single purchase, what would be the merchandise total?
3. Determine the price for one can of soda when a six-pack sells for $2.17.
4. Determine the price for two rolls of film when three rolls sell for $12.25.

● What You'll Learn

- The various types of sales transactions
- The math calculations necessary to fill out sales checks

● Why It's Important

Although cash is used for payment in many transactions, an ever-greater proportion of sales involves the use of a debit card or a credit card. Understanding how to handle such sales will be necessary on many sales jobs, and this section explains how it is done.

● Key Terms

- cash sale
- debit card
- floor limit
- layaway
- on-approval sale
- cash on delivery (COD) sale
- return
- exchange
- allowance
- sales tax
- parcel post

Chapter 16 ■ *Using Math in Sales* **279**

FOCUS

 Bell Ringer Activity

Describe Have students share the various types of sales transactions that they perform at their co-op work stations or ones they have observed as customers. *(Answers should include cash sales, credit card sales, layaway sales, on-approval sales, and COD sales.)* Generate a board list of these transactions during the discussion.

Have co-op students describe how they were trained to perform each type of transaction. Ask:
- Who supervised your training?
- What did you find easiest to learn during the training process?
- What was most difficult to learn?
- What skills are you still developing in order to better conduct sales transactions?

Introducing the Section

Sales Transactions Explain to students that this section will discuss the various types of sales transactions. Conducting sales transactions may look relatively simple, but there are many skills involved in this essential customer service. These include knowledge of how to make change, knowledge of company policies and procedures, efficient use of cash registers and credit card readers, attention to the customer, and taking various safety precautions.

Classroom Resources

For the Teacher
- Teacher Editions for all workbooks
- Assessment Package
- PowerPoint Presentation Software
- Interactive Lesson Planner
- ILP Block Scheduling, p. 5
- ILP Lesson Plans, p. 34
- ILP Internet Resources, p. 51

- ILP Blackline Masters, p. 29
- ILP *BusinessWeek* Case Studies, p. 103
- ILP Marketing Career Portfolio, p. 35
- *Marketing Essentials* Web site (**www.marketing.glencoe.com**)

For the Student
- Student Activity Workbook, p. 133
- Marketing Math Workbook, p. 31

- Marketing Research Project Workbook, p. 65
- ILP School-to-Work Activity Workbook, p. 65
- Virtual Business simulation
- *Marketing Essentials* Web site (**www.marketing.glencoe.com**)

ILP These resources are available in print and on the Interactive Lesson Planner (ILP)

TEACH

📊 Technology Resources

PowerPoint The *Marketing Essentials* PowerPoint Presentation CD-ROM provides visual lecture aids for every chapter section.

Concept Development

1. Read Section 16.2 with students.
2. Have students read aloud the Case Study on page 282 and review the answers in class.
3. Assign and review the Chapter 16 Activity in the *School-to-Work Activity Workbook*.
4. Have students "buy" change for the cash drawer. Ask them how much currency they would need to purchase a roll of quarters (*$10*), dimes, (*$5*), nickels (*$2*), and pennies (*$.50*).

FIGURE 16-3 ANSWER
Multiple Purchase Sales Check It is important to check your work when you are finished and use a calculator when necessary.

FIGURE 16-3

Sales Check—Multiple Purchases

Step 1—Multiply unit price times quantity for each item and extend the amounts to the last column. Remember that the last two digits on the right are cents. Place a decimal point to their left, or enter them to the right of the vertical line dividing the last column into two unequal parts.

Step 2—Add item amounts to arrive at a merchandise subtotal. Enter this figure on the appropriate line.

Step 3—Calculate sales tax or look it up in a tax table. Sales tax must be paid by the buyer on all retail sales. It is calculated as a percentage of the merchandise subtotal. In most states, food and prescription medicine are exempt from sales tax, as are shipping charges.

Step 4—Calculate shipping charges. You need to decide if you will use Parcel Post or a specific express mail carrier.

Step 5—Add subtotal, tax, and shipping to get the purchase total. This is the amount the customer will pay.

■ **Multiple Purchase Sales Check** Customers often buy more than one item and more than one unit of each item, which creates a more complicated sales check. *What can you do to ensure that the sales check is correct in the end?*

■ Debit Card Sales

Many businesses offer customers the option of using their automatic teller machine (ATM) cards to purchase products. When a customer uses an ATM card to make a purchase at a store, the card becomes a debit card. This means that the amount of the purchase is debited (or subtracted) from the customer's bank account.

A customer slides his or her ATM card through a device that reads the information from the magnetic strip on the card. After the sale is totaled on the cash register, the cardholder enters his or her *personal identification number (PIN)* into a keypad to authorize the debit. If there is money in the customer's bank account to cover the purchase, the sale is approved electronically. The customer then receives a receipt.

Debit cards provide advantages for both customers and businesses. The business has access to money much sooner than with a check. Customers benefit from not having to carry large amounts of cash or checkbooks. It is also harder for thieves to use a debit card because they can't make a purchase without knowing the cardholder's PIN number.

THE DECA CONNECTION

COMPETITIVE EVENTS AND MARKETING ESSENTIALS

Using Math in Sales As you present the material in this chapter, you can use DECA's Learn and Earn Project Event to enhance the lessons of using math in sales. This project provides your students with the opportunity to apply entrepreneurial skills to a sales or service project to be run as a real business venture in your community. This sales/services project is like a business. Your students will use their sales math while preparing the proposed budget (Section IV D) for the project. They will also use their math skills while preparing Section V C as they document the project earnings and compare them to the projected budget.

■ **Debit or Credit** Card readers such as this make it easier and easier to use a credit card to complete retail sales. *Why would retailers want to make it easier for people to use credit cards?*

REAL WORLD MARKETING

Plastic Fantastic

Have you ever polished off a huge meal only to realize that you are just short of money for the bill? That happened to Frank McNamara while dining in Manhattan in 1950. Based on this experience, McNamara created the Diners' Club—the first American credit card. The idea caught on and was followed with more cards, such as American Express, marketed as a benefit to traveling salespeople for use on the road. As credit card mania increased in the 1970s, Congress had to ban such common practices as the mass-mail distribution of active credit cards to individuals who did not request them.

Thinking Critically
Why would Congress want to stop the mass mailing of active credit cards?

Discussion Starter

Return/Exchange/Allowance Policies Have students discuss the various return/exchange/allowance policies at their co-op training stations or at stores they frequent as customers. Some stores, such as Nordstrom, have a nonrestrictive return policy and will take back any merchandise at any time. Other stores state that merchandise must be returned within a certain period of time and that the exchange will be made for store credit only. Have students discuss the uses and abuses they have observed of such policies. *(Answers will vary.)*

■ Credit Sales

Most businesses today accept one or more of the major credit cards, such as Visa, MasterCard, and American Express. Many large oil companies and department stores issue their own cards in addition to accepting the major ones. The goal is to make it easier for the general public to shop. This, of course, increases sales.

In many businesses now, the amount of each credit card sale is electronically deposited to the business's bank account as the sale is made. A combination credit card sales check and receipt is issued by the cash register. With this procedure, the credit card company is able to deduct its service charge from the store's bank account immediately. The store normally has access to its funds the next day. This is much faster than if credit card sales checks had to be delivered to a bank.

GETTING CREDIT AUTHORIZATIONS Credit cards have become an efficient, popular alternative to more traditional forms of payment. Some people, however, abuse the privilege of using a credit card by charging more than they can pay. Thus, many businesses (especially retail stores) have a set limit on credit card charges. The floor limit is the maximum amount a salesperson may allow a customer to charge without getting special authorization. Usually, the manager or someone in the credit department must approve charges that exceed the floor limit.

To confirm that a customer has been approved to charge the amount of a sale, most businesses use electronic credit authorizers. Many POS systems, in fact, include an integrated credit authorizer. Other electronic credit authorizers are separate pieces of equipment. These devices, smaller than a telephone, read data encoded on credit cards. The sales clerk inputs the amount of the sale into the device. The data is transmitted to a computer, which offers approval or disapproval in less than a minute.

Companies that do not use electronic credit authorizers obtain approval of charges in other ways. With a major credit card, for example, you may wait while a salesperson calls a central authorization telephone number for approval of charges. The salesperson may also look for your credit card number on a list of delinquent account numbers.

Chapter 16 ■ *Using Math in Sales* **281**

CAPTION ANSWER
Debit or Credit An increased use of credit cards usually leads to an increase in sales.

REAL WORLD MARKETING

Plastic Fantastic
Answer Fraud, stolen cards, and uneducated consumer usage were main reasons for the ban.

Procedures and Policies Divide students into groups of four or five. Have each group of students discuss their employers' procedures and policies (or ones they have observed as customers) for accepting and cashing checks, traveler's checks, foreign currency, special store redemptions such as bonus points that count toward the purchase of merchandise, and $50 and $100 bills.
Also ask:

- Who must approve checks—a senior sales associate? a department manager?
- What type of identification do the various companies require of customers—picture ID? driver's license number?
- Are third-party checks allowed? Why or why not?

Have each group report their findings to the class.

Case Study

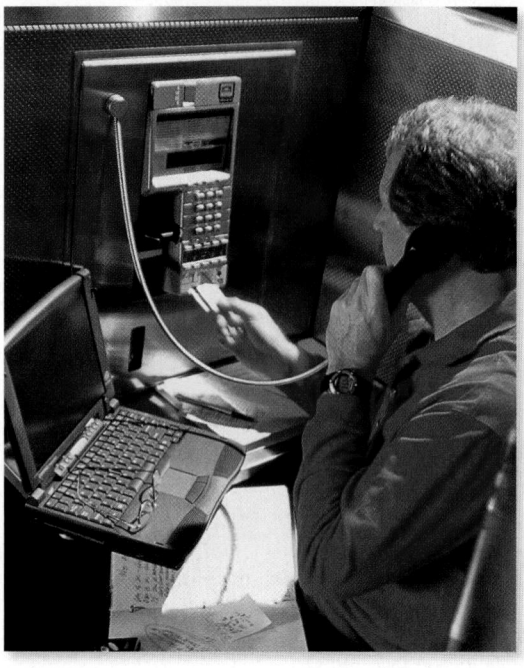

Get Smart!

Everyone is familiar with ATM and credit cards, but are you familiar with smart cards? By the year 2010, smart cards are likely to be as familiar as paper money—and maybe even more common. While they have been popular in Europe and Asia since their invention in France 25 years ago, smart cards are gaining momentum the United States.

Although smart cards look like credit or debit cards, there is a big difference. Credit and debit cards have a magnetic strip with identifying information, while smart cards have computer chips embedded in the plastic. What this means is that a smart card is much more closely related to your personal computer than to your regular VISA card. The tiny microchips embedded in the plastic of a smart card are electronics capable of memory and processing.

The simplest cards have a dollar value attached to them, and the chip records the amount spent and the balance after every purchase. With a more powerful chip, a smart card can be used to download money from a customer's bank account directly into the card's memory. Instead of getting cash from a machine, you "fill up" your card by inserting it into a card reader on a computer or specially equipped phone. Then it can be used like cash to shop in stores or to pay bills over the telephone. The card stores the account information, which you can download into your computer later. Smart cards can also be used for payment of telephone calls, payment of parking and tolls, storage of identification and medical records, and access to satellite television. The use of smart cards addresses many security issues that people have regarding using their credit cards or debit cards when shopping online. Because the smart card stores account information on a computer chip rather than through an account number embossed on a card, it is much more secure from theft.

In 2000, Visa U.S.A. introduced the first smart credit card, which combines the purchasing power of traditional payment cards with smart chip technology. With the growth in e-commerce, technologically enhanced payment products such as the smart credit card will meet the evolving needs of consumers for greater convenience and control over their account information.

Case Study Review

1. Why would online marketers be interested in increasing customer security?
2. How would it benefit banks to have people use smart cards rather than write checks or use cash?

A MATTER OF ETHICS

3. Some smart cards allow marketers to collect data about the customer's spending habits. What ethical concerns does this bring up?

Case Study Review Answers

Get Smart!

1. Increased customer security could lead to an increase in sales—if people are not worried about credit card information being misused, they are more likely to shop online.
2. Smart cards cost banks less, require no paper storage, and allow for faster transactions.

A MATTER OF ETHICS

3. Answers will vary, but students should raise privacy issues regarding smart cards and collecting data about customers' spending habits.

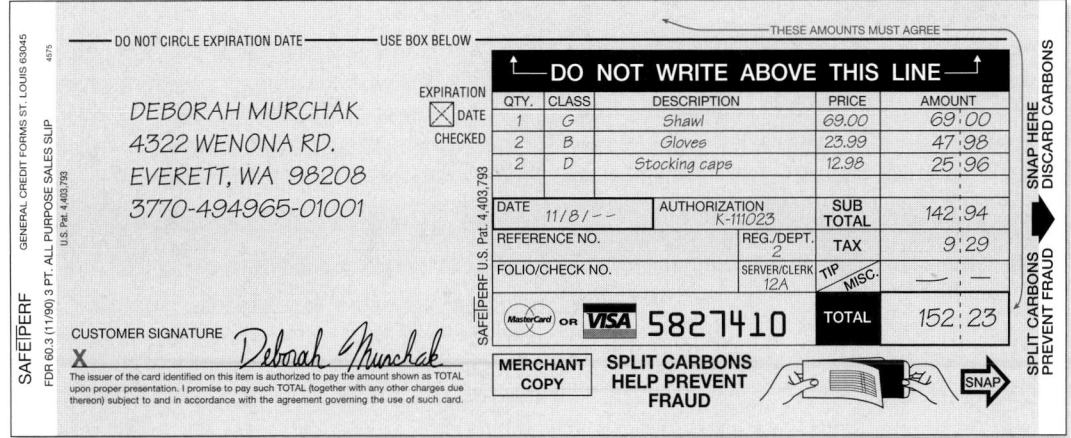

■ **Credit Card Slip** A credit card slip provides information not usually seen on a cash sales check or receipt. *What is that information?*

RECORDING SALES As a salesperson in retail business, you will probably sell merchandise to customers who want to charge their purchases on a credit card. In this case, you will have to know how to complete credit card sales checks. This is not very difficult, since the math calculations are identical to those for a cash transaction.

There are usually at least three copies of each sales check—one for the customer, one for the seller, and one for the bank or credit card agency. You might use a mechanical imprinter to transfer the customer's name and account number to the sales slip, or you might write the information on the sales check by hand.

Some businesses do not use credit card sales checks at all, but instead record all necessary information electronically. Electronic recording of credit card sales is becoming more common.

OBTAINING PAYMENT Credit card sales checks for charges to bank cards (VISA, MasterCard, etc.) may be deposited when you deposit checks in your company account. A special deposit slip must be prepared for the bank so that your accounts are credited quickly.

Copies of sales checks for travel and entertainment cards and oil company credit cards are sent for payment to the company that originated them. It takes longer to turn these charges into cash.

If your company accepts credit cards, it pays a fee to the bank or agency that handles the billing and record keeping. This fee is a percent of credit sales based on a sliding scale. Suppose your store had VISA sales of $100,000 during the same period that another store had VISA sales of only $2,000. Your company would pay a smaller percentage for handling. The handling fee for travel and entertainment cards is usually slightly higher than for bank cards.

PRACTICE 3

Calculate the impact credit card fees would have on the business described below.

1. At Rachel's Gifts, VISA sales are usually between $13,000 and $15,000 per month. The VISA handling charge for $10,000–$14,999 is 3 percent of sales; for $15,000–$19,999, 2.5 percent; and for $20,000–$29,999, 2 percent.

   a. Rachel had $15,500 in VISA sales one month. How much more would she net than if sales were $14,300?

   b. How much would Rachel net in that month if her shop did $21,000 in VISA sales?

2. Rachel has decided to accept the Diner's Club card in her shop. The handling charges are 1 percent higher than for VISA at each sales level. If Rachel had $21,000 in Diner's Club sales, how much more would she pay in handling fees than she does for VISA sales?

3. Rachel had $13,600 in cash sales, $14,800 in Diner's Club sales, and $15,200 in VISA sales one month. What were her net sales after handling charges?

Chapter 16 ■ *Using Math in Sales* **283**

Independent Practice

Research and Discuss Have each student contact two local retailers to find out whether or not they have layaway plans. If the retailers contacted do not offer layaway, have students ask if they have replaced it with such plans as deferred payment or "90 days same as cash." Have students share their findings in class. Afterwards conduct a discussion dealing with how such payment plans increase sales and what problems, if any, they present for retailers.

Did You Know?
What protects electronic payment such as credit or electronic checks against theft? Encryption technology can prevent computer hackers from stealing your account number when you make an online purchase. Merchants and card issuers get the information they need, but the public is prevented from accessing your account number through electronic scrambling.

CAPTION ANSWER
Credit Card Slip The information on a credit card slip includes the name and signature, credit card number, and phone number of the buyer.

Human Relations Skills

L1 Pose this problem to students: You are in a movie theater management training program, and it's a busy Saturday night. A customer tries to use a movie ticket that was included in an entertainment coupon book he recently purchased. However, the book states that such tickets are not to be used on a Saturday night. When you point this out, he says he was unaware of the restriction and wants to see the movie anyway. How would you handle this situation? *(Answers will vary. In this situation, you might allow the customer to use the ticket but explain that you cannot allow this again.)*

L2 Tell students that some people refuse to show identification when asked. Pose this problem: At your co-op training station, you ring up a sale for a man who writes a check for his purchase. When you ask to see his identification, he refuses. How would you handle this situation? *(Answers will vary. Tell the customer that you are following standard store policy and that you must see his ID. If he still refuses, tell him you will take cash. If he says he has no cash and protests, call a manager.)*

▪ Layaway Sales

Merchandise is removed from stock and kept in a separate storage area until the customer pays for it with **layaway**, or will-call. Layaway appeals to many shoppers and increases sales. The customer will make a deposit on the merchandise and agree to pay for the purchase within a certain time period. The customer may have the merchandise when it is fully paid for; if it is not paid for within the agreed-upon time, the goods are returned to stock. Any money paid need not be returned to the customer.

▪ On-Approval Sales

Some department and specialty stores extend a special privilege to their regular customers —**on-approval sale**. This agreement permits a customer to take merchandise (usually clothing) home for further consideration. If the goods are not returned within an agreed-upon time, the sale is final. The customer must then send a check or return to the store to pay for the merchandise. Credit card information may be taken from the customer so that the sale can be processed if the customer keeps the item. This practice is a safe way for retailers to handle on-approval sales because there is much less risk involved.

▪ COD Sales

A **cash on delivery (COD) sale** is a transaction that occurs when a customer pays for merchandise at the time of delivery. Because the customer must be on hand when the merchandise is delivered, however, COD sales are not as efficient as other types of sales transactions.

▪ Returns, Exchanges, and Allowances

A **return** is merchandise brought back for a cash refund or credit. Gifts that do not suit the recipient's taste are one of the most common categories of returns.

An **exchange** is merchandise brought back to be replaced by other merchandise. Items of clothing that are the wrong size or color are commonly exchanged.

An **allowance** is a partial return of the sale price for merchandise that the customer has kept. These are usually given when there is a defect in the merchandise, such as a missing button.

Each of these situations will require you to do a different type of sales transaction. Some businesses adopt a policy of no returns; however, most feel that accepting returns is an important part of good customer relations. Some businesses accept returns

FIGURE 16-4

Refund Slip

Nicky's Dress Shop			REFUND SLIP		
STORE NO.	DATE		ITEM RETURNED	AMOUNT	
	10/20/--		DRESS	89	90
NAME	Deborah Murchak				
ADDRESS	4322 Wenona Rd.				
CITY & STATE	Everett, WA 98208				
TELEPHONE NO.	206-882-0252		TAX	5	84
CUSTOMER'S SIGNATURE	Deborah Murchak		TOTAL AMOUNT	95	74
EMPLOYEE NO. 12A	AUTHORIZED BY K. Allen		REASON FOR RETURN Too small		
			No refunds after 30 days; No refunds without receipt.		

▪ **Refund Slip** Most businesses give customer refunds or exchanges under certain circumstances. *Why would the store insist the customer have a sales receipt before giving a refund?*

FIGURE 16-4 ANSWER
Refund Slip A sales receipt is necessary to be sure the merchandise was purchased at that store and to be sure of the price the customer originally paid.

Fly with the Web

In the "new economy," the nation's airlines are facing more and more competition as Web-based airline ticket brokers, such as Travelocity.com, Expedia.com, and Priceline.com, sell discounted airline tickets online. Airlines have realized that they need to hit the Web to stay competitive. Loyalty marketing programs offering incentives to frequent flyers have become widespread. Many airlines regularly send out e-mails about special fares and sales to frequent fliers and loyal customers. Many airlines now also offer last minute deals, or e-savers, which are fights that customers can book online at discounted prices only days before flying!

Thinking Critically

How can airlines benefit from offering discounts or mileage to customers who book online?

---

but issue credit slips that can be used to pay for other merchandise purchased from the same business instead of a cash refund.

Most businesses are happy to make exchanges because they want their customers to be satisfied. Transactions that involve returning an item for a replacement that is priced the same is an even exchange; if not, it is an uneven exchange.

Suppose Nigel decides he needs a calculator for his personal use but wants a less expensive one than he was given for his birthday. The original calculator was priced at $90 (excluding sales tax), and Nigel wants to exchange it for one priced at $60. You would refund the difference, $30, plus the sales tax on $30. The procedure would be reversed for a customer who wants to exchange an item for one that is more expensive. The customer would pay the extra cost of the exchanged item and the extra sales tax on that amount.

Consider how a sales check is prepared. Each item is not taxed individually in multiple purchases; instead the subtotal is used to calculate the sales tax. When looking at the sales check, simply find the

item being returned, calculate the difference between that item and the item the customer is taking in exchange for the item returned, and tax the difference between the two amounts. The customer already paid tax on the original item. The tax due is on the difference between the two items and is paid by the customer if the customer wants a more expensive item or by the store if the customer wants a less expensive item.

When you refund cash to a customer on a return or an exchange, you will probably have to fill out a refund slip. One of these is shown in Figure 16-4 on page 284.

■ Sales Tax

A sales tax is a fee placed on the sale of goods and services. These rates differ from state to state and combine local and state charges. Local sales and use taxes in addition to the state tax cannot exceed 2 percent. The state tax rate in Texas is 6.25 percent, making the highest possible tax rate 8.25 percent in Texas.

Sales tax is only paid once by the final user; in other words, it does not apply to goods bought for resale. Customers handle the costs of sales taxes. Problems arise with this because the sales tax is *regressive*, meaning that there is a flat rate to be paid by all income levels. It is more of a challenge for a lower-income individual to pay this fee than for someone who makes a higher salary. Sometimes certain items, such as food, clothing, or drugs, may be exempt from sales tax for this reason.

New challenges have developed with the sales tax with the rise in e-commerce. The Federal Commission on Electronic Commerce was created by the Internet Tax Freedom Act of 1998. This limits new laws taxing Internet access and sets standards for taxes for online purchases.

PRACTICE 4

1. Assuming a sales tax rate of 6 percent, find the tax and total amount due for each purchase listed below. Round the tax to the nearest cent.

Item	Price
Tires	$315
Ski Boots	$185
Clock	$105
Books	$110
Washer	$429

Chapter 16 ■ *Using Math in Sales* **285**

Individualized Practice

Human Relations Skills (continued)

L3 Pose this problem to students: You do not work on commission in your co-op job as a retail sales associate. One of the full-time employees, who works on a base salary and commission, constantly asks you to ring your sales on her cash register key so she can get the credit for your sales and thus earn more commission. When you balk at this, she says, "What does it matter to you? You're paid hourly. It doesn't matter how much you sell." How would you handle this situation? *(Answers will vary. However, the employee is asking you to do something dishonest. She would be earning money because of your work. Also, your supervisor is probably monitoring your sales performance which, in turn, will be considered for any future raises or promotions.)*

Electronic Frontiers — Fly with the Web

Answer Airlines benefit from offering discounts to online customers because traffic and business may increase on their Web sites. Airlines stay competitive by offering special fares and mileage on the Web.

Reteaching

1. **Vocabulary** Assign and review the vocabulary terms for this section.
2. **Fact and Idea** Assign and review Fact and Idea Review questions 5–8 from the Chapter Assessment.
3. **Section Concepts** Review with students the major concepts in this section so they understand the various types of sales transactions.

Enrichment

1. **Review** Assign and review the appropriate Thinking Critically questions from the Chapter Assessment.
2. **Review** Assign and review the following Chapter Assessment activities: Building Workplace Skills, Applying Marketing Concepts, Linking School to Work Activities, DECA Connection, and Internet Connection.
3. **Extend** Assign and review the corresponding activities from the *School-to-Work Activity Workbook.* iLP
4. **Calculate** Have each student create one math problem related to any of the concepts in this lesson (for example, multiplying unit price by quantity, figuring sales tax, or determining the unit price on one item when merchandise is sold in multiple quantities). Have students work in pairs to solve each other's problems.

■ Shipping Charges

Most retailers use the United Parcel Service (UPS), Federal Express, or the U.S. Postal Service to deliver merchandise. Because delivery charges are generally exempt from sales tax, they are added after the sales tax has been calculated.

PARCEL POST The cost of shipping merchandise depends on the service used, the weight of the shipment, and the distance it is being sent. Parcel post is one type of standard surface package delivery that is offered by the U.S. Postal Service. Parcel post is a good option if you take your packages to the post office and your customer is willing to wait for delivery.

When you ship COD, the postal carrier will collect the amount due and forward it to your company. Your company must prepay the shipping charges; however, the amount due to the customer may include both the totals for merchandise and shipping costs. The customer must pay a fee for the COD service, which varies depending on the amount collected. Up to $500 may be collected on delivery by a postal carrier.

Many businesses prefer using United Parcel Service for COD shipments. This is because UPS does not limit the amount that can be collected at delivery to $500 and the shipping charges do not have to be prepaid.

EXPRESS MAIL When you need to ship something fast, you may use the express mail service provided by the U.S. Postal Service. This faster delivery service, of course, costs more. A number of private parcel carriers also provide such service. They include Federal Express, UPS, Airborne Express, DHL Worldwide Express, and Emery Worldwide Courier.

All of these private package delivery companies compete vigorously with each other and with the U.S. Postal Service for the overnight delivery market. This market is extremely competitive, and the various package delivery firms try to outdo each other in regard to price, pickup and delivery time and speed, tracking technology, and customer service.

PRACTICE 5

How much will be returned to or paid by the customer in each of the following cases? Assume a sales tax rate of 7 percent.

1. Mrs. Smith returned a $150 dress that was too large and selected a smaller size in another style priced at $115. How much will you return to her?

2. Mr. Jordan returned a $45 radio because it was apparently defective. He selected another model priced at $75. How much more will you charge him?

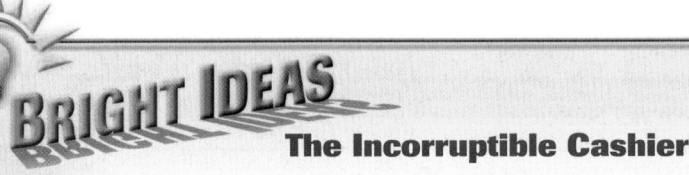

BRIGHT IDEAS

The Incorruptible Cashier

Cash registers are commonplace in most businesses, from large retail stores and neighborhood ice cream shops; but, it wasn't always this way. James Ritty invented the first mechanical cashier in 1884, receiving a patent under his company name of National Manufacturing. That same year, John H. Patterson recognized that Ritty's invention provided security and saved time. He bought out Ritty and the patent rights, then launched the National Cash Register Company (NCR) to manufacture and sell cash registers. The invention—nicknamed the "Incorruptible Cashier"— came complete with the familiar bell ringing referred to in advertising as "The Bell Heard Round the World". Patterson improved upon the patent by attaching a paper roll that kept track of transactions. In 1906, an electronic motor was added to the cash register to increase efficiency.

Thinking Creatively

The "Incorruptible Cashier" was revered for time saving and security. How might employers screen applicants to be able to meet their security needs?

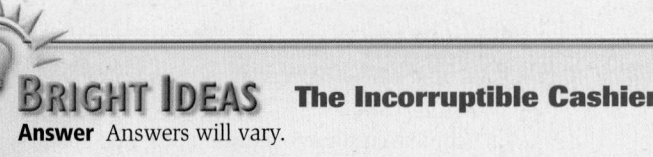

BRIGHT IDEAS   The Incorruptible Cashier
Answer Answers will vary.

Answers to Practice Sets

PRACTICE 1 (PAGE 276)

1. Four pennies, a dime, a quarter, two $1 bills (or a $2 bill), a $5 bill, and a $20 bill. Note: If customer has the penny (for the $.61), then a nickel could substitute for the four pennies.

2. Ask if customer has $.09 in change or at least a dime.

3. By disregarding the exact change provided, the cashier is less likely to get confused. Disregard the $.15 and simply say "That's $27 out of $40; $28, $29, $30 (giving back three $1 bills, one at a time); and $40 (giving back $10).

4. "That's $13.63 out of $20.75; $.64, $.65 (handing off two pennies), $.75 (handing a dime)"; then say, "That leaves $13 out of $20; $14, $15 (handing off two $1 bills), and $20 (handing off a $5 bill)." By tendering the $.75, the customer reduces the amount of small change to be returned to him.

PRACTICE 2 (PAGE 279)

1. Vests $850; footballs $79.75; clocks $291.50; irons $799

2. $2,020.25

3. $.37

4. $8.17

PRACTICE 3 (PAGE 283)

1. a. $1,241.50

   b. $20,580

2. $210

3. $42,628

PRACTICE 4 (PAGE 285)

1. Tires $333.90; boots $196.10; clock $111.30; books $116.60; washer $454.74

PRACTICE 5 (PAGE 286)

1. $37.45

2. $32.10

SECTION 16.2

Evaluation
Assign and review the Section 16.2 Assessment.

Technology Resources

Assessment Resources
Go to the *Marketing Essentials* Web site (**www.marketing.glencoe.com**) for resources to teach and assess occupation-specific vocabulary.

CLOSE

Section Wrap-Up
Have students summarize in at least 50 words why they feel that conducting retail sales transactions accurately and efficiently is good customer service.

16.2 ASSESSMENT

Reviewing Key Terms and Concepts

1. How is a credit card sale different from a debit card sale? A will-call sale? An on-approval sale?

2. What is the difference between a return and exchange?

3. Kim is considering the purchase of a new guitar for $950, plus $24 shipping. The state sales tax is 8 percent. How would Kim go about figuring the total purchase amount?

Thinking Critically

4. People have suggested that as more buyers use debit cards, checks will become obsolete. Do you think this is likely? Why or why not?

Integrating Academic Skills

5. **MATH** A department store offers a 20 percent discount to senior citizens. If your grandmother purchased items at $17.99, $15.95, and $3.59, what would be her total bill, assuming the sales tax rate is five percent?

16.2 ASSESSMENT ANSWERS

Reviewing Key Terms and Concepts

1. Credit sale involves later payment; debit sale creates immediate deduction from bank account. Credit sale gives immediate possession with later payment; will-call sale gives later possession after gradual payment. Credit sale involves deciding to buy before possession; on-approval sale involves deciding after possession.

2. A return is merchandise returned for a cash refund or credit; an exchange is merchandise replaced with other merchandise.

3. $950 x 0.08 = $1,026 + $24 = $1,050

Thinking Critically

4. Answers will vary.

Integrating Academic Skills

5. **MATH** ($17.99 + $15.95 + $3.59) – .20 = $30.02.

SECTION 16.3

Purchase Orders and Invoices

What You'll Learn

- To calculate and verify extensions on purchase orders and invoices
- To use appropriate tables to determine shipping charges

Why It's Important

In this section, you will learn some math applications that are regularly used by buyers and vendors. In many marketing jobs, including sales, you will need to understand the costs and methods of shipping.

Key Terms

- purchase order
- extension
- invoice

Business-to-Business Sales

Much of the math that a buyer does in business-to-business sales is for purchase orders; for vendors, the comparable form is the invoice. The calculations for both forms are very similar to those performed by retail salespeople on sales checks.

■ Purchase Orders

To place an order, most companies prepare a **purchase order (PO)**, a legal contract between the buyer and the supplier. The PO lists the quantity, price, and description of the products ordered, along with the terms of payment and delivery. In Figure 16-5 on page 289, notice the information routinely included in a purchase order:

- *Item number*—the vendor's catalog designation that identifies the merchandise being ordered
- *Quantity*—the number of units ordered
- *Description*—what is being ordered
- *Unit*—how the item is packaged and priced (individually, by the dozen, by the ream, etc.)
- *Unit cost*—the price per unit
- *Total*—the **extension**, or result of multiplying the number of units by the cost per unit

Note that if you order several items on the same purchase order, the total of all extensions is entered at the bottom of the Total column. This amount is used to compute any sales tax.

■ Invoices

When filling an order based on a PO, a vendor will include an **invoice** with the delivered merchandise. The invoice in Figure 16-6 on page 290 uses check marks to indicate that the information has been checked for accuracy. The invoice numbers and amounts are correct when they match the PO and other documents, as are the extensions.

Notice the entries at the bottom of the invoice. In addition to the merchandise total (or subtotal), there are also places for sales tax, shipping charges, and the amount to be paid by the customer.

In Figure 16-6, Mountain-Air pays the tax because its purchases are clearly intended for business purposes; if it purchased ten bikes for resale, however, there would be no sales tax entry. The sales tax would be paid by the customers.

Regardless of the nature of its purchases, Mountain-Air is entitled to take advantage of the specified payment terms (2/10, N30). Note, however, that discounts apply only to merchandise—shipping charges are not discounted.

FIGURE 16-5

Purchase Order

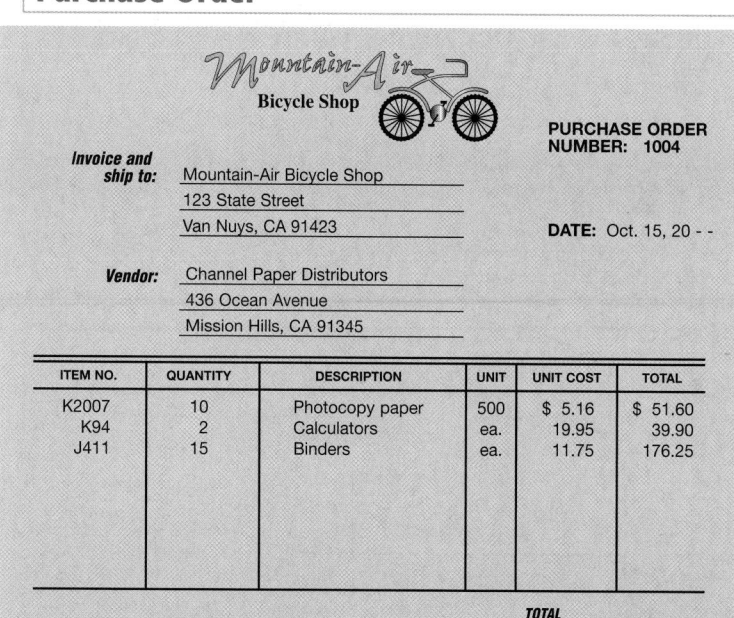

Concept Development

1. Read Section 16.3 with students.
2. For those students still experiencing difficulties with basic math skills, your procedure for teaching should include a great deal of guided practice and comprehension checking.
3. You may wish to have representatives of the U.S. Postal Service, FedEx, and UPS talk to students as a panel about the various services that each company provides, including corporate discount rates.

Discussion Starter

Shipping Have students discuss some ways that such services as Express Mail, UPS, and FedEx have changed the way companies do business. *(Answers will vary. Express mail services have enabled companies to do business more efficiently. They can send and receive merchandise more quickly. It generates more business by better satisfying customers' wants and needs.)*

Thinking Critically

Post Office Service Ask students why post-office-to-post-office service costs less. *(It saves the carrier the trip to the addressee's home or place of business.)*

Cooperative Learning

Design and Calculate Design a worksheet with problems in each of the areas covered in this lesson. Have students complete the worksheets in cooperative groups, including below-level, on-level, and above-level students in each group. Reward the groups whose members are all able to describe the steps taken to calculate each problem.

■ **Purchase Order** A purchase order is a legal contract between buyer and seller. *How would you determine the extension cost of an item from its unit cost?*

■ Dating Terms

Dating terms state when a bill must be paid and the discount permitted for paying early. Ordinary dating occurs when the dating terms are based on the invoice date. Consider, for example, ordinary dating of 2/10, net 30. It specifies the percent of discount permitted for paying early (2 percent), the number of days the buyer has to take advantage of the discount (10 days), and the number of days within which the invoice must be paid (30 days).

■ Shipping

Part of the selling arrangement negotiated between the buyer and seller involves delivery—specifically who will pay and when change of title (ownership) will take place. Both of those issues are part of the agreement between the buyer and seller in business-to-business sales.

The terms for delivery are all variations of F.O.B. (free on board). There are four options:

- *F.O.B. destination*—The title or ownership of the goods remains with the seller until the goods reach their destination. The seller pays transportation charges and is responsible for the condition of the goods until they arrive to the buyer.
- *F.O.B. shipping point*—The buyer pays the shipping costs and is responsible for losses for damages that occur in transit.
- *F.O.B. factory freight prepaid*—The goods become the buyer's property. However, the seller pays for shipping.
- *F.O.B. destination charges reversed*—The merchandise becomes the buyer's when goods are received. The buyer pays for transportation, but if the goods are lost or damaged in transit, the buyer's investment is protected.

Chapter 16 ■ *Using Math in Sales* **289**

FIGURE 16-5 ANSWER
Purchase Order You can multiply the number of units by the unit cost to determine the extension cost.

ASSESS

Reteaching

1. **Vocabulary** Assign and review the vocabulary terms for this section.
2. **Fact and Idea** Assign and review Fact and Idea Review questions 9–10 from the Chapter Assessment.

Enrichment

1. **Review** Assign and review the Chapter 16 activities in the *Student Activity Workbook*.
2. **Review** Assign and review the appropriate Thinking Critically questions from the Chapter Assessment.

Evaluation

Assign and review the Section 16.3 Assessment.

Technology Resources

 Assessment Resources Go to the *Marketing Essentials* Web site (**www.marketing.glencoe. com**) for resources to teach and assess occupation-specific vocabulary.

CLOSE

Section Wrap-Up

Have students complete these statements: (1) Much of the math that a buyer does is for . . . *(purchase orders.)* (2) Much of the math that a vendor does is for . . . *(invoices.)*

FIGURE 16-6 ANSWER
Invoices The terms of the sale, including any discounts, shipping information, and the date and place of shipment.

FIGURE 16-6

Invoice

 CHANNEL PAPER DISTRIBUTORS

SOLD TO: Mountain-Air Bicycle Shop
123 State Street
Van Nuys, CA 91423

INVOICE NO: K5005
DATE: Oct. 24, 20 - -

YOUR ORDER NO.	DATE SHIPPED	SHIPPED VIA	FOB	TERMS
1004	10/24/- -	UPS	M. HILLS	2/10, N30

ITEM NO.	QUANTITY	DESCRIPTION	UNIT	UNIT COST	TOTAL
K2007 ✓	10 ✓	Photocopy paper ✓	500	$ 5.16 ✓	$ 51.60 ✓
K94 ✓	2 ✓	Calculators ✓	ea.	19.95 ✓	39.90 ✓
J411 ✓	15 ✓	Binders ✓	ea.	11.75 ✓	176.25 ✓

TOTAL AMOUNT:	$ 267.75 ✓
TAX	22.09 ✓
UPS	14.22 ✓
TOTAL:	$ 304.06 ✓

■ **Invoices** The vendor (seller) prepares an invoice based on the buyer's purchase order. *What categories of information does an invoice include that are missing from a purchase order?*

16.3 ASSESSMENT

Reviewing Key Terms and Concepts

1. Who prepares a purchase order?
2. A customer orders six triple packs of adhesive tape at $1.79 each—6 × $1.79 on your invoice. What term describes this calculation?
3. What is the meaning of the letters F.O.B. in terms of delivery?

Thinking Critically

4. How could using a computer to generate invoices save time?

Integrating Academic Skills

5. **COMMUNICATION** You are the buyer for a men's retail clothing store. There have been repeated requests for a certain brand of trousers, but your manager doesn't like doing business with the company that makes them. Use your word processing program to write a memo to your manager describing the increased sales that would result if you were allowed to buy these trousers.

16.3 ASSESSMENT ANSWERS

Reviewing Key Terms and Concepts

1. A purchase order is prepared by a buyer and supplier.
2. extension
3. free on board

Thinking Critically

4. A computer can calculate the extensions, subtotals, and totals, and merge information from various databases, instantly updating customer records.

Integrating Academic Skills

5. **COMMUNICATION** Memos will vary depending on student hypotheses.

Careers in Marketing

FOOD MARKETING

Danielle Ellis
Cashier
Fresh Fields

What does your job entail?

"I handle money—ringing up groceries, making change, and processing credit and debit cards. I must always greet customers with a smile and ensure customer satisfaction. In the year that I have worked here, I have mastered the register, which is especially important during the 'crunch times.' Saturdays, Sundays, and Mondays are our busiest days, and with the number of people that we have coming through the lines, things can get crazy. It is necessary to keep your focus. I also have to be comfortable handling the customer service desk and bagging groceries when we are short-staffed."

What kind of training did you have?

"I started working here bagging groceries for customers. I volunteered often, which helped me learn the skills required for working as a cashier. I also showed enthusiasm and learned all of the codes for the register on my spare time. When it came my time to train as a cashier, my supervisors found that I didn't need much training at all."

What skills are most important?

"Two of the most important skills to my job are math and problem solving. When things are hectic, you must concentrate on the numbers and make sure you give out the right change. There are also times when a customer might disagree with a price on a certain item and you have to make sure that they don't think that you don't know how to do your job."

What is your key to success?

"The secret to my success is 'the customer is always right, even when they are wrong.' You have to be strong and handle rude comments when they come your way. You encounter many different customers every day, which can be draining. Despite that, working here is a wonderful experience because while you occasionally encounter mean people, you also work with some truly wonderful people."

Thinking Critically
How might technology affect those who work as cashiers?

Career Facts

Education and Training: Employers prefer high school graduates with experience in cash handling and clerical skills. Recommended courses include marketing, business math, accounting, data processing and communication. Training on the job is usually informal, but some employers may have established programs; vocational schools also provide formal training.

Aptitudes, Abilities, and Skills: Good arithmetic skills, ability to work well with the public, a friendly personality, and appropriate hand-eye coordination skills are a must. Cashiering involves standing for long hours in a confined area and performing repetitive tasks.

Career Outlook: The outlook is expected to be average through the year 2006. Jobs will be affected by technological changes, including online shopping and self check-out equipment.

Career Path: Many cashiers begin working at lower-level jobs, stocking shelves or carrying groceries, or working part-time while attending school. Cashiers may be promoted to supervisory positions, or with further education, to management positions.

Careers in Marketing

Ask a student to read the Careers in Marketing feature aloud to the class. Discuss the skills and aptitudes required for a career in food marketing. Ask students whether they think they would like or dislike a career in food marketing. Discuss the pros and cons of such a career.

Thinking Critically Answer
It may simplify the job with electronic scanning wands, computerized cash registers, and other innovations.

Guest Speakers
Invite a cashier to class to discuss his/her job and factors he/she considers when making marketing decisions.

Exploring Careers

Discounts and Sales Tax
Explain to students that math is one of the skills salespeople must use every day. Have students calculate the discounted prices with sales tax for the following items:
1. Model Clothing is offering $50 casual shirts on sale at 10 percent off during the Back-to-School Daze Sale. Local sales tax is 8.5 percent. How much will the customer have to pay for two shirts? *($50 x .10 = $5; $50 - $5 = $45; $45 x 2 = $90; $90 x 1.085 = $97.65)*
2. The once-a-year holiday sale at X-treme Outfitters is being advertised in the local newspaper. All snowboards, surfboards, and skateboards are on sale at a 25-percent discount. Local sales tax is 7 percent. How much will the customer pay for a Zoom Baby skateboard that usually sells for $65? *($65 x .25 = $16.25; $65 - $16.25 = $48.75; $48.75 x 1.07 = $52.16)*

Lifelong Learning

Using Math in Sales
Most students are already active retail purchasers, but the information in this chapter acquaints them with the seller's side of the process. Learning the math involved in a sales transaction can help students audit the work of salesclerks before they leave a check stand or register. They can also develop lifelong habits of double-checking receipts.

Meeting Individual Needs

Students with Learning Disabilities
Students with learning disabilities may have trouble with symbols, such as numbers. Some students can more easily access the information when it is read aloud in-person or on tape. Students who have difficulty communicating through printing or cursive writing may prefer to use a computer to perform calculations or to dictate their work to another person.

Vocabulary Review

Explanations will vary. See Glossary for definitions.

Fact and Idea Review

1. information about department, type of transaction, salesperson, amount of sale, amount tendered, and change due
2. manual key entry, electronic wand entry, and optical scanning
3. It is a bar code that can be read by a scanner.
4. accuracy and speed
5. driver's license and one other form of identification
6. It authorizes the amount of a purchase to be debited from one's bank account.
7. It is an electronic device that reads data encoded on credit cards and transmits it for immediate approval or disapproval of a purchase.
8. In most states, food, prescription drugs, and shipping charges are exempt from sales taxes.
9. quantity, price, prescription of the products, and terms of payment and delivery
10. Dating terms usually state when a bill must be paid and the discount permitted for paying early.

Thinking Critically

1. A store might use it as a basis for relationship marketing—to announce sales, or target certain merchandise to specific customers. It could also be used as a marketing research tool.
2. It could constantly update inventory status with sales check data and eliminate the need for a physical count.
3. It might make customers more cautious in their purchase decisions and thus may discourage sales.
4. Some advantages are: stations reduce labor costs and crime risk; customers don't have to carry cash; and customers can fill up more quickly. Some disadvantages are: stations become more dependent on computer technology that could break down; business may lose money as a result of discounting; and customers might miss human touch.
5. saved time and less paperwork

VOCABULARY REVIEW

Study each pair of terms and then, in your own words, tell how they are related to each other.

- UPC—UVM code
- till—opening cash fund
- layaway—will-call
- sales transaction—exchange
- cash sale—personal check
- debit card—PIN
- credit sale—floor limit
- return—allowance
- on-approval sale—COD sale
- purchase order—invoice

FACT AND IDEA REVIEW

1. What information does a cash register provide about a sale? (16.1)
2. List the three methods of entering information into electronic cash registers. (16.1)
3. What is a UPC? (16.1)
4. What two factors are important to the customer about the way you make change? (16.1)
5. When a customer pays for a purchase by check, what else is he or she usually asked to supply? (16.2)
6. How is an ATM card used as a debit card? (16.2)
7. What is an electronic credit authorizer? (16.2)
8. What items are usually exempt from sales tax? (16.2)
9. What information is usually listed on a purchase order? (16.3)
10. What are dating terms? (16.3)

THINKING CRITICALLY

1. Why would a store want a list of all its customers' names and addresses?
2. How could having a POS system make taking inventory easier?
3. How do you think a no-return policy would affect sales in a store?
4. A gas station allows customers to pay for gas using debit or credit cards. Customers pump their own gas and use an electronic pay point near the pump to pay. They never directly interact with a station employee. What advantages and disadvantages might there be to allowing customers to complete sales without help?
5. Some businesses use combination purchase order/invoice forms. What advantages would there be to this?

BUILDING WORKPLACE SKILLS

1. **Human Relations** You work as a cashier, and today has been exceptionally busy. You give change to a woman for a $10 bill. She claims she gave you a $20 bill. Unfortunately, you neglected to leave the bill out while making change. How would you handle this situation?
2. **Technology** You work as a cashier in a children's clothing store where an old-fashioned cash register requires entering the amount of each sale by hand. The owner of the store has asked you to research what POS systems would be appropriate for the store and how much these systems cost. Use the Internet to do this research. Then use your word processing program to prepare a report.

Building Workplace Skills

1. Answers will vary depending on store policy.
2. Reports will vary.

Applying Marketing Concepts

1. Increased labor costs and better inventory control could contribute to profit.
2. Reports will vary; however, the following ideas should be included. When a scanner's laser beam hits the light reflected by the white spaces in a bar code, a photo diode in the scanner decodes the reflected light into an electric signal. This is translated into a digital code by the scanner's microprocessor. That code is then fed into the store's main computer, which finds the price. There are 12 digits in a U.P.C. code. The first represents the general category of the product; the next five, the product's manufacturer; the next five the individual item, and finally, a 'check digit' that is used to make sure the code has been scanned correctly.
3. Reports will vary.
4. Spreadsheets will vary.
5. Answers will vary.

APPLYING MARKETING CONCEPTS

1. **Researching Optical Scanners** Use the Internet to research information on grocery store conversion to optical scanners. Use a word processor to write a report that describes how the increased speed and accuracy of these systems affect a grocery store's profits.

2. **Understanding UPC Codes** Use the World Wide Web to research what the bars and numbers in a UPC represent. Prepare an oral report using presentation software to present your findings to the class.

3. **Preventing Profit Loss** Discuss the ways that a store manager might train employees to prevent loss through credit card fraud, bad checks, and counterfeit currency. Use presentation software to prepare an oral report on this topic.

4. **Comparing Purchase Order and Invoice Forms** Ask several local businesses for copies of their purchase orders and invoice forms. Use a spreadsheet program to compare the formats based on ease of use.

5. **Comparing Sales Tax Rates** Choose five different states and research the sales tax rates that are applied there. See if you can find any states that don't have any sales tax. Create a chart using a spreadsheet program comparing these rates.

LINKING SCHOOL TO WORK

Basic and Thinking Skills Inquire about the payment methods customers prefer at local businesses. Specifically, try to determine what percentage of customers use cash, debit cards, personal checks, and credit cards. Compare your findings with other class members, and discuss why you think different payment methods are used depending on the type of business.

Role Play: Cashier

Situation You are to assume the role of newly hired cashier at a music and video store. Your job will include completing sales using cash, checks, and credit and debit cards.

Activity You must demonstrate to the store manager (judge) that you are competent at accurately completing transactions. Assume a customer purchased a DVD movie for $29.95 and there is a 6% sales tax on that item.

Evaluation You will be evaluated on how well you meet the following performance indicators:
- Calculate charges
- Process sales documentation
- Prepare simple written reports

inter **NET** CONNECTION

Selling Online
You are in charge of setting up the retail sales end of your company's Web site.

Connect
- Research the ease of buying and customer privacy protection at a variety of popular e-tailers.
- Select the company with the most customer-friendly procedure.
- Write a report detailing your findings, focusing on the strategies you thought were the most successful.

Chapter 16 ■ *Using Math in Sales* **293**

Students should be evaluated on the performance indicators noted in the Role Play.
- For another DECA Role Play, go to the *Student Activity Workbook,* p. 133.
- For more in-depth Role Play practice, refer to DECA's *Essential Competitive Events Handbook.* To order, contact DECA at www.deca.org.

*inter*NET CONNECTION

Results will vary.

Mini Quiz
Administer the Mini Quiz orally. For an expanded chapter quiz, go to page 85 of the *Reproducible Tests* book.

1. Two types of widely used codes for electronic entry are the UPC and the UVM.
2. Coins and currency designated for the register for a given day's business are collectively called the opening cash fund.
3. The floor limit is the maximum amount a salesperson may allow a customer to charge without getting special authorization.
4. A(n) purchase order is a legal contract between the buyer and the supplier.
5. In ordinary dating of 2/10, net 30, the 2 represents percent of discount permitted for paying early.

Linking School to Work
Answers will vary.

1. **Assessment** Have students complete the Reproducible Tests for Chapter 16 and Unit 5 or construct your own tests using the ExamView software.
2. **Enrichment** Have students complete the corresponding activities in the following workbooks:
   - *Marketing Math Workbook,* p. 31
   - *Marketing Research Project Workbook,* p. 65

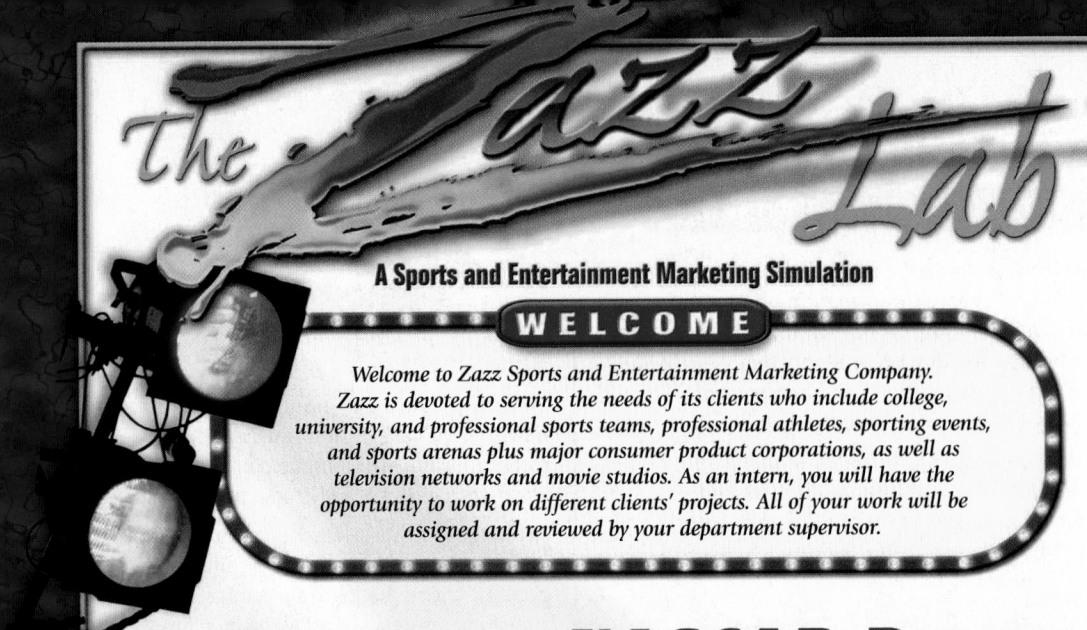

the Zazz Lab...

A Sports and Entertainment Marketing Simulation

WELCOME

Welcome to Zazz Sports and Entertainment Marketing Company. Zazz is devoted to serving the needs of its clients who include college, university, and professional sports teams, professional athletes, sporting events, and sports arenas plus major consumer product corporations, as well as television networks and movie studios. As an intern, you will have the opportunity to work on different clients' projects. All of your work will be assigned and reviewed by your department supervisor.

SPONSOR A NASCAR DRIVER

SITUATION

Jose Ramirez, a professional race car driver involved with NASCAR, is one of Zazz's newest clients. Your job is to secure a primary sponsor or several companies that will sponsor the Jose Ramirez Car. NASCAR hopes to attract new spectators and Hispanic fans with this outgoing, charismatic, bilingual race car driver.

ASSIGNMENT

Your challenge is to raise a minimum of $1 million for the new client, the cost for him to race in this year's racing series. Jose will be driving a Ford Taurus as a member of the Tony Pessolano Race Team. You can sell space on any part of the driver's suit, pit crew's uniforms, or auto (hood, dashboard, spoiler, doors, front fender, rear quarter panels). You can also sell sponsored merchandise and arrange personal service contracts, including retail point-of-purchase material, TV commercials, or public appearances. Sponsors must be category exclusive (you cannot sell McDonald's and Burger King sponsorships on the same car) and must represent different categories of goods and services.

Your supervisor wants you to develop a sales training manual with a Ramirez-specific feature-benefit table and script for telephone solicitation of potential sponsors. Additionally, you have been asked to generate a list of potential sponsorship leads, taking into consideration the demographics of Jose's and NASCAR's fan base. To demonstrate your selling skills, your supervisor expects you to role play your complete sales presentation. Use your sales training manual as the basis of the role play and incorporate a computer presentation.

Tools and Resources

To complete this assignment you will need to conduct research at a library or on the Internet. You will also need a word processing program, a spreadsheet program, and presentation software. Helpful trade publications include *Brandweek*, *Advertising Age*, *Sports Business Journal*, *Sports Business Daily*, *Team Marketing Report*, *Motorsports Sponsor FactBook*, and *National Speed Sport News*.

Research

Research NASCAR drivers, sponsorships, and fans. To generate a list of potential sponsors, research consumer products and companies that target the same market, as well as identify untapped markets. Research sponsorship agreements for other race car drivers so you can develop selling points that you can use to create a feature-benefit chart.

MORE ABOUT MOTORSPORT

Motorsport is growing in popularity both nationally and internationally. Currently it is the largest and fastest growing spectator sport in the USA and is surpassed only by soccer internationally. Over 40 percent of the spectators are women; 53 percent of the spectators earn over $50,000 a year; and fans often travel as much as 300 miles one way to attend a race.

Historically, international venues have included Monaco, Le Mans, and Brands Hatch. Some sponsors spend upward of $10 million domestically and $20 million internationally for team sponsorship rights—but those figures do not include the price of driver product endorsements.

Report

Prepare a written sales training manual, a computer presentation for the sales presentation, and a telephone script to qualify prospects. Use a word processing program to prepare the double-spaced documents. The feature-benefit chart in the sales training manual should be in table format. Arrange your written report around the following headings:

- Plan to generate $1 million
  - Strategy (one sponsor vs. many sponsors)
  - What's for sale?
- Prospecting
  - Rationale for selection of prospects
  - List of suggested leads (minimum of 20)
  - Telephone script for use in qualifying prospects
- Sales training manual
  - Introduction
  - Feature-benefit chart for Jose Ramirez
  - Sample approach dialogue
  - Determining needs
    - Observations that should be made
    - Sample dialogue to demonstrate good listening skills and effective questioning techniques
  - Product presentation
    - Two sample selling sentences
    - Suggested sales aids
    - Demonstration of selling points
    - Involvement of customer in presentation
  - Handling objections
    - Two potential objections
    - Suggested answers to potential objections
  - Closing the sale
    - Suggested closing methods (minimum of two)
    - Sample dialogue to demonstrate closing methods
  - Suggestion selling
    - Suggested products or services
    - Sample dialogue to suggest additional product or service
  - Relationship marketing
    - Suggested follow-up strategies

Using computer presentation software, prepare a presentation of your ideas for the client that includes:

- Key selling points
- Graphic illustrations and/or figures
- Very little text
- A minimum of 10 slides

Presentation and Evaluation

Present your ideas in a written report and an oral presentation. In your oral presentation, conduct a role play that demonstrates how to utilize the telephone script to qualify prospects and a role play for a salesperson calling on a prospective sponsor. You will be evaluated on your selling and oral presentation skills, including:

- Knowledge of motorsports, especially NASCAR
- Demonstration of effective selling techniques
- Ability to communicate with prospects
- Ability to handle questions and objections
- Continuity of presentation
- Voice quality
- Body language and eye contact

 Portfolio . . . .

Print a copy of your completed report and presentation for your Portfolio.

CONNECTION

DECA Business Services Marketing Series
Selling sponsorships for a professional race car driver could be a potential role play in this event.

DECA Marketing Management Series
Developing a sales training plan for the sale of sponsorships could be a role play in this event.

DECA Hospitality and Recreation Marketing Research Event
Researching potential sponsors and developing an effective sales presentation for the sale of sponsorships could be a topic for this event.

DECA Sports and Entertainment Marketing Management Team Decision-Making Event
Working on this project with a partner will make the experience similar to what is expected in a DECA Team Decision-Making Event.

The Zazz Lab **295**

COOPERATIVE LEARNING

Teamwork This unit lab lends itself to working in teams of three to four students. Have teams collaborate on preparing the written report by assigning each member part of the research required to understand NASCAR and its drivers, as well as its fans and sponsors. Have teams brainstorm ideas for preparation of the sales plan and sales training manual, as well as the computer presentation to be used as part of the actual sales presentation.

Promotion

Chapter 17
Promotional Concepts and Strategies

Chapter 18
Visual Merchandising and Display

Chapter 19
Advertising

Chapter 20
Preparing Print Advertisements

Unit Objectives

After completing this unit, students will be able to:

- Explain the promotional mix concept and its role in marketing.
- Discuss trade and consumer sales promotions.
- Explain the nature and scope of public relations.
- Write a news release.
- Discuss the elements of visual merchandising and the artistic aspects of creating a display.
- Explain the purpose and importance of advertising.
- Identify the different types of advertising media.
- Calculate media costs.
- Prepare print advertising.

Enrichment Resources

Books
50 Trade Secrets of Great Design Retail Spaces by Stafford Cliff
Hey, Whipple, Squeeze This: A Guide to Creating Great Ads by Luke Sullivan
Truth, Lies, and Advertising: The Art of Account Planning by Jon Steel

Magazines/Journals
Advertising Age
AdWeek
Promo: The Magazine for Promotional Marketing

Associations
Advertising Research Foundation
641 Lexington Avenue
New York, NY 10022
(212) 751-5656
www.arfsite.org

Direct Marketing Association
1120 Avenue of the Americas
New York, NY 10036-6700
(212) 768-7277
www.the-dma.org

Journal Writing Activity

1. You may provide a supply of magazines and newspapers for this activity. Ask students to find a magazine or newspaper ad that they consider to be persuasive. Have each student copy or paste the ad in their journal. Ask students to write in their journals and identify the target audience of their chosen ads. Then have students evaluate the strengths of their ads according to these elements: headline, good copy or selling message, illustration or photo, signature, and overall layout of the ad. Have students share their journal entries with the class.

2. Ask students to find a magazine or newspaper ad that they think is ineffective. Have each student copy or paste the ad in their journal. Ask them to write in their journals and identify the target audience of their ads. Then have students evaluate the shortcomings of their ads according to these elements: headline, good copy or selling message, illustration or photo, signature, and overall layout of the ad. Have students share their journal entries with the class.

TEACHER CLASSROOM RESOURCES

Program Resources	Chapter 17	Chapter 18	Chapter 19	Chapter 20
Student Activity Workbook	p. 141	p. 149	p. 159	p. 169
Marketing Math Workbook	p. 45	p. 45	p. 45	p. 45
Marketing Research Project Workbook	p. 85	p. 85	p. 85	p. 85
School-to-Work Activity Workbook	p. 69	p. 77	p. 81	p. 85
BusinessWeek Case Studies	p. 109	p. 115	p. 121	p. 127
Marketing Career Portfolio	p. 36	p. 36	p. 36	p. 36
Reproducible Tests	p. 95	p. 99	p. 105	p. 111
ExamView User's Guide and Testbank	p. 17-1	p. 18-1	p. 19-1	p. 20-1
Internet Resources	p. 53	p. 55	p. 57	p. 59
Blackline Masters	p. 33	p. 34	p. 35	p. 37
Lesson Plans	p. 36	p. 39	p. 41	p. 43
Block Scheduling	p. 6	p. 6	p. 6	p. 6
Impact! Simulation	p. 61	p. 61	p. 61	p. 61

 Each of these resources is available in print and on the Interactive Lesson Planner CD-ROM.

Technology Resources

- **Interactive Lesson Planner (ILP) CD-ROM**
- **PowerPoint Presentation CD-ROM**
- **Marketing Essentials Web site**
- **ExamView! CD-ROM**
- **Impact! Simulation**

Virtual Business

Virtual Business is a fully visual marketing and business simulation that introduces students to the principles of marketing by letting them start and run their own virtual businesses. In *Virtual Business*, students have the power to control all aspects of a retail convenience store. Students strategize marketing decisions using a powerful learning tool in the guise of a video game. They learn by experiencing how their decisions affect their virtual business.

Key to Individualized Academics Activities

L1 Level 1 activities are basic activities and should fall within the range of all students.

L2 Level 2 activities are average activities and should be within the range of average and above average students.

L3 Level 3 activities are challenging activities designed for the ability range of above average students.

National Marketing Education

CHAPTER	SECTION	PERFORMANCE INDICATOR
Chapter 17 Promotional Concepts and Strategies	17.1	Explain the role of promotion as a marketing function (PRO)
		Identify the elements of the promotional mix (PRO)
	17.2	Develop sales promotion plans (PRO)
		Analyze the use of specialty promotion (PRO)
	17.3	Develop public relations plan (PRO)
		Analyze costs/benefits of company participation in community activities (PRO)
		Obtain publicity (PRO)
Chapter 18 Visual Merchandising and Display	18.1	Explain the use of visual merchandising (PRO)
		Explain the use of visual merchandising to create an image (PRO)
		Explain the types of display arrangements (PRO)
	18.2	Explain the relationship of merchandising and visual merchandising (display) (PRO)
		Prepare merchandise for display (PRO)
		Maintain displays (PRO)
Chapter 19 Advertising	19.1	Explain the types of advertising media (PRO)
		Evaluate the effectiveness of advertising (PRO)
	19.2	Calculate media costs (PRO)
		Select advertising media (PRO)
Chapter 20 Preparing Print Advertisements	20.1	Explain the use of advertising agencies (PRO)
		Explain the components of advertisements (PRO)
	20.2	Describe the use of technology in the promotion function (PRO)
		Demonstrate appropriate creativity (PD)

CIS Communication, Interpersonal Skills   **DIS** Distribution   **FIN** Financing   **PRI** Pricing   **SEL** Selling

Standards Assessment Correlation

SECTION ASSESSMENT			CHAPTER ASSESSMENT						UNIT LAB
Reviewing Key Terms and Concepts	Thinking Critically	Integrating Academic Skills	Fact and Idea Review	Thinking Critically	Building Workplace Skills	Applying Marketing Concepts	Linking School to Work	Internet Connection	Zazz Lab
1, 3, 4, 5	●	●	1	1, 2		2, 3		●	●
2, 5	●	●	2	1		2, 3		●	●
1, 2	●	●	3		2	1, 2, 3, 4	●	●	●
3, 4, 5	●	●	3	2	2	1, 2, 3, 4	●		●
1, 2, 4, 5		●	5, 6, 7, 8	3		1, 2, 3, 4		●	
3	●	●	5, 6	4	1				
4, 5		●	7, 8	3, 4, 5		2, 4		●	●
1, 2, 3, 4, 5	●	●	1, 2, 3	1, 3	1			●	●
2, 3, 5	●	●	1, 2, 3, 4, 5	1, 2, 3, 4	2	2, 3		●	●
4, 5			4, 5, 6			1, 2, 3, 4	●		
1, 3, 5	●		8	2, 3, 4	1	2, 3, 4	●	●	●
1, 2, 4			8	1	1, 2	1, 2			
5		●	9	1					
1, 2, 3, 4, 5	●	●	1, 2, 3, 4, 5	1, 2 ,3	1, 2	1, 2, 3, 4	●	●	
	●	●	2, 3, 5	1, 2, 3, 4	1, 2	2, 3, 4	●	●	
1, 2, 3, 4	●	●	6, 8, 9						●
5	●		7, 9	1		3			●
1			1	1, 4		4		●	
1, 2, 3, 4, 5	●	●	2, 3, 4, 5, 6, 7, 8, 9	5	2	1, 2, 3, 4	●		●
1, 2, 3, 4, 5	●	●	9, 10	1, 2, 3, 4	1, 2	1, 3, 4			●
		●			1, 3	1, 2, 3			●

UNIT 6

Unit Overview

Businesses spend a phenomenal amount of money annually on promotional activities. Thus, this marketing function is a key unit in *Marketing Essentials.* Students will learn about the importance of promotional strategies when selling goods and services or developing a business image.

Chapter 17 describes the concept of promotion and how promotion strategies must be coordinated using an appropriate promotional mix. The chapter focuses on two promotional strategies—sales promotion and public relations. Students also learn how to write news releases. Chapter 18 gives an overview of visual merchandising and display concepts. Chapter 19 explains the different types of advertising media and teaches students how to calculate media costs. Chapter 20 explains how advertising campaigns are developed and discusses the role of advertising agencies. Lastly, students will learn about the essential elements of print advertisements and techniques for developing effective ad layouts.

Introducing the Unit

Present students with an array of ads, specialty items, press kits, news releases, and pictures of displays. On the board, have them make a list of the skills needed to create these promotional pieces. Then ask students to look at the board list and identify some of their own personal abilities and aptitudes.

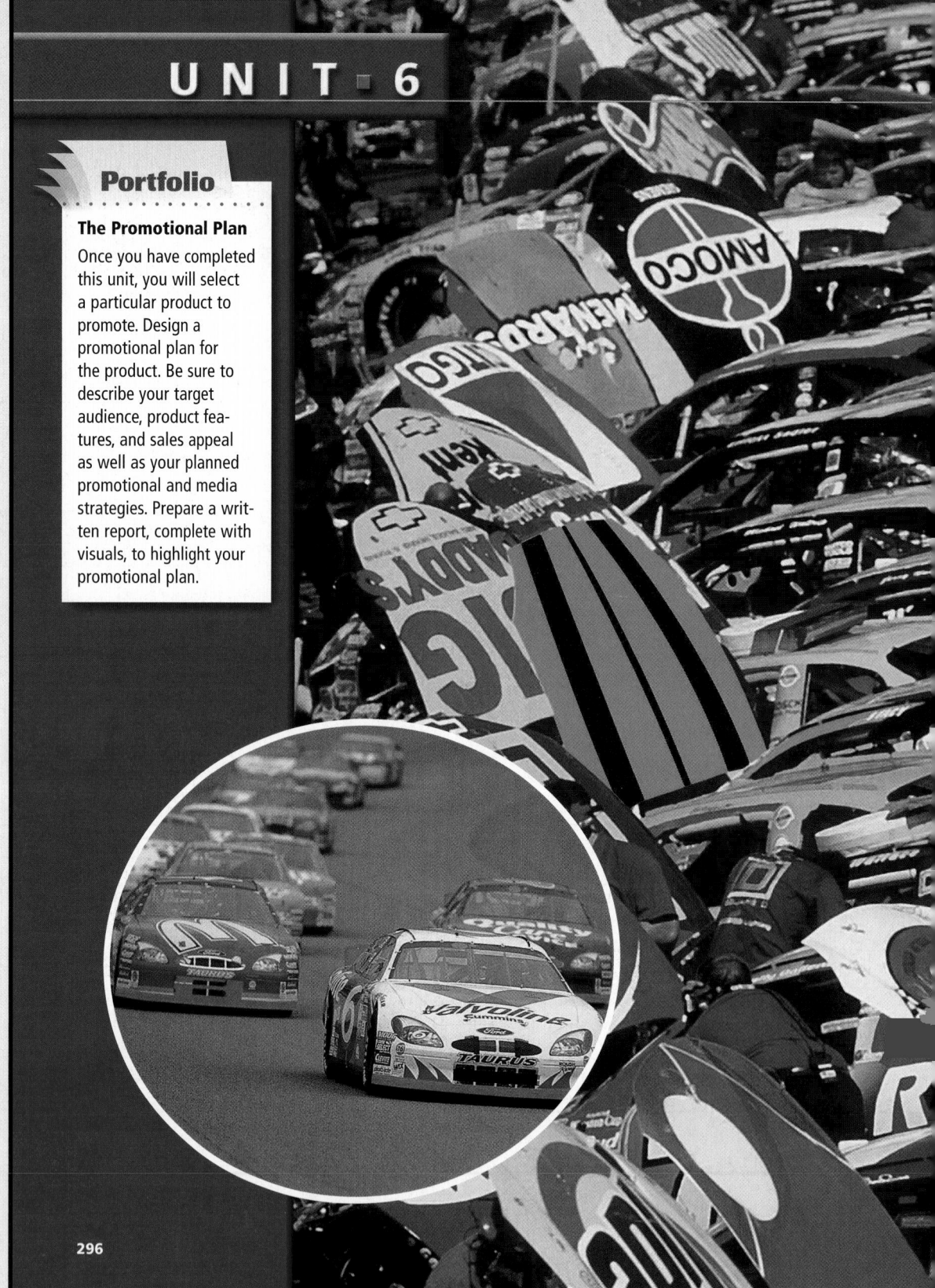

UNIT · 6

Portfolio

The Promotional Plan
Once you have completed this unit, you will select a particular product to promote. Design a promotional plan for the product. Be sure to describe your target audience, product features, and sales appeal as well as your planned promotional and media strategies. Prepare a written report, complete with visuals, to highlight your promotional plan.

296

Field Trip Suggestions

Observe Mall Promotions Have your students visit a local mall during a mall-wide promotion. They should observe the theme of the promotion and how the stores in the mall carry out the promotion. The students should also note any other promotion-related activities at the mall. You could make this an ongoing project and have the students observe the promotions at that mall for the entire school year.

UNIT 6

Promotion

Unit Overview

Businesses spend large amounts of money annually on promotional activities. In this unit you will learn about promotion and promotional strategies.

Through your exploration of Chapter 17, you will learn the importance of promotional strategies when selling goods and services or developing an image. Chapter 18 explains the importance of visual merchandising and display. Chapter 19 details the different types of advertising media used for product and institutional promotion. Chapter 20 highlights the essential parts of print advertisements and explains how to create effective advertising layouts.

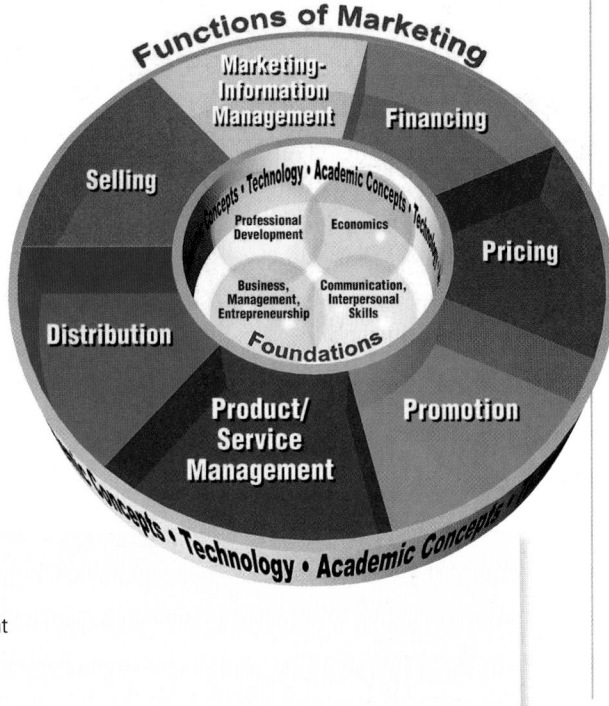

In this Unit:

Foundations of Marketing
○ Professional Development

Functions of Marketing
◢ Promotion

DECA Unit Project

Have each chapter member interview three people involved in different aspects of promotion—for example, an advertising copywriter, an artist, and a marketing manager—and write a report comparing and contrasting the duties, career paths, and job satisfaction levels of each. The report should conclude with a statement as to whether the student would or would not consider these professions as potential careers.

www Go to the *Marketing Essentials* Web site (**www.marketing.glencoe. com**) for resources to teach and assess occupation-specific vocabulary.

Unit Closure

Have students choose a job in the field of promotion that interests them and job shadow a professional for part of the person's work day. (Students can do this at their co-op training stations.) Have each student write a summary after the experience. If time permits, discuss the job shadowing experiences in class.

Guest Speaker Suggestions

Visual Merchandising Manager Invite the visual merchandising manager for a local department store to talk to your class about how he or she plans seasonal display themes that relate the store's image throughout the store.

Advertising Agency Account Executive Ask an account executive from an advertising agency to talk to your class about how advertising campaigns are planned and executed. Have the speaker discuss how media is selected, the media mix, and how ad campaign budgets are decided.

Chapter Overview

This chapter explores the concept of the promotional mix as well as the four basic types of promotion—advertising, selling, sales promotion, and public relations.

 Springboard

Brainstorm Bring to class rival brands of two similar products. Tell students to imagine that they want to buy the product, but there is little information available to help them decide—no ads, salespeople, sales promotions, or public relations activities. Students must decide based on the items in front of them. Have them jot down some factors that would influence their decision.

Prereading

List the section objectives to discuss with students. Have students skim the chapter, looking at the pictures, reading the captions, and noting the heads. Ask questions to ensure that the students have a minimal understanding of the chapter structure.

Preteaching Marketing Vocabulary

List and review the vocabulary terms with the students. Acknowledge students' correct answers by writing a brief definition next to the terms they know. Place an asterisk by terms they do not know and return to the vocabulary list later when you come across these unfamiliar terms.

Marketing: What It Takes

Answer You must evaluate how well your promotional mix reaches your audience. These activities include advertising, special promotions, and public relations to raise awareness.

Promotional Concepts and Strategies

Marketing: What It Takes

Attracting Young Professionals

You thought your promotional plan for a new line of baseball hats was exciting, organized, and complete. The manager of the advertising department, however, was not as enthusiastic. He questioned your promotional mix of advertising, sales promotions, and public relations activities to reach young professionals in the city.

WHAT WILL YOU DO?
How will you evaluate this difference of opinions to determine the most effective promotional plan?

298

THE DECA CONNECTION **ADVISOR CORNER**

Photo Op Promotion To increase your chapter's visibility and promote DECA, keep a camera handy in the classroom and in your student store (if applicable). Assign each student one or more public relations activities for the semester, such as taking pictures, videotaping activities, creating a display for your school's open house, or writing articles for your local or school newspaper. To enhance this activity, have DECA members create a theme for the year, and use that theme throughout all public relations activities. The photos, videos, and displays can be displayed on parents' nights and used as recruitment tools. *(Mike Karpie, Central H.S., Hamburg, NY)*

The Promotional Mix

[handwritten: Please look at the top of page 299. The book says promotion is "any form of communication"]

The Concept of Promotional Mix

Promotion is any form of communication a business or organization uses to inform, persuade, or remind people about its products. Promotion is also used to improve the public image of an organization.

To achieve promotional goals, it is important to decide on the right promotional mix. **Promotional mix** is a combination of the different types of promotion. A business decides on the promotional mix that will be most effective in persuading potential customers (wholesalers, retailers, and consumers) to purchase and support its products. *[handwritten: who can recall what a promotional mix is?]*

The purpose of any promotion may be directly related to the product or to the image of the business. A business uses **product promotion** to convince potential customers to buy products instead of buying from a competitor. The business also explains the major features and benefits of its products, identifies where those products are sold, advertises product sales, answers customer questions, and introduces new products. *[handwritten: Next, the book mentions the difference between product promotion and institutional promotion]*

Institutional promotion is used by a business to create a favorable image for itself, as opposed to promoting a product or service. Businesses may maintain Web sites to provide news, product information, and answers to questions as part of institutional promotion. While institutional promotion does not directly sell a certain product, creating a favorable image may result in increased sales for a company. *[handwritten: promotion. Who can remember what the difference between these two types of promotion is?]*

■ Types of Promotion
[handwritten: The book mentions that there are four basic types of promotion. Please tell me what they are. And if you recall from the reading: Advertising, Public relations, and sales promotion are nonpersonal. Personal selling, on the other hand is personal.]

There are four basic types of promotion: personal selling, advertising, sales promotion, and public relations. Each plays a vital role in promoting businesses and their products. Figure 17-1 on page 300 illustrates how the Oscar Mayer Division of the Kraft Foods company uses all four types of promotion.

Advertising, public relations, and sales promotion are forms of non-personal selling—communicating with customers in ways other than through direct contact. Personal selling, on the other hand, requires direct personal contact with the customer. *[handwritten: The first type of promotion is personal selling.]*

PERSONAL SELLING Personal selling is one of the largest forms of promotion. It requires individuals to make contact with potential buyers, making it the most expensive form of promotion. Personal selling is designed to complete a sale once a customer is attracted to a business by advertising, sales promotion, or public relations. You learned more about personal selling in Unit 5.

[handwritten: As we just said, Personal selling requires the salesperson to make direct contact with the customer. Therefore, it is the most expensive form of personal selling. Can anybody explain why this is so?]

● What You'll Learn

[handwritten: It is an important section. In this section, you'll learn "The role of promotion"]

- The role of promotion in marketing
- The concept of promotional mix
- The characteristics of personal selling and advertising
- The nature and scope of publicity

[handwritten: It's an important section because]

● Why It's Important

[handwritten: "since businesses must continually"]

Since businesses must continually promote their organizations, products, and policies to gain customer acceptance, you will need to learn successful promotional strategies.

Key Terms

- promotion
- promotional mix
- product promotion
- institutional promotion
- advertising
- sales promotion
- public relations
- publicity
- push policy
- pull policy

[handwritten: Who can explain the difference between personal and nonpersonal selling?]

[handwritten: • ONE-WAY COMMUNICATION • TWO-WAY COMMUNICATION]

FOCUS

Bell Ringer Activity

Brainstorm Returning to the Springboard Activity, have the students list the ways they would make their buying decision. Ask them to also list any limitations they encounter in making this decision.

Introducing the Section

The Promotional Mix Ask students what this activity taught them about the value of promotion. Tell them that a common complaint about promotion is that its cost is absorbed into the price of the product and thus is passed on to the consumer through higher product prices. However, they should be able to see that promotion and the right kind of promotional mix can help consumers make better buying decisions.

TEACH

📊 Technology Resources

PowerPoint The *Marketing Essentials* PowerPoint Presentation CD-ROM provides visual lecture aids for every chapter section.

[handwritten: Dave will get you these materials]

[handwritten: Types of Promotion on Eisel]
[handwritten: Video Superbowl Commercials]

Classroom Resources

For the Teacher
- Teacher Editions for all workbooks
- Assessment Package
- PowerPoint Presentation Software
- Interactive Lesson Planner
- ILP Block Scheduling, p. 6
- ILP Lesson Plans, p. 36
- ILP Internet Resources, p. 53

- ILP *BusinessWeek* Case Studies, p. 109
- ILP Marketing Career Portfolio, p. 36
- *Marketing Essentials* Web site (**www.marketing.glencoe.com**)

For the Student
- Student Activity Workbook, p. 141
- Marketing Math Workbook, p. 45

- Marketing Research Project Workbook, p. 85
- ILP School-to-Work Activity Workbook, p. 69
- Virtual Business simulation
- *Marketing Essentials* Web site (**www.marketing.glencoe.com**)

ILP These resources are available in print and on the Interactive Lesson Planner (ILP)

SECTION 17.1

Concept Development

1. Read Section 17.1 with students.
2. Have students read aloud the Case Study on page 303 and review the answers in class.
3. Have students refer to the info-graphic on the promotional mix. Call on students to give some examples of each type of promotional strategies. *DO NOW*

Discussion Starter

1. **Local Businesses** Give some examples of local businesses. Ask the following questions about each identified business:
   - What kind of advertising is done by the business?
   - Does the business use personal selling to sell its products?
   - Does the business use any sales promotions?
   - How could the business use public relations to build and promote itself or its products? *DO NOW*
2. **Promotional Mix** Why does a business use a promotional mix instead of relying on one form of promotion only? *(Different types of promotion appeal to and reach different members of a target audience. By using several types of promotion, a business can thus appeal to and reach a wider audience.)*

Let's take a minute to notice "The concept of promotional mix" on page 300.

FIGURE 17-1

THE CONCEPT OF PROMOTIONAL MIX

It say" Promotion involves a total approach to selling a product. The *Share the Smiles* promotion by Kraft's Oscar Mayer division included advertising, personal selling, sales promotion, and public relations.

Bologna makes me happy up to here!

Please read sales promotion

Cara Owada our 1998 Talent Search winner!

for the name you trust & the taste they love *Just Whistle!*

SALES PROMOTION

Manufacturers frequently provide incentives to both the retailer and the customer to promote sales. Retailers who placed large orders received plush toys to give to customers and to use as gifts in a customer raffle.

ADVERTISING

Please read advertising

Oscar Mayer's Weinermobiles advertise Oscar Mayer products in a unique and fun way. Local and national advertising announced the arrival of the Weinermobile and brought large crowds of onlookers.

PUBLIC RELATIONS

Promotions that benefit the community generate positive publicity toward the company and its products. Customers who donated $1 to Second Harvest National Food Bank received consumer incentives.

SELLING

Manufacturer sales representatives convince supermarket owners to support the promotion by purchasing additional quantities of hot dogs, bologna, and bacon products. Shared advertising, consumer promotions, and point-of-purchase displays are designed to boost sales for both the manufacturer and the retailer.

300 Unit 6 ■ Promotion

GREAT IDEAS from the Marketing Classroom

Jay Walker
James W. Robinson Secondary School
Fairfax, VA

Joining your DECA members to the local Chamber of Commerce is one of the best suggestions I can offer. The benefits as a résumé builder and classroom resource have been incredible for our school. The chamber can give your students a higher profile in your community and provide special recognition throughout the year. One of our special events organized with the Chamber is a marketing student one-day internship. The Chamber Internship is introduced through the Chamber newsletter, and then each DECA member writes three letters of introduction requesting the internship using the chamber directory.

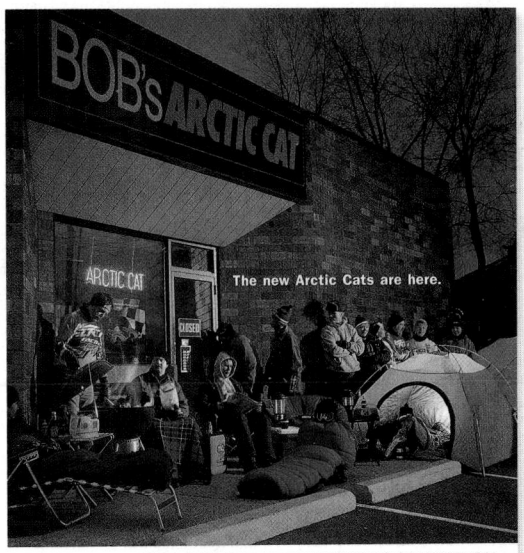

And if you plan to get one, you may want to do it before April 15, 2000. That way, you're sure to get the exact sled you want. You don't want to miss out on the hot new 2001 models. Sleds with unbelievable innovations that you just have to see to believe. Including our all-new Limited Edition sleds with great customized features. Plus you'll find awesome deals on all models you won't want to miss. Just remember to see your dealer and order before April 15. Or there may be nothing left to wait for. Call 1-800-3-ARCTIC for a dealer near you or visit www.arctic-cat.com.

ARCTIC CAT *What Snowmobiling's All About.*

tread lightly!®   See dealer for details. Always wear a helmet and don't drink and ride. ©2000 Arctic Cat Sales Inc., ®™ Trademarks of Arctic Cat Inc., Thief River Falls, MN 56701. (218) 681-4999. Printed in the U.S.A.

■ **Attention Grabber** Advertising is a form of non-personal presentation and promotion. *How does advertising differ from other forms of promotion?*

[handwritten: Please look at the top of page 301 "Real World Marketing" Touchdown. I-I say "football teams"]

REAL WORLD MARKETING

Touchdown!

Football teams aren't the only ones who struggle to score a touchdown during the Superbowl. Advertisers hope to score by spending big money to sell to a huge TV audience. What happened when more than a dozen Internet-based companies spent an average of $2.2 million for 30-second spots during the 1999 Superbowl? Several of the companies ran into financial troubles by fumbling through their cash reserves, and some were forced to close. For example, despite spending $1.6 million on Superbowl advertising in 1999, Epidemic Marketing ran out of capital and left the business market in 2000.

Thinking Critically
How can a business formulate an effective promotional strategy within budget?

[handwritten: 2. The second type of promotion is advertising. I expect everyone to be able to tell me what advertising is?]

ADVERTISING Advertising is any paid form of non-personal presentation and promotion of ideas, goods, or services by an identified sponsor. Advertising can be found everywhere, from magazines and newspapers to television and Web sites. Advertising involves one-way communication, whereas personal selling is communication between seller and buyer. Nationally, businesses spend approximately $200 billion annually on various types of advertising. A more detailed explanation of the various forms and purposes of advertising is given in Chapter 19.

[handwritten: Remember the three elements of advertising ① Paid ③ Identified Sponsor ② Non-Personal]

SALES PROMOTION According to the American Marketing Association, sales promotion represents all marketing activities, other than personal selling, advertising, and public relations, that are used to stimulate consumer purchasing and sales effectiveness. The objectives of sales promotions are to increase sales, to inform customers about new products, and to create a positive store or corporate image. Later in this chapter, you will study specific sales promotion activities.

[handwritten: 3. The third type of promotion is sales promotion. The book say that sales promotion represents all marketing activities, other than personal selling, advertising, and public relations. Examples of sales promotion include 1.) Games 2.) Contests 3.) Rebates 4.) Sweepstakes]

PUBLIC RELATIONS AND PUBLICITY Public relations refers to any activity designed to create a favorable image toward a business, its products, or its policies. Public relations activities and the audiences to which they are targeted will be covered in the last section of this chapter.

Publicity is a specific kind of public relations that involves placing positive and newsworthy information about a business, its products, or its policies in the media. Publicity differs from advertising as a promotional tool because it is free. A one-minute story on the evening news about a company or one of its products costs nothing. Fifteen seconds of advertising time on the same broadcast costs thousands of dollars.

Cost is not the only advantage of publicity. Newspapers, news programs, and news reporters are usually viewed as more objective than advertisers. People are more likely to pay attention to and believe news stories than advertisements. Publicity often appears as a media story, which makes the information appear more credible to many people.

Chapter 17 ■ *Promotional Concepts and Strategies* **301**

[handwritten right margin: The fourth type of promotion is public relations and publicity. Who can tell me what Public Relations is?]

[handwritten: Publicity, on the other hand is a type of public relation. It involves placing positive and newsworthy information about a business into the media. I think people figure "Oh, publicity and advertising are the same thing." That is incorrect. Can anyone tell me how the two differ?]

[handwritten: Publicity vs. Advertising

Advantages   Disadvantages
Free   Uncontrolled (What, When)
Objective   How
Credible   Can create
Can create Positive negative
Image   image]

REAL WORLD MARKETING

Touchdown!
Answer Businesses can determine where advertising dollars may be most effective by testing and measuring response rates to a variety of campaigns and advertising mediums.

Individualized Practice

Communication Skills

Divide students into groups of four to six. Have each group determine the image it wants to portray to the student body, to students' parents and guardians, and to the community about your school's marketing education program.

L1 Have students make a list of how the program benefits both students and the community. Students should compose a list of five to ten benefits of the program.

L2 Have each group create a first draft of a two- to four-page brochure that can be used as a publicity tool to generate interest in your marketing program and present a positive image to parents and guardians, to prospective marketing education students, and to the community.

L3 Have each group create a first draft of a two- to four-page brochure to generate interest in your marketing program. Give every student a copy of each group's draft of a brochure so that students can see each other's work. Working with the entire class, have students arrive at a consensus for the organization and wording of the final brochure. Encourage students to be creative! Help them by supplying photos of classes or projects, or any other information that will contribute to the overall design of the publication.

■ **Positive Publicity** Awarding scholarships is one way a company generates good publicity. Here, Best Buy Co., Inc. Divisional Human Resources Manager Daniel Fleischman awards a scholarship to Colin Eide. *Why is this good publicity?* I think a lot of people don't understand this so listen up. Companies don't award scholarships because they want to be nice. They award scholarships to generate good publicity.

The disadvantage of publicity is that its content, unlike paid advertising, cannot be controlled by the business. The media selects the content, as well as deciding when and how that content is presented. Negative stories, such as an accident or an unsafe product, are as likely to get publicized as positive stories about company successes or work in the community. Businesses work to generate positive publicity through public relations activities whenever possible. Please notice the last line here. It says businesses.

The principal function of publicity is building an image. Image is the way a business or organization is defined in people's minds. It is an impression based on a combination of factors including physical surroundings, personal experiences, and media exposure. The right kind of publicity can create and maintain a company's positive image. People like to do business with companies that have a respectable and positive image. Some business activities that can be great image-builders include sponsoring cultural events, awarding scholarships, and donating land or equipment for public use. In the book, it says "People like to do business with..."

302 Unit 6 ■ Promotion

■ Coordination of Promotional Mix

Most businesses use more than one type of promotion to achieve their promotional goals. The Oscar Mayer division of the Kraft Foods company uses a combination of local and national advertising, personal selling in the form of manufacturer sales representatives, sales promotions, and public relations. This assures them that their product will be widely recognized. There is a good explanation in the book of how each type of promotion is.

Each type of promotion is designed to complement the other types. Advertising creates awareness of a business's product, while public relations creates a favorable image for the business itself. Sales promotion efforts stimulate sales, reinforce advertising, and support selling efforts. Finally, personal selling builds on all of these previous efforts by helping the individual customer and completing the sale. Please read the next ¶.

All types of promotion must be coordinated. National advertising should be accompanied by local promotional efforts. Many consumer products manufacturers will give or sell retailers decorations

---

CAPTION ANSWER
Positive Publicity Awarding scholarships builds a positive image, and people like to do business with companies with such an image.

Case Study

Action in the Toy Stores

Bright costumes! Superpowers! X-Treme Sports! When you think of action figures, what comes to mind? Star Wars? X-Men? Pokemon? How about a snowboarding college student? That is exactly what toy makers Hasbro and Mattel want you to think, when you think of action figures!

Even the most popular action figures have short-lived fame. The most successful superheroes of the 1980s—Masters of the Universe, Teenage Mutant Ninja Turtles, and Power Rangers—had great initial popularity but faded quickly.

Research shows that boys age two to five fantasize about Batman-like heroes; by age six, however, they focus on more realistic heroes. In an attempt to capitalize on these results, Mattel, Inc., and Hasbro are shaping new products for development.

Mattel's *Action Man* and Hasbro's *Max Steel* action figures rely on less fantasy and are designed to be more "real." Competing for the same target market, each company hopes to generate sales of $100–$150 million, and success will be primarily based upon promotion.

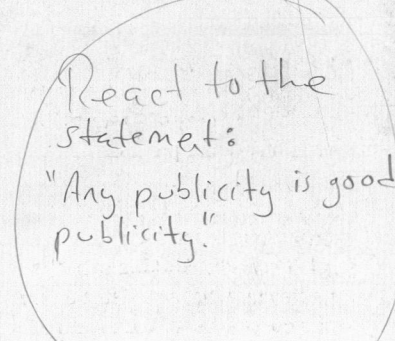

Mattel's *Action Man* will star in a computer-animated TV show on Fox's Kids Network. In addition, the company is sending CD-ROMs with "game missions" to three million boys whose families own computers and have purchased action figures before.

Hasbro's *Max Steel* action figure will have a Saturday morning TV show produced by Sony Pictures and will also be on Time-Warner's Kids WB Network. Mattel is also planning to sponsor extreme sporting events, like snowboarding, around the country.

Case Study Review

1. **What are unique challenges to toy companies marketing to this age group?**
2. **What other promotional strategies would you suggest to the companies to reach this target market?**

A MATTER OF ETHICS

3. **Is it ethical to use children in marketing research activities? Does your opinion change depending on the toys that are developed? Why or why not?**

ASSESS
Reteaching

1. **Vocabulary** Assign and review the vocabulary terms for this section.
2. **Fact and Idea** Assign Fact and Idea Review questions 1–2 from the Chapter Assessment.
3. **Promotion and Promotional Mix** To reteach the concept of promotion and the promotional mix, have the students draw a concept map on a sheet of paper or poster board with the words *promotional mix* in the middle of the page. Have the students draw four lines to each corner. Ask students to identify all four types of promotional tools in a different corner of the paper. Ask the students to identify through words or symbols at least three ideas that they have learned about each type of promotion.

React to the statement:
"Any publicity is good publicity."

Case Study Review Answers

Action in the Toy Stores
1. Unique challenges include the short product life cycle, price sensitivity, sales based upon popularity of TV show characters, narrow range of target market, and extensive TV promotion.
2. Answers will vary but could include consumer promotions tied-in with TV show characters, advertisements on products used by target audience, point-of-sale displays, etc.

A MATTER OF ETHICS
3. Answers will vary. One factor is the aspect of parental approval. If parental approval is granted, there is less of an ethical problem.

Enrichment

1. **Review** Assign and review the appropriate Thinking Critically questions from the Chapter Assessment.
2. **Extend** Assign and review the corresponding activities from *BusinessWeek Case Studies* and *Internet Resources.* **ILP**

Evaluation

Assign and review the Section 17.1 Assessment.

Technology Resources

Assessment Resources
Go to the *Marketing Essentials* Web site (**www.marketing.glencoe. com**) for resources to teach and assess occupation-specific vocabulary.

CLOSE

Section Wrap-Up

Have students complete this statement: Promotion is . . . *(any form of communication a business or organization uses to inform, persuade, or remind people about its products and improve its public image.)*

304

---

or in-store displays that promote a national campaign. At the local retail level, the national and local efforts need to be communicated to the store personnel. Sales personnel should be made aware of coupons, rebates, contests, and any other featured promotional tools so that they can encourage customer participation. Sales are lost and customer dissatisfaction is created when advertised products are not available or the sales staff is uninformed about the promotion. *In other words, the promotion must be unified and coherent*

PROMOTIONAL BUDGET In large companies, the marketing department has many roles. It establishes a promotion budget, allocates resources, coordinates the campaign, and determines the right promotional mix for the company. It is important to consider all aspects of promotional activities when designing the promotional budget. Determining the ideal amount for the promotional budget can be difficult because there is no precise way to measure the exact results of spending promotional dollars. Promotional budgeting methods are discussed in further detail in Chapter 19. *If you remember from the reading, the marketing department "establishes a budget, allocates resources, coordinates"*

THE PUSH-PULL CONCEPT When deciding on a promotional mix, manufacturers often need to develop a promotional mix for each member of the distribution channel. To promote a product to its larger retailers, a manufacturer might want to use a mix of personal selling, advertising (direct mail and/or trade publications), and buying discounts. This type of promotion—known as the **push policy** of promotion—is used only with the next partner in the distribution channel. It is helpful when a manufacturer is trying to "push" a product through a channel. The main purpose of the promotion is to convince a retailer to stock the products being promoted. A push strategy relies heavily on personal selling and sales promotion, especially at trade shows. It is a helpful strategy for manufacturers of business products and consumer goods that do not have strong brand identity.

The manufacturer *pushes* the product in to the retailer. The same manufacturer might use a different promotional mix of local and national advertising, in-store displays, sales promotions, and public relations to reach consumers. The pull policy directs promotion towards customers. This **pull policy** of promotion is designed to create consumer interest. Consumer demand can *pull* or encourage retailers to carry the product being promoted. This strategy relies on heavy advertising geared toward consumers, in addition to premiums, samples, and demonstrations.

How many have parents that work in the marketing department of organizations? Can anybody tell me who is in charge of the marketing department?

Organizational Chart on easel pg. 648

Next, your book mentions the difference between push policy and pull policy. Does anybody know what the difference is?

17.1 ASSESSMENT

Reviewing Key Terms and Concepts

1. What is promotion?
2. Describe the concept of promotional mix.
3. What is the difference between product and institutional promotion?
4. Why is personal selling the most expensive form of promotion?
5. What is the difference between publicity and advertising?

Thinking Critically

6. Some people think that advertising is a waste of money and needlessly raises the prices of goods and services. What do you think? Is the money spent on advertising justified? Provide an argument to support your position.

Integrating Academic Skills

7. **COMMUNICATION** Find stories about local or national companies in a local newspaper. Identify each company and then categorize the publicity in the newspaper as either positive or negative. Support your conclusions in each case with a paragraph or two explaining what the facts are and how the publicity may help or harm the business.

Manufacturer (make/manufacture product)
Retailer (middleman/sells to retailer)
Consumer (user of the product)
Distribution Chain
Please read "the Push-Pull Concept"

17.1 ASSESSMENT ANSWERS

Reviewing Key Terms and Concepts

1. Promotion is any form of communication a business uses to inform, persuade, or remind people about its products and its image.
2. It is a combination of different types of promotion used to persuade potential customers to purchase and support the business's products.
3. Product promotions convince people to buy or use a certain product. Institutional promotion does not directly sell product, but is used to create a favorable image.
4. Individuals must contact potential buyers.
5. Publicity is free with no control over content; advertising has control over cost and content.

Thinking Critically

6. Answers will vary.

Integrating Academic Skills

7. **COMMUNICATION** Answers will vary.

Sales Promotion

Sales Promotion

Sales promotion is a short-term incentive offered to encourage buying a good or service. The purpose of sales promotions is to increase demand and stimulate sales. Sales promotions can be <u>directed toward manufacturers, wholesalers, retailers, and consumers</u>. Sales promotions can also be directed toward a company's employees, encouraging a sales force to sell products aggressively. Sales promotions are usually supported by advertising activities.

Sales promotions may be either trade (business-to-business) oriented or consumer oriented. Let's take a closer look at the different types of promotions.

■ Trade Promotions

Trade promotions are sales promotion activities designed to gain manufacturers', wholesalers', and retailers' support for a product. More money is actually spent on promoting to businesses than to consumers. Major trade promotions include slotting allowances, buying allowances, trade shows and conventions, and sales incentives.

SLOTTING ALLOWANCES A slotting allowance is a cash premium paid by the manufacturer to a retail chain for the costs involved in placing a new product on its shelves. Slotting allowances can range from a few thousand dollars to more than $100,000 per product. In addition to buying space in the store, slotting allowances also pay for a retailer's discount specials on a product, charges for store shelves, penalties for poor sales, and store advertising and display costs.

BUYING ALLOWANCES A buying allowance is a price discount given by manufacturers to wholesalers and retailers to encourage the purchase of a product. It is sometimes used to encourage buying a larger quantity of a product. The price discount results in more money for wholesalers and retailers for each sold product. They are more likely, therefore, to promote the product to customers.

TRADE SHOWS AND CONVENTIONS Trade shows and conventions are designed to reach wholesalers and retailers. They provide businesses with opportunities to introduce new products, encourage increased sales of existing products, and gain continued company and product support.

SALES INCENTIVES Sales incentives are awards given to managers and employees who successfully meet or exceed a sales quota. Such quotas can apply to a specific period of time, such as a month, one-day sale, or a year, or for a particular product or line of products.

● What You'll Learn

- The characteristics of sales promotion
- The concept of trade promotions
- The different kinds of consumer sales promotions

● Why It's Important

To be successful, a business must continually promote its products. This section introduces you to the concept of sales promotion and to the techniques used to increase sales and inform customers about a company's products.

Key Terms

- sales promotion
- slotting allowance
- sales incentives
- premiums
- incentives
- promotional tie-ins

FOCUS

Bell Ringer Activity

Describe Have students consider promotional activities in relation to product or institutional promotion. Ask students: How have they been induced to buy merchandise, been informed about new products, or changed or upgraded their image of a store or corporation? What promotional tools were used? What are the similarities between selling a program or an idea, and selling merchandise?

Introducing the Section

Sales Promotion Tell students that this section looks at trade and consumer promotional activities designed to increase sales, to inform customers about new products, and to create a positive store image or corporate image. They will also look at personal selling and how promotional goals are achieved with the proper promotional mix.

Classroom Resources

For the Teacher
- Teacher Editions for all workbooks
- Assessment Package
- PowerPoint Presentation Software
- Interactive Lesson Planner
- ILP Block Scheduling, p. 6
- ILP Lesson Plans, p. 37
- ILP Internet Resources, p. 53

- ILP *BusinessWeek* Case Studies, p. 109
- ILP Marketing Career Portfolio, p. 36
- *Marketing Essentials* Web site (www.marketing.glencoe.com)

For the Student
- Student Activity Workbook, p. 141
- Marketing Math Workbook, p. 45

- Marketing Research Project Workbook, p. 85
- ILP School-to-Work Activity Workbook, p. 69
- Virtual Business simulation
- *Marketing Essentials* Web site (www.marketing.glencoe.com)

ILP These resources are available in print and on the Interactive Lesson Planner (ILP)

Handwritten annotations:

If you recall from section 17.1, sales promotion are short-term incentives offered to encourage buying a good or service.

The book says that "sales promotions may be either trade oriented or consumer oriented. (ON EISEL)

Who can recall what a slotting allowance is?

Who can tell me what a slotting allowance is?

This is important to understand. Slotting allowances get very competitive.

Next, the book mentions buying allowances. Who can explain that?

Next, the book mentions trade shows/conventions. What is that? Please look at the picture on page 306 of a trade show.

The last trade promotion mentioned in the book are sales incentives. Sales incentives are awards given to managers and employees who successfully meet or exceed a sales quota. Notice that sales incentive can be very motivating to employees.

Examples of sales Incentive

At the top of page 305, let's look at "What You'll Learn". It says, "The characteristics of sales promotion."

This section is important because, "To be successful, a business must continually be..."

Notice that the major trade promotion include...

Raise
Bonus
Vacation Get-Away
Car

Concept Development

1. Read Section 17.2 with the students.
2. If possible, schedule a field trip to a local trade show so that students have a better understanding of the purpose of trade shows. (Those students who go to state and national DECA competitions will have the opportunity to visit the trade show at the convention in which textbooks and other educational materials, DECA merchandise, and school store merchandise will be displayed.)
3. Invite a promotional events coordinator from a local shopping mall to discuss how the mall uses promotion to attract shoppers.

Discussion Starter

Ask students: Why does a business use different sales promotions instead of relying on one form of promotion? *(Sales promotions increase demand and simulate sales.)*

■ **Business-to-Business Promotion** Trade shows and conventions are forms of business-to-business promotion. *What are other examples of trade promotions?*

Sales contests may also be used to provide incentives for a company's own staff or even for a company's channel partners. In the latter case, a manufacturer's distributor may win points for the sales generated for that manufacturer's products. The points may then be redeemed for prizes. Sales incentive awards vary from business to business but may include prizes such as merchandise, travel, or cash.

A manufacturer of housing units might offer its top dealer (distributor) a group travel award to motivate the dealer's sales force. The prize for selling a certain number of housing units could be an all-expense-paid vacation for the entire sales force. On a smaller scale, a distributor's top salesperson may win a weekend getaway for two.

■ Consumer Sales Promotions

Sales promotion efforts designed to encourage customers to buy a product are called consumer promotions. More than half the households in the United States take advantage of sales promotions each year.

Major consumer sales promotion devices include premiums, incentives, product samples, loyalty marketing programs, promotional tie-ins, product placement, and visual merchandising and displays.

PREMIUMS Premiums are low-cost items given to consumers at a discount or for free. They are designed to increase sales by building product loyalty and attracting new customers. They also can persuade nonusers to switch brands.

The fundamental concept behind premium marketing is that people will be more motivated to buy a product when they are offered an "added value" gift in exchange. While viable, worthy

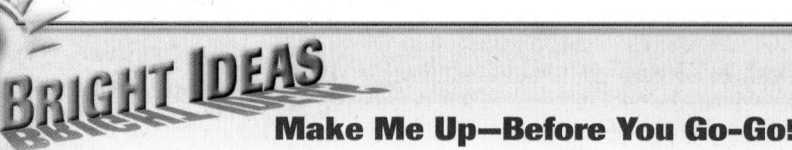

BRIGHT IDEAS

Make Me Up—Before You Go-Go!

Have you ever been on a plane ride that seemed to last forever? How did you feel when you finally reached you destination? Dirty? Tired? Sweaty? Low humidity and poor air circulation in the cabin dry out the skin, making it look chapped and fatigued. Not only is traveling stressful on your body, it is hard on your skin–and cosmetic companies are honing in on that truth! Guerlain, a French cosmetic company, has developed a skin-care line for travelers. Their line, Blue Voyage, includes a moisturizer to be used in-flight and a recovery cream to be used upon arrival. Their packages are designed to not break or spill in transit. So far, the in-flight beauty therapy seems to be very popular with both male and female business travelers. So now, when you are jetlagged, at least you won't look like you are!

Thinking Creatively

What other types of cosmetics would be good for business travelers?

CAPTION ANSWER
Business-to-Business Promotion Other examples of trade promotions include slotting allowances, buying allowances, and sales incentives.

BRIGHT IDEAS
Make Me Up—Before You Go-Go!

Answer Other items that would be convenient for travelers are travel-size items, unbreakable containers, perfumes and shampoos in leak-proof bottles, stress-relief masks, and products to reduce puffiness in the eyes.

products may sell themselves, the element of competition increases the need for differentiation. While in many instances price is the determining factor in the consumers' decision to purchase a product, a well planned and targeted premium can override price considerations. When planning premiums, consider the following:

- Premiums should be low cost.
- Premiums should provide added value.
- Premiums should aim to negate the targeted audience's price issue.
- Premiums should effectively differentiate the product from the competition.
- Premiums should create an immediate need to buy.

Four types of popular consumer premiums are coupons, factory packs, traffic builders, and coupon plans. Let's take a closer look at each of these four types of consumer premiums.

Coupons are certificates which entitle customers to cash discounts on goods or services. Manufacturers use coupons to introduce new products, to enhance the sales of existing products, and to encourage retailers to stock and display both. Retailers and service businesses use coupons to introduce a grand opening, to acknowledge new customers, and to encourage repeat business by current customers. Coupons reach potential customers through a variety of routes. They are placed on or inside product packages, sent through regular mail, made available on a business's Web site, and printed in newspapers and magazines. Sometimes they are placed by themselves into newspapers as free-standing inserts. Coupons are probably the most popular type of premium.

Despite the popularity of coupons, coupon distribution has been steadily declining in recent years. Although billions of coupons are distributed each year through freestanding newspaper inserts, most are not actually redeemed by consumers. Part of the problem is that coupons are often wasted on consumers who have no interest in the product–for example, dog food coupons that reach those without pets. Another problem is that most coupons expire before the consumer has the opportunity to use them.

Because of their high cost and low redemption rates, many businesses are reevaluating their use of coupons. Procter & Gamble, for example, has cut coupon distribution in half and shifted to a lower-price strategy. Similarly, Kraft has opted to distribute a single, all-purpose coupon good on any of its cereal brands.

Factory packs, or in-packs, are free gifts placed in product packages, on product packages, or as a container premium. This form of premium is especially popular with cereal manufacturers, who use it to increase their products' appeal to children. The prize in the box of Cracker Jacks is a classic example of an in-pack premium. A container premium is a product container which, when empty, may be used as a container for other items.

Traffic builders are low-cost premiums, such as pens, key chains, and calendars, which are given away free to consumers for visiting a new store or for attending a special event.

Coupon plans are ongoing programs offering a variety of premiums in exchange for labels, coupons, or other tokens from one or more purchases. A customer might send a manufacturer three specific soup can labels in exchange for a recipe book. Available premiums are often shown in special catalogs. A variation of this program is called the part-cash redemption, whereby a customer returns proof-of-purchase seals from a product plus a cash amount in exchange for a gift.

There are costs involved in using premiums. These costs are ultimately paid by the businesses offering them. Stores accepting manufacturers' coupons send them to their company headquarters or to a clearinghouse to be sorted and passed along to redemption centers. The centers, in turn, reimburse the stores for the face value of each coupon plus a handling charge of about eight cents per coupon. They then bill the manufacturers.

INCENTIVES Businesses use incentives to promote many products because they create customer excitement and increase sales. **Incentives** generally are higher-priced products earned and given through contests, sweepstakes, and rebates. Let's take a closer look at each of these types of consumer incentives.

Contests are games or activities that require the participant to demonstrate a skill. This can include writing a short story or essay about a product, naming a new product, or creating a new advertising slogan. Contest winners are awarded such prizes as scholarships, vacations, and money.

Thinking Critically

Types of Promotion Bring in a product familiar to students that is currently being promoted using several different types of promotion. Ask the students how the item is currently being promoted and how each type of promotion contributes to the sale of the product.

Independent Practice

1. **Research and Write** Using such publications as *Advertising Age, Supermarket News, Mass Market Retailers, Stores, Chain Store Age, Business Week,* and *Inc.,* have students research the latest trends in sales promotion. They may need to focus on one area only, such as trends in promoting entertainment, clothing, or jewelry. Have them develop an outline of their findings and then write a 250-word report based on their outlines.

2. **Research, Describe, and Write** Have students choose one local company and list five characteristics of its image. Then have them write a 50-word summary of the company's image.

Reteaching

1. **Fact and Idea** Assign and review Fact and Idea Review questions 3–4 from the Chapter Assessment.
2. **Vocabulary** Have students write a one-sentence statement using each vocabulary term in Section 17.2.

Enrichment

1. **Review** Assign and review the appropriate Thinking Critically questions from the Chapter Assessment.
2. **Extend** Assign and review the corresponding activities from the *School-to-Work-Activity Workbook.* **ILP**
3. **Design** Have students work together to prepare a promotional calendar for your school store for each month of the school year. They should try to incorporate all four types of promotion into the calendar.

Try **New**
Curél Nutrient Rich

Breakthrough formula ends your severe dry skin once and for all

Free Sample & $1.00 Coupon Enclosed

■ **A Small Sampling** Product samples are free trial size products sent through the mail. *Why do manufacturers use product samples?*

Sweepstakes are games of chance. One example is customers at fast-food restaurants receiving a game card with or without a purchase. By law in most states, customers cannot be required to make a purchase in order to enter a contest or sweepstakes. Their game card might earn them a small prize or a chance at a bigger prize.

Rebates are discounts offered by manufacturers to customers who purchase an item during a given time period. Auto and household appliance manufacturers frequently use rebates to encourage customers to buy their products.

PRODUCT SAMPLES Another form of consumer sales promotion is the product sample. A product sample is a free trial size of a product sent through the mail, distributed door-to-door, or given away at retail stores and trade shows. Detergents, toothpastes, shampoos, deodorants, and colognes are frequently promoted this way.

Samples are especially important in promoting new products. Drug manufacturers frequently give samples to doctors and dentists to try with their patients. Teachers sometimes receive sample textbooks to encourage them to buy classroom sets.

PROMOTIONAL TIE-INS Promotional tie-ins involve sales promotional arrangements between one or more retailers or manufacturers. They

308 Unit 6 ■ *Promotion*

combine their resources (advertising and sales promotional activities) to do a promotion that creates additional sales for each partner. Promotional tie-ins can be complex and involve several companies. An example is the link between McDonald's *Happy Meal*, Disney studios, and Fisher-Price Toddler Toy promotion of the *Goofy* Movie. Successful tie-ins can also be done on a regional, state, or local basis with only a single partner. Tie-ins are designed to stimulate customer response to a product or products offered and combine the resources of each partner in the arrangement.

PRODUCT PLACEMENT When Apple introduced the iMac in 1999, the new computer popped up in television shows from Ally McBeal to the X-Files. This is known as *product placement.* An organization can develop product recognition by making sure that it is featured in special events, on television, or in the movies. One of the most well-known merges for product placement took place between Warner Brothers movie studios and America Online (AOL) for the film "You've Got Mail." The onscreen exposure in this movie is said to have cost AOL between $3 and $6 million. The benefits: Warner Brothers cut down on production costs and created a realistic aspect of the film, and AOL received international film exposure.

The hope is that the strategic placement of an item will increase or enhance the public's knowledge about a particular product. James Bond is known as much for his Rolex watch and BMW as he is for his espionage and fancy footwork. Product placement in movies, television, or on the sports field may reach a wider audience for a reduced cost.

VISUAL MERCHANDISING AND DISPLAYS *Visual merchandising* refers to the coordination of all physical elements in a place of business so that it projects the right image to its customers. *Displays* refer to the visual and artistic aspects of presenting a product to a target group of customers. Window, floor, counter, and other in-store display techniques are all forms of visual merchandising.

By exposing potential customers firsthand to a company's products, visual merchandising stimulates sales and serves as in-store advertising. A complete discussion of visual merchandising and display can be found in Chapter 18.

CAPTION ANSWER
A Small Sampling Manufacturers use product samples to promote new products. They can be free trial sizes of a product sent in the mail, distributed door-to-door, or given away at retail stores and trade shows.

[Handwritten note at top: The book says that loyalty marketing rewards customers for making multiple purchase.]

LOYALTY MARKETING PROGRAMS Loyalty marketing programs, also called frequent buyer programs, reward customers for making multiple purchases. Loyalty marketing was popularized in the 1980s by the airline industry, which instituted frequent flier programs. These programs reward customers with free air travel after accumulating a set amount of paid travel. The hotel industry has adopted similar programs in which consumers can win free lodging after spending a set amount on paid lodging.

[Handwritten: Please read]

Loyalty exists when a customer, because of past experience, is sufficiently satisfied with a particular brand or retailer that he or she buys that brand or from that retailer when the need arises without considering other alternatives. Loyalty marketing offers consumers incentives not to consider other alternatives.

[Handwritten: explain / Remember this is Routine Decision-making]

Other industries have adopted loyalty marketing programs. Sears has a program called Kidvantage in which parents are rewarded with discounts after purchasing a certain amount of children's clothing. Online versions of loyalty marketing programs have also become popular. The Internet search engine Yahoo! awards points to Web surfers who buy from certain retailers or visit certain Web sites. Yahoo! has negotiated with the airline industry to allow consumers to convert their points into frequent flier miles.

[Handwritten: Example: Air line Industry, Credit Cards, Oil Cards]

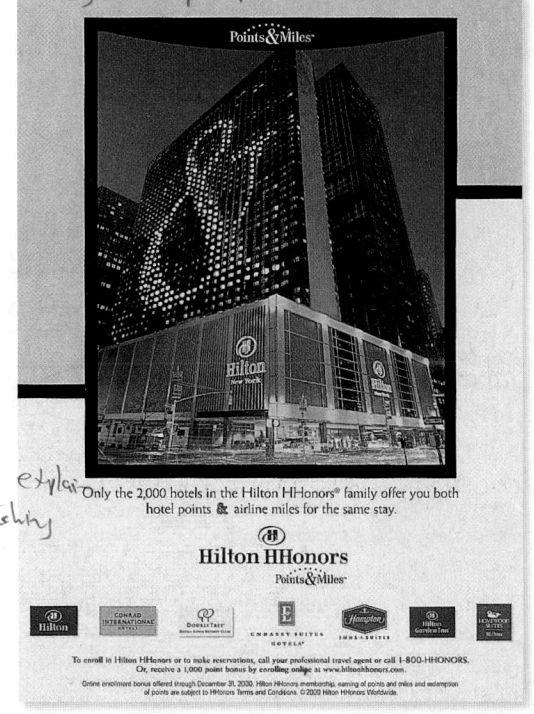

Points&Miles

Only the 2,000 hotels in the Hilton HHonors® family offer you both hotel points & airline miles for the same stay.

Hilton HHonors
Points&Miles

■ **Frequent Flier** Loyalty marketing programs reward customers for making multiple purchases. *Why would a business institute a loyalty marketing program?*

17.2 ASSESSMENT

Reviewing Key Terms and Concepts

1. Why do businesses use sales promotions?
2. What unique characteristics do sales promotions have?
3. What are trade promotions?
4. What are consumer promotions?
5. Explain the difference between a sweepstakes and a contest.

Thinking Critically

6. Why don't manufacturers who issue coupons simply lower the price of their products to attract customers? What is the value of coupons to such businesses?

Integrating Academic Skills

7. **MATH** Promotional discounts are given to stores by manufacturers to place products in preferred locations or to pay for ads, displays, or in-store demonstrations. Calculate the store's cost to stock the following items and the percentage of the discount given.

Item	Purchase Amount	Discount Amount	Net Cost to Store	Percent Discount
Snowboards	$5,650	$847.50	_____	_____
CD Players	$535	$42.80	_____	_____

Chapter 17 ■ *Promotional Concepts and Strategies* **309**

17.2 ASSESSMENT ANSWERS

Reviewing Key Terms and Concepts

1. to generate sales and increase market share
2. short-term activities with incentive to purchase; are used with all channel members
3. sales promotion activities designed to gain manufacturers' wholesalers' and retailers' support
4. activities to encourage customers to buy a product
5. A contest requires participants to demonstrate a skill, and a sweepstakes is a game of chance.

Thinking Critically

6. to introduce new products, to enhance sales of existing products, and to encourage retailers to stock and display both

Integrating Academic Skills

7. **MATH** snowboards: $4,802.50 net costs, 15%; CD players: $492.20 net costs, 8%

Public Relations

FOCUS

Bell Ringer Activity

Organize and Brainstorm Have a marketing education open house to show students, parents and guardians, and the business community the advantages of participating in a marketing education program. In addition to press releases to announce the event, give students a few minutes to generate a list of other things they could do to induce people to come to the marketing education open house.

Introducing the Section

Public Relations Generate a board list of students' answers from the Bell Ringer Activity. Answers will vary but could include the following:

- selling raffle tickets for a prize that will be given away during the open house
- advertising the availability of school store merchandise or DECA related items to be given away at the open house
- sponsoring a contest or a sweepstakes, the winner of which is announced at the open house
- offering samples of food items sold as DECA fund-raisers

Ask students: Why is it important to get people to come to the open house? *(People can see the activities instead of just hearing about them. Their attendance will help build loyalty and goodwill toward the program, attract more students, and garner more support from the business community.)*

• What You'll Learn

- The nature and scope of public relations
- The different audiences for public relations
- The duties of public relations specialists
- How to prepare a news release

• Why It's Important

Public relations is image-building. A company is concerned with how its employees, customers, and the general public (including its stockholders) view it. This section explains how the public relations department of a company fosters goodwill among the public.

Key Terms

- customer advisory boards
- consumer affairs specialists
- community relations
- news release
- press kit
- press conference

The Nature and Scope of Public Relations

Businesses want to present a positive image to their customers, employees, and the general public. Public relations specialists attempt to create goodwill for their companies by creating public relations events. Here are some examples:

- Grand opening of a new mall
- Interview with a company official about hiring plans
- Launch of a new product or product line
- Announcement of employee promotions or retirements
- Presentation of an award to the company or to one of its employees
- Company-sponsored sports event
- Community activity, such as a scholarship program sponsored by the business
- Charitable activity, such as a walkathon for a local charity, in which the business participates
- Cultural activity, such as support for a new exhibit at a museum

The goodwill generated by such public relations events benefits the business in many ways. Well-planned and organized public relations efforts can increase sales, reinforce a good reputation, and increase the willingness of consumers to respond to advertising efforts for the company's products.

■ Customer Relations

Good communication between employees and customers is vital in promoting a favorable business image. Courtesy, helpfulness, interest, tolerance, and friendliness help make customers come back. This repeat business is what makes a company successful.

Many businesses, however, go further than just friendliness and courtesy. They offer special services and amenities in order to maintain good customer relations. These services and amenities might include on-premise restaurants, child-care facilities, gift wrapping, check-cashing services, fax and copying services, and free delivery.

Other public relations efforts are less obvious. **Customer advisory boards** are panels of consumers who make suggestions about products and businesses. Manufacturers, wholesalers, and retailers use customer advisory boards to test new products. A supermarket might want to learn about customer preferences regarding store hours and preferred cultural or health food products to stock. It may also want to learn whether customers like in-store promotional devices, such as electronic coupons and videocarts. By consulting with

Classroom Resources

For the Teacher
- Teacher Editions for all workbooks
- Assessment Package
- PowerPoint Presentation Software
- Interactive Lesson Planner
- ILP Block Scheduling, p. 6
- ILP Lesson Plans, p. 38
- ILP Internet Resources, p. 53

- ILP Blackline Masters, p. 33
- ILP *BusinessWeek* Case Studies, p. 109
- ILP Marketing Career Portfolio, p. 36
- *Marketing Essentials* Web site (**www.marketing.glencoe.com**)

For the Student
- Student Activity Workbook, p. 141
- Marketing Math Workbook, p. 45

- • Marketing Research Project Workbook, p. 85
- ILP School-to-Work Activity Workbook, p. 73
- • Virtual Business simulation
- • *Marketing Essentials* Web site (**www.marketing.glencoe.com**)

ILP These resources are available in print and on the Interactive Lesson Planner (ILP)

[Handwritten margin notes:]
Notice the objectives of Section 17.3. It says "You'll learn"

Please read "Why It's Important"

Make a list of Good PR vs. Bad PR

Next the book mentions customer advisory boards. Does anybody remember what these are?

The book says that

How does good public relations benefit the company? How does negative PR impact the company?

The book says, "by

an advisory board, the supermarket can adjust or change policies, products, or promotional efforts to meet customers' needs.

Some larger department stores also hire consultants to assist customers with their purchases. Fashion, cosmetic, travel, bridal, and interior decorating consultants, as well as personal shoppers are examples of employees with specialized training who are hired by some retail firms.

National companies often employ consumer affairs specialists to handle customer complaints and to serve as consumer advocates within the firm. **Consumer affairs specialists** design programs to reflect customer needs for information on topics such as nutrition, health and wellness, and product safety.

■ Employee Relations

Successful businesses have loyal and well-motivated employees who feel they are important to the company. The public relations staff works with management and employees to design programs that foster positive attitudes. Some examples include providing:

- Tuition reimbursement for college courses
- Newsletters for and about the company and its employees
- Recreational programs
- Employee recognition programs for improvements in performance and efficiency

Positive employee relations are necessary for all companies. They are the building block for developing a good reputation—made up of positive public and community relations.

■ Community Relations

Community relations refers to the activities that a business uses to acquire or maintain the respect of the community. Businesses foster good community relations by participating in and sponsoring activities that benefit the civic, social, and cultural life of a community. Some examples of community relations activities include sponsoring Special Olympics, providing mentors for marketing students, and matching employee donations to local charities.

Companies encourage employees to join and remain active in civic organizations, such as the Optimists, Rotary Club, or the Lions. In addition,

GOOD HANDS.

IN AN ERA THAT'S SHORT ON POSITIVE ROLE MODELS, ALLSTATE AGENT ANTHONY SAMPSON STANDS OUT. HE

SPENDS 10-15 HOURS A WEEK WORKING WITH YOUTH GROUPS, AND BELIEVES THAT A THRIVING COMMUNITY BENEFITS EVERYONE WHO'S PART OF IT. **AT WORK.**

AMERICA'S PROMISE
THE ALLIANCE FOR YOUTH

Allstate
You're in good hands.

■ Part of the Community Businesses need to be actively involved in community activities. *How does this ad publicize Allstate's commitment to gain the goodwill and respect of community members?*

involvement with school and community organizations, such as business advisory committees, business and school partnership programs, or the local chamber of commerce, provide recognition for individual employees and present a favorable image for the business. Some companies release employees from normal job responsibilities for limited time periods to chair important charitable fund-raising efforts, such as United Way campaigns.

Effective businesses need to be active participants in their communities. Although the primary aim of community relations work is to promote civic pride and help the local residents, these events also help create goodwill for their business participants. Customers and the general public pay attention to the sponsors of community-wide activities.

TEACH

📊 Technology Resources

PowerPoint The *Marketing Essentials* PowerPoint Presentation CD-ROM provides visual lecture aids for every chapter section.

Concept Development

1. Read Section 17.3 with students.
2. Invite a public relations specialist to speak about public relations and related duties.

Discussion Starter

Public Relations What kinds of public relations activities can a business do in an attempt to avoid bad publicity? *(By treating customers and employees properly and engaging in community events, a positive image can be created.)*

CAPTION ANSWER
Part of the Community By contributing to charitable organizations, businesses seek to assist the community in providing valuable service activities, and hope to gain the goodwill and respect of community members.

■ The Role of Public Relations Specialists

Companies often hire public relations firms or establish public relations departments. Public relations specialists work with more than just customers, employees, and the media. They also consult with civic and professional groups, legislators, government officials, consumer activists, stockholders, environmentalists, and suppliers. Public relations specialists work in both the public and the private sector. The public sector includes schools, hospitals, universities, government agencies, charitable organizations, and the military. Like private businesses, public agencies also have a need to project a favorable image.

The principal task of a public relations specialist is to publicize the good news about a company and its products—and to control the damage done by any negative news.

In 1999, two different production problems in Belgium affected the taste, quality, and external odor of some Coca-Cola products. This prompted the Belgium health minister to take precautionary measures. Although no health or safety issues were discovered, the negative publicity affected the overall image and sales of Coke products in Europe. Coca-Cola Belgium removed all old products from the marketplace and destroyed them in an environmentally safe manner. The company also took steps to restart production with all new ingredients, performed more rigorous testing on all production lines, added new equipment, and improved monitoring systems. By acting quickly and responsibly, Coca-Cola was able to overcome the bad publicity.

WRITING NEWS RELEASES The public relations specialist's principal publicity tool is the news release. A **news release** is a prewritten story about a company that is sent to the various media. It usually contains information about the company's employees, stores, operations, products, corporate philosophy, or participation in an event or program. Publicity projects should be selected for multiple uses. Information gathered for a news release should also be appropriate for use in a new company brochure or ad.

A news release must contain a certain amount of newsworthy information in order to be picked up

Life In The Diverse MARKETPLACE

Naming Names

For Westerners, addressing someone in Malaysia can be complex. Malaysia is a constitutional monarchy with nine royal houses, so it is quite possible that you could meet royalty in Malaysia! When addressing people, use their titles (Teacher, Doctor, Engineer, etc.) and their names. To further complicate matters—each of the three main groups in Malaysia (Chinese, Muslim, and Indian) have different naming conventions. To ask a Malaysian what to call him or her, be direct and polite—he or she may be just as confused about what to call you!

Thinking Critically

What U.S. naming standards might cause confusion to a visitor from abroad?

and carried by the media. There are certain guidelines that public relations personnel must observe in planning and carrying out publicity projects.

A public affairs staff should send only important news releases to the media. A news release telling of a shopping mall expansion that will result in many new jobs created in a community has a good chance of being run by the media. When a media source is overwhelmed with submissions, it will tend to disregard them. By sending significant news releases periodically, a business has a better chance of having its material published. It is also helpful to send news releases to all media, both print and broadcast, at the same time. The chances that one will use the material are greater when all are contacted.

News releases should have a continuity of theme extending over many months or even years. Similar repeat messages will achieve maximum impact on an audience. A consistent message might be that a business is community minded. Such is the case with the Dayton Corporation community involvement program. Since 1946, the company has

FIGURE 17-2

NEWS RELEASES

News releases sent through regular mail to the media should be double-spaced and written on letterhead stationery. Margins should be about $1\frac{1}{2}$ inches to allow the editor to make notes. Always type or word process copy, and be sure it is clean and free of spelling errors. News releases published through electronic means on the World Wide Web are limited by the design of the Web site, but still must identify the company and follow the rules listed below.

I will read this

1
The first paragraph should answer the Who, What, When, Where, and Why questions.

Please read the buble #1 #2 #3

Adidas' Olympic Mission: More Sports, More Athletes

Colorado Springs, May 16—Why would a company spend a lot of time and resources developing a fencing shoe for the 2000 Olympics in Sydney? For Adidas, the answer is simple: They are committed to more athletes and more sports than any other brand.

Adidas' roots and heritage are linked to the Olympic Games. Adi Dassler, founder of Adidas, was producing track shoes for Olympic athletes as early as the 1928 Games in Amsterdam. Since then, the company has consistently been making advances in technologies specifically designed for Olympic competitors.

Adidas is committed to producing revolutionary products to enhance the performance of all athletes at all levels. Throughout every stage of the development and testing process, Adidas works closely with athletes. The athletes' requirements and preferences, coupled with Adidas' expertise and knowledge, produce the most technologically advanced shoes and apparel available.

For more information, please contact Adidas Public Relations:
Nigel Wright
Phone: (818) 555-2609
Fax: (818) 555-2674
Mobile: (818) 555-4064
E-mail: nigel.wright@yourname.com

# # #

2
The story with important facts should be developed within the next few paragraphs.

3
More information that is slightly less important can follow. This information could be cut by an editor without losing vital information.

4
When identifying people in a news release include the full name and title or position of the person, but avoid using Mr., Ms., Mrs., Dr., etc. After you have used the complete name refer only to the last name in the remaining part of the news release.

5
The news release should always include the name, address, and phone number of the contact person sending out the release. All pages should be numbered except for the first page.

6
The entire news release should be brief—usually one or two pages is enough. If the news release runs more than one page, write "more" at the bottom of each page except the final one. Identify and number each succeeding page at the top. On the last page, put "---30---" or "###" at the bottom to signify the end of the news release.

Place on board ---30--- ###

ASSESS

Reteaching

1. **Vocabulary** Assign and review the vocabulary terms for this section.
2. **Fact and Idea** Assign and review Fact and Idea Review questions 5–10 from the Chapter Assessment.
3. **News Releases** Give each student a copy of a news release that they can write on and keep. Have them turn to the section of their texts which lists the five basic questions that should be answered in a news release. Have them indicate on the news release where each of the questions is answered. Review their answers in class.

THE DECA CONNECTION

COMPETITIVE EVENTS AND MARKETING ESSENTIALS

Seasonal Sales Promotion Plan You can use DECA's Fashion Merchandising Promotion Plan Event as a way to illustrate the competencies presented in this chapter. This event allows your students to develop a seasonal one- to four-week sales promotion plan using apparel and accessory items for a retail store. Your students will develop objectives for the promotional plan, schedule promotional activities, and prepare a promotional budget. The students compile that information into nine Fashion Merchandising Promotion Plan fact sheets to present in competition. Students then explain their promotional plan ideas to a businessperson/judge during a 20-minute presentation/interview.

Enrichment

1. **Review** Assign and review the Chapter 17 activities in the *Student Activity Workbook.*
2. **Review** Assign and review the appropriate Thinking Critically questions from the Chapter Assessment.
3. **Review** Assign and review the following Chapter Assessment activities: Building Workplace Skills, Applying Marketing Concepts, Linking School to Work, The DECA Connection Role Play, and Internet Connection.

Evaluation

Assign and review the 17.3 Section Assessment.

Technology Resources

Assessment Resources

Go to the *Marketing Essentials* Web site (**www.marketing.glencoe.com**) for resources to teach and assess occupation-specific vocabulary.

CLOSE

Section Wrap-Up

Have students complete this statement: As a public relations specialist, your principal task is to . . . *(publicize the good news about your company and its products, and control the damage done by any bad news.)*

314

---

contributed over $200 million to the communities where it operates stores. The money goes to support local job training and dropout prevention programs, dance, music, theater, and arts groups. As a result, Dayton and its family of stores (Target, Mervyns, Hudson's, Dayton's, and Marshall Field's) are recognized as good corporate citizens and respected in the community.

Remember that the media are interested in news, not publicity. The word publicity should never be used when communicating with media personnel.

[handwritten: Please reread] A news release should be properly formatted. It also must answer five basic questions: *who, what, where, when,* and *why*. Try to avoid editorial comment and personal opinion; your focus should remain on the facts and details, not personal commentary. When an opinion must be included, attribute it to the originator by using quotes. Use simple and accurate words. Words that are unfamiliar or jargon used in a business might confuse news personnel. Be as brief as possible but be sure to cover important facts about the event. Figure 17-2 on page 313 illustrates the necessary components of an effective news release. It gives all of the necessary information regarding dates and places and offers contact names for further information. It also has an enthusiastic tone.

[handwritten: Please turn the page back to page 313]

[handwritten top margin: Lastly, let's look at press kits and press conferences]

OTHER PUBLIC RELATIONS DUTIES News releases are the major written documents for which public relations specialists are responsible, but they are not the only ones. Public relations staff members also prepare annual reports for investors and interested customers. They also prepare brochures and responses to customer inquiries. Occasionally, they even write short feature articles for trade magazines. Public relations staff members may help keep a company web site updated with noteworthy and interesting news. They also develop press kits. A **press kit** is a folder containing articles, news releases, feature stories, and photographs about a company, product, or person. Press kits are given to the media to assist them in reporting on the intended news item. These save time for public relations specialists because frequently asked questions can be covered in one place.

[handwritten: I think a lot of people don't understand that public relation specialists do so much more than news releases]

Public relations personnel frequently meet customers and the public face-to-face. They attend public relations events and organize press conferences. A **press conference** is a meeting in which a business or organization invites media members to hear an announcement about a newsworthy event. Examples of announcements usually covered in press conferences include corporate officer changes, reorganizations of corporate divisions, or mergers with different corporations. They also include new product developments, expansions, and closings of company plants or offices.

17.3 ASSESSMENT

Reviewing Key Terms and Concepts

1. Name three ways in which the goodwill generated by public relations can benefit a company.
2. What are customer advisory boards?
3. What is meant by community relations?
4. What is the primary task of public relations specialists?
5. What are three reasons why a company may call a press conference?

Thinking Critically

6. What is meant by the statement, "To the customer, the employees are the company"?

Integrating Academic Skills

7. **COMMUNICATION** Write a news release announcing the attendees of a DECA Leadership Development Conference.

17.3 ASSESSMENT ANSWERS

Reviewing Key Terms and Concepts

1. increase sales, reinforce good reputation, increase customers' response to advertising.
2. panels of customers who make suggestions about new products
3. activities a business uses to acquire or maintain respect of the community
4. They publicize the good news about a company, its products, and policies, and attempt to control damage from any negative publicity.
5. corporate officer changes, reorganizations, new products, expansions, or closings.

Thinking Critically

6. Image customers have of company's employees reflect feelings about their products.

Integrating Academic Skills

7. **COMMUNICATION** News releases may vary.

Careers in Marketing

PUBLIC RELATIONS

Beth Gillespie
Public Relation Specialist
Edelman Public Relations Worldwide

How does your workload vary?

"It's actually a consistent workload and doesn't vary all that much, though the Internet has been cause for adjustment. Our Internet-based clients want things yesterday, so we have had to learn new skills to make us better, smarter, and faster. We work with editorial services to develop the content for the press releases, and must ensure that all outgoing information is 100 percent correct."

What kind of training would you recommend for students?

"Communications and journalism are the most commonly recommended subject areas. I was lucky enough to get into a good PR department in college. Getting into any kind of writing program is very important—the written word is our best form of communication. Don't just stock up on newspaper writing courses—take creative writing classes as well. Strong writers make great PR people!"

What is your favorite part of your job?

"I enjoy the account management elements of my job, but my favorite part is when we get a 'hit', which is when the media picks up a story. Behind every story, there are weeks of hard work trying to convince the media that it is a story worth picking up. In addition, when it 'hits,' it's an amazing feeling to say, 'I was responsible for that!'"

What is your key to success?

"My product is my communication skills—it is my job to determine the needs of my clients and the best way to communicate and articulate the value of their product to the media. I am a press person, and at the end of the day, my client wants to see clips of their product in the news."

Thinking Critically
How could a course in Creative Writing improve your skills as a PR Specialist?

Career Facts

Education and Training: Increased competition raises the need for a college degree. Coursework in journalism, English, speech, communications, marketing, media production, and computer applications is recommended. Working on high school and college publications and in clubs provides valuable experience.

[handwritten: Does anybody write for a publication? parents. friends.]

Aptitudes, Abilities, and Skills: The ability to relate well to people is the primary required skill. Strong communication abilities, good listening and persuasion skills, assess confidence, quick decision-making skills, and strong management and supervisory skills are necessary.

[handwritten: whether skills important?]

Career Outlook: Employment is expected to grow faster than average through the year 2006. It is not known how the use of the Internet will affect job growth.

Career Path: Media workers, public relations production workers, and public relations assistants are all entry positions into public relations work. Experienced public relations specialists may advance to administrative positions such as Director of Public relations for government or private organizations.

[handwritten: Extra Fixture Envo-]

315

Vocabulary Review

Sentences will vary. See Glossary for definitions.

Fact and Idea Review

1. Businesses use promotion to explain features and benefits of products, tell where products are sold, advertise sales, answer customer queries, introduce new products, and create a favorable image.
2. personal selling, advertising, sales promotion, and public relations
3. Trade promotions are incentives provided in business-to-business transactions; consumer promotions are aimed at individual purchasers of a particular product or service.
4. Contests and sweepstakes are different kinds of games. Contests require participants to demonstrate a skill; sweepstakes are games of chance. Rebates are discounts offered by manufacturers to customers who purchase a product or service during a given time period.
5. Employee relations are programs and activities conducted by a business to promote goodwill among employees. Customer relations are amenities, programs, services provided to a business's customers. Community relations are activities that may acquire or maintain the respect of the community.
6. tuition reimbursement, newsletters, recreation, health and wellness programs
7. grand opening of a new business, interview with a company official, and introduction of a new product or product line
8. A news release is a prewritten story about a company sent to the media. It may contain information about the company's employees, managers, stores, operations, products, or philosophy.

Thinking Critically

1. Answers will vary, but students should indicate that the company uses all four types of promotional tools.
2. Retailers make sure that the products they carry will sell. Since there are more stock keeping units (SKUs) than most stores can handle, retailers can't afford to have slow-moving inventory.
3. The principal reason is to communicate good news about the company and its products and to control the damage done by bad news.

316

Chapter 17 ASSESSMENT

VOCABULARY REVIEW

Write one correct sentence for each of the following terms.

- promotion
- promotional mix
- product promotion
- institutional promotion
- advertising
- sales promotion
- public relations
- publicity
- push policy
- pull policy
- slotting allowance
- sales incentives
- premiums
- incentives
- promotional tie-ins
- customer advisory boards
- consumer affairs specialists
- community relations
- news release
- press kit
- press conference

FACT AND IDEA REVIEW

1. For what specific purposes do businesses typically employ promotion? (17.1)
2. List the four basic types of promotion. (17.1)
3. Explain the differences between trade promotions and consumer sales promotions. (17.2)
4. Explain the difference between contests, sweepstakes, and rebates. (17.2)
5. Distinguish between employee, customer, and community relations. (17.3)
6. List three programs or policies that businesses use to improve their image to employees. (17.3)

---

7. Give three examples of public relations events. (17.3)
8. What is a news release? (17.3)

THINKING CRITICALLY

1. Saturn has a good promotional mix for their cars. What does this statement mean?
2. Some manufacturers are upset that they are forced to pay slotting allowances. Why do retailers feel that they are justified in charging manufacturers these fees?
3. Besides working with customers and the media, public relations specialists also consult with civic and professional groups, legislators, government officials, consumer activists, stockholders, environmentalists, and suppliers. Explain why public relations specialists should respond to these groups.
4. The Dayton Corporation gives five percent of its taxable profits to communities where it does business. The contributions are made in social service programs and local arts. Analyze the reasons why the company gives to these causes.
5. Why is it important to keep news releases brief and to the point?

BUILDING WORKPLACE SKILLS

1. **Human Relations** Each month a certain amount is automatically deducted from a manager's paycheck at your company and donated to established charities. Your boss has asked you to participate. You are reluctant because you already donate to your own given charities and you prefer to pick where your money goes. How would you explain your position?
2. **Technology** Research and prepare a brief report on the advantages of electronic coupon machines as promotional devices.

---

4. Answers may include that the company wants stores located in healthy, thriving neighborhoods. Grants for social service programs encourage young people and adults to complete their education, become self-reliant, and find good jobs.
5. Answers will vary but should suggest that the information needs to be communicated quickly, and that it may also be used for an ad or brochure.

Building Workplace Skills

1. Answers will vary but should tactfully handle the situation presented.

2. Answers should mention customer convenience and increased product sales.

Applying Marketing Concepts

1. Outlines will vary. Some advantages of coupons are that they build brand awareness; reward purchasers of the product; encourage large purchases; and tell the manufacturer what market was reached. Disadvantages include misredemption and fraud; low success rates for attracting new consumers; and a bad image is created for stores that do not carry the product.

APPLYING MARKETING CONCEPTS

1. **Understanding Promotional Devices** Research the advantages and disadvantages of coupons as promotional devices. Prepare a one-page outline using a word-processing program.

2. **Planning Promotions** Plan a promotion for a product of your choice. Use a word processing program to write a report about your plan. Describe your target market, as well as the public image you would like for your product. Choose a product name and explain why it will appeal to your audience. Describe where you will sell your product (catalog, retail store, discount store, or industry). Discuss any premiums you might offer to promote your product and what kind of premiums would not be suitable.

3. **Analyzing Promotions** Choose a product that is heavily promoted in the marketplace. Prepare an oral analysis of the product using presentation software. Answer the following questions in your analysis: What market is being targeted? What type of image is the company trying to project? What types of promotion are used? Are the promotions effective? Why or why not?

4. **Researching Publicity** Identify an event that brought a business negative publicity. Could the business have avoided the outcome? Could it have limited the damage? Explore your answers in a word-processed one-page report.

LINKING SCHOOL TO WORK

Information Skills Visit a local store or cooperative education training station to review products offered for sale. Photograph or bring examples to class of consumer sales promotions being used to sell products at the store.

Role Play: Promotion Planner

Situation You are to assume the role of assistant manager of a local bookstore. Your manager (judge) has recently asked you to develop a promotional mix to attract people aged 16 to 24 to your business.

Activity You must identify the proper promotional mix for your store by using various promotional devices (advertising, publicity, sales promotions, and personal selling) available in your area and explain your ideas for the promotional mix.

Evaluation You will be evaluated on how well you meet the following performance indicators:

- Identify elements of the promotional mix
- Coordinate activities in the promotional mix
- Develop a sales promotion plan
- Analyze use of specialty promotions
- Explain the nature of a promotional plan

*inter*NET CONNECTION

About Our Company
As public relations specialist for a national consumer products company, you are required to develop a Web site to assist customers in understanding company events, products, and services.

Connect
- Find three consumer products company sites on the Web.
- Identify at least three elements on each Web site that can be described as public relations tools.

THE DECA CONNECTION

Students should be evaluated on the performance indicators noted in the Role Play.
- For another DECA Role Play, go to the *Student Activity Workbook,* p. 141.
- For more in-depth Role Play practice, refer to DECA's *Essential Competitive Events Handbook.* To order, contact DECA at www.deca.org.

*inter*NET CONNECTION
Answers will vary.

Mini Quiz

Administer the Mini Quiz orally. For an expanded chapter quiz, go to page 95 of the *Reproducible Tests* book.

1. A promotional mix is a combination of different types of promotion used to sell a product. T/F? True

2. Any form of paid non-personal presentation and promotion of ideas, goods, or services by an identified sponsor is called advertising.

3. Any activity designed to create goodwill toward a business is called public relations.

4. Publicity differs from advertising, as a promotional tool because it is not paid by the business.

5. A pre-written story about a company that is sent to the various media is called a(n) news release.

2. Reports will vary.
3. Analyses will vary.
4. Reports will vary.

Linking School to Work
Answers will vary depending on work situation.

1. **Assessment** Have students complete the Reproducible Test for Chapter 17 or construct your own tests using the ExamView software.
2. **Enrichment** Have students complete the corresponding activities in the following workbooks:
   - *Marketing Math Workbook,* p. 45
   - *Marketing Research Project Workbook,* p. 85

Chapter Overview

This chapter explains the importance of visual merchandising as a promotional strategy to attract potential customers and to create a desired business image. The chapter explains the concepts of visual merchandising and display. It discusses the different types of store displays, the key steps in display preparation, required artistic elements contained in displays, and basic display maintenance principles.

Springboard

Brainstorm Ask students to imagine that they're in a local shopping mall. Have them list the interior and exterior elements of a store that indicate the type of merchandise carried (discount—low priced, specialty, prestige—high priced). List students' answers on the board and include the store location, storefront, signage, exterior window displays, store entrance, store layout, and interior displays. Tell students that these elements comprise visual merchandising.

Prereading

List the section objectives to discuss with students. Have students skim the chapter, looking at the pictures, reading the captions, and noting the heads. Ask questions to ensure that the students have a minimal understanding of the chapter structure.

Preteaching Marketing Vocabulary

Randomly call on different students to define in their own words the chapter's vocabulary words. Clarify any misconceptions about the definition of each term.

Marketing: What It Takes
Answer Answers will vary but should show creativity and consideration of consumers' buying interests in the season.

Chapter 18

Visual Merchandising and Display

Marketing: What It Takes

Matching the Season
You work as a sales associate for an apparel and accessories store. You have been asked by the assistant manager to design a visually appealing interior display for a spring promotion. You must suggest a possible plan for the display to match the store's image.

WHAT WILL YOU DO?
What ideas will you use to plan an appropriate seasonal display for your store?

THE DECA CONNECTION — **ADVISOR CORNER**

Business Fashions on Display After a lesson on professional dress, bring in an expert from the retail industry to talk about general rules of thumb when dressing for work and/or professional DECA conferences. One way to further focus students on professional dress is to partner with area retailers by having them lend clothing to be displayed at school. Have small groups of students approach local retailers and explain the program and ask to borrow some professional clothing for display. Display cases could be changed weekly to showcase professional clothes from a variety of retailers for different kinds of jobs. This is a service your chapter can perform for the benefit of the entire student body.

Display Features

What Is Visual Merchandising?

Visual merchandising refers to the coordination of all of the physical elements in a place of business that are used to project the right image to its customers. The "right" image is one that invites interest in the merchandise or services being offered, encourages purchasing, and makes the customer feel good about where he or she is doing business. It creates the whole vision of an organization and draws in the customer.

Successful businesses create distinct, clear, and consistent images for their customers. A good image sets a business apart from the competition. This image is a unique blend of store characteristics, location, products, prices, advertising, public relations, and personal selling. A store's image should highlight what sets it apart from the competition. Its most important component, however, is sales promotion. While this chapter primarily focuses on visual merchandising in retail stores, manufacturers and wholesalers also use visual merchandising to sell their products. Visual merchandising is used extensively at manufacturers' showrooms, trade shows, and conventions.

The term *visual merchandising* is sometimes used interchangeably with the term *display* even though the two are not the same. Display is a much narrower concept and makes up only one part of visual merchandising. Display refers to the visual and artistic aspects of presenting a product to a target group of customers. Visual merchandising, by contrast, involves the visual and artistic aspects of the entire business environment.

Visual merchandising has increased tremendously in importance because of the growth of self-service, superstores, and box stores. There is little personal selling in the warehouse environment of the box store—products must sell themselves. This has spurred box stores to develop giant signs, graphics, and banners to designate areas within the store. Individual displays are set off the main or drive aisles with merchandise presented on fixtures behind each display. Home Depot, an example of a box store, has over 100,000 square feet and specializes in home improvement products. These visual merchandising activities have had a strong influence on the promotional activities of other self-service and full-service retailers.

It is the visual merchandisers that are responsible for the total merchandise or service presentation, the overall business image, and even the building and placement of design elements. They are active members of the decision-making team that promotes a business and its products.

What You'll Learn

- The concepts of visual merchandising and display
- The important display features that contribute to a store's image
- The various types of displays

Why It's Important

Since visual merchandising helps sell products and build store image, you will need to know about the different types of store displays and how to create them.

Key Terms

- visual merchandising
- display
- storefront
- marquee
- store layout
- fixtures

FOCUS

Bell Ringer Activity

Describe and Analyze Have students choose one of the stores they frequent and write answers to the following questions:

- Where is the store located? What does its location say about its exclusivity or lack thereof?
- What image does the store sign project?
- What does the store's entrance look like?
- What is the quality and sophistication of these window displays?
- What type of merchandise is displayed in the windows?
- How is the store laid out?
- How are the fixtures, walls, and floors treated?
- What is the lighting like?
- What is the quality of the interior displays?
- What types of customer services are available?

Introducing the Section

Display Features Review students' answers to the Bell Ringer Activity. Were there any disagreements among students regarding their perceptions? Explain that students should not judge a store negatively because it carries discount merchandise. Some of the most successful retailers in the United States, such as Wal-Mart and Kmart, do some of the heaviest discounting.

TEACH

Technology Resources

PowerPoint The *Marketing Essentials* PowerPoint Presentation CD-ROM provides visual lecture aids for every chapter section.

319

Classroom Resources

For the Teacher
- Teacher Editions for all workbooks
- Assessment Package
- PowerPoint Presentation Software
- Interactive Lesson Planner
- ILP Block Scheduling, p. 6
- ILP Lesson Plans, p. 39
- ILP Internet Resources, p. 55

- ILP *BusinessWeek* Case Studies, p. 115
- ILP Marketing Career Portfolio, p. 36
- *Marketing Essentials* Web site (**www.marketing.glencoe.com**)

For the Student
- Student Activity Workbook, p. 149
- Marketing Math Workbook, p. 45

- Marketing Research Project Workbook, p. 85
- ILP School-to-Work Activity Workbook, p. 77
- Virtual Business simulation
- *Marketing Essentials* Web site (**www.marketing.glencoe.com**)

ILP These resources are available in print and on the Interactive Lesson Planner (ILP)

Concept Development

1. Read Section 18.1 with students.
2. Show the class photographs or slides of store layouts. Have students identify and define selling space, merchandise space, personnel space, and customer space. Ask students to study each photo or slide and make suggestions for improving the layout of the store.

Discussion Starter

Promotional Displays

Promotional displays promote the sale of one product, a line of related products, or a storewide sale of a variety of the store's products. Have students give some creative examples of special lighting, signs, and/or props you would find in displays for the following items:

- luggage *(maps, a globe, a miniature airplane or train, sunglasses or anything evocative of a beach, a sunlamp, signs for certain cities or destinations)*
- fine crystal goblets displayed during the holiday season *(the goblets could be filled with confetti or clear marbles, a sign that says Happy Holidays or Happy New Year, streamers in various colors, party favors, holiday ornaments or wrapped gifts)*
- a vacuum cleaner *(a thick square of carpeting with [fake] dirt sprinkled on it)*

Have students generate other examples of products and display ideas.

CAPTION ANSWER

The Superstore Phenomenon
They are often referred to as category killers because they do "kill off" smaller stores because of their greater selection, better prices, and easy-to-shop space.

■ **The Superstore Phenomenon** Superstores are often 20,000- to 100,000-square-foot buildings of concrete, cement, steel and glass with a vast assortment of one specific kind of product. *Why are these types of stores often called category killers?*

Elements of Visual Merchandising

Visual merchandising is used to create a positive shopping experience—and that makes customers want to return. Stores may consider four key elements to achieve this: *storefront, store layout, store interior,* and *interior displays.*

■ Storefront

The total exterior of a business is known as the storefront. The storefront includes the store's sign, marquee, outdoor lighting, banners, planters, awnings, windows, and the building itself (its design and setting). Consider K-Mart superstores, which are typically large buildings with bold graphics, signage, and colorful facades that are conveniently located near a main highway with a large, well-lit parking lot to attract customers.

The importance of an effective storefront cannot be overestimated. It projects the image of the store as discount or expensive or conservative or trendy. It can also attract potential customers by making the business stand out from its competitors.

SIGNS The store sign offers the first impression and therefore should make a statement about the business. It should be original and easily recognizable. The letters, building materials, and colors that are used help create the store's image. An upscale department store might use an elegant script, while

a discount merchandiser, such as Wal-Mart, uses bold, block-like capital letters in signage. Signs are designed primarily to attract attention and help to advertise a business.

MARQUEE A marquee is an architectural canopy that extends over a store's entrance. Marquees can be found over most theater entrances, where the times and dates of the latest plays or movies are highlighted. Older stores and some specialty stores also use marquees to display the store's name. A marquee extends out over an entrance and is highly visible. This gives greater prominence than other store signs.

ENTRANCES Entrances are usually designed with customer convenience and store security in mind. Smaller stores normally have only one entrance, while larger stores (such as department stores) have several. The average midsize business probably needs at least two entrances—one leading in from the street for pedestrians and another adjacent to the parking lot for patrons who drive to the business.

There are several types of entrances, including revolving, push-pull, electronic, and climate-controlled entrances. Climate-controlled entrances are most frequently found in enclosed shopping malls. Each of these projects a certain image. Electronically controlled sliding doors, for example, suggest a practical, self-service business. Push-pull doors, which often have fancy metal or wooden push plates or bars, suggest a full-service establishment.

GREAT IDEAS from the Marketing Classroom

Patricia D. King
Windham High School
Willimantic, CT

Many high school students love to spend free time shopping or hanging out in the mall. Use this interest to enhance their understanding of visual merchandising and display techniques. Have students visit three different types of retail

establishments. Students should observe the merchandise in the windows, the entrance of the building, and the store layout. How would they classify the overall image of the establishment? Is the merchandise easily accessible? Do the window displays conform to the overall image of the store? Have students prepare a written evaluation of each display in terms of artistic elements.

■ **It's One of a Kind** A unique store-front can attract customers by being different from its competitors. *What features make this store stand out from its competitors?*

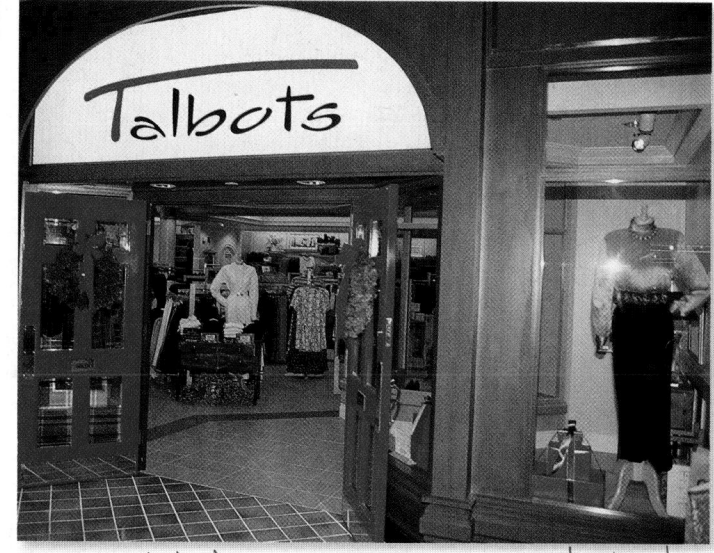

[handwritten: It's important to point this out]

WINDOW DISPLAYS Display windows, when available on a building's exterior, are especially useful for visual merchandising. Displays placed in these windows can begin the selling process even before the potential customer enters the store.

Window displays are designed to attract the customer by suggesting both the type of merchandise and the type of atmosphere inside the store. Two basic kinds of window displays are promotional displays and institutional displays. *[handwritten: the book says there are two types, window displays. Who can tell me the difference?]*

Promotional displays promote the sale of one product, a line of related products, or a variety of products. They do so by presenting items with special lighting, signs, and props. Promotional displays frequently are used to sell a particular product or related product line, such as athletic clothing for golfers. Often promotional displays emphasize a particular theme, such as Mother's Day or Labor Day. Promotional displays are also used to promote storewide events, such as anniversary, pre-season, or end of season sales.

Institutional displays promote store image rather than specific products. Such displays are designed to build customer goodwill and enhance store image by showing that the business is interested in the welfare of the community. Institutional displays focus on public causes, worthy ideas, or community organizations. They might feature the activities of the national groups, such as the American Cancer Society, or local volunteer efforts.

■ **Store Layout** *[handwritten: Next the book mentions store layout. What is store layout?]*

Store layout refers to the way store floor space is used to facilitate and promote sales and to best serve the customer. A typical store layout divides a store into four different kinds of space: *[handwritten: Please read]*

- *Selling space* assigned for interior displays, product demonstrations, and sales transactions
- *Merchandising space* allocated to items that are kept in inventory for selling
- *Personnel space* assigned to store employees for lockers, lunch breaks, and restrooms
- *Customer space* assigned for the comfort and convenience of the customer, including a café or food court, dressing rooms, lounges, and recreation areas for children

Once selling space has been allocated, visual merchandising personnel work closely with store layout specialists to decide the best locations for particular kinds of merchandise. In conjunction with management, visual merchandisers have input about where each product category area will be located. They also help to determine which products and services should be located closest to doors, exits, elevators, and parking lots.

Decisions are made about how much selling space to have and the type of interior and window displays to use for various products and related items. Store layout planners and visual merchandisers design traffic patterns to promote extended shopping within the store. *[handwritten: This is interesting. It says]*

Chapter 18 ■ *Visual Merchandising and Display* **321**

Independent Practice

1. Interview and Summarize
Have students interview your co-op supervisor or manager of a local retail store. Have them ask him or her how the decisions are made to create the store's image through visual merchandising. Have them ask what recent image changes have been made or are planned. Why was the decision made to change the store's image? Have students summarize the findings in a 250-word report, and if possible, include photos of the store's visual merchandising.

2. Research, Photograph or Draw, and Discuss Have students make up a display rating sheet addressing the criteria discussed in this chapter. Tell them to take the rating sheet to the local mall and use the sheet to rate various displays in a variety of stores. If possible, have them photograph the displays. Have them pick the best display and present the photo or a sketch to the class along with a brief discussion of why they rated the display as the best.

■ Store Interior

Once the general placement of merchandise has been determined, store personnel can develop the visual merchandising approaches for the building's interior. The selection of floor and wall coverings, lighting, colors, and store fixtures can powerfully affect the store image.

Take flooring, for example. Many supermarkets use linoleum or tile floors to project an inexpensive, practical image. Specialty stores often use thick carpeting to send the opposite message to their customers.

Colors and lighting can be used in a similar fashion. Bright colors and light pastels (or plain white) appeal to different types of customers. Stores catering to teens might favor bright colors and lighting. Stores catering to adults often choose pastels and soft, subtle lighting effects. Superstores choose fluorescent or high-intensity discharge lighting, while prestige retailers might install expensive chandeliers.

The principal installations in a store, however, are the fixtures. **Fixtures** are permanent or movable store furnishings, such as display cases, counters, shelving, racks, and benches.

A business seeking an upscale image might enhance its fixtures by painting them or covering them with textured materials (carpeting, fabric, cork, or reed, for example). A business catering to discount buyers would most likely leave its fixtures plain.

Walls are interior features that can be covered to reinforce store image. Women's specialty stores often use small or subtly patterned paper, while department stores tend to favor soft pastels. Walls are also used to display merchandise. Clothing can be pinned to the surface. This technique has the advantage of both saving space and attracting customers with higher-than-eye-level displays.

The width of a store's aisles may influence behavior more directly than any other element of visual merchandising. Different aisle widths create different images for a store.

Finally, the size, variety, and quality of the merchandise assortment carried by a store affects its clientele. Brand name merchandise conveys a different image from generic goods; each will attract (or put off) a different kind of customer.

■ **Supporting the Arts and Education** Institutional displays promote public causes, institutions, and organizations. *How do stores benefit from institutional displays?*

■ Interior Displays

Interior or in-store displays are technically part of the general store interior. As elements of visual merchandising, however, they are so significant that they are commonly considered in a category of their own. This is because such displays generate one out of every four sales. If interior displays are done exceptionally well, they enable customers to make a selection without personal assistance. Thus, they occupy an important place in today's selling environment, where many stores are self-service.

Five types of interior displays are closed displays, open displays, architectural displays, point-of-purchase displays, and store decorations. Figure 18-1 illustrates the five types of interior displays.

Interior displays use fixtures and props to showcase merchandise. The types of fixtures and props visual merchandisers use will vary depending on the merchandise displayed.

CAPTION ANSWER
Supporting the Arts and Education Institutional displays build goodwill for the sponsoring store and show that the store is interested in worthy causes, public organizations, and educational endeavors. The photo indicates support for education by Mobil.

FIGURE 18-1

TYPES OF INTERIOR DISPLAYS

Retailers use interior displays to show merchandise, provide customers with product information, get customers to stop and shop at the store, reinforce advertising, and promote the store's image.

ARCHITECTURAL DISPLAYS

Architectural displays consist of model rooms that allow customers to see how merchandise might look in their homes. Area rugs or the arrangement of the furniture itself can be used to suggest the setting instead of walls or partitions.

STORE DECORATIONS

Store decorations are displays that coincide with specific seasons or holidays. Banners, signs, props, and similar items used to invoke the spirit of Valentine's Day, Halloween, summer, or fall are examples.

OPEN DISPLAYS

Open displays allow customers to handle and examine merchandise without the help of a salesperson. Hanging racks for suits and dresses or countertop and shelf displays for cosmetics are examples.

CLOSED DISPLAYS

Closed displays allow customers to see but not handle merchandise. They are found in catalog showrooms or businesses such as jewelry stores where security or breakage is a concern.

POINT-OF-PURCHASE DISPLAYS

Point-of-purchase displays are displays designed mainly to promote impulse purchases. Point-of-purchase displays are usually more effective at supporting new products than established ones. Point-of-purchase displays are usually supplied by a product manufacturer for use at or near the cash register.

More About . . .

Fixtures

A current trend in fixtures is "ambiance" displays. For example, sporting goods retailers might create waterfalls, complete with the sights and sounds of an actual fishing location to complement fishing goods displays.

Did You Know?

PC Week reports that as many as 85 percent of consumer purchases are influenced by what consumers see in the store. This opens a new era for computer retailers who in the past have relied heavily on sales staff rather than point-of-purchase displays to sell computers and related items. Interactive displays have also become more popular for the industry.

SECTION 18.1

ASSESS

Reteaching

1. **Vocabulary** Assign and review the vocabulary terms for this section.
2. **Fact and Idea** Assign and review Fact and Idea Review questions 1–6 from the Chapter Assessment.
3. **Visual Merchandising** Ask students to explain why display is only one part of visual merchandising. Then, for reteaching purposes, have them identify all aspects of visual merchandising that they have learned.

Enrichment

1. **Review** Assign and review the appropriate Thinking Critically questions from the Chapter Assessment.
2. **Extend** Assign and review the corresponding activities from *BusinessWeek Case Studies, Internet Resources,* and the *School-to-Work Activity Workbook.* ILP
3. **Report** Have students write a report that compares and contrasts two types of retailers who sell the same types of items but have two totally different images.

Evaluation

Assign and review the Section 18.1 Assessment.

Technology Resources

GO TO **Assessment Resources**
Go to the *Marketing Essentials* Web site (**www.marketing.glencoe. com**) for resources to teach and assess occupation-specific vocabulary.

SECTION 18.1

VIRTUAL BUSINESS

Merchandising
Introduce the concept of merchandising and principles of store layout to students using Knowledge Matters' Virtual Business visual simulation, "Marketing—Merchandising." Students change the floor plan for their store, observe customer traffic patterns, and analyze the overall effect on sales. If needed, have students run the Virtual Business tutorial before beginning this simulation. For additional instructions and teaching tips for this activity, go to the *Marketing Essentials* Web site (**www.marketing.glencoe.com**).

CLOSE

Section Wrap-Up

Have students complete this statement: Visual merchandising refers to . . . *(the coordination of all physical elements in a place of business so that it projects the right image to its customers.)*

One Stop Shop

Answer *Loppi* could act as an ATM, sell products too large for a Japanese convenience store to shelve, or even provide horoscopes.

It is important to create a clean and organized visual display regardless of which type of display you choose. It is also helpful to group merchandise by type or with related items to simplify the shopping experience for customers.

As you can see in Figure 18-1, different sales situations call for different types of displays. Items like clothing would be difficult to showcase in a closed display. One typical department store department that often combining many different displays is the cosmetic department. Some items may be part of an open display, such as brushes or accessories; other items could be contained in a closed display to prevent customers from sampling goods other than the tester; finally, a point-of-purchase display may feature a computerized touch screen terminal that can evaluate the best cosmetics for each customer's preferences, coloring, and skin type. These different types of displays all compliment each other and create a positive, interactive buying experience.

Props used with interior displays are generally classified as *decorative* or *functional*. Decorative props include background scenery used to indicate a season or to create an interesting setting. Functional props include functional items for holding merchandise, such as mannequins and shirt forms. Display designers often look for unusual props or unusual ways to use common items as props. Imaginative jewelry display designers, for example, may use open candy boxes to display colored stone.

One Stop Shop

A loaf of bread, a carton of milk, tickets to the symphony—in Japan, a trip to the convenience store can yield much more than groceries or a newspaper. In a country where physical space is extremely limited, product display and delivery have become a major concern. Enter *Loppi*. *Loppi* is a computer terminal located in convenience stores that increases product offerings. Using a touch-pad screen, shoppers can order concert tickets, make travel reservations, or order meals online to be delivered. Need a book? Order online, then pay and pick it up at your local 7-Eleven the next day. This seems like a perfect fit for Japanese consumers, who are more reluctant than their American counterparts to use their credit cards online.

Thinking Critically
What other products might *Loppi* offer to its customers?

18.1 ASSESSMENT

Reviewing Key Terms and Concepts

1. What is visual merchandising?
2. Why is a display considered part of visual merchandising?
3. How do exterior and interior features help a store's image?
4. List two different types of window displays.
5. Describe the five different types of interior displays used by retailers.

Thinking Critically

6. Is it necessary for staff members who work with visual merchandising to know basic sales promotion techniques? Justify your response.

Integrating Academic Skills

7. **COMMUNICATION** You work as a visual merchandiser for a large department store. You would like to devote one of the main display windows to a public service, rather than using a less visible space within the store as suggested by the manager. Write a formal proposal detailing your views. Be sure to name the public service, describe the display, and indicate how you believe the store will benefit.

18.1 ASSESSMENT ANSWERS

Reviewing Key Terms and Concepts

1. It involves the visual artistic elements of the entire business environment.
2. It relates to visual and artistic elements of product presentation to target customers.
3. They can project an appropriate image and help attract customers by making the business stand out from its competition.
4. promotional displays and institutional displays
5. closed displays, open displays, architectural displays, point-of-purchase displays, and store decorations

Thinking Critically

6. Yes. Visual merchandising is a form of sales promotion.

Integrating Academic Skills

7. **COMMUNICATION** Answers will vary.

Artistic Design

SECTION 18.2

Display Design and Preparation

In the retail environment, a display has about three to eight seconds to attract a customer's attention, create a desire, and sell a product. This limited time frame means that a business must target its displays carefully to appeal to its customers. Failing to do this not only risks losing sales but may ruin a business's image as well. The traditional clothing store that suddenly begins showing abstract displays of trendy merchandise is likely to attract some new style-conscious customers. It also might alienate many of its regular customers.

A business needs to identify its customers, the desired image, and the kind of merchandise concept that it wants to promote before building displays. Display design and selection involves the following five steps.

■ Step 1: Selecting Merchandise for Display

The first important step when preparing a display is to select the right merchandise. Merchandise selected for display must have sales appeal. New, popular, and best-selling products are often selected for display for this reason. Display merchandise must also be visually appealing and current to attract customers. It must be appropriate for the season and for the store's geographic location. Displays often address the latest fashion, fad, or trend.

■ Step 2: Selecting the Display

The merchandise selected largely determines the type of display that is used. There are four kinds of displays.

A *one-item display* is used to show a single item. An example would be an Anne Klein shoe displayed on a show box with a promotional logotype. One-item displays are usually constructed for a single product promotion or an advertised special.

A *line-of-goods* display shows one kind of product but features several brands, sizes, or models. An example would be a display unit showing tennis shoes by different manufacturers, such as Reebok and Nike, or a display of styles of shoes put out only by Nike.

A *related-merchandise* display features items that are meant to be used together. In an apparel store, a related-merchandise display might feature casual wear—shirts, pants, sweaters, and shoes. Related-merchandise displays are designed primarily to entice the customers to buy more than one item.

An *assortment display* features a collection of unrelated items. Such displays usually emphasize price and tell customers that a wide variety of merchandise is available for sale. They are typically used by variety stores, discounters, and supermarkets to have a special appeal to bargain hunters.

Chapter 18 ■ *Visual Merchandising and Display* **325**

• What You'll Learn

- The steps used in designing and preparing displays
- The artistic considerations involved in display preparation
- The maintenance considerations for displays

• Why It's Important

Visual merchandisers must know the rules of artistic design for displays that attract customers and keep them coming back.

• Key Terms

- complementary colors
- adjacent colors
- proportion
- formal balance
- informal balance

SECTION 18.2

FOCUS

Bell Ringer Activity

Brainstorm Ask students this question: If you only had three to eight seconds to attract attention in a nonverbal way, how would you do it?

Introducing the Section

Artistic Design Review students' answers from the Bell Ringer Activity. Some of the things they mentioned might include using dramatic or loud colors, using signs, or using physical motion—all things that are used in display to attract attention.

Tell students that in the retail environment, a display has about three to eight seconds to attract a customer's attention, create a desire, and sell a product. Thus, a business must create its displays carefully to appeal to its target customers. Ask students to describe displays that made a particularly lasting impression on them and tell why.

TEACH

Technology Resources

PowerPoint The *Marketing Essentials* PowerPoint Presentation CD-ROM provides visual lecture aids for every chapter section.

Classroom Resources

For the Teacher
- Teacher Editions for all workbooks
- Assessment Package
- PowerPoint Presentation Software
- Interactive Lesson Planner
- ILP Block Scheduling, p. 6
- ILP Lesson Plans, p. 40
- ILP Internet Resources, p. 55

- ILP Blackline Masters, p. 34
- ILP *BusinessWeek* Case Studies, p. 115
- ILP Marketing Career Portfolio, p. 36
- *Marketing Essentials* Web site (**www.marketing.glencoe.com**)

For the Student
- Student Activity Workbook, p. 149
- Marketing Math Workbook, p. 45

- Marketing Research Project Workbook, p. 85
- ILP School-to-Work Activity Workbook, p. 77
- Virtual Business simulation
- *Marketing Essentials* Web site (**www.marketing.glencoe.com**)

These resources are available in print and on the Interactive Lesson Planner (ILP)

325

Concept Development

1. Read Section 18.2 with students.
2. Have students read aloud the Case Study on page 329 and review the answers in class.
3. Show slides or pictures to illustrate the various types of displays. Have students identify the type in each picture. Also have them tell what kind of store uses each type of display. Use slides or pictures to illustrate the use of realistic, semirealistic, and abstract settings for displays. Ask students to evaluate the settings shown.
4. Magazines such as *Visual Merchandising and Store Design, Display and Design Ideas, Retail Store Image,* and *Inspiration,* a European trade publication, feature current national and international trends in visual merchandising. Have several copies available in your classroom for students to peruse.

Discussion Starter

Types of Lines Draw various types of lines on the board (straight, curved, diagonal, vertical, horizontal) and ask students what moods they evoke.

[handwritten]
1. line
2. color
3. shape
4. direction
5. texture
6. proportion
7. balance
8. motion
9. lighting

[handwritten top] Next, the book mentions "choosing a setting"

■ Step 3: Choosing a Setting

[handwritten] This states that there are 3 types of settings

Displays can be presented in a number of different types of settings. The setting a business selects will depend largely on the image it wants to project. *[handwritten] Please read each one.*

A *realistic setting* depicts a room, area, or recognizable locale. The scene could be a restaurant, a park, or a party. Props, such as tables, chairs, plants, risers, books, dishes, and mannequins provide the details.

A *semirealistic setting* suggests a room or locale but leaves the details to the viewer's imagination. A cardboard sun, beach towel, surfing poster, and a sprinkling of sand would be enough to invoke the rest of the scene—an oceanfront beach—in the viewer's mind. Businesses use semirealistic settings when either space or budgets do not permit realistic settings. *[handwritten] Recall that businesses use semirealistic settings when either space or budgets are...*

An *abstract setting* does not imitate (or even try to imitate) reality. It focuses on form and color rather than reproducing actual objects. Wide bands of torn colored paper used as an accent behind or around merchandise can create an attractive visual image that has little or nothing to do with reality.

Abstract settings are gaining popularity, mainly because they are inexpensive and do not require large amounts of storage space for accumulated props. Display specialists are increasingly accenting products with items such as cardboard, paper, string, yarn, ribbon, and paint instead of more traditional items. *[handwritten] It says that "Abstract settings are gaining popularity..."*

■ Step 4: Manipulating Artistic Elements

[handwritten] Next, the book mentions "Manipulating Artistic Elements"

The artistic elements of a display include *line, color, shape, direction, texture, proportion, balance, motion,* and *lighting*. These elements influence your perception of a display in ways that you are probably not aware of. *[handwritten] Recall that the (9) artistic elements are*

LINE As you know, people read English from left to right. They also tend to read displays the same way. Lines are created within displays to travel from left to right over featured products. *[handwritten] Notice that lines are created to travel left to right*

Various types of lines create different impressions. Straight lines suggest stiffness and control; curving lines suggest freedom and movement; diagonal lines give the impression of action; vertical lines offer height and dignity; and horizontal lines give width and confidence.

[handwritten] stiffness + control / freedom, movement / action / height dignity / width, confidence

---

■ Creating a Brand Image A single item display is designed to promote the sale of a particular product and create a distinct image. *What techniques are used to create a brand image for this product?*

REAL WORLD MARKETING

Targeting Teens

Chasing teen dollars has reinvented the way traditional malls treat some of their most valued customers. Most teens visit a mall 54 times annually—each spending nearly $2,000 on clothes, CDs, and gadgets per year. Competing with the Internet is the mall's biggest challenge; however, malls are making strides for two reasons—many teens don't have credit cards, and they prefer shopping with friends. Capitalizing on these facts, malls like the Glendale Galleria in California are unveiling teen zones, complete with live DJs, big screen TVs, and Internet kiosks. Older patrons aren't enthused; but many retailers are asking to be moved closer to the center of activity.

Thinking Critically

What types of stores would benefit from being nearest to teen zones?

CAPTION ANSWER
Creating a Brand Image The product's distinctive and bold logotype is pictured on the display. The sleek design of the display complements the design of the product. In addition, the product information aspect of the display prominently features the product's slogan.

REAL WORLD MARKETING

Targeting Teens
Answer Answers will vary but may include electronics, music, and clothing stores.

FIGURE 18-2

The Color Wheel

■ **The Color Wheel** The color wheel is structured to show similarities and differences in colors. *Which colors are most like each other? Which show the greatest contrast?*

COLOR can make or break a display. Displays whose colors match their surroundings too closely may not catch the customer's eye. Displays whose colors are too bright or contrasting may overwhelm the merchandise.

The colors selected for a display should contrast with those used on the walls, floors, and fixtures around them. A store decorated in pastels should have displays featuring darker, stronger colors.

Which colors make the most effective contrasts? The answers can be found in the standard color wheel (see Figure 18-2), which illustrates the relationships among colors. Complementary colors are found opposite each other in the color wheel and create the greatest contrasts. Red and green, blue and orange, and violet and yellow are examples of complementary colors.

Adjacent colors, also called analogous colors, are located next to each other in the color wheel and contrast only slightly. Successive adjacent colors (such as blue-green, blue, and blue-violet) form families, or groups of colors that blend well with each other.

Effective displays use color groupings to create visual calm or excitement. Colors from the warm side of the color wheel, such as red and yellow, convey a festive, party mood that works well with lower-priced merchandise. These colors must be used cautiously. Their contrast is so great that it can detract from the merchandise and even irritate customers. This problem can usually be avoided by varying the shades of the colors somewhat to lessen their contrast yet still retain their warmth and friendliness. Colors from the cool side of the color wheel, such as blue and green, represent calm and refinement. They are often associated with higher-priced merchandise.

Customers' expectations about color are also important in planning displays. People have come to expect certain color schemes at certain times of the year, such as earth tones in the fall and bright colors in the spring. Finally, customers' reactions to color also figure into planning displays. Red evokes excitement, so you would not use it in a display designed to convey tranquillity.

Thinking Critically

Related Display Items Have students describe related merchandise that could be displayed with the following items:

- ten-speed bicycles (*bicycle locks, carrying pouches, additional reflectors, bicycle clothing*)
- flower seeds (*gardening supplies, books on planting flowers, flower pots, sun hats, gardening clogs*)
- computers (*printers, dust covers, paper, paper holders, software, "how to" books such as DOS for Dummies, disks, and disk cases*)

Cooperative Learning

Types of Display Divide students into four to six groups. Using things they find in the classroom, have each group design and create a one-item, line-of-goods, or variety display. Each group should agree on answers to the three questions that must be asked before a display is built (potential customers? desired business image? merchandising concept?). Have them create a setting type, and use whatever artistic elements available to them in the classroom. Have each group self-critique its display and the other groups' displays.

CAPTION ANSWER
The Color Wheel The colors that are most alike are adjacent colors like blue and blue-green, red and violet, and yellow and yellow-orange. The greatest contrast is found in complementary colors like red and green, blue and orange, and violet and yellow.

THE DECA CONNECTION — **COMPETITIVE EVENTS AND MARKETING ESSENTIALS**

Role Play and Visual Merchandising While presenting the material in this chapter, you can return to DECA's Individual Series Events and utilize the role-play situations. Each of the eleven series events evaluates promotion competencies; many of those deal with visual merchandising or display. You can use those to give your students an opportunity to role-play as a means of exhibiting their newly acquired knowledge in both of those areas. You can most likely find suitable role-play situations for Visual Merchandising and Display in the areas of Food Marketing or Quick-Serve Restaurant Marketing.

Independent Practice

Draw and Identify Have students draw a color sketch of the following: a one-item display, a line-of-goods display, a related-merchandise display, and a variety display. They should identify the products in each display.

Individualized Practice

Math Skills

Tell your students: You will be decorating a holiday window display. The store's window measures 13 feet by 10 feet.

L1 You know that you need 15 yards of ribbon to complete your window display. The length of each spool of ribbon you intend to purchase is 9 feet. How many spools will you need to finish your display? How much ribbon will you have left over? *(You need 6 spools to complete the display, and you will have 7.5 feet left over. First, you need 46.5 feet of ribbon [15.5 x 3 = 46.5 feet]. 46.5 ÷ 9 feet per spool = 5.16 or 6 spools. 6 spools x 9 feet of ribbon on each spool = 54 feet of ribbon. 54 - 46.5 = 7.5 feet remaining.)*

L2 The ribbon will be fastened around the perimeter of your store's display window. What is the perimeter of the window? *(46 feet. P = 2 x [13 + 10])*

L3 What is the square footage of the store window? *(130 square feet. Width x length = A. 13 feet x 10 feet = 130 feet.)*

SHAPE Shape refers to the physical appearance, or outline, of a display. It is important to consider shape when selecting display units and the merchandise used in a display.

Shape is determined by the props, fixtures, and merchandise used in the display. Squares, cubes, circles, and triangles are some of the shapes that display units may resemble. Displays that have little or no distinct shape—called *mass displays*—are also possible. Mass displays are used to display large quantities and to convey a message of low price.

DIRECTION A good display guides the viewer's eye over all the merchandise, moving smoothly from one part of the display to another. It does not skip around. This smooth visual flow is called *direction*. Good displays create direction by using color, repetition, lighting patterns, and ribbons. This is done by arranging merchandise in a pattern to guide the customer's eye.

Displays should have a focal point. A good method of creating a focal point is to build a display around an imaginary triangle (having more merchandise at the bottom of the display than at the top, for example). This arrangement helps keep the eyes moving up and center.

Displays that lack direction are said to be *unfocused*. Typically, an unfocused display contains too many unrelated items, too many colors, or too many lines that confuse the customer and detract from the merchandise.

TEXTURE The way the surfaces in a display look together is texture. These surfaces can be either smooth or rough. The contrast between them creates visual interest. Products that are smooth, such as flatware, should be placed against backgrounds or props that are rough.

PROPORTION Proportion refers to the relationship between and among objects in a display. The merchandise should always be the primary focus of a display. Props and signs should be in proportion to the merchandise—they should never overshadow it in importance.

BALANCE Placing large items with large items and small items with small items in a display is called formal balance. When a large item is placed on one side of a display, an equally large item should be placed on the other side for balance.

The opposite technique can also be exciting in a display. Balancing a large item with several small ones is called informal balance. An example would be a display in which an adult mannequin is juxtaposed with several shallow baskets of flowers raised to the mannequin's height.

MOTION Motion can be made part of a display through the use of motorized fixtures and props. Animated figures, such as mechanical mannequins, have been used for years in holiday displays. Motion should be used sparingly to accentuate merchandise.

BRIGHT IDEAS

I Smell Sales!

When you walk into the Rainforest Café, you are greeted by tropical noises, simulated rainstorms, and what is that . . . the smell of wildflowers? Just your imagination? Probably not. The latest addition to retail purchasing is "environmental fragrancing." This innovation is now believed by many to be as important as traditional design elements such as lighting, layout, and music. Retailers are looking to enhance their customers' shopping experiences and influence purchasing. The Christmas Store at Walt Disney World pumps in scents of evergreen and spiced apple cider to put shoppers in the right mood year round. The Rainforest Café infuses fresh-flower extracts into its retail section in an effort to open consumers' minds, make them curious, and drive sales. Shoppers at Jordan's Furniture in Massachusetts smell bubble gum in the children's room displays or a hint of pine in the country-style section.

Thinking Creatively

What type of "environmental fragrancing" would be appropriate in other retailing outlets?

BRIGHT IDEAS   I Smell Sales!

Answer Answers will vary, but the type of "environmental fragrancing" used would depend on the kind of business considered.

Case Study

Redefining Nordstrom

In early 2000, Nordstrom department stores set out to create a fresh new look in the company's stores, fashion lines, and advertising. The venerable Seattle-based national retailer undertook the image makeover to attract a trendier clientele and boost sagging sales. The company redesigned stores to make them brighter, more fun, and easier to navigate. Store displays were made flashier and casual clothes more prominently displayed. Even the piano players relaxed, losing their tuxedoes after customer surveys deemed the look too formal and rigid. The company also undertook a $40 million advertising campaign, the largest in company history.

Nordstrom developed the makeover strategy after an extensive 18-month study, complete with customer interviews and focus groups. However, the redefining of Nordstrom eventually proved to have been more controversial than the company's management estimated. The approach was somewhat lost on the store's traditional audience. Some loyal customers, accustomed to a more genteel and upscale shopping experience, were alienated by the "Reinvent Yourself" campaign and found the new store layouts confusing. Although the company said it was not trying to attract the young market at the expense of its loyal customer base, the Nordstrom family halted the campaign in September 2000.

With the Nordstrom family members as focused as ever on the quality and customer service, the company is likely to prosper even in the face of shifting trends.

Case Study Review

1. Why did Nordstrom undertake a campaign to reinvent its image?
2. Why did the Nordstrom makeover fail?

A MATTER OF ETHICS

3. Is it ethical for an established company to change its image?

LIGHTING Proper lighting makes merchandise appear more attractive in displays. It is recommended that display lighting be two to five times stronger than a store's general lighting. Colored lighting can be used in displays to create dramatic effects.

It is important to consider lighting when displaying delicate, reflective items such as crystal, jewelry, and fine china. The lighting that would be used to create an elegant atmosphere in the fine housewares department would be very different than the lighting that would be used to make a bold statement in the teen clothing department. Although the lighting in the dressing rooms is technically not part of a display, it should be considered as well. Dressing room lighting that is glaring and unflattering will negatively affect a consumer buying decisions.

Chapter 18 ■ *Visual Merchandising and Display* **329**

ASSESS

Reteaching

1. **Vocabulary** Assign and review the vocabulary terms for this section.
2. **Fact and Idea** Assign and review Fact and Idea Review questions 7–10 from the Chapter Assessment.
3. **Types of Display** Show photographs and slides of displays. Have the students tell you what type of display each is, the setting type, and whether it exhibits formal or informal balance. Also discuss whatever is appropriate about the line, use of color, shape, direction, texture, lighting, and proportion.

Enrichment

1. **Review** Assign and review the Chapter 18 activities in the *Student Activity Workbook*.
2. **Review** Assign and review the appropriate Thinking Critically questions from the Chapter Assessment.
3. **Review** Assign and review the following Chapter Assessment activities: Building Workplace Skills, Applying Marketing Concepts, Linking School to Work, The DECA Connection Role Play, and Internet Connection.
4. **Design and Build** If your program has a school store, assign a team of students to design and build an interior or window display promoting merchandise available through the store.
5. **Research and Discuss** Have the students visit the display area of a local retail store to see where and how fixtures and props are stored. Discuss how they are reused in various displays throughout the year.

SECTION 18.2

Evaluation

Assign and review the Section 18.2 Assessment.

Technology Resources

 Assessment Resources
Go to the *Marketing Essentials* Web site (**www.marketing.glencoe.com**) for resources to teach and assess occupation-specific vocabulary.

CLOSE

Section Wrap-Up

Have students write or orally summarize the five steps in display design and selection. (*Steps are listed in the chapter.*)

Colors of Success

Answer While consumers' perceptions of color may change from country to country, it is not likely that the color wheel will change because it is based on the relationships between colors, not between colors and consumers.

330

■ Step 5: Evaluating Completed Displays

Visual merchandisers should evaluate completed displays by checking to see if they enhance the store's image, appeal to customers, and promote the product in the best possible way. Other factors that should be evaluated include whether the display is creatively and appropriately themed, artistically pleasing, and clean and orderly.

Display Maintenance

Once a display has been constructed, it needs to be maintained and eventually dismantled. Individual businesses have different policies regarding the duration of displays. Most businesses check displays daily for damage, displacements, or missing items caused by customer handling. Clothing items that are folded and stacked in a display should be organized and restocked frequently.

Proper display maintenance can keep the merchandise fresh and attractive to customers. Poor maintenance can create a negative image not only of the merchandise but of the store as well. Display units and props should be cleaned and merchandise dusted on a regular basis. Customers are not likely to be enthusiastic about purchasing items that are dusty or displayed on dirty shelves.

MARKETPLACE
Colors of Success

As you have already learned, serious thought must go into planning color schemes. When working in a global marketplace, the importance of colors becomes an even greater priority. A company that chooses to highlight the marketing of its new product with the color white might run into some trouble in Japan and other Asian countries. In contrast to the clean, pure image that white represents in the United States, it is the color of mourning for most Asian countries. Red may be a better choice, as it is considered a lucky color in many of the same countries.

Thinking Critically

Will the color wheel change in different countries?

18.2 ASSESSMENT

Reviewing Key Terms and Concepts

1. What decisions must be made before displays are prepared?
2. Name the five steps involved with display preparation.
3. How does a business select the display setting it desires?
4. Describe five of the artistic elements used in displays.
5. How should displays be evaluated?

Thinking Critically

6. Manufacturers often provide point-of-purchase displays to retailers. If you were a retailer, what criteria would you use in deciding whether or not to accept such a display?

Integrating Academic Skills

7. **MATH** You must recondition a half dozen mannequins (two adult and four youth). If reconditioning a youth mannequin costs $150 and reconditioning an adult mannequin costs 50 percent more, what amount should you budget for the entire job?

18.2 ASSESSMENT ANSWERS

Reviewing Key Terms and Concepts
1. Identify customers, desired business image, and kind of merchandise concept.
2. select merchandise for display, select display, choose display setting, manipulate artistic elements, and evaluate display
3. It is selected based on the image a business wants to project to potential customers.
4. line, color, shape, direction, texture, proportion, balance, motion, and lighting
5. enhance store's image, appeal to customers, and promote product

Thinking Critically
6. Answers will vary.

Integrating Academic Skills
7. **MATH** $1,050.

Careers in Marketing

RETAIL MANAGEMENT

Robin Kramer
Visual Merchandising Coordinator
KramerHutchison

Career Facts

Education and Training: Degrees in design and marketing are excellent preparation for visual merchandising coordinators, as well as classes in graphic arts and architecture.

Aptitudes, Abilities, and Skills: Creativity and an eye for design are important, as well as organizational skills, the ability to work under pressure, and strong communication skills.

Career Outlook: The overall outlook for visual merchandising is good but will likely vary according to the general economy and geographical location.

Career Path: Visual merchandising managers may be promoted to visual merchandising directors, or creative directors, assuming responsibility for several locations.

What does your job entail?

"I communicate the designer's image using plastic, metal, and wood in the arrangement of shelves, mannequins, and other fixtures upon which clothes or items are displayed. The smallest nuances—ranging from where a purse is placed on a shelf to the lighting used in a department—come together to create the atmosphere. Creating a lifestyle and an environment that speaks to the customer gives him or her a reason to choose one store over another. My company works not only with the visual display but also with the architecture, graphics, and packaging for our clients. I've helped create a brand image for companies such as Tommy Hilfiger, Donna Karan, Coach, Narciso Rodriguez, and Barneys New York."

What kind of training did you have?

"I graduated from Syracuse University and the Fashion Institute of Technology before working for Calvin Klein for seven years. As the vice president of store planning and visual display, I learned the art of carrying an image through even the smallest details. In 1996, I went into business with a single client (Isaac Mizrahi) and a single employee (my mother). KramerHutchison now has 60 employees with an ever-growing client list."

What skills are most important?

"It is imperative to have an eye for design and a flair for innovation."

How does your workload vary?

"My workload varies depending on the client's needs—some clients need one freestanding store and some need 1,500 shops in department stores."

What is your key to success?

"The key to success is to maintain a happy, motivated team while developing good relationships with clients. It is important to understand your clients and to be able to interpret their goals and wishes on the design floor."

Thinking Critically

Why are good communication skills particularly important in visual merchandising?

Chapter 18 ▪ *Visual Merchandising and Display* **331**

Vocabulary Review

See glossary for definitions.

Fact and Idea Review

1. Visual merchandising provides a clear, consistent image for a store in physical terms; shows merchandise clearly and with excitement; and creates an atmosphere that convinces people to buy products and services.
2. It is the way floor space is allocated to facilitate sales and serve customers.
3. selling space, merchandise space, personnel space, and customer space
4. Interior displays generate one out of every four sales.
5. point-of-purchase displays
6. Decorative props include background scenery to indicate a season or create an interesting setting. Functional props include items for holding merchandise, such as mannequins, racks, and shirt forms.
7. A business needs to identify its customers, the desired business image, and the kind of merchandise concept it wants.
8. Complementary colors oppose each other in the color wheel and create the greatest contrast. Adjacent colors are next to each other on the color wheel and contrast only slightly.
9. Formal balance is achieved by placing large items with large items and small items with small items. Informal balance is achieved by balancing a large item with several smaller ones.

Thinking Critically

1. Answers will vary but should include a person who has related education and/or experience in design layout, lighting, or animation; a good work history; initiative, creativity, and flexibility; and good basic skills.
2. Display windows should appeal to the store's customers and also be reflective of the community's values.
3. Answers will vary but might include stationing greeters or security personnel at the entrances, keeping merchandise near entrances in closed displays, or placing alarm mechanisms near the entrances/exits.
4. Answers will vary, but students should suggest types of displays,

---

Chapter 18 ASSESSMENT

Chapter 18 ASSESSMENT

VOCABULARY REVIEW

Organize the class into two teams for a game of "Marketing Tic-Tac-Toe." Team members will give the definition for the terms and will place an "X" or "O" on the board for each correct definition.

- visual merchandising
- display
- storefront
- marquee
- store layout
- fixtures
- complementary colors
- adjacent colors
- proportion
- formal balance
- informal balance

FACT AND IDEA REVIEW

1. What is visual merchandising? (18.1)
2. What is "store layout"? (18.1)
3. Name the four types of space found in most store layouts. (18.1)
4. Why are interior displays important? (18.1)
5. Which interior display type is most effective for new product introductions? (18.1)
6. Explain the difference between decorative and functional props. (18.1)
7. What three issues must every business address before constructing displays? (18.2)
8. Locate complementary and adjacent colors on the color wheel. How do the colors contrast with each other? (18.2)
9. How is formal and informal balance achieved in a display? (18.2)

THINKING CRITICALLY

1. Assume you are in charge of hiring visual merchandisers for a large department store. What basic skills would you require in any display specialist you hired?
2. Explain why it is important to know your community and your customers when designing store displays.
3. Retailers in some locations are limiting the number of customer entrances due to concern over shoplifting and theft. Discuss what could be done to reduce theft risks around or near store entrances.
4. The trendy colors this season, hot pink, lime green, and iridescent orange, clash with your store's conservative, beige-on-brown decor. How can you creatively display the merchandise without creating jarring or irritating effects?

BUILDING WORKPLACE SKILLS

1. **Human Relations** Your store installed lock racks for all leather merchandise, which are secured with locks, keys, and metal cords that must be removed by store personnel before an item can be tried on. The fixtures have cut theft losses by half but are unpopular with customers. Unfortunately, it is the salespeople who are taking the brunt of the criticism. How would you respond to customers if you were a salesperson?
2. **Science** Using the library or the Internet, conduct research about color. Use a word processing program to write a report detailing the physical properties that determine various colors and the psychological uses of color as an artistic element in visual merchandising.

---

settings, and artistic elements that can be manipulated to create a pleasing effect.

Building Workplace Skills

1. Students should explain that retailers must take measures to curtail shoplifting and should be readily available to assist customers by unlocking merchandise and showing it to them.
2. Reports should show thorough research into the effects of using different colors.

Applying Marketing Concepts

1. Floor plans and critiques will vary based on type of business selected.
2. Descriptions will vary, but the window displays, theme, and merchandise selected must match the image of the business.
3. Sketches, charts, and evaluations will vary.
4. Photos and presentations will vary based on the displays selected.

APPLYING MARKETING CONCEPTS

1. **Designing Store Layouts** Use a computer aided design program (CAD) to draw a floor plan showing the layout of a local business (or one floor of a department store). Code those areas provided for merchandise, selling, customers, and personnel. Then critique the layout in terms of ease of entry, traffic flow, utilization of display space, and availability of customer conveniences.

2. **Planning Holiday Displays** Select a holiday or season, and use a word processing program to describe an effective window display based on that theme for both an apparel and accessories store and an auto parts store. Specify five kinds of merchandise you would feature in each store.

3. **Comparing Display Technique** Visit a department store to observe and rate five different displays. After creating a simple sketch for each display, use a spreadsheet program to create a chart indicating color, the featured merchandise, and apparent theme. Evaluate each display in terms of the artistic elements from this chapter.

4. **Recognizing Display Tactics** Visit a local pharmacy to observe the point-of-purchase displays. Use a camera to photograph at least five different displays. Scan these into your computer and create a slide show using presentation software.

LINKING SCHOOL TO WORK

Thinking Skills Visit a cooperative education training station or a business in your community. Identify at least eight different types of interior displays, and specify the kinds of merchandise featured.

THE DECA CONNECTION

Role Play: Display Designer

Situation You are to assume the role of sales associate in an apparel and accessories department. Your department manager (judge) has asked you to create an interior display for the department. You will be given an assortment of merchandise to be displayed and the following supplies: scissors, fish line, straight pins, safety pins, foam board, a small iron, and white tissue paper.

Activity You must construct an effective display within a specified time period using the materials and merchandise provided.

Evaluation You will be evaluated on how well you meet the following performance indicators:

- Demonstrate appropriate creativity
- Demonstrate product
- Demonstrate initiative
- Demonstrate orderly and systematic behavior
- Persuade others

inter NET CONNECTION

About Our Company
As an assistant display manager, you are required to develop a list of prospective suppliers of store fixtures, mannequins, and props.

Connect
- Use the Internet to find five suppliers of store fixtures.
- Write a summary of the products and services provided by each supplier.
- Research visual merchandising trade shows and conventions for the upcoming year.

THE DECA CONNECTION

Students should be evaluated on the performance indicators noted in the Role Play.
- For another DECA Role Play, go to the *Student Activity Workbook*, p. 149.
- For more in-depth Role Play practice, refer to DECA's *Essential Competitive Events Handbook*. To order, contact DECA at **www.deca.org**.

inter NET CONNECTION
Answers will vary.

Mini Quiz

Administer the Mini Quiz orally. For an expanded chapter quiz, go to page 99 of the *Reproducible Tests* book.

1. The coordination of all physical elements to project the right image in a place of business is called <u>visual merchandising</u>.

2. The visual and artistic aspects of promoting a product to a target group of customers are known as <u>display</u>.

3. The store sign is important because it <u>makes the first impression</u>.

4. The way a store's floor space is allocated to facilitate sales and best serve customers is called its <u>store layout</u>.

5. <u>Complementary</u> colors are found opposite each other on the color wheel and create the greatest contrasts.

Linking School to Work
Answers depend on the business visited.

1. **Assessment** Have students complete the Reproducible Test for Chapter 18 or construct your own tests using the ExamView software.

2. **Enrichment** Have students complete the corresponding activities in the following workbooks:
   - *Marketing Math Workbook*, p. 45
   - *Marketing Research Project Workbook*, p. 85

Chapter Overview

This chapter introduces advertising and its purposes, and explains the different types of print, broadcast, and specialty media. The chapter also gives an overview of how advertising rates are determined for newspaper, magazine, and online advertising. Key reasons for selecting a promotional media are also reviewed.

 Springboard

Analyze Post several print ads around the classroom. Include a mix of promotional and institutional ads with different target markets. Have students look at the ads, then close their eyes and say which ads they remember best. Ask them what attracted their attention or aroused their interest. Tell students they have just discovered the purpose of advertising: to attract attention and arouse interest so people will buy a product or accept an idea.

Prereading

List the section objectives to discuss with students. Have students skim the chapter, looking at the pictures, reading the captions, and noting the heads. Ask questions to ensure that the students have a minimal understanding of the chapter structure.

Preteaching Marketing Vocabulary

Ask students to define the word *media*. Point to the ads in the room that feature products and ask about the purpose of these ads. Then point to a few of the institutional ads and ask about their purpose. Students have identified the two types of advertising.

Marketing: What It Takes

Answer Answers will vary, but because it is a national chain, the owner may advertise on television, newspapers, and use magazine advertising.

334

Chapter **19**

Advertising

Marketing: What It Takes

A Master Media Plan
Imagine that you work as an account executive for an advertising agency. Your supervisor has asked you to design a media plan for a new client. The client, a national chain of sports-themed restaurants, wants to use different types of advertising media to reach different target markets. It is your job to review the different types of advertising media and make recommendations based on your research and the client's needs.

WHAT WILL YOU DO?
How will you determine the best ways to advertise the restaurant chain?

334

THE DECA CONNECTION — ADVISOR CORNER

Advertising Your DECA Chapter Don't be shy—advertise yourself! Your chapter will blossom, and DECA can become one of the hottest activities at your school. During the year make sure that significant chapter events are videotaped. At the end of the year, your chapter can produce a 10- to 20-minute video for looking back at the year. The video can also also be used to recruit future members. Video segments might include in-school events (ceremonies, banquets, chapter work sessions), conferences, competitions, chapter projects, and community involvement (fund raising, civic activities). This video can serve as a valuable public relations tool and will be fun, too!
(Allen Gancarz, Easy Syracuse-Minoa H.S., New York)

Advertising Media

Advertising and Its Purpose

Advertising is everywhere—television, radio, magazines, newspapers, stores, the World Wide Web, billboards, and even on buses. The average person is exposed to more than 2,000 advertisements a week.

Recall from Chapter 17 that *advertising* is any paid form of non-personal promotion of ideas, goods, or services by an identified sponsor. Advertising is different from other forms of promotion because the time or allotted space is paid for. In advertising, a message is carried by a set format rather than by personal selling. Advertising usually identifies the sponsor of the message.

There are two main types of advertising—promotional and institutional. Advertising designed to increase sales is known as **promotional advertising**. It introduces new products and businesses, encourages an interest in products, and explains product and service features. Promotional advertising also supports personal selling efforts and creates new markets for a business.

Institutional advertising attempts to create a favorable impression and goodwill for a business or an organization. It does this by providing positive information about a business. Support of community projects and community-endorsed ideas about important public topics such as the environment, public health, and education can create a favorable image.

Advertising allows large numbers of people to see the advertiser's message. The main purpose of advertising is to present a message that encourages the customer to buy the product or accept the ideas. Advertising identifies the good, service, or idea and special features such as price, benefits, location, and business hours. Advertising costs per potential customer (whether that customer is a viewer, reader, or listener) are usually lower than other forms of promotion. Businesses must choose the most appropriate advertising for their target market, for example, billboards, newspapers, radio, or television; a business then prepares the content of an advertisement. This differs from publicity because it can be controlled. Advertisements are subject to repeat viewing, which keeps the advertiser's message in people's minds. Finally, advertising can "presell" products—influencing people's decisions about a product or service before they even go shopping!

■ Advertising Drawbacks

While there are advantages to advertising, it does have its drawbacks. Advertising cannot focus on individual needs because the same message is conveyed to all customers. Some forms of advertising, such

Chapter 19 ■ *Advertising* 335

What You'll Learn

- The concept and purpose of advertising
- The different types of advertising media

Why It's Important

Advertising is an important element of promotion. You need to know the different ways a business can use advertising media to promote its image and products.

Key Terms

- promotional advertising
- institutional advertising
- media
- print media
- broadcast media
- online advertising
- banner ad
- specialty media

FOCUS

Bell Ringer Activity

Discuss and Identify Ask students how many of them watch infomercials. Discuss the types of products generally featured in infomercials, such as exercise equipment, makeup, skin care products, and kitchen appliances. Ask students the following questions:

- What is an infomercial?
- Why are the above-mentioned products (and others that students generate) suited to infomercial advertising as opposed to print advertising or 30-second radio or TV ads?
- At what times of the day and on what days of the week are infomercials run?
- Why are infomercials appropriate for today's viewing audience?
- Are infomercials effective advertising tools?

Introducing the Section

Advertising Media Review student answers to the Bell Ringer Activity. Explain to students that infomercials were developed in response to the lifestyle trends of the 1990s. They are appropriate to our times because people are staying at home more and are watching much more television at odd hours of the day, seven days a week. Celebrities are ideal infomercial spokespeople because they are credible in the eyes of a large portion of our society. Home shopping has become a popular way to purchase products. Thus, infomercials, have become effective advertising tools. Have students make predictions about other types of advertising that might be developed in the next century, given current societal trends.

Classroom Resources

For the Teacher
- Teacher Editions for all workbooks
- Assessment Package
- PowerPoint Presentation Software
- Interactive Lesson Planner
- **ILP** Block Scheduling, p. 6
- **ILP** Lesson Plans, p. 41
- **ILP** Internet Resources, p. 57

- **ILP** Blackline Masters, p. 35
- **ILP** *BusinessWeek* Case Studies, p. 121
- **ILP** Marketing Career Portfolio, p. 36
- *Marketing Essentials* Web site (**www.marketing.glencoe.com**)

For the Student
- Student Activity Workbook, p. 159
- Marketing Math Workbook, p. 45

- Marketing Research Project Workbook, p. 85
- **ILP** School-to-Work Activity Workbook, p. 81
- Virtual Business simulation
- *Marketing Essentials* Web site (**www.marketing.glencoe.com**)

ILP These resources are available in print and on the Interactive Lesson Planner (ILP)

TEACH

TEACH

📊📶 Technology Resources

PowerPoint The *Marketing Essentials* PowerPoint Presentation CD-ROM provides visual lecture aids for every chapter section.

Concept Development

1. Read Section 19.1 with students.
2. Have students read aloud the Case Study on page 343 and review the answers in class.
3. As you review ads throughout this lesson, have students identify whether the ads appeal to people's wants, needs, or both. Discuss the societal trends reflected in advertising.
4. Advertising Services by Wray, available from Glencoe, (800) 334-7344, is an excellent supplement to this chapter and a good independent study aid for students preparing for DECA competition in advertising.

FIGURE 19-1 ANSWER
U.S. Advertising Expenditures
The percentage spent on television is 38.39 percent.
(*$42.347 billion ÷ $110.282 billion = .3839 = 38.39%*)

CAPTION ANSWER
Get the Picture? This advertisement attempts to create a favorable impression and goodwill for Texaco by sponsoring the U.S. Women's Soccer Team.

---

as television, can be too expensive for many businesses. Advertising can be inefficient—not everyone who reads a magazine ad is a potential customer. Advertising messages are often very short. A page of advertising or a few words on a billboard cannot inform a potential buyer in the same way that other forms of promotion, such as a personal sales presentation, can.

Types of Media

Remember that media are the agencies, means, or instruments used to convey

Media are the agencies, means, or instruments used to convey advertising messages to the public. The four general categories of advertising media are print, broadcast, online, and specialty. Figure 19-1 illustrates media expenditures and Figure 19-2 on page 340 illustrates the different types of media.

■ Print Media

First, the book mentions print media. Who can tell me what print media is

Print media is written advertising that may be included in everything from newspapers and magazines to direct mail, signs, and billboards. They are among the oldest and most effective types of advertising.

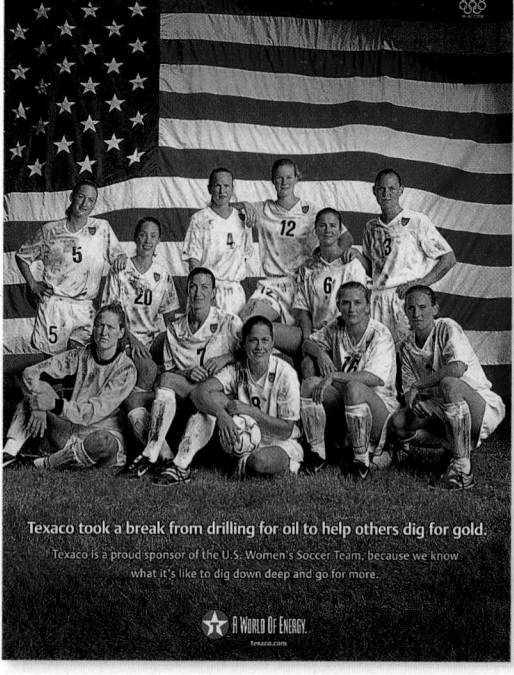

Texaco took a break from drilling for oil to help others dig for gold.
Texaco is a proud sponsor of the U.S. Women's Soccer Team, because we know what it's like to dig down deep and go for more.

⭐ A WORLD OF ENERGY. texaco.com

■ **Get the Picture? Institutional advertising creates good relationships between a business and the public.** *How does this advertisement seek to accomplish this?*

FIGURE 19-1

Media Advertising Expenditures

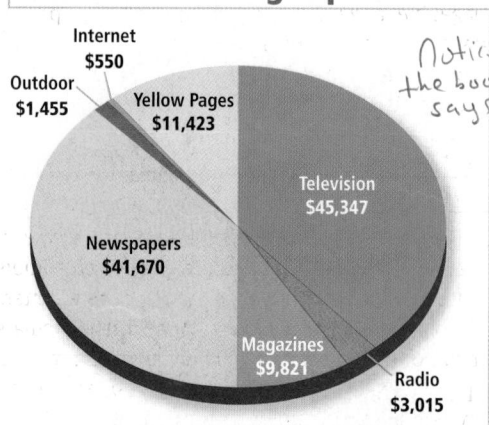

Notice " the book says

Internet $550
Outdoor $1,455
Yellow Pages $11,423
Television $45,347
Newspapers $41,670
Magazines $9,821
Radio $3,015

■ **U.S. Advertising Expenditures** Advertising is a multibillion-dollar business. Given the 1999 figures shown in the pie chart, calculate the total spent on advertising among all types of media. *What percentage was spent on television advertising?*

NEWSPAPER ADVERTISING Newspapers are the main form of print media for many businesses. Newspapers can be daily or weekly and may be local, regional, or national in scope.

Local newspapers are sold to community subscribers. National newspapers, such as *USAToday* and *The Wall Street Journal,* are distributed to regional markets and throughout the country.

Daily and weekly newspapers feature local news and advertising about area businesses. One type of community paper is called a *shopper.* Shoppers contain little editorial content, but are delivered free to persons who live in certain areas.

Advantages of newspaper advertising include large readership and a high level of reader involvement. Newspapers carry high interest content that attracts readers. It is estimated that 55 percent of U.S. adults read a newspaper every day. Since newspaper circulation is known, advertisers can target their advertising to people living in certain areas or with certain interests. The cost of newspaper advertising is relatively low because the quality of reproduction (paper and print) is less than that used in magazines

Can anybody give me examples of local + national newspapers

Boston Globe/ NY Times / Washington Post / USA Today

GREAT IDEAS from the Marketing Classroom

Jim Konrad
Cherry Creek High School
Englewood, CO

One problem I have encountered teaching a first-period class is getting kids to school on time. Tardies seem to be a problem especially during the first hours of the day. Each morning after the bell rings to start class, I recite a "Thought for the Day,"

a motivational quote from a famous person or a favorite quote from a student in class. The "thought" must be written down by the students and turned in periodically for points. This encourages students to show up on time. This simple idea was used by my own high school Marketing teacher, Steve Urban of Thornton High School in Colorado; it has proven to be very effective for me.

and direct mail. Subscribers pay for some of the publishing costs. Newspaper ads are timely and advertisers can easily change ads, often up to 24 hours before the paper goes to print.

Newspaper advertising does have some limitations. Wasted circulation can occur, as when papers are sent to a wider area than the target market. Advertising life is short, because newspapers are thrown away. Finally, the black-and-white format of most newspapers makes ads less appealing than other print media. This can be overcome with the use of freestanding inserts and supplements.

MAGAZINE ADVERTISING Magazines can be classified as local, regional, or national, as well as weeklies, monthlies, and quarterlies. Local and regional magazines are often developed for cities or metropolitan areas to promote businesses in their immediate geographical area. Many national magazines have regional editions and rates. *Field and Stream,* for example, has seven regional editions. Examples of national weeklies include news magazines such as *U.S. News and World Report, Time,* and *Newsweek.*

Magazines can also be classified as consumer or business (trade) magazines. Consumer magazines are read for personal pleasure or interest and include such publications as *Reader's Digest, Vogue,* and *Sports Illustrated.*

Business magazines appeal to people with an interest in general business or a particular business field. Examples of general business publications include *Business Week, Fortune,* and *Forbes.* Some business magazines or trade journals, such as *Supermarket News, Advertising Age,* or *Stores,* are directed at individuals in a certain field of business. Special interest magazines are important to smaller companies selling products to specialized markets because they reach target audiences with little wasted circulation or irrelevant editorial content.

Magazine advertisers, like newspaper advertisers, can target their audiences because they know the circulation and characteristics of regular readers. Magazines have a longer life span and are often read more slowly and thoroughly than newspapers. The information in a magazine ad is more likely to be remembered. The print quality in magazines is generally better than that in newspapers. People tend to keep magazines for a more extended period of time, increasing the chance that they (and the ads in them) may be reread. Magazines offer a variety

of presentation formats, including full page ads, two-page spreads, gatefolds (a page folded into itself), return cards, and heavy stock inserts.

Despite these advantages, there are drawbacks to magazine advertising. Compared to newspapers, magazines have less mass appeal within a geographical area and are more expensive. Deadlines for inserting magazine ads are often many months before actual publication, which makes them less timely.

DIRECT-MAIL ADVERTISING Direct-mail advertising, as its name suggests, is sent by businesses directly through the mail to prospective customers. Types of direct-mail advertising include newsletters, catalogs, coupons, samplers, price lists, circulars, invitations to special sales or events, postage-paid reply cards, and letters. Businesses often enclose direct-mail advertising with their monthly bills and statements. Large retailers and manufacturers send direct-mail catalogs and price lists to prospective customers.

Mailing lists are assembled by the advertiser from current customer records. They may also be purchased from a direct mail specialty firm that offers lists of potential customers. Mailing lists must be accurate or using them is a waste of a resources.

Not Just the ABCs

Imagine creating a typewriter with over 3,000 keys! The Japanese language, containing over 3,000 separate characters, or ideographs, creates a challenge for keyboard and typewriter manufacturers. The ancient Chinese symbols—known as *kanji*—are the symbols upon which Japanese is based. And that's not all! The Japanese also use two other alphabets—*katakana* for English and foreign words and *hiragana* for Japanese grammar and pronunciation. Creating more work for advertising typesetters, most billboards in Japan combine both alphabets to communicate with everyone!

Thinking Critically

Why is it important to use both alphabets in Japan?

Discussion Starter

Inducement to Buy Ask students: Have you ever made a purchase based largely on an advertising campaign? What was the product, and what factors induced you to buy?

[Handwritten notes:]

Characteristics of Magazines
- longer life span
- read slowly/thoroughly
- better print quality And variety of ad format

Can anybody give me examples of local/regional/national magazines

Sports Illustrated
Time
Newsweek
Business Week

Limitations
- less mass appeal
- more expensive
- advertising can be inflexible

Characteristics of Newspapers

Advantages
- large readership (55% of US adults do we think this is high or low?)
- high level of reader involvement
- circulation is known
- advertising in newspapers is relatively inexpensive + flexible

Limitations
- Advertising life is short
- Black-and-white format unappealing

LA Times/Chicago Tribune

Life In The Diverse **MARKETPLACE**

Not Just the ABCs

Answer Representing both alphabets is not only culturally sensitive but practical, since both are common in the Japanese culture.

■ **Drive-by Advertising** Billboards are outdoor signs that advertise. *Do you think this is a local or national advertisement?*

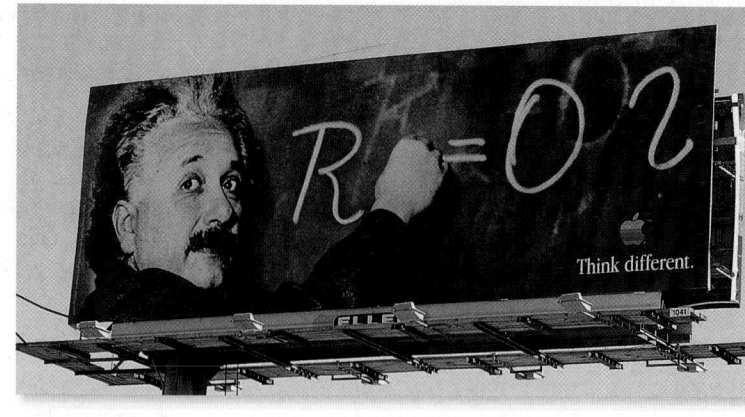

Direct mail advertisers can be highly selective about who will receive their mailing. They control the timing of the mailing and prevent competitors from seeing the initial mailing. The advertiser has a wide choice of advertisement sizes and formats—such as letters, catalogs, and postcards—limited only by certain postal regulations. Direct mail advertisers can use coupons or other incentives to get customers to try the product. The advertiser can use direct mail, such as product catalogs or magazine or music club subscriptions, to actually make the sale. Customers can order or subscribe directly using an order form or a toll-free number.

There are some disadvantages to direct-mail advertising. There is a low level of response in relation to the number of items sent—usually less than one percent. Many people think of direct-mail advertising as "junk mail" to be discarded without opening or careful reading. This problem is compounded when customer lists become dated and items are sent to the wrong target audience. The cost of direct mail is high, including producing and printing each piece of the mailing, maintaining and buying mailing lists, processing, and postage.

DIRECTORY ADVERTISING Directory advertising is an alphabetical listing of households and businesses. The best known of these listings are telephone *directories*, which are commonly divided into the White Pages (alphabetical listings) and the Yellow Pages (categorical and alphabetical listings).

In the White Pages, businesses receive a free alphabetical listing along with noncommercial telephone customers. In the Yellow Pages, businesses pay for an alphabetical listing and, if desired, a larger display ad. These appear under general headings, such as florists, physicians, recreational vehicles, or travel agencies. The Yellow Pages help consumers find suppliers of goods and services.

Directory advertising has some unique advantages. It is relatively inexpensive and can be used with all demographic groups (telephone directories are found in 98 percent of American households). Directories are usually kept for at least a year until another is provided. One advantage, however, is also a disadvantage—directories are usually printed yearly. Advertisers cannot adjust their prices, advertise sales, or change their message easily.

Service businesses like to use directory advertising, which is illustrated in the local Yellow Pages. You will see ads for such service providers as accountants, electricians, plumbers, and physicians. These are all businesses that you are likely to call only when you have a particular need. These services are used infrequently; therefore, such businesses often combine directory advertising with other forms of advertising to attract customers before there is a service need.

OUTDOOR ADVERTISING Both local and national businesses use outdoor signs, or billboards, for advertising. There are two types of outdoor signs—*nonstandardized* and *standardized*.

Nonstandardized outdoor signs are used by local firms at their places of business or in other locations throughout the community. Businesses usually pay rent to the owners on whose property the signs are displayed for the off-site signs.

Standardized outdoor signs are available to local, regional, or national advertisers. These signs, which are purchased from outdoor advertising companies in standard sizes, are placed near highly traveled roads and freeways where there is high visibility.

■ **E-billboards** E-billboards are digital video screens that display advertising. *Why is a train station a good place to put these screens?*

Three types of standardized outdoor signs are *posters, painted bulletins,* and *spectaculars. Posters* are pre-printed sheets put up like wallpaper on outdoor billboards. They are changed three to four times each year. *Painted bulletins* are painted billboards that are changed about every six months to a year. *Spectaculars* are outdoor advertising signs which use lights or moving parts and are situated in high traffic areas, such as densely populated metropolitan cities.

Outdoor advertising is highly visible and relatively inexpensive. It provides a 24-hour a day message and can be located to reach specific target markets. However, despite its popularity with some advertisers, its use is becoming more restricted. In fact, four states (Alaska, Hawaii, Maine, and Vermont) have completely banned billboards on the premise that the signs mar scenic views and distract drivers. In many urban areas, outdoor billboards have size restrictions and spacing requirements. They also have to be a specified number of feet away from schools, parks, and playgrounds. Outdoor advertising is primarily used along roadways in areas zoned for commercial and industrial uses.

Some limitations for outdoor advertising include limited viewing time, a largely unknown audience of viewers, and increasing government regulations.

TRANSIT ADVERTISING *Transit advertising* uses public transportation facilities to bring advertising messages to people. It includes:

- Printed posters found inside business and commuter trains
- Exterior posters on the outside of taxis and buses
- Station posters located near or in subways and in railroad, bus, and airline terminals

Transit advertising reaches a wide and (in the case of bus and train passengers) captive audience. It is economical and has a defined market, usually an urban area. Unfortunately, transit advertising is often unavailable in smaller towns and cities, is subject to defacement, and is restricted to predetermined travel routes.

A new type of popular advertising in bus stops, train stations, and gas stations are *e-billboards.* These are video screens that advertisers use to promote their products. E-billboards can also be used in stores, lobbies of hotels or buildings, elevators, and even at lines in amusement parks.

■ Broadcast Media

Broadcast media includes radio and television. The average person will spend nearly ten years watching television and almost six years listening to the radio over a lifetime of 70 years. You can see why advertising through broadcast media is popular.

People use television and radio not only for entertainment, but also to get information. In fact, people are more likely to believe the information they get from television than the information they get from print media. Since they can both see and hear the television message, it comes alive for them.

In the United States, there are approximately 10,000 AM and FM radio broadcast stations. Most of the 1,200 commercial television stations are affiliated with one of the major networks—ABC, CBS, NBC, or FOX. In addition, there are about 11,600 cable systems. Over 66 percent of the estimated 98 million TV households are cable television subscribers.

Given the tremendous availability and the popularity of broadcast media, it is no surprise that many businesses use it to sell their products, despite the higher advertising costs involved.

Chapter 19 ■ *Advertising* **339**

More About . . .

Outdoor Advertising
The latest gimmick offered by a company called Space Marketing Concepts, Inc., is the opportunity for companies to advertise on a large inflatable billboard that will orbit in space with a brand name or logo clearly visible to an observer on earth. The cost ranges from $15 to $30 million. Insurance is available to cover any disasters.

SECTION 19.1

Cooperative Learning

Advertising Poster Divide students into groups. Have each group develop an advertising poster for National DECA Week, Free Enterprise Week, or for your school's marketing program.

Independent Practice

1. **Research and Report** Have students select a magazine that they like, and use it to do some research on magazine advertising. Ask students to determine the characteristics of the magazine's readership. Have students look at a few issues to see the kinds of goods and services that are advertised in the magazine. Students should write a brief report summarizing their findings.

2. **Research and Critique** Have students find an example of a print ad that they do not like, or write a description of a television commercial or radio spot that they do not like. Have them answer the following questions:
   - What elements of the ad don't you like?
   - What would you do to improve the ad?
   - Despite your dislike of the ad, do you think it is effective?

FIGURE 19-2
ADVERTISING MEDIA

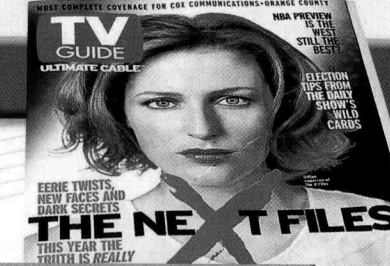

A business can use different types of advertising media to promote its image and products in different ways. Media are the agencies, means, or instruments used to convey advertising messages to the public. The four general categories of advertising media are print, broadcast, online, and specialty media. The advertising media should be determined much in the same way as the advertising message, by the appeal and the target audience. *How would you categorize each of these specific advertising mediums?*

MAGAZINES

Magazines generate a high level of reader involvement and the messages can be seen repeatedly. *TV Guide* and *People* have been ranked first and second, respectively, in gross revenues for the past several years among the top 300 magazines with advertising revenues of $1,080,118 in 1998 (dollars in thousands).

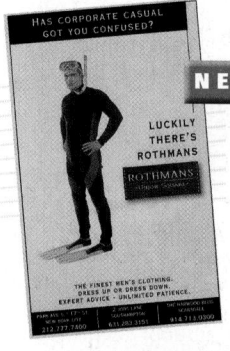

NEWSPAPERS

Newspapers are a convenient way for a local advertiser to present a message in selected geographical areas.

TELEVISION ADVERTISING

Television advertising combines audio, visual, and live action effects to present an often-entertaining message.

DIRECT MAIL

Direct mail advertising sends a message right to your home. Direct mail items encourage customers to try new products, since they are convenient and can be used with little effort.

TRANSIT ADVERTISING

Transit advertising uses public transportation facilities and vehicles to bring advertising messages to people.

FIGURE 19-2 ANSWER
Advertising Media Television advertising is broadcast; magazine advertising is print; newspaper advertising is print; transit advertising is print; and direct mail is print.

More About . . .

Television Advertising
Television advertising influences what gets seen on television. The absence of soccer on major networks is due in part to the fact that soccer only has two periods of play. Unlike football or basketball, soccer has no time-outs, leaving little time for commercials. Instead, billboards are placed around the arena to be viewed.

TELEVISION ADVERTISING Television is the ultimate advertising medium for many businesses because it can communicate a message with sound, action, and color. Prime time for network and cable television is between 8 p.m. and 11 p.m., when millions of viewers are watching.

Most television commercial advertisements are 30- or 60-second spots. An exception is the infomercial, which is a 30-minute advertisement. Infomercials promote products such as cookware, exercise equipment, and appliances using a talk-show type setting. Viewers can order the advertised merchandise by calling a phone number or writing to an address.

Perhaps more than any other medium, television can pull together all the elements necessary to produce a creative advertising message. Television is also great for demonstrating a product's features and benefits. Television advertising is very appealing to large companies with widespread distribution. Think of the catch phrases and jingles you know by heart simply from hearing them on TV commercials.

Television can be directed to an audience with a specific interest—such as news, comedy, history, movies, sports, or science—through cable networks. A televised advertising message can be adapted to take advantage of holidays, seasonal changes, and special-events programming, such as the Super Bowl, the NCAA basketball tournament, or entertainment specials.

There are drawbacks to using television as an advertising medium. Television has the highest production costs of any type of media and a high

■ **Would You Like to Have Something to Eat?** HomeGrocer.com is one company that uses a catchy jingle in its television ads. *What are the benefits of this?*

dollar cost for the time used. Prime-time costs, in particular, are sometimes prohibitive. They keep many smaller companies from using television advertising or force them to buy time in less desirable periods when fewer people are watching. Actual audience size is not assured, and many viewers consider television commercials to be an opportunity to leave the room. As a result, advertising dollars don't always pay off.

RADIO ADVERTISING It is estimated that radio reaches 96 percent of all people age 12 and over in a given week. This ability to reach a wide audience makes radio an extremely effective advertising medium.

The best times for radio advertising are when people are driving to work in the morning and when they are coming home during the afternoon or early evening. These are called prime times or "drive times" for radio advertising because advertisers are guaranteed a concentrated audience.

Radio advertisements are presented in 15-, 30-, or 60-second time periods. The messages are effective in encouraging people to buy because the announcer or actors—along with background music, jingles, slogans, and sound effects—add excitement, drama, or humor.

Radio advertisers can select an audience, such as teenagers, various ethnic groups, and professionals, by advertising on stations targeting that particular market. Radio is more flexible than print advertising because messages can be changed easily. An advertiser can make changes in the script for an advertising message a few days, or even just a few minutes, before the message is recorded. Radio is a mobile medium that can be taken just about anywhere—shopping, jogging, hiking, or driving.

There are also several disadvantages to radio advertising. Radio advertisements have a short life span. When a message is broadcast, it is over—unless the business pays to have it rebroadcast later. In fact, radio advertisers usually buy several time slots instead of just one. In larger markets with many stations, several stations often compete for the same audience. Potential advertisers must decide on which radio station to advertise, or advertise on several.

The lack of visual involvement causes some listeners to become easily distracted and miss some, most, or all of the message. That is why the catchy jingle is so useful.

ASSESS

Reteaching

1. **Vocabulary** Assign and review the vocabulary terms for this section.
2. **Fact and Idea** Assign and review Fact and Idea Review questions 1–5 from the Chapter Assessment.
3. **Full-Page Advertising** Bring in a magazine and a section of the newspaper that both contain a great deal of full-page advertising. Choose several ads and ask the following questions about each one:
   - Is this a promotional ad or an institutional ad?
   - Is it appealing to a want, a need, or both?
   - Who is the target audience for this ad?
   - How do the elements in the ad (for example, color, visual images) appeal specifically to the target audience?
   - If the product is a familiar one, can you recall prior advertising campaigns for it? How does that ad campaign differ from this one? How does the current advertising reflect current societal trends?

CAPTION ANSWER
Would You Like to Have Something to Eat?
Using jingles that are catchy and easy to remember increase product awareness.

Enrichment

1. **Review** Assign and review the appropriate Thinking Critically questions from the Chapter Assessment.

2. **Extend** Assign and review the corresponding activities from *BusinessWeek Case Studies, Internet Resources,* and the *School-to-Work Activity Workbook.* **ILP**

3. **Research and Report**
Advertising offers many career-sustaining job opportunities. Have students research the field of advertising and write a 150- to 200-word report that outlines the job responsibilities of three positions in advertising. Have them tell what educational, extracurricular, and volunteer activities will help students prepare now for each job. If there are time and resources, have students contact people who are actually doing these jobs and ask them to discuss some of the things they do and do not like about the job. Many school resource centers have computer-based occupational information systems that can provide information on careers. Print resources include *The Career Directory* series, the *Dictionary of Occupational Titles,* the *Occupational Outlook Handbook,* and the *Encyclopedia of Careers and Vocational Guidance.* They will also find many career books in the business or reference section of their local bookstores.

4. **Identify** Television and radio advertising both set their rates based on the time of day and the programming (which determine the target audience). Ask students to identify the advertising, which appears during their favorite television show and on their favorite radio station in general. Is the advertising similar? Are there similarities in the audience that advertisers are trying to reach?

■ Online Advertising

Online advertising involves placing advertising messages on the Internet. Online advertising is still a small part of overall advertising spending, but it is growing quickly. Estimates call for spending to go up to $10 billion by 2002. Most online advertising appears as banner ads. A **banner ad** is usually a wide shallow rectangle seen at the top or bottom of Web pages, which takes the user to the advertiser's Web page if clicked with a mouse. Banner advertisements that use technology known as "rich media" include animation, sound, and even video. Similar to banner ads, but smaller in size, are button ads placed in a strategic position on a Web page. Both banner and button ads are designed to attract viewers to click through to the advertiser's Web site. Some advertisers use *interstitial ads,* which are screens that pop up to interrupt Web surfing. A viewer must click on the billboard to get to the Web site or close the ad window to resume surfing.

Unlike other forms of print advertising, online advertisers can easily measure effectiveness by the number of *click-throughs,* or times the ad has been visited. Online advertisers have found that bold colors, top-of-page placement, animation, calls to action, and limited frequency of exposures help increase that number of click-throughs. Even using these techniques, online advertisers report response rates as low as one percent. In other words, for every 100 banner ads, only one in one hundred Web users click the ad. Although online advertising is now part of the advertising media mix, its overall selling effectiveness is still uncertain.

REAL WORLD MARKETING

The Outer Limits of Advertising

These are the voyages of the Starship Radio Shack!?! Radio Shack, in an effort to brand itself as a leader in consumer technology, is joining forces with a space mission. In exchange for an undisclosed dollar amount, LunaCorp will allow Radio Shack to place its logo on the new moon rover, scheduled to land on the moon in 2003. The mission's objective is to explore ice on the moon. The marketing endeavor will allow Radio Shack customers to participate in the mission via the Internet. Radio Shack's marketing department believes the effort will be an effective way to stimulate brand interest.

Thinking Critically
Are there any areas that should be considered safe from advertising? What are the pros and cons?

Some people find online advertisements an annoyance or a distraction from the Web page that they are visiting. Other Internet users may be concerned about the reliability or privacy issues associated with unfamiliar Web sites that may appear in banner ads.

■ **Banners Galore** Online advertising involves placing advertising messages on the Internet. *What characteristics of banner ads cause the viewer to click to the advertiser's Web site?*

CAPTION ANSWER
Banners Galore Animation, audio, and attractive visual effects might cause the viewer to visit a particular Web site.

REAL WORLD MARKETING

The Outer Limits of Advertising
Answer Perhaps national parks and playgrounds should be considered safe habitats from advertisers. However, large companies' sponsorships help these programs to continue.

Case Study

A Free Ticket on the Internet Express

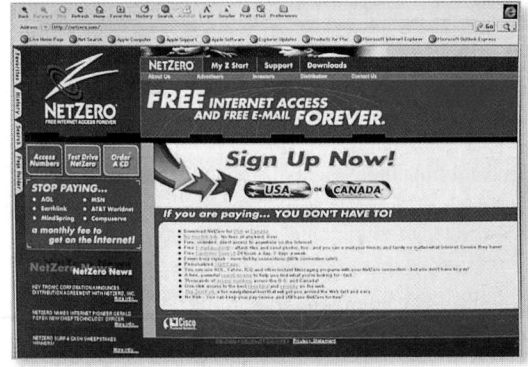

How would you like free unlimited Internet access? Companies such as AltaVista, Blue Light, Juno, and NetZero offer customers just that. But there is a catch. After signing on, you'll be required to fill out a personal questionnaire. This information helps advertisers target advertising messages to you.

Free Internet services are popular in the United States with teenagers and their parents. They are also immensely popular overseas, like in Great Britain where people have to pay a "per-minute" fee for local phone calls. Other individuals avoid free Internet service providers because they worry about their privacy. They are concerned about how the information they would submit about themselves will be used. All free Internet companies have privacy policies and promise to keep any personal information private. Free Internet access works well for people who don't mind the questionnaires and aren't bothered by the advertisements.

Case Study Review

1. What factors should a potential user consider in evaluating free Internet service providers?
2. Why are free Internet services popular with teenagers and their parents?

A MATTER OF ETHICS

3. Is it possible for Internet providers to uphold a privacy code on the Internet? Why or why not?

Are you concerned with Internet privacy? The workplace viewing your emails, putting credit card info. into the computer?

◼ Specialty Media

Specialty media are relatively inexpensive, useful items with an advertiser's name printed on them. The items are usually given away with no obligation attached to receiving and keeping them.

To be successful as advertising tools, specialty items must be practical, subject to frequent use, and likely to be placed in locations with high visibility. Common items that fit this description include bottle openers, calendars, magnets, pens and pencils, memo pads, and key chains. When designed well, specialty items carry the name and address of the business sponsoring them and an advertising message urging the reader to action. Sometimes, however, the size of the item prevents the use of a message, and there is only room for the name and address of the business.

Specialty advertising has some limitations. The distribution of the items is usually limited. In addition, the items might be given to people who would never consider buying the product or patronizing the business.

◼ Other Advertising Media

Businesses are constantly creating innovative means of transmitting their messages to potential customers. Examples include sports arena billboards, ads in movie theaters and home video rentals, ads placed on hot air balloons and blimps, skywriting, and airplanes pulling advertising banners. Increasingly, advertising techniques, such as electronic shelf ads, supermarket cart advertising displays, and instant coupon machines, are being used to advertise products in the store.

Technology Resources

Assessment Resources
Go to the *Marketing Essentials* Web site (**www.marketing.glencoe. com**) for resources to teach and assess occupation-specific vocabulary.

▶ VIRTUAL BUSINESS ◀

Promotion
Explore the concept of promotion to students using Knowledge Matters' Virtual Business visual simulation, "Marketing—Promotion." Students advertise with four types of media and have the option of computing the cost effectiveness of each type in their simulated town. If needed, have students run the Virtual Business tutorial before beginning this activity. For additional instructions and teaching tips for this activity, go to the *Marketing Essentials* Web site (**www.marketing.glencoe.com**).

Case Study Review Answers

A Free Ticket on the Internet Express

1. When considering a free Internet service, individuals should consider the ease of use, the ad annoyance factor, and the risk of privacy invasion.
2. They are popular because people don't want to pay the monthly access fee.

A MATTER OF ETHICS

3. Although all of the free Internet service providers promise to uphold a privacy code, many people do not trust Internet providers to keep information private and confidential. The information collected has the potential to be misused.

The Ad is in the E-Mail

Answer A musician could send an e-mail ad in the form of a music video that had a link to his or her Web site. The benefit would be the convenience to the customer.

Selection of Promotional Media

The choice of an advertising medium ultimately depends on the product to be advertised, the habits and lifestyles of the target audience, and the types of media available in the area.

To determine the type of promotional media to use advertisers need to address three basic questions:

- *Does the medium have the ability to present the product and the appropriate business image?*
- *Does the medium have the ability to target the desired customers?*
- *Does the medium have the ability to obtain the desired response rate?*

The selected advertising medium ideally illustrates the company's product or product line well. It provides the opportunity to present an effective selling message, which stirs excitement for a customer to buy. The advertising medium should portray the desired business image with an appropriate measure of prestige and distinction.

It is important that the medium reaches the targeted audience and covers the appropriate geographical area. Flexibility, in terms of making last-minute changes, can allow the advertiser to take advantage of special promotions and events more easily.

The medium must have the capability to reach the greatest number of potential customers. Hopefully, the selected medium will also generate high response rates for the business at the lowest possible cost per customer.

The Ad is in the E-mail

In May 2000, CBS officials were worried that their newest show—a departure from their typical target market—wouldn't catch on with audiences. In fact, CBS was so worried about promoting its new show that it e-mailed a miniature television commercial to over 29,000 viewers. It was CBS's hope that even if they didn't tune in, recipients would forward the e-mail to their friends. The show—Survivor—became a critical financial success for CBS. E-commercials have become popular not only because they are cheaper than television commercials but also because (unlike radio and television advertising) marketers can track who watches the commercial and for how long. Who knows . . . your next e-mail message just might be from your favorite television network!

Thinking Critically

How could e-mail ads help a musician sell albums? What would the benefit be?

19.1 ASSESSMENT

Reviewing Key Terms and Concepts

1. What is advertising?
2. What is the main purpose of advertising?
3. List the six different types of print media.
4. What are two forms of broadcast advertising?
5. What is online advertising?

Thinking Critically

6. If response rates are very low with online advertising, why do some advertisers continue to use it?

Integrating Academic Skills

7. **COMMUNICATION** Gather information about one product from three different types of media. Use a word processor to create a one-page summary of how these sources differ from each other in their presentation of the products.

Media Rates

Media Costs

To reach customers, advertising uses a set format that is defined in terms of time (a 30-second television commercial) or space (a half-page newspaper ad). Media costs vary greatly, not just with type of media but with geographical location as well. For example, a quarter-page newspaper ad in a large-city daily newspaper could cost four to eight times more than the same size ad in a small-town weekly. Given such variations, it is virtually impossible to quote exact rates for each type of media advertising. It is possible, however, to generalize about how those rates are set.

When businesses want to access rates for the various media, they can look up the rates in the publications of Standard Rate and Data Service. It publishes rate cards for most major media according to general categories, such as print media or broadcast media.

Another advertising industry service important to both advertisers and print media is the Audit Bureau of Circulation (ABC). Print media publishers subscribe to the ABC to have it verify their circulation figures. This is important in print media because advertising rates are based on circulation. Circulation figures are important selling points for the media to use when trying to attract advertisers to the publication.

■ Newspaper Rates

Newspaper advertising rates are classified into two categories depending on whether the ad is a *classified ad* or a *display ad*. Classified ads can advertise everything from services to houses for sale to job openings. They are called *classified* because they are grouped or classified into specific categories, such as help wanted, real estate, personals, and auto sales. People or businesses that buy classified ads usually pay by the word or line of type.

Display ads involve the creative illustration of the product being advertised. They are a mix of art or photographs, headlines, copy, and a signature or logo of the product or business. Display ads are generally larger than classified ads and their cost is based upon the amount of space used.

Newspapers quote display advertising rates by the column inch. A column inch is an area that is one column wide by one inch deep. If a newspaper quotes a column inch rate, you simply multiply the number of inches by the number of columns to determine the total number of column inches. Then you multiply the total column inches by the rate. An example is if the rate for a column inch is $17, then an ad that measures four inches long by three columns will cost $204.

$$\$17 \times 4 \text{ inches} \times 3 \text{ columns} = \$204$$

What You'll Learn

- How various media rates are set
- The costs of print media
- The standards for selecting promotional media

Why It's Important

Since businesses need to reach as many customers as possible within limited budgets, you will need to know how to calculate media costs to best reach your potential audience.

Key Terms

- cost per thousand (CPM)
- network radio advertising
- national spot radio advertising
- local radio advertising
- cooperative advertising

FOCUS

Bell Ringer Activity

Brainstorm Ask students how they think print publications and broadcast stations pay for the bulk of their publication costs and programming, respectively. Then write two headings on the board: *Print* and *Broadcast*. Ask students to help you list the factors that would influence advertising rates for each.

Introducing the Section

Media Rates Advertising rates vary so much that it's impossible to quote exact rates for each type of media advertising. However, tell students that this section will give them a better understanding for the cost of advertising and the formulas used to calculate advertising rates.

Concept Development

1. Read Section 19.2 with students.
2. Some students may work on the school newspaper, the school yearbook, or at the school radio station. If any one of these charges for advertising, ask students how ad rates are set.
3. Some students may have co-op jobs in print or broadcast media. If they do, make sure they discuss what they know or can find out about how their publication or station sets its advertising rates. For those students working in advertising, ask if they can get rate information from the agency about commissions it charges for ad placement.

Discussion Starter

Advertising Rate Computations
Ask students which advertising rate computations discussed in this section do they understand the best. Which computations do they feel they need to understand better? What course of action would best help them become familiar with the computations they need to understand better?

A number of factors can change the regular newspaper rates charged to advertisers. Display ads are usually sold at *run-of-paper* rates. Run-of-paper allows the newspaper to choose where to run an ad in the paper. However, for a higher rate advertisers can run ads in guaranteed or preferred locations, such as the last page of a section.

The use of color also affects the advertising rate. Color ads are sold at a higher rate than those done in black and white. The frequency of advertising lowers the rate charged for display ads. The more a business advertises, the lower the rate charged.

Businesses that advertise in a newspaper generally pay an *open rate*. The open rate, often referred to as the noncontract rate, is the basic charge for a minimum amount of advertising space. The open rate varies depending on when an advertisement will appear in a paper. A newspaper may charge a Monday through Thursday rate of $28 per column inch, a Friday rate of $29, a Saturday rate of $31, and a Sunday rate of $35 per column inch.

Businesses that advertise in the newspaper more frequently may contract with a newspaper to guarantee that they will use a certain amount of space for a specified time period. They are granted *contract rates*, which are discounted from the open rate. Contracts can be written in a number of ways. A yearly frequency contract guarantees that an advertiser will use a minimum number of column inches each week for 52 weeks. A bulk space contract guarantees that a minimum number of inches will be used when the advertiser chooses, within a 12-month period.

Another important rate is the **cost per thousand (CPM)** rate, which is the media cost of exposing 1,000 readers to an ad. It is useful in comparing the cost of advertising to reach 1,000 readers in one newspaper to the cost of advertising to reach 1,000 readers in another newspaper. The comparison is made by using the following formula:

$$\text{Cost of the ad} \times 1{,}000/\text{Circulation} = \text{cost per thousand (CPM)}$$

Suppose the cost of an ad in the *Times* is $500 and the paper has a circulation of 500,000. Its cost per thousand rate would be calculated as follows:

$$\$500 \times 1{,}000/500{,}000 = \$500{,}000/500{,}000 = \$1 \text{ per } 1{,}000 \text{ readers.}$$

The cost of an ad in the *Tribune*, a competing paper, is $600, and the paper has a circulation of 300,000. Its cost per thousand rate would be calculated as follows:

$$\$600 \times 1{,}000/300{,}000 = \$600{,}000/300{,}000 = \$2 \text{ per } 1{,}000 \text{ readers}$$

All other things being equal, an advertiser would probably choose the *Times* over the *Tribune* because it would cost less per 1,000 readers. Of course, all other things might not be equal. The *Tribune's* circulation could include more of the advertiser's target market, or the paper could offer a special ad placement. The point is that the CPM is a convenient measure that allows you to compare costs among newspapers.

■ Magazine Rates

Magazine rates are based on circulation, quality of readership, and production technique. To calculate the actual cost of magazine advertising, you need to become familiar with some terms found on magazine advertising rate cards, including *bleed, black-and-white rates, color rates, premium position, discounts,* and the *cost per thousand rate (CPM)* discussed earlier.

Bleed means that half- or full-page ads are printed to the very edge of the page, leaving no white border. Magazines generally charge between 15 to 20 percent extra for bleeds.

The lowest rate magazines offer for display ads are black-and-white rates for black-and-white advertisements. *Color rates* are offered for color ads. Each time the magazine adds color to the ad, the rates increase. Four-color advertisements, also called *full-color,* are the most expensive magazine ads.

Premium position refers to where ads are placed in the magazine. Ads placed in premium positions, such as on the back cover or the inside first page, are more expensive to run. The back cover is considered the highest premium position because people will see the ad whenever the magazine is placed cover down. The inside front cover and first page are also premium positions because most people begin reading a magazine from the first page.

Frequency discounts are offered to advertisers who run the same ad several times during the year. The magazine may publish an entire schedule of rates for the number of times during the year an advertiser contracts to advertise. The rate per issue decreases as the frequency increases.

Did You Know?
Why is cost per thousand referred to as CPM instead of CPT? In this case, M stands for *mille,* the Latin word for thousand. The word *millennium* comes from the same word, as does the word *millenary,* meaning a group of 1,000 units or things.

FIGURE 19-3

Magazine Rate Card

General Rates

RATE BASE: Rates based on a yearly average of 1,100,000 net paid A B C
A member of the Audit Bureau of Circulation

SPACE UNITS	BLACK & WHITE	BLACK & ONE COLOR	FOUR COLOR
1 page	$16,000	$19,630	$23,300
2 columns	11,620	14,560	18,170
½ page	10,130	13,550	17,200
1 column	5,920	9,530	12,180
½ column	3,020		
Covers			
Second Cover			$25,520
Third Cover			23,300
Fourth Cover			27,020

BLEED CHARGE: 15%
AGENCY COMMISSION: 15%
CASH DISCOUNT: 2% 10 days, net 30 days

Bleed accepted in color, black & white, and on covers, at an additional charge of 15%. No charge for gutter bleed in double-page spread.

Premium Positions: A 10% premium applies to advertising units positioned on pages 1, 2, and 3. A surcharge of 5% applies to bleed units in premium positions.

Rate Change Announcements will be made at least two months in advance of the black & white closing date for the issue affected. Orders for issues thereafter at rates then prevailing.

ISSUANCE AND CLOSING DATES

A. On sale date approximately the 15th of month preceding date of issue.

B. Black & white, black & one color, and four-color closing date, 20th of the 3rd month preceding date of issue. Example: Forms for August issue close May 20th.

C. Orders for cover pages noncancellable. Orders for all inside advertising units are noncancellable 15 days prior to their respective closing dates. Supplied inserts are noncancellable the 1st of the 4th month preceding month of issue. Options on cover positions must be exercised at least 30 days prior to four-color closing date. If order is not received by such date, cover option automatically lapses.

■ **Ad Rates** Ad rates are based on color. *Based on this magazine rate card, what is the cost of a four-colored ad paid in ten days from the issuance of the invoice?*

Another discount is a *commission*—a percentage of sales given by the magazine to the advertising agency for placing the ad for the advertiser. A typical commission is 15 percent.

Finally, a cash discount may be offered for paying the bill earlier than its due date (this may be written 2/10, net 30). This cash discount would permit the advertiser or ad agency to take a two percent discount if the bill is paid within ten days from the date of the invoice. The payment, if the discount is not taken, is due 30 days from the date of the invoice.

Take a look at the rate card in Figure 19-3. You would calculate the cost of a full-page, four-color advertisement with bleed as follows:

$23,300	1 page, four-color rate
× .15	bleed
$ 3,495	extra for bleed

$23,300	1 page, four-color rate
+ 3,495	bleed
$26,795	for 1 page, four color, with bleed

An ad agency placed the ad and it took the commission and the cash discount. The total cost of the above ad to the agency would be:

$ 26,795	1 page, four color, with bleed
× .15	ad agency's commission
$ 4,019.25	

$26,795.00	1 page, four color, with bleed
− 4,019.25	agency's commission
$22,775.75	net cost of ad to agency after commission
× .02	cash discount percentage if paid within 10 days of invoice
$ 455.52	cash discount

$22,775.75	net cost of ad to agency after commission
− 455.52	cash discount
$22,320.23	net cost to advertising agency for one full-page, four-color ad, with bleed after cash discount and agency commission.

As with newspapers, the CPM can be used to compare the cost of advertising in several magazines. A magazine that has a circulation of 2 million and a full-page, black-and-white ad rate of $35,000, would have a CPM rate $17.50.

$35,000 × 1,000/2,000,000 = $17.50

Independent Practice

1. **Research, Analyze, and Report** Have students select a magazine that they like. They should first determine the circulation of the magazine.
   - Has the circulation decreased or increased over the past few years? Why?
   - What are the characteristics of the magazine's readership?
   - What kinds of products are advertised in the magazine?
   - Generally, how do the products advertised match the publication's target market? Students' findings should be summarized in 100 to 150 words.

FIGURE 19-3 ANSWER
Ad Rates The ad would cost $16,856. *($17,200 − [$17,200 x .02] = $17,200; $17,200 − $344 = $16,856)*

THE DECA CONNECTION

COMPETITIVE EVENTS AND MARKETING ESSENTIALS

Advertising Campaign DECA's Advertising Campaign Event is a fun and exciting tool to use to teach advertising. The event provides students with the opportunity to prepare an advertising campaign for a real product, service, company, or business, and to present the campaign to a prospective client/advertiser. The students indicate an appropriate budget and select media. This event allows from one to three students to complete the advertising campaign. The students prepare nine pages of fact sheets about their ad campaign, then give a 15-minute oral presentation explaining their proposal. During the final five minutes, the students respond to questions from the businessperson/judge.

Individualized Practice

Math Skills

Tell students that they are considering advertising a business in a local newspaper.

L1 The *Williamstown Gazette* quotes a column-inch, non-contract rate of $23 for Monday through Thursday placement, and $25 for Friday placement. If you want to run one 6-inch by 3-column ad on Thursday and one 6-inch by 3-column ad on Friday, how much will you pay? *($864. Thursday's ad is $414. $23 x 6 inches x 3 columns = $414. Friday's ad is $450. $25 x 6 x 3 = $450. $414 + $450 = $864.)*

L2 You decide that you want to run a 6-inch by 3-column ad in the *Gazette* on the first Thursday and Friday of each month. Your *Gazette* salesperson offers you a 12-month contract for $7,257.60. What percentage discount has she given you? *(30%. $864 x 12 = $10,368 [cost without discount]. $10,368 - $7,257.60 = $3,110.40. $3,110.40 ÷ $10,368 = 0.3 or 30%.)*

L3 The cost of an ad in the *Gazette* is $650; it has a circulation of 475,000. The cost of an ad in the *Herald-News* is $600; it has a circulation of 560,000. Which has the lowest CPM rate? *(The Herald-News at $1.07 per 1,000 readers versus the Gazette's CPM rate of $1.37 per 1,000 readers. Gazette: [$650 x 1,000] ÷ 475,000 = $650,000. $650,000 ÷ 475,000 = $1.37. Herald-News: [$600 x 1,000] ÷ 560,000 = $600,000. $600,000 ÷ 560,000 = $1.07.)*

■ Online Rates

Online advertising rates are based upon the type of format the customer desires. Banner ads, rich-media enhanced banner ads, button/text links, and interstitial ads are some of the options. Online advertising rates are set on a CPM rate of page views. Rates vary based on the volume of monthly page views.

Like newspapers and magazines, online advertisers also look at the CPM rate to determine the medium's effectiveness. A recent study by AdKnowledge of approximately 1200 Web sites found that the average CPM rate was about $40 per thousand or $.04 per banner ad. However, there is a wide range for individual sites. Some very popular sites targeted to high-income professionals averaged over $100/CPM, others were as low as $10/CPM. Discounts are offered to high volume advertisers. Last-minute purchasers of unused advertising space are able to buy banner ads at as low as $1/CPM.

Many online advertisers also engage in barter arrangements, whereby each advertiser agrees to run banner ads for the other. Companies that have the same target market or that sell complimentary products can benefit from such a relationship. Barter arrangements can lead to more traffic for each business and is another method to use unsold advertising capacity.

■ Radio Rates

When purchasing radio time, a business needs to decide what kind of radio advertising to use. There are three options—network radio advertising, national spot radio advertising, and local radio advertising.

Businesses with a national scope usually choose network radio advertising or national spot radio advertising. **Network radio advertising** is a broadcast from a studio to all affiliated radio stations throughout the country. Network radio advertising allows an advertiser to broadcast an ad simultaneously to several markets through sponsorship of a special program, activity, or radio personality.

National spot radio advertising is used by national firms to advertise on a local station-by-station basis. It is used to target select markets in the country. **Local radio advertising** is done by a local business for its target market. It is limited to a specific geographical area.

When selecting advertising, it is important to know the difference between spot radio and spot commercials. Spot radio refers to the geographical area an advertiser wants to reach with its advertising. Spot commercials are advertising messages of one minute or less that can be carried on network or spot radio.

BRIGHT IDEAS

Wouldn't You Like to Be a Pepper, Too!

Have you ever wondered what flavor Dr. Pepper is? Some say it is grape juice, others say cherry juice and still others claim it is prune juice! In truth, Dr. Pepper's flavor is a closely guarded secret created by Charles Alderton, who combined soda flavors to serve customers of Morrison's Old Corner Drug Store in Waco, Texas. One soda combination in particular became very popular. Alderton and store owner Wade Morrison were overwhelmed by demand for the drink and had trouble making enough soda to supply customers. Morrison spoke to the owner of Circle "A" Ginger Ale Company about bottling the drink. Alderton, not wanting to pursue the business of soft drink manufacturing, dropped out while Morrison got help from the Artesian Manufacturing and Bottling Company. In 1904, the company introduced Dr. Pepper to 20 million people at the World's Fair Exposition.

Thinking Creatively

Dr. Pepper has changed its advertising campaign several times. Develop an advertising slogan for the company appropriate for the next decade.

BRIGHT IDEAS
Wouldn't You Like to Be a Pepper, Too!
Answer Ad slogans will vary.

Each radio station determines actual advertising rates by time of day. Rates are higher during peak listening times, also called "drive times" (early mornings and late afternoons). Radio stations also offer less costly, run-of-schedule (ROS) airtimes. ROS airtime allows a radio station to decide when to run the ad spot. Target audiences, audience size, rates, weekly package plans, and discounts vary from station to station; therefore, a business should carefully review and compare the rates of the radio stations on which it might advertise.

■ Television Rates

Advertising rates for television also vary with time of day. It is more expensive, for example, to advertise during the hours of 8 p.m. to 11 p.m. (known as Class AA time) than during other hours. The rates charged for other time slots, such as Class A, Class B, Class C, and Class D, are lower based on diminishing viewership. Businesses try to place their advertisements in time slots during which their potential customers will most likely see them.

A business considering the purchase of television time contacts a television media representative. The representative helps the business determine coverage times available. He or she also arranges package deals that can be developed to give the advertiser more advertising spots, volume, or seasonal discounts.

Cooperative Advertising

Cooperative advertising is a cost-sharing arrangement whereby both a supplier and a local advertiser pay for advertising. Cooperative advertisements feature both the supplier's (typically a manufacturer's) product name and the name of the local advertiser. In a cooperative advertising campaign, a variety of advertising and promotional materials are usually supplied to the local advertiser. These might include print newspaper ads with space for the advertiser's name and address, scripts for television and radio ads with time allotted for the local advertiser's name and location, in-store advertising displays, and posters. An example of a cooperative advertisement might be a newspaper display promoting Calvin Klein products at Lord & Taylor. This ad tells people that Lord & Taylor carries the Calvin Klein line and also encourage shoppers to come to the Lord & Taylor to shop. Both parties benefit from this.

To participate in cooperative advertising campaign, a local advertiser must follow certain guidelines and sign an agreement with the supplier. The guidelines include specific conditions for featuring the supplier's product or service in the media, such as size of a print ad and its placement.

Each time a local advertiser purchases a supplier's goods or services, a certain number of advertising credits are earned—usually three to five percent of the total purchase price. A local advertiser can use these credits to offset advertising that meets with the supplier's approval. Sometimes, the local advertiser pays for all the advertising and then presents the ads to the supplier to receive reimbursement. Up to 50 percent of the total pre-approved advertising expenses are normally reimbursed to the local advertiser.

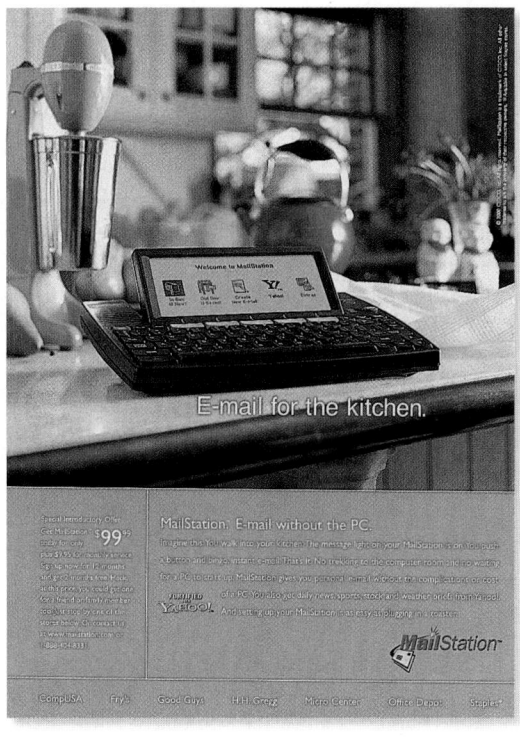

■ **Cooperative Advertising** Cooperative advertising displays a manufacturer's products along with the name of the local advertiser. *How do cooperative advertisers share in costs and benefits?*

Chapter 19 ■ *Advertising* **349**

ASSESS

Reteaching

1. **Vocabulary** Assign and review the vocabulary terms for this section.
2. **Fact and Idea** Assign and review Fact and Idea Review questions 6–10.
3. **Magazine Rates** Go over each of the formulas for calculating newspaper and magazine rates. Stress to students that they should not hesitate to talk to you privately if they need more help in understanding the content of this section.

Enrichment

1. **Review** Assign and review the Chapter 19 activities in the *Student Activity Workbook*.
2. **Review** Assign and review the appropriate Thinking Critically questions from the Chapter Assessment.
3. **Review** Assign and review the following Chapter Assessment activities: Building Workplace Skills, Applying Marketing Concepts, Linking School to Work, The DECA Connection Role Play, and Internet Connection.
4. **Research and Report** Have students watch television or listen to the radio for 20 minutes at three different intervals during the day: in the morning before school or on the way to school; in the early afternoon from 2:00 to 6:00; and in the evening from 7:00 to 10:00. Have students write down what types of products are advertised during these three different time periods, and answer these questions: Did the commercials differ at all in their general presentation or length of time from one time period to another? Why were these time periods chosen for these specific products? Have students bring their findings to class for discussion.

Evaluation

Assign and review the Section 19.2 Assessment.

Technology Resources

 Assessment Resources

Go to the *Marketing Essentials* Web site (**www.marketing.glencoe. com**) for resources to teach and assess occupation-specific vocabulary.

CLOSE

Section Wrap-Up

Have students complete this statement: The choice of advertising media depends on . . . *(the product to be advertised, the habits and lifestyles of the target audience, and the types of media available in the area)*

There are advantages and disadvantages to cooperative advertising for the manufacturer and retailer. Advantages to cooperative advertising may include shared advertising expenses (between supplier and local advertiser) and pre-prepared print advertisements, in-store displays, and TV and radio scripts for local use. Retailers specifically benefit from cooperative advertising as they gain access to greater amounts of promotional funding. Manufacturers benefit specifically as they can gain local recognition—people are made aware of where they can purchase their products nearby. Disadvantages may include loss of control over content, placement in various media, and the need for local advertisers to follow guidelines of suppliers.

Promotional Budget

Once a company decides on promotional methods, it must create a budget. The promotional budget considers not only the cost for the advertising, but for the staff necessary to make it all happen as well. This budget must be considered not only in short-term, but also in the long-term benefits that advertising brings about. There are numerous methods that a company might use when deciding on a budget. Four common promotional budgeting methods are *percentage of anticipated sales, all you can afford, following the competition,* and *objective and task.*

In the *percentage of anticipated sales* method the budget is decided based on a percentage of past or anticipated sales. An example of this might be that the budget for advertising this year is five percent of last year sales. An advantage of this is that there is little financial risk. On the other hand, if sales are down, the promotional budget may be decreased. As you know, it is advertising and promotional effects that could boost sales.

The *all you can afford method* turns all monies to promotional activity only after all other company expenses are paid. The objective is to build sales and reputation in the beginning. This method is often used for only a short period of time. It is popular in small businesses, especially Internet start-up companies.

In the *following the competition* method, the competitor's promotional expenditures are matched or spending is planned in proportion to market share. This is generally considered to be a weak promotional budgeting method because it is based on the competition's promotional objectives.

In the *objective and task* method, the company determines goals, considers the necessary steps to meet goals, and determines the cost for these promotional activities. This method considers the current situation that a company is in and where they want to be going. This is the most effective of the three methods as it considers what the company wants and how it will get there. It is an efficient use of company funds.

19.2 ASSESSMENT

Reviewing Key Terms and Concepts

1. Name three factors that affect newspaper rates.
2. What is the difference between an open rate and a contract rate?
3. What is the formula for figuring cost per thousand?
4. What determines the rate television and radio stations charge for advertising?
5. Name three factors that affect the selection of promotional media.

Thinking Critically

6. Will a prime-time television slot always guarantee an advertiser the best results in selling a product? Why or why not?

Integrating Academic Skills

7. **MATH** Calculate the per thousand rate for a magazine that has a circulation of 1.5 million and charges $25,000 for a full-page black-and-white advertisement.

19.2 ASSESSMENT ANSWERS

Reviewing Key Terms and Concepts
1. location, color, and frequency
2. An open rate is the basic charge; a contract rate provides a discount based upon volume.
3. cost of ad x 1,000 = cost per thousand (CPM)
   circulation rate
4. time of day
5. product, lifestyles of the target audience, and types of media available

Thinking Critically
6. No. While prime-time viewership is the largest potential viewing audience, it may not be the right target market.

Integrating Academic Skills
7. **MATH** CPM is $16.67.
   ([$25,000 x 1,000] ÷1,500,000 = $16.67)

Careers in Marketing

ADVERTISING

George Karaleks
Advertising Producer

What does your job entail?

"Advertising producers create media commercials. They select scripts and directors, and handle the financial arrangements for the project, which includes drawing up a budget, negotiating with unions, contracting with staff, and securing investors. Part of my job is to give recommendations to companies about how best to spend their money when given an array of statistics, demographics, and channels."

What do you recommend for students who want to go into advertising production?

"No one gets into advertising production fresh out of college. In business, the more specific the job function, the harder it is to get into. You need to build a reputation first. My advice is to become an assistant and take a low-level job that you can move up from."

What skills are most important?

"The ability to organize and prioritize is vital. It's my role to bring everyone together—from the actors to the person bidding on the music. I am the person to whom everyone turns when there is a problem. This requires thinking on your feet and doing what is best for both you and the client."

What kind of training did you have?

"I originally wanted to be an actor, because I knew that I wanted to communicate and convey a message. When I realized that I was not getting far in my acting career, I decided to go behind the camera. I went on to work for Grey Advertising and was made vice-president of the company within three years. I currently work on my own with many different clients, troubleshooting when problems come up in an advertising campaign."

What is the secret to your success?

"In this business, you have to be a jack-of-all-trades and master of all of them."

Thinking Critically

Why is it difficult to immediately get a job as an advertising producer?

Career Facts

Education and Training: Coursework in communication technologies, photographic arts, English, drama, speech, media, business management, and accounting is helpful. A bachelor's degree in dramatic arts also provides a good background.

Aptitudes, Abilities, and Skills: Ability to coordinate people, money, ideas, and resources, and above average communication skills for negotiating good business deals. The ability to multitask, and foresight to visualize the finished project are helpful.

Career Outlook: Faster than average growth is expected through the year 2006 due in part to increased use of Internet advertising.

Career Path: Advertising producers may first gain recognition as advertising copywriters. One can advance from associate producer to line producer to executive producer.

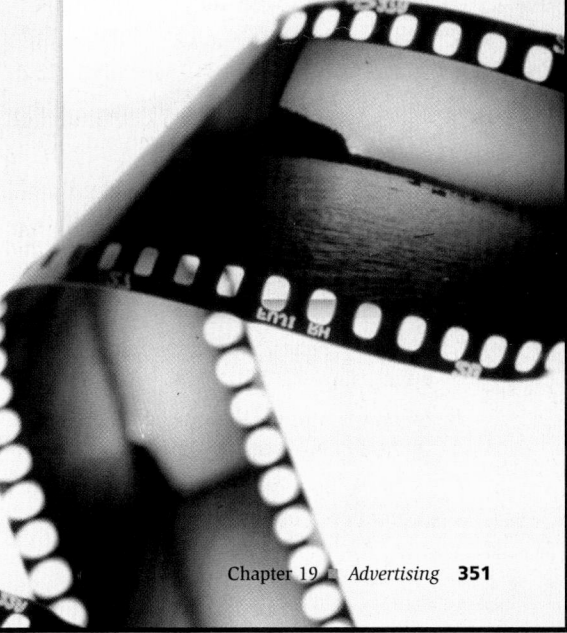

SECTION 19.2

Careers in Marketing

Ask a student to read the Careers in Marketing feature aloud to the class. Discuss the skills and aptitudes required for a career in advertising. Ask students whether they think they would like or dislike a career in advertising. Discuss the pros and cons of such a career.

Thinking Critically Answer

It is necessary to develop a positive reputation and gain experience before building a steady clientele.

 Guest Speakers

Invite an advertising producer or executive to class to discuss his/her job and factors he/she considers when making marketing decisions.

Exploring Careers

Advertised Jobs

1. Ask students what sources might provide job leads.

2. Write the following sources for job/volunteer leads on the board:

- school
- newspaper
- Web sites
- radio or TV
- calling businesses listed in the *Yellow Pages*
- talking to counselors at school or people in the work world (called networking)

3. Ask students to choose a job and research it using three sources for job leads listed on the board.

4. Have students write down their findings and discuss them in class.

Lifelong Learning

Advertising

Since advertising affects so many decisions that students will make during their lifetimes, they can benefit from understanding its uses and applications. After taking this class, they can keep up with trends in advertising by reading a variety of publications, including *Adweek, Advertising Age, Marketing News,* and other general interest publications.

Meeting Individual Needs

Students with Orthopaedic Impairments

If your class involves field research, encourage students with orthopaedic impairments to participate in site selection and transportation planning to ensure access to all sites. Access issues are a major concern for students who use wheelchairs. Barriers, such as stairs, curbs, narrow walkways, heavy doors, etc., must be taken into account when planning an event.

Vocabulary Review

Papers will vary. See Glossary for definitions.

Fact and Idea Review

1. print media, broadcast media, specialty media
2. Advantages of newspaper advertising are large readership; high level of reader involvement; circulation is known, so businesses can target advertising to geographical areas; lower costs due to lower quality of paper and print; lead time can be 24 to 48 hours. Some disadvantages are wasted circulation; short life of ads since newspapers are thrown away; and poorer quality.
3. Magazine advertising can target an audience because circulation and characteristics of regular readers are known. Magazines are often read more slowly and have a longer life, so information in an ad is more likely to be grasped and retained. Print quality is higher in magazines.
4. Direct-mail advertising is sent by businesses directly to prospective customers. Examples include newsletters, catalogs, and coupons.
5. It is said to mar scenic views and cause traffic safety concerns.
6. They are useful for comparing the relative advertising costs of different media.
7. Broadcast advertising is widely available and popular.
8. time of day
9. Use the objective and task method.

Thinking Critically

1. Answers will vary. Without the help of advertising, it would be difficult to compare the availability of desired products and to make price comparisons.
2. Institutional advertising attempts to create a favorable impression and goodwill for a company. Answers will vary.
3. Answers will vary but should focus on determining what is junk mail and what is legitimate, useful advertising.
4. Answers will vary.

Chapter 19 Assessment

VOCABULARY REVIEW

Use the following vocabulary terms in a 250-word paper on advertising media.

- promotional advertising
- institutional advertising
- media
- print media
- broadcast media
- online advertising
- banner ads
- specialty media
- cost per thousand (CPM)
- network radio advertising
- national spot radio advertising
- local radio advertising
- cooperative advertising

FACT AND IDEA REVIEW

1. Identify advertising media categories. (19.1)
2. What are some advantages and disadvantages of using newspaper advertising? (19.1)
3. In what respect is magazine advertising superior to newspaper advertising? (19.1)
4. What is direct-mail advertising? Give five examples of direct-mail advertising. (19.1)
5. Why is outdoor advertising losing popularity in some areas of the country? (19.1)
6. Why is a knowledge of cost per thousand rates helpful to newspaper, magazine, and online advertisers? (19.2)
7. Why is broadcast media popular for advertising? (19.2)
8. What determines the rates charged for television advertising? (19.2)
9. What is the most effective way to create a promotional budget? (19.2)

THINKING CRITICALLY

1. How might consumer buying habits be different if advertising in all of the forms discussed in this chapter did not exist?
2. Why do companies use institutional advertising? Do you think that this is an effective method of advertising?
3. Assume you are a member of a legislative committee considering a ban on "junk mail" advertising. What information would you like to have from people on both sides of the issue before making your decision?
4. As more television and cable network channels develop, television advertisers are confronted with the problem of "channel surfers." These are people who use their remote control to switch channels to avoid viewing advertising commercials. Come up with one creative way that advertisers can try to limit the amount of channel surfing.

BUILDING WORKPLACE SKILLS

1. **Science** Environmentalists believe that advertising conducted on the Internet and online shopping will have positive effects on the environment. They believe that valuable resources can be saved or recycled. Develop a one-page outline (use broad topic headings such as Energy, Resources, Social Costs, etc.) on possible ways that electronic advertising and online shopping can preserve the environment.
2. **Language Arts** Why do some parents and school administrators believe that advertising should not occur within school buildings? Do you personally believe there should be limits on in-school advertising? Why or why not? Write a one-page paper explaining your position.

Building Workplace Skills

1. Outlines will vary.
2. Papers will vary, but answers may suggest that administrators and parents are concerned that advertising interferes with learning process and allows for commercialization of the educational process.

APPLYING MARKETING CONCEPTS

1. **Identifying Different Types of Advertising** Look through newspapers and magazines to find examples of promotional and institutional advertising. Clip four appropriate ads, convert them into electronic form using a scanner, and create a computer presentation to show to the class.

2. **Analyzing Television Viewing** Use a spreadsheet computer program to prepare an advertising log for one hour of your television viewing. List the products advertised, characterize the advertising approach taken, and identify the sponsor as either national or local.

3. **Creating an Advertising Plan** Develop an advertising plan for a product of your choice. Use a word processing program to write a report about your plan that identifies what media you will use, your target audience, and times you want the ad to run. Decide whether you will use institutional or promotional advertising or a combination of both. Research the costs of each advertising medium and your estimated advertising budget per month and per year.

4. **Writing a Direct-Mail Piece** Using a word processing program, write a direct-mail marketing piece to promote either a Caribbean cruise adventure or a charity or special interest group of your choice. As you write your letter, think about your target market. Decide what other pieces should go into the package with the letter, such as reply cards, incentive discounts, or testimonial letters from famous people.

LINKING SCHOOL TO WORK

Information and Basic Skills Bring examples of the print advertisements produced by a local business to class. Be prepared to explain how often the print ads are run and in what types of print media they appear.

THE DECA CONNECTION

Role Play: Direct Advertising Strategist

Situation You are to assume the role of sales associate in a newly opened apparel and accessories store. Since your store is new, procedures need to be established to create a customer mailing list.

Activity Your store manager (judge) has asked you to develop a plan for a direct-mail campaign to target new and current customers.

Evaluation You will be evaluated on how well you meet the following performance indicators:
- Explain the types of advertising media
- Write informative messages
- Write persuasive messages
- Explain the nature of written communications
- Explain the nature of direct advertising strategies

interNET CONNECTION

About Our Company
You work for an advertising firm that develops online advertisements specializing in travel. You are required to review various banner ads developed by companies.

Connect
- Identify three travel-related Web sites that use banner advertisements.
- Write a report summarizing the features of each ad.
- Identify which banner ad you think is the best and explain why.

Chapter 19 ■ Advertising **353**

Mini Quiz
Administer the Mini Quiz orally. For an expanded chapter quiz, go to page 105 of the *Reproducible Tests* book.

1. Advertising designed to increase sales is known as promotional advertising.
2. Advertising designed to create a favorable impression is known as institutional advertising.
3. The main purpose of advertising is to present a message so well that a customer buys the products or accepts the idea presented.
4. Agencies, means, or instruments used to convey messages are called media.
5. The cost per thousand or CPM rate is the cost of exposing 1,000 readers to an advertisement.

Applying Marketing Concepts
1. Presentations will vary depending on ads selected.
2. Spreadsheets will vary depending on television viewing.
3. Advertising plans will vary but should be appropriate for the type of product.
4. Direct mail marketing pieces will vary.

Linking School to Work
Answers will vary.

 1. Assessment Have students complete the Reproducible Test for Chapter 19 or construct your own tests using the ExamView software.
2. Enrichment Have students complete the corresponding activities in the following workbooks:
- *Marketing Math Workbook*, p. 45
- *Marketing Research Project Workbook*, p. 85

Chapter Overview

Chapter 20 introduces the concept of advertising campaigns and how they are developed. The chapter explains different roles that advertising agencies can play in assisting businesses with advertising campaigns. Next, cooperative advertising arrangements between suppliers and advertisers are detailed. The chapter also describes the essential elements of print advertisements.

 Springboard

Brainstorm and Describe Write the following on the board: Lincoln Navigator, IBM or Apple Computer, Nike or Reebok athletic shoes, Rolex watches. Ask students to describe how a print ad should look for each product. Ask: Is it usually in color or in black and white? What is the basic appeal of the ad? What types of slogans are used?

Prereading

List the section objectives to discuss with students. Have students skim the chapter, looking at the pictures, reading the captions, and noting the heads. Ask questions to ensure that the students have a minimal understanding of the chapter structure.

Preteaching Marketing Vocabulary

Write the vocabulary terms for the parts of a print ad in one column on the board and the rest of the terms in another column. Display several print ads and ask students to identify the four parts of each ad and generate definitions for each term. Help students generate definitions for the second column of terms, using the Glossary as needed.

Marketing: What It Takes
Answer Include a headline, illustration, copy with special offers, and signature.

Chapter 20

Preparing Print Advertisements

Marketing: What It Takes

Advertising 101
As the manager of a new travel agency, you must prepare an ad layout announcing the agency's grand opening. Be sure to include the following: a headline, an illustration, copy that includes any introductory offers and special pricing that will be featured, and a signature plate including the location and hours.

WHAT WILL YOU DO?
What steps can you take to make sure you develop a great print advertisement?

354

THE DECA CONNECTION

ADVISOR CORNER

Online Competitions Reinforce students' computer and advertising skills by getting them involved in one of DECA's online advertising competitions, like the 7UP Challenge. Guidelines for the competitions are on National DECA's Web site (**www.deca.org**). DECA's online advertising competitions encourage DECA members to seek knowledge beyond traditional advertising media, and to develop a working appreciation of the potential for advertising on the World Wide Web. This can be a great learning experience for your chapter members to enter individually. You can also involve your whole chapter by doing a chapter entry with students assigned to teams.
(Lucinda Mason, Demopolis H.S., Demopolis, AL)

Essential Elements of Advertising

Advertising (On Board)
• Determine the target audience
• Determine resources available

The Advertising Agency

• develop advertising campaign

To advertise a product, a company must first determine the target audience it wants to reach and how much money it can spend. The next step is to develop an advertising campaign. An **advertising campaign** involves the creation and coordination of a series of advertisements (both broadcast and print) around a particular theme to promote a product. The size and the financial resources of a business determines whether an advertising campaign is developed by an "in-house" advertising department, a few designated individuals, or an advertising agency.

Remember that "the size and the financial resources of a business..."

Advertising agencies work jointly with business clients to develop advertising campaigns. Depending on the scope and size of the advertising campaign and the needs of the business, agencies can serve as a *full-service agency* or a *limited-service agency*. Full-service agencies perform advertising research, media selection, copy development, and artwork for an advertising campaign. Larger advertising agencies employ specialists, such as copywriters, artists, media experts, marketing researchers, and legal advisers to assist with advertising campaigns.

Notice the book mentions full-service agencies and limited-service agencies. What is the difference?

Limited-service agencies specialize in one aspect of the campaign, such as creative services. *In-house agencies* provide full or limited advertising services based upon the size of the company.

Frequently, larger businesses select an advertising agency to be an *agency of record* to handle all aspects of the advertising campaign. The agency of record does all necessary research, media selection, copy development, and artwork. Increasingly, larger companies are selecting from specialists to develop different aspects of the advertising campaign. In addition, technology and e-commerce opportunities have caused many businesses to employ their own people to perform certain aspects of advertising, such as Web site development and maintenance.

Is anybody interested in a career in Web site development and maintenance?

■ Agency Organization

Advertising agencies are usually organized into four service departments: client, creative, research, and media.

Client service departments work with agency groups and individual businesses to identify opportunities for advertising. Employees—called account executives—look at client needs, create advertising plans, and coordinate advertising with other promotion activities related to the account.

I think people figure, "Ohh, advertising is done only in private business." That is incorrect. Agency could promote candidate, presidential visit, etc., legislation. (give example)

IRS e-file

• What You'll Learn

There is a lot of information in Sec. 20.1 such as

- How advertising campaigns are developed
- The creation of advertising headlines
- The preparation of advertising copy
- The selection of advertising illustrations
- The significance of advertising signatures

Does anybody have parents involved in advertising?

It's an important section because...

• Why It's Important

In order to understand how successful advertising campaigns help sell products, you need to know how essential advertising elements are used to develop effective advertisements.

Key Terms

- advertising campaign
- advertising agencies
- headline
- copy
- illustration
- clip art
- signature
- slogan

Next, who can tell me how advertising agencies are usually organized?

FOCUS

Bell Ringer Activity

Brainstorm Tell students to imagine that they manage a creative services department of an advertising agency. The department, which includes graphic artists and copywriters, is responsible for developing the advertising message and producing the ads. Your client, Palm Computing, Inc., has called a meeting for late this afternoon. Your job is to generate some ideas for a magazine ad campaign that promotes a palm-size (handheld) platform computer.

Have students name the product and come up with an idea for a photo or illustration, copy, and a catchy slogan. Ask: What predominant colors would they use? Would they have a great deal of written copy explaining the product, or very little? Who is the target audience?

Introducing the Section

Essential Elements of Advertising Review students' answers from the Bell Ringer Activity, which should start them thinking in terms of how the elements of an ad combine to create message, sales appeal, and image. Tell students to keep the information they generate for the Bell Ringer Activity. They may wish to use it in conjunction with the Linking School to Work Activity in the Chapter Review or with the Building Academic Skills Activity in Section 20.2.

Classroom Resources

For the Teacher
- Teacher Editions for all workbooks
- Assessment Package
- PowerPoint Presentation Software
- Interactive Lesson Planner
- **ILP** Block Scheduling, p. 6
- **ILP** Lesson Plans, p. 43
- **ILP** Internet Resources, p. 59

- **ILP** Blackline Masters, p. 37
- **ILP** *BusinessWeek* Case Studies, p. 127
- **ILP** Marketing Career Portfolio, p. 36
- *Marketing Essentials* Web site (**www.marketing.glencoe.com**)

For the Student
- Student Activity Workbook, p. 169
- Marketing Math Workbook, p. 45

- Marketing Research Project Workbook, p. 85
- **ILP** School-to-Work Activity Workbook, p. 85
- Virtual Business simulation
- *Marketing Essentials* Web site (**www.marketing.glencoe.com**)

ILP These resources are available in print and on the Interactive Lesson Planner (ILP)

TEACH

📊 Technology Resources

PowerPoint The *Marketing Essentials* PowerPoint Presentation CD-ROM provides visual lecture aids for every chapter section.

Concept Development

1. Read Section 20.1 with students.
2. Have students read aloud the Case Study on page 362 and review the answers in class.
3. Invite a representative from a local advertising agency to visit your class to explain the depth and breadth of the agency's business and to discuss the types of advertising (particularly print) it does for various client accounts. Discuss the creative teamwork involved in developing ads.

You may wish to ask the agency to send representatives from more than one department (for example, an account rep, a copywriter, and a graphic artist) to discuss the various aspects of their work.

If there are no advertising agencies in your area, invite an independent small business owner to discuss the procedures that are used to develop print ads for the local newspaper.

To further extend students' learning, have them take notes on the presentation, or respond to a list of teacher-developed guest speaker questions and word process the notes or answers to the pre-written script as an assignment.

Stamping Out Unwanted E-mail

Everyone loves getting e-mail, right? Wrong! It might be nice to get an e-mail from a family member, coworker, or long lost friend, but what about unwanted junk e-mail? In an effort to limit unwanted e-mail, Congress approved the Unsolicited Electronic E-mail Act in 2000. The bill places restrictions on e-mail marketers. These restrictions include requiring "spam e-mail," or unsolicited e-mail, to include a valid reply-to-address. It also forces people and companies to stop spamming consumers upon request. Internet Service Providers, also referred to as "ISPs," are allowed to establish their own spam policies either accepting, limiting, or charging companies for sending spam. Those ISPs that are compensated for accepting spam must offer their subscribers the ability to opt out of spam e-mail.

Thinking Critically

Why would the government place restrictions on Internet advertising?

Creative service departments develop the advertising messages and produce the ads. Graphic artists, copywriters, commercial designers, and art directors work together in this department to create advertisements. *I think a lot of people don't understand that art majors have a valuable role in business*

Research service employees study the target markets, the attitudes of potential customers, and buying behaviors toward a company's products. This department helps determine the type of message that will have the greatest appeal for a particular market segment. *Questionnaires, surveys, interviews, etc. Matt you too*

Media service departments advise clients on their media choices. This department suggests an advertising budget for television, radio, newspapers, magazines, and other forms of advertising, such as billboards and direct mail. This department also coordinates the timing, placement, and frequency of various advertisements. The media plans developed by this department for a company's products are based on the region, city, population, gender income, education, and the reading and television viewing habits of people in the target market. *This is based largely on marketing research*

356 Unit 6 ■ Promotion

■ New Models for Advertising Agencies

Please read the "New Models for Ad Agencies"

Advertising experts predict that new models for advertising agencies will be used in the future. These new models will include business formats, such as creative boutiques, project team agencies, and virtual agencies.

A *creative boutique* is a specialized service agency where creative production is sent outside the business, but copy is provided by the business. This results in faster layout and production.

Project team agencies provide copywriting, creative execution, and media placement without larger agency overhead. Teams can come together to do one project, and then move on to the next project when the ad campaign is complete.

Virtual agencies provide services coordinated by an individual who works with a network of experienced freelancers. A *freelancer* is a self-employed person who sells work or services by the hour, day, or job, rather than working on a regular salary basis for one employer. *The book talks about freelancers. What does a freelancer do?*

Developing Print Advertisements

Jess doing this on side for restaurant (Adobe Photoshop)

Although they are only one part of an advertising campaign, print advertisements are very important to most campaigns. Print advertisements must contain four key elements, which include *headline, copy, illustrations,* and *signature* (see Figure 20-1 on page 360). Some advertisements also include the company's slogan, which is often presented with or near the signature. Each of the four key elements enhances the overall theme of a product promotion. The four fundamental elements of a print advertisement are applicable for ads in other media. As you read this section, think of ways these concepts would apply to preparing television and radio commercials, as well as online advertising. *Who can tell me the four key elements that a print advertisement must contain?*

■ Headline

The **headline** is the saying that gets the readers' attention, arouses their interest by providing a benefit, and leads them to read the rest of the ad. Headlines are responsible for the overall effectiveness of most advertising campaigns, so many experts consider them the most important part of an advertisement. *Who can recall what a headline is?*

Stamping Out Unwanted E-mail

Answer The government places restrictions on Internet advertising to protect consumers from unsolicited e-mail.

PURPOSES OF A HEADLINE The purposes of a headline are to attract readers' attention, select an audience, provide a benefit to the reader, and lead to the illustration and copy.

Headlines must be attention-getters, or the advertisement may not be read. More than 80 percent of the people who look at a print advertisement just read the headlines. Headlines that use words such as *new, now,* and *free* universally attract attention.

Effective headlines select an audience. They must have advertising appeal and provide a reason for purchasing a product or service. The motivation for purchase is what will help to identify a targeted group of potential customers. Headlines can appeal to people for a variety of reasons including profit, love, fear, fun, and vanity. Effective headlines can create the image a product wants to project toward a specific type of customer.

A headline provides a benefit to the reader. You want to promise the reader something that matches a need or want. Some benefits include free offers, more miles per gallon, better service, or fewer cavities.

Headlines are used to lead to the copy and illustration. Headlines are often written so that a reader can grasp the entire point of the ad by simply viewing the headline, seeing the illustration, and reading a few words of the copy. Other times, headlines have a subheadline to clarify or expand on the main idea expressed in the headline. Subheadlines are usually found in smaller type close to the headline. Headlines should be powerful enough to draw potential customers into reading the copy.

WRITING EFFECTIVE HEADLINES Most headlines are brief because many people cannot take in more than seven words at one time. One effective and short headline is that for Charmin bath tissue— "Ultra Soft. Ultra Strong." This headline utilizes an illustration to tell the rest of the story.

Ultra soft. Ultra strong.

Charmin's a great combination of softness and strength. Maybe that's why it's the number one bath tissue today. Everyone wants that Charmin feeling. **Charmin** *Ultra*

■ **Effective Headlines** A brief, catchy headline is often an effective method of attracting a reader's attention. *Why are most headlines brief?*

Chapter 20 ■ *Preparing Print Advertisements* **357**

Discussion Starter

Advertising Agencies Ask students: In which department of an ad agency would they prefer to work and in what capacity? Why? Based on their answers, what skills will they need to develop for this type of work?

CAPTION ANSWER
Effective Headlines Most headlines are brief because most people cannot absorb more than seven words at one time.

GREAT IDEAS from the Marketing Classroom

Keith Smith
Pendleton Memorial High School
Falmouth, KY

Our Principles of Marketing class prepares a creative marketing research project. We devise a survey tool to use for our research project, complete the interviews, compile and analyze the results, and prepare charts and graphs to represent the results.

While we discuss preparing a research survey tool, each student creates a questionnaire, charts, and graphs, as well as an analysis of the results. Past projects have included identifying target markets for new businesses, identifying needs and wants of the community, checking the effectiveness of the advertising plan of a business, and doing a price comparison of our only grocery store.

SECTION 20.1

Thinking Critically

Effectiveness of Print Advertisements Ask students: What techniques can businesses use to track the effectiveness of print advertisements?

Cooperative Learning

Newspaper Display Advertisements Organize the class into teams of three to five students, and make each team responsible for preparing a newspaper display advertisement for a new or an existing store that the instructor selects. Ask students to use examples from stores in your community. Have each group include the following in their ad layout:

- headline
- illustration
- copy, including any introductory offers, special pricing, etc.
- signature plate including store location and hours

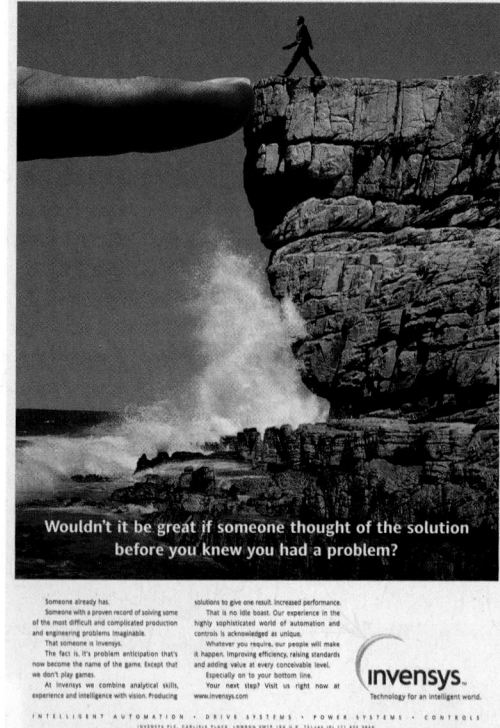

Wouldn't it be great if someone thought of the solution before you knew you had a problem?

invensys.
Technology for an intelligent world.

■ Creative Writing This ad uses a paradox in the headline. *Why is the headline a paradox?*

It is possible to create longer headlines that are effective if they are provocative. In a recent study, creative directors from major advertising agencies analyzed award-winning print ads to determine what their headlines had in common. They discovered that 32 percent of the headlines used familiar sayings with a twist. About 23 percent of the headlines made use of opposites such as "up/down" and "lie/truth." For example, a headline used by a boot manufacturer made the following statement: "After a Day of Downhill Skiing, Getting a Fine Meal Shouldn't Be an Uphill Battle."

Every headline should have a single focus or main idea. Before writing a headline, try to sum up the main idea in a single sentence. This technique will help you stay focused on the subject and produce a headline with impact.

Here are some other techniques you can use when writing headlines:

- *Alliteration* (repeating initial consonant sounds)—Win with Wireless (Samsung)
- *Paradox* (a seeming contradiction that could be true)—It's an environmental movement all by itself. (Honda Insight)
- *Rhyme*—Bounty. The Quicker Picker-Upper
- *Pun* (a humorous use of a word that suggests two or more of its meanings or the meaning of another word similar in sound)—Beauty and the Beef (Ball Park Franks)
- *Play on Words*—For Soft Babies and Baby Soft Hands

■ Copy

The **copy** is the selling message in a written advertisement. It directly expands on the information in the headline or the product shown in the illustration. It should also stress the benefits and features of the product advertised to encourage customers to try this product or service.

Good copy, like a good headline, is simple and direct. Copy can vary from a few words to several paragraphs. Copy does not need to be extensive to get a message across. As with all aspects of advertising, a few well-chosen words will intrigue the customer while not bombarding them with information.

Copy might be a conversation, an educational tool, a testimonial to the benefits of using the product, or a description of how an institution can help you. Your copy will be competing with hundreds of other advertisers for the reader's attention; therefore, it must be noticeable or dramatic.

Copy should appeal to the senses. Through the words, the customer should be able to see, hear, touch, taste, or even smell a product. This can be done through using descriptive adjectives.

Give your copy news value by providing specific information. Tell the *who, what, when, why, where,* and *how* of your product. Remember that facts about your product are more powerful than claims. Use case histories, statistics, performance figures, dates, and quotes from experts whenever possible. While it is helpful to include quotes from satisfied customers, facts are most helpful when trying to win new customers.

CAPTION ANSWER

Creative Writing A paradox is a seeming contradiction that could be true. The contradiction in the headline concerns the idea that a problem usually precedes a solution, instead of a solution preceding a problem.

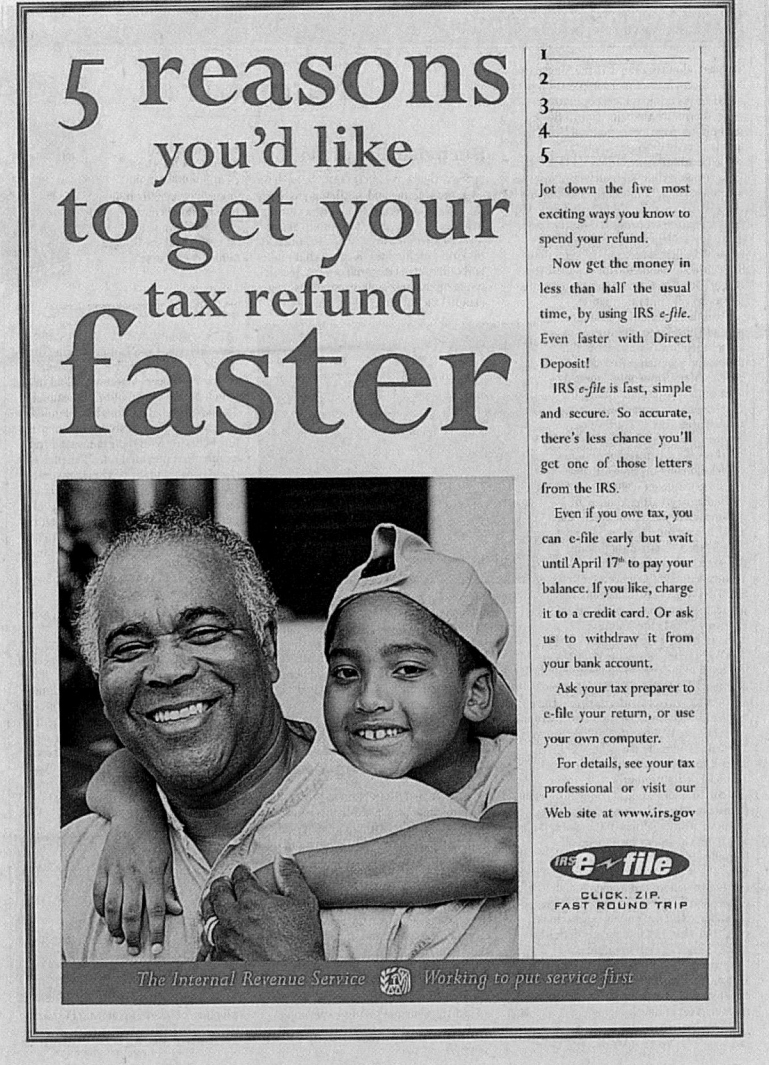

■ **A Call to Action** The Internal Revenue Service ad shown here is an example of an ad with well written copy. *In what ways does this ad demonstrate effective copy techniques?*

5 reasons you'd like to get your tax refund faster

Jot down the five most exciting ways you know to spend your refund.

Now get the money in less than half the usual time, by using IRS *e-file*. Even faster with Direct Deposit!

IRS *e-file* is fast, simple and secure. So accurate, there's less chance you'll get one of those letters from the IRS.

Even if you owe tax, you can e-file early but wait until April 17th to pay your balance. If you like, charge it to a credit card. Or ask us to withdraw it from your bank account.

Ask your tax preparer to e-file your return, or use your own computer.

For details, see your tax professional or visit our Web site at www.irs.gov

IRS *e-file*
CLICK. ZIP.
FAST ROUND TRIP

The Internal Revenue Service — Working to put service first

Key words used in copy, such as *compare, introducing, now, price, save, easy,* and *new,* establish immediate contact with the reader. They arouse interest, encourage awareness, and create desire. Customers enjoy knowing that they are on the cutting edge when trying new products, and words such as *improved* and *introducing* offer this impression.

Advertising copy should provide a call to action to shoppers. It should always be written in the active voice. You would write, "This item will help you," rather than "You will be helped by this item."

Including a penalty for not acting now—such as *before it's too late* or *without delay*—help create this sense of action.

Asking for action is especially important in local advertising, which generally seeks immediate action. On the other hand, most national advertising is not looking for immediate action; its purpose is to keep the name of the product in front of the public. It is trying to build brand awareness for new prospects and brand loyalty for current customers. In this case, no action is requested in the print ad.

Chapter 20 ■ *Preparing Print Advertisements* **359**

Independent Practice

Research and Identify Have each student review your local newspaper for one example of cooperative advertising. Tell students to look for retail ads where only products from one manufacturer are included in the ad. For each ad, they should identify the type of business, the local merchant, and the manufacturer who sponsored the ad. They should also identify each element of the ad (headline, copy, illustration, and signature).

CAPTION ANSWER
A Call to Action The ad urges readers to list five ways to spend the refund. The copy is simple and direct, and written in the active voice. It is dramatic, establishes contact with the reader, creates awareness, and arouses interest. Most importantly, it tells readers how to take action.

Individualized Practice

Communication Skills

Tell students that advertising copy should always be written in the active voice.

L1 Have students rewrite the following sentences in the active voice:

1) SensorExcel™, the next revolution in shaving closeness, is brought to you by Gillette.

2) One Hundred Twenty images selected from Corel Professional Photos are profiled in The World's Best Digital Photographs (coffee-table book and companion CD-ROM).

3) A 3800 V engine, air conditioning, and many other luxury appointments are included as standard features of the Buick LeSabre.

FIGURE 20-1
PARTS OF A PRINT ADVERTISEMENT

Print advertisements must contain four key elements: *headline, copy, illustrations,* and *signature.* Some advertisements also include the company's *slogan,* which is often presented with or near the signature. Each of the key elements enhances the overall theme of a product promotion.

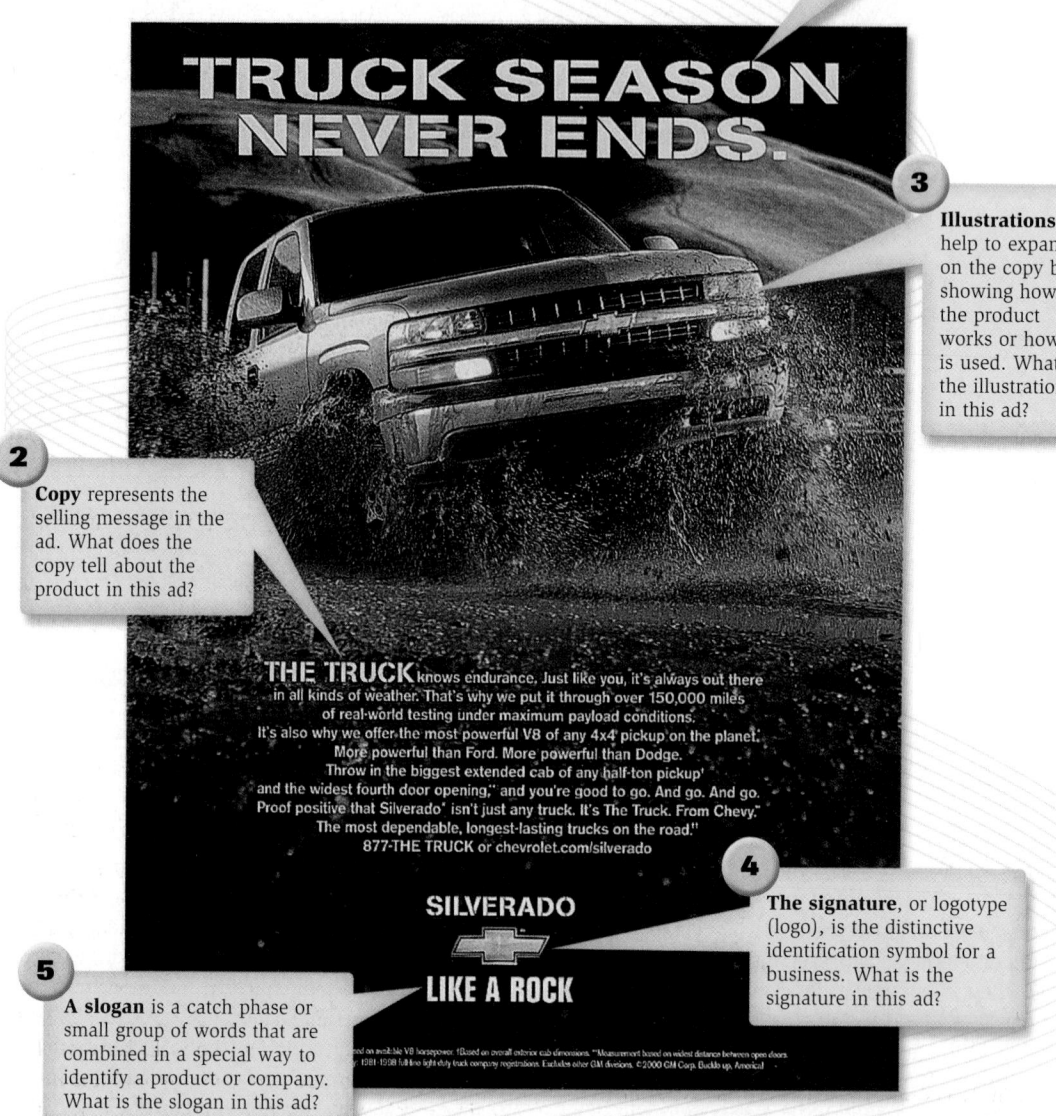

1 **Headlines** attract readers, arouse interest and get them to look at the illustration and copy. What is the headline?

3 **Illustrations** help to expand on the copy by showing how the product works or how it is used. What is the illustration in this ad?

2 **Copy** represents the selling message in the ad. What does the copy tell about the product in this ad?

4 **The signature**, or logotype (logo), is the distinctive identification symbol for a business. What is the signature in this ad?

5 **A slogan** is a catch phase or small group of words that are combined in a special way to identify a product or company. What is the slogan in this ad?

DECA CONNECTION
COMPETITIVE EVENTS AND MARKETING ESSENTIALS

Print Advertisements Continue using the Advertising Campaign Event as a tool to assist in teaching the preparation of print advertisements. The guidelines for the advertising campaign allow nine fact sheets about the ad campaign; item IV asks the student for a list of advertising media selection necessary for the campaign. You can assign your students to prepare one or more print advertisements they plan to use in their campaign. Students can use the mock-up print advertisements and present them during the oral presentation to illustrate their ideas to the businessperson/judge.

■ Illustration

The illustration is the photograph or drawing used in a print advertisement. Its primary function is to attract attention and to encourage a purchase of the advertised product. It should also tie into the headline and copy. The illustration, together with the headline, should lead the potential customer to read at least the first sentence of the copy.

The illustration should transmit a total message that would be hard to communicate just with words. Illustrations should show the product, how the product works, and safety features. Illustrations should also project the appropriate image desired for the product, such as convenience, entertainment, leisure, or status. Sometimes it is necessary for customers to see the product in use, such as models wearing the featured clothing items. Businesses also want to be careful when choosing an image that it will not become outdated quickly. Once a business selects an illustration, it normally does not change for a period of time. To maintain its image, therefore, a business should not only carefully select its illustrations, but also periodically evaluate them for consistency.

MARKETPLACE

The Way of the Words

Attempting to produce print ads for Arabic-speaking Middle Eastern countries can be a disorienting experience for the novice. Where does the challenge lie? The placement of words! Arabic is read from right to left, not left to right as is English. Pictorial sequences must also be shown in that order, therefore, because that is how the mind reads—words on a page or pictures on an ad. One U.S. laundry detergent manufacturer learned this the hard way. An ad for an Arab client showed a step-by-step illustration of doing laundry. When the client "read" the ad, it appeared that clean clothes became dirty after being exposed to the detergent!

Thinking Critically
What are some other goods that could be mistranslated if the ad was read the opposite way?

■ **Advertising Transmittal** The purpose of advertising illustrations is to transmit a message. *What kind of message does the above ad transmit? Do you like it? Why or why not?*

Photographs should be used in advertisements when a sense of reality is necessary. Sometimes it's important for the customer to know exactly what the product looks like or how it's used. Consumer products such as cars, computers, cosmetics, electronic equipment, furniture, and sporting equipment should be illustrated with photographs.

Drawings are often used to show a part of a product that the reader would not normally see. Cutaway drawings and illustrations of constructed or manufactured products and equipment can help show important features not visible in a photograph.

SOURCES FOR ILLUSTRATIONS Businesses often use clip art in their print advertisements. Clip art takes the form of images, stock drawings, and photographs. It is often provided by suppliers, manufacturers, or trade associations for print advertisements. Clip art can also be found in published books, compact disks, and on the Web. Because clip art is ready for reproduction and printing, it is inexpensive, quick, and easy to use. When stock art work is not sufficient, professionals may be hired to photograph situations or products.

Chapter 20 ■ *Preparing Print Advertisements* **361**

The Way of the Words
Answer Answers will vary but other goods that could be mistranslated may include food products or a hair dryer.

SECTION 20.1

Individualized Practice

L2 Ask students to combine each group of sentences to create one sentence that is written in the active voice:

Group 1

1) The finest selection and quality of internationally sourced leather sofas and sectionals are now offered by Jennifer Leather.

2) Jennifer Leather also offers internationally sourced loveseats, chairs, and ottomans.

Group 2

1) Esquire is an extensive collection of handsome timepieces.

2) These timepieces have quality features and details.

3) The features and details of Esquire timepieces are rarely found in watches so affordable.

L3 Have students collect and critique a variety of print ads discussing the use of active and passive voices.

CAPTION ANSWER
Advertising Transmittal Apple desires to transmit a new and different image for its line of computers through design and color. Students' answers will vary as to like and dislike of the ad.

Reteaching

1. **Vocabulary** Assign and review the vocabulary terms for this section.
2. **Fact and Idea** Assign and review Fact and Idea Review questions 1–8 from the Chapter Assessment.
3. **Ads** Show students several ads from a magazine and a newspaper. Have them identify the parts of each ad and answer the following questions about each ad:
   - What technique does the headline use to get the reader involved?
   - What figurative techniques were used to create the headlines?
   - (Read the ad copy to the students.) Is it written in the form of a conversation or written to educate the consumer?

Enrichment

1. **Review** Assign and review the appropriate Thinking Critically questions from the Chapter Assessment.
2. **Extend** Assign and review the corresponding activities from *BusinessWeek Case Studies, Internet Resources,* and the *School-to-Work Activity Workbook.* **ILP**
3. **Research and Discuss** Have students research the evolution of print advertising with respect to such things as illustrative style, style of typeface used, amount of copy in the ad, and trends in layout. Discuss their findings in class. *(Ads in the early part of this century contained a great deal of copy in very small typeface compared to modern ads; they were elaborately illustrated and appeared to be more like art; and copy was often written to educate.)*

Case Study

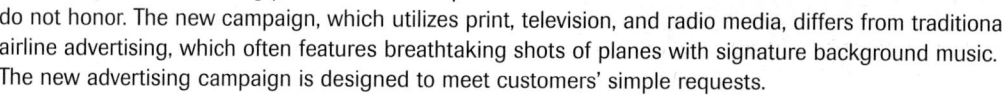

How Do You Want to Fly?

Delta Airlines recently unveiled a new $100 million advertising campaign created by the full-service advertising agency Leo Burnett. The old slogan "On Top of the World?" did not produce the results that Delta's management wanted.

Delta's reputation suffered during the 1990s when cost-cutting measures reduced customer service and satisfaction. When Delta realized that it was time to develop a new advertising campaign, they turned to the The Leo Burnett Company, which is responsible for the advertising for seven out of the 25 most valuable global brands, according to Interbrand. The new advertising campaign slogan entitled "How Do You Want to Fly?" is turning things around.

Burnett researchers conducted airport interviews with travelers and found out that most flyers simply want hassle-free travel. Many consumers find that advertising often makes big promises that companies do not honor. The new campaign, which utilizes print, television, and radio media, differs from traditional airline advertising, which often features breathtaking shots of planes with signature background music. The new advertising campaign is designed to meet customers' simple requests.

The campaign's print advertisements will feature luggage tags with flyer requests printed on them, such as "Fly with more magazines," "Fly efficiently," and "Fly according to schedule." These ads will be featured in 20 business publications. Television ads will feature real-life experiences of passengers, with no slogan, musical jingle, or big name announcers.

In place of an ending tagline, all new ads will end with a customer travel request on a Delta baggage tag. In conjunction with the new ad campaign, Delta has revamped its Web site to make it more user and customer friendly. Delta Airlines is betting that the new campaign will improve its image for service by placing importance on the airline traveler's time and keeping travel hassles to a minimum.

Case Study Review

1. **How can Delta ensure that the new advertising campaign is successful?**
2. **Why is Delta relying on providing simple service?**

A MATTER OF ETHICS

3. **Do you think that Delta implies in this advertising theme that all service requests will be honored? If yes, is this ethical for the company to do? Why or why not?**

Mention
- *Knowledge of Southwest (Low Cost, Regional, Food Service, Turn Around Time, Ticketless Transaction)*
- *Painted Planes*
- *Marketing Research*

Case Study Review Answers

How Do You Want to Fly?

1. Delta must convince customers that their on-time performance and service have improved. They need to focus on meeting frequent fliers' needs and incorporate airline "success stories" into their campaign.
2. Delta found that most passengers really want hassle-free, on-time travel.

A MATTER OF ETHICS

3. Answers will vary, but most may say no. Delta is not implying the company will honor the different requests. This is probably recognized by most customers. Advertising research confirms that customers allow Delta to place a priority on the requests that occur most frequently.

Signature

No advertisement is complete without naming its sponsor. The **signature**, or logotype (logo), is the distinctive identification symbol for a business. A well-designed signature gets instant recognition for a business.

In national ads, the signature is the name of the firm. It may also include the corporate symbol and slogan. The signature in local advertisements usually includes the business's name, address, telephone number, business hours, or slogan. Many advertisers also include their Web addresses in the signature.

SLOGAN To support a firm's signature, many businesses create and use slogans that help customers identify with the firm and its image. A **slogan** is a catch phase or small group of words that are combined in a special way to identify a product or company.

Slogans create a distinct image for the company, its products, or its corporate mission. Headlines frequently become the slogan for an advertising campaign. An example of an advertising slogan is *Melts in your mouth, not in your hand.*

Figure 20-2 highlights some of the most popular slogans of the twentieth century. Each of these advertising slogans had the power to attract attention and arouse interest. It is important to notice how all of these slogans used fewer than seven words to get their point across.

FIGURE 20-2

Top slogans of the 20th Century

1	Diamonds are forever.	A	Maxwell House
2	The pause that refreshes.	B	Nike
3	Good to the last drop	C	public service
4	Does she . . . or doesn't she?	D	Crest
5	Where's the beef?	E	Clairol
6	Let your fingers do the walking.	F	Wendy's
7	Just do it!	G	General Electric
8	We try harder.	H	Yellow Pages
9	Breakfast of champions.	I	Avis
10	When it rains, it pours.	J	Wheaties
11	Look ma, no cavities!	K	Morton Salt
12	Loose lips sink ships	L	DeBeers
13	We bring good things to life.	M	Coca-Cola

■ **Super Slogans** These advertising slogans were judged to be some of the best of the 20th century. *Can you match the slogan to the product?*

1-L; 2-M; 3-A; 4-E; 5-F; 6-H; 7-B; 8-I; 9-J; 10-K; 11-D; 12-C; 13-G

SECTION 20.1

Evaluation

Assign and review the section 20.1 Assessment.

Technology Resources

GO TO **Assessment Resources**
Go to the *Marketing Essentials* Web site (**www.marketing.glencoe. com**) for resources to teach and assess occupation-specific vocabulary.

CLOSE

Section Wrap-Up

Have students complete this statement: The four essential elements in a print ad are . . . *(headline, copy, illustration, and signature.)*

FIGURE 20-2 ANSWER
Super Slogans See the upside down answer key below the caption for correct responses.

20.1 ASSESSMENT

Reviewing Key Terms and Concepts

1. How are advertising campaigns developed?
2. Why are headlines considered by many to be the most important part of print advertisements?
3. What is the main purpose of advertising copy?
4. What should illustrations show about a product?
5. What is the signature in an advertisement?

Thinking Critically

6. What is a problem with a well-designed ad that does not have a signature?

Integrating Academic Skills

7. **COMMUNICATION** Identify five household or consumer products you are familiar with and develop advertising headlines for each. Assume that the product is being advertised by the manufacturer. Base your headlines on opposite words such as up/down, hot/cold, or inside/outside.

20.1 ASSESSMENT ANSWERS

Reviewing Key Terms and Concepts

1. Often smaller firms develop the campaign "in-house." Larger businesses within national or international markets may also use full or limited service advertising agencies.
2. 80 percent of the people who look at a print advertisement just read the headlines.
3. selling message and product features
4. show product, how product works, safety features, and present appropriate image
5. It is the distinctive identification symbol for the business.

Thinking Critically

6. Customers might not immediately recognize company or product being advertised.

Integrating Academic Skills

7. **COMMUNICATION** Answers will vary.

SECTION 20.2

Ad Layouts

FOCUS

Bell Ringer Activity

Proofread In Chapter 8 students did proofreading exercises in the Communications Skills Activities in Section 8.2. Give each student a copy of a print ad that you have rewritten to contain several errors, including an error in the price of the product. Allow 15 minutes for students to proofread the ad.

Introducing the Section

Ad Layouts Review the Bell Ringer Activity. Tell students that proofing ads for correctness is essential. Ask students to tell you some of the negative consequences of errors printed in ads. *(Customers might demand to be given a product at the advertised price if the price is incorrectly printed at a lower price.)*

In this section, students will look at how layout contributes to the overall print advertising message. They will also discover the critical importance of proofing print ads.

TEACH

Technology Resources

PowerPoint The *Marketing Essentials* PowerPoint Presentation CD-ROM provides visual lecture aids for every chapter section.

Concept Development

1. Read Section 20.2 with students.

What You'll Learn

[handwritten: On page 364, it says, "What You'll Learn"]

- The importance of advertising layouts
- The principles of preparing an ad layout
- The advantages and disadvantages of using color in advertising
- How typefaces and type sizes can be changed to add variety and emphasis to print advertisements *[handwritten: Please read the second P]*
- How to check advertising proofs

Why It's Important

[handwritten: Please read why this section is important]

Since print advertisements have only a few seconds to reach a reader, you'll want to learn how to develop an advertising layout that will attract your target audience.

Key Terms

- ad layout
- advertising proof

*[handwritten: On Board — Let's look at the advantages of using color
- ad stands out
- more realistic
- higher response rates
Disadvantage
- cost increase ≈ 35%]*

Developing Print Advertising Layouts

[handwritten: Does anybody recall what the ad layout is?]

An **ad layout** is a rough draft that shows the general arrangement and appearance of a finished ad. It clearly indicates the position of the headline, illustration, copy, and signature. There are different sources of ad layout services, including newspaper salespeople, a magazine representative, or a printer. You submit a rough draft of your idea and the provider will create the ad based on your information.

Ad layouts should be prepared in exactly the same size as the final advertisement. The illustrations should be large enough to show all product features. The ad should make generous use of white or unused space for an uncluttered look. A proper balance of white space and color highlights the image or drawing that you want the consumer to focus on. White space also helps to make copy legible and creates an eye flow for the ad. The image projected in the layout should be appropriate for the target audience. The typeface, style of printing type, and size should be easy to read and appropriate for the target audience. A car dealership may use bold block letters to draw customer's attention, while an antique store or Victorian bed and breakfast may utilize a gothic print or fancy script. *[handwritten: Notice typeface is italicized. Who can explain typeface for...]*

When designing advertisements, pay careful attention to where the reader's eyes will be directed. The best ads contain lines of force that guide the reader to the copy through illustrations. The models in photos or drawings should be facing or looking at the copy. A model in an illustration that looks out of the ad space moves the reader's eyes away from the copy. *[handwritten: The book also mentions lines of force. Has to do with eye movement and focal points]*

■ Using Color in Print Advertisements

[handwritten: focal points]

Color makes an advertisement stand out on the printed page. Color ads draw higher response rates than black-and-white ads do because they are more realistic. A color ad is also more visually appealing and commands the reader's attention more than a black and white advertisement does. In fact, research has proven that color newspaper ads can increase the reading of copy by as much as 80 percent over black-and-white ads. Studies have also shown that because of the response rates full-color ads are usually more cost effective than two-color ads (usually black plus a color).

Although color adds excitement and realism, each added color raises the cost of the advertisement. Adding another color can increase costs by as much as 35 percent. Therefore, when businesses use color in advertisements, the added cost must be continually measured against the desired results.

Classroom Resources

For the Teacher
- Teacher Editions for all workbooks
- Assessment Package
- PowerPoint Presentation Software
- Interactive Lesson Planner
- ILP Block Scheduling, p. 6
- ILP Lesson Plans, p. 44
- ILP Internet Resources, p. 59

- ILP *BusinessWeek* Case Studies, p. 127
- ILP Marketing Career Portfolio, p. 36
- *Marketing Essentials* Web site (**www.marketing.glencoe.com**)

For the Student
- Student Activity Workbook, p. 169
- Marketing Math Workbook, p. 45

- Marketing Research Project Workbook, p. 85
- ILP School-to-Work Activity Workbook, p. 85
- Virtual Business simulation
- *Marketing Essentials* Web site (**www.marketing.glencoe.com**)

ILP These resources are available in print and on the Interactive Lesson Planner (ILP)

SHE CLICKED **Print**

WHICH SENT THE IMAGE

THAT PRINTED WITH SUCH DEPTH AND CLARITY

THAT IT EXQUISITELY CAPTURED

EVERY SINGLE SLIMY DETAIL.

XEROX PRINTERS MAKE IT HAPPEN.

THE DOCUMENT COMPANY
XEROX

XEROX
BETWEEN PRINTERS

■ **Color Excitement** Color photos often receive better reception than black and white. *How has Xerox used color to illustrate its product and corporate image?*

■ Selecting Typefaces and Type Sizes for Print Advertisements

There are a variety of typefaces and type sizes available for use in print ads. Advertisers make sure that the size of the type and the typefaces they select are distinctive, yet appropriate for the business and target audience. Large, bold type is usually chosen when the words contained in a headline are to be shouted. Smaller, lighter type is usually chosen when the words in a headline are to be whispered. Different typefaces and type sizes can affect the way a reader feels about an advertisement. A typeface that is too small or difficult to read will lower the readership of an ad. A study done by the Newspaper Advertising Bureau found that nearly one-third of readers over 65 had trouble reading newspaper type. This means that some one-third of newspaper readers over 65 may not be reading ads at all unless they have large, simple type and an uncluttered design.

In general, print advertisers should use one typeface for headlines and prices and another typeface for copy. You can add variety and emphasis by using different sizes, italics, and boldface versions of the two basic typefaces selected for the advertisement. A variety of combinations of capital and lowercase typefaces can be used to create different effects. The message may remain the same; however, the effect may be changed by capitalizing different words.

Notice you can use sizes, italics, boldface, etc.

It's important to remember US demographics and the baby-boomers.

BRIGHT IDEAS

Slinking Its Way to Success

What walks down stairs alone or in pairs and makes a slinkity sound? Everyone knows it's Slinky! How did everyone come to love the Slinky? Richard James invented the Slinky by accident while trying to develop an antivibration device for the Navy. Knocking some experimental springs off a shelf, he was surprised at how they 'slinked' down, as opposed to just falling. In 1945, James first demonstrated the Slinky at the Gimbles department store in Philadelphia. Afraid no one would buy the product because it was so simple, James gave a friend a dollar so that at least one person would buy one. Within 90 minutes of the demonstration, James sold 400 Slinkys! To date, over 250 million Slinkys have been sold!

Thinking Creatively

Can you think of any other products that might have been invented "by accident"?

Chapter 20 ■ *Preparing Print Advertisements* **365**

BRIGHT IDEAS   Slinking Its Way to Success
Answer Answers will vary.

SECTION 20.2

Discussion Starter

Typefaces A serif typeface, such as Times New Roman, has a short light line projecting from the top and bottom of a main stroke of a letter. A sans serif typeface, such as Modern, is plain with lines of uniform thickness and no serifs. Ask students if they can tell the difference between serif and sans serif.

Thinking Critically

Using Colors Reds, oranges, and yellows are considered aggressive, intense, warm colors that make things appear to advance. Greens, blues, and violets are considered tranquil, cool colors that make things appear to recede. Ask students what colors they would use to create a four-color ad for the following products, and why:
- sports car that goes from 0 mph to 60 mph in a matter of seconds
- boxed chocolate candy advertised as "fit for royalty"
- computer that is advertised as being something "different"

ASSESS

Reteaching

1. **Vocabulary** Assign and review the vocabulary terms for this section.
2. **Fact and Idea** Assign and review Fact and Idea Review questions 9–10 from the Chapter Assessment.

CAPTION ANSWER
Color Excitement
Xerox used a vivid color photograph to illustrate its photographic-quality color printer.

SECTION 20.2

■ Checking Advertising Proofs

When advertisements are given to a newspaper or magazine staff for preparation, an **advertising proof** is developed. The advertising proof shows exactly how an ad will appear in print.

The advertising proof is sent to the advertiser for review and approval. The advertiser carefully checks the proof to make sure that the ad was done exactly as planned. It is particularly important to make sure that all prices are accurate and all brand names and company names are correctly spelled. Any errors found in the proof must be marked and returned to the newspaper or magazine publisher for correction.

Before giving final approval to a written advertisement, the advertiser performs an evaluation of each advertisement. The evaluation should be based on the following criteria.

- The ad should be bold enough to stand out on a page, even if it is placed next to other ads.
- The overall layout should look clean and uncluttered and should guide the reader through the copy.
- The typefaces and type sizes should be easy to read and help further develop the image of the company.
- The signature plate should be apparent and distinctive.
- The intended message and image projected must be appropriate for the target audience.

[handwritten: Who can to explain me what the advertising proof is?]

[handwritten: Remember to check and re-check]

[handwritten: Please read RP #3 "Before giving...]

REAL WORLD MARKETING

Fingerhut: Making it Great!

How can you shop from a catalog if there is not one available in your language? Fingerhut Companies, one of the nation's largest retailers, considered this obstacle. The result was a new advertising campaign of 300,000 Spanish-language catalogs. The campaign included a series of newspaper, television, radio, and outdoor advertisements. The response rate more than doubled when Fingerhut used what is called a "push-pull complementary strategy." They pushed catalogs, while at the same time pulling in customers through ads aimed to educate consumers about catalog shopping. Fingerhut's ads also stressed the convenience of mail order and the reliability of delivery from the U.S. Postal Service.

Thinking Critically
Why was it important for Fingerhut to use advertising to promote its catalogs?

20.2 ASSESSMENT

Reviewing Key Terms and Concepts

1. What is an ad layout?
2. Why is color important in print advertisements?
3. How can variety be added to the type selected for print advertising?
4. What is the purpose of an advertising proof?
5. What should an advertiser review before submitting an advertising proof to a newspaper?

Thinking Critically

6. In what ways are online banner ads similar to print advertisments?

Integrating Academic Skills

7. **MATH** Your office supply store has a cooperative arrangement with a computer manufacturer. The store receives a 3.5 percent advertising credit on total yearly computer purchases. What is your advertising credit on purchases totaling $42,000?

20.2 ASSESSMENT ANSWERS

Reviewing Key Terms and Concepts
1. It is a rough draft that shows the general arrangement and appearance of the finished ad.
2. Color is used to make an ad stand out on a page and draws a higher response rate.
3. Variety can be added by using different sizes, italics, and boldface versions of typefaces.
4. The purpose is to provide information to newspaper and magazine staff as to how the ad should appear.

5. The advertiser should make sure that all prices are accurate and words are spelled correctly.

Thinking Critically
6. Both ads are designed to reach a target market and attract attention by headlines and copy. Some banner ads are interactive.

Integrating Academic Skills
7. **MATH** $1,470 ($42,000 x .035 = $1,470)

Careers in Marketing

ADVERTISING

Deborah Brumfield
Illustrator
Brumfield Studios, Inc.

What do you like the most about your work?

"I am self-employed and enjoy setting my own course. I like the creative aspect of my job—I bring an idea to life on paper. The reason for working is to either bring you fame, fortune or fun. When a job meets all three criteria, it's heavenly!"

How did you get into art?

"I have wanted to be an artist since kindergarten. I went to a college and got a two-year degree in Advertising Art (now called Graphic Design). Competition was rough and I spent time working in unrelated fields while looking for work. I searched the phone book and made appointments with every printer, ad agency, and photographer to show my portfolio. I got my first break as Art Director at a local television station."

What training do you recommend for students?

"I recommend a four-year degree in illustration, fine art, graphic design, photography, or another major that emphasizes creative expression as well as business courses. An internship at an ad agency, magazine, or related business shows how companies work from the inside. Students should seek out a mentor—most artists are happy to take the time to talk to someone who is starting out."

What is your key to success?

"Success takes persistence, confidence, thick skin, flexibility, and creativity. Never take rejection of your art personally—it means that you haven't found the right person or company to appreciate your work yet. Remember that there are record companies that turned down the Beatles, and movie companies that turned down *Titanic*. Be willing to try to new things, learn new skills, and tap new markets. Finally, look at things in your own unique way."

Thinking Critically

Why is it essential to maintain a positive attitude in any job?

Career Facts

Education and Training: An art or design degree, and classes in computer design, communication skills, business, advertising, and marketing are recommended.

Aptitudes, Abilities, and Skills: Illustrators must be creative and artistic, as well as detail-oriented and capable of working with precise tools. Ability to visualize two-dimensional representations is necessary, in addition to flexibility and good people skills to work with clients.

Career Outlook: The need for illustrators is expected to grow rapidly, but competition for the best jobs is likely to be high.

Career Path: Work as a layout artist or paste-up artist may lead to the position of illustrator. Illustrators and designers may advance to art or design directors.

Careers in Marketing

Ask a student to read the Careers in Marketing feature aloud to the class. Discuss the skills and aptitudes required for a career in advertising illustration. Ask students whether they think they would like or dislike a career in advertising illustration. Discuss the pros and cons of such a career.

Thinking Critically Answer

If you can maintain a positive attitude and look on the bright side, it will be easier to persevere and handle challenges when work is difficult.

 Guest Speakers

Invite an advertising illustrator to class to discuss his/her job and factors he/she considers when making marketing decisions.

Exploring Careers

Promoting a Business

1. Ask students to consider the following business ideas for young entrepreneurs:

- Baby-sitting
- Tutoring
- Party planning
- House-sitting
- Videotaping events
- Catering
- Car washing/detailing
- Plant-sitting
- Lawn or garden care
- Pet bathing and grooming
- Grocery shopping
- Repairing bicycles
- Making and selling holiday gifts
- Pet-sitting
- Garage cleaning
- Delivery or messenger service
- Snow shoveling
- Computer tutoring

2. Have students pick one business they might be interested in starting and create a visually appealing flyer for the business.

Lifelong Learning

Preparing Print Advertisements

Having the ability to dissect a written advertisement can be useful to students in a wide variety of situations both on and off the job. Knowing the components of written advertisements can help individuals evaluate a variety of products fairly and teach them not to rely on the visual content alone.

Meeting Individual Needs

Students with Visual Impairments

Due to the visual nature of print advertising, you may want to plan for some of the challenges faced by your students with visual impairments. When discussing print ads that include photos and/or illustrations, describe aloud the complete ad as well as the pictorial portion, giving verbal descriptions of the shapes and sizes in the picture.

Vocabulary Review

Crossword puzzles will vary.

Fact and Idea Review

1. Full-service agencies perform advertising research, media selection, copy development, and artwork for an advertising campaign. Limited service agencies specialize is just one aspect of a campaign, such as creative execution.
2. headline, copy, illustration, and signature
3. The purposes are to attract attention, select an audience, offer a benefit, and lead the reader to the rest of the ad.
4. Most people cannot absorb more than seven words at a time.
5. Answers may include alliteration, paradox, rhyme, pun, and play on words.
6. Its purpose is to stress the product features and benefits, and to appeal to the wants and needs of a potential customer.
7. Photos are used when sense of reality is necessary. Drawings are used to show part of a product or technical features that customers would normally not see in a photo.
8. The signature in a local ad usually includes the business's name, address, telephone number, hours of operation, and slogan. In national ads, a signature includes name of firm and possibly the trademark, slogan, and Web address.
9. 1) Layouts should be prepared the same size as the final advertisement; 2) illustrations should be large enough to show all of the product's features; 3) ad should make generous use of white space for an uncluttered look; 4) image projected in the layout should be appropriate for the target audience; and 5) typeface should be appropriate and easy to read.
10. Errors should be marked and returned for correction.

Thinking Critically

1. The new models will include business formats, such as creative boutiques, project team agencies, and virtual agencies.
2. The primary trading area is well known, which allows these businesses to target customers effectively. Many people read print

Chapter 20 ASSESSMENT

VOCABULARY REVIEW

Construct a crossword puzzle using the following vocabulary terms. Below the puzzle, include appropriate clues for each term.

- advertising campaign
- advertising agencies
- headline
- slogan
- copy
- illustration
- clip art
- signature
- ad layout
- advertising proof

FACT AND IDEA REVIEW

1. Compare a full-service and a limited-service advertising agency. (20.1)
2. What are the four essential elements of a written advertisement? (20.1)
3. What are the purposes of headlines? (20.1)
4. Why should headlines consist of no more than seven words? (20.1)
5. Identify three techniques you can use to develop attention-getting headlines. (20.1)
6. What is the purpose of advertising copy? (20.1)
7. What are the two types of illustrations used in print ads and when should each be used? (20.1)
8. What is included in an ad signature? (20.1)
9. List five principles that should be followed in developing print advertising layouts. (20.2)
10. What should an advertiser do if there is an error on an advertising proof? (20.2)

THINKING CRITICALLY

1. What are some of the predictions for advertising agency models of the future?
2. Why do you think local supermarkets, banks, pharmacies, and department stores frequently use print advertising?
3. Why would a business develop different print ads for the same product if it advertised the same product in both newspapers and magazines?
4. Why are some businesses beginning to employ their own specialists to develop and maintain their Web sites?
5. Advertisers often debate whether the price of the product should be included in an ad. How would you determine when price should or should not be included in print advertisements?

BUILDING WORKPLACE SKILLS

1. **Human Relations** A customer wishes to purchase an item that was advertised improperly in a print advertisement. The item actually costs more than the advertised price. When told about the higher price the customer is upset and angry, but still wants the product. What procedures would you use to calm the customer and still complete the sale?
2. **Technology** Using a graphics design program, select a product to advertise. Develop an advertising layout with computer-generated clip art. The ad should appeal to a customer's need for convenience, vanity, or health. Then write a paragraph describing how your advertising layout creates a particular appeal.

media, so there is an immediate response. These businesses mass market their products, and print advertising can reach all classes of consumers.
3. Newspapers are mass marketed and are read by all types of people in a certain area; magazines tend to attract certain target segments based on the magazine's content.
4. Since e-activity is expanding rapidly and evolving, specialists would ensure that the latest information is provided and that the technology to support the Web site is maintained properly.

5. When you want customers to buy a product now, include the price; when you are presenting an image for a business or product, do not include the price.

Building Workplace Skills

1. The student should act professionally and try to meet the customer's needs, telling the customer that he or she will find the manager to help rectify the problem.
2. Ad layouts will vary.

368

APPLYING MARKETING CONCEPTS

1. **Preparing a Display Advertisement** As an advertising account executive for a newspaper, you have been asked by a potential advertiser (a local flower shop) to prepare a display advertisement. Use a word processing program to prepare the sample ad, including a headline, copy, illustration, and signature.

2. **Addressing Advertising Concepts** Use a word processing program to prepare a one-page summary of special concerns that need to be addressed when advertising to senior citizens.

3. **Developing Headline Writing Techniques** There are five techniques that can help you write memorable headlines. They are alliteration, paradox, rhyme, puns, and plays on words. Develop a headline for each of these techniques.

4. **Summarizing Key Elements of Print Advertisements** Using a presentation software program, prepare a slide presentation with at least 10 slides summarizing the key elements of a print advertisement.

5. **Identifying Popular Slogans** Conduct Internet research on five companies. Write each company's name and slogan on an index card. Read each slogan aloud and have your classmates identify the business using it.

LINKING SCHOOL TO WORK

Speaking and Information Skills Collect a print advertisement from a place of business and evaluate the headline, copy, illustration, and signature for completeness and appropriateness. Be prepared to present your findings orally to the class.

THE DECA CONNECTION

Role Play: Marketing Coordinator

Situation You are to assume the role of assistant marketing coordinator for a restaurant chain. Currently your restaurant is running a print ad that features a pair of absentminded elderly spinsters. The general public apparently finds the ad both amusing and persuasive (purchase of the specials is up by 30 percent). However, members of a local senior citizens group are not amused and have complained about the ad. Your marketing manager (judge) has asked you to create a new ad that targets senior citizens.

Activity You must develop a layout of your ad and present it to the marketing manager explaining the strengths of the ad.

Evaluation You will be evaluated on how well you meet the following performance indicators:
- Explain the components of advertisements
- Write promotional messages
- Address needs of individual personalities
- Evaluate effectiveness of advertising
- Demonstrate appropriate creativity

interNET CONNECTION

Understanding Advertising Agencies
Advertising agencies assist businesses with product promotions. They frequently perform market research, perform creative work, and coordinate advertising campaigns for their clients.

Connect
- Investigate an advertising agency online and write a one-page report detailing the name of the company and summarizing the types of services it provides to clients.

Chapter 20 ■ *Preparing Print Advertisements* **369**

THE DECA CONNECTION

Students should be evaluated on the performance indicators noted in the Role Play.
- For another DECA Role Play, go to the *Student Activity Workbook*, p. 169.
- For more in-depth Role Play practice, refer to DECA's *Essential Competitive Events Handbook*. To order, contact DECA at www.deca.org.

interNET CONNECTION

Answers will vary based upon each advertising agency selected.

Mini Quiz

Administer the Mini Quiz orally. For an expanded chapter quiz, go to page 111 of the *Reproducible Tests* book.

1. The creation and coordination of a series of both broadcast and print advertisements around a theme to promote a product is called a(n) advertising campaign.

2. The lettering, slogan, or saying that gets the reader's attention is called a(n) headline.

3. Copy does not have to be extensive as long as it gets the message across.

4. The photograph or drawing used in a print advertisement is known as the illustration.

5. A rough draft that shows the general arrangement and appearance of a finished ad is called the ad layout.

Applying Marketing Concepts

1. Sample ads will vary.
2. Summaries will vary.
3. Headlines will vary.
4. Presentations will vary.
5. Answers will vary, but each student should identify at least five slogans.

Linking School to Work

Answers depend on the work situation.

1. **Assessment** Have students complete the Reproducible Tests for Chapter 20 and Unit 6 construct your own tests using the ExamView software.

2. **Enrichment** Have students complete the corresponding activities in the following workbooks:
   - *Marketing Math Workbook*, p. 45
   - *Marketing Research Project Workbook*, p. 85

Unit Lab Overview

In this Zazz Lab, students will use their knowledge of promotional concepts and strategies to plan a Super Bowl promotion.

Bell Ringer Activity

Identify Ask students: What is McDonald's or Burger King's most recent promotion? *(Answers will vary depending on the current promotions.)*

Discussion Starter

Capitalize on students' answers to the Bell Ringer Activity by asking: Who was the promotion targeting? Do you think it was successful? Why or why not? What promotions do you recall that were successful? Why? *(Answers will vary, but most will suggest that the premium offers were things customers wanted, such as Beanie Babies or glasses/mugs imprinted with popular characters.)*

Thinking Critically

1. **Special Promotions** Ask students: Can a special promotion be so unique, funny, or exciting that it negates its primary goal of selling the advertiser's product? *(Yes. Some customers may be able to recall the entire commercial but not know what product is advertised.)*
2. **Broadcast Promotion** Ask students: Why would a fast food chain or an airline want to spend so much money advertising during the Super Bowl? *(The number of people viewing the Super Bowl permits tremendous exposure for the advertiser.)*

The Zazz Lab

A Sports and Entertainment Marketing Simulation

WELCOME

Welcome to Zazz Sports and Entertainment Marketing Company. Zazz is devoted to serving the needs of its clients who include college, university, and professional sports teams, professional athletes, sporting events, and sports arenas plus major consumer product corporations, as well as television networks and movie studios. As an intern, you will have the opportunity to work on different clients' projects. All of your work will be assigned and reviewed by your department supervisor.

PLAN A SUPER BOWL PROMOTION

SITUATION

Two major corporations—Crystal Airlines and J.T. Burgers—want to run special promotions to tie in with the Super Bowl. Crystal Airlines, a Midwest airline known for on-time flights and friendly staff, has just started coast-to-coast service. J.T. Burgers is a Southern fast food restaurant that has been quickly expanding its popular franchise across the United States. Both companies are looking for national exposure which Zazz can make happen by affiliating them with the Super Bowl. To capitalize on the popularity of this major event, the promotional plan will be carried out throughout the local level, as well as in the national media.

ASSIGNMENT

You have been asked to prepare a promotional plan for one of the above companies. Your supervisor wants you to prepare a complete promotional package, as well as a budget and calendar of events. Begin with your idea for a unique special promotion, such as a contest or sweepstakes. You will need to explain any contest rules and any prizes (Super Bowl tickets, etc.). You will need to promote through product packaging, in-store displays, various advertising media, and the company's Web site. Create a product package design for food and drinks served in J.T. Burgers restaurants or refreshments served on the airline. Design an in-store display, which would be placed in the airline terminal or inside the restaurant. Plan the promotion's ads for television, radio, direct mail, magazine and/or newspaper, and the company Web site. Determine the costs for every promotional idea and create a promotional budget. Prepare a promotional calendar of events with deadline dates for insertion and publication. You also want to generate free publicity if possible.

Tools and Resources

To complete this assignment you will need to conduct research at the library or on the Internet. You will also need a word processing program, a spreadsheet program, and presentation software. Trade publications that may be helpful include *Brandweek*, *Advertising Age*, *Sports Business Journal*, and *Sports Business Daily*.

Research

Research previous Super Bowl promotions. Investigate promotions run by the client's competitors in the past. What qualities or characteristics of the promotions were successful? Research the cost of television commercials aired during the Super Bowl, as well as all other suggested advertising media. You also will need research regarding how much money is normally spent on a promotional mix of this magnitude.

THE FIRST SUPER BOWL

Originally dubbed the AFL-NFL World Championship Game, the very first Super Bowl was played on January 15, 1967 at the Los Angeles Coliseum and was a matchup between the Kansas City Chiefs and the Green Bay Packers. The Green Bay Packers won with a score of 35–10. By throwing touchdown caliber passes, Bart Starr of the NFL Packers became the first Super Bowl MVP (Most Valuable Player). This battle on the football field was the culmination of over six years of the fledgling American Football League vying for position against the 40-year-old National Football League. In 1966 the AFL struck a deal with the NFL for a common draft and regular season play, but what fans remember is the birth of the championship game, better known as the Super Bowl.

Report

Prepare a written report and a computer presentation for the client. Use a word processing program to prepare a double-spaced report. Use a spreadsheet program to create a promotional budget. To prepare the promotional calendar, use a table format found in your word processing program or a spreadsheet program. Arrange your written report around the following headings:

- Market analysis
  - Competitors
    - Participation in other Super Bowl promotions
    - Current promotions and their costs
  - Previous Super Bowl promotions
    - Characteristics of successful promotions
    - Cost of television advertising
- Suggested promotional mix
  - Special promotion
    - Type (contest, sweepstakes) and rationale
    - Theme, rules, and prizes
  - Advertising media rationale and design samples
    - Broadcast
    - Print
    - Direct mail
    - Internet
  - Product packaging rationale and design samples
  - In-store displays rationale and design samples
  - Publicity
  - Promotional calendar of events
  - Promotional budget
- Conclusion

Using computer presentation software and other visual aids (sample ads, etc.), prepare a presentation for the client that includes:

- Key topics covered in your written report
- Graphic illustrations that are relevant to each slide's topic
- Very little text
- A minimum of 10 slides
- Samples of all promotional materials suggested

Presentation and Evaluation

Present your ideas in a written report and an oral presentation. The presentation will later be shown to the client. You will be evaluated on your oral presentation skills, including:

- Proposed promotional plan
- Creativity
- Ability to meet the customer's needs
- Continuity of presentation
- Enthusiasm
- Voice quality
- Eye contact

Portfolio

Print a copy of your completed report and presentation for your Portfolio.

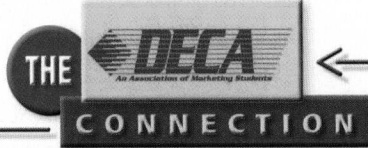

THE DECA CONNECTION

DECA Business Services Marketing Series
Planning a promotional campaign for a client is part of this occupational area because it is a business service.

DECA Marketing Management Series
Planning a promotional campaign for any type of business is a possible role play situation in this event.

DECA Quick Serve Restaurant Management Event
Developing a Super Bowl promotional campaign for a quick serve restaurant could be a potential role play for this event.

DECA Advertising Campaign Event
Developing a promotional campaign and presenting it to a client/advertiser is the essence of this DECA competition.

DECA Sports and Entertainment Marketing Management Team Decision-Making Event
Working on this project with a partner will make the experience similar to what is expected in a DECA Team Decision-Making Event.

The Zazz Lab **371**

Distribution

Chapter 21
Channels of Distribution

Chapter 22
Physical Distribution

Chapter 23
Purchasing

Chapter 24
Stock Handling and Inventory Control

Unit Objectives

After completing this unit, students will be able to:

- Select the appropriate channels of distribution to effectively sell consumer and industrial products.
- Explain the nature and scope of transportation systems and services.
- Distinguish between purchasing agents and buyers.
- Describe the buying process and the effect the Internet has had on the purchasing function.
- Calculate the major entries in a merchandise plan.
- Explain the stock-handling process.
- Figure stock turnover rates.
- Discuss the nature and the impact of technology on inventory management and inventory systems.

Enrichment Resources

Books

Basics of Inventory Management: From Warehouse to Distribution Center (Fifty Minute Series) by J. David Viale and Christopher Carrigan, Editors
Quick Response: Managing the Supply Chain to Meet Consumer Demand by Bob Lowson, R. King, and A. Hunter

Magazines/Journals
American Shipper
Distribution and Traffic

Associations
Air Transport Association
1301 Pennsylvania Avenue, NW,
 Suite 1100
Washington, DC 20004-1707
(202) 626-4000
www.air-transport.org

Council of Logistics Management
2805 Butterfield Road, Suite 200
Oak Brook, IL 60523
(630) 574-0985
www.clm1.org

Journal Writing Activity

1. Ask students to write their own definitions of *distribution* in the their journals. Remind them to consider the steps it takes to distribute a product from manufacturer all the way to the consumer. Have some students share their journal entries with the class.

2. Ask students to write a paragraph in their journals identifying what they think are various types of physical distribution for specific products, such as appliances, food, sports equipment, clothing, and computers and software. In class discussion, ask students to share their entries. Write their types of physical distribution on the board. Then lead the class in a discussion evaluating the advantages and disadvantages of different kinds of transportation systems.

TEACHER CLASSROOM RESOURCES

Program Resources	Chapter 21	Chapter 22	Chapter 23	Chapter 24
Student Activity Workbook	p. 177	p. 187	p. 195	p. 203
Marketing Math Workbook	p. 59	p. 59	p. 59	p. 59
Marketing Research Project Workbook	p. 111	p. 111	p. 111	p. 111
ILP School-to-Work Activity Workbook	p. 89	p. 93	p. 97	p. 101
ILP *BusinessWeek* Case Studies	p. 133	p. 139	p. 145	p. 151
ILP Marketing Career Portfolio	p. 37	p. 37	p. 37	p. 37
Reproducible Tests	p. 125	p. 129	p. 133	p. 137
ExamView User's Guide and Testbank	p. 21-1	p. 22-1	p. 23-1	p. 24-1
ILP Internet Resources	p. 61	p. 63	p. 65	p. 67
ILP Blackline Masters	p. 38	p. 42	p. 43	p. 45
ILP Lesson Plans	p. 45	p. 47	p. 49	p. 51
ILP Block Scheduling	p. 7	p. 7	p. 7	p. 7
Impact! Simulation	p. 75	p. 75	p. 75	p. 75

ILP Each of these resources is available in print and on the Interactive Lesson Planner CD-ROM.

Technology Resources

- Interactive Lesson Planner (ILP) CD-ROM
- PowerPoint Presentation CD-ROM
- Marketing Essentials Web site
- ExamView! CD-ROM
- Impact! Simulation

Virtual Business

Virtual Business is a fully visual marketing and business simulation that introduces students to the principles of marketing by letting them start and run their own virtual businesses. In *Virtual Business*, students have the power to control all aspects of a retail convenience store. Students strategize marketing decisions using a powerful learning tool in the guise of a video game. They learn by experiencing how their decisions affect their virtual business.

Key to Individualized Academics Activities

L1 Level 1 activities are basic activities and should fall within the range of all students.

L2 Level 2 activities are average activities and should be within the range of average and above average students.

L3 Level 3 activities are challenging activities designed for the ability range of above average students.

National Marketing Education

CHAPTER	SECTION	PERFORMANCE INDICATOR
Chapter 21 **Channels of Distribution**	21.1	Explain the nature of channels of distribution (DIS)
		Explain the nature of channel members relationships (DIS)
	21.2	Explain the nature and scope of distribution (DIS)
		Explain the nature of channel strategies (DIS)
		Select channels of distribution (DIS)
Chapter 22 **Physical Distribution**	22.1	Explain the nature and scope of distribution (DIS)
		Explain the shipping process (DIS)
	22.2	Explain storing considerations (DIS)
		Explain the nature of warehousing (DIS)
		Explain marketing and its importance in a global economy (BME)
Chapter 23 **Purchasing**	23.1	Explain the nature and scope of purchasing (BME)
		Plan purchases (BME)
	23.2	Explain the nature of the buying process (BME)
		Conduct vendor search (BME)
Chapter 24 **Stock Handling and Inventory Control**	24.1	Explain the receiving process (DIS)
		Explain stock handling techniques used in receiving deliveries (DIS)
	24.2	Explain the nature of inventory control systems (DIS)
		Explain the types of inventory control systems (DIS)

CIS Communication, Interpersonal Skills   **DIS** Distribution   **FIN** Financing   **PRI** Pricing   **SEL** Selling

Standards Assessment Correlation

	SECTION ASSESSMENT		CHAPTER ASSESSMENT						UNIT LAB
Reviewing Key Terms and Concepts	Thinking Critically	Integrating Academic Skills	Fact and Idea Review	Thinking Critically	Building Workplace Skills	Applying Marketing Concepts	Linking School to Work	Internet Connection	Zazz Lab
1, 2, 3, 4, 5	•	•	1, 3, 4, 5	1, 2	1, 2	1, 3	•	•	•
2, 3		•	1, 2, 4, 5	1, 4		1, 3	•	•	•
1, 3, 4, 5	•	•	6, 7, 8, 9	1, 2, 3, 4	2			•	•
2, 3, 4	•	•	7, 8, 9, 10	1, 3, 4	2	2, 3	•	•	
5	•	•	8	1, 3	1				•
1, 2, 3	•	•	1, 2, 6	1, 4, 5	2	1, 3, 4, 5	•	•	•
2, 3, 4, 5	•	•	1, 2, 3	1, 2a, 2b, 2c, 2d	2	1, 3, 4, 5	•	•	
1, 2, 4, 5	•	•	9	3, 4	1	3, 4			
2, 3, 4			8	3	1	3, 4			
5			9	2a, 5	2				•
1, 2, 3, 4, 5	•	•	1, 2, 3, 4	1, 2	2	1	•		•
4, 5	•	•	2, 3, 4	1, 2, 3	1	1, 3	•	•	
1, 2, 4, 5	•	•	5, 6, 7, 9	5	1, 2	1	•		
3		•	8	4, 5		3		•	
1, 3, 4, 5	•	•	1, 2, 3, 4	1, 3, 4, 5	1	3	•		
2		•	2, 4	5	1	4, 5	•		
1, 2, 3, 4, 5	•	•	5, 6	1, 2, 3, 4, 5	2	1, 2, 3, 4, 5			•
3, 4		•	5, 6, 7, 8	5	2	1, 4, 5		•	•

Unit Overview

Unit 7 presents the "nuts and bolts" of buying and distribution. Chapter 21 explores the place decision of the marketing mix—how products will be distributed and sold in domestic and foreign markets. Chapter 22 concentrates on the nature and scope of physical distribution—transportation systems, storage, etc. Chapter 23 considers the purchasing function in depth. Finally, Chapter 24 looks at the critical importance of stock handling, inventory control, and stock management.

Introducing the Unit

Have students speculate about how your school cafeteria purchases food, supplies, equipment, and utensils. Ask students: Who is responsible for purchasing? Where and how was the merchandise stored prior to distribution? By what means of transportation did it arrive at its final destination? How was the merchandise checked in and stored once it arrived? How often is merchandise reordered? As you discuss each aspect of the distribution process, write it on the board.

UNIT 7

Portfolio

Choosing a Distribution Plan

To demonstrate mastery of the content in this unit, select a consumer or industrial product to investigate. Using the library, media, Internet, and company resources such as annual reports, press releases, and publications, prepare a detailed research report, using a word processing program, on the manufacturing and distribution process for the selected product. Be prepared to present the information in an oral report to demonstrate what you learned by creating your distribution plan.

372

Field Trip Suggestions

Visit a Local Supermarket Arrange for your students to visit a local supermarket to observe receiving and check-in practices, price marking of goods, and routing of goods to the sales floor. Have students note the differences in handling of perishable and non-perishable goods.

Visit an Automotive Parts Store Have students visit a local automotive parts store to observe the inventory system and how the store handles the stocking of a new parts shipment.

UNIT 7

Distribution

Unit Overview

In this unit, you will learn about the various aspects of distribution. Chapter 21 discusses the concept of distribution planning and channels of distribution. The effect of the Internet on distribution planning is covered, as well as challenges in foreign market distribution. Chapter 22 explains that physical distribution involves the transportation of the product or its physical movement to various locations. The nature and scope of purchasing is detailed in Chapter 23. An explanation of how purchasing is conducted in both the industrial market and the resale market is included, along with vendor analysis and the effect of business-to-business e-commerce. Chapter 24 concentrates on the process of stock handling, inventory control, and stock management, all of which are essential for efficient control of products in industrial and consumer markets.

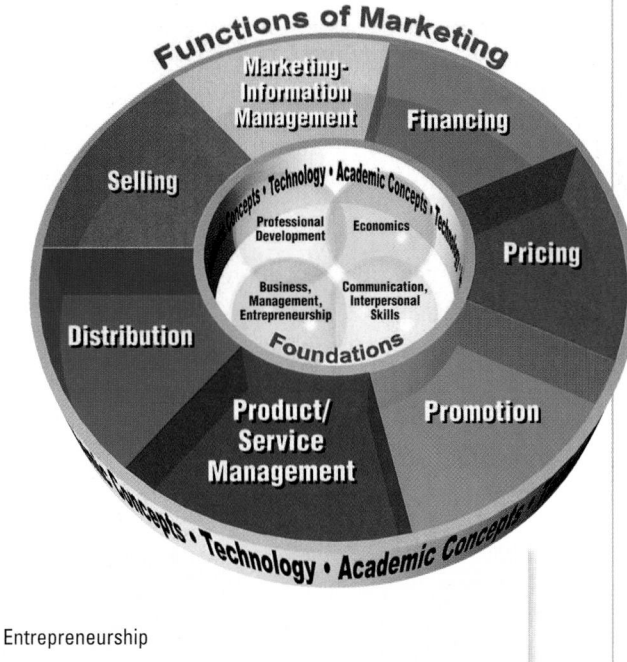

In this Unit:

Foundations of Marketing

● Business, Management, Entrepreneurship

Functions of Marketing

◗ Distribution

DECA Unit Project

Have chapter members investigate the policies, forms, and procedures used to receive, check, and route merchandise within a local business of their own choice. Students should prepare a written report based on their research. They should evaluate the effectiveness of the policies, forms, and procedures used, and then draw conclusions and make recommendations for improvement.

www Go to the *Marketing Essentials* Web site (**www.marketing.glencoe. com**) for resources to teach and assess occupation-specific vocabulary.

Unit Closure

Have students select one product (e.g., apples, meat, or auto parts) and trace on a large posterboard its route from manufacturer to storage to distribution to final inventory before sale.

Guest Speaker Suggestions

Florist Ask a florist to speak to the class about how he or she purchases flowers as well as how the flowers are received and handled on the channel of distribution from grower to supplier to shop. The florist should also explain any differences in handling cut flowers and potted plants.

Chapter Overview

Chapter 21 presents fundamental information about channels of distribution. It also distinguishes the types of channels typical of the consumer and industrial markets. Distribution planning involving e-commerce and foreign markets are also discussed.

 Springboard

List Hold up a 100-percent cotton T-shirt. Tell students to assume it's their latest purchase. Then have them write down the steps that were necessary to transform raw cotton from a farmer's field into a garment. Their list can be used for later reference to cover channels of distribution.

Prereading

List the section objectives to discuss with students. Have students skim the chapter, looking at the pictures, reading the captions, and noting the heads. Ask questions to ensure that students have a minimal understanding of the chapter structure.

Preteaching Marketing Vocabulary

Dictate each of the vocabulary terms and ask students to write them on a sheet of paper. When they finish, write the terms on the board. Then have students guess at the meaning of each. Write their guesses next to each term. Leave this list on the board so students can see how close their guesses were to the actual definitions as they work through the chapter.

Marketing: What It Takes

Answer All direct and indirect channels may be used. Direct channels use online sales on Web sites, infomercials, or advertising on television or in magazines or direct mail. Indirect channels use agents, wholesalers, and/or retailers.

374

Channels of Distribution

Marketing: What It Takes

Changing Channels

The Research and Development department in your toy company just designed a new line of toys for pets. You know that your company's current customers (toy wholesalers and retailers) do not want to carry this new line. Since your company has never produced pet toys before, you have been asked to suggest the most effective channels of distribution for selling the new products.

WHAT WILL YOU DO?

What channels of distribution should be considered for the new line of pet toys?

374

THE DECA CONNECTION — ADVISOR CORNER

Make a Video If your school has Channel One, create a custom video for your DECA chapter with the aid of your school's communications or technology class, and incorporate the national membership video into your video. Airing the video on Channel One throughout the school will allow other students to learn about DECA and where to go for more information. If you are unable to create a video, much can be gained from airing the national video on Channel One as a recruiting tool. If your school does not have Channel One, you can use the video when you talk to student groups about your DECA chapter and program. *(Janet Stinson, C.E. Byrd H.S., Shreveport, LA)*

Distribution

Distribution—How It Works

How do you get somebody to buy your product? By marketing it! Now the question is who do you market to, or who is your target audience? This is the place decision, one of the four Ps of the marketing mix. Shampoo manufacturers, for example, know that customers like to buy personal convenience items in supermarkets, drugstores, or hair salons. A shampoo manufacturer would therefore want its products to be sold to these stores.

To make a place decision, marketers must decide on their channel of distribution. The channel of distribution is the path a product takes from producer or manufacturer to final user. When the product is purchased for use in a business, the final user is classified as an industrial user. When the product is purchased for personal use, the final user is classified as a consumer.

Using the shampoo example, you can see how the same product may be classified as both a consumer and an industrial product. Manufacturers of shampoo sell their product to the customer through retail operations but may sell it as an industrial product for use in a business too. Hair salons buy shampoo in bulk to wash their customers' hair, while hotel chains buy small bottles of shampoo for customers to use during their hotel stay.

■ Channel Members

All the businesses involved in sales transactions that move products from the manufacturer to the final user are called intermediaries or middlemen. Intermediaries provide value to producers because they often have expertise in certain areas that producers do not have. Intermediaries that sell to the final consumer are experts in displaying, merchandising, and providing convenient shopping locations and hours for customers. Intermediaries reduce the number of contacts required to reach the final user of the product. In a case of four customers who wanted to buy a digital camera, a producer would have to make four sales transactions. By using an intermediary (such as Computer City), the number of contacts is reduced to one. This is illustrated in Figure 21-1 on page 376.

Intermediaries are classified on the basis of whether or not they take ownership (or title) to goods and services. Merchant intermediaries take title; agent intermediaries do not. Agent intermediaries, usually called agents, are paid a commission to help buyers and sellers get together. The two major types of merchant intermediaries are wholesalers and retailers.

• What You'll Learn

- The concept of a channel of distribution
- Who channel members are
- The different non-store retailing methods
- How channels of distribution differ for consumer and business-to-business products

• Why It's Important

As you know, the marketing mix includes decisions about product, price, place, and promotion. In this chapter you will explore the place decision—that is, how the product will be distributed and sold in the marketplace. Making the correct place decision has an impact on the entire operation of a business.

• Key Terms

- channel of distribution
- intermediaries
- wholesalers
- rack jobbers
- drop shippers
- retailers
- brick and mortar retailers
- e-tailing
- agents
- direct distribution
- indirect distribution

Chapter 21 ■ *Channels of Distribution* **375**

FOCUS

Bell Ringer Activity

Review Have students recall the four P's of the marketing mix they learned in Chapter 2. *(product, place, price, and promotion)* Ask what they recall about the place decision.

Introducing the Section

Distribution Ask students where they buy their clothing, CDs, shampoo, and shoes. Remind students that in order to reach them, manufacturers of those products would have to include those businesses in their place decisions. Tell them that the place decision in the marketing mix is the focus of this chapter.

TEACH

ılıl Technology Resources

PowerPoint The *Marketing Essentials* PowerPoint Presentation CD-ROM provides visual lecture aids for every chapter section.

Classroom Resources

For the Teacher
- Teacher Editions for all workbooks
- Assessment Package
- PowerPoint Presentation Software
- Interactive Lesson Planner
- ILP Block Scheduling, p. 7
- ILP Lesson Plans, p. 45
- ILP Internet Resources, p. 61

- ILP Blackline Masters, p. 38
- ILP *BusinessWeek* Case Studies, p. 133
- ILP Marketing Career Portfolio, p. 37
- *Marketing Essentials* Web site (**www.marketing.glencoe.com**)

For the Student
- Student Activity Workbook, p. 177
- Marketing Math Workbook, p. 59

- Marketing Research Project Workbook, p. 111
- ILP School-to-Work Activity Workbook, p. 89
- Virtual Business simulation
- *Marketing Essentials* Web site (**www.marketing.glencoe.com**)

ILP These resources are available in print and on the Interactive Lesson Planner (ILP)

SECTION 21.1

Concept Development

1. Read Section 21.1 with students.
2. Remind students of the T-shirt example used in the Springboard activity and the lists they made. Ask how many channels of distribution were involved there. *(four: cotton farmer to thread manufacturer, thread manufacturer to fabric manufacturer, fabric manufacturer to clothing manufacturer, and clothing manufacturer to retailer.)*
3. To teach the concept of agents, ask students to explain the job of a real estate agent. *(Agents find buyers for sellers and sellers for buyers, tasks for which they receive a commission.)* Then ask students if, in general, the real estate agents own the properties. *(No, they are sales agents for people who wish to sell their property.)*
4. To teach the concept of channels of distribution in the consumer market, put a diagram on the board (producer to consumer), and identify it as direct distribution. Then ask students to name products they have purchased directly from producers, and have them describe the circumstances of the purchase.

FIGURE 21-1
Intermediaries

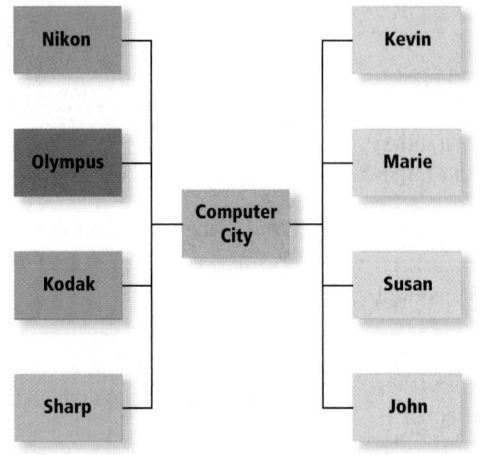

Contracts with one intermediary
4 producers + 4 buyers = 8 contracts

■ **Intermediary Role** Intermediaries reduce the number of transactions required by manufacturers to reach their final customers. *What expenses of doing business are lowered by this reduction in transactions?*

■ **Wholesalers** Some large mass merchandisers have specialized wholesalers manage certain product lines they carry, like health and beauty aids. *What type of specialized wholesaler is the person in this photo?*

376 Unit 7 ■ *Distribution*

WHOLESALERS Generally, wholesalers buy large quantities of goods from manufacturers, store the goods, and then resell them to other businesses. They are called wholesalers and their customers are called retailers. They may be called distributors when their customers are professional or commercial users, manufacturers, governments, institutions, or other wholesalers. In either case, they take title to the goods they buy for resale.

Two specialized wholesalers are rack jobbers and drop shippers. Rack jobbers are wholesalers that manage inventory and merchandising for retailers by counting stock, filling it in when needed, and maintaining store displays. As the name implies, they provide the racks for display of the product in a retail store and manage that product for the retailer. They bill the retailer only for the goods sold, not for all the items on display. Products that are handled by rack jobbers include compact discs, hosiery, health products, and beauty aids.

Drop shippers own the goods they sell but do not physically handle the actual products. They deal in large quantities of items in bulk, such as coal, lumber, and chemicals that require special handling. Drop shippers sell the goods to other businesses and have the producer ship the merchandise directly to the buyers. The products are owned, but never handled by the drop shipper.

RETAILERS Retailers sell goods to the final consumer for personal use. Traditional retailers, called brick and mortar retailers, sell goods to the customer from their own physical stores. These retail stores display, store, and merchandise the products they buy from manufacturers or wholesalers. They serve as the final link between the manufacturer and consumer. They often provide special services, such as offering credit or providing delivery to help solidify customer relationships.

Aside from brick and mortar retailers, there are a number of non-store retailing operations that serve the customer. They include automatic retailing, direct mail and catalog retailing, TV home shopping, and online retailing.

Vending service companies buy manufacturers' products and sell them through machines that dispense goods to consumers. These companies often place their vending machines in stores, office buildings, restaurants, hospitals, schools, and other institutions for free. They make their money from the items sold through the machines, which are regularly stocked. You can purchase a variety of food

FIGURE 21-1
Intermediary Role Some expenses that are reduced are the paperwork and staff that would be needed to process the orders, as well as the cost of invoicing, shipping, and handling.

CAPTION ANSWER
Wholesalers The person in this photo is a rack jobber, a type of specialized wholesaler.

and snacks—sandwiches, fresh fruit, cookies, candy, soda, and hot drinks—from vending machines.

Direct mail and catalogs also reach the final consumer. Many large brick and mortar retailers produce their own catalogs to reach those consumers who prefer shopping at home. There are catalog houses that buy goods from different manufacturers and display them in a catalog for sale to the customer. Sometimes these catalog businesses have their names put on the products they sell in the catalog. This makes it appear as though they manufactured all the items in the catalog.

Television home shopping networks are TV stations that sell products to consumers. These companies buy the products in set quantities and sell them via television programs. Consumers phone in their orders while watching shows. One example of this is the Home Shopping Network.

Online retailing, or e-tailing, involves retailers selling products over the Internet to the customer. People with computers equipped to access the Internet can buy goods directly from e-tailers' Web sites. Some of the big e-tailing companies are solely found on the Internet, such as Amazon.com or the music seller CD-NOW.

Not to be left out of the technology revolution, many brick and mortar retailers, such as Toys R Us and Barnes & Noble, have created Web sites. Some of the top e-tailing sectors with high sales volume are depicted in Figure 21-2, with air travel, books, and hardware leading the list. This list can change quickly based on new competitors in the market and time of year.

AGENTS Unlike wholesalers and retailers, agents do not own the goods they sell. Agents act as intermediaries by bringing buyers and sellers together. You may be familiar with real estate agents who sell people's homes for them. They are paid a commission for that service, which is a percentage of the sale price of the home. This type of agent is called a *broker*. A broker's principal function is to bring buyers and sellers together in order for a sale to take place. They usually do not have a continued relationship with either party. They negotiate the sale and then look for other customers. Brokers are found in seasonal industries, where they represent producers of items such as fruits and vegetables, as well as in the real estate business.

FIGURE 21-2

Shopping on the Web

Buying plane tickets on the Web has taken off. January 2001 shopping revenues:

Top e-tailing sectors	MILLIONS OF DOLLARS
Air Travel	$318
Books	224
Hardware	224
Software	187
Apparel	182
Hotels	164
Toys/games	146
Music	143
Health, beauty	143
Electronics	126

Source: Dow Jones

■ **Shopping on the Web** Note the millions of dollars attributed to online sales by e-tailers in January 2001. *Which three sectors lead the list? How might this list be changed if the month was December?*

■ **Brick and Mortar** Brick and mortar retailers sell goods to consumers through their own physical stores. *In what ways do these intermediaries help manufacturers?*

Discussion Starter

Wholesalers and Distribution
Ask students if they think the Hershey Foods Corporation in Hershey, Pennsylvania, would be willing to distribute their school store candy. *(Most students will recognize that Hershey would not want to deal with such a small operation because the paperwork and shipping would be too costly and time-consuming. The only way the school store could buy from the Hershey Company might be to buy a truckload, which would be impractical.)* This example will help introduce the need for wholesalers and their role in the distribution process.

Thinking Critically

1. **E-Tailing** Ask students: Do you think that by the year 2030 electronic retail outlets will replace traditional retail store outlets? Have them support their opinions. *(Answers will vary.)*

2. **Intermediaries** Have students try to imagine what it would be like if all intermediaries were to disappear overnight. Ask students: What would happen within a year to the variety of goods available to consumers? to production capabilities? *(The former would be reduced, and the latter limited, unless the Internet is able to generate enough business for manufacturers.)*

3. **Wholesalers** Ask students why small retailers tend to use the services of wholesalers. *(Small retailers lack the storage space, capital, and customers to buy in large quantities.)*

CAPTION ANSWER
Brick and Mortar These intermediaries help manufacturers by displaying, storing, and merchandising the products they buy from manufacturers. They also serve as the final link between the manufacturer and consumer, and provide special services (e.g., credit, long hours of operation, delivery, and gift-wrapping).

FIGURE 21-2 ANSWER
Shopping on the Web Air travel, books, and hardware lead the list; toys and games might be higher due to the holiday season.

Independent Practice

1. **Interview** Have students interview a local broker, wholesaler, or retailer. Have them develop questions that relate to current problems and/or challenges these business-people face today.

   For example, many wholesalers and brokers have the problem of being left out of the distribution channel for very large retail operations like Wal-Mart, because they buy only directly from the manufacturer. Small retailers are also getting hurt because they cannot command the deep discounts that operations like Wal-Mart can. Therefore, they can't offer their customers the same low prices.

2. **Research and Report** Have students research the new forms of interactive channels of distribution in the consumer and industrial markets. Specifically, tell them to see how e-commerce impacts the way business is being done. Have students report their findings on the trends and types of electronic equipment necessary for e-commerce to work.

FIGURE 21-3

DISTRIBUTION CHANNELS FOR CONSUMER PRODUCTS AND SERVICES

Historically, most consumer goods have not been marketed using direct distribution (channel A) because consumers have become accustomed to shopping in retail stores. Of the indirect channels available, Manufacturer/Producer to Retailer to Consumer (channel B) is the most commonly used in the consumer market.

CHANNEL A

There are five ways in which direct distribution is used for consumer goods.

1. Selling products at the production site. Examples include a farmer's roadside stand or a factory outlet.

2. Having a sales force call on consumers at home. Examples include Avon and Tupperware.

3. Using catalogs or ads to generate sales. One example is an Infomercial, which is a 30- or 60-minute television commercial that explains a product in detail and tells viewers how to order it directly from the manufacturer.

4. Having a sales representative call a consumer on the telephone (telemarketing). Examples include magazine subscriptions and telecommunications services.

5. Using the Internet to make online sales. Examples include manufacturers' Web sites where they sell their products to consumers without help from retailers.

CHANNEL B

This is the most commonly used channel for merchandise that dates quickly or needs servicing. Fashion apparel and automobiles are sold this way. Chain stores also use this channel because they handle the physical distribution of the products they buy. Online retailers will use this method, too; however, they must handle the distribution of products to the final consumer as well.

CHANNEL C

This is the most common distribution method for staple goods, which are items that are always carried in stock and whose styles do not change frequently. The manufacturer sells to the wholesaler, who then handles the sales, warehousing, and distribution of the goods to retailers. Consumer goods sold this way include supermarket items, flowers, candy, and stationery supplies.

CHANNEL D

This is the channel for manufacturers who wish to concentrate on production and leave sales and distribution to others. The agent sells to wholesalers who are involved in storage, sale, and transportation to retailers. The retailer then sells to consumers.

CHANNEL E

This is the channel chosen by manufacturers who do not want to handle their own sales to retailers. The agent simply brings the buyer and seller together. Expensive cookware, meat, cosmetics, and many supermarket items are sold this way.

Manufacturers/Producers

A B C D E

Agents

Wholesalers

Retailers

Consumers

GREAT IDEAS from the Marketing Classroom

Lois Farese
Northern Highlands Regional High School
Allendale, NJ

This activity will help students understand the reasons for and consequences of channel conflict. Divide your class into three groups and assign each group a distribution channel identity: manufacturers, wholesalers, and retailers. Then ask each group to develop a list of conflicts that might arise between their own group and the other groups. After they have developed their lists, ask each group to air their grievances. Allow the groups to respond to each other. Students will quickly realize how blame can get passed, and that channel relations can break down if conflict escalates.

FIGURE 21-4

DISTRIBUTION CHANNELS FOR INDUSTRIAL PRODUCTS AND SERVICES

Because industrial users shop differently and have different needs than consumers, they use different channels of distribution. In fact, the least commonly used channel in the consumer market—direct distribution (channel A)—is the most commonly used in the industrial market.

CHANNEL A

This is the most common method of distribution for major equipment used in manufacturing and other businesses. The manufacturer's sales force calls on the industrial user to sell goods or services. For example, a Xerox sales representative sells copiers directly to manufacturers and commercial businesses. Note: All methods of direct distribution listed for the consumer market are used in the industrial market as well.

CHANNEL B

This channel is used most often for small standardized parts and operational supplies needed to run a business. Industrial wholesalers (distributors) take ownership of the products, stock them, and sell them as needed to industrial users. For example, a restaurant supply wholesaler buys pots, pans, utensils, serving pieces, and paper products from various manufacturers to sell to restaurant owners.

CHANNEL C

Small manufacturers who do not have the time or money to invest in a direct sales force may prefer this channel. The agent sells the goods to the industrial wholesaler who stores, resells, and ships them to the industrial user. The advantage of this arrangement is that both agent and industrial wholesaler are likely to be experts well known in the industry. Their reputation and services may be impossible for a small manufacturer to duplicate on its own.

CHANNEL D

This is another channel used when a manufacturer does not want to hire its own sales force. The agent represents the manufacturer for sale of the goods but does not take possession or title. The merchandise is shipped directly from the manufacturer to the industrial user. Construction equipment, farm products, and dry goods are often marketed this way.

Math Skills

Pose this problem to students: A manufacturer sells an item to a discount chain store at 50 percent off the list (or suggested retail) price.

L1 If the item has a list price of $75.59, what does the discount chain store pay for it? *($75.59 x .50 = $37.80)*

L2 Tell students to assume that the same manufacturer that sells the item to the discount chain store for 50 percent off the list price gives a regular retailer only 40 percent off. Ask students to determine the dollar savings enjoyed by the chain store over a regular retailer. *(retailer cost: $75.59 x .60 = $45.35; difference: $45.35 - $37.80 = $7.55)*

L3 Tell students to assume that the chain store does not get 50 percent off the list price, but rather the standard 40 percent off and an additional 10 percent for doing its own distribution. Ask students if this arrangement is the same as a 50 percent discount, and have them explain their answers. *(No, it's not the same because the discounts apply in sequence: $75.59 x .60 = $45.35; $45.35 x .90 = $40.82.)*

More About . . .

Manufacturers

Manufacturers provide retailers with more than just goods. Because they are the best authorities on the use, quality, and content of their own products, they often supply retailers with valuable product information, display materials, and advertising ideas. This can be important to small retailers or those with limited budgets for advertising.

Reteaching

1. **Vocabulary** Assign and review the vocabulary terms for this section.
2. **Fact and Idea** Assign and review Fact and Idea Review questions 1–5 from the Chapter Assessment.
3. **Agent Intermediaries** To reteach the concept of agent intermediaries, have students think about professional athletes, actors and actresses, and other celebrities. Ask students if they have ever heard that such people have agents. Invite students to speculate about what an agent's job might be in such circumstances. **(An agent's job would be to find work and negotiate contracts for their clients.)**
   Tell students that some manufacturers are just like those actors and athletes. They want to sell their goods but don't want to go out and find customers. They, too, hire agents to do it for them.

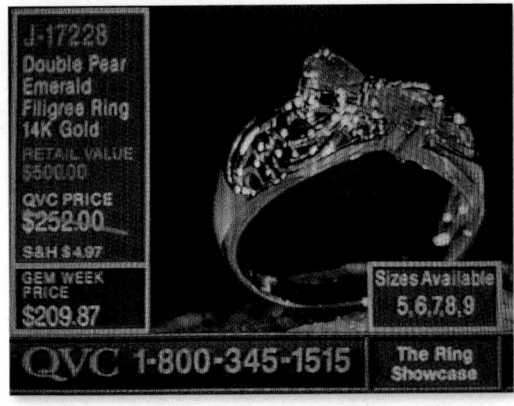

■ **Shop From Home** Retailers can take many different forms. *Why is the Home Shopping Network considered a non-store retailer?*

■ **Retailing Giants** Home Depot is a retailing giant. As such, it has a lot of clout in the channel of distribution. *If you were a manufacturer of lighting fixtures, would you want to sell your products to Home Depot? Why or why not?*

Food brokers, however, are an exception to this rule. Food brokers represent several manufacturers of products sold in supermarkets, convenience stores, and other specialty food stores. Most food brokers sign agreements with their principals (manufacturers they represent) that outline their responsibilities. A food broker may be responsible not only for selling the goods, but for merchandising them as well. Food brokers' employees are often expected to follow plans from their principals regarding shelf position and other merchandising requirements when displaying and stocking the products in supermarkets.

Another type of sales agent is an *independent manufacturer's representative*. Independent manufacturers' representatives represent several related (but noncompeting) manufacturers in a specific industry. They are not on any manufacturer's payroll. They work independently, running their own businesses. An independent manufacturers' agent might carry a line of fishing rods from one manufacturer, lures from another, insulated clothing for

hunters from a different manufacturer, and outdoor shirts from still another manufacturer. This manufacturers' agent would sell the merchandise to sporting goods wholesalers and retailers who specialize in hunting and fishing.

■ Direct and Indirect Channels

Channels of distribution are classified as direct or indirect. Direct distribution occurs when the goods or services are sold from the producer directly to the customer; no intermediaries are involved. Indirect distribution involves one or more intermediaries.

Direct and indirect distribution are both common in marketing goods. The channel of distribution is more often direct when services are performed by the service business itself. Employees in a hair salon actually perform such services as cutting customers' hair. Sometimes the channel for services can be indirect, for example, when an independent insurance agent sells insurance policies from different insurance companies to consumers or businesses.

CAPTION ANSWER
Shop from Home The Home Shopping Network performs the basic function of a retailer, which is to buy products for resale to consumers. Since they sell the products via television programs, they are considered non-store retailers.

CAPTION ANSWER
Retailing Giants Answers will vary. Those who want to sell to Home Depot would stress the huge volume of products that could be sold to such a big chain. Those who would not want to sell products to Home Depot would note that there are problems, such as selling products for lower prices due to the quantities retailing giants buy and being financially dependent on their business.

Channels in the Consumer and Industrial Markets

To get a clearer picture of how channels are structured in the consumer and industrial markets, study Figures 21-3 and 21-4 on pages 378–379. Note that while the individual channels may be different, both markets make use of direct and indirect channels of distribution.

Different channels of distribution are generally used to reach the customer in the consumer and industrial markets. A manufacturer of paper products might sell napkins to both markets by using two different and distinct channels. When selling to the industrial market, the company would sell napkins to industrial distributors who, in turn, would sell the napkins to restaurants. When selling to the consumer market, the company would sell napkins to a wholesaler or use food brokers to sell to retailers. The retailers would then sell the napkins to consumers for personal use at grocery stores or party supply shops.

It is important for any manufacturer, whether industrial or consumer, to weigh all of its options when selecting the best channels of distribution. Not every option works best for every kind of product or company. Despite the potential for success that any product may seem to have, it can fail if the wrong channels of distribution are used.

REAL WORLD MARKETING

Make-up to Go

The main channel of distribution for high-end make-up brands has long been the upscale department store. That is fine for a New Yorker, but what if you live in Lewiston, Idaho, and can't get to a Bloomingdale's? Enter Sephora. Between its flagship stores and online marketplace, Sephora is changing the face of shopping for beauty supplies. Customers have access to make-up without having to wait at counters or peer through the glass. All tubes and containers are within sight and reach, or are just a mouse click away. In addition to marketing its original products, Sephora carries high-end products such as Shiseido, Christian Dior, and Stila.

Thinking Critically
How do expensive make-up companies benefit from Sephora's services?

21.1 ASSESSMENT

Reviewing Key Terms and Concepts

1. What is a channel of distribution?
2. Name two major types of merchant intermediaries.
3. What type of intermediary is a rack jobber? A drop shipper?
4. Distinguish between brick and mortar and online retailers.
5. Which type of distribution channel—direct or indirect—is used more frequently for consumer products? For industrial products?

Thinking Critically

6. Do you think e-tailing will eventually replace brick and mortar retailers? Explain.

Integrating Academic Skills

7. **COMMUNICATION** Prepare and deliver a three-minute speech on the value created by intermediaries for producers in a specific channel of distribution.

21.1 ASSESSMENT ANSWERS

Reviewing Key Terms and Concepts

1. It is the path a product takes from producer or manufacturer to final user.
2. wholesalers and retailers
3. Both are specialized wholesalers.
4. Brick and mortar retailers sell goods to the ultimate consumer through their own physical stores. Online retailers sell over the Internet.

5. Indirect distribution is used for consumer goods; direct is used for industrial products.

Thinking Critically

6. Answers will vary. Some students will say no because people want to see and touch the items they buy. Speed and convenience are also advantages.

Integrating Academic Skills

7. **COMMUNICATION** Speeches will vary.

Enrichment

1. **Review** Assign and review the appropriate Thinking Critically questions from the Chapter Assessment.
2. **Extend** Assign and review the corresponding activities from *BusinessWeek Case Studies*, *Internet Resources*, and the *School-to-Work Activity Workbook*. **ILP**
3. **Display** Have students prepare a bulletin-board display showing the channels of distribution used to get a product to final consumers. They can select something as simple as a pencil or as complex as an automobile.

Evaluation

Assign and review the Section 21.1 Assessment.

Technology Resources

 Assessment Resources
Go to the *Marketing Essentials* Web site (**www.marketing.glencoe.com**) for resources to teach and assess occupation-specific vocabulary.

CLOSE

Section Wrap-Up

Have students complete the following statement: The path a product takes from producer or manufacturer to final user is called . . . *(a channel of distribution.)*

REAL WORLD MARKETING

Make-up to Go

Answer Expensive make-up brands benefit because it gives them greater exposure while keeping an upscale reputation.

381

SECTION 21.2

Distribution Planning

Bell Ringer Activity

Identify Ask students to name some nonfood products that have found their way into supermarkets. *(Examples include videotapes, carpet cleaners, flower arrangements.)*

Introducing the Section

Distribution Planning Use the answers from the Bell Ringer Activity to introduce the concept of multiple channels of distribution. Then have students think about hotels and how they target business travelers.

Tell students that whenever a business expands the sale of its goods or services to a different market, it must use multiple channels of distribution. Ask why that is necessary. *(Each market may have a distinct way in which goods and services are sold and distributed.)*

What You'll Learn

- The key considerations in distribution planning
- When to use multiple channels of distribution
- How to compare the costs and control involved in having a direct sales force versus using independent sales agents
- The three levels of distribution intensity
- The effect of the Internet on distribution planning
- The challenges involved in distribution planning for international markets

Why It's Important

Distribution decisions affect the entire company, so it is important for you to know how these decisions are made. It is also helpful to know how these decisions are carried out in different markets, including international and e-marketplaces.

Key Terms

- exclusive distribution
- integrated distribution
- selective distribution
- intensive distribution
- e-marketplace

Understanding Distribution Planning

Distribution planning involves decisions about a product's physical movement and transfer of ownership from producer to consumer. In this chapter, we address only transfer of ownership concerns. You will study physical distribution concerns in Chapter 22.

Distribution decisions affect a firm's marketing program. Some of the major considerations are the use of multiple channels, control versus costs, intensity of distribution desired, and involvement in e-commerce.

■ Multiple Channels

Multiple channels are used when a product fits the needs of both industrial and customer markets. Consider Greenfield's Healthy Foods, a company that produces fat-free cookies and brownies. Presently Greenfield's sells its fat-free snacks to supermarkets and convenience stores, as well as to airlines. It is also looking to expand into other markets, such as schools and hospitals. Each new market poses questions regarding the exact channel of distribution needed to reach it.

Retailers also use multiple channels. A retail stationery store, for example, generally carries stationery supplies, greeting cards, and some convenience items for consumers. Much of its business, though, may involve selling office supplies to businesses in the local area. To cater to this industrial market, the stationery store might offer credit, trade discounts, and delivery services.

■ Control vs. Costs

All manufacturers and producers must weigh the control they want to keep over the distribution of their products against costs and profitability. This means deciding between using an in-house sales force or independent sales agents, in some cases. It can also mean accommodating one's business to the dominant member in a particular channel of distribution.

WHO DOES THE SELLING? A manufacturer must make decisions regarding the amount of control it wants over its sales function. It can decide to use its own sales force or hire agents to do the selling.

A direct sales force is costly. In-house sales representatives are on the company payroll, receive employee benefits, and are reimbursed for expenses. The manufacturer, though, has complete control over them. It can establish sales quotas and easily monitor each sales representative's performance.

Classroom Resources

For the Teacher
- Teacher Editions for all workbooks
- Assessment Package
- PowerPoint Presentation Software
- Interactive Lesson Planner
- ILP Block Scheduling, p. 7
- ILP Lesson Plans, p. 46
- ILP Internet Resources, p. 61

- ILP Blackline Masters, p. 40
- ILP *BusinessWeek* Case Studies, p. 133
- ILP Marketing Career Portfolio, p. 37
- *Marketing Essentials* Web site (**www.marketing.glencoe.com**)

For the Student
- Student Activity Workbook, p. 177
- Marketing Math Workbook, p. 59

- Marketing Research Project Workbook, p. 111
- ILP School-to-Work Activity Workbook, p. 89
- Virtual Business simulation
- *Marketing Essentials* Web site (**www.marketing.glencoe.com**)

ILP These resources are available in print and on the Interactive Lesson Planner (ILP)

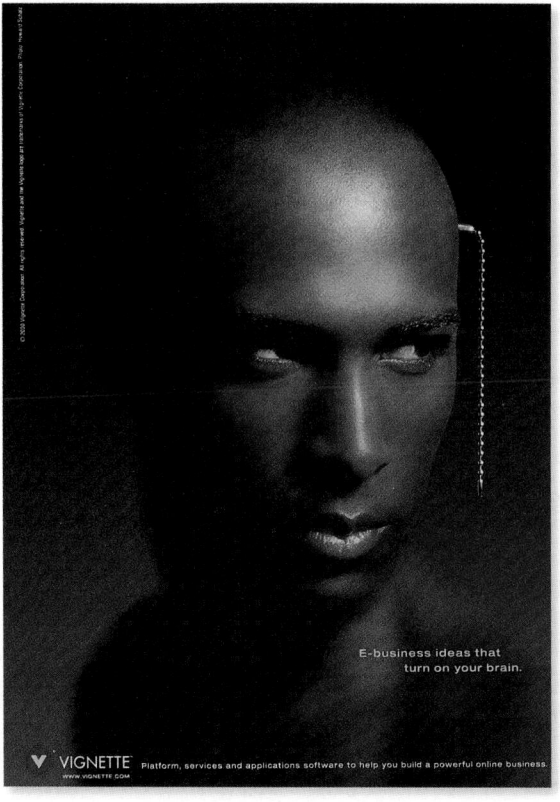

E-business ideas that turn on your brain.

▼ VIGNETTE   Platform, services and applications software to help you build a powerful online business.
www.vignette.com

■ **Getting Started** E-business is so big that there are companies that will help businesses become established on the Internet. *What types of services would you expect a company like Vignette to offer to help you start your own e-business?*

When sales volume is very high and a company is well established in the marketplace, it may be less costly to use an in-house sales force. That is because the selling effort is minimal, and the company can hire sales representatives on a salary basis to service established accounts.

With an agent, a manufacturer loses some of its control over how sales are made. An agent serves primarily as the independent selling arm of producers. There are two different types of agents: manufacturer's agents and selling agents. Manufacturer's agents, or manufacturer's representatives, work for several producers and carry non-competitive, complementary merchandise in an exclusive territory. Selling agents represent a single producer. However, the relative cost of using agents can be lower than hiring an in-house sales staff. No employee benefits or expenses must be paid because agents are independent businesspeople. Another benefit is that agents are paid a set percentage of sales, assuring that the cost of sales is always the same in relation to the sales generated.

WHO DICTATES THE TERMS? A cost and control consideration that has emerged in recent years is the increasing power of retail giants like Wal-Mart and Home Depot. Manufacturers that want to do business with such retailers must often adhere to strict criteria. These criteria relate to selling direct and offering special services in areas like shipping, pricing, packaging, and merchandising. These added services cost manufacturers money. Despite that, most manufacturers adhere to these wishes because of the large volume of business generated by the retail giants.

There are those manufacturers, however, that cannot or do not get involved with the giants. They distribute their products through smaller retailers instead. They follow such a policy so they don't become totally dependent on one customer as their main source of revenue.

More About . . .

Multiple Channels

The trend toward manufacturers opening their own stores is on the upswing. Sony Corporation has two such stores—Sony Style in New York City and Sony Gallery in Chicago, Illinois. Analysts claim that the trend helps independent retailers, rather than harms them, by increasing product awareness.

CAPTION ANSWER

Getting Started Companies might offer e-business software for managing content, gathering and analyzing customer data, and integrating with suppliers.

Case Study

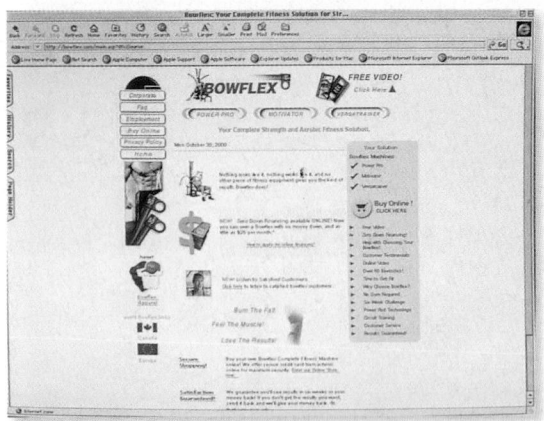

Getting Fit & Trim

Direct Focus is making strides in the exercise equipment industry. The company manufactures and sells Bow-flex exercise rod-resistance equipment. They do it through direct marketing channels, using 30-minute infomercials and spot cable TV ads that target baby boomers interested in health and fitness. Industry reports note that the average sale is between $1,150 and $1,200. Another direct channel of distribution Direct Focus uses is the Internet. Direct Focus has its own Web site, which generated $5 million in sales in its first three months of operation. The Web site stresses the satisfaction guarantee, which encourages customers to trust Direct Focus. It also offers a free video to customers demonstrating the different machines that are available.

The commercial market for exercise equipment is ten times larger than the home exercise equipment market. To compete in that arena, Direct Focus bought Nautilus International Inc., a brand of commercial (weight resistance) fitness equipment. To sell this new line, Direct Focus plans to use its current direct marketing channels, as well as through indirect channels, including specialty retailers and sporting goods stores. Some of the problems that Direct Focus will face with this indirect method of distribution are meeting shipping demands, pricing pressures, and competing for shelf space.

Case Study Review

1. Explain Direct Focus's channels of distribution for its home exercise equipment and for its Nautilus commercial equipment.
2. Why do you think Direct Focus is using multiple channels of distribution?

A MATTER OF ETHICS

3. How ethical is it for a company to target the same market with two different brands of exercise equipment?

▪ Distribution Intensity

Distribution intensity has to do with how widely a product will be distributed. There are three levels of distribution intensity—exclusive, selective, and intensive.

EXCLUSIVE DISTRIBUTION Exclusive distribution involves protected territories for distribution of a product in a given geographic area. Dealers are assured that they are the only ones within a certain geographic radius that have the right to sell the manufacturer's or wholesaler's products. Prestige, image, channel control, and a high profit margin for both the manufacturer and intermediaries are characteristic of this distribution strategy. When there is an exclusive distribution agreement, the retailer is usually tied by contract to the manufacturer. Franchised operations are examples of exclusive distribution planning. This is because only licensed franchises can sell the product.

384 Unit 7 ▪ *Distribution*

Case Study Review Answers

Getting Fit and Trim

1. The channel is manufacturer to consumer for home exercise equipment; for its Nautilus commercial brand, it is manufacturer to retailer to consumer.
2. Answers may suggest that Direct Focus wants to see which channel is more profitable.

A MATTER OF ETHICS

3. Most students will say it is okay, especially since each piece of equipment is different: One is rod-resistance equipment and the other is weight-resistance equipment.

Wholesalers may also sponsor voluntary groups in which a retailer agrees to buy and maintain a minimum inventory of the wholesaler's products. The wholesaler services the account regularly. This includes checking inventory, telling the retailer what needs to be reordered, and sponsoring special promotions to sell those products to customers. One example of a voluntary group sponsored by a wholesaler is the National Auto Parts Association (NAPA). Retailers affiliated with NAPA buy most of their stock from NAPA and participate in its promotions.

Guidelines given by the manufacturer, franchiser, or the wholesaler cooperative ensure exclusivity of the product line to the retailer. The retailers have limited competition in the sale of the product. The product's image is maintained through the exclusivity of distribution. It is assumed that buyers will seek the outlets that carry these products.

A variation on exclusive distribution is found in manufacturers that own and run their own retail operations. This is called integrated distribution. The manufacturer acts as wholesaler and retailer for its own products. Sherwin-Williams sells its paints in company-owned retail stores.

SELECTIVE DISTRIBUTION Selective distribution means that a limited number of outlets in a given geographic area are used to sell the product. The objective is to select channel members that can maintain the image of the product and are good credit risks, aggressive marketers, and good inventory planners. The manufacturer may exert some pressure on intermediaries to move the product with this type of distribution strategy. Frequent local advertising may be required of the intermediaries, as well as maintenance of a well-stocked and well-balanced inventory.

The intermediaries chosen are selected for their ability to cater to the final users that the manufacturer wants to attract. Ralph Lauren selects only top department and specialty stores to appeal to the affluent target market that will buy its clothing and dry goods. They would not choose to sell their goods in a chain megastore or a variety store for different reasons. The cost of Ralph Lauren goods is in line with those goods carried by fine department stores or specialty shops. This makes it more likely that customers will purchase their goods. The company also chooses top quality stores to ensure that their high quality image is maintained.

Life In The Diverse MARKETPLACE

Going Global

It's not just the big names that head overseas for international expansion. Sure, McDonald's and Pepsi are known worldwide, but many smaller companies have learned the art of business abroad as well. For example, the dry cleaning franchise One-Hour Martinizing opened its first business outside of the United States in Ecuador. Why Ecuador? The heat and sticky humidity require some business people to change shirts three times a day! It looks like One-Hour Martinizing has found its international niche.

Thinking Critically

What are some challenges that smaller companies face with international expansion?

INTENSIVE DISTRIBUTION Intensive distribution involves the use of all suitable outlets to sell a product. The objective is complete market coverage, and the ultimate goal is to sell to as many customers as possible, wherever they choose to shop. Motor oil is marketed in quick-lube shops, farm stores, auto parts retailers, supermarkets, drugstores, hardware stores, warehouse clubs, and other mass merchandisers to reach the maximum number of customers.

Industrial supplies fall into this category. One such product manufactured by 3M is a facial respirator. To reach all possible users of facial respirators, 3M has included welding supply channels, farm supply distributors, and specialty chemical channels in its distribution planning.

With the use of the Internet, businesses are opting for their own Web sites to make their products available to final users in consumer and industrial markets. This creates more intensive product distribution. Individuals who might not have had access to a brick and mortar store in their town can shop online to find any specialized or hard-to-find products.

Cooperative Learning

Distribution Planning Tell students that a new computer company has developed a revolutionary new laptop computer that is less expensive than those on the market today. Although the company is running short on funds, the owners believe that once the benefits of this new laptop are publicized, the laptop will be in demand.

Have students break into groups. Ask them to develop a comprehensive distribution plan that is realistic and fits the circumstances described. Tell them to concentrate on key factors used in distribution planning, costs, and expenses involved in their plans, and the level of distribution intensity suggested.

At the end of fifteen minutes, ask each group to share its plan with the class. Be sure they provide a rationale for each component offered. *(Plans will vary depending on the level of distribution intensity they suggest. Since cost is a factor, they may suggest using manufacturers' sales agents in the channel of distribution to reach businesses directly or to reach wholesalers and retailers in the computer field.)*

Independent Practice

Research and Present Have students research distribution planning required in a country of their choice. Tell them to access their public or school library databases to find articles that deal with the challenges and opportunities involved in selling goods abroad using foreign distributors. Ask them to prepare a PowerPoint presentation to report their findings in class.

Life In The Diverse MARKETPLACE

Going Global

Answer Some challenges might include the lack of resources and funds as well as the lack of international product recognition.

Decision-Making Skills

Tell students to assume that they work for a perfume manufacturer that wants to expand the market for its scents beyond perfumes and colognes for consumers. Company marketers are giving consideration to selling the firm's chemical formulas to the manufacturers of other products that require scents. They are also looking to place their existing products with businesses other than retail outlets. Have students brainstorm two lists—the first, all the different types of products that require scents; the second, other businesses that could be markets for perfumes and colognes. *(Some possibilities include: products— soaps, detergents, and other cleaning products; markets— hotels and motels, cruise ships and airlines, all businesses that use employee gifts.)*

L1 Have students review the lists generated and select one product/market they think has the most potential.

L2 Have students select one product/market from their lists that they think has potential. Have them provide a written rationale for their choice.

L3 Have students decide exactly how they would pursue one product/market they select from their lists. Tell them to develop a plan that includes selling points for that product/market, as well as strategies to inform their new target customers that they are in a new line of business.

FIGURE 21-5 ANSWER
Reservations Online Airfare sales have the largest share of the market with 36 percent.

FIGURE 21-5

Jet Set

Led by airline tickets, online travel sales are expected to reach $29 billion by 2003, or more than double the total online travel sales in 2000.

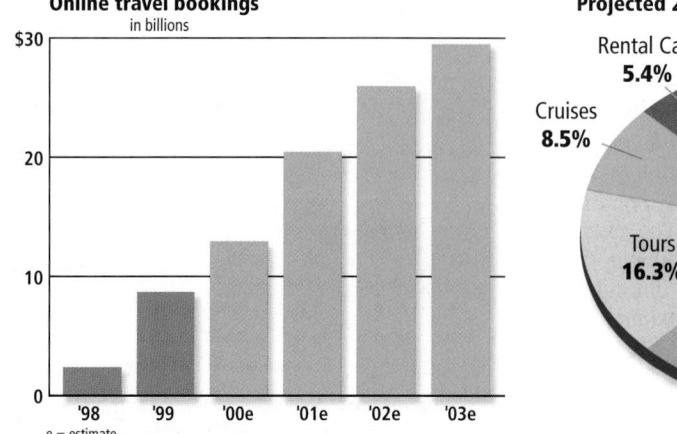

Online travel bookings in billions

Projected 2003 Online Travel Market

- Rental Cars 5.4%
- Cruises 8.5%
- Air Fare 36%
- Tours 16.3%
- Hotels 33.8%

e = estimate

■ **Reservations Online** Online travel is a growing Internet industry. *Which area of the industry has the largest share of the travel market?*

E-COMMERCE E-commerce is the means by which products are sold to customers and industrial buyers through use of the Internet. You already learned that e-tailing is when retailers sell over the Internet. This online shopping location is called **e-marketplace**. In 2000 almost half of America's top retailers sold online. To get an idea of how significant the Internet business is for consumer products, consider Ticketmaster.com, which has over $1.5 million in Internet ticket sales daily. Online travel is also becoming increasingly popular, which is illustrated by the interest in Web sites such as Travelocity.com, Priceline.com, and Expedia.com, all of which offer vacation planning services online. The increasing popularity of online travel planning is illustrated in Figure 21-5.

Over 2.2 million small businesses were online in 1999. According to market researcher Forrester Research Inc., business e-commerce sales are expected to reach $2.7 trillion by 2004. The conclusion is that the Internet is here to stay as a channel of distribution for consumer and industrial products.

Panasonic, a consumer electronics maker, provides a business-to-business (B2B) Web site for its retail dealers. The Web site enables them to check on orders, products, pricing, and promotions, in addition to purchasing goods. On Panasonic's business-to-consumer (B2C) Web site, its dealers are able to add their store locations so consumers can find them. Panasonic is not selling directly to the consumer; it is simply using its consumer Web Site for informational purposes.

E-marketplaces for B2B operations provide one-stop shopping and substantial savings for industrial buyers. Online catalogs of products supplied by different companies make it easier for corporate buyers to compare prices and get the best deal. E-marketplaces provide smaller businesses with the exposure that they could not get elsewhere. An e-marketplace company in the chemical industry is ChemConnect. ChemConnect allows companies in the chemical market to sell goods and services and buy supplies over the Web. Even a large company like Dow Chemical, which has its own Web site to sell to its business customers, has signed up with ChemConnect for those customers that want to go to a central site where other products are sold as well. According to Forrester Research, 17 percent of all B2B trade will take place via the Internet by 2004. Figure 21-6 on page 387 illustrates the projected explosion of growth in the sales of goods and services via electronic marketplaces.

386 Unit 7 ■ *Distribution*

COMPETITIVE EVENTS AND MARKETING ESSENTIALS

Role Play and Channels of Distribution As you teach this chapter you can use the role-play situations from DECA's Individual Series Events to illustrate this material for your students. Select distribution role-play situations from several of the eleven occupational areas. You can then lead a discussion on how channels of distribution relate to each of the occupational areas.

You can also have your students role play with one another to reinforce the chapter material. As students practice role-playing, they will also be preparing for DECA competition. This preparation offers advantages, such as lessening the fear of presenting, increasing familiarity with the event format, and reinforcing knowledge of content.

Distribution Planning for Foreign Markets

Distribution planning takes on a new dimension when businesses get involved in international trade.

Different environments in foreign markets require that businesses adjust their distribution systems. This situation also gives businesses the opportunity to experiment with different distribution strategies. For example, in the United States, General Motors distributes automobiles through franchised retail car dealerships. However, in Taiwan, GM owns its own retail dealers and sells cars directly to consumers. In that nation, GM is free from franchise dealer constraints and has been able to test systems for selling cars to consumers directly over the Internet.

Cultural considerations should also be weighed when planning distribution in foreign markets. For example, when Reebok owners wanted to sell their athletic shoes in Europe, they studied European culture and found that Europeans visit sporting goods stores far less often than Americans. This led them to decide to distribute Reebok's shoes through hundreds of traditional retail shoe outlets. Within one year of adopting this distribution strategy, Reebok's sales in France doubled.

FIGURE 21-6

Going To Market

Sales of goods and services via electronic marketplaces are projected to skyrocket

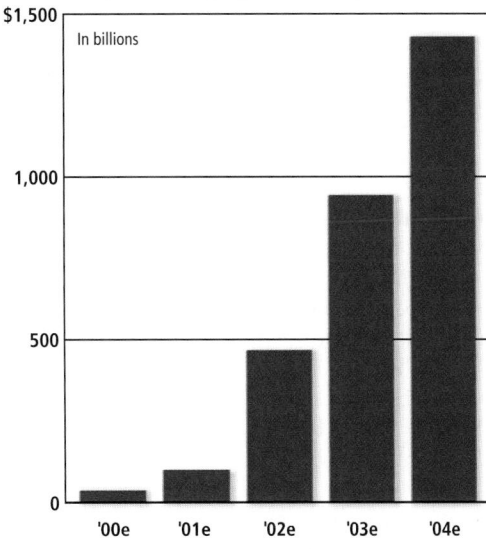

■ **E-Marketplace or Private Web Site?** E-marketplaces for B2B operations provide one-stop shopping and savings for industrial buyers. *Why would a business opt to be part of an e-marketplace rather than having its own Web site?*

SECTION 21.2

ASSESS

Reteaching

1. **Vocabulary** Assign and review the vocabulary terms for this section.
2. **Fact and Idea** Assign and review Fact and Idea Review questions 6–10 from the Chapter Assessment.
3. **Distribution Intensity** To reteach distribution intensity, ask students where they have seen chewing gum sold. They should be able to identify a variety of locations, including but not limited to supermarkets, convenience stores, diners, candy stores, service station stores, etc. This will help reinforce the concept of intensive distribution.
4. **Exclusive Distribution** To reteach exclusive distribution, ask students how many Ford or Chevrolet dealerships they can name in the immediate area. The students will come to realize that the manufacturer offers those retailers the exclusive right to serve a certain geographic area of the community based on population density.

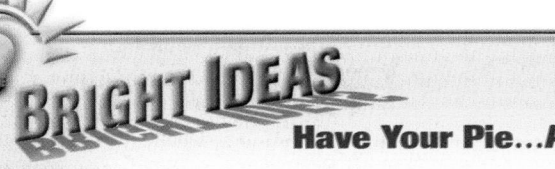

Have Your Pie...And The Tin Too

What to do with the pie tin when the pie is all gone? New England college students in the mid-1900s found that empty pie tins made excellent toys for flinging back and forth across college lawns. Talk about creative recycling! These pie tins came from Frisbie Baking Company of Bridgeport, Connecticut, which sold pies to many New England colleges between 1871 and 1958. In 1948, W. F. Morrison and Warren Franscioni invented a plastic version of the pie tin "Frisbie" that could fly farther with better accuracy. The two men went separate ways before their product had achieved any success. Morrison later marketed the toy as the "Pluto Platter," feeding into America's growing fascination with UFOs. Morrison sold his design rights to Wham-O in 1957 but retained the patent. Wham-O named the product Frisbee and promoted it as a new sport. Sales soared, and Morrison received more than $1 million in royalties for his invention.

Thinking Creatively

What household products might be given new life and reinvented as possible toys?

Chapter 21 ■ *Channels of Distribution* **387**

FIGURE 21-6 ANSWER
E-Marketplace or Private Web Site A business may lack the expertise to set up their own Web site and may feel more secure going with an established Internet company with a following.

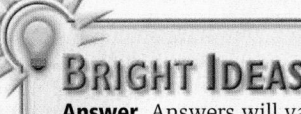

Have Your Pie . . . And the Tin Too

Answer Answers will vary. An example might be using the design for an egg carton as a jewelry case.

1. **Review** Assign and review the Chapter 21 activities in the *Student Activity Workbook*.
2. **Review** Assign and review the appropriate Thinking Critically questions from the Chapter Assessment.
3. **Review** Assign and review the following Chapter Assessment activities: Building Workplace Skills, Applying Marketing Concepts, Linking School-to-Work, The DECA Connection Role Play, and Internet Connection.

Evaluation

Assign and review the Section 21.2 Assessment.

Technology Resources

 Assessment Resources Go to the *Marketing Essentials* Web site (**www.marketing.glencoe. com**) for resources to teach and assess occupation-specific vocabulary.

CLOSE

Section Wrap-Up

Ask students to recall the three levels of distribution intensity that a business can consider in its distribution planning. *(intensive, selective, and exclusive)*

Pick, Pack, and Ship

Answer Companies can outsource almost anything, including labor, fulfillment, manufacturing, and information technology.

A look at Japan's system of doing business can serve as an example of challenges companies face when doing business abroad. Japan has a unique distribution system, called *keiretsu* (which means alignment), in which intermediaries have strong social and economic bonds with producers. They are often groups of anywhere from 20 to 45 companies that are all connected to one bank. Keiretsu are groups of closely related companies that do business with one another on a regular basis. Through distribution keiretsu, the manufacturer dominates the marketing channels for its products. Understanding these relationships and becoming a part of them is important for any business wanting to do business successfully in Japan. The Japanese Fair Trade Commission estimated that 90 percent of domestic business takes place between parties in a relationship such as the keiretsu. Warner Lambert needed to utilize a Japanese wholesaler in order to sell its Schick razors and blades in Japan.

Why are wholesalers so important in Japan? One reason is simply tradition and the other is a lack of storage space. As a comparison, it may take five intermediaries to sell soap in Japan and only one or two in the United States. Thus, distributors remain the main links into the marketplace. Foreign business approaching the Japanese market should study the players and their relationships with each other very carefully.

Pick, Pack, and Ship

In addition to marketing and selling their products, most Internet companies ship more than 1,000 packages a day. Amazon.com usually ships 10,000 packages; during the holiday season, however, numbers rise to as high as 60,000 packages. This task is too large for even the dot.com giant Amazon. The cost of hiring employees alone would be a challenge, but building a one-million square-foot warehouse would take two years and cost between $60 million and $80 million. To solve this problem, third-party distribution organizations, also known as pick, pack, and ship fulfillment specialists, help to meet demand, and receive roughly ten percent per order. Outsourcing, or looking outside of your own resources to fill needs, is a practical alternative for time-, space-, or cash-strapped companies.

Thinking Critically
What other services can a company outsource?

21.2 ASSESSMENT

Reviewing Key Terms and Concepts

1. What key factors are considered when developing an effective distribution plan?
2. When are multiple distribution channels used?
3. Give two reasons for using a direct sales force instead of independent sales agents.
4. What are the levels of distribution intensity?
5. Explain the challenges businesses face when getting involved with distribution planning in Japan.

Thinking Critically

6. What problems might be created by a clothing manufacturer that establishes its own Web site to sell to the final consumer, while it also sells the same items to retailers for resale to consumers?

Integrating Academic Skills

7. **MATH** Assuming a manufacturer's sales were $2,000,000 last year and the commission paid to independent sales agents was 8 percent, what was the company's yearly sales expense? What would be the difference in its yearly sales expense if that company hired its own sales force at a cost of $600,000? Assuming the projected expenses for an in-house sales force remained the same, determine the sales volume at which point the manufacturer could switch from independent sales agents to an in-house sales force without being hurt financially.

21.2 ASSESSMENT ANSWERS

Reviewing Key Terms and Concepts
1. use of multiple channels, control vs. costs, intensity of distribution, and involvement in e-commerce
2. They are used when a product fits the needs of both industrial and ultimate consumers.
3. A manufacturer may use direct sales force when it wants complete control or when they only need to service existing accounts.
4. exclusive, selective, and intensive
5. Japan's system, *keiretsu*, creates strong bonds between intermediaries and producers.

Thinking Critically
6. Its supplier would become its competitor.

Integrating Academic Skills
7. **MATH** $160,000 ($2,000,000 x .08 = $160,000); $440,000 ($600,000 − $160,000 = $440,000); $25,000,000 ($2,000,000 ÷ .08 = $25,000,000)

Careers in Marketing

FOOD MARKETING

Sheryl Modesti
Watson and Associates
Food Broker

What does your job entail?

"I assess operators' needs, identifying their concepts and target markets and taking into consideration their food costs. I get to know all people responsible for making decisions in each facility—ranging from the owner or the purchasing director to the kitchen staff and the wait staff. I train food facility staff and distributor sales representatives in my products. I am the link between the manufacturer, the operator, and distributor."

What kind of training did you have?

"I have no formal training in the food industry, only a love of food and cooking. It is very important to your success that you have a passion for what you do. I was a national sales manager, copywriter, and national trainer for a skincare, cosmetic, and nutrition line for 11 years. I traveled 70 percent of the time, hiring, training, selling, and establishing accounts. This gave me a background in sales and marketing and paved the way for my current career. I recommend that students keep focused on their dream."

What do you like most about your work?

"Meeting chefs and absorbing information from them is my favorite part of the job, and it makes me a better consultant. I also enjoy the manufacturer training at our brokerage facility, where we have a test kitchen to experiment with recipes."

What is your key to success?

"Developing good relationships with operators and distributors is the key to my success. Without cultivated relationships, you will not be able to accomplish your end result—closing the sale!"

Thinking Critically
What kinds of research can food brokers do to keep up with the industry?

Career Facts

Education and Training: Many more companies are requiring college degrees in business or marketing. Sales experience and familiarity with brands are also valuable. Many companies have training programs for new sales representatives.

Aptitudes, Abilities, and Skills: Good organizational skills to prepare reports, analyze data, maintain expense accounts, and schedule appointments are required. Food brokers must be goal oriented and able to work independently or on a team, in addition to having a pleasant personality and strong desire to sell.

Career Outlook: Opportunities are expected to grow more slowly than average through 2008.

Career Path: Successful food brokers may be assigned to larger territories or advance to sales supervisors, district managers, or sales trainers.

SECTION 21.2

Careers in Marketing

Ask a student to read the Careers in Marketing feature aloud to the class. Discuss the skills and aptitudes required for a career in food marketing. Ask students whether they think they would like or dislike a career in food marketing. Discuss the pros and cons of such a career.

Thinking Critically Answer
Research can be done through getting information from chefs, distributors, and operators.

 Guest Speakers
Invite a food broker to class to discuss his/her job.

Exploring Careers

Finding a Career Interest
1. Read to students the 12 different career interests areas from the *Guide for Occupational Exploration*:
- Artistic—creative expression of feelings or ideas
- Scientific—discovering, collecting, analyzing information about the natural world
- Plants and animals—outdoor activities involving plants/animals
- Protective—use of authority to protect people/property
- Mechanical—using machines, tools, techniques
- Industrial—repetitive and specific activities
- Business detail—activities requiring attention to detail
- Selling—using personal persuasion, sales, and promotion techniques to sell products or services
- Accommodating—providing services to others
- Humanitarian—helping others
- Leading-influencing—guiding actions of others
- Physical performing—activities performed before an audience

2. Discuss with students their three favorite career areas.

Lifelong Learning

Channels of Distribution
Knowing about distribution channels can make students better consumers and marketers. As technology makes home shopping easier, consumers need to evaluate products and their usefulness. Perceiving the pros and cons of each channel can help students determine the best one for each product.

Meeting Individual Needs

Gifted
Gifted students often finish work more quickly than others and have above average ability, task commitment, and creativity. Have these students work individually or as a group to research channels of distribution in foreign markets. Ask them to imagine that they are U.S. manufacturers who are considering a new market for a product.

389

Chapter 21 ASSESSMENT

Vocabulary Review

Stories will vary. See Glossary for definitions.

Fact and Idea Review

1. Intermediaries are classified on the basis of whether they take title to the goods they sell. Those that take title are merchant intermediaries, and those that don't are agents.
2. They carry non-competing lines to avoid conflict of interest.
3. Direct distribution has no intermediaries involved; indirect has one or more intermediaries involved.
4. direct distribution
5. In the consumer market, the channel of distribution would be from manufacturer to agent to wholesaler to retailer to consumer. In the industrial market, the channel of distribution would be from manufacturer to agent to industrial distributor to industrial user.
6. Giant retailers often require from manufacturers strict criteria about selling direct and offering special services in the areas of transporting, pricing, packaging, and merchandising.
7. A business may use intensive distribution to sell to as many customers as possible.
8. It would assure a protected territory for the products, as well as a high profit margin.
9. E-commerce is the means by which products can be sold to final consumers and industrial buyers through the use of the Internet.
10. In Japan, intermediaries have strong bonds with producers through vertical integration and other social and economic ties.

Thinking Critically

1. They use wholesalers' services because they provide the racks for display of the product and manage that product for the retailer. They bill the retailer only for the goods sold, not for all the items on display.
2. Answers will vary but should question if traditional retailers should join the interactive shopping movement or fight it since they've put a great deal of money into making their stores pleasant shopping environments.

VOCABULARY REVIEW

Working in a group, choose a company and tell how it sells products to consumers and industrial buyers. Include the following terms:

- channel of distribution
- intermediaries
- wholesalers
- retailers
- e-tailing
- agents
- direct distribution
- indirect distribution
- exclusive distribution
- selective distribution
- intensive distribution
- integrated distribution
- e-marketplace

FACT AND IDEA REVIEW

1. How are intermediaries classified? (21.1)
2. Do independent sales agents carry competing products from different manufacturers? Why or why not? (21.1)
3. What is the difference between direct and indirect distribution? (21.1)
4. What channel of distribution is generally used for services? (21.1)
5. A manufacturer wants to concentrate solely on production. What channel of distribution would be used in the consumer market? In the industrial market? (21.1)
6. How are giant retailers becoming powerful in the channels of distribution? (21.2)
7. Why would a business opt for intensive distribution of it product(s)? (21.2)

8. Why would retailers want to be part of an exclusive distribution agreement with a manufacturer? (21.2)
9. What is e-commerce and what effect is it having on how businesses sell their products? (21.2)
10. Explain why the *keiretsu* system of distribution makes it difficult for foreign businesses to sell their products in Japan. (21.2)

THINKING CRITICALLY

1. Why do you think that small retailers tend to use the services of wholesalers?
2. How much do you think e-tailing will change the way brick and mortar retailers operate?
3. Under what circumstances would an established business replace its independent sales representative with a direct sales force?
4. Which level of distribution (intensive, selective, or exclusive) would you chose for personal computers, expensive imported sweaters, a new brand of hair spray, and an automobile? Why?

BUILDING WORKPLACE SKILLS

1. **Writing** A new sporting goods equipment company wants to sell its products through infomercials. The vice president of marketing has asked your opinion. As the new marketing manager, you think the Internet would be more effective. Prepare a memo addressing this.
2. **Human Relations** You are a salesperson for Fanny Farmer candies. A customer complains that the selection is small and that she would like to see candy made by other manufacturers sold in the store. What would you say to the customer?

3. A business might establish a direct sales force if business were so good that the independent reps were making more than in-house sales personnel on straight salary.
4. Personal computers would be elective or exclusive; expensive imported sweaters would be selective or exclusive; a new brand of hair spray could use any of the three distribution channels depending on rationale; and automobiles would be exclusive because of franchising agreements.

Building Workplace Skills

1. Memos will vary. Students should stress the need to be on the Internet and could even suggest that a video be part of the Web site to show the sporting goods equipment in action, as an infomercial would do.
2. Answers will vary but should include a tactful explanation of integrated distribution and its benefits.

Applying Marketing Concepts

1. Summaries will vary.

APPLYING MARKETING CONCEPTS

1. **Summarizing Key Concepts** Summarize an article that demonstrates any of the key concepts discussed in this chapter. In the summary, identify the specific concepts in parentheses. Use business publications, such as *BusinessWeek, Fortune, Forbes, Marketing News,* and *Nation's Business,* to find an applicable article.

2. **Defining Channels of Distribution** Using design software, diagram the channel of distribution for two products—one that is meant for the final consumer and one that is sold to industrial buyers. Prepare a written report that depicts and explains each channel of distribution.

3. **Analyzing Sales Costs** Using a spreadsheet program, prepare an analysis of the sales costs associated with hiring independent sales agents to sell your company's products. Assume that the sales of your company are $15,000,000 and that the percentage paid to independent sales agents range from five percent to ten percent in your industry. Show what the effect is at each percentage point from five percent to ten percent.

4. **Understanding E-Commerce** Using presentation software, prepare an oral presentation that addresses e-commerce and its effects on channels of distribution.

LINKING SCHOOL TO WORK

Information, Thinking, and Interpersonal Skills
Ask an employer to tell you from whom it buys selected goods. Trace those goods back to the manufacturer or producer in order to diagram the channels of distribution to the final user. Share your findings with your class in both oral and written reports.

THE DECA CONNECTION

Role Play: DECA Fundraiser

Situation You are to assume the role as chairperson of your DECA chapter's fund-raising efforts this year. You have developed a unique board game based on trivia about your state. You have identified two target markets within your state—consumers age 12 and over and businesses, which might be able to use the game as a premium for customers. A local businessperson, John Ruiz, has given you a quote on manufacturing the game, but you need to present your marketing teacher (judge) with a thorough distribution plan before you can ask people to invest.

Activity Present your distribution plan to your marketing teacher (judge).

Evaluation You will be evaluated on how well you meet the following performance indicators:

• Explain the nature of channels of distribution
• Explain the nature and scope of distribution
• Explain the relationship between customer service and distribution
• Select channels of distribution
• Demonstrate orderly and systematic behavior

inter NET CONNECTION

E-Everything
Brick and mortar businesses are establishing Web sites to sell their products directly to consumers.

Connect
• Find the Web sites for three competing catalog companies.
• Analyze the purpose of each company's Web site and how it fits into the company's channels of distribution.
• Prepare a written report that provides a comparison of the three companies' channels of distribution.

THE DECA CONNECTION

Students should be evaluated on the performance indicators noted in the Role Play.
• For another DECA Role Play, go to the *Student Activity Workbook,* p. 177.
• For more in-depth Role Play practice, refer to DECA's *Essential Competitive Events Handbook.* To order, contact DECA at **www.deca.org**.

inter NET CONNECTION

Web sites, analyses, and written reports will vary depending on catalog companies selected.

Mini Quiz

Administer the Mini Quiz orally. For an expanded chapter quiz, go to page 125 of the *Reproducible Tests* book.

1. The path a product takes from producer or manufacturer to final user is called its <u>channel of distribution</u>.

2. All the business involved in sales transactions that move products from the manufacturer to the final user are called <u>intermediaries or middlemen</u>.

3. Two types of agent intermediaries are <u>brokers and manufacturers' sales representatives</u>.

4. When one or more intermediaries are involved in a channel, the distribution is considered <u>indirect</u>.

5. The three levels of distribution intensity are <u>exclusive, selective, and intensive</u>.

---

2. Diagrams and reports will vary depending on the products.
3. The figures on the spreadsheet should be: $750,000 (at 5%); $900,000 (at 6%); $1,050,000 (at 7%); $1,200,000 (at 8%); $1,350,000 (at 9%); and $1,500,000 (at 10%).
4. Presentations will vary, however all should address the fact that some businesses feel compelled to have a Web site because their competitors have one. Online sales become a direct channel of distribution.

GO TO
1. **Assessment** Have students complete the Reproducible Test for Chapter 21 or construct your own tests using the ExamView software.
2. **Enrichment** Have students complete the corresponding activities in the following workbooks:
   • *Marketing Math Workbook,* p. 59
   • *Marketing Research Project Workbook,* p. 111

Linking School to Work

Answers depend on the work situation.

Chapter 22

Physical Distribution

Chapter Overview

Chapter 22 examines physical distribution, which is the process of transporting, storing, order processing, stock handling, and inventory control of materials and products on the way from seller to customer.

Springboard

List and Define Read the chapter introduction aloud with students. Ask them to list the methods of transportation used in physical distribution and write this list on the board. Finally, ask students to define product storage and tell where most products are usually stored.

Prereading

List the section objectives to discuss with the students. Have the students skim the chapter, looking at the pictures, reading the captions, and noting the heads. Ask questions to ensure that the students have a minimal understanding of the chapter structure.

Preteaching Marketing Vocabulary

Assign an equal number of vocabulary terms to each row of students. Have each row look up their terms in the chapter, write a short definition in their own words, and generate one symbol that will serve as a mnemonic to help students remember the term. Have one student from each row write abbreviated definitions and symbols on the board, and review with the class.

Marketing: What It Takes

Answer Answers will vary. A common carrier provides transportation in its operating area to any business. Its rates are published, and they carry less-than-full loads. Private carriers allow businesses to maintain total control, but they require a large investment.

Marketing: What It Takes

A Decision to Make: Common Carriers, Private Carrier, or Both? You have been asked to evaluate the current transportation system for your company. The company is deciding between a common carrier, its own private fleet, or a combination of both to transport its products. Management has asked you to identify the pros and cons of each transportation alternative.

WHAT WILL YOU DO? What advantages and disadvantages will you present for each type of transportation choice?

392

THE DECA CONNECTION — ADVISOR CORNER

***USA Today* and DECA** In partnership with DECA, *USA Today's* Student Business Program allows students first-hand knowledge of the marketing, distribution, sales, and advertising functions of the nation's newspaper. Additionally, your chapter can make up to $30 per annual subscription sold and for each individual paper sold. Your chapter creates only one marketing plan, which can be entered in two competitions—*USA Today's* Special Marketing Project and DECA Competitive Events. You can use this excellent program to reinforce many marketing functions—and raise funds at the same time.

Transportation Systems and Services

The Nature and Scope of Physical Distribution

After a company decides on its channels of distribution, it must plan for actually moving the products through those channels. Physical distribution comprises all the activities that help to ensure that the right amount of product is delivered to the right place at the right time. Physical distribution is also known as *logistics*. Physical distribution or logistics involves order processing, transporting, storing, stock handling, and inventory control of materials and products. Figure 22-1 on page 394 presents an overview of the functions of physical distribution. Physical distribution is an important link between a business and its customers.

Physical distribution involves moving products quickly with minimal handling to reduce costs and maximize customer satisfaction. Marketing experts believe that between 20–25 percent of the value of a product can be assigned to physical distribution expenses.

Businesses try to make the physical distribution system as efficient and cost effective as possible. At the same time, physical distribution needs to be coordinated with other business functions, such as purchasing, finance, production, packaging, and promotion. Promotional activities are planned in advance, therefore the distribution system must be able to deliver the correct products at the right time and to the right place.

As you can imagine, transporting, storing, and handling products is expensive—physical distribution is the third largest expense for most businesses. It is surpassed only by the costs of material and labor.

Types of Transportation

Once something has been sold, it usually needs to be moved from the seller to the buyer. Transportation is the marketing function of moving products from a seller to a buyer. Transportation costs are a significant part of each sale; therefore, manufacturers, wholesalers, and retailers look for the most efficient and cost-effective delivery methods.

There are five major transportation forms that move products, including motor carriers, railroads, waterways, pipelines, and air carriers. Figure 22-2 on page 395 shows the percentage of freight carried by each transportation mode. Most businesses that transport goods are subject to federal and state regulations of the rates they charge and their operating procedures.

What You'll Learn

- The nature and scope of physical distribution
- How transportation systems are used to move products
- The different kinds of transportation services

Why It's Important

To gain a competitive advantage and succeed in today's business environment, you will want to learn how businesses are delivering products to buyers around the country and the world.

Key Terms

- physical distribution
- transportation
- common carriers
- contract carriers
- private carriers
- exempt carriers
- ton-mile
- carload
- freight forwarders

FOCUS

Bell Ringer Activity

Identify and Explain Write the following products on the board. Ask students to tell you which method of transportation they would use to transport them from seller to consumer, and the factors that would influence their decision.

- coal *(train, because it's a heavy, bulky freight)*
- a small overnight parcel *(air or transportation service company, depending on the dollar value of the parcel and the time value of delivery)*
- fruit *(train or truck, depending on distance and time value of delivery)*
- coffee to be shipped abroad *(waterway, since it will not spoil in storage and thus doesn't need to be shipped by air)*
- live fish from Maine to California *(air, because of the time value of delivery)*
- roses from France *(air, because of the time value of delivery)*
- computer equipment *(air, because of its fragility and dollar value)*

Introducing the Section

Transportation Systems and Services Based on their answers to the Bell Ringer Activity, have students generate the main reasons for selecting certain types of physical distribution. Tell students that in this section they will look at the advantages and disadvantages of the various methods of physical distribution and the factors that influence the usage of each.

Classroom Resources

For the Teacher
- Teacher Editions for all workbooks
- Assessment Package
- PowerPoint Presentation Software
- Interactive Lesson Planner
- ILP Block Scheduling, p. 7
- ILP Lesson Plans, p. 47
- ILP Internet Resources, p. 63

- ILP Blackline Masters, p. 42
- ILP *BusinessWeek* Case Studies, p. 139
- ILP Marketing Career Portfolio, p. 37
- *Marketing Essentials* Web site (**www.marketing.glencoe.com**)

For the Student
- Student Activity Workbook, p. 187
- Marketing Math Workbook, p. 59

- Marketing Research Project Workbook, p. 111
- ILP School-to-Work Activity Workbook, p. 93
- Virtual Business simulation
- *Marketing Essentials* Web site (**www.marketing.glencoe.com**)

ILP These resources are available in print and on the Interactive Lesson Planner (ILP)

Concept Development

1. Read Section 22.1 with students.
2. Have students read aloud the Case Study on page 401 and review the answers in class.
3. When discussing water transportation, make sure to indicate on a map the key shipping routes, such as the St. Lawrence Seaway, the Mississippi and the Ohio Rivers, the Great Lakes, etc.

FIGURE 22-1

PHYSICAL DISTRIBUTION

Physical distribution involves the functions of order processing, transportation, storage, stock handling, and inventory control.

ORDER PROCESSING

The purchase of a product initiates the movement of products through a physical distribution system.

TRANSPORTATION

Transportation involves the actual physical movement of products. It is estimated that up to 8 percent of a company's sales are spent on the transportation function.

STORAGE

The storage function facilitates the actual movement of products through the distribution channel as products are sold.

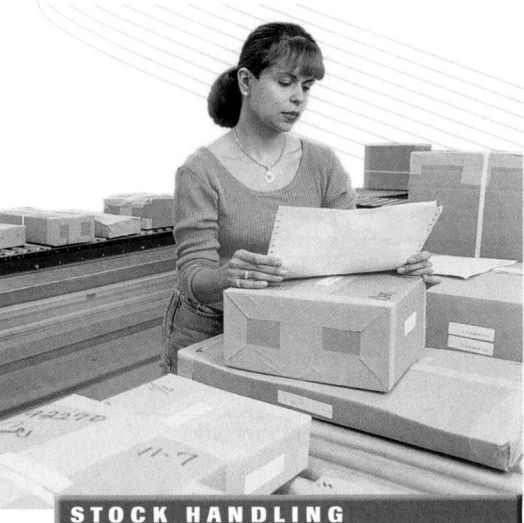

STOCK HANDLING

Receiving, checking, and marking items for sale are an important step in the physical distribution system.

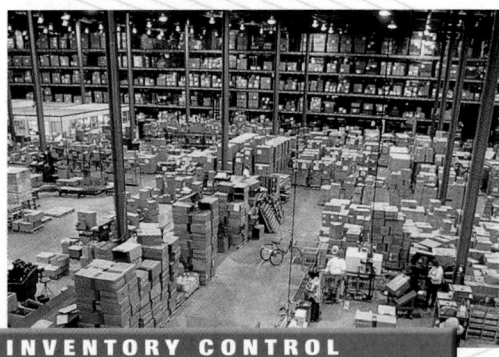

INVENTORY CONTROL

Proper inventory control ensures that products are kept in sufficient quantities and available when requested by customers.

394 Unit 7 ■ *Distribution*

GREAT IDEAS from the Marketing Classroom

Lanette Duncan
Daniel Webster High School
Tulsa, OK

Divide students into groups and assign each group a mode of transportation. I provide a list of questions to research about local, regional, and national companies, and their policies and prices. Students also interview someone locally who works in the industry. Each group prepares a 10-minute presentation, using either PowerPoint, video, or both. Students dress professionally for their presentation, which is accompanied by a written report. When the groups finish, we combine the information as a class and graph the various modes of distribution. Each student may transfer their project onto a CD to keep in their marketing portfolios.

■ Trucking

Trucks (or motor carriers) are the most frequently used form of transportation. They carry higher-valued products that are expensive to carry in inventory. Lightweight shipments transported over moderate distances are generally handled by trucks—nearly 80 percent of those shipments weigh less than 1,000 pounds each. Businesses use trucks for virtually all *intracity* (within a city) shipping and for 26 percent of the *intercity* (between cities) freight traffic in the United States.

State and federal transportation agencies regulate motor carriers used for interstate commerce. State transportation agencies regulate fuel taxes, safety issues, and rates charged for *intrastate* (within a state) trucking. The Interstate Commerce Commission (ICC), a former federal agency, regulated transportation of goods between states from 1887 to 1995. In 1995, the ICC was abolished and most of its responsibilities were assigned to the U.S. Department of Transportation Surface Transportation Board.

TYPES OF CARRIERS Businesses that use trucks to move their products have different options from which to choose. They can use *for-hire carriers, private carriers,* or a combination of both. For-hire carriers include common carriers and contract carriers.

Most motor carriers are for-hire or common carriers. Common carriers provide transportation services to any business in its operating area for a fee. A common carrier receives a "certificate of convenience and necessity" from the state and federal governments.

A common carrier must publish its freight rates to prevent discrimination against shippers. Carriers can change their rates or geographical areas, as long as they do not charge rates that are different from their published rates or provide different services. More than one-third of all motor freight is handled by common carriers. Common carriers are primarily used for less-than-full truckloads to several long distance locations over infrequently traveled roads or for full-truckload shipments over major highways.

Contract carriers are for-hire carriers that provide equipment and drivers for specific routes, according to agreements between the carrier and the shipper. A contract carrier can provide services on a one-time basis or on a continuing basis.

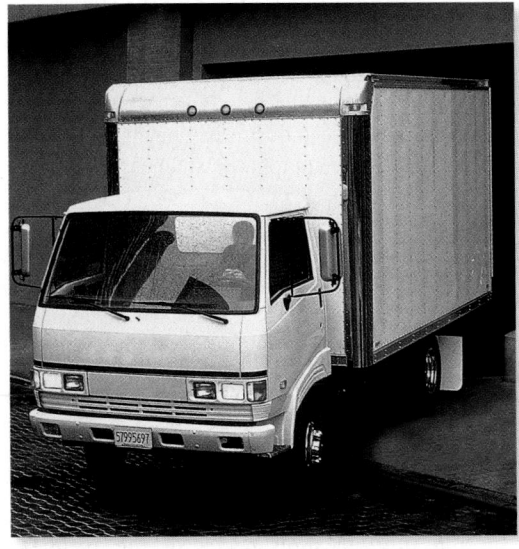

■ **Delivering the Goods** Common carriers handle different commodities but often specialize in handling a single commodity. *Why are common carriers important to the trucking industry?*

FIGURE 22-2

Transportation Systems

SOURCE: BUREAU OF CENSUS, 1997

■ Railroads
■ Trucks
■ Pipelines
■ Waterways
■ Airways

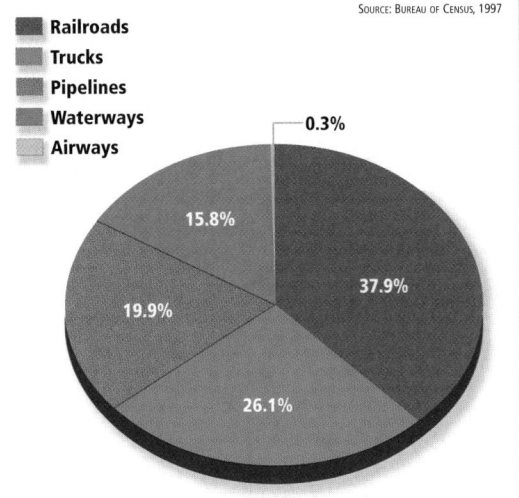

0.3%
15.8%
37.9%
19.9%
26.1%

■ **The Importance and Size of Transportation Systems** The chart shows the percent of freight in ton miles shipped by each form of transportation. *Why is the percentage shipped by air transportation small in relation to other types of transportation?*

CAPTION ANSWER
Delivering the Goods More than one-third of all motor freight is handled by common carriers.

FIGURE 22-2 ANSWER
The Importance and Size of Transportation Systems Airlines generally handle high value, lightweight items versus other forms of transportation.

Cooperative Learning

Physical Distribution Divide the class into two groups: Team #1 and Team #2. Have each team generate a list of 20 products and the type of physical distribution appropriate for each product.

When students have finished, toss a coin to see which team goes first. The winner of the coin toss starts by giving the other team its first product. If the other team correctly identifies the method of distribution for the product, it gets a point and gets a turn. If it incorrectly identifies the method of distribution, it loses its turn, and the querying team gets the point. Go through each team's 20 products. The team with the most points wins.

Contract carriers negotiate their fees with each customer, and the fees may differ from agreement to agreement. Contract carriers often transport goods for more than one business, and they can charge different rates to each business. They must file their contracts with the appropriate state or federal regulatory agency.

A business that uses for-hire common or contract carriers does not need to invest in transportation equipment; however, its shipments are subject to the carriers' schedules, routes, and available equipment. For-hire carriers also offer less flexibility for special pick-ups or handling, rush deliveries, and direct shipments.

PRIVATE CARRIERS Private carriers transport goods for an individual business. The transportation equipment can be owned or leased to meet the specific transportation needs of the business. Transportation companies, such as the Ryder System, Inc., make a variety of private carrier options available to a business. These options include full service leasing, finance leasing, and dedicated contract logistics. Significant capital investment is required if a business decides to own and maintain its own private fleet.

Cost is certainly a major factor in selecting transportation. Starting a private carrier operation involves a large investment in equipment and facilities. A business that regularly ships a large amount of merchandise may like the flexibility of owning its own means of transporting its products.

Private carriage lets a business maintain total control over equipment, maintenance, availability, routes, delivery times, and handling procedures. Private carriage also allows a business to rapidly change schedules, routes, and delivery times to meet customers' needs.

Many businesses use a combination of for-hire and private carriers. They may use their own trucks for local deliveries and common or contract carriers for shipments beyond their local service areas.

Exempt carriers, which commonly carry agricultural products, are free from direct regulation of rates and operating procedures. In most cases, they carry agricultural products. Their rates are lower than those charged by common carriers because of their exempt status. Exempt carrier status can also be granted to local transportation firms that make short-distance deliveries within specified trading areas in cities.

At 1500 ... Or 3:00?

Aside from the different time zones that one must be familiar with, different countries also utilize different methods of telling time. What is known in the United States as "military time" is just plain time for our global partners. 8:00 a.m. in U.S. time is 800 hours; 3:00 p.m. is 1500 hours. The trick? Add 12 to the p.m. hours. While in casual conversation all people might not use the 24-hour system. In fact, many Europeans drop the "hours," calling the time just by the number. Don't be surprised if your international travel agent reminds you that your flight leaves at 2200!

Thinking Critically

What are some benefits of the 24-hour time system?

ADVANTAGES AND DISADVANTAGES OF TRUCK TRANSPORTATION Trucks are a convenient form of transportation. They can pick up products from a manufacturer, wholesaler, or retailer and deliver them door-to-door to any geographical location. Trucks help reduce the packaging costs for some products because goods require less protective packaging. Trucks can make rapid deliveries of large amounts of goods and therefore reduce the need to carry large inventories between shipments.

The disadvantages of using motor carriers include susceptibility to delays due to traffic jams, equipment breakdowns, and traffic accidents. Trucks are also subject to size and weight restrictions enforced by states.

■ Rail Transportation

Railroads are a major type of transportation in the United States. Trains transport nearly 38 percent of the total intercity *ton-miles* of freight. A ton-mile is the movement of one ton of freight one mile.

Trains are important for moving heavy and bulky freight, such as coal, steel, lumber, chemicals, grain, farm equipment, and automobiles over long distances. To compete with motor carriers, railroads have aggressively advertised the benefits of shipping by rail.

More About . . .

Trucking

In August 1991 Congress eliminated state regulation and interstate tariffs on motor carriers, except for carriers of household goods. Now the states only regulate insurance and safety, so there are fewer distinctions between common or private carriers and exempt carriers than previously.

At 1500 . . . Or 3:00?

Answer Answers will vary but may include that the 24-hour time system doesn't create confusion about the hour being in the morning, afternoon, or night.

Independent Practice

Draw and Identify Have students create a map of the United States with the key waterway shipping routes marked as both internal and intracoastal. Also on this map, they should identify at least two products likely to be transported over each major waterway.

PRICING AND DELIVERY SERVICES Railroads offer several specialized and innovative pricing and delivery services, including *piggyback service, fishyback service, specialized service, package cars, diversion-in-transit,* and *processing-in-transit.*

PIGGYBACK AND FISHYBACK SERVICE *Piggyback service* gets its name from carrying (piggybacking) loaded truck trailers over land on railroad flatcars. *Fishyback service* is shipping loaded truck trailers over water on ships and barges. Piggyback and fishyback services combine the advantages of truck transportation with the lower costs of rail and water transportation.

Some products need to be hauled in special railroad cars. Refrigerated cars keep perishable products such as milk or fresh vegetables from spoiling over long distances. Other specially designed freight cars haul combustible or hazardous materials, such as chemicals.

Shippers pay lower rail transportation rates if they fill an entire boxcar. A **carload** is the minimum number of pounds of freight needed to fill a boxcar. Carload weights are established for different classifications of goods. Once a shipment reaches the minimum weight, the shipper pays the lower rate, regardless of the size of the car. A *less than carload* is a shipment that falls short of minimum weight requirements for filling a freight car. Rates charged for less than carload shipments are more expensive because partial carloads have to be unloaded at each destination. Unloading time and the extra effort involved increase the rates charged to shippers.

Package (or pool) arrangements allow several shippers who are sending their items to a common destination to combine their items to fill an entire carload. If sold separately, each shipper would have to pay a higher rate since it would be shipping less than a carload. *Diversion-in-transit* service allows the redirection of carloads already en route. A vegetable grower in the South can send vegetables north and find the best price for them while they are en route. The railroad will divert the shipment to the buyer for a fee—even if the buyer is not at the originally anticipated destination. *Processing-in-transit* permits shippers to have products processed, repackaged, and assembled while in transit to their final destination.

ADVANTAGES AND DISADVANTAGES OF RAIL TRANSPORTATION Railroads can ship at relatively low costs by handling large quantities. Trains are seldom slowed or stopped by bad weather.

The biggest disadvantage of train transportation is the lack of flexibility. Trains can pick up and deliver goods only at stations along designated rail lines, and therefore can not reach as many places as motor carriers are able to.

■ Water Transportation

Shipment over water is one of the oldest methods of transporting merchandise. Ships carry merchandise from one part of the United States to others, as well as around the world. The United States Maritime Commission regulates U.S. water transportation.

Chapter 22 ■ *Physical Distribution* **397**

CAPTION ANSWER
The Best of Both Worlds Piggybacking service combines the advantages of truck transportation with the lower costs of rail transportation. Some products require special rail cars, such as refrigerated cars for perishables.

Math Skills

L1 Motor carriers ship 24 percent of the ton-miles of freight transported in the United States. If railroads ship one and one-half times more than this, what percentage of the ton-miles is shipped by train? *(36%. 1.5 x .24 = 0.36 = 36%)*

L2 Pipelines carry about 24 percent of the ton-miles of freight transported in the United States. Air transportation is less than 1 percent of the ton-miles of freight shipped. Motor carriers ship 24 percent of the ton-miles of freight shipped; railroads ship one and one-half more. Have students make a pie chart titled "Freight Shipment by Carrier" that shows the percentage of ton-miles shipped by motor carrier, railroad, pipelines, air transportation, and waterways/other. They will have to determine the percentage for waterways/other, given the other statistics. *(Graphs should reflect these percentages: motor carriers, 24%; railroads, 36%; pipelines, 24%; air transportation, 1%; waterways/other, 15%.)*

INTERNAL AND INTRACOASTAL WATERWAYS

Internal shipping is shipping from one port to another on connecting rivers and lakes. The St. Lawrence Seaway, the Mississippi River, the Ohio River, and the Great Lakes are important internal shipping routes. The St. Lawrence Seaway, which is a combination of rivers, canals, and lakes, and the Mississippi and Ohio Rivers all give ocean-going vessels access to the heartland of America. Agricultural and industrial products of the Midwest are regularly shipped from the Great Lakes to other parts of the world.

Intracoastal shipping is the shipping of goods between ports along the Atlantic or Pacific coasts or from one coast to the other. Shipments can be sent from the New York Port Authority to the San Francisco Port Authority through the Panama Canal.

INTERNATIONAL WATERWAYS
International waterways are the oceans and rivers that connect continents and countries. Transportation by water is particularly important for international product shipments. Almost all overseas freight is transported by ships and barges because of the low cost. Products commonly shipped by international waterways include heavy equipment, steel, ore, forest products, grain, and petroleum. As international trade continues to increase, so will the use of shipping by international waterways.

■ **Waterways** Waterways are a transportation method of choice for many companies. *Why is this true?*

ADVANTAGES AND DISADVANTAGES OF WATER TRANSPORTATION
The biggest advantage of waterway transportation is low cost—ships and barges are the cheapest form of freight transportation. However, they are also the slowest form of transportation. Speed is not a problem when shipping bulky, non-perishable items, such as coal, forest products, and cement. Perishable goods such as dairy products, however, require shippers to use other forms of transportation so they can reach their destination before they perish.

Water transportation has some other disadvantages. Buyers that are located far from the port city must have products off-loaded from ships onto railroad cars or motor carriers to reach their destination. This added cost of distribution reduces the cost advantages of water transportation.

Water transportation is affected by bad weather. Great Lakes shipping, for example, is generally closed for two to three months in the winter.

■ Pipelines

Pipelines are normally owned by the company using them, so they are usually considered private carriers. There are more than 200,000 miles of pipelines in the United States.

Pipelines are most frequently used to transport oil and natural gas. They move crude oil from oil field to refinery, where it is processed. The refined products, such as gasoline, are then trucked to retail outlets such as your local gasoline station.

Pipelines are more important in the physical distribution process than most people know. They carry approximately 20 percent of the ton-miles of freight transported in the United States.

ADVANTAGES AND DISADVANTAGES OF PIPELINE TRANSPORTATION
The construction of pipelines requires a high initial investment, but operational costs are small. The risk of a pipeline leak is small, but when a leak does occur the damage to the environment can be extensive. The National Transportation Safety Board and the U.S. Department of Transportation have determined that pipelines have the best safety record among all major transportation systems. Products carried through pipelines move slowly but continuously, suffer minimal product damage or theft, and are not subjected to delivery delays due to bad weather.

■ **Overnight Delivery** Air transportation is a growing segment of the transportation industry. *What items are generally sent by air?*

■ Air Transportation

Currently, air transportation is less than one percent of the total ton-miles of freight shipped. High-value, low-weight items such as overnight mail are often shipped by air. Certain high-value products, such as emergency parts, instruments, medicines, flowers, and perishable food products are also shipped by air.

Air freight is the most costly form of distribution. However, its speed may create some savings in lower inventory. Because air freight has space constraints, the items usually carried are valuable, light-weight, and time sensitive. Products transported in containers are also well-suited to this form of shipment. There are specialized firms that offer ground support to businesses that use air freight. These specialized firms collect shipments and deliver them to the air terminal.

When air freight is handled by a major airline such as United, Delta, or Air Canada, it is often carried as cargo in the luggage space of passenger flights. This allows passenger airlines to use excess capacity that would otherwise be lost. When air freight is carried by specialized air freight companies, it is usually carried in the body of the plane.

The Federal Aviation Administration (FAA) regulates air transportation. It does not regulate charges for air freight. Airlines and air transport companies set their own rates. Air freight carriers offer such things as wide-bodied jets that can ship more goods and specialized packaging designed to help prevent

REAL WORLD MARKETING

Changing Channels

What happens when manufacturers suggest to customers where to buy their goods? Baume & Mercier, the luxury Swiss watchmaker, took out a full-page ad in the Wall Street Journal warning consumers not to buy their goods through the discount retailer Ashford.com. This cut-throat competition isn't exactly fashionable. The e-tailing sector has a term for the trouble that Ashford.com is stirring up—channel conflict. It happens when a manufacturer threatens its existing retailers by selling products through a more efficient channel like the Web. Is this really bad news for Baume & Mercier? On the day the ad ran, Ashford's sales of the $1,000-plus Swiss watches doubled!

Thinking Critically
What are the pros and cons of Baume & Mercier not doing business with certain retailers?

damage. Specialized freight planes now under development will soon allow air carriers to reach and serve even more markets.

ADVANTAGES AND DISADVANTAGES OF AIR TRANSPORTATION The greatest advantage to air transportation is its speed. Many companies, such as Airborne, DHL, Federal Express, United Parcel Service, and the U.S. Postal Service advertise overnight delivery. This fast delivery time allows businesses to satisfy customers who need something quickly. It also reduces inventory expenses and storage costs for warehousing products.

The greatest disadvantage of air transportation is its cost. It is the most expensive form of distribution. Air shipment rates are usually twice as costly as truck rates. For some shippers, however, the advantage of greater speed of delivery may outweigh the extra costs. Other disadvantages of air transportation include mechanical breakdowns and delays in delivery caused by bad weather.

Chapter 22 ■ *Physical Distribution* **399**

SECTION 22.1

Individualized Practice

L3 Parcel post is used for shipping small packages weighing between 16 ounces and 70 pounds. Have students tell whether the following packages would be shipped by parcel post:

- 1,200 ounces *(No. This is 75 pounds. 1,200 oz. x 16 oz = 75 pounds)*
- 928 ounces *(Yes. This is 58 pounds. 928 oz. x 16 oz = 58 pounds)*
- 1,088 ounces *(Yes. This is 68 pounds. 1,088 oz. x 16 oz = 68 pounds)*
- 32 ounces *(Yes. This is 2 pounds. 32 oz. x 16 oz = 2 pounds)*
- 1,120 ounces *(Yes. This is 70 pounds. 1,120 oz. x 16 oz = 70 pounds)*

CAPTION ANSWER
Overnight Delivery High value, lightweight items, such as overnight mail, specialty parts, and certain food products are often sent by air.

REAL WORLD MARKETING

Changing Channels
Answer Baume & Mercier works very hard at protecting its image as a reputable manufacturer of luxury items. By limiting its distribution to only the retailers they choose, Baume & Mercier retains control of its image. However, they lose distribution in other areas.

Reteaching

1. **Vocabulary** Assign and review the vocabulary terms for this section.
2. **Fact and Idea** Assign and review Fact and Idea Review questions 1–7 from the Chapter Assessment.
3. **Methods of Transportation** List on the board the five methods of transportation used in physical distribution and have students generate at least five products normally transported by each.

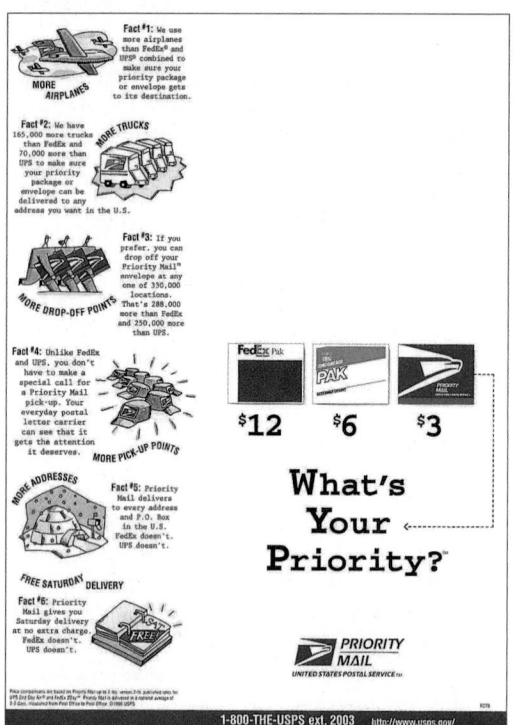

■ **Through Rain, Hail, Sleet, or Snow** The U.S. Postal Service competes with other transportation service companies. *After looking at the advantages in the ad, why do shippers use other express companies?*

Transportation Service Companies

Transportation service companies handle small- and medium-size packages. Some examples of these companies are the *U.S. Postal Service, express carriers, bus package carriers,* and *freight forwarders.*

■ U.S. Postal Service

The U.S. Postal Service ships small packages by parcel post or fourth-class mail. This includes packages weighing more than 16 ounces, as well as newspapers and magazines and printed matter that weighs less than 16 ounces (but not postcards and letters). Parcel post is used most often for shipping large and oversized packages weighing less than 70 pounds and not more than 130 inches in combined length and girth (distance around). Parcel post can be insured against loss or damage or sent COD (cash on delivery). Parcel post can also be express-mailed at higher rates to guarantee next-day delivery.

In recent years the U.S. Postal Service has seen tremendous growth with its *Priority Mail* product. *Priority Mail* is marketed as a quick, convenient, reliable, and cost-effective way to deliver important correspondence within a two–three day period or for an extra charge, overnight delivery.

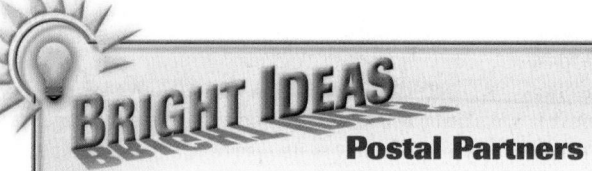

BRIGHT IDEAS
Postal Partners

When there is a task at hand that someone else can handle better, it is best to delegate. LeShop, the first online store of its kind in Europe, heeds this lesson well! LeShop sells packaged food and personal products, such as soaps, diapers, and toothpaste, to Swiss customers. Next morning delivery is guaranteed for orders received by 4:30 p.m. LeShop knew that meeting this guarantee would be a challenge and found an outside business partner in a most ingenious place—the Swiss Post Office. The Post Office controls the logistics for the entire distribution. Validated orders are electronically transmitted to postal employees who fill LeShop's boxes with the requested inventory. Boxes are then placed into the traditional mail postal circuit. Customers are charged an additional 10 Swiss francs (about $7.00), but demand keeps rising. Convenience is worth the price in a country where things are expected to run like fine Swiss clockwork.

Thinking Creatively

What other products could LeShop offer with its timely delivery to attract customers?

CAPTION ANSWER
Through Rain, Hail, Sleet, or Snow They may use other companies because of convenience. Other transportation service companies pick up packages directly from the shipper location. The U.S. Postal Service lacks sophisticated computer systems to track customers and packages effectively.

BRIGHT IDEAS   Postal Partners
Answer Answers will vary, but Le Shop may offer items that are needed within certain time frames, such as prescriptions, meals, and video rentals.

Case Study

From Your Computer to Your Home

Federal Express—a company known for its business-to-business next-day air express service—is looking at a new market. The company is starting a new division called FedEx Home Delivery, which will handle delivery of products ordered online.

E-tailing is changing physical distribution systems. More customers are beginning to order products online and have them delivered directly to their homes or apartments. A study by Ernst & Young states that approximately 50 percent of online shoppers state convenience as their motivation to shop on the Web. FedEx Home Delivery hopes to make this process even easier for customers. FedEx Home Delivery faces keen competition from United Parcel Service (UPS) and the U.S. Postal Service. UPS handled about 55 percent and the U.S. Postal Service about 30 percent of the holiday 1999 deliveries ordered over the Web. Only 10 percent was handled by the existing Federal Express ground-based system.

Experts feel that UPS is currently more focused on the business-to-consumer market than Federal Express is. The U.S. Postal Service already delivers mail to every household in the country.

Federal Express is interested in securing a bigger piece of the action. In 1999, $20 billion in goods was ordered and shipped over the Internet. Internet sales are expected to rise to $180 billion by 2004. Although delivering to homes is more costly than business-to-business deliveries, it still adds to profits. Schedules can be maximized because air express work can be done in the morning, business-to-business deliveries in the afternoon, and residential deliveries in the evening.

FedEx Home Delivery will use smaller trucks to deliver packages in the evening and on Saturdays when most people are home. Federal Express is also offering customers the option of scheduling an appointment at a time that is convenient for the customer. Federal Express plans to provide a Web site that will allow both shippers and customers to track their orders. This service aids not only consumers but also telecommuters who work from home. As an increasing number of employees work from home, there is a greater need for guaranteed and timely home delivery.

Case Study Review

1. Why does Federal Express want to enter the home delivery market?
2. Why are home deliveries more expensive?

A MATTER OF ETHICS

3. Is it ethical for a government agency to compete with private companies for business? Why or why not?

Enrichment

1. **Review** Assign and review the appropriate Thinking Critically questions from the Chapter Assessment.
2. **Extend** Assign and review the corresponding activities from *BusinessWeek Case Studies, Internet Resources,* and the *School-to-Work Activity Workbook.* **ILP**
3. **Identify** If your school has a school store, have students identify how various merchandise arrived at the store. They should give the name of the carrier and also indicate the type of carrier—common, private, exempt, or contract.
4. **Identify and Research** Identify several of the common carriers in your state. Have students investigate the scope of each business and the number of employees that each company has. Have students share their findings with the class.

Chapter 22 ■ *Physical Distribution* **401**

Case Study Review Answers

From Your Computer to Your Home

1. More customers are ordering products online and having them delivered to their homes and apartments.
2. Answers will vary, but may include increased overhead.

A MATTER OF ETHICS

3. Answers will vary.

Evaluation

Assign and review the Section 22.1 Assessment.

Technology Resources

 Assessment Resources
Go to the *Marketing Essentials* Web site (**www.marketing.glencoe. com**) for resources to teach and assess occupation-specific vocabulary.

CLOSE

Section Wrap-Up

Have students complete these statements:

1. Physical distribution is . . . *(the process of transporting, storing, order processing, stock handling, and inventory control to make materials and products available to customers.)*

2. Physical distribution includes . . . *(freight transportation, warehousing, materials handling, protective packaging, inventory control, warehouse site selection, order processing, and customer service.)*

3. Physical distribution is a key link between . . . *(a business and its customers.)*

■ Express Carriers

Express carriers specialize in delivering small, lightweight packages and high-priority mail usually weighing less than 150 pounds. Express parcel carriers, such as Federal Express, DHL, and United Parcel Service, offer door-to-door pickup, delivery, and COD service. Express shipments may be made nationally or internationally by airplane, truck, bus, or train. Rates are based on speed, weight, distance to be sent, size of package, and type of service used. Regular service usually takes from two to three days; more expensive, next-day service is also available.

Over the last 30 years, express carriers have become a more important part of physical distribution. Federal Express, which began operations in 1973, now transports more than 3.3 million packages daily. It has a worldwide fleet of more than 650 aircraft, 150,000 employees, and 1200 service centers serving 210 countries.

DHL, another popular express carrier, started in 1969 shipping from San Francisco to Honolulu. They were the first to introduce express international shipping via airplane to the Eastern Bloc in 1983 and to China in 1986. Today, DHL Worldwide Express is the largest company that specializes in international express shipping. They can send packages to approximately 635,000 destinations in over 233 countries and territories.

■ Bus Package Carriers

Bus package carriers provide transportation services for packages weighing less than 100 pounds. Bus package carriers, such as Greyhound, can provide same-day or next-day service to cities and towns along their scheduled routes. As with other forms of shipping, the cost of bus package transportation depends on the weight of the package and the distance it will travel.

Greyhound may run numerous buses daily to major cities, such as New York, Boston, Chicago, or San Francisco. This is attractive to shippers as they have many options to deliver their products quickly, while at a reasonable rate.

■ Freight Forwarders

Freight forwarders are private companies that combine *less-than carload* or *less-than truckload* shipments from several different businesses and deliver them to their destinations. They accumulate small shipments into larger lots and then hire a carrier to move them, usually at reduced rates. By combining shipments, freight forwarders can often obtain truckload or carload rates and lower transportation costs for shippers. Freight forwarders also provide logistical services that help businesses select the best transportation methods and routes.

22.1 ASSESSMENT

Reviewing Key Terms and Concepts

1. What is physical distribution?
2. What function does transportation play in marketing a product?
3. Identify five transportation systems for the distribution of products.
4. What is the difference between a common and a contract carrier?
5. List four different examples of transportation service companies.

Thinking Critically

6. Many retail distribution and transportation executives support federal legislation that would reduce state trucking regulations. What do you see as potential benefits and disadvantages of this effort?

Integrating Academic Skills

7. **COMMUNICATION** Research and write a 100-word paper about the advantages and disadvantages of federal deregulation of the trucking industry.

22.1 ASSESSMENT ANSWERS

Reviewing Key Terms and Concepts

1. It involves the transporting, storing, order processing, stock handling, and inventory control of materials and products.
2. movement of products from a seller to a buyer
3. motor carriers, railroads, waterways, pipelines, air carriers, transportation service companies
4. Common carriers provide transportation services to any business in its operating area for a fee; a contract carrier is a "for hire" carrier that provides equipment and drivers for specific routes.
5. express carriers, bus package carriers, freight forwarders, and the U.S. Postal Service

Thinking Critically

6. Answers may vary.

Integrating Academic Skills

7. **COMMUNICATION** Papers will vary.

Inventory Storage

The Storage of Goods

Storage is the marketing function of holding goods until they are sold. The amount of goods stored is called an inventory. We will talk more about inventories in Chapter 24.

Storing goods is an essential activity for most businesses. Each business member in a channel of distribution needs to store its products until orders are received from customers.

Products might also need to be stored because production has outpaced consumption or demand decreases. Sometimes, certain agricultural commodities such as corn, wheat, and soybeans may be available only during certain times. Commodity storage helps to stabilize prices for the product. Some purchasers buy in quantity to get discounts on their purchases and then store the items until they are needed. Finally, products are stored at convenient locations to provide faster delivery to customers.

Storing goods adds time and place utility to products. Products should be available for customers when and where they want them. The costs involved in storing products include space, equipment, and personnel. Storage also involves the cost of tying up money (or capital) in inventory rather than investing it in an activity that could provide a larger return. Businesses must balance the costs of holding merchandise in inventory against the possibility of not having merchandise available for customers when they want to purchase it.

Determining where to store goods is an important decision. Products are stored in a number of ways. Cars and trucks are frequently stored in outdoor lots, petroleum products in specialized storage tanks, and grain in grain elevators. Efficient, adequate storage reduces the storage costs for a business and helps assure good customer service. Most products are stored in warehouses—facilities in which goods are received, identified, sorted, stored, and dispatched for shipment. Let's take a closer look at the type of warehouses businesses use.

■ Private Warehouses

A private warehouse is a facility designed to meet the specific needs of its owner. Any producer, wholesaler, or retailer has the option of owning its own private warehouse. A private warehouse is valuable for companies that move a large volume of products. Specialized conditions, such as a temperature-controlled environment, may be built into the facility. Private warehouses often house other parts of the business operation, such as offices.

• What You'll Learn

- The concept and function of inventory storage
- The types of warehouses
- How distribution planning works for international markets

• Why It's Important

Most products must be kept for a time in a safe location until they are needed or ready to be sold. In this section, you will be introduced to the concept of inventory storage and learn about the places where products are kept until they are distributed to customers.

Key Terms

- storage
- private warehouse
- public warehouse
- distribution center
- bonded warehouses

Chapter 22 ■ *Physical Distribution* **403**

FOCUS

Bell Ringer Activity

Storage Have students generate reasons why products need to be stored until they are sold, taking into consideration the needs of a producer, manufacturer, a wholesaler, and a retailer.

Introducing the Section

Inventory Storage Based on the list students generated in the Bell Ringer Activity, ask them how storage adds time and place utility to products. Tell students that in this section they will look at the marketing function of storage.

TEACH

📊 Technology Resources

PowerPoint The *Marketing Essentials* PowerPoint Presentation CD-ROM provides visual lecture aids for every chapter section.

Concept Development

1. Read Section 22.2 with students.
2. As you discuss the contents of this section, encourage students to identify the various types of storage facilities in your community and the types of goods each holds.
3. Assign and review the Chapter 22 Activity in the *School-to-Work Activity Workbook*.

Classroom Resources

For the Teacher
- Teacher Editions for all workbooks
- Assessment Package
- PowerPoint Presentation Software
- Interactive Lesson Planner
- **ILP** Block Scheduling, p. 7
- **ILP** Lesson Plans, p. 48
- **ILP** Internet Resources, p. 63

- **ILP** *BusinessWeek* Case Studies, p. 139
- **ILP** Marketing Career Portfolio, p. 37
- *Marketing Essentials* Web site (**www.marketing.glencoe.com**)

For the Student
- Student Activity Workbook, p. 187
- Marketing Math Workbook, p. 59

- Marketing Research Project Workbook, p. 111
- **ILP** School-to-Work Activity Workbook, p. 93
- Virtual Business simulation
- *Marketing Essentials* Web site (**www.marketing.glencoe.com**)

ILP These resources are available in print and on the Interactive Lesson Planner (ILP)

403

■ **Ensuring a Rapid Turnaround** Distribution centers are designed to speed delivery of products while minimizing the time that they are stored. *Why is moving the product quickly so important?*

Private warehouses are costly to build and maintain. In a recent survey, large retailers reported spending 51 percent of their total physical distribution costs on warehouse expenses; transportation costs accounted for the remaining 49 percent. Larger retailers, such as Sears, Radio Shack, and Kmart link their private warehouses to the purchasing and distribution activities of their retail outlets. Private warehouses should be considered only when a significant amount of merchandise needs to be stored, and the total operating costs are lower than those of public warehouses.

■ Public Warehouses

A public warehouse offers storage and handling facilities to individuals or companies. It is a facility available to any company that will pay for its use. Public warehouses not only rent space but also provide services to businesses. These services include shipment consolidation, receiving, unloading, inspecting, reshipping, order filling, and truck terminal operation services. Public warehouses are helpful to businesses that have low volume storage needs or seasonal production.

There are five types of public warehouses:

- *Commodity warehouses* are used primarily for agricultural products, such as tobacco, cotton, or grain.

- *Bulk storage warehouses* keep products only in bulk form, such as chemicals and oil.
- *Cold storage warehouses* store perishables such as fruits, vegetables, and frozen products.
- *Household goods warehouses* handle personal property storage, household articles, and furniture.
- *General merchandise warehouses* store any item that does not require specialized handling.

■ Distribution Centers

A variation of the private and public warehouse is the distribution center—a warehouse designed to speed delivery of goods and to minimize storage costs. The main focus in a distribution center is on moving products, not on storing them. Distribution centers are planned around markets rather than transportation requirements. They can cut costs by reducing the number of warehouses and cutting excessive inventory. Because companies are in business to sell goods, not to store or ship them, warehousing and delivery times must be cut to a minimum. Distribution centers help in this regard. Since warehousing adds 5 to 7 percent to the cost of merchandise, there is no value added in keeping merchandise stored for very long. Goods in storage do not make money for a business.

Some distribution centers also assist in physically changing the final customer product by changing its appearance, mixing ingredients, labeling, and repackaging it. Sherwin-Williams and Benjamin Moore are paint companies that use their distribution centers in this way.

Distribution centers consolidate large orders from many sources and redistribute them as separate orders for individual accounts or stores within a chain. Merchandise normally stays only a short time in a distribution center.

■ Bonded Warehouses

Bonded warehouses, either public or private, store products that require the payment of a federal tax. Imported or domestic products cannot be removed from a bonded warehouse until the required federal tax is paid. Businesses save on taxes by taking goods out of storage only when they are needed.

■ **Challenges of International Distribution**
Distribution planning for an international
marketplace has several unique challenges.
What are some of the challenges?

ORDERING CHINESE?

© 2000 FedEx. See FedEx Service Guide for terms of carriage.

FedEx provides direct service from the U.S. to the most Asian cities, including Hong Kong,
Beijing, Shanghai and Shenzhen. From Taipei to Tokyo, from Seoul to Singapore, FedEx
is your gateway to the Far East. And now FedEx introduces the International Resource Center,
the one stop for all your international trade needs. Let our International Document Assistance
program guide you through the customary red tape of international shipping. Find out
more about the International Resource Center and our full menu of FedEx services at
fedex.com or call 1-800-Go-FedEx. Be absolutely sure.®

FedEx Express

■ Distribution Planning for International Markets

Distribution is of critical importance in global marketing. Exports now support one-sixth of the manufacturing and agricultural output of the United States. International trade will continue to expand along with the need for worldwide physical distribution systems. This is because of the growing importance of electronic commerce, the increasing popularity of free-market economics, the sweeping away of global trade barriers, and the establishment of regional trading blocs such as the European Union, the Association of South East Asian Nations, and the North American Free Trade Agreement (NAFTA).

Selling to customers in the international marketplace requires even more planning than for selling within domestic markets. Businesses that sell internationally must follow U.S. export laws as well as the import laws of the countries to which they are selling. Some countries also have legal restrictions about how products may be transported. Businesses frequently have to deal with bureaucratic regulations, language barriers, and tedious negotiations.

The need for extensive planning becomes even more obvious when you consider that parts for many products are made in different countries. Car manufacturers often use parts made in several countries. The parts are shipped to assembly plants in other countries where the final product is put together and ultimately shipped to still other destinations. Planning for the best method of transporting parts from each country for each step of the process is the key to keeping the assembly lines running and the final products getting to buyers like you.

To deliver their goods successfully, businesses must understand other countries' physical transportation systems. Once a product reaches a foreign

ASSESS

Reteaching

1. **Vocabulary** Assign and review the vocabulary terms for this section.
2. **Fact and Idea** Assign and review Fact and Idea Review questions 8–10 from the Chapter Assessment.
3. **Identify and Brainstorm** Write these products on the board, then have the students tell you in which type of public warehouse each would likely be stored:
   - broccoli *(cold storage)*
   - cotton *(commodity)*
   - chemicals *(bulk)*
   - personal bicycle and skis *(household goods)*
   - apples *(cold storage)*
   - washing machines (general merchandise)
   - wheat *(commodity)*
   - furniture *(household goods)*
   - oil *(bulk)*
   - toys *(general merchandise)*

Enrichment

1. **Review** Assign and review the Chapter 22 activities in the *Student Activity Workbook.*
2. **Review** Assign and review the appropriate Thinking Critically questions from the Chapter Assessment.
3. **Review** Assign and review the following Chapter Assessment activities: Building Workplace Skills, Applying Marketing Concepts, Linking School to Work, The DECA Connection Role Play.
4. **Research and Report** Have the students use library resources and personal interviews to research a career-sustaining job in distribution. Have the students share their findings with the class.

CAPTION ANSWER
Challenges of International Distribution Some challenges include language barriers, bureaucratic red tape, and differing physical distribution networks.

THE ◀DECA▶ CONNECTION   **COMPETITIVE EVENTS AND MARKETING ESSENTIALS**

Learn and Earn Project DECA's Learn and Earn Project Event serves as a tie-in to this chapter's content. The guidelines specify that the project your class conducts be operated using marketing and management skills. Section IV B asks for specific information about suppliers and inventory policies, providing a real-life illustration of this chapter's competencies.

The primary focus of the Learn and Earn Project is the learning outcomes in the form of enhanced marketing and management skills through first-hand experience. Additionally, the favorable publicity generated by the Learn and Earn Project will reflect positively on your students and program.

Evaluation

Assign and review the Section 22.2 Assessment.

Technology Resources

GO TO **Assessment Resources**
Go to the *Marketing Essentials* Web site (**www.marketing.glencoe.com**) for resources to teach and assess occupation-specific vocabulary.

CLOSE

Section Wrap-Up

Have students complete this statement: Storage is . . . *(the marketing function of holding goods until they are sold.)*

Digital Distribution

Answer Answers will vary, but may include music videos, motion pictures, and games.

---

nation, that country's distribution channels take over. The sophistication of a country's distribution channels increases as its economic infrastructure develops. In some less developed nations, the postal system may not be reliable enough to assure delivery of small packages by mail. Other countries may not have well-developed roads and highway systems to support dependable motor carrier deliveries. In China, for example, much of the distribution of goods is done through human labor. Most goods are carried by hand, in handcarts or via bicycle.

Another consideration is how retail institutions in other countries differ from American retail institutions. In most of the world, retailers have little or no capacity for refrigeration. For example, when Coke and Pepsi entered China, both had to create direct-distribution channels, investing in trucks and refrigerator units for small retailers. American-style supermarkets are rare in developing countries. In Japan, the term supermarket refers to a type of retail outfit that is very different from an American supermarket. They are often multi-story buildings that sell food as well as clothing, furniture, and appliances.

As global trade becomes more important to the success or failure of firms of all types and sizes, a well-planned global logistics strategy becomes increasingly important. Uncertainty regarding international distribution channels is the number one reason companies stay out of international markets.

Digital Distribution

Who would have thought that physical distribution would become a "dinosaur" in the music industry? As technology adjusts how basic things are done, there are new ways to listen to and receive music. Digital technology now allows music to be sent and received over the Internet. Anyone with a powerful computer, speakers, and an Internet connection can hear music electronically. Streaming audio allows for radio-like Web casts or songs to be played online. Advances in technology such as satellite or cable modems and MP3 players have made for quicker and broader distribution of music. Unfortunately, digital distribution also allows for the "piracy" or trading of music without payment. This loophole has the recording industry fuming.

Thinking Critically
With the evolution of technology, what other products could evolve from physical to digital distribution?

22.2 ASSESSMENT

Reviewing Key Terms and Concepts

1. What is the function of storage?
2. Give four reasons why merchandise is stored.
3. What is a warehouse? List the four types of warehouses.
4. How does a distribution center differ from a warehouse?
5. Describe at least three reasons why planning is important for distribution in international markets.

Thinking Critically

6. Most of the inland waterways were developed with federal funds, while the oil companies built pipelines themselves. Why do you think the federal government supports one mode of transportation and not the other?

Integrating Academic Skills

7. **MATH** The George A. Stinson is the second largest freighter on the Great Lakes. Normally, it carries 57,000 tons of taconite ore each voyage between Superior, Wisconsin, and Detroit, Michigan. Due to lower lake levels, it can only carry 50,000 tons per trip. At $5 per ton, how much revenue is lost per trip?

22.2 ASSESSMENT ANSWERS

Reviewing Key Terms and Concepts
1. to hold goods until they can be sold
2. Merchandise is stored to facilitate delivery to purchaser, when production has outpaced demand, for seasonal storage, and to take advantage of quantity purchases.
3. It is a facility in which goods are received, identified, sorted, stored, and dispatched. private, public, bonded, distribution

4. Distribution centers focus on moving products; warehouses focus on storing them.
5. language difficulties, bureaucratic regulations, and different legal customs

Thinking Critically
6. Inland waterways had few improvements.

Integrating Academic Skills
7. **MATH** $35,000

Careers in Marketing

SERVICE MARKETING

Eddie Habbaz
Logistics Manager, International
Warehouse Logistics Association

What does your job entail?

"My job is to ensure the availability of the specified product, in the correct quantity, at the right place and time. It is necessary to get the product to the customer in good condition and at the best cost. Logistics managers work with managers who are responsible for the operation of the company. The job requires evaluating company systems that handle the acquisition, transportation, storage, and distribution of supplies, materials, and finished products. By analyzing the systems controlling the flow of materials and products, they propose improvements to increase profitability and customer satisfaction."

What skills are most important?

"Logistics managers must use observational and analytical skills to assess the efficiency of existing distribution systems. Logistics managers gather information from staff and customers and communicate their findings with those in charge of management systems. Logistic managers work with many different people; this requires good people skills."

What kind of training do you recommend for students?

"Students should take business courses in high school and seek an internship. It is recommended to go on to college for business administration or industrial engineering. Experience with a company working in such areas as project management, planning, inventory control, purchasing, or customer relations is valuable."

What is your key to success?

"My key to success lies in the understanding that each customer must be made to feel that his or her business is the single most important business in the universe. If customers do not feel valued, they may take their business somewhere else."

Thinking Critically
What other professionals do you think logistics managers work with frequently?

Career Facts

Education and Training: Logistics managers generally have a minimum of a bachelor's degree in business administration or industrial engineering. Five to six years of experience in areas such as project management, planning, inventory, purchasing, or customer relations provide valuable background experience for logistics managers. Coursework in statistics, economics, and quantitative mathematics is recommended.

Aptitude, Abilities, and Skills: Strong observational and analytical skills, in addition to mathematical skills, are required. Good communication skills, ability to delegate, effective management, and computer familiarity are vital.

Career Outlook: The outlook for logistics managers is excellent, with the demand exceeding the supply.

Career Path: Because logistics managers are exposed to many operations within an organization, they can advance to supervisory and management positions.

Chapter 22 Physical Distribution **407**

Careers in Marketing

Ask a student to read the Careers in Marketing feature aloud to the class. Discuss the skills and aptitudes required for a career in service marketing. Ask students whether they think they would like or dislike a career in service marketing. Discuss the pros and cons of such a career.

Thinking Critically Answer
Answers will vary.

Guest Speakers
Invite a logistics manager to class to discuss his/her job and factors he/she considers when making marketing decisions.

Exploring Careers

Words to Know on the Job
1. Explain to students that the work environment has its own vocabulary. On the board, write the following list of terms: salary, entry-level, commission, minimum wage, and discriminate.
2. Then read the following sentences to students, and ask them to fill in the blanks with the correct term from the list.
1) *Salary* is a fixed amount of money paid for a certain period of time, such as a month.
2) A lower-level, full-time job is called an *entry-level* job.
3) If you work on *commission*, you earn your pay based on how much you sell.
4) The *minimum wage* is the lowest hourly wage an employer can pay for a worker's services.
5) To say that an employer cannot *discriminate* against you means you cannot be treated unfairly because of race, age, gender, religion, nationality, or physical appearance.

Lifelong Learning

Physical Distribution
Students who are not planning careers in the physical distribution area of marketing might not be aware of innovations in methods of transportation or new regulations. However, these factors will impact students through prices they pay. Students can keep informed by reading business magazines, such as *BusinessWeek* and *The Wall Street Journal*.

Meeting Individual Needs

Students with Speech Impairments
Students with speech impairments benefit from contributing to the class through activities other than in-class discussion. Students might prepare a bulletin board display or a report on a topic that can be distributed to the class. The opportunity to participate is the key, and involvement can grow if students are given regular opportunities.

Vocabulary Review

1. carload
2. physical distribution
3. common carrier
4. private carrier
5. transportation
6. exempt carriers
7. ton-mile
8. storage

Fact and Idea Review

1. Transportation function is an important function because once something has been sold, it must be moved.
2. Differences will vary.
3. Some advantages may include convenience, reduction in packaging costs, and reduced inventory costs. The possible disadvantages could be higher prices for longer distances and delays due to traffic jams, equipment breakdowns, and traffic accidents.
4. Two advantages are relatively low costs for items in large quantities and few delays for bad weather. One disadvantage is the lack of flexibility.
5. agricultural, industrial, and mineral products for domestic and international shipments
6. Pipelines are usually owned by the company using them.
7. An advantage is the speed of delivery.
8. A private warehouse is a facility owned by a company, manufacturer, wholesaler, or retailer for its own use. A public warehouse is a facility available to any business that will pay for its use.
9. International businesses must follow not only U.S. export law but also relevant import law.

Thinking Critically

1. Answers will vary.
2. (a) air carrier, (b) waterways, (c) pipelines
3. The business may receive the following benefits: direct control over the facility, its inventory, its record keeping, its employees, and its service functions.
4. Answers will vary but may include personal services, such as accounting, consulting, and legal services.
5. Exports support one-sixth of the manufacturing and agricultural output of the United States. International trade will continue to grow.

VOCABULARY REVIEW

Write the term that best matches each definition given below.

1. Minimum number of pounds of freight to fill a boxcar
2. Process of transporting, storing, and handling goods
3. Provide transportation services to any business for a fee
4. Owned and operated by an individual business to provide transportation services
5. Marketing function of moving goods from sellers to buyers
6. Free from direct regulation with respect to rates and operating procedures
7. The movement of one ton of freight one mile
8. Marketing function of holding goods

FACT AND IDEA REVIEW

1. What is the transportation function and why is it important to physical distribution? (22.1)
2. Explain the differences among the four types of motor carriers. (22.1)
3. Identify the advantages and disadvantages of motor carriers. (22.1)
4. What are two advantages and one disadvantage of railroads? (22.1)
5. What types of products are typically shipped by water? (22.1)
6. Why are most pipelines classified as private carriers? (22.1)
7. What is an advantage of air transportation? (22.1)
8. What is the difference between private and public warehouses? (22.2)
9. How might international distribution differ from distribution in the United States? (22.2)

THINKING CRITICALLY

1. Identify six examples of merchandise that would be shipped by motor carrier, rail carrier, air carrier, and water carrier. Tell whether this mode of transportation would be the only one used and support your answer.
2. Identify the primary mode of physical transportation for each of these items:
   a. flowers transported from Holland to Detroit
   b. iron ore shipped from Duluth, Minnesota to New Jersey
   c. gasoline to be delivered to a local retailer
3. Why would a business use a public warehouse rather than a private warehouse?
4. Give five examples of businesses that do not require product storage.
5. Why is distribution planning for international markets increasingly important?

BUILDING WORKPLACE SKILLS

1. **Human Relations** You are a clerk in a warehouse. A carton of snack items has been damaged during a shipment. As you are filling out a report for the damaged merchandise, a coworker suggests you have some of the snacks because the warehouse will never miss them. What would you say to your coworker? How do you believe management would view your coworker's suggestion?
2. **Technology** Use trade professional journals such as *Air Cargo World, Air Transport,* and *American Shipper,* or information from the *American Trucking Association, Association of American Railroads,* or the *National Transportation Library* to research the latest technologies used by shipping companies to track merchandise from place of origin to final delivery.

Building Workplace Skills

1. Management would view this incident as possible grounds for dismissal, particularly if no attempt were made to properly record the damage.
2. Answers may include a discussion of Internet services, just-in-time pick up and delivery scanning equipment, bar codes, electronic data interchange and voice response, quick response delivery, and integrated logistics planning and control.

APPLYING MARKETING CONCEPTS

1. **Analyzing Transportation Methods** Talk to a local businessperson about why the company uses a particular type of transportation for physical distribution. Use a word processing program to prepare a 150-word report and share it with your class.

2. **Comparing Transportation Methods** Your company is shipping out samples of a new product to potential buyers around the United States. Research the least expensive and most effective way to distribute these goods if delivery time is not an issue. Create a table using a spreadsheet program comparing the different options that you have, including rail, bus, truck, or air.

3. **Visiting a Warehouse** Visit a warehouse and observe its receiving, storing, and shipping processes. Use a presentation software program to develop at least five visuals about your observations during the field trip.

4. **Finding a Warehouse** Research a warehouse business in your area using the Internet. Develop a word-processed outline identifying the Internet address, where the business is physically located, services offered, number of employees, and the type of merchandise stored there.

5. **Investigating Small Package Express Carriers** Investigate a small package express carrier (i.e. FedEx, RPS, UPS) or the U.S. Postal Service using the Internet. Prepare a report on online services and technologies available to shippers.

LINKING SCHOOL TO WORK

Systems Skills Research the transportation systems used at cooperative education training stations or places of employment. Prepare a written report on your findings, including a description of the method(s) used most frequently and the rationale for using it.

THE DECA CONNECTION

Role Play: Traffic Manager

Situation You are to assume the role of assistant traffic manager for a large company that grows oranges. Your plant superintendent (judge) has asked you to assist in the training of new employees.

Activity You must give a 15-minute talk on various types of distribution methods approved for shipping oranges. You are to explain the advantages of each method, including the methods most appropriate and most inappropriate for shipping oranges.

Evaluation You will be evaluated on how well you meet the following performance indicators:
- Explain the nature and scope of distribution
- Describe the use of technology in the distribution function
- Explain shipping procedures
- Explain storage considerations
- Explain the relationship between customer service and distribution

inter NET CONNECTION

Fly Like an Eagle
The U.S. Postal Service maintains a Web site for business and household use.

Connect
- Locate the U.S. Postal Service Web site.
- Find the business "Domestic Rate Calculator" page on the Web site.
- Calculate the cost to send a large package (length plus girth more than 84″ and less than or equal to 108″) from your city to Chicago, Illinois.

THE DECA CONNECTION

Students should be evaluated on the performance indicators noted in the Role Play.
- For another DECA Role Play, go to the *Student Activity Workbook,* p. 187.
- For more in-depth Role Play practice, refer to DECA's *Essential Competitive Events Handbook.* To order, contact DECA at **www.deca.org**.

*inter*NET CONNECTION
Answers will vary based upon location of city.

Mini Quiz
Administer the Mini Quiz orally. For an expanded chapter quiz, go to page 129 of the *Reproducible Tests* book.

1. Physical distribution is also known as <u>logistics</u>.
2. The marketing function of moving products from a seller to a buyer is called <u>distribution</u>.
3. Most motor carriers are for hire or <u>common</u> carriers.
4. The function of holding goods until they are sold is called <u>storage</u>.
5. A variation of the private and public warehouse is the <u>distribution</u> center.

Applying Marketing Concepts

1. Reports will vary depending on the business that was investigated.
2. Research and tables will vary.
3. Presentations will vary.
4. Outlines will vary.
5. Reports will vary.

Linking School to Work

Reports will vary depending on the work situation.

GO TO

1. **Assessment** Have students complete the Reproducible Test for Chapter 22 or construct your own tests using the ExamView software.
2. **Enrichment** Have students complete the corresponding activities in the following workbooks:
   - *Marketing Math Workbook,* p. 59
   - *Marketing Research Project Workbook,* p. 111

Chapter Overview

Chapter 23 examines the duties of organizational buyers, both in the industrial market and the reseller market. How buyers plan and calculate purchases is covered in Section 23.1. Section 23.2 provides an overview of other purchasing duties and a discussion of how the purchasing function is changing due to the Internet.

Springboard

Brainstorm Have students generate a board list of all the things they would need to purchase if they were to open a retail gift store. *(Examples might include lighting fixtures, counters, and a cash register.)* Help students determine which items would be purchased by the store's buyer.

Prereading

List the section objectives to discuss with students. Have students skim the chapter, looking at the pictures, reading the captions, and noting the heads. Ask questions to ensure that students have a minimal understanding of the chapter structure.

Preteaching Marketing Vocabulary

Dictate each of the vocabulary terms and ask students to write them on a sheet of paper. Then write the terms on the board and have students guess at their meanings. Write the guesses next to each term. Leave this list on the board so students can see how close their guesses were to the actual definitions as they work through the chapter.

Marketing: What It Takes

Answer Factors are what functions the buyer presently performs, such as planning purchases, types of purchase situations involved in the items purchased, how suppliers are selected, and how terms are negotiated.

Chapter 23

Purchasing

Marketing: What It Takes

Online Purchasing
You have been asked to conduct research on online purchasing for a manufacturer of mountain climbing gear. You need to prepare a written analysis of how purchasing is presently being conducted and your recommendation on how the Internet may be used to reduce costs.

WHAT WILL YOU DO?
What factors will you consider when conducting your analysis and making your recommendation?

410

THE DECA CONNECTION — ADVISOR CORNER

Leadership Development Leadership skills, an impressive portfolio documenting specific accomplishments, and a system of recognition reaching from local to national level—these are the rewards you can offer your chapter members through the Leadership Education Action Program (LEAP). LEAP, DECA's newest leadership development program, is the most exciting approach yet developed for teaching effective leadership skills. This activity-based program keeps reading and writing to a minimum and does not require a great deal of management by the instructor. Students are encouraged to participate at their own pace and on their own time. To learn more about LEAP, contact DECA at www.deca.org.

The Role of the Buyer

Planning Purchases

Who does the shopping in your household? How does that person know what to buy, how much to buy, and when and where to shop? Those questions are not very different for the people who do the purchasing for businesses. What is different is what they buy and the quantity purchased.

Organizational buyers buy goods for business purposes, usually in much greater quantities than the average consumer. Much of what they buy requires technical knowledge and knowledge of the operations of the firm, especially in manufacturing and service operations. Having a handle on the business trends that affect their industry is also important, especially when buying for resale purposes. Let's look at industrial and reseller markets to see how each plans its purchases.

■ Industrial Markets

In manufacturing and service businesses, the people responsible for purchasing may be called purchasing managers, industrial buyers, or procurement managers. Although the job titles may differ, the key function is to buy goods and services for use in the business.

To plan purchases in manufacturing businesses, industrial buyers are often directly involved with production planning. To get an idea of the responsibilities this entails, consider the case of a purchasing manager for an outerwear apparel manufacturer.

The company's master production schedule would provide the purchasing manager with details of production needed to meet sales requirements. Let's say that the marketing department predicts the company will sell 500 Style No. 1900 jackets in the coming season. The purchasing manager must know how much fabric, insulation, and thread and how many zippers it takes to produce one Style No. 1900 jacket. This is called a *bill of materials*. The total of all the materials necessary to make one jacket can be multiplied by 500 to determine exactly what needs to be purchased to meet the sales goal.

To determine *when* to buy those items, the purchasing manager would be responsible for materials requirement planning (MRP). MRP includes an analysis of when to make the purchases so they are available when needed according to the production schedule. The purchasing manager must therefore know the capacity of the manufacturing facility. He or she must be sure the company has room for the supplies, raw materials, and inventory of finished goods.

Time lines and delivery of all supplies must be followed and checked on a regular basis to maintain the master production schedule. This ensures that everything is as it should be for manufacturing to progress at an appropriate rate.

• What You'll Learn

- The terms used to describe organizational buyers
- How planning purchases differs between an industrial market and a reseller's market
- The six-month merchandise plan and its calculations
- The concept of chain store buying

• Why It's Important

The purchasing function in any business is important because the costs associated with running a business are often a direct result of the competence of the person responsible for buying the goods and services required to run the business.

Key Terms

- organizational buyers
- wholesale and retail buyers
- six-month merchandise plan
- open-to-buy
- centralized buying
- decentralized buying

Discuss Ask students if they would enjoy going shopping—with someone else's money. Then ask if any of them have ever considered becoming a buyer, either one who buys goods for a retail store or one who buys goods used to operate a business.

Introducing the Section

Role of the Buyer Once you have the students' responses to the Bell Ringer Activity, you can continue your questioning to help introduce the two types of buyers—industrial and resale buyers. Ask:

- What do you think that type of job would be like? Would it be fun? interesting? challenging? *(Answers will vary.)*
- Which type of buying appeals to you more—buying for resale or buying materials and supplies for use in the operation of a business? Why? *(Answers will vary.)*

TEACH

📊 Technology Resources

PowerPoint The *Marketing Essentials* PowerPoint Presentation CD-ROM provides visual lecture aids for every chapter section.

Classroom Resources

For the Teacher
- Teacher Editions for all workbooks
- Assessment Package
- PowerPoint Presentation Software
- Interactive Lesson Planner
- ILP Block Scheduling, p. 7
- ILP Lesson Plans, p. 49
- ILP Internet Resources, p. 65

- ILP Blackline Masters, p. 43
- ILP *BusinessWeek* Case Studies, p. 145
- ILP Marketing Career Portfolio, p. 37
- *Marketing Essentials* Web site (**www.marketing.glencoe.com**)

For the Student
- Student Activity Workbook, p. 195
- Marketing Math Workbook, p. 59

- Marketing Research Project Workbook, p. 111
- ILP School-to-Work Activity Workbook, p. 97
- Virtual Business simulation
- *Marketing Essentials* Web site (**www.marketing.glencoe.com**)

ILP These resources are available in print and on the Interactive Lesson Planner (ILP)

Concept Development

1. Read Section 23.1 with students.

2. Ask students to think about the resale and industrial buying situations. How would they be similar or different? What general kinds of tasks would be involved in both? (*Both must plan purchases and evaluate vendors before making purchases. They differ in their purpose: Industrial buyers purchase materials used in the making goods or providing services.*)

3. To lead the students through the six-month merchandise plan, provide different scenarios as you introduce each section of the plan:

   • For planned sales, tell students that the economy appears to be in a period of recovery and continued growth is expected. Unemployment figures have dropped from 6.9 percent to 4.5 percent, and inflation is low at 3 percent. Ask students how they would use this general economic information to project planned sales for the next six months. (*Most students will recognize that there should be an increase in sales for the coming season.*)

   • For BOM inventory, ask students how much inventory must be on hand to meet sales of $10,000 in a given month in a local retail store. Ask if $10,000 in inventory would be sufficient. (*You would have to have more than that on hand. Otherwise, the shelves would be bare.*)

   • For retail reductions, ask students what they think would be included in this figure. (*employee discounts, markdowns, and shortages*)

412

■ **Industrial Buyers** Industrial buyers in manufacturing businesses buy the materials required to make products the company sells. *What does an industrial buyer have to know in order to purchase the correct quantity at the right time?*

■ Resellers

The resellers' market is found in wholesaling and retailing operations, where the person responsible for purchasing is simply called a buyer. Wholesale and retail buyers purchase goods for resale—they forecast customers' needs and buy the necessary products. Buyers must plan far in advance of the selling season to know how much of each item to purchase.

SIX-MONTH MERCHANDISE PLAN Buyers plan their purchases by preparing a six-month merchandise plan—or the budget that estimates planned purchases for a six-month period. Let's look at how the figures on a six-month merchandise plan are calculated and what factors are taken into consideration to arrive at those figures.

The first figure calculated on a merchandise plan is the *planned sales* figure. In most cases, this is determined by using the previous year's monthly sales figures and adjusting them to reflect the firm's current-year sales goal.

Suppose sales for a particular month last year were $100,000 and this year's goal is to increase sales by 10 percent. This year's planned sales for the month would be calculated as follows:

Desired increase: $100,000 × .10 = $10,000
Planned sales: $100,000 + $10,000 = $110,000
You could also reach the same result in a single step: $100,000 × 1.10 = $110,000

A firm's goal for the current year is derived from a study of last year's sales, current market and economic conditions, and an analysis of the competition. Projection of accurate planned sales figures is important because all other figures on the merchandise plan are computed on the basis of this figure.

Buyers must ensure that there is enough stock to accommodate the sales volume planned; this is also known as *beginning-of-the-month (BOM) inventory*. To project this figure, a buyer checks the previous year's records for how much stock was needed in relation to monthly sales. Sales were $40,000 in a given month and the BOM stock for that month was

---

GREAT IDEAS from the Marketing Classroom

Miranda Nixon Blocker
Heyward Career and
Technology Center
Columbia, SC

"Let Your Students Do the Ordering" is a helpful teaching tool that gives students a chance to plan inventory control of materials and supplies needed to complete classroom projects.

Some suggested activities include:

• Students review projects, goals, and guidelines and submit a list of supplies and materials needed for classroom projects.

• Students update classroom inventory spreadsheets of materials and supplies available.

• Students develop a plan for receiving, checking and distributing classroom supplies.

■ **Planning Ahead** Employee pilferage and customer shoplifting must be considered when planning purchases in a six-month merchandise plan. *If your business upgraded its security system, how would you adjust your planned reductions figure for the coming season?*

$120,000; therefore, the stock-to-sales ratio is 3 to 1. The buyer can apply that same ratio to the planned figure for another month if economic and market conditions are similar.

Here is how the BOM figure on the merchandise plan would be calculated. Suppose the stock-to-sales ratio is 2:1 (usually reported as 2). This means that to accommodate a given sales volume it is necessary to keep twice that amount of stock on hand. BOM inventory should be twice the amount of anticipated sales—if sales are $5,000, then the BOM would be $10,000.

There is also an EOM (end-of-the-month) stock figure, which is closely related to the BOM stock figure. The BOM stock figure for any given month is the EOM stock figure for the previous month.

Planned retail reductions take into account reductions in the selling price and shortages of merchandise caused by clerical mistakes, employee pilferage, or customer shoplifting. Such reductions in earnings and merchandise shortages ultimately affect the amount of money that must be planned for purchases.

Planned retail reductions can be calculated in two different ways. One is to calculate reductions as a percentage of planned sales. Suppose planned reductions have historically been 10 percent of planned sales; if planned sales for the month are $25,000, planned reductions for that month would be calculated as follows:

$25,000 × .10 = $2,500

Some firms set goals of reducing planned reductions from the previous year. Assume a firm's goal is to reduce this year's planned reductions by 5 percent from last year's figure. Last year's reductions were $700; therefore this year's planned reductions would be figured this way:

Desired decrease: $700 × .05 = $35

Planned reductions: $700 − $35 = $665

This result could also be reached in a single step: $700 × .95 = $655

The planned purchase entry shows the retail-dollar purchase figures a firm needs in order to achieve its sales and inventory projections for each month. All of the figures discussed above—planned sales, BOM stock, and reductions—are needed to determine planned purchases (P). That includes planned sales (PS), planned EOM/BOM stock, and planned reductions (R). The formula for planned sales is

(PS + EOM stock + R) − BOM stock = P

Assume that planned sales are $10,000, planned EOM stock $25,000, planned reductions $500, and BOM stock $20,000. Using the formula, planned purchases would be arrived at this way:

($10,000 + $25,000 + $500) − $20,000 = $35,500 − $20,000 = $15,500

Figure 23-1 on page 414 shows a nearly completed merchandise plan. Study it carefully, then duplicate the buyer's computations based on what you have learned in this section.

Discussion Starter

1. **Planning Purchases** Ask students if they think large chain stores should allow local branches to buy some of the goods they sell, or if they think central buyers should do all the buying for all the stores. *(Answers will vary. Supporters of centralized buying will cite the need for a unified image. Supporters of local buying will suggest the need for freedom to make each store unique and to cater to its particular customers.)*

2. **Planned Sales** When introducing planned sales on the merchandise, ask students, "What social, economic, and market factors would you consider when determining a percentage increase with which to adjust your firm's current-year sales goals?" *(Answers will vary, but possibilities include the following:*
   - *new and/or improved products that you intend to offer*
   - *an increased focus on customer service*
   - *an increase in the population in your area and/or a change in demographics*
   - *a new business location that is more accessible*
   - *an increase in the prices of your products*
   - *greater use of advertising and promotion*
   - *a decrease in competition*
   - *good word-of-mouth from your established customer base)*

Thinking Critically

Planning Purchases Ask students: Whose job is easier in terms of planning purchases—an industrial buyer's or a retail buyer's? *(Answers will vary. Each job has its difficulties, depending on the scope of the job's responsibilities.)*

More About . . .

Trade Journals

Progressive Grocer and *Frozen Food Digest* are examples of trade journals read by buyers in the supermarket industry. In the field of sporting goods, buyers read *Sporting Goods Dealer, Sports Style,* and *Outdoor Retailer.* Industrial buyers can keep abreast of their field by reading a trade journal called *Purchasing.*

CAPTION ANSWER
Planning Ahead You would reduce your planned reductions figure, under the assumption that improved security will lower the incidence of pilferage and shoplifting.

Independent Practice

1. **Research and Report** Have students research the career of buyer by reading about it in the *Dictionary of Occupational Titles*, by clipping help-wanted ads for buyers in their local newspaper, and by interviewing buyers in their community. Have them determine the positive and negative aspects of buying jobs, the recommended educational requirements, experience that would be helpful, and projections for employment in the field for the next five years. Have students present their findings in written reports.

2. **Research, Summarize, and Present** Ask students to research the names of trade journals that are read by wholesale and retail buyers in given fields. There are trade journals for each area of specialization, such as *Women's Wear Daily* and *Sporting Goods Dealer*. If possible, have students read one article that reports a trend that would be important to a buyer/purchasing agent. Ask students to write a summary and present oral summaries of the articles.

OPEN-TO-BUY During the buying season, a buyer may want to know the open-to-buy (OTB). This is the amount of money left for buying goods after all other expenses have been considered. It is calculated as follows:

P − (goods received + goods ordered) = OTB

Assume that merchandise received against the planned purchase figure computed above is $6,500 thus far and merchandise on order against it is $2,000. The present OTB would be as follows:

$15,500 − ($6,500 + $2,000) = OTB

$15,500 − $8,500 = $7,000

This $7,000 figure represents the retail value of the goods that the buyer may purchase at the time. However, the problem is not solved here. If a buyer did not continue to work this problem, he or she would have an incorrect estimation of potential funds available to spend.

There is a way to determine the actual money the buyer has to spend. You must calculate the markup percentage used by the buyer and deduct that figure from the retail value. Assuming that the markup percentage is 45 percent based on the retail value of the merchandise, the buyer would actually be able to spend $3,850. The formula for determining the OTB at cost is shown below:

100% − markup % = % attributed to cost of the item

% attributed to cost × retail value = OTB at cost

100% − 45% markup = 55% (cost)

55% (cost) × $7,000 (retail) = $3,850 OTB at cost

Therefore in the end, the buyer has $3,850 to spend with all other costs considered. You can see how this extra step makes a big difference in the final amount.

FIGURE 23-1

Six-Month Merchandise Plan

Spring Season 20____ Department ___Toys___ No. ___6124___

		February	March	April	May	June	July	Total
Sales	Last year	82,000	96,000	90,000	100,000	94,000	80,000	
	Plan	90,200	105,600	99,000	110,000	103,400	88,000	
	Actual							
Retail Stock BOM	Last year	328,000	336,000	297,000	360,000	291,400	224,000	
	Plan	360,800	369,600	326,700	396,000	320,540	246,400	
	Actual							
Retail Reductions	Last year	12,300	14,400	13,500	15,000	14,100	12,000	
	Plan	11,685	13,680	12,825	14,250	13,395	11,400	
	Actual							
Retail Purchases	Last year	N/A	N/A	N/A	N/A	N/A	N/A	
	Plan	110,685	76,380	181,125				
	Actual							

■ **Making Merchandise Plans** This nearly completed model merchandise plan is based on the following assumptions: sales are expected to increase by 10 percent over last year; last year's stock-to-sales ratios should be used to compute this year's BOM stock figures; this year's planned reductions should be 5 percent lower than last year's; and the planned BOM for August is $264,000. *What are the planned purchase figures for May through July?*

FIGURE 23-1 ANSWER
Making Merchandise Plans The planned purchase figures are as follows: May—$48,790; June—$42,655; and July—$117,000.

PLANNING PURCHASES FOR A CHAIN STORE OPERATION Buying for all branches in a chain store operation is usually done in a central location (company headquarters) and is called centralized buying. Buyers involved in centralized buying generally buy all the items for a department or part of a department. There may be three buyers for women's shoes—one in charge of casual shoes, another of traditional shoes, and still another of better shoes. To coordinate the efforts of those three buyers, there would be a merchandise or division manager. This person would oversee all shoe buyers, which may include those for men's, children's, and women's shoes.

Chain stores use centralized buying in order to create a unified image for the chain. Customers can expect to find the same goods in every branch. How can centralized retail buyers for national chains adjust for slight variations in customer preferences? Computers allow buyers to study sales daily. They can determine where goods are selling quickly and slowly. A certain style of shoe may be selling well in one branch store but poorly in another.

Do It Yourself Furniture

Where can you buy a futon, a rice paper lamp, and a dresser, all for approximately $750? Ikea, of course. What's the catch? The reasonable prices come with a catch—self-assembly. Since 1985, Ikea has kept customers coming back for more with their minimalist attitude and do-it-yourself style. Stressing safe construction, simple design, and good prices, Ikea has held customers' attention since 1985. Consumers can browse the catalog or check out simulated rooms in stores, copying down the item numbers to pick up in the self-serve warehouse. The unassembled products are stored easily, and Ikea can stock large quantities of items packaged in flat boxes.

Thinking Critically
What are the benefits to Ikea of stocking do-it-yourself furniture kits?

PRACTICE

On a separate sheet of paper, do the following merchandise plan calculations for Granny's Gift Shoppe:

1. Last March the shop had sales of $4,200. The owner's goal is to increase sales by 7 percent. What would be the planned sales for this March?

2. Last year's stock-to-sales ratio for March was 1.5:1. What should be the BOM stock figure for this March?

3. The owner would like to cut planned reductions by 5 percent this year. Last year's reductions for the month were $500, therefore what would be this year's target figure?

4. Using the figures already given or calculated and an EOM stock figure of $5,000 for March, determine planned purchases for the gift shop.

5. Assuming merchandise received and ordered amounted to $1,200, what would be the open-to-buy position at retail?

6. The customary markup percentage for an item is 60 percent. What is OTB at cost?

Note: The answers to this practice set are on page 416.

The buyer can have the shoes transferred from the store with poor sales to the other store. Another benefit of centralized buying is the quantity discounts that chain stores can negotiate with vendors because of the large volume of goods that they purchase at one time.

There are a few instances, however, when chain stores want to have special goods in their stores that are not available elsewhere in the chain. In these cases, local store managers or their designated buyers are authorized to make special purchases for their individual stores. This would be considered decentralized buying. Decentralization is when authority for retail decisions is made at low levels in the organization.

Each approach for coordinating buying has limitations. Retailers constantly make trade-offs between the efficiency gained through centralized buying and the greater sales potential obtained through decentralized buying decisions that tailor merchandise to local markets.

ASSESS

Reteaching

1. **Vocabulary** Assign and review the vocabulary terms for this section.
2. **Fact and Idea** Assign and review Fact and Idea Review questions 1–4 from the Chapter Assessment.
3. **Types of Buyers** To reteach the different types of buyers, provide examples of several buying situations, and ask students to classify the type of buyer involved. Tell them that Toys R Us has employees who are located in the central office. One group of employees buys all the toys for the chain. The other group of employees buys all the bags, tape for the sales registers, shelving, and display equipment needed in the operation of those stores. Ask: Which one is the resale buyer and which one is the industrial buyer? *(toys: resale buyer; supplies and equipment: industrial buyer)*
4. **Merchandise Plan Calculations** When working on the merchandise plan calculations, it may help students with comprehension if you write each of the basic formulas on the board.

Do It Yourself Furniture
Answer Ikea saves money on employees because furniture does not need to be assembled in-house and stored. A flat box is easier to store than a standing desk.

SECTION 23.1

Enrichment

1. **Review** Assign and review the appropriate Thinking Critically questions from the Chapter Assessment.

2. **Extend** Assign and review the corresponding activities from *BusinessWeek Case Studies, Internet Resources,* and the *School-to-Work Activity Workbook.* **ILP**

3. **Research and Write** Have students investigate buying trends in college bookstores and the application to high school bookstores. Ask them to identify at least one new product to be added to the existing line of goods carried in their own school store. Students should base their suggestion on a careful investigation of students' needs and possible supply sources. Tell them to present their findings and the rationale for their suggestion in a written report.

Evaluation

Assign and review the Section 23.1 Assessment.

 GO TO **Assessment Resources**
Go to the *Marketing Essentials* Web site (**www.marketing.glencoe. com**) for resources to teach and assess occupation-specific vocabulary.

Technology Resources

CLOSE

Section Wrap-Up

The formula for calculating planned purchases is _____.
(Planned Sales + EOM stock + reductions - BOM stock = Planned purchases)

416

■ Government Markets

In the same way that there are special markets such as industrial or reseller, there are also buyers for government markets. *Government Units* are the federal, state, or local agencies that are responsible for purchasing goods and services for their specific markets. There are approximately 85,000 government units in the United States. These would include the Federal Aviation Administration (FAA), the Department of Sanitation, the Public Library, or the local school board.

Government markets make up one of the largest single markets for retail goods and services in the world. In the United States, the federal government is a huge consumer of goods, ranging from food for school lunches to equipment for the military and the U.S. Postal Service. A large portion of the federal government's buying is centralized. However, there is not one federal agency that is entirely responsible for all government buying.

Government markets are not unique to the United States. As we see a global marketplace expanding trading networks, we see many international government agencies doing business with U.S. organizations. For example, the world's second-largest aircraft manufacturer—Europe's Airbus Industries—purchases mechanical goods from the U.S. company Pratt & Whitney.

■ Institutions

There is one final segment of the market that cannot be overlooked when discussing buying power. This market includes institutions and non-profit organizations that do not compete in the business world in the same way that retailers and wholesalers do. These institutions include hospitals, schools, colleges, churches, civic clubs, and foundations that do not work solely for profit. Institutions and nonprofit organizations may have unique buying requirements. They often provide specialized marketing needs.

23.1 ASSESSMENT

Reviewing Key Terms and Concepts

1. What are the differences between organizational buyers and consumers?
2. What products might an industrial buyer purchase?
3. What do wholesale and retail buyers purchase?
4. In a retail buying situation, what does a buyer prepare in advance of the selling situation?
5. Why do chain stores use centralized buying?

Thinking Critically

6. What would happen if a buyer computed a planned sales figure for the next planning period that was 20 percent too high?

Integrating Academic Skills

7. **COMMUNICATION** As an employee of a chain store operation, you have been told to call other branch stores if a customer requests something that is not in stock. Your customer wants a particular dress you carry, but prefers a different color. Role play your telephone conversation with a branch store that has the dress in the color the customer requested. Include all necessary information such as model number, size, color, and make arrangements for getting the dress to your customer.

23.1 ASSESSMENT ANSWERS

Reviewing Key Terms and Concepts

1. Organizational buyers buy goods and services for use in a business in much greater quantities than consumers do; what they buy requires technical knowledge and/or knowledge of the operations of the firm, and industry trends.
2. raw materials and parts used in manufacturing, office supplies and equipment
3. goods for resale.
4. a six-month merchandise plan
5. It creates a unified image for chain stores.

Thinking Critically

6. It might cause overstocking of goods that cannot be sold.

Integrating Academic Skills

7. **COMMUNICATION** Telephone conversations will vary.

The Purchasing Function

The Buying Process

Planning purchases is the preliminary step in the buying process. Now it is time to look at how that function is actually performed. Let's review the types of purchase situations, the way suppliers are selected, how terms are negotiated, and how the Internet is changing the entire process.

■ Types of Purchase Situations

How difficult is the task of a purchasing manager or a buyer? The answer depends on which type of purchase situation is considered. Let's review the three types of purchase situations: new-task purchase, modified rebuy, and straight rebuy.

NEW-TASK PURCHASE In a new-task purchase situation, a purchase is made for the first time, possibly triggered by a formerly unrecognized need. This can be the most complicated buying situation, as it involves a first time purchase. In a retail or wholesale operation, salespeople prepare want slips, like the one shown in Figure 23-2 on page 418. These are customer requests for items that are not carried in the store.

Another reason for a new-task purchase may be a desire to change an existing operation in a firm. Let's say a manufacturer may be considering a new way to make its product, such as using robots instead of people to handle one phase of the manufacturing process. In this new-task purchase, many people in the organization may be responsible for determining the characteristics of the equipment needed. In both the industrial market and the reseller market, it is quite common to see buying committees. Some of the people who may be asked to serve on the committee might be people who will use the equipment, as well as top executives in the manufacturing division. Other influential people, such as the president of the company, may get involved too, because they may be the ones who make the final buying decision. The purchasing manager will generally be part of the team and will most likely be responsible for doing research into possible supply sources.

MODIFIED REBUY In a modified-rebuy situation, the buyer has had experience buying the good or service, but some aspect of the purchase changes. Perhaps the buyer is purchasing from a new vendor because the previous vendor went out of business or increased prices significantly. Other reasons for investigating new vendors may come from an analysis of the competition (through comparison shopping) or from current trade information (found in trade journals or trade shows).

● What You'll Learn

- The three types of purchase situations
- The criteria for selecting suppliers
- The factors involved in negotiating terms of a sale
- The various Internet purchasing methods

● Why It's Important

Knowing the details of the purchasing function will give you a better idea of what is involved in the overall job description. It is especially important to recognize the impact of the Internet on the purchasing function. You can expect changes in job descriptions for buyers in the near future due to the significant increase in online purchasing.

● Key Terms

- want slips
- resident buying offices
- consignment buying
- memorandum buying
- reverse auction

FOCUS

Bell Ringer Activity

Describe and Discuss Have students recount their experiences making their own purchases or participating in a family purchase decision. If necessary, suggest the following types of purchases to get the discussion going: jeans, athletic shoes, dress shoes, CD player, CDs, television, family automobile, and a family vacation. Ask students what makes certain buying decisions easier than others.

Introducing the Section

The Purchasing Function Write the students' answers to the Bell Ringer Activity on the board. This line of questioning will help to introduce the types of purchase situations—new-task, modified re-buy, and straight re-buy. Ask students to project how these three purchase situations would affect the way resale buyers and purchasing agents purchase goods for their businesses. *(Answers will vary but should recognize the need for a lot more research prior to purchase for a new-task and modified re-buy than with a straight re-buy.)*

Classroom Resources

For the Teacher
- Teacher Editions for all workbooks
- Assessment Package
- PowerPoint Presentation Software
- Interactive Lesson Planner
- ILP Block Scheduling, p. 7
- ILP Lesson Plans, p. 50
- ILP Internet Resources, p. 65

- ILP Blackline Masters, p. 44
- ILP *BusinessWeek* Case Studies, p. 145
- ILP Marketing Career Portfolio, p. 37
- *Marketing Essentials* Web site (**www.marketing.glencoe.com**)

For the Student
- Student Activity Workbook, p. 195
- Marketing Math Workbook, p. 59

- Marketing Research Project Workbook, p. 111
- ILP School-to-Work Activity Workbook, p. 97
- Virtual Business simulation
- *Marketing Essentials* Web site (**www.marketing.glencoe.com**)

ILP These resources are available in print and on the Interactive Lesson Planner (ILP)

TEACH

📊 Technology Resources

PowerPoint The *Marketing Essentials* PowerPoint Presentation CD-ROM provides visual lecture aids for every chapter section.

Concept Development

1. Read Section 23.2 with students.
2. Have students read aloud the Case Study on page 421 and review the answers in class.
3. Ask students what criteria they would use for selecting a vendor. (For example, tell them to imagine that they are in charge of buying T-shirts for a DECA fund-raiser, and they have a choice of three local and three out-of-state firms.) Keep soliciting responses until you have covered the key criteria—production capabilities; past experience with the vendor; product offerings; and buying arrangements.

FIGURE 23-2

Want Slip

Item requested _____ Brand name _____
Size _____ Style _____ Quantity _____
Item description _____
_____
Your name _____
Address _____
(Street)   (City)   (State)   (Zip code)
Telephone ( ) _____

EMPLOYEE: PLEASE FORWARD IMMEDIATELY TO YOUR SUPERVISOR.

Employee Signature _____

Store No. _____ Dept. No. _____ Date _____

■ **Want Slip** Salespeople often prepare want slips and give them to the buyer for their department. *Why are want slips so valuable to a buyer?*

Comparison shopping involves researching competing businesses in order to see what goods and services they offer. Buyers in retail operations will note and compare brands carried, prices, and quantities of items. In a modified-rebuy situation, the buyer usually gets proposals from several vendors before making a buying decision.

To stay abreast of industry trends, reading trade journals and general business publications is a must. A trade journal is a business publication that covers a specific business. *Women's Wear Daily* covers the women's apparel industry. Other good sources of business information are general business publications, such as *Forbes, Business Week,* and *Investor's Business Daily.* Attending trade shows to see what is current is another means of learning about new products and vendors. At trade shows, suppliers for a given industry present their goods for buyers to see. Many trade shows publish a directory of all participating vendors to make it easy for buyers to contact them at a later date.

Finally, retail buyers may hire the services of a resident buying office. **Resident buying offices** are retailers' representatives in a central market. A central market is a geographic area where many suppliers of a given product are located. New York

■ **Factory Issues** Sweatshops are often in the news and create poor publicity for a company. *Why do you think social issues are part of the vendor evaluation process for clothing and toy manufacturers?*

418 Unit 7 ■ *Distribution*

City's garment district, for example, is a central market for apparel. Resident buying offices send information to retail buyers on a regular basis. They inform buyers about new merchandise offerings, closeouts, fashion trends, special buys in the market, and market conditions.

STRAIGHT REBUY In a straight-rebuy situation, the buyer routinely orders the goods and services purchased from the same vendor(s) as in the past. Staple goods such as office supplies fall into the straight-rebuy category for wholesale and retail buyers. The purchase of certain manufacturing supplies may be considered a straight rebuy for most purchasing managers.

Some manufacturing companies purchase all materials and parts in a straight-rebuy situation. This is because of an inventory control system called just-in-time (JIT), which you will learn more about in Chapter 24. JIT links a company via computer to its supplier so the supplier knows exactly what, how much, and when to deliver to meet production needs. Suppliers deliver parts and raw materials just before they are needed for production. Computerized orders are placed when parts and supplies run low. The company is essentially in a partnership with suppliers to guarantee frequent shipments of goods that keep pace with production needs.

■ Selecting Suppliers

The criteria for selecting suppliers fall into a few key categories. They include production capabilities, past experience, product and buying arrangements, and special services.

PRODUCTION CAPABILITIES When dealing with a source for the first time, buyers may request specific information about the source's production capabilities. They may even visit a facility in person to see it in operation. Buyers may solicit business references to determine the source's reputation in the industry. These factors would be extremely important when selecting suppliers and transportation firms as partners in a just-in-time production arrangement.

Production capabilities for some companies go beyond the actual physical plant into social issues, such as review of facilities to ensure that they are not sweatshops. *Sweatshops* are factories characterized by poor working conditions and negligent treatment of employees. Production costs are reduced because factory owners underpay staff workers. Companies may require suppliers to sign a contract stating that they will follow a fair code of conduct. Factory audits performed by human-rights groups may be conducted to ensure that these rules are being followed.

Companies, such as Reebok and Liz Claiborne, often hire the services of manufacturing facilities outside the United States to produce their goods. To show social responsibility and to avoid abuse of workers, these companies require foreign manufacturers to adhere to specific labor standards.

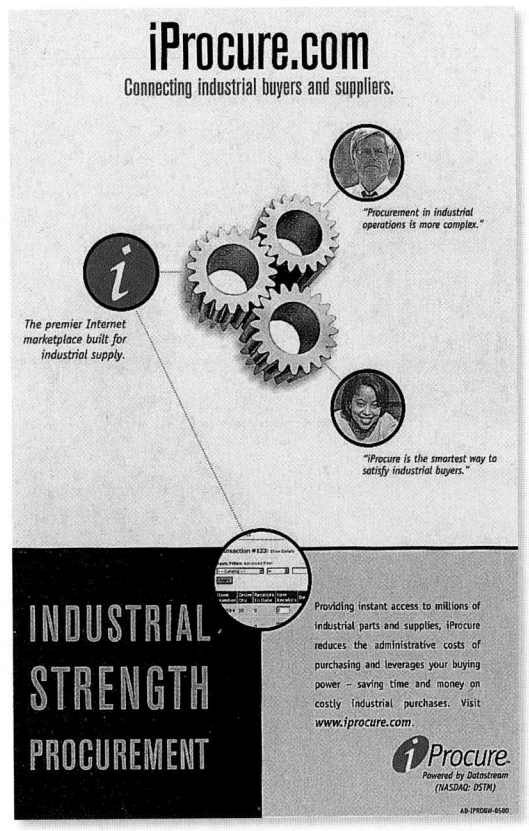

■ **Going Electronic** This dot-com company is an example of an electronic exchange in a specific industry. *How might this e-business change the role of an industrial buyer?*

Discussion Starter

Purchasing Agents Present this situation to students for their consideration: They are purchasing agents for a bicycle manufacturer. They buy the components that go into bikes. They have two principal vendors that offer the same quality components. Vendor A offers low prices with no shipping charges but is unreliable when it comes to meeting delivery schedules. Vendor B charges higher prices (also with no shipping charges) and guarantees its delivery dates.

Thinking Critically

Selecting Suppliers Some socially conscious companies require vendors to supply proof that they employ or do business with minorities. For example, Ben & Jerry's Ice Cream company requires its suppliers to furnish proof that they are either minority-owned or that the vendors with whom they do business are minority-owned. Ask how such a requirement impacts on an industrial buyer's ability to negotiate the best deal for its company. *(Answers will vary. Most will realize that in some cases the buyer may not be able to get the lowest price if in fact the lowest price is from a vendor that does not meet that requirement.)*

Independent Practice

Purchasing Decisions Tell students that their local DECA chapter wants to buy a camcorder to record all their activities for the year. They will also use the camcorder to videotape role plays done by students in preparation for DECA competition. Some of their videotapes will be used for presentations to the administration and parents, and as recruitment tools for DECA.

Have students research the camcorders available and recommend the best product for the chapter's needs. They should also be prepared to recommend the best vendor and back up that choice with a suitable rationale.

PAST EXPERIENCES Many buyers maintain resource files that document past experiences with vendors. All basic information, such as products carried, prices, delivery and dating terms, and the names of sales representatives, is recorded. Also noted are evaluations of products, delivery performance, and customer service. A major factor in selecting a supplier is the quality of goods it offers. Retail buyers keep accurate records of customer returns and the reasons for them. Returns relating to the quality of the goods may cause a vendor to be dropped as a supplier.

SPECIAL BUYING ARRANGEMENTS Suppliers may have special policies regarding merchandise returns and sales arrangements. Two special types of sales and return policies are called consignment buying and memorandum buying.

In consignment buying, goods are paid for only after they are purchased by the final customer. This special arrangement is applicable to wholesale and retail buying situations. The supplier owns the goods until the wholesaler or retailer sells them. Many suppliers offer consignment buying as an incentive when introducing a new line of goods. No money is tied up in inventory because the buyer pays for goods after they are sold. This is virtually a no-risk situation. The problem with consignment buying occurs when merchandise is stolen or damaged, which raises the question of who is responsible and who must pay.

Memorandum buying occurs when the supplier agrees to take back any unsold goods by a certain preestablished date. The buyer pays for all of the goods purchased but is later reimbursed for all of the goods returned in accordance with the agreement. This buying arrangement allows for returns. Each agreement may be a little different from other similar agreements with regard to the time lines for accepting returns.

SPECIAL SERVICES Businesses today demand more services from their suppliers than just the basic return policy. Suppliers must keep up with these services to stay competitive.

One special service that many retailers are requesting or demanding is the placement by manufacturers of Universal Product Codes (UPCs) on goods. Having the codes on all products saves the retailer time because individual items do not have to be marked with a price. It also helps retailers keep track of what they have in stock.

Even the large boxes that hold products now have bar codes on them to identify the contents. Machines that read those codes can use them to route the products to various departments within a business or, in the case of a chain store, to branch stores within a chain.

BRIGHT IDEAS
Smart Cart

Silicon Valley inventor George Cokely has a modern solution to one of the supermarket industry's oldest problems—stolen shopping carts. His invention, Stop Z-Cart, consists of a small computer chip inside one of the cart's wheels. The system is activated when the cart rolls over a special mat. Once the cart is a certain distance away from the store, the wheels lock. After the store retrieves the stolen cart they can easily release the locked wheels with a Stop Z-Cart magic wand. Why are supermarkets interested in Stop Z-Cart? Supermarkets lose up to 25 percent of their shopping carts every year to theft. This leaves supermarkets with major additional purchasing costs. Carts can cost up to $200 each, which adds up pretty quickly to $80 million annually industry wide. Stop Z-Cart is worth the extra cost, since it virtually eliminates shopping cart theft.

Thinking Creatively

Retail stores lose millions of dollars in theft. What are other creative ways that stores can prevent stealing?

BRIGHT IDEAS Smart Cart

Answer Answers will vary. Stores may be able to prevent stealing by embedding computer chips in clothing labels.

Case Study

FreeMarkets.com

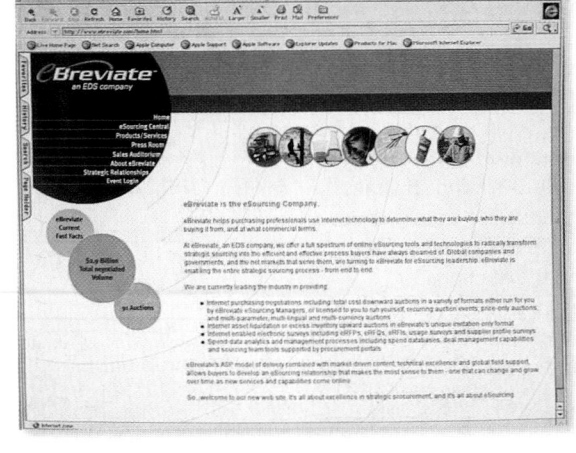

FreeMarkets.com was one of the first Internet companies to link industrial buyers and sellers through computerized auctions. In addition to overseeing online trading, it also helps buyers find and qualify new suppliers.

Online bartering is becoming so popular that there are many more companies that are carving a niche in this expanding market. To compete against FreeMarkets.com, eBreviate.com offers flat rates rather than the industry standard cut of one percent to six percent from each sale.

At one time, FreeMarkets.com only catered to large companies, while other auction companies targeted mid-sized and smaller firms. To counter that competition, FreeMarkets.com began offering software to let buyers and sellers set up their own online transactions. This action makes one wonder how soon companies may reject third-party auction service providers and simply do it themselves.

Case Study Review

1. In the business-to-business e-marketplace, how are new companies competing with FreeMarkets.com?
2. Why would companies prefer to register with a B2B e-marketplace provider instead of conducting an online auction by themselves?

A MATTER OF ETHICS

3. Is it ethical for a company that was registered with an online auction company to set up its own company-run online auction?

SECTION 23.2

Individualized Practice

Communication Skills

Pose this problem for students: The T-shirts you ordered for a DECA fund-raiser have arrived along with a bill charging you $7 per shirt. The price you were quoted before placing the order was $6.50 per shirt. The shirts have been unpacked and readied for silk screening, which will be handled by another firm.

L1 What will you say when you contact the vendor about the price discrepancy? *(Answers will vary. However, students should first establish whether the pricing is the result of misunderstanding or mistake. If it is not, then they should state firmly that the pricing must be corrected if the vendor ever expects to do school business again.)*

L2 Tell students to write an outline of exactly what they would say to the vendor.

L3 Have students role-play the negotiation to settle the dispute with the vendor.

■ Negotiating Terms

To evaluate suppliers, buyers must negotiate their prices, dating terms, delivery arrangements, and discounts. You have already learned about dating terms and delivery arrangements in Chapter 16. Discounts are any reductions from the quoted price. Such reductions are generally granted for the buyer's performance of certain functions. These will be discussed in Chapter 26.

Dating terms involve when a bill must be paid and the discount permitted for paying early. You learned about ordinary dating (2/10, net 30) in Chapter 16, but you should also know that there are several variations for specific situations. A company may allow the dating terms to take effect later than the invoice date. This type of dating, which is known as advance dating, is sometimes offered to businesses as an incentive to buy before the buying season. An invoice may be dated January 15 and include the following advance dating terms: 2/10, net 30—as of March 1.

In other situations, additional days may be granted for the discount (called extra dating). This special dating may be used to encourage a buyer to purchase new merchandise. In still another situation, the terms begin when the buyer's firm receives the goods, which is called "ROG dating" (receipt of goods).

Chapter 23 ■ *Purchasing* **421**

Case Study Review Answers

FreeMarkets.com

1. They are competing by offering flat rates rather than the industry standard cut of 1 percent to 6 percent from each sale, as well as stressing its user-friendly software and flexibility in trade.

2. Third party B2B e-marketplace providers have a large number of suppliers registered so there are more possible contacts.

A MATTER OF ETHICS

3. Answers will vary.

Reteaching

1. **Vocabulary** Assign and review the vocabulary terms for this section.
2. **Fact and Idea** Assign and review Fact and Idea Review questions 5–10 from the Chapter Assessment.
3. **Buying Online** To reteach the concept of buying online, ask if anyone has purchased anything online. Ask students who purchased online what they purchased. Then ask if businesses could to the same thing to buy goods they need to run their businesses. *(Answers should recognize that they can.)*
4. **Auctions** To differentiate between an auction and a reverse auction, have half the class decide on an item they would like to sell and the other half decide on an item they want to buy. Have each group conduct an auction with the other half of the class. After the two auctions are completed, ask students which group was performing a regular auction and which one was performing a reverse auction. *(regular auction: when the group was selling an item; reverse auction: when the group was asking for bids on an item to be purchased)*

FIGURE 23-3

HOW BUSINESS E-COMMERCE WORKS

By 2004, estimates for online trade among businesses range from $2.7 trillion to $7.3 trillion. Business-to-business e-commerce covers everything from online auctions to electronic exchanges among manufacturers and suppliers.

2 BIDS SUBMITTED

Chem-One bids to fill order

Chemical-Plus bids to fill order

Chemicals Unlimited bids to fill order

Chem-One Inc., Chemical Plus, and Chemicals Unlimited all bid to fill the order.

1 BIDS REQUESTED

XYZ company requests bids

XYZ company needs an order of chemicals. The director of procurement goes to Chembuyer.com and puts out a request for bids.

3 BIDS REVIEWED

XYZ company downloads the bids and reviews each one.

XYZ company reviews bids

6 ORDER RECEIVED

XYZ receives order and processes the records

Back at XYZ company, the order is received and the records associated with it go through its computer network—recording information in inventory, sales, and production departments.

4 ORDER AWARDED

At Chemicals Unlimited, the order is recorded electronically with the information going through its computer network to inventory, sales, and production departments for processing.

Chemicals Unlimited is awarded the order

5 ORDER SHIPPED

The order is shipped.

THE DECA CONNECTION

COMPETITIVE EVENTS AND MARKETING ESSENTIALS

Role Plays for Buying and Pricing DECA's Individual Series Events provide many role-play scenarios to enhance this chapter on purchasing. A number of role-play events from the Buying and Pricing instructional area require the student to solve purchasing problems that relate very closely to this chapter. The student will then explain how they arrived at their decision. You can use these role-play situations as a class assignment. The Quick Serve Restaurant Management Event and the Apparel and Accessories Marketing Event are also excellent sources for appropriate role-play situations.

Internet Purchasing

Business-to-business, or B2B, electronic commerce has revolutionized the purchasing function for businesses in the industrial and reseller markets. Figure 23-3 on page 422 illustrates how B2B e-commerce works. Estimates for online trade among businesses range from $2.7 trillion to $7.3 trillion by 2004, according to *Investor's Business Daily*. Organizational buyers account for 80 percent of the total dollar value of all online transactions.

The popularity of online buying is expected to continue to grow into the twenty-first century. This is partly because organizational buyers have come to depend heavily on timely supplier information, and such information can be easily and quickly conveyed via the Internet. Another reason is that businesses have found that online purchasing dramatically reduces marketing costs for many types of products and services.

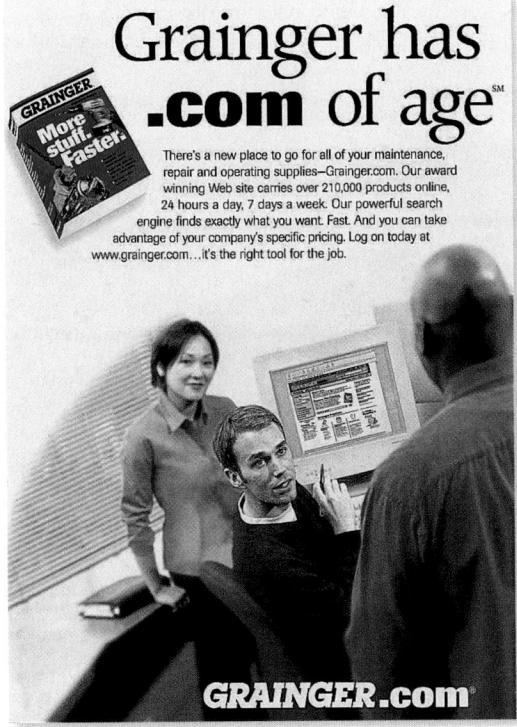

■ Grainger.com Business-to-business electronic commerce has changed the way buyers conduct business. Some vendors have established their own Web sites, like Grainger.com. *Why might a buyer buy supplies like those noted in this ad?*

MARKETPLACE

Don't Whistle While You Work

As the soccer team scores the winning goal, the stadium erupts in shouts, cheers, and…whistles? Maybe in the United States, but in other countries this would be offensive. While whistling is a sign of appreciation or approval at U.S. sporting events or concerts, it is a symbol of disrespect in other countries. In Europe, it is the equivalent of being booed, whether the setting is a stadium, opera house, or political gathering. In the Middle East, whistling at a woman is not only rude, but it breaks political and social rules!

Thinking Critically
Are there times when whistling is considered inappropriate in the United States?

The bulk of B2B e-commerce transactions are routine purchases made more efficient by the Internet. For example, the sale of standardized products, such as office supplies, and commodities such as stock steel, require little or no buyer-seller interaction. An increasing number of businesses are using the Internet to facilitate the buying of such standardized goods.

Some companies have their own Web sites from which other companies may make purchases directly. The company W. W. Grainger sells over $40 million worth of maintenance, repair, and operating supplies annually through its Web site to other businesses.

Growing in popularity are electronic exchanges where registered users can buy and sell their goods online. Most of these electronic exchanges are in specific industries, such as NECX Global Electronics Exchange (necx.com), which is an electronic exchange for electronic components, computer products, and networking equipment. According to its Web site, NECX has over ten billion items available and access to $30 billion in inventory. Medibuy.com connects buyers and sellers of medical equipment, while Chemdex Corporation maintains an electronic exchange for the biotech and drug industries.

Chapter 23 ■ *Purchasing* **423**

CLOSE

Section Wrap-Up

Ask students to answer the following sentence: What factors do buyers consider when evaluating a vendor? *(past experience with the vendor; product offerings; and buying arrangements, including price, dating terms, shipping terms, return policy, and any special services available)*

To Order ... Don't Dial Now

Answer Answers will vary, but some may say convenience would be an advantage of using this type of cell phone.

424

Another Internet purchasing trend involves online auction companies, which register those parties interested in selling an item or service. An auction usually involves having a seller set an asking price and buyers try to outbid each other. This type of auction is found in online exchanges in farming and other industries. In other cases, a reverse auction takes place. In a **reverse auction**, companies post what they want to buy and suppliers bid for the contract.

There are advantages and disadvantages of purchasing online through third parties. The biggest advantage is lower prices; however, as with most businesses on the Internet, privacy is a problem. Some companies fear that competitors will know how much was paid for materials and supplies. To combat that problem, some big companies, like Intel and General Electric, have decided to run their own reverse auctions. GE only spent $15,000 to write its own reverse auction software. This has inspired other companies to follow.

GE's Trading Process Network (TPN) enables GE buyers to post requests for quotes, negotiate, and place orders with global suppliers. The TPN has lowered GE's purchasing costs by over 20 percent.

Another problem with the online purchasing process, especially in a reverse auction, is that unknown companies could artificially deflate prices by bidding low prices. Such a practice would benefit buyers, but cause bad relationships with suppliers.

To Order...Don't Dial Now

We've seen cellular phones develop from a communication tool used merely to make phone calls to a tool that displays e-mail and stock quotes as well as messages. Cell phone technology is going further as unique bar codes are developed that make ordering by telephone even easier. These codes will be embedded on products, in ads, or even shown on television. Next time you see an infomercial for that must-have product or CD, you may just be a click away from being its proud owner. When a consumer clicks on the code with his or her phone, the product is ordered instantly at the advertised price. Using the personal data stored on the device, the selection, purchase, and shipment will take place via the Internet—completely invisible to the user. This technology is expected to be available in hand-held computing devices as well as traditional television remote controls.

Thinking Critically
Would you like to have a cellular phone with this capability? Why or why not?

23.2 ASSESSMENT

Reviewing Key Terms and Concepts
1. List the three types of purchase situations.
2. What four things can buyers do to stay abreast of industry trends?
3. Name four criteria buyers use in selecting supply sources.
4. What is the difference between consignment and memorandum buying?
5. What are electronic exchanges and in what types of industries are they found?

Thinking Critically
6. How do you see the job description of a buyer or procurement manager changing with the advent of Internet purchasing?

Integrating Academic Skills
5. **MATH** Assuming all discounts are taken, determine which vendor is granting a better deal based on the following facts. Vendor A offers to sell you 1,500 stuffed animals at a unit cost of $3.45 and will pay for shipping. Dating terms are 2/10, net 30. Vendor B's offer is $3.35 per stuffed animal, shipping charges of $65, and payment must be made COD for all 1,500 stuffed animals.

23.2 ASSESSMENT ANSWERS

Reviewing Key Terms and Concepts
1. new-task purchase, modified rebuy, and straight rebuy
2. Buyers can read trade journals, and general business publications, attend trade shows, and hire the services of a resident buying office.
3. production capabilities, past experience, product and buying arrangements, and special services
4. Consignment buying—goods paid for after purchase; memorandum buying—supplier to take back any unsold goods by a certain date.
5. online registered users to buy and sell goods in industries that sell standardized goods

Thinking Critically
6. Answers will vary.

Integrating Academic Skills
7. **MATH** Vendor A: $5,071.50; Vendor B: $5,090

Careers in Marketing

RETAIL MANAGEMENT

Bob Ricketts
Buyer
Barney Greengrass

What skills are most important to you?

"A buyer needs to be knowledgeable about trends and products. My job is to select and purchase merchandise from a number of different sources. I need to be at the nexus of everything, and so communication skills are very important. I must be able to relate to sellers and know the difference between the hype and the reality. This is an extremely stressful job at times, and you need to handle your customers and coworkers well. My job requires a good deal of creativity!"

What kind of training did you have?

"I have been in food service all of my life. My family had a restaurant business in Chicago. I did not go to college for restaurant management; instead I worked my way up the ladder, developing my sales skills along the way. I took some short-term classes in culinary school. The growing importance of computers in my line of business has encouraged me to broaden my horizons."

Why did you focus on a career in retail buying?

"This job allows me to combine my retail knowledge with my personal communication skills. Knowledge is useless without application and I have been able to apply all of my knowledge in my work. The sky is the limit as long as you apply the knowledge that you have gained."

What is your key to success?

"My key to my success is to know my product. I need to recognize quality and turn down inferior products that are not up to our standards."

Thinking Critically
How does a job as a retail buyer differ from that of a retail salesperson?

Career Facts

Education and Training: High school courses in marketing, accounting, business, and consumer education help to develop skills needed to become a retail purchaser. Two-year as well as four-year college programs in business administration, marketing, or finance provide good preparation for becoming a buyer. Some companies offer in-store training.

Aptitudes, Abilities, and Skills: Ability to organize and coordinate goods, attention to detail, computer skills, and accuracy are necessary. Buyers must be able to discern quality, recognize trends, work well with people, negotiate terms, manage budgets, and make decisions.

Career Outlook: Slower than average growth is projected through the year 2006.

Career Path: A typical career path begins as a sales clerk or trainee and proceeds through assistant to head buyer. Some individuals may advance to business executive and manager positions.

Careers in Marketing

Ask a student to read the Careers in Marketing feature aloud to the class. Discuss the skills and aptitudes required for a career in retail buying. Ask students whether they think they would like or dislike a career in retail buying. Discuss the pros and cons of such a career.

Thinking Critically Answer
A retail buyer selects and purchases merchandise from a number of different sources.

Guest Speakers
Invite a buyer to class to discuss his/her job.

Exploring Careers

Researching Qualifications
1. Ask students what qualities and skills they think are necessary to be a clothing buyer for a department store.
2. Have them write their ideas on a separate sheet of paper.
3. Have students find at least three newspaper job ads for a clothing buyer (or another type of buyer).
4. Have students write down the qualifications and job requirements for each advertised job.
5. Then tell them to compare their initial ideas about qualifications for a clothing buyer with those found in the ads.

Lifelong Learning

Purchasing

Consumers can be thought of as purchasing agents for their homes and/or businesses. Many steps mentioned in this chapter can help students plan major purchases, as well as analyze and understand their own needs. Tips such as keeping track of purchased items can encourage students to become astute and well-informed consumers.

Meeting Individual Needs

Students with Behavior Disorders

Students with behavior disorders require a class environment with support and structure so they know what to expect and what will be expected of them. Determine the best learning modality for each student, and structure activities accordingly. For example, a visual learner would benefit from viewing photographs or computer graphics.

Chapter 23 ASSESSMENT

VOCABULARY REVIEW

Write one sentence per each group of vocabulary terms.

- Organizational, retail, and wholesale buyers
- Six-month merchandise plan and OTB
- Centralized vs. decentralized buying
- Consignment and memorandum buying
- Electronic exchange and reverse auctions

FACT AND IDEA REVIEW

1. In manufacturing and service businesses, what are three job titles that people responsible for purchasing might have? (23.1)

2. How do industrial buyers use materials requirement planning (MRP) in their purchasing function, and how is it related to the master production schedule? (23.1)

3. What is the main role of wholesale and retail buyers? (23.1)

4. Why are projected accurate planned sales figures important in a merchandise plan? (23.1)

5. Explain three buying situations in which all buyers may find themselves. Provide an example of each. (23.2)

6. What is the significance of want slips to retail buyers? (23.2)

7. What is a resident buying office, and how might it help a local retail buyer? (23.2)

8. Explain the importance of one special service that retailers may demand from suppliers. (23.2)

9. What are customer advantages and disadvantages of online purchasing through third parties? (23.2)

THINKING CRITICALLY

1. Why wouldn't you prepare a new merchandise plan every month? What is a planning method that is more effective?

2. Why is it a good idea to keep a stock-to-sales ratio low?

3. Your high school is purchasing a new copier. Who in the school system might influence the purchasing decision?

4. In recent years, there has been an increased effort to put an end to employing individuals in sweatshops. Why do you think this is so?

5. As a result of online purchasing, are face-to-face negotiations between suppliers and industrial and retail buyers a thing of the past? Why or why not?

BUILDING WORKPLACE SKILLS

1. **Writing** You work in a men's clothing store. A customer approaches you and asks for a sweater that the store does not carry. Design and prepare a want slip for this request.

2. **Human Relations** Top level management has instructed you to speak with a buyer who has been with the company for twenty years. The purpose of the meeting is to let the buyer (who is not computer literate) know that management wants him to purchase online.

Answer Key

Vocabulary Review

Paragraphs will vary. See Glossary for definitions.

Fact and Idea Review

1. purchasing managers, industrial buyers, or procurement managers
2. The company's master production schedule would provide the purchasing manager with details of production needed to meet sales requirements. To determine when to buy those items, the purchasing manager would be responsible for materials requirement planning, which includes an analysis of when to make the purchases so they are available when needed.
3. They forecast the needs of their firms' customers and buy products that will meet those needs.
4. Accurate planned sales figures are necessary because all other figures are computed on the basis of those figures.
5. Three buying situations are: new-task purchase—a first-time purchase of a new product line; modified rebuy—prior purchase that has changed in some respect, such as purchasing from a new vendor; and straight-rebuy—purchase made repeatedly without change such as routinely ordering goods from the same vendor.
6. Want slips help retail buyers identify unrecognized needs of the store's customers.
7. Resident buying offices are retailers' representatives in a central market. They send information to retail buyers on a regular basis, informing them about new merchandise offerings, closeouts, fashion trends, special buys in the market, and market conditions.
8. They may request the placement by manufacturers of Universal Product Codes on goods, saving the retailer time because individual items do not have to be marked with a price.
9. The biggest advantage is lower prices. Privacy is a problem because the Internet puts a lot of information in the public domain. Another problem is that unknown companies could artificially deflate prices by bidding low prices in a reverse auction.

Thinking Critically

1. Such a short lead time hardly allows for "planning." The Six-Month Merchandise Plan is more effective.
2. Keeping a low stock-to-sales is a good idea so that too much money is not tied up in inventory.
3. principal, superintendent, or business administrator
4. Answer will vary but may include that human rights violations harm a company's image and may affect sales.
5. Answers will vary. Some will say it is over for the industrial buyers and retail buyers who deal in staple items that easily can be purchased online. Others may say retail buyers that deal in fashionable merchandise may not be as easily replaced because the fashion industry changes constantly.

Building Workplace Skills

1. Want slip designs will vary but should include basic information about the item requested, the customer, the salesperson, and department.
2. Answers will vary.

Applying Marketing Concepts

1. Planned purchases are: Jan. $192,500; Feb. $250,800; March $206,250; April $212,575; May $152,900; and June $133,925.

APPLYING MARKETING CONCEPTS

1. **Preparing a Six-Month Plan** Use a spreadsheet program to prepare a six-month merchandise plan (from January to June) based on the following information. Last year's sales figures are: January $100,000; February $120,000; March $150,000; April $155,000; May $160,000; and June $145,000. July's sales were $130,000 (needed to calculate planned EOM figure). Sales are expected to increase 10 percent this year. The stock-to-sales ratio for each month is the same as last year at 3:1. Reductions are done at 15 percent of planned sales.

2. **Selecting a Vendor** You have been asked to select a vendor for the purchase of 150 pairs of jeans. Using a word-processing program, prepare a memo that includes your analysis of the two potential vendors and your recommendation for one of them. Provide calculations used in determining the final price for one pair of jeans for each vendor (taking into consideration all available discounts and shipping charges), as well as a rationale for your recommendation.
   - Vendor A has a reputation for late deliveries. The price per pair of jeans is $20, and there is a one percent quantity discount on all purchases over 100. Vendor A has dating terms of 2/10, net 30 and delivery charges of $79 (FOB shipping point).
   - Vendor B has an excellent reputation for delivering on time. The price per pair of jeans is $22 with dating terms of 2/10, net 60 and free delivery (FOB store).

LINKING SCHOOL TO WORK

Personal and Information Skills Interview someone who is responsible for purchasing supplies or merchandise for resale. Ask about his or her job responsibilities and the skills required. Share your findings with your classmates.

THE DECA CONNECTION

Role Play: Buying Intern

Situation You are an intern for the buyer of bicycles for a chain store operation. The buyer has asked that you show a new intern how to do the calculations for a merchandise plan.

Activity You will need to explain the basis for planned sales percentage increases. The standard stock-to-sales ratio for your store is 4, and retail reductions are generally 10 percent of sales.

Evaluation You will be evaluated on how well you meet the following performance indicators:
- Compute the figures found on a merchandise plan
- Use current economic information to project the rate of increase, if any, in planned sales
- Communicate knowledge and use of a merchandise plan

interNET CONNECTION

Paper, Pens, and Pencils

Since your business purchases office supplies on a regular basis, you decide to check out e-commerce as a means for purchasing them.

Connect
- Find five different Internet sources for purchasing office supplies.
- Evaluate the prices for one item found on all five sites.
- Present your findings in a memo along with your recommendation.

Chapter 23 ■ *Purchasing* **427**

2. Calculations to support each vendor are: Vendor A: $20 x 150 = $3,000 x .99 (one percent quantity discount) = $2,970 x .98 (cash discount) = $2910.60 + $79 for shipping = $2989.60 divided by 150 = $19.93 unit price for Vendor A. Vendor B: $22 x 150 = $3,300 x .98 (cash discount) = $3234 divided by 150 = $21.56 unit price for Vendor B. Arguments for selecting either vendor can be made.

Linking School to Work

Oral presentations will vary.

1. **Assessment** Have students complete the Reproducible Test for Chapter 23 or construct your own tests using the ExamView software.

2. **Enrichment** Have students complete the corresponding activities in the following workbooks:
   - *Marketing Math Workbook*, p. 59
   - *Marketing Research Project Workbook*, p. 111

Chapter Overview

Chapter 24 discusses the key functions in the distribution system of stock handling and inventory control—including the steps in the receiving process for merchandise, the concept of inventory control, and the types of inventory systems. Students are exposed to the concepts of unit and dollar control of inventory, stock turnover, and stock management. Finally, the impact of technology on inventory systems is explored.

 Springboard

Brainstorm Ask students to imagine they own a business. How would they know what merchandise is on order, is on hand, has been sold, and needs to be ordered? A process to receive merchandise and storage is needed to be able to answer these questions.

Prereading

List the section objectives to discuss with students. Have the students skim the chapter, looking at the pictures, reading the captions, and noting the heads. Ask questions to ensure students have a minimal understanding of the chapter structure.

Preteaching Marketing Vocabulary

Ask students to define the vocabulary. Write the most accurate definitions on the board. Then list the terms with which they are unfamiliar and write the correct definitions as you come to them in the chapter.

Marketing: What It Takes

Answer Selection criteria may include use of computerized inventory tracking systems and electronic data interchange.

Stock Handling and Inventory Control

Marketing: What It Takes

Planning and Controlling Your Inventory

You work for a manufacturer that ships products for the domestic as well as international markets. You have been asked by management to identify the criteria to be used when selecting a freight carrier to move your products to market quickly and help your company better manage its inventory.

WHAT WILL YOU DO?
What selection criteria will you identify for the freight carrier?

428

THE DECA CONNECTION

ADVISOR CORNER

Advisory Committee Support The importance of having a good advisory committee cannot be stressed enough. Advisors who rely on an advisory committee run successful chapters with the support of business professionals. When establishing your advisory committee, choose about five members with diverse marketing backgrounds. This group can provide guidance for the marketing program, assist with fund raising, help with media contacts, serve as classroom speakers, provide editing assistance with written projects, and more. Consider organizing a group of adults who might want to lend their expertise on an advisory committee. *(Jay Walker, Robinson Secondary School, Fairfax County, VA)*

The Stock Handling Process

Stock Handling

Manufacturers and suppliers all receive many different parts or raw materials for use in making finished products. These items are received in stock and must be tracked just as retailers track the merchandise they receive.

Whether a business receives raw materials, parts, or merchandise, a process is needed for handling items received. The steps in the stock handling process include receiving goods, checking them, marking the goods with information, and delivering them to their selling location.

■ Receiving Merchandise

Merchandise ordered by a store is received, checked, and marked with a selling price before it is transferred to the sales area. In larger businesses, several people do this job. In smaller businesses, a salesperson, manager, or even the owner may perform this function.

Where merchandise is received depends on the type and size of the business. Smaller businesses may have a back room or may even use store aisles for receiving merchandise. Most stores, however, have enough space to devote a part of the basement, upstairs, or first floor to receiving.

Large businesses and chain stores usually have separate warehouses or distribution centers to receive and store merchandise before it is routed within the company. The specific area where deliveries are made by carriers is called a *dock*. Docks usually have covered or enclosed platforms to protect the merchandise from weather damage. They are large enough to accommodate the type and size of shipment the business normally receives.

RECEIVING RECORDS Every business records the goods it receives in a receiving record or log. A **receiving record** is a form that is used to describe the goods received by a business. The items on a receiving record depend on the needs of the business. They can include the following:

- Person who received the shipment
- Shipper of the merchandise
- Place from which the goods were shipped
- Name of the carrier
- Number of the carrier
- Number of items delivered
- Weight of items delivered
- Shipping charges
- Department or store that ordered the merchandise
- Date the shipment was received

What You'll Learn

- The need for a stock handling process
- How merchandise is received and checked
- The methods and procedures used to mark merchandise
- The procedures used for transferring merchandise

Why It's Important

To be successful, businesses must have systems in place to handle and organize their stock. This helps control costs and ensure that operations can continue without interruption.

Key Terms

- receiving record
- blind check method
- direct check method
- spot check method
- quality check method
- source marking
- preretailing marking method

Classroom Resources

For the Teacher
- Teacher Editions for all workbooks
- Assessment Package
- PowerPoint Presentation Software
- Interactive Lesson Planner
- ILP Block Scheduling, p. 7
- ILP Lesson Plans, p. 51
- ILP Internet Resources, p. 67

- ILP *BusinessWeek* Case Studies, p. 151
- ILP Marketing Career Portfolio, p. 37
- *Marketing Essentials* Web site (**www.marketing.glencoe.com**)

For the Student
- Student Activity Workbook, p. 203
- Marketing Math Workbook, p. 59

- Marketing Research Project Workbook, p. 111
- ILP School-to-Work Activity Workbook, p. 101
- Virtual Business simulation
- *Marketing Essentials* Web site (**www.marketing.glencoe.com**)

ILP These resources are available in print and on the Interactive Lesson Planner (ILP)

FOCUS

Bell Ringer Activity

Study and Discuss Receiving goods is the first step in inventory management. Copy a receiving record or an apron (from a local business such as a fast food restaurant or a retail store), and give each student a copy. Explain to students the basic usage of the record or apron. Have them study the categories on each and discuss why the information on the forms is essential for receiving merchandise.

Introducing the Section

The Stock Handling Process
Have students think about how they might receive inventory in the school store. How would they check it to verify quantity and condition? How would they mark it and move it to the sales area? If you do not have a school store, ask how students would verify quantity, condition, and perhaps mark various items used for a DECA fund-raising sale.

Ask students why receiving, checking, and marking inventory are considered part of the physical distribution process. *(Distribution includes handling and storing products.)*

In Chapter 22 students looked at the general physical distribution process, which included warehousing. In this section they will further explore the physical distribution process by looking at receiving, checking, marking, and transferring merchandise.

TEACH

Technology Resources

PowerPoint The *Marketing Essentials* PowerPoint Presentation CD-ROM provides visual lecture aids for every chapter section.

429

Concept Development

1. Read Section 24.1 with students.
2. Have students visit a local business, warehouse, or distribution center, which receives a substantial amount of merchandise daily. Ask them to observe and talk with those who receive, check, and mark merchandise. Have students ask if these procedures have changed and/or been streamlined over the years. Why or why not? If so, what changes have occurred? How do the procedures vary by type of merchandise received? How has technology changed inventory management practices?

Discussion Starter

Handling Inventory Have students think of some ways that receiving, checking, marking, and transferring merchandise would be handled on these products: flowers and plants; produce such as fruits and vegetables; seafood and fresh fish; and animals, birds, and aquarium fish received at a pet store. *(All of these products would probably be more closely inspected than other products that are easier to check, such as canned goods.)*

CAPTION ANSWER
Receiving Stock—An Important First Step It depends on the size of the business. Specially trained employees called receivers are responsible for checking merchandise in larger businesses, while smaller businesses may use sales associates, a manager, or even the owner to perform this activity.

Some businesses use a short type of receiving record called an *apron*. An apron is a form attached to the invoice before the merchandise moves through checking and marking. The apron system helps prevent the payment of duplicate invoices because the apron is made out only when the shipment is received.

The receiving number may be called an apron number for businesses using this system. In retail business, the apron is prepared by a store's buyers. Apron forms stay with the merchandise until it reaches the sales floor. They list the steps the merchandise takes to reach the selling floor. The information found on the apron includes the receiving number, the department number, the purchase order number, any terms on the purchase order and on the invoice, routing information, and the date the shipment was checked.

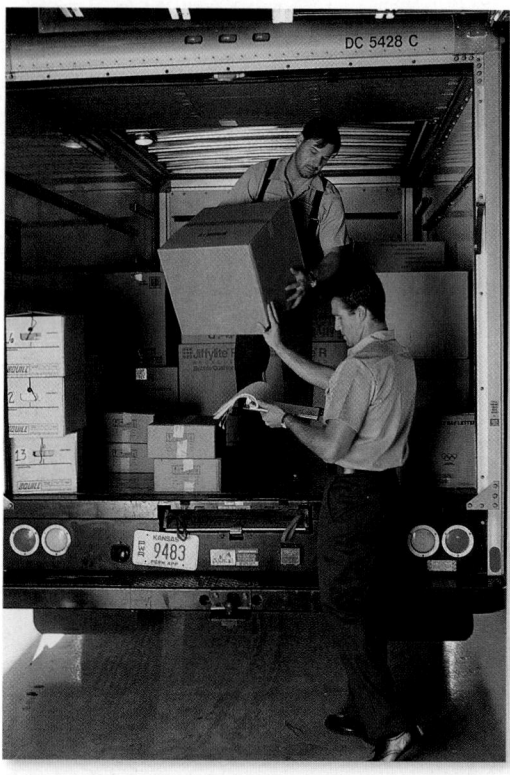

■ **Receiving Stock—An Important First Step** Newly arrived merchandise is inspected and recorded. This activity represents the first step in the stock handling process. *Who is responsible for this activity in a business?*

Electronic Elimination

Excess and obsolete equipment is a big problem for big businesses. U.S. industries generate about $18 billion in excess inventory a year that they cannot sell, which is nearly ten percent of all finished goods produced. Manufacturers attempting to get to the bottom of this big problem and sort out their extra-large trash are looking to a new source—the Internet. New commercial Internet software will allow companies to run their own auctions and generate revenue by selling excess and outdated merchandise. This software saves companies the time and effort of creating such marketplaces themselves. Now a clothing company can sell surplus fabric on an online auction to an interested retail company, or a car manufacturer can find a home for unused parts. This saves companies money and saves the environment some space!

Thinking Critically
What types of companies could benefit from online auction software?

■ Checking Merchandise

Checking is the process of going through the goods upon receipt to make sure they arrived undamaged and that the merchandise ordered was the merchandise received. Merchandise must be checked to verify quantity and condition once it is received. All cartons are checked for damage, and the merchandise is sorted and counted. Some businesses use specially trained employees called *receivers* to inspect and record newly arrived merchandise. In larger businesses, checking is usually done in the receiving area. In small retail stores, it may be done in the aisles.

In the past, checking merchandise was a time- and labor-intensive process. Today, however, many distribution systems use electronic data interchange systems that considerably minimize the time required for this process. The distribution center can pre-notify the retailer regarding what should be in each box. UPC coded shipping box labels can be electronically scanned, identifying the carton's

 Electronic Elimination

Answer All companies that have a surplus of goods or raw materials can benefit from the use of an online auction. Larger manufacturers with extra-large excess inventory would especially benefit by generating revenue with the time-saving software that runs online auctions.

contents, and the information is automatically transferred to an inventory management computer system.

There are other merchandise checking methods, as well. Invoices and shipping tickets should always be verified against physical counts. The physical count is also verified against the purchase order. There are four methods that are frequently used to check merchandise. These methods include the blind check, direct check, spot check, and the quality check.

The blind check method requires the receiver to write the description of the merchandise, count the quantities received, and list them on a blank form or dummy invoice. The list or dummy invoice is then compared to the actual invoice after the blind check is made. The blind check method is considered the most accurate checking method, but it can be time-consuming. The blind check method is used when the merchandise needs to be moved quickly to the sales floor and the actual invoice has not yet been received from the seller. Invoices often follow the shipment of goods by two or more days.

With the direct check method, the merchandise is checked directly against the actual invoice or purchase order. This procedure is faster than the blind check method, but errors may not be found if the invoice itself is incorrect. Some receivers do not completely check the total number of items once they see the amount listed on the invoice—if the amount looks correct, they may not bother to take an actual count.

The spot check method is a random check of one carton in a shipment (such as one out of every twenty). The carton is checked for quantity, and then one product in the carton is inspected for quality. When the contents are as stated on the invoice, the remaining cartons are assumed to be the same. Spot checking is often used for products such as canned goods, paper products, and pharmaceuticals.

The quality check method is done to inspect the workmanship and general characteristics of the received merchandise. Although a receiver can do a quality check, a buyer often performs this check. The merchandise is checked to determine whether the quality of the goods received matches the quality of the products which were ordered. If the goods are damaged, a damage report is prepared. Damaged goods should not be discarded without the authorization of the supplier.

REAL WORLD MARKETING

Tracking Time

Do you send documents to a new client for next-day delivery? Do you keep track of the shipper's guarantees for timely delivery? For a monthly fee of $9.95, a Web service will track the status of a regular customer's FedEx and United Parcel Service shipments. The program alerts the sender whenever a package arrives later than the time guaranteed by the delivery company. Once alerted, the shipper can use that information to ask FedEx or UPS to fulfill its on-time guarantee by paying a full refund for the cost of shipping the package, usually between $10 and $20.

Thinking Critically
Why might this service be of value to a business?

RETURNING MERCHANDISE Careful checking practices can save a business large amounts of money. All incorrect items, damaged merchandise, and items ordered but not received are identified and reported according to the policies of the business. When this is done, the business can get proper credit or adjustments from the carrier or the seller.

Apart from damage, there are many other reasons a business might return merchandise. Perhaps it received something it did not order or decided to cancel an order after it was shipped. Sometimes orders get mixed up and delivered to the wrong clients. It is also possible that the seller sent too many items or that the merchandise arrived late.

Upon return of the merchandise, the seller issues a *credit memorandum*. A credit memorandum is notification that the buyer's account has been credited for the value of the returned merchandise.

Thinking Critically

Damaged Merchandise Have students think of some reasons why merchandise sometimes arrives damaged at a business. *(Some possibilities are: poor packing of the product, either in its packaging or in the carrier itself; mishandling merchandise before or after it is shipped; and bad weather conditions that made the physical transport of the merchandise unusually rough.)*

Cooperative Learning

Receiving/Checking/Marking Systems If you have a school store, have students work as a team to receive, check, and mark merchandise for a defined period of time (perhaps one month) in the store. After that time they should assess how they could improve on the process of doing all three tasks and present a written report on how they would implement changes in the current receiving/checking/marking system.

Independent Practice

Research and Report Have students check with a store that has more than one outlet in your area and determine why and how stock is transferred between stores. Students should present their findings to the class as an oral report.

REAL WORLD MARKETING

Tracking Time
Answer This service is valuable because it saves a company money and ensures that deliveries are made on time.

■ **Marking Merchandise** Different methods are used for marking merchandise depending on the product. *Why are UPCs often used for source marking?*

■ Marking Merchandise

After it has been received and checked, merchandise must be marked with the selling price and other information. Different methods may be used for various kinds of merchandise. The most common method of marking price is with a UPC, however a hand-operated pricing machine or pricing tickets can be used as well.

Universal Product Codes (UPCs) are widely used in business today for tracking merchandise. Many businesses receive goods that are preticketed with prices and UPCs. As you learned in Chapter 16, UPCs are made up of parallel vertical bars and a row of numbers printed on a package or a label. These codes describe the merchandise and price information. The UPC codes are scanned into a computer for use in tracking sales and inventory levels.

UPCs are often used for **source marking**. With this method, the seller or manufacturer marks the price before delivering the merchandise to the retailer. Merchandise can be moved directly from the receiving area to the sales floor. The UPCs are scanned at the checkout area, and the price stored in the computer for that code is entered for the sale.

Some businesses use a *preretailing marking method* of marking merchandise. With the **preretailing marking method**, pricing information is marked in advance on the purchase order. This information is entered in the buyer's computer system, and prices are available for marking merchandise as soon as it is received. Preretailing marking is normally used for staple items that are

unlikely to have price changes between the time of the order and receipt of the merchandise. It saves time because merchandise can be price marked immediately.

Merchandise can also be marked at the store with an electric or hand-operated pricing machine. Few stores use this method today because of the wide use of bar code scanners.

Finally, merchandise can be marked with the familiar price tickets. In large stores, price tickets are prepared by hand or by machine in a marking room or in a stock room. Gum labels are used on merchandise with a flat, hard surface such as books. Pin tickets are used on merchandise that will not be damaged by the pinholes, such as socks or scarves. String or plastic tags are used for larger articles, such as dresses, shirts, and suits. The pricing ticket also helps when a customer needs to return an item to a store as it is difficult to return an item that has no tags.

PRICE TICKET INFORMATION Price marking on the price ticket identifies the price of the merchandise. Other important information may also be included on the price ticket. Many businesses include information such as store numbers, model or style numbers, color, sizes, fabrics, manufacturer's number, and lot numbers. This information is useful for tracking merchandise. It helps a business determine which items, sizes, and colors are popular with customers. This information may also simplify the shopping process for consumers as necessary information is contained in one place.

■ Transferring Merchandise

Once merchandise is received, checked, and marked, it is ready to be moved to the sales area. From there it is often transferred to different departments within the business.

Stock is generally transferred from a department or store to a warehouse at the beginning of each season. Old merchandise must be removed from the department sales area to make room for new merchandise. The old merchandise is put on sale for a short time, and the merchandise that does not sell is transferred to a warehouse or distribution center.

Transferred merchandise is accompanied by a form describing the items, style numbers, colors, sizes, cost, and retail prices. Duplicate copies of the transfer forms are retained as a record of merchandise on hand.

Stock transfers between departments can occur when merchandise is carried by more than one department or when the demand for merchandise in one department creates a need for additional merchandise. Stock transfers can also occur when the merchandise is used for sales promotions, such as displays, advertising illustrations, or fashion shows or when the merchandise is used for installation or repairs in various departments.

Stock transfers between stores can occur to meet unexpected demand or to fill requests by customers. A customer may find the perfect pair of pants, but find that the branch of the store is sold out. Some stores will call another local store to have it send

over the right size. Finally, stock transfers from store to distribution outlet can occur when off-season and nonsaleable merchandise is sold to surplus or discount stores. A store may choose to transfer all of its bathing suits to a discount store if the stock doesn't clear out during after-season sales.

Swimwear in Winter

Managing inventory is difficult enough for most businesses. When selling to international customers, this job becomes even harder. This is especially true if the clients are in Chili or the far south of South America. Geographic differences find those areas entering the heat of summer while we enter winter—seasons are reversed. While shoppers are snatching up warm coats and snow shovels in the United States, their South American counterparts are trying on bathing suits and new suntan lotions.

Thinking Critically
How can a business maintain storage room if stocking for both summer and winter simultaneously?

24.1 ASSESSMENT

Reviewing Key Terms and Concepts

1. Describe the stock handling process.
2. What is the purpose of a receiving record?
3. What are the four methods used for checking merchandise?
4. Explain two methods used for marking merchandise.
5. What are some reasons for transferring merchandise between various store departments?

Thinking Critically

6. Retailers often code their actual cost of merchandise on price tickets. Do you think this information should be kept from customers? Why or why not?

Integrating Academic Skills

7. **COMMUNICATION** Use word processing software to write a two-page report detailing how an effective receiving process can benefit a business's sales, goods, expenses, and image.

Chapter 24 ■ *Stock Handling and Inventory Control* **433**

CLOSE

Section Wrap-Up

Have students work in pairs to explain to each other, in their own words, the methods of receiving, checking, marking, and transferring merchandise. When students have finished, review these concepts with the class.

Swimwear in Winter
Answer A business can use a Quick Response Delivery program or use warehouse storage space.

Inventory Control

Bell Ringer Activity

Define and Brainstorm Ask students to define *inventory management*. Then ask students to imagine they manage a store that offers different products (for example, a video rental store, a sporting goods store, a restaurant). Have them think of some reasons why inventory management would be challenging in this store.

Introducing the Section

Inventory Control Businesses must anticipate customer demand for various types of merchandise, as well as balance the cost of inventory with the benefits of maintaining a large inventory.

In this lesson, students will look at inventory management and how technology has made the process easier and more efficient.

What You'll Learn

- The concept of inventory management
- Different types of inventory systems
- Unit and dollar control of inventory
- How to calculate stock turnover
- The concept of stock management of basic, model stock, and never-out lists
- The impact of technology on inventory systems

Why It's Important

The inventory a business owns represents money tied up in products until the inventory is sold. Since inventory is a large part of the total investment of a business, well-managed and controlled inventories increase the profits of a business.

Key Terms

- inventory
- inventory management
- just-in-time (JIT) inventory system
- perpetual inventory system
- physical inventory system
- tickler control
- dollar control
- unit control
- stockkeeping unit (sku)
- stock turnover
- basic stock list
- model stock list
- never-out list
- real time inventory system

Inventory Management

Inventory is one of the most costly parts of business operations for many businesses. **Inventory** refers to an amount of goods stored, including raw materials, purchased components, manufactured subassemblies, works in process, packaging materials, and finished goods. Finished goods are often subdivided to reflect the stock at a manufacturing plant and the stock in distribution centers and warehouses. Retail inventory includes all goods for resale. It is important to maintain a certain level of inventory to meet supply and demand needs.

Inventory management is the process of buying and storing products for sale while controlling costs for ordering, shipping, handling, and storage. This is usually the responsibility of the supply chain manager. Unnecessarily high inventories can create many problems for a business. In addition to using up valuable storage space, they increase personnel costs for security, production, and warehouse staff, cause higher inventory insurance premiums, and may lead to increased interest expenses for a business. Businesses lose money and reduce profits when they manage their inventories poorly. They may have the wrong merchandise in stock, holding too many slow-selling items or too few fast-selling ones.

Inventory management has been greatly affected by the just-in time (JIT) inventory management system. This system originated in the 1980s in the auto manufacturing industry and has since been adopted by the other manufacturers. A **just-in-time (JIT) inventory system** is an arrangement in which suppliers deliver parts and raw materials just before they are needed for production. Orders are placed when parts and supplies run low. Plants keep only small stocks on hand to avoid tying up money and inventory space.

Computer link-ups tell suppliers and transportation companies which items are needed and when to deliver them to meet production needs. Parts are delivered on a schedule—just in time for use in the production process. A late shipment can bring an entire manufacturing operation to a standstill.

In this system, parts go straight to production, where they are assembled immediately. No parts are stored. Finished goods are shipped to customers as soon as they are assembled. Inventories of completed or partially completed products are kept to a minimum.

In essence, the manufacturer enters into a partnership with suppliers to guarantee frequent shipments of goods that keep pace with production needs. JIT inventory management reduces inventory investment and improves cash flow for a business. This type of inventory management system is particularly useful when there is reliable forecasting for goods that will be used quickly.

434 Unit 7 ■ *Distribution*

Classroom Resources

For the Teacher
- Teacher Editions for all workbooks
- Assessment Package
- PowerPoint Presentation Software
- Interactive Lesson Planner
- ILP Block Scheduling, p. 7
- ILP Lesson Plans, p. 52
- ILP Internet Resources, p. 67

ILP Blackline Masters, p. 45
ILP *BusinessWeek* Case Studies, p. 151
ILP Marketing Career Portfolio, p. 37
- *Marketing Essentials* Web site (**www.marketing.glencoe.com**)

For the Student
- Student Activity Workbook, p. 203
- Marketing Math Workbook, p. 59

- Marketing Research Project Workbook, p. 111
ILP School-to-Work Activity Workbook, p. 101
- Virtual Business simulation
- *Marketing Essentials* Web site (**www.marketing.glencoe.com**)

ILP These resources are available in print and on the Interactive Lesson Planner (ILP)

Inventory management is complex because a business has to correctly anticipate demand for its products while trying to keep overall inventory investment as low as possible. Retail businesses are expected to:

- Maintain the right quantities of merchandise without running out of stock
- Keep a wide product assortment (with low inventory investment) without compromising on customer needs and wants
- Purchase merchandise at large volumes to gain the lowest prices while not buying more than it will sell
- Keep a current inventory on hand

Good inventory management balances the costs of inventory with the benefits of maintaining a large inventory. The costs of inventory include not only the cost of the items in stock, but also storage, insurance, and taxes. Inventory ties up a business's working capital—money that could be used for other purposes. It is not effective for a company to maintain large inventory holdings if that money could be spent more effectively somewhere else or invested. Effective inventory management helps increase working capital and allows a business to use its savings to pay for other business expenses.

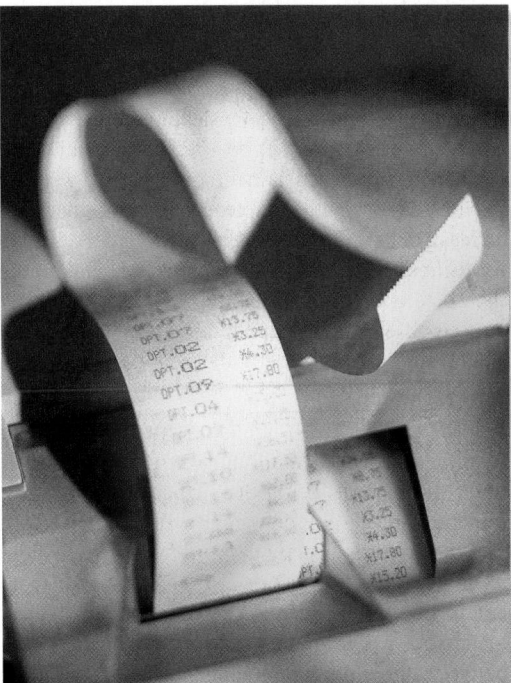

■ **Manual Systems** With manual inventory control systems, employees gather paper records of sales information to track inventory. *What are some examples of paper records that can be used to track inventory?*

BRIGHT IDEAS

Bar Codes: Bionic Fingerprints

Bar codes are everywhere today, on product packages and goods. They are so common you probably don't even think twice about them. Where did they come from? In 1948, a local food chain store owner asked the Drexel Institute of Technology in Pennsylvania to research a method of automatically reading product information during checkout. Graduate students Bernard Silver and Norman Joseph Woodland were assigned to work on a solution. Woodland first used ultraviolet light sensitive ink, which was unsuccessful. Their second attempt, however, proved more fruitful! The duo filed for a patent, and in 1966, the bar code was first used commercially. The first scanner was installed at March's supermarket in Troy, Ohio, in 1974. What was the revolutionary product to carry the first bar code? Wrigley's gum!

Thinking Creatively

Why are bar codes so important today?

Chapter 24 ■ *Stock Handling and Inventory Control* **435**

Inventory Systems

All merchandise bought and sold must be tracked to gain the information needed for effective inventory management (see Figure 24-1 on page 437). Two methods of tracking inventory are the perpetual inventory system and the physical inventory system.

Perpetual Inventory System

A perpetual inventory system tracks the number of items in inventory on a constant basis. The system tracks all new items purchased and returned, as well as sales of current stock. An up-to-date count of inventory is maintained for purchases and returns of merchandise, sales and sales returns, sales allowances, and transfers to other stores and departments. With a perpetual inventory system, a business keeps track of sales as they occur.

MANUAL SYSTEMS Employees gather paper records of sales and enter that information into the inventory system in a manual system. These records can include receiving department records, sales checks, price tickets, cash register receipts, stock transfer requests, and other documents used for coding and tabulation.

Merchandise tags are used to record information about the vendor, date of receipt, department, product classification, color, sizes, and style. The merchandise tags from items sold are sent in batches to a company-owned tabulating facility or to an independent computer service organization where the coded information is analyzed through the use of computer software.

COMPUTER BASED SYSTEMS Computer based systems to control inventory are increasingly popular even among smaller businesses. They are also faster and more accurate than manual systems. As you learned in Chapter 16, a *point-of-sale terminal* uses hand-held laser guns, stationary lasers, light pens, or slot scanners to feed sales transaction data directly from Universal Product Codes (UPCs), sales checks, or merchandise tags into a computer. Businesses then use computer-generated information printouts at different times for review and action.

Offline point-of-sale terminals can also relay sales information directly to a supplier. The supplier then uses the sales transaction data to ship additional items automatically to the business.

Physical Inventory System

Under a physical inventory system, stock is visually inspected or actually counted to determine the quantity on hand. A physical inventory can be conducted periodically or on a regular annual basis.

Even if a perpetual inventory system is used, businesses normally complete a physical inventory at least once a year. A physical inventory allows a business to calculate its income tax, determine the correct value of its ending inventory, identify any stock shortages, and plan future purchases. There are several methods used for physical inventory control.

VISUAL CONTROL Visual control is used to monitor physical inventory levels. Hardware stores often place stock cards on pegboards with stock numbers and descriptions for each item displayed. The stock cards specify the number of each item to be kept in stock. It can also be somewhat inaccurate because it does not account for misplaced merchandise. The amount to reorder is the difference between the number on hand and the specified number to be stocked.

Although a visual control system is easy for stock clerks and ordering personnel to use, it does not tell the rate of sales for each item. It can also be somewhat inaccurate because it does not account for misplaced merchandise. The number to stock may be an estimate of sales for a typical period of time.

TICKLER CONTROL Another method of physical control is called tickler control. In the tickler control method, a small portion of the inventory is physically counted each day so that the entire inventory is accounted for on a regular basis. The entire inventory is never counted at one time. Manufacturers' representatives do a variation of the tickler control method. The representative visits a business on a regular basis, takes the stock count, and writes the order. Unwanted merchandise is removed from stock and returned to the manufacturer through a predetermined, authorized procedure.

ANNUAL INVENTORY COUNT Most businesses physically count inventory at least once a year. In many cases, the business will close so employees can count the inventory. Employees usually work in pairs—one counts merchandise while the other records the count. After the counting is finished, the total value of the inventory is determined. This value is reported on the business's financial statements.

More About . . .

Inventory Management
In some industries, such as grocery and dry goods, it can take 60 days to move a product through distribution channels. According to an article in the *Journal of Commerce*, the grocery sector could save $30 billion annually by reducing inventory cycle time, and the dry goods industry could save $10 billion a year.

FIGURE 24-1

TIPS FOR BETTER INVENTORY MANAGEMENT

All merchandise that is bought and sold must be tracked to gain the information needed for effective inventory management.

1 AT TIME OF DELIVERY

At the time of delivery, it is important to verify counts and carefully inspect for damage. If damage is visible, note it on the delivery receipt and have the driver sign the business's copy.

2 WHEN DAMAGE IS DISCOVERED

When damage is discovered, retain the items in the receiving area and contact the carrier to report the damage and request an inspection.

3 DOCUMENT DAMAGES

Retain the damaged goods in the receiving area until the carrier prepares a damage report, which is checked for accuracy before signing.

4 AFTER INSPECTION

After inspection, the damaged items should not be disposed of without carrier permission and should not be returned without written authorization from the supplier.

Chapter 24 ■ *Stock Handling and Inventory Control* **437**

SECTION 24.2

Thinking Critically

Inventory Management Without using the textbook, have students independently answer these questions: Why do you think inventory management is so difficult? What expectations are placed on a business that complicates inventory management? Then open the questions for general discussion. *(Refer to Section 24.2 for some possible answers.)*

THE DECA CONNECTION
COMPETITIVE EVENTS AND MARKETING ESSENTIALS

Individual Series Event Chapter 24 is enhanced by the use of one of DECA's eleven Individual Series Events. The distribution instructional area provides the performance indicators that match the material in this chapter. The Full Service Restaurant Management Event and the Vehicles and Petroleum Marketing Event both provide several relevant role-play situations. The Individual Series Events are so named because one student participates in a series of activities. The student first takes a comprehensive exam, then completes two different role-play situations from the occupational area he or she has chosen.

Types of Inventory Have students work in pairs to generate lists of the types of goods that each of the following businesses would keep in its inventory: manufacturing *(raw materials, component parts such as motors and computer chips)*, wholesaling *(packaged products for resale and bulk products for resale)*, retailing *(merchandise for resale)*, service *(products used to provide services, such as auto accessories in a car repair business and hair-care products in a beauty salon)*, and extraction *(extracted materials such as ore, crops, fish, and semi-processed materials)*.

■ Using Both Systems

A business does not have to choose between a physical inventory system and a perpetual inventory system. Many businesses find it most effective to use both systems. The perpetual system gives an up-to-date inventory record throughout the year. The physical system gives an accurate count that can be compared to the perpetual records to identify any errors or problems. The two systems actually compliment each other.

The perpetual inventory records are used to help the business track sales and manage its merchandise. After a physical inventory is taken, the ending inventory amount becomes the beginning inventory for the year that follows. Purchases during the year are added to this amount, while sales are subtracted. Ending inventory is calculated in the example that follows.

Number of Items for 1/1/00 to 6/30/00	
Beginning inventory, 1/1/2000	1,000
Net purchases (purchases less purchases and allowances returned)	+ 300
Merchandise available for sale	1,300
Less net sales (sales less returns and allowances)	− 1,050
Ending inventory 6/30/19	250

Sometimes the ending inventory shown in the perpetual inventory system does not match the physical count of inventory. When the physical count shows less merchandise than is supposed to be in inventory, a *stock shortage* or *shrinkage* has occurred. Theft, incorrect counting, and errors at the cash register or point-of-sale terminal can cause stock shortages for a business.

Using the previous example, all records for purchases and sales are ongoing in a business; therefore the data represents a perpetual inventory system. The ending inventory figure of 250 items is the perpetual inventory. However, as you know, it is possible that this is not the most accurate count. If the physical inventory system showed ending inventory of 225, a stock shortage of 25 would have occurred (250 − 225 = 25). It isn't until the physical inventory is taken that the company really knows if its ending inventory records are correct. It is still helpful, however, to use the perpetual inventory as a good estimation.

■ Stock Control

Stock control involves monitoring stock levels and investments in stock so that a business is run efficiently. Planning those stock levels and monitoring them requires the use of several different systems. They include dollar vs. unit control methods, stock turnover calculations, and three stock lists (model, basic, and never-out).

DOLLAR VS. UNIT CONTROL Inventory management involves both dollar control and unit control of merchandise held in inventory. **Dollar control** represents the planning and monitoring of the total inventory investment that a business makes during a stated period of time. A business's dollar control of inventory involves information about the amount of purchases, sales, dollar value of beginning and ending inventory, and stock shortages. This information helps a business determine the cost of goods sold and the amount of gross profit or loss during a given period of time. By subtracting operating expenses from the gross profit, the business can determine its net profit or loss. Additional information about developing profit and loss statements is found in Chapter 36.

Unit control refers to the quantities of merchandise that a business handles during a stated period of time. Unit control allows the business to keep stock adjusted to sales and lets the business determine how to spend money available under a planned budget. In a unit control inventory system, each item or a group of related items is referred to as a **stockkeeping unit (sku)**. A unit control inventory system tracks merchandise by the merchandise's sku. Tracking the skus gives valuable sales information on those items that are successful and those that are not selling. A business can use this information to make better merchandising decisions. Sales promotions can be run to sell slow-moving items or to spotlight popular ones.

Unit control records also allow purchasing personnel to see what brands, sizes, colors, and price lines are popular. By keeping track of this information, buyers can understand customer preferences and order accordingly. Finally, unit control records specify when items need to be ordered. When a minimum stock amount is reached, an order is placed for more stock. This system ensures that adequate assortments are available and helps avoid out-of-stock situations.

STOCK TURNOVER The most effective way to measure how well inventory is being managed is to look at stock turnover. Stock turnover is the number of times the average inventory has been sold and replaced in a given period of time. The higher the stock turnover rate, the more times the goods were sold and replaced. In retailing and wholesaling operations, the key is moving inventory so there is cash available to buy more fast-selling merchandise. High turnover rates mean that merchandise is selling quickly. That means higher profit for the business because its money is not tied up in inventory. Stock turnover is also a good measure of success for businesses to use in evaluating vendors and products from year to year.

Businesses use *stock turnover rates* to compare a particular store's entire operation with the operations of similar stores. The stock turnover rate for a supermarket can be compared with rates of other supermarkets, but not with those of a furniture store.

Stock turnover rates for selected retailers are available from trade associations and commercial publishers. One such publisher is Dun & Bradstreet, which publishes *Industrial Norms* and *Key Business Ratios*.

Stores that keep records of the retail value of stock compute their stock turnover rates as follows:

$$\frac{\text{Net sales (in retail dollars)}}{\text{Average inventory on hand (in retail dollars)}}$$

When net sales during a period are $49,500 and average inventory is $8,250, the stock turnover is 6:

$$\frac{\$49,500}{\$8,250} = 6$$

To determine the average inventory, use inventory amounts for each of the months included in the time period being considered. Total these, as shown in the second column below, and then calculate the average.

Month	Average Inventory	Net Sales
January	$ 50,000	$ 10,000
February	55,000	15,000
March	68,000	20,000
April	64,000	19,000
May	63,000	21,000
June	60,000	20,000
Totals	$360,000	$105,000

To get the average inventory for the six-month period, divide by the number of months.

$$\frac{\$360,000}{6} = \$60,000$$

Finally, to calculate stock turnover, divide total net sales (see the third column above) by average inventory).

$$\frac{\$105,000}{\$60,000} = 1.75$$

This figure means that the average inventory was sold and replaced 1.75 times during the six-month period.

When only cost information about stock is available, stock turnover can be calculated with this formula:

$$\frac{\text{Cost of goods sold}}{\text{Average inventory on hand (at cost)}}$$

When a store wants to look at the number of items carried in relation to the number of items sold, it calculates its stock turnover rates in units with this formula:

$$\frac{\text{Number of units sold}}{\text{Average inventory on hand in units}}$$

STOCK LISTS There are three plans used to monitor different types of goods—staple items, fashionable items, and very popular items. They are the basic stock list, model stock list, and never-out list.

A basic stock list (see Figure 24-2 on page 440) is used for those staple items that should always be in stock. This list specifies products that a store should always carry based upon the type of business. A basic stock list in a men's clothing store would include items such as tee shirts, underwear, and dress socks. The basic stock list at a card store would include birthday cards, blank cards, thank you cards, and cards for general occasions, such as weddings and anniversaries. Based on expected sales for a given period, a basic stock list specifies the minimum amount of merchandise that should be on hand for particular products. It shows the quantity of items that should be reordered, as well as the colors, styles, and sizes that should be carried. Retailers assign each product a code for ease in recording those products when they are purchased and sold. That code is commonly referred to as its sku (*stock-keeping unit*). An sku is the smallest available unit for keeping inventory control.

Independent Practice

1. **Read and Summarize** Have students read an article on advances in inventory systems from one of the following sources: *American Shipper, Traffic World, Mass Market Retailers, Supermarket News, Chain Store Age Executive, Progressive Grocer, International Business,* or *Stores.* They should write a 250-word summary of the article, including the title of the article, the magazine source, and the date of the issue.

2. **Count Inventory and Write** If your school has a store, do the following: Assign students in pairs to count inventory, and have students develop written procedures to be followed in the store when taking inventory. (If you already have written procedures, have students compare their suggested procedures to the existing ones and combine the two documents to create a more efficient inventory-taking process.)

Individualized Practice

Human Relations Skills

You are looking for a prospective employee to receive, check, mark, and transfer goods.

L1 What skills, abilities, and personal qualities would you look for in such a candidate? *(Answers could include: honesty; attention to detail; the ability to concentrate for extended periods of time; accuracy and efficiency in recording information; tact in dealing with suppliers whose goods arrive damaged; physical stamina and the ability to lift potentially heavy merchandise; and being bilingual if the business receives merchandise from a foreign country with transmittal forms in another language.)*

L2 How would you test the candidate to determine his or her suitability for the job? *(Possibilities include having the person do the following: demonstrate the ability to record goods on a receiving record or an apron; tell you how he or she would check merchandise; pass a physical exam; and pass a test that assesses the depth of his or her second language skills. There are standardized tests for potential employees that assess honesty and level of attention to detail.)*

L3 What factors would influence your hiring decision if you found two equally qualified candidates for the position? *(You may wish to consider each candidate's familiarity with the type of goods your business receives; how well you think each candidate will work with you and your employees; the candidates' personal references; and how long each candidate might stay in the job and possibly assume more responsibility.)*

FIGURE 24-2

Basic Stock List

Stock	Description	Size	Packing Units	Cost	Retail	Min. Stock	October Sales This Year	October Sales Last Year	November Sales This Year	November Sales Last Year	December Sales This Year	December Sales Last Year
1381	Skippy Peanut Butter	32 oz.	24			4						
1382	Skippy Peanut Butter	18 oz.	24			8						
1383	Skippy Peanut Butter	12 oz.	24			8						
1384	Jif Peanut Butter	32 oz.	24			4						
1385	Jif Peanut Butter	18 oz.	24			8						
1386	Jif Peanut Butter	12 oz.	24			8						

■ **Basic Stock List** Buyers use basic stock lists to plan purchases and keep track of items that should always be in stock. *Where on this list is the SKU?*

FIGURE 24-3

Model Stock List

PRODUCT CLASS __Misses Sportswear__   SEASON __Spring__

General Style	Specific Style	Price Range	Color	Total Units	Size 6	Size 8	Size 10	Size 12	Size 14
Blouse	Sleeveless Tailored	$25	White	12	1	3	3	3	2
			Black	12	1	3	3	3	2
			Blue	12	1	3	3	3	2
Blouse	Short-sleeve Oversize	$35	Pink	24	2	6	6	6	4
			Orange	24	2	6	6	6	4

■ **Model Stock Lists** Buyers use model stock lists for fashion merchandise. *How and why does this type of list differ from a basic stock list in form and content?*

A model stock list (see Figure 24-3) is used for fashionable merchandise. Fashion items change relatively rapidly; therefore, these lists are less specific than basic stock lists. The information contained in model stock lists identifies goods by general classes (blouses, skirts, dresses, slacks) and style categories (short sleeve, long sleeve), sizes, materials, colors, and price lines. Style numbers are not included because each manufacturer's style numbers change each year. Although model stock lists identify how many of each type of item should be purchased, the buyer must actually select specific models at the market.

A never-out list is used for best-selling products that make up a large percentage of sales volume. Items are added to or taken off the list as their popularity increases or declines. A video rental store will keep a popular movie on the never-out list and keep a large quantity of the videocassettes in the store. After the movie declines in popularity, only regular quantities of it will be maintained. It will be taken off the never-out list and more popular titles will replace it. When a popular new toy is first introduced, a toy store may keep a large amount of the toy in stock. As it decreases in popularity, a smaller inventory will be held.

440 Unit 7 ■ Distribution

FIGURE 24-3 ANSWER
Basic Stock List The first column shows the stockkeeping unit code, or SKU.

FIGURE 24-4 ANSWER
Model Stock Lists This list contains general descriptions of merchandise rather than codes. It lacks cost data, space for sales totals (past or present), and minimum stock figures. This is done because some items change so quickly that they are unlikely to ever be re-ordered.

Case Study

From New Car Order to Delivery—All Within Eight Days

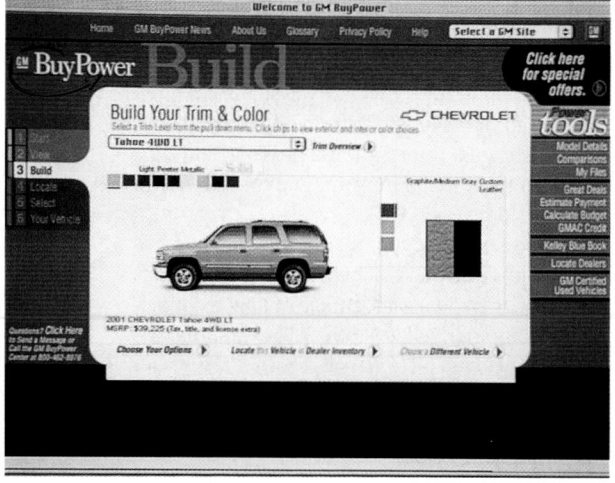

Something revolutionary is happening with the General Motors (GM) Corporation, the world's largest industrial company. Faced with using new information technologies or losing market share to competitors, GM executives are changing their way of doing business. GM executives are recognizing what an important tool the Internet has become for car shoppers. Potential buyers can do their browsing and price comparing online. Now GM wants to take that a step further on their company Web site with e-GM.

The company is creating a new business model, e-GM. Company officials hope to integrate electronic car and supplier orders into its manufacturing operations and existing GM dealer network. A company Web site receives over 4.5 million hits a day from customers and dealers. GM has joined with partners such as AOL and NetZero to help lead Web users to their Web site where they can find out more information about GM products and buying their cars online.

GM also plans to implement a Web-based system that will facilitate the delivery of a customized vehicle to car owners within eight days of an electronic order for a car. E-commerce technologies should save $3,700 on the cost of a new car by reducing inventories, cutting paperwork, and improving communication with suppliers.

The company also plans to save money by ordering parts electronically from its suppliers. This will improve the purchasing process and lead to material cost reductions for the company. Reduced inventories and less paperwork will shorten delivery times to transport the vehicle to dealers and ultimately to the customer.

Reductions in inventory will save GM billions of dollars. The savings will be passed along as increased earnings to shareholders and reduced car prices to customers.

Case Study Review

1. Why did GM feel that it needed to change its way of doing business?
2. How will GM be able to enter other business fields by using this new approach?

A MATTER OF ETHICS

3. Would it be ethical for General Motors to sell its cars directly to customers without involving GM dealers? What are the advantages and disadvantages of this approach?

Case Study Review Answers

From a New Car Order to Delivery—All Within Eight Days

1. GM was feeling pressure from companies marketing cars via the Internet. This potentially could have destroyed GM's dealer and distribution network.
2. Because of huge projected savings in more efficient inventory management, the company will have additional assets to invest in non-traditional business fields.

A MATTER OF ETHICS

3. Answers will vary. GM could lower the final price to consumers but would lose an efficient system for distributing and servicing vehicles. Automobile dealers have much local, state, and national clout.

ASSESS

Reteaching

1. **Vocabulary** Assign and review the vocabulary terms for this section.
2. **Fact and Idea** Assign and review Fact and Idea Review questions 5–10 from the Chapter Assessment.
3. **Inventory Management** Have students list the reasons for inventory management and describe the difference between physical and perpetual inventory systems.
4. **Stock Turnover** Have the students explain the significance of stock turnover. Discuss reasons why the stock turnover rates often differ for similar businesses.

The Impact of Technology on Inventory Management

Electronic data processing using UPC product codes and computerized inventory systems are often used today to manage and improve inventory control. Sophisticated information-gathering software systems can track items from the purchase order to the final customer sale.

Technology is quickly changing the way stock is handled and controlled. The retail industry has created standards to take advantage of new technologies and computerized systems. These standards include:

- UPCs with standard product identifier bar code symbols to capture sku-level information at the point of sale
- Standard electronic data interchange (EDI) transactions to communicate electronically from business to business
- Standardized shipping container marking (SCM) as a way to identify case and case contents

EDI can shorten order cycles by as much as five days. Savings of two days are possible for manual orders. This time-saving between reorders allows businesses to carry one week less of inventory at their stores. SCM also enables distribution centers to reduce processing time by about two days.

Manufacturers and retailers are teaming up to implement Quick Response Delivery programs. Some *Quick Response Delivery* programs utilize a consolidation facility as a hub to receive, sort, and consolidate materials prior to delivery. This improves inventory control in the retail store, shortens the order cycle, and reduces excess inventory carried in stores.

Even small stores can get low-cost, computer-generated reports containing sales and inventory figures by product classifications. This information improves stock turnover and increases profits by pinpointing inventory that is too high or too low.

The Future of Inventory Management

In the early days of e-commerce, most e-tailers did not check stock until after an order was received. Because most customers who buy online expect their orders to be filled immediately, the ability to process and ship orders without delay has become essential to the success of e-businesses. This has brought about real time inventory systems. Real time inventory management capability lets a company constantly track every product it sells from when it's manufactured, or when it arrives in its warehouse, to when the customer orders it online, and to when it arrives at the buyer's door.

The theory behind real-time inventory management is that by integrating a Web site with such a system, a company will never disappoint an online customer, because its Web site will list only products actually in the warehouse, ready to be shipped, and would reserve those products right when the customer places the order. In the ultra-competitive world of e-commerce, real-time inventory management will make the difference between e-tailers who succeed and those who fail.

24.2 ASSESSMENT

Reviewing Key Terms and Concepts

1. What is inventory management and why is it important?
2. Explain the concept of just-in-time inventory.
3. Name the two different types of inventory systems used for inventory management.
4. What is the difference between dollar control and unit control as they relate to inventory management?
5. What is stock turnover?

Thinking Critically

6. Do you think a just-in-time inventory control system could be used in a retail or wholesale operation? Why or why not?

Integrating Academic Skills

7. **MATH** What is the amount of the ending inventory if beginning inventory was $280,000, net purchases were $756,000, and net sales were $872,000?

24.2 ASSESSMENT ANSWERS

Reviewing Key Terms and Concepts

1. It is the process of buying and storing products for sale while controlling costs for ordering, shipping, handling, and storage. Businesses can lose money without it.
2. Suppliers deliver parts and raw materials just before they are needed for production.
3. physical and perpetual
4. Dollar control: planning and monitoring total inventory investment. Unit control: merchandise quantities handled in period of time
5. It is the number of times the average inventory is sold and replaced in a period of time.

Thinking Critically

6. Yes. Computers already keep track of daily inventory in grocery and department stores.

Integrating Academic Skills

7. **MATH** $164,000

Careers in Marketing

CUSTOMER SERVICE

Alisha Eads
Manager of Customer Service
E-Toys.com

How does your workload vary?

"You will never be bored in customer service and you will always be provided with challenges. Your work will never be complete and you will never stop striving to 'do better' for the customer. There are always improvements that can be made in customer service so you are always thinking of new and creative ways to motivate staff to achieve your goals."

What skills do you find most important?

"Strong interpersonal skills and relationship building skills are vital. It is important to have relationships in all areas of the company. You must work hard to build the respect and confidence of your peers and coworkers."

Why do you like managing a customer service team?

"I like the challenge of working with many different personality types. You learn to become a better leader by working with such a variety of individuals. You also learn to adjust your personality style to get the best out of each person you work with. Achievements are team achievements, not just individual achievements."

What is your key to success?

"Recognizing the potential of every staff member is my key to success. A rule to live by in this job is that you will only be as successful as your staff. Once you assess what people are capable of, your job will become much easier. Recognizing and utilizing that 'special something' in each person who reports to you will make you successful. Every person has something that they do well and every person can add value to your organization. It is your job as a manager to ensure that you know what those areas are in each of your employees."

Thinking Critically
What is meant by the statement "You will only be as successful as your staff"?

Career Facts

Education and Training: A college degree with course work in business administration, operations management, public relations, marketing, or communications provides valuable background. Experience supervising personnel and handling sensitive customer problems is required.

Abilities, Aptitudes, and Skills: Strong leadership skills and the ability to motivate employees are necessary. Strong goal orientation, skill and productivity promoting efficiency, and the ability to maintain excellent service standards are needed.

Career Outlook: Job availability is projected to increase rapidly, but competition for the best jobs is expected to be keen.

Career Path: Work as an entry-level customer service employee may lead to customer service training jobs or assistant supervisor positions, and then to customer service management. Customer service managers may advance to public relations work.

Careers in Marketing

Ask a student to read the Careers in Marketing feature aloud to the class. Discuss the skills and aptitudes required for a career in customer service. Ask students whether they think they would like or dislike a career in customer service. Discuss the pros and cons of such a career.

Thinking Critically Answer
Recognizing and using the potential of each staff member will make you successful as a manager and your job easier.

 Guest Speakers
Invite a customer service manager to class to discuss his/her job.

Exploring Careers

Taking Inventory on Your Goals
1. Read the following questions to students to help them discover their career goals. Have them answer these questions on a separate sheet of paper:

- What careers do you think you might have in your lifetime? Give three examples. *(Answers will vary.)*
- What do you think will be your first full-time job? *(Answers will vary.)*
- Why do you think you would want to change positions after a period of time? *(Answers will vary.)*
- Why should you make a habit of reviewing your career plan and progress from time to time? *(It allows you to continue exploring your interests and expand your skills.)*
- Why do you need to be flexible regarding career changes? *(Many people change careers often in their lifetimes.)*

2. Discuss the students' answers in class.

Lifelong Learning

Stock Handling and Inventory Control
One benefit of taking a marketing course is discovering that so many steps and people are involved in getting a product to consumers. This chapter's information on stock handling and inventory control illustrates that. Reading the business section of a daily newspaper, the *Wall Street Journal,* or *Business-Week* can help students be informed consumers.

Meeting Individual Needs

Students With Hearing Impairments
Students who wear hearing aids can be distracted by background noise. It is important to restrict unneeded interference. Hearing aids have a limited range of use, so you need to learn where to stand to be heard. Comments from the back of the room may be inaudible. Repeat questions or comments, or include a question in your answer.

Vocabulary Review

See the Glossary for definitions.

Fact and Idea Review

1. It describes the goods received by a business. It is important because it provides essential shipping, quantity, ordering, and delivery information.
2. Checking merchandise documents the quantity and condition of products and merchandise received by a business.
3. They can determine whether the quality of the goods received matches the quality of the merchandise that was ordered.
4. Stock is carried by more than one department; it has been used in a display or sales promotion; or it has been used for installation and repairs.
5. Inventory can be tracked by using a manual system or a computer based system.
6. visual control, tickler control, and an annual physical inventory
7. They help a business keep stock adjusted to sales and lets a business determine how to spend money.
8. Developments include UPC codes, electronic data interchange (EDI) transactions, standardized Shipping Container Markings (SCM), and Quick Response Delivery programs.

Thinking Critically

1. It reduces the retailers' costs.
2. Some businesses rely on high sales volumes with low profit margins for their success while other businesses rely on high profit margins for each item sold. Examples will vary.
3. A business would have no way of identifying inventory losses. It can be avoided by using a physical inventory system.
4. They can assist with inventory management by keeping track of items at every stage from the purchase order to the customer sale.
5. Businesses are expected to purchase merchandise in large volumes to get lowest prices, and keep a current inventory on hand.

VOCABULARY REVIEW

Pair up with another student and quiz each other on the following vocabulary words.

- receiving record
- blind check method
- direct check method
- spot check method
- quality check method
- source marking
- preretailing marking method
- inventory management
- just-in-time (JIT) inventory system
- perpetual inventory system
- physical inventory system
- dollar control
- unit control
- stockkeeping unit (sku)
- stock turnover
- basic stock list
- model stock list
- never-out list

FACT AND IDEA REVIEW

1. What is a receiving record? Why is it an important document? (24.1)
2. Why must merchandise be checked after it has been received? (24.1)
3. Why do buyers perform quality checks? (24.1)
4. Identify three reasons for transferring merchandise between departments. (24.1)
5. How can inventory be tracked in a perpetual inventory system? (24.2)
6. What is a point-of-sale terminal? What are some of its advantages? (24.2)
7. What advantage does unit control provide? (24.2)
8. Name three recent developments in the retail industry that take advantage of computerized systems and new technologies. (24.2)

THINKING CRITICALLY

1. Explain why source marking is important for a small business.
2. Why do stock turnover rates vary by the type of business? Give examples of businesses with high and low turnover rates.
3. What problems might occur if a business used only a perpetual inventory system and never made an actual count of its inventory? How can this be avoided?
4. How does computer technology assist in inventory management?
5. What expectations should be placed on a business that oversees inventory management?

BUILDING WORKPLACE SKILLS

1. **Human Relations** You work in a receiving room of a large department store. You know that a coworker has been damaging incoming merchandise through deliberate and careless behavior. Unfortunately, your manager suspects that you are at fault and has approached you regarding this. Explain how you would handle this situation.
2. **Technology** Find an article about just-in-time inventory management at the library or on the Internet. Use a word processing program to prepare a summary focussing on the article's main points. Identify the name of the article, the author, source, and date of publication.

Building Workplace Skills

1. Responses should be well thought out and tactful.
2. Summaries will vary.

Applying Marketing Concepts

1. Rates will vary based upon type of retail institution.
2. Charts will vary as slow and peak sales times will depend on the school store hours of operation.
3. Spreadsheets will vary.
4. Presentations will depend on the selected companies.
5. Questions will vary but might ask how to establish a computer-based inventory system; how often inventories are updated; and whether the system will ship expired or on-hold products?

APPLYING MARKETING CONCEPTS

1. **Understanding Stock Turnover Rates** Research why stock turnover rates vary by type of retail institution. Use a word processing program to list five different types of retail institutions and their stock turnover rates.

2. **Analyzing Sales Patterns** Use a design software program to make a sales chart for your school store for each hour of the business day or for each day in a month. Analyze the slow and peak sales times.

3. **Making Inventory Purchases** Research catalogs of merchandise to be sold in a school store. Use a spreadsheet program to list ten items and make a description of each by type, brand, style, cost, and retail price. Decide the quantities to stock for each item chosen.

4. **Improving Inventory Management** Research business magazines to find an example of a company that has improved its inventory management system. Use presentation software to create an oral presentation describing the situation and how the solution increased profit.

5. **Researching Inventory Management Systems** Research computer-based inventory management systems on the Internet. Develop a list of five to ten questions you would ask a company representative if you were converting from a physical inventory system to a computer-based system.

LINKING SCHOOL TO WORK

Systems Skills Investigate the receiving process used at a place of employment or at your cooperative education training station. List the job tasks that a receiver would perform from the time the stock is delivered until it is placed on the sales floor.

Role Play: Store Manager

Situation You are to assume the role of store manager of a large discount store. A problem has come up with inventory shortages. Your department manager (judge) has asked you to prepare a presentation about inventory control for an upcoming associates' meeting.

Activity You must make a presentation about the possible causes of inventory shortages as well as specific inventory control procedures that could be used to reduce inventory shortages.

Evaluation You will be evaluated on how well you meet the following performance indicators:

- Explain the possible causes for inventory shortages
- Identify unit inventory control systems that are appropriate for your company
- Develop a plan identifying specific procedures to reduce inventory shortages
- Make oral presentations

interNET CONNECTION

Inventory Management
There are currently many companies that sell software programs for computer-based inventory management systems.

Connect
- Research the Internet to identify a software company specializing in inventory management programs.
- Use a word processing program to write a report detailing the company's Web site address, name, and physical location, as well as at least five advantages that the company advertises about its inventory management software applications.

Students should be evaluated on the performance indicators noted in the Role Play.
- For another DECA Role Play, go to the *Student Activity Workbook*, p. 203.
- For more in-depth Role Play practice, refer to DECA's *Essential Competitive Events Handbook*. To order, contact DECA at **www.deca.org**.

interNET CONNECTION
Answers will vary depending on selected company.

Mini Quiz
Administer the Mini Quiz orally. For an expanded chapter quiz, go to page 137 of the *Reproducible Tests* book.

1. A form used to describe the goods received by a business is called a(n) <u>receiving record</u>.

2. The <u>spot check</u> method involves a random check of a shipment in which the contents are assumed to be accurate for the entire shipment.

3. <u>Inventory</u> refers to the amount of goods stored.

4. A(n) <u>perpetual inventory</u> system tracks the number of items in inventory on a constant basis.

5. Under a(n) <u>physical inventory</u> system, stock is visually inspected or counted to determine the quantity on hand.

Linking School to Work
Answers will depend on the selected employer or work situation.

1. **Assessment** Have students complete the Reproducible Tests for Chapter 24 and Unit 7 or construct your own tests using the ExamView software.
2. **Enrichment** Have students complete the corresponding activities in the following workbooks:
   - *Marketing Math Workbook*, p. 59
   - *Marketing Research Project Workbook*, p. 111

Unit Lab Overview

In this Zazz Lab, students will use their knowledge of the distribution (place) decision of the marketing mix to establish distribution for a teen sport magazine.

 Bell Ringer Activity

Explain Ask students: How did you purchase the most recent issue of your favorite magazine? *(Answers will vary but may include a paid or gift subscription.)*

Discussion Starter

Ask students: What factors contribute to the success of a new magazine? *(current and interesting editorial content for target audience; positive publicity; availability to targeted audience; offering trial issues; effective advertising to target market; generating sales)*

Thinking Critically

1. **Place Decision** Ask students: What are the pros and cons of publishing an entire magazine on a Web site instead of printing hard copies for distribution? *(Pros include: no printing so costs are lower. Cons include: loss of revenue from people who prefer hard copies to read, and advertisers may be reluctant to buy into the new concept.)*
2. **Web Publishing** Ask students: Why publish magazines at all when sports news can be found on many Web sites? *(At most Web sites, you will only find current news; magazines offer special feature articles and more variety.)*

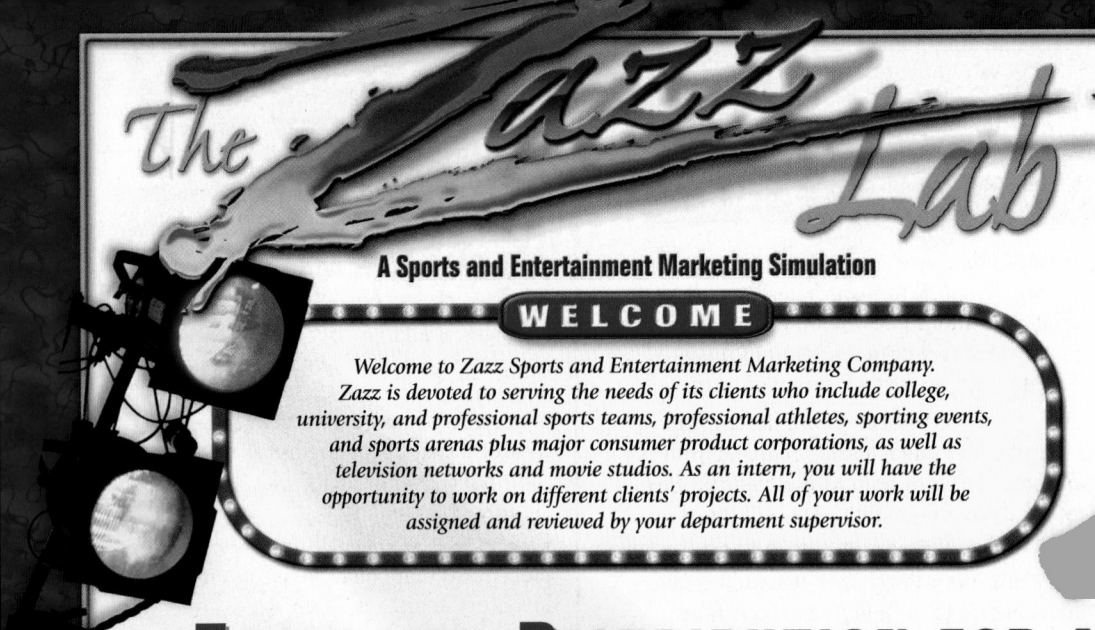

The Zazz Lab

A Sports and Entertainment Marketing Simulation

WELCOME

Welcome to Zazz Sports and Entertainment Marketing Company. Zazz is devoted to serving the needs of its clients who include college, university, and professional sports teams, professional athletes, sporting events, and sports arenas plus major consumer product corporations, as well as television networks and movie studios. As an intern, you will have the opportunity to work on different clients' projects. All of your work will be assigned and reviewed by your department supervisor.

ESTABLISH DISTRIBUTION FOR A TEEN SPORTS MAGAZINE

SITUATION

A new Zazz client is *MW* Sports Magazine, a monthly magazine geared to teenage sports enthusiasts. *MW* covers football, baseball, volleyball, soccer, ice hockey, track and field, golf, tennis, and extreme sports, including special amateur events. Zazz has been hired to come up with a new name for the magazine and to establish an effective distribution system. The client is also interested in establishing a Web site.

ASSIGNMENT

Your supervisor wants you to consider the purchasing habits of buyers for magazines of *MW's* target market. Review all possible channels of distribution for the new magazine. Decide on the desired intensity of distribution (intensive, selective, exclusive) and provide your rationale. Provide a sales plan to include the type of sales personnel that should be used to sell to resellers and individual subscribers. Suggest methods of physical distribution, and explain inventory control methods that will be used to keep all customers supplied on a monthly basis. Design the subscription order form that will be inserted in the magazine. Finally, build a Web site for the magazine and make recommendations for online publishing.

Tools and Resources

To complete this assignment you will need to conduct research at a library or on the Internet. You will also need a word processing program, a spreadsheet program, and presentation software. Helpful trade publications include *BrandWeek, Advertising Age, Sports Business Journal,* and *Sports Business Daily.*

Research

Research sports magazines that target teens to determine the market share of competitors. Research all possible outlets for distribution of the magazine to determine what intermediaries may be needed to get this new magazine into the hands of the final customer. Investigate physical distribution methods used to transport these magazines to intermediaries and individual subscribers. Research magazines on the Internet to determine how they are sold and find about about the required links for resellers and individual subscribers.

TEEN ZINES

Since the Internet and World Wide Web became accessible to the public in the late twentieth century, Web sites have grown exponentially. In fact, there seems to be a Web site for almost everything—including teen magazine directories. These sites provide direct links to all kinds of magazines for teens, including sports, education, fashion, entertainment, health, etc. They offer an alternative, relatively low-cost distribution method for start-up and established Web publishers. A few suggested sites to visit are:

www.nanana.com/teenslinks.html
www.centerofweb.com/teenzone/magazines.htm
www.linapuzzles.com/teens.html
(Note: Web site addresses may change.)

Presentation and Evaluation

Present your ideas in a written report and an oral presentation. The presentation will later be shown to the client. You will be evaluated on your oral presentation skills, including:

- Knowledge of distribution, sales, and inventory control used in publishing
- Knowledge of e-commerce and online publishing
- Continuity of presentation
- Voice quality
- Eye contact

Report

Prepare a written report and a computer presentation for the client. Use a word processing program to prepare a double-spaced report. Use a spreadsheet program to create a pie chart illustrating the current market share enjoyed by the major competitors in the teen sports magazine market. Arrange your written report around the following headings:

- The teen sports magazine market
- Possible outlets for distribution
- Physical distribution methods
- New name for magazine
- Suggested channel(s) of distribution
- Channel(s) for resellers and individual subscribers
- Intensity of distribution
- Use of the Internet
- Physical distribution (for intermediaries and individual subscribers)
- Sales methods
- Sales staff vs. agents
- Sample subscription order form
- Web site design
- Inventory control

Using computer presentation software, prepare a presentation of your ideas for the client that includes:

- Key topics covered in your written report
- Graphic illustrations that relate to each slide's topic
- Very little text
- Minimum of 10 slides

Portfolio

Print a copy of your completed report and presentation for your Portfolio.

THE **DECA** CONNECTION

DECA Business Services Marketing Series
Consulting is an occupational area in this event, so the concept of suggesting a channel of distribution for a new sports magazine is a possible role play.

DECA Marketing Management Series
Deciding on the channels of distribution, physical distribution, sales methods, and inventory control are all areas of marketing management.

DECA Hospitality and Recreation Research Event
Researching current distribution methods used for sports magazines and then developing a Web site and the channels of distribution for it could be a topic for this event.

DECA Sports and Entertainment Marketing Management Team Decision-Making Event
Working on this project with a partner would make the experience similar to what is expected in a DECA Team Decision-Making Event.

COOPERATIVE LEARNING

Teamwork This unit lab lends itself to working in teams of two to four students. Teams can compete with one another to come up with the best name and distribution plan for the new sports magazine.

Independent Practice

Research and Write Ask students to research the Web sites of three sports-related magazines and write a short report on their layout, links, special offers, and subscription methods.

ASSESS

Enrichment

Research and Analyze Have students go to **www.magazines.com** or a similar Web site that sells magazine subscriptions online. Have them research becoming a sales affiliate, earning a commission for the sale of magazines purchased from their Web site or through e-mail links to the online magazine retailers. Ask them to analyze using a fund-raiser for DECA or another school activity.

Evaluation

The rubrics for evaluation of the written, oral, and computer presentation are included in the student text. (See the outline and guidelines for the written report, the computer presentation, and the skills' assessment for oral presentations.) It might be best to replicate those rubrics to evaluate the students' work. A separate rubric could be created to evaluate the work of a team.

CLOSE

Lab Wrap-Up

Have students name the various channels of distribution and related sales methods that may be used to sell magazines. *(Channels and methods include: publisher to final consumer through the Internet, order card in the magazine, or own telemarketing sales staff; publisher to intermediary, such as a subscription service that may use telemarketers, the Internet, or sweepstakes to reach consumer; publisher to wholesaler to retailers, such as bookstores.)*

Pricing

Chapter 25
Price Planning

Chapter 26
Pricing Strategies

Chapter 27
Pricing Math

Unit Objectives

After completing this unit, students will be able to:

- Explain the nature and scope of price planning.
- Explain factors affecting pricing decisions.
- Discuss the legal considerations of pricing.
- Describe pricing concepts and policies for products in various stages of the life cycle.
- Use pricing terminology and techniques correctly and effectively.
- Use pricing math to calculate markups and markdowns.
- Plan and implement a pricing strategy.

Enrichment Resources

Books

Power Pricing: How Managing Price Transforms the Bottom Line by Robert J. Dolan and Hermann Simon (Contributor)

Pricing: Concepts & Methods for Effective Marketing by Andre Gabor

2001 Professionals Guide to Value Pricing by Ronald J. Baker

Magazines/Journals

Discount Store News
Wholesale Source

Associations

Professional Pricing Society
3277 Roswell Road, Suite 620
Atlanta, GA 30305
(770) 509-9933
www.pricing-advisor.com

Journal Writing Activity

1. Ask students to make a list in their journals of ten words that come to mind when they think of pricing. Have students share their pricing-related words with the rest of the class. Write the words on the board. Categorize the words into psychological, cost, demand, and competition pricing, as well as markup, markdown, and discount-related pricing. Write on the board any aspects of pricing that were not identified and explain their importance.

2. Ask students to write two paragraphs in their journals about what they think it takes to price effectively. Then ask them to share their answers with the class. Explain to students that the basic formulas for determining various types of prices are valuable methods for successful pricing.

TEACHER CLASSROOM RESOURCES

Program Resources	Chapter 25	Chapter 26	Chapter 27
Student Activity Workbook	p. 213	p. 223	p. 233
Marketing Math Workbook	p. 71	p. 71	p. 71
Marketing Research Project Workbook	p. 131	p. 131	p. 131
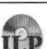 School-to-Work Activity Workbook	p. 105	p. 109	p. 113
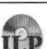 *BusinessWeek* Case Studies	p. 157	p. 163	p. 169
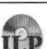 Marketing Career Portfolio	p. 38	p. 38	p. 38
Reproducible Tests	p. 147	p. 153	p. 157
ExamView User's Guide and Testbank	p. 25-1	p. 26-1	p. 27-1
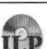 Internet Resources	p. 69	p. 71	p. 73
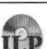 Blackline Masters	p. 47	p. 50	p. 53
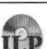 Lesson Plans	p. 53	p. 55	p. 57
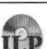 Block Scheduling	p. 8	p. 8	p. 8
Impact! Simulation			

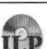 Each of these resources is available in print and on the Interactive Lesson Planner CD-ROM.

Technology Resources

- **Interactive Lesson Planner (ILP) CD-ROM**
- **PowerPoint Presentation CD-ROM**
- **Marketing Essentials Web site**
- **ExamView! CD-ROM**
- **Impact! Simulation**

Virtual Business

Virtual Business is a fully visual marketing and business simulation that introduces students to the principles of marketing by letting them start and run their own virtual businesses. In *Virtual Business*, students have the power to control all aspects of a retail convenience store. Students strategize marketing decisions using a powerful learning tool in the guise of a video game. They learn by experiencing how their decisions affect their virtual business.

Key to Individualized Academics Activities

L1 Level 1 activities are basic activities and should fall within the range of all students.

L2 Level 2 activities are average activities and should be within the range of average and above average students.

L3 Level 3 activities are challenging activities designed for the ability range of above average students.

National Marketing Education

CHAPTER	SECTION	PERFORMANCE INDICATOR
Chapter 25 **Price Planning**	25.1	Explain the nature and scope of the pricing function (PRI)
		Select approach for setting a base price (PRI)
		Determine cost of product (break-even, ROI, markup, price) (PRI)
	25.2	Explain factors affecting pricing decisions (PRI)
		Calculate break-even point (PRI)
		Explain legal considerations for pricing (PRI)
Chapter 26 **Pricing Strategies**	26.1	Explain the nature and scope of the pricing function (PRI)
		Explain the principles of supply and demand (ECO)
		Identify strategies for pricing new products (PRI)
	26.2	Determine cost of product (PRI)
		Explain factors affecting pricing decisions (PRI)
		Select approach for setting a base price (PRI)
		Set prices (PRI)
Chapter 27 **Pricing Math**	27.1	Explain the nature and scope of the pricing function (PRI)
		Describe the nature of profit-and-loss statements (BME)
		Set prices (PRI)
	27.2	Determine discounts and allowances that can be used to adjust base prices (PRI)

CIS Communication, Interpersonal Skills   **DIS** Distribution   **FIN** Financing   **PRI** Pricing   **SEL** Selling

Standards Assessment Correlation

	SECTION ASSESSMENT			CHAPTER ASSESSMENT					UNIT LAB
Reviewing Key Terms and Concepts	Thinking Critically	Integrating Academic Skills	Fact and Idea Review	Thinking Critically	Building Workplace Skills	Applying Marketing Concepts	Linking School to Work	Internet Connection	Zazz Lab
1, 2, 3, 4	●	●	1, 2, 3, 4	1, 2	1, 2	1, 2, 3	●	●	●
3	●	●	4			1	●		●
5	●		3	2	1	1	●		●
1, 2, 3	●		5, 6, 7, 8, 10			1, 3, 4	●	●	●
2		●		1	1	1	●		
4			9, 10			2, 4		●	
1, 2, 3, 4	●	●	1, 2, 3, 4	1, 2		2	●	●	●
2, 4		●	2	2		1, 2			●
5	●		3	2					●
2, 4, 5	●	●	6, 7, 8, 9	4	1, 2	1		●	●
2, 3, 5	●		5, 6, 8, 9	2, 3, 4		1, 2	●	●	●
1, 2, 3, 4			8	3	1	1			●
5			7, 8		2	1, 2	●		●
1, 2	●	●	1, 2	1, 2		1, 2	●	●	●
1				1					
2, 3	●	●	1, 2, 3, 4, 5, 6	2	1, 2, 3, 4, 5, 6, 7	1, 2	●	●	●
1, 2, 3	●	●	7, 8, 9, 10	1, 2	2	1, 2	●		

Unit Overview

Unit 8 examines pricing principles and practices. Chapter 25 addresses the importance of price and broadens students' awareness of the various factors that affect it. Chapter 26 contains many basic pricing strategies that students will recognize, from various forms of psychological pricing to cost-, demand-, and competition-oriented pricing. Chapter 27 focuses on the computational skills needed for pricing. Students are taught the basic formulas for determining markups, markdowns, and various kinds of discounts.

Introducing the Unit

Ask students what would happen to a local business that charged its customers the same amount it paid for the goods it sold. *(Some students may say that the business would break even, while others will recognize that it would be losing money because there would be nothing left to pay operating expenses.)* This example should help students recognize how important price planning is to the financial success of a business.

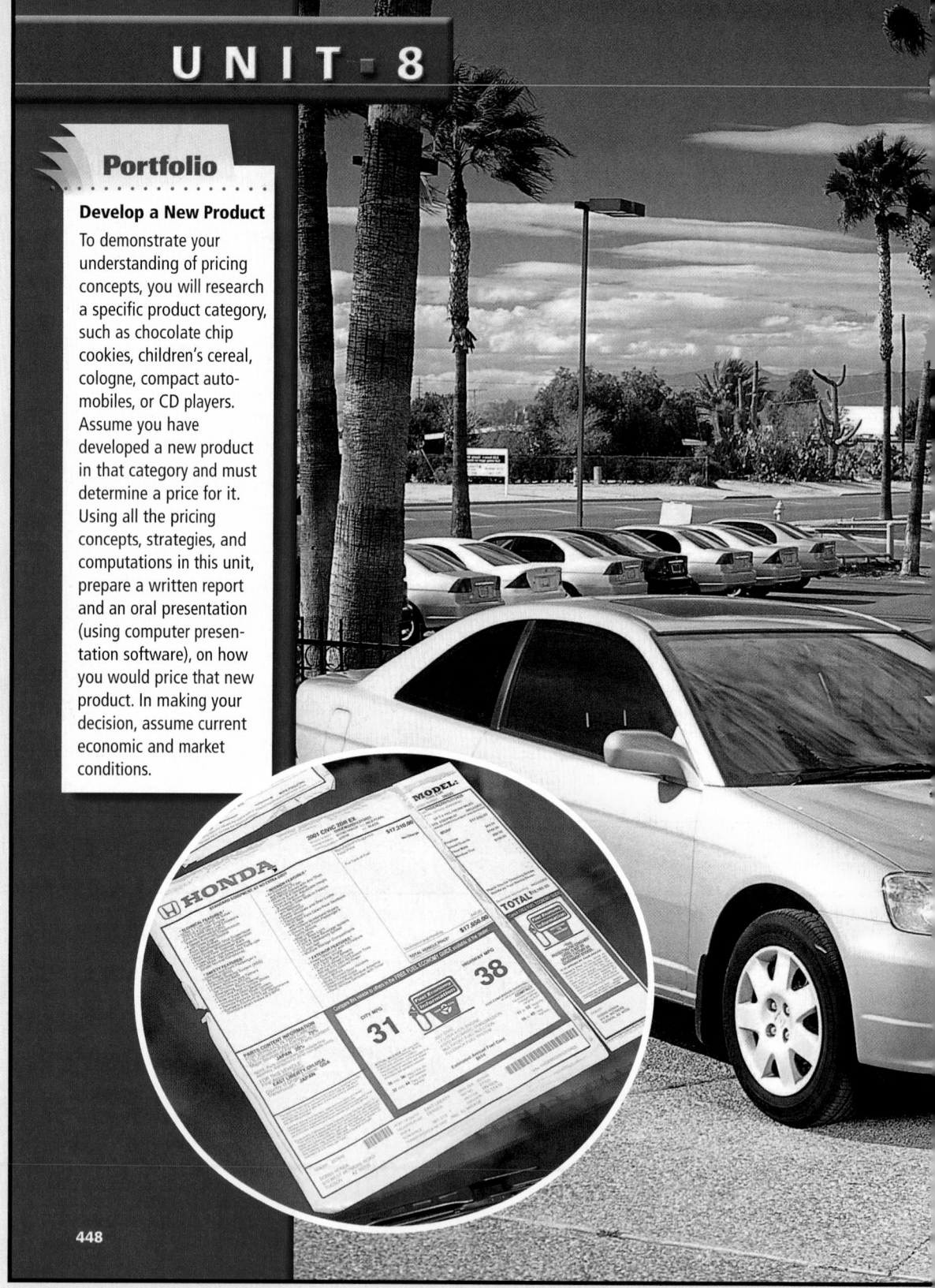

UNIT 8

Portfolio

Develop a New Product

To demonstrate your understanding of pricing concepts, you will research a specific product category, such as chocolate chip cookies, children's cereal, cologne, compact automobiles, or CD players. Assume you have developed a new product in that category and must determine a price for it. Using all the pricing concepts, strategies, and computations in this unit, prepare a written report and an oral presentation (using computer presentation software), on how you would price that new product. In making your decision, assume current economic and market conditions.

448

Field Trip Suggestions

Plan a Trip to a Bookstore Have your students visit a bookstore to observe the varying pricing strategies there. They should look at hardback and paperback best-sellers, magazines, books on tape, damaged books, and publishers' over-stock items. Have students report on the pricing strategies they observed.

Pricing

Unit Overview

As you recall from Chapter 2, the four Ps of the marketing mix are product, place, price, and promotion. Unit 8 addresses the marketing mix decision regarding price. Throughout the unit you will see how essential price is to a company's marketing plan and its ultimate success or failure.

Chapter 25 explores the importance of price and all the factors that affect the pricing decision. In Chapter 26 various pricing policies and strategies provide a wide range of ideas on how one goes about deciding on a price for products. Pricing computations, including how to calculate markups, markdowns, and discounts are explained in Chapter 27. You will learn the relationship between pricing and a company's profitability based on pricing calculations. Chapter 27 ties the profit and loss statement to the concept of pricing.

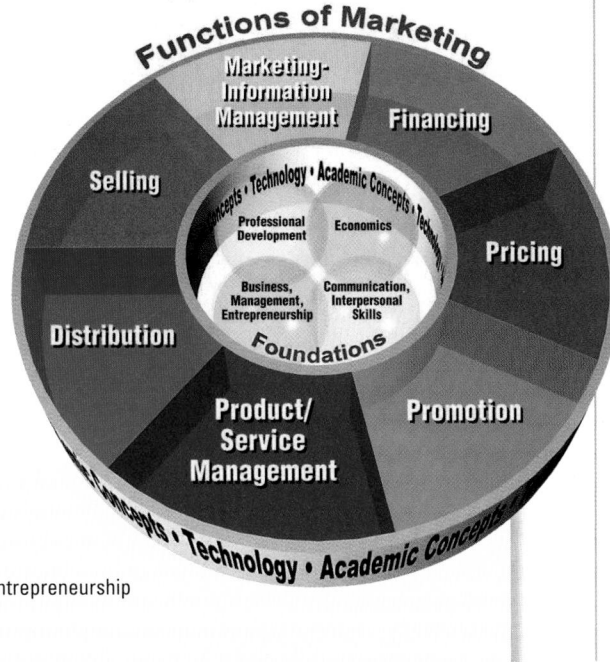

In this Unit:

Foundations of Marketing

◉ Economics

◉ Business, Management, Entrepreneurship

Functions of Marketing

◥ Pricing

⬧ DECA Unit Project

Have chapter members prepare a video or computer presentation (i.e., PowerPoint) on pricing principles and practices. Prepare a rubric for evaluation that includes time limits, number of topics, variety and coverage of topics, real-life examples, continuity, and quality of oral presentation. The presentation should be between five and ten minutes long, logically organized, and cover the key points from the unit. Students can work in groups to decide what they should include in the presentation.

Go to the *Marketing Essentials* Web site (**www.marketing.glencoe. com**) for resources to teach and assess occupation-specific vocabulary.

Unit Closure

Have students revisit the work they did in determining the retail, wholesale, and manufacturer's price for Delectable Delights (boxed candy) in Chapter 26. Have them write a short report on the steps they would suggest for pricing another new company product. Tell students to include calculations to cover concepts such as markup and break-even point.

👤 Guest Speaker Suggestions

Antique Dealer Have an antique dealer talk to the class about how he or she determines the prices of items purchased from individuals and auctions, as well as how pricing considerations affect buying decisions. The antique dealer should address specific factors considered when deciding upon a selling price once the goods have been acquired by the store.

Chapter Overview

Chapter 25 introduces students to price planning. The chapter discusses the goals of pricing, as well as the market factors that affect it. Government regulations that deal with pricing are also considered.

 ## Springboard

Brainstorm and Compare Have students think of items they would buy even if it meant foregoing other purchases. Ask students to take turns asking their classmates how much they would be willing to pay for these goods or services. Have them list answers on sheets of paper. Then have students compare their answers.

Prereading

List the section objectives to discuss with students. Have students skim the chapter, looking at the pictures, reading the captions, and noting the heads. Ask questions to ensure that students have a minimal understanding of the chapter structure.

Preteaching Marketing Vocabulary

Dictate each of the vocabulary terms and ask students to write them on a sheet of paper. When they finish, write the terms on the board. Then have students guess at the meaning of each. Write their guesses next to each term. Leave this list on the board so students can see how close their guesses were to the actual definitions as they work through the chapter.

Marketing: What It Takes

Answer They might affect profit, gaining market share, return on investment, meeting the competition, and projecting a quality image. Other considerations might include costs and expenses, supply and demand, demand elasticity, consumer perceptions, competition, and government regulations.

Price Planning

Marketing: What It Takes

Arts and Crafts

You have designed a line of stuffed animals that your friends think you should sell at arts and crafts shows. The problem is that you don't know how to go about pricing your creations.

WHAT WILL YOU DO? How will your pricing goals affect the price you charge customers? What other considerations are important in pricing your unique stuffed animals?

450

THE **◄DECA** CONNECTION

ADVISOR CORNER

Highlighting DECA Week One approach to DECA Week is to highlight a different aspect of DECA each day during that week. Brainstorm with chapter members to plan specific activities for each day during National DECA Week, and use this suggested structure based on the DECA Diamond, the conceptual foundation of the organization:

- Monday: Vocational Understanding Day
- Tuesday: Social Intelligence Day
- Wednesday: Advisor/Educator Appreciation Day
- Thursday: Civic Consciousness Day
- Friday: Leadership Development Day

The Steps of Price Planning

What Is Price?

Price is the value of money (or its equivalent) placed on a good or service. It is usually expressed in monetary terms, such as $5.50 for a pen. It may also be expressed in nonmonetary terms, such as free goods or services in exchange for the purchase of a product. The oldest form of pricing is the barter system. *Bartering* involves the exchange of a product or service for another product or service, without the use of money. For example, a business might exchange some of its products for advertising space in a magazine or newspaper. Some companies also will exchange advertising spots on their Web pages as a form of bartering, or an equal trade.

■ Relationship of Product Value

The key to pricing is understanding the value that buyers place on a product. The value that a customer places on an item makes the difference in his or her spending $100 on a new bicycle or $500. If the buyer is an avid cyclist, it is likely that he or she will pay a high price for the desired quality. If the buyer is merely looking into purchasing a bike as a new hobby or to get around on the weekends, he or she may not place as high of a value on the item. Value is a matter of anticipated satisfaction—if consumers believe they will gain a great deal of satisfaction from a product, they will place a high value on it. They will also be willing to pay a high price.

A seller must be able to gauge where a product will rank in the customer's estimation—whether it will be valued much, valued little, or valued somewhere in between. This information can then be considered in the pricing decision. The seller's objective is to set a price high enough for the firm to make a profit and yet not so high that it exceeds the value potential customers place on the product.

■ Various Forms of Price

Price is involved in every marketing exchange. The fee you pay a dentist to clean your teeth, the amount you pay for a new pair of shoes, and minor charges such as bridge tolls and bus fares are all prices. Rent is the monthly price of an apartment. Interest is the price of a loan. Dues are the price of membership. Tuition is the price you pay for an education. Wages, salaries, commissions, and bonuses are the various prices that businesses pay workers for their labor. Price comes in many forms and goes by many names.

> ### ● What You'll Learn
> - The different forms of price
> - The importance of price
> - The goals of pricing
> - The difference between market share and market position

> ### ● Why It's Important
> Price—one of the four Ps of the marketing mix—is an essential element in marketing a product to the correct target market. The goals of company and government regulations are two issues that must be considered in that process. Understanding the steps involved in determining the price of a product is essential for business success.

> ### ● Key Terms
> - price
> - market share
> - market position
> - return on investment

Chapter 25 ■ *Price Planning* **451**

FOCUS

Bell Ringer Activity

Define and Discuss Ask students to define the term *price*. Use the discussion to consider the many ways we use price when spending money or putting value on something. Conclude by having students name all the forms price takes in situations other than purchasing goods. *(rent, dues, tuition, interest, wages, salaries, etc.)*

Introducing the Section

The Steps of Price Planning As students generate responses to the Bell Ringer Activity, write them on the board. This exercise will help the class refine their concept of price or value of money placed on a good or service.

TEACH

Technology Resources

PowerPoint The *Marketing Essentials* PowerPoint Presentation CD-ROM provides visual lecture aids for every chapter section.

Concept Development

1. Read Section 25.1 with students.
2. To introduce the importance of price, ask students to characterize the prices of the following products as high, medium, or low: products sold in Wal-Mart stores *(low)*, Mercedes Benz automobiles *(high)*, clothing sold in GAP stores *(medium)*. Ask students why it was so easy for them to identify those price levels. *(The image of the product or company makes clear what kind of pricing each one uses.)*

451

Classroom Resources

For the Teacher
- Teacher Editions for all workbooks
- Assessment Package
- PowerPoint Presentation Software
- Interactive Lesson Planner
- ILP Block Scheduling, p. 8
- ILP Lesson Plans, p. 53
- ILP Internet Resources, p. 69

- ILP Blackline Masters, p. 47
- ILP *BusinessWeek* Case Studies, p. 157
- ILP Marketing Career Portfolio, p. 38
- *Marketing Essentials* Web site (**www.marketing.glencoe.com**)

For the Student
- Student Activity Workbook, p. 213
- Marketing Math Workbook, p. 71

- Marketing Research Project Workbook, p. 131
- ILP School-to-Work Activity Workbook, p. 105
- Virtual Business simulation
- *Marketing Essentials* Web site (**www.marketing.glencoe.com**)

ILP These resources are available in print and on the Interactive Lesson Planner (ILP)

Importance of Price

Price is an important factor in the success or failure of a business. It helps establish and maintain a firm's image, competitive edge, and profits.

Many customers use price to make judgments about products and the companies that make them. A higher price means better quality from an upscale store or company to some customers; to other customers, a lower price means more for their money. Price is a vital component of a business's image.

Price is sometimes the main thrust of a firm's advertising strategy. Some retailers stress that they offer the lowest prices in town or promise that they will beat any other store's prices. In such cases, price plays an important role in establishing the edge a firm enjoys over its competition.

Finally, price helps determine profits. Marketers know that sales revenue is equal to price times the quantity sold. Sales revenue can be increased either by selling more items or by increasing the price per item, in theory. The number of items sold may not increase or even remain stable if prices are raised. Figure 25-1 shows what may happen.

It is also important to remember that an increase in price can increase profits only if costs and expenses can be maintained. You will explore this limitation later in the chapter.

Goals of Pricing

While marketers are concerned primarily with earning a profit, they do have other pricing goals. They include gaining market share, achieving a certain return on investment, and meeting the competition.

Gaining Market Share

A business may forgo immediate profits for long-term gains in some other area. One goal, for example, might be to take business away from competitors. The business is trying to increase its market share in this case. Market share is a firm's percentage of the total sales volume generated by all competitors

---

FIGURE 25-1

Projected Effects of Different Prices on Sales

Price per Item	×	Quantity Sold	=	Sales Revenue
$50		200		$10,000
$45		250		$11,250
$40		280		$11,200
$35		325		$11,375
$30		400		$12,000
$25		500		$12,500

■ **Increased Price or Increased Sales?** An increase in the price of an item may not produce an increase in sales revenue. *Why is this true?*

---

in a given market. Businesses constantly study their market share to see how well they are doing with a given product in relation to their competitors.

Visualize the total market as a pie. Figure 25-2 on page 453 depicts the total market for digital cameras. Each slice of the pie represents each competitor's share of that market. The biggest slice of the pie represents the firm that has the largest percentage of the total sales volume. In addition to market share, marketers are interested in their relative standing in relation to their competitors, or their market position. To monitor market position, a firm must keep track of the changing size of the market and the growth of its competitors. According to market position, the number one cookie brand in the United States is Oreo (see Figure 25-3 on page 453).

Pricing may play a role in establishing and maintaining a firm's market share and market position. Businesses must watch their competitors to maintain or improve their market share and position. A company that wants to increase its market share will engage in price competition in order to take business away from its competitors. This may be accomplished by increasing advertising or using new advertising media and messages.

■ Return on Investment

Return on investment is a calculation that is used to determine the relative profitability of a product. The formula for calculating return on investment is as follows:

Profit/Investment

Profit is another word for return, which explains the expression return on investment.

Assume your company sells trash cans for $8 each. Your cost to make and market the trash cans is $6.50 per unit. Remember that profit is money earned by a business minus costs and expenses, so that your calculation on investment is:

$8 − $6.50 = $1.50/$6.50 = .23

This means that your rate of return on investment is 23 percent.

A company may price its products to achieve a certain return on investment. Let's say that your trash can company wants to achieve a return on investment of at least 15 percent on a new model. To determine the price at which the new trash can would have to sell, you would work backward. Start with a target price, the price at which you want to sell the new trash cans. Then, determine how your company can get costs down so that that price will generate your target return. You will learn more about target pricing in Chapter 26.

FIGURE 25-2

Digital Camera Market Share

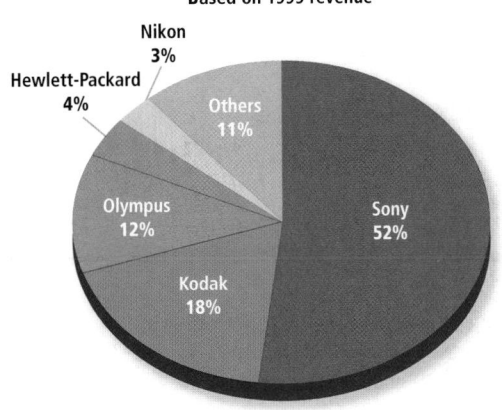

Based on 1999 revenue

Nikon 3%
Hewlett-Packard 4%
Others 11%
Olympus 12%
Sony 52%
Kodak 18%

■ **Market Share** Market share is a firm's percentage of the total sales volume generated by all competitors in a given market. *Which brand has the largest share of the digital camera market? If total sales for this market are $3 billion, what is the sales revenue for the market leader?*

FIGURE 25-3

Cookies—The U.S. Market

$510 million

$396 million

$172 million

$143 million

■ **Market Position** Market position is the relative standing a competitor has in a given market in comparison to its competitors. *Which brand is the market leader in the U.S. cookie market? Given total sales of $1,221 (in millions) for the U.S. cookie market, what is the leader's market share?*

Chapter 25 ■ *Price Planning* **453**

■ **At What Price?** The concept of price comes in a variety of ways. *Besides paying money for products or services, what other means is there to exchange products and services?*

■ Meeting the Competition

Some companies simply aim to meet the prices of their competition. They either follow the industry leader or calculate the average price and then position their product close to that figure. Two products priced in this manner are automobiles and soft drinks. Competing products in both these categories tend to be very similar and are therefore priced closely to one another. Prices may vary slightly, but the figures are in the same ballpark. It is unlikely that you would find a can of soda priced over $1.00 if the rest of the soft drinks in that category match that price. Manufacturers want to ensure that they match their competition in price and quality.

How does one compete when there is no price competition? You compete on the basis of other factors in the marketing mix. These might include quality or uniqueness of product, convenience of business location or hours, and level of service. A television manufacturer might offer a longer term or more comprehensive warranty than its competitors. A bookstore might engage a local drama group to do weekly readings from popular titles. A local restaurant may offer luncheon specials for certain businesses within a certain zip code. Businesses would try to meet competition based on a marketing strategy that takes more than price into consideration in these situations.

25.1 ASSESSMENT

Reviewing Key Terms and Concepts

1. What is bartering?
2. Why is price an important factor in the success or failure of a business?
3. Name three goals of pricing in addition to making a profit.
4. Distinguish between market share and market position.
5. Define and show the formula for return on investment.

Thinking Critically

6. Setting prices higher than the competition will put your business on a fast track to failure. Is this statement true or false? Explain the reasons for your answer.

Integrating Academic Skills

7. **COMMUNICATION** Deliver a two-minute talk explaining why knowledge of the consumer is so important in pricing decisions.

25.1 ASSESSMENT ANSWERS

Reviewing Key Terms and Concepts

1. It is the exchange of a product or commodity for another product or commodity.
2. It plays a big role in a firm's image, competitive edge, and profits.
3. to secure a share of the market, to achieve a return on investment, and to meet competition
4. Market share reflects the percentage of total sales volume a competitor has in a market.

Market position reflects each competitor's rank in order of sales volume in a market.

5. It is a calculation to determine profitability of a product. profit ÷ investment

Thinking Critically

6. False. Some businesses succeed on nonprice basis.

Integrating Academic Skills

7. **COMMUNICATION** Talks will vary.

Factors Involved in Price Planning

Market Factors Affecting Prices

How do businesses make price decisions? The answer is not an easy one, as you have probably already realized.

Most price planning begins with an analysis of costs and expenses, many of which are related to current market conditions. The cost of raw materials may increase a manufacturer's costs to make an item. Passing that increase on to customers may seem an easy remedy for the situation; however, it is not that simple. An organization's goals must be considered. When a firm's goal is to increase market share, pricing decisions must be in line with that goal. The manufacturer must fully consider the effect the higher price will have in the marketplace.

■ Costs and Expenses

In today's competitive economic environment, businesses constantly monitor, analyze, and project prices and sales in the light of costs and expenses. They do this because sales, costs, and expenses together determine a firm's profit.

RESPONSES TO DECLINING PROFIT MARGINS What do marketers do when costs or expenses increase or when sales decline? Some pass the costs to their customers. When oil prices go up, you will often see an increase in rates charged by airlines, shipping companies, and at the gas stations. How else could businesses maintain their profit margins? Let's look at other options available to improve a firm's profit picture.

Some businesses have found that price is so important in the marketing strategy of a product that they will hesitate to make any price changes. They will reduce the size of an item before they will change its price. A candy manufacturer might reduce a candy bar from 4 to 3.5 ounces rather than increase its price. This would reduce the cost of making the candy bar, so the manufacturer could still make a profit at the established price.

Manufacturers drop features their customers don't value. Some airlines have stopped serving meals and offer only beverages. Eliminating a small portion of its service helps the company to compete more effectively based on price.

Some manufacturers respond to higher costs and expenses by improving their products. They add more features or upgrade the materials in order to justify a higher price. The increase caused by higher costs or expenses is merged with the increase resulting from improvements in the product. For example, the Ford Motor Company designed more comfortable supercabs on some of their trucks and charged more for those models.

● What You'll Learn

- The four market factors that affect price planning
- What demand elasticity is in relation to supply and demand theory
- The government regulations that affect price planning

● Why It's Important

Pricing a product may seem like an easy task, until you take all the factors affecting that decision into consideration. Skipping even one aspect of this process could cost a business millions of dollars in lost sales, or even in fines or lawsuits from not following the laws governing pricing.

● Key Terms

- break-even point
- elastic demand
- law of diminishing marginal utility
- inelastic demand
- price fixing
- price discrimination
- loss leader
- unit pricing

FOCUS

Bell Ringer Activity

Analyze To open discussion of this section and address the market factors affecting price, ask students to consider the following scenario:

A family wins a raffle sponsored by a charitable organization. The prize is a sports car that the family doesn't want. For legal reasons, however, the charity cannot take it back. So, the family decides to sell the car. Ask students what the family should charge for the car. Have them consider what factors would play a part in setting the price for the car.

Introducing the Section

Factors Involved in Price Planning The students' responses to the Bell Ringer Activity will help you introduce the market factors affecting price. They include the following:

- **Costs and Expenses** In the Bell Ringer Activity, the family will have to pay income taxes on the car they won. They may also incur charges to register the vehicle with the state.
- **Supply and Demand** The amount the family can get for the car will depend in part on the popularity and general availability of the car in the marketplace. Consumers' perceptions of the car will also play a role.
- **Competition** The amount auto dealers are asking for the same type of car will also influence how much the family can get for it.

Virtual Yard Sale!

Aiming to mimic the pricing deals available at yard sales, where prices tend to decline as the day wears on, an e-commerce site called WebSwap.com has introduced an online service in which prices decline over time. Sellers set starting prices and minimum prices for items they want to sell. WebSwap automatically decreases the starting price by a set amount each hour. The price continues to decline over the course of a week, until it hits the minimum price the seller is willing to accept. Buyers must decide whether to risk losing the item and wait for a lower price or pay a slightly higher price and get their item for sure.

Thinking Critically

How would a seller determine the starting and minimum prices for a virtual yard sale?

RESPONSES TO LOWER COSTS/EXPENSES Prices may occasionally drop because of decreased costs and expenses. Aggressive firms are constantly looking for ways to increase efficiency and decrease costs. Improved technology and less expensive materials may help create better-quality products at lower costs. Personal computers have fallen in price because of the improved technology.

BREAK-EVEN POINT Manufacturers are always concerned with making a profit. They are especially concerned, however, in two situations—when marketing a new product and when trying to establish a new price. In these circumstances manufacturers carefully analyze their costs and expenses in relation to unit and dollar sales. To do this they calculate their break-even point.

The break-even point is the point at which sales revenue equals the costs and expenses of making and distributing a product. After this point is reached, businesses begin to make a profit on the product.

Suppose a toy manufacturer plans to make 100,000 dolls that will be sold at $6 each to retailers

456 Unit 8 ▪ *Pricing*

and wholesalers. The cost of making and marketing the dolls is $4.50 per unit, or $450,000 for the 100,000 dolls. How many dolls must the toy manufacturer sell to cover its costs and expenses? To calculate the break-even point, the manufacturer divides the total amount of costs and expenses by the selling price:

$$\$450,000 \div 6 = 75,000$$

To break even, the firm must sell 75,000 dolls. After 75,000 are sold, the firm will begin to make a profit.

▪ Supply and Demand

In Chapter 3, you learned about supply and demand theory. You might recall that demand tends to go up when price goes down and down when price goes up. This statement is accurate as a general rule. However, demand for some products does not respond readily to changes in price. The degree to which demand for a product is affected by its price is called *demand elasticity*. Products are said to have either elastic demand or inelastic demand.

Elastic demand refers to situations in which a change in price creates a change in demand. Changes in the price of steak can serve as an example. If the price of steak were $8 per pound, few people would buy steak; if the price were to drop to $5, $3, and finally $2 per pound, however, demand would increase at each price level.

These increases would not continue indefinitely, however. At some point, they would be limited by another economic law—the law of diminishing marginal utility, which states that consumers will buy only so much of a given product, even though the price is low. Let's say that detergent went on sale, and you bought two cases of it. Three weeks later a new sale is announced for the same detergent, but you already have enough to last for months; therefore, you don't take advantage of the new sale.

Inelastic demand refers to situations in which a change in price has very little effect on demand for a product. Certain food products, such as milk and bread, fall into this category. Most people would not buy less milk or bread if prices were to increase sharply. The same holds true if the prices were to decrease sharply—there would be only so much bread and milk that we could use.

What determines whether demand for a product is likely to be elastic or inelastic? Figure 25-4 suggests some answers.

 Virtual Yard Sale!

Answer Sellers would have to consider costs and expenses, supply and demand, consumer perceptions, and competition. For a new item, the cost would be what the seller paid for the item. For a used item, the cost paid would have to be adjusted. If the seller wants to break even, then the total of the cost and expense of selling the item would be the minimum price. To determine the ceiling price, demand and competition would come into play. If this item were in demand or one-of-a-kind, the seller could charge more.

FIGURE 25-4

DEMAND ELASTICITY

Demand elasticity varies with five factors. Most depend on the consumer's personal situation or attitudes about the purchase.

BRAND LOYALTY

Some customers will not accept a substitute product, even though there are many competing brands. In such situations, demand becomes inelastic.

AVAILABILITY OF SUBSTITUTES

When substitutes are readily available, demand becomes more elastic. In the case of detergents, there are many competing brands, most of which will clean your clothes equally well. Demand for detergents would therefore be elastic.

LUXURY VS. NECESSITY

When a product is a necessity (such as medicine for a sick person), demand tends to be inelastic. When a product is a luxury, just the opposite is true. Note that here again the classification is relative. What is perceived as a luxury by one person may be perceived as a necessity by another.

PRICE RELATIVE TO INCOME

Changes in price are relative to the income of the customer. If a price increase is slight and does not have a major impact on the customer's budget, he or she will probably buy the product. If the increase is large and far more than the customer's budget allows, he or she will probably not buy it. Thus, if the increase is significant relative to one's income, demand is likely to be elastic.

URGENCY OF PURCHASE

If you are running out of gasoline and the next gas station charges $.15 more per gallon than you usually pay, you will probably still stop and buy gas. If a purchase must be made immediately, demand tends to be inelastic.

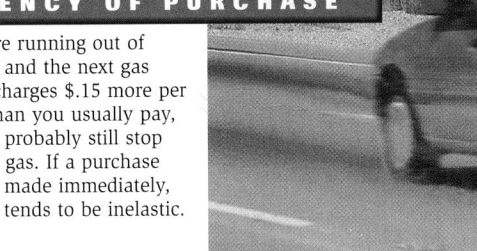

Discussion Starter

Price Planning Tell students to assume they can manufacture and distribute perfume for $5 an ounce. Then ask: If you wish to sell this product in upscale department stores, is a suggested retail price of $10 appropriate? Why or why not? *(It is not appropriate because patrons of such stores expect to pay much more.)*

Thinking Critically

Supply and Demand Curves Ask students to ponder the following: If suppliers are always willing to produce more at higher prices, and buyers are always willing to buy more at lower prices, what does this suggest about the general configuration of supply and demand curves? If students are perplexed by the abstract nature of this question, refer them to the supply and demand schedules and graph in Chapter 3, to help them visualize it. *(Supply curves will move higher from left to right; demand curves will move lower.)*

THE *DECA* CONNECTION

COMPETITIVE EVENTS AND MARKETING ESSENTIALS

Role-Play Pricing You can utilize any of DECA's Individual Series Events to illustrate the lessons of this chapter. There are many role-play situations available to provide students with practical experience planning the pricing of items and services across the nine occupational areas. Role plays might ask for students to explain factors a business owner must consider when determining the prices of goods. Others might ask students to calculate mark-up for several items in order to attain a specified average mark-up or break-even point. Practicing role play scenarios will provide your students with a review of this chapter's material and preparation for competition.

SECTION 25.2

Cooperative Learning

Price Setting Have students form groups to discuss this situation: The students run a company that manufactures cookies. They have just been informed by the company purchasing agent that the cost of flour will be going up. They must now decide how they can absorb the increase without raising prices to their customers.

Give students about ten minutes to brainstorm ideas, and then have each group report their suggestions. Have the class vote on the most creative, yet realistic, solution offered.

Independent Practice

Research and Report Have students select three products that are advertised at very low prices in their local newspaper. Have them go to the stores in question and explore the situations. Were the prices listed in the paper real, or were they misrepresented? Were the products with the low prices being used as loss leaders? Was this a case of bait-and-switch? Students should present their findings as an oral report.

■ Consumer Perceptions

Consumer perceptions about the relationship between price and quality or other values also play a role in price planning. Some consumers equate quality with price. They believe a high price reflects high quality. A high price may also suggest status, prestige, and exclusiveness.

Some businesses create the perception that a particular product is worth more than others by limiting the supply of the item in the market. They do this by coming out with a limited edition of a certain model and charging a higher price. Why? The reasoning is that the value of the item will increase as a result of its exclusiveness.

Personalized service can add to the consumer's perceptions about price. Many consumers are willing to pay more for items purchased from certain businesses because of the service those businesses might offer. Marketers can charge slightly higher prices because consumers are willing to pay for the added service.

A marketer must be concerned with subjective price—that is, the price consumers see as the value they are getting for what they are buying. The perception of the price is what counts.

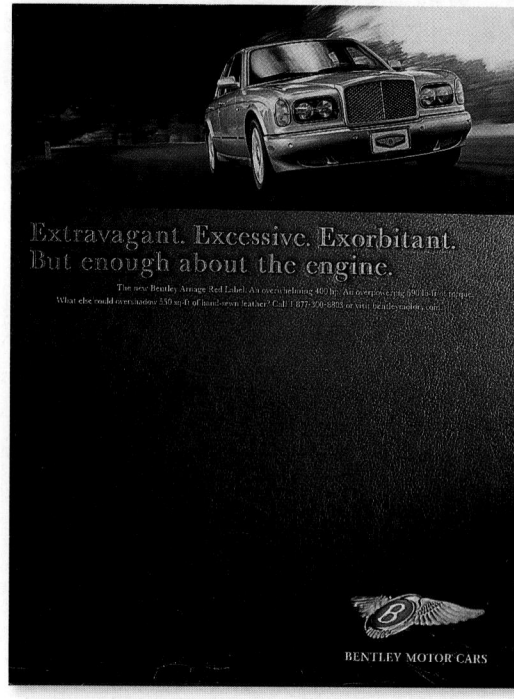

Extravagant. Excessive. Exorbitant. But enough about the engine.

BENTLEY MOTOR CARS

■ **Presenting Quality** Some businesses want to establish a quality image for their company and products. *What does a high price for this car suggest?*

BRIGHT IDEAS

The Pet Rock—Selling Nothing for Something

You're planning a big vacation. Only problem—you can't find someone to feed your parakeets. A California advertising man had this in mind when he created the infamous fad—the pet rock. Gary Dahl argued to his friends one evening that pets misbehaved, cost too much money, and made a mess. His idea of a great pet was a rock—something with a nice personality and low maintenance. Dahl spent the next two weeks writing the "Pet Rock Training Manual," which included instructions on the essentials of house-training and teaching your new pet to play dead. Dahl packaged the manual in a cardboard case resembling a small pet carrier along with an individual stone, purchased for one penny. In one month's time, a million rocks sold for $3.95 each, making Dahl an overnight star (and millionaire)!

Thinking Creatively

For what inexpensive items could you recreate other uses?

Unit 8 ■ *Pricing*

CAPTION ANSWER
Presenting Quality A high price for the car suggests status, prestige, and exclusiveness.

The Pet Rock—Selling Nothing for Something
Answer Answers will vary.

458

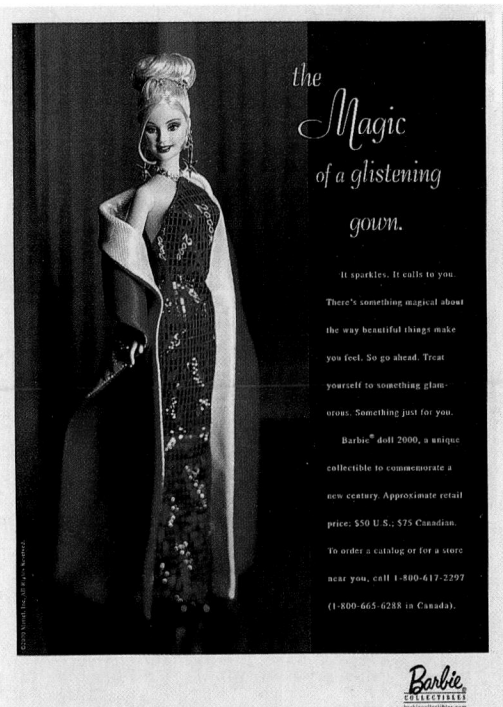

Special Editions Special editions of a product are limited in quantity to create an exclusivity for the item. *How do most businesses price special editions?*

▪ Competition

Price must be evaluated in relation to the target market and is one of the four Ps of the marketing mix. A company can use a lower price to appeal to that market when its target market is price conscious. When its target market is not price conscious, a company can resort to various forms of *nonprice competition*.

Nonprice competition minimizes price as a reason for purchase; instead, it creates a distinctive product through such means as product availability and customer service. The more unusual a product is perceived to be by consumers, the greater the marketer's freedom to set prices above those of competitors.

Marketers change prices to reflect consumer demand, cost, or competition. When products are very similar, price often becomes the sole basis on which customers make their purchase decisions. Shoppers are more likely to buy the less expensive brand if they see no difference between Maxwell House coffee and Hills Brothers coffee.

Because of this, competitors must watch each other closely. When one company changes its prices, others usually react. When the manufacturer of Tide detergent reduces its price, its competitors are likely to do the same. The benefit of this kind of competition is lower prices for consumers.

When competitors engage in a fierce battle to attract customers by lowering prices, a price war is the result. The problem with price wars is that firms reduce their profits while trying to undercut their competitors' prices and attract new customers. This may result in excessive financial losses and, in some cases, actual business failure. According to *PC World*, it took two years for the home scanner market to stabilize after a two-year price war. The battle put many vendors out of business.

Government Regulations Affecting Prices

Federal and state governments have enacted laws controlling prices. Marketers must be aware of their rights and responsibilities regarding price fixing, price discrimination, resale price maintenance, minimum pricing, unit pricing, and price advertising.

Same Price for All . . . Sometimes

Imagine that you are a Russian citizen living and working in Germany. While looking for a flight home, you are quoted $2,500 on an airline's Web site. That same flight is available to you for $1,000 if you go through a "gray market." This technique, known as ethnic pricing, offers reduced rates and discounts to nationals living abroad. Gray markets—usually in the form of discount specialized travel agencies—offer cheaper flights. While not legal in the United States and most of Europe, ethnic pricing has been a common practice in countries such as China, India, and Russia.

Thinking Critically

Why do you think that ethnic pricing is illegal in most countries?

Chapter 25 ▪ *Price Planning* **459**

Individualized Practice

Math Skills

L1 Ask students to explain in their own words the formula for determining the break-even point. (*Divide the total costs and expenses of making a product by the selling price. The result is the point at which the business begins to make a profit.*)

L2 Have students calculate the number of backpacks All Outdoors, Inc., (AOI) must sell to break even if the cost of making one backpack is $15 and AOI plans to produce 60,000. The selling price AOI would charge its customers per backpack is $24. (*[$15 x 60,000] ÷ $24 = $900,000, $900,000 ÷ $24 = 37,500 backpacks*)

L3 Tell students that All Outdoors, Inc., has learned that its chief competitor is charging only $20 for a backpack similar to its $24 model. So, AOI has decided to reduce the price of its backpack to $19.50. Have students calculate the new break-even point. (*[$15 x 60,000] ÷ $19.50 = 46,154 backpacks*)

CAPTION ANSWER
Special Editions Special editions are priced higher than the rest of the products in the same line.

Same Price for All . . . Sometimes
Answer Ethnic pricing is a form of pricing discrimination.

Individualized Practice

Problem-Solving Skills

Tell students they work for a jeans manufacturer that wants to keep its prices low in order to be competitive. However, the firm has been losing money because its expenses and cost of doing business have been rising. If the company has another bad year, employees may be laid off, and the company may go bankrupt. The management team has asked employees for suggestions on how they as employees can reduce the company's expenses.

In groups, have students brainstorm ideas to reduce the company's expenses.

L1 Tell students to select the three ideas they think are most feasible to reduce the company's expenses.

L2 Tell students to select three ideas they think are most feasible. Have them identify the pros and cons of those ideas in a jointly written memo.

L3 Tell students to select the three ideas they think are most feasible. Have one student from each group defend the group's ideas to the rest of the class. The class will represent the firm's corporate board of directors.

REAL WORLD MARKETING

Too Cool For Cola

On a chilly day could you be persuaded to buy a cold soda at 20 cents off? Would you be willing to pay 20 cents more for the same soda on a sweltering summer day? Coca-Cola Co. found out the hard way that the answer is no. The beverage company experimented with the idea of "smart" vending machines that priced sodas according to inventory levels. After conducting research however, Coke found that customers felt that they were being taken advantage of. Marketing specialists determined that Coke would damage its brand image by focusing on price.

Thinking Critically?
Why didn't Coke's fluctuating pricing scheme work?

Price Fixing

Price fixing occurs when competitors agree on certain price ranges within which they set their own prices. Price fixing can be proved only when there is evidence of collusion. This means that there was communication among the competing firms to establish a price range. Price fixing is illegal because it eliminates competition—the cornerstone of the free enterprise system.

The federal law against price fixing is the Sherman Antitrust Act of 1890, which outlawed monopolies. In 1999, Hoffman-LaRoche and BASF (Badische-Anillin & Soda-Fabrik) were found guilty of price fixing in the human and animal vitamin industry and they paid a $725 million fine.

Price Discrimination

Price discrimination occurs when a firm charges different prices to similar customers in similar situations. The Clayton Antitrust Act of 1914 defines price discrimination as creating unfair competition. The Robinson-Patman Act was passed in 1936 to strengthen the provisions of the Clayton Act. The

Robinson-Patman Act prohibits sellers from offering one customer one price and another customer a different price if both customers are buying the same product in similar situations.

The Robinson-Patman Act was intended to help smaller retailers compete with the large chain stores. It was presumed that bigger stores would be in a position to demand lower prices because of the volume of goods they could purchase. Smaller retailers who could not buy large quantities of product to sell would be at a competitive disadvantage.

The Robinson-Patman Act created restrictions on pricing and other price-related options, such as rebates, credit terms, warehousing, premiums, coupons, guarantees, discounts, and delivery. There are a few exceptions, however. Price discrimination within a channel of distribution is permissible if:

- Products purchased are physically different
- Non-competing buyers are involved
- Prices do not hurt competition
- Costs justify the differences in prices
- Production costs go up
- Prices are changed to meet another supplier's bid

Discounts are permitted if the sellers can demonstrate that they are available to all channel members on a proportional basis, graduated to allow small and large buyers to benefit and qualify, or justified by savings incurred. Price discrimination is obviously a complicated matter that must be studied carefully to be sure pricing is in line with the provisions of the Robinson-Patman Act.

Resale Price Maintenance

Manufacturers' resale price maintenance policies have come under scrutiny by legal authorities. Historically, manufacturers would set a retail price for an item and force retailers to sell it at that price. The manufacturer would punish retailers that sold the item for a lower price by withholding deliveries or refusing promised discounts or allowances. This practice of punishing retailers was outlawed in 1975 in the Consumer Goods Pricing Act.

Nine West Group Inc., one of the largest suppliers of women's shoes, was found guilty of such practices in 2000. Nine West divisions made agreements with retailers that create a fixed retail price for their shoes. They also limited the time when retailers could run promotional sales at discount prices.

REAL WORLD MARKETING

Too Cool for Cola
Answer Customers didn't like the idea of paying different prices for Coke on different days. They felt they were being taken advantage of.

Case Study

The Price of Gas

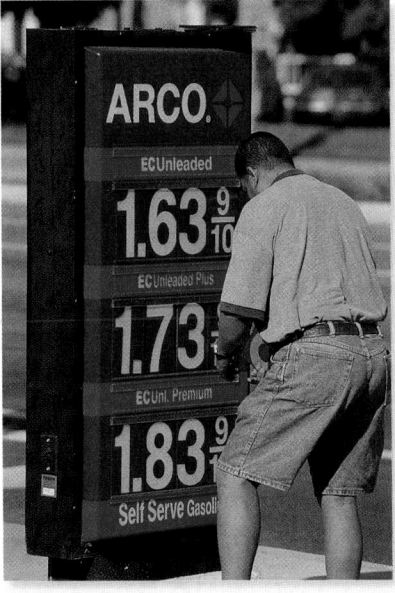

In June 2000, gasoline prices escalated to over $2.00 per gallon, especially in the Midwest. Everyone wanted to know why.

One reason is that oil refiners use a "just-in-time" inventory system so they do not maintain a lot of reserves. Unprepared for increased demand, refiners had to pay higher prices for crude oil.

A second reason involved increased expenses that refiners incurred due to new environmental requirements. The mandate for cleaner air has prompted state legislatures to require different formulas for gasoline to meet requirements in their respective states. That meant a refiner had to create several different versions of reformulated gasoline for each state it served, costing refiners more money. The concept of special formulas for gasoline is not new. In 1996, California auto drivers experienced a 30-percent increase in gasoline prices when that state mandated its own special formula.

The higher prices led to a federal government investigation and new exploration to increase supplies by oil companies. Until supply meets demand, however, you can expect higher gasoline prices.

Case Study Review

1. How are gasoline prices related to the supply and demand theory and to the theory of demand elasticity?
2. Besides a shortage of inventory, what other factor caused higher gasoline prices for consumers?

A MATTER OF ETHICS

3. Is it ethical for oil refineries to pass the higher cost of fuel on to the consumer, when they were the ones who did not anticipate the increased demand?

Those retailers who did not follow these rules were penalized by Nine West. The State Attorney General called for Nine West Group to pay a fine of $34 million. They also may not threaten a stop in shoe supply if retailers don't comply with their rules.

A manufacturer may suggest resale prices in its advertising, price tags, and price lists. There can even be an agreement to fix the maximum retail price as long as the price agreement is not an "unreasonable restraint of trade" or considered "anti-competitive." A business cannot coerce current customers into adhering to such prices. It can tell customers in advance that they will not be permitted to sell its

products if they break the established pricing policy. The difference between "coercing customers" and "telling them in advance" is the fine line manufacturers with such policies must walk.

■ Minimum Price Laws

Very closely related to resale price maintenance laws is the practice of selling goods at a very low price. Many states have enacted minimum price laws (also known as unfair sales laws). The laws were enacted to prevent retailers from selling goods below cost plus a percentage for expenses and profit. Some states have passed such laws that cover all

Chapter 25 ■ *Price Planning* **461**

ASSESS

Reteaching

1. **Vocabulary** Assign and review the vocabulary terms for this section.
2. **Fact and Idea** Assign and review Fact and Idea Review questions 5–10 from the Chapter Assessment.
3. **Pricing Factors** To reteach the factors affecting price, provide various examples in story form. After each story, have students identify the pricing factor being illustrated.

Enrichment

1. **Review** Assign and review the Chapter 25 activities in the *Student Activity Workbook*.
2. **Review** Assign and review the appropriate Thinking Critically questions from the Chapter Assessment.
3. **Review** Assign and review the following Chapter Assessment activities: Building Workplace Skills, Applying Marketing Concepts, Linking School to Work, The DECA Connection Role Play, and Internet Connection.
4. **Research and Report** Have students research five products that have gone down in price over the last ten years. Tell students to write a report that uncovers the reasons for the reductions and explain them in relation to the concepts presented in this section.

Case Study Review Answers

The Price of Gas

1. If supply goes down and demand goes up, prices will go up. Regarding demand elasticity, answers will vary depending upon gasoline being classified as a necessity vs. a luxury, and price increase relative to income.
2. increased expenses of refiners due to state legislation mandating cleaner air

A MATTER OF ETHICS

3. Answers will vary, but some may say that oil refiners cannot predict the future so they cannot be expected to absorb the higher costs of crude oil. Others may say that oil refiners should be responsible.

Technology Resources

Assessment Resources
Go to the *Marketing Essentials* Web site (**www.marketing.glencoe. com**) for tools to teach and assess occupation-specific performance indicators.

VIRTUAL BUSINESS

Monopoly
Introduce the concept of monopoly pricing to students using Knowledge Matters' Virtual Business visual simulation, "Economics—Monopoly." Go to the *Marketing Essentials* Web site (**www.marketing. glencoe.com**) to download this classroom activity. Students will change price to maximize profit in a town with one other competitor. Then they will run the same simulation but with ownership of the competitor. If needed, have students run the Virtual Business tutorial before beginning this activity.

CLOSE

Section Wrap-Up

Ask students to recall the laws governing price discrimination and price fixing. *(The Clayton Antitrust Act covers price discrimination; the Sherman Antitrust Act covers price fixing. The Robinson-Patman Act covers both.)*

CAPTION ANSWER
Compare and Contrast The customer could compare the price per ounce of similar goods packaged differently.

---

products, while others have included only specific products.

In states where minimum price laws are not in effect, an item priced at cost to draw customers into a store is called a **loss leader**. This means the business takes a loss on the item to lead customers into the store. Retailers select highly popular, well-advertised products to use as loss leaders, such as disposable diapers.

■ Unit Pricing

A number of states have passed laws to make it easier for consumers to compare similar goods that are packaged in different sizes or come in different forms (such as frozen and canned foods). **Unit pricing** allows consumers to compare prices in relation to a standard unit or measure, such as an ounce or a pound. Food stores have been most affected by these laws and have responded with shelf labels and computer records of unit prices.

■ Price Advertising

The Federal Trade Commission (FTC) has developed guidelines for advertising prices. The FTC's price advertising guidelines forbid a company from advertising a price reduction unless the original price was offered to the public on a regular basis for a reasonable and recent period of time. Another rule says that a company may not say that its prices are lower than its competitors' without proof of such comparison based on a large number of items. Also,

■ **Compare and Contrast** A number of states have passed laws to make it easier for consumers to compare similar goods that are packaged in different sizes or come in different forms. *How would a customer determine which is a better buy?*

a premarked or list price cannot be used as the reference point for a new sale price unless the item has actually been sold at that price.

Bait-and-switch advertising, in which a firm advertises a low price for an item it has no intention of selling, is illegal. When a customer comes in and asks for the advertised item, salespeople switch the customer to a higher-priced item by saying that the advertised product is out of stock or of poor quality.

25.2 ASSESSMENT

Reviewing Key Terms and Concepts

1. Name four market factors that affect price planning.

2. In response to increased costs and expenses, what three pricing options might a business consider to maintain its profit margins?

3. What is demand elasticity, and how does it alter the theories of supply and demand?

4. What is the difference between price fixing and price discrimination? What laws govern each?

Thinking Critically

5. Many people with diabetes depend on insulin. If the price of insulin went up $10, would the demand for insulin go down as is suggested by the theory of supply and demand? Explain your answer in terms of demand elasticity.

Integrating Academic Skills

6. **MATH** Calculate the break-even point for a notebook that costs a business $1 to make and market and that will be sold for $1.50. The total quantity that will be sold at that price is 60,000.

25.2 ASSESSMENT ANSWERS

Reviewing Key Terms and Concepts

1. cost and expense; supply and demand; consumer perceptions; and competition

2. reduce size of item and keep same price; produce less expensive model by eliminating some features; improve product to charge a higher price

3. It is the degree to which demand for a product is affected by its price. Price changes have no effect on inelastic demand.

4. Price fixing: collusion among competitors to agree on prices (Sherman Act). Price discrimination: firm charges different prices to similar customers (Clayton, Robinson-Patman Acts).

Thinking Critically

5. Insulin is a necessity; demand would be inelastic.

Integrating Academic Skills

6. **MATH** 40,000 ($1 x 60,000 = $60,000, $60,000 ÷ $1.50 = 40,000)

Careers in Marketing

PROFESSIONAL SALES

Dennis Spiegel
Manufacturer's Agent
Spiegel & Spiegel Sales Associates LLC

What does your job entail?

"My job involves the direct selling of furniture to various corporations. Manufacturers' agents are also known as marketing or wholesale sales representatives. They are the contact between the manufacturers of products and the customers. I travel to customers' business locations and demonstrate new products, write orders, and solve any problems between the customers and the manufacturers. I also communicate special requests from customers to manufacturers. Sales agents help customers to display a manufacturers' merchandise or to write advertising copy to increase retail sales of the merchandise they represent. In addition to traveling to the customers' locations, they conduct sales by phone and at special manufacturers' showrooms."

What skills are most important to you?

"I believe that it is extremely important to offer the customer extraordinary service. To do this you must have excellent product knowledge, as well as the ability to persuade the customer. Sometimes, you might need to overcome objections before you can close the deal. All of this requires very strong communication skills."

What kind of training do you recommend?

"High school students interested in sales should take courses in business, marketing, economics, consumer education, accounting, and English. This will give you a good background for the specialized training programs that are available on the job."

What is your key to success?

"I enjoy the interaction with my customers. I am persistent in meeting my personal goals and corporate goals. In this business, it is necessary to stay flexible and maintain a broad perspective. Enthusiasm and a positive attitude are what will help you stay on top!"

Thinking Critically
Why is on-the-job training vital in this career?

Career Facts

Education and Training: Most employers require a two to four-year college degree involving some technical training related to the product.

Aptitudes, Abilities, and Skills: Self-motivation, high energy, ability to work with little direct supervision, good people skills, excellent sales skills, and a pleasant personality are vital, in addition to average clerical, arithmetic, and computer skills.

Career Outlook: Average growth is projected for manufacturers' agents through the year 2006. New Internet marketing techniques may reduce the need for agents as fewer agents are able to cover sales territories with less traveling.

Career Path: Many manufacturers' sales agents have previous sales experience. Successful sales agents may advance to sales supervisor positions or to account executives.

Chapter 25 ■ *Price Planning* **463**

463

Vocabulary Review

Explanations will vary. See Glossary for definitions.

Fact and Idea Review

1. If consumers believe they will get a great deal of satisfaction from certain product features, they will place a higher value on the product and will be willing to pay a high price for it.
2. Market share is a firm's percentage of the total sales volume generated by all competitors in a given market. (e.g., Sony has a 52 percent market share in the digital camera market.) Market position is a business's relative standing in relation to its competitors. (e.g., Oreo cookies are ranked number one among U.S. cookie brands in terms of sales volume.)
3. Divide profit by investment, which is price less cost divided by cost.
4. Businesses can compete on the basis of quality or uniqueness of goods and services, extra consumer benefits, and convenience of business location or hours.
5. In the personal computer business, prices dropped because of decreased costs and expenses.
6. Factors include: the availability of substitutes, the price relative to customer's income, brand loyalty, luxury vs. necessity, and urgency of purchase.
7. Consumers may perceive a product to be worth more because of a high price, a limited supply, or the quality of service provided by the firm selling the product.
8. Firms can compete on either a price or nonprice basis. (The latter emphasizes things like availability and customer service over price.)
9. Minimum price laws—laws that prevent retailers from selling goods below cost plus a percentage for expenses and profit—are considered unfair sales laws.
10. Unit pricing allows consumers to compare prices in relation to a standard unit or measure, such as an ounce or pound. This helps consumers compare similar goods that are packaged differently.

Chapter 25 ASSESSMENT

VOCABULARY REVIEW

Explain the difference between each pair of words listed below.

- price—unit price
- market share—market position
- return on investment—break-even point
- elastic demand—inelastic demand
- price fixing—price discrimination
- loss leader—bait and switch

FACT AND IDEA REVIEW

1. How does the role of product value play a part in price planning? (25.1)
2. Provide one example each of market share and market position. (25.1)
3. How is return on investment calculated? (25.1)
4. Once businesses meet each other's prices, how else can they compete? (25.1)
5. Name one business situation in which prices dropped because of decreased costs and expenses. (25.2)
6. Name five factors that indicate if a product is likely to have elastic or inelastic demand. (25.2)
7. How do consumers' perceptions play a role in price planning? (25.2)
8. What is the role of competition in price planning? (25.2)
9. What are unfair sales laws? (25.2)
10. What is unit pricing? Why have some states passed laws requiring businesses to post the unit prices of items? (25.2)

THINKING CRITICALLY

1. A firm is selling 10,000 shower curtains at $10 each. The cost of manufacturing and marketing the shower curtains is $7.50 each. Calculate the break-even point for the shower curtains. How is this significant to the manufacturer?
2. Determine the return on investment for the following two video games:

	Morris Mania	Berto's Revenge
Manufacturing costs	$10.00	$ 8.75
Selling/marketing expenses	$ 4.00	$ 3.25
Selling price	$17.00	$14.75

Based on return on investment, which video game is more profitable for the company?

BUILDING WORKPLACE SKILLS

1. **Human Relations** A regular customer approaches you at the snack shop where you work to ask about a new package of chewing gum. The ten-stick package for $.50 replaces the six-stack pack for $.25. The customer is not happy with this change. What do you say to maintain her good faith?
2. **Technology** Use a spreadsheet program to prepare a pie chart depicting market shares for the $800 million sports drink market. Use these fictional figures to represent each brand's sales.

Brand	Sales (× 1,000)
Thirstade	$570,000
Drinkade	93,000
Nautilus	55,000
Everlast	33,500
Energade	24,500
Hy-5	15,000
Other	9,000

Thinking Critically

1. ($7.50 – 10,000) ÷ $10 = $75,000, $75,000 ÷ $10 = 7,500. The figure means that the firm will begin to make a profit after selling 7,500 shower curtains. This can help the firm set sales goals.
2. Morris Mania: [$17 – ($10 + $4)] ÷ ($10 + $4) = ($17 – $14) ÷ $14 = $3 ÷ $14 = 21.4%.
   Berto's Revenge: [$14.75 – ($8.75 + $3.25)] ÷ ($8.75 + $3.25) = ($14.75 – $12) ÷ $12 = $2.75 ÷ $12 = 22.9%.
   Berto's Revenge is more profitable.

Building Workplace Skills

1. Answers will vary but should include references to any improvements that could justify the increased unit price.
2. The finished pie chart should show Thirstade with close to three-fourths (71 percent) of the total market, Drinkade with 12 percent, and all the others with pie chart "slices" representing single-digit percentages.

APPLYING MARKETING CONCEPTS

1. **Identifying Price** You must determine the customer price (wholesalers and retailers) for your new shampoo called Hair Joy. Visit two local beauty supply stores and compare the retail prices and unit prices (per ounce) of four comparable shampoos. Assume that your cost of manufacturing and distributing Hair Joy to wholesalers and retailers will be $1.85 per ten-ounce bottle. Assume that retailers double the price they pay for shampoo from the manufacturer. What would you suggest as the price retailers should be charged? You expect to make 200,000 bottles of shampoo at the chosen price. What will be your break-even point? Use a word processing program to prepare a written report.

2. **Researching Pricing Violations** Use the Internet to research recent legal cases of companies accused of breaking federal or state laws that govern pricing practices. Use a word processing program to write a 200-word report of your findings.

3. **Reviewing Influences on Price** Use presentation software to prepare an oral report on market factors affecting price. Be sure to include examples and appropriate graphics.

4. **Understanding Price Advertising** Research the Federal Trade Commission's guidelines for advertising prices. Using presentation software, prepare a summary of the rules and their effects on manufacturers.

LINKING SCHOOL TO WORK

Basic and Information Skills Investigate the pricing goals of your firm. Ask your supervisor to identify the goals according to the importance for your business. Prepare a written report.

THE DECA CONNECTION

Role Play: Management Trainee

Situation You are to assume the role of management trainee for a unisex clothing store that specializes in jeans and trendy clothing. The store's buyer (judge) wants your opinion about whether or not to carry a new brand of jeans that would sell for $10 more than your most expensive brand. Even at the $80 retail price, you think they will sell.

Activity In ten minutes, you will be meeting with the store buyer to share your thoughts and opinions. What will you say?

Evaluation You will be evaluated on how well you meet the following performance indicators:

- Explain the nature and scope of the pricing function
- Explain factors affecting pricing decisions
- Identify strategies for pricing new products
- Explain the nature of sales forecasts
- Persuade others

interNET CONNECTION

A Fair Price?
Supply and demand theory is alive on the World Wide Web with Web sites such as Priceline.com, where customers name their prices for air fares and other products.

Connect
- Determine the positive and negative features of a Web site that allows customers to buy goods and services online through a bidding system.
- Determine if such a system constitutes price discrimination.

THE DECA CONNECTION

Students should be evaluated on the performance indicators noted in the Role Play.
- For another DECA Role Play, go to the *Student Activity Workbook,* p. 213.
- For more in-depth Role Play practice, refer to DECA's *Essential Competitive Events Handbook.* To order, contact DECA at **www.deca.org**.

interNET CONNECTION

Answers will vary depending on the Web sites visited. Many will say that the Web site companies are not breaking the law.

Mini Quiz

Administer the Mini Quiz orally. For an expanded chapter quiz, go to page 147 of the *Reproducible Tests* book.

1. The key to pricing is understanding the <u>value</u> buyers place on a product.

2. A firm's percentage of the total sales volume generated by all competitors in a given market is called its <u>market share</u>.

3. To start, most price planning begins with an analysis of <u>costs</u> and <u>expenses</u>.

4. The <u>break-even point</u> is the point at which sales revenue equals the costs and expenses of making and distributing a product.

5. Price fixing can be proved only when there is evidence of <u>collusion</u>.

Applying Marketing Concepts

1. The competition's prices, students' retail prices, and students' break-even points will vary.
2. Reports will vary.
3. Presentations will vary.
4. Presentations will vary.

Linking School to Work

Answers depend on the work situation.

1. **Assessment** Have students complete the Reproducible Test for Chapter 25 or construct your own tests using the ExamView software.

2. **Enrichment** Have students complete the corresponding activities in the following workbooks:
   - *Marketing Math Workbook,* p. 71
   - *Marketing Research Project Workbook,* p. 131

Pricing Strategies

Chapter Overview

Chapter 26 considers a wide variety of pricing strategies: cost-, demand-, competition-oriented strategies, product life cycle strategies, psychological strategies, and discount-based strategies.

Springboard

Brainstorm Have students read the opening paragraph of this chapter. Tell them that while working on this chapter they will have to decide on a price for Delectable Delights, a new boxed candy product. Suggest they begin now by listing information they think they will need or questions to be answered in order to reach a decision.

Prereading

List the section objectives to discuss with students. Have students skim the chapter, looking at the pictures, reading the captions, and noting the heads. Ask questions to ensure that students have a minimal understanding of the chapter structure.

Preteaching Marketing Vocabulary

Dictate each of the vocabulary terms and ask students to write them on a sheet of paper. Then write the terms on the board and have students guess at the meaning of each. Write their guesses next to each. Leave this list on the board so students can see how close their guesses were to the actual definitions as they work through the chapter.

Marketing: What It Takes

Answer Review cost-oriented, demand-oriented, and competition-oriented approaches to pricing. Decisions should be made regarding the use of a one-price policy vs. a flexible-price policy and skimming pricing vs. penetration pricing.

466

Marketing: What It Takes

At What Price?

You have just been hired as a product manager for a candy company. Your first assignment is to review the pricing structure used for all current products and to develop a price for a new box of candy called "Delectable Delights"— chocolate covered dried fruits, nuts, and crackers, packaged in a fancy tin.

WHAT WILL YOU DO?

What pricing concepts and strategies will you use to arrive at a price for the new box of candy?

466

THE DECA CONNECTION

ADVISOR CORNER

Mini-Evaluations For mini-evaluations within the curriculum, invite members of the business community into the classroom to role-play with each class member. Advisors should select or develop a case study and give to students a few days in advance. Students will then present their results to the visiting business people in a role-play format. The business volunteers write a formal appraisal of the student's performance on a form similar to DECA's evaluation sheet, but they also deliver an oral evaluation on the spot, which is a good way to correct presentation blemishes regarding voice quality, etc.
(Karen Brettingen, Eden Prairie H.S., Eden Prairie, MN)

Pricing Concepts

Basic Pricing Concepts

A major factor in determining the profitability of any product is price. You need to find the right price for your target market. Only then will you have a chance of being successful.

There are three basic concepts that you will want to consider in determining the price for any given product. They are cost-oriented pricing, demand-oriented pricing, and competition-oriented pricing.

■ Cost-Oriented Pricing

In cost-oriented pricing, marketers first calculate the costs of acquiring or making a product and their expenses of doing business; then they add their projected profit margin to these figures to arrive at a price. Markup pricing and cost-plus pricing are two of the most common methods of cost-oriented pricing.

MARKUP PRICING Markup pricing is used primarily by wholesalers and retailers who are involved in acquiring goods for resale. A markup is the difference between the price of an item and its cost that is generally expressed as a percentage. The markup on products must be high enough to cover the expenses of running the business and must include the intended profit. Details and calculations related to markup pricing are given in Chapter 27.

COST-PLUS PRICING In cost-plus pricing, all costs and expenses are calculated, and then the desired profit is added to arrive at a price. Very similar to markup pricing, cost-plus pricing is used primarily by manufacturers and service companies. The method is more sophisticated than markup pricing because all fixed and variable expenses are calculated separately for different goods and services. When a manufacturer is running at full capacity, the fixed expenses become a smaller percentage of total sales. This permits the manufacturer to charge a lower unit price for goods. Figure 26-1 on page 468 illustrates how cost-plus pricing can be used to calculate price.

■ Demand-Oriented Pricing

Marketers who use demand-oriented pricing attempt to determine what consumers are willing to pay for given goods and services. The key to this method of pricing is the consumer's perceived value of the item. The price set must be in line with this perception or the item will be priced too high or too low for the target market. Inappropriate pricing could cause the product to fail.

Another aspect of demand-oriented pricing involves demand differentials. Demand-oriented pricing is effective when there are few substitutes for an item and there is demand inelasticity. Consumers

● What You'll Learn

- The three basic pricing concepts involving cost, demand, and competition
- The concepts of pricing forward vs. pricing backward
- The idea of one-price policy vs. a flexible-price policy
- The two polar pricing policies for introducing a new product

● Why It's Important

After deciding on pricing goals, marketers must establish pricing strategies that are compatible with the rest of the marketing mix. Understanding the various options helps businesses effectively execute the difficult task of pricing products.

● Key Terms

- markup pricing
- cost-plus pricing
- one-price policy
- flexible-price policy
- skimming pricing
- penetration pricing

FOCUS

Bell Ringer Activity

Brainstorm Tell students to assume that their DECA chapter has decided to raise funds by making and selling decorative wreaths (or design-your-own T-shirts or costume jewelry). Have them list all the factors that must be considered to arrive at a price for the item they want to make.

Introducing the Section

Pricing Concepts On the board list the factors students came up with in the Bell Ringer Activity. Then group the factors into cost-oriented, demand-oriented, and competition-oriented categories. Ask students why all three kinds of factors need to be considered when deciding on the price of the product. *(All factors should be considered to be sure the price is not so high or low that the company does not make enough money.)*

Chapter 26 ■ *Pricing Strategies* **467**

Concept Development

1. Read Section 26.1 with students.
2. To introduce the influence of wholesalers and retailers, take the DECA scenario in the Bell Ringer Activity one step further. Suggest that instead of having a fund-raiser, the local DECA chapter will sell the wreaths, T-shirts, or jewelry that members create to other DECA chapters and to local retailers. That would make the club a manufacturing business. Ask students what additional factors would have to be considered in determining prices. Ask: Who besides the manufacturer would need to make a profit?
3. To introduce the choice between a one-price policy and a flexible-price policy, continue to use the DECA scenario in the Bell Ringer Activity. Suggest that the club's products be sold in the school store as well. Ask students if they think the club should put price tags on the items, or if customers should be allowed to bargain. Encourage students from cultures in which bargaining is the norm to explain the process and the rationale for it.
4. To introduce pricing and the product life cycle, continue to use the DECA scenario in the Bell Ringer Activity. Tell students to consider the choice that must be made when introducing a new product to the market. Should the product's price be higher, lower, or in line with competing products? Have students discuss each pricing option.

FIGURE 26-1

Cost-Plus Pricing

Suburban Research Consultants

Questionnaire Design and Printing	$3,500
Postage	400
Labor (40 hours at $30)	1,200
Refreshments	100
Expenses	350
Profit	950
Final Price to customer	**$6,500**

■ **Cost-plus Pricing** Cost-plus pricing breaks a price down into its component parts. *How might you relabel these entries to show the similarity between markup pricing and cost-plus pricing?*

are generally willing to pay higher prices because they believe an item is different from that offered by competitors. Companies try to achieve this status by developing brand loyalty.

Sometimes prices do not reflect major differences in the good or service, but reflect only the demand for the good or service. Theaters often charge different prices for tickets on the basis of the location of the seats. Front row seats may be significantly more expensive than those located high in a balcony. Everyone who buys a ticket will see the same performance but from a different vantage point. Telephone companies may charge higher rates for long-distance calls made during peak times. The cost of providing that service may not change, but the demand for the service increases.

Manufacturers may also create prices for different styles on the basis of a demand differential that is not a reflection of the cost of making the item but of the demand for a given style. White refrigerators may be priced at $360, but the same refrigerator in yellow or beige might sell for $450. A similar refrigerator with a stylish stainless steel exterior, while functionally identical to the other refrigerators, could command over $1,000. The difference in price is not based on an increase in the cost of producing refrigerators; rather, it is based on consumer demand for fashionable colors.

FIGURE 26-1 ANSWER

Cost-Plus Pricing You can divide the list into Cost Elements (Questionnaire Design and Printing, Postage, Labor, and Refreshments) and Markup Elements (Expenses and Profit).

■ Competition-Oriented Pricing

Marketers who study their competitors to determine the prices of their products are using competition-oriented pricing. These marketers may elect to take one of three actions after learning their competitors' prices: price above the competition, price below the competition, or price in line with the competition (going-rate pricing). There is no relationship between cost and price or between demand and price in this pricing method—marketers simply set prices based on what their competitors charge.

Competitive-bid pricing, one type of competition-oriented pricing strategy, determines the price for a product based on bids submitted by competitors to a company or government agency. Laws require most government agencies to request bids based on certain specifications so they can select the company that offers the lowest prices. In such cases, some companies will elect to enter a very low bid in order to obtain the contract. They will accept a smaller profit in order to keep their employees working.

REAL WORLD MARKETING

The Power of Pricing

$7.2 billion in 1999! How did Ford manage to make more than any other automaker in history? With the help of a new pricing strategy. Even though Ford's U.S. market share fell almost two percent, it concentrated on selling cars that provided the most profit. Ford informed dealers which cars, options, and model packages made the most profit so they would stop pushing low-profit vehicles. The Ford Escort and Aspire, two low-margin vehicles, decreased in sales by 420,000 units, while the high-margin Crown Victorias and Explorers increased in sales by 600,000. Ford cut prices on its most profitable vehicles to spur demand, but not so much that it lost attractive margins.

Thinking Critically

How did Ford realize its best year in sales?

REAL WORLD MARKETING

The Power of Pricing

Answer Ford concentrated on selling the right cars that provided the most profit, and it informed dealers about which cars, options, and model packages made the most profit.

Combining Pricing Considerations

Most marketers use all three pricing policies to determine prices. Cost-oriented pricing helps marketers determine the price floor for a product—the lowest price for which it can be offered to still make a profit. Demand-oriented pricing determines a price range for the product that is defined by the price floor and the ceiling price (the highest amount consumers would pay). Competition-oriented pricing may be used to assure that the final price is in line with the company's pricing policies. Combining pricing considerations offers a good range within which a company can establish its selling price. If a company decides to go with the competition-oriented pricing strategy, they still know how much they can lower their prices if necessary based on the cost-oriented pricing figures.

Manufacturers may also consider the prices they will charge wholesalers and retailers for their products. This can be done in one of two ways. You can work backward from the final retail price to find the price for the wholesalers. You can also do this in reverse, working forward from costs and expenses to the final retail price. Figures 26-2 and 26-3 illustrate these two methods.

In Figure 26-2, which describes the steps in working backward, the retail price is set first, on the basis of consumer demand and competition. Next, the markups desired by the wholesalers and retailers are deducted based on the suggested retail price. Finally, the price that the manufacturer will charge the wholesaler is determined. Note that the price to the wholesaler must be high enough to cover the manufacturer's costs, any expenses, and the intended profit. Figure 26-3 illustrates the steps to working forward from the manufacturer's cost. Expenses and intended profit must be considered, and then the wholesalers' and retailers' markups are added to the manufacturer's price to arrive at the final selling price. Competition and consumer demand may be left out of the pricing decision if the price is set at this point. When the marketer does not consider these two factors, the final retail price may be higher than a competitor's and higher than the price consumers are willing to pay. You may have noticed that the methods used in Figures 26-2 and 26-3 produced the same final result. This is not always the case when using these techniques.

FIGURE 26-2

Pricing Backward from Retail Price

Estimated retail price	$50
Retailer's markup (40% of retail)	− $20
Wholesaler's price to retailer	**$30**
Wholesaler's markup (30% of wholesale)	− $9
Manufacturer's price to wholesaler (must cover costs, expenses, and profit)	**$21**

■ **Wholesale Price** To arrive at a wholesale price, a manufacturer can subtract all markups for channel members from the suggested retail price. *What problem would the above manufacturer have if its costs and expenses totaled $22? What might this manufacturer have to do?*

FIGURE 26-3

Pricing Forward from Manufacturer's Cost

Cost of producing item	$16.80
Manufacturer's expenses and profit (25% of cost)	+ $4.20
Manufacturer's price to wholesaler	**$21.00**
Wholesaler's markup (42.9% of cost)	+ $9.00
Wholesaler's price to retailer	$30.00
Retailer's markup (66.67% of cost)	+ $20.00
Retailer's price to consumer	**$50.00**

■ **Markups** Adding markups to cost is another way manufacturers can price their goods. Suppose in the example given here market research had shown that consumers would pay as much as $60 for the item. *What would the manufacturer's options be?*

Discussion Starter

Skimming or Penetration Pricing Tell students that their company, Realrock, is introducing a walking shoe for people who want jogging shoe construction without all the high-impact features. Ask students if they would use skimming or penetration pricing. (*Answers will vary. With the proper rationale, either type of pricing would be acceptable.*)

Thinking Critically

Price Setting Have students support this statement: To some degree, price setting is beyond the control of the manufacturer. (*Students should note that consumers ultimately determine the price by what they are willing to pay. Students could also cite the repeal of price maintenance laws. Wholesalers and retailers can raise or lower the price beyond what the manufacturer feels is ideal by adding their own markups.*)

FIGURE 26-2 ANSWER

Wholesale Price The manufacturer would lose $1 on each item. The manufacturer may have to find some way to lower production costs or convince the retailer, wholesaler, or both to lower their markups.

FIGURE 26-3 ANSWER

Markups The manufacturer could raise the price to wholesaler to approximately $25.20 (increase of $4.20), which would allow each channel member to also make more money on the item ($10.80 wholesaler's markup, an increase of $1.80; $24.00 retailer's markup, an increase of $4). The other option is to use the lower price and count on the appeal of the relative bargain to increase sales volume.

Independent Practice

1. **Research and Report** Have students identify a product that is new on the market and research its price. Have them also research the prices of similar competing products to see if prices are higher, lower, or the same as the new product. When their research is complete, have students prepare a report stating their findings and conclusions regarding the pricing strategy used to introduce the new product. Part of those conclusions should include an explanation of whether penetration or skimming pricing was used.

2. **Interview and Report** Have students interview the owner or manager of an antique store or automobile dealership regarding the pricing policy used by their sales staff. Do they use a one-price or a flexible-price policy? Have students ask their interview subjects to explain why the chosen method is effective in their type of business. Have students report their findings in written form.

CAPTION ANSWER
Name Your Price Priceline.com uses a flexible-price policy, in which customers pay different prices for the same type or amount of merchandise, thus permitting bargaining.

■ **Name Your Price** Priceline.com was one of the first Internet companies to conduct auctions for consumer goods and services. *What kind of pricing policy does such an Internet site have?*

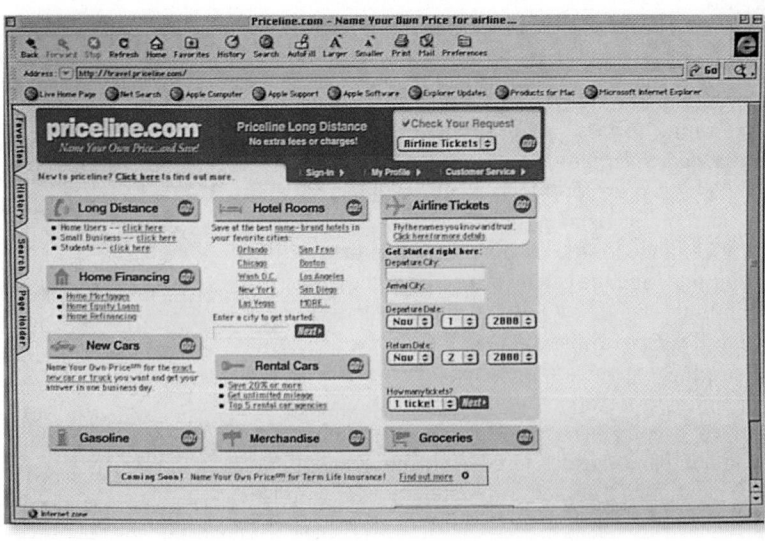

Pricing Policies and Product Life Cycle

A basic pricing decision every business must make is to choose between a one-price policy and a flexible-price policy. A business also needs to consider how a new product will be introduced into the marketplace. That choice will determine the pricing decisions that follow as the product moves through its life cycle.

■ One-Price vs. Flexible-Price Policy

A one-price policy is one in which all customers are charged the same price for the goods and services offered for sale. Prices are quoted to customers by means of signs and price tags and no deviations are permitted. Most of the retail stores that you are familiar with employ this policy.

A flexible-price policy is one in which customers pay different prices for the same type or amount of merchandise. This kind of policy permits customers to bargain for merchandise. The buyer or seller quotes a price and the bargaining begins. Most retail stores avoid using flexible pricing because it can cause legal problems. While many customers do not like the bargaining method, most expect to find a flexible-price strategy in effect with such goods as used cars, antiques, furniture, and selected jewelry.

The concept of flexible pricing is gaining popularity with the rise of e-tailing. Some Internet companies host auctions where buyers state the price they want to pay for an item and wait to see if they find a match. In other situations, sellers note the items they want to sell and let buyers bid on those items. Both situations employ a flexible-pricing policy. There are many advantages and disadvantages to consider when choosing a price policy. A one-price policy offers consistency and reliability. It also allows for retailers to estimate sales and profit because they know the set price. The flexible-price policy, on the other hand, is appealing to customers. It can be used by sellers to generate new customers. It also allows the seller to adjust its prices to meet the competition. On the other hand, a flexible-price policy does not offer consistent profits. It also may turn off some customers who prefer not to haggle to get the best price.

■ Product Life Cycle

Products move through four stages: introduction, growth, maturity, and decline. When products are no longer profitable to a company, they may be dropped from the line. Pricing plays an important role in this sequence of events.

NEW PRODUCT INTRODUCTION A business may elect to price a new product above, in-line, or below its competitors depending on the philosophy of the business and market conditions. When a going-rate strategy is not used to introduce a new product, two polar methods may be used—skimming pricing or penetration pricing.

GREAT IDEAS from the Marketing Classroom

Grady Kimbrell
Educational Consultant
Santa Barbara, CA

To stimulate interest in pricing, ask students to visit three different types of retail stores (i.e., large chain grocery store, small independent grocery store, convenience store, drug store) to document the different prices charged for ten common products.

The products must be clearly defined, including weight, brand, and any special features. Have students prepare a chart or spreadsheet for documenting the prices. Discuss students' findings and talk about the factors that influence price variations. Select a few examples to write on the board. This exercise provides great real-life examples for pricing concepts.

Skimming pricing is a pricing policy that sets a very high price for a new product. This kind of policy can be used any time demand is greater than supply. Such a policy is designed to capitalize on the high demand for a product during its introductory period. Laptop computers were originally very expensive when they were available from relatively few retailers. When they were first introduced, the target market was technology aficionados and people with high incomes who were willing to pay for the convenience of having a very small computer. At this stage, the high price is geared toward trendsetters, who are generally willing to pay higher prices in order to have or use a new product.

Businesses that use this method recognize that the price will have to be lowered once the market for the product changes to more price-conscious customers. While the product is hot, the business will enjoy a high profit margin. This profit may cover the research and development costs incurred in designing the product and creating a prestigious image. Another advantage of skimming pricing is that the price may be lowered without insulting the target market.

One disadvantage of skimming pricing is that the high initial price generally attracts competition. Once other firms begin to compete successfully, the price will have to be lowered. Another disadvantage becomes apparent if the initial price is far above what consumers (even the trendsetters) are willing to pay. In that case, sales will be lost and profits diminished because the market will not take the item seriously.

Penetration pricing is the opposite of skimming pricing—the initial price for a new product is set

very low. The purpose of penetration pricing is to encourage as many people as possible to buy the product and thus penetrate the market. This type of pricing is most effective in the sale of

Price Adjusting Using the Extranet

Need to communicate a price change quickly to clients and manufacturers? Help is on the way in the form of the "extranet." Companies are creating private networks, or extranets, that electronically link them with their suppliers and customers. These systems make it possible to get precise information on inventory, costs, prices, and demand at any given moment. In the past, companies with a large product line were literally "at a loss" when making price adjustments. It could take months for price adjustments to filter down to distributors, retailers, and salespeople. Changing prices resulted in a significant cost known as the "menu cost." Research, market share, and potential lost sales are all factors of menu cost. Streamlined networks, like extranets, reduce menu cost and time to near zero. The best news—it's already benefiting consumers.

Thinking Critically
Why would reducing menu costs be important to consumers?

■ **The Pricing Cycle** A product's life cycle stage has a bearing on its price. *When these products were first introduced in the marketplace, which type of pricing policy do you think the company used—skimming or penetration pricing? Why? How are the older models priced now?*

Chapter 26 ■ *Pricing Strategies* **471**

SECTION 26.1

ASSESS

Reteaching

1. **Vocabulary** Assign and review the vocabulary terms for this section.
2. **Fact and Idea** Assign and review Fact and Idea Review questions 1–4 from the Chapter Assessment.
3. **Demand-Oriented and Competition-Oriented Pricing** To reteach demand-oriented and competition-oriented pricing, ask students to recall some of their favorite toys from childhood. Ask if those toys were very popular at the time in the same way that Power Rangers and Beanie Babies were popular in the 1990s. Ask if there were many other toys that were similar to their favorites. Finally, ask if anyone remembers the price of their favorite toy—whether it was more or less than the price of the similar toys? This line of questioning should help reteach how demand can increase the price of an item and how competition can help to keep prices of similar products in line with each other.
4. **Product Life Cycles** To reteach product life cycles, have students suggest other examples of established (or even aging) products that have been given a new lease on life by an appeal to a new market segment. If students have difficulty generating their own ideas, suggest some products, and ask students how the manufacturer appealed to new market segments. *(Possibilities include oatmeal, aspirin, cake mixes, and baking soda.)*

price-sensitive products (items with elastic demand). Sony used a penetration pricing strategy when it introduced its first PlayStation game console in 1995. The company's strategy was to saturate the market with low priced PlayStation consoles in an effort to gain market share. Such a strategy deterred competitors and attracted price-conscious customers.

In order to penetrate the market quickly with penetration pricing, mass production, distribution, and promotion must be incorporated into the marketing strategy. The product should take hold in a short period of time. This allows the marketer to save on fixed expenses (through mass production) and to increase the profit margin (through volume sales).

The biggest advantage of penetration pricing is its ability to capture a large number of customers in a relatively short period of time. This blocks competition from other companies. Another advantage is its ability to move into a market in which the leaders are offering higher prices and lure away large numbers of customers.

A major disadvantage of penetration pricing becomes apparent if the product is not in high demand. In that case, the lower price will cause the marketer to suffer a bigger loss than it would have if a higher initial price had been set.

Understanding where a product is in its life cycle is useful in predicting sales. The decision regarding whether to use a penetration pricing strategy during the introductory stage willl influence the product's sales throughout the rest of its life cycle.

OTHER PRODUCT STAGES Pricing during subsequent periods in a product's life cycle is determined by which pricing method was originally used—skimming or penetration. Sales increase rapidly during the penetration stage, and total costs per unit decrease because volume absorbs fixed costs. The main goal of marketers is to keep products in this stage as long as possible.

Sales of products introduced with skimming pricing should be monitored closely. Once sales begin to level off, the price should be lowered to appeal to the price-conscious target market. Prices may lower drastically if the product is considered a fad.

Very little price change will be made in the growth stage for products introduced with penetration pricing. Other promotions will be used to keep sales high.

When demand decreases and sales begin to level off, competition is generally very keen. At this stage, marketers look for new market segments to hold the prices for their products. A baking soda marketer may stress non-cooking uses for baking soda, such as deodorizing or cleaning refrigerators.

The marketer's principal goal during the maturity stage is to stretch the life of a product. Some companies revitalize products in this stage by adding new

BRIGHT IDEAS
Priced to Sell on eBay

How great it would be if one could collect Pez dispensers and interact with other collectors over the Internet? That question, posed by an avid Pez dispenser collector and wife of an early Internet enthusiast, gave birth to eBay. Pierre Omidyar ran with his wife's idea to give people a central location to buy and sell unique items and to meet other users with similar interests. Omidyar lauched eBay in September 1995 and it has since grown to become the world's largest online trading community. It has successfully developed an efficient one-to-one online auction trading system in which buyers determine their own prices. eBay features more than 4,320 categories of merchandise and some 4 million new auctions daily.

Thinking Creatively
Auctions allow users to determine pricing. Why is this pricing strategy effective?

BRIGHT IDEAS   Priced to Sell on eBay

Answer Auctions take place when a group of interested buyers gather to bid on items. Buyers feel that they have control of the amount they prefer to pay for an item. They can determine when they do not want to bid any higher on a product. The interaction between buyers can help drive up prices on products, however, which is a benefit to the seller.

features or improvements. Another option is to seek new markets in other nations in the global marketplace. Products that have been made obsolete in the U.S. by technological advances may be in the introductory or growth stage in other places. Photocopiers and fax machines are examples. Older or superseded models are reconditioned and sold in other countries. By using techniques like these, marketers can significantly extend a product's life cycle. When such efforts are not successful, however, a product moves into its decline.

Sales decrease and profit margins are reduced in the decline stage. Companies are forced to reduce the price to generate sales. To maintain profitability, marketers try to reduce manufacturing costs or cut back on advertising and other promotional activities. Once a product is no longer profitable, it is phased out.

You can see how important pricing is during every stage of a product's life cycle. If all of the stages aren't well considered, a company can lose profits or see a new product experience failure instead of success. On the other hand, if a company implements a well-thought out pricing plan and carries it through, it is much more likely to experience success.

Life In The Diverse MARKETPLACE

Same Snacks, Different Price

How much would you guess that someone would pay for a snack-size bag of Doritos? $.50? Maybe even $.75? How about $.16? That is the strategy that PepsiCo Inc. took when they took their goods to Mexico. When pricing goods for sales internationally, it is important to keep in mind the income of those consumers and the exchange rate. In most developing nations, income levels and personal spending money is limited compared to the United States. PepsiCo Inc. is just one company that has responded to this with low prices and high availability.

Thinking Critically

Is it fair to U.S. consumers that prices are lower in other countries?

26.1 ASSESSMENT

Reviewing Key Terms and Concepts

1. Name the two most common methods of cost-oriented pricing.

2. Explain how cost-oriented, demand-oriented, and competition-oriented pricing concepts can be combined to determine price.

3. What two methods may manufacturers use when considering the price to charge wholesalers and retailers? How do they differ?

4. What is the difference between a one-price policy and a flexible-price policy?

5. Name and explain two polar pricing methods that may be used when a new product is introduced into the market.

Thinking Critically

6. Would you use skimming pricing or penetration pricing to introduce a new cookie called Coconut Surprise? Why?

Integrating Academic Skills

7. **COMMUNICATION** Prepare a two-minute speech on the pros and cons of a new Internet company using either a one-price policy or a flexible-price policy. Explain why you think the particular policy will be most effective.

Enrichment

1. **Review** Assign and review the appropriate Thinking Critically questions from the Chapter Assessment.

2. **Extend** Assign and review the corresponding activities from *BusinessWeek Case Studies, Internet Resources,* and the *School-to-Work Activity Workbook.* **ILP**

Evaluation

Assign and review the Section 26.1 Assessment.

Technology Resources

GO TO

Assessment Resources
Go to the *Marketing Essentials* Web site (**www.marketing.glencoe.com**) for resources to teach and assess occupation-specific vocabulary.

CLOSE

Section Wrap-Up

Have students complete this statement: Going-rate pricing involves studying the competition's pricing to be sure that . . . *(one's own prices are in line with them.)*

Life In The Diverse MARKETPLACE

Same Snacks, Different Price

Answer Some students will say that it is fair because prices are based on percentage of salary; others may say it's not because the same product is being sold for less.

26.1 ASSESSMENT ANSWERS

Reviewing Key Terms and Concepts

1. markup pricing and cost-plus pricing

2. Cost-oriented provides price floor; demand-oriented provides price range; competition-oriented provides final consideration.

3. Pricing backward begins with the price you assume customers are willing to pay and considers competition. Pricing forward does not involve demand or competition orientations.

4. One-price: same price paid; flexible-price: different prices for same merchandise.

5. Skimming pricing sets a very high price. Penetration pricing sets the initial price very low.

Thinking Critically

6. penetration if product is price-sensitive and competitive.

Integrating Academic Skills

7. **COMMUNICATION** Speeches will vary.

SECTION 26.2

Setting Prices

● What You'll Learn
- The various pricing techniques
- The steps in setting prices

● Why It's Important
Now that you have studied pricing concepts and policies, it is time to look at the special pricing techniques that help companies achieve their business goals. Then you will put all of that information into a single process: the steps for determining price.

Key Terms
- psychological pricing
- odd-even pricing
- prestige pricing
- multiple-unit pricing
- bundle pricing
- promotional pricing
- everyday low prices (EDLP)
- price lining
- discount pricing
- trade discounts
- seasonal discounts

Pricing Techniques

Marketers use specific pricing techniques to determine pricing. These techniques include psychological pricing and discount pricing.

■ Psychological Pricing

Psychological pricing refers to techniques that create an illusion for customers or that make shopping easier for them. In either case, psychological pricing techniques appeal to particular market segments because of their shared perceptions and buying habits. Among common psychological pricing techniques are odd-even pricing, prestige pricing, multiple-unit pricing, bundle pricing, promotional pricing, everyday low prices (EDLP), and price lining.

ODD-EVEN PRICING A technique that involves setting prices that all end in either odd or even numbers is known as odd-even pricing. The psychological principle on which the technique is based is that odd numbers ($.79, $9.95, $699) convey a bargain image. Even numbers ($10, $50, $100) convey a quality image. Whether or not this is true, you will find that many marketers follow the odd-even technique in an effort to project a certain image.

PRESTIGE PRICING Prestige pricing sets higher-than-average prices to suggest status and prestige to the consumer. As noted in Chapter 25, many customers assume that higher prices mean higher quality and are willing to pay more for certain goods and services. Rolls Royce automobiles, Waterford crystal, and Lenox china are all prestige priced.

MULTIPLE-UNIT PRICING Some businesses have found that pricing items in multiples, such as 3 for $.99, is better than selling the same items at $.33 each. Multiple-unit pricing suggests a bargain and helps to increase sales volume.

BUNDLE PRICING Including several complementary products in a package that is sold at a single price is bundle pricing. The one price for all the complementary products and the main item is lower than if a customer purchased each item separately. Computer companies use bundle pricing when they include software and Internet service in the sale of a computer. Travel services use bundling when a single price is offered for a package that includes airfare, hotel accommodations, and meals. Bundling helps businesses sell items (parts of the package) that they may not have sold otherwise, which increases their sales and revenue.

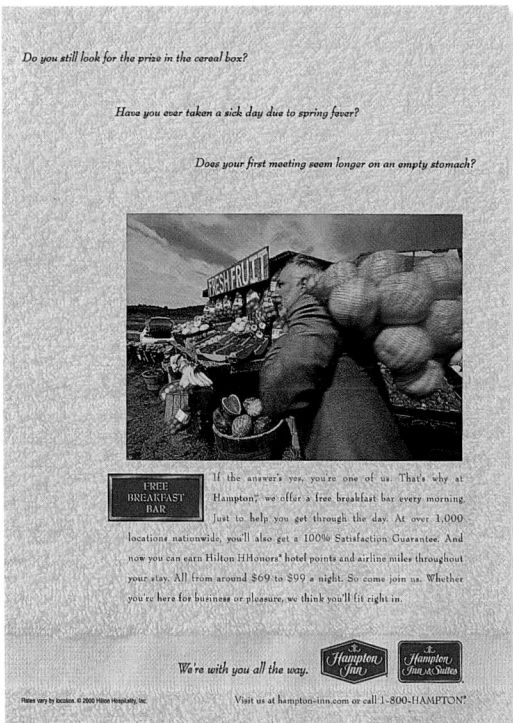

Do you still look for the prize in the cereal box?

Have you ever taken a sick day due to spring fever?

Does your first meeting seem longer on an empty stomach?

FREE BREAKFAST BAR

If the answers yes, you're one of us. That's why at Hampton,® we offer a free breakfast bar every morning. Just to help you get through the day. At over 1,000 locations nationwide, you'll also get a 100% Satisfaction Guarantee. And now you can earn Hilton HHonors® hotel points and airline miles throughout your stay. All from around $69 to $99 a night. So come join us. Whether you're here for business or pleasure, we think you'll fit right in.

We're with you all the way.

Hampton Inn   Hampton Inn & Suites

Visit us at hampton-inn.com or call 1-800-HAMPTON®

■ **Even or Odd?** Pricing techniques include psychological pricing in odd numbers. *Why is it referred to as psychological pricing?*

PROMOTIONAL PRICING The psychological technique of promotional pricing is generally used in conjunction with sales promotions when prices are lower than average. Two basic types of promotional pricing are loss-leader pricing (discussed in Chapter 25) and special-event pricing.

As you recall, loss-leader pricing is used to increase store traffic by offering very popular items of merchandise for sale at low prices. In special-event pricing, items are reduced in price for a short period of time, based on a specific happening. Some examples of this technique can be found in back-to-school specials, Presidents' Day sales, dollar days, or anniversary sales. At the end of a season, businesses also run clearance sales to get rid of old merchandise and make room for new merchandise.

Other promotional pricing techniques involving rebates, coupons, and special discounts, will be covered later in this chapter. All types of businesses may offer special promotional discounts to help boost sales at any time. The main characteristic of promotional pricing is that it is temporary—after the promotion ends, prices go back to normal.

EVERYDAY LOW PRICES (EDLP) Everyday low prices (EDLP) are low prices that are set on a consistent basis with no intention of raising them or offering discounts in the future. Everyday low prices are not as deeply discounted as promotional prices might be, which creates sales stability. Other benefits include reduced promotional expenses and reduced losses due to discounting. Wal-Mart is known for its EDLP policy.

PRICE LINING Price lining is a special pricing technique that requires a store to offer all merchandise in a given category at certain prices. A store might price all of its blouses at $25, $35, and $50.

When deciding on price lines, marketers must be careful to make the price differences great enough to represent low, middle, and high prices for the category of goods being offered. Price lines of $25, $26, $27, and $28, for example, would confuse customers because they would have difficulty discerning their basis. (Slight price differences translate into equally slight quality differences.) When price lines are properly drawn, customers can easily compare items.

An advantage of price lining is that the target market is fully aware of the price range of products in a given store. This helps the store maintain its image. In addition, price lining makes merchandising and selling easier for salespeople, who can readily draw comparisons between floor and ceiling prices. The technique also helps salespeople trade up, or offer a higher-priced, better-quality item to a customer to better satisfy the customer's needs.

Manufacturers use a variation of price lining in that they offer three tiers of prices for various models or brands in the same product category. The upper tier is for better quality premium brands, the middle tier for average priced brands, and the lower tier for price-conscious customers.

■ **Discount Pricing**

Discount pricing involves the seller's offering reductions from the usual price. Such reductions are generally granted for the buyer's performance of certain functions. These discounts include cash, quantity, trade, and seasonal discounts, as well as promotional discounts and allowances.

Chapter 26 ■ *Pricing Strategies* **475**

TEACH

Technology Resources

PowerPoint The *Marketing Essentials* PowerPoint Presentation CD-ROM provides visual lecture aids for every chapter section.

Concept Development

1. Read Section 26.2 with students.
2. Have students read aloud the Case Study on page 477 and review the answers in class.
3. Ask students to recall the Bell Ringer Activity:
   • Ask students if they would change their price to an odd or even price now that they know about the psychological affect of odd-even pricing.
   • Ask students if they would change their price now that they know about prestige pricing, multiple pricing, bundle pricing, promotional pricing, everyday low prices, and price lining.
   • Ask students if they would offer discounts to their school store customers, other DECA chapters, and local retailers. If so, ask what those discounts would be—cash, quantity, trade, seasonal, and/or promotional. Have students provide written rationales for their decisions.

CAPTION ANSWER

Even or Odd? Because it creates an illusion for customers or makes shopping easier for them. Odd numbers convey an illusion of a bargain image.

More About . . .

Pricing Techniques
When Dillard's Department Stores, Inc., adopted an "everyday low pricing" policy in the 1980s, it was in contrast to the way other department stores priced merchandise (with markdowns at sale time). Since then Dillard's has suffered declining revenues. Customers seem to want cyclically reduced prices. The thrill of the bargain wins in this case.

The New 2000 7 Series. Bristling with a host of ingenious technological features amid sophisticated elegance, the 7 Series continues to live by the credo that no amount of refinement can ever compensate for a lack of pure driving zeal. Starting at $62,970. Call 1-800-334-4BMW. Or visit www.bmwusa.com

The Ultimate Driving Machine®

■ **Prestige Pricing** The practice of setting higher-than-average prices to suggest status and prestige to the consumer is called prestige pricing. *Do you think prestige pricing is being employed in this ad?*

CASH DISCOUNTS Cash discounts are offered to buyers to encourage them to pay their bills quickly. Terms are generally written on the invoice, for example, 2/10, net 30 means that a 2 percent discount is granted if the bill is paid in 10 days. The buyer who does not take advantage of the discount must pay the full amount within 30 days.

QUANTITY DISCOUNTS Quantity discounts are offered to buyers for placing large orders. Sellers benefit from large orders through the lower selling costs involved in one transaction as opposed to several small transactions. Quantity discounts also offer buyers an incentive to purchase more merchandise than they originally intended to purchase.

There are two types of quantity discounts—noncumulative and cumulative. Noncumulative quantity discounts are offered on one order, while cumulative quantity discounts are offered on all orders over a specified period of time. Cumulative discounts may be granted for purchases made over six months, for example, in which case all purchases for that period are used to determine the quantity discount offered. In other cases, buyers may be required to sign a contract that guarantees a certain

level of business. Advertisers who agree to use a specified number of column inches in their newspaper ads might be charged contract rates that reflect usage. Generally, the more you advertise, the less you pay per column inch.

TRADE DISCOUNTS Trade discounts are not really discounts at all but rather the way manufacturers quote prices to wholesalers and retailers. Many manufacturers establish suggested retail prices, or list prices, for their items. They grant members of the channel of distribution discounts from the list price for performing their respective functions. A manufacturer might grant wholesalers a 40 percent discount from the list price and retailers a 30 percent discount.

The manufacturer might also quote the discounts in series, such as 25 and 10 percent for retailers and wholesalers, respectively. Series, or chain, discounts are calculated in sequence, as shown below. The example is based on a list price of $50.

Retailer's discount	$50 × .25 = $12.50
Cost to retailer	$50 − $12.50 = $37.50
Wholesaler's discount	$37.50 × .10 = $ 3.75
Cost to wholesaler	$37.50 − $3.75 = $33.75

Case Study

Cleaning Up With Promotional Pricing

Dirty laundry makes money—proven by the $4.7 billion laundry detergent market. Procter & Gamble departed from its everyday low price policy to regain market share when it offered off-invoice allowances to retailers for Downy fabric softener and detergent brands Tide, Cheer, Era, and Gain.

This six-month promotional pricing special increased orders, and retailers passed the discounts to their customers through special promotions and more consistent lower prices. Since detergents are often used as loss leaders, the off-invoice discounts allow retailers to run their own promotions without taking a loss on the sale of those items.

In addition to the promotional pricing, Proctor & Gamble also used coupons by dropping FSIs (free standing inserts) during the same period.

Stiff competition from competitor Unilever followed, as it slashed prices on Surf, Wisk, and All brands from 6 percent to 18 percent. Unilever's actions, which made reductions directly to the price, varied greatly from the actions of Procter & Gamble. While Procter & Gamble ran promotions to gain customers, Unilever changed prices permanently. As pricing changes spur more companies into action, it is the consumer who wins—with low prices and fresh-smelling clothes!

Case Study Review
1. What prompted Procter & Gamble to depart from its EDLP pricing policy?
2. What else did Procter & Gamble do to boost sales during that six-month period?

A MATTER OF ETHICS
3. Which pricing policy is more ethical—Procter & Gamble's special time-limited promotional pricing or Unilever's permanent price reductions?

SECTION 26.2

Cooperative Learning

Auction Have some students form groups of 4-6 members to generate a list of items they would be willing to sell. They should record the opening bid they would accept for the item. The list could consist of favorite CDs, electronics, and electronic games. Another group of students will be a dot-com auction company that conducts the auction and takes a percentage of each sale. The rest of the class will be buyers who will bid on the items.

To make the auction realistic, have a record keeper keep track of each transaction. Have students draw from a number from a hat to determine which items will be auctioned first, second, etc. Then let the bidding begin. After a few minutes, calculate total charges earned by the auction company (i.e., 5 percent on each transaction), the bill for each student who bought something during the auction, and the money made by the group that put their items up for sale.

Have students discuss what they liked and disliked about the bargaining process. Ask: Would auctioning be easier on the Internet than in person? *(Answers will vary.)* What limited the negotiations in the class simulation? *(limited number of items and buyers)*

Independent Practice

Research and Report Have students visit several different retail stores in their community to investigate psychological pricing strategies discussed in this section. Ask them to write a report with examples of products and their prices.

In series discounts, note that the wholesaler's discount is based on the retailer's discount, not the original list price.

SEASONAL DISCOUNTS Seasonal discounts are offered to buyers willing to buy at a time outside the customary buying season. Manufacturers offer discounts to obtain orders for seasonal merchandise early so that production facilities and labor can be utilized throughout the year.

Other businesses use seasonal discounts to cut anticipated costs. Many retailers, for example, drastically reduce prices on Christmas cards and decorations the day after Christmas. Such retailers prefer to sell this merchandise at a lower markup than pay the costs of warehousing it until the following year. A variation on this device is used by vacation resorts. They offer vacationers lower rates to encourage use of resort facilities during the off-season.

Chapter 26 ■ *Pricing Strategies* **477**

Case Study Review Answers

Cleaning Up With Promotional Pricing
1. Stiff competition from Unilever and private label brands prompted Procter & Gamble.
2. Proctor & Gamble used coupons by dropping FSIs during the same six-month period.

A MATTER OF ETHICS
3. Answers will vary. Promotional pricing, used by Procter & Gamble to boost sales, is ethical in all business circles. However, permanently lowering prices by Unilever may appear to be more ethical because of the commitment made to the lower price.

FIGURE 26-4
THE SIX STEPS FOR DETERMINING PRIC

Individualized Practice

Communication Skills

L1 Ask students to recall the text found on most pricing signs. Specifically, ask them what most signs look like when the store uses prestige pricing. *(script or small print for the price, or no price at all)* Ask what such signs look like when the store uses promotional pricing. *(big, bold letters)* Ask what such signs look like when the store uses multiple pricing. *(big, bold lettering with savings noted)* Finally, ask what such signs look like when pricing lining is used. *(There is one sign for each rack stating that all items on the rack are one particular price.)*

L2 Ask students to design a pricing sign to go on top of a rounder (circular rack) of sweat pants and sweatshirts. Tell them that the items are on sale for $15 each, but if customers buy two, they pay only $25— a savings of $5.

L3 Ask students to develop a system for having all salespeople remind their customers of a special on sweat pants and sweatshirts. They are to prepare a memo to all salespeople explaining exactly what they want them to do to encourage the sale of the specially priced merchandise.

Marketers usually follow six steps in setting the price of a new product. They determine pricing objectives, study costs, estimate consumer demand, study the competition's prices, decide on a pricing strategy, and set the price. Now that you have studied pricing concepts, policies, and techniques, you should be able to establish a price for a given good or service. Imagine that you are the product manager for a candy company and you have been assigned the task of pricing a new box of candy called "Delectable Delights." Evaluate the relevant factors and set an initial price for a box of Delectable Delights.

1 DETERMINE PRICING OBJECTIVES

What is your purpose in setting a price for your product? Do you want to increase sales volume or sales revenue? Establish a prestigious image for your product and your company? Increase your market share and market position? Answering these questions will help you keep your prices in line with other marketing decisions.

2 STUDY COSTS

Since the main reason for being in business is to make a profit, give careful consideration to the costs involved in making or acquiring the goods or services you will offer for sale. Determine whether and how you can reduce costs without affecting the quality or image of your product.

3 ESTIMATE DEMAND

Employ market research techniques to estimate consumer demand. The key to pricing goods and services is to set prices at the level consumers expect to pay. In many cases, those prices are directly related to demand.

Did You Know?

Would you believe that the price of an accounting software program called *Simply Money* was "no charge" for the first million copies sold? Computer Associates International, Inc., dared to risk the lowest price ever to encourage users to buy future upgrades and related programs.

4 STUDY COMPETITION

Investigate your competitors to see what prices they are charging for similar goods and services. Study the market leader. What is the range of prices from the ceiling price to the price floor? Will you price your goods lower than, equal to, or higher than your competitors'?

5 DECIDE ON A PRICING STRATEGY

You may decide to price your product higher than the competition's because you believe your product is superior. You may decide to set a lower price with the understanding that you will raise it once the product is accepted in the marketplace.

6 SET PRICE

After you have evaluated all the foregoing factors, apply the pricing techniques that match your strategy and set an initial price. Be prepared to monitor that price and evaluate its effectiveness as conditions in the market change.

Chapter 26 ■ *Pricing Strategies* **479**

Individualized Practice

Human Relations Skills

Have students assume that they work for a local retailer who is running a special end-of-season sale. All seasonal merchandise is reduced 25 percent or 50 percent off the original price. Unfortunately for the salespeople, some prices reflect markdowns that were taken prior to the sale. This confuses customers because some expect the 25 percent or 50 percent discount to be taken off the ticketed price, instead of the original price.

L1 Ask students how they would handle the confused customers. *(Explain that even though some merchandise was marked down previously, today's sale stipulates that the markdown is a percentage off the original price, not a prior sales price.)*

L2 Tell students that some of non-seasonal merchandise has been found on the special sale racks. Customers, belatedly seeing the rack with specially priced goods, have been leaving non-sale goods on the sale racks when they pick up sale items. A customer who selected a misplaced item has asked to receive the 25 percent discount. Have students role-play this situation. The customer should get very annoyed when told that she has selected an item that is not on sale, even though she found it on the sale rack.

L3 Tell students to assume that they have observed a salesperson giving a customer a 25 percent discount on a non-sale item because the customer complained about finding it on the sale rack. Have students role-play the part of the salesperson's superior (assistant manager or store manager) who must address the mistake this employee is making, which is costing the store money.

THE DECA CONNECTION

COMPETITIVE EVENTS AND MARKETING ESSENTIALS

Learn and Earn Pricing Strategies Pricing strategies can be worked on through DECA's Learn and Earn Project. Section IC asks for proposed product/service and marketing strategies, including pricing strategies. If your students are preparing the Learn and Earn Project around a fund raising activity, they will learn a great deal about the importance of pricing their products or services in relationship to the other expenses they will incur while completing the proposed project. They can delineate the lesson learned about pricing strategies in Section VC, the Earnings Outcomes.

ASSESS

Reteaching

1. **Vocabulary** Assign and review the vocabulary terms for this section.
2. **Fact and Idea** Assign and review Fact and Idea Review questions 5–10 from the Chapter Assessment.

Enrichment

1. **Review** Assign and review the Chapter 26 activities in the *Student Activity Workbook.*
2. **Review** Assign and review the appropriate Thinking Critically questions from the Chapter Assessment.
3. **Review** Assign and review the following Chapter Assessment activities: Building Workplace Skills, Applying Marketing Concepts, Linking School to Work, The DECA Connection Role Play, and Internet Connection.

Evaluation

Assign and review the Section 26.2 Assessment.

Technology Resources

Assessment Resources
Go to the *Marketing Essentials* Web site (**www.marketing.glencoe. com**) for resources to teach and assess occupation-specific vocabulary.

CLOSE

Section Wrap-Up

Have students list the six steps in setting price. *(determine pricing objectives, study costs, estimate demand, study competition, decide pricing strategy, set price.)*

CAPTION ANSWER
Promotional Pricing
It is temporary.

480

PROMOTIONAL DISCOUNTS AND ALLOWANCES

Promotional discounts are offered to wholesalers and retailers willing to advertise or promote a manufacturer's products. The discount may take the form of a percentage reduction in price or free merchandise. Another alternative, discussed in Chapter 19, is cooperative advertising in which the manufacturer and the retailer share the costs of advertising, with the manufacturer paying the lion's share.

Some kinds of promotional discounts are offered directly to the consumer. As you learned in Chapter 17, a rebate is a partial refund on the cost of a particular item from the manufacturer. To receive the rebate, a customer buys the product and then sends in a rebate form along with the product proof of purchase and a store receipt. Manufacturers offer rebates to wholesalers, and retailers too, for purchasing certain quantities of goods during special promotions.

Trade-in allowances also go directly to the buyer. Customers are offered a price reduction if they sell back an old model of the product they are purchasing. Consumers are generally offered trade-in allowances when purchasing new cars or major appliances. Companies are usually granted such allowances when purchasing machinery or equipment.

■ **Promotional Pricing** Often pricing is tied to special promotional events, such as the 4th of July. *What is the main characteristic of promotional pricing?*

26.2 ASSESSMENT

Reviewing Key Terms and Concepts

1. How are odd-even, prestige, multiple-unit, and bundle pricing related? Different?
2. What is the main difference between promotional pricing and everyday low prices?
3. What is the key factor in deciding on price lines?
4. Name five types of discount pricing techniques.
5. List the six steps in setting prices.

Thinking Critically

6. Johnson & Johnson promoted its baby shampoo to adult male athletes by touting the product's gentleness, even when used every day. At what stage in the shampoo's life cycle do you think this promotion took place? What do you think Johnson & Johnson was trying to accomplish by promoting its baby shampoo to adult males?

Integrating Academic Skills

7. **MATH** Determine the price a wholesaler would pay for an item with a list price of $100 if the series trade discounts were 40 percent and 10 percent for retailers and wholesalers, respectively.

26.2 ASSESSMENT ANSWERS

Reviewing Key Terms and Concepts
1. All are psychological pricing techniques. Odd-even prices end in odd (bargain) or even (quality) numbers. Prestige prices suggest status. Multiple-unit prices items in multiples. Bundle pricing has several products in package.
2. Promotional pricing temporarily lowers prices; EDLP is consistent low pricing with no future price increase/discount.
3. low, middle, high prices for category
4. cash, quantity, trade, seasonal, promotional
5. determine pricing objectives, study costs, estimate demand, study competition, decide pricing strategy, and set price

Thinking Critically
6. Shampoo was at maturity stage. The company was trying to open a new market: adult males.

Integrating Academic Skills
7. **MATH** Retailers: $60; Wholesalers: $54

Careers in Marketing

RETAIL MANAGEMENT

Mike McKenzie
Store Manager
Alternate World Comics

What does your job entail?

"I manage a small business, so I am responsible for all phases of that business. I control inventory, manage employees, create shipping schedules, and most importantly, keep the customers happy. As companies grow, they tend to become less efficient; my job is to impart a 'shared vision' to the employees, so that we are all on the right track. Enthusiasm is an important quality in this job."

What training would you recommend for students?

"When you are the best at something, for example chemistry, you might keep getting promoted until you are the head chemist. The best chemist in the world, however, doesn't necessarily make the best manager. Managers need training, and anyone who wants to go into business needs to know that."

What do you like most about your job?

"I enjoy the daily interaction with the customers. It is really interesting, especially at this time in the comic book industry. The excitement is contagious and it is hard to not be a part of it. It is a great feeling to be able to impart 'industry buzz' to fans. Assuring that people are getting what they want and helping them pursue their hobby is the truly exciting part of selling. People visit stores for more than just a product—and with comics, you can actually talk about the product in the store and develop some really interesting conversations and friendships."

What is your key to success?

"If I knew what that was, I would put it in a bottle and sell it! I would have to say luck and preparation have been my greatest assets. As a manager, you also have to pay attention to every detail of a business. As companies grow, they tend to forget the basics, which are always important!"

Thinking Critically

Your boss tells you that to become a successful store manager you must be a "Jack of all trades." What does she mean?

Career Facts

Education and Training: A store manager should have a minimum of a high school diploma and good sales experience. Courses in marketing, business administration, consumer education, accounting, psychology, and data processing are recommended. Many companies provide on-the-job training and instruction.

Aptitudes, Abilities, and Skills: Above average communication skills, a good understanding of advertising and display concepts, and average clerical and numerical skills are necessary. Many store managers are required to work weekends and evenings, often working more than 40 hours per week.

Career Outlook: Faster than average growth is expected for store management positions in the next five years.

Career Path: Experience at related jobs such as sales or buying may lead to management positions within a store. It may be necessary to move from a small store to a larger store to advance. Some store managers become divisional or regional managers.

Lifelong Learning

Pricing Strategies
Knowledge of how and why manufacturers and retailers set prices can motivate students as consumers to find the best products they can for the money. It can also convince them of the need to stay informed about the more technical aspects of marketing. Combined with good consumer habits, this knowledge can save students both time and money.

Meeting Individual Needs

Students with Orthopaedic Impairments
Students who use wheelchairs do so as a result of a variety of disabilities. Most wheelchairs are electric or manually operated, but some students with limited use of hands or arms may have an aide. Most students needing other assistance will ask for it. Don't assume that assistance is required, and refrain from "helping" if your offer is turned down.

Vocabulary Review

Stories will vary. See Glossary for definitions.

Fact and Idea Review

1. Marketers calculate the costs of acquiring or making a product and their expenses of doing business. They add their projected profit margin to these figures to arrive at a price. Markup pricing and cost-plus pricing are the most common methods of cost-oriented pricing.
2. Competition-oriented pricing does not take into account costs or customer demand.
3. It should be lowered to appeal to the next target market.
4. Marketers hold the price by trying to attract new market segments.
5. Odd numbers present a bargain image; even numbers present a quality image.
6. Advantages for customers are: They are fully aware of the price range of products, which helps the store maintain its image. Advantages for salespeople are: It makes merchandising easier and helps salespeople trade up so they can better satisfy customers' needs.
7. Cash discounts encourage buyers to pay quickly.
8. No, trade discounts are the way manufacturers quote prices to wholesalers and retailers.
9. Seasonal discounts are offered to buyers who are willing to buy at a time other than the customary buying season. Manufacturers offer them so production facilities and labor can be utilized throughout the year. Retailers offer them to cut anticipated costs of warehousing seasonal products until the following year.

Thinking Critically

1. Customers may wonder if they received the lowest possible price and if other customers paid less. Customers may also feel uncomfortable haggling.
2. Answers will vary.
3. Unless the package is exactly the same from other competitors, it is difficult to determine the value of all the items included in the package deal.
4. It would be cumulative, because you would not have to purchase and store all the goods at one time.

482

Chapter 26 ASSESSMENT

VOCABULARY REVIEW

Write a one-page paper about a fictitious company's pricing practices using ten terms from the list below.

- markup pricing
- cost-plus pricing
- one-price policy
- flexible-price policy
- skimming pricing
- penetration pricing
- psychological pricing
- odd-even pricing
- prestige pricing
- multiple-unit pricing
- bundle pricing
- promotional pricing
- everyday low prices (EDLP)
- price lining
- discount pricing
- trade discounts
- seasonal discounts

FACT AND IDEA REVIEW

1. Name two common methods of cost-oriented pricing. (26.1)
2. How does competition-oriented pricing differ from demand-oriented pricing? (26.1)
3. Once sales level off after product introduction with skimming pricing, what happens to price? (26.1)
4. During the maturity stage of a product's life cycle, what do marketers do to hold the price? (26.1)
5. What psychological principle is associated with odd-even pricing? (26.2)

6. What are the advantages of price lining to customers and to salespeople? (26.2)
7. Why are cash discounts offered to buyers? (26.2)
8. Are trade discounts really discounts? Explain. (26.2)
9. What are seasonal discounts? Why are they offered by manufacturers? By retailers? (26.2)

THINKING CRITICALLY

1. What ill effects could a flexible pricing policy have on customer relations?
2. Select a product and decide what product life cycle stage it is in at the present time. Provide rationale based on its price history and the industry.
3. Why does bundling discourage comparison shopping?
4. If you were a small business with little storage space, which type of quantity discount would be better for you—cumulative or noncumulative? Why?

BUILDING WORKPLACE SKILLS

1. **Human Relations** You work for a retail jeweler who has a flexible-price policy for selected customers. You are alone in the store and ring up the sale of a steady customer. The customer tells you that you did not deduct the customary 20 percent discount. What would you do?
2. **Technology** Set up a spreadsheet that will automatically calculate 20 percent, 30 percent, and 50 percent discounts during special promotions. Assume this will be input into the sales terminal so salespeople will not have to do the calculations in their heads.

Building Workplace Skills

1. Answers will vary. The salesperson could offer to credit the customer's account after speaking with the owner.
2. The formula for 20 percent discount is: retail price x .80 = sale price; for 30 percent discount: retail price x .70 = sale price; and for 50 percent discount: retail price x .50 = sale price.

Applying Marketing Concepts

1. Answers will vary, depending on how the students interpret the high demand for the product and whether

they choose a skimming or penetration pricing strategy. The basic mathematical calculations should be: The manufacturer would sell the box of candy to wholesalers for $5 ($4 cost of making and marketing x 1.25 = $5). The wholesaler would sell it to retailers for $7 ($5 x 1.40 = $7). Retailers would mark it up 40 percent to $9.80 ($7 x 1.40 = $9.80). The actual retail price using odd/even pricing would be $9.99 for odd pricing or $10 using even pricing. A $9.99 or $10 price would be a going-rate price. If they elect skimming, the price would be at the higher end and should reflect a higher margin for the manufacturer,

APPLYING MARKETING CONCEPTS

1. **Determining Suggested Retail Price** You are product manager for Delectable Delights candy company. The cost to make and market a one-pound tin of Delectable Delights is $4, and the manufacturer hopes to make at least 25 percent profit on the product. Wholesalers and retailers both use a 40 percent markup but are happy when it is higher. Competitors have suggested retail prices between $8.99 and $12.99 per pound. You need to establish the suggested retail price for the product. Use a word processing program to write a memo to your boss exploring your decision. Tell if you are using skimming or penetration pricing, and odd or even pricing. Include the math calculations and prices for the wholesalers.

2. **Understanding Pricing Strategies** The student council purchased 300 tee shirts at $2.50 each as a fund raiser. There are 100 shirts each in three different styles (popular, average, not popular). You need to decide the suggested price for the tee shirts that will generate at least $700. Decide what psychological pricing techniques would be most appropriate. Anticipate how your plan would change if you knew 50 shirts would not sell at all. Use a spreadsheet program to generate possible prices and profits. Use a word processing program to prepare a report with your final pricing plan and rationale.

LINKING SCHOOL TO WORK

Basic Thinking and Information Skills Review the psychological and discount pricing techniques in this chapter in relation to the practices you have observed on your, or a friend's, job. Cite examples of every concept used by the firm. Prepare written and oral reports on your findings.

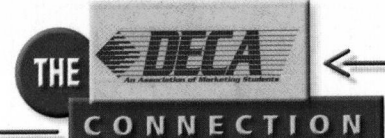

THE DECA CONNECTION

Role Play: Product Manager

Situation You are to assume the role of product manager. The toy department buyer (judge) has asked for your opinion of a new dinosaur electronic game. There are three models, with the cost (what the retail store pays) ranging from $15.75 to $20.25.

Activity At what retail price(s) should the new items sell? Support your position with known pricing strategies.

Evaluation You will be evaluated on how well you meet the following performance indicators:
- Set prices
- Explain factors affecting pricing decisions
- Explain the nature and scope of the pricing function
- Select promotional pricing strategies used to adjust base prices
- Persuade others

interNET CONNECTION

What Price to Charge?
You want competitive prices at the electronics store you own. Competition has been keen with brick and mortar retailers, mass merchandisers, and online shopping Web sites. You need to review your prices in relation to competition.

Connect
- Research your competition in your local market and on the Internet.
- Identify the price for three specific products sold by all of your competitors.
- Determine the pricing strategies used by two of your competitors.

THE DECA CONNECTION

Students should be evaluated on the performance indicators noted in the Role Play.
- For another DECA Role Play, go to the *Student Activity Workbook*, p. 223.
- For more in-depth Role Play practice, refer to DECA's *Essential Competitive Events Handbook*. To order, contact DECA at **www.deca.org**.

interNET CONNECTION
Answers will vary depending on competitors used.

Mini Quiz

Administer the Mini Quiz orally. For an expanded chapter quiz, go to page 153 of the *Reproducible Tests* book.

1. <u>Markup</u> pricing and <u>cost-plus</u> pricing are two of the most common methods of cost-oriented pricing.

2. A(n) <u>one-price</u> policy is one in which all customers are charged the same price for goods offered for sale.

3. A(n) <u>flexible-price</u> policy permits customers to bargain for merchandise.

4. When the ending number in a price is an even number, the image conveyed is a(n) <u>quality</u> image.

5. <u>Price lining</u> is a special pricing technique that requires stores to offer all merchandise in a given category at certain prices that reflect a low, middle, and high price strategy for its goods.

---

wholesaler, and retailer. Using a 50 percent margin for the manufacturer, wholesaler, and retailer, the calculations would be as follows: $4 x 1.50 = $6 price to wholesaler; $9.00 price to retailer; and $13.50 price to consumer.

2. Spreadsheets and reports will vary. Regardless of the actual price(s) suggested, the students' plans must provide a profit of $700.

Linking School to Work
Answers depend on the work situation.

1. **Assessment** Have students complete the Reproducible Test for Chapter 26 or construct your own tests using the ExamView software.

2. **Enrichment** Have students complete the corresponding activities in the following workbooks:
- *Marketing Math Workbook*, p. 71
- *Marketing Research Project Workbook*, p. 131

Chapter Overview

Chapter 27 presents the various mathematical formulas used to determine prices. It focuses on three principal areas—markup calculations, markdown calculations, and discount calculations.

 Springboard

Calculate Tell students Ollie's Gifts buys designer phones for $27.50 each and prices them at twice that amount. Cathy wants to buy one of the phones but can't spend more than $50. Have students determine the retail price of the phone (*$55*), how much Cathy will pay after a 15 percent discount (*$46.75*) and 4 percent sales tax (*$48.62*).

Prereading

List the section objectives to discuss with students. Have students skim the chapter, looking at the pictures, reading the captions, and noting the heads. Ask questions to ensure that students have a minimal understanding of the chapter structure.

Preteaching Marketing Vocabulary

Dictate each of the vocabulary terms and ask students to write them on a sheet of paper. When they finish, write the terms on the board. Then have students guess at the meaning of each. Write their guesses next to each term. Leave this list on the board so that students can see how close their guesses were to the actual definitions as they work through the chapter.

Marketing: What It Takes

Answer Subtract the discount percentage from 100 percent. Multiply the percentage and retail price to get net price. The relationship between the store's profitability and retail prices is seen in a comparison of a profit and loss statement with the formula for calculating retail price.

Pricing Math

Marketing: What It Takes

Pricing for Profitability

As the new assistant manager of a bookstore, you have been assigned the task of checking retail prices, handling markdowns for sales events, and approving employee discounts. You realize that in this position, you are now responsible for the profitability of the store.

WHAT WILL YOU DO?
How will you calculate the new sale prices and the amount employees will pay for purchases? How will you communicate the relationship between the store's profitability and retail prices?

484

THE DECA CONNECTION

ADVISOR CORNER

Learn By Earning Use the guidelines for DECA's Learn and Earn Event for planning the following activity, but you do not have to enter it into DECA competition unless it serves the needs of your chapter. Select something the students will be excited about for a major fund raising activity (school dance, 5K run, community auction, golf tournament, etc.). Choose a worthy charity to receive the proceeds from your event, and set a fee for participation. Students will use their math skills in projecting how much the project will gross for your charity.

Calculating Prices

Profit vs. Markup

A businessperson says "We made a profit of $50—buying the radio for $100 and selling it for $150." The businessperson is only partially correct. The difference between the retail price of $150 (which is equal to 100 percent) and the $100 cost ($66\frac{2}{3}$ percent) is the markup of $50 ($33\frac{1}{3}$ percent), not the profit. Profit is the amount left from revenue after the costs of the merchandise and expenses have been paid. The markup on an item, however, is similar to gross profit. **Gross profit** is the difference between sales revenue and the cost of goods sold. Expenses must still be deducted in order to get net (actual) profit. Therefore, a business must have a markup high enough to cover expenses and provide the profit sought to be successful.

Let's compare a profit and loss statement to retail markup by using the above figures and sales of 300 items. On a profit and loss statement, sales revenue would be $45,000 (100 percent), less cost of goods sold of $30,000 ($66\frac{2}{3}$ percent), which would equal gross profit of $15,000 ($33\frac{1}{3}$ percent). If expenses were $9,000, the gross profit ($33\frac{1}{3}$ percent) would be enough to cover expenses (20 percent) and earn a net profit of $6,000 or $13\frac{1}{3}$ percent ($6,000 divided by $45,000 or $33\frac{1}{3}$ percent − 20 percent = $13\frac{1}{3}$ percent).

■ Basic Markup Calculations

Retailers and wholesalers use the same formulas to calculate markup. We will use only retail prices here to make these formulas easier to understand. Note, however, that wholesale prices can be substituted in any of the formulas.

The most basic pricing formula is the one for calculating retail price. It states in mathematical terms a relationship that has been discussed in the last two chapters—retail price is a combination of cost and markup. Knowing these two figures will enable you to calculate retail price. Here's how.

$$\text{Cost (C)} + \text{markup (MU)} = \text{retail price (RP)}$$
$$\$14 \quad + \quad \$6 \quad = \quad \$20$$

Two other formulas can be derived from this basic formula—cost and markup, respectively.

$$\text{Retail price (RP)} - \text{markup (MU)} = \text{cost (C)}$$
$$\$20 \quad - \quad \$6 \quad = \quad \$14$$

$$\text{Retail price (RP)} - \text{cost (C)} = \text{markup (MU)}$$
$$\$20 \quad - \quad \$14 \quad = \quad \$6$$

You will rely on these three formulas throughout this chapter. The formulas and their terms will be cited in abbreviated form (as C + MU = RP) from this point on.

• What You'll Learn

- How a firm's net profit or loss is related to pricing
- How to calculate dollar and percentage markup based on cost or retail
- How to calculate markdown in dollars and how to determine sale price and maintained markup

• Why It's Important

Now that you understand the principles of pricing, it is time to learn how to perform the mathematical calculations needed to determine prices. You learned earlier that pricing is related to a company's profitability; now you will learn how they are related.

• Key Terms

- gross profit
- maintained markup

Chapter 27 ■ *Pricing Math* **485**

FOCUS

Bell Ringer Activity

Distinguish Ask students if profit and markup are one and the same.

Introducing the Section

Calculating Prices Have students decide and commit to their answer for the Bell Ringer Activity. Then put an abbreviated profit and loss statement on the board. Next to it, put the retail price parts that correspond to items on the profit and loss statement. For example, next to *Sales Revenue*, put an arrow and note *Price*; next to *Cost of Goods Sold*, put an arrow and note *Cost*; and next to *Gross Profit*, put an arrow and note *Markup*.

Have students study the board comparison and decide if they want to change or keep their original response to the Bell Ringer Activity. Once you have all students committed to the correct answer, ask them how the markup of a product is related to the profit that the company expects to make. *(Markup must be high enough to cover expenses and include profit if the company is to be financially successful.)*

TEACH

Technology Resources

PowerPoint The *Marketing Essentials* PowerPoint Presentation CD-ROM provides visual lecture aids for every chapter section.

Classroom Resources

For the Teacher
- Teacher Editions for all workbooks
- Assessment Package
- PowerPoint Presentation Software
- Interactive Lesson Planner
- ILP Block Scheduling, p. 8
- ILP Lesson Plans, p. 57
- ILP Internet Resources, p. 73

- ILP Blackline Masters, p. 53
- ILP *BusinessWeek* Case Studies, p. 169
- ILP Marketing Career Portfolio, p. 38
- *Marketing Essentials* Web site (**www.marketing.glencoe.com**)

For the Student
- Student Activity Workbook, p. 233
- Marketing Math Workbook, p. 71

- Marketing Research Project Workbook, p. 131
- ILP School-to-Work Activity Workbook, p. 113
- Virtual Business simulation
- *Marketing Essentials* Web site (**www.marketing.glencoe.com**)

ILP These resources are available in print and on the Interactive Lesson Planner (ILP)

Concept Development

1. Read Section 27.1 with students.
2. To introduce the basic markup calculations, draw a circle on the board, and label it *Retail Price*. Then divide the circle into two parts, and label these parts *Costs and Markup*. Start assigning figures to these two parts. For example, make the markup 40 percent and the costs of the item 60 percent. Make the markup $2 and the costs $8. Provide several more variations to demonstrate that retail price equals cost plus markup.

   Once students understand that basic formula, provide them with two of the three numbers, and have them identify the third. For example, if the cost is $14 and the retail price $30, the markup is . . . ***($16.)***

PRACTICE 1

Use the retail price formula and its variations to do the following problems.

1. A calculator costs AB Products $15, and the markup is $10. What is its retail price?

2. A tennis racket retails for $175, and its markup is $85. What is its cost?

Note: Answers to all practice sets in this chapter are on page 496.

■ Percentage Markup

In the examples shown, markup was expressed as a dollar amount. In most business situations, however, the markup figure is generally expressed as a percentage. We will distinguish between these two forms of markup (dollar and percentage) throughout the rest of the chapter. In calculations, dollar markup will be represented with the abbreviation MU($) and percentage markup with the abbreviation MU(%).

Expressing markup in either dollar or percentage form is not the only choice that wholesalers and retailers have in making markup calculations. They may also elect to compute their markup on either cost or retail price if they choose to use the percentage form.

Most choose to base the markup on retail price for three reasons. First, the markup on the retail price sounds like a smaller amount. This sounds better to customers and may encourage customers to buy because the price seems reasonable. Second, future markdowns and discounts are calculated on a retail basis. Third, profits are generally calculated on sales revenue. It makes sense to use markup on retail prices when comparing and analyzing data that play a role in a firm's profits.

Here are the steps that are used to calculate the percentage markup on retail. They will be easier to follow if we have an example to work with. Assume that you want to calculate the percentage markup on a pair of bookends that Wright's Department Store stocks for $49.50 (cost) and sells for $82.50 (retail price).

STEP 1 Determine the dollar markup.
RP − C = MU($)
$82.50 − $49.50 = $33.00

STEP 2 To change the dollar markup to the percentage markup, divide it by the retail price. The result will be a decimal.
MU($)/RP = MU(%) on retail
$33.00 divided by $82.50 = .4

STEP 3 Change the decimal to a percentage. This figure is the percentage markup on retail.
.40 = 40%
Shift decimal point two places right.

Retailers may find the percentage markup on cost to be helpful. The calculation is the same, except for Step 2. Using the same facts from above, you calculate the percentage markup on cost as follows:

STEP 1 Determine the dollar markup.
RP − C = MU($)
$82.50 − $49.50 = $33.00

STEP 2 To change the dollar markup to the percentage markup, divide by cost.
MU($)/C = MU(%) on cost
$33.00 divided by $49.50 = .6667

STEP 3 Change the decimal to a percentage. This figure is the percentage markup on cost.
.6667 = 66.67%
Shift decimal point two places right.

PRACTICE 2

Calculate the percentage markup in each of these situations.

1. The retail price of a coffee mug is $10.99 and the cost is $6.50. What is the percentage markup based on cost price? Based on retail price?

2. An electric sander costs $69.74, and its markup is $23.25. Find its percentage markup on cost price. Calculate the retail price, and then calculate its percentage markup on retail price.

3. A gallery sells a framed print for $100, and its markup is $50. What is its percentage markup on cost price? On retail price?

GREAT IDEAS from the Marketing Classroom

Carl Woloszyk
Western Michigan University
Kalamazoo, MI
To enhance the teaching of contemporary marketing issues, select a topic of current interest in marketing and require each student to keep a scrapbook on that topic. The scrapbook should contain any relevant news articles or news analyses of the topic.

Students can use periodicals, such as *BrandWeek*, *Advertising Age*, and *BusinessWeek*, as well as newspapers such as *The New York Times* and *The Wall Street Journal*. Periodically evaluate students' scrapbooks, and require a written essay on the topic in question at the end of the course. This essay should summarize the topic's key points, counterpoints, and developments.

FIGURE 27-1

Markup Equivalents

Markup on Retail	Markup on Cost	Markup on Retail	Markup on Cost
4.8%	5.0%	25.0%	33.3%
5.0	5.3	26.0	35.0
6.0	6.4	27.0	37.0
7.0	7.5	27.3	37.5
8.0	8.7	28.0	39.0
9.0	10.0	28.5	40.0
10.0	11.1	29.0	40.9
10.7	12.0	30.0	42.9
11.0	12.4	31.0	45.0
11.1	12.5	32.0	47.1
12.0	13.6	33.3	50.0
12.5	14.3	34.0	51.5
13.0	15.0	35.0	53.9
14.0	16.3	35.5	55.0
15.0	17.7	36.0	56.3
16.0	19.1	37.0	58.8
16.7	20.0	37.5	60.0
17.0	20.5	38.0	61.3
17.5	21.2	39.0	64.0
18.0	22.0	39.5	65.5
18.5	22.7	40.0	66.7
19.0	23.5	41.0	70.0
20.0	25.0	42.0	72.4
21.0	26.6	42.8	75.0
22.0	28.2	44.4	80.0
22.5	29.0	46.1	85.0
23.0	29.9	47.5	90.0
23.1	30.0	48.7	95.0
24.0	31.6	50.0	100.0

■ **Markup Equivalents Table** A markup equivalents table, one page of which is shown here, allows users to quickly convert markups on retail to markups on cost and vice versa. *A 37.5% markup on retail is equal to what markup percentage on cost?*

■ Markup Equivalents Table

You would notice a correlation between the two figures if you calculated enough problems using the formulas for computing percentage markup based on cost and retail. This correlation led marketers to develop a calculation aid called a markup equivalents table, a portion of which is shown in Figure 27-1. The table lists markup percentages based on retail and the equivalent percentages based on cost. To use the table, you locate the percentage markup on retail and read its cost equivalent in the adjacent column or vice versa.

> **PRACTICE 3**
>
> Use the markup equivalents table to answer the following questions.
>
> 1. When the markup on retail is 28.5 percent, what is its equivalent markup on cost?
>
> 2. The markup on cost is 60 percent; what is its equivalent markup on retail?

■ Cost Method of Pricing

Sometimes marketers know only the cost of an item and its markup on cost. In such a situation, they use the cost method of pricing.

Consider a board game that a toy store buys for $8.50 and sells for cost plus a 40-percent markup on cost. To arrive at the retail price, follow these steps:

STEP 1 Determine the dollar markup on cost. Multiply the cost by the percentage markup on cost in decimal form.

$C \times MU(\%) = MU(\$)$
$\$8.50 \times .40 = \$3.40$

STEP 2 Add the dollar markup to the cost to get the retail price.

$C + MU(\$) = RP$
$\$8.50 + \$3.40 = \$11.90$

Often, the situation isn't that simple. Suppose you have the cost, but the only markup figure you know is the markup on retail. What will you do? You cannot use the markup percentage on retail to calculate the markup in dollar unless you know the retail price. This is the perfect time to use the Markup Equivalents Table (see Figure 27-1). You can

Chapter 27 ■ *Pricing Math* **487**

Discussion Starter

Cost and Retail Figures Remind students that they learned about the distinction between cost and retail figures in Chapter 23. To be sure they understand the significance of the distinction, help them cite some analogies.

Begin by noting that the percentage markup on retail must only be applied to or used with other retail figures. Likewise, the percentage markup on cost must only be applied to or used with other cost figures. The two types of figures cannot be mixed. Ask students to suggest some other math situations in which the same general rule applies. *(For example, if you were figuring the area of a rectangle, you would have to convert all dimensions to the same unit of measure; you wouldn't multiply inches by feet, only inches by inches or feet by feet. If you were adding fractions, you would convert them all to the lowest common denominator.)*

> **FIGURE 27-1 ANSWER**
> **Markup Equivalents Table** A 37.5 percent markup on retail is equivalent to a 60 percent markup percentage on cost.

Thinking Critically

1. **Markup Percentage** Ask: If you are given the markup percentage on retail and the only other figure you have is what an item cost the business, what options do you have to figure out the markup in dollars and the retail price? *(Use the markup equivalents table or the retail method of pricing.)*

2. **Markup Equivalents Table** To prove the reliability of the markup equivalents table, have students calculate the markup percentage on retail and the markup percentage on cost for three different situations:

   • RP $100 and C $80 [MU($) = $20; $20 ÷ $100 = .2 = 20%; $20 ÷ $80 = .25 = 25%]

   • RP $85 and C $68 [MU($) = $17; $17 ÷ $85 = .2 = 20%; $17 ÷ $68 = .25 = 25%]

   • RP $95 and C $76 [MU($) = $19; $19 ÷ $95 = .2 = 20%; $19 ÷ $76 = .25 = 25%]

   Ask students what they noticed about the three problems they calculated. *(When the markup on retail is 20%, its equivalent markup on cost is always 25%.)*

Independent Practice

Research and Write Have students skim trade journals to find articles that reveal industry markup percentages. Have them report their findings in a written report.

FIGURE 27-2 ANSWER
Markup Percentages Use markup equivalents table to determine markup percentage based on retail (30 percent markup on cost equals 23.1 percent markup on retail). Subtract percentage (23.1 percent) from 100 percent to get percentage of retail price that represents costs (100 − 23.1 = 76.9) percent and apply to retail price to get cost in dollars ($159.99 x 76.9 = $123.03).

FIGURE 27-2

Typical Markup Percentages

Product Category	Typical Markup Percentage Based on Cost
Small Appliances (microwave, coffee maker)	30%
Large Appliances (refrigerator, dryer)	15%–20%
Automobiles	5%–10%* (*note dealers make money on factory incentives and sale of accessories)
Automobile Accessories (sunroof, CD player)	15%–25%
Clothing	100%

■ **Markup Percentages** Markup percentages vary with the type of product and business. *How would you determine how much a microwave whose retail price was $159.99 cost when all you know is the markup percentage based on cost noted in the above table? What would be its cost in dollars?*

---

convert the markup on retail to the markup on cost and apply it to the cost of the item to arrive at the markup in dollars. (See Figure 27-2.)

Here's an example: A marketer knows that the customary markup for a particular cosmetics firm is 33.3 percent on retail and that the cost of its most popular lipstick is $8.00. To project the lipstick's retail price, follow these steps:

STEP 1 Use the markup equivalents table to get all the information in the same (cost) form. Find the cost equivalent of a 33.3 percent markup on retail.

Markup on Retail	Markup on Cost
32.0	47.1
33.3	50.0
34.0	51.5

STEP 2 Apply the cost method to determine the retail price. First calculate the dollar markup on cost.

C × MU(%) = MU($)
$8.00 × .50 = $4.00

STEP 3 Then calculate the retail price.

C + MU($) = RP
$8.00 + $4.00 = $12.00

The Drive-In Inventor

Richard M. Hollingshead, Jr. had two interests—cars and movies. It is no irony that he invented the first drive-in movie theater. Hollingshead combined his hobbies to develop a movie theater where movie-goers could watch from their own cars. He experimented in his driveway in New Jersey, projecting movies from a 1928 Kodak projector on to a screen nailed to trees in his backyard. The original Drive-In Theater opened on June 6, 1933, in Camden, New Jersey, charging 25 cents per car and per person.

Thinking Creatively

Drive-ins were once the rage. Today, their popularity has declined. What are some marketing tactics you might employ to bring back the popularity of the drive-in?

BRIGHT IDEAS   **The Drive-In Inventor**

Answer Answers will vary. Tactics to bring back the popularity of drive-in theaters might include offering prices that are lower than movie theater prices and including new forms of entertainment, such as utilizing high definition screens and high quality sound.

FIGURE 27-3

Retail Box

	$	%		$	%
Retail Price	M	J 100	Retail Price	M 11.25	J 100
Markup	N	K	Markup	N 4.50	K 40
Cost	O	L	Cost	O 6.75	L 60

Computation: $L = J - K$ $L = 100 - 40 = 60\%$
                    $M = O \div L$ $M = \$6.75 \div .60 = \$11.25$
                    $N = M - O$ $N = \$11.25 - \$6.75 = \$4.50$

Check: $M \times K = N$ $11.25 \times .40 = \$4.50$

■ **The Retail Method** To compute the retail price using the retail method, fill in the boxes following the letter sequence (J-O). Note that the box labeled "J" (RP%) is always 100%. The amounts that go in the boxes labeled K (MU%) and O (C$) are usually known. *Why is this retail box an example of the retail method for calculating markup?*

■ Retail Method of Pricing

Another way to compute the retail price when all you know are cost and the markup on retail is to use the retail method. This method is based on changing the information that you already have into retail figures.

Let's consider an example: The owner of a sporting goods store wants to know what the markup and retail price should be for a sun visor that costs $6.75. His customary markup on retail is 40 percent. Thus, in algebraic terms 40 percent of "X" equals the retail price. The steps that he follows in his calculation are as follows:

STEP 1 Determine what percentage of the retail price is equal to cost. This is a matter of subtracting the known retail markup figure from 100 percent, which represents the retail price.

$RP(\%) - MU(\%) = C(\%)$
$100\% - 40\% = 60\%$

STEP 2 To determine the retail price, divide the cost by the decimal equivalent of the percentage calculated in Step 1.

$6.75 divided by .60 = \$11.25$

STEP 3 Calculate the dollar markup.

$RP - C = MU(\$)$
$\$11.25 - \$6.75 = \$4.50$

STEP 4 Check your work by multiplying the retail price you calculated in Step 2 by the percentage markup on retail given originally. The answer will match the dollar markup you calculated in Step 3, if your retail price is correct.

$RP \times MU(\%) = MU(\$)$
$\$11.25 \times .40 = \$4.50$

You can use a visual device called the retail box (Figure 27-3) to help you remember this sequence of calculations. This retail box organizes your information and makes it simple to check your work.

PRACTICE 4

Calculate retail price and markup in these two problems by using the retail method.

1. Find the retail price and dollar markup for a hand-made sweater that costs the Woolens Closet $90 and has a 40-percent markup on retail.

2. A machine-made sweater costs the Woolens Closet $30 and has a 60 percent markup on retail. Calculate this sweater's retail price and dollar markup.

Individualized Practice

Math Skills

A product costs a business $75.49 and has a mark-up of $38.51.

L1 Have students determine the retail price of the product. *($75.49 + $38.51 = $114)*

L2 Have students determine the markup percentage of the product. *($38.51 ÷ $114 = .3378 = 33.78%)*

L3 Tell students that the cost of purchasing the product has gone up 10 percent, and the selling price must be increased accordingly. Have students determine the new selling price and markup by using the original retail markup percentage. *(new C: $75.49 x 1.10 = $83.04; MU(%) on cost: 100 − 33.78% = 66.22%; new RP: $83.04 ÷ .6622 = $125.40; new MU($): $125.40 − $83.04 = $42.36)*

Chapter 27 ■ *Pricing Math* **489**

FIGURE 27-3 ANSWER
The Retail Method This is an example of the retail method for calculating markup because all figures are converted to retail figures to do the computations.

Reteaching

1. **Vocabulary** Assign and review the vocabulary terms for this section.
2. **Fact and Idea** Assign and review Fact and Idea Review questions 1–6 from the Chapter Assessment.
3. **Profit and Markup** To reteach the relationship between profit and markup, go through some hypothetical situations. Use play money to demonstrate how expenses reduce gross profit and how markup must be high enough to cover expenses and leave a residual amount, which is net profit.
4. **Pricing Formulas** Use flash cards to reteach the basic pricing math formulas. Show students a formula, and have them identify what that formula is for. Then provide students with a problem related to the formula they have just identified.
5. **Markdowns** To reteach how to calculate markdowns, have students draw on their personal experience in buying things on sale. Ask them how they calculate markdowns when they select something from a rack posted "20% Off Ticketed Prices." Show them that their methods are similar to, if not exactly the same as, the methods described in the text for calculating markdowns.

Calculations for Lowering Prices

When a business lowers its prices, a new sale price must be calculated, as well as a new markup. Let's look at the steps used in calculating markdowns (lowered prices), maintained markups (new markup), and the actual sales prices derived from these calculations.

■ Markdowns

To reduce the quantity of goods in stock, a business will sometimes mark down merchandise by a certain percentage [MD(%)]. This reduction is based on the retail price. Consider as an example a record store that wants to mark down by 25 percent compact disks that originally sold for $16. The steps for calculating the sale price (SP) are as follows:

STEP 1 Determine the dollar markdown. Multiply the retail price by the percentage markdown.

$$RP \times MD(\%) = MD(\$)$$
$$\$16 \times .25 = \$4$$

STEP 2 To determine the sale price, subtract the markdown from the retail price.

$$RP - MD(\$) = SP$$
$$\$16 - \$4 = \$12$$

Another way to arrive at the same answer is to consider what percentage of the original price will equal the sale price. The procedure is still two steps long, but the percentage calculation is so easy that you can probably do it in your head and save some time. Here are the steps involved.

STEP 1 Determine what percentage of the original price will equal the sale price. This is simply a matter of subtracting the markdown percentage from 100 percent.

$$RP(\%) - MD(\%) = SP(\%)$$
$$100\% - 25\% = 75\%$$

STEP 2 To find the sale price, multiply the retail price by the decimal equivalent of the percentage calculated in Step 1.

$$RP \times SP(\%) = SP$$
$$\$16 \times .75 = \$12$$

■ Maintained Markup

When a marketer marks down goods, the markup and markup percentage change. The difference between an item's final sale price and its cost is called the maintained markup.

Businesses must plan for markdowns, as they are part of being profitable and competitive in the marketplace. Reductions in the original retail price include employee discounts, damaged goods allowances, and special sales events. For businesses to enjoy the profit margin they need to be successful, these factors must be considered. Thus, the concept of maintained markup becomes extremely important in planning the original price of the item and all future markdowns.

Life In The Diverse MARKETPLACE

Driving Others Crazy

When traveling, you expect changes in language, customs, and food. But how about driving? You may be a confident and skilled driver in the United States, but that may change abroad. Other countries often have road standards different from those in the United States. In England, motorists drive on the left side of the road, instead of on the right as in the United States. Speed limits in Canada are based on the metric system, listed in kilometers per hour, not miles per hour. Common rules of the road are nearly disregarded in Brazil, where driving can be a very risky endeavor to an unfamiliar visitor!

Thinking Critically
How can you find out about the driving rules before traveling to another country?

More About . . .

Markup
Keystone markup is a term commonly used in retailing circles. It refers to a 100 percent markup on cost. Because the retail price is determined by adding a fixed percentage to the cost of the merchandise, keystone markup is a form of cost-oriented pricing. Its strength is that it's designed to achieve target levels of profits.

Life In The Diverse MARKETPLACE

Driving Others Crazy
Answer Before traveling you can contact a tourist office, the Department of Motor Vehicles, a car rental agency, or consult the Internet for online travel guides to find out about driving rules.

Let's consider an example. Assume that a cassette recorder that cost Zap Electronics $25 and originally sold for $50 is marked down 20 percent. The maintained markup (expressed in both dollars and as a percentage) is calculated as follows:

STEP 1 Calculate the new sale price.

$100\% - 20\% = 80\%$
$\$50 \times .80 = \$40$

STEP 2 To determine the maintained markup in dollars (MM$), subtract the cost from the sale price.

$SP - C = MM(\$)$
$\$40 - \$25 = \$15$

STEP 3 To determine the maintained markup percentage, divide the maintained markup in dollars by the sale price.

$MM(\$)$ divided by $SP = MM(\%)$
$\$15 \div \$40 = .375$
$.375 = 37.5\%$

PRACTICE 6

Now try the same type of computation on your own.

A hand-held computer that costs Compco Industries $126 to stock sells for $350 (retail price). The firm wants to mark down the computer 20 percent. Determine the sale price and maintained markup in dollars, and then calculate the maintained markup percentage.

Hot Bot

You are purchasing a new camera, but don't know the best value available on the market. You can read consumer magazines, hit the mall, take your best guess, or let someone else do the work for you. Now with the help of a "bot" you can type a request into a Web site and wait for a reply. Most consumers don't have time to comparison shop on the Internet. That's why shopping services with helpers—or "bots"—are popping up all over the Web. These bots comb Web sites for prices. Once a request is made, the agents hunt down product information and prices. Excite.com's shopping service tracks products from over 500 merchants. While these programs offer plenty of bargains for consumers, they also cause many headaches for merchants. Product margins are being pushed down and prices must stay competitive, because shoppers can be directed to another company.

Thinking Critically
How might you use bots for price comparisons?

27.1 ASSESSMENT

Reviewing Key Terms and Concepts

1. Explain how a firm's net profit or loss is related to pricing.

2. How are the dollar and percentage markups calculated based on cost and based on retail? Illustrate the formulas for a book that costs $13.99 and has a retail price of $19.99.

3. Assume that an item that cost $125 and currently retails for $279.99 (RP) is going to be marked down 40 percent for a special sale. Calculate the new sale price, as well as the maintained markup in dollars and as a percent.

Thinking Critically

4. If a buyer wanted to buy goods that cost $100 and the customary markup on retail was 40 percent, what two methods could the buyer use to calculate the retail price? Explain.

Integrating Academic Skills

5. **COMMUNICATION** Your supervisor has requested that you train your coworkers on markdowns that are not automatically deducted at the sales terminal. How should they manually calculate the net price a customer pays in those cases?

27.1 ASSESSMENT ANSWERS

Reviewing Key Terms and Concepts

1. A successful firm has markup high enough to cover its expenses and profit.
2. Dollar markup is difference between cost and retail price. Percentage markup is calculated by dividing dollar markup by cost/retail price. MU($) $19.99 - $13.99 = $6.00; MU(%) on cost: $6.00 ÷ $13.99 = .4288 = 42.9%; MU% on retail: $6.00 ÷ $19.99 = .3001 = 30%.

3. markdown: 100% – 40% = 60%; $279.99 x .60 = $167.99 sale price; $167.99 – 125 = $42.99 MM$; $42.99 ÷ $167.99 = .2559 = 25.6% MM%

Thinking Critically

4. cost method using equivalents table; retail method equating all figures to retail.

Integrating Academic Skills

5. **COMMUNICATION** Multiply retail price and discount %; deduct dollar figure from retail price.

SECTION 27.1

Enrichment

1. **Review** Assign and review the appropriate Thinking Critically questions from the Chapter Assessment.
2. **Extend** Assign and review the corresponding activities from *BusinessWeek Case Studies*, *Internet Resources*, and the *School-to-Work Activity Workbook*. **ILP**
3. **Research** In *Consumer Reports* have students find out how much a dealership pays to put a car on its lot (the cost). Have students get a sticker price for the car (the retail price) and calculate dealer's dollar and percentage markup.

Evaluation

Assign and review the Section 27.1 Assessment.

Technology Resources

GO TO **Assessment Resources**
Go to the *Marketing Essentials* Web site (**www.marketing.glencoe.com**) for resources to teach and assess occupation-specific vocabulary.

CLOSE

Section Wrap-Up

Ask students to complete the following statement: Retail price equals cost . . . *(plus markup.)*

Hot Bot

Answer Consumers can type in a request to a Web site with the help of a "bot" while shopping. The bot will comb Web sites for prices. Bots help to keep the prices in the marketplace competitive.

491

Calculating Discounts

FOCUS

Bell Ringer Activity

Discuss Ask students if any of them work for a business that offers employee discounts, or if they know someone who does. Ask what conditions or stipulations are attached to using the discount privilege.

Introducing the Section

Calculating Discounts Compile students' answers to the Bell Ringer Activity on a board list and use it to introduce the section. *(Common conditions or stipulations might be discounts can only be applied to the employee and his/her immediate family. A manager must authorize or initial the purchase sales check.)*

● What You'll Learn

- The general procedure for figuring discounts
- How to calculate various kinds of discounts

● Why It's Important

Discounts affect the final price a customer will pay. Therefore, it is essential that you learn how to calculate discounts and the net price payable.

Key Terms

- employee discounts

Discounts

Recall that a discount is a reduction in the price of goods and services sold to customers. Retailers may offer discounts to their employees as a job benefit or to encourage their employees to purchase their goods. Manufacturers and distributors offer discounts to their customers to encourage prompt payment and stimulate business.

The general procedure for calculating discounts involves two steps:

STEP 1 Multiply the price (P) by the discount percentage [D(%)] to get the dollar amount of the discount [D($)].

$$P \times D(\%) = D(\$)$$

STEP 2 Subtract the discount from the price to get the net price (NP), or the amount that the customer will actually pay.

$$P - D(\$) = NP$$

Here is an example. A business is offering a 35 percent discount on an item that sells for $150.

$150 \times .35 = \$52.50$ D($)
$150 - 52.50 = \$97.50$ NP

You can simply subtract the discount percent from 100 percent to determine net price's equivalent percentage to determine the net price. Then multiply the original price by that percentage to get the net price. Using the above example, those calculations would be as follows:

$100\% - 35\% = 65\%$
$150 \times .65 = \$97.50$ NP

■ Employee Discounts

Businesses offer **employee discounts** to encourage workers to buy the products they sell or manufacture. Employees who buy and use their company's products project confidence in and enthusiasm about the products. Employee discounts can range from 10 percent to 30 percent for entry-level employees and as high as 50 percent or more for top-level executives.

■ Discounts from Manufacturers and Distributors

Some common types of discounts offered by manufacturers and distributors are cash, trade, quantity, seasonal, and promotional discounts, all of which were already explained in Chapter 26. This section is devoted to explaining how each of these types of discounts is calculated.

Classroom Resources

For the Teacher
- Teacher Editions for all workbooks
- Assessment Package
- PowerPoint Presentation Software
- Interactive Lesson Planner
- **ᴵᴸᴾ** Block Scheduling, p. 8
- **ᴵᴸᴾ** Lesson Plans, p. 58
- **ᴵᴸᴾ** Internet Resources, p. 73

- **ᴵᴸᴾ** *BusinessWeek* Case Studies, p. 169
- **ᴵᴸᴾ** Marketing Career Portfolio, p. 38
- *Marketing Essentials* Web site (**www.marketing.glencoe.com**)

For the Student
- Student Activity Workbook, p. 233
- Marketing Math Workbook, p. 71

- Marketing Research Project Workbook, p. 131
- **ᴵᴸᴾ** School-to-Work Activity Workbook, p. 113
- Virtual Business simulation
- *Marketing Essentials* Web site (**www.marketing.glencoe.com**)

ᴵᴸᴾ These resources are available in print and on the Interactive Lesson Planner (ILP)

CASH DISCOUNTS Recall from Chapter 26 that a cash discount is a discount offered to buyers to encourage them to pay their bills quickly. Consider the invoice terms 3/15, net 60. Recall that the first number (3) represents the percentage of the discount applicable to the invoice total. When that total is $1,000 and the customer takes advantage of the discount, the calculations are as follows:

STEP 1 Determine the dollar discount.

$$P \times D(\%) = D(\$)$$
$$\$1,000 \times .03 = \$30$$

STEP 2 Determine the net price.

$$P - D(\$) = NP$$
$$\$1,000 - \$30 = \$970$$

Cash discounts can also be calculated on a unit basis. The net unit price for 100 items at $10 each listed on the invoice is determined as follows:

STEP 1 Determine the dollar discount.

$$P \times D(\%) = D(\$)$$
$$\$10.00 \times .03 = \$.30$$

STEP 2 Determine the net price.

$$P - D(\$) = NP$$
$$\$10.00 - \$.30 = \$9.70$$

The net amount payable by the customer would still be the same, of course—$970 ($9.70 × 100).

TRADE DISCOUNTS You may recall from Chapter 26 that trade discounts are based on manufacturers' list prices. They are really not discounts at all, but rather the way manufacturers quote prices to wholesalers and retailers. Trade discounts are called trade discounts because different prices are offered to different lines of trade (i.e., wholesalers vs. retailers). They are calculated in the same way as cash discounts. To figure a 40-percent trade discount for an invoice totaling $5,789, you would do the following:

STEP 1 Determine the dollar discount.

$$P \times D(\%) = D(\$)$$
$$\$5,789.00 \times .40 = \$2,315.60$$

STEP 2 Determine the net price.

$$P - D(\$) = NP$$
$$\$5,789.00 - \$2,315.60 = \$3,473.40$$

Invoices containing several items have a trade discount that is applied to each item separately to determine its net unit price to the business.

PRACTICE 7

Determine the amounts payable by the following customers.

1. Southbend Trucking receives an invoice in the amount of $225,000 showing the terms 2/10, net 30. The invoice lists five trucks at $45,000 each. If Southbend takes advantage of the discount, what will be the net amount due on the invoice? The net price per truck?

2. A manufacturer gives retailers a 55-percent trade discount. The invoice received by Wright's Department Store totals $180,775; what is the amount of the store's discount? What is the amount payable to the manufacturer?

QUANTITY DISCOUNTS You may recall from Chapter 26 that quantity discounts are offered to buyers for placing large orders. Sellers benefit from large orders from the lower selling costs involved in one transaction as opposed to several small transactions. They are meant to encourage buyers to buy in bulk and purchase more merchandise than they originally intended to purchase. Quantity discounts may be quoted as either a percentage of price or as part of a quantity price list like this:

No. of items	1–24	25–48	49–72
Unit price	$.95	$.90	$.85

Using the above table, if you purchased 50 items, you would pay $.85 each. Your total bill would be $42.50 ($.85 × 50).

Sometimes businesses offer cumulative quantity discounts, whereby a certain minimum purchase must be made during a specified period of time for the discount to be activated. A firm may offer a 2-percent cumulative quantity discount to any company that purchases $3,000 worth of products in a six-month period. In the case that a firm's purchases total $2,500 during that period, no discount is permitted; if they total $4,000, however, the discount is allowed. It would be calculated in the following manner:

STEP 1 Determine the dollar discount.

$$P \times D(\%) = D(\$)$$
$$\$4,000 \times .02 = \$80$$

STEP 2 Determine the net price.

$$P - D(\$) = NP$$
$$\$4,000 - \$80 = \$3,920$$

Chapter 27 ■ *Pricing Math* **493**

SECTION 27.2

TEACH

📊 Technology Resources

PowerPoint The *Marketing Essentials* PowerPoint Presentation CD-ROM provides visual lecture aids for every chapter section.

Concept Development

1. Read Section 27.2 with students.
2. Have students read aloud the Case Study on page 495 and review the answers in class.
3. To introduce discounts from manufacturers and distributors, ask students to recall what they learned about them in Chapter 26. Have students identify the principal types of discounts (cash, quantity, trade, promotional, and seasonal) and write the terms on the board. Then have students explain how each type of discount is used.

THE DECA CONNECTION

COMPETITIVE EVENTS AND MARKETING ESSENTIALS

Competitive Events and Pricing Math There are several competitive events that you can use to enhance the importance of pricing math. The Learn and Earn Project is one. Your students will be explaining their earnings outcomes resulting from pricing decisions they made earlier in the project planning. Many of the role-play situations in the Individual Series Events require correct calculations and use of pricing formulas in order to complete the requirements of the event. The Fashion Merchandising Promotion Plan Event is another that makes use of pricing math when figuring the budget need component of this event.

Employee Discounts Tell students that in retail situations, employee discounts often compensate for relatively low hourly wages. Ask students if they would take such a job and why. Encourage students who already hold such jobs to comment on the value of the discounts.

Cooperative Learning

Quantity Discounts Have students work in groups to develop their own quantity discount plan for the school store. Tell them that the markets they will be targeting are school sports teams and the parents sport association.

Tell students to begin their plan with specialized T-shirts designed for each targeted group. Note that the cost per T-shirt to the school store is $10. Finally, suggest that they first determine the retail price for one T-shirt and then work out the details for the quantity discounts.

Groups should summarize their discount pricing plans in chart form. They should prepare a written report as well, spelling out the rationale for the plan.

Independent Practice

Interview and Report Have students sign up to interview the managers or personnel directors of selected retail stores in the community to learn about their employee discount policies. Areas of inquiry should include the discount percentage for entry-level employees, conditions of the discount, and what the store gains by offering discounts. Students should present their findings in a written report.

Case Study

Costco's Business Plan

Costco Corporation is a unique enterprise that offers low prices in a warehouse setting to businesses and individual consumers. To be eligible to shop at Costco, you must become a member. Originally this membership was only available to small businesses; however, this service has been extended to individuals. Once nonbusiness members began to seek membership at Costco, the first warehouse store opened in Seattle in 1983. Its success is based on several factors, one of which is its low markup on products (about 10 percent above cost), compared with full-service retailers whose markups are 25 percent or more.

Costco keeps expenses low with bare-bones warehouse facilities, few salespeople, tight control on inventory, and a limited selection of brands and sizes (i.e., two brands of mustard in two sizes) in a product category. To offset its

low markup on goods, Costco charges membership fees ranging from $35 to $100. There are different membership categories that require different membership fees—Executive, Business, and Gold Star.

Another part of Costco's success is the variety of goods offered at low prices. You will find high-end items like Waterford crystal and common consumer items like bottles of ketchup. Costco also offers one-hour photo labs, optical centers, pharmacies, and food courts. They also carry business supplies, household products, clothing, electronic equipment, and fresh grocery items. Executive members may also establish health care for small businesses as well as lease business equipment and establish payroll services. Members can even shop online at Costco.com and have deliveries sent to their home or office.

Costco's rivals include Wal-Mart, a subsidiary Sam's Club, and BJ's Wholesale Club, Inc. Even though all three follow the same basic business plan, Costco's average store generates more sales ($94 million) than its competitors ($55 million for Sam's and $44 million for BJ's).

Case Study Review

1. Why is Costco able to mark up its goods only around 10 percent above cost, while other full-service retailers must mark up their products 25 percent or more to be profitable?
2. Who are Costco's rivals, and how does each compare to Costco in average sales revenue generated?

A MATTER OF ETHICS

3. Do you think it is ethical for Costco to charge different customers different membership fees?

Case Study Review Answers

Costco's Business Plan

1. Costco's bare-bones warehouses, small sales staff, tight control on inventory, few brands and sizes in a category, and membership fees help generate revenues.
2. Rivals are Wal-Mart and BJ's. One Costco unit generates more sales than its competitors' average units.

A MATTER OF ETHICS

3. Answers will vary, but some may say that if each customer is a different type of customer (i.e., business and non-business), it is not unethical.

PROMOTIONAL DISCOUNTS Promotional discounts are given to businesses that agree to advertise or in some other way promote a manufacturer's products. When the promotional discount is quoted as a percentage, it is calculated the same way as a cumulative discount.

Sometimes, marketers are granted a dollar amount as a promotional discount. In such cases, they may want to determine the net purchase price or the percentage of the promotional discount for themselves. Consider an example. The Cycle Shop buys Speedo bicycles for $10,000 and is granted a $250 promotional discount for displaying the bikes in its store window during the month of March. To determine the percentage discount, follow these steps:

STEP 1   Divide the dollar discount by the original price. The answer will be a decimal.

D($) divided by P = D(%)
$250 ÷ $10,000 = .025

STEP 2   Change the decimal to a percentage. This figure is the percentage discount.

.025 = 2.5%
Shift decimal point two places right.

SEASONAL DISCOUNTS Sellers offer seasonal discounts to encourage buyers to purchase goods long before the actual consumer buying season. Purchasing Halloween costumes before July 27 or ski apparel before May 1 might qualify retailers for seasonal discounts.

Seasonal discounts are calculated in the same way as other discounts. Here is an example. Lobo Inc. offers an 8-percent seasonal discount to all buyers who purchase Christmas decorations before August 1. An order placed on July 20 for $1,500 worth of decorations has a net purchase price that is calculated as follows:

STEP 1   Determine the dollar discount.

P × D(%) = D(S)
$1,500 × .08 = $120

STEP 2   Determine the net price.

P − D($) = NP
$1,500 − $120 = $1,380

MARKETING
REAL WORLD

Priced to Fly

Think only first-class passengers can fly in style? Think again! Richard Branson, founder of Virgin Atlantic, is changing this with his price-sensitive service with style. Virgin Atlantic airline soared by selling discount air travel with plush amenities like shower facilities at airport lounges, massages and manicures in flight, and goodie packs with Virgin socks and toothbrushes. But he's no longer flying solo. JetBlue, marketed by ex-Virgin Atlantic employees, offers cheap fares out of New York City's JFK airport. Its hook—economy class with leather seats and personal satellite television. You certainly do get what you pay for!

Thinking Critically
Why do these airlines use price-sensitive services?

PRACTICE 8

Now try these problems involving quantity, promotional, and seasonal discounts.

1. Suppose a firm is required to buy $10,000 worth of goods by September 15 in order to qualify for a 10-percent cumulative quantity discount. Would a firm that purchased $5,000 worth of goods on September 1 get the discount? What about one that purchased $10,500 worth on September 20?

2. A manufacturer offers a retailer $750 as a promotional discount for advertising a certain product. What is the percentage discount if the total invoice was $37,500?

3. Regal Shoe Company offers retailers a 5-percent discount for placing orders by May 1. A retailer takes advantage of the offer and purchases $78,290 worth of shoes by the cutoff date. What is the net amount payable on the invoice?

ASSESS
Reteaching

1. **Vocabulary** Assign and review the vocabulary terms for this section.
2. **Fact and Idea** Assign and review Fact and Idea Review questions 7–10 from the Chapter Assessment.
3. **Discounts** To reteach the various kinds of discounts, give students clues associated with each type of discount. Use their responses to create a list on the board. For example:
   - 1–12 items at 8 cents each, 13–20 items at 6 cents each (quantity discount)
   - 15 percent off if you buy your back-to-school stock in May (seasonal discount)
   - 30 percent off anything you can wear on the job (employee discount)

More About . . .

Promotional Discounts
To secure shelf space for new food products, manufacturers are charged a stocking (or slotting) fee by some supermarket chains. Even an older product may have such a fee, especially if the manufacturer wants it in a specific shelf location. The supermarket industry refers to these fees as promotional discounts from the manufacturer.

MARKETING
REAL WORLD

Priced to Fly
Answer In today's competitive market, these types of strategies help to set the airlines apart from the others in order to stay competitive.

1. **Review** Assign and review the Chapter 27 activities in the *Student Activity Workbook*.
2. **Review** Assign and review the appropriate Thinking Critically questions from the Chapter Assessment.
3. **Review** Assign and review the following Chapter Assessment activities: Building Workplace Skills, Applying Marketing Concepts, Linking School to Work, The DECA Connection Role Play, and Internet Connection.
4. **Research and Report** Have students visit or call a stationery store, an auto parts store, a building supply company, or any retailer that sells goods to trades people. Have students inquire if the business offers trade discounts. If so, ask about the rate and any proof required to obtain them. Have students to prepare an oral report for the class.

Evaluation

Assign and review the Section 27.2 Assessment.

Technology Resources

Assessment Resources
Go to the *Marketing Essentials* Web site (**www.marketing.glencoe.com**) for resources to teach and assess occupation-specific vocabulary.

CLOSE

Section Wrap-Up

Have students name as many of the discounts associated with pricing as they can think of. (*employee, cash, trade, quantity, seasonal, and promotional*)

496

Answers to Practice Set Problems

PRACTICE 1 (PAGE 486)
1. $25 ($15 + 10 = $25)
2. $90 ($175 − 85 = $90)

PRACTICE 2 (PAGE 486)
1. 69.0% cost ($10.99 − 6.50 = $4.49; $4.49 divided by 6.50 = .690); 40.9% retail ($10.99 − 6.50 = $4.49; $4.49 divided by $10.99 = .4085)
2. 33.3% cost ($23.25 divided by $69.74 = .333); $92.99 RP ($69.74 + 23.25 = $92.99 RP); 25% retail ($23.25 divided by $92.99 = .25)
3. 100% cost ($50 divided by 50 = 1); 50% retail ($50 divided by $100 = .5)

PRACTICE 3 (PAGE 487)
1. 40%
2. 37.5%

PRACTICE 4 (PAGE 489)
1. $150 ($90 divided by .60 = $150)
2. $75 ($30 divided by .40 = $75); $45 ($75 − $30 = $45)

PRACTICE 5 (PAGE 490)
$135 (100% − 40% = 60%; $225 × .60 = $135)

PRACTICE 6 (PAGE 491)
$280 sale price ($350 × .80 = $280); $154 MM$ ($280 − 126 = $154); 55% MM% ($154 divided by $280 = .55)

PRACTICE 7 (PAGE 493)
1. Net amount on invoice $220,500 ($45,000 × 5 = 225,000 × .98) Net amount per truck $44,100 ($45,000 × .98)
2. $99,426.25 discount ($180,775 × .55); $81,348.75 amount payable ($180,775 − $99,426.25)

PRACTICE 8 (PAGE 495)
1. No, because the minimum quantity is $10,000. No, because the deadline date was September 15.
2. 2 percent ($750 ÷ $37,500 = .02)
3. $74,375.50 ($78,290 × .95)

27.2 ASSESSMENT

Reviewing Key Terms and Concepts
1. What procedures are used to calculate the dollar amount of a discount and the final selling price?
2. Carlo's Ice Cream Specialties gives all of its employees a 15-percent discount on ice cream cakes. What would an employee pay for a chocolate ice cream cake that is $13.75?
3. Why do sellers offer seasonal discounts to customers?

Thinking Critically
4. Assume you are given a trade discount of 30 percent and a seasonal discount of 10 percent. You also take advantage of a cash discount of 2 percent. Would you be entitled to a 42-percent discount? Explain.

Integrating Academic Skills
5. **MATH** The dating terms on a $3,000 invoice are 3/10, net 30. If the buyer takes advantage of the cash discount, what will be the net amount due?

27.2 ASSESSMENT ANSWERS

Reviewing Key Terms and Concepts
1. You can multiply price by discount percentage to get dollar amount of discount. You can also subtract discount amount from the price to get net price.
2. The discount amount is $2.06. ($13.75 x .15 = $2.0625) The employee pays $11.69 ($13.75 − $2.06 = $11.6875)
3. They encourage buyers to purchase goods long before the consumer buying season.

Thinking Critically
4. No, because discounts are taken in a series.

Integrating Academic Skills
5. **MATH** $2,910 ($3,000 x .03 = $90; $3,000 − $90 = $2,910)

Careers in Marketing

CUSTOMER SERVICE

Mary Shipman
Creative Management, Inc.
Customer Service Representative

What does your job entail?

"My job is to find solutions for customer concerns and problems with our software, in addition to training customers on software use. Customers will call with questions regarding how to run their software or general computer troubleshooting. Sometimes customers will call in with complaints about the software. I generally deal with customers on the phone for our software hotline, and I make decisions based on company policy and the facts of each situation. Sometimes it is necessary to send company representatives to the client's company or home to amend the problem, but sometimes it can be handled over the phone."

What skills are important to you?

"Good communication skills are vital. It is impossible to register customer complaints or explain the software's functions without strong verbal communication and problem solving skills. I must listen to concerns and act as a liaison between customers and the company in order to develop changes in a product to meet a customer's specific need. All customer service representatives must have the ability to understand both the customers' need and corporate policies."

What do you like most about your job?

"My job involves a great deal of social interaction, which is rare in computer-based positions. My duties vary daily, ranging from customer training to calming down an unhappy customer. I find it gratifying when I am able to solve someone's problems."

What is your key to success?

"My key to success lies in my ability to remain patient even in stressful situations. There are times when I will be dealing with back-to-back phone calls involving lengthy explanations and sometimes customers become frustrated if there is not a simple answer. It is necessary to always keep a professional attitude—I represent my entire company."

Thinking Critically

What kind of on-the-job training do you think is necessary for a customer sales representative?

Career Facts

Education and Training: High school courses in marketing, accounting, business, office procedures, English, and communications are good preparation for customer service work. Clerical experience and training provide preparation for customer service clerks. Most employers have on-the-job training programs for customer service clerks and professional customer service representatives.

Aptitudes, Abilities, and Skills:
Good communication skills, ability to work efficiently under pressure, and good problem-solving skills are necessary. Customer service representatives must be able to gather information accurately in order to arrive at appropriate decisions.

Career Outlook: Faster than average growth is expected through the year 2006.

Career Path: Many customer service representatives gain experience in some area of clerical work, then complete an on-the-job training program in customer service. Experience in customer service is a good preparation for promotion to management.

Chapter 27   *Pricing Math*   **497**

Lifelong Learning

Pricing Math
Understanding and performing basic pricing calculations enhances students' confidence as future employees and consumers. Encourage students to use these equations at school or work. Repetition will increase familiarity, speed, and accuracy. Checking the math on invoices at home or on the job provides good practice.

Meeting Individual Needs

Students with Visual Impairments
Students with visual/spatial difficulties may have difficulty working with accounting-oriented content. Describe the accounting procedures and operations. Do not assume they follow what you are saying while you perform calculations. Name categories and explain calculations. Encourage students to ask questions or request assistance.

Vocabulary Review

Examples will vary. See Glossary for definitions.

Fact and Idea Review

1. Cost plus markup equals retail price.
2. Markup on retail sounds like a smaller amount and, thus, sounds better to customers; future markdowns and discounts will be calculated on retail basis; and profits are generally calculated on sales revenue.
3. retail price: RP – C = MU($); MU($) ÷ RP = MU(%) on retail; Cost: RP – C = MU($); MU($) ÷ C = MU(%) on cost
4. Determine the dollar markup on cost by multiplying the cost by the percentage markup on cost in decimal form. Then add the dollar markup to the cost to get the retail price.
5. Subtract the known retail markup percentage figure from 100 percent. Next, divide the cost by the decimal equivalent of the percentage calculated in Step 1 to get the retail price. Calculate the dollar markup by subtracting the cost from the retail price. Check by multiplying the retail price calculated in Step 2 by the percentage markup on retail given originally.
6. Subtract cost from the sale price. To determine the maintained markup percentage, divide the maintained markup in dollars by the sale price.
7. Multiply price by discount percentage to get the dollar amount of the discount, and then subtract the dollar amount of the discount from the price to get the price the customer pays.
8. $40 x .02 = $.80; $40 – $.80 = $39.20
9. Company B would receive $600 in discounts ($400 on the first order and $200 on the second) posted retroactively to its account at the end of the six-month period.
10. Discount in dollars divided by price equals the discount percentage. D($) ÷ P = D(%)

Thinking Critically

1. Net profit or loss is related to pricing because both profit and loss depend on markups.
2. Yes, the initial markup may be the same as the maintained markup when no markdowns have been taken and no price increases have been made.

498

Chapter **27** ASSESSMENT

VOCABULARY REVIEW

Explain the meanings of the following terms by giving an example of each.

- gross profit
- maintained markup
- employee discounts

FACT AND IDEA REVIEW

1. What is the most basic formula you need in order to calculate retail price? (27.1)
2. List three reasons why most wholesalers and retailers elect to compute their markup on the selling price. (27.1)
3. What is the formula for calculating the percentage markup on retail price? On cost? (27.1)
4. What steps are used to calculate prices according to the cost method? (27.1)
5. What steps do marketers follow when using the retail method to determine the retail price and dollar markup? (27.1)
6. What steps do you follow to calculate maintained dollar markup and maintained percentage markup? (27.1)
7. What is the two-step procedure for calculating a discount? (27.2)
8. Calculate the price for a $40 item with a 2-percent cash discount. (27.2)
9. Company A offers a cumulative discount of 5 percent on orders of $10,000 in a six-month period. Company B purchases $8,000 in one order and $4,000 in another. What would be the dollar discount to Company B? (27.2)
10. What is the formula for determining the percent of a promotional discount? (27.2)

THINKING CRITICALLY

1. Why is a firm's net profit or loss related to pricing?
2. Is the initial markup calculated for an item sometimes the same as the maintained markup? Explain.

BUILDING WORKPLACE SKILLS

1. **Math: Determining Retail Price** A dress costs a business $72, and the markup is $45. What is the retail price?
2. **Math: Calculating Markup** A pair of slacks retails for $110, and the cost is $50. What is the markup?
3. **Math: Calculating Cost** A hammer sells for $16.95, and its markup is $6.75. What is the cost?
4. **Math: Calculating Percentage Markup** A wallet costs a business $27 and sells for $45. What is the percentage markup on cost? The percentage markup on retail?
5. **Math: Calculating Percentage Markup** A stationery store buys greeting cards for $1.90 and puts a $1.60 markup on each of them. What is the percentage markup on cost? The percentage markup on retail?
6. **Math: Calculating Equivalent Markup** What is the equivalent markup on cost for the following percentage markups on retail?
   a. 25.0%   d. 50.0%
   b. 23.1%   e. 40.0%
   c. 33.3%   f. 28.5%
7. **Math: Determining Retail Price** A pencil sharpener that costs a business $12.50 has a markup of 62 percent on retail price. Use a retail box to calculate the sharpener's retail price and check your answer.

Building Workplace Skills

1. $72 (C) + $45 (MU) = $117 (RP)
2. $110 (RP) – $50 (C) = $60 (MU)
3. $16.95 (RP) – $6.75 (MU) = $10.20 (C)
4. Percentage markup on cost: $45 (RP) – $27 (C) = $18 (MU$) $18 (MU$) ÷ $27 (C) = 66.7%.
   Percentage markup on retail: $45 – $27 = $18; $18 (MU$) ÷ $45 (RP) = 40%.
5. Percentage markup on cost: $1.60 (MU$) ÷ $1.90 (C) = .8421 = 84.2 percent.
   Percentage markup on retail: $1.60 (MU$) + $1.90 (C) = $3.50 (RP). $1.60 (MU) ÷ $3.50 (RP) = .4571 = 45.7 percent.
6. a. 33.3% b. 30% c. 50% d. 100% e. 66.7% f. 40%
7. Retail price: $12.50 (C) ÷ .38 = $32.89 (RP).
   Check: $32.89 x .62 = $20.39 (MU$); $32.89 (RP) – $20.39 (MU$) = $12.50 (C).

APPLYING MARKETING CONCEPTS

1. **Preparing a Quantity Price List** Use a spreadsheet program to prepare a quantity price list for cookies you sell in your school store in order to increase sales volume. Assume your cost to make and market one cookie is $.25. At present, you sell one cookie for $.50. Be sure your quantity prices still generate a profit for the store. Provide a written rationale for your list.

2. **Understanding Markdowns** Research the different ways businesses present markdowns to consumers. Some run sales and advertise those sales in newspapers and direct mail pieces. Others use coupons and rebates. Compare the methods, language, and calculations used to demonstrate the savings a consumer is getting with these markdowns. Contrast those consumer markdown methods with the types of discounts manufacturers and distributors offer retailers (cash discount, trade discount, quantity discount, promotional discount, and seasonal discount). Report your findings in an oral presentation to the class, using presentation software.

LINKING SCHOOL TO WORK

Basic, Information, and Thinking Skills Interview the owner/manager of a business about the use of computers to calculate prices. Ask if the firm uses special software to determine the price for an item or a job for a manufacturing or service concern. Ask what information must be input for the system to work. In a retail concern, ask if markups and markdowns are incorporated into the firm's computer system. Ask who is responsible for inputting the information and checking it for accuracy. Report your findings in both a written and oral report.

Role Play: Sales Associate

Situation You are to assume the role of sales associate in the men's department. Your department manager (judge) asks you to input the prices of newly arrived slacks into the computer inventory system. You notice that the price of $26 appears to be incorrect. According to the invoice, the slacks cost the store $18, not including shipping and handling. You know the customary markup in your store is 50 percent of the retail price.

Activity What will you do and what will you say to your department manager?

Evaluation You will be evaluated on how well you meet the following performance indicators:
- Select approach for setting a base price
- Determine discounts and allowances that can be used to adjust base prices
- Explain factors affecting pricing decisions
- Persuade others
- Foster positive working relationships

*inter*NET CONNECTION

Comparison Shopping
To establish competitive prices for your athletic shoe department, you need to see what rival companies are charging.

Connect
- Locate the Web sites of two manufacturers of athletic shoes and select two different shoes from each one.
- Find three online sporting goods stores that sell those models.
- Create a table depicting the price comparison for the four pairs of shoes. Include the prices manufacturers charge if they sell their shoes online.

Chapter 27 ■ *Pricing Math* **499**

*inter*NET CONNECTION
Answers will vary depending upon athletic shoes researched.

Mini Quiz
Administer the Mini Quiz orally. For an expanded chapter quiz, go to page 157 of the *Reproducible Tests* book.

1. The difference between the retail price and the cost of an item is the markup.
2. In comparing a profit and loss statement with pricing of an individual item, the markup is related to the gross profit on a profit and loss statement.
3. To calculate the markup percentage based on cost, you divide the markup by the cost.
4. The difference between an item's final sale price and its cost is called the maintained markup.
5. To determine the promotional discount percentage, you divide the dollar discount by the price and then change the decimal to a percentage.

Students should be evaluated on the performance indicators noted in the Role Play.
- For another DECA Role Play, go to the *Student Activity Workbook*, p. 233.
- For more in-depth Role Play practice, refer to DECA's *Essential Competitive Events Handbook*. To order, contact DECA at www.deca.org.

Applying Marketing Concepts
1. Quantity price lists will vary.
2. Presentations will vary.

Linking School to Work
Answers depend on the work situation.

1. Assessment Have students complete the Reproducible Tests for Chapter 27 and Unit 8 or construct your own tests using the ExamView software.
2. Enrichment Have students complete the corresponding activities in the following workbooks:
- *Marketing Math Workbook*, p. 71
- *Marketing Research Project Workbook*, p. 131

499

FOCUS

Unit Lab Overview

In this Zazz Lab, students will market a golf resort using their knowledge of pricing principles and practices, and pricing strategies, such as psychological pricing and cost-, demand-, and competition-oriented pricing.

Bell Ringer Activity

Discuss Ask students if they have even been to, seen advertised, or heard about resorts that specialize in golf, tennis, or other sports-related activities.

Discussion Starter

Ask students: Why are sports-related resorts so popular? *(Answers will vary but may suggest they provide leisure-time entertainment and recreation. Corporations often hold conferences at resorts.)*

TEACH

Thinking Critically

1. **Package Pricing** Ask students: Would the package deals for a golf resort in Florida be in competition with those for a golf resort in Scottsdale, Arizona, or any other geographic area here or abroad? *(Most will say "yes" because golfers may research various options available if air travel is involved.)*
2. **Psychological Pricing** Ask students: What psychological pricing techniques might be employed when deciding on the pricing structure for all aspects of the new golf resort in Florida? Provide examples. *(Some options may include: odd-even pricing; prestige pricing; bundle pricing—golf packages; promotional pricing—special rates for groups or time periods; seasonal discounts; and a one-price policy for pro and gift shops, spa services, and food.)*

500

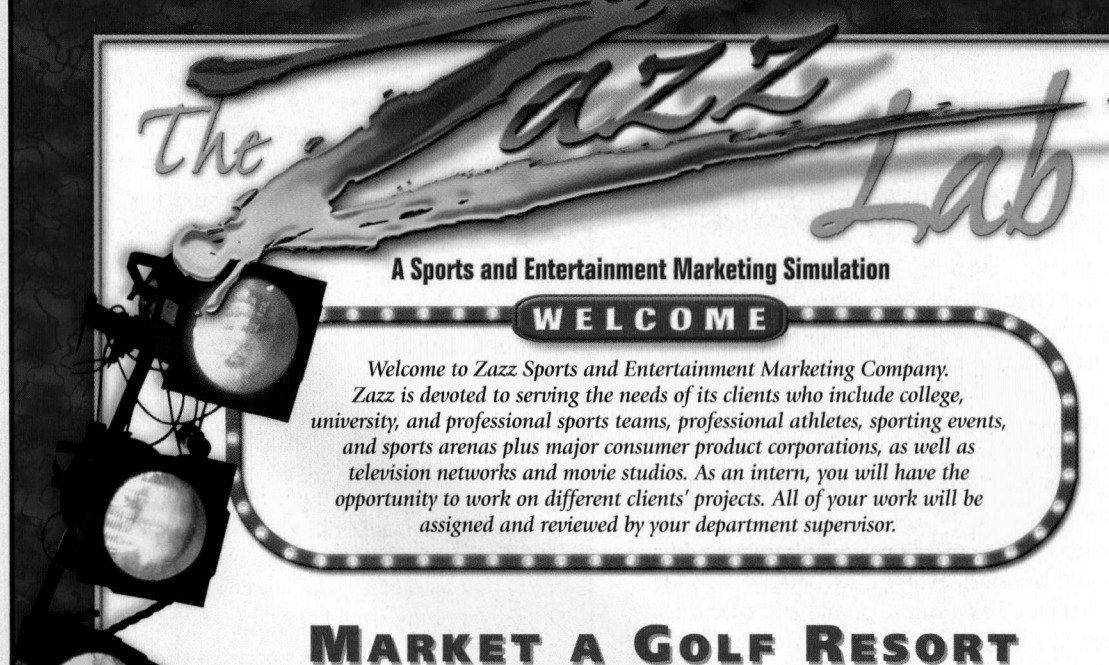

The Zazz Lab

A Sports and Entertainment Marketing Simulation

WELCOME

Welcome to Zazz Sports and Entertainment Marketing Company. Zazz is devoted to serving the needs of its clients who include college, university, and professional sports teams, professional athletes, sporting events, and sports arenas plus major consumer product corporations, as well as television networks and movie studios. As an intern, you will have the opportunity to work on different clients' projects. All of your work will be assigned and reviewed by your department supervisor.

MARKET A GOLF RESORT

SITUATION

A new golf resort in Florida would like Zazz to help market its facility and determine its pricing structure. The resort features two 72 par, 18-hole championship golf courses with rolling hills. Additional amenities include a comprehensive practice facility with a driving range and areas to practice putting, chipping, and sand bunker shots. A pro shop is stocked with golf apparel, equipment, and accessories and a gift shop offers apparel, collectibles, resort logo items, and personal sundries. There are three restaurants in the resort: formal, casual, and a snack bar. The hotel has 250 rooms and suites, as well as 12 conference rooms. There are two swimming pools, ten tennis courts, and a health spa offering fitness equipment, classes, trainers, as well as other personal services such as facials and massages.

ASSIGNMENT

Your supervisor wants you to determine the rates for hotel accommodations, golf greens fees, golf carts, eateries, health spa services, and shop merchandise. Separate seasonal rates for each aspect of the complex need to be established. Design comprehensive golf packages that include breakfast, greens fees, admission to the spa, and any other special features. The pricing structure for the gift and pro shop merchandise should include merchandise examples and reflect the desired markup on items. All restaurant operations will require a name, sample menu, and prices.

Tools and Resources

To complete this assignment, you will need to conduct research at a library or on the Internet. You will also need a word processing program, a spreadsheet program, and presentation software. Trade publications that may be helpful include *Golf Market Today, Golf Digest, Golf Magazine, Restaurant News, Fitness Management, Food Service and Hospitality, Hospitality News,* and *Hotel Management.*

Research

Research competing golf resorts located in Florida, around the United States, and abroad. Compare our client's facilities with its competitors. Analyze the pricing strategies used by comparable competitors. Analyze seasonal supply and demand. Research economic factors, weather, and psychographic trends, such as the type and length of vacations generally taken by various age groups or sports enthusiasts. Research common markup practices for specialty and sports-related merchandise in resorts. Obtain various restaurant menus and research the methods used to determine prices for food service and personal spa services.

ORIGINAL GOLF

The first American golf course, St. Andrews Golf Club, opened in Yonkers, New York, in 1888. That was over 100 years ago, but the origins of the game have been traced to the 14th century in northern France where *chole* was played with a stick and a ball aimed at a tree or door. *Het kolven* was a variation played in the open country. In southern France, *jeu de mail* required a stick resembling a croquet mallet. In 1421 Scottish soldiers returning home from France brought *chole*, which became golf with a new element—the hole. Controversy developed in 1457 when King James II prohibited golf due to its popularity among archers. Finally, the legendary Society of St. Andrews Golfers in Scotland inscribed the first rules of the game in 1754.

Report

Prepare a written report and a computer presentation for the client. Use a word processing program to prepare a double-spaced report. Prepare a spreadsheet to illustrate the formulas and calculations used to arrive at the suggested prices. Arrange your written report around the following headings:

- General background on golf resorts and recreation
  - Economic and psychographic trends
- Pricing principles
  - Suggested pricing objectives for client
  - Researched costs for gift and pro shop and food service operations
  - Estimated demand
  - Competition
    - Major competitors
    - Pricing plan to meet competition
  - Appropriate pricing strategies and techniques
    - Client's image
    - Skimming vs. penetration pricing
    - Use of psychological pricing techniques
- Suggested price structure and rationale
  - Rates for hotel accommodations (fall, winter, and spring; single and double occupancy)
  - Rates for golf
    - Greens fees and cart fees
  - Rates for spa facilities
    - Use of facility
    - Services
  - Packages for sports enthusiasts
  - Gift and pro shop
    - Suggested markup policy (show calculations and provide product examples)
    - Suggested markdown policy (show calculations and provide product examples)
  - Restaurants
    - Names, sample menu items and prices, and calculations and rationale for prices

Using computer presentation software, prepare a presentation of your ideas for the client that includes:
- Key topics covered in your written report
- Graphic illustrations that are relevant to each slide's topic
- Very little text
- Minimum of 10 slides

Presentation and Evaluation

Present your ideas in a written report and an oral presentation. The oral presentation will be shown to the client. You will be evaluated on your oral presentation skills, including:
- Knowledge of pricing principles and practices
- Continuity of presentation
- Voice quality
- Eye contact

 Portfolio
....

Print a copy of your completed report and presentation for your Portfolio.

THE DECA CONNECTION

DECA Business Services Marketing Series
Analyzing research on competitors' pricing and making recommendations for a client could be the basis for a role play in this event.

DECA Marketing Management Series
Pricing is a major function of marketing management and as such could be a topic for a role play in this event.

DECA Hospitality and Recreation Research Event
Researching and developing a pricing structure for a hotel and golf resort could be the basis for a research project in this event.

DECA Sports and Entertainment Marketing Management Team Decision-Making Event
Working on this project with a partner would make the experience similar to what is expected in a DECA Team Decision-Making Event.

Independent Practice

Targeted Pricing Students can research how golf resorts target businesses to hold conferences and meetings at their facilities. Ask students what hotel rates and package deals are offered to businesses.

ASSESS

Enrichment

Research Have students conduct research and write a report on the pros and cons of having a golf school associated with the new golf resort. Have them include the names and locations of other golf schools in the country. Then have them suggest one golf school that would be the most appropriate. Have them research the amenities that would have to be included in the resort.

Evaluation

The rubrics for evaluation of the written, oral, and computer presentation are included in the student text. (See the outline and guidelines for the written report, the computer presentation, and the skills' assessment for oral presentations.) It might be best to replicate those rubrics to evaluate the students' work. A separate rubric could be created to evaluate the work of a team.

CLOSE

Lab Wrap-Up

Ask students: How are the steps of pricing a product demonstrated in the pricing structure of a new golf resort? *(1. Determine pricing objectives, such as profit, market share, return on investment, and meeting competition. 2. Study costs involved with employee salaries, supplies required for golf, food, personal spa, and hospitality services. 3. Estimate demand for golf market, seasons, and vacationing in general. 4. Study competition for golf resorts. 5. Decide on a pricing strategy, should it be skimming or penetration. 6. Set the price after taking into consideration psychological pricing techniques.)*

COOPERATIVE LEARNING

Teamwork You may want to assign teams of two to four students to each of the following areas: golf (fees and carts), spa services, pro shop, gift shop, formal restaurant, two casual dining restaurants, hotel accommodations, and package deals. The entire class can work together to prepare the final report.

Marketing Information Management

Chapter 28
Marketing Research

Chapter 29
Conducting Marketing Research

Unit Objectives

After completing this unit, students will be able to:

- Discuss the nature, importance, and usage of marketing research in planning and implementing marketing strategies.
- Explain the function of marketing information systems.
- Describe four important types of marketing research.
- Describe the steps used in conducting marketing research.
- Construct effective marketing research questionnaires.

Enrichment Resources

Books

Market Research: A Guide to Planning, Methodology, and Evaluation by Paul Hague and Peter Jackson

State of the Art Marketing Research by George Edward Breen, Alan Dutka, and Albert Breneman Blankenship

Magazines/Journals

Advertising Age
Journal of Marketing Research

Associations

Advertising Research Foundation
641 Lexington Avenue
New York, NY 10022
(212) 751-5656
www.theARF.org

Council of American Survey Research Organizations
3 Upper Devon
Port Jefferson, NY 11777
(631) 928-6954
www.casro.org

ESOMAR
World Association of Opinion and Marketing Research Professionals
1054 GV Amsterdam
The Netherlands
31-20-664-21-41
www.esomar.nl

Journal Writing Activity

1. Ask students to write a short paragraph in their journals about why marketing research is important for the success of a product. Then have them discuss their ideas with the class. During the discussion, remind students that there are five steps in the marketing research process—problem definition, obtaining data, data analysis, recommending solutions to the problem, and implementing the findings.

2. Ask students to think of a product they like and either use or would use. Have them write the name of the product in their journals and identify a potential problem in marketing that particular product. Also ask them to explain how doing a survey could enhance the marketing of that product.

TEACHER CLASSROOM RESOURCES

Program Resources

Program Resources	Chapter 28	Chapter 29
Student Activity Workbook	p. 241	p. 251
Marketing Math Workbook	p. 95	p. 95
Marketing Research Project Workbook	p. 151	p. 151
School-to-Work Activity Workbook	p. 117	p. 121
BusinessWeek Case Studies	p. 175	p. 181
Marketing Career Portfolio	p. 39	p. 39
Reproducible Tests	p. 167	p. 171
ExamView User's Guide and Testbank	p. 28-1	p. 29-1
Internet Resources	p. 75	p. 77
Blackline Masters	p. 56	p. 62
Lesson Plans	p. 59	p. 61
Block Scheduling	p. 9	p. 9
Impact! Simulation		

Each of these resources is available in print and on the Interactive Lesson Planner CD-ROM.

Technology Resources

- **Interactive Lesson Planner (ILP) CD-ROM**
- **PowerPoint Presentation CD-ROM**
- **Marketing Essentials Web site**
- **ExamView! CD-ROM**
- **Impact! Simulation**

Virtual Business

Virtual Business is a fully visual marketing and business simulation that introduces students to the principles of marketing by letting them start and run their own virtual businesses. In *Virtual Business*, students have the power to control all aspects of a retail convenience store. Students strategize marketing decisions using a powerful learning tool in the guise of a video game. They learn by experiencing how their decisions affect their virtual business.

Key to Individualized Academics Activities

L1 Level 1 activities are basic activities and should fall within the range of all students.

L2 Level 2 activities are average activities and should be within the range of average and above average students.

L3 Level 3 activities are challenging activities designed for the ability range of above average students.

National Marketing Education

CHAPTER	SECTION	PERFORMANCE INDICATOR
Chapter 28 **Marketing Research**	28.1	Describe the need for marketing information (MIM)
		Explain the nature of marketing research in a marketing-information function (MIM)
		Explain the nature and scope of the marketing-information management function (MIM)
	28.2	Identify information monitored for marketing decision making (MIM)
		Identify the nature of sales forecasts (MIM)
Chapter 29 **Conducting Marketing Research**	29.1	Explain the nature and scope of the marketing-information management function (MIM)
		Describe sources of secondary data (MIM)
		Use data for information analysis (MIM)
	29.2	Collect marketing information from others (MIM)
		Describe the use of technology in the marketing-information management function (MIM)

CIS Communication, Interpersonal Skills   **DIS** Distribution   **FIN** Financing   **PRI** Pricing   **SEL** Selling

502C

Standards Assessment Correlation

SECTION ASSESSMENT			CHAPTER ASSESSMENT						UNIT LAB
Reviewing Key Terms and Concepts	Thinking Critically	Integrating Academic Skills	Fact and Idea Review	Thinking Critically	Building Workplace Skills	Applying Marketing Concepts	Linking School to Work	Internet Connection	Zazz Lab
1, 2, 3	●	●	3, 4	1, 2, 3, 4, 5	1, 2	1, 2, 3	●		●
1, 2, 3	●	●	1, 2	1, 2, 3, 4, 5	1, 2	1, 2, 3, 4, 5	●	●	●
2, 3, 4, 5	●	●	3, 4	1	1	1, 2, 5		●	●
1, 2, 3, 4, 5	●	●	5, 6, 7, 8, 9	1, 2, 3, 4, 5	2	1, 2, 4	●		●
2, 3						1			●
1, 2, 4	●	●	1, 2, 3, 4, 5, 6	2, 5	1, 2		●	●	●
3		●	1, 2, 5	1	1	1, 2, 3	●	●	●
5	●	●	6	1	2	2, 3	●	●	●
1, 2, 3, 4, 5	●	●	7, 8, 9	1, 2, 3, 4, 5	1, 2	2, 3	●		●
5	●			3, 4, 5	2	1, 2, 3	●	●	●

Unit Overview

Unit 9 explores marketing information management—its importance, the major areas of marketing research, the steps performed in the marketing research process, and how marketing information systems can assist in solving problems that businesses face today. Chapter 28 introduces marketing research—the process of getting the marketing information needed to make sound business decisions through systematic gathering, recording, and analyzing of data. Chapter 29 defines the five steps in the marketing research process—problem definition, obtaining data, data analysis, recommending solutions to the problem, and implementing the findings. The chapter also shows students how to develop, format, and administer survey instruments. The impact of computer technologies on marketing research is also detailed.

Introducing the Unit

Ask students how they think their co-op training stations make decisions about when to introduce new products and discontinue old ones. For example, what factors made McDonald's consider adding low-calorie salads to its menu? Have students speculate on the ways companies get information about their markets; list students' answers on the board.

Portfolio

Performing Market Research

To demonstrate mastery of the content in this unit, you will conduct a marketing research study on a topic of your choice or for a business of your choice. One idea might be to develop a customer profile for a business based on a survey of its current customers. Prepare a written report that includes a discussion of the secondary research conducted (background information), target population, steps taken to create the survey, steps taken to administer the study, findings, and conclusions. Be sure to include a copy of the survey instrument in your report.

502

Field Trip Suggestions

Visit a Marketing Research Company

Arrange for your students to visit a marketing research company and participate in consumer focus groups. They can then compare the types of marketing research questions asked and speculate on the purpose and outcome of the research.

■ **Chapter 28** *Marketing Research*

■ **Chapter 29** *Conducting Marketing Research*

Marketing Information Management

Unit Overview

Marketing information management is an organized attempt by a business to gather information to make better decisions about marketing issues, strategies, and problems. This unit explains how marketing information systems can assist in finding solutions to problems businesses face today.

Chapter 28 introduces marketing research—the process of getting the marketing information needed to make sound business decisions. You will learn the importance of marketing research and the function of a marketing information system. Chapter 29 identifies the five steps in the marketing research process. The chapter also explains how to construct, format, and administer survey questionnaires and explores the effect of computer technologies on marketing research activities.

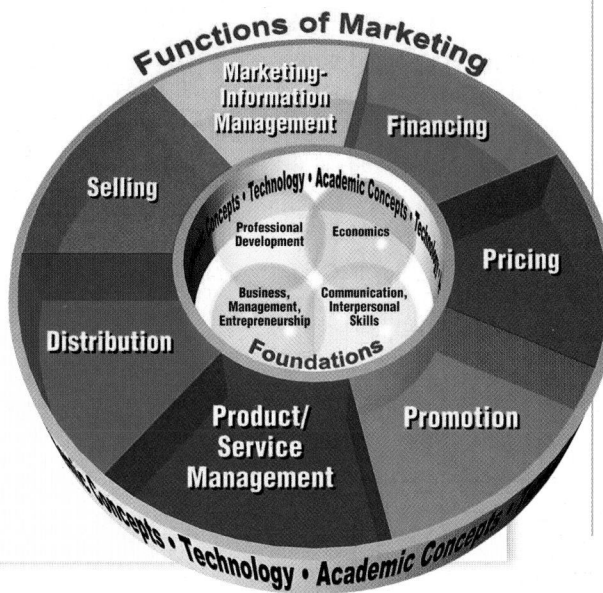

In this Unit:

Foundations of Marketing

● Business, Management, Entrepreneurship

Functions of Marketing

◣ Marketing Information Management

◀DECA Unit Project

If your program has a school store, have chapter members develop a research study to determine the market potential for products to be offered in the store. Students should develop the survey, conduct the research, analyze the data, and write a report on the findings to give to the school administration.

Go to the *Marketing Essentials* Web site (**www.marketing.glencoe. com**) for resources to teach and assess occupation-specific vocabulary.

Unit Closure

Make sure students understand the importance of marketing research for making sound business decisions, and that marketing research is a process in which the steps must be followed sequentially to obtain the best results. Have students create a visual representation of the marketing research process and the various types of marketing research. Display their work on the bulletin board.

 Guest Speaker Suggestions

Small Business Owner Ask a small business owner to speak about the types of marketing information they consider important for their business, how they obtain that information, how they use the information, and how it helps them make other business decisions.

Chapter Overview

Chapter 28 introduces the world of marketing research and its increasing importance in our competitive marketplace.

 Springboard

Identify and Explain Bring in several different brands of a commonly used product such as shampoo. Have students tell you the features, benefits, and target market of each. Ask students how the marketers of these products determined a marketplace need. *(They use marketing research.)*

Prereading

List the section objectives to discuss with students. Have students skim the chapter, looking at the pictures, reading the captions, and noting the heads. Ask questions to ensure that the students have a minimal understanding of the chapter structure.

Preteaching Marketing Vocabulary

Write the remaining vocabulary words that were not introduced in the Springboard Activity on the board. Have students generate definitions for each.

Marketing: What It Takes

Answer Answers will vary, but students should include such elements as parking, mall cleanliness, politeness, efficiency, and appearance of custodial and security staff, cleanliness and convenience of public restrooms, quality of food and appearance of dining area, and quality of service.

Marketing Research

Marketing: What It Takes

Designing a Customer Service Survey

You are working as an assistant to the marketing manager of a recently opened shopping mall. Your manager has asked you to devise a survey to measure whether shoppers have had a pleasant shopping experience and are satisfied with the level of services at the new mall.

WHAT WILL YOU DO?

What important customer service elements would you include in your survey of shopping mall customers?

504

THE DECA CONNECTION **ADVISOR CORNER**

Information through Technology Acquaint your chapter members with National DECA and reinforce the importance of using technology in acquiring information with the following activity. Pair up members of your chapter and give them a list of questions that can be answered by viewing DECA's Web site (www.deca.org). Have students describe DECA's home page; identify the national officers; list ten National Advisory Board members; find the name of the president of DECA's National Board of Directors; name ten of the competency-based competitive events; discover DECA's mission; and find out how many state associations have their portion of the Web site up and running.

Marketing Information Systems

Defining Marketing Research

According to the American Marketing Association, **marketing research** involves the marketing function that links the consumer, customer, and public to the marketer through information. Marketing information is used to identify marketing opportunities, solve marketing problems, implement marketing plans, and monitor marketing performance. Marketing research involves the methods used to gather information, analyze it, and report findings related to marketing goods and services. Marketing research can apply to any aspect of marketing. Kellogg's, a cereal manufacturer, might research the potential sales and market for a new product line of breakfast snacks. Marriott Hotels, Resorts, and Suites might conduct customer satisfaction research on the quality of its guest services.

The primary emphasis of marketing research is to obtain information about the preferences, opinions, habits, trends, and plans of current and potential customers. This information helps marketers in many ways. Before developing a product, marketers can conduct research to determine the type of product customers want. The research can minimize potential losses when introducing the new product. Consumers accept only one out of every ten new products introduced into the marketplace; therefore, gaining information about consumer likes and dislikes is significant.

Why Is Marketing Research Important?

Given the high failure rate of new products on the market, marketing research can make or break a business. The major goal of any business is to increase sales and profits. Businesses that do not pay attention to what consumers are buying are likely to make costly marketing mistakes.

The information obtained from research helps businesses plan their future operations to increase sales and profits. Research answers questions such as what products should be produced, where the products should be sold, how the products will be promoted, and at what price the products will sell.

Research also helps businesses solve marketing problems or anticipate future marketing potential. It took Stouffer's almost 13 years of marketing research and development to start its Lean Cuisine product line. Stouffer's studied consumers' interest in health and dieting. It

• What You'll Learn

- The importance of marketing research
- The function of a marketing information system

• Why It's Important

Successful companies must be able to understand the needs and wants of their customers. Marketing research can provide the necessary information to help a business while planning, solving problems, and making decisions regarding its products and services.

Key Terms

- marketing research
- marketing information system
- database

Chapter 28 ■ *Marketing Research* **505**

FOCUS

Bell Ringer Activity

Brainstorm Tell students that consumers accept only one out of every ten new products introduced into the marketplace. Ask them to brainstorm a written list of reasons for this. *(Possibilities include poor and/or unsafe product design, customer loyalty to a well-established product that is already on the market, inferior product quality, poor packaging, a misleading or offensive product name, high price, and an unclear image of the product's intended use.)*

Introducing the Section

Marketing Information Systems Review students' answers from the Bell Ringer Activity. Tell students that, given the many things that could go wrong when introducing a product, marketing research can greatly reduce the chances of product failure by doing the following: (1) answering such questions as what products should be produced, where, how, and at what price, (2) helping businesses solve marketing problems and anticipate future marketing problems, and (3) helping a company keep track of what has happened in its markets.

TEACH

Technology Resources

PowerPoint The *Marketing Essentials* PowerPoint Presentation CD-ROM provides visual lecture aids for every chapter section.

Classroom Resources

For the Teacher
- Teacher Editions for all workbooks
- Assessment Package
- PowerPoint Presentation Software
- Interactive Lesson Planner
- ILP Block Scheduling, p. 9
- ILP Lesson Plans, p. 59
- ILP Internet Resources, p. 75

- ILP Blackline Masters, p. 56
- ILP *BusinessWeek* Case Studies, p. 175
- ILP Marketing Career Portfolio, p. 39
- *Marketing Essentials* Web site (**www.marketing.glencoe.com**)

For the Student
- Student Activity Workbook, p. 241
- Marketing Math Workbook, p. 95

- Marketing Research Project Workbook, p. 151
- ILP School-to-Work Activity Workbook, p. 117
- Virtual Business simulation
- *Marketing Essentials* Web site (**www.marketing.glencoe.com**)

ILP These resources are available in print and on the Interactive Lesson Planner (ILP)

505

Concept Development

1. Read Section 28.1 with students.
2. Have students read aloud the Case Study on page 509 and review the answers in class.

Discussion Starter

Identify Ask students to determine what kind of customer information the following companies would maintain in their databases:

- mail-order company offering gardening supplies and seeds *(the seasonal climate where customers live; what types of seeds they buy at certain times of the year; whether they buy more flower seeds than vegetable seeds and vice versa; what types of supplies they buy most; what additional merchandise they request most)*
- small publisher that specializes in producing works of fiction *(the type of fiction customers are buying—poetry, novels, mysteries, or short stories; which authors' books they buy most; whether they're buying softcover or hardback texts; how often they purchase books and in what quantities)*
- real estate office *(customers' average incomes; the prices of their current homes; length of time in and size of their current homes; number of people in each family; the number of times they have purchased a new home in the past several years)*

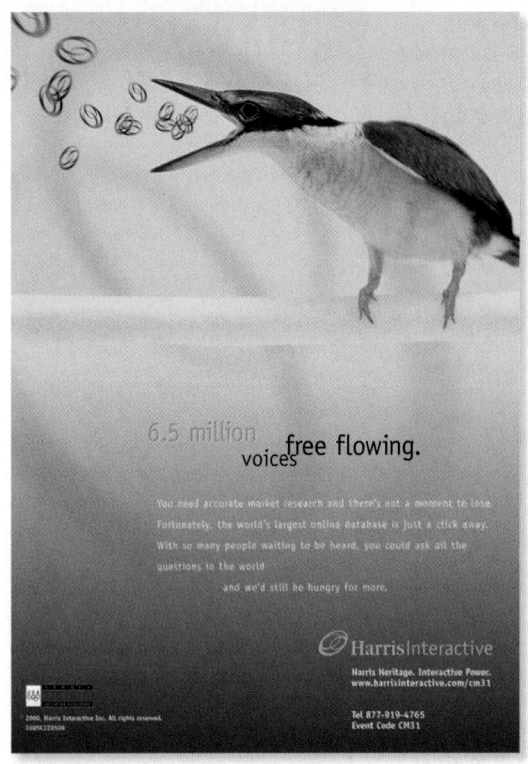

6.5 million voices free flowing.

You need accurate market research and there's not a moment to lose. Fortunately, the world's largest online database is just a click away. With so many people waiting to be heard, you could ask all the questions in the world and we'd still be hungry for more.

⦿ HarrisInteractive

Harris Heritage. Interactive Power.
www.harrisinteractive.com/cm31

Tel 877-919-4765
Event Code CM31

© 2000, Harris Interactive Inc. All rights reserved.

■ **Marketing Research Information Is Critical** Marketing research is essential for all companies regardless of size. *How can smaller companies obtain necessary marketing information?*

conducted consumer panels to find out what dieters liked and disliked about diet meals. Using the information, the company developed its product, tested its package design, and piloted sales of the product in several large cites before national distribution. The product was a tremendous success, with over $125 million in sales after the first year of national distribution.

Research also helps a company keep track of what is happening with its current markets. Through research, a company can determine its major competitors, what its competitors are offering, and which products consumers prefer.

Who Uses Marketing Research?

Marketing research is valuable for organizations of any size. The size of the business, though, may affect how it conducts the research. Small businesses that do less than $5 million in annual sales usually do not have separate research departments. Here, marketing research is done informally by the owners, managers, or employees. Marketing research is conducted by a variety of business groups and the government (see Figure 28-1).

FIGURE 28-1

Marketing Research Revenues by Industry Groups

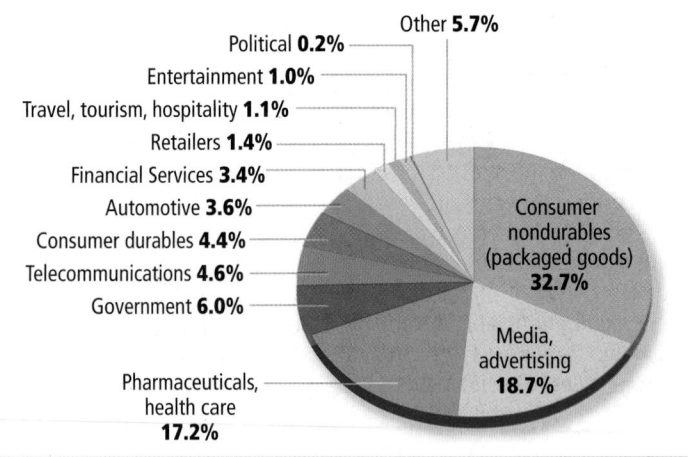

Other **5.7%**
Political **0.2%**
Entertainment **1.0%**
Travel, tourism, hospitality **1.1%**
Retailers **1.4%**
Financial Services **3.4%**
Automotive **3.6%**
Consumer durables **4.4%**
Telecommunications **4.6%**
Government **6.0%**
Pharmaceuticals, health care **17.2%**
Consumer nondurables (packaged goods) **32.7%**
Media, advertising **18.7%**

■ **Marketing Research Revenues by Industry Groups** Over $3 billion is spent annually by client industry groups for marketing research. *Why does the government spend money on marketing research?*

CAPTION ANSWER
Marketing Research Information is Critical
Owners, managers, and employees of smaller businesses can do informal marketing research. Business groups and the government also conduct marketing research.

FIGURE 28-1 ANSWER
Marketing Research Revenues by Industry Groups Many governmental agencies have regulatory or legislative mandates to conduct research on matters such as the safety of products, transportation issues, the operation of the postal service, and the services of the Internal Revenue Service. Other agencies need research support to improve their service for the good of the general public.

FIGURE 28-2

Consumer Product Survey of America

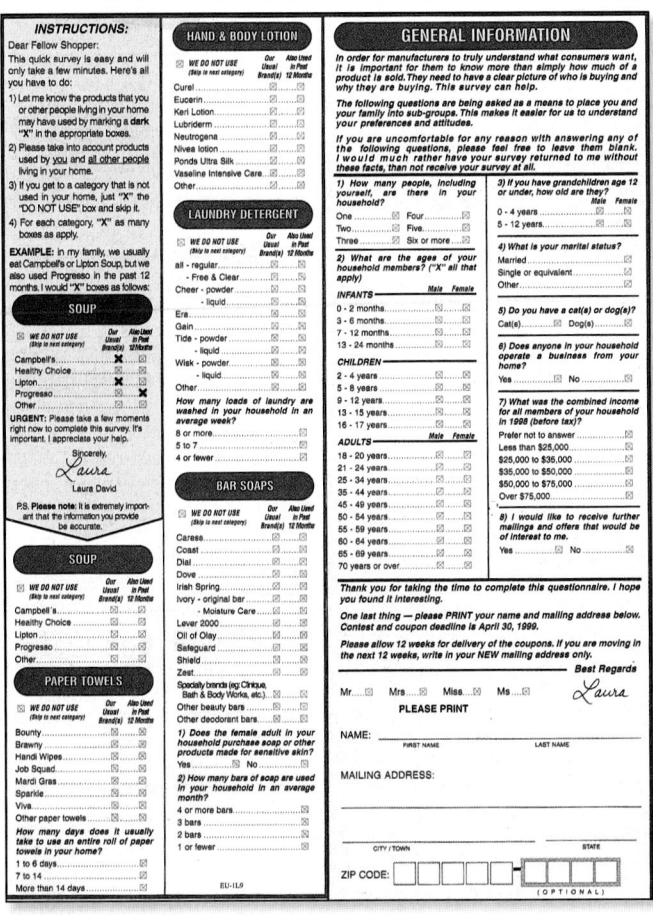

■ **Consumer Product Research** The largest category of marketing research is for nondurable consumer products. *What information is provided to businesses from the general information section of the survey pictured?*

Thinking Critically

Adapting Consumer Goods Have the entire class brainstorm at least ten consumer goods that will require adaptation because of a generally aging population. Describe how the products will need to be adapted.

Cooperative Learning

New or Changed Products Have the class work in pairs to identify at least ten new or changed products that resulted from the change in consumers' attitudes toward products that are safer for the environment. Randomly select students each day to review their answers with the entire class.

Larger companies have formal research departments and specialists to plan and conduct marketing research. Some larger companies contract with marketing research companies to investigate special marketing related problems.

In 1997 $3.3 billion was spent on research in the United States in connection with public opinion polls, marketing, and advertising campaigns. The largest percentage of marketing research dollars was spent on consumer nondurables (packaged products).

Individual businesses are not the only organizations that find marketing research valuable. Several departments in state and federal governments, plus

trade associations representing various manufacturers, wholesalers, and retailers, conduct marketing research. Industry trade associations, such as the National Retail Merchants Association, collect industry data to help their members understand the markets for their products.

The Consumer Product Safety Commission, a U.S. government agency, tests products to make certain they are safe for consumer use and to give consumers product information. An example of a customer service survey is shown in Figure 28-2. The U.S. Postal Service conducts annual surveys designed to gain input about needed improvements and services (see Figure 28-3 on page 508).

Chapter 28 ■ *Marketing Research* **507**

FIGURE 28-2 ANSWER

Consumer Product Research Demographic information (age, children in household, marital status, etc.) is provided in the general information section of the survey. In addition, the popularity of various products based upon the demographic profile is useful to businesses for product promotions and advertising.

More About . . .

Marketing Research

To locate trade associations for class projects or to conduct actual marketing research, ask a librarian to locate a copy of *Encyclopedia of Associations* published by Gale Research, Inc., of Detroit, Michigan. This source annually publishes an alphabetical list of trade associations, both domestic and international.

Independent Practice

Research and Write Have students contact a local small business which is not their co-op work station to determine what type of marketing research information the business maintains *(for example, company records, competitors' records, customer profile data, and government data)*, and how this information is stored and used. Have students write their findings in 150 to 200 words and share them with the class. Did they find that small businesses kept significantly less or significantly more information than they expected?

FIGURE 28-3

The U.S. Postal Survey

■ **Providing Better Postal Services** Government agencies seek ideas to improve customer services. *What information will the U.S. Postal Service gain from an annual survey?*

Marketing Information Systems

The data collected in marketing research must be sorted and stored so that the results can be put to good use. Many businesses have implemented sophisticated marketing information systems to organize, collect, and store marketing research data for future decisions. A marketing information system is a set of procedures and methods that regularly generates, stores, analyzes, and distributes marketing information for use in making marketing decisions. Most marketing information systems rely heavily on internal data, such as sales reports and inventory figures. However, they also often include information from outside sources such as trade reports and marketing research studies. Both managers and salespeople can use marketing information systems.

Data that should be a part of a marketing information system include:

- Company records, such as sales results, expenses, supplier data, and production schedules

- Competitors' records, such as their prices, products, location, and market share

- Customer profile data, such as the results of previous marketing studies regarding buying behavior, shopping patterns, customer demographics, and lifestyles research

- Government data, such as price trends, new regulations and laws, and future projections for the economy

- Marketing research reports that are produced and sold by research firms

508 Unit 9 ■ *Marketing Information Management*

FIGURE 28-3 ANSWER
Providing Better Postal Services The Postal Service will obtain measures about overall customer satisfaction rates on several variables including the delivery of mail, courtesy of postal workers, and other existing services. They will also gain information about the feasibility of offering new products and services.

Did You Know? If students need the U.S. Census for a class project, and the document is not carried at a local library, instruct students to ask the local librarian for the location of the closest government depository library.

Case Study

Keep Away From My Cookies!

Large companies, like Procter & Gamble, are concerned about Internet advertising services companies using their data, or their "cookies." Cookies are tiny data files that a marketer can download onto the hard drive of a user's computer after the user connects to a Web site. Many Web sites require that a visitor accept a cookie as a condition of access. Cookies hold a log of the user's activities, and this information can be read by the owner of an individual Web site and by the advertising services company used by that site.

Ad service companies help individual advertisers by storing individual company ads on their central computer. This process saves large individual advertisers the trouble of placing their own Internet advertisements, which are often placed into hundreds of different Web pages. However, this arrangement also gives the ad service companies access to the data files. Cookies are extremely helpful to an advertiser because they measure what works and what does not work based on visitors' activity on the Web site.

Procter & Gamble is one company that has banned its advertising service providers from using any data obtained from its popular "Pampers Parenting Institute." On the Parenting Institute Web site, Procter & Gamble has visitors register with their names, address, and children's ages to receive a free newsletter on parenting, information about products, and free coupons. All of this information is logged in cookies.

Case Study Review

1. Why do you think Procter & Gamble has banned its ad service company from using its Web site user's data?
2. What benefits can a company obtain by using cookies collected from a company Web site?

A MATTER OF ETHICS

3. Is it ethical for Procter & Gamble to provide visitors with free information regarding parenting skills in exchange for personal information on its Web site? Why or why not?

■ Marketing Databases

Information technologies have made the collection and analysis of data for marketing decision-making much easier. Bar code scanners at point-of-sale terminals provide information on the merchandise that sells and on inventory levels. Many supermarkets have even gone further in data collection by furnishing "valued customer cards," which add the customer's identity to the purchase. Customers complete an application for this card, which entitles them to special discounts. The store in turn collects data on household demographics, lifestyles, and purchase behavior.

Information about consumers and their buying habits are stored in computer databases. A database is a collection (or file) of related information about a specific topic. L. L. Bean, a sportswear and outdoor products retailer, has a database of the people to whom it sends its catalogs. American Express maintains a database of its card members and their addresses, plus what they buy, where they buy it, where they eat out, and how much money they spend. The company uses the information to send its card members special offers on hotels, restaurants, and travel.

Chapter 28 ■ *Marketing Research* **509**

Case Study Review Answers

Keep Away From My Cookies!

1. Companies are afraid of valuable marketing information falling into the hands of their competitors.
2. Companies can tell what is most interesting to consumers and then customize the site to match a consumer's needs. This information is helpful to determine demographics, age, salary, and buying patterns.

A MATTER OF ETHICS

3. Answers will vary but may suggest that the company does incur costs in providing the parenting information and parents have a choice in deciding whether to use the Web site.

Evaluation

Assign and review the Section 28.1 Assessment.

Technology Resources

GO TO **Assessment Resources**
Go to the *Marketing Essentials* Web site (**www.marketing.glencoe. com**) for resources to teach and assess occupation-specific vocabulary.

CLOSE

Section Wrap-Up

Have students complete this statement: Marketing research involves . . . *(the systematic gathering, recording, analyzing, and presentation of information related to marketing goods and services.)*

Honesty is the Best Policy . . .

Answer Participants may lie to give the answer that they think is right or expected, or because they are uncomfortable telling the truth.

510

Many companies that collect information about their customers sell that information to others. Banks that provide mortgage loans often sell the names and addresses of the borrowers to insurance companies that then send information on buying mortgage insurance to the borrower. This exchange of information among businesses has led to complaints of invasion of privacy. Consumers don't know what information about them is contained in various databases. This information can be passed on or sold to other companies without the consumers knowledge or permission. The government has stepped in to create laws regarding protecting the privacy of consumers. Marketers defend the need to have information about their customers and their buying habits to better serve them.

■ Difficulties of Marketing Information Systems

Setting up a marketing information system requires a significant investment of time and money. Trained personnel are needed to maintain and analyze the data collected in the system. Vast amounts of data can be readily obtained with computerized systems; therefore, businesses sometimes have to prioritize the kind of information that is most useful to them.

Even smaller businesses that cannot afford to establish their own management information department recognize the need for marketing information. *Sales and Management,* a monthly magazine, publishes a directory of 200 companies that specialize in sales and marketing software to help businesses obtain marketing information.

Honesty Is the Best Policy...

Researching a new product with a focus group is a great idea, right? Sure it is, as long as everyone is telling the truth. That is the catch in marketing research—there is no "Pinocchio's growing nose" or litmus test to detect lying. Media Direct Partners became acutely aware of this problem when hosting a focus group on advertising for a surgical hair replacement company. The participants of the focus group—all bald men—insisted that they were not bothered by their hair loss. Yet most of them were wearing hats in the middle of August! When you can't trust the responses of your research participants, your research is no good—especially not in the billion-dollar advertising business. To solve this problem, new research methods are being developed with tools that track brain waves and measure the skin's reaction to questions.

Thinking Critically

Why would focus group participants lie in a research setting?

28.1 ASSESSMENT

Reviewing Key Terms and Concepts

1. What is marketing research?
2. How does marketing research help businesses?
3. Who uses marketing research?
4. What is a marketing information system?
5. What is a database?

Thinking Critically

6. Supermarkets often require the use of a "valued customer" card to obtain special discounts on the store's products. Do you think that supermarkets should give special bargains in exchange for personal shopping information?

Integrating Academic Skills

7. **COMMUNICATION** Write a business letter to your local chamber of commerce or a state trade association to ask how the organization assists its members in conducting marketing research.

28.1 ASSESSMENT ANSWERS

Reviewing Key Terms and Concepts

1. Marketing research involves the marketing function that links the consumer, customer, and public to the marketer through information.
2. It helps businesses to plan their future operations to increase sales and profits.
3. government, small and large businesses in a variety of business sectors
4. It is a set of procedures and methods that regularly generates, stores, analyzes, and distributes marketing information.
5. A database is a collection (or file) of related information about a specific topic.

Thinking Critically

6. Answer will vary.

Integrating Academic Skills

7. **COMMUNICATION** Letters will vary.

Types, Trends, and Limitations of Marketing Research

Types of Marketing Research

The type of research businesses conduct depends on the problem that they are trying to solve. Some of the most significant areas of research are attitude research, market research, media research, and product research.

■ Attitude Research

Attitude research, also known as opinion research, is research designed to obtain information on how people feel about certain products, ideas, or companies. The Gallup Organization conducts opinion research polls on politics, elections, business and the economy, social issues, and public policy. Through interviewing techniques using random samples of the population, opinion poll results can be generalized to the entire population. A business considering a major expansion might be interested in the attitude of the general population toward the economy. For example, knowing the attitude of Americans who currently wear glasses but would consider laser surgery is important information for companies considering a marketing strategy for corrective laser surgery.

■ Market Research

Market research involves the systematic gathering, recording, analyzing, and presentation of information related to marketing goods and services. Market research is concerned with the size, location, and makeup of the market for a particular product or service. It uses market analysis to obtain the necessary data.

Market research is needed before a product is introduced to the market and on a regular basis throughout a product's life. Research, however, is not limited only to products; it is also conducted to answer questions about market segments, stores, brands, advertising strategies, prices, and every other aspect of marketing.

Market analysis is the study of particular consumer and industrial markets. The goal of market analysis is to investigate the potential markets for a product and to define characteristics of the target market.

Existing and projected sales data are used in performing market research. Sales data helps businesses project the potential sales for a product and anticipate problems related to future sales. Sales trends for various products may also be compared to determine whether a product's sales are increasing or declining.

• What You'll Learn

- The four important areas of marketing research
- The important trends affecting marketing research
- The limitations of marketing research

• Why It's Important

Sometimes more than one type of research is needed to solve a particular problem. In addition, data collected from one research study can often be used to solve other business problems relating to marketing. This section will introduce you to the major types of marketing research, the latest trends in this field, and the limitations of marketing research.

• Key Terms

- attitude research
- market research
- media research
- product research
- test marketing

FOCUS

Bell Ringer Activity

Analyze Tell students to imagine that they are a marketing research panel of consumers who will evaluate the effectiveness of package design. Hold up two different brands of the same product, each with different packaging. Ask students the following questions about each package: What do you like about the package: color or lack of it; artistic treatment? Do you like the fact that you immediately know the product's features and benefits? What specifically do you dislike about this packaging? Would you change anything about the packaging? If so, what? Would this packaging induce you to pick up this product over the other brands next to it? Why or why not?

Introducing the Section

Types, Trends, and Limitations of Marketing Research Discuss students' answers to the Bell Ringer Activity. Consumer panels are used to test reactions to products, product packaging, and advertising. This exercise shows how subjective customer preferences can be. Some of these panel members may offer entirely different responses to the marketers' questions on a different day. This is why marketers rely on three other types of marketing research in addition to product research.

Write the names of each type of research on the board: attitude or opinion research, market research, media research, and product research. Tell students that in this section they will learn in detail about each of these areas.

Classroom Resources

For the Teacher
- Teacher Editions for all workbooks
- Assessment Package
- PowerPoint Presentation Software
- Interactive Lesson Planner
- ILP Block Scheduling, p. 9
- ILP Lesson Plans, p. 60
- ILP Internet Resources, p. 75

- ILP Blackline Masters, p. 59
- ILP *BusinessWeek* Case Studies, p. 175
- ILP Marketing Career Portfolio, p. 39
- *Marketing Essentials* Web site (**www.marketing.glencoe.com**)

For the Student
- Student Activity Workbook, p. 241
- Marketing Math Workbook, p. 95

- Marketing Research Project Workbook, p. 151
- ILP School-to-Work Activity Workbook, p. 117
- Virtual Business simulation
- *Marketing Essentials* Web site (**www.marketing.glencoe.com**)

ILP These resources are available in print and on the Interactive Lesson Planner (ILP)

SALES FORECASTING *Sales forecasting* is an effort to estimate the future sales of a product. A total estimate of a market is calculated, and then an individual share is predicted for a business.

The share that is assigned to a business is called its *market share* or *sales penetration* of the market. Based on its research findings, the business can then try to increase its market share through changes in the product, pricing, promotion, or distribution strategies.

ECONOMIC FORECASTING *Economic forecasting* is an attempt to predict the future economic conditions of a city, a region, the country, or another part of the world. This research requires extensive knowledge of economic statistics and trend indicators.

Several federal agencies collect information on key economic indicators, such as new building construction, inflation rates, money supply, and consumer and producer price indexes. Most businesses rely on government data to predict economic conditions and to adjust their business activities depending on the economic outlook.

Businesses use research on general economic conditions to help plan for long-range expansion. This research helps to determine whether to cut costs when unfavorable economic conditions, such as higher interest rates or raw materials costs, are predicted.

Private companies, such as Woods and Poole Economics, Inc., also specialize in long-term economic and demographic projections. The Woods and Poole database for every county, state, and metropolitan statistical area (MSA) in the United States contains projections through 2020 for more than 550 variables. This information helps marketing researchers to analyze the makeup of the economy, population changes, households, and retail sales potential (see Figure 28-4 on page 513).

■ Media Research

Media research focuses on issues of media selection and frequency. It measures the effectiveness of the advertising message and media placement. Media research is done on various forms of media such as print, broadcast, and online.

Businesses often conduct research to determine which media or mix of media are most effective for getting an advertising message to a particular market. To conduct that research, businesses may request information from the print, broadcast, and online media of interest to them. In most cases information received would include a rate card, which lists the advertising costs, as well as its circulation or viewership figures, deadline dates, and other requirements for submission of an advertisement. Other information might be about the readers, subscribers, or viewers with regard to age, income, interests, hobbies, occupations, and attitudes. Another means of conducting research on the various media available would be to subscribe to a publication called *Standard Rate and Data Services* (SRDS), which publishes rates and data for the advertising industry.

BRIGHT IDEAS

Bubbles with Attitude

Bubbles are always in style—and popular everywhere from children's parties to fancy weddings. Looking to re-market a time-tested product, Germany's Swetland family used research and development to find success in the bubble market. They hoped to create bubbles that glowed in the dark, but found that the idea was already taken. Instead they developed Tekno Bubbles. These bubbles look like regular bubbles in the light, but under ultra violet or black lights they take on a special quality—they glow! Tekno bubbles, which are available in a variety of colors and scents, are sold at novelty stores.

Thinking Creatively

Choose an already existing product and determine product enhancements that would improve and extend the life of that product.

BRIGHT IDEAS Bubbles with Attitude
Answer Answers will vary depending on product chosen.

FIGURE 28-4

Economic and Demographic Projections

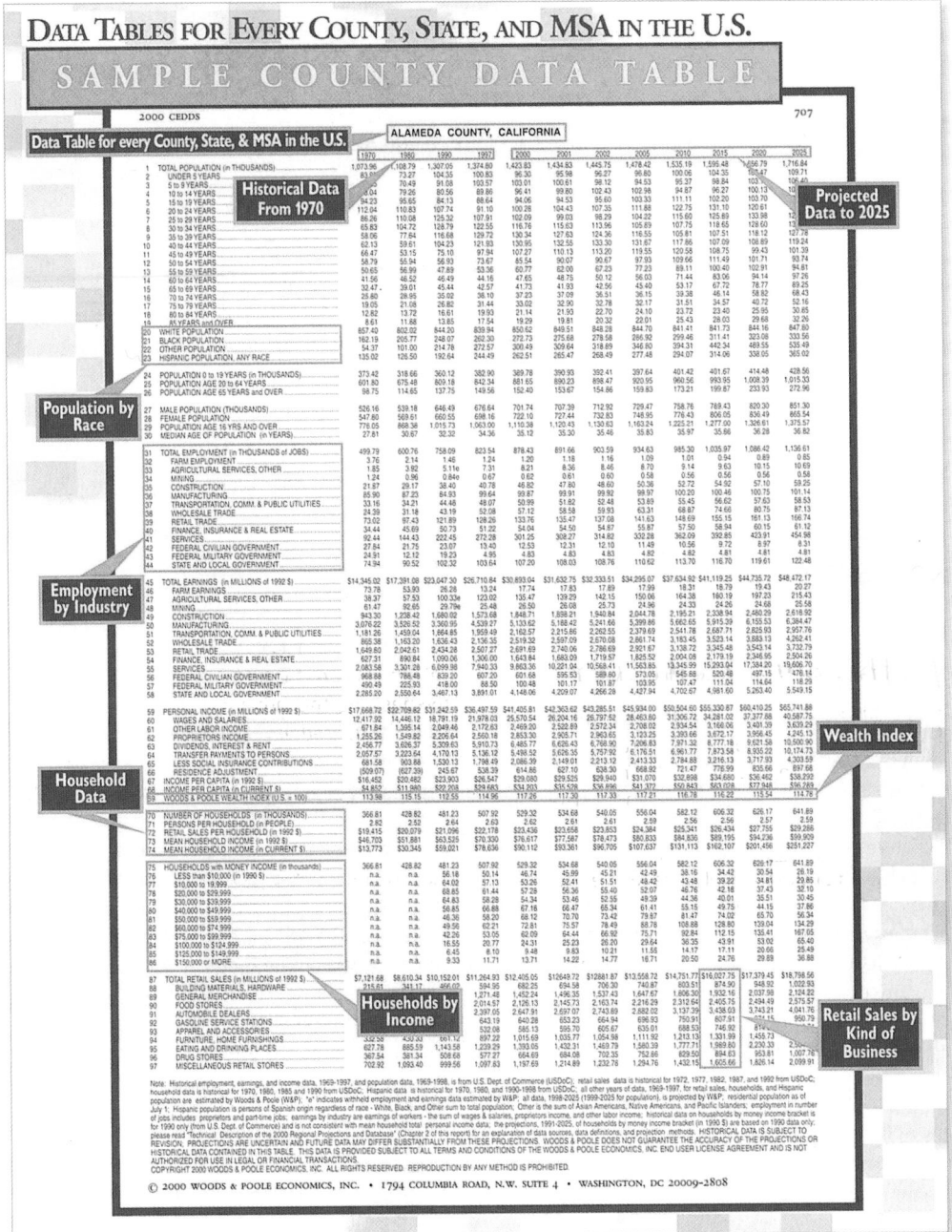

■ **Obtaining Market Research Data** Public and private organizations provide valuable information for exploring the market potential for products and services. *Why is data such as that found in the chart above important for market research?*

Chapter 28 ■ *Marketing Research* **513**

SECTION 28.2

Discussion Starter

Marketing Research Have students imagine that they own a small business and don't have enough money to pay a marketing research firm. How would they conduct marketing research on their advertising? On trends in the community that they could address with their marketing mix? On demographics? On customer satisfaction with their product? *(Answers could include casually talking to customers as they find merchandise in the store, asking customers to fill out comment cards or surveys before they leave the store, sending out informal customer surveys with an incentive to return them, such as a percentage off of a product, or asking customers as they check-out how they learned of the business.)*

FIGURE 28-4 ANSWER
Obtaining Market Research Data The data provide information on population trends, employment, household data, household income, and retail sales, which is helpful for a business exploring the market potential for its products.

GREAT IDEAS from the Marketing Classroom

Greg Gregoriou
Parkside High School
Dundas, Ontario
Canada

To introduce the concept of marketing research, have the class brainstorm and name some everyday items (gum, chocolate bars, toothbrush, etc.). Then write each item on pieces of paper and put them in a hat or a box. Divide the class into pairs. Each pair selects an item out of the box. Have each pair interview 50 people randomly, noting gender and brand preference for each person surveyed. Have them tabulate their findings. (Percentages work the best.) Once they are finished tabulating their findings, teach students how to use a spreadsheet program to graphically display their data.

Thinking Critically

Economic Indicators Have students name some positive and negative economic indicators in your community. Based on their answers, have them make some predictions about the future economic conditions in your town or city and region. What products are people in your community and in your region likely to need more of and less of in one year? In five years?

Cooperative Learning

1. **Types of Marketing Research**
   Divide students into four groups: *attitude research, market research, media research,* and *product research.* Each group will contribute to a marketing research bulletin board, which features key terms, phrases, and visuals that combine to explain and illustrate the purpose of each type.

   Allow each group to generate five to ten key terms and visuals for the bulletin board. Give them magic markers and paper. Allow them to cut pictures and ads from magazines and newspapers. For example, to illustrate advertising research, they could (1) cut out an ad and (2) write the phrases *effectiveness of the advertising message* and *effectiveness of media placement.*

   After all the information has been placed on the bulletin board, a spokesperson from each group should explain why each written element and visual element was chosen.

2. **Test Marketing** Have groups of 4–5 students each prepare a report on the advantages and disadvantages of test marketing with different products which were test marketed over the past five years. Each group will be responsible for completing a written report on the products that were test marketed and the city(ies) where the test marketing occurred.

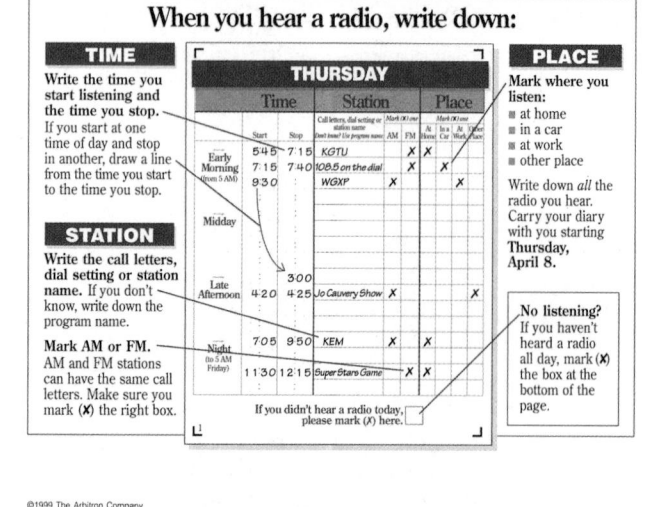

© 1999 The Arbitron Company

■ **Researching Radio Advertising** Businesses need to research the effectiveness of their radio advertisements. *What information can be provided through radio diaries?*

RESEARCHING PRINT ADVERTISEMENTS The effectiveness of a printed advertising message can be tested on its recall, communication, and persuasive abilities. Marketing researchers can use different techniques to get people's reactions to an advertisement. In one technique, readers are shown ads from not-yet-released general distribution magazines such as *People, Newsweek,* and *Better Homes and Gardens.* They are queried regarding the ad's effectiveness as to the extent it was noticed, remembered, and associated with the advertised brand. The ad is also measured on its ability to change the consumer's beliefs, attitudes, or intended behavior.

Another technique to measure print advertising effectiveness is through the use of consumer panels. Consumer panels, also called focus groups, are groups of people who are questioned periodically to provide information on research issues. A consumer panel can be comprised of a cross section of people or of people who share common characteristics— senior citizens, single parents, college-educated adults, or teenagers, for example. Oral, written, or observed behavioral responses are recorded to indicate panel members' reactions to an advertisement.

RESEARCHING BROADCAST MEDIA Businesses also want to find out information about various types of broadcast media. The Arbitron Ratings Company, a subsidiary of the Ceridian Corporation, assembles important data on radio advertising. Arbitron produces radio audience measurements and sells software that analyzes advertising expenditure data. Continuous audience measurement in 267 local markets serving 2,300 radio stations makes it the largest radio audience service in the world. Arbitron radio contacts more than 2 million consumers a year and collects more than 1 million diaries to compile its radio station rating reports. *Diaries* are records on which people report such viewer data as who is watching or listening to a station and what programs are tuned in.

Nielsen Media Research, Inc. provides audience measurement information for the television industry. Unlike a magazine or newspaper, where the number of subscribers is known, there is no simple way to know exactly how many people are watching a television program. Nielsen estimates the audience by drawing a sample. It counts the number of viewers in the sample to get a particular television

514 Unit 9 ■ *Marketing Information Management*

CAPTION ANSWER
Researching Radio Advertising A business can receive audience measures for the most popular radio stations and when the most popular advertising times are for a company's potential customers.

program's rating. The ratings information is generated from a National People Meter Sample of 5,000 homes measuring the viewing habits of 13,000 people.

In meter-equipped households, devices attached to television sets automatically monitor program viewing. Broadcast and cable network providers, program developers, distributors and advertisers use this information to decide on which television programs to advertise (see Figure 28-5).

RESEARCHING ONLINE ADVERTISING As online advertising increases in popularity, researchers have developed marketing research techniques for online copy testing. One technique uses a mock environment similar to traditional copy testing and live testing in an interactive environment. Another aspect to online marketing research is tracking of ad recall and copy effectiveness, as well as evaluation of Web site elements that attract users.

■ Product Research

Product research centers on evaluating product design, package design, product usage, and consumer acceptance of new and existing products. Many new products and their packages are designed, tested, changed, and introduced each year. Product research is also conducted to collect information about competitive products.

NEW PRODUCT ACCEPTANCE Product tests are a way of measuring new product acceptance. One product test has consumers try a product and give their opinions. Product testers are asked questions about specific aspects of the product. A tester of body lotion may be asked about the lotion's texture, scent, consistency, oiliness, and absorption into the skin. Sometimes, two different products are given to test and compare. The products are packaged generically and identified by letter or number. Consumer panels (focus groups) are also used extensively to give feedback on new products.

Have you or your family ever received a small sample box of cereal in the mail? Companies often send samples, usually accompanied by a coupon, to consumers to determine whether they like a product well enough to buy it. You have probably been part of a test market and did not even realize it. Test marketing occurs when a new product is placed in one or more selected geographic areas. Test

FIGURE 28-5

TV Ratings

RATINGS FOR WEEK OF 10/2/00 – 10/8/00

RANK	PROGRAM	NETWORK	RATING	DAY
1	The West Wing	NBC	16.3	Wed
2	Everybody Loves Raymond	CBS	14.6	Mon
3	Who Wants to Be a Millionaire	ABC	14.1	Tue
4	Who Wants to Be a Millionaire	ABC	13.7	Thu
5	Who Wants to Be a Millionaire	ABC	13.4	Wed
6	Who Wants to Be a Millionaire	ABC	13.1	Sun
7	60 Minutes	CBS	12.8	Sun
8	CSI: Crime Scene Investigation	CBS	11.8	Fri
9	Monday Night Football	ABC	11.4	Mon
10	Dark Angel	FOX	11.2	Tue

SOURCE: NIELSEN

■ **Measuring TV Ratings** Advertisers who prepare television advertisements are interested in TV ratings. *What information can TV ratings provide for a television advertiser?*

Peace of mind

FOCUS Suites
We focus on you.

The pressure is on. Your clients are waiting; the group participants are checking in. The last thing you want is an unpleasant surprise. The first thing you need is a responsive staff that supports you.

Focus Suites staff has the experience to anticipate your needs and be flexible when they change. You need to be at your best. From recruitment to project management, Focus Suites does our best to put you there.

visit our website www.focussuites.com

■ **Getting into Focus** Consumer panels are used extensively to give feedback on new products. *What is another term for consumer panel?*

Chapter 28 ■ *Marketing Research* **515**

FIGURE 28-5 ANSWER
Measuring TV Ratings Information about the most popular TV shows, time periods, their ratings, and share of the viewing audience can influence when and where advertisers run TV ads.

CAPTION ANSWER
Getting into Focus A consumer panel is also called a focus group.

Individualized Practice

Math Skills

Provide students with the total gross domestic revenue in a particular industry for the most recent calendar year. Also provide them with the total gross domestic revenues for the major companies in that industry during the same year. (For example, if you choose the rental car industry, obtain figures for Hertz, Avis, Dollar, Thrifty, and Budget.)

L1 Have students do a bar graph or a line graph to visually show the total annual revenue for each firm.

L2 Based on the statistics you give students, have them calculate the market share percentage of each firm and show these percentages on a circle graph.

L3 Convert each of the market share percentages to a decimal.

FIGURE 28-6 ANSWER
Providing Information on Existing Products and Services The information collected will allow a business to know how customers view its merchandise and services. In addition, information about how the business compares to its competitors is helpful in designing promotional activities and advertising campaigns.

---

marketing allows marketers to gauge customers' response and to observe a product's sales performance. In the new product development stage, products are test marketed in limited areas. The company monitors the product's sales performance in retail stores that are located in the test market. The results of the test marketing help the manufacturer determine whether the product needs changes before it is introduced to the entire country.

A concern about test marketing is that it offers competitors a chance to see new products before they are ready for national introduction. Competitors can also try to influence the test results by running special advertising and promotions on their own products. Technology has offered one solution to that problem. A company called MarketWare Simulation Services has introduced a program called Visionary Shopper. A computer program allows individuals in a research group to see many different products on screen, including existing products and the new test product. Viewers make choices about which products to put in their on-screen shopping carts.

The program tallies the group's responses to different products and gives its clients test market results via computer.

Another marketing research technique to test new products is a product rating board. The Consumer Report magazine for young people, *Zillions*, established a "Z-Team" nationwide rating board. This 100-member board of 8- to 14-year-olds was asked to serve for a year and to evaluate various products such as pizza and 35mm cameras.

EXISTING PRODUCT RESEARCH Satisfaction questionnaires and interviews gather information about existing products and services for both the industrial and consumer markets. *Industrial satisfaction surveys* focus upon products and services utilized by business and manufacturing firms. *Customer satisfaction surveys* provide a rich data source for businesses interested in retail customer attitudes toward existing products and services (see Figure 28-6).

FIGURE 28-6

J.C. Penney Customer Survey

■ **Providing Information on Existing Products and Service** Businesses frequently survey their customers about products and services. *How is this information useful to a business?*

THE DECA CONNECTION

COMPETITIVE EVENTS AND MARKETING ESSENTIALS

Marketing Research and Local Businesses Any of DECA's Marketing Research Events can be used as a class project to reinforce the concepts of this chapter. The specific event will depend upon the students' choice of business. Students working alone, or in teams of up to three, conduct basic research about their community and a local business for studying a local business of their choice. The *Marketing Essentials Marketing Research Project Workbook* offers a detailed, step-by-step procedure for students to plan, conduct, and report on their own marketing research project. It provides the details for reporting, analyzing, and presenting findings of a marketing research study.

Trends in Marketing Research

The nature and scope of marketing research are rapidly changing to keep pace with a changing marketplace. The United States is a huge market with many goods and services for almost any consumer need or want. The trend toward a global marketplace means increased international competition for U.S. companies, which must improve or change products frequently to hold on to their customers. In this environment, product quality and customer satisfaction are the keys to business success. Research that measures these qualities has become the fastest growing form of marketing research. It is becoming increasingly important for companies to consider the needs of international consumers.

The basic measure of business success in the future will be customer relationship management, which is measured in continued sales. To maintain a high level of customer satisfaction, companies will need a thorough understanding of their customers' needs and information that tells them how well they are meeting those needs. This can be achieved through effective use of marketing research.

Life In The Diverse MARKETPLACE

Next Door...to the North

Canada may be right next door, but there are many differences to consider when marketing to Canadian citizens. Don't be fooled by the common border and the strong trade history—the cultural makeup is quite different than in the United States. Approximately 25 percent of Canadians call French their first language, 80 percent in the province of Quebec. These French-speaking Canadians are not the only nationals with a foreign influence. Canada was settled by a variety of people from around the world, including France, Britain, Ireland, Germany, Scandinavia, Asia, the Netherlands, Ukraine, Italy, and Poland. How's that for diversity?

Thinking Critically
How can marketers use this information when directing product promotion in Canada?

Another important trend is the use of both internal and external information in managing a business. *Total Quality Management* programs, or *TQM*, place a premium on gathering marketing and other information for use in improving business operations.

As the need and technology for marketing research increases, marketers are faced with a new set of ethical concerns. Some of these concerns include privacy in data collection, privacy in data use, excessive intrusiveness, and deceptive research practices. Such concerns have spurred efforts by the American Marketing Association to discourage unethical research practices among its members.

■ **Research Trends** Advances in technology have resulted in the increased use of marketing research technologies, such as point-of-sale data collection, Internet research, fax broadcasting of surveys to a select group of fax numbers, automated dialing, prerecorded digital surveys, and computerized database management programs. *What effect will the trend toward a global marketplace have on marketing research?*

Chapter 28 ■ *Marketing Research* **517**

ASSESS

Reteaching

1. **Vocabulary** Assign and review the vocabulary terms for this section.
2. **Fact and Idea** Assign and review Fact and Idea Review questions 5–10 from the Chapter Assessment.
3. **Concept Mapping** Conduct a concept mapping activity by having students use a poster board or newsprint to draw a map with the term "marketing research" in the center of the poster. Have students identify key concepts underlying marketing research that students learned about after reading the information in the chapter. Post the maps on the walls of the classroom and the board and have a number of students orally explain their map. Add instructor comments after each student presentation to connect the concepts to the chapter reading.

CAPTION ANSWER
Research Trends The trend toward a global marketplace means increased international competition for U.S. companies, which will increasingly depend on marketing research to improve their products and keep their customers.

Life In The Diverse MARKETPLACE

Next Door . . . to the North
Answer It is important to be familiar with the heritage and cultural make-up of any nation in which you want to market goods or services because products can be advertised or marketed directly toward that group.

1. **Review** Assign and review the Chapter 28 activities in the *Student Activity Workbook.*
2. **Review** Assign and review the appropriate Thinking Critically questions from the Chapter Assessment.
3. **Review** Assign and review the following Chapter Assessment activities: Building Workplace Skills, Applying Marketing Concepts, Linking School to Work, The DECA Connection Role Play, and Internet Connection.

Evaluation

Assign and review the Section 28.2 Assessment.

Technology Resources

 Assessment Resources
Go to the *Marketing Essentials* Web site (**www.marketing.glencoe. com**) for resources to teach and assess occupation-specific vocabulary.

CLOSE

Section Wrap-Up

Have students complete this statement: The four major areas of marketing research are . . . *(attitude or opinion research, market research, media research, and product research)*

What's in a Name?
Answer Answers will vary.

518

Limitations of Marketing Research

Each of the major types of marketing research information is used to help businesses make sound business decisions. Few companies, however, can conduct as much marketing research as they would like. The amount of information that can be gathered is limited by the amount of money a company can afford to spend on the equipment and personnel needed to do the research. Often, there is too little time to do the research because decisions must be made before all possible data can be obtained.

Marketing research information also has its limitations. Customers in a test market situation may say they want a particular product, but there is no guarantee they will actually buy the product when it is sold. In addition, fast-changing markets may not allow time for research. There is a time lag between identifying the need for a product, collecting the marketing research, and presenting the findings so the business can decide whether to produce the product. Business conditions, customer buying habits, and customer preferences can change.

Despite these limitations, marketing research provides valuable information. Businesses will continue to rely on marketing research to obtain the best possible information about customers and the marketplace.

What's in a Name?

Sometimes a change of names can be all it takes to help a product sell. This was the case in 2000 when the California Prune Board (CPB) requested that the Food and Drug Administration (FDA) grant it permission to use the name "dried plums" as an alternative to "prunes." The name change was determined necessary after market research showed that "dried plums" offers a more positive mental image than "prune." The CPB hopes the name change will help to attract its target audience—women age 35 to 44. California prunes aren't the only fruit to change names—the popular kiwifruit was previously called a Chinese gooseberry!

Thinking Critically
Can you think of any products that might benefit from a name change?

28.2 ASSESSMENT

Reviewing Key Terms and Concepts

1. What are the four major areas of marketing research?
2. What is the difference between sales and economic forecasting?
3. What is test marketing?
4. List at least four trends facing marketing researchers today.
5. What are two limitations of marketing research?

Thinking Critically

6. Should every type of business engage in marketing research? Why or why not?

Integrating Academic Skills

7. **MATH** Assume that your company plans to send a marketing questionnaire to 30 percent of the names on a mailing list of 5,000 people. The mailing list was purchased from another company for $0.30 per name. Each questionnaire costs $0.10 to print; mailing costs are $0.36 (including the envelope and return envelope) each; and the cost of writing the questionnaire, analyzing the information, and preparing the report is $15,000. What is the total cost?

28.2 ASSESSMENT ANSWERS

Reviewing Key Terms and Concepts
1. attitude research, market research, media research, and product research
2. Sales forecasting estimates future sales of a product. Economic forecasting predicts future economic conditions of a region.
3. Product is placed in one or more geographical areas; sales are monitored before distribution.
4. emphasis on customer satisfaction; total quality management; integrating marketing research data with other sources; quality assurance
5. The amount of information that can be gathered is limited by the amount of money. Time constraints may force premature decisions.

Thinking Critically
6. It is valuable for every type of business.

Integrating Academic Skills
7. **MATH** $17,190

Careers in Marketing

MARKETING RESEARCH

Martin Saperstein
Research Analyst
Saperstein Associates, Inc.

What does your job entail?

"Research analysts use statistical data to study potential markets for new products and services. I gather data on customer buying habits, prices, and other market factors. I organize focus groups to help companies make decisions. These focus groups provide information to reduce the possibility of a business making a mistake. We use inferential data, but our sampling error by no means eliminates the chance of being wrong. This information is used to prepare recommendations to management personnel."

What skills are most important?

"Being a good listener is a very important skill. A good analyst can listen and discover what is needed—we find out what the questions are and choose a format for the best answers for a company's research project. We have to be able to collect the data, process it, and share the results with clients. We do not make their decisions, but we offer them recommendations based on the data."

What kind of training did you have?

"I received my undergraduate degree from George Washington University and I have a doctorate in political science from Ohio State University. The rest of the training came from working on the job."

What is the key to your success?

"There are four elements to my success. The first is education, which is the price of admission to this kind of career. The second element is hard work. A strong focus on anticipated goals is the third important element. Many people start businesses and change the direction on a whim, or do too many things at once with no plan. The fourth essential element is my understanding spouse. I cannot overestimate the importance of having a partner who is equally committed, as well as a nonwork environment where I can unwind and be myself. Removing any one of these four aspects would diminish my ability to be successful."

Thinking Critically

Why do you think that being a good listener is important when analyzing research data?

Career Facts

Education and Training: College preparatory classes in advanced math, economics, marketing, merchandising, computer science, English, and psychology are helpful. A bachelor's degree is usually required, and knowledge of current research techniques and online research is helpful.

Aptitudes, Abilities, and Skills: Above-average ability in mathematics, interest in problem solving, ability to plan and develop strategies for gathering and interpreting information, good decision-making skills, strong communication skills, and developed interpersonal skills are necessary.

Career Outlook: Employment opportunities are expected to grow at an average rate through the year 2006. A strong economy and online marketing may increase demand.

Career Path: Senior research analysts begin their careers as interviewers, research assistants, or junior analysts. Some work part-time on these jobs while still in school.

Vocabulary Review

See Glossary for definitions.

Fact and Idea Review

1. It involves the methods used to gather information related to marketing goods and services, analyze it, and report the findings.
2. The major emphasis is obtaining information about the preferences, opinions, habits, trends, and plans of potential customers.
3. It generates, stores, analyzes, and distributes marketing information.
4. It is a collection of information on a specific topic. Examples will vary.
5. It is research conducted to obtain information on how people feel about certain products, ideas, or companies.
6. It is the collection of information about the customer and the market for a product. An example is to calculate the total market for a type of product, then find the amount of that market held by a particular company to find the market share.
7. Media research focuses on issues related to media selection and frequency. Research on print media is done on known subscribers and readers, while broadcast media research is done by ratings drawn from samples.
8. Product research evaluates consumer acceptance and collects information about competitive products. An example is asking a consumer panel to describe what they like or dislike about a product.
9. Answers will vary but could include product tests, test marketing, ratings boards, and satisfaction surveys.
10. International competition is forcing U.S. companies to constantly improve products.

Thinking Critically

1. Individual companies must assure their consumers that the information collected will not be used in unscrupulous ways.
2. Answers will vary, but legislators have viewed telemarketing efforts more critically and in some cases have limited telemarketing efforts.
3. A car wash would benefit from all the major types of marketing research.
4. Businesses are better able to suit their goods and services to consumers.

Chapter 28 ASSESSMENT

VOCABULARY REVIEW

Write the following vocabulary terms and their definitions on index cards. Review the terms and definitions by quizzing a classmate.

- marketing research
- marketing information system
- database
- attitude research
- market research
- media research
- product research
- test marketing

FACT AND IDEA REVIEW

1. What is involved in marketing research? (28.1)
2. What is the major emphasis of marketing research? (28.1)
3. What is the primary function of a marketing information system? (28.1)
4. What is a marketing database? Give an example. (28.1)
5. What is attitude research? (28.2)
6. What is market research? Give an example. (28.2)
7. What is media research? How does research on print media differ from research on broadcast media? (28.2)
8. What is product research? Give an example. (28.2)
9. What are two techniques for researching new product acceptance? (28.2)
10. How has the global economy affected marketing research? (28.2)

THINKING CRITICALLY

1. Surveys indicate that only 34 percent of consumers surveyed trust marketers with regard to their use of consumer marketing information. What can be done to counteract consumer fears about invasion of privacy?
2. Is legislation necessary to make a distinction between legitimate research and telemarketing sales? Explain.
3. Explain what kind of marketing research should be done by a coin-operated car wash.
4. Why are marketing researchers concerned about consumer attitudes and lifestyles?
5. What do you think marketing research would reveal about the differences between the lifestyles of dual-income families with children and the lifestyles of dual-income families without children?

BUILDING WORKPLACE SKILLS

1. **Human Relations** You have a part-time job in the marketing research department of a large corporation. You and three coworkers are gathering information through telephone surveys. Your supervisor wants each of you to complete at least 30 surveys a day, which can be difficult. One coworker makes rude comments to people who do not participate and has told others that the survey is government-sponsored and mandatory. What should you do?
2. **Technology** Investigate database management computer software programs used for marketing research by reviewing advertisements in business publications. Write a letter requesting additional information.

5. Answers will vary, but students may suggest that families without children may have more time to shop and have more discretionary income.

Building Workplace Skills

1. Students' responses will vary.
2. Business letters should be written according to the specifications in Chapter 8.

520

APPLYING MARKETING CONCEPTS

1. **Summarizing Key Concepts** Summarize an article that demonstrates any of the key concepts in this chapter. In the summary, identify the specific concepts in parentheses. Use business publications such as *BrandWeek, Adweek, BusinessWeek, Fortune, Forbes,* and *Marketing News* to find an applicable article.

2. **Identifying Market Factors** Use the Internet to research your city or state's population, income, education, trading area, and purchasing power. Consult city or state offices for additional market information. Create an oral report using presentation software highlighting these marketing factors.

3. **Evaluating Research Agencies** Investigate companies that provide customer research, online database searching, and information-brokering services on the Internet. Identify four questions that you would ask of a large research agency before you would use its services for media research.

4. **Meeting Consumer Needs** Search the Internet for an existing consumer product that you think needs to be changed to raise consumer appeal. Research the product and propose changes. Present your proposal and rationale in an oral report.

5. **Analyzing Marketing Trends** Use presentation software to present an oral report on the trends affecting marketing research within a particular industry, such as electronics.

LINKING SCHOOL TO WORK

Basic Skills Interview your training sponsor or current supervisor to find out how research is conducted at your place of employment. Report your findings orally to the class.

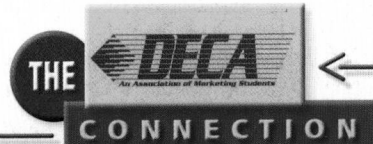

THE DECA CONNECTION

Role Play: Research Consultant

Situation You are to assume the role of employee at a sporting goods store. You have been asked by your store manager (judge) to present your ideas for conducting research on the feasibility of adding a new line of in-line skates and related accessories.

Activity You must make an oral presentation to your store manager (judge) explaining the types of research that will need to be conducted to determine whether the new product line and accessories should be added.

Evaluation You will be evaluated on how well you meet the following performance indicators:

• Explain the nature of marketing research in a marketing information management system
• Assess marketing information needs
• Interpret descriptive statistics for marketing decision making
• Explain the nature of sales forecasts
• Describe the need for marketing information

interNET CONNECTION

Researching Market Researchers
Visit the Web site for the American Marketing Association and select one of the top 50 U.S. research organizations to investigate.

Connect
• Write a summary of the company in 150–200 words, describing the company's history, number of employees, and the marketing research that it conducts.

Chapter 28 ■ *Marketing Research* **521**

Mini Quiz

Administer the Mini Quiz orally. For an expanded chapter quiz, go to page 167 of the *Reproducible Tests* book.

1. <u>Marketing research</u> is the marketing function that links the consumer, customer, and public to the marketer through information.

2. A set of procedures and methods that regularly generates, stores, analyzes, and distributes marketing information is called a(n) <u>marketing information system</u>.

3. A collection (or file) of related information on a specific topic is known as a(n) <u>database</u>.

4. <u>Attitude</u> or opinion research is designed to obtain information on how people feel about certain products, ideas, or companies.

5. <u>Market</u> is concerned with the size, location, and/or make-up of the market for a particular product or service.

Applying Marketing Concepts

1. Summaries will vary depending on selected articles.
2. Reports will depend on the students' city or state.
3. Students might ask about the company's data sources, computer technology, research services offered, and references.
4. Reports will vary.
5. Reports will vary.

Linking School to Work

Answers depend on the work situation.

1. **Assessment** Have students complete the Reproducible Test for Chapter 28 or construct your own tests using the ExamView software.
2. **Enrichment** Have students complete the corresponding activities in the following workbooks:
   • *Marketing Math Workbook,* p. 95
   • *Marketing Research Project Workbook,* p. 151

Chapter Overview

This chapter introduces students to the process of conducting marketing research. The chapter explains the difference between primary and secondary data and the methods used for collecting each type of data. Students learn how to construct survey questionnaires and how technology is used in marketing research.

 Springboard

Brainstorm Remind students that marketing research is a process in which many elements are brought together to arrive at a final product. Ask students how they think their co-op training stations make decisions to introduce new products and delete old ones. For example, what factors made McDonald's investigate the possibility of adding low-calorie salads to its menu? Make a list of their answers on the board.

Prereading

Have students skim the chapter, looking at the pictures, reading the captions, and noting the heads. Ask questions to ensure that the students have a minimal understanding of the chapter.

Preteaching Marketing Vocabulary

Have students skim through the chapter before class, paying attention to the boldface vocabulary terms. Read the definitions for this chapter's vocabulary terms (but not in order). Have students match the terms to the definitions.

Marketing: What It Takes

Answer Carefully consider the needs and preferences of the population you want to survey in order to determine the best manner of gaining data. To ensure a high response rate, conduct personal interviews and offer an incentive for participation.

Chapter **29**
Conducting Marketing Research

Marketing: What It Takes

Surveying Citizens
Imagine that you are surveying people in the community to obtain feedback about government services and ideas for improvements.

WHAT WILL YOU DO?
How will you determine the best way to gain data? How will you ensure a high response rate?

THE **◆DECA** CONNECTION

ADVISOR CORNER

DECA Writing Events Encourage members to participate in either individual or chapter written events. Assigning participants due dates for each section of the written paper will make the entire process easier. Form a support network/advisory panel for the students to utilize during the research and writing process. Appropriate business professionals and other teachers make excellent members of advisory panels to guide and support students. It is also helpful for students to be able to read winning entries from past years. To obtain previous years' winning entries, contact National DECA at **www.deca.org**.

Marketing Research

The Marketing Research Process

The five steps that a business follows when conducting marketing research are *defining the problem, obtaining data, analyzing the data, recommending solutions,* and *applying the results.* Each step is performed sequentially to arrive at solutions to a problem or research issue. Figure 29-1 on page 524 provides more details on each of these steps in the research process.

Step 1: Defining the Problem

The most difficult step in the marketing research process is defining the problem. Problem definition occurs when a business clearly identifies a problem or research issue and the information that is necessary to solve it. An example of a problem may be declining sales. The business needs to decide what it can do to improve sales. It will want to know who is buying its products, who are its present competitors, and why past customers stopped buying. The business will also need to know where, when, and why the product sells or does not sell.

Research issues can focus on any aspect of the marketing process. To study the problem of declining sales, marketers might pose questions such as:

- Are customers satisfied with the present product?
- Are prices competitive?
- Are the products distributed efficiently in the marketplace?
- Are promotion activities effective?

Because money and time are limited, each business has to determine which problems and issues are the most important to address at a given time.

Step 2: Obtaining Data

The second step in the marketing research process is to obtain data. During this second step, data are collected and examined in terms of the problem or problems being studied.

The word *data* means facts. There are two types of data used in marketing research: *primary* and *secondary*. Primary data are data obtained for the first time and used specifically for the particular problem or issue under study. Secondary data have already been collected for some purpose other than the current study. Secondary data are less expensive to collect than primary data. It is most effective for a company to decide what secondary data it will use before collecting any primary data.

What You'll Learn

- The steps in conducting marketing research
- The difference between primary and secondary data
- The various methods used to collect primary and secondary data

Why It's Important

Businesses that want to increase their customer base must have information about the attitudes and behaviors of current and prospective customers. Marketing research can provide information for strategies that will increase sales and profits.

Key Terms

- problem definition
- primary data
- secondary data
- survey method
- sample
- observation method
- point-of-sale research
- experimental method
- data analysis

TEACH

📊 Technology Resources

PowerPoint The *Marketing Essentials* PowerPoint Presentation CD-ROM provides visual lecture aids for every chapter section.

Concept Development

1. Read Section 29.1 with students.
2. Have students read aloud the Case Study on page 531 and review the answers in class.
3. For further information on data collection and analysis, contact the Marketing Research Association, 1344 Silas Deane Hwy., Suite 306, Rocky Hill, CT 06067-0230.
4. The following publications are good supplemental resources to use in teaching this chapter:
   - *Advances in Consumer Research,* Association for Consumer Research, Brigham Young University, Graduate School of Management, 632 TNRB, Provo, UT 84602, (801) 378-2080 (scholarly journal of new marketing research techniques and findings)
   - *AMA Complete Guide to Marketing Research for Small Business,* American Marketing Association, 250 S. Wacker Dr., Ste. 200, Chicago, IL 60606, (312) 648-0536
   - *"Alert!",* Marketing Research Association, 1344 Silas Deane Hwy., Suite 306, Rocky Hill, CT 06067-0230 (newsletter that informs readers about industry news, research technology and management techniques)

FIGURE 29-1

THE MARKETING RESEARCH PROCESS

There are five steps in the problem solving process. They start with defining the problem and involve collecting and analyzing data until a potential solution can be found and applied. Following each step in the proper order helps businesses reach effective business decisions.

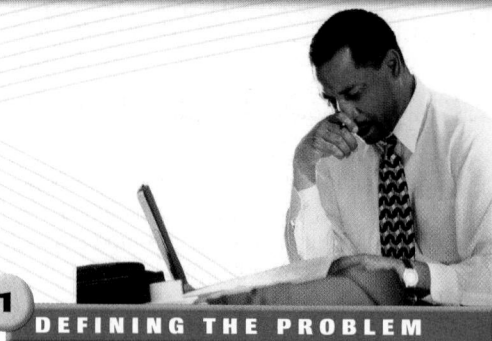

1 DEFINING THE PROBLEM

The problem or research issue is identified and goals are set to solve the problem.

3 ANALYZING DATA

Researchers compile, analyze, and interpret the data.

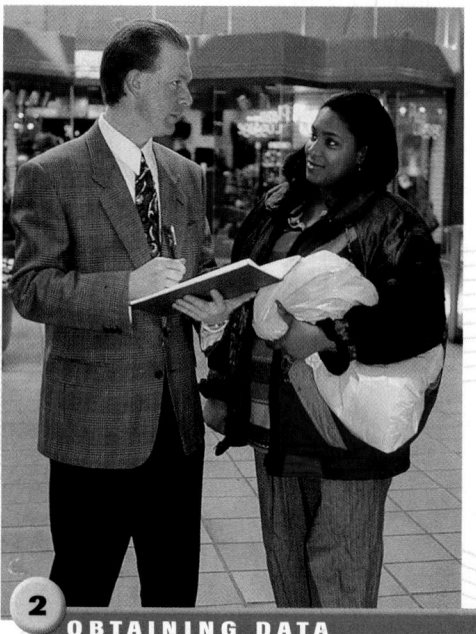

2 OBTAINING DATA

Researchers obtain data from primary and secondary sources.

4 RECOMMENDING SOLUTIONS

Researchers come up with potential solutions to the problem and present them in a report.

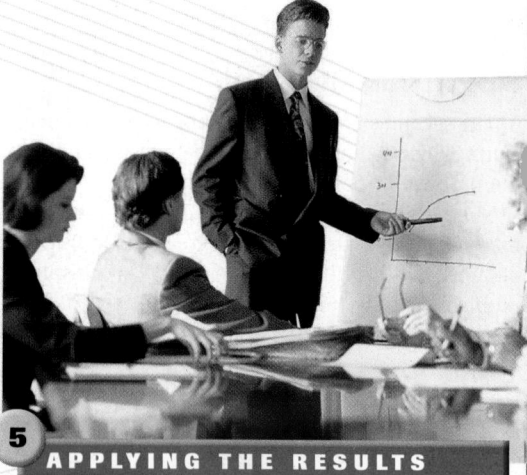

5 APPLYING THE RESULTS

The research results are put into action.

GREAT IDEAS from the Marketing Classroom

Dennis Sweetapple
Spanish River Community
High School
Boca Raton, FL

The backbone of marketing is research, so I introduce my first-year students to marketing research at the beginning of the school year. Each student receives a copy of the current DECA Marketing Research Guidelines and is assigned Unit 9, Chapters 28 and 29 of the *Marketing Essentials* textbook for the first three weeks of the school year. Students get a calendar noting when each section of the marketing research project is due for a grade. I encourage students whose projects show promise to expand their projects for DECA competition. However, no student is required to compete.

How Secondary Data Are Obtained

Secondary data are obtained from both internal sources (sources within the company) and external sources (sources outside the company). An excellent source of internal secondary data is the marketing information system of a business. As explained in Chapter 28, a marketing information system is an internal method of getting data used to measure monthly sales, determine the geographic distribution of customers, track customer buying patterns, and identify popular items on the market.

INTERNET SOURCES The Internet has increased the availability of secondary data from a variety of sources. *Digital dossiers,* which provide company profiles on public corporations, income statements, and balance sheets, are available online. These reports can be purchased for a fee from online databases such as *Hoover, Fortune 500,* and *Inc. 500.*

Online business clearinghouses such as *Starting Point* and the *Competitive Intelligence Guide* offer commercial directories and company resources.

■ **Obtaining Secondary Data** Government data are an excellent source of secondary data for businesses. *Why should a business review government data sources before launching into a marketing research project?*

U.S. GOVERNMENT SOURCES Federal government studies can provide useful information and statistics about markets, people, and business activities. Data collected by U.S. government agencies regarding population demographics, specific markets, industries, products, economic news, export information, and legislative trends can be accessed on the Internet for free or for a nominal cost. *FedWorld* and *The Federal Web Locator* are two Web directories with links to most government Web sites that provide such data.

The Small Business Administration, U.S. Department of Commerce, U.S. Census Bureau, U.S. Security and Exchange Commission, and the Bureau of Labor Statistics can also be excellent sources for secondary data. Publications such as the *Census of the Population* and the *Statistical Abstract of the United States* contain hundreds of tables, graphs, and charts that can be useful when analyzing various business situations.

CONSUMER AND BUSINESS INFORMATION COMPANIES An active and growing number of specialized research companies or *syndicated services* also offer secondary data for business needs. Specialized companies sell demographic data, five-year forecasts, consumer purchase information, business data, census information, and consumer classification reports to businesses. An example is Audit & Surveys Worldwide (ASW), which provides continuous monthly national measures of retail sales by brand. ASW also provides an annual update of the universe for all U.S. retail and service outlets from the National Retail Census, which is the largest in-person distribution measurement program conducted in the United States, as well as many other types of market research services. Syndicated service companies make data available in print and electronic formats.

BUSINESS AND TRADE PUBLICATIONS Secondary data can also be obtained in publications such as *Forbes, Business Week, The Wall Street Journal,* and *Sales and Marketing Management.* Trade association publications often publish secondary data through articles, reports, and books. Examples of trade associations for marketing research include the American Association for Public Opinion Research, Council of American Survey Research Organizations, and the Marketing Research Association.

- *Findex,* Cambridge Information Group Directories, Inc., 7200 Wisconsin Ave., Bethesda, MD 20814, (301) 961-6750 (directory and description of thousands of published marketing research studies and reports about companies and industries)
- *Journal of Marketing Research,* American Marketing Association, 250 S. Wacker Dr., Ste. 200, Chicago, IL 60606, (312) 648-0536 (offers detailed information about the methods and analyses used in marketing research)
- *Marketing Research: A Magazine of Management and Applications,* American Marketing Association, 250 S. Wacker Dr., Ste. 200, Chicago, IL 60606, (312) 648-0536 (magazine source for how ideas are applied in business)
- *Marketing Tools Sourcebook,* American Demographics, P.O. Box 10580, Riverton, NJ 08076-0580, (800) 529-7502 (covers tools and services used by marketing research professionals)

Discussion Starter

Brainstorm Have students brainstorm five or six problems that need to be addressed in your school. By group consensus, choose the four most pressing problems.

Then divide students into four groups and assign one problem to each group. Have each group brainstorm types of primary and secondary data they would use in order to obtain information on the problem.

CAPTION ANSWER

Obtaining Secondary Data The data the business needs may already have been collected and may be available in free or low cost publications and reports.

Thinking Critically

Identify Ask students whether the following are examples of primary or secondary data:

- measuring three groups' responses to a new cereal packaging design *(primary data)*
- a U.S. government demographics report *(secondary data)*
- statistics from the SBA on the number of small business start-ups *(secondary data)*
- IBM's five-year sales figures *(secondary data)*
- marketing research conducted by Procter & Gamble for a new dishwashing liquid *(primary data)*
- a jewelry store's customer buying records *(secondary data)*
- census data from the State of Ohio *(secondary data)*
- an opinion research poll conducted by IBM for a new computer it plans to introduce two years from now *(primary data)*
- a table from the *Statistical Abstract of the United States* *(secondary data)*
- a personal interview conducted in a supermarket by a representative of a new ice cream manufacturer *(primary data)*
- a questionnaire sent to new home owners by their real estate agent's realty company *(primary data)*
- statistics from *Newsweek* on population growth in the Southwest *(secondary data)* and
- observing customers interacting with salespeople in the housewares department of a local department store *(primary data)*

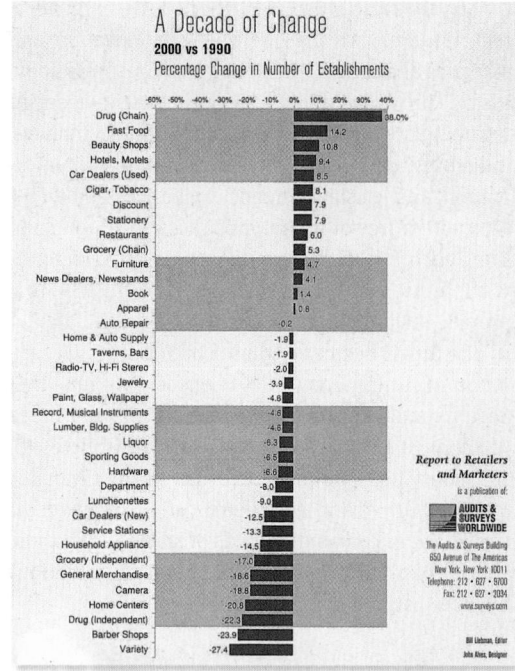

A Decade of Change
2000 vs 1990
Percentage Change in Number of Establishments

Report to Retailers and Marketers

■ **Call the Specialists** Syndicated service companies provide specialized data to other businesses. *Why would a company want to receive information about their competitors?*

ADVANTAGES OF SECONDARY DATA The greatest advantage of secondary data is that it can be obtained easily because the data are either on the Internet, in corporate, public, and college libraries, or for purchase from syndicated services. In addition, some types of secondary data, such as nationwide population figures, are available through the U.S. Bureau of the Census. Any firm trying to collect similar population data would have to spend a great deal of time and money.

DISADVANTAGES OF SECONDARY DATA There are two major disadvantages associated with secondary data. First, the existing data may not be suitable or available for the problem under study. This situation is most common for new and innovative products. In 1999, secondary data available from *PC Data* showed that Sony's original PlayStation platform had 29 percent of the video game market in the United States. When Sony developed the PlayStation2 video game console, however, no secondary data on this new category of "networked digital entertainment" was available.

526 Unit 9 ■ *Marketing Information Management*

The other disadvantage is that secondary data may sometimes be inaccurate. Federal census data are collected every ten years. As a result, projections based on the census most recently completed may not be correct for the current year.

Despite these limitations, a business should first try to find free or low-cost secondary data to avoid the cost and time of collecting primary data.

■ How Primary Data Are Obtained

When marketing researchers cannot find the information they need from secondary data, they collect primary data. Primary research data can be obtained through company research projects or commercial research organizations. Large companies frequently have their own marketing research staff to conduct primary research for the company. Smaller companies that don't have a research staff rely on commercial research organizations. National research organizations often provide attitude and opinion, market, media, and product research services under contract for other businesses and organizations. AC Nielsen, Arbitron, Market Facts, IMS Health, and Westat are some of the leading research organizations in the U.S. In addition, many advertising agencies have research departments that will conduct research for clients.

Primary data may be collected using three methods. These include the survey method, the observation method, and the experimental method.

THE SURVEY METHOD The survey method is a research technique in which information is gathered from people through the use of surveys or questionnaires. It is the most frequently used method of collecting primary data.

When designing a survey, marketers must determine the number of people to include in their survey. Researchers can survey the entire population if the target population is small. This is called a census. Usually, though, the target population is too large, and time and money are too limited to allow researchers to survey the entire population. In this case, researchers would use a sample of the entire target population to get survey results. A sample is a part of the target population that is assumed to represent the entire population. The size of the sample depends upon the amount of money the company has to spend and the degree of accuracy that is needed. Generally speaking, the larger the sample, the greater the accuracy of the results.

CAPTION ANSWER
Call the Specialists These syndicated service companies allow marketers to track a variety of data by product, product line, and market share for an industry. This data can be used for many purpose, including helping to measure a specific company's performance against industry averages.

Did You Know?
The *Marketing Research Project Workbook* provides a step-by-step approach for students to conduct their own marketing research studies. This textbook-workbook provides directions for reporting, analyzing, and presenting the findings of a marketing research study, complete with rationale for all decisions, and a report of the findings, conclusions, and recommendations.

After determining the size of the population to survey, you must decide what type of survey to conduct and create the data collection instrument. Surveys can be conducted in person, by phone, (personal and prerecorded), by mail (regular and e-mail), or by using Internet technologies. The decision on how to conduct the survey must be made before the questionnaire is created so that the questions can be written according to the specific needs of each survey type. You will learn more about how to create a survey questionnaire in Section 29.2.

The *personal interview* involves questioning people face-to-face. Since door-to-door interviews are expensive, researchers often conduct interviews in central locations, such as shopping malls and airports. Because this type of interview began in shopping malls, it is called a *mall intercept* interview.

A form of personal interview is the focus group interview. A *focus group interview* involves eight to twelve people who are brought together to evaluate advertising, a particular product, package design, or a specific marketing strategy under the direction of a skilled moderator.

The moderator must direct the discussion to accomplish the objectives of the study. He or she is also responsible for stimulating the group's thinking about the idea or concept. Focus group facilities usually include conference rooms, observation rooms, and audiotape and videotape equipment.

A major advantage of personal interviews is that it is often easier to get people to respond to personal interviews than to mail, phone, or Internet surveys. Interviewers are able to obtain more complete answers to the survey questions. A disadvantage, however, is the cost associated with personal interviews. Personal interviews are generally more expensive than mail, telephone, or Internet surveys because they require hiring experienced interviewers who are skilled at asking nonbiased questions and interpreting the answers correctly. Personal surveys are easy to administer, but it takes time to get survey responses tabulated for data analysis.

The telephone interview is quick, efficient, and relatively inexpensive. A disadvantage of telephone interviews, however, is that some people are unwilling to respond to questions over the telephone. People sometimes resist this approach to data collection because they do not know the caller, dislike responding to a prerecorded digital survey, resent the intrusion on their personal time, or question how their answers will be used.

■ **Mall Intercept Interviews** Mall intercept interviews involve questioning people face to face. *What are some advantages of personal interviews?*

A mail survey is a relatively inexpensive way to reach a potentially large audience. With a direct mail survey a business can use visual presentation techniques. Respondents are generally honest with their responses and find mail surveys to be less of a personal intrusion.

Unfortunately, the average return rate for mail surveys is only 10 percent. Techniques aimed at improving response rates include pre- and post-survey reminders encouraging people to respond to the survey. Average response rates can be improved for questionnaires by offering some type of incentive to complete them. In recent years, some researchers have found that including incentives with the questionnaire, such as discounts on future purchases or pre-paid minutes on a telephone card gets better results. Offering a copy of the results might encourage participation, especially if the survey is of professionals in a given area.

Research information can also be obtained through Internet technologies. *Internet survey* methods include wide-open polls, anybody-can-answer polls, invitation-only surveys, password protected research sites, and Internet-based panels. While

Cooperative Learning

Displays Divide the class into teams of 4–5 students to develop a list of questions for a survey on the impact of window displays. Appoint a presenter from each group to share the best question to ask of shoppers. Continue this process until every group has had an opportunity to share their responses.

CAPTION ANSWER
Mall Intercept Interviews The response rates are generally higher than with other forms of survey research. In addition, more complete answers can be obtained, and further questioning can occur for clarification of a respondent's answers.

Independent Practice

Research and Report Have students use library and other resources to research careers in marketing research. They should gather the following information:

(1) types of businesses that hire market researchers
(2) qualifications and training required for this job
(3) starting salary range
(4) projected job availability in this field over the next five to ten years
(5) what students can do now to prepare for a career in marketing research

Have students write reports between 250 to 500 words about careers in marketing research.

■ **Taking the Mystery Out of Customer Service** Mystery shopping is an observation technique that can improve customer service. *How can the results of a mystery shopping experience improve customer service?*

online research will never completely replace traditional survey methods, the Council of America Survey Research Organizations estimates that by 2005 online research will represent 30–50 percent of the research volume.

Computer-administered surveys are quick and eliminate data entry because the responses are automatically tabulated when the survey is completed. Internet-based research allows for real-time data collection, multiple-choice, and open-ended text-based answers. A drawback is that the use of Internet surveys is limited to individuals who have access to the Web.

THE OBSERVATION METHOD The observation method is a research technique in which the actions of people are watched and recorded either by cameras or observers. Properly performed and recorded observations supply better results than those from survey techniques.

Another use of observation called *mystery shopping* is used to view the interaction between customers and employees. A *mystery shopper* is a researcher who poses as a customer and goes into retail stores to observe employees. A manufacturer, for example, may want to know whether retail employees who sell its products are demonstrating

FIGURE 29-2

Rating Quality of Service

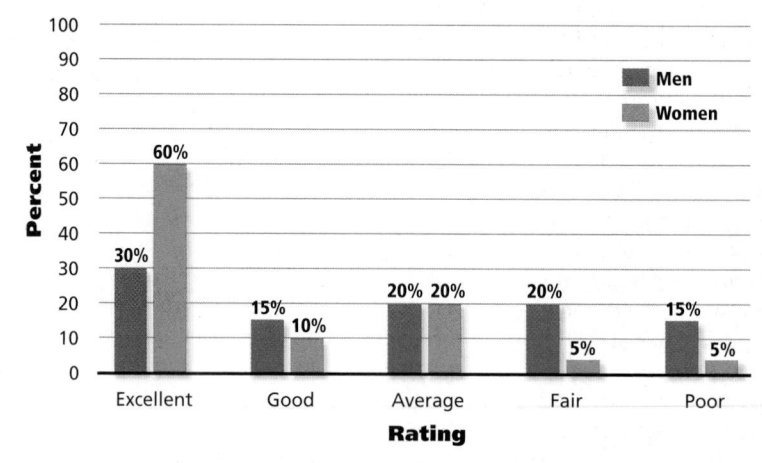

■ **Presenting the Research Results** Charts such as this one representing research results are typically included in a research report. *Why are charts often included?*

CAPTION ANSWER
Taking the Mystery Out of Customer Service A marketing researcher can share the data with a manufacturer or retailer to improve employee-training programs dealing with customer approach, sales presentation, product knowledge, and suggestion selling.

FIGURE 29-2 ANSWER
Presenting the Research Results Charts are typically included because they help to illustrate research results.

them properly and answering customers' questions correctly. The salespeople are observed on approach, sales presentation, product knowledge, and suggestion selling.

One disadvantage of the observation method is that it cannot measure attitudes or motivation. Observation provides information on what the person does, but not why the person does it. Since there is no direct interview of the individuals being observed, a researcher can only speculate on the motives behind the behavior. When knowledge of motivation is important to the business research, another research method may be more useful.

The observation technique may use either *contrived* or *natural* situations. The researcher sets up contrived observations. To decide which toys to market, a toy manufacturer may bring in a group of children to play with the toys. Observers note which toys the children choose and how long they play with them. This is often done using a one-way mirror through which observers can see the children, but the children cannot see the observers. The popular toys are the ones that get marketed. Contrived observations allow researchers to control a testing situation, but respondents may not make the same choices as they would in a real buying situation. Children faced with an entire store of toys might not choose the same toys as they would in the contrived observation.

In natural observation customers or employees are viewed as they would normally act in a given situation. An example of natural observation is when people or hidden cameras observe customers as they enter, shop, or leave a store. Another form of natural observation is the *traffic count*—a count of people or cars as they pass by a store. A traffic count might tabulate the number of people who pass without looking, look and then pass, or stop, look, and enter.

Observation research is faster than personal interviews because participants do not have to be screened by telephone or scheduled for a particular time. Usually people are unaware that they are being observed, which suggests that they are acting how they normally would in a given situation. This type of research can be cost-effective because businesses do not pay for postage or telephone costs, participant fees, or special interviewing facilities.

REAL WORLD MARKETING

Making Tweens Feel At Home

They say that home is where the heart is and furniture designers are stressing that the bedroom is where the heart is for tweens. Tweens—8-to-14 year olds—are one of the hottest consumer groups, and the latest trend is home furnishings. Traditionally adult furniture stores—such as IKEA, Ethan Allen, and Pottery Barn—have expanded their lines to include designer beds, rugs, and dressers that are guaranteed to provide sweet dreams. As more people have children later in life, there is more disposable income; this equals more money to spend on a place where kids like to hang—their rooms. Look out Martha Stewart!

Thinking Critically
How might research firms track the number of tweens in the U.S.?

Point-of-sale research is a powerful form of research that combines natural observation with personal interviews to get people to explain buying behavior. Point-of-sale researchers observe shoppers to decide which ones to choose as research subjects. Researchers may look for shoppers buying a specific type of product, product brand, or who inspect a product but do not buy it.

After observation, researchers approach the selected shoppers and ask them questions. Point-of-sale research combines observation with personal interviews, which offers many benefits to researchers. All participants in the research study are "qualified" respondents because they have been selected by observation. Participants can be chosen based on variables such as shopping time (morning, afternoon, or evening), product price, or any other variable that can be observed. Researchers can also get input from other family members or shopping companions. Participants can easily remember the reason why they purchased a product because the purchase has just been made.

Chapter 29 ■ *Conducting Marketing Research* **529**

Individualized Practice

Math Skills

Here are Kmart Corporation's sales figures for 1995–2000:

1995: $25,822,000

1996: $27,496,000

1997: $29,736,000

1998: $32,281,000

1999: $34,792,000

2000: $37,942,000

L1 What percentage of the highest sales figure is the lowest sales figure? *(68%. $25,822,000 ÷ $37,942,000 = 0.68)*

L2 By what percentage did the company increase its sales from 1997 to 1998? From 1998 to 1999? *(From 1997 to 1998, 8%. $32,281,000 – $29,736,000 = $2,545,000. $2,545,000 ÷ $32,281,000 = .078 or 8%. From 1999 to 1998, 7%. $34,792,000 – $32,281,000 = $2,511,000. $2,511,000 ÷ $34,792,000 = .072 or 7%)*

L3 Have students make a bar graph or a line graph of Kmart Corporation's sales statistics. What conclusions can they draw about Kmart's growth from 1995 to 2000? *(Kmart experienced steady growth with no decline in sales.)*

REAL WORLD MARKETING

Making Tweens Feel At Home
Answer Research firms use private and public records to arrive at statistics and can track the number of tweens in the U.S.

Reteaching

1. **Vocabulary** Assign and review the vocabulary terms for this section.
2. **Fact and Idea** Assign and review Fact and Idea Review questions 1–6 from the Chapter Assessment.
3. **Marketing Research Steps** Write each step in the marketing research process as a column heading on the board. Divide students into five groups and assign each group one of the five steps. Have each student write one fact on the board about his or her groups' marketing research step. Have the students in each group explain their respective step in the marketing research process.

THE EXPERIMENTAL METHOD The *experimental method* is a research technique in which a researcher observes the results of changing one or more marketing variables while keeping certain other variables constant under controlled conditions. The experimental approach is often used to test new package designs, media usage, and new promotions.

A candy company, for example, may want to compare the effectiveness of two different package color designs for its new candy bar. The company researcher will select two similar groups of consumers. The first group is shown a proposed package for the candy bar. The other group is shown an identical package containing the same product information, except the colors of the package have been changed. Each group's response is measured and the results are determined. The researcher had control over the test environment and only the color of the packaging changed, therefore if one package gets a better response, the company can attribute it to the color.

The experimental method is infrequently used for marketing research. One reason for this is the cost of setting up the research situation. In addition, people respond differently under controlled conditions in contrast to actual buying situations. This difference can make the research data collected less valuable. In situations where different approaches or ideas need to be compared, the experimental method offers an excellent source of information.

Step 3: Analyzing the Data

The third step in the marketing research process is data analysis. **Data analysis** is the process of compiling, analyzing, and interpreting the results of primary and secondary data collection.

Rupert's Autos surveyed customers about the quality of the dealership's repair service. The number of customers returning the survey was 120. Answers to questions were organized so that the percentage of men and women responding to each question could be shown clearly. Data were cross-tabulated to determine such things as how men and women differ in their perceptions of the service. The answers to a question about the quality of service might be presented as follows. The number of respondents is given in parentheses after the question to tell the reader how many people responded.

Changing Focus

Focus groups—informal discussion sessions of current or potential customers—help companies receive feedback on products and see how they stack up against competition. Now, they are even more effective with the help of technology. In the past, focus groups took place in specially designed boardrooms, with marketers gathered behind a one-way mirror to observe the progress. Today, these rooms are wired with video cameras and satellite networks that allow close-ups or full-group views of focus groups live to interested companies across the country. Online focus groups are becoming more popular, using e-mail to screen and qualify possible focus group candidates. The focus group then operates in an environment similar to an online chat, with all participants seeing all questions and responses. The companies have simplified their research procedures and participants still receive the customary $30–$50 payment sometimes without ever leaving their home!

Thinking Critically

What are some benefits of online chats for market researchers?

Question: *How would you rate the quality of service provided by Rupert's Autos? (N = 120)*

Rating	Men	Women
Excellent	30%	60%
Good	15%	10%
Average	20%	20%
Fair	20%	5%
Poor	15%	5%

As you can see in Figure 29-2 on page 528, female customers of Rupert's Autos generally have a more favorable impression of the quality of service than the male customers do. This information shows that the dealership's image among its male customers needs to be improved.

Changing Focus

Answer Speed, cost effectiveness, broad geographic scope, accessibility, and honesty could all be benefits to online chats for market researchers.

Case Study

It's a Hit!

All professional baseball teams have Web sites for ticket information, merchandise, and statistics. The new baseball stadiums in Detroit, Houston, and San Francisco have taken technology a step further.

Each new stadium is equipped with advanced fiber optic networks that handle data from voice and data links, concession stands, scoreboards, security cameras, sound systems, interactive kiosks, and video production centers. The data measures attendance, improves services, supports modern sound systems, monitors interactive services, and provides video displays on stadium scoreboards.

In return, owners gather information on fans through fan loyalty programs that provide incentives and rewards for attending games and buying food and merchandise. A condition for receiving fan loyalty cards is that fans must fill out a questionnaire.

Fans receive a card with a magnetic strip that stores personal information. This card is swiped each time the fan attends a game or purchases an item. Points are accumulated which can then be used for free or discounted tickets or team merchandise. Loyalty cards allow owners to capture information such as arrival times, gate access, and purchase habits of each fan. Even the turnstiles use bar code readers, which store information on attendance counts and traffic patterns for stadium entrances. The computer also can invalidate lost or stolen tickets and issue new tickets.

Case Study Review

1. Why is computerized data collection becoming a part of baseball?
2. How can baseball owners use bar coded ticket information to improve customer service?

A MATTER OF ETHICS

3. Is it ethical to ask for background information before issuing a fan loyalty card? Why or why not?

Step 4: Recommending Solutions to the Problem

Successful research results in information that helps businesses make decisions on how to solve a problem. The conclusions drawn from the research are usually presented in an organized and well-written report. Recommendations must be clear and well supported by the research data.

Let's use the example of the auto dealership. Looking at the table of percentages, the researcher would conclude that 55 percent of the male customers thought service was average or worse. The 55 percent is calculated by adding the percentages for average, fair, and poor. The percentage of women who answered that service was average or below was 30 percent. The conclusion to be drawn from these percentages is that service needs to be improved. A recommendation might be to provide additional training for repair staff or to develop a program to communicate better with customers about their repairs.

Enrichment

1. **Review** Assign and review the appropriate Thinking Critically questions from the Chapter Assessment.
2. **Extend** Assign and review the corresponding activities from *BusinessWeek Case Studies, Internet Resources,* and the *School-to-Work Activity Workbook.* ILP
3. **Invite Guest Speaker** Invite the marketing research director of a shopping mall, department store, or advertising agency to discuss recent marketing research studies conducted in their business or organization, data-gathering methods used, and solutions to marketing problems. You may also wish to have this person discuss careers in marketing research.
4. **Brainstorm** If you know any small business owners, see if one of them has a marketing research issue that the class could work on as a project. For example, perhaps the business would like to open a second branch, but does not know where the best new location would be; or, a new product line is being considered in a sporting goods store, and customer response is critical because a large cash outlay is necessary to bring the new line into the store. Have students work in teams to propose surveys, questionnaires, and other marketing research tools that the business could use to get a handle on the information needed to make a decision.

Case Study Review Answers

It's a Hit!

1. Technology simplifies the process of purchasing tickets, checking schedules, subscribing to mailing lists, and obtaining latest team news and information. Marketing to customers and tracking customer patterns can be more effective.

2. Owners can track attendance counts and traffic patterns, reassign ushers and concession workers, and order food items.

A MATTER OF ETHICS

3. Answers will vary. If fan loyalty programs are optional, most fans may be comfortable with them. Requiring personal information would pose ethical concerns.

Evaluation

Assign and review the Section 29.1 Assessment.

Technology Resources

 Assessment Resources
Go to the *Marketing Essentials* Web site (**www.marketing.glencoe.com**) for resources to teach and assess occupation-specific vocabulary.

CLOSE

Section Wrap-Up

Have students complete this statement: The most difficult and yet the most important step in the marketing research process is . . .
(defining the problem.)

A typical research report includes the following:
- Title page
- Acknowledgments to people who assisted in the research effort
- Table of contents
- Tables, figures, charts, and graphs
- Introduction (includes the problem under study, its importance, definitions, limitations of the study, and basic assumptions)
- Review of the research information (including the results of any secondary data reviewed for the research effort)
- Procedures used (research technique or techniques used to obtain primary data)
- Findings
- Recommendations
- Summary and conclusions
- Appendices
- Bibliography

Step 5: Applying the Results

Managers use the research report to make decisions about marketing strategies in relation to the researched problem or issue. In evaluating the research, managers may find that the research was inconclusive, additional research may be needed, or the research suggests specific courses of action.

The results are inconclusive if the data gathered by research does not help to solve the problem. Inconclusive results generally require more research. Sometimes the research also points out new areas of a problem that had not been anticipated. That situation may also call for additional research.

After the research has been completed and recommendations acted upon, a business should carefully monitor the results. A business needs to know whether the specific actions taken are successful. The research effort has been a success if decisions made as a result lead to increased profits through better sales, increased efficiency, or reduced expenses.

Marketing research is an ongoing process of problem solving. The results obtained through marketing research should become a part of the total information available to a business for making future decisions.

It is possible that management may choose to not use the findings of a research study. There might have been problems that made the results inconclusive. It may turn out the problem was misdefined from the beginning or it may have disappeared during the research. Sometimes the results and solutions are identified too late to be of any help. The follow-up process helps to determine when and how these problems occurred. It also identifies how research can be better planned in the future.

29.1 ASSESSMENT

Reviewing Key Terms and Concepts

1. What are the five steps in designing and conducting a research study?
2. Explain the difference between primary and secondary data.
3. Name the methods used most frequently to collect secondary data.
4. Name the methods used most frequently to collect primary data.
5. What is meant by the term data analysis?

Thinking Critically

6. Many retail stores ask customers to give their phone number or ZIP code after each sale. Do you support this type of data collection? Why or why not?

Integrating Academic Skills

7. **COMMUNICATION** Write a 100-word memo to your instructor explaining what method of marketing research should be conducted prior to the introduction of new merchandise for your school store. Provide the rationale for your method.

29.1 ASSESSMENT ANSWERS

Reviewing Key Terms and Concepts
1. problem definition, obtaining data, analyzing the data, recommending solutions to the problem, applying the results
2. Primary data are obtained for the first time for particular issues. Secondary data have already been collected, for other purpose(s).
3. Secondary data can be obtained internally or externally. External sources are Internet sources, government reports, information companies, business/trade publications.
4. survey, observation, and experimental methods
5. compiling, analyzing, and interpreting results of primary and secondary research.

Thinking Critically
6. Answers will vary.

Integrating Academic Skills
7. **COMMUNICATION** personal interviews

The Marketing Survey

Constructing the Questionnaire

Questionnaires should provide data with validity. **Validity** exists when the questions asked measure what was intended to be measured. A researcher designs a questionnaire to measure a restaurant's customer service. Questionnaires that feature poorly written questions or do not address customer service will not have validity.

Research questionnaires should also have reliability. **Reliability** exists when a research technique produces nearly identical results in repeated trials. Reliability requires that the questions ask the same type of information from all the respondents. Questions should be clear and easily understood so that all participants understand the question in the same way. Questions that are unclear and poorly written will not gain reliable responses. Asking a respondent in a restaurant survey, "Was your food hot?" would not yield a reliable answer. "Hot" could be interpreted as either the level of spiciness or food temperature.

To be valid and reliable, a questionnaire must be properly written, formatted, and administered. There are guidelines that can be followed to ensure that a questionnaire is effective.

■ Writing Questions

Survey questions can be either open ended or forced choice. **Open-ended questions** ask respondents to construct their own response to a question. "How can we serve you better?" is an example of an open-ended question. Some surveys have a space for "general comments" or "suggestions" on the survey instrument. This is also a type of open-ended question. Open-ended questions generate a wide variety of responses that are sometimes difficult to categorize and tabulate. As a result, most researchers prefer forced-choice questions.

Forced-choice questions ask respondents to choose answers from possibilities given on a questionnaire. Forced-choice questions are the simplest questions to write and the easiest to tabulate. They can be two-choice questions, multiple choice questions, rating or ranking scales, and level of agreement scales.

YES/NO QUESTIONS Two-choice questions give the respondent only two options, usually yes or no. Yes/No questions should be used only when asking for a response on one issue. You could use a Yes/No question to ask "Was our facility clean?" but not to ask "Was our facility clean and well-maintained?" The customer may have conflicting answers for the two issues that the question addresses. This would decrease validity and reliability.

● What You'll Learn

- How to construct a survey
- The ways that technology is used in marketing research

● Why It's Important

Businesses need valid and reliable data to make good decisions. Marketing researchers need to know how to construct survey instruments that provide the necessary information to assist in the decision-making process.

● Key Terms

- validity
- reliability
- open-ended questions
- forced-choice questions

FOCUS

Bell Ringer Activity

Brainstorm Have students brainstorm a list of three problems for which a business might use marketing research. Write each problem as a column heading on the board. Have each student choose one of the three problems and write three questions that could be asked about it on a research questionnaire.

Introducing the Section

The Marketing Survey Solicit students' answers from the Bell Ringer Activity. Write their questions under the appropriate headings. Ask students to identify the various types of questions they generated, categorizing each question on the board list as open-ended or forced-choice question. Have students discuss the value and the disadvantages of each type of question.

In this section students will look at how to construct, format, and administer a marketing research questionnaire, including how to write good questions. They will also look at how the computer is used in research.

Chapter 29 ■ *Conducting Marketing Research* **533**

Classroom Resources

For the Teacher
- Teacher Editions for all workbooks
- Assessment Package
- PowerPoint Presentation Software
- Interactive Lesson Planner
- **ILP** Block Scheduling, p. 29
- **ILP** Lesson Plans, p. 62
- **ILP** Internet Resources, p. 77

- **ILP** Blackline Masters, p. 63
- **ILP** *BusinessWeek* Case Studies, p. 181
- **ILP** Marketing Career Portfolio, p. 39
- *Marketing Essentials* Web site (**www.marketing.glencoe.com**)

For the Student
- Student Activity Workbook, p. 251
- Marketing Math Workbook, p. 95

- Marketing Research Project Workbook, p. 151
- **ILP** School-to-Work Activity Workbook, p. 121
- Virtual Business simulation
- *Marketing Essentials* Web site (**www.marketing.glencoe.com**)

ILP These resources are available in print and on the Interactive Lesson Planner (ILP)

The following is an example of a Yes/No questionnaire that a bakery and restaurant might administer to customers.

Please answer Yes or No to the following questions:

Did you receive a pleasant greeting upon entering?	Yes	No
Was our facility clean?	Yes	No
Was your server courteous?	Yes	No
Was your menu selection prepared to your liking?	Yes	No
Other comments or suggestions _____		

Yes/No questions are most often used as filter questions. Filter questions help to guide respondents to answer only those questions that apply. Question #5 on the Ford Automobile Ownership Survey in Figure 29-3 serves as a filtering question.

Have you for any reason taken your vehicle to have it serviced (maintenance or repair) during the last year?

Yes   No—Go to question 15

Respondents who answer *No* may skip to other survey questions. While respondents who answer *Yes* are asked a series of questions following

Question #5 related to the quality of repair services that they did receive at the car dealership. In cases where there is a range of choices and yes/no questions are not appropriate, you would use multiple choice questions, rating scale questions, or level of agreement questions.

MULTIPLE CHOICE QUESTIONS Multiple choice questions give the respondent several choices. When constructing multiple choice questions, it is important that the options are made comprehensive enough to include every possible response. Multiple choice options must be mutually exclusive and all encompassing. In order to be sure that all options are covered, many surveys have a space for the option "other."

An outdoor clothing manufacturer might ask its customers the following question.

What is your primary intended use of this product? (check only one)
- ☐ **A.** Backpacking/Mountaineering
- ☐ **B.** Camping/Hiking
- ☐ **C.** Fishing
- ☐ **D.** Hunting
- ☐ **E.** Other_____

FIGURE 29-3

Ford Automobile Ownership Survey

Please tell us about your most recent service visit.

ABOUT YOUR SERVICE EXPERIENCE

5 Have you for any reason taken your vehicle to have it serviced (maintenance or repair) during the past year?
☐ Yes   ☐ No → *Go to 15*

a. For the **most recent service**, what kind of work was done? Mark all that apply.
☐ Routine maintenance (e.g., oil change, lube, tune-up)   ☐ Recall work
☐ Body work (e.g., collision repairs, paint)   ☐ Other repairs
☐ Engine, transmission or axle repairs

b. Where did you go for your **most recent service visit?** Mark one box.
☐ Grand Ledge Ford, Inc. → *Go to 6*
☐ Another Ford/Lincoln–Mercury Dealer
☐ Independent garage/mechanic   ☐ Some other place (e.g., Goodyear, Sears, Midas, Jiffy Lube)

c. If you did not return to your selling dealer for this most recent service visit, please tell us why. Mark all that apply.
☐ Dealer location   ☐ Quality of prior service   ☐ Other_____
☐ Convenience   ☐ Price   _____
☐ Treatment by service personnel   ☐ Parts not available   _____

0017780   *(Please Go To Next Page)*

■ **Importance of Yes/No Questions** Yes/No questions are known as forced-choice questions because there are only two choices. *How can Yes/No questions be used as filtering questions?*

534   Unit 9 ■ *Marketing Information Management*

FIGURE 29-3 ANSWER
Importance of Yes/No Questions Yes/No questions can direct respondents to go to or skip a question or questions that don't apply. This can shorten the survey process and helps to individualize the surveying process.

Offering the choice of "other" increases reliability. Respondents who purchased the product for another reason may choose not to answer at all or may choose to pick an inaccurate answer from the list just to give an answer if "other" was not provided. This would cause misleading results.

RATING SCALE QUESTIONS Other forced-choice questions may ask respondents to rate a product based on a scale (see Figure 29-4). A variety of scales may be used, such as a rating scale from *very satisfied* to *very dissatisfied*, or from *excellent* to *poor*. The following is an example of a rating question that might be used by a hotel.

FIGURE 29-4

Holiday Inn Customer Service Survey

■ **Rating Scales** Some forced-choice questions have respondents reply with a rating scale. *Why do businesses often use rating scales to measure customer satisfaction?*

Please rate the following:

Reservations	Excellent	Good	Average	Fair	Poor
Concierge Services	Excellent	Good	Average	Fair	Poor
Check-In Process	Excellent	Good	Average	Fair	Poor
Message Service	Excellent	Good	Average	Fair	Poor
Parking	Excellent	Good	Average	Fair	Poor

LEVEL OF AGREEMENT QUESTIONS When assessing attitudes or opinions, it is often a good idea to write statements that reflect those attitudes or opinions. Then you can ask respondents for their level of agreement with the statements. Commonly used options include *strongly agree* (SA), *agree* (A), *neutral* (N), *disagree* (D), and *strongly disagree* (SD). The following are examples of statements that might be used in a health-related questionnaire.

Indicate your level of agreement with the following statements based on your personal preference:

"I am extremely health conscious."

    SA   A   N   D   SD

"I do not like vegetables."

    SA   A   N   D   SD

"Eating low cholesterol foods is important to me."

    SA   A   N   D   SD

"The cafeteria should serve heart-healthy foods."

    SA   A   N   D   SD

As you can see, if someone had to answer Yes or No to these questions, the researcher may not get an accurate picture. That is why it is often easier to use statements for research on attitudes and opinions.

■ Basic Guidelines for Writing Questions

When writing the specific questions you should follow some basic guidelines. Each question should be written clearly and as briefly as possible. Use the same ranking or rating scales for all similar questions. It is important not to ask leading questions, which suggest a correct answer. An example of a leading question is: "Do you prefer X or the more reasonably priced Z?" The phrase "more reasonably priced" could cause respondents to answer Z.

Discussion Starter

Discuss Have students discuss the types of questionnaires they have seen and/or filled out. Ask the students: What was the general nature of the questions? What problems do they think were being researched? (You might bring to class several surveys, duplicating them, and asking students to determine the types of problems being researched.)

Cooperative Learning

Write Have half the class develop a questionnaire that Patty Morris of Patty Cakes (in the 29.1 Bell Ringer Activity) could send to her target market. Have the other half of the class develop a questionnaire that Patty Morris could send to people outside her target market area.

Independent Practice

1. **Write and Wordprocess** Have students use a word processing program to create a two-page questionnaire, and ask them to specifically focus on page format. (They can input a questionnaire developed for one of the activities in this section.)
2. **Research and List** Have students research companies that provide online marketing research. Ask them to prepare a list of five companies with addresses for companies that perform this type of research.

FIGURE 29-4 ANSWER
Rating Scales Rating scales measure the degree of satisfaction with products and services. Rating scales are more objective than using a simple number scale or ranking scale from one to five.

Reteaching

1. **Vocabulary** Assign and review the vocabulary terms for this section.
2. **Fact and Idea** Assign and review Fact and Idea Review questions 7–10 from the Chapter Assessment.
3. **Marketing Research Problems** Identify one marketing research problem in your community, or have students identify a research problem for a local business. Write the problem on the board and have the class generate survey questions for this problem. Make sure students generate samples of each type of question discussed in this section.

FIGURE 29-5 ANSWER
Identifying the Purpose of a Survey This information details the purpose of the research and explains how the results will be used to improve the operation of the business.

FIGURE 29-5

Century 21 Quality Service Survey

■ **Identifying the Purpose of a Survey** The purpose of a survey should be identified on the survey itself or in a cover letter mailed with the survey. *Why is this information important?*

You should avoid any *bias*, which is a systematic error introduced by encouraging one outcome or answer over the others. It is also important to avoid questions that might cause a respondent to guess at the meaning of your question. The following is an example of a question that might cause a respondent to guess:

"How many students in your high school drink coffee on a daily basis?"

☐ Less than 10
☐ 10–49
☐ 50–99
☐ 100–149
☐ 150–199
☐ over 200

Without asking every student, the respondent can't answer the question without guessing.

When a survey questionnaire is finished, it is a good idea to pretest the wording of the questions. This pretest allows for correction of any misleading questions, directions, or problems on the questionnaire.

536 Unit 9 ■ *Marketing Information Management*

■ Formatting

Questionnaires must have excellent visual appearance and design to appeal to respondents. You should use dark ink (usually black) on light paper and type that is easy to read. Shading sections for contrast and using arrows to lead the reader through the questionnaire are other ways to improve the visual look of the questionnaire.

Section headings or numbers should be placed on all individual survey sections. In addition, numbers should be placed on all individual questions. Respondents are more likely to respond to all sections and questions if they are identified and numbered. Numbered questions are also easier to tabulate. When your questionnaire requires more than one page, place a message at the bottom of each page to continue to the next page.

Directions for completing the questionnaire must be clear for each section or group of questions. Do not assume that respondents will know how you want them to complete the questionnaire.

THE DECA CONNECTION — COMPETITIVE EVENTS AND MARKETING ESSENTIALS

Creative Marketing Project DECA's Creative Marketing Project competitive event is a great tie-in for this chapter. The Creative Marketing Project is part of the Chapter Team Events and encourages participation by all or most of your chapter members. The marketing research your students will conduct as part of this event should be designed to benefit your community or a large segment of your community. This is a great way for your students to observe local marketing. To help your students conduct their marketing research, use the *Marketing Essentials Marketing Research Project Workbook*. This textbook-workbook offers a detailed step-by-step procedure for students to plan, conduct, and report on their own marketing research project.

General demographic questions about gender, age, ethnic background, education are typically grouped together at the end of a questionnaire. This is because respondents are more likely to answer personal questions after completing the other questions. Some people may take offense to personal questions when they are placed at the beginning of the questionnaire. They may choose not to take part in the survey. The only time such information is placed at the beginning of a questionnaire is to qualify a respondent. Here is an example: "Are you between the ages of 20 and 30?" If yes, the interviewer would administer the survey. If no, then the person would not be included in the study.

To increase the response rate the survey should have a variety of question types. It may have a mix of 25 percent yes and no questions, 25 percent agree/disagree items, and 50 percent scaled-response questions.

■ Administering the Questionnaire

All surveys should have deadlines for completion. A mailed questionnaire should be sent first-class with a hand-signed cover letter (attached or part of the survey) and personalized if the potential respondent is known. Figure 29-5 is an example of a survey with a clearly identified purpose. The cover letter should explain the purpose of the survey and give the deadline for returning the questionnaire. A postage-paid return envelope should be included with the questionnaire for the respondent's convenience.

Questionnaires that are not mailed should have a brief explanation of the survey's purpose placed on the questionnaire itself. When conducting personal interviews, the actual selection of the participants for the study is an important issue. It is important that the selection process is unbiased, so a plan should be established for selecting participants. The plan could be as simple as interviewing every third person to exit a store, regardless of age, gender, or appearance. Personal interviews provide a degree of flexibility in collecting data. In a personal interview, probing questions can be asked and reactions to visual materials such as ads or actual product samples can be collected.

To conduct an interview, dress in a businesslike manner and carry a clipboard to hold your questionnaires. Be sure to approach people politely and don't take offense if some individuals don't wish to participate. You may want to hire a marketing research firm, which will have trained professional interviewers on staff.

BRIGHT IDEAS

From Junk Mail to Direct Mail Success

Junk mail received its name aptly—most people throw it out immediately after taking it out of their mailboxes. With the help of mathematician Yuri Galperin this may become a thing of the past for direct-mail marketing companies! This Russian mathematician has used his math skills to create software that tells direct-mail marketers the best avenue to take when marketing new products. His company—MarketSwitch—uses a company's market research on buying patterns and demographics to determine how to best target direct mail campaigns. Why can't these mathematical problems be solved with pen and paper? A large customer database can create ten million different variables to be accounted for. Galperin, with the help of his math expertise, has scaled this down to create manageable equations that produce fast results.

Thinking Creatively
Galperin has merged his math skills to apply to marketing. What other academic areas are useful in marketing? Why?

Chapter 29 ■ *Conducting Marketing Research* **537**

BRIGHT IDEAS — From Junk Mail to Direct Mail Success
Answer Answers may include sociology or psychology skills to understand people's buying habits, English/writing skills to create creative ad campaigns, and foreign languages to expand your market.

Technology Resources

GO TO **Assessment Resources**
Go to the *Marketing Essentials* Web site (**www.marketing.glencoe. com**) for resources to teach and assess occupation-specific vocabulary.

VIRTUAL BUSINESS

GO TO **Market Research**
Introduce marketing research to students using Knowledge Matters' Virtual Business visual simulation, "Market Research." Go to the *Marketing Essentials* Web site (**www.marketing.glencoe.com**) to download the Virtual Business "Market Research" classroom activity designed for the *Marketing Essentials* program. In this simulation, students discover how to use surveys to learn about their potential customers and their competitors. If needed, have students run the Virtual Business tutorial before beginning this activity.

CLOSE

Section Wrap-Up

Have students complete this statement: Research questionnaires should have two key things: *(validity and reliability.)*

Vacation Time

Answer Some countries require long vacations because it is assumed that well-rested and happy workers work better.

538

The Impact of Computer Technologies on Marketing Research

Computer technologies have had a tremendous impact on marketing research. Software programs allow researchers to analyze huge amounts of information. They also allow researchers to find secondary data in computer databases, prepare surveys, and generate lists of potential questionnaire respondents.

Information can be stored, sorted, and used to improve processes in the future. Computerized databases are a source of *data collection* for researchers. Computer programs are available that analyze the information collected, such as competitive, demographic, site, and location data. Finally, specialized software programs can assist with *forecasting*. These programs analyze current market data and use this information to predict future sales.

Survey research can now be conducted through online surveys and focus group chat sessions on the Internet. *Fax broadcasting* allows businesses to send questionnaires to a select group of fax numbers. *Automated dialers* increase the number of telephone survey responses by placing multiple calls and automatically rejecting those with busy signals and answering machines. *Digital surveys* allow a prerecorded voice to qualify a respondent and then ask

a series of survey questions. *Interactive voice response* is similar to voicemail as callers are greeted by a recorded voice that leads them through a series of questions. Responses can be given using the telephone keypad.

Vacation Time

While working with companies abroad, you may be pleasantly surprised to see how seriously most other nations take vacation. Vacation time is often referred to as a benefit in the United States and the average allotted time is two weeks. In most European countries, six weeks is the average! In Germany, even those who are unemployed have the right to three weeks of paid vacation. And this is a right that can't be taken away—or replaced with payment—as it falls under labor laws.

Thinking Critically

Why would labor laws require up to six weeks of vacation for employees?

29.2 ASSESSMENT

Reviewing Key Terms and Concepts

1. Why should questionnaires provide data that have validity?

2. Why should research questionnaires have reliability?

3. What are three steps that must be taken to construct a valid and reliable questionnaire?

4. What are some methods of administering a questionnaire?

5. Name six research activities that computers can help researchers perform.

Thinking Critically

6. Can business risks be eliminated by marketing research? Why or why not?

Integrating Academic Skills

7. **MATH** Research indicates that 80 percent of the customers for a pizza store live within one mile of the store, another 15 percent live within two miles of the store, and the remaining five percent live within five miles of the store. Compute the number of customers who live within the various trading areas if the population of the area is 12,540.

29.2 ASSESSMENT ANSWERS

Reviewing Key Terms and Concepts
1. Validity means that the survey will measure what it was designed to measure.
2. Reliability insures that the same type of information is collected from each respondent.
3. properly written, formatted, and administered
4. personal interview, mail, electronically, phone
5. data collection, data analysis, forecasting, interviewing, survey research, media research

Thinking Critically
6. No. Some products and services fail.

Integrating Academic Skills
7. **MATH** 10,032 (12,540 x .80 = 10,032) within one mile; 1,881 (12,540 x .15 = 1,881) between one–two miles; 627 (12,540 x .05 = 627) within five miles; 11,913 (10,032 + 1,881 = 11,913) within two miles

Careers in Marketing

MARKETING RESEARCH

Robert W. Cuzner
Research Director
Digital Research, Inc.

What does your job entail?

"Digital Research, Inc. (DRI) is a full-service research firm. As research director, I am responsible for assuring that all clients are satisfied with our services. This involves direct client contact through every stage of the research process. My job includes defining research objectives, recommending the appropriate methodology (telephone, mail, in-person, online), designing the questionnaire, analyzing data, and reporting results. On other projects, I may supervise, train, and mentor the project managers. DRI's areas of specialization are e-commerce, publishing, and tourism."

Why do you like working as a Research Director?

"I enjoy working as a research director because every day offers new and interesting challenges. The process of designing questionnaires and interpreting the results is creative and fulfilling. There are a variety of problems that occur that need to be solved, such as finding eligible survey respondents. One of DRI's major studies is the annual 'Toy of the Year' program for *FamilyFun* magazine. Children test new toys which helps DRI know in advance what each year's hot sellers will be."

How did you get into marketing research?

"I was intrigued by a marketing research course that I took in college. Upon graduation, I sought an entry-level position in research and began doing store location research for a supermarket chain, later moving into consumer research. I then worked for a publishing company where I created a research department and conducted studies for media. After 17 years in that position, I went into consulting."

What is your key to success?

"The key to success is the ability to communicate effectively, not only with the client, but also with the internal staff assigned to work on the project. This includes defining research objectives, reporting survey results clearly, and providing insightful conclusions based on the research."

Thinking Critically

What aspect of this career do you find most appealing?

Career Facts

Education and Training: A college degree in business, marketing, or communications is required, and a master's degree in one of these fields is highly recommended. A minimum of eight years of marketing experience with an emphasis in research and research design is necessary.

Aptitudes, Abilities, and Skills: Excellent communication skills and outstanding analytical and decision-making skills are necessary in this career.

Career Outlook: Employment opportunities are expected to grow through the year 2008.

Career Path: Many directors of research begin their careers as interviewers, research assistants, or junior analysts. They may move up to senior analysts before attaining the position of director.

Chapter 29 ■ *Conducting Marketing Research* **539**

Vocabulary Review

Paragraphs will vary. See Glossary for definitions.

Fact and Idea Review

1. Secondary data are readily available at little or no cost.
2. Advantages of using secondary data are that they can be obtained quickly and are less expensive. Disadvantages include that the data may be unsuitable, out-of-date, or unavailable.
3. It is a research technique in which information is gathered from people directly through the use of questionnaires. Surveys can be conducted by mail, telephone, Internet, or by personal interview.
4. In a natural observation, customers or employees are viewed as they would normally act in a given situation. The situation is not natural in a contrived observation where observers pose as customers.
5. Survey research involves asking people directly, while the observation method involves observing people in certain situations.
6. title page, acknowledgments, table of contents, lists of illustrations, introduction, review of the literature, procedures used to obtain primary data, findings, recommendations, summary and conclusions, appendices, and bibliography
7. Validity exists when the questions that are asked actually measure what was intended to be measured.
8. Open-ended questions ask respondents to construct their own response to a question. Forced-choice questions ask respondents to choose answers from listed possibilities.
9. It increases reliability. Someone might not find their ideal choice and need to choose "other" or answer inaccurately.

Thinking Critically

1. Answers should reflect a combination of primary and secondary data.
2. Answers will vary. Some students will feel that this is an invasion of privacy. Others may feel that the customer or employee is in public so there is no invasion of privacy.
3. Data collection with telephones is quicker and relatively inexpensive. Automated calling equipment has contributed to reduced expenses for telephone surveys. There has

540

Chapter 29 ASSESSMENT

VOCABULARY REVIEW

Write three paragraphs on conducting marketing research using these vocabulary terms.

- problem definition
- primary data
- secondary data
- survey method
- sample
- observation method
- point-of-sale research
- experimental method
- data analysis
- open-ended questions
- forced-choice questions

FACT AND IDEA REVIEW

1. Why should secondary data be used first when trying to solve marketing research problems? (29.1)
2. What are two advantages and disadvantages of using secondary data? (29.1)
3. What is the survey method of research? Describe four ways to conduct surveys. (29.1)
4. What is the difference between a natural and contrived observation? (29.1)
5. How does survey research differ from observation research? (29.1)
6. Identify the elements in a final marketing research report. (29.1)
7. What is validity? (29.2)
8. What is the difference between an open-ended question and a forced-choice question? (29.2)
9. Why is the answer choice "other" important in multiple choice questions? (29.2)

THINKING CRITICALLY

1. What sources of information would you use to identify the market for a new automated car wash in your community?
2. Under natural observation, customers or employees do not know they are being observed. Do you think that this research technique is an invasion of privacy? Why or why not?
3. Compared to mail surveys, why have telephone surveys become so popular?
4. Why is Internet survey research increasingly important?
5. A small business owner wants to conduct a focus group interview, but is unwilling to pay several thousand dollars to an outside company to conduct one. What could the owner do to reduce costs, but still conduct the focus group?

BUILDING WORKPLACE SKILLS

1. **Human Relations** You work for the manager of a marketing research department. You and five other employees conduct a number of surveys by telephone. Getting people to respond to questions over the telephone is increasingly difficult. The manager has asked each of you to provide suggestions for how the response rates to telephone surveys could be improved. What suggestions would you make?

2. **Social Studies** Review your local newspaper or a weekly magazine for an article dealing with an opinion poll on a local, state, or national issue or election campaign. Write a 100-word summary of when and how the poll was conducted, and what the results indicated.

---

been a growing customer aversion to print surveys. Lastly, mail surveys lack the interactive element of telephone research.

4. Internet research is cheaper, faster, and easier than surveys done in person, by mail, or over the telephone, and many U.S. households now have access to the Internet.
5. To reduce costs but still conduct a focus group, the small business could write its script, let someone from the business serve as moderator, use its own conference rooms, and do its own data analysis.

Building Workplace Skills

1. Responses will vary.
2. Summaries will differ based upon the type of opinion poll investigated.

Applying Marketing Concepts

1. Answers will vary based upon specialty and the state where the students are located.
2. Answers will vary.

APPLYING MARKETING CONCEPTS

1. **Finding a Marketing Research Firm** Locate the Web page of *Quirk's Marketing Researcher Sourcebook*. Search for a marketing research firm in your state. Search by research specialty area and identify one firm in your state that performs the specialty research. Make a print-out of the company's home page to share with your class.

2. **Researching Market Information** Choose a business to research. Use a word processing program to prepare a report on at least two secondary data sources for each of the following items: size of the business's market, characteristics of its customers, income of its customers, present sales volume of its competitors, and information about trends in its industry.

3. **Analyzing Census Data** Locate the U.S. Census Bureau's Web site. Find the following information about your community: population, number of restaurants, retail stores, and gas stations; and the total sales for each number of households, average family size, average income, estimated average age of the population, and average education level. Use the research information you found to prepare a 200-word report on what new type of business might be successful in your community, including how the research supports your recommendation.

LINKING SCHOOL TO WORK

Basic and Information Skills Research a company in your community or where you are currently employed to find out how it collects demographic information about its customers. Write a 250-word report on how customer information (name, address, phone, occupation, age, etc.) is collected and used.

THE DECA CONNECTION

Role Play: Marketing Research Consultant

Situation You are to assume the role of a marketing research consultant. The owner (judge) of a small floral shop has asked you to identify whether the shop should add a large assortment of greeting cards. The owner knows very little about marketing research.

Activity You must explain the steps used in marketing research and recommend a research method to determine the feasibility of adding greeting cards.

Evaluation You will be evaluated on how well you meet the following performance indicators:
- Identify information monitored for marketing decision making
- Describe sources of secondary data
- Describe the need for marketing information
- Explain the nature of marketing research in a marketing-information management system
- Collect marketing information from others

interNET CONNECTION

Secondary Data Online
Locate the U. S. Census Bureau's Web site to obtain secondary data about business activity in your county.

Connect
- Locate the *County Business Patterns Economic Profile* for your county.
- Identify the total number of employees in your county and the annual payroll (in $1,000) in your county.
- Find the total estimated employment by size of business and locate the industry area in your county that employs the most people.

THE DECA CONNECTION

Students should be evaluated on the performance indicators noted in the Role Play.
- For another DECA Role Play, go to the *Student Activity Workbook*, p. 251.
- For more in-depth Role Play practice, refer to DECA's *Essential Competitive Events Handbook*. To order, contact DECA at **www.deca.org**.

interNET CONNECTION
Answers will vary depending on the county.

Mini Quiz
Administer the Mini Quiz orally. For an expanded chapter quiz, go to page 171 of the *Reproducible Tests* book.

1. The most difficult step in the marketing research process is problem definition.
2. When conducting marketing research on a problem or issue, a business should always try to find secondary data first.
3. Specialized research companies that provide secondary data for businesses are known as syndicated services.
4. The most popular method of collecting primary data is the survey method.
5. A part of the population that is assumed to represent a part of the population is called a(n) sample.

---

3. Information will depend on the community that the students live in. Types of businesses will depend on the results of students' research.

Linking School to Work
Answers depend on the work situation.

 GO TO
1. **Assessment** Have students complete the Reproducible Tests for Chapter 29 and Unit 9 or construct your own tests using the ExamView software.
2. **Enrichment** Have students complete the corresponding activities in the following workbooks:
   - *Marketing Math Workbook*, p. 95
   - *Marketing Research Project Workbook*, p. 151

Unit Lab Overview

In this Zazz Lab, students will use their knowledge of marketing information management and marketing research to conduct a marketing research study to assess the viability of a new Minor League Baseball franchise.

Bell Ringer Activity

Explain Ask students: As a spectator, what do you like most and least about baseball? *(Answers will vary from not liking baseball at all to positive responses, such as going to the stadium, following the statistics of a favorite player or team, home runs, great plays, stadium hot dogs and other refreshments.)*

Discussion Starter

Ask students: Would a Minor League Baseball team take fans away from a nearby Major League team? Why or why not? *(Answers will vary. Most will recognize that Minor League teams are not targeting the same audiences. Also, they may be affiliated with Major League teams.)*

Thinking Critically

1. **Competition** Ask students: What forms of family entertainment are in competition with Minor League Baseball franchises? *(Answers may include: miniature golf, movies, bowling, or another inexpensive form of family outing, like going to the beach.)*

2. **Features** Ask students: What amenities would you like to see in a new baseball stadium? *(Answers will vary but may include food service, good seating, and a domed stadium.)*

542

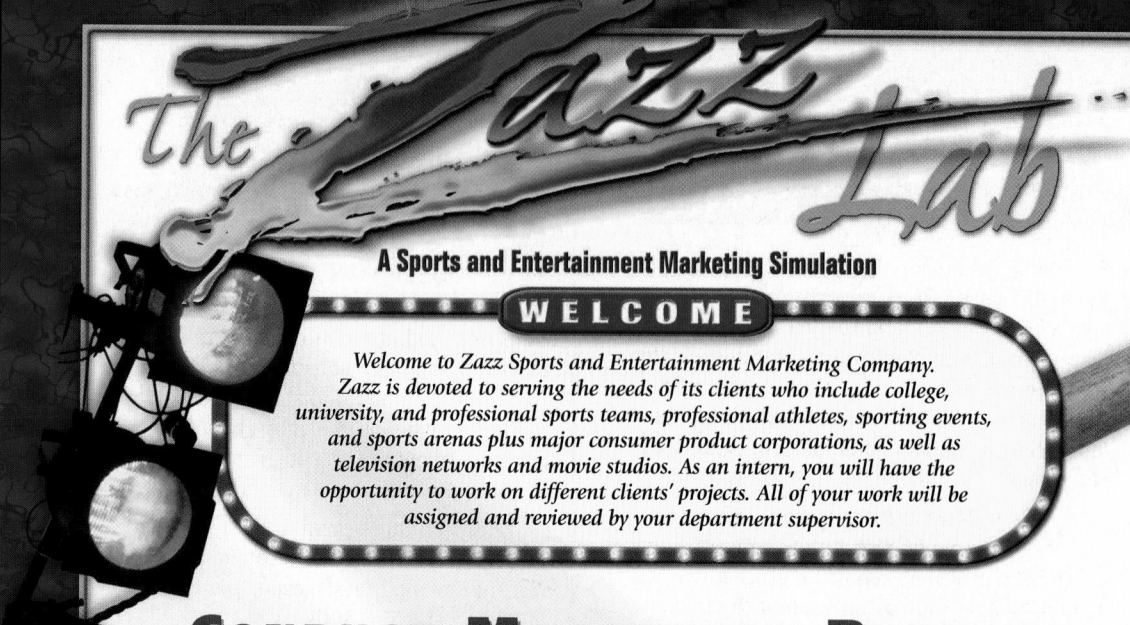

The Zazz Lab

A Sports and Entertainment Marketing Simulation

WELCOME

Welcome to Zazz Sports and Entertainment Marketing Company. Zazz is devoted to serving the needs of its clients who include college, university, and professional sports teams, professional athletes, sporting events, and sports arenas plus major consumer product corporations, as well as television networks and movie studios. As an intern, you will have the opportunity to work on different clients' projects. All of your work will be assigned and reviewed by your department supervisor.

CONDUCT MARKETING RESEARCH FOR A NEW MINOR LEAGUE BASEBALL FRANCHISE

SITUATION

A current Zazz client would like to build a Minor League Baseball team and stadium in your community. Our client wants to assess community support, potential target market(s) needs and wants, and how to promote this new source of entertainment.

ASSIGNMENT

Your supervisor wants you to design and administer a marketing research study regarding the creation of a Minor League Baseball team and stadium. You need to address the 4 *P*s of the marketing mix for the new team by conducting primary and secondary research. *Product* decisions may include the name of the new team, stadium design and facilities, and amenities for families and corporate audiences. *Promotional* strategies may include special events, special corporate promotions, advertising media, trade character, and Web site. *Place* decisions would include how tickets are sold. *Price* strategies for tickets, food, and merchandise would also be important. Establish the methodology for the primary research and indicate how the survey should be conducted. Explain how you will ensure a valid and reliable study. Create a questionnaire that includes one open-ended question and a variety of forced-choice questions. Prepare a table to show that your questionnaire items correlate with the objectives of the study. Develop a customer profile of who is likely to use the facility.

Tools and Resources

To complete this assignment, you will need to conduct research at a library or on the Internet. You will also need a word processing program, a spreadsheet program, and computer presentation software. Other resources include local newspapers, real estate agencies, and your local Chamber of Commerce.

Research

Study the demographics and psychographics of the community to determine potential attendance. Demographic information should include population, average household income, household size, number of families with children under 21 years old, level of education, and types of occupations. Research the marketing mix of Minor League Baseball franchises to determine what has made them successful.

THE BALLPARK BOOM

With attendance at Minor League Baseball games doubling since the early 1980s, Minor League stadiums have proliferated. Close to 100 new stadiums have been built. Costs to construct the more recent stadiums have ranged from $19 million for HarborYard in Bridgeport, Connecticut, to as much as $30 million for Riverfront Stadium in Newark, New Jersey. Complete with luxury boxes, these stadiums boast all the amenities of the majors without the price tag. The best seats average $8 per ticket. Affordability combined with the chance to be close to the players and action are sure to bring the Minor League a long winning streak!

Report

Prepare a written report and a computer presentation. Use a word processing program to prepare a double-spaced report. Use a spreadsheet program to create tables illustrating your research findings. Arrange your written report around the following headings:

- Background information
  - Target population demographics and psychographics
  - Minor League Baseball franchises
  - Significant trends
- Primary research design
  - Selected method and rationale
  - Questionnaire design
    - Correlation with objectives of the study
    - Measures taken to prevent instrumental bias
    - Sample questionnaire
  - Administration of the questionnaire
    - Sample vs. census
    - Measures taken to prevent sample bias
- Study's findings and conclusions
  - Customer profile
  - Product
    - Stadium design and amenities
    - Baseball franchise
  - Price
  - Place
  - Promotion
- Recommendations and plan for implementation

Using computer presentation software and other visual aids (sample promotional materials, team name and logo, etc.), prepare a presentation of your ideas for the client that includes:

- Key topics covered in your written report
- Graphic illustrations that are relevant to each slide's topic
- Very little text
- Minimum of 10 slides

Presentation and Evaluation

Present your ideas in a written report and an oral presentation. The oral presentation will later be shown to the client. You will be evaluated on your oral presentation skills, including:

- Secondary research conducted
- Primary research design and administration
- Research findings, conclusions, and recommendations
- Continuity of presentation
- Enthusiasm
- Voice quality
- Eye contact

 Portfolio

Print a copy of your completed report and presentation for your Portfolio.

THE DECA CONNECTION

DECA Business Services Marketing Series
Conducting marketing research for a client is part of this occupational area, because it is a business service.

DECA Marketing Management Series
Designing and administering a marketing research study is a possible role play situation in this event.

DECA Hospitality and Recreation Research Event
Since a Minor League Baseball franchise is a form of entertainment and recreation, conducting a marketing research study for such a business is a possible topic for this event.

DECA Sports and Entertainment Marketing Management Team Decision-Making Event
Working on this project with a partner would make the experience similar to what is expected in a DECA Team Decision-Making Event.

COOPERATIVE LEARNING

Teamwork Have students role play exactly what they would say when asking a person to participate in their marketing research study, then have them administer the questionnaire to classmates. Then have students work in teams to administer the questionnaires. Students can work together to tabulate the results, prepare the necessary tables and charts, and orally present the research findings.

UNIT 9
ZAZZ LAB

Independent Practice

Brainstorm, Identify, and Write
Have students brainstorm ideas for group ticket sales for the new Minor League Baseball team. Have them also identify groups that would be interested in attending games. Once they have their list, ask them to generate a minimum of five questions that they might include in a telephone survey targeting the groups and write a complete telephone script that also solicits group ticket sales.

ASSESS

Enrichment

Write and Survey Have students write a telephone script to conduct a survey for businesses in the area to see if they would use the facility as perks for top executives and/or to entertain guests. Have them find out how much they would pay for a luxury box, what amenities they would want, and what other features they would want in the stadium.

Evaluation

The rubrics for evaluation of the written, oral, and computer presentation are included in the student text. (See the outline and guidelines for the written report, the computer presentation, and the skills' assessment for oral presentations.) It might be best to replicate those rubrics to evaluate the students' work. A separate rubric could be created to evaluate the work of a team.

CLOSE

Lab Wrap-Up

Ask students: What are the five steps in the marketing research process that are demonstrated in doing research for a Minor League Baseball franchise? *(The five steps are: defining the problem; obtaining data; analyzing the data; recommending solutions to the problem; and applying the results.)*

Product and Service Management

Chapter 30
Product Planning

Chapter 31
Branding, Packaging, and Labeling

Chapter 32
Extended Product Features

Unit Objectives

After completing this unit, students will be able to:

- Explain how businesses plan what products to produce and sell and how they position and manage these products.
- Explain the nature and scope of product planning, product mix, and product development.
- Explain the concept of a product life cycle.
- Identify strategies to position products in various life cycles.
- Explain the nature and scope of branding, packaging, and labeling in product planning.
- Identify the importance of branding, branding elements, and branding strategies to product/service management.
- Explain the importance of warranties and credit to product planning.
- Discuss the importance of warranties as extended product features.

Enrichment Resources

Books

Emotional Branding: How Successful Brands Gain the Irrational Edge by Daryl Travis and Richard Branson

4D Branding: Creating the Corporate Code of the New Economy by Thomas Gad, Richard Branson, and Richard Stagg (Editor)

Successful Product Management: A Guide to Strategy, Planning, and Development by Stephen Morse

Magazines/Journals

New Product News
Packaging Digest

Associations

Consumer Federation of America
1424 16th Street, NW, Suite 604
Washington, DC 20036
(202) 387-6121
www.consumerfed.org

Institute of Packaging Professionals
P.O. Box 861588
4143 Weeks Drive
Warrenton, VA 20187
(540) 428-2092
www.iopp.org

Journal Writing Activity

1. Have students list five reasons why planning which new products to produce and sell is a good strategy for a company. Ask students to be sure to consider the importance of including branding and product labeling in the product planning stages. Have students share their journal entries with the class. Write students' responses on the board.

2. Remind students that companies must consider warranties and consumer rights when creating and planning a new product line. Ask students to write the name of a popular product in their journals. Then have them analyze in writing how this particular product might hypothetically affect a consumer's rights or safety. Ask them what precautions the manufacturer might take in order to insure consumer satisfaction.

TEACHER CLASSROOM RESOURCES

Program Resources	Chapter 30	Chapter 31	Chapter 32
Student Activity Workbook	p. 261	p. 269	p. 277
Marketing Math Workbook	p. 101	p. 101	p. 101
Marketing Research Project Workbook			
ILP School-to-Work Activity Workbook	p. 123	p. 127	p. 131
ILP *BusinessWeek* Case Studies	p. 187	p. 195	p. 201
ILP Marketing Career Portfolio	p. 40	p. 40	p. 40
Reproducible Tests	p. 179	p. 183	p. 189
ExamView User's Guide and Testbank	p. 30-1	p. 31-1	p. 32-1
ILP Internet Resources	p. 79	p. 81	p. 83
ILP Blackline Masters	p. 66	p. 68	p. 69
ILP Lesson Plans	p. 63	p. 65	p. 67
ILP Block Scheduling	p. 10	p. 10	p. 10
Impact! Simulation			

ILP Each of these resources is available in print and on the Interactive Lesson Planner CD-ROM.

Technology Resources

- **Interactive Lesson Planner (ILP) CD-ROM**
- **PowerPoint Presentation CD-ROM**
- **Marketing Essentials Web site**
- **ExamView! CD-ROM**
- **Impact! Simulation**

Virtual Business

Virtual Business is a fully visual marketing and business simulation that introduces students to the principles of marketing by letting them start and run their own virtual businesses. In *Virtual Business*, students have the power to control all aspects of a retail convenience store. Students strategize marketing decisions using a powerful learning tool in the guise of a video game. They learn by experiencing how their decisions affect their virtual business.

Key to Individualized Academics Activities

L1 Level 1 activities are basic activities and should fall within the range of all students.

L2 Level 2 activities are average activities and should be within the range of average and above average students.

L3 Level 3 activities are challenging activities designed for the ability range of above average students.

National Marketing Education

CHAPTER	SECTION	PERFORMANCE INDICATOR
Chapter 30 **Product Planning**	**30.1**	Explain the nature and scope of the product/service management function (PSM)
		Explain the concept of product mix (PSM)
		Plan product mix (PSM)
	30.2	Identify the impact of product life cycles on marketing decisions (PSM)
		Describe factors used by marketers to position products/businesses (PSM)
Chapter 31 **Branding, Packaging, and Labeling**	**31.1**	Explain the nature of branding (PSM)
		Explain branding strategies
	31.2	Explain the functions of packaging
		Explain labeling laws
Chapter 32 **Extended Product Features**	**32.1**	Explain warranties and guarantees (PSM)
		Identify consumer protection provisions of appropriate agencies (PSM)
	32.2	Explain the purposes and importance of credit (FIN)
		Explain the purposes and importance of obtaining credit (business) (FIN)
		Describe legal issues affecting businesses (BME)

CIS Communication, Interpersonal Skills   **DIS** Distribution   **FIN** Financing   **PRI** Pricing   **SEL** Selling

Standards Assessment Correlation

SECTION ASSESSMENT			CHAPTER ASSESSMENT						UNIT LAB
Reviewing Key Terms and Concepts	Thinking Critically	Integrating Academic Skills	Fact and Idea Review	Thinking Critically	Building Workplace Skills	Applying Marketing Concepts	Linking School to Work	Internet Connection	Zazz Lab
1, 4	●	●	1, 2, 3, 5	1, 3, 4	1, 2	2, 3, 4	●	●	●
2, 3, 4	●	●	2, 3, 4, 5	2		1, 3, 4	●		
4, 5	●	●	3, 4, 5	2		1, 4	●		
1	●		6, 7	1				●	
2, 3, 4, 5	●	●	6, 7	1, 3, 4	1, 2	2	●	●	●
1, 2, 4	●	●	1, 2, 3, 4	4		1, 2, 3	●	●	●
2, 3, 4	●	●	3, 4, 5			1, 2, 3	●	●	
1, 2, 3, 4	●		6, 7, 8	1, 2, 3	2	1, 4			●
4	●		8, 9	5	1	1, 4			●
1, 2, 3, 5		●	1, 2, 3, 4, 5	1, 2	2	1	●		●
4, 5	●		5	3	2	3	●		
1, 2, 3	●	●	6, 7, 8, 9	4	1	2, 4, 5		●	
4	●		9			2, 4		●	
5	●		10	4					

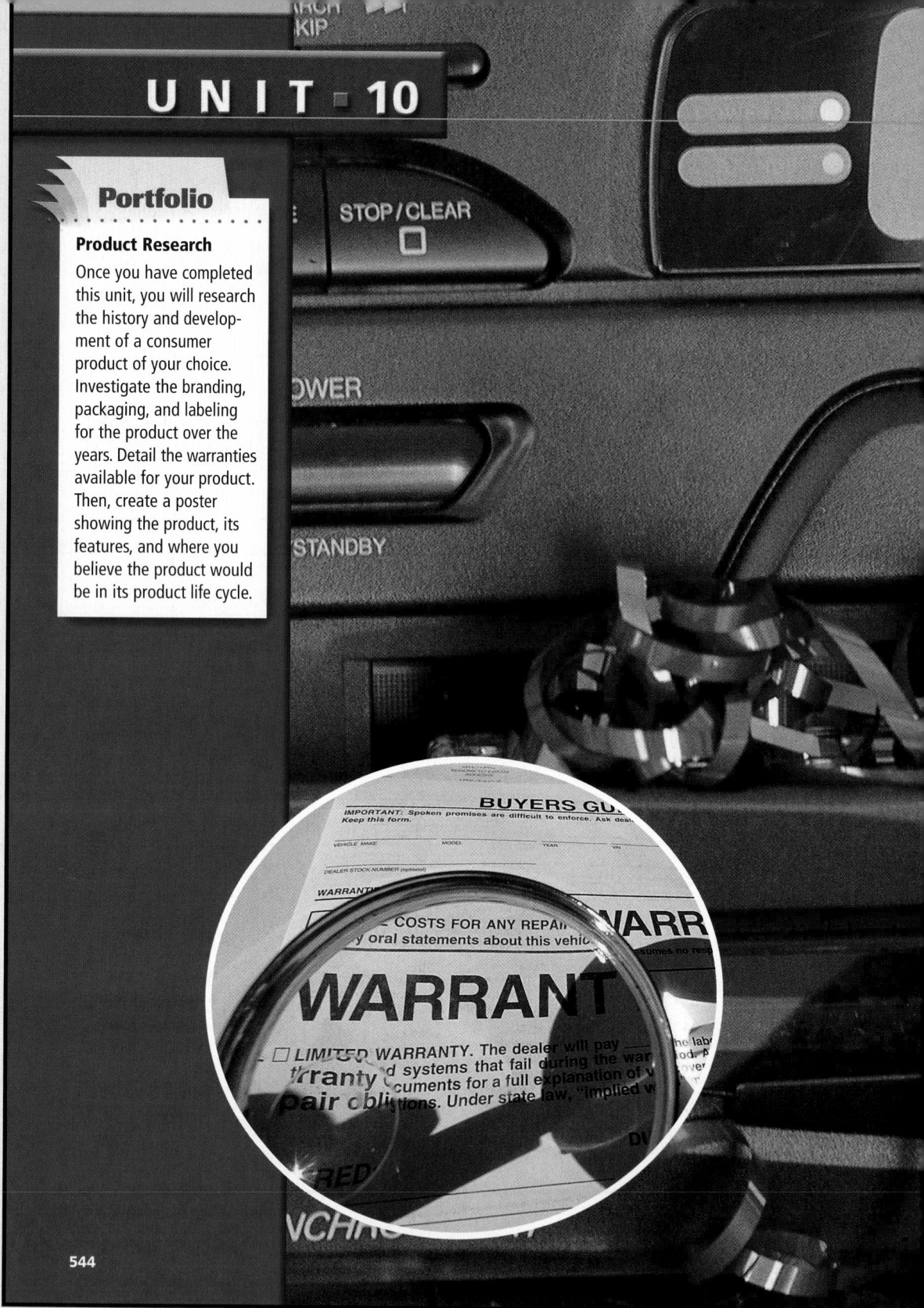

Unit Overview

Product and service management involves all of the decisions a business makes in the production and sale of its products. Chapter 30 shows how businesses plan what products to produce and sell. Chapter 31 introduces the nature and scope of branding in product planning. The chapter explores how branding, packaging, and labeling are incorporated into product planning strategy to create perceived product differences. Chapter 32 discusses the various types of warranties and credit offerings provided by businesses to support products and services. Consumer rights and responsibilities affecting product usage and credit protection are also explained.

Introducing the Unit

The day you begin this unit, bring to class some "classic" products that have been on the market for a long time, such as Arm & Hammer Baking Soda, Quaker Oats oatmeal, Ivory soap, Kleenex tissues, Coke, or Lipton Tea. Place these products next to some new products. Have students speculate on why the classic products have survived and what marketing activities the manufacturers have done to ensure their place in today's market.

Portfolio

Product Research

Once you have completed this unit, you will research the history and development of a consumer product of your choice. Investigate the branding, packaging, and labeling for the product over the years. Detail the warranties available for your product. Then, create a poster showing the product, its features, and where you believe the product would be in its product life cycle.

Field Trip Suggestions

Plan a Trip to an Advertising Agency

Arrange for your students to visit an advertising agency during the planning of a product packaging design. Have the students observe how colors are decided upon for packaging and labeling as well as the "look" the product should have to best appeal to its target market.

Product and Service Management

Unit Overview

Product and service management involves all of the decisions a business makes in the production and sale of its products.

Through your study of Chapter 30, you will see how businesses plan, position, and manage the products and services they will produce and sell. This chapter also discusses the concept of product mix, product mix strategies, and new product development. Chapter 31 explores how branding, packaging, and labeling are incorporated into product planning strategy to create perceived product differences. Chapter 32 discusses extended product features with an emphasis on the use of warranties and the use of credit in product planning as well as consumer rights and responsibilities affecting product usage and credit protection.

In this Unit:

Foundations of Marketing

 Business, Management, Entrepreneurship

Functions of Marketing

 Product/Service Management

■ Financing

◆*DECA* **Unit Project**

Have chapter members complete a 15-minute sales presentation for an item to be sold to a company for resale. Students should stress the product features, brands, warranties, packaging, labeling, and related extended product features. Refer to your guidelines or guidelines developed by the National DECA Delta Epsilon Chi division for the Sales Representative Event. Use the rating form provided by National DECA or develop your own.

Go to the *Marketing Essentials* Web site (**www.marketing.glencoe. com**) for resources to teach and assess occupation-specific vocabulary.

Unit Closure

Conclude this unit with a general review of all elements of product planning, including new product development, product mix, branding, packaging, labeling, warranties, and credit. Have products available in your classroom to use as specific examples.

Guest Speaker Suggestions

Bank Credit Representative Invite a bank credit representative to speak to your class about the considerations they make when deciding to extend credit. Ask the speaker to explain the various types of business and consumer credit available and the qualifications involved for each.

Chapter Overview

This chapter introduces students to the nature and scope of product planning. The concept of product mix is discussed. The importance of product mix strategies and their impact on product planning is also detailed. The strategies used in each stage of the product cycle are provided along with a discussion of product positioning and category management.

 Springboard

Read, Write, and Present Have students read through the chapter and write down the vocabulary definitions. Provide small groups of students with magazines and newspapers, large sheets of paper, and colored markers. Have each group look through the magazines and newspapers, and choose product shots that illustrate the key term concepts. Have each group present their product shots/drawings.

Prereading

List the objectives from the *What You'll Learn* sections of Chapter 30 to discuss with the students. Have the students skim the chapter, looking at the pictures, reading the captions, and noting the heads. Ask questions to ensure that the students have a minimal understanding of the chapter structure.

Preteaching Marketing Vocabulary

Have students ask you to define unfamiliar vocabulary words. If no one asks for definitions, choose students to define each term.

**Marketing:
What It Takes**

Answer Students may address product planning, product mix, product lines, product items, product width and depth, new product development, existing product development, and product positioning.

546

Chapter 30

Product Planning

Marketing: What It Takes

Great Products Boost the Bottom Line
As part of the summer internship program at XYZ company, you are required to prepare a written report on the company's product mix. Your analysis must demonstrate your understanding of product planning and product strategies used by companies to achieve success.

WHAT WILL YOU DO?
What major topics will you evaluate in your analysis of the company's product mix?

546

THE DECA CONNECTION — **ADVISOR CORNER**

Your School-Based Enterprise If you have a DECA operated, school-based enterprise, now is a good time to analyze how your products are selling to determine if products need to be added or deleted from your selection. Have chapter members conduct research among your school's population to determine their interests. Also have your students go to National DECA's School-Based-Enterprise Web site to explore potential products/product lines. In addition to being able to order from many different vendors at DECA discount prices, students can gain valuable information for operating a successful school-based enterprise.

Product Planning, Mix, and Development

Product Planning

A product is anything a person receives in an exchange. A product can be a tangible item (car), a service (haircut), an idea (a good education), or a combination of all of these concepts. A product, therefore, includes its physical features, the seller's reputation, the seller's services, warranties, and the way the product is viewed by people. Product planning involves making decisions about those features that are needed to sell a business's products, services, or ideas. These decisions relate to product features, such as packaging, labeling, and branding, as well as the services, such as product warranties, necessary to support the product. Product planning allows a business to coordinate existing products and features offered to customers, add new products, and delete products that no longer appeal to customers. Product planning requires creativity as well as the ability to interpret current customer needs and forecast new trends.

Product Mix

Product mix includes all the different products that a company makes or sells. A large manufacturer, such as Kraft Foods, the second-largest packaged-foods company in the world, may have hundreds of different products. Some of Kraft's key brands include Kraft, Maxwell House, Oscar Mayer, and Post products.

A retailer has a product mix that is made up of all of the different products the store sells. Retail stores must plan their product mix carefully because they cannot offer all of the products that customers may want. Stores need to offer a good selection of merchandise. Adding more products, though, may not result in increased sales if those products are not popular. In fact, sometimes adding too many new products can take away from existing sales.

The type and number of products to be carried must be based on the objectives of the business, the image the business wants to project, and the market it is trying to reach. This makes product mixes unique to each business. Even similar types of businesses can offer different product mixes. Gap and Brooks Brothers are both apparel stores, yet they have different product mixes. While Brooks Brothers carries a product mix of classic clothing and accessories for business-people, the Gap carries a product mix of trendsetting, fashion-conscious clothing for the youth market. Each store serves a different market and projects a different image.

What You'll Learn

- The nature and scope of product planning
- The concept of product mix
- The different product mix strategies
- The steps in new product development

Why It's Important

Product planning allows a business to make or sell products that are wanted by customers. Product planning also is used to design appropriate marketing programs that help create increased sales and profit opportunities.

Key Terms

- product planning
- product mix
- product line
- product item
- product width
- product depth
- product modification

FOCUS

Bell Ringer Activity

Brainstorm Have students imagine that they are going to open a retail business and they must determine the types and number of products to be carried. Have them write the following on a separate sheet of paper:
(1) Type of retail business they would like to open (for example, a beauty supply store)
(2) Four general categories of merchandise they would like to carry (for example, shampoo, hair coloring, nail polish, and cosmetic brushes)
(3) Factors that would determine the type and number of products they will carry

Introducing the Section

Product Planning, Mix, and Development Review students' answers to #1 and #2 from the Bell Ringer Activity. From their prior reading of the chapter, students should be able to recall the types and number of products to be carried, which must be based on the objectives of the business, the image the business wants to project, and the market it is trying to serve. List these factors on the board and leave them there for the remainder of this chapter.

Classroom Resources

For the Teacher
- Teacher Editions for all workbooks
- Assessment Package
- PowerPoint Presentation Software
- Interactive Lesson Planner
- ILP Block Scheduling, p. 10
- ILP Lesson Plans, p. 63
- ILP Internet Resources, p. 79

- ILP Blackline Masters, p. 66
- ILP *BusinessWeek* Case Studies, p. 187
- ILP Marketing Career Portfolio, p. 40
- *Marketing Essentials* Web site (**www.marketing.glencoe.com**)

For the Student
- Student Activity Workbook, p. 261
- Marketing Math Workbook, p. 101

- Marketing Research Project Workbook
- ILP School-to-Work Activity Workbook, p. 123
- Virtual Business simulation
- *Marketing Essentials* Web site (**www.marketing.glencoe.com**)

ILP These resources are available in print and on the Interactive Lesson Planner (ILP)

TEACH

📊 **Technology Resources**

PowerPoint The *Marketing Essentials* PowerPoint Presentation CD-ROM provides visual lecture aids for every chapter section.

Concept Development

1. Read Section 30.1 with students.
2. Have students read aloud the Case Study on page 555 and review the answers in class.
3. If possible, invite a person from the product development division of a local company to discuss product development with your class. He or she may not be allowed to discuss products currently under development but should be able to give information on products developed and introduced in the recent past. Before the speaker comes to your class, tell students that product development in any company is a highly confidential process, so they should understand the speaker's limitations in discussing current products under development.
4. It may be helpful to obtain copies of past issues of *Advertising Age* and *Brandweek* for students to peruse in your classroom.

■ Product Items and Lines

A **product line** is a group of closely related products manufactured and/or sold by a business. Examples include all the car models produced by the Saturn division of General Motors, all the cereals produced by Kellogg's, and all the computers produced by IBM.

Retailers frequently sell more than one product line. A motorcycle dealer, for example, might carry both Honda and Kawasaki product lines. A supermarket might stock both the Libby and Del Monte canned fruit lines. A camera and electronics store might sell the JVC, Panasonic, Sharp, and Sony digital camcorder product lines.

A **product item** is a specific model, brand, or size of a product within a product line. Typically, retailers carry several product items for each product line they sell. A computer dealer handling hand-held organizers might carry several Palm Computer models. These models might include the Palm3, Palm3C, Palm 3X, and Palm 3Xe.

■ **A Look at Product Mix** A company like Frito Lay is able to succeed while carrying a large product mix. *Is it a good idea for all companies to expand their product lines?*

■ **What Is My Target Market?** Similar businesses often have different images and serve different markets. Because of this, they also offer different product mixes. *What is the primary target market for this store?*

CAPTION ANSWER
What is My Target Market? Answers will vary, but students should note that this store is targeted at working professionals.

CAPTION ANSWER
A Look at Product Mix No. Adding too many products to a product line might cause a company to lose focus and overwhelm customers. This would lead to a decrease in sales.

FIGURE 30-1

The Concept of Product Mix

Width of the Gillette Product Mix			
Blades and Razors	**Toiletries**	**Writing Instruments**	**Lighters**
MACH 3	Series	Paper Mate	Cricket
Sensor	Adorn	Flair	S.T. Dupont
Trac II	Toni		
Atra	Right Guard		
Swivel	Silkience		
Double-Edge	Soft and Dri		
Lady Gillette	Foamy		
Super Speed	Dry Look		
Twin Injector	Dry Idea		
Techmatic	Brush Plus		

(Left labels: **Product** ▶, **Depth of the Product Lines** ▶)

■ **Product Mix** The width and depth of product lines define product mix. *What does product depth tell you about the importance of a given product line?*

■ Product Width and Product Depth

The width and depth of its product offerings define a product mix. **Product width** refers to the number of different product lines a business manufactures or sells. **Product depth** refers to the number of product items offered within each product line.

As you can see in Figure 30-1, Gillette has a product width of four different product lines including blades and razors, toiletries, writing instruments, and lighters. Product depth for the Gillette product mix is ten product items under blades and razors, ten items under toiletries, and two each under writing instruments and lighters.

A retailer that sells several brands of jeans, such as Levi's, Lee, and Guess? is demonstrating product width. The product depth is the number of sizes, price ranges, colors, and styles for each brand.

Product mix strategies vary with the type of business. Red Lobster restaurants, which specialize in seafood dinners, have product depth within a narrow product line (seafood-related entrees). Other restaurants offer broader menus that include steak, chicken, pork, and pasta dinners, as well as seafood. Their product mix shows greater width but less depth than Red Lobster's.

Both manufacturers and retailers must decide on the width and depth of their product mix. To determine its product mix, a business needs to identify its target market, its competitors, and the image the business wants to project. After a target market and an image are determined, a business must determine its product lines and items to manufacture or sell. Periodically a business also must review whether its existing product lines need to be expanded, modified, contracted, or deleted.

Product Mix Strategies

A product mix strategy is the plan for how the business determines which products it will make or stock. Businesses can use different product mix strategies depending upon their resources and their objectives. Some businesses develop completely new products to add to their existing product lines. Others expand or modify their current product lines. Sometimes businesses drop existing products to allow for new product offerings.

To make these decisions, a business must take an objective look at sales as well as other factors such as current trends. A product that has experienced success in the past may not continue to thrive if consumers' wants and needs are changing.

Chapter 30 ■ *Product Planning* **549**

GREAT IDEAS from the Marketing Classroom

Rhonda Cmerek
Taylor High School
Taylor, TX

Applying product planning makes the subject matter more personal to students and can promote their presentation skills. After studying product planning, branding, packaging, and labeling, group students in two- or three-person teams and assign a generic product (soap, soft drink, bubble gum, etc.). Ask students to develop a new and improved product, design the packaging, give the product a brand name, label the product, and then present the product to the class. Give the assignment overnight so that they can develop the appropriate "props" and any necessary artwork. Display the finished projects for the whole class to see and discuss.

Cooperative Learning

New Products and Modifications

Divide the class into 3–5-member groups. Assign each group a general concept, such as housing, transportation, health care, food and nutrition, recreation, travel, etc. Have each group develop a list of new product ideas or product modifications that address the assigned concept for their group. The new product ideas must be appropriate for the needs of an increasingly older population. Have each group identify their top five product ideas to share with the entire class.

■ Developing New Products

New products can add substantially to a company's overall sales and boost its market share. Often a slight variation of the original or existing product can lead to increased sales.

Packaged-goods giant Procter & Gamble, with such venerable brands as Tide, Crest, and Pampers in its lineup, devotes roughly 15 percent of its research and development budget to developing new products. Innovative products that have created consumer-goods categories include P&G's Febreze odor remover for fabrics, the Swiffer dry-mop system, and the Dryel home dry-cleaning kit. Other P&G brands introduced in 2000 include Mr. Clean Antibacterial Wipes, Fit Fruit and Vegetable Wash, Thermacare heat wraps, and Impress food wrap.

According to one study, new products (those less than five years old) account for about 35 percent of total sales for major consumer and industrial goods companies. New products also can help a company's image by providing it with a reputation as an innovator and leader with its customers.

New products also increase markups and profits to sellers. This happens when new products are successful because they tend to be priced 10–15 percent higher than older, comparable products.

New products often become a major part of a company's product line. The Sensor for Women Razor, first introduced in July 1992, has become an ongoing product for Gillette. More than 100 million razors and one billion refills have been sold since its introduction.

New product development generally involves seven key steps:

1. Generating ideas
2. Screening ideas
3. Developing a business proposal
4. Developing the product
5. Testing the product
6. Introducing the product (commercialization)
7. Evaluating customer acceptance

Let's take a closer look at these steps (see Figure 30-2 on page 551).

GENERATING IDEAS New product ideas come from a variety of sources, including customers, competitors, channel members, and company employees. Larger companies establish research and development departments that work with marketing staff, marketing research staff, and outside research companies to develop and test new products.

■ **Dirty Work** Procter and Gamble developed "Fit Fruit and Vegetable Wash" after the company's market research found that although nine out of ten consumers wash their fruits and vegetables, 61 percent feel they're not getting them clean enough. *How can new products help a company's image?*

Creativity is essential for new product development. Some companies sponsor idea sessions, which are designed to generate new ideas and new product concepts in as many product categories as possible.

SCREENING IDEAS During the screening process, ideas for products are evaluated. They are matched against the company's overall objectives to see if they fit. Consider the example of a company that comes up with a new idea to develop a home blood-pressure machine. The company's objective, however, is to disband the consumer products division of the company in the next three years. There would be no reason to continue evaluating that new product idea. During the screening process, the new idea would be evaluated on its potential conflict with existing products. What would a manufacturer of digital thermometers do if a new way of taking body temperature was invented? Let's

Did You Know?

Some good product ideas come from deep space. Due to the special needs of astronauts, product innovations have developed by necessity. Cordless home power tools, such as those developed by Black and Decker, actually came out of the Apollo space program because astronauts had to have tools they could use both in and out of the spacecraft.

CAPTION ANSWER

Dirty Work New products can give a company a reputation as an innovator, and can possibly boost a company's overall sales and market share.

FIGURE 30-2

THE STEPS IN NEW PRODUCT DEVELOPMENT

Developing new products involves several key steps.

1 GENERATING IDEAS

This involves tracking cultural trends and observing customer behaviors to generate ideas.

2 SCREENING IDEAS

Ideas for new products are screened and evaluated. Some ideas are eliminated while the best ideas are put through further evaluation. Finally, one or two ideas are selected for development and a business proposal is written.

3 DEVELOPING THE PRODUCT

During the development stage, a prototype is made. The prototype is tested, and adjustments are made to improve the final product.

4 TESTING THE PRODUCT

Newly developed products are test marketed to obtain customers' responses.

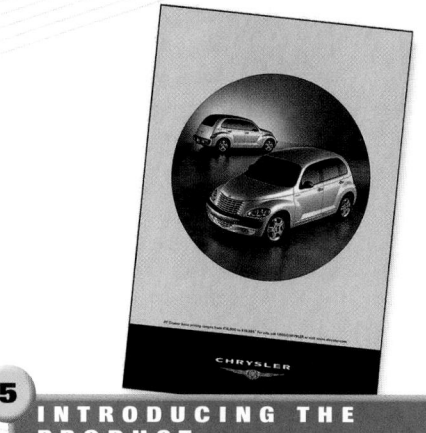

5 INTRODUCING THE PRODUCT

If customer response is favorable, the product is introduced into the marketplace.

The mark PT Cruiser® is a registered trademark of DaimlerChrysler Corporation and the PT Cruiser reprints are used with permission from the DaimlerChrysler Corporation.

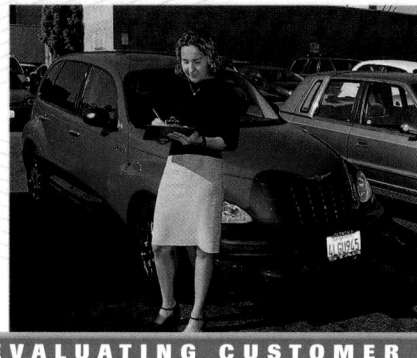

6 EVALUATING CUSTOMER ACCEPTANCE

After the product has been introduced, marketers track customer acceptance.

SECTION 30.1

Independent Practice

Research and Discuss Have students research the product mix of one of these corporations: American Home Products Corp., Borden, Inc., Bristol-Myers Squibb Co., H.J. Heinz Co., PepsiCo, Inc., Proctor & Gamble, and Sara Lee Corp. (or of any other corporation of their choice that offers an extensive product mix).

Students should list at least ten different brand-name products carried by each company. They should also research the history and background of the company to determine how and when the company came to produce such different types of products. (For example, PepsiCo acquired Frito-Lay in 1965 and thus got into the snack food business.) Students may be surprised at the variety of products these companies carry.

A good resource to use for this assignment and an excellent reference to have in your classroom is *Hoover's Handbook of American Business,* The Reference Press, 6448 Highway 290 East, Suite E-104, Austin, Texas 78723, (512) 454-7778. Other resources include *Directory of Corporate Affiliations, Million Dollar Directory, Standard and Poor's Register of Corporations, Thomas Register of American Manufacturers,* and *Macmillan Directory of Leading Private Companies.*

Review students' findings in class. Discuss the fact that many companies end up producing products far afield from their original product lines due to such things as mergers and acquisitions.

More About . . .

Generating Ideas

There are computer software programs that are designed specifically to help companies generate new product ideas. These programs allow marketers to review a large database of ideas. They also include problem-solving questions to help marketers screen possible ideas.

Individualized Practice

Communication Skills

Have students research the product development of a now popular product. It could be a toy such as a Barbie Doll, a food product such as a popular snack food, a car, or any product each student finds interesting. Students should take notes on the following:

(1) How the idea for the product came about

(2) How ideas were evaluated, eliminated, and selected for development

(3) How adjustments were made to the prototype

(4) How the product was tested

(5) How the product was introduced in the market

(6) How customer acceptance was evaluated and continues to be evaluated

L1 Allow students library research time to choose a product. Discuss with each student his or her chosen product. Ask them to avoid repetition—each student should have a different product.

(continued on next page)

---

say a disposable plastic strip that turned different colors based on body heat could be used instead of the standard thermometer. Would that new product be in conflict with the standard thermometer?

Take this idea a step further and screening might involve concept testing with consumers to see if they would actually use a thermometer that provided colored readings instead of digital numbers. Focus groups could be conducted at this stage to see how consumers felt about the new concept of taking one's temperature in this manner. A description of the product would be presented in writing. Consumers would be asked to identify attributes they liked and disliked about the new concept, and their willingness to buy such a product. The purpose of this stage is to find the products that deserve further study. A large number of products are rejected in the screening stage, making it an important preliminary step.

DEVELOPING A BUSINESS PROPOSAL A product idea that makes it through the screening process would then be evaluated in terms of its profit potential. A business proposal would be developed to evaluate the new product in terms of the size of the

MARKETING REAL WORLD

Marketing to Kids: Icing on the ...Chocolate Bar?

Kids can now design their own candy bars! Hershey Food Corporation is letting kids do the "dirty work" of filling and decorating their own chocolate treats. Hershey's Candy Bar Factory contains a cleverly designed chocolate bar with four ready-to-fill sections. Kids can use the kit to fill or decorate the bar with Reese's peanut butter filling, colored sprinkles, chocolate cookie bits, and white frosting. Although each candy bar costs nearly $2 per package, people buy them as a special treat. The kits provide kids with creative entertainment and "incr-edible" results!

Thinking Critically
Why do you think personalizing a product leads consumers to believe the value is higher?

---

market, potential sales, costs, profit potential, technological trends, overall competitive environment, and level of risk. During this stage, production requirements must be considered. How long will it take to produce and introduce the new product? Can it be produced efficiently and at a competitive price? A program to develop the product is planned and someone is assigned the responsibility of studying the feasibility of making and marketing the new product.

DEVELOPING THE PRODUCT During product development, the new product idea takes a physical shape, and marketers develop a marketing strategy. Plans relating to production, packaging, labeling, branding, promotion, and distribution are made.

During this product planning stage, technical evaluations are made to see if the company can produce the new product and if it is practical to do so. Ben & Jerry's ice cream company had difficulties when it first developed Cherry Garcia ice cream. The original idea was to use whole chocolate-coated cherries. The whole cherries were too large to go through the production machinery, which caused the chocolate to break off the cherries. After numerous tests, the company finally separated the cherries and the chocolate; the rest is history.

In addition to detecting difficulties with product production, tests are conducted on products to see how they will hold up during normal and not-so-normal use by the consumer. A new product may be tested for durability in the lab by machines that will reproduce the actions or motions that the product will endure during use. It is at this stage that technical problems should be detected so that they can be corrected before full-scale production begins.

Sometimes millions of dollars can be spent at this stage of development for testing, prototypes, and research. A *prototype* is a model of the product. Usually, only a few models are made at first, as the business tests the idea and makes changes to improve the final product. Companies can experience long delays during this stage of product planning. The government requires extensive testing in various stages for some products, such as prescription drugs and genetically engineered food products. These tests end with testing on human beings to determine side effects and problems with the product's safety. Getting final approval from the government for use by the general public can take years.

MARKETING REAL WORLD

Marketing to Kids: Icing on the . . . Chocolate Bar?

Answer Extra steps to make a product unique, such as monogramming initials on a pillowcase or choosing the size of a hard drive, add uniqueness. A consumer who has control over the final product is willing to pay more.

TESTING THE PRODUCT After the product is tested in the lab, consumer acceptance of the product is the next step. As you learned in Chapter 28, new products frequently are test marketed in certain geographic areas to see whether consumers will accept them. PepsiCo developed a new soft drink for the European market to try to increase its market share. The new soft drink is called Pepsi Max, a one-calorie cola, and it was made specifically for non-American tastes. International consumers typically do not like diet beverages, so the company spent more than two years testing different flavor combinations on the European market. Finally, one version met the company's goal of having at least 40 percent of the consumers in a taste test choose the new product over Coke.

Not every new product is test marketed in geographic areas. Frequently a focus group evaluation during development can provide additional input into final product design and uncover potential problems before production.

In some cases, the costs of test marketing, focus group evaluations, or direct marketing tests to sample households may be too high. In others, marketers may forgo testing because they would need to ask people to evaluate something that for them does not even exist. Sometimes companies fear that a time delay will allow competitors to enter the market before their product is ready.

INTRODUCING THE PRODUCT When a new product has been researched successfully, it is ready for full market introduction. This stage also is called commercialization. The costs of introducing a new product often are quite high. The product must be advertised to introduce its benefits to consumers. A new or revised distribution network may be needed. The company may need to develop training programs for its sales force. To pay for these costs, the company needs to get its new products into the market as quickly as possible.

The earlier a product can be brought to market, the greater the chance that revenues and profits will be high. The first company to introduce a new product has an advantage in acquiring customers and in building brand loyalty.

EVALUATING CUSTOMER ACCEPTANCE After products have been introduced, marketers track new product performance. This step is done to evaluate customer acceptance of the product and the marketing strategies used to introduce the product.

One way to obtain customer responses is to study sales information. Scanning equipment and computer systems can be used to compile large amounts of sales and market data on existing and new products. From this information, customized reports can be prepared. These reports help answer key questions such as:

- *Who are the best customers for our new product?*
- *What new products are customers buying?*
- *How often do customers buy the new product?*
- *When did customers last buy the new product?*

■ Developing Existing Products

Companies constantly review their product mix to see if they can further expand their product lines or modify existing products. They do this in order to build on an already established image, to appeal to new markets, and to increase sales and profits. Companies that have successful product lines often add products to those lines to take advantage of customers' positive attitude toward the brand name. Sony built on its image as a producer of high-quality

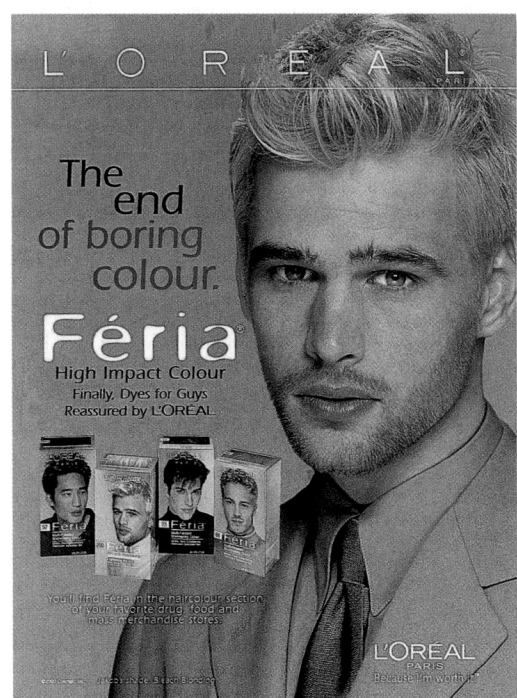

■ **Appealing to New Markets** A business must always look at new markets for its products. *How can new ideas for products or product expansions help a business?*

Chapter 30 ■ *Product Planning* **553**

Individualized Practice

Communication Skills
(continued)

L2 Have students write a 150- to 200-page report summarizing their findings.

L3 Have students present their findings in a five-minute oral presentation. Encourage students to use illustrations to augment their oral reports. All students should take notes on each presentation. Their notes should be typed into a final draft copy.

Reteaching

1. **Vocabulary** Assign and review the vocabulary terms for this section.
2. **Fact and Idea** Assign and review Fact and Idea Review questions 1–6 from the Chapter Assessment.
3. **Product Mix** To determine its product mix, a business must decide on the width and depth of the product offerings. Review the process for developing a product mix explained in this section (identify a target market, competitors, and the image a business wants to project). Then choose two or three local businesses (for example, a fast-food restaurant, a retail store, and a service business), and have the students identify the target market for each business, its competitors, and the image it wants to project.

---

electronics products when it added the original PlayStation video game to its product line. Sony was able to capitalize on its image and brand awareness when it introduced PlayStation2, a technically more advanced version of the game, in 2000. To appeal to new markets, a hair color line for men was introduced by L'Oréal, which up until that time only sold hair color for women. In these examples, the companies utilized their knowledge of existing products to expand their businesses.

One disadvantage of adding new products to a company's product mix is the cost factor. Adding products or product lines increases inventory, promotion, storage, and distribution costs. New products also may take sales away from existing products and may require additional training for sales representatives who sell the products to suppliers. Finally, when a brand or corporate name is placed on a new product and the product proves harmful or defective, all products with the corporate name suffer.

Even though these disadvantages exist, they are often not significant enough to keep a company from developing its products. Two ways of developing existing products are line extensions and product modifications. Let's look at both options.

LINE EXTENSIONS Companies can expand product offerings by adding new product lines, items, or services, which may or may not be related to current products. To illustrate this strategy, think of all the varieties of Tylenol, such as Tylenol Flu, Tylenol Cold, and Tylenol Allergy/Sinus. Also think about the different forms they come in, such as tablets, caplets, and gelcaps. Each of these products is a line extension of the original Tylenol product.

A line extension is designed to be a different product that appeals to somewhat different needs of consumers. In essence, the company wants to provide a wider range of choices to increase product depth within a line. Line extensions are easy to market because customers are already familiar with the original product on which the extension is based.

In some cases, the line extension may be a product that is not directly related to the original product, but the brand name is used nonetheless. You see Bic pens and Bic disposable lighters. In this case, the company is building a new product line based on an existing brand name that is familiar to consumers.

PRODUCT MODIFICATIONS A product modification is an alteration in a company's existing product. Modified products may be offered in new

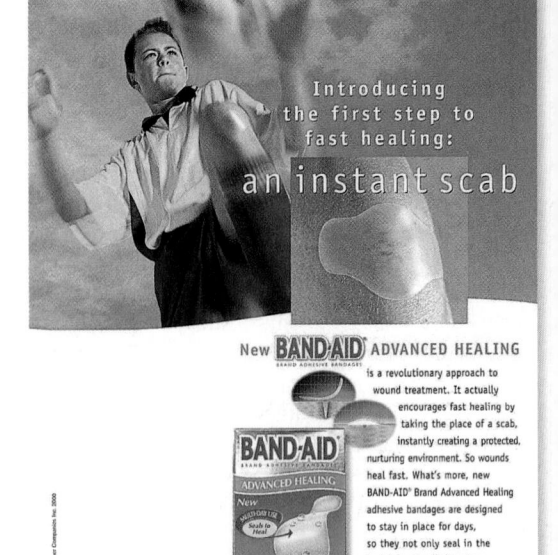

■ **Ouch!** Product modifications are a relatively easy and inexpensive way to add new products to a company's product line. *How did BAND-AID modify its traditional bandages to create a new product?*

and different varieties, formulations, colors, styles, features, or sizes. Product modifications are a relatively quick and easy way to add new products to a company's product line.

When modifying a product, the old product often is phased out. Packaging may be modified to appeal to consumers and attract them to the product. One of the best examples of a product modification is the classic story of Coca Cola.

A few years ago Coke decided to make its cola slightly sweeter to compete for the market that prefers sweeter colas. While the sweeter coke drew new customers, Coke's traditional drinkers responded to the sweeter product with protest. They preferred their old, original Coke. The company soon decided to market two products instead of one. Coke Classic used the old formula, and Coke became the new, sweeter version. The company was able to increase its sales by holding on to its traditional market while gaining new customers for the new product. In this case a product modification actually became a line extension because both products were kept in the product mix.

Case Study

Nike Gear

Hoping to build on the success of its digital Triax Sports Watch launched in 1998, Nike is developing a new line of electronic products for sports. Its goal is to create technologically advanced products that can enhance athletes' workouts. The oversized digital Triax Sports Watch, which is easy to read while running or jogging, has sold 2.5 million units worldwide.

Nike has formed a new division called Tech Lab, which is introducing a line of sports-focused products including a digital audio player, a high tech walkie-talkie, and portable heart monitors. These new products will be marketed globally.

The new products will bear the trademark swoosh symbol. The portable audio player will be the first product released. It will play MP3 files and Microsoft's Windows Media audio files. These lightweight players will have the software needed to let users mix their own music. An added attraction is that the player will not skip when jogged. To avoid potential problems with digital copyrights and royalties, Nike will get permission from artists and record companies for any songs downloaded from the company's Web site.

Other new products include a heart-rate and speed-distance monitor, a digital compass, and hand-held walkie talkies. The company will also sell related accessories, such as holsters and fanny packs to carry the new gadgets.

Nike will sell the new electronic line and accessories at NikeTown stores, Nike's Web site, sporting goods chains, and retail stores, such as Circuit City. The company will face tough competition in this $2 billion market from Sony, which already has a Sports Walkman unit.

Case Study Review

1. Why does Nike want to enter a new market for its products?
2. Discuss the psychographic trends that have created demand for Nike's new electronic sports accessories.

A MATTER OF ETHICS

3. What steps has Nike taken to avoid copyright infringements by the users of its product?

Enrichment

1. **Review** Assign and review the appropriate Thinking Critically questions from the Chapter Assessment.
2. **Extend** Assign and review the corresponding activities from *BusinessWeek Case Studies, Internet Resources,* and the *School-to-Work Activity Workbook.* **ILP**
3. **Research and Write** Have the students interview the manager or owner of a local retail store, discussing with him or her the choices made in the product mix. The manager or owner should give examples of product lines that have been added and deleted in the particular store, and tell why. Have students ask: How do the types and brands of products carried reflect the objectives of the business, the image the business wants to project, and the market the business is trying to serve? Students should summarize their findings in a 250-word report. Each student's report should tell what things are taken into consideration when new product lines are added, and when product lines are deleted.

Case Study Review Answers

Nike Gear
1. Nike views electronic sports equipment as a growing area with sales potential.
2. Increased concern about and attention to physical fitness was one psychographic factor that has helped to create demand for Nike's electronic sports accessories.

A MATTER OF ETHICS
3. Nike is getting permission from record companies and artists for any songs downloaded from Nike's Web site.

Evaluation

Assign and review the Section 30.1 Assessment.

Technology Resources

Assessment Resources
Go to the *Marketing Essentials* Web site (**www.marketing.glencoe.com**) for resources to teach and assess occupation-specific vocabulary.

CLOSE

Section Wrap-Up

Choose one local business with which all students are familiar—a business that you have not already discussed in class. Have students describe its product mix in light of the objectives of the business, the image it wants to project, and the market it is trying to serve.

■ Deleting a Product or Product Line

Sometimes companies decide that they will no longer produce or sell a particular product or perhaps even a whole product line. Let's take a look at other reasons to drop a product or a product line.

OBSOLESCENCE Changing interests and technology have caused many products to be dropped. For example, older models of desktop computers have been dropped because newer models are faster and less expensive to produce. Early computer games have been replaced by games that have life-like graphics.

LOSS OF APPEAL As consumer tastes change, companies drop products that no longer appeal to the old tastes. Products popular with older generations, such as Brylcreem hair cream and Ovaltine hot chocolate, have lost much of their original customer appeal. These products may have some lasting loyalties that generate revenue, so the manufacturers must decide whether to keep them in their product mixes.

CONFLICT WITH CURRENT COMPANY OBJECTIVES Sometimes a product does not match a company's current objectives. Sears sold one subsidiary, Caldwell Banker real estate company, for this reason. Over the past several years, Sears stores had lost market share to other retailers. The company sold some unrelated businesses to focus on its retail objectives.

REPLACEMENT WITH NEW PRODUCTS Supermarkets, drugstores, department stores, and other retail outlets may change product mix frequently. Shelf space is limited, so retailers must make shelf or display space for new products. Products may be dropped because the store decides that it can make more money selling a different brand. One manufacturer might offer better buying terms because the store can buy in volume.

LACK OF PROFIT Seeking to increase profits, retailers will handle only fast-moving and profitable items. Often retailers will carry only those products whose stock turnover exceeds a certain number of turns per month.

Product developers may drop products when sales reach such a low level that the return on sales does not meet company objectives. Examples of products that have been dropped because they were no longer profitable are items such as Beeman's Black Jack gum, bite-size Oreos, Pepsi Crystal soda, and Powerhouse candy bars.

CONFLICT WITH OTHER PRODUCTS IN THE LINE Sometimes products take business away from other products in the same product line. Increased sales of one product can cause decreased sales of another product. In the 1990s, Procter & Gamble dropped many of its "unproductive" products, such as White Cloud tissue and Gleem toothpaste. The company was willing to give up market share to improve its return on similar products.

30.1 ASSESSMENT

Reviewing Key Terms and Concepts

1. What is product planning?
2. What is product mix?
3. Name four product mix strategies.
4. Identify the steps for new product development.
5. Name one advantage and one disadvantage to expanding a product line.

Thinking Critically

6. Suppose a company is developing a new product when a competitor introduces a new product that is similar. What are some things the company should consider in deciding whether to proceed with the development of its new product?

Integrating Academic Skills

7. **COMMUNICATION** Develop a 200-word written product plan for a truck manufacturer that is planning to diversify into the building and selling of buses. Identify possible target markets and product features.

30.1 ASSESSMENT ANSWERS

Reviewing Key Terms and Concepts

1. decisions about packaging, labeling, warranties, guarantees, branding, product mix
2. It is the different products a company makes or sells.
3. developing new product, expanding, modifying, contracting, deleting product line
4. generating ideas, screening ideas, developing business proposal, developing, testing, introducing, evaluating the product
5. New products can add to company sales and boost market share. Disadvantages include increasing inventory, promotion, storage, and distribution costs.

Thinking Critically

6. The company can study competitor's product and compare features to new product.

Integrating Academic Skills

7. **COMMUNICATION** Product plans will vary.

Sustaining Product Sales

The Product Life Cycle

A product life cycle represents the stages that a product goes through during its life. There are four stages of the life cycle: introduction, growth, maturity, and decline (see Figure 30-3 on page 558). As each stage in the product life cycle is reached, marketers must adjust their product mix and their marketing strategies to ensure continued sales.

■ Managing During the Introduction Stage

When the product is introduced to the market, the focus of the company's efforts is on promotion and production. The major goal is to draw the customer's attention to the new product. The company works to build its sales by increasing product awareness. Special promotions may get the customer to try the new product. As you know, the costs of introducing a product are high. Therefore, this is usually the least profitable stage of the life cycle.

■ Managing During the Growth Stage

During the growth phase of the product life cycle, the product is enjoying success as shown by increasing sales and profits. Much of the target market knows about and buys the product. Advertising may now focus on consumer satisfaction, rather than on the new product benefits. By this time, the competition is aware of the success of the product and is likely to offer new products in order to compete. To keep its product sales growing, the company may have to introduce new models or modify the existing product to offer more than the competition.

Consider the example of the market for video game consoles. Sales of improved video game players now amount to several million units a year and several companies offer competing products.

■ Managing During the Maturity Stage

A product reaches the maturity stage when its sales level off or slow down. The product may have more competition now, or most of the target market may already own the product. When a large proportion of potential buyers have the improved video game platforms, sales will slow and the product will enter the maturity stage.

During this stage, a company spends more of its marketing dollars fighting off the competition. Advertising expenses may climb, and the company may have to decide whether it can continue to improve the product to gain additional sales.

● What You'll Learn

- The product life cycle
- The concept of product positioning
- The purpose of category management

● Why It's Important

After products are introduced in the marketplace, they go through different stages of growth and decline. It is important to understand the different marketing strategies used to sustain product sales over time.

● Key Terms

- product life cycle
- product positioning
- category management
- planogram

Chapter 30 ■ *Product Planning* **557**

FOCUS

Bell Ringer Activity

Identify and Write Write the stages of the product life cycle on the board. Review the meaning of each. Then have students identify five products that can be found in your classroom or in the possession of the students, and then write on a separate sheet of paper where they think each product is in its product life cycle.

Introducing the Section

Product Life Cycles and Product Positioning Review students' answers from the Bell Ringer Activity. Explain that product planning allows a business to create sales opportunities, design appropriate marketing materials, develop effective advertising campaigns, coordinate the product mix, add new products, and delete older products when necessary.

Point out that product planning is one of the broadest areas of marketing students will encounter. If a product plan is well structured, a company can maintain successful products over a longer period of time than would be possible without product planning.

Ask students to imagine what happens to companies that ignore this step. *(They can fold or go bankrupt even though they may have had an initially good product.)* Relating product life cycle to products that students use daily will help them understand this concept.

Classroom Resources

For the Teacher
- Teacher Editions for all workbooks
- Assessment Package
- PowerPoint Presentation Software
- Interactive Lesson Planner

ILP Block Scheduling, p. 10
ILP Lesson Plans, p. 64
ILP Internet Resources, p. 79

ILP Blackline Masters, p. 67
ILP *BusinessWeek* Case Studies, p. 187
ILP Marketing Career Portfolio, p. 40
- *Marketing Essentials* Web site (**www.marketing.glencoe.com**)

For the Student
- Student Activity Workbook, p. 261
- Marketing Math Workbook, p. 101

- Marketing Research Project Workbook
ILP School-to-Work Activity Workbook, p. 123
- Virtual Business simulation
- *Marketing Essentials* Web site (**www.marketing.glencoe.com**)

ILP These resources are available in print and on the Interactive Lesson Planner (ILP)

FIGURE 30-3

The Product Life Cycle

Introduction   Growth   Maturity   Decline

■ **Understanding the Product Life Cycle** The life cycle of a product can be divided into four stages: introduction, growth, maturity, and decline. *Why are sales not at their highest during the introduction stage?*

■ Managing During the Decline Stage

During the decline stage, sales fall. Profits may reach the point where they are smaller than the costs. Management will need to decide how long it will continue to support the product.

Besides dropping the product, the company can use other product mix strategies to try to gain further sales from a declining or failing product. These strategies include selling or licensing the product, recommitting to the product line, discounting the product, regionalizing the product, and modernizing or altering the product.

SELL OR LICENSE THE PRODUCT Many companies sell or license their poorly performing products to risk-taking companies. Risk-taking companies try to rejuvenate the product by changing the product's image or introducing it to a new market.

A Virtual Test with Real Results

As you walk down the supermarket aisle, you see a box of cereal that looks interesting. You take the box off the shelf and realize that it's one of your favorites—but with a new box design. You turn the box around and read its sides. When you decide to buy the cereal, you click on the shopping cart and lean back in your chair. You are a test shopper in a virtual supermarket! Many marketers use simulation software to see how their products will fare in the real world. Using this technology, marketers can test packaging changes or discount-price promotions. Before spending the money to create prototypes, product engineers can see how consumers like their efforts. Simulation software "virtually" changes the way products are tested.

Thinking Critically

A simulated test can cost up to five times more than conventional testing. Why would a company pay more for a software-simulated test?

RECOMMIT TO THE PRODUCT LINE Some companies decide that a declining product has other uses that can help improve sales. Knox gelatin lost sales as people spent less time cooking and stopped making fancy gelatin desserts. The company found a new use for the product that appeals to a different market. Adding Knox gelatin to Jell-O mixes allows people to make gelatin desserts that can be held in the hand. The new desserts are especially popular with children. Creating this new use helped Knox to improve sales.

Even with recommitment and advertising of new product uses, there is no guarantee that a product will continue to have enough sales. Eventually it may need to be discontinued.

FIGURE 30-3 ANSWER
Understanding the Product Life Cycle A product is at its infant stage in its introduction. At this stage the product is new and unfamiliar to consumers. A great deal of money must be spent to get customers to accept the product. Production, pricing, promotion, and distribution of the product are adjusted in this stage to ensure that the product gains recognition and becomes popular.

 A Virtual Test with Real Results

Answer Although the costs of the test may be expensive, they may be less costly than going through the expense of making prototypes or fully engineering a working product.

DISCOUNT THE PRODUCT Many declining product lines can be saved from deletion by discounting them to compete with cheaper store or private brands. Lever Brothers discounted Pepsodent toothpaste and Lifebuoy soap and advertised the products with phrases such as "compare and save."

REGIONALIZE THE PRODUCT Sometimes companies decide to sell declining products only in the geographical areas where there is strong customer loyalty. The Nabisco Food Group only markets its My-T-Fine soups in northeastern states because it still has a significant customer base there. By marketing its product only in that area, the company saves the money of national advertising and distribution costs.

MODERNIZE OR ALTER THE PRODUCT OFFERING Some products can be altered or modernized to avoid deletion. Products can be completely redesigned, packaged differently, or reformulated. Tide laundry detergent—available in powder form in a box—was redesigned as New Tide. The product was also introduced in liquid form and repackaged in a plastic bottle. The new product now has a different appeal to existing consumers and a completely different look to new consumers who never used the original Tide.

Companies spend large amounts of money to develop and promote consumer and industrial products. As a result, they are reluctant to delete products without trying one of the above strategies. When products must be dropped, a company needs to plan the move carefully to avoid disappointing customers and damaging the company's overall image.

Product Positioning

The *focus* of product positioning is the image a product projects. The *goal* of product positioning is to set the product apart from the competition. Al Ries and Jack Trout, authors of *Positioning: The Battle for Your Mind,* explain positioning as the way you get into your customer's mind. Product positioning refers to the efforts a business makes to identify, place, and sell its products in the marketplace. It is an attempt to create an image of a product that appeals to customers. Changing the image or repositioning unsuccessful products is costly. To position their products, businesses identify customers' needs and determine how their product compares to the competition. A number of strategies are used to position products in the marketplace. Let's take a closer look at each of these strategies.

BRIGHT IDEAS
FUN, Inc.

Who might like lip gloss with a mirror on the bottom, or makeup and a fortune in a miniature Chinese-food container? How about a line of temporary tattoos that come off with soap and water? Kristin Penta knows what's hot. She dreamed up these and other new products to create and market to teenage girls. How did Penta get started? She teamed with a pencil manufacturer, Pentech International, who helped transform Penta's lip and eye pencils into a line of makeup for teens. Penta's ideas for low-cost—and fun—cosmetics led her to find investors for her start-up company, FUN Cosmetics, Inc. FUN is now expanding its product line and marketing to women in their twenties. Penta's new products and promotions keep her company one step ahead of the competition. For Penta, work truly is fun!

Thinking Creatively
How might Penta plan which products will be future trends?

BRIGHT IDEAS FUN, Inc.

Answer Penta can conduct research to screen ideas for future trend; then develop, test, introduce, and evaluate products to generate ideas throughout a product's life cycle.

Discussion Starter

Product Positioning Have each student generate a list of three products. (They should not use the products they generated for the Bell Ringer Activity.) Then have them discuss whether they think their products are positioned: (a) by price and quality, (b) by product features and benefits, (c) in relation to competition, and/or (d) in relation to other products in a line. You may wish to let them look through magazines or newspapers to generate their product ideas.

As this textbook went to press, the following experimental products had been introduced into the market:

- Cars powered by electricity
- Virtual reality, head-mounted displays which plug into PCs and TV sets (They immerse the wearer in the images they see. As the wearer moves his or her head, the images move.)
- Extremely user-friendly software from Microsoft entitled "Bob" that gives easy instructions to the licensee and can be customized to anticipate the licensee's use patterns
- Videophones and video watches
- Edible slime called *Glop,* manufactured by Catco, a specialty toymaker (You may wish to add to this discussion by including other recently introduced test products.)
- Alert bikes with home pager and radio signals mounted on bicycles to let children detect traffic problems
- Home medical boxes with video links to the doctor
- Smart cards for medical record keeping

Have students make some predictions about how these products will perform over the next few years.

SECTION 30.2

Thinking Critically

Customer Taste The text states that as consumer tastes change, companies drop products that no longer appeal to the old tastes. Ask students what things influence changes in customer taste. *(Changes in customer taste are influenced by such things as (1) trends in hair style and clothing; (2) a need for more technologically advanced products and/or products with more features and benefits; (3) a need for products that can be prepared quickly (such as microwave dinners); and (4) a desire for products that reflect one's racial/cultural heritage.)*

Cooperative Learning

Product Life Cycle Divide the class into four groups. Give each group colored markers and large sheets of paper. Have each group collaborate to create a visual/verbal representation of the phases of the product life cycle and how advertising and promotion are managed during each phase. Allow each group to display its completed work in your classroom.

Independent Practice

Diagram and Identify Select a product line from a business of your choice. Create a diagram of all the product items in one product line carried by the store. Identify each item by name, price, and at least two other distinguishing features.

> **CAPTION ANSWER**
> **A Facial A Day** They are promoting the product based on features to the buyer. The cleansing cloths are disposable, and they wash and moisturize.

560

■ **A Facial A Day** Olay used research to determine how to best place its new product. *How is Olay focusing on product placement?*

■ Positioning by Price and Quality

Companies frequently position their products in a product line based upon price and quality. A company may offer an economy line, a mid-priced line, and a luxury line. Positioning by price and quality stresses high price as a symbol of quality or low price as an indication of value.

The Ford Motor Company deliberately positions its Focus as an economical compact car while still emphasizing quality. It positions its Taurus as a full-size passenger car. Promotional efforts are aimed at creating a price and quality image for each of these Ford products. This strategy enables Ford to give each of its products a unique position in the marketplace.

■ Positioning by Features and Benefits

Companies frequently position products by stressing their features and benefits to the buyer. Products are often associated with a feature, attribute, or customer benefit. For example, Rockport shoes are positioned as comfortable shoes, whether dress or casual.

Olay Daily Facials were introduced in 2000 to appeal to younger women. Research had indicated that consumers would use the product to get rid of damp washcloths next to bathroom sinks. The thin

disposable cleaning cloths are designed to remove makeup, wash, and moisturize. They also offer convenience and portability. Olay promoted the new product by emphasizing its benefits using the theme, "a little bit of a facial every day."

Companies frequently position products to highlight the products' unique characteristics. When Palm Computing introduced the Palm Pilot, it tried to position the product as a user-friendly tool for people to access, manage, and communicate information. The Palm Computer was unique from the other personal digital assistants on the market because it could easily fit in a pocket or purse. By 2000, Palm had 72 percent of the world market for hand-held computers.

■ Positioning in Relation to the Competition

Some businesses position their products to compete directly with the products of other companies. Positioning in relation to the competition is a common strategy that is often used when a firm is trying to solidify an advantage over another firm.

When the Warner-Lambert Company introduced Cool Mint Listerine, it did so by positioning its product against the competition. Traditionally, customers of mouthwashes chose between the "therapeutic" benefits of strong tasting, original

560 Unit 10 ■ *Product and Service Management*

THE DECA CONNECTION — **COMPETITIVE EVENTS AND MARKETING ESSENTIALS**

Learn and Earn with Product Planning This chapter lends itself to DECA's Learn and Earn Project. This project requires that students conduct a fund raising project along the lines of a real business. Section IV B asks for details of the product to be offered, including potential suppliers and inventory policies (if applicable). As your students conduct the Learn and Earn

Project, you can use this section the competitive event to tie in the information learned in this chapter. DECA's Entrepreneurship and International Marketing events also contain product planning sections. For more information and official guidelines of the Learn and Earn Project, go to the DECA Web site at **www.deca.org**.

Listerine or the "cosmetic" benefits of other brands like Scope. With its "cool mint" flavor, Listerine hoped to compete directly with other cosmetic brands. The company also hoped to retain those customers who believed that Listerine could fight germs, plaque, and gum infection better than other products.

It is not always a good idea to compete head-to-head with the industry leader. It might be better to compete by showing that you are the underdog. Southwest Airlines does a good job of that by telling potential customers that they are the low-fare alternative to full-service airlines.

■ Positioning in Relation to Other Products in a Line

Individual products may be positioned in relation to other products in the same line. Binney & Smith introduced washable crayons and positioned them as a specialty item in the company's Crayola crayon line.

Life In The Diverse MARKETPLACE

The Customer's Choice

When Coca-Cola first moved into the Indonesian soft-drink market, it was sadly surprised to find low customer interest levels. Carbonated beverages were not popular or well-known to Indonesians, who preferred tea and fruit juices. The solution? Coke started again, keeping customers' preferences in mind. To slowly introduce carbonated beverages, Coke developed strawberry-, pineapple-, and banana-flavored soft drinks. It hoped that once customers developed a taste for these products, they may be more apt to try other Coke products. Building the market share will help build recognition of the Coke name and brand!

Thinking Critically
What are possible disadvantages of the technique that Coke used?

■ **The Scope of Listerine** Products can be positioned to compete directly with other brands. *How did Warner-Lambert position the new, mintier Listerine?*

ASSESS

Reteaching

1. **Vocabulary** Assign and review the vocabulary terms for this section.
2. **Fact and Idea** Assign and review Fact and Idea Review questions 7–10 from the Chapter Assessment.
3. **Product Life Cycle** Create a bulletin board display by first placing each of the four stages of the product life cycle on a separate sheet of paper and tacking each paper to the board. Have each student bring in a picture of one product from a magazine or newspaper, tell the class where the product is in its life cycle, tell how the product is positioned in the marketplace, and then place the picture under its appropriate category on the board.

Enrichment

1. **Review** Assign and review the Chapter 30 activities in the *Student Activity Workbook*.
2. **Review** Assign and review the appropriate Thinking Critically questions from the Chapter Assessment.
3. **Review** Assign and review the following Chapter Assessment activities: Building Workplace Skills, Applying Marketing Concepts, Linking School to Work, The DECA Connection Role Play, and Internet Connection.
4. **Research and Write** Have the students interview the manager of a local store to review a planogram for particular products in a category and discuss the management strategy behind the product placement. Students should write their findings in 150 to 200 words.

Life In The Diverse MARKETPLACE

The Customer's Choice

Answer Some possible disadvantages of the technique that Coke used are that customers may not adapt their tastes, and the process may take long.

CAPTION ANSWER
The Scope of Listerine The new flavors of Listerine compete with the more cosmetic mouthwashes while providing the same germ-killing benefits as original Listerine.

Evaluation

Assign and review the Section 30.2 Assessment.

Technology Resources

Assessment Resources
Go to the *Marketing Essentials* Web site (**www.marketing.glencoe. com**) for resources to teach and assess occupation-specific vocabulary.

VIRTUAL BUSINESS

Merchandising
Introduce the concept of merchandising and product planning to students using Knowledge Matters' Virtual Business visual simulation, "Marketing— Merchandising." In this activity, students change the floor plan for their store, observe customer traffic patterns, and focus on extensive product reporting available by category, brand, and week. If needed, have students run the Virtual Business tutorial before beginning this simulation. For additional instructions and teaching tips for this activity, go to the *Marketing Essentials* Web site (**www.marketing.glencoe.com**).

CLOSE

Section Wrap-Up

Have students complete this statement: A product life cycle represents . . . *(the stages that a product goes through in its life.)*

562

Category Management

Many manufacturers and retailers are adopting a new process for marketing and selling their products known as category management. **Category management** is a process that involves managing product categories as individual business units. A category may include a group of product lines that have the same target market and distribution channels. The process is designed to put manufacturers and retailers in closer touch with customer needs.

The position of *category manager* is one that is relatively new. This person is responsible for all of the profits or losses for one specific product line. The position of category manager evolved out of the position of brand manager. The difference between the two job titles is that a category manager is responsible for only one category and has more interaction with the sales force, whereas a brand manager manages an entire brand and has little direct interaction with the sales force.

The manufacturer can customize this category's product mix, merchandising, and promotions according to customer preference on a store-by-store basis. Using scanned data on product sales and other market data, manufacturers assist retailers with their product mix. In examining product mix, a manufacturer determines which of its products a particular retailer does not carry. It also identifies products that would have strong sales potential for both the retailer and the manufacturer. This analysis helps the manufacturer to recommend an optimum product mix by projecting sales volume and profits for a retailer. Suggestions are then made to add or delete certain items to its product mix. If the category manager feels as if one product is taking away from other products in the same category, this product will be discontinued.

Another way manufacturers can help retailers is through planograms. A **planogram** is a computer-developed diagram that shows retailers how and where products within a category should be displayed on a shelf at individual stores. This is important to maximize a product's potential. Placement can also be used to highlight other products that can be used in conjunction with a product. Manufacturers can even customize planograms for specific types of stores. Each store then can stock more of the products that appeal to people in its trading area and fewer products that do not appeal to its customers.

30.2 ASSESSMENT

Reviewing Key Terms and Concepts

1. What is a product life cycle? Name the four stages in the product life cycle.

2. Explain the concept of product positioning. Why is it important?

3. List and describe four strategies used to position products in the marketplace.

4. What is category management?

5. How can manufacturers use category management to assist a retailer?

Thinking Critically

6. Identify a possible product modification or product extension for an electric shaver, a toothbrush, and animal crackers.

Integrating Academic Skills

7. **MATH** The Griffin Company has two declining products and is considering deleting one of them from its product line. Product A costs $68 per unit to produce and sells for $105. The storage, distribution, and promotion costs average $5.40 a unit. Last year, 18,000 units were sold. Product B costs $46 to produce and sells for $67. Its storage, distribution, and promotion costs average $8.50 a unit. Last year, 80,000 units were sold. Of the two products, which is the less profitable and should be deleted?

30.2 ASSESSMENT ANSWERS

Reviewing Key Terms and Concepts

1. stages a product goes through during its life span: introduction, growth, maturity, decline
2. Businesses identify, place, and sell products to appeal to consumers.
3. stress price and quality; stress product features and benefits; compare product to competition; show relationship to other products in the line
4. managing product categories as individual business units

5. Manufacturers can customize product mix, merchandising, and promotions according to customer preference on a store-by-store basis.

Thinking Critically

6. electric shaver that sharpens its blades; toothbrush with toothpaste; vehicle-shaped crackers

Integrating Academic Skills

7. **MATH** Product B is more profitable, so product A should be dropped first.

Careers in Marketing

PRODUCT MANAGEMENT

Frederick Hacket
Product Planner
London Fog

What does your job entail?

"My job requires me to set the blueprint for the designers. You have to have an understanding of the market on a creative and sales level. You need to know a little bit of everything. I try to travel to the major fashion shows in Paris. I need to have an eye for colors, directions, and trends in Europe, so that when I visit our retail stores I can determine their needs. I love my job because every day offers new opportunities! Every day leads to new learning and new challenges."

What training did you have?

"I have spent my entire working career in retail, which helps me understand the needs of retailers. I also spent two years merchandising for a product group called Façonnable. I was responsible for an entire product line from conception to creation. I have worked my way up through the industry."

Why did you focus on a career in product planning?

"Product planning is the only thing I have ever really wanted to do. In high school geometry, when the teacher asked us to draw different geometric shapes, I drew Argyle socks. I have always dressed pretty normally, but with a small twist here and there. While I don't consider myself a fashion maven, I love doing what I do."

What is your key to success?

"I think the key to success in this business is understanding what customers want and need. I also have the ability to interpret trends and apply them to the product and the personality of brand."

Thinking Critically

What challenges might a product planner face when dealing with a retailer?

Career Facts

Education and Training: A minimum of a BS in engineering along with several years of product marketing experience is necessary. An MBA is highly desirable.

Aptitudes, Abilities, and Skills: Product planners must have exceptional analytical skills to present their assessments to many different groups including management, engineers, and customers. Strong leadership, the ability to promote teamwork, good communication skills, and the ability to work with little supervision are all necessary.

Career Outlook: Opportunities are linked to the growth in the consumer market and vary as the demand for new products increases or decreases.

Career Path: Experience in marketing or engineering design may lead to a career as a product planner, who can move into executive management levels.

Chapter 30 ■ Product Planning 563

Chapter 30 ASSESSMENT

Vocabulary Review

Papers will vary. See the Glossary for definitions.

Fact and Idea Review

1. A product item is a specific model, brand, or size of product within a product line. A product line is a group of closely related products manufactured and/or sold by a business.

2. Product width is the number of different product lines a business carries. Product depth is the number of product items offered within each product line.

3. New products are matched against the company's overall objectives to see if they fit. They are evaluated for potential conflict with existing products. Products might also be consumer tested.

4. Marketers use marketing research techniques during product development and continued monitoring of product performance after introduction.

5. Manufacturers may expand a product line to build on an already established image, to increase sales and profits, to offer customers complementary products, and to appeal to new markets.

6. Product modification is an alteration in a company's existing product. Product modifications are low-risk and low-cost ways to develop new products.

7. During a product's introduction stage, a company may use heavy advertising and other means of promotion, such as in-store displays, to draw customers' attention. A company should be prepared to counter the effects of competitors' new products by offering new features during a product's growth stage.

8. Advertising would focus on customer satisfaction. The company might introduce new modules or modify the existing product.

9. A business must allocate more of its advertising budget to promote the product during the product's maturity stage. During a decline stage, a company may sell or license, recommit, discount, regionalize, modernize, or alter the product.

10. Sell or license the product; recommit to the product line; discount the product; regionalize the product; and modernize or alter the product.

564

VOCABULARY REVIEW

Using all of the vocabulary terms below, write a 150-word paper on product planning.

- product planning
- product mix
- product line
- product item
- product width
- product depth
- product modification
- product life cycle
- product positioning
- category management
- planogram

FACT AND IDEA REVIEW

1. Explain the difference between a product item and a product line. (30.1)

2. Explain the difference between product depth and product width. (30.1)

3. Summarize the types of criteria that marketers use to screen new product ideas. (30.1)

4. How do marketers evaluate customer acceptance of a new product? (30.1)

5. Identify four reasons for expanding a product line. (30.1)

6. What is a product modification? (30.1)

7. What strategies might a business use during a product's introduction and growth stages? (30.2)

8. What strategies might a business use during a product's growth stage? (30.2)

9. What strategies might a business use during a product's maturity and decline stages? (30.2)

10. List the strategies that a company can use during a product's decline stage. (30.2)

THINKING CRITICALLY

1. Hometown Favorites is a company that will ship over 400 old-time favorite food items, which are largely unavailable on a regular basis at local supermarkets. Why do certain brands of cereal, candy, and staple products have such appeal that consumers will order them specially?

2. You own a small retail store that sells party supplies. What are ten items you should have in your product mix?

3. In response to the "green movement," manufacturers are designing products that are safe for the environment. Choose a type of company, and suggest ways it could modify one of its products to be environmentally friendly.

4. Explain the strategies you would use to manage a computer product, video game, or cosmetic product during each stage of its life cycle.

BUILDING WORKPLACE SKILLS

1. **Technology** Select a favorite sport in which you are either an active spectator or a participant. Investigate how technological improvements have impacted at least one product used in the sport. Using a word-processor, prepare a written report between 150–200 words about the technology and its effect on the sport.

2. **Human Relations** You are a buyer of clothing for a large department store. You are confronted by an exasperated customer who is ready to walk out of the store because of the cluttered merchandise. She complains that too many sizes, colors, and styles are jammed together on too many racks. What might you say or do to pacify the customer and cause her to stay in the store to buy merchandise?

Thinking Critically

1. Answers will vary but may argue that some individuals develop a brand loyalty for products that cause them to purchase them even when they are not readily available. They might evoke pleasant experiences or memories that the purchasers want to relive.

2. Answers may include paper plates, cups, napkins, gift wrap, balloons, party invitations, party favors, table cloths, greeting cards, and decorations.

3. Answers will vary but may include design packages that are recyclable and use less harmful contents.

4. Answers will vary based on choice of product items.

Building Workplace Skills

1. Reports will vary.

2. Answers will vary, but the students should be tactful in their responses to the customer.

APPLYING MARKETING CONCEPTS

1. **Identifying Product Mix** Explore a Web site for a car manufacturer, such as Chevrolet, Pontiac, Saturn, or another one of your choice. Identify the product mix offered by the car manufacturer. Write an outline detailing each product in the product line and the primary market for each product.

2. **Finding Product Line Extensions** Find a consumer product manufacturer's Web site (Kellogg's, Quaker Oats, Nabisco, Procter & Gamble, Kraft, etc.) to obtain five examples of product line extensions. Use presentation software to give an oral report on the name of the original product and the line extensions for the product.

3. **Investigating Width and Depth of a Product Line** Investigate a consumer product, such as cameras, computers, a line of clothing, or sporting equipment. Evaluate the width and depth of each product line. Use a word processor to prepare a 150-word report on how the selection increases or decreases the potential sales of those products.

4. **Representing a Product Line** Use a spreadsheet program to represent visually a product line carried in a store of your choice. Identify the product line, each item in the product line, its price, and product features.

LINKING SCHOOL TO WORK

Basic Information and Thinking Skills Analyze the product mix of a place of employment. Determine the target market and write a 250-word report on how the product mix appeals to the target market.

Role Play: Ad Agency Employee

Situation You are to assume the role of an employee at an advertising agency. A representative of Consolidated Union Foods (judge) has approached you regarding its High Brow brand of decaffeinated coffee. High Brow's coffee sales are flat, while the industry's sales figures are going up. A possible reason is that High Brow only carries regular and decaffeinated coffee in traditional tin cans.

Activity You have been asked to review High Brow's product mix and make suggestions to position the product in order to increase sales.

Evaluation You will be evaluated on how well you meet the following performance indicators:
- Explain the concept of product mix
- Plan product mix
- Develop strategies to position product/businesses
- Describe factors used by marketers to position products/businesses
- Make oral presentations

*inter*NET CONNECTION

Product Life Cycles for Services
Locate one of the following Web sites: United States Postal Service, Federal Express, or United Parcel Service.

Connect
- Write a report on the delivery service features offered by the business that you visited.
- Develop a product life cycle for one service that you investigated.
- Indicate in what stage the particular service would fall on your product life cycle.

Chapter 30 ■ Product Planning **565**

Students should be evaluated on the performance indicators noted in the Role Play.
- For another DECA Role Play, go to the *Student Activity Workbook,* p. 261.
- For more in-depth Role Play practice, refer to DECA's *Essential Competitive Events Handbook.* To order, contact DECA at **www.deca.org**.

*inter*NET CONNECTION
Reports will vary.

Mini Quiz
Administer the Mini Quiz orally. For an expanded chapter quiz, go to page 179 of the *Reproducible Tests* book.

1. Making decisions about the product and service features needed to sell a business's products, services, or ideas is called product planning.
2. The different products a company makes or sells is known as its product mix.
3. A group of closely related products manufactured and/or sold by a business is called its product line.
4. The stages a product goes through is called its product life cycle.
5. The efforts a business makes to identify, place, and sell its products in the marketplace is called product positioning.

Applying Marketing Concepts
1. Answers will vary.
2. Presentations and reports will vary. Some examples include Frito-Lay potato chips, Frito-Lay barbecue, sour cream and onion, salt and vinegar potato chips, and Baked Lays.
3. Reports will vary.
4. Spreadsheets will vary based upon selected products.

Linking School to Work
Answers will depend on the work situation.

 1. **Assessment** Have students complete the Reproducible Test for Chapter 30 or construct your own tests using the ExamView software.
2. **Enrichment** Have students complete the corresponding activities in the following workbooks:
- *Marketing Math Workbook*, p. 101

Chapter Overview

Chapter 31 introduces the nature and scope of branding for product planning. The chapter details the elements of branding, explains the different types of brands, and discusses branding strategies. The major functions of packaging and labeling are also explained.

 ## Springboard

Brainstorm Write these products across the board as column headings: breakfast cereal, hand soap, laundry detergent, instant coffee, toothpaste, cookies, and packaged meat. Assign one product to each row of students and have each row generate five manufacturer and private distributor brands for each product. Write them in the appropriate column on the board. Tell students that in this chapter they will look at each of elements that make up a brand name.

Prereading

List the objectives in the *What You'll Learn* section and discuss them with students. Have the students skim the chapter, looking at the pictures, reading the captions, and noting the heads. Ask questions to ensure that the students have a minimal understanding of the chapter structure.

Preteaching Marketing Vocabulary

List the vocabulary terms on the board. Have the class reach a consensus on a definition for each term.

Marketing: What It Takes

Answer Answers will vary, but students should realize that the first step in brand building for a dot-com company is generating Web site awareness and visits to the site. Initial investment must be made in advertising using mass media. Then the brand must be built through customer relationships.

Chapter 31
Branding, Packaging, and Labeling

Marketing: What It Takes

Brand Building on the Internet

You are employed in a leading advertising and media agency that offers a variety of branding services. You have been assigned to develop a brand building campaign for a new dot-com company.

WHAT WILL YOU DO?
What recommendations would you give to your new dot-com company to help with its brand building efforts?

THE DECA CONNECTION — ADVISOR CORNER

Presenting DECA to Marketing Classes Invite a state officer or former DECA members to your school and/or chapter meeting to make presentations to your marketing classes. They will get your members excited about DECA and can share exactly what DECA has done for them. While they are there, ask them to assist with recruiting efforts outside the classroom. They can speak to other classes, to your co-op sponsors, or to fellow educators. This is a first-hand method of demonstrating the vast role that DECA plays in developing leadership, marketing, and management skills in America's youth.

Branding Elements and Strategies

Branding

A **brand** is a name, term, design, or symbol (or combination of them) that identifies a business or organization and its products. Brands are divided into two categories—corporate brands and product brands.

Corporate brands, such as Coca-Cola, McDonald's, and Citibank, are used not only to identify the business but also to reflect quality, value, and reliability. Corporate brands build relationships with customers and support the product brands offered by the company.

Effective brands have tremendous value and are well known worldwide. A 1999 brand valuation study by Interbrand, a leading international branding company, identified 60 global brands worth more than $1 billion. The Coca-Cola brand was valued at $83.8 billion, Microsoft at $56 billion, and IBM at $43 billion. U.S. companies dominated the ranking, accounting for the top ten brands and two-thirds of the 60 brands analyzed. Figure 31-1 on page 568 identifies some of the best-known worldwide brands.

Product brands, such as Pepsi, Coke, Barbie, Whopper, and Big Mac, also are used to connote quality and reliability. Almost every product has a brand. Product brands are among a company's most important assets and are powerful in the selling process.

Brands can include a number of elements. Some examples of these are brand name, brand mark, trade name, trade character, and trademark.

A **brand name** is the word, group of words, letters, or numbers representing a brand that can be spoken. Some brand names for products include PT Cruiser, Mountain Dew, SnackWells, and K2. Brand-name products usually cost more than similar unbranded merchandise because of higher advertising costs. A **brand mark** is the part of the brand that is a symbol or design. It may include distinctive coloring or lettering. A brand mark is the element of the brand that usually is not spoken. Some examples of brand marks are the U.S. Postal Service's eagle, Apple Computer's apple, and Greyhound Bus Company's greyhound.

A **trade name** identifies the company or a division of a particular corporation. This is the legal name that a company uses when it does business. Dell, Kellogg's, and Xerox are all examples of trade names. A **trade character** is a brand mark with human form or characteristics. Some examples include Birds Eye's Jolly Green Giant, Kellogg's Tony the Tiger, the Pillsbury Doughboy, and the Keebler Elves. A **trademark** is a brand name, brand mark, trade name, trade character, or a combination of these that is given legal protection by the federal government.

What You'll Learn

- The nature, scope, and importance of branding in product planning
- The various branding elements
- The different types of brands
- How to classify branding strategies

Why It's Important

The right name is an important part of every successful business. The name of a business or a product projects the personality of the company, product, or service.

Key Terms

- brand
- brand name
- brand mark
- trade name
- trade character
- trademark
- manufacturer brands
- private distributor brands
- generic brands
- brand extension
- brand licensing
- mixed-brand strategy
- co-branding strategy

FOCUS

Bell Ringer Activity

Collect and Identify The day before you begin this section, tell students to bring a magazine with ads to class for the next day's lesson. On the day of the class, write the correct definitions on the board from the vocabulary list that you created for Preteaching Marketing Vocabulary. Using the definitions as guidelines, have each student cut out one ad from his or her magazine and label the brand name, brand mark, trade name, trade character, and/or trademark.

Introducing the Section

Branding Elements and Strategies You may not have time to review each student's ad with the entire class, but review as many as you can. It's important that students start the identification process immediately to avoid confusing the concepts. Have them make a classroom bulletin board of their labeled ads.

TEACH

📊 Technology Resources

PowerPoint The *Marketing Essentials* PowerPoint Presentation CD-ROM provides visual lecture aids for every chapter section.

Classroom Resources

For the Teacher
- Teacher Editions for all workbooks
- Assessment Package
- PowerPoint Presentation Software
- Interactive Lesson Planner
- ILP Block Scheduling, p. 10
- ILP Lesson Plans, p. 65
- ILP Internet Resources, p. 81

- ILP Blackline Masters, p. 68
- ILP *BusinessWeek* Case Studies, p. 195
- ILP Marketing Career Portfolio, p. 40
- *Marketing Essentials* Web site (**www.marketing.glencoe.com**)

For the Student
- Student Activity Workbook, p. 269
- Marketing Math Workbook, p. 101

- Marketing Research Project Workbook
- ILP School-to-Work Activity Workbook, p. 127
- Virtual Business simulation
- *Marketing Essentials* Web site (**www.marketing.glencoe.com**)

ILP These resources are available in print and on the Interactive Lesson Planner (ILP)

567

Concept Development

1. Read Section 31.1 with students.
2. Have students read aloud the Case Study on page 572 and review the answers in class.
3. After you finish reading this section, have students list products they often buy, and write the brand of each product they buy most frequently. Ask why each particular brand appeals to them.

Discussion Starter

Private Brands As the text states, private distributor brands are now more accepted by the buying public. Have students name some private brands that are available locally. Ask: Why were people in past decades sometimes reluctant to buy private brands? Why are private brands so popular now?
(In the past, many private brands—particularly food products—were inferior in quality to manufacturer-brand products. However, many private distributor brands now rival the quality of manufacturer brands and are usually lower priced than manufacturer brands. Thus, consumers in our increasingly tough economy feel that private brands are a bargain.)

Ask students to name some products to which they are brand loyal. Why?

FIGURE 31-1

Top Ten Brands

Rank	Brand	Company	1999 Advertising (in millions of dollars)
1	Chevrolet vehicles	General Motors Corp.	762.4
2	AT&T telephone services	AT&T Corp.	711.4
3	Dodge vehicles	Daimler-Chrysler	651.7
4	Ford vehicles	Ford Motor Co.	629.5
5	McDonald's restaurants	McDonald's Corp.	627.2
6	Toyota vehicles	Toyota Motor Corp.	569.4
7	Sears department stores	Sears, Roebuck & Co.	556.1
8	Sprint telephone services	Sprint Corp.	470.1
9	Chrysler vehicles	Daimler Chrysler	426.5
10	Nissan vehicles	Nissan Motor Co.	416.9

■ **The World's Most Valuable Brands** Brands are often a company's most valuable asset. *What is the total 1999 advertising spending for these top ten brands?*

■ **Branding** Brands include brand name, brand mark, and trademark. *Can you find these elements on this bottle of Gatorade?*

568 Unit 10 ■ *Product and Service Management*

Trademark branding of products and services has been expanding to include additional elements of sound, color, and smell. Harley-Davidson has applied for a sound trademark consisting of the exhaust sound from its V-Twin motorcycle engine. Every motorcycle that Harley-Davidson sells is in effect a sound billboard for its products. Boston Duck Tours, a sightseeing tour company, received a sound trademark for the sound of a human voice making duck-like quacking noises.

Trademarks are followed by a registered trademark symbol (®). Examples include Frito-Lay's *Doritos*®, Kellogg's *Rice Krispies Treats*® cereal, and *VISA*®. When brand names, brand marks, trade characters, and other elements of branding are registered, they cannot be used or misused by other companies.

Brand names, brand marks, trade names, trade characters, and trademarks are often combined to form a firm's *corporate symbol* or name.

■ Importance of Brands in Product Planning

The use of brands is important in product planning for several reasons.

Branding helps build customer loyalty. Satisfied customers can easily recognize a company's products when they want to make repeat purchases. Nine out of ten people will pay 25 percent more to buy GE Soft White light bulbs. The GE Soft White brand is perceived by customers to be better than competitors.

Branding assures customers that products carrying the same brand are of a consistent quality. Branding identifies the firm that manufactures the product, and reduces the risk of customer dissatisfaction.

Branding is vital as it addresses new target markets. By simply extending the brands, different markets can be reached. Branding also helps when introducing new product lines and categories. Customers are more willing to try new products that carry a familiar brand name. When Burger King announced its Big Kids Meals, aimed at kids 7 to 12, they capitalized on customer familiarity with kids' meals.

Finally, branding establishes an image for a product or company. The company's brand becomes a reflection of its target customers. The Volkswagen Company reinvented its VW image in 2000 by focusing on youth and vitality. They decided to place less emphasis on the traditional engineering approach. The new image has proven very successful with the younger market.

FIGURE 31-1 ANSWER
Top Ten Brands The total advertising spending is just over $5.82 billion.

CAPTION ANSWER
Branding Students should locate the brand name, brand mark, and trademark on the Gatorade label.

Generating Brands

According to an Interbrand survey for the first six months of 1998, 93 publicly-traded companies registered corporate name changes. It is estimated that 75 percent of all companies introduce a new product name on an annual basis. Some companies find it increasingly difficult to secure the right corporate or product names because so many names are already taken. This fact is not surprising when in 1999 over 79,000 trademarks were registered by the U.S. Patent and Trademark Office.

Some companies with global brands such as Mars, Inc. and Kellogg's Company are doing the opposite. They are reviewing whether they should rename their similar products that have different names. The *3 Musketeers* candy bar is called the *Mars Bar* in England, which may cause confusion. The Coca-Cola Company has already adopted this worldwide approach. Procter & Gamble has reduced the number of brand names from 600 to 400 to take advantage of increased worldwide exposure caused largely by the Internet.

Brand names are often generated internally by employees. There are computer software programs that specialize in generating brand names. Some programs will check to see if a name is already owned and trademarked by another company. Companies hire branding agencies, naming consultants, or public relations firms to generate brand names. Branding is so important to product planning that 50 percent of all marketing firms do research to test new brand names before they are released.

Despite the high costs involved, marketers sometimes must change brand names. Names may change when a business adds new product lines, seeks new markets, or modifies its image. Approximately 50 percent of all corporate name changes occur because of company mergers and acquisitions. Brand names also are changed as a result of lawsuits and court decisions.

Types of Brands

Manufacturers, wholesalers, and retailers often brand their own products. These products are classified by who owns them. Three classifications of brands are manufacturer brands, private distributor brands, and generic brands.

REAL WORLD MARKETING

The Booming Itsy Bitsy Market

Kenn Viselman's company, Itsy Bitsy Entertainment, is growing larger and larger. The company sells merchandise targeted at preschoolers. Viselman takes characters from television programs and well-known children's books and licenses their images to manufacturers of everything from dolls to underwear to shampoo. Some of the characters that Viselman licenses are Thomas the Tank Engine, the Teletubbies, and Eloise. The big money is in licensing, according to Viselman. While a successful movie might bring in $100 million, "a successful licensing program can make $1 billion in its first year."

Thinking Critically
What propels classic books such as *Eloise* into the mainstream years after their first introductions?

MANUFACTURER BRANDS Manufacturer brands, also called *producer brands*, are owned and initiated by manufacturers. Examples of manufacturer brands include General Electric, Heinz, and Motorola.

Manufacturer brands generate the majority of sales for most product categories. Approximately 70 percent of all food products, 65 percent of all appliances, 80 percent of all gasoline, and 100 percent of all automobiles are sold under manufacturer or producer brands.

Manufacturer brands not only identify a given product but also indicate a standard quality and price. They appeal to customers who want consistent quality, dependable product performance, and status.

PRIVATE DISTRIBUTOR BRANDS Private distributor brands—also called *private brands, store brands,* or *dealer brands*—are owned and initiated by wholesalers and retailers. The manufacturer's name does not appear on the product. Some examples of private distributor brands are Radio Shack and Kmart.

Chapter 31 ■ *Branding, Packaging, and Labeling* **569**

SECTION 31.1

Thinking Critically

Generic Products Generic drugs are some of the most popular generic products available today. Some generic medicines contain the same formulas and ingredients as brand-name medicines, but the generics are considerably cheaper. Ask students why this is the case. (*Companies that research, develop, and manufacture medicine recoup their development and manufacturing costs in their product price. However, once a patent on the formula for a particular medicine expires, other pharmaceutical companies can reproduce the formula, manufacture the product, and offer a generic version at a lower price because they do not have to put money into the original R & D. Generics have become so widely accepted that many medical insurance companies will now only pay for patients' prescriptions if generics are used, or if no generics are available.*)

Cooperative Learning

Trade Characters Divide students into four groups. Assign each group one trade character. Have students research the changes this character has undergone over the years. Trade character examples might include Betty Crocker the Pillsbury Doughboy, and the Campbell's kids.

REAL WORLD MARKETING

The Booming Itsy Bitsy Market
Answer The exposure generated from becoming a media property, such as a film or television series, is what causes a licensed product to grow. As audience numbers increase, so does the potential for increased distribution and profit.

Independent Practice

Research and Identify

Using business magazines, such as *Adweek*, *BrandWeek*, *BusinessWeek*, *Fortune*, *Inc.*, *Grocery Marketing*, *Supermarket News*, *Mass Market Retailers*, and *Stores*, or an Internet search engine, have students identify five new products being introduced into the market. Have them identify the brand name, brand mark, trade name, trade character, and trademark.

What's in a Domain Name?

Looking for a name for your new business? Before the "Technology Revolution," finding a name for a business was commonplace. You could file a name with a local county government as a "DBA" (doing business as) and forge into your business activities. Now, with the increase of Internet businesses, people must register for domain names. Over 10,000,000 entrepreneurs have registered dot-com domain names. This means that many memorable domain names already are taken! Some entrepreneurs register names in order to sell them in the future — and make a great profit. One entrepreneur registered the name Business.com and sold the domain name for $7.5 million! Although new top-level domain name extensions, such as dot shop and dot banc are in the works, the original dot com is expected to be most valuable.

Thinking Critically

What problems might occur with the introduction of new top-level domain name extensions?

■ **Same Store, Different Brands** You will find different types of brands in many retail stores. *Why might a supermarket carry all of these types of macaroni and cheese dinners?*

GENERIC BRANDS Generic brands represent a general product category and do not carry a company or brand name. The packaging for generic products carries only a description of the product, such as "pancake mix" or "paper towels." They are generally sold in supermarkets and discount stores. Unbranded products are often priced 30 to 50 percent lower than manufacturer brands and 10 to 15 percent lower than the private distributor brands. Generic brands come with a lower price because they are not heavily advertised or promoted.

The Jewel supermarkets in Chicago were the first to introduce generic products in the 1970s. Generic products have expanded to include more than 300 product categories, including vitamins, auto parts, food staples, and pharmaceuticals. Generic products are now offered in more than 250 retail chains throughout the United States, and more than 75 percent of all U.S. supermarkets carry generic items.

■ Branding Strategies

Branding strategies are the ways companies use brands to meet sales and company objectives. Some of these strategies include brand extensions, brand licensing, mixed branding, and co-branding. Effective use of different brand strategies can increase sales of branded products and maximize company profits.

Private distributor brands appeal to customers who want the quality and performance of manufacturer brands at a lower price. Many large supermarket and retail chains have private distributor brands. At some major department stores, private brands amount to more than 40 percent of all merchandise carried.

Private brands are popular with retailers because they usually carry higher gross margins (and are thus more profitable for the seller) than manufacturer brands. They are better controlled by retailers because they cannot be sold by competitors and thus can lead to retailer, rather than to manufacturer, loyalty. Some private distributor brands, such as the Sears' Kenmore line of appliances and Craftsman tools, have become so popular and respected that they rival manufacturer brands in sales and customer recognition.

What's in a Domain Name?

Answer The consumer might become confused if new top-level domain name extensions are introduced. Also, brand dilution might occur, with the original brand losing strength and identity.

CAPTION ANSWER
Same Store, Different Brands A supermarket would want to appeal to a wide range of customer needs. The store could reach several target markets, maintain brand loyalty, and increase product mix.

BRAND EXTENSION Brand extension is a branding strategy that uses an existing brand name for an improved or new product in the product line. For example, Ocean Spray Cranberry juice extended its product line by adding Cran®Apple, Cran®Raspberry, Cran®America, and various other fruit blends. Other examples of brand extension include Ann Taylor personal-care products and Starbucks ice cream. As you learned in Chapter 30, launching new products is costly, and the failure rate for new products is high. Companies can reduce the risk of failure by using an already established brand name.

A potential problem with brand extensions is that over-extending a product line may cause *brand dilution*. Brand dilution occurs when the original brand loses its strength in brand identity because it has been stretched to include too many products. The original brand may lose its appeal with customers. Some marketing specialists believe that the Arm & Hammer brand was diluted when the brand was extended to laundry detergent, antiperspirant, toothpaste, and cat litter.

BRAND LICENSING Brand licensing is the legal authorization by a trademarked brand owner to allow another company (the licensee) to use its brand, brand mark, or trade character for a fee. The licensee pays the brand owner a royalty for the use of the product name.

Companies license their brands to enhance their company image and to sell more of their core products. Caterpillar Corporation of Peoria, Illinois has licensed its name to more than 700 products, from marine apparel to scaled replicas of the company's tractors and other machinery.

McDonald's paid a $75 million licensing fee to associate its *Happy Meals* with Disney's 2000 movie, *Dinosaurs.* Licensed products must always support the core product's marketing strategy.

MIXED BRANDS Some manufacturers and retailers use a mixed-brand strategy to sell products. A mixed-brand strategy involves simultaneously offering a combination of manufacturer, private distributor, and generic brands. In mixed branding, a firm markets products under its own name and that of a reseller because the market segment attracted to the reseller is different from their own market. Michelin manufactures tires for Sears and with the Sears brand name as well as under its own brand name. Union Carbide produces and sells generic and national brands of garbage bags. It advertises Glad bags, its national brand, as "superior to the thin, bargain bags." Union Carbide can maximize its profits by selling a generic product without damaging the reputation and the sales of its brand product. A mixed-brand strategy allows a business to reach several target markets, maintain brand loyalty, and increase its overall product mix.

■ **Brand Extension Helps Sell Products** Developing brand extensions is an effective branding strategy. *What are some advantages of using brand extensions?*

Chapter 31 ■ *Branding, Packaging, and Labeling* **571**

Individualized Practice

Communication Skills

L1 Hand write the label copy for a common product. Then produce a typed version of this same copy on your computer, but include several errors. Give a copy of your handwritten and your typeset copy to each student for a proofreading exercise. Students should use the proofreader's marks they entered in their notebooks when they studied Chapter 10.

L2 Have each student bring a product label to class. Divide students into pairs. Have each student read his or her label to the other student, who will take notes on the key information in the label's contents. How accurate was each student's note-taking? (If you want to make this a memory skills activity, do not allow students to take notes.)

L3 Have each student find one product label that contains at least 100 words and keyboard it. Students should type the label exactly as it's typeset, using caps, caps/lower case, italic, and boldface. When students are finished, have them proofread their own work, or have them proofread each other's work.

Reteaching

1. **Vocabulary** Assign and review the vocabulary terms for this section.
2. **Fact and Idea Review** Assign and review Fact and Idea Review questions 1–5 from the Chapter Assessment.
3. **Terms** Have students write the terms *manufacturer brands, private distributor brands,* and *generic brands* as three column headings across a sheet of paper. To help reinforce their understanding of each, have them review these three sections in the chapter and write down key points underneath each heading.

Case Study

Building Brand Loyalty on the Internet

PepsiCo has started to experiment with the Internet as a tool for building brand loyalty by promoting its brand on the Web. As the interest for Internet use continues to grow, especially among teens, it seems that cyberspace is the place to build brand awareness.

In August 2000, PepsiCo began jointly co-branding and co-promoting its drink products with the Web site Yahoo! Pepsi will feature Yahoo! on 1.5 billion soft drink labels, while Yahoo! will promote Pepsi products on a co-branded site called PepsiStuff.com. In order to take advantage of the services of this Web site, you need to first register with Yahoo! The desired result is that newly registered users will take advantage of other Yahoo! services.

A joint promotional campaign will involve coded bottle caps of Pepsi's products that can be redeemed online for merchandise discounts and prizes. Companies such as The Sports Authority and Sony Pictures offer merchandise that can be "purchased" using PepsiStuff points.

The expenditures of online advertising are smaller than non-Internet advertising. However, consumer product manufacturers prefer to advertise on television and do not feel that Internet banner ads will build brand loyalty. They believe that Internet advertising is limited in what it can convey through sound and video. In 1999, consumer products companies spent only 2 percent of their advertising budgets on Internet advertising.

Promoting and advertising branded products on the Internet does have some potential advantages for manufacturers. Direct feedback can be obtained through e-mail, by tracking respondent behavior. Experimenting with sponsorships and contests can bring fast results. Good results with these types of activities might convince other manufacturers to use the Internet to promote brand loyalty.

Case Study Review

1. How do Pepsi and Yahoo! expect to build brand loyalty through the Internet?
2. Why do consumer product manufacturers prefer television advertising to online advertising?

A MATTER OF ETHICS

3. Is it ethical for consumer product manufacturers to alter promotional campaigns to address changing lifestyles? Why or why not?

Case Study Review Answers

Building Brand Loyalty on the Internet

1. Pepsi and Yahoo! hope that co-branding on the labels of Pepsi products and the PepsiStuff.com Web site will promote brand loyalty for each company. Discounts and prizes will be used to encourage consumers to visit the co-branded Web site.
2. Manufacturers believe that television spots build emotional attachments to products. They believe that most banner ads are too limited in what they can convey through sound and video.

A MATTER OF ETHICS

3. It is ethical because businesses need to develop products to address customer needs or they will not be successful in the competitive marketplace.

CO-BRANDING Have you ever noticed that Kellogg's Pop-Tarts are made using only Smucker's fruit filling? Sometimes companies use a co-branding strategy to sell their products. A co-branding strategy combines one or more brands to increase customer loyalty and sales for each individual brand. For example, the Ford Motor Company wanted to find a marketing tool that would strengthen customer loyalty among Harley-Davidson riders and create a distinctive vehicle for potential owners of Ford trucks. Therefore, they created the Limited Edition 2000 Harley-Davidson F-150 pickup truck. This strategy draws on the customer base for both separate products.

Co-branding can also work when two or more retailers share a location. Starbucks Coffee Co. has an agreement with Barnes & Noble bookstores to open coffee shops inside the store. Book shoppers know that they can buy Starbucks coffee in the bookstore. This helps to draw customers into Barnes & Noble and away from other bookstores that don't offer brand name coffee bar services. The Barnes & Noble/Starbucks partnership is advertised throughout the bookstore's promotional materials to increase customer awareness.

Co-branding strategies primarily build brand recognition for each business. Co-branding works well if both companies' brands complement each other and each brand receives equal billing in

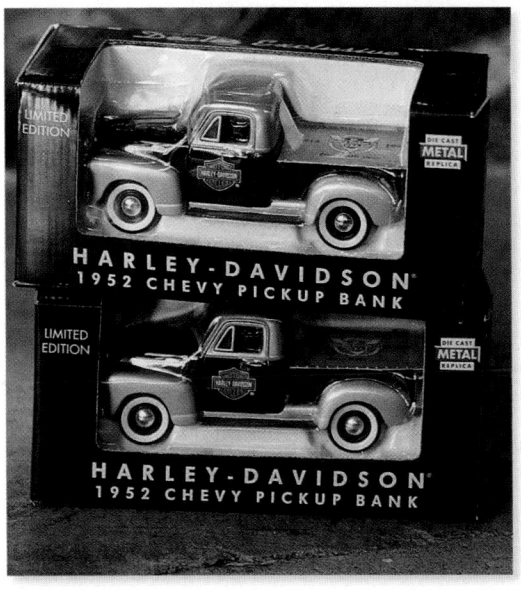

■ **Co-Branding Creates a Winning Combination**
Co-branding techniques work well with well-respected products. *How does co-branding help each business partner?*

advertisements, direct mail, and other promotions. Customer benefits will assure that the arrangement will succeed.

31.1 ASSESSMENT

Reviewing Key Terms and Concepts

1. What is the difference between a brand name and a brand mark?
2. Why is branding important to product planning?
3. Name three types of brands.
4. List four different branding strategies.

Thinking Critically

5. Internet service providers are teaming with airlines, financial institutions, media outlets, celebrities, and non-profit groups to offer private-label Web access. Do you think that individuals want to receive their Internet access from the New York Yankees, David Bowie, Pepsi, or their local bank? Why or why not?

Integrating Academic Skills

6. **COMMUNICATION** Kellogg's sells a cereal called Frosted Flakes in the United States, Frosties in most European countries, and Zucaritas in Italy. Write a 150-word paper explaining why the company uses different product names in various countries.

Enrichment

1. **Review** Assign and review the appropriate Thinking Critically questions from the Chapter Assessment.
2. **Extend** Assign and review the corresponding activities from *BusinessWeek Case Studies, Internet Resources,* and the *School-to-Work Activity Workbook.* ILP

Evaluation

Assign and review the Section 31.1 Assessment.

Technology Resources

 Assessment Resources
Go to the *Marketing Essentials* Web site (**www.marketing.glencoe. com**) for resources to teach and assess occupation-specific vocabulary.

CLOSE

Section Wrap-Up

Have students once again go through a magazine, choose an ad, and point out the following: the brand name, brand mark, trade name, trade character, trademark, and whether it's a manufacturer or a local distributor brand.

CAPTION ANSWER
Co-Branding Creates a Winning Combination Co-branding builds brand recognition, increases customer loyalty to both brands, and hopefully increases the sales of the co-branded product.

31.1 ASSESSMENT ANSWERS

Reviewing Key Terms and Concepts

1. A brand name is the name, design, or symbol that identifies the products of a company. A brand mark is a symbol or design with distinctive coloring or lettering.
2. It makes it easy for consumers to identify the product.
3. manufacturer, private distributor, and generic
4. brand extension, brand licensing, co-branding, and mixed brands

Thinking Critically

5. Answers will vary but might argue that private-label Internet service providers could grab a substantial share of the market in the future. This could happen because the service is often free or discounted.

Integrating Academic Skills

6. **COMMUNICATIONS** Papers will vary.

573

SECTION 31.2

Packaging and Labeling

FOCUS

Bell Ringer Activity

Describe and Explain Place the following on a table in front of the class: 12 pencils, 6 to 12 cookies, 4 rolls of tape, 25 paper clips or rubber bands, 20 to 30 loose Kleenex, 6 to 12 pickles or olives, and a glob of toothpaste—or display several products that are packaged differently. Also provide the packaging for all of these products.

Ask students to tell you how each of these products are normally packaged for retail sale. Then place each product's package in front of the product. Ask students why each type of packaging material is used. Why, for example, are rubber bands packaged in cardboard boxes instead of in glass jars? Why are pickles and olives packaged in glass or plastic jars instead of in cellophane pouches? Why are pencils packaged in cardboard boxes or cardboard wrappers instead of in plastic bags?

Introducing the Section

Packaging and Labeling Have students help you generate a board list of the purpose of packaging. Allow students to look closely at the product packaging and tell you the information contained on each product label. Then have students brainstorm the reasons for product labels. Given all the uses for packaging and product labels, it should be easy for students to see why both are so important in product planning.

• What You'll Learn

- The principal functions of product packaging
- The main functions of labels

• Why It's Important

While branding gives a specific brand personality, packaging puts a face on a product. Effective packaging creates a good impression, helps to sell the product, and communicates benefits to customers.

• Key Terms

- package
- label

Packaging

A **package** is the physical container or wrapping for a product. A package represents the size, shape, and final appearance of a product at the time of sale which makes it important to product planning. It is estimated that 10 percent of a product's retail price is spent on the actual package as well as package development and design.

■ Functions of Packaging

A package does much more than hold a product—it is a selling tool. Companies take great care in designing or redesigning the packages for their products. When Coca-Cola created a new embossed 8-ounce "Georgia green" glass bottle in 2000, the company did a lot of research and promotion. Sampling stations were set up in malls, movie theatres, concerts, skating rinks, and ski areas in more than 75 cities across the country. The green glass contour bottle was also made the focus of new packaging graphics, featuring a visual of the cap popping off of the top of the bottle.

The functions of packaging include promoting and selling the product, defining product identity, providing information, meeting customer needs, ensuring safe use, and protecting the product (see Figure 31-2 on page 575).

PROMOTING AND SELLING THE PRODUCT Customer reaction to a product's package and brand name is an important factor in determining marketplace success or failure. This function is especially important as more stores focus on a self-service layout. Attractive, colorful, and artistic packages have promotional value. The brand name on a package reminds the customer of the product's manufacturer.

A better container can even create new sales or minimize the sales lost to competitors for the same products. Pump soap containers were designed to be neater, cleaner, easier to use, and more germ-free than bar soaps. The new containers have not replaced bar soaps; instead, they provide a choice for customers. Pump type dispensers create new sales and encourage competitors to offer similar new products.

DEFINING PRODUCT IDENTITY Packages are often used to invoke prestige, convenience, status, or another positive product attribute. An example of convenience packaging is Breakaway Foods "Push N' Eat" IncrEdibles. This line of food products including macaroni and cheese and scrambled eggs with cheese and sausage comes in a microwavable cylinder similar to a push-up ice cream bar. The company's slogan is "No forks, no spoons, no plates, no mess!" This food product's packaging was specially designed to allow the food to be frozen and then microwaved.

Classroom Resources

For the Teacher
- Teacher Editions for all workbooks
- Assessment Package
- PowerPoint Presentation Software
- Interactive Lesson Planner
- ILP Block Scheduling, p. 10
- ILP Lesson Plans, p. 66
- ILP Internet Resources, p. 81

- ILP *BusinessWeek* Case Studies, p. 195
- ILP Marketing Career Portfolio, p. 40
- *Marketing Essentials* Web site (**www.marketing.glencoe.com**)

For the Student
- Student Activity Workbook, p. 269
- Marketing Math Workbook, p. 101

- Marketing Research Project Workbook
- ILP School-to-Work Activity Workbook, p. 127
- Virtual Business simulation
- *Marketing Essentials* Web site (**www.marketing.glencoe.com**)

ILP These resources are available in print and on the Interactive Lesson Planner (ILP)

FIGURE 31-2
THE FUNCTIONS OF PACKAGING

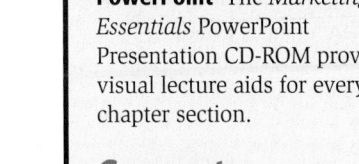

Packaging actually serves many purposes, ranging from product protection to attracting customer's attention. It is a selling tool that should promote and sell the product by catching customers' attention, defining the product's identity, providing information, ensuring safe use, and protecting the product.

PROMOTING AND SELLING THE PRODUCT

A well-designed package is a powerful point-of-purchase selling device because it can make a product stand out from its competition.

DEFINING PRODUCT IDENTITY

Packaging can be a crucial part of an overall marketing strategy for a product—particularly its advertising component.

PROVIDING INFORMATION

Some packages contain preprinted prices and UPC symbols to assist with inventory control.

ENSURING SAFE USE

Proper packaging helps to eliminate potential injuries or misuse of a product. Protective packaging prevents the contamination of products and also makes it difficult for a child to have access to potentially harmful substances.

PROTECTING THE PRODUCT

Packaging can protect a product from damage or spoilage.

Chapter 31 ■ Branding, Packaging, and Labeling **575**

SECTION 31.2

TEACH

Technology Resources

PowerPoint The *Marketing Essentials* PowerPoint Presentation CD-ROM provides visual lecture aids for every chapter section.

Concept Development

1. Read Section 31.2 with students.
2. After you have finished reading this section, have students look again at the product packaging you used for the Bell Ringer Activity. Have them speculate about why the colors and typeface were used on each label, and what total product image each label conveys. Remind them that a product label acts as an ad for a product; have them recall some of the fundamentals of good written ad preparation from Chapter 20.

GREAT IDEAS from the Marketing Classroom

**Lisa Jones
Centennial High School
Franklin, TN**

Students can understand packaging techniques by creating a product and packaging it. Bubble Jelly, for making bubbles, is a simple product to make and package right in the classroom. After completing lessons on packaging, have students cre-ate a package for Bubble Jelly, including labels. If you have a classroom computer, use a label program to create labels. The recipe for Bubble Jelly is: Melt one envelope of unflavored gelatin in 2/3 cup hot water. Add 1/2 cup of unscented dish washing liquid and mix. Don't stir vigorously. Add 1–2 drops of food coloring and 5–6 drops of fragrance. Pour into a package and let set uncovered overnight.

■ **Finger Foods Become Popular** New packages are created to address customer needs. *Why are hand-held foods becoming more popular?*

PROVIDING INFORMATION The package provides information for the customer. Many packages give directions for using the product and information about its contents, product guarantees, nutritional value (where applicable), and potential hazards.

MEETING CUSTOMER NEEDS Product packages often come in various sizes to meet the needs of different market segments. Family packs are designed to meet the needs of larger families, while smaller packages are made for individuals. Specific examples include multipacks of beverages such as soda and juice, bulk sizes of paper packages, single-serving cans of soup, and family meals at fast-food outlets.

Packages and package design must also keep up with changing lifestyles. Lunch kits with sliced meats and snack kits with cookies did not exist fifteen years ago. Now, this product category is a $1 billion business. Such products are especially popular with time-strapped consumers who purchase these products for their children. Tostitos Snack Kits are another example of product packaging that seeks to meet a consumer need. These snack kits contain a single serving of chips and salsa that can be conveniently eaten on the run.

ENSURING SAFE USE A package can improve product safety for the customer. Many products formerly packaged in glass now come in plastic containers. To avoid misuse or product tampering, many nonprescription drugs, cosmetics, and food items are now sold in tamper-resistant packages. These include jars and plastic containers with sealed lids and blisterpacks. *Blisterpacks* are packages with preformed plastic molds surrounding individual items arranged on a cardboard backing.

Countless other products are packaged in child-proof containers. These have lids that make them more difficult to open to reduce the chances of accidental spills and poisonings.

PROTECTING THE PRODUCT A package must protect a product during shipping, storage, and display. The package design should prevent tampering with the product while on display. The package design also might help prevent shoplifting of the product. It must protect the product from breakage and, in the case of food items, from spoilage.

Product planners must consider many factors when designing packaging. A poorly designed package that does not protect the product will cause a business to lose money. Additionally, a damaged or spoiled product creates a bad image and leads to a reduction in sales.

■ **Safety Directions Included** Packaging also encourages the safe use of individual products. *Why are safety directions often placed on a product package?*

CAUTION: KEEP OUT OF REACH OF CHILDREN. IF SWALLOWED, GIVE A GLASSFUL OF WATER. CALL A PHYSICIAN. IN CASE OF EYE CONTACT, FLUSH WITH WATER. DO NOT REUSE THIS PACKAGE FOR DISPENSING BEVERAGES OR OTHER LIQUIDS. Ingredients include biodegradable surfactants (anionic and nonionic) and enzymes. Made in U.S.A. by PROCTER & GAMBLE, Cincinnati, Ohio 45202 under one or more of the following U.S. Patents: D267,631; D292,491; D292,492; 4,318,818; 4,446,042; 4,515,705; 4,537,706; 4,537,707; 4,550,862; 4,561,998; 4,597,898; 4,968,451; 5,194,639; 5,288,431; 5,458,809; 5,458,810; 5,460,752; 5,466,802; 5,470,507; and 5,565,145. ©2000 P&G

CAPTION ANSWER
Finger Foods Become Popular Hand-held foods eliminate the need for utensils, are easy to use, and involve little clean up.

CAPTION ANSWER
Safety Directions Included Safety directions help to ensure the safe use of the product and avoid possible liability on the part of the manufacturer.

Basic protective materials for packages include cardboard, foam, and plastic. Many food items are packaged in airtight containers with resealable foil or plastic covers to prevent spoilage. This is especially important with perishable food products such as cheese, yogurt, or lunchmeat.

■ Contemporary Packaging Issues

Product packaging offers companies unique opportunities to address lifestyle changes and social and political concerns. Companies must consider using environmentally friendly types of packaging as well as packaging that makes social and political statements.

ENVIRONMENTAL PACKAGING The condition of the environment is an important issue facing product planners today. Recent public opinion surveys show that most Americans support less wasteful packaging. They are even willing to pay more for products that reduce waste. In response to consumer concern, companies are making more packages that are reusable, recyclable, less wasteful, and safer for the environment.

Celestial Seasonings, a specialty tea company, uses recycled paperboard for its boxes. Most of Procter & Gamble's plastic laundry detergent containers are made with at least 25 percent recycled plastic. *Budget Gourmet* frozen dinners are packaged in molded paper containers. The molded package eliminates the need for plastic trays,

■ **Sealed for Protection** Some packages have special protective material surrounding the product. *Why are blisterpacks often used in product packaging?*

aluminum tops, and cardboard boxes that would otherwise be used to package frozen dinners.

Many compact disc manufacturers have switched from plastic jewel cases to recycled cardboard packaging to hold CDs. On the same note, many companies that manufacture spray products such as hair products, air freshener, and paint have switched from using aerosol cans to pump dispensers, which do not release ozone-destroying cholorflurocarbons, or CFCs, into the atmosphere.

Cooperative Learning

Domestic and Foreign Product Packaging and Labeling Organize students into groups of three to five students to compare the product packaging and labeling of a domestic product and an identical foreign product (for example, a domestic and a foreign brand of tea, cookies, or rice).

Using the information in this section as a guide, have students compare and contrast the quality of the packaging and the amount and type of information on the label, and then speculate on the reasons for the similarities and differences. For example, ask students if foreign brands offer less or more product and nutritional information than domestic brands. Have students discuss their findings in class.

BRIGHT IDEAS
Cool Placement

Have you ever enjoyed a nice big brownie and a tall glass of . . . soymilk? To make its products more appealing to consumers, White Wave, the Boulder, Colorado, maker of soymilk and soy-based foods, changed its product packaging. Its sealed boxes of soymilk that were tucked away in health-food shelves just weren't "making waves." White Wave changed the look of its product by packaging it in traditional-looking milk cartons in the dairy cases of grocery stores. The company distributed coupons and free samples to shoppers during in-store giveaways in an effort to bring back its followers and find new ones. The result: White Wave obtained 30 percent of the soymilk product market and 78 percent of the refrigerated soy milk category, a $300 million market.

Thinking Creatively

Why did White Wave change its product packaging?

CAPTION ANSWER
Sealed for Protection Blisterpacks are used to prevent product tampering, improper use of the product by children, and theft.

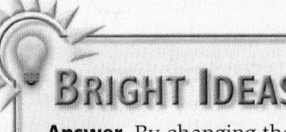

BRIGHT IDEAS
Cool Placement

Answer By changing the package to look like a familiar milk carton, people's perception of the product changed. The company also added the health benefits of soy on its packaging.

Independent Practice

Research, Compare, and Contrast Have students use a search engine to find the Web sites for two popular lines of clothing (i.e., Levi's, Dockers, etc). Ask students to compare and contrast the target markets for brand names, the elements of the product's corporate symbol, the packaging materials used, and any required labeling elements (health warnings, for example). Then have students write a one- to two-page, word-processed description about how each product's package performs the basic package functions listed in this chapter.

CAUSE PACKAGING As you learned earlier, packages perform a variety of functions to promote products. Packages also can be used to promote non-product issues. Some companies are using their packages to promote social and political causes. This practice is known as *cause packaging*. The issues on the packages may be totally unrelated to the product you buy. Ben & Jerry's Homemade ice cream cartons promote saving the rain forests and oppose the use of bovine growth hormone to stimulate milk production in cows. Body Shop products feature packaging that promotes social justice and environmental responsibility issues.

Stonyfield Farm yogurt company prints "call-to-action" messages on the lids of its yogurt containers. The messages include pleas to protect the rain forests, stop child labor, preserve the environment, end hunger, promote wildlife research, and defend human rights. The company, whose slogan is "Stonyfield Farms. Yogurt on a Mission," hopes to promote commendable causes and link such causes to the company's desire to change the world and make a profit.

Printing messages on packages, bags, and bills encourages consumers to participate in politics. Some marketers believe that companies using cause-packaging take an enormous risk promoting causes that not every consumer may agree with. Others feel that their views on social and political causes may actually help sell the product.

(6g sugars), and 4g protein.

**Percent Daily Values are based on a 2,000 calorie diet. Your daily values may be higher or lower depending on your calorie needs:

		Calories:	2,000	2,500
Total Fat	Less than		65g	80g
Sat Fat	Less than		20g	25g
Cholest	Less than		300mg	300mg
Sodium	Less than		2,400mg	2,400mg
Potassium			3,500mg	3,500mg
Total Carb			300g	375g
Fiber			25g	30g

INGREDIENTS: WHEAT FLOUR, MALTED BARLEY FLOUR, SALT, YEAST.
VITAMINS AND MINERALS: REDUCED IRON, NIACINAMIDE, ZINC OXIDE (SOURCE OF ZINC), VITAMIN B6, VITAMIN A PALMITATE, RIBOFLAVIN (VITAMIN B2), THIAMIN MONONITRATE (VITAMIN B1), FOLIC ACID, VITAMIN B12, VITAMIN D.

© KRAFT FOODS, INC., BOX GN-64, TARRYTOWN, NY 10591, USA

KRAFT *Good Food & Good Food Ideas!* ™

EXCHANGE: 3 Starch/Bread. Exchange calculations based on *Exchange Lists for Meal Planning*. ©1995, American Diabetes Association, Inc. and The American Dietetic Association.

578 Unit 10 ■ *Product and Service Management*

Labeling

A **label** is an information tag, wrapper, seal, or imprinted message that is attached to a product or its package. Labeling plays a major role in product planning strategy. The information on labels helps customers decide if the product is right for them.

The main function of a label is to inform customers about a product's contents and give directions for use. Labels also protect businesses from legal liability for mishaps involving their products. Fear of litigation, consumer pressure, government regulation, and concern for consumer safety are all factors that have led manufacturers to place more detailed information on labels.

There are three kinds of labels. These are the brand label, descriptive label, and grade label.

The brand label gives the brand name, trademark, or logo. Some bananas are stamped with the Chiquita brand label. Although this is an acceptable form of labeling, it doesn't supply sufficient information alone.

A descriptive label gives information about the product's use, construction, care, performance, and other features. A descriptive label usually includes statements describing the precise type of product. Descriptive labels do not necessarily always contain all of the information wanted by a customer in making a buying decision.

A grade label states the quality of the product. Eggs are grade-labeled, AA, A, and B; corn and wheat are grade-labeled 1 and 2; canned fruit is often grade labeled A, B, or C.

Labels often contain a brand name, logo, ingredients, directions, and special promotional messages. Food labels include product illustrations, weight statements, dating and storage information, a universal product code, product guarantees, and the manufacturer's name and address.

Product illustrations must represent what is in the package. Weight statements give the "net weight" of the entire product minus the package or liquid in which it is packed.

■ **Food Labels Contain Nutritional Information** Food products are required to have ingredients displayed on the label. *What agency regulates the labeling of food products?*

CAPTION ANSWER
Food Labels Contain Nutritional Information The U.S. Food and Drug Administration regulates the labeling of food products.

Date and storage information is necessary for food items. Date information includes the packed on date (date food was packed), the sell by date (last date product should be used), the best if used by date (last date for use for top quality), and the expiration date (date after which the product should not be used). Storage information tells how the product should be stored to have the least waste and best quality.

Nonfood labels usually provide consumers with instructions for the proper use and care of products. They also give manufacturers a convenient place to communicate warranty information and product-use warnings. Notices of electrical hazard, flammability, and poisonous ingredients are required on the labels of certain categories of products. Due to increased international business, labels might contain symbols in addition to words. These symbols give graphic instructions on how to wash, cook, or care for the product.

The manufacturer's name and address are provided so consumers can write for more information or to register a complaint. Many packages include the company's Web address, where consumers can find more product information if desired. Some labels include a customer service phone number that can be called regarding any questions or problems with a product.

■ Labeling Laws

In the past, the public has criticized product labeling for failing to offer complete and truthful information. Public complaints about the lack of uniformity in labeling on packages encouraged the government to establish labeling laws. Many package labels must now meet local, state, and federal standards. Federal mandates require the name and address of the manufacturer, packer, or distributor, and the quantity of contents. These standards prevent manufacturers from misleading consumers with deceptive or incomplete packaging labels.

The Fair Packaging and Labeling Act (FPLA) of 1966 requires mandatory labeling requirements and provides the authority to the U.S. Food and Drug Administration (FDA) and the Federal Trade Commission (FTC) to establish packaging regulations. A 1992 amendment to the FPLA requires

that the packaging of selected products include metric measurements. The amendment, which went into effect in 1994, mandates that product weight is listed not only in traditional American weights and measures, but also in metric weights and measures.

Careful consideration must also be taken when planning package labeling for foreign markets. Care must be taken to meet all local labeling laws. Some countries require that labeling is bilingual. Other countries require that every ingredient in a product is listed on the label. In the late 1990s, this became a problem for Coca-Cola. An Italian judge ordered all Coca-Cola pulled from store shelves because Coca-Cola keeps part of its recipe a secret.

Labeling is becoming a highly regulated and complex part of product planning. Marketers face the challenge of planning product packaging and labeling that conforms to regulations.

If The Name Fits . . .

How many different ways are there to say "beans" in Spanish? More than you would think, as realized by Goya Foods, Inc. Goya makes over 800 food products that are popular in the Hispanic food market. The nuances of the Spanish language in different cultures causes obstacles when labeling. Beans are called *frijoles* in Cuba and *habichuelas* in Puerto Rico. Goya already makes bilingual labels for those customers who do not speak Spanish. It also relies on a clear product photo to ensure that different groups know exactly what they are buying—despite any language barriers.

Thinking Critically

What are the benefits of creating bilingual labels for a company?

SECTION 31.2

ASSESS

Reteaching

1. **Vocabulary** Assign and review the vocabulary terms for this section.
2. **Fact and Idea** Assign and review Fact and Idea Review questions 6–10 from the Chapter Assessment.
3. **Package Design** Have students list all of the reasons for the package design and the information presented on the package for a consumer product of their choice. Have them classify each feature under one of the functions of packaging.

If the Name Fits . . .

Answer Bilingual labels increase a company's target market and encourage higher sales.

THE DECA CONNECTION

COMPETITIVE EVENTS AND MARKETING ESSENTIALS

Create an Advertising Campaign You can use DECA's Advertising Campaign Event to reinforce the material in this chapter. If your students decide to create their advertising campaign around a particular product, then branding, packaging, and labeling of the product can all be brought into focus through the advertising and promotion sections of this event. You can use these sections as a class assignment, allowing the students to work alone or in groups of up to three. The event guidelines allow teams of up to three students to participate in creating the advertising campaign and presenting it to a businessperson/judge.

Enrichment

1. **Review** Assign and review the Chapter 31 activities in the *Student Activity Workbook*.
2. **Review** Assign and review the appropriate Thinking Critically questions from the Chapter Assessment.
3. **Review** Assign and review the following Chapter Assessment activities: Building Workplace Skills, Applying Marketing Concepts, Linking School-to-Work, The DECA Connection Role Play, and Internet Connection.

Evaluation

Assign and review the Section 31.2 Assessment.

Technology Resources

Assessment Resources
Go to the *Marketing Essentials* Web site (**www.marketing.glencoe. com**) for resources to teach and assess occupation-specific vocabulary.

CLOSE

Section Wrap-Up

Have students complete the following statements:
1. The purposes of packaging are . . . *(to hold the product, to promote it, to help define its identity, to provide product information, to meet customer needs with various sizes available, to ensure safe use, and to protect the product.)*
2. The main functions of labels are . . . *(to give product content and directions for use, and to protect businesses from legal liability for mishaps involving their products.)*

580

THE FEDERAL FOOD AND DRUG ADMINISTRATION The Federal Nutrition Labeling and Education Act passed in 1990 and enacted in 1994 protects consumers from deceptive labeling. This act, which is administered by the FDA, requires that labels give nutritional information on how a food fits into an overall daily diet. Labels must clearly state the amount of calories, fat, carbohydrates, sodium, cholesterol, and protein in each serving, as well as the percentage of a daily intake of 2000 calories. The act also regulates health claims and defines descriptive terms to make them consistent on all products. These terms include *light* and *lite; free* (as in fat free, salt free, cholesterol free); *low; reduced;* and *good source.*

The FDA also requires the manufacturers of certain products to place health warnings on their packages. Beginning in 1989, all alcoholic beverage labels had to carry the following statement: "According to the Surgeon General, women should not drink alcoholic beverages during pregnancy because of the risk of birth defects. Consumption of alcoholic beverages impairs the ability to drive a car or operate machinery and may cause health problems." Similar warnings of health risks are required on cigarette package labels.

The FDA also has proposed new regulations on genetically modified foods. The FDA is developing guidelines for voluntary labeling as to whether food products contain genetically modified organisms.

THE FEDERAL TRADE COMMISSION Another federal agency involved with product labeling is the Federal Trade Commission (FTC). The FTC is also responsible for monitoring for deceptive advertising that is false or misleading.

The Care Labeling Rule, first passed by the Federal Trade Commission in 1972, requires that care labels be placed in textile clothing. The care labeling rules ensure that specific detailed information about the care of garments related to washing, drying, and ironing are placed on labels.

The FTC released guidelines in 1992 for companies to use when making environmental claims on product labels. Many environmental terms previously had loose definitions and could be used freely on labels and in advertisements. When using the term *recycled content,* the FTC requires that proof be given about the amount of material in a product or package that has been kept from a landfill or retrieved as manufacturing scraps. The term *recyclable* can be used only if the product or package can be reused as raw material for a new product or package. The terms *ozone safe* and *ozone friendly* can be used only if the products do not contain any ozone-depleting chemicals. The terms *degradable, biodegradable,* and *photodegradable* can be used only if the product will decompose into elements found in nature within a reasonably short period of time after disposal.

31.2 ASSESSMENT

Reviewing Key Terms and Concepts

1. What is a package?
2. List the principal functions of product packaging.
3. What is a product label?
4. What are the main functions of labels?

Thinking Critically

5. Many popular products have symbols on their packages telling consumers how to cook, clean, and wash. Why have symbols and graphic directions been placed on many packaged products?

Integrating Academic Skills

6. **MATH** Robinson & Perry Advertising Agency billed Sky High Air Cargo Service $3,500 for the development of Sky High's corporate symbol. Robinson & Perry's designer was paid $1,500 for her creative work on this project. Her salary was what percentage of the entire amount?

31.2 ASSESSMENT ANSWERS

Reviewing Key Terms and Concepts

1. physical container or wrapping for product
2. promoting and selling the product, defining product identity, providing information, meeting customer needs, ensuring safe use, and protecting the product
3. It is an information tag, wrapper, seal, or imprinted message on a product or package.
4. to inform customers about product contents, give directions for use, and to protect businesses from legal liability for product mishaps

Thinking Critically

5. International business, multi-national corporations, trade, and travel have grown.

Integrating Academic Skills

6. **MATH** 42.85 percent ($1,500 ÷ $3,500 = 42.85%)

Careers in Marketing

SPORTS MARKETING

Liam Mooney
Athletic Horizons
Talent Manager

What does your job entail?

"I am a sports agent for international European football (or soccer in the United States) players. I represent individual athletes in the international football market. It is my responsibility to negotiate contracts and fees, and schedule public appearances both in the United States and around Europe and Latin America. I have to look out not only for my clients' income, but also their public image. My clients look to me for advice on business matters."

What do you like most about your job?

"I have been a huge football fan since I was a child and grew up watching the matches. It is an exciting field to be in—I'm doing what I love. Not only do I get to attend games all over the world, but I'm also on the cutting edge of new talent in soccer."

What skills are important to you?

"A thorough understanding of the media and how to use them to the best advantage is essential for my success. I need to know how to troubleshoot when there is bad press, but also be ready for good opportunities to promote my clients and their successes. I have also worked hard to develop my ability to oversee, supervise, and manage people and budgets."

What is your key to success?

"My key to success is keeping my client's best interests at heart. It is important for me to set standards, but in the end I have to remember that behind each athlete is an individual who needs personal attention and consideration."

Thinking Critically
Is it necessary to have a love of sports to work in this field?

Career Facts

Education and Training: High school students interested in becoming talent managers should take college preparatory classes. Courses in English, journalism, communication and marketing, psychology, media, computer science, and graphic art classes are good choices. Many employers now require applicants to have a college degree or related work experience, especially in public relations, journalism, or communications.

Aptitudes, Abilities, and Skills: Talent managers must have excellent communication skills, both verbal and written. They must be able to "size up" a situation quickly and offer advice based on experience. A talent manager must understand each client's strengths and weaknesses and have the ability to present each client in a good light.

Career Outlook: Job growth is expected to be greater than average through the year 2006. Opportunities increase as the numbers of star athletes increase.

Career Path: Talent managers come from varied educational and professional backgrounds. Many have played on college athletic teams, and often have worked in some area of public relations, business, or sales.

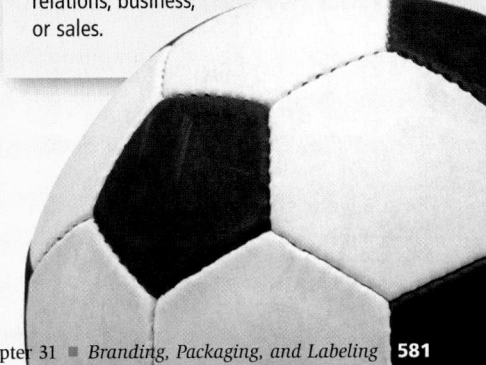

Careers in Marketing

Ask a student to read the Careers in Marketing feature aloud to the class. Discuss the skills and aptitudes required for a career in sports marketing. Ask students whether they think they would like or dislike a career in sports marketing. Discuss the pros and cons of such a career.

Thinking Critically Answer
Answers will vary but include that a love of sports might be an advantage.

Guest Speakers
Invite a sports talent manager to class to discuss his/her job.

Exploring Careers

Marketing and Distribution Careers

1. Tell students that package designers fall under the Marketing and Distribution careers cluster. The career outlook for package designers is faster than average, and the job requires a bachelor's degree.
2. Ask students what other occupations might be included in the Marketing and Distribution career cluster.
3. Then ask students: What skills are needed to work in the Marketing and Distribution cluster? After discussion, write the following skills on the board:
  • interpersonal skills
  • self-starting skills
  • creativity skills
  • communication skills
  • business skills
  • sales skills
4. Read to the students the following examples of careers in this cluster: salesperson, sales manager, buyer, package designer, market research analyst, and broker. Ask students to research at least one job in this cluster that interests them.

Lifelong Learning

Branding, Packaging, and Labeling
Having the ability to understand brand, packaging, and labeling issues will allow students to enter the marketplace as savvy consumers. Labels are designed to help the consumer make informed decisions and to promote the product. If students are interested in working in this area, they will need to take further classes in marketing and graphic arts.

Meeting Individual Needs

Students with Orthopaedic Impairments
Having students with orthopaedic impairments in your class gives you the opportunity to educate other students about people with physical impairments. Speak with your students who have orthopaedic impairments, discuss issues you feel uncertain about, and read educational journals about students with physical impairments who succeed in the world.

Vocabulary Review

Paragraphs will vary. See Glossary for definitions.

Fact and Idea Review

1. Employees, software programs, branding agencies, public relations firms, and naming consultants generate brands.
2. The manufacturer owns a manufacturer brand. Wholesalers and retailers own private distributor brands.
3. Brand extension uses a familiar or original brand name for other items in the product line. Brand licensing is the legal authorization by a brand owner to allow another company to use the brand, logo, or trademark for a fee.
4. Co-branding works well if the company's brands complement each other; there is a customer benefit to the arrangement; and each brand receives equal billing in promotions.
5. It is the simultaneous offering of manufacturer, private, and generic brands. This allows a business to reach several target markets, maintain brand loyalty, and increase the overall product mix offered to customers.
6. A package is the physical container or wrapping for a product. A label is an information tag, wrapper, seal, or imprinted message that is attached to a product or its package.
7. cause packaging and environmental packaging
8. Labels often contain a brand name, logo, ingredients, directions, and special promotional messages.
9. The guidelines include definitions for environmental terms that could be used on labels.

Thinking Critically

1. Students may say the clear bags will allow customers to check their orders quickly to see if they were filled properly and improve drive-through accuracy.
2. Students might indicate that larger lids and protective packaging that is easier to remove would appeal to older consumers.
3. Salad packages that fit in a car cup holder are effective for customers who want to buy a salads to eat while "on the go."

Chapter 31 ASSESSMENT
Chapter 31 ASSESSMENT

VOCABULARY REVIEW

Select two products that your family uses regularly. Write one paragraph on each product describing the product characteristics by incorporating these vocabulary terms.

- brand
- brand name
- brand mark
- trade name
- trade character
- trademark
- manufacturer brand
- private distributor brand
- generic brands
- brand extension
- brand licensing
- mixed-brand strategy
- co-branding strategy
- package
- label

FACT AND IDEA REVIEW

1. Describe how brands are generated. (31.1)
2. What is the difference between a manufacturer brand and a private distributor brand? (31.1)
3. How does brand extension differ from brand licensing? (31.1)
4. When does a co-branding strategy work well for companies? (31.1)
5. What is a mixed-brand strategy? Why is it used? (31.1)
6. What is the difference between a package and a label? (31.2)
7. Name two contemporary packaging issues. (31.2)
8. Identify three kinds of information commonly found on product labels. (31.2)
9. Summarize the FTC label guidelines concerning environmental claims. (31.2)

THINKING CRITICALLY

1. Burger King is testing see-through bags for its stores. Do you think that this is a good idea? Why or why not?
2. Some childproof packages tend to be adult proof, too. Do some product planning for an over-the-counter drug (such as a pain reliever) that is packaged to be childproof. Address the problems that older people have opening these packages and suggest some ways that product manufacturers can help.
3. McDonald's has designed a salad package that will fit into car cup holders. Explain the rationale behind this product packaging concept.
4. Time-Warner Inc. introduced a new Internet business magazine in 2000 called *E-Company Now.* The company added the word "now" at the last minute. Why do you think they added the word?
5. Why are consumer advocates promoting the labeling of food products that have been genetically altered?

BUILDING WORKPLACE SKILLS

1. **Science** Investigate genetically engineered plants for human consumption. Prepare a two-page research report on a word processor identifying the advantages and disadvantages of gene-altered plants and their impact on food labeling.
2. **Technology** Research the process used to recycle paper, cardboard, glass, plastic, wood, or other packaging materials. Create a chart that illustrates and describes the type of recycling process for the material selected.

---

4. Adding the word "now" to the Internet magazine title might make it easier to trademark and implies that it is on the cutting-edge of technology.
5. It is important because of the possibility of allergic reactions to the food or the potential harm to the environment.

Building Workplace Skills

1. Reports will vary, but advantages could include more disease-resistant plants and animals, better tasting food, and increased production. Disadvantages could include concern over unforeseen effects on health and the environment.
2. Charts will vary, but students should show the recycling process used for the packaging material.

APPLYING MARKETING CONCEPTS

1. **Summarizing Key Concepts** Summarize an article that demonstrates any of the key concepts discussed in this chapter. In the summary, identify the specific concepts in parentheses. Use business publications, such as *BrandWeek, Adweek, BusinessWeek, Fortune, Forbes, Marketing News,* and *Nation's Business,* to find an applicable article.

2. **Understanding the Whole Package** Locate the Web site of a consumer products company of your choice, such as Johnson & Johnson, Gillette, Heinz, or Procter & Gamble. Review the Web site and determine the company image, as well as the branding elements and strategies that are used on products. Use presentation software to create a report based on your research.

3. **Identifying Brand Extensions** Locate the Web site for one of the companies in the "billion dollar league" (refer to Figure 31-1 on page 568). Use a spreadsheet program to identify and display the brand extensions that exist for three product lines.

4. **Researching Packaging Trends** Research new packaging trends that respond to changing lifestyles, changing demographics, legislation, or environmental concerns. Identify one product and use word processing software to prepare a report explaining how the product's packaging addresses at least one or more of these concerns.

LINKING SCHOOL TO WORK

Information Skills Select one line of product sold by a business. Identify the various brands sold in that product line. Use product brochures to create a posterboard presentation of the product features of the various brands sold in the product line.

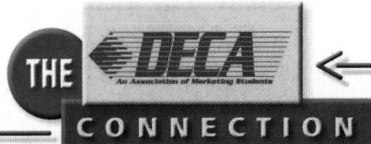

THE DECA CONNECTION

Role Play: Brand Manager

Situation You are to assume the role of a brand manager for a large company. Your supervisor (judge) has asked you to develop a brand name, brand mark, trade character, and corporate symbol for a new type of hand-held food product: a frozen, chocolate-covered banana on a stick. You have also been asked to develop a package and label for your product.

Activity You must present all of the elements of your new brand in a meeting.

Evaluation You will be evaluated on how well you meet the following performance indicators:
- Explain the nature of branding
- Describe factors used by marketers to position products/businesses
- Develop strategies to position product/business
- Develop appropriate branding, package, and label elements for your product
- Make oral presentations

inter NET CONNECTION

Brand Games
Locate the Nabiscoworld Web site and play one of the several games sponsored by a Nabisco product.

Connect
- Write a one-page report using a word processing program about the game, how it could be improved, and why Nabisco might sponsor a Web site for games.

Chapter 31 ■ *Branding, Packaging, and Labeling* **583**

interNET CONNECTION
Reports will vary, but each student should identify the game and ways to improve on the game.

Mini Quiz
Administer the Mini Quiz orally. For an expanded chapter quiz, go to page 183 of the *Reproducible Tests* book.

1. A(n) <u>trade</u> name identifies the company or a division of a particular corporation.

2. A personified brand mark (that is, one given human form or characteristics) is known as a(n) <u>trade character</u>.

3. A <u>co-branding</u> strategy combines one or more brands to increase customer loyalty and sales for each individual brand.

4. The physical container or wrapping for a product is called a(n) <u>package</u>.

5. An information tag, wrapper, seal, or imprinted message that is attached to a product or its package is called a(n) <u>label</u>.

Applying Marketing Concepts

1. Summaries will vary.
2. Presentations will vary.
3. Spreadsheets will vary. Brand extensions will depend on the product. Examples for Coca-Cola include Diet Coke, Cherry Coke, and Caffeine Free Coke.
4. Reports will vary.

Linking School to Work

Answers will depend on the work situation.

GO TO

1. **Assessment** Have students complete the Reproducible Test for Chapter 31 or construct your own tests using the ExamView software.
2. **Enrichment** Have students complete the corresponding activities in the following workbooks:
   - *Marketing Math Workbook,* p. 101

Chapter Overview

Chapter 32 introduces the concept of extended product features used in product planning. Emphasis is placed on the use of warranties and credit to sell products and services as the various types of warranties and credit are discussed. The chapter also explains the laws and agencies involved with product safety and the use of credit.

 ## Springboard

Brainstorm Ask students to recall the definition for the term *product feature;* write this on the board. Have students define the word *extend;* write their answers on the board. Then have students define the term *extended product features.* Have students brainstorm ways a product's features could be extended.

Prereading

List the objectives in the *What You'll Learn* sections to discuss with the students. Have the students skim the chapter, looking at the pictures, reading the captions, and noting the heads. Ask questions to ensure that the students have a minimal understanding of the chapter structure.

Preteaching Marketing Vocabulary

Write the vocabulary list on the board and ask if students are familiar with any of the terms. If they are, have them give brief definitions. As you study the chapter, have students choose phrases and/or symbols that will help them remember each term, and write these on the board list.

Marketing: What It Takes
Answer Answers will vary.

Chapter **32**

Extended Product Features

Marketing: What It Takes

Understanding Warranties
You have been hired to work in the service department of an automobile dealership. Your dealership offers warranties with its car sales. To assess your knowledge of product and service planning, your supervisor has asked you to explain the importance of warranties in product planning.

WHAT WILL YOU DO?
What sources will you use to research and verify your report on service warranties?

584

THE DECA CONNECTION

ADVISOR CORNER

Developing Leadership Skills DECA affords members many opportunities to build leadership skills. Students with leadership skills are more likely to be involved in community affairs and better able to establish professional contacts. Break students into small groups and ask them to discuss and answer the following questions: 1) What are the most important skills for tomorrow's leaders? 2) How has technology changed leadership? 3) How can we further develop the leadership skills of our members? 4) How can high school students today further develop their own leadership skills? After allowing time for group discussions, ask a spokesperson from each group to share their thoughts with the entire group.

Warranties

Warranties

A warranty is a promise, or guarantee, given to a customer that a product will meet certain standards. Typically, these standards apply to materials, workmanship, and/or performance.

A *guarantee* is another term for warranty. The major difference in the use of the two terms is in the promotion of goods and services. The term guarantee (or guaranteed) is usually used for promotional phrases, such as "money-back guarantee," "results guaranteed," "guaranteed for 1,000 average hours," or "satisfaction guaranteed."

Warranty text is usually framed as a series of specific promises. An example is "D & A Auto Body will repair any defects in workmanship billed on the repair invoice unless caused by or damaged from unreasonable use, maintenance, or care of the vehicle, excluding paint work if the vehicle's original finish is defective."

Most warranties set time or use limits for coverage and limits the seller's liability. The most familiar language is usually found in auto warranties—"Warranty ends at 36 months or 36,000 miles, whichever occurs first." The typical warranty limits the seller's liability to some degree.

Businesses are not required by law to issue warranties, though most do to convince their customers of their quality products and services. Some companies, notably automobile manufacturers, make warranties a key component of their product advertising.

Warranties come in two different forms—*express* and *implied*. These forms, in turn, can be divided into specific types.

■ Express Warranties

An express warranty is one that is explicitly stated, in writing or spoken words, to induce a customer to buy. A written warranty can appear in a number of places—on the product packaging, in the product literature, in an advertisement, or as part of a point-of-purchase display. All that is required is that the location of the warranty is easily accessible to customers before purchase. The warranty must always be clearly worded so that customers can easily understand its terms. Spoken warranties, however, even if clearly worded, may not be enforceable unless they are in writing.

Here is an example of how an express warranty works. A print ad states that a portable stereo headset will operate while the user jogs. You purchase a headset and discover almost immediately that it shorts out when you jog. You are entitled to whatever relief the warranty specifies. Now imagine that the headset package features a runner using the product in the rain. You find that the product shorts out in the rain. Once again, you are entitled to warranty relief because

What You'll Learn

- The different types of warranties
- The importance of warranties to product planning
- Additional extended product features
- The major provisions of product safety legislation
- Consumer responsibilities and rights related to product performance

Why It's Important

Warranties are used by sellers to encourage customers—whether a wholesaler, retailer, or final consumer—to purchase a product or service. Depending on how warranties are used and the quality of the product or service, they can either boost sales or become a major problem for a business.

Key Terms

- warranty
- express warranty
- full warranty
- limited warranty
- implied warranty
- warranty of merchantability
- warranty of fitness for a particular purpose
- disclaimer

Chapter 32 ■ *Extended Product Features* **585**

Classroom Resources

For the Teacher
- Teacher Editions for all workbooks
- Assessment Package
- PowerPoint Presentation Software
- Interactive Lesson Planner
- ILP Block Scheduling, p. 10
- ILP Lesson Plans, p. 67
- ILP Internet Resources, p. 83

- ILP Blackline Masters, p. 69
- ILP *BusinessWeek* Case Studies, p. 201
- ILP Marketing Career Portfolio, p. 40
- *Marketing Essentials* Web site (www.marketing.glencoe.com)

For the Student
- Student Activity Workbook, p. 277
- Marketing Math Workbook, p. 101

- Marketing Research Project Workbook
- ILP School-to-Work Activity Workbook, p. 131
- Virtual Business simulation
- *Marketing Essentials* Web site (www.marketing.glencoe.com)

ILP These resources are available in print and on the Interactive Lesson Planner (ILP)

■ **A Guarantee or Warranty?** A guarantee is another term for warranty. *What is the major difference between the two terms?*

FIGURE 32-1

Limited Warranty

ANDERSEN WINDOWS, INC.
Windows and Patio Doors Limited Warranty

Glass
Twenty (20) Year Transferable Limited Warranty
   The glass in Andersen factory glazed sash and patio door panels glass *(including annealed double pane, High-Performance™ glazing, High-Performance Sun™ glazing, FineLight™ grilles, full divided light grilles, High-Performance tempered glazing, and High-Performance Sun tempered glazing)* is warranted to be free from defects in manufacturing, materials, and workmanship for twenty (20) years from the date of purchase from the retailer/dealer. It is also warranted not to develop, under normal conditions, any material obstruction of vision resulting from manufacturing defects or as a result of premature failure of the glass or organic seal for twenty (20) years from the date of purchase from the retailer/dealer. This limited warranty on glass does not apply to special glazings, Andersen® art glass and glass that is not factory installed by Andersen.
   In the event a glass failure occurs as a result of a defect in manufacturing, materials, or workmanship within the limited warranty period, Andersen, at its option, will: (1) provide the appropriate replacement glass product to the Andersen retailer/dealer you specify—installation labor is not included; or (2) provide a factory authorized repair to the existing glass at no cost to you; or (3) refund the purchase price or the retailer's/dealer's price at the time of the original purchase, whichever is less. Such replacement or repair is warranted for the remainder of the original warranty period.

Components Other Than Glass
Ten (10) Year Transferable Limited Warranty
   Non-glass portions of Andersen windows and patio doors *(including non-electric operators, locks, lifts, balance systems, hinges, handles, insect screens, weather-stripping, sash and frame members)* are warranted to be free from defects in manufacturing, materials and workmanship for a period of ten (10) years from the date of purchase from the retailer/dealer. This limited warranty does not apply to Andersen electric window operators, retractable insect screens and solid bright brass patio door hardware.
   In the event a component other than glass fails as a result of a defect in manufacturing, materials, or workmanship within the limited warranty period, Andersen, at its option, will: (1) provide replacement parts to the Andersen retailer/dealer you specify—installation labor is not included; or (2) provide a factory authorized repair to the existing component at no cost to you; or (3) refund the original purchase price or retailer's/dealer's price at the time of the original purchase, whichever is less. Such replacement parts and repairs are warranted for the remainder of the original warranty period.

■ **Stating the Specifics** A limited warranty states the time period and specific ways products are warranted. *What does this long-term warranty tell you about the company and its products?*

the illustration constitutes a promise of performance, even though the promise is not a written one.

There are two types of written warranties—a *full warranty* and a *limited warranty.* A **full warranty** guarantees that if a product is found to be defective within the warranty period, it will be repaired or replaced at no cost to the purchaser. A manufacturer that offers a full warranty agrees to repair a defective product "within a reasonable time and without charge." A defective product must be replaced or a full refund offered if the product does not work after a reasonable number of repair attempts. Full warranties are rarely offered on consumer goods as they incur high costs for the manufacturer.

A **limited warranty** may exclude certain parts of the product from coverage or require the customer to bear some of the expense for repairs resulting from defects. It is not uncommon, for example, for a limited warranty to specify that the manufacturer will pay for replacement parts but charge the customer for labor or shipping. See Figure 32-1 for an example of a limited warranty.

CAPTION ANSWER
A Guarantee or Warranty? The major difference is in the use of the two terms when promoting goods and services. The term *guarantee* is used in promotional phases, such as seen in the Chemlawn ad that states, "Results Guaranteed!" A warranty states the actual conditions of a product guarantee.

FIGURE 32-1 ANSWER
Stating the Specifics Andersen Windows, Inc., has specialized for over 90 years in the manufacture of quality windows and patio doors. These long-term warranties represent a statement of confidence in the company's products and its desire to provide customers with total satisfaction.

Implied Warranties

Most major purchases that customers make are covered by written warranties provided by manufacturers. Where there is no written warranty, implied warranty laws apply.

An implied warranty is one that exists automatically by state law whenever a purchase takes place. There are two types of implied warranties—a warranty of merchantability and a warranty of fitness for a particular purpose.

A warranty of merchantability is a promise from the seller that the product sold is fit for its intended purpose. Some examples are that an automatic coffee maker will make coffee or a washing machine will clean clothing.

A warranty of fitness for a particular purpose arises when the seller advises a customer that a product is suitable for a particular use and the customer acts on that advice. A customer, for example, might buy a small truck based on a salesperson's recommendation that it will pull a trailer of a certain weight. The dealership must take back the truck and refund the buyer's money if it turns out that the truck cannot tow the anticipated load.

Warranty Disclaimers

Warranties often have disclaimers to protect the businesses issuing them. A disclaimer is a statement that contains exceptions to and exclusions from a warranty. Disclaimers are used to limit damages that can be recovered by a customer. A common form of disclaimer limits recovery to a refund of the purchase price. It can specifically exclude any other costs that may have been incurred by the owner as a result of product failure. Another common disclaimer waives customers' rights under implied-warranty laws.

Role of Warranties in Product Planning

Warranties are an important element of product planning. Customers may make their decisions to purchase based on the extended product feature. Warranties are significant to a business because they:

- Force a company to focus on customer needs
- Set clear standards of performance
- Generate customer feedback
- Encourage quality control
- Boost promotional efforts

FIGURE 32-2

Extended Warranty

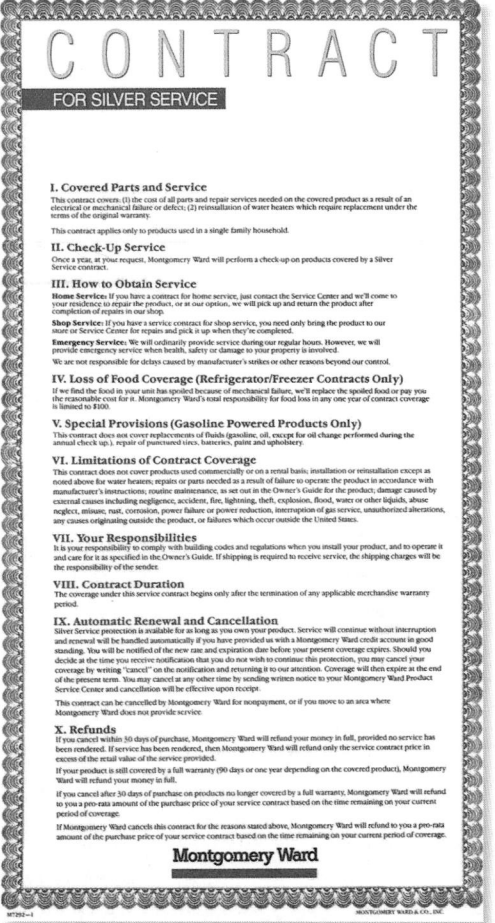

■ **Increasing Sales Revenue** Extended warranties and service contracts provide repair and maintenance service beyond the life of the original product warranty. *How does a business benefit from extended warranties?*

Extended warranties or *service contracts* provide repairs or preventative maintenance for a specified length of time beyond a product's normal warranty period (see Figure 32-2). Customers pay extra for such a contract at the time of purchase. Costs range from a few dollars on a low-cost item to hundreds of dollars on a higher-priced item, such as a car. There is often a deductible amount, which the customer pays before work is performed.

Chapter 32 ■ *Extended Product Features* **587**

Thinking Critically

Certification Why does a state's Department of Education require teachers to be certified? Does this process guarantee a good teacher? Why or why not? If not, should teacher certification be required? *(Answers will vary, but requiring teachers to be certified is the state's attempt to insure that teachers are technically competent in their subject area and have mastered entry-level teaching skills.)*

FIGURE 32-3

THE IMPORTANCE OF WARRANTIES TO PRODUCT PLANNING

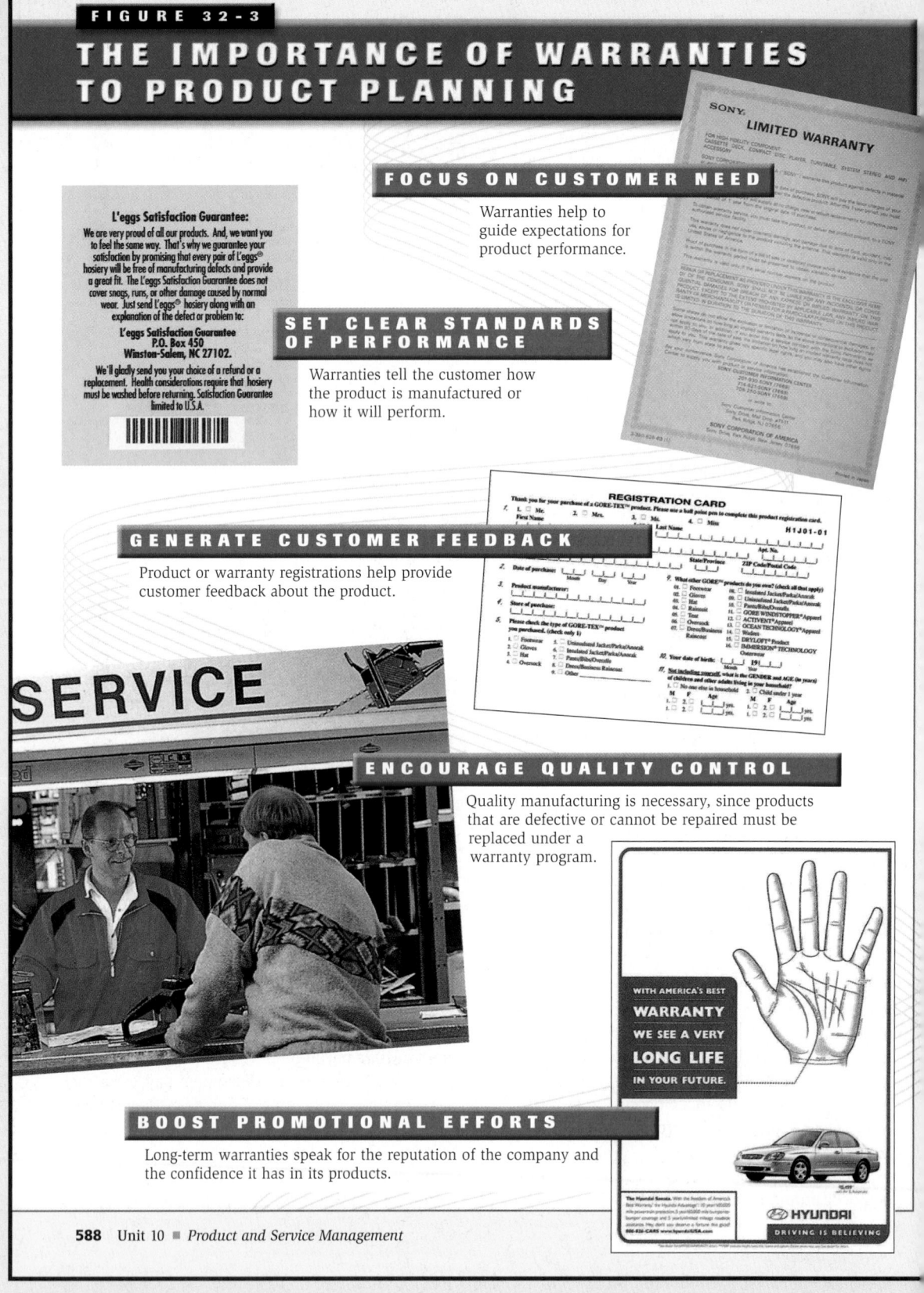

FOCUS ON CUSTOMER NEED

Warranties help to guide expectations for product performance.

SET CLEAR STANDARDS OF PERFORMANCE

Warranties tell the customer how the product is manufactured or how it will perform.

GENERATE CUSTOMER FEEDBACK

Product or warranty registrations help provide customer feedback about the product.

ENCOURAGE QUALITY CONTROL

Quality manufacturing is necessary, since products that are defective or cannot be repaired must be replaced under a warranty program.

BOOST PROMOTIONAL EFFORTS

Long-term warranties speak for the reputation of the company and the confidence it has in its products.

Extended warranties, or service contracts, are beneficial to both businesses and customers. Businesses benefit by receiving additional money (and more profit, if the product performs as expected) on the original sale of a product. Customers benefit from the assurance of long-term satisfaction with their purchase.

There are also disadvantages to service contracts. *Consumer Reports* magazine estimates that only 12 to 20 percent of people who buy extra repair or service protection ever use it. This happens because some service contracts overlap existing warranty coverage—the consumer is paying for something that is already available. It is also common for customers to forget that they have the service contract. Figure 32-3 on page 588 shows how important warranties are in product planning.

■ Other Extended Product Features

Product planners provide additional extended product features, in addition to warranties, to help create customer satisfaction. These features include delivery, installation, billing, service after the sale, directions for use, technical assistance, and training.

Product planners must constantly evaluate a product's extended features from a customer's viewpoint. They should be able to answer yes to questions such as these:

- *Was the product delivered on time?*
- *If installation was necessary, was it done properly?*
- *Was the bill for the good or service accurate and timely?*
- *If needed, was the service provided promptly, courteously, and correctly?*
- *If needed, were technical assistance and training provided?*
- *Were directions clearly written?*

Consumer Laws and Agencies

A working knowledge of relevant federal, state, and local laws is essential for businesspeople. Manufacturers must be sure that their products meet all the requirements of the law. They must be safe, adequately labeled, and accurately advertised; if they are not, the manufacturer could face fines or product recalls.

A DVD That's Book Smart

Graduate students at some dental schools across the country are lightening the load—of their backpacks, that is. Their coursework remains the same, but they'll be spared lugging heavy textbooks around campus. They don't even need any of the usual 400 pounds of books and manuals that previous classes used. Each incoming student purchases a DVD containing the four-year curriculum—including all textbooks, manuals, and lecture slides. Each DVD will replace more than two million pages of printed matter and costs roughly the same as the four-year total for books, roughly $3,000 to $6,000 paid over time. In order for financial aid programs to cover the costs, the dental schools are making the DVD and a laptop with a DVD player requirements for all students.

Thinking Critically

What are the benefits and disadvantages of changing the product features of a traditional print textbook to a DVD format?

Larger companies often employ consumer affairs or legislative specialists to advise management on requirements. Smaller companies often join trade associations to stay informed on existing and pending laws that affect their products.

■ Federal Statutes

Many of the warranty features discussed in this chapter have their origins in a federal statute called the *Magnuson-Moss Consumer Product Warranty Act* of 1975. This statute governs written warranties for all consumer products costing $15 or more. It sets minimum standards for such warranties, rules for making them available before a product is sold, and provisions for lawsuits against manufacturers if a warranty is not fulfilled.

Other federal statutes protect consumers by forcing companies to manufacture and sell safe products. The *Consumer Product Safety Act* of 1972, for example, established the Consumer Product Safety Commission (CPSC). This agency monitors

Cooperative Learning

Extended Product Features
Divide students into four groups. Have each group brainstorm at least four extended product features (in addition to a warranty) for one product. Have each group make its presentation to the class; have the entire class generate additional extended product features.

A DVD That's Book Smart

Answer Advantages might include better images, animation and video, and search capacity. Disadvantages might include difficulty in reading and inability to alter content.

Independent Practice

Research and Explain Find a warranty for a small appliance and read the document carefully. Then answer the following questions:

- Is the warranty full or limited? How do you know?
- To what remedy is the purchaser entitled if a manufacturer's defect is found?
- What is the required procedure for obtaining warranty repairs? Include the name and address of the nearest service center and note what, if any, charges the customer must pay.
- What disclaimers does the warranty contain?

the safety of more than 11,000 nonfood items, such as toys, televisions, and appliances. The agency is empowered to issue standards for the construction, testing, packaging, and performance of these products.

When the CPSC finds any product that it believes to be defective or dangerous, it can:

- Require that warning labels be attached to the product
- Recall the product and order repairs
- Prohibit the product's sale

The CPSC recalled about seven million infant swings manufactured by Graco in April 2000. The swings were made from 1970 until 1998. During its investigation, the CPSC found that the swings were often sold second-hand without a strap necessary for protection. The absence of this strap caused injury and even death of many infants. Under the Graco recall, swing owners received a new safety attachment that ensured that the strap is used.

To ensure consumer awareness of product recalls, notices for unsafe children's products, appliances, toys, and other items are placed in all 33,000 U.S. Post offices since April 2000. The CPSC had found that less than 5 percent of recalled toys were being returned for repairs or replacement, 60 percent for child safety seats, and 90 percent for major appliances.

The *Food, Drug, and Cosmetic Act* of 1938 is another federal statute designated to assure consumers that the products they buy will be safe. "Safe" in this case means pure, wholesome, and effective, as well as informatively labeled and truthfully advertised. The Food and Drug Administration, which certifies new drugs and inspects drug and food processing plants, enforces the act. The agency also regulates the advertising and sale of imported and exported foods, drugs, cosmetics, medical devices, animal drugs, animal feed, and products that emit radiation.

Some products are regulated by more than one agency. Cars and trucks, for example, have their emission standards set by the Environmental Protection Agency (EPA), their price stickers regulated by the Federal Trade Commission, and any potentially dangerous design flaws investigated by the National Highway Traffic Safety Administration. Making sure products meet this multiplicity of standards is an important function of product planning.

■ State Statutes

Many states have passed their own consumer protection laws. Most are aimed at poorly made or poorly serviced products. Nearly all states have passed lemon laws to protect customers.

Sealing In Success

Sitting around a living room discussing the virtues of Tupperware might sound boring to you. The marketing movement of the Tupperware party, however, has revolutionized the concept of in-house selling. Earl Tupper created the infamous Tupperware in his home lab, while working with a new substance named plastic at the DuPont Chemical Company. Tupper molded plastic to create non-breakable, lightweight cups, plates, bowls, and lids. Tupper's wares hit the market in 1946, but hardware and department stores were not successful sales places. With no demonstrations, consumers were confused by the lids and uninterested in the potential. Tupper ingeniously pulled all merchandise from store shelves in 1951, and developed the sale of his products through in-home demonstrations known as Tupperware Parties. Today, a Tupperware demonstration begins approximately every two seconds with yearly sales exceeding $1.2 billion.

Thinking Creatively

What other product sales might benefit from in-home demonstrations? What product features of this product would you highlight?

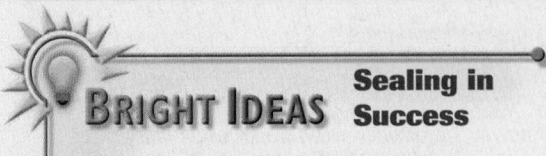

Answer Answers will vary.

Lemon laws are statutes designed to protect consumers from poorly built cars. Under most lemon laws, a car is a "lemon" if it is out of service at least 30 days during the first year of ownership or if four attempts have been made to fix the same problem. Lemon owners are entitled to a refund or a comparable replacement car.

Many states have incorporated *arbitration programs* into their lemon laws. In arbitration, an impartial third party, such as a representative of the Better Business Bureau, decides the crucial issues—for example, whether a vehicle is a lemon and how much the refund should be. In most cases, the arbitrator's ruling is not binding on the parties. The owner can sue the carmaker in a court of law if he or she is not satisfied with the outcome. The principal benefit of arbitration is that it saves all parties long delays and excessive costs often associated with a lawsuit.

The most common form of state regulation mainly affects service businesses. Most states require certain individuals—for example auto mechanics, realtors, building contractors, barbers, and police officers—to meet training requirements. It is necessary to hold a license or state certification before legally practicing in their professions. The process frequently involves testing and the payment of a substantial fee.

Consumer Rights and Responsibilities

Consumers have a right to expect quality products at fair prices. What happens when the extended features that a business has placed on a product or service fail? What happens when, for example, buyers do not feel that the warranty has protected them adequately?

Consumers can take several steps when they have not been adequately protected by a warranty.

- The consumer should contact the business that sold the product or the product manufacturer.
- If the problem is still unresolved, the consumer should contact the local, state, or federal offices that can assist with consumer complaints. These numbers can be found on the World Wide Web or in a telephone directory.
- Finally, if the problem is still not resolved, consumers can take legal action.

REAL WORLD MARKETING

Yesterday

The classic retro Volkswagen Beetle is back, and some might say, better than ever. Modern conveniences such as four air-bags and power outlets for cell phones appeal to a new generation of "bug" drivers. Its familiar bubble shape symbolizes carefree youth for most consumers, even those who weren't around for the original. By developing an advertising strategy using symbols of the 1960s, Volkswagen has hit a home run and other companies are following suit. Maxwell House has rolled their old ads into their new TV spots, while Charlie Tuna has once again returned from the sea. Consumers can't seem to get enough of the good old days and nostalgia marketing!

Thinking Critically
What other products have reinvented themselves with a hint of the past?

Because part of being a consumer is getting the best value for your money, you must be compensated for products that are defective.

Consumers can sue manufacturers or retailers on at least three grounds—breach of federal law (written warranty), breach of state law (implied warranty), and negligence. When a company does not hold up its end of a warranty or when it shows carelessness, consumers have the right to take a case to court. *Negligence* means failure to take proper or reasonable care. Courts have held manufacturers and retailers liable for defects in products, or when injury is caused by use of the product. Individuals can also bring food suppliers to court if sickness is caused by unhealthy practices or bad food. Class action suits—filed by more than one party—can be filed by consumers, cities, and states against manufacturers for making unsafe products. Some states brought a class-action suit against tobacco companies for health-related costs caused by smoking. This led to a $206 billion settlement in November 1998.

Chapter 32 ■ *Extended Product Features* **591**

ASSESS

Reteaching

1. **Vocabulary** Assign and review the vocabulary terms for this section.
2. **Fact and Idea** Assign and review Fact and Idea Review questions 1–5 from the Chapter Assessment.
3. **Concepts** If the students are having a difficult time remembering these concepts, divide them into pairs and have them explain the concepts to each other, using their texts for reference.

Enrichment

1. **Review** Assign and review the appropriate Thinking Critically questions from the Chapter Assessment.
2. **Extend** Assign and review the corresponding activities from *BusinessWeek Case Studies, Internet Resources,* and the *School-to-Work Activity Workbook.* **ILP**
3. **Write and Discuss** Have the students look at product packaging at home or in local stores for product warnings and write at least three of the warnings in full. They should discuss these warnings in class. Ask students: Do some or most of the warnings seem ridiculously obvious? Discuss the need for even obvious warnings. If the warning is not included, a customer can always say that he or she did not know about the potential hazards in using a product and can then sue the manufacturer if injured while using the products. Product warnings are included with food products for this reason.

REAL WORLD MARKETING

Yesterday
Answer Answers will vary but may include bell-bottom jeans, retro handbags, and baseball stadiums designed after the classic stadiums.

Evaluation

Assign and review the Section 32.1 Assessment.

Technology Resources

Assessment Resources
Go to the *Marketing Essentials* Web site (**www.marketing.glencoe. com**) for resources to teach and assess occupation-specific vocabulary.

CLOSE

Section Wrap-Up

Have students write a summary (without looking at their texts) of the key concepts they can recall from reading this section and doing the activities.

CAPTION ANSWER
Protecting the Consumer
Aside from avoiding fines and penalties for violating specific legal requirements on some products, such as tobacco, medicine and alcoholic beverages, businesses place warnings on products to help protect them from possible product liability lawsuits.

592

Businesses can take steps to minimize liability suits during product planning. Manufacturers should examine product design and consider what might go wrong. Products should be tested thoroughly. Items such as cars are repeatedly tested before they are put on the market. Besides federally mandated tests, there are extensive-use tests that manufacturers can do to make suggestions for recommended product use. It is more effective to spend money on precaution measures ahead of time instead of risking lawsuits and a ruined reputation. Manufacturers should give special attention to package design and provide warnings on the package and labels about any potential hazards involved in using the product. When a manufacturer suspects a problem with a product, it is often more cost efficient to recall that product than to risk liability.

Private distributors can limit their liability by questioning manufacturers before accepting a product for sale. They should obtain the manufacturer's test data and determine the company's ability to stand behind the product before it is put on store shelves.

As a final line of defense against product liability, businesses should encourage their customers to be responsible consumers. They should take every

■ **Protecting the Consumer** Product warnings are often printed on packages to make the consumer aware of potential health concerns and to protect the consumer from unsafe product use. *What are some other benefits for businesses of putting warnings on products?*

opportunity to remind customers of their duty to be informed. Customers are responsible for reading and following the safety directions provided with products. This is especially important with items for children, such as car seats, cribs, and even toys.

32.1 ASSESSMENT

Reviewing Key Terms and Concepts

1. What are two types of warranties?
2. Why are warranties important for product planning?
3. Identify three additional extended product features that are frequently part of product planning.
4. What are the basic provisions that product safety legislation requires of manufacturers?
5. What can consumers do when they do not feel that a product's warranty has protected them adequately?

Thinking Critically

6. Many unsafe and potentially dangerous toys enter the country from other countries. What should the federal government do to prevent this from happening?

Integrating Academic Skills

7. **COMMUNICATION** While warranties are supposed to be written in clear, simple language, many consumers still find them hard to understand. Find an example of a detailed warranty for a household appliance, electronic equipment, or a motor vehicle. Rewrite the warranty in your own words.

32.1 ASSESSMENT ANSWERS

Reviewing Key Terms and Concepts
1. express and implied warranties
2. Warranties focus on customer needs, set clear standards of performance, generate customers, encourage quality control, and boost promotional efforts.
3. delivery, installation, billing, service after sale, directions, technical assistance, training

4. Products must be safe, adequately labeled, and accurately advertised.
5. Customers can sue.

Thinking Critically
6. It can involve the U.S. Customs Service and Consumer Product Safety Commission to prevent dangerous toys from entering the country.

Integrating Academic Skills
7. **COMMUNICATION** Answers will vary.

Credit

Credit and Its Importance

Credit allows businesses or individuals to obtain products or money in exchange for a promise to pay later. The use of credit is essential to our economy. In 2000 there were over 500 million credit cards in circulation. Visa USA—the nation's largest credit card system—had over $724 billion in transactions in 1999. There are over 6,000 individual credit card issuers and the average household receives about two dozen credit card solicitations every year.

Credit allows most people to buy major purchases such as homes, autos, appliances, furniture, and recreational vehicles. Credit is also used by individuals for less costly purchases, such as meals, clothing, groceries, and movies. Credit cards can be used to purchase just about any good or service. Even the Internal Revenue Service now accepts credit cards for payment of taxes.

Credit is used by businesses to purchase goods and services, which are ultimately sold to consumers. Credit is also used between manufacturers, wholesalers, and retailers to buy materials, equipment, supplies, and services for use either within their business or to sell to other businesses.

Millions of people and thousands of businesses would not be able to buy necessary goods and services without credit. This is because income (business or personal) often does not match buying needs when they occur. When buying a new car, you will probably need to use some of your savings; however, it is often difficult to save enough to buy a car. Credit allows you to purchase a car on regular monthly payments—you can buy a car and pay for it over a period of time. Extending credit to customers gives consumers an incentive to purchase, which increases businesses' sales and profits.

Credit helps build long-term relationships with customers. J.C. Penney has incorporated special programs for customers who use a store credit card. The company sends mail-order catalogs, notices of special sales, and postcard mailings with special product offerings to these customers.

■ Consumer Credit

Companies who offer credit to consumers, such as banks, department stores, and oil companies, typically issue credit cards. Customers fill out credit applications that ask about customers' sources of income and credit history. If they meet the company criteria, they are issued a credit card.

Credit cards are issued with a *credit limit* based upon customers' ability to pay and their payment history. A credit limit is a preapproved dollar amount, which customers can use to purchase items on credit.

• What You'll Learn

- The importance of credit
- The five sources of consumer credit
- The four types of credit accounts extended to consumers
- How businesses use trade credit
- The most important credit legislation

• Why It's Important

Extending credit to customers or accepting credit cards for purchases is an important part of product planning. The wise use of credit can be a great benefit to a business and its customers.

Key Terms

- credit
- regular, or 30-day, charge accounts
- installment accounts
- revolving accounts
- budget accounts

Chapter 32 ■ *Extended Product Features* **593**

FOCUS

 Bell Ringer Activity

Define and Brainstorm First ask students to define the term *credit*. Ask them to brainstorm two lists: (1) things that people normally buy on credit and (2) things that businesses buy on credit. They may have a more difficult time with the latter since they may not have considered the fact that businesses buy things on credit.

Introducing the Section

Credit and Its Importance Tell students that credit—both consumer credit and business credit—is essential to our economy. Without it, many people and businesses would not be able to buy products when they need them. Ultimately, extending credit to consumers can give them an incentive to buy and thus increase a business's profits.

Classroom Resources

For the Teacher
- Teacher Editions for all workbooks
- Assessment Package
- PowerPoint Presentation Software
- Interactive Lesson Planner
- ILP Block Scheduling, p. 10
- ILP Lesson Plans, p. 68
- ILP Internet Resources, p. 83

ILP *BusinessWeek* Case Studies, p. 201
ILP Marketing Career Portfolio, p. 40
- *Marketing Essentials* Web site (**www.marketing.glencoe.com**)

For the Student
- Student Activity Workbook, p. 277
- Marketing Math Workbook, p. 101

- Marketing Research Project Workbook
- ILP School-to-Work Activity Workbook, p. 131
- Virtual Business simulation
- *Marketing Essentials* Web site (**www.marketing.glencoe.com**)

ILP These resources are available in print and on the Interactive Lesson Planner (ILP)

Concept Development

1. Read Section 32.2 with students.
2. Have students read aloud the Case Study on page 597 and review the answers in class.
3. Invite the following people to be part of a panel to talk to your students about credit and its wise use: (1) a credit manager from a local bank, who can talk to students about the types of credit that banks commonly offer; (2) a credit manager from a local department store or other retail establishment to tell students how the store issues credit cards; (3) a representative from a consumer credit service; and (4) a representative from a local business to discuss which types of products his or her firm buys on trade credit.

Credit limits can range from several thousand dollars per card to as little as $250 for first time card-holders.

Purchases made by credit cards go through a computerized preapproval process prior to the purchase. This assures a customer has not exceeded the credit limit. A point-of-sale terminal typically scans the approved card and prints sales receipts for the customer and business.

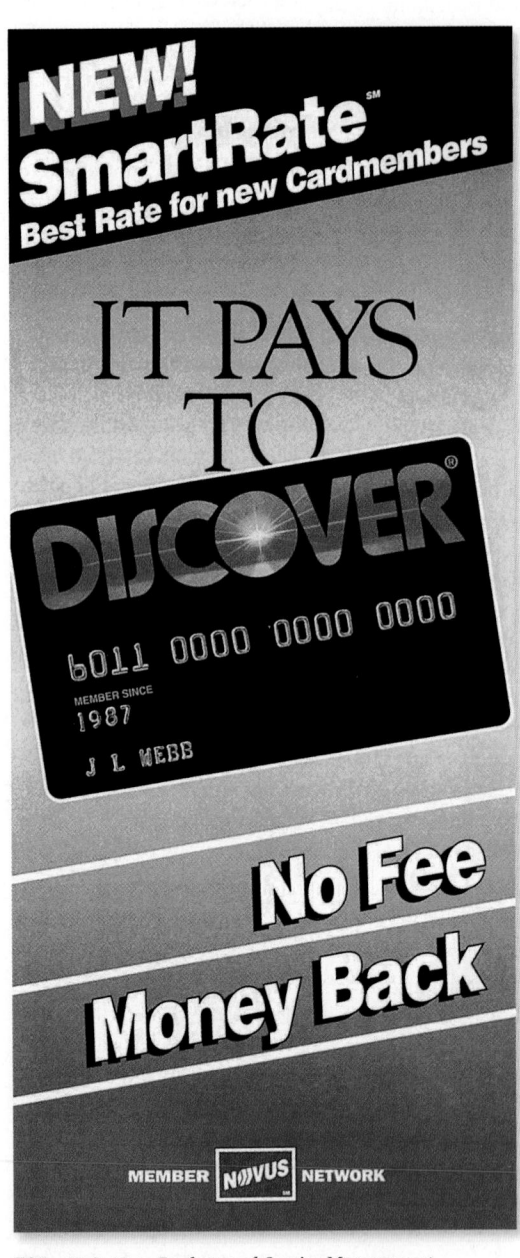

BANK CREDIT CARDS Bank credit cards are issued by banks and their subsidiaries. VISA, MasterCard, and Discover sponsor bank credit cards but do not issue them directly. Banks that issue credit cards, such as Bank One, Citibank, or First USA, set their own interest rates and fees. An *annual fee* is a flat yearly charge similar to a membership fee. Some credit card interest rates are tied to other rates such as the prime rate or the treasury bill rate and are called *variable rate* plans. Others are not explicitly tied to changes in other rates and are called *fixed rate* plans. Banks frequently issue *gold* or *platinum* cards for people earning higher incomes. Depending on the type of card, different credit limits and services are available. Originally, special bank cards carried a certain amount of prestige with owning them, but today they are used as a promotional tool. First USA bank recently issued a *titanium* card. *Standard* or *classic* bank cards, issued for people with lesser incomes, may carry a higher annual percentage rate (APR) and higher fees.

Retailers who belong to a bank credit card system either electronically process credit card sales or mail the credit card forms to the bank for payment. The bank charges a service fee to process the amount of the purchase and sends the balance to the retailer. Often the service fees can be lowered for a business by letting a third party, such as a trade association, process the credit card sales.

After the credit card sales are processed, the bank bills the customer for credit card purchases. Banks that issue bank cards receive their income from finance charges, annual membership fees, and servicing fees.

STORE AND GASOLINE CREDIT CARDS Some businesses are large enough to offer their own credit cards, known as proprietary cards. Some store and gasoline credit cards include those issued by J.C. Penney, Sears, Target, Sunoco, and Shell. Usually proprietary cards do not have an annual fee, but instead have very high interest rates. The individual company handles the processing and billing of all customer purchases.

■ **Do You Qualify for a Credit Card?** Credit applications are completed to determine credit worthiness and to establish a credit limit for customers. *What general types of information are normally collected on a credit application?*

Charge your Gas - Save your Cash!

3 Credit Cards...

THE GASOLINE CARD
Primarily for gas. $250 credit line.
No revolving charges. No annual fee.

THE SUNOCO CARD
Higher credit limits for gas and other
products or auto repairs and services.
No annual fee.

THE PRESTIGE CARD
All the advantages of The Sunoco Card PLUS
towing and roadside insurance. Low annual fee.

4 ways to apply!

PHONE
1-800 2 SUNOCO
(1-800-278-6626)
FAX
1-918-586-6066
ONLINE
www.SunocoCreditCard.com
MAIL
Postage paid

The Choice is Yours

■ **A Card for Every Customer** Retail stores and gasoline companies often issue different types of credit cards. *Why do businesses issue different credit cards?*

Businesses that issue credit cards receive their income from finance charges. Finance charges on unpaid credit card balances are very expensive. In most states, the legal annual percentage rates can not exceed 18 percent, but in some states they can be as high as 21.6 percent.

TRAVEL AND ENTERTAINMENT CARDS Travel and entertainment companies include American Express, Discover, and Diners Club. Travel and entertainment credit card companies require that payments be made in full each month, in addition to an annual fee or service charge.

These types of cards are often accepted for non-travel and entertainment-related goods and services. American Express's main business is travel, which makes up more than two-thirds of its sales.

Travel and entertainment credit card companies also charge retailers a service fee when retailers submit customers' charge slips to the credit card companies. This fee is payment for the service provided by the travel and entertainment card company. Because some businesses are unwilling to pay the service fee, these cards are not accepted everywhere.

REBATE CARDS Rebate cards offer some type of reward or incentive to use their credit. Rebate cards are frequently co-branded and offer rewards in cash, airline miles, long distance service, or special merchandise offers. Individuals who carry a balance on a credit card should look for the card with the lowest interest rate. Those who use a credit card for convenience, however, and pay the balance every month may find the best deal in a rebate card.

Rebate cards have higher interest rates because they are subsidizing the membership costs by offering special incentives on future purchases. The General Motors Mastercard, for example, allows you to transfer 5 percent of your purchases toward the purchase or lease of a new GM vehicle. You can accumulate up to $500 a year toward the rebate.

AFFINITY CARDS Affinity Cards are credit cards issued by issuing banks to show your loyalties to a particular sports team, university, charity, or other organization. The issuer gives a small percentage (usually less than 1%) of the interest toward the organization that is supported by the customer.

DEBIT CARDS A variation of the credit card is a *debit card*. These cards look like credit cards and allow the funds to be withdrawn directly from a checking account and applied to the place of purchase. The customer receives a receipt showing the transfer and the transfer appears on your bank statement as a withdrawal. The ATM machine automatically deducts a customer's purchase from his or her bank checking or savings account.

SPECIAL CUSTOMER CARDS While not really a credit card, many stores are using plastic *special customer cards* as part of product planning. Special customer cards are offered to frequent shoppers.

They allow customers to receive reduced prices on items purchased or reward certificates for cash discounts on future purchases. These cards provide customers with an incentive to shop at the store, and for the business, they provide marketing research information about customers and their purchase patterns.

Chapter 32 ■ *Extended Product Features* **595**

Discussion Starter

Credit Cards as Status Symbols
Discuss with students the fact that credit card companies have promoted their cards as status symbols. American Express offers three tiers of membership: the green card, the gold card, and the platinum card. While green card holders must pay off their charges each month and pay extra for flight insurance when booking airline tickets, gold and platinum card members receive flight insurance as a benefit of membership.

Ask students: Does using credit encourage people to live beyond their means? *(Answers will vary but may suggest that some people definitely abuse credit cards. Others use credit cards responsibly. Some people over-spend on credit cards because they use them in financial emergencies. For example, medical emergencies may cause some people to spend beyond their means.)*

Thinking Critically

Minimum Purchase Amount Ask students why some businesses set a minimum total dollar amount (for example, $15 or $20) before they will allow you to charge a purchase to a bank credit. *(Banks charge the business a service fee for processing each bank card purchase. By setting a dollar minimum on bank card purchases, businesses are hoping to reduce their service fee costs.)*

Independent Practice

Research Have students call credit representatives at three local business establishments (retail stores, gas stations, department stores, etc.) to determine what types of credit accounts they offer. Have students report their findings to the class.

Individualized Practice

Decision-Making Skills

L1 Many credit card issuers send out solicitations to students after high school graduation. Ask students if they were to receive such a solicitation in the near future, what factors would determine whether or not they would apply for the card? *(Answers should include consideration of employment situation, financial obligations, and personal needs.)*

L2 Tell students: You need to purchase a couch, a television set, and a refrigerator, and you plan to buy them all at one store on a credit account. What factors would determine whether you would decide to put them on a 30-day account, an installment account, a revolving account, or a 90-day account? *(Answers should include a consideration of other financial obligations and ability to pay over a certain period of time, an ability to make a down payment on the merchandise, the finance charge of the account, etc.)*

L3 Suppose that a business owner wants to purchase goods from you on trade credit. You do not know this business owner or his business. How will you decide whether or not to extend trade credit? *(You could do the following: (1) obtain information about the business from a relevant trade organization, (2) contact a local bank, (3) talk to other people who have done business with this person, and (4) contact the Better Business Bureau.)*

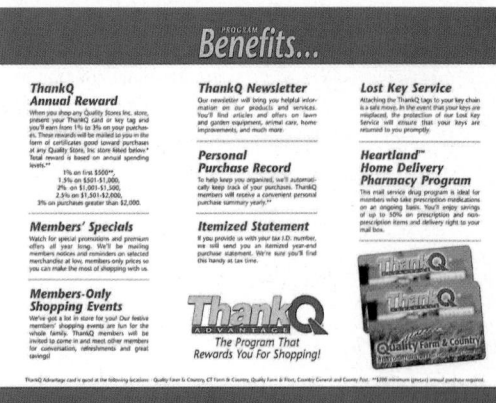

■ **Rewarding Special Customers** Special plastic customer cards are given to loyal shoppers and the sales are recorded for each purchase. *What are the benefits of these special cards for customers and the business?*

SECURED AND UNSECURED LOANS Loans are also a form of credit. Consumers and businesses can obtain *secured loans* and *unsecured loans* for the purchase of goods and services. In secured loans, something of value, such as property, motor vehicles, machinery, or merchandise is pledged as collateral, or security. The collateral helps to ensure that a loan will be repaid; if the loan is not repaid, the lender can keep the secured items to repay the debt.

Consumers and businesses can also obtain unsecured loans, which represent a written promise to repay a loan. Unsecured loans do not require any security. They rely on the excellent credit reputation of the borrower who pledges to repay the loan.

■ Types of Accounts

There are four major consumer credit plans in use today. They are:
- Regular, or 30-day accounts
- Installment accounts
- Revolving accounts
- Budget accounts

The dollar amount a customer pays to use credit is called the finance charge. A *finance charge* may include interest costs and other charges associated with transactions. Let's take a closer look at each type.

REGULAR Regular charge accounts or 30-day accounts allow customers to charge purchases during a month and pay the balance in full within 30 days after they are billed. There is no finance charge for this type of credit plan as long as the bill is paid on time.

INSTALLMENT ACCOUNTS Installment accounts, or time payment plans, allow for payment over a period of time. Installment accounts are normally used for large purchases, such as a college education, travel, automobiles, appliances, and furniture. Installment accounts offer a certain interest rate over a set period of time. Installment accounts sometimes require a down payment and a separate contract for each purchase.

REVOLVING ACCOUNTS The retailer determines the credit limit and when payments are due with a revolving account. The minimum payment is usually a certain percentage on the balance owed or a minimum dollar amount, such as $15. The customer can choose to pay more than the minimum payment to reduce the balance owed. An interest charge is added to the unpaid balance for the billing period.

Customers can make purchases up to the credit limit when using a revolving account. Under most credit card arrangements, regular accounts become revolving accounts if the full amount is not paid for the billing period. Most billing cycles are 25-day periods.

BUDGET ACCOUNTS Budget accounts allow for the payment of a purchased item over a certain time period without a finance charge. The most typical interest-free time period is 90 days, but some businesses have extended the time period to as much as one year. Some retailers who handle expensive products, such as furniture and appliances, offer budget accounts. Budget accounts do not require the customer to pay an interest charge if the amount owed is paid within the interest-free time period. Finance charges are applied if not paid within the specified time period. Offering budget accounts is one way that a company can stay competitive. Customers are attracted to this because they don't have to pay large amounts up front and can budget their money accordingly.

THE DECA CONNECTION
COMPETITIVE EVENTS AND MARKETING ESSENTIALS

Role Plays for Warranties and Guarantees
DECA's Individual Series Events can be helpful in working with this chapter on Extended Product Features. The areas of warranties and guarantees can be found in role-play situations especially in the competitive event occupational areas of Business Services Marketing or Marketing Management.

Typical role-play situations might require students to explain to a businessperson/judge the meaning of a warranty or provisions of a product guarantee. The Financial Services Management Team Decision Making Event provides some case study situations relating to the topic of business credit and the extension of credit.

Case Study

A New Kind of Bank

Commerce Bancorp, based in New Jersey, is a different kind of bank. Unlike many banks, Commerce Bancorp provides a variety of extended product features to its banking customers. As more retail banks consolidate, creating impersonal service and higher fees, consumers are looking for better banking features.

Commerce Bancorp gives free checking for the first year and requires only a $100 minimum balance for free checking after the first year. Other banks frequently have several different fees for a variety of checking accounts. Commerce also offers free money orders, keeps extended hours and has branches open on Saturdays, Sundays, and holidays.

Commerce Bancorp has adopted many of the same branding and service concepts used in quick-serve restaurants. All of the bank's 150 branches have a big red "C" on the front of the bank, open glass architecture, and red and gray design.

Commerce Bancorp spends about $100,000 on marketing each new branch opening. Grand openings for the new branches are special. Magicians, disk jockeys, sports celebrities, raffles, and free food and gifts are all part of the event.

Case Study Review

1. How can Commerce Bancorp provide free checking services when other banks have different fees for different checking accounts?
2. Why does Commerce Bancorp make all of the branches look the same?

A MATTER OF ETHICS

3. Do you think that so much money should be spent on marketing new branches? Why or why not?

▪ Business Credit

Business credit, or trade credit, is similar to consumer credit in that money is lent for goods and services. Suppliers provide raw materials, equipment, and inventory to businesses under an arrangement to pay later. Businesses often use credit for the same reasons that individual consumers do.

Unlike consumer credit, trade credit does not involve the use of credit cards. Credit memorandums, letters of credit, and credit drafts are used in trade credit arrangements. Money is lent with an agreement to pay later. As you learned in Chapter 16, cash discounts are frequently offered to businesses that promptly pay their bills.

Chapter 32 ▪ *Extended Product Features* **597**

Evaluation

Assign and review the Section 32.2 Assessment.

Technology Resources

GO TO **Assessment Resources**
Go to the *Marketing Essentials* Web site (**www.marketing.glencoe. com**) for resources to teach and assess occupation-specific vocabulary.

CLOSE

Section Wrap-Up

Have students write a short statement that tells why credit is an extended product feature. *(Answers should include the idea that credit allows consumers and businesses to buy goods and services when they are needed.)*

Kids Today!
Answer This trend is apparent in many different cultures because of the prevalence of global competition.

Legislation Affecting Credit

There are many government regulations that protect consumers and their credit standing while providing information on the proper use of credit. The following are some of the principal credit laws:

The *Truth in Lending Act* of 1968 requires that lenders disclose information about annual percentage rates, the name of the company extending credit, and the amount financed. It also requires lenders to provide the total purchase price minus any down payments and taxes, the actual finance charge in dollars, a payment schedule, and late payment penalties.

The *Fair Credit Reporting Act* of 1971 requires that a lender report the name and address of the credit bureau that was used by the lender when a consumer is denied credit. The Act gives consumers the opportunity to check their credit histories for errors that prevent them from obtaining credit.

The *Equal Credit Opportunity Acts* of 1975 and 1977 set guidelines for the review of applications for credit. These acts also prohibit discrimination based upon age, gender, race, religion, or marital status.

The *Fair Debt Collection Act* of 1980 prevents businesses from harassing or abusing bad-debt customers in order to collect from them.

The *Credit and Charge Card Disclosure Act* of 1988 helps consumers by requiring credit card issuers to provide information about card costs.

Life In The Diverse MARKETPLACE

Kids Today!

"I walked eight miles to school" will soon be replaced with "When I was a kid, we rode bikes and played outside!" This strange concept of outdoor play and free time to children in the future could be true globally if trends continue in the pattern that market researchers are finding. Studies of children ages 6 to 11 from several countries, including Brazil, Germany, and the United States, find that kids today just don't play. From London to Singapore, the rise in technology, accessibility to computers, popularity of video games, and the push to get into the right college find more kids clicking a mouse than tossing a football.

Thinking Critically
Why is this trend apparent in many different cultures?

32.2 ASSESSMENT

Reviewing Key Terms and Concepts

1. Why is credit important to our economy?
2. List the types of consumer credit.
3. Identify the four major credit plans extended to consumers.
4. How do businesses use trade credit?
5. Why do federal and state governments pass legislation regulating credit?

Thinking Critically

6. More and more banks are issuing credit cards that offer low interest six-month "teaser" rates. What are some possible disadvantages of accepting these offers?

Integrating Academic Skills

7. **MATH** The average American charges $2,800 per year on a card. How many years would it take to earn 25,000 miles for a free airline trip, if the rebate was 1 mile earned per $1 spent?

32.2 ASSESSMENT ANSWERS

Reviewing Key Terms and Concepts

1. Credit allows consumers and businesses to buy goods and services when they are needed in exchange for a promise to pay later.
2. bank credit cards, store and gasoline credit cards, travel and entertainment cards, secured and unsecured loans
3. regular or 30-day accounts, installment accounts, revolving accounts, and budget accounts

4. purchase raw materials; equipment; inventory for manufacturers, wholesalers, and retailers
5. It is necessary due to the tremendous impact credit has on the economy and individuals.

Thinking Critically

6. Some interest rates increase if a customer pays late or exceeds credit limit.

Integrating Academic Skills

7. **MATH** 8.9 years

Careers in Marketing

RESTAURANT MANAGEMENT

Joe O'Brien
Executive Chef
H2O Inc.

What does your job entail?

"I'm responsible for managing the business to success in both profitability and recognition. The chef's reputation and specialties are very important marketing tools for a dining establishment. I develop menus, set prices, design the presentation of the food, oversee the preparation of the food, hire and train kitchen staff, and educate the service staff about menu offerings. Other tasks include ordering food and accounting for and controlling food costs."

What kind of training did you have?

"I started out in this business at the age of 14, working in a restaurant as a dishwasher. I later got a position as a cook, and after I got my speed and coordination, I became a line cook in a full-service restaurant. My life changed when I got an apprenticeship with a master French chef. Over the course of three years, I got a solid European-style education in true cooking. Then I was able to get a position at Lutèce, a first-rate French restaurant in New York City. Three years later, I opened my own restaurant. I designed the kitchen, staffed it, and ran it for two years. After that, I accepted my first 'multi-unit' executive chef position, supervising several operations at a private resort in Florida. I went on to work as chef of the Blue Door restaurant at the Delano Hotel in Miami, and I later moved to Las Vegas to open, staff, and design the menus for four new restaurants. Now I'm the director of operations for an eight-unit restaurant operation in Las Vegas."

What skills are most important?

"You truly have to train your palate to develop a strong sense of taste and a sense of smell. It is also important to have an eye for presentation and design. You have to be able to use both hands at once."

What is your key to success?

"The most important key to my success is hard work. After hard work, the key to advancement is asking questions and listening. Not just hearing, but truly listening, to the answer and to the person."

Thinking Critically

Why would a solid background in business education be important for an Executive Chef?

Career Facts

Education and Training: Valuable college courses include health and nutrition, botany, consumer education, marketing, and business math. French is also recommended. Most chefs receive formal training in culinary schools, while some train through apprenticeships. Some four-year colleges offer culinary programs.

Aptitudes, Abilities, and Skills: The ability to work under stress is important. Good communication, interpersonal, and listening skills are needed. Organizational skills are very important. Chefs must be able to prioritize many tasks, and move from one to another quickly. It is also important to know how to give directions effectively.

Career Outlook: Average growth is projected in this field. Competition for the best jobs is likely to be high.

Career Path: Many chefs begin their careers as apprentices to experienced chefs. They often advance to supervisory or management positions. Some become entrepreneurs by opening their own restaurants.

Chapter 32 ■ *Extended Product Features* **599**

Careers in Marketing

Ask a student to read the Careers in Marketing feature aloud to the class. Discuss the skills and aptitudes required for a career in restaurant management. Ask students whether they think they would like or dislike a career in restaurant management. Discuss the pros and cons of such a career.

Thinking Critically Answer
Answers will vary but may say that a chef's tasks, such as setting prices and ordering and accounting for food, might be addressed in business education.

 Guest Speakers
Invite an executive chef to class to discuss his/her job.

Exploring Careers

Career Advice and Assistance

1. Read to students the following descriptions of the four types of career service companies:

- *Career Counselors* help clients develop career plans, give career interest and psychological tests and interpret results, and teach job-hunting and interview tactics.
- *Career-Marketing (Job Search) Firms* offer job-search services to individuals. Employment agencies fall in this category.
- *Outplacement Firms* offer career and psychological testing, career planning, assistance with preparing a résumé and letters, mail and word-processing services, interview preparation, and individual counseling.
- *Résumé-Writing Companies* Specialize in creating individual résumés and writing cover letters and other job-search correspondence.

2. Have students research companies specializing in career services and share findings.

Lifelong Learning

Extended Product Features
Becoming aware of the rationale behind extended product features is a significant step in the marketing education of every student. Students should take with them the habit of reading the fine print and asking about anything they don't understand. Reading publications, such as *Consumer Reports* and other business publications, can help.

Meeting Individual Needs

Second Language Learners
Students whose native language is not English may find the legal terms used in extended warranty features or in credit applications overwhelming. You may wish to spend extra time going over this vocabulary, and provide examples for students to read. Allow time for students to ask questions and receive clarification of any unfamiliar terminology.

Vocabulary Review

See Glossary for definitions.

Fact and Idea Review

1. A warranty is a promise, or guarantee, given to a customer that a product will meet certain standards.
2. An express warranty is explicitly stated, in writing or in spoken words. An implied warranty exists automatically by state law when a purchase takes place.
3. Under a full warranty, a product found to be defective within the warranty period would be repaired or replaced at no cost. A limited warranty offers less coverage than a full warranty.
4. Some advantages are the assurance of continued satisfactory product performance and peace of mind. Some disadvantages are: Some contracts overlap existing coverage while the manufacturer's warranty is in effect, meaning that a consumer is paying for something that is already available; most people either never need them or forget to use them.
5. The consumer should contact the seller; if the seller does not resolve the problem, the consumer should contact the manufacturer. Local, state, or federal offices that assist with consumer complaints can be contacted next.
6. Credit is an arrangement whereby businesses or individuals can obtain products or money in exchange for a promise to pay later. A credit limit is a preapproved maximum dollar amount of credit.
7. Banks receive their income from finance charges, annual membership fees, and retailer servicing fees. Store and gasoline companies that issue credit cards receive their income from finance charges.
8. Travel and entertainment cards require the payment in full of charges made during the month; bank credit cards do not.
9. Business or trade credit is similar to consumer credit in that money is loaned for goods and services. Trade credit does not involve the use of credit cards.
10. The Truth in Lending Act requires that lenders disclose credit information.

600

Chapter **32** ASSESSMENT

VOCABULARY REVIEW

Create four-member teams. Use the vocabulary terms below to create hangman puzzles. Each team takes turns guessing the missing letters until the term is identified. The team that correctly identifies and defines the term gets a point.

- warranty
- express warranty
- full warranty
- limited warranty
- implied warranty
- warranty of merchantability
- warranty of fitness for a particular purpose
- disclaimer
- credit
- regular, or 30-day, charge accounts
- installment accounts
- revolving accounts
- budget accounts

FACT AND IDEA REVIEW

1. What is a warranty? (32.1)
2. How does an express warranty differ from an implied warranty? (32.1)
3. Is a full warranty different from a limited warranty? (32.1)
4. What are consumer advantages and disadvantages regarding extended warranties or service contracts? (32.1)
5. What steps should consumers take to remedy a problem they have with a product? (32.1)
6. Explain the difference between credit and credit limits. (32.2)
7. Summarize how bank, store, and gasoline credit card issuers receive income. (32.2)

8. How do travel and entertainment charge cards differ from bank credit cards? (32.2)
9. Compare consumer and business credit. (32.2)
10. What does the Truth in Lending Act of 1968 require of lenders? (32.2)

THINKING CRITICALLY

1. In your opinion, what criteria should be part of a good guarantee?
2. Why does a company sell extended warranties to its customers if its advertising stresses product quality? Doesn't this imply that the company's products are subject to failure?
3. Federal legislation has been proposed to place a product liability limit of $250,000 on small businesses for selling a defective product. What are the pros and cons of this proposal?
4. Many credit card issuers provide new college students free tee shirts, Frisbees, and other gifts to apply for credit cards. Do you think college students should be targeted for credit card offerings? Why or why not?

BUILDING WORKPLACE SKILLS

1. **Communication** Write a business letter to the Federal Reserve Board requesting informational material regarding how to choose a credit card. In your letter, ask if it has information on how to maintain good credit. Find the address on the World Wide Web, or use a telephone directory.
2. **Science** Investigate the recent recall of three consumer products by the Consumer Products Safety Commision (www.cpsc.gov) or the National Highway Traffic Safety Commission (www.nhtsa.dot.gov). Prepare a chart of the reasons that the products were recalled.

Thinking Critically

1. A good guarantee should be unconditional and easy for the customer to use.
2. They guard against rising repair costs after a product is used for several years and to assure the customer of worry-free service and repairs. Answers will vary.
3. A pro may be that a small business would be protected from losing all of their money in a lawsuit. The cons would be that the limit may harm consumers and hamper government efforts to collect money for environmental damage.
4. Answers will vary. Some students are unaware of credit and how to effectively handle it, and they may ruin their credit. On the other hand, college students might find the opportunity to have a credit card helpful for emergencies.

Building Workplace Skills

1. Letters will vary.
2. Charts will vary, but each chart should list the type of testing that occurred and the results of the tests.

APPLYING MARKETING CONCEPTS

1. **Obtaining Warranty Quotes** Use the Internet to find a direct marketer of extended warranties. Obtain a quote for an automobile, recreational vehicle, motorcycle, or boat.

2. **Researching Credit Advice** Use the library or the Internet to investigate how to use credit wisely. Prepare a one-page report using a word processing program.

3. **Finding the Better Business Bureau** Find a Better Business Bureau located in your state. Use presentation software to create an oral report that summarizes the various services it provides and where it is located.

4. **Protecting Your Credit** Use the Internet to search for "credit repair services." Investigate how to prevent identity theft. Write a one-page report using a word processing program.

5. **Comparing Credit Cards** Locate the Federal Reserve Board Web site and find information about comparison shopping for bank credit cards. The Board's site provides information on interest rates, grace periods, annual fees, and telephone numbers for the 150 largest banking institutions offering credit cards. Prepare a spreadsheet using computer software that compares the advantages and disadvantages of three credit cards. Compare annual fees, annual percentage rates, and other pertinent information.

LINKING SCHOOL TO WORK

Interpersonal and Basic Skills Develop a one-page written report on the process used at your or another's place of employment to honor product or service guarantees.

THE DECA CONNECTION

Role Play: Service Manager

Situation You are to assume the role of service manager in an auto dealership. An angry customer (judge) is complaining about rattles and noises, which are occurring in his/her car. The customer's (judge's) new car warranty has recently expired. The customer (judge) is complaining that prior to expiration, he/she requested the necessary repairs, but they were not completed correctly.

Activity Your task is to represent the warranty conditions to the customer (judge) and to resolve the situation to the satisfaction of the customer (judge).

Evaluation You will be evaluated on how well you meet the following performance indicators:
- Explain warranties and guarantees
- Handle customer/client complaints
- Demonstrate problem-solving skills
- Interpret business policies to customers/clients
- Show empathy for others

interNET CONNECTION

Finding Great Rates
Locate the *Consumers Digest* Web site for the best credit card rates.

Connect
- Use a spreadsheet program to create a table showing the bank and the best annual percentage rates for each type of credit card.

THE DECA CONNECTION

Students should be evaluated on the performance indicators noted in the Role Play.
- For another DECA Role Play, go to the *Student Activity Workbook*, p. 277.
- For more in-depth Role Play practice, refer to DECA's *Essential Competitive Events Handbook*. To order, contact DECA at www.deca.org.

interNET CONNECTION

Answers must include the best annual percentage rate for type of bank card and the name of the particular institution.

Mini Quiz

Administer the Mini Quiz orally. For an expanded chapter quiz, go to page 189 of the *Reproducible Tests* book.

1. A promise to a customer that a product will meet certain standards is called a(n) warranty.

2. A(n) express warranty is one that is explicitly stated, in writing or spoken words to induce a customer to buy.

3. A(n) warranty of merchantability amounts to a promise from the seller that the product is fit for its intended purpose.

4. A service contract that provides service or preventative maintenance for a specified period beyond a product's normal warranty period is called a(n) extended warranty.

5. An arrangement whereby businesses or individuals can obtain products or money is exchanged for a promise to pay later is called credit.

Applying Marketing Concepts

1. Answers will depend on the direct marketer.
2. Answers will vary.
3. Presentations will vary.
4. Reports will vary.
5. Spreadsheets will vary, but should contain pertinent information related to credit cards.

Linking School to Work

Answers depend on the work situation.

1. **Assessment** Have students complete the Reproducible Test for Chapter 32 and Unit 10 or construct your own tests using the ExamView software.
2. **Enrichment** Have students complete the corresponding activities in the following workbooks:
   - *Marketing Math Workbook*, p. 101

FOCUS

Unit Lab Overview

In this Zazz Lab, students will create a sports product using their knowledge of product planning, branding, packaging, and labeling, as well as warranty and consumer protection.

Bell Ringer Activity

Discuss Ask students: Has anyone ever heard of a Hula Hoop, a Slinky, or a Frisbee? Tell students about each one, and then ask if they have ever said to themselves, "Why didn't I think of that?"

Discussion Starter

Ask students to identify different variations of bicycles. *(tricycles—small ones for children and larger ones for senior citizens; two-wheelers with training wheels; unicycles; tandem bicycles made for two; 10-speed racing bikes, dirt bikes, mountain bikes; stationary bicycles for working out, etc.)* Ask students: Why there are so many variations of bicycles? *(Answers will vary but should recognize that different types were created based on various needs identified by different target populations.)*

TEACH

Thinking Critically

Consumer Rights Ask students: How do federal and state laws affect design and promotion of new sports apparel or sporting goods equipment? *(Clothing labels have to include the garment's fabric content and care instructions; sporting goods have implied warranties regarding what the product is "supposed to do," as described in promotional literature and packaging. If something is dangerous, age restrictions may have to be placed on the product, and warnings on its package.)*

602

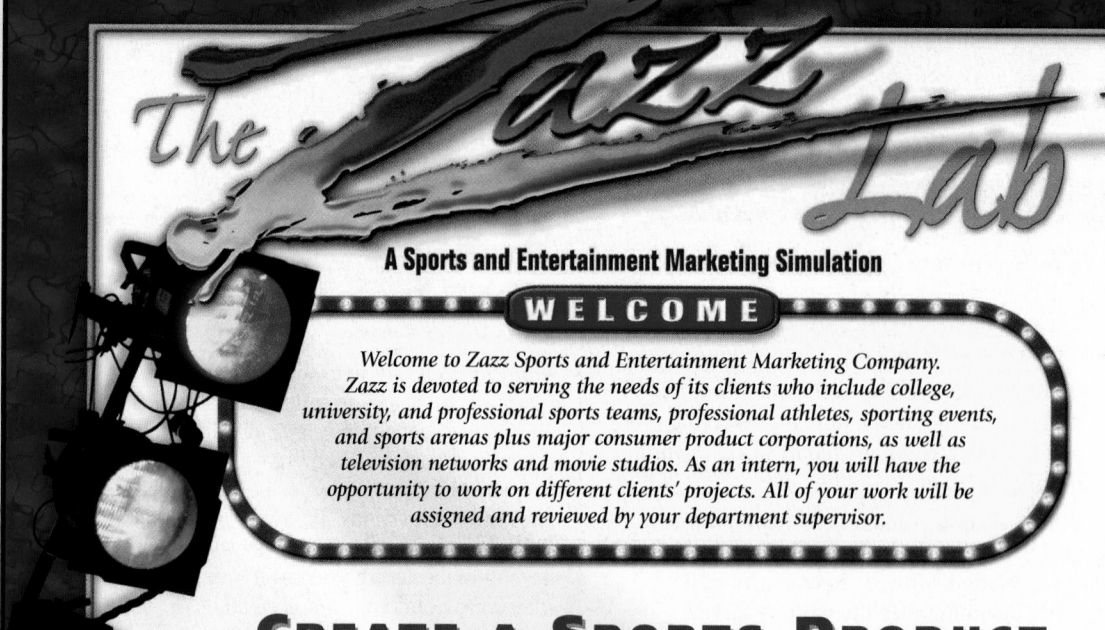

the Zazz Lab

A Sports and Entertainment Marketing Simulation

WELCOME

Welcome to Zazz Sports and Entertainment Marketing Company. Zazz is devoted to serving the needs of its clients who include college, university, and professional sports teams, professional athletes, sporting events, and sports arenas plus major consumer product corporations, as well as television networks and movie studios. As an intern, you will have the opportunity to work on different clients' projects. All of your work will be assigned and reviewed by your department supervisor.

CREATE A SPORTS PRODUCT

SITUATION

Zazz's client, Good Sports, would like to develop a new piece of sports equipment and/or apparel for teens. The client's research and development department has not come up with any satisfactory ideas. Zazz has volunteered to take on the challenge. Think of how surfing was the impetus for snowboarding and skateboarding. Consider how in-line skating transformed regular roller skating into a new dimension. This is the kind of creative new idea that Good Sports is looking for.

ASSIGNMENT

Your supervisor wants you to develop your ideas using the steps for new product planning. You may want to create an entire product line or just one item. Create a prototype of your product if possible, or draw your design. If it's not a new concept, decide what will differentiate your product from others like it. Identify the product positioning, brand name, and packaging, including any warnings that should be part of the package design. Develop a warranty for the product and note any other extended product features. Design a brand mark or trade character to attract attention.

Tools and Resources

To complete this assignment, you will need to conduct research at a library or on the Internet. You will also need a word processing program, spreadsheet program, and presentation software. Trade publications that may be helpful include *Brandweek, Sports Business Journal, Sports Business Daily, Women's Wear Daily,* and *Sporting Goods Dealer.*

Research

Research traditional and current trends in sports, such as extreme sports, to identify an unfulfilled equipment or apparel need. Once you have a solid product design, conduct a small-scale marketing research study among your peers to test your concept. Use your findings to make adjustments to your original plan. Research the target market for this product, identifying characteristics and numbers in the population who may buy such an item. Research any laws that may pertain to the use of your product, as well as labeling laws. Research other similar products or product lines to determine how best to position your new product idea. Finally, research your competition to find out how you can differentiate your product.

WHAM-O'S HULA HOOP

The Hula Hoop is the one product by which all other fads are compared due to the tremendous excitement it created in the late 1950s. Within six months of its introduction in 1958, Hula Hoop's sales topped 25 million, and after two years, exceeded 100 million. Demand for these large plastic rings was so great that toy manufacturers couldn't keep up. Its popularity grew with competitions in which contestants would swing the brightly colored plastic hoops around their waists, legs, and arms. The Hula Hoop was inspired by a bamboo exercise hoop used in Australian elementary schools. The hoop's origin can be traced back to more than 3,000 years ago, when children in Egypt played with large hoops of dried grapevines.

Report

Prepare a written report and a computer presentation for the client. Use a word processing program to prepare a double-spaced report. Arrange your written report around the following headings:

- Product idea
  - Concept and design
  - Target market
  - Features and benefits
  - Brand name, brand mark, and/or trade character
- Market and business analysis
  - Sporting goods trends
  - Market demand (number of potential customers in target market)
  - Competition (market share enjoyed by each competitor)
  - Product's potential profitability (selling price, estimated cost, estimated sales)
  - Product development program
- Packaging, labeling, and extended product features
  - Package design
  - Pertinent labeling laws
  - Label design
  - Warranty
- Product positioning
  - Relation to competition
  - Differentiation
  - Positioning methods
- Distribution
  - Identified retail markets
  - Rationale for distribution method

Using computer presentation software, prepare a presentation of your ideas for the client that includes:

- Key topics covered in your written report
- Graphic illustrations that are relevant to each slide's topic
- Very little text
- Minimum of 10 slides

Presentation and Evaluation

Present your ideas in a written report and an oral presentation. The oral presentation will be shown to the client. You will be evaluated on your oral presentation skills, including:

- Knowledge of market and business analysis for the proposed product
- Product design
- Creativity
- Ability to meet the customer's needs
- Program to develop the product (packaging, labeling, positioning, distribution)
- Continuity of presentation
- Enthusiasm
- Voice quality
- Eye contact

 Portfolio

Print a copy of your completed report and presentation for your Portfolio.

THE CONNECTION

Apparel and Accessories, Management Level
Designing a new piece of apparel and determining how to position it in the marketplace could be a topic for this event.

DECA Business Services Marketing Series
Designing a new product, package design, extended features, and positioning for a client is a possible role play topic for this event.

DECA Hospitality and Recreation Research Event
Since the product involved in this unit lab is a sporting goods product, the research involved in developing a new product and its design is a potential topic for this research event.

DECA Sports and Entertainment Marketing Management Team Decision-Making Event
Working on this project with a partner would make the experience similar to what is expected in a DECA Team Decision-Making Event.

COOPERATIVE LEARNING

Teamwork This unit lab lends itself to working in teams of four to six students. Have teams compete with one another to come up with the best new product idea and program to develop it. Another option is to assign all students the task of researching a new product idea, and then have the class select the best three ideas for the lab. Assign teams of four to six students to complete specific aspects of the project, such as market and business analysis, packaging and labeling, warranty, positioning, and distribution.

Independent Practice

Research, Write, and Present
Students can research products unrelated to sports to see how they were invented and promoted. Have them select products such as hair products, electronics, household appliances, etc. Have students write reports and give oral presentations on their findings.

ASSESS

Enrichment

Research, Write, and Present
Have students take an existing product and find a new use for it. You may want to share the following examples of such products: The breathable fabric trademarked as Gortex was first used by surgeons as a conduit to connect organs to arterial supplies. Gortex is now found in boots, gloves, jackets, and rain wear. Baking soda is now used for toothpastes, detergents, fire suppressants, and deodorizers. Have students prepare a written report and make an oral presentation. Internet sites, such as **www.ideafinder.com/** may be helpful.

Evaluation

The rubrics for evaluation of the written, oral, and computer presentation are included in the student text. (See the outline and guidelines for the written report, the computer presentation, and the skills' assessment for oral presentations.) It might be best to replicate those rubrics to evaluate the students' work. A separate rubric could be created to evaluate the work of a team.

CLOSE

Lab Wrap-Up

Ask students: What are the major product development steps? *(Steps include generating ideas, screening ideas, business proposal, developing the product, market testing, and commercialization.)*

Unit 11

Entrepreneurship and Finance

Chapter 33
Entrepreneurial Concepts

Chapter 34
Risk Management

Chapter 35
Developing a Business Plan

Chapter 36
Financing the Business

Unit Objectives

After completing this unit, students will be able to:

- Identify the risks, rewards, advantages, and disadvantages of entrepreneurship.
- Identify the different forms of business ownership.
- Explain the types of business risks and different methods used to handle them.
- Identify the three major sections of a business plan.
- Develop a business plan with appropriate documentation.
- Prepare financial statements used by entrepreneurs to report income and analyze a business's financial status.

Enrichment Resources

Books

The Entrepreneurial Mindset by Rita Gunther McGrath and Ian MacMillan
Entrepreneurship and Small Business Management, Glencoe/McGraw-Hill

Magazines/Journals

Entrepreneur Magazine
Young Entrepreneur

Associations

National Small Business United
1156 15th Street, NW, Suite 1100
Washington, DC 20005
(202) 293-8830
www.nsbu.org

Small Business Administration
409 3rd Street, SW
Washington, DC 20416
(800) 8-ASK-SBA
www.sba.gov

Journal Writing Activity

1. Ask students to make a list in their journals of ten words that come to mind when they think of *entrepreneurship.* Ask them to share their entrepreneurship-related words with the rest of the class. Write the words on the board. Then write the words *economic risk, natural risk,* and *human risk* on the board. Ask students to continue writing in their journals and briefly explain what they think each term means in relation to entrepreneurship. Remind students that entrepreneurs manage risk by careful planning.

2. Ask students to write two paragraphs in their journals about what they think it takes to be a successful entrepreneur. Then ask them to share their answers. Remind students that entrepreneurs must not only manage risk, they must also create a solid business plan, identify potential investors and lenders, as well as develop an effective financial plan to meet capital needs.

TEACHER CLASSROOM RESOURCES

Program Resources	Chapter 33	Chapter 34	Chapter 35	Chapter 36
Student Activity Workbook	p. 287	p. 297	p. 307	p. 317
Marketing Math Workbook	p. 111	p. 111	p. 111	p. 111
Marketing Research Project Workbook				
School-to-Work Activity Workbook	p. 135	p. 139	p. 143	p. 147
BusinessWeek Case Studies	p. 207	p. 213	p. 219	p. 225
Marketing Career Portfolio	p. 41	p. 41	p. 41	p. 41
Reproducible Tests	p. 197	p. 203	p. 207	p. 213
ExamView User's Guide and Testbank	p. 33-1	p. 34-1	p. 35-1	p. 36-1
Internet Resources	p. 85	p. 87	p. 89	p. 91
Blackline Masters	p. 71	p. 72	p. 73	p. 75
Lesson Plans	p. 69	p. 71	p. 73	p. 76
Block Scheduling	p. 11	p. 11	p. 11	p. 11
Impact! Simulation				

ILP Each of these resources is available in print and on the Interactive Lesson Planner CD-ROM.

Technology Resources

- **Interactive Lesson Planner (ILP) CD-ROM**
- **PowerPoint Presentation CD-ROM**
- **Marketing Essentials Web site**
- **ExamView! CD-ROM**
- **Impact! Simulation**

Virtual Business

Virtual Business is a fully visual marketing and business simulation that introduces students to the principles of marketing by letting them start and run their own virtual businesses. In *Virtual Business,* students have the power to control all aspects of a retail convenience store. Students strategize marketing decisions using a powerful learning tool in the guise of a video game. They learn by experiencing how their decisions affect their virtual business.

Key to Individualized Academics Activities

L1 Level 1 activities are basic activities and should fall within the range of all students.

L2 Level 2 activities are average activities and should be within the range of average and above average students.

L3 Level 3 activities are challenging activities designed for the ability range of above average students.

National Marketing Education

CHAPTER	SECTION	PERFORMANCE INDICATOR
Chapter 33 **Entrepreneurial Concepts**	33.1	Explain the concept of private enterprise (ECO)
		Identify speculative business risks (BME)
		Explain the types of business risk (BME)
		Identify desirable personality traits important to business (PD)
	33.2	Explain employment opportunities in business (PD)
		Explain the types of business ownership (BME)
		Explain legal issues affecting business (BME)
Chapter 34 **Risk Management**	34.1	Explain the nature of risk management (BME)
		Explain types of business risk (BME)
	34.2	Explain routine security precautions (BME)
		Describe the concept of insurance (BME)
Chapter 35 **Developing a Business Plan**	35.1	Explain the nature of a business plan (BME)
		Explain external planning considerations (BME)
	35.2	Develop business plan (BME)
		Plan and organize the work efforts of others (BME)
		Explain the nature of marketing plans (BME)
	35.3	Explain the nature and scope of financing (FIN)
		Determine financing needed to start a business (FIN)
		Describe sources of financing for businesses (FIN)
Chapter 36 **Financing the Business**	36.1	Explain the nature and scope of financing (FIN)
		Explain the nature of business plans (BME)
		Interpret financial statements (BME)
	36.2	Explain the concept of accounting (BME)
		Explain the nature of balance sheets (BME)
		Describe the nature of cash-flow statements (BME)

CIS Communication, Interpersonal Skills   **DIS** Distribution   **FIN** Financing   **PRI** Pricing   **SEL** Selling

Standards Assessment Correlation

SECTION ASSESSMENT			CHAPTER ASSESSMENT						UNIT LAB
Reviewing Key Terms and Concepts	Thinking Critically	Integrating Academic Skills	Fact and Idea Review	Thinking Critically	Building Workplace Skills	Applying Marketing Concepts	Linking School to Work	Internet Connection	Zazz Lab
1, 2, 3, 5	●	●	1, 2, 3	3	1, 2	1		●	
2, 3	●		1, 2, 3	3	1, 2	1, 2, 4		●	●
3	●		3	3	1, 2	1, 2, 4		●	
4	●	●	1	1, 3	1	1, 3, 4, 5		●	
1	●	●		1		4, 5			
2	●	●	4, 5, 6, 7, 8, 9	2, 3	2	1, 3, 4	●	●	
3, 4, 5	●		4, 5, 7, 8, 10	2		4			●
2	●	●	1	1, 2, 4	1, 2	1, 2, 4, 5	●	●	
1, 3, 4, 5	●	●	2	1	1	2, 3	●	●	
1, 2, 3, 4, 5		●	3, 10	2, 3, 4	1	1, 2, 4	●	●	
1, 2, 3, 4	●		3, 5, 6, 7, 8, 9	2, 3, 4	1, 2	3, 4		●	
1, 2, 3	●	●	1, 5	2, 4		1, 2, 3		●	●
4, 5	●	●	2, 3, 4	2	1, 2	2		●	●
1, 4	●		7	4		1, 3, 4		●	●
2, 3	●		6	1, 3, 4		2			
5						2			●
4		●					●		●
1, 4			8	4		2, 4			●
1, 2, 3, 4, 5	●	●	8, 9, 10	5		2	●	●	
1, 4, 5	●		1	1	1	1, 4	●	●	●
1, 3, 4, 5	●		1, 2, 3	1, 2, 3, 4, 5	1, 2	1, 2, 3		●	●
2				3, 5			●		●
1, 2, 3		●	4, 5, 7, 8, 9	1, 2, 5		3, 4			
4			6, 9						
5	●		9			2			

Unit Overview

Entrepreneurship is stressed to marketing students because it is so important to the U.S. economy. Chapter 33 introduces students to the process of starting and managing a business. Chapter 34 discusses the economic, natural, and human risks inherent in business ownership, as well as the steps business owners take to reduce and manage risk by careful planning. Chapter 35 discusses how potential business owners create a business plan to give an overall picture of a proposed business to potential investors and lenders. Chapter 36 shows students how to identify capital needs for a business and develop a financial plan that will meet those needs.

Introducing the Unit

Ask students if they can generate the names of some modern-day entrepreneurs. Have them speculate on why some people prefer to work for themselves and initially sacrifice a great deal of security. Ask what skills and abilities it takes to be your own boss. Also ask students if any of them have already participated in some type of entrepreneurial endeavor, and would they consider working for themselves as a career move.

UNIT·11

Portfolio

Preparing a Business Plan

Once you have completed this unit, you will prepare a business plan for a business of your choice. A good business plan describes every part of a proposed business to potential investors and lenders. It also helps you develop your ideas and provides a way for you to evaluate your results. To ensure that all required elements are present, follow the outline detailed in Chapter 35.

604

Field Trip Suggestions

Visit the School or Local Library Plan a visit to the school or local public library to use the Internet to explore the resources available online to individuals wishing to start their own business and create a business plan. Have them also research online resources for identifying capital needs and sources.

Entrepreneurship and Finance

Unit Overview

Entrepreneurship is highly stressed in marketing education because it is so important to the U.S. economy. Chapter 33 introduces you to the process of starting and managing a business. Chapter 34 discusses the economic, natural, and human risks inherent in business ownership and the steps business owners take to reduce and manage risk by careful planning. Chapter 35 explains how potential business owners create a business plan to give an overall picture of a proposed business to potential investors and lenders. Chapter 36 shows how to identify capital needs for a business and develop a financial plan that will meet those needs.

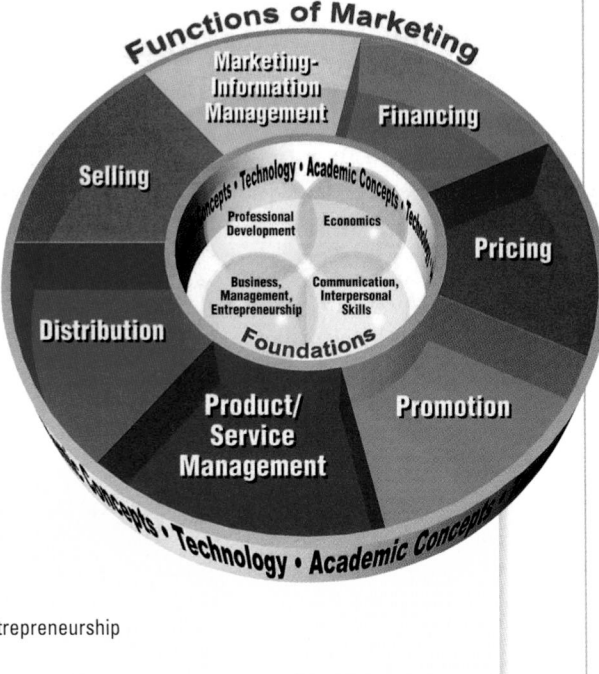

In this Unit:

Foundations of Marketing

◯ Professional Development

◯ Economics

◯ Business, Management, Entrepreneurship

Functions of Marketing

◣ Financing

DECA Unit Project

Have students research the role of small business ownership in our society since the 1700s. What role did small business play in the society of the late 1990s? What role will it probably play in the early twenty-first century? How is small business ownership reflective of current economic and sociological trends in our society?

www Go to the *Marketing Essentials* Web site (**www.marketing.glencoe. com**) for resources to teach and assess occupation-specific vocabulary.

Unit Closure

Ask students if they were inspired by studying this unit to pursue an entrepreneurial endeavor. Were they influenced to consider entrepreneurship as a career? What conclusions can they draw about entrepreneurship from their study of this unit?

🎙 Guest Speaker Suggestions

Franchise Business Owner Invite a franchise business owner to discuss with your class the types of business support available from his or her franchisor. Have him or her explain what duties the franchisor is responsible for, such as management training, advertising, and merchandising.

Chapter Overview

This chapter introduces entrepreneurial concepts including the meaning of entrepreneurship and its risks, advantages, and disadvantages. The chapter identifies the characteristics and skills needed by entrepreneurs, and details the importance of small business to our economy. The types of business ownership and legal steps in establishing a business are also explored.

 ### Springboard

Analyze Ask students if any of them have worked as entrepreneurs. Cite some examples of entrepreneurial work, such as providing childcare, mowing lawns, cleaning pools, and developing Web sites. Ask them what the rewards and drawbacks were of working for themselves. Tell students that by working for themselves, they were acting in an entrepreneurial manner.

Prereading

List the section objectives to discuss with students. Have them skim the chapter, looking at the pictures, reading the captions, and noting the heads. Ask questions to ensure that the students have a minimal understanding of the chapter structure.

Preteaching Marketing Vocabulary

Flip through the chapter with students. When you come to a bold-face key term, have a student read the definition aloud. Have students develop a visual symbol to illustrate each term. Draw each symbol next to its term that you write on the board.

Marketing: What It Takes

Answer Answers will vary but may include friends or family members who are entrepreneurs as well as professional organizations.

Chapter **33**

Entrepreneurial Concepts

Marketing: What It Takes

Entrepreneurship 101
Look seven years into the future. You've graduated from college and worked in computer software sales for three years. You've dreamed of having your own business. You're ready to pursue your dream, but you have many questions.

WHAT WILL YOU DO?
How will you know where to find the answers you need as you prepare to start up a business?

606

THE DECA CONNECTION   **ADVISOR CORNER**

Virtual Business Challenge Have students learn fundamental marketing and business principles with Knowledge Matters' *Virtual Business Challenge,* a new tool for a new century. *Virtual Business* is a fully visual marketing and business simulation that introduces students to the principles of marketing by letting them start and run their own virtual business. In *Virtual Business* students have the power to control all aspects of a retail convenience store. Students strategize marketing and business decisions using a powerful tool in the guise of a video game.

Entrepreneurship

What Is Entrepreneurship?

Entrepreneurship is the process of starting and managing your own business. Everyone in the United States is free to start, own, and operate a business. **Entrepreneurs** are people who organize, manage, and take the risk of owning and operating a business. You are an entrepreneur if you have provided baby-sitting services or cut someone's lawn.

Entrepreneurs have made major contributions to our economy. Henry Ford introduced the mass production of automobiles, thus making them affordable to the average person. Ray Kroc made McDonald's the largest fast-food restaurant chain in the world. Bette Graham, a secretary, developed Liquid Paper to cover errors in typed, printed, or photocopied documents; the product is now sold worldwide. Steven Jobs and Steven Wozniak began Apple Computer, Inc., working mostly from their homes, and soon turned it into an international business.

These entrepreneurs became famous and wealthy; however, there are many entrepreneurs who do not dream of fame and riches. They are people who want to be their own bosses and to make their own business decisions. They are willing to put in the effort and dedication it takes to be successful at running their own businesses.

■ The Risk of Entrepreneurship

Starting a new business is a risk because it requires a major commitment of time, money, and effort. New business owners must be risk takers. It is often necessary to quit a job, work long hours, invest savings, and borrow money—all with no guarantee that the new business will succeed.

Approximately 60 percent of those who start a business are between the ages of 25 and 40. People between these ages usually have the work experience, the personal drive, the financial resources, and the willingness to take business risks. People over the age of 40 are usually established in life. They may have the money and experience it takes to start a business, but they may be reluctant to do so because of family commitments or the fear of losing what they have achieved.

The threat of losing money or of not making enough money with a new business venture is very real. Most new businesses that survive employ only a few people and provide a living only for the business owner and his or her family. More than 3,000 new businesses are started each week in the United States. Studies show that two out of three new firms close their doors within four years.

● What You'll Learn

- The meaning of entrepreneurship
- How to identify the risks involved in entrepreneurship
- The advantages and disadvantages of entrepreneurship
- How to identify the personal characteristics and skills necessary for entrepreneurs
- The scope of small business in the American economy

● Why It's Important

In this section, you will learn some important advantages and disadvantages of business ownership.

● Key Terms

- entrepreneurship
- entrepreneurs

FOCUS

 Bell Ringer Activity

Write Give students five minutes to write a list of what they would consider to be the advantages and disadvantages of entrepreneurship.

Introducing the Section

Entrepreneurship Review with the class students' answers from the Bell Ringer Activity. In this section they will look at the pros and cons of entrepreneurship and begin the process of exploring entrepreneurship as a career option.

Chapter 33 ■ *Entrepreneurial Concepts* **607**

Classroom Resources

For the Teacher
- Teacher Editions for all workbooks
- Assessment Package
- PowerPoint Presentation Software
- Interactive Lesson Planner
- ILP Block Scheduling, p. 11
- ILP Lesson Plans, p. 69
- ILP Internet Resources, p. 85

- ILP Blackline Masters, p. 71
- ILP *BusinessWeek* Case Studies, p. 207
- ILP Marketing Career Portfolio, p. 41
- *Marketing Essentials* Web site (**www.marketing.glencoe.com**)

For the Student
- Student Activity Workbook, p. 287
- Marketing Math Workbook, p. 111

- Marketing Research Project Workbook
- ILP School-to-Work Activity Workbook, p. 135
- Virtual Business simulation
- *Marketing Essentials* Web site (**www.marketing.glencoe.com**)

ILP These resources are available in print and on the Interactive Lesson Planner (ILP)

■ Small to Big Business McDonald's started out as a single drive-in restaurant in California. *What other big businesses began as small entrepreneurial ventures?*

■ Advantages of Entrepreneurship

You can see that owning and operating your own business can be risky. There are no guarantees of success. Nevertheless, being an entrepreneur has its advantages.

There are many reasons why people choose to start their own businesses despite the risks. If you become your own boss, you can enjoy great benefits. Some of these advantages include personal freedom, personal satisfaction, increased income, and increased self-esteem.

Entrepreneurs are not controlled by any other managers in their organizations. They set their own work schedules and control their own fate. They make their own decisions, try out their own new ideas, and direct their energies into business activities as they see fit.

Personal freedom leads to the satisfaction of doing what you enjoy each day. By being in control of their businesses and their work settings, entrepreneurs are much more in control of their lives.

Personal satisfaction usually leads people to work hard at what they enjoy. Working hard generally results in making more money. The incentive to make money—coupled with the personal satisfaction that comes from doing so—is always present.

Freedom, satisfaction, and increased income add up to a greater feeling of self-esteem. People who work hard and are well rewarded for it, both personally and financially, are truly successful people.

■ Disadvantages of Entrepreneurship

The advantages of being an entrepreneur are definitely exciting and motivating. There are also some disadvantages. These include the potential loss of income, long and irregular hours, and the necessity for strong self-discipline.

New businesses usually have a restricted cash flow because of start-up costs. This may mean that an entrepreneur's first year or more of operation does not meet his or her personal financial needs. Entrepreneurs enjoy improved earnings only if the business is successful. If they do not have the necessary personal or technical skills, their businesses will probably fail. The failure of a business may cause the loss of employment, status, and invested money.

Entrepreneurs are not 40-hour-a-week people. It is quite possible that a new business will demand 12 to 16 hours a day in addition to weekends and holidays. New business owners often do not take vacations until the business proves successful.

Running a business requires doing many tedious, time-consuming tasks. The business owner may do general cleaning and maintenance because there is not enough money to hire someone else to do it. There is usually a lot of paperwork. Accounts payable, accounts receivable, payroll, and forms to fill out for all levels of government regulations require precise record keeping.

GREAT IDEAS from the Marketing Classroom

Pam Naylor
Shades Valley High School
Birmingham, AL

Have students research an entrepreneur who has had a major impact on U.S. business and/or lifestyle. Students may use the Internet, library or classroom materials, and other sources, such as the television series *A&E Biographies.* The project is worth 100 points: 50 points for research paper, 35 points for poster/visual, and 15 points for oral presentation. A list of sources must be included, as well as a discussion of risks involved, how the business was affected by supply and demand, and any advice the student would have offered to the entrepreneur. The poster or visual should have photos or illustrations and include relevant information on the subject.

■ **Satisfaction Guaranteed** The satisfaction of working for yourself is a great advantage for entrepreneurs. *What other advantages are there to owning and managing your own business?*

From Germany to eBay...And Back

Based on the quick success of eBay, it was only a matter of time before the trend went international. Brothers Oliver, Marc, and Alexander Samwer saw their opportunity as eBay interns and ran with it—back to their native Germany. They returned to Berlin to model their own auction site—Alondo.de—on eBay's. In three months, the twenty-somethings sold Alondo.de to eBay for $43 million. The young entrepreneurs have become German celebrities. Alondo.de, now called eBay Germany, has set off a wave of young start-up companies throughout their country.

Thinking Critically
What are some advantages of an unpaid internship for people who want to start their own businesses?

It takes a great deal of self-discipline to keep up with all these things on a daily, weekly, and monthly basis. They are just as important as selling the product or service.

Despite these disadvantages, the lure of being one's own boss attracts countless people each year. Those who are successful at it have certain personal characteristics that enable them to succeed where others fail. What are these personal qualities? Are you a budding entrepreneur?

To be a successful entrepreneur, you must have strong organizational skills, tremendous drive, and very good leadership ability. You must have the special skills and knowledge necessary to operate the business you have chosen. You must also be in good physical and mental condition to work the necessary hours.

It helps to have parents or relatives who are already in business for themselves. Studies have shown that the family is a major influence on who becomes an entrepreneur. Being around people who are successful entrepreneurs influences children to

feel that they can be successful entrepreneurs, too.

People who become entrepreneurs usually feel that they are in control of their career and daily work activities. They think that their hard work and determination—not luck or fate—will make their business successful. They also have a spirit of adventure. They get a great deal of satisfaction from taking risks and achieving goals.

■ Do You Have What It Takes?

Being an entrepreneur is a huge responsibility. You are responsible not only for your own welfare but also for the welfare of your company and employees. An entrepreneur is responsible for owning the business and for managing the basic functions as well. Without the proper skills or training, entrepreneurs can quickly go out of business and lose all of the money that they invested. Being a smart entrepreneur requires not only strong business skills but also tremendous dedication to the vision of the company. Entrepreneurs have many personal skills and characteristics that their job demands of them.

Chapter 33 ■ *Entrepreneurial Concepts* **609**

SECTION 33.1

Discussion Starter

Altruism Many people have strong altruistic motives for becoming entrepreneurs. First, make sure students understand the term *altruism* (unselfish regard for the welfare of others). Then have them discuss why altruism plays a part in some people's desire to be an entrepreneur. *(Some people feel they are contributing to the local labor force and are thus making the community a better place in which to work and live.)*

Thinking Critically

Small Business Ownership Have students discuss why small business ownership has become so important in our society.

Cooperative Learning

Entrepreneurs Many major corporations, such as Ford Motor Company, Microsoft, J.C. Penney, Wendy's International, Inc., The Walt Disney Company, and William Wrigley, Jr. Company, were started by entrepreneurs who had a dream of achieving a goal, created a product to fill a market need, or simply discovered or created a product accidentally and began to market it. Have students form 3-member teams to research, write, and present information about the founder of one of these or any other U.S. corporation. Each team should prepare an oral presentation using transparencies or a presentation software program.

CAPTION ANSWER
Satisfaction Guaranteed Advantages to owning and managing your own business may include a chance for increased income, more personal freedom, and higher self-esteem.

From Germany to eBay ... And Back
Answer Interns can begin to prove themselves and gather information about business practices, career styles, leadership, as well as make necessary contacts. Internships are a great way to learn from the ground up.

Independent Practice

Interview and Discuss Have students interview a business owner or supervisor on the advantages and disadvantages of being an owner/manager and the type of preparation and/or training required for the position. Discuss the interviews in class.

ASSESS

Reteaching

1. **Vocabulary** Assign and review the vocabulary terms for this section.
2. **Fact and Idea** Assign and review Fact and Idea Review question number one from the Chapter Assessment.
3. **Advantages and Disadvantages of Entrepreneurship** Have students rank the advantages and disadvantages of entrepreneurship and explain why they ranked the items.

Enrichment

1. **Review** Assign and review the appropriate Thinking Critically questions from the Chapter Assessment.
2. **Extend** Assign and review the corresponding activities from *BusinessWeek Case Studies, Internet Resources,* and the *School-to-Work Activity Workbook.* ILP
3. **Research and Brainstorm** Have students research the structure of the workforce and where employment growth is predicted to be the greatest. Discuss with the class their findings and brainstorm ideas for entrepreneurial endeavors based on the information. *(The U.S. Department of Labor predicts that the greatest employment growth will be in health services, retail trade, and business services.)*

Before you think about owning your own business, you have to ask yourself if you have what it takes to go into business for yourself. This may seem like an obvious question to ask, but committing to owning your own business requires serious thought.

You can answer this question by doing a self-evaluation—an assessment of your personal qualities, abilities, interests, and skills. The self-evaluation in Figure 33-1 was developed by the Small Business Administration. Take a few minutes to answer each question and write your answers on a piece of paper. Think before you answer—and be honest with yourself.

As you can see from answering the questions in Figure 33-1, starting a business requires careful self-evaluation. Answering "yes" to most or all of these questions should be an indication that you may have the right characteristics for success. You should also consider the experiences of family, friends, and other businesspeople who are in the same or a similar business. Find out about their experiences. Do research on the type of business you want to start. All this information taken together should give you a good indication of whether you are ready and able to join the millions of small business owners in the United States.

FIGURE 33-1

Self-Evaluation

	YES	NO
The first seven questions relates to your personality characteristics.		
1. Do you like to make your own decisions?	___	___
2. Do you enjoy competition?	___	___
3. Do you have willpower and self-determination?	___	___
4. Do you plan ahead?	___	___
5. Do you like to get things done on time?	___	___
6. Can you take advice from others?	___	___
7. Can you adapt to changing conditions?	___	___
The next series of questions relates to your physical, emotional, and financial well-being.		
8. Do you understand that owning your own business may entail working 12 to 16 hours a day, probably six days a week and maybe on holidays?	___	___
9. Do you have the physical stamina to handle a business?	___	___
10. Do you have the emotional strength to withstand the strain?	___	___
11. Are you prepared to lower your living standard for several months or years?	___	___
12. Are you prepared to lose your savings?	___	___
13. Do you know which skills and areas of expertise are critical to the success of your business?	___	___
14. Do you have these skills?	___	___
15. Does your idea for a business use these skills?	___	___
16. Can you find the people who have the expertise you lack?	___	___
17. Do you know why you are considering this business?	___	___
18. Will your business meet your career aspirations?	___	___

■ **Self-Evaluation** Be honest as you answer each of these self-evaluation questions. Being clear about where you stand is the only way to learn what improvements you need to make. *What do your answers say about you?*

FIGURE 33-1 ANSWER
Self-Evaluation Answers will vary.

More About . . .

The SBA and Business Opportunities
Founded in 1953, the SBA is the federal agency that assists small businesses by providing information and counseling services, as well as loan programs. It serves as a representative and advocate of small businesses, and collects small business data. The SBA has helped launch many familiar corporations, such as Apple Computer, Nike, and FedEx.

The Importance of Entrepreneurship in Our Economy

Small businesses are those with less than 500 employees in manufacturing and less than 100 in retailing. As you learned in Chapter 4, small businesses make up the majority of U.S. businesses. In addition, they provide jobs for about 55 percent of the labor force. Eighty percent of the new jobs created annually come from businesses that are less than five years old.

Small businesses produce 50 percent of the Gross Domestic Product (GDP). As you may recall from Chapter 4, the GDP is a measure of the goods and services produced using labor and property in this country.

Small businesses benefit the economy and society in other ways, too. They offer consumers more choices of goods and services. They help improve products and processes. They challenge existing businesses to become more efficient and provide better goods and services. They also offer on-the-job training to many students who then use this valuable experience to open small businesses of their own. In addition to providing goods and services people need, small businesses generate jobs and create income for the community.

Life In The Diverse MARKETPLACE

What Time Was That Meeting?

From lunchtime to siesta time, there are many rules that govern when to call a business meeting around the world. Don't schedule a breakfast meeting when in France or Germany—anything before 10:00 A.M. is absurd! Most of the real business gets taken care of in a social setting in China, so don't be shocked if your deals are made during dinner or drinks. Finally, it's best not to schedule more than two appointments in one day in Latin America, as the clock does not hold the same almighty power that it might elsewhere.

Thinking Critically

Why is it important to schedule a meeting at the best time for all participants?

33.1 ASSESSMENT

Reviewing Key Terms and Concepts

1. What is entrepreneurship?
2. Why is starting a new business such a risk?
3. What are four advantages and three disadvantages of being an entrepreneur?
4. What are three characteristics of a successful entrepreneur?
5. What are three reasons small businesses are important to the economy?

Thinking Critically

6. Do you think money and material gain are the most important reasons for becoming an entrepreneur? Explain. If your answer is no, what do you consider the most important reasons for becoming an entrepreneur?

Integrating Academic Skills

7. **COMMUNICATION** Using this book and other sources, write a 250-word paper on why the entrepreneur is so important to the U.S. economy.

Chapter 33 ■ *Entrepreneurial Concepts* **611**

SECTION 33.1

Evaluation

Assign and review the Section 33.1 Assessment.

Technology Resources

Assessment Resources
Go to the *Marketing Essentials* Web site (www.marketing.glencoe.com) for resources to teach and assess occupation-specific vocabulary.

VIRTUAL BUSINESS

Venture Capital
Introduce entrepreneurship and the concept of venture capital to students using Knowledge Matters' Virtual Business visual simulation, "Entrepreneurship—Venture Capital." This exciting activity highlights two hot career areas as students take on the roles of entrepreneurs and venture capitalists. For additional instructions and teaching tips for this activity, go to the *Marketing Essentials* Web site (www.marketing.glencoe.com).

CLOSE

Section Wrap-Up

Have students complete this statement: At this time, entrepreneurship interests me (or doesn't interest me) as a potential career option because . . . *(Answers will vary.)*

Life In The Diverse MARKETPLACE

What Time Was That Meeting?

Answer People work best when they meet during normal working hours. Scheduling during those hours is a sign of respect for the culture.

SECTION 33.2

Logistics of Business Ownership

FOCUS

Bell Ringer Activity

Brainstorm Clip several "business for sale" ads for sole proprietorships, franchises, and corporations from a local or national newspaper, or from business magazines. Read the ads to students. Ask them to help you generate a board list of things they would consider before buying each one of the enterprises mentioned.

Introducing the Section

Logistics of Business Ownership
Students' answers from the Bell Ringer Activity will vary but should include the following: (1) the amount of money they would have to invest in the business; (2) their general level of interest in and knowledge of the product(s) the business sells; (3) the legal requirements involved in business start-up and in taxation; (4) whether or not they want to have stockholders; (5) whether or not they want to answer to a corporate parent; and (6) the location of the business and its prior reputation and financial success.

In this section, students will look at the various forms of business ownership and the advantages and disadvantages of each.

What You'll Learn

- How to discuss business ownership opportunities
- How to identify forms of business ownership
- The legal steps to take in establishing a business

Why It's Important

Considering whether and how to become an entrepreneur requires knowledge of the several forms of business organization, along with the legal steps for establishing a business.

Key Terms

- franchise
- sole proprietorship
- unlimited liability
- partnership
- general partnership
- limited partnership
- corporation
- stockholders
- foreign corporation
- Subchapter S corporation
- DBA
- Articles of Incorporation

Business Ownership Opportunities

According to Dun & Bradstreet, some 150,000 businesses are started each year. There are four ways to enter business: 1) develop a new business, 2) purchase a franchise business, an agreement to operate a business in the name of a recognized company, 3) purchase an existing nonfranchise business, or 4) take over the family business (See Figure 33-2 on page 613).

Forms of Business Organization

Just as you can choose which good or service to provide, you can also choose the legal organization or structure your business will take. The legal form of business organization you select may make the difference between success and failure. It determines how fast you implement your business decisions, how well you compete in the marketplace, and how quickly you can raise money for expansion.

As an entrepreneur, your choices of business organization are sole proprietorship, partnership, or corporation. The one you select depends on circumstances such as your financial condition, the type of business you want to start, the number of employees you will hire, the business risk involved, and your tax situation.

You can change your initial decision about the type of business organization you choose. As your business grows and prospers, your financial and tax situations may require you to change organization.

■ Sole Proprietorship

A sole proprietorship is a business owned and operated by one person. This is the most common form of business ownership. Approximately 70 percent of all U.S. businesses fall into this category. People usually become sole proprietors when they have a special skill by which they can earn a living. Plumbers, auto mechanics, and writers are often sole proprietors.

The sole proprietor must provide the money and management skill to run the business. In return for all this responsibility, the sole proprietor is entitled to all the profits.

There are several other advantages to a sole proprietorship. It is relatively easy to start, and all business decisions are made on your own. It is generally taxed less than other forms of business, and there is more freedom from government regulation.

Choosing this form of ownership offers you complete control over

Classroom Resources

For the Teacher
- Teacher Editions for all workbooks
- Assessment Package
- PowerPoint Presentation Software
- Interactive Lesson Planner

ILP Block Scheduling, p. 11
ILP Lesson Plans, p. 70
ILP Internet Resources, p. 85

ILP *BusinessWeek* Case Studies, p. 207
ILP Marketing Career Portfolio, p. 41
- *Marketing Essentials* Web site (**www.marketing.glencoe.com**)

For the Student
- Student Activity Workbook, p. 287
- Marketing Math Workbook, p. 111

- Marketing Research Project Workbook
ILP School-to-Work Activity Workbook, p. 135
- Virtual Business simulation
- *Marketing Essentials* Web site (**www.marketing.glencoe.com**)

ILP These resources are available in print and on the Interactive Lesson Planner (ILP)

FIGURE 33-2

WAYS TO ENTER BUSINESS

The manner by which you choose to enter business will depend on your experience, needs, and financial resources.

PURCHASING AN EXISTING BUSINESS

When you buy an existing nonfranchise business, you usually receive little or no help from the previous owner. You must investigate why the business is being sold. You must carefully examine the business records and the condition of the property and inventory. You must also determine the reputation of the business in the community.

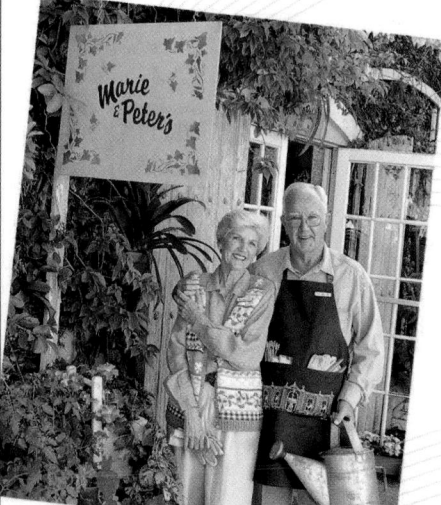

TAKING OVER THE FAMILY BUSINESS

Some of the same considerations for purchasing an existing business also apply for a family business. You must review business records and the overall condition of the property and inventory. You must determine the reputation of the business in the community. In addition, you need to explore potential conflicts and concerns with family members.

STARTING YOUR OWN BUSINESS

Starting your own business allows you to start the business of your choice. You can decide where to locate your business and how you will set it up. You do not have to take on old debts, a bad reputation, or a poor location that you may inherit when you buy an existing business. However, you must establish every aspect of your business from ground up. In addition, you must create and build a reputation with your customers.

PURCHASING A FRANCHISE BUSINESS

A franchise is a legal agreement to operate a business in the name of a recognized company. The *franchisee* (the person purchasing the franchise) buys an existing business operation. All business planning is done by the *franchisor*, the owner of the recognized company. Planning generally includes management training and assistance with advertising, merchandising, and day-to-day operations. The biggest disadvantages of franchising are the large amount of capital needed to purchase most franchises and the high initial fees charged to begin operations. Also, the franchisor may limit the franchisee's choices as to how the business is run.

Chapter 33 ■ *Entrepreneurial Concepts* **613**

SECTION 33.2

TEACH

📊 Technology Resources

PowerPoint The *Marketing Essentials* PowerPoint Presentation CD-ROM provides visual lecture aids for every chapter section.

Concept Development

1. Read Section 33.2 with students.
2. Have students read aloud the Case Study on page 616 and review the answers in class.

Discussion Starter

1. **Networking** Discuss with students the value of networking. Entrepreneurs network constantly to keep up on innovations in their field, to keep building their list of resources and contacts, and to keep themselves visible in the community. Have students discuss ways that they can network now.
2. **Professional Associations** Discuss the value, as a professional, of belonging to associations that sponsor national and regional conferences, provide publications, and act as a clearinghouse of information for members.

More About . . .

Franchises

Franchise costs don't end when the business is up and running, but continue through the life of the agreement. The franchisee pays a percentage of sales or profits to the franchiser. Many franchise agreements contain "buy back" language specifying when the franchiser can "buy back" the franchise and the pay out to the franchisee.

Thinking Critically

Corporations Ask students: Why are many professionals, such as doctors, attorneys, and other professionals forming corporations? *(Answers will vary but could include the following: to limit liability, share costs of doing business, share work responsibilities, etc.)*

Cooperative Learning

Entrepreneurial Opportunities
Divide the class into four to six groups. Have each group choose one of the following career clusters: Agribusiness and Natural Resources Environment; Business and Office; Communication; Construction; Consumer and Homemaking; Fine Arts and Humanities; Health; Hospitality and Recreation; Manufacturing; Marine Science; Marketing and Distribution; Personal Services; Public Services; Transportation; and Technology.

Have each group research entrepreneurial opportunities in their chosen career cluster by listing the following: (1) several small business opportunities; (2) what the demand will be for jobs in the cluster; (3) emerging occupations in the cluster; (4) the skills, knowledge, and experience one needs to enter the field; (5) physical demands of working in the area; (6) work environment; (7) education and training necessary; and (8) part-time, volunteer, and/or summer work that would help students prepare now for the entrepreneurial endeavor. Have each group present their its findings to the class.

the business. However, you are also responsible for all business debts or legal judgments against the business.

In the event that the debts of your business exceed its assets (that is, all of its resources), your creditors can claim all of your own personal assets, such as your car, home, and savings. This is called **unlimited liability,** which means that your financial liability is not limited to your investment in the business, but extends to your total ability to make payments.

Problems can develop in a sole proprietorship when it becomes necessary to expand business operations but the only money available is the owner's personal assets. This is why making all the decisions yourself, without the input and advice of others, can be difficult.

■ The Partnership

A partnership is a legal agreement between two or more people to be jointly responsible for the success or failure of a business. The least common form of U.S. business, partnerships represent just 10 percent of U.S. businesses. A partnership agreement, usually prepared by an attorney, specifies the responsibilities of each partner. Profits in a partnership are usually divided in a proportion equal to the amount of time and money invested. Partners share

the profits if the business is a success and share the losses if it fails. Common partnerships in your community may include real estate agencies, law offices, and medical offices.

Like a sole proprietorship, a partnership is subject to relatively little regulation and is fairly easy to establish. Partnerships are more complicated than sole proprietorships because more than one person is involved.

There are two types of partnerships: general and limited. In a **general partnership**, each partner shares in the profits and losses. As in the sole proprietorship, each partner has unlimited liability for the company's debts. Also, each partner's share of the profits is taxed as personal income.

Based on the unlimited liability that you face as a member of a general partnership, you might want to establish a limited partnership. In a **limited partnership,** each limited partner is liable for any debts only up to the amount of his or her investment in the company.

Every limited partnership, however, must have at least one general partner who has unlimited liability. In exchange for their limited liability, limited partners have no voice in the management of the partnership. The withdrawal of a limited partner does not dissolve the partnership if you and your partners decide to continue doing business.

When establishing a limited partnership, you

Strumming Success

Have you ever tried to learn the guitar, but given up frustrated? You need to get in touch with Nicholas Ravagni from Seattle. At only eleven years old, he created and marketed a device that helps people learn how to play the guitar. Nicholas began playing the guitar when he was five years old. He came up with his invention one year later, while watching another child struggle while practicing musical scales. His device, a self-adhesive strip of plastic that fits under the strings, allows a player to see exactly where to place his or her fingers. It uses a color-coded and letter system to teach where the notes are. Nicholas has marketed his device up and down the West Coast and on the Internet.

Thinking Creatively
Nicholas's invention was the result of trying to simplify a process. Brainstorm some ideas that might simplify some of your everyday chores.

Strumming Success
Answer Answers will vary depending on students' everyday chores.

■ **Inc.** Most small businesses are not incorporated because of complicated legal requirements. *What are some advantages of corporate ownership?*

Independent Practice

Research and Report Have each student contact one company that offers franchises and write a 250-word report that summarizes: (1) the amount of money it takes to buy a franchise outlet and breakdown of the total cost; (2) training provided by the franchiser; (3) restrictions on the types of products one can sell in the franchise outlet; and (4) any other relevant information one would need to know about buying a franchise from this corporation.

must give public notice stating that one or more partners have limited liability. Otherwise, it is assumed that a general partnership exists, and all partners have unlimited liability. You can get additional information regarding limited partnerships by contacting your state department of commerce.

There are several advantages to a partnership. It combines the skills of the owners. Partnerships may offer more money, which allows easier operation and expansion. It allows each partner a voice in the management of the business. A partnership is taxed and regulated less heavily than a corporation.

Despite these advantages, there are some disadvantages to partnerships. The owners may not always agree on business decisions, yet the actions of one partner are legally binding on the other partners. This means that all partners must assume their share of the business debt. They must also be responsible for the shares of the other partners if they cannot pay. Finally, the business is dissolved if one partner dies. It can be reorganized as a new partnership, but the process is time consuming and costly.

■ The Corporation

A corporation is a business that is chartered by a state and legally operates apart from the owner or owners. It is the most complicated form of business organization we've looked at in this chapter.

Although a corporation can be any size, larger firms are usually organized as corporations. Those who work for a corporation are not necessarily the people who own it. Corporations form governing bodies called *boards*, who hire directors and officers to manage the affairs of the business and the interests of the stockholders.

The value of a corporation is divided into equal units called shares of stock. These shares of stock are sold through the *stock market* to individual investors called stockholders. The stockholders are the people who actually own the corporation with limited liability. The liablity for the losses of the corporation belong to the stockholder only to the extent of his or her individual investment. Stockholders are not responsible for debts incurred by the corporation.

A corporation can own assets, borrow money, and perform business functions without directly involving the shareholders. Therefore, it is subject to more government regulation than a sole proprietorship or a partnership.

Corporations can be *incorporated* (established) in the state where they will do business or in another state. It is best for most small businesses to incorporate in the state where they are going to do business. Otherwise, they may have to do business as a foreign corporation. A foreign corporation is incorporated under the laws of a different state from the one in which it does business. Foreign corporations must seek approval from and register with each state in which they intend to do business.

Some new businesses can also be established as Subchapter S corporations. A Subchapter S corporation is a small business that is taxed like a partnership or proprietorship.

There are strict provisions for Subchapter S cor-

Chapter 33 ■ *Entrepreneurial Concepts* **615**

CAPTION ANSWER

Inc. Some advantages of corporate ownership are limited liability, greater access to investment capital, ease of entering and leaving business, and professional management of each area of business.

Math Skills

L1 Tell students that the National Federation of Independent Business Foundation conducted a study of small business owners to determine where the idea for their small businesses originated. 45 percent said their business idea came from prior work experience. 6 percent said it came from a family business. 5 percent said it came from friends and relatives. 16 percent said it came from a personal interest/hobby. 7 percent said it came from a suggestion. 6 percent said it came from their education. 11 percent said it came from a chance happening. 4 percent of the ideas came from other sources. Have students create a pie chart of these statistics.

L2 Tell students that in the early 1990s, it would cost $75,000 to obtain a franchise for a Pro Image sporting goods store. The franchise fee would cost $13,500; inventory, $35,000; fixtures and equipment, $6,500; leasehold improvements, $15,000; and working capital, $5,000. Ask students: What percentage of the $75,000 would go to the (a) franchise fee, (b) the inventory, (c) figures and equipment, (d) leasehold improvements, and (e) working capital? *((a) 18%. 13,500 ÷ 75,000 = .18. (b) 47%. 35,000 ÷ 75,000 = 0.466 or 0.47. (c) 9%. 6,500 ÷ 75,000 = .086 or .09. (d) 20%. 15,000 ÷ 75,000 = .2. (e) 7%. 5,000 ÷ 75,000 = .066 or .07.)*

L3 Read aloud the percentages from the L2 answers, and have students create a pie chart, labeling the chart and each slice of the pie.

Case Study

Finding Your Niche

Seeing a need that's not being met and turning it into a business—that's an entrepreneur's dream. That is exactly what the Yee sisters of Columbus, Ohio did and now they are enjoying their success.

The Yees are Chinese-American women who never tired of looking for make-up tints that flattered their complexions. When the eldest, Susan, came out of a cosmetic counter makeover looking "awful," the five sisters decided to pool their savings and start a company to serve the Asian-American market.

The big cosmetic companies have developed lines for African-American skin tones, but none had addressed the Asian-American market. The Yees realized their frustration trying to find cosmetics was shared by millions of other Asian-American women.

They found a chemist to develop make-up formulas, designed their catalog themselves, and modeled for the photographs. Susan's husband developed and sent out press kits. Zhen Cosmetics was born. An employee at a local Asian-language newspaper saw their ad and told a contact at Nordstrom's who was immediately interested. Nordstrom was Zhen's first retail customer.

The operation, which began in 1994 in Susan's home has grown to include 24 employees, a suite of offices, a warehouse, cosmetics counters in 47 J.C. Penney's locations, and a Web site for sales online. They expanded their product line from make-up products to include facial cleansers and other skin care products. They have even developed a line of personal care products for men, including after shave and moisturizer. Their Web site includes beauty tips as well as a forum where product users can interact with each other.

Zhen cosmetics holds an estimated 2 percent of the ethnic cosmetics market, with about $8 million in revenues in 2000. The next move? Asia, of course!

Case Study Review

1. **What characteristics of entrepreneurs do the Yee sisters have?**
2. **Does it make sense to invest your life savings in a new business? Why or why not?**

A MATTER OF ETHICS

3. **Do large cosmetics companies have an ethical responsibility to create makeup for all skin colors? Defend your position.**

Case Study Review Answers

Finding Your Niche
1. Many answers are possible, including willingness to take risks, work hard, and be competitive.
2. Answers will vary. Students must weigh the risks and possible losses against the advantages.

A MATTER OF ETHICS
3. Answers will vary.

porations. The business, for example, can have no more than 35 shareholders. It must be incorporated in the United States. It can have no more than 20 percent of its gross revenues from investment income and no more than 80 percent of its gross revenues from foreign sources. You can learn more information about Subchapter S corporations by consulting Internal Revenue Service (IRS) publication number 589 or by calling your IRS office.

Whether or not you choose to file as a Subchapter S corporation, you must show your internal corporate organization when forming a corporation. This requirement includes the development of corporate bylaws, the selection of a board of directors, and the election of officers who will actually run the corporate operations. In small corporations, the members of the board of directors frequently are elected as the officers of the corporation. There are four key advantages to this form of business organization.

- Each owner has limited liability.
- It is easier for a corporation to raise money for expansion than it is for other forms of business.
- People can easily enter or leave the business simply by buying or selling their shares of stock.
- Each operation area of the business can be professionally managed by an expert in that area.

As you can see, there are many advantages of forming a corporation. There are times when this is not the best option, however. Among the disadvantages to the corporation are:

- The complexity of forming it
- Increased government regulation
- Higher taxes on the profits of the corporation and on each stockholder
- Intricate accounting and record keeping

It is important to be flexible in approaching the legal form of ownership when establishing a new business. A business may start out as a sole proprietorship, grow into a partnership, and ultimately end up as a corporation. The entrepreneurs you read about at the beginning of the chapter—Henry Ford, Ray Kroc, Bette Graham, Steven Jobs, and Steven Wozniak—watched their businesses grow from sole proprietorships or partnerships to major corporations.

Legal Steps in Establishing Your Business

Before you can officially open the doors of your business, you will need to take specific legal steps to establish your business. These will vary if you form a sole proprietorship, partnership, or corporation.

When you establish a sole proprietorship or partnership, you must file for a DBA (Doing Business As) at your local county clerk's office. A **DBA** is a registration process by which your county government officially recognizes that your business exists. This legitimizes your business.

There is usually a filing fee for registration, but the process protects the name of your business for a certain number of years. This name protection applies only to the county where your business is registered.

You must check with the county clerks in your trading area and with your state department of commerce to see if any other business is using your chosen business name. This reduces the chances that someone will sue later if you are using his or her same business name.

When forming a corporation, you must file **Articles of Incorporation** with the corporation and securities bureau in your state department of commerce. Articles of Incorporation identify the name and address of your business, its purpose, the names of the initial directors, and the amount of stock that will be issued to each director.

There is a filing fee, but your business becomes protected and no other business may register under your business name. The necessary forms, applications, and information on filing fees can be obtained from your state department of commerce.

The type of business organization that you choose is important to the overall success of your business. The decision is somewhat complicated, so you must get the best advice possible before starting operations. Discuss the advantages and disadvantages of each business form with an accountant, an attorney, or another business advisor. Do your research and investigate all of the options. When forming a corporation, the laws of your state may require you to hire an attorney. Check your state laws for specific

ASSESS

Reteaching

1. **Vocabulary** Assign and review the vocabulary terms for this section.
2. **Fact and Idea** Assign and review Fact and Idea Review questions 2–10.
3. **Types of Business Ownership** Have the students create a chart that compares each type of business ownership regarding initial investment of capital, level of risk involved, taxation, and ease or difficulty of starting the business.

Enrichment

1. **Review** Assign and review the Chapter 33 activities in the *Student Activity Workbook*.
2. **Review** Assign and review the appropriate Thinking Critically questions from the Chapter Assessment.
3. **Review** Assign and review the following Chapter Assessment activities: Building Workplace Skills, Applying Marketing Concepts, Linking School to Work, The DECA Connection Role Play, and Internet Connection.
4. **Research and Write** Have the students review the Web site of one of the following national organizations and write a paragraph on the benefits of membership in the organization:
   - National Small Business Association (**www.nsba.net**)
   - Small Business Service Bureau (**www.sbsb.com**)

THE DECA CONNECTION
COMPETITIVE EVENTS AND MARKETING ESSENTIALS

Entrepreneurship and Business Plans DECA's Competitive Events program includes four events with strong entrepreneurial components. The Entrepreneurship Participating Event with independent or franchising business options allows students to create the outline of a business plan and present it in a nine-page prospectus. The Entrepreneurship Written Event requires a full business plan presented in a 40-page written manual. The International Marketing Event involves setting up a business to either import or export a product. This project is presented in a 30-page manual. The Learn and Earn Project is a chapter project presented by up to three chapter members. For more information, go to **www.deca.org**.

Assessment Resources

Go to the *Marketing Essentials* Web site (**www.marketing.glencoe. com**) for resources to teach and assess occupation-specific vocabulary.

CLOSE

Section Wrap-Up

Have students complete this statement: There are four main ways to enter business . . . *(start your own business, purchase an existing franchise, purchase an existing business, or take over a family business.)*

Send the Work Out

Answer Thoroughly review an MSP's operation and experience. Look at its support center, the people who work for it, and its confidentiality policy.

---

requirements regarding incorporating a business. These may vary from state to state.

Depending on what business you enter and where you locate, you may have to obtain one or more licenses. Individual states license many businesses and occupations, such as doctors, accountants, cosmetologists, barbers, marriage counselors, and pharmacists. Licensing is done to protect the public from unqualified people practicing in a business and to maintain the health and welfare of the citizens. Licenses establish minimum standards of education and training for people who practice in a particular profession. They also regulate where businesses can locate, and protect neighborhoods and the environment.

In addition to state licenses, your community may require special local licenses or permits to comply with zoning ordinances, building codes, and safety standards. Local governments use licensing as a way to regulate people who plan to enter certain types of businesses. Most communities require you to obtain a license before you open a hotel, restaurant, or movie theater. Check with your local government and your state department of licensing and regulation prior to starting your business.

As an entrepreneur, it is important to protect yourself and your ideas—other legalities may include safeguarding your intellectual property. Patents, trademarks, or copyrights can protect these products and ideas.

Send the Work Out

While small- to mid-size companies have many advantages over larger companies, available resources is not one of them. MSPs, or management service providers, are a new type of business that assists these businesses with a level of help that only large corporations have had in the past. Limited financial or human resources can sometimes undermine a small entrepreneurial company's ability to implement successful information technology management programs. MSPs evaluate technology management to find out where companies need the most help. MSPs are able to monitor clients' computer networks and perform network maintenance, upgrades, and fixes off-site. This allows in-house labor to focus on more pressing work.

Thinking Critically
Before hiring an MSP, what qualifications might a company check for?

33.2 ASSESSMENT

Reviewing Key Terms and Concepts

1. What are four ways to enter into a business?
2. What are the three basic forms of business ownership?
3. What legal steps must you take to establish a sole proprietorship or partnership?
4. What legal steps must you take to establish a corporation?
5. What is a Subchapter S corporation?

Thinking Critically

6. Which of the four ways to enter a business would you use to start your own business? Explain your decision.

Integrating Academic Skills

7. **MATH** An entrepreneur works 11 hours a day, five days a week, 52 weeks a year. How many hours is the person working annually?

33.2 ASSESSMENT ANSWERS

Reviewing Key Terms and Concepts

1. Start own business; purchase existing franchise business; purchase existing non-franchise business; take over family business.
2. sole proprietorship, partnership, and corporation
3. File for a DBA at county clerk's office. Pay filing fees. Before filing, check with county clerks and Department of Commerce to see if another business uses your business name.
4. File Articles of Incorporation with the Corporation and Securities Bureau. Pay filing fee.
5. small business taxed as partnership or proprietorship

Thinking Critically

6. Answers will vary.

Integrating Academic Skills

7. **MATH** $(11 \times 5) \times 52 = 2,860$

Careers in Marketing

ENTREPRENEUR

Ron Wilson
Chief Executive Officer
Big Bang Products

What does your job entail?

"I started Big Bang Products with my partner Brian Le Gette when we were MBA students at the Wharton School of Business (University of Pennsylvania) in 1993. While in school, Brian and I developed a product called Arctic 180s—earwarmers that wrap around the back of the head. We handled every aspect of the business in the beginning, including product design, finding contract manufacturers, standing on street corners selling the product, collecting market research, making cold calls to retailers, designing packaging, creating logos, raising money, and even assembling the product on occasion. As CEO, my role is now focused on shaping our vision and market strategy to clearly define and maintain focus on our customers."

What do you like most about your work?

"I still remember the first person I saw on the streets of Philadelphia wearing our earwarmers. The realization that a stranger was wearing something that I worked hard to create, was amazing."

How does your workload vary?

"The first few years my workload was extremely heavy with an average of 80+ hours a week. The workload is still heavy, but it's now about 60 hours a week. This seems like a lot, but when you love what you do you don't notice. Every day I get up and can't wait to get to work. If you like marketing, the entrepreneurial environment can provide a demanding, yet satisfying career."

What is your key to success?

"Most successful entrepreneurs I know have two common traits: tenacity and love of their job. My other key to success has been education. After earning a bachelor's degree in Industrial Engineering, I went on to business school. The results paid off! In 1996, we launched the product on QVC, selling over 5000 units in four minutes, and we are now a $10 million dollar company."

Thinking Critically

What are some things that you can do to make work more manageable when starting on an entrepreneurial venture?

Career Facts

Education and Training: Business courses and experience are helpful, especially in the small business field.

Aptitudes, Abilities, and Skills: Creativity, willingness to take risks, resilience, good people skills, strong leadership skills, and a good understanding of economics and government policies are necessary.

Career Outlook: The number of small businesses is growing and is expected to continue to grow.

Career Path: Many entrepreneurs have some experience working in a line of business similar to the type they plan to enter as an owner.

Chapter 33 ■ *Entrepreneurial Concepts* **619**

Vocabulary Review

See Glossary for definitions.

Fact and Idea Review

1. It helps you assess whether you have the personal qualities, abilities, interests, and necessary skills to be an entrepreneur.

2. The franchiser does all the business.

3. Some advantages are that it is easy to start, generally taxed less than other forms of business, allows more freedom from government regulation; all business decisions are the owner's who is entitled to all profits. Disadvantages are that it is harder to raise capital with only the owner's funds; making decisions can be difficult; and the owner must provide the money and management skills and work long hours.

4. Unlimited liability applies to sole proprietorships and general partnerships. To limit your liability, consider the limited partnership or corporate form.

5. In a general partnership, each partner shares the profits and losses of the business, and has unlimited liability. In a limited partnership, each partner is liable for any debts up to the amount of his or her investment in the company. Limited partners have no voice in management.

6. Advantages are that it combines skill of the owners, allows access to more money, and improves the ability to operate and expand easily. Disadvantages are that owners may not always agree, the actions of one partner are binding on the others, and the business is dissolved if one partner dies.

7. Advantages are that each owner has limited liability; it is easy to raise money for expansion; and people can enter and leave simply by buying or selling shares. Some disadvantages are that it is harder to establish; increased government regulation; and higher taxes on the corporation and each shareholder.

8. shareholders, directors, and officers

9. A foreign corporation is incorporated under the laws of a different state from the one in which it does business.

10. Some reasons include: to protect the public from unscrupulous people; establish minimum

---

Chapter 33 ASSESSMENT

VOCABULARY REVIEW

Divide the class into teams for a Marketing Quiz Bowl. Your teacher will call out the terms below. Teams should raise their hands when they feel they know the correct definition for the term. The team that raises a hand first has ten seconds to respond; if they incorrectly define the term, the other team then has ten seconds to respond. The team that correctly defines the term first gets a point.

- entrepreneurship
- entrepreneurs
- franchise
- sole proprietorship
- unlimited liability
- partnership
- general partnership
- limited partnership
- corporation
- stockholders
- foreign corporation
- Subchapter S corporation
- DBA
- Articles of Incorporation

FACT AND IDEA REVIEW

1. Why should you do self-evaluation if you want to become an entrepreneur? (33.1)

2. How does franchising work? (33.2)

3. List three advantages and three disadvantages of the sole proprietorship. (33.2)

4. How does unlimited liability affect the type of business organization selected by an entrepreneur? (33.2)

5. Explain the difference between the two kinds of partnerships. (33.2)

6. List three advantages and three disadvantages of a partnership. (33.2)

7. List three advantages and three disadvantages of a corporation. (33.2)

8. What three groups of people are involved with the corporate form of ownership? (33.2)

9. What is a foreign corporation? (33.2)

10. What are five reasons for licensing certain occupations and businesses? (Sec. 33.2)

THINKING CRITICALLY

1. What are the disadvantages of working for others as opposed to being your own boss? Are the disadvantages enough to make you consider starting your own business? Why?

2. A franchisee has a new product idea. Who should get credit for it—the franchisee or the franchisor?

3. Imagine you are starting a restaurant. Which type of business organization would you choose? Explain the reasons for your decision.

BUILDING WORKPLACE SKILLS

1. **Human Relations** A very good friend of yours has an idea to start a small video rental business. You have heard, however, that small video stores are being replaced by video rental superstores. You have also heard that the cost of opening a store has risen from $50,000 a few years ago to between $150,000 and $200,000 today. What would you tell your friend to do before she invests in this kind of business?

2. **Technology** You have always wanted to own a small sporting goods store. You have a friend who is interested in joining you in a partnership. Use the library or the Internet to research how much competition you would have in your geographical area.

---

standards of education and training for people who practice a particular profession; maintain the health and welfare of all citizens; regulate where businesses can locate; and protect neighborhoods and the environment.

Thinking Critically

1. Answers will vary based on students' opinions.
2. Answers will vary.
3. Students' answers should be based on the advantages and disadvantages discussed in the chapter and on their own personalities and work experience.

Building Workplace Skills

1. Students should discuss the advantages and disadvantages of being an entrepreneur.
2. Answers will vary.

Applying Marketing Concepts

1. You can obtain a copy of DECA's Entrepreneurship Written or Participating Event by writing National DECA, 1908 Association Drive, Reston, VA 22091-1594 (www.deca.org).
2. Debates will vary.

APPLYING MARKETING CONCEPTS

1. **Opening Your Own Business** Using a word processing program, write a description of a business you might want to open in preparation for DECA's Entrepreneurship Written or Participating Event.

2. **Understanding Risk** Work with a partner to prepare a debate on the advantages and disadvantages of entrepreneurship. Stage the debate for your class.

3. **Investigating Small Business** Interview a small business owner in your community to find out why that person started his or her own business. Present an oral report about the job duties and tasks typically performed by the business owner on a daily, weekly, and/or monthly basis.

4. **Buying a Franchise** Use the Internet to research and identify factors you need to know when you buy a franchise. Use presentation software to create a report on what you have learned.

5. **Identifying New Market Possibilities** Entrepreneurs often look into the future to see new market possibilities. Use a word processing program to explain the kinds of businesses that you think will boom in the next 25 years. Explain how you would go about getting the knowledge or training to enter one of them.

LINKING SCHOOL TO WORK

Resources and System Skills Research whether a local business was originally organized as a proprietorship, partnership, or a corporation. Write a 300-word report on how the business got started and whether it has changed its type of ownership over the years.

THE DECA CONNECTION

Role Play: Bookstore Manager

Situation You are to assume the role of manager of a local bookstore that is operated as a sole proprietorship. The owner (judge) is interested in changing the ownership to either a partnership or a corporation.

Activity You have been appointed to research the benefits of each. You must report to the store owner (judge) about your findings.

Evaluation You will be evaluated on how well you meet the following performance indicators:
- Explain the types of business ownership
- Describe legal issues affecting businesses
- Explain the nature of tax regulations on businesses
- Describe the nature of legally binding contracts
- Explain types of business risk

inter NET CONNECTION

Entrepreneurs Online
Knowing that many new companies start up every day, you want to discover what makes a successful startup.

Connect
- Locate information online about successful entrepreneurs.
- E-mail entrepreneurs and ask if they are willing to share what factors they think led to their success.
- Hold an "Entrepreneurship Week" at your school and invite entrepreneurs to come and talk to your marketing class.

THE DECA CONNECTION

Students should be evaluated on the performance indicators noted in the Role Play.
- For another DECA Role Play, go to the *Student Activity Workbook,* p. 287.
- For more in-depth Role Play practice, refer to DECA's *Essential Competitive Events Handbook.* To order, contact DECA at www.deca.org.

inter NET CONNECTION
E-mails and speakers will vary.

Mini Quiz

Administer the Mini Quiz orally. For an expanded chapter quiz, go to page 197 of the *Reproducible Tests* book.

1. <u>Entrepreneurs</u> attempt to earn money and make profits by taking the risk of owning and operating a business.

2. A business owned and operated by one person is called a(n) <u>sole proprietorship</u>.

3. A legal agreement between two or more people to be jointly responsible for the success of a business is called a(n) <u>partnership</u>.

4. A <u>corporation</u> is chartered by a state and legally operates apart from its owners.

5. The people who actually own a corporation are known as its <u>stockholders</u>.

---

3. Students should share their findings with the class.
4. Reports will vary.
5. Presentations will vary.

Linking School to Work
Answers depend on the work situation.

1. **Assessment** Have students complete the Reproducible Test for Chapter 33 or construct your own tests using the ExamView software.
2. **Enrichment** Have students complete the corresponding activities in the following workbooks:
   - *Marketing Math Workbook,* p. 111

Chapter Overview

This chapter introduces students to the concept of business risk and risk management, and identifies the different economic, natural, and human risks faced by businesses. The chapter also explains how businesses limit risk.

Springboard

Write Write the word *risk* on the board and have students define the term. Divide the class into groups that will compose their own tales about Sad Sam's Service Station—a business in which everything goes wrong. Encourage students to incorporate a wide variety of disasters with employees, customers, the weather, etc. Have each group share its story. Categorize the risks in their stories into three columns on the board—economic, natural, and human—but do not label the columns.

Prereading

List the section objectives in *What You'll Learn* to discuss with students. Have students skim the chapter, looking at the pictures, reading the captions, and noting the heads. Ask questions to ensure that the students have a minimal understanding of the chapter structure.

Preteaching Marketing Vocabulary

Write the terms for this chapter on the board. Have each group from the Springboard activity generate definitions for each term. Review all terms in class.

Marketing: What It Takes

Answer Answers will vary but may include: Place a surveillance camera on the pumps; hire a person to pump gasoline; require prepayment of gas during peak theft periods; train employees in procedures to use in the event of theft; and post signs saying pumps are monitored.

Chapter 34

Risk Management

MATHEWS DELI-MARKET · SHORT STOP VIDEO · STATE FARM · VALLEY CLEANERS

Marketing: What It Takes

Stopping "Drive-offs"
You work as an assistant manager for a 24-hour a day self-service gas station and convenience store. Because of rising gasoline prices, you are experiencing an increasing amount of "drive-offs." More individuals are filling their tanks and driving away without paying. Your manager has asked for your input in designing a plan to reduce external theft at your gas station.

WHAT WILL YOU DO?
How will you find a solution that doesn't offend your regular customers, but will help lower gasoline theft for your store.

622

THE DECA CONNECTION — ADVISOR CORNER

Employer Appreciation Breakfast Hold an employer appreciation breakfast. Invite your business supporters, key teachers, school administrators, and chapter members. A student presentation about DECA should be the main component of the agenda. Include the current year's membership video and/or your own video highlights of the year. Many advisors utilize this time to recognize their employers with a certificate of appreciation. Others have chapter members come forward and say thank you to those for helping to make the DECA year a success. This event will reap benefits of professional support for years to come.

Risk Management

What Is Risk Management?

As a business owner, one of your primary goals will be to make a profit. Unfortunately, there is no guarantee that this will happen. Your business may realize a lower return on investment than you expected or may experience a loss after you have paid all your expenses. The possibility of financial loss is called risk.

A business cannot eliminate all risks, but marketers can reduce and manage risks. According to the American Risk and Insurance Association, risk management is the systematic process of managing an organization's risk exposure to achieve objectives in a manner consistent with public interest, human safety, environmental factors, and the law. Risks are managed by using the best available marketing information, analyzing opportunities, and making wise decisions.

Kinds of Risks

Business risks are the possibility of business loss or failure. There are three kinds of business risks—*economic, natural,* and *human.* Let's take a closer look at each of these types of risks.

■ Economic Risks

Economic risks occur from changes in overall business conditions. These changes can include the amount or type of competition, changing consumer lifestyles, population changes, limited usefulness or style of some products, product obsolescence, government regulation, inflation, or recession.

Businesses that fail to change their products when competitors offer more features and benefits lose sales and experience economic risk. Foreign competition is also an economic risk for many U.S. companies, because foreign products can often be produced and sold for less than similar domestic products. The positive aspect of foreign competition is that it forces U.S. companies to improve productivity and efficiency to compete successfully in the marketplace.

Consumer lifestyles and population changes are other economic risks facing modern businesses. More single-parent households, dual-income families, the aging of the Baby Boom generation, and the increasing number of single individuals delaying marriage all present potential risks for businesses that fail to adapt products to meet changing needs.

The limited usefulness or style of some products is another potential economic risk. Prices have to be reduced on unsold products at the end of the season to sell them. This obviously reduces profits.

• What You'll Learn

- The nature and scope of risk management
- The various types of business risks

• Why It's Important

Businesses must manage risks in ways that accommodate public interest, human safety, the environment, and state and federal laws. Risk management is necessary for effective financial, marketing, production, and human resource management decisions. Risk management reduces the adverse effects of risk on business resources, cash flow, and profits.

Key Terms

- risk
- risk management
- business risks
- economic risks
- natural risks
- human risks

Chapter 34 ■ *Risk Management* **623**

FOCUS

 Bell Ringer Activity

Identify Have students remain in the same groups they formed for the Springboard activity and Preteaching Marketing Vocabulary. Have students study the three board lists generated during the Springboard activity and now identify the categories of the three columns of risks (economic, natural, and human).

Introducing the Section

Risk Management Review students' Bell Ringer Activity answers. Tell students that while no business owner can eliminate all the risks of doing business, he or she can reduce and manage risks through careful planning, analysis, and decision making.

TEACH

📊 Technology Resources

PowerPoint The *Marketing Essentials* PowerPoint Presentation CD-ROM provides visual lecture aids for every chapter section.

Concept Development

1. Read Section 34.1 with students.
2. Have students discuss natural disasters of the last few years and how they have affected the economy in your area or in other areas of the country. Review the table of natural and other disasters found on page 625 for ideas on how these events have affected the specific area and economies of the country.

Classroom Resources

For the Teacher
- Teacher Editions for all workbooks
- Assessment Package
- PowerPoint Presentation Software
- Interactive Lesson Planner
- ILP Block Scheduling, p. 11
- ILP Lesson Plans, p. 71
- ILP Internet Resources, p. 87

- ILP Blackline Masters, p. 72
- ILP *BusinessWeek* Case Studies, p. 213
- ILP Marketing Career Portfolio, p. 41
- *Marketing Essentials* Web site (www.marketing.glencoe.com)

For the Student
- Student Activity Workbook, p. 297
- Marketing Math Workbook, p. 111

- Marketing Research Project Workbook
- ILP School-to-Work Activity Workbook, p. 139
- Virtual Business simulation
- *Marketing Essentials* Web site (www.marketing.glencoe.com)

ILP These resources are available in print and on the Interactive Lesson Planner (ILP)

623

Natural Risks The text states that natural causes, such as floods, tornadoes, hurricanes, fires, lightning, droughts, earthquakes, and unexpected changes in normal weather conditions, can create risks. How can these natural causes financially ruin a business? *(They can physically destroy the place of business, destroy off-site equipment like delivery trucks and service lines or cables, and destroy the homes or businesses of customers.)*

Thinking Critically

Risk Management Read aloud this statement: "It's insured, so don't worry about it." Ask: What's wrong with this statement? *(The cost of replacing individual losses is made up through higher premiums charged to all policyholders.)*

Cooperative Learning

Business Risks Divide the class into 3–5 member teams to each create a chart, using drawings, photos, and illustrations that show types of business risks. Next to each illustration, have each team provide a written explanation about how businesses can manage the risks.

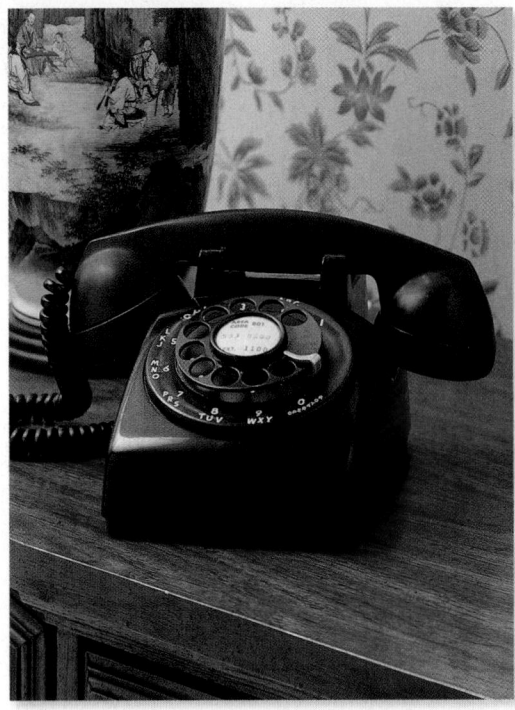

■ **Keeping Up with the Times** Products that were once successful often become outdated and obsolete in time. *Why do some products experience product obsolescence?*

Some products inevitably become obsolete or outdated. Known as *product obsolescence*, this represents another type of economic risk for businesses that depend on fashion and the latest trends to market goods and services. This is because new products are constantly being developed. When a new product is faster, more efficient, or more convenient than its predecessor, the predecessor becomes obsolete.

Changes in the general business environment caused by inflation or recession can present economic risks. All businesses in an area experiencing high unemployment will suffer through reduced product sales.

Government laws and regulations can also result in economic risks. Laws requiring businesses to pay for such things as street and sewer improvements, or parking and general maintenance, reduce profits.

Product recalls, or even the threat of recalls, by government agencies can affect sales and profits. Companies that have to recall products often face high legal costs and expensive repairs and replacements. DaimlerChrysler AG recalled 380,000 Dodge Ram 1998–2000 model year pickup trucks in 2000 to reinforce trailer hitches that had shown signs of cracking. The company incurred costly expenditures because it had to notify all owners by mail, provide free inspections, and then make the needed repairs on the vehicles.

BRIGHT IDEAS

If the Shoe Fits...

How would you feel if you made a product and everyone walked all over it? If you were Mark Thatcher—inventor of the Teva sports sandal—you would be feeling good! For Thatcher, the saying "You don't know a man until you've walked in his shoes," has truth! Thatcher spent some time living as a nomad in the deserts of Israel. On his return, he became an engineering student in Arizona, but found his zest for life was working the summers as a river guide, or "boatman," on the Colorado River in the Grand Canyon. Thatcher decided to return to his love for river rafting with a business concept. He knew there was no adequate footwear for boatmen who traveled by river. Tennis shoes never dried out, and flip-flops seemed to always slip off. Thatcher came up with Teva (the Hebrew word for nature) as the first modern sport sandal. Thatcher's sandals are available in 140 styles and have generated $106 million in sales.

Thinking Creatively

Think of other types of sports that could benefit from new equipment. What new type of product would suit that sport?

BRIGHT IDEAS   If the Shoe Fits . . .

Answer Cargo pants with pockets, fleece vests, and all-terrain sneakers are all popular innovations that turned camping, hiking, and outdoor sports into an arena for a range of high-technology fashion-conscious products.

FIGURE 34-1

The Top Catastrophes of 1999

1. Winter Storm Lothar	Western Europe	$4.5 billion
2. Typhoon Bart	Southern Japan	$2.98 billion
3. Hurricane Floyd	Eastern United States	$2.36 billion
4. Winter Storm Martin	Southwest France	$2.2 billion
5. Earthquake	Izmit, Turkey	$2 billion
6. Tornadoes	Midwest United States	$1.49 billion
7. Earthquake	Nantou, Taiwan	$1 billion
8. Hailstorm	Sydney, Australia	$982 million
9. Snowstorm	Midwest United States	$755 million
10. Explosion	Ford Motor Company plant, Dearborn, Michigan	$650 million

■ **The Top Catastrophes of 1999** Businesses face natural risks from floods, hurricanes, fires, and other natural causes. *How many times greater were the damages caused by Hurricane Floyd compared to the Ford Motor Company plant explosion and fire?*

■ Natural Risks

Natural risks are risks resulting from natural causes such as floods, tornadoes, hurricanes, fires, lightning, droughts, earthquakes, and even unexpected changes in normal weather conditions.

Businesses can insure against unexpected losses from some natural risks, but not all. Some businesses and products depend on predictable weather conditions for success. Unexpected weather conditions can often spell financial ruin or reduced profits for a business. Ski resorts depend on a season of normal to above-normal snowfall levels so they can operate ski lifts, sell ski packages, and fill restaurants. A mild or below-normal winter represents lost revenues and a natural risk to the business (see Figure 34-1).

Conversely, a hot summer will have a positive effect on sales of certain products like air conditioners, cooling fans, boats, and swimming pools. Protecting your business against the natural risk of fire is simpler. Smoke detectors and fire sprinklers will protect your staff and your property. Cash and important documents should be stored in a fireproof safe.

■ Human Risks

Human risks are caused by human mistakes, as well as the unpredictability of customers, employees, or the work environment. They range from the negative effects of thefts to the issues involved with injury on the job.

Customer dishonesty, such as theft, fraudulent payment, or nonpayment, is a human risk. Additional examples of customer dishonesty include the nonpayment of accounts or paying for goods and services with fraudulent checks or credit cards.

Employees represent another human risk for business. Employee error, negligence, incompetence, and theft also pose a human risk. Another employee risk can be seen when employees take advantage of employee discounts by extending his benefit to non-employees.

In a restaurant, failing to properly cook or handle food can lead to customers becoming ill or hospitalized. To lessen risks of this type, many companies have instituted food safety programs that stress the importance of proper food handling. Employees must be *competent*. They must possess the skills and direction to do their jobs well.

Chapter 34 ■ *Risk Management* **625**

GREAT IDEAS from the Marketing Classroom

Mark Rael
Cooper City High School
Cooper City, FL

Traditionally, risk management was thought of as a matter of purchasing the right insurance. However, comprehensive risk management has become increasingly important. Ask students to undertake a comprehensive assessment of potential risks to their school store or a local business. Have students cover all the major functions of business (administration, production, marketing) and include solutions to the most common business risks (good management and personnel policies; insurance and legal protection; and resource management). Then discuss how instituting standards for ethics, planning, and problem solving might reduce a business's risk.

SECTION 34.1

Independent Practice

Research, Write, and Present
Using the Internet, the *Reader's Guide to Periodical Literature*, and/or the newspaper/magazine database in your media center or library, have students research and obtain a copy of an article on risk management. (The article should be at least 150 words.) Have students write a 50- to 100-word abstract of the article and develop an outline of it. Ask students to prepare a five-minute oral presentation on the contents of the article. Students can report on how businesses respond to a natural disaster and steps being taken to prevent shoplifting.

ASSESS

Reteaching

1. **Vocabulary** Assign and review the vocabulary terms for this section.
2. **Fact and Idea** Assign and review Fact and Idea Review questions 1–2 from the Chapter Assessment.
3. **Risks** Write the terms economic risk, natural risk, and human risk on the board. Have each student give you one example of whatever type of risk you indicate.

FIGURE 34-1 ANSWER
The Top Catastrophes of 1999 Damages from Hurricane Floyd were approximately 3.6 times greater than the Ford plant explosion (*$2.36 billion ÷ 650 million*).

Enrichment

1. **Review** Assign and review the appropriate Thinking Critically questions from the Chapter Review.
2. **Extend** Assign and review the corresponding activities from *BusinessWeek Case Studies, Internet Resources,* and the *School-to-Work Activity Workbook.*

Evaluation

Assign and review the Section 34.1 Assessment.

Technology Resources

GO TO **Assessment Resources** Go to the *Marketing Essentials* Web site (**www.marketing.glencoe. com**) for resources to teach and assess occupation-specific vocabulary.

CLOSE

Section Wrap-Up

Have students complete this statement: There are three kinds of business risks: . . .*(economic, natural, and human.)*

If the Gift Fits

Answer When going to dinner with business associates in Ecuador, you may bring flowers (appropriate ones), or special food items from your state or country, or an American item.

626

The business environment or work setting itself often becomes a risk. Customer or employee accidents are potential human risks. Airlines train crews to prepare for emergencies caused by mechanical problems, but to consider human factors as well. A customer might fall on the premises, break an arm, and sue the store. Businesses must be especially careful during inclement weather when rain or ice may cause injuries in the building or on the property. An employee might be injured in a work-related accident caused by faulty machinery or improperly built structures. Another risk is employee illness caused by toxic fumes or other hazards at the workplace. Asbestos in old buildings is an ongoing issue that companies must deal with.

Over the past decade, computer crime has emerged as a significant new human risk that businesses must protect against. Employees may pass along confidential information through an e-mail, either intentionally or unintentionally. Computer criminals penetrate the security of computer systems for mischievous or criminal purposes. This type of crime can be committed by a disgruntled employee or by an outsider. The simplest and least expensive way to protect your business from computer crime is to secure the computer network using passwords, encoding programs, and virus detectors. It is also necessary to train employees on the proper handling of computers and the proper use of software.

If the Gift Fits

In some countries, gift giving in business can be a sensitive event. Even the most well-intentioned gifts can be offensive. Never give a clock as a present in Hong Kong, as it connotes death. In Ecuador, bring flowers when invited to someone's home—but avoid lilies and marigolds, which are used in funerals. The only article of clothing that is appropriate to give in Germany is a scarf—items such as perfume, soap, and other clothing are considered too personal.

Thinking Critically

What might you bring as a gift when invited for dinner to a client's home in Ecuador?

34.1 ASSESSMENT

Reviewing Key Terms and Concepts

1. What is a business risk?
2. What is risk management?
3. What are the three kinds of business risks?
4. Why does product obsolescence represent an economic risk?
5. Give three examples of human risks.

Thinking Critically

6. A business faces risks daily. Why are business owners willing to assume risks when it would be much easier to work for someone else?

Integrating Academic Skills

7. **COMMUNICATION** Write a 100-word paper on parents' responsibilities to instill honesty and respect for personal property in their children so they do not shoplift.

34.1 ASSESSMENT ANSWERS

Reviewing Key Terms and Concepts
1. the possibility of business loss or failure
2. It is the systematic process of managing an organization's risk exposure to achieve objectives consistent with public interest, human safety, environmental factors, and law.
3. economic, natural, and human
4. If products are not sold before a new model year or before the new styles or colors are introduced, prices have to be reduced.
5. unpredictability of customers, employees, and the environment or work setting

Thinking Critically
6. Answers will vary, but some take risks because there may be a larger profit.

Integrating Academic Skills
7. **COMMUNICATION** Papers will vary.

Handling Business Risks

Ways of Handling Business Risks

There are four basic ways that businesses can handle risks: risk prevention and control, risk transfer, risk retention, and risk avoidance (see Figure 34-2 on page 628). Let's take a closer look at each of these.

■ Risk Prevention and Control

Business risks can be handled through prevention and control. Risks can be prevented and controlled by screening and training employees, providing safe conditions and safety instruction, preventing external theft, and deterring employee theft.

SCREENING AND TRAINING EMPLOYEES The best way to prevent the human risk of employee carelessness and incompetence is through effective employee screening, orientation, and training. Many businesses have human resource development departments to screen, test, and train new and existing employees to minimize the risk caused by improperly trained personnel.

Most larger companies and some smaller ones now require prospective employees to undergo drug testing before being hired. Drug abuse can lead to increased human risk by making employees careless and more likely to forget safety rules.

When employees begin a new job, some form of orientation, training, and instruction is normally provided. The training may be brief verbal instruction or extensive training that lasts several weeks or months.

Effective orientation and training programs are essential in minimizing business risk. Properly trained personnel are better able to meet customer needs and wants and to prevent the risk of lost sales through human error.

Chapter 11 outlines the basic necessities of an effective orientation. In addition to these, workers should be trained in rules and regulations relating to safety. Many companies support continuing education for all of their employees through individual company training activities or support for college training and education related to the field.

PROVIDING SAFE CONDITIONS AND SAFETY INSTRUCTION According to the National Safety Council, each year U.S. businesses lose over $42 billion to work-related illness and injuries. The financial impact of workplace accidents is staggering. Based on these numbers, it seems clear that safety and health information needs to improved.

What You'll Learn

- The ways businesses handle risks

Why It's Important

Businesses use certain strategies to help prevent, avoid, and protect against accidents, injuries, fires, thefts, defective products, and environmental disasters.

Key Terms

- insurance policy
- extended coverage
- fidelity bonds
- performance bonds

FOCUS

Bell Ringer Activity

Define There are four basic ways that businesses can handle risks: risk prevention and control, risk transfer, risk retention, and risk avoidance. Write these terms on the board. Have students write a definition for them and give examples of each.

Introducing the Section

Handling Business Risks Review students' Bell Ringer Activity answers. Make sure they understand the concept behind each method of risk transfer. Write the examples on the board under each type of risk management. You can use the lists for reinforcement as you read through this section with students.

Classroom Resources

For the Teacher
- Teacher Editions for all workbooks
- Assessment Package
- PowerPoint Presentation Software
- Interactive Lesson Planner
- ILP Block Scheduling, p. 11
- ILP Lesson Plans, p. 72
- ILP Internet Resources, p. 87

- ILP *BusinessWeek* Case Studies, p. 213
- ILP Marketing Career Portfolio, p. 41
- *Marketing Essentials* Web site (**www.marketing.glencoe.com**)

For the Student
- Student Activity Workbook, p. 297
- Marketing Math Workbook, p. 111

- Marketing Research Project Workbook
- ILP School-to-Work Activity Workbook, p. 139
- Virtual Business simulation
- *Marketing Essentials* Web site (**www.marketing.glencoe.com**)

ILP These resources are available in print and on the Interactive Lesson Planner (ILP)

FIGURE 34-2

HANDLING BUSINESS RISKS

There are four basic ways that businesses can handle risks: risk prevention and control, risk transfer, risk retention, and risk avoidance.

RISK PREVENTION AND CONTROL

Risk prevention and control are important ways to handle business risks. Effective employee screening and orientation can help a business.

RISK TRANSFER

Risk transfer attempts to place some or all of the risk on other parties. Product warranties transfer the risk to the manufacturer.

RISK RETENTION

Risk retention frequently occurs when a company is unaware of the risks, underestimates the risk, or anticipates a profit by taking a risk. A risk is often held by a business in hopes of a future profit.

RISK AVOIDANCE

Risk avoidance attempts to minimize risk through good information and research. Marketing research on a new product is carried out to reduce risk exposure.

628 Unit 11 ■ *Entrepreneurship and Finance*

Did You Know?

There are many ways that companies can educate their employees on safe working techniques. One way is with the help of OSHA (Occupational Safety and Health Association), which is in charge of investigating violations of workplace safety. OSHA is ready to help employers plan workplace safety programs, and best of all, their service is free of charge.

When employees receive safety instruction and are provided with safe work conditions, the potential for on-the-job accidents is greatly reduced. In marketing jobs, for example, common accidents include falls that occur while moving merchandise, or injuries due to improper lifting techniques.

To prevent such risks, businesses can design stock and selling areas for efficient foot traffic and merchandise storage. They can also provide training on proper ways to lift and store merchandise.

Many companies address workplace safety by developing accident management programs which include:

- Creating a safety committee to check for hazards
- Correcting hazards before accidents occur
- Developing procedures to comply with all state and federal health and safety regulations
- Investigating and recording all workplace accidents
- Providing employees with protective clothing and equipment
- Placing first aid kits near work stations
- Posting the address and phone number of the nearest hospital and clinic
- Offering employee classes in first aid and cardiopulmonary resuscitation (CPR)
- Keeping track of how many work days were missed due to accidents or injuries
- Scheduling regular safety meetings
- Preparing written safety plans and circulating them to all employees
- Offering incentives for improved safety records, such as prizes or bonuses for accident-free months

PREVENTING EXTERNAL THEFT One of the largest and most costly forms of human risk is internal and external theft from stores. It has been estimated that total theft from retail stores costs the American public between $20–30 billion every year.

Shoplifting is a form of external theft that involves stealing merchandise from a business. Shoplifting is one of the fastest-growing crimes against property in the country. According to the Federal Bureau of Investigation (FBI), about 15 percent of all thefts committed in the United States involve shoplifting.

While shoplifting losses vary by store type, it is estimated that one-third of the total inventory shrinkage is caused by shoplifting. According to an annual Price Waterhouse *Shrinkage Survey,* 1.5 to 1.9 percent of mass merchandisers retailers' net sales and 2.4 percent of apparel specialty retailers' net sales are lost to shoplifting. This means that if a specialty retailer's net sales are $100 million, approximately $2.4 million are lost to shoplifters!

There are many ways to deter shoplifting. Businesses can educate store employees about shoplifting prevention guidelines. Effective store layouts, with adequate lighting, orderly displays, and expensive items stored in locked display cases or tagged with electronic devices can cut down on shoplifting. In clothing stores, employees typically monitor how many items are brought in and returned. Many stores use security personnel and security devices such as two-way mirrors, closed circuit television, and wall and ceiling mirrors to cut down on the risk of theft.

Many states have passed strict legislation regarding shoplifting. Still, apprehending shoplifters is not without its own risks. Aside from any necessary physical contact, merchants can be sued for allegations of false arrest, false imprisonment, malicious prosecution, excessive use of force, or assault. To limit their liability, retailers must know acceptable shoplifter detention policies, and be sure that employees are trained in this.

Robbery is the stealing of money or merchandise by violence or threat. No matter where a business is located, it has a chance of being robbed. Many local police departments provide instruction on how to prevent and handle robberies. Sometimes businesses band together to form business watch programs that are similar to neighborhood watch programs.

Businesses can lower their risk from robberies by:

- Limiting the amount of money kept on hand and handling bank deposits discreetly
- Installing video cameras to help identify robbers
- Hiring extra employees so that no one is alone in a business at any time
- Hiring security guards
- Installing bulletproof glass in cashier cubicles
- Opening back doors only for freight or trash
- Installing switches near cash registers that allow employees to lock outside doors
- Increasing lighting inside and outside of the establishment
- Making sure doors are locked and alarms are set at night

Discussion Starter

1. **Risk Prevention** Have students discuss the type of safety training they have received at their co-op training stations.
2. **Screening Employees** Someday students who open their own businesses or who are in a position to hire employees for a company may have job applicants who have been convicted of and served prison time for a felony. Make sure that students understand the difference between a felony and a misdemeanor. A felony is a serious crime, such as auto theft or bank robbery; a misdemeanor is a less serious crime, such as shoplifting. State laws differ in their definitions of what constitutes a felony. Some states have more stringent parameters than other states.

Thinking Critically

1. **Screening Employees** Ask students why some states have banned lie detectors for job screening. *(Possibilities include unreliability of equipment, misinterpretation of test results, invasion of privacy, and constitutional limits on self-incrimination.)*
2. **Preventing Theft** Tell students employee theft can take many forms. Have students generate some types of employee theft, other than outright stealing money from the business. *(Answers could include theft of office supplies, parts, and/or raw materials; use of the telephone, photocopier and/or FAX machine for personal use; or use of the office mail for personal use.)*

THE DECA CONNECTION — COMPETITIVE EVENTS AND MARKETING ESSENTIALS

Assessing Business Risk You can use DECA's Entrepreneurship Written Event to tie into this chapter. This event is a full business plan developed into a 40-page written manual. Part III Analysis of the Business Situation requires that the participant assess his/her willingness to take risks and to assess his/her business strengths and weaknesses. The remainder of that section requires Analysis of the Trading Area, Market Segment, and Trading Areas. The process of analysis will help the student determine how best to deal with the business risks uncovered. Section IV, Planned Financing, covers financial risks and their management. In competition, students also request financing in a judged role play.

Cooperative Learning

1. **Types of Insurance** Divide the class into four groups and assign each group one or two types of insurance: (1) property insurance, (2) personal liability insurance and product liability insurance, (3) life insurance and credit insurance, and (4) workers' compensation insurance.

   Give each group several magazines, a large sheet of poster board, several large sheets of paper, colored markers, and tape. Have each group use its materials to create a poster on the types of insurance assigned to them. If students cannot find appropriate pictures in the magazines, they can draw the pictures.

   Have each group write a definition for each type of insurance on the poster board, tape the relevant pictures on the board, and write words or phrases that illustrate the type of insurance.

2. **Preventing External Theft** Divide the class into 3- to 5-member teams to work on an anti-shoplifting campaign for your community and school. Have each team develop ideas and an action plan for the campaign. Document the entire effort by following the guidelines of the Civic Consciousness Project provided by National DECA.

■ **Helping to Deter Shoplifting** Businesses often use a variety of techniques to reduce the threat of shoplifting. *How do electronic article surveillance systems deter shoplifters?*

CONTROLLING EMPLOYEE THEFT Employee theft—stealing merchandise, funds, or other company property—is another problem businesses face. Most employee theft occurs at the point-of-sale (POS) terminal, or cash register. To protect themselves from employee theft, many businesses have installed closed-circuit television systems and POS terminals that generate computerized reports.

POS computerized reports monitor void transfers, cash discrepancies, sales reports, refunds by employees, employees' discounts, and cash register transactions. By carefully analyzing these data, businesses improve the chances of apprehending dishonest employees.

Closed-circuit television systems used in conjunction with POS terminals lower the risk of employee theft. Closed-circuit systems include cameras concealed in mannequins, ceilings, or walls. Usually operated by security personnel in a control room, they are backed up with a video recorder.

It is important to set internal business standards regarding dishonest behavior and incorporate polices to prosecute dishonest employees. Open discussion about employee honesty and company policies keeps

all employees aware of expectations. Another prevention techniques is preemployment testing to detect attitudes about honesty. Some states, however, have banned the use of lie detectors for preemployment screening.

■ Risk Transfer

Some business risks can be handled by transferring the risk to another business or to another party. Three common risk transfers are insurance, product and service warranties, and the transference of risks through business ownership.

PURCHASING INSURANCE Businesses can insure property and people against potential loss by purchasing insurance policies. An **insurance policy** is a contract between a business and an insurance company to cover a certain business risk. A business can buy an insurance package that includes several types of insurance policies.

Insurance companies estimate the probability of loss due to such natural risks, such as fire, lightning, and wind damage, and human risks, such as theft and vandalism. The insurance company then looks at the business's location, past experience, and type of business, and determines an insurance rate depending on the degree of risk.

A business located in a neighborhood with a high risk of robbery will be charged higher rates for adequate coverage against theft. This business has a higher likelihood of being robbed and therefore of making a claim against the insurance company for coverage of its losses.

One of the most common forms of business insurance is property insurance. *Property insurance* covers the loss of, or damage to, buildings, equipment, machinery, merchandise, furniture, and fixtures. Coverage can be purchased for the full replacement value of the building, merchandise, and other items, or for a portion of the replacement value in the case of fire.

In addition, property insurance often covers off-premise accidents, outdoor property, loss of valuable papers and records, fire department service charges, and the personal property losses of others. Some policies provide added coverage for theft of personal property. Property insurance typically includes the following features:

CAPTION ANSWER
Helping Deter Shoplifting EAS devices trigger an alarm if the item has not been purchased. The alarm notifies store personnel and calls attention to a potential theft.

More About . . .

Purchasing Insurance
Insurance companies not only sell insurance, but also educate their clients about ways to reduce risk. They typically will assist business owners in identifying potential risks by conducting a walk-through and recommending changes that can be easily made to warn customers and employees of potential hazards.

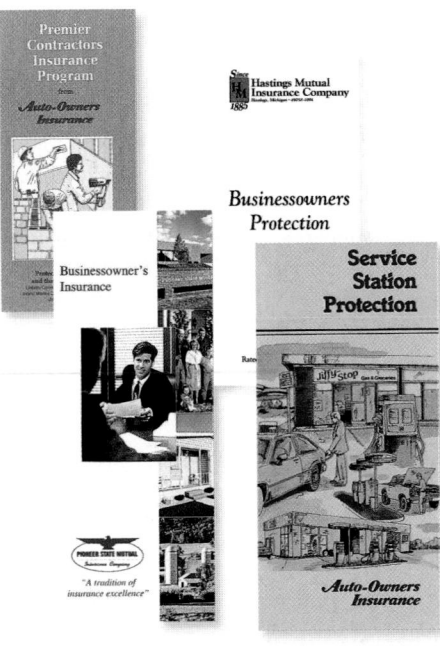

■ **Transferring Risks Through Insurance** Businesses often purchase insurance to transfer some of the risks of doing business. *What does an insurance policy represent?*

- *Replacement Cost Coverage* This covers the replacement cost of buildings and other personal property. A *coinsurance policy* has the insured business and the insurance company both sharing the risk if there is a loss. A business may be insured for 80 percent of the replacement value. This means that in case of a loss, the insurance company pays 80 percent of the covered items and the business pays 20 percent.
- *Automatic Increase Protection* This policy feature automatically adjusts the coverage to compensate for inflation on both the building and the personal property.
- *Loss of Income* This feature compensates a business for loss of income during the time that repairs are being done to a building or property after a natural disaster. Loss of income coverage also covers certain expenses that continue during the repair period, such as interest on loans, taxes, rent, advertising, telephone, and salaries.

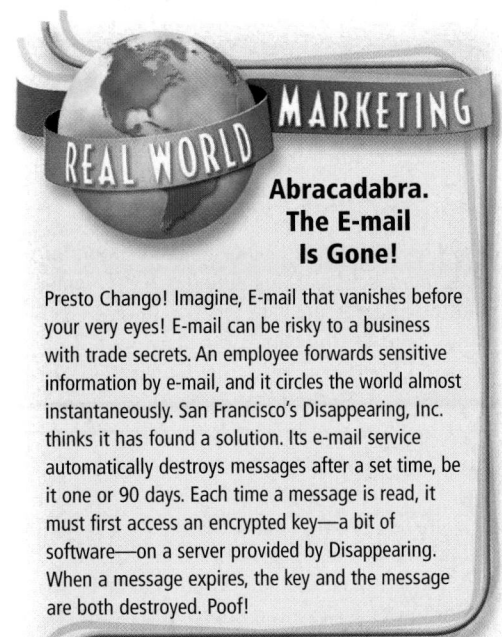

Property insurance policies can be purchased with **extended coverage**, which represents optional coverage on a basic property coverage policy. Extended coverage can be purchased to cover items that may not be covered on the basic property insurance policy, such as employee dishonesty, exterior glass, outdoor signs, rented cars, and valuable paper and records.

Business liability insurance protects a business against damages for which it may be held legally liable, such as an injury to other persons or damage to others' property. Business liability insurance is usually provided with limits up to $1 million. This type of insurance includes features such as premises and operations coverage, medical expense, personal injury coverage, employee and advertising liability.

Personal liability insurance covers damage claims made by customers and employees. The damages must have occurred near or in the business establishment.

Product liability insurance protects against business loss resulting from personal injury from

Independent Practice

1. **Research and Report** Some students may one day have to be bonded. Have students research this process. Ask: What must you do to become bonded? How does the bonding company determine how much money it will reimburse to a person who makes a claim against a bonded employee? Who is not eligible to become bonded? Under what circumstances is bonding revoked? Students should present their findings in a 250-word report.
2. **Report** Write a report on the 200- to 250-word report on the orientation program used at your place of employment. Discuss the strengths and weaknesses in the program and any suggestions that you may have for improving it.

Chapter 34 ■ *Risk Management* **631**

CAPTION ANSWER
Transferring Risks Through Insurance An insurance policy represents a contract between the business and the insurance company to cover certain business risks in the event of a loss.

REAL WORLD MARKETING

Abracadabra. The E-Mail Is Gone!
Answer Companies or individuals that need to have private conversations about sensitive topics using e-mail would benefit from disappearing e-mail.

Individualized Practice

Communication Skills

L1 The SBA offers numerous publications on crime prevention in small business. Have each student acquire one of these publications (or have several copies of each publication available in your classroom), read it, and write a summary of the information. Have students review this information in class.

L2 Have students use a dictionary and write the phonetic spelling of these words from Section 34.2:

- beneficiary
- compensate
- deter
- discrepancy
- fraudulent
- guarantee
- insurance
- legislation
- liability
- orientation
- warranty

L3 Have students write the dictionary definitions for the words listed in L2. Then have them write each word in a sentence that is related to chapter content.

Case Study

Fighting the Cyberpirates

While major companies seek to expand and increase their commitments to e-commerce and the Internet, they are faced with new business risks. Companies now have to fight cyberpirates. Cyberpirates make their Web site's domain name similar to an established company's Web domain name. The similarity can cause customers to be directed to the cyberpirate's Web site.

DaimlerChrysler AG recently won a trademark infringement case against a Web site that used a domain site similar to their foradodge.com. Ford Motor Company has also been aggressively fighting the cyberpirates. In February 2000, Ford won an injunction against a Cleveland man who tried to sell 52 domain names, including ford-quality.com on eBay's auction Web site.

The pirating of established brand names has become such a big problem that the federal government passed the *Anticybersquatting Consumer Protection Act* in November 1999. Pirates may be other companies or individuals who want to make a fast buck by trading on the brand name of an established company.

Other risks force companies to protect themselves from rumors, product disparagement, and false accusations against top executives. Stock swindlers have used the Internet to spread rumors about a company that affect the price of its stock. The Internet has proven to be a tremendous marketing tool for companies, but it also creates new and different types of business risks.

Case Study Review

1. Why are companies concerned about Web site cyberpirates?
2. What can companies do about rumors and false accusations that occur on the Internet?

A Matter of Ethics

3. Is it ethical for companies and individuals to develop Web sites that sound similar to established companies and brands? Why or why not?

---

products manufactured or sold by a business. Many businesses purchase product liability insurance to guarantee against losses even after products have been tested extensively by private companies and government agencies.

Fidelity bonds protect a business from employee dishonesty. Businesses usually require employees who handle money, such as bank tellers and cashiers, to be bonded. If a bonded employee steals money, the bonding company pays the loss. Individuals who are bonded undergo personal character reviews and background checks before they are bonded.

Performance bonds (also called surety bonds) insure against losses that might occur when work or a contract is not finished on time or as agreed. A

Case Study Review Answers

Fighting the Cyberpirates
1. Companies desire to protect their intellectual property and reputations.
2. They can ask employees to report any information about their company that they see on the Internet and work with law enforcement officials to investigate cybersquatting.

A Matter of Ethics
3. Answers will vary. It is not only unethical but possibly illegal to develop a Web site that is too similar to an established company's name and brand name.

building contractor might be required to purchase a performance bond to guarantee completion of the job on time and according to specifications. The company that issues the performance bond is responsible for damages if the contract is not completed.

Life insurance is often purchased to protect the owners or managers of a business. A sole proprietor (sole business owner) is usually required to have life insurance in order to borrow money. The policy will guarantee that there will be money to pay off the sole proprietor's debts and obligations if he or she dies. Life insurance on a deceased partner can provide the money needed for other partners to continue the business if the partners are named as *beneficiaries* —those who will receive the money from the policy.

Credit insurance protects a business from losses on credit extended to customers. *Credit life insurance* pays the balance of any loans granted by banks, credit unions, and other financial agencies in the event the borrower dies.

Workers' compensation insurance is a type of insurance paid by employers to cover employees that suffer job-related injuries and illness and to protect employers from being sued by an employee who is injured on the job. Most states require all public employers, and those private employers who regularly employ a predetermined minimum number of employees for prescribed time periods, to have workers' compensation insurance coverage.

PRODUCT AND SERVICE WARRANTIES *Warranties* are promises made by the seller or manufacturer with respect to the performance and quality of a product and protection against loss. Product and service warranties were discussed in depth in Chapter 32.

TRANSFERRING RISKS THROUGH BUSINESS OWNERSHIP As you learned in Chapter 33, the amount of risk a business must handle depends in part on the type of business ownership. In a sole proprietorship, the individual owner assumes all risks. Partnerships enable the partners to share in the business risks. Corporations allow the stockholders, as owners, to share the business risks. The corporate form of ownership offers the most protection from losses.

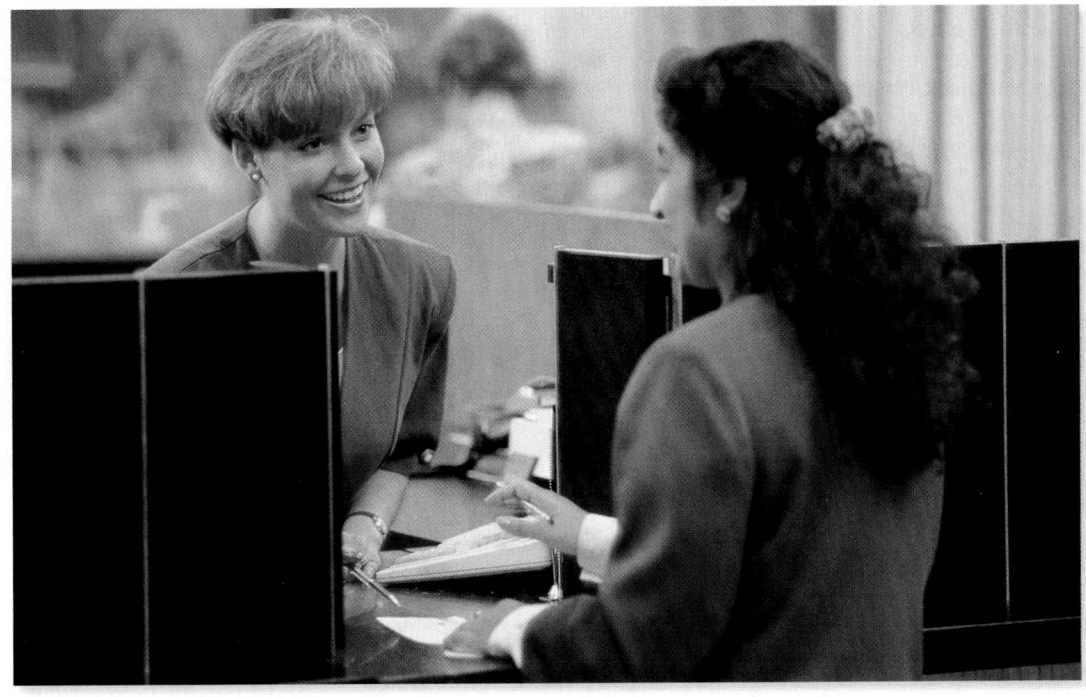

■ **Protecting the Business** Businesses can purchase insurance to protect themselves against many forms of risk. *What type of insurance would help protect a bank from employee theft?*

Chapter 34 ■ *Risk Management* **633**

ASSESS

Reteaching

1. **Vocabulary** Assign and review the vocabulary terms for this section.
2. **Fact and Idea** Assign and review Fact and Idea Review questions 3–10 from the Chapter Assessment.
3. **Section Content** Divide students into six groups. Assign each group one of the following topics: (1) things included in employee orientation/ training programs; (2) things included in accident management programs; (3) how businesses can deter shoplifting; (4) how businesses can lower their risk from robberies; (5) techniques for controlling employee theft; and (6) types of insurance and guarantees and warranties. Give each group five minutes to review its assigned information, then have all students close their texts while each group reteaches its assigned content.

Enrichment

1. **Review** Assign and review the Chapter 34 activities in the *Student Activity Workbook*.
2. **Review** Assign and review the appropriate Thinking Critically questions from the Chapter Assessment.
3. **Review** Assign and review the following Chapter Assessment activities: Building Workplace Skills, Applying Marketing Concepts, Linking School to Work, The DECA Connection Role Play, and Internet Connection.

> **CAPTION ANSWER**
> **Protecting the Business** Fidelity bonds could protect the bank from employee theft.

Risk Retention

In some cases, it is impossible for businesses to prevent or transfer risks so they *retain* or assume responsibility for them. This is called *risk retention*. A business has to assume the loss—or retain the risk—if customer trends change and merchandise remains unsold. Most retail shops assure they will assume the loss of a certain percentage of goods to damage or theft.

Businesses and businesspeople may retain certain business risks because they are unaware of the risk. It is also possible to underestimate the risk, such as when merchandise is purchased in anticipation of high sales, but weather, trends, and customers' habits change. A business could anticipate a profit by taking a risk, such as purchasing land for development and future sale for a subdivision.

Risk Avoidance

Certain risks can be avoided by anticipating them in advance. Market research can lead businesses to conclude that investment in a product is not worth the risk. All business decisions should be made with the consideration of both potential benefits and potential risks. Risk avoidance should be a key consideration in any marketing decision.

As you can see, businesses have several ways of handling risks. Owning and operating a business, however, always involves a degree of risk. The way a business manages its risks determines its success or failure.

Electronic Frontiers

When Computers Get Sick!

"An apple a day keeps the doctor away," or so the adage goes. It means, "Prevention is the best medicine." Companies are always seeking ways to immunize themselves against computer viruses. Disabling executable files that can carry viruses into corporate e-mail networks is a major focus. Hackers have used e-mail messages with subject lines such as "I Love You" or "Jokes," which seemed to be harmless. However, many people opened the messages to realize they were part of a virus that shut down some of the largest e-mail systems around the world. A virus attacks by installing itself in a computer system and can spread by mailing itself to all of the addresses registered in a computer's electronic address book. This can reduce system performance and clog mail servers. The best way to avoid viruses is to check with the sender and not open any unknown file attachments.

Thinking Critically

What kind of corporate e-mail policy might a shipping company develop to help reduce the risk of spreading computer viruses?

34.2 ASSESSMENT

Reviewing Key Terms and Concepts

1. Identify the four ways businesses handle risk.
2. Name four ways that companies prevent and control risks.
3. How can businesses reduce the human risk of on-the-job injuries?
4. What are the three principal ways to transfer risk?
5. What is the difference between risk retention and risk avoidance?

Thinking Critically

6. What important factors should a business consider when selecting an insurance company?

Integrating Academic Skills

7. **MATH** Calculate the amount of net sales lost to shoplifting in a discount store with sales of $400 million and a shoplifting rate of 1.5 percent.

Careers in Marketing

SERVICE MARKETING

Heather Lowry
Insurance Agent
GEICO

What does your job entail?

"I spend most of the day on the phone. My job is to keep customers happy and to make sure that they have the coverage they need and want. I also prepare reports, maintain records, and assist clients in making insurance claims. Insurance agents need to be able to analyze data and make recommendations. I must be familiar with insurance policies and be able to communicate the details of these policies clearly. It's important that I do my job well and always treat the customer with respect."

What kind of training did you have?

"The GEICO training process took approximately six months. The first six weeks are spent learning all of the commands on the computer. After that, I learned about the phone system and I studied for a state government mandated certification course. My calls were monitored to ensure that I was providing the right information to customers. GEICO offers training seminars and continuing education."

What skills are most important?

"Communication is the most important skill; I must be able to articulate the details of policies to my customers, and I have to listen carefully to their concerns. It is important to be equally comfortable working alone and as part of a team."

What is your key to success?

"Persistence—you have to keep learning every day. Problem solving is also very important; you need to know how to adapt to any given situation."

Thinking Critically
Why is it important to know the insurance laws and policies for different states?

Career Facts

Education and Training: Most insurance companies require a college degree. High school and college courses in accounting, economics, marketing, business law, investments, psychology, and communication are recommended.

Abilities, Aptitudes, and Skills: The ability to analyze data, make recommendations, understand different policies, and communicate clearly are helpful. Successful agents are self-motivated, self-disciplined, and self-confident.

Career Outlook: Because of the increasing popularity of online insurance agencies, the number of positions is expected to grow more slowly than average.

Career Path: Some apprenticeship opportunities exist that prepare employees for state insurance agent exams. Insurance agents may advance to sales managers of local offices, to district or regional executive positions, or to establish their own businesses.

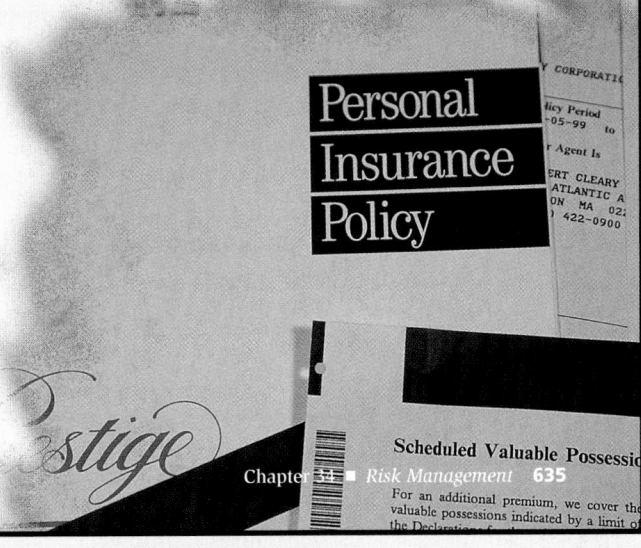

Chapter 34 ■ *Risk Management* **635**

Lifelong Learning

Risk Management
Risk management is a specialty that offers great employment opportunity. Workplace safety can be managed by many different departments, including Human Resource Management. Students interested in this field will benefit from taking courses in human resources, industrial and/or labor relations, as well as risk management.

Meeting Individual Needs

Students with Visual Impairments
Students with visual challenges may require special tools in order to participate in academic and workplace environments. The tools can vary from reading machines and Braille texts to the use of guide dogs. Some students benefit from working with a peer "visual translator" who is able to verbally describe visual images, such as photos in the textbook.

Vocabulary Review

Songs will vary. See Glossary for definitions.

Fact and Idea Review

1. Risk management is necessary for effective financial, marketing, production, and human resource management decisions. It reduces the adverse effects of risk on business resources, cash flow, and profits.
2. It is costly to notify customers about recalls, replace and/or repair defective products, and pay possible legal fees. Product recalls also create bad publicity for a company's products.
3. They reduce the human risk of carelessness through employee screening, effective initial training, and support for on-going continued education.
4. Drug abuse can make employees careless and more likely to forget safety rules.
5. An insurance policy is a contract between a business and an insurance company to cover a certain business risk.
6. Property coverage includes loss of or damage to buildings and property. Business liability insurance covers damages for which a business may be held legally liable, such as injury to other persons or damage to others' property.
7. Property coverage policies include replacement cost coverage, automatic increase protection, and loss of income.
8. It covers claims for damages suffered by customers and employees near or in the business establishment. Product liability insurance protects against business loss resulting from personal injury from products manufactured or sold by a business.
9. It is insurance paid by employers to cover employees that suffer job-related injuries and illness and to protect employers from being sued by an employee who is injured on the job.
10. In a sole proprietorship, the owner assumes all risks; in the partnership, partners share in the risk; in a corporation, the stockholders, as owners, share the business risks.

636

Chapter 34 Assessment

VOCABULARY REVIEW

Use the following vocabulary terms to write a song on how businesses can manage risks.

- risk
- risk management
- business risks
- economic risks
- natural risks
- human risks
- insurance policy
- extended coverage
- fidelity bonds
- performance bonds

FACT AND IDEA REVIEW

1. Why is risk management an important marketing function? (34.1)
2. Why do companies fear product recalls? (34.1)
3. How can businesses reduce the human risk of carelessness and incompetence? (34.2)
4. Why can drug abuse lead to increased human risk? (34.2)
5. What is an insurance policy? (34.2)
6. Compare property coverage and business liability coverage. (34.2)
7. Identify some features and types of coverage found in property coverage policies. (34.2)
8. Explain the difference between personal and product liability insurance. (34.2)
9. What is workers' compensation insurance? What are its two basic purposes? (34.2)
10. How can the type of business ownership affect the risks of the business owners? (34.2)

THINKING CRITICALLY

1. Some people think that shoplifting only affects retailers. Explain the consequences of shoplifting to individuals and society.
2. Identify some factors that may affect the insurance rates a retailer pays for fire protection.
3. How does a business decide what kinds of insurance it needs? Do you think it's possible for a business to carry too much insurance? Explain your answer.
4. Insurance rates are partially based on past experience. Do you think it is appropriate to deny auto insurance to companies that have employees with poor driving records or robbery insurance to businesses that are located in high crime areas? Analyze the two situations and defend your answer.
5. How can warranties and guarantees transfer business risks to other parties?

BUILDING WORKPLACE SKILLS

1. **Human Relations** You are planning to start a small arts and crafts shop with a friend. You believe that the business should be free from risk through the purchase of insurance coverage on the building, vehicles, merchandise, staff, etc. Identify the types of insurance you will need.
2. **Social Science** Jury judgments on personal and product liability cases have led to huge cash settlements for injured parties. How do these claims affect businesses? How do they affect you? Should there be limits on the cash amounts given for injury or death? How would you determine the settlement amounts?

Thinking Critically

1. It causes higher prices, affecting society as a whole. It can lead to a criminal record with fines and imprisonment.
2. type of business; the age, condition, and type of construction of the building in which the business is housed; the location of the business relative to fire protection services; and any past experience the business may have had with fires
3. A business must look at the degree of risk associated with each insurable feature. Answers will vary.
4. Some may say businesses should be entitled to some form of insurance without higher rates. Others might say customers should pay additional costs.
5. The risk is transferred to the seller or manufacturer.

Building Workplace Skills

1. Include types of insurance discussed in chapter.
2. Answers will vary, however, claims made against a business are passed along to consumers in the form of higher prices. Some cases have led to deaths and serious injuries requiring compensation.

APPLYING MARKETING CONCEPTS

1. **Understanding Workplace Safety** Locate the address of the National Safety Council (NSC) at the library or the Internet. Write a letter requesting business safety information for your class. Prepare an oral report using presentation software based on the materials.

2. **Researching Shoplifting** Locate the Web site of your local chamber of commerce, Retail Merchants Association, police department, or state retail trade association. E-mail a request for information about your state's legislation on shoplifting. Report your findings orally.

3. **Comparing Life Insurance** Research life insurance on the Internet or at the library. Use a word processing program to write a two-page report. Explain the various forms of life insurance and how rates are established. Present your oral report to your class.

4. **Evaluating Insurance Policies** Locate the Web site of a local insurance agency. E-mail a request to obtain sales brochures on business operations protection policies. Bring any brochures you receive to class, and display them on posterboard for your classmates.

5. **Understanding Product Recall Reasoning** Locate the Web site of the Federal Consumer Information Center. Search for product recall information and identify three recent recalls. Create a spreadsheet using computer software outlining the reasons for recall.

LINKING SCHOOL TO WORK

Writing Systems Skills Write a report on an employer's company policies when observing a shoplifting incident. Explain the procedures and actions taken at your place of business when dealing with a shoplifter.

THE DECA CONNECTION

Role Play: Assistant Manager

Situation You are to assume the role of assistant manager for a large department store. Your store manager (judge) has assigned you a special assignment to develop a risk management plan for your store.

Activity You are to describe the risks your business faces and develop a checklist of ways to handle these risks.

Evaluation You will be evaluated on how well you meet the following performance indicators:
- Explain the types of business risk
- Explain the nature of risk management
- Explain routine security precautions
- Describe the concept of insurance
- Follow safety precautions

*inter*NET CONNECTION

Business and the Environment
There are often environmental risks involved with conducting a business. The U.S. Environmental Protection Agency plays a significant role in preventing and correcting environmental damages caused by businesses.

Connect
- Perform a search of the EPA Web site for information about a recent case involving a business.
- Identify the actions taken by the EPA and the impact on public interest.

THE DECA CONNECTION

Students should be evaluated on the performance indicators noted in the Role Play.
- For another DECA Role Play go to the *Student Activity Workbook*, p. 297.
- For more in-depth Role Play practice, refer to DECA's *Essential Competitive Events Handbook*. To order, contact DECA at **www.deca.org**.

*inter*NET CONNECTION

Answers will vary, but each student should identify a case involving a business, the actions taken by the EPA to penalize and/or correct the problem, and how the EPA's actions affected the public interest.

Mini Quiz

Administer the Mini Quiz orally. For an expanded chapter quiz, go to page 203 of the *Reproducible Tests* book.

1. The possibility of financial loss is called risk.
2. The systematic process of managing an organization's risk exposure is known as risk management.
3. Insurance, product and service warranties, and business ownership are ways to transfer risk.
4. A strategy used when it is impossible for a business to prevent or transfer risks is known as risk retention.
5. Anticipating certain risks to prevent them from happening is known as risk avoidance.

Applying Marketing Concepts

1. Presentations will vary.
2. Reports will vary.
3. Reports will vary.
4. Displays will vary.
5. Spreadsheets will vary.

Linking School to Work

Answers depend on the work situation.

1. **Assessment** Have students complete the Reproducible Test for Chapter 34 or construct your own tests using the ExamView software.
2. **Enrichment** Have students complete the corresponding activities in the following workbooks:
   - *Marketing Math Workbook*, p. 111

Chapter Overview

This chapter introduces students to the business plan. It stresses the importance of business planning in developing a business idea and in evaluating results. The chapter details how to conduct a self and marketing analysis for a new business and ways to obtain capital to start a business.

 ## Springboard

Discuss Ask: Which method would be the best to reach a destination: (1) using a road map, or (2) pointing your car in the general direction of your destination, relying on intuition, and following road signs? Write *business plan* and *road map* on the board. Tell students that a business plan is a road map that helps them choose the best route, mark progress, and avoid futile side trips. The business plan helps you determine whether your business idea will work.

Prereading

List the section objectives to discuss with students. Have students skim the chapter, looking at the pictures, reading the captions, and noting the heads. Ask questions to ensure that the students have a minimal understanding of chapter structure.

Preteaching Marketing Vocabulary

Give students ten minutes to look through this chapter, find each vocabulary term, and make notes. Review each term with students.

Marketing: What It Takes

Answer Develop a business plan that explains, describes, and analyzes your proposed business, and details your organization, marketing, and financial plan for your business. Then convince a lending agency that your plan is worthy of financial backing.

Developing a Business Plan

Marketing: What It Takes

Realizing Your Dream

You have worked part-time at a small market during your high school years and have really enjoyed the job. You have an idea for a unique type of fish market you could successfully operate. This market would be different from the other franchise operations. You will need financing to lease a building and the necessary equipment.

WHAT WILL YOU DO? How will you determine what kind of capital you will need? How will you learn where to find the right kind of financing?

638

THE DECA CONNECTION

ADVISOR CORNER

Preparing a Business Prospectus Utilizing the guidelines for the Entrepreneurship Participating Event from the DECA Guide, have each student develop a business prospectus for starting their own business as directed in the event guidelines. This is an excellent way to reinforce those entrepreneurship lessons from the classroom and an opportunity for students to experience a practical application in a specific entrepreneurial situation. The advisor can put together a panel of judges (economics, business, and English teachers, local business people, etc.) and have local competition to decide which business plans will be entered in state competition.

The Business Plan

Developing the Business Plan

Once you have determined that you want to establish your own business, you need to develop a business plan. A business plan is a proposal that describes a new business to potential investors and lenders. Although business plan formats vary somewhat, the outline in Figure 35-1 on page 640 is an excellent model.

It is expensive to open a business, and you will probably need financial assistance. A business plan maps out the course of your business and helps you to obtain financing, guide the opening of a business, and plan the successful management of the business.

Your business plan should convince investors and lenders that your business idea is profitable; identify procedures necessary to legally establish the business; and, work as a management tool to identify the month-to-month steps necessary to operate a profitable business.

A business plan must be well organized and easy to read. It should contain three main sections:
- Description and analysis of the proposed business situation
- Organizational and marketing plan
- Financial plan

Description and Analysis of the Proposed Business

The description and analysis section introduces the proposed business concept. This section should clearly identify the products and services the business will sell. It includes your personal business philosophy, as well as a self-analysis that describes your business experience, education, and training. This section of your business plan also includes a trading area analysis, a market segment analysis, and an analysis of potential locations.

■ Type of Business, Business Philosophy, and Type of Products

Begin your business plan with a description of the type of business you plan to open. In this section you will present marketing research data or significant trends that will influence the success of your business. Explain how a current or changing situation has created an unfulfilled consumer want that your business will address.

Next, give your business philosophy, which tells how you think the business should be run and shows your understanding of your business's role in the marketplace. It reveals your attitude toward your customers, employees, and competitors.

● What You'll Learn
- The purpose and importance of a business plan
- The major sections of a business plan
- How to describe and analyze a proposed business situation

● Why It's Important

It takes financing to start a new business. To obtain financing you must have a well-developed business plan. A business plan is an invaluable tool that helps an entrepreneur plan business goals, determine necessary resources, and clearly identify how the new business will operate and be managed.

● Key Terms
- business plan
- business philosophy
- trading area
- buying behavior

FOCUS

Bell Ringer Activity

Analyze Have several copies of fairly detailed business plans available in your classroom. Allow students to sit in groups of three or four to thumb through several of the plans and get a feel for the contents of each. Then get students' reactions to the plans. Ask them: Does business planning seem like a great deal of perhaps unnecessary work? Would students rather jump into a business without taking the time to create the type of detailed plans they just reviewed?

Ask students to help you brainstorm a board list of reasons why business planning is important.

Introducing the Section

The Business Plan Business planning is important for three reasons:
1) It helps to obtain financing. Most potential lenders and investors will want to see a detailed business plan before lending or investing money.
2) A business plan serves as a guide in opening a business. New business owners need a guide during business start-up to identify the legal procedures required for starting a business.
3) Finally, a business plan helps in business management because it lays out the steps you must take to ensure profitable operation. Business owners review their business plans regularly to compare current business operation with original planning and projected financial information.

In this section, students will look at the first key section of a business plan: description and analysis of the proposed business.

Classroom Resources

For the Teacher
- Teacher Editions for all workbooks
- Assessment Package
- PowerPoint Presentation Software
- Interactive Lesson Planner
- ILP Block Scheduling, p. 11
- ILP Lesson Plans, p. 73
- ILP Internet Resources, p. 89

ILP *BusinessWeek* Case Studies, p. 219
ILP Marketing Career Portfolio, p. 41
- *Marketing Essentials* Web site (**www.marketing.glencoe.com**)

For the Student
- Student Activity Workbook, p. 307
- Marketing Math Workbook, p. 111

- Marketing Research Project Workbook
- ILP School-to-Work Activity Workbook, p. 143
- Virtual Business simulation
- *Marketing Essentials* Web site (**www.marketing.glencoe.com**)

ILP These resources are available in print and on the Interactive Lesson Planner (ILP)

Concept Development

1. Read Section 35.1 with students.
2. MarkED Resource Center in Columbus, Ohio, (800) 448-0398, offers materials appropriate for use with this chapter, including *The Small Business Planning Guide.*
3. Some other references include: (1) *How to Set Up Your Own Business,* M. Fallek, 1995; (2) *The McGraw-Hill Guide to Starting Your Own Business: A Step-by-Step Blueprint for the First-time Entrepreneur.* S.C. Harper, 1991; (3) *Young Entrepreneur,* a bi-monthly magazine for teens; (4) E. Meyer and K. Allen, 2000, *Entrepreneurship and Small Business Management,* Glencoe/McGraw-Hill; (5) *PACE Level 1, II, and III* instructional materials, The International Consortium for Entrepreneurship Education, Center on Education and Training for Employment, Ohio State University.
4. In the third Applying Marketing Concepts in the Chapter Assessment, students are asked to create a business plan. Help them to organize and prioritize information by developing a notebook that has one section devoted to each section of the business plan. Or they can create a 3" x 5" card file, writing one or two related thoughts per card.

FIGURE 35-1

OUTLINE FOR A BUSINESS PLAN

A business plan details every part of a proposed business to potential investors and lenders.

1 Section 1 describes the general concept of the proposed business, outlines the entrepreneur's special skills, and analyzes the potential market.

2 Section II discusses how the business will be organized, describes the product or service to be offered, and details the marketing plan.

3 Section III identifies the sources of capital and projects income and expenses.

I. **Description and analysis of the proposed business situation**
   A. Type of business
   B. Business philosophy
   C. Description of good or service
   D. Self-analysis
      1. Education and training
      2. Strengths and weaknesses
      3. Plan for personal development
   E. Trading area analysis
      1. Geographic, demographic, and economic data
      2. Competition
   F. Market segment analysis
      1. Target market
      2. Customer buying behavior
   G. Analysis of potential location

II. **Organization and marketing plan**
   A. Proposed organization
      1. Type of ownership
      2. Steps in establishing business
      3. Personnel needs
   B. Proposed good/service
      1. Manufacturing plans and inventory policies
      2. Suppliers
   C. Proposed marketing plan
      1. Pricing policies
      2. Promotional activities

III. **Financial plan**
   A. Sources of capital
      1. Personal sources
      2. External sources
   B. Projected income and expenses
      1. Personal financial statement
      2. Projected start-up costs
      3. Projected personal needs
      4. Projected business income
      5. Projected business expenses
      6. Projected income statement(s)
      7. Projected balance sheet
      8. Projected cash flow

GREAT IDEAS from the Marketing Classroom

Elizabeth S. Pitts
Cass High School
Cartersville, GA

Students studying demographics can gain a greater understanding of the concept through "The Decades Project." Based on the theory that beliefs and habits formed during teen years influence later actions in life, students study each decade in the last century. Divide students into groups of two or three and assign a decade from the 1900s through the 1990s. Have them create an overview of their decade through research, and prepare a display and PowerPoint presentation. Information can include trends, movies, television, music, clothing, inventions, and headlines. The students may also dress in clothing of their decade.

■ Self-Analysis

The next part of your business plan includes a self-analysis. A *self-analysis* is a description of your personal education, training, strengths, weaknesses, and a plan for personal development in the field of marketing.

Imagine that you are interested in apparel and accessories marketing and want to start a related business. You must be able to accurately predict current fashion trends. You also must be able to buy, display, price, and advertise your merchandise correctly. In this part of the business plan, highlight your strengths and skills in this area. Describe how you will acquire the skills you need through training or hiring a professional.

Indicate the education and training you have had so far to prepare you for operating your new business. In addition to mentioning your marketing education program, you should discuss other courses that you have taken and related job experience that will benefit you in your endeavor. Your education and work experience shows potential lenders that you can understand and interpret your business's financial statements.

Discuss any future educational plans, such as attending a community college, technical institute, or university. Plans for continuing education show that you intend to improve on your existing skills for operating your business.

Some businesses require applying for a special license. In this section, you should explain if you already have this license or are in the application process. Some businesses that require licensing are adult and childcare facilities; automotive, electrical, and mechanical repair businesses; construction companies; and, styling salons and barbershops.

Finally, include the special personal traits and work habits you possess that will help you to operate the proposed business. Examples of past leadership activities, personal initiatives, and willingness to work hard, all add strength to your business plan.

■ Trading Area Analysis

Following an explanation of your personal strengths and skills, you should begin to define your trading area. A trading area is the geographical area from which a business draws its customers. Before going into business, you must analyze the trading area with respect to geographic, demographic, and economic data, as well as competition.

■ **Having the Required Skills** Some types of businesses require special training and education. *Why does the government require special licensing for certain occupations?*

Your business philosophy will help you attract new customers and maintain existing customers once you start a business. Wal-Mart's business philosophy states that the company will match the advertised sale prices of any competitor. The principal pricing policy is that Wal-Mart will not be undersold and the return policy is that customers can always return merchandise if they are dissatisfied with it. This business philosophy has earned Wal-Mart a loyal following of customers.

After identifying your business philosophy, describe the product or service you will offer. Explain the potential consumer benefits and why your product or service will be successful. Include as many facts as you can—speculation and statements of belief do not convince investors and lenders to lend you money. For regional and national business information, consult recent issues of *Business Week, Entrepreneur, Fortune, Inc., Money, The Wall Street Journal,* and other business publications.

Discussion Starter

Business Philosophies As the text mentions, part of Wal-Mart's business philosophy is that the customer should always be happy with merchandise purchased at the lowest possible price. Discuss with students the business philosophies of other businesses in your area. Also, have students compare the business philosophies of two similar businesses.

Thinking Critically

Services Services are intangible and, therefore, are more difficult to describe than goods. Ask students what types of things they would include in a product description of a service such as a hair salon. *(Possibilities include: special techniques or equipment which will be used to provide the service that other similar service providers might not offer, descriptions of the service providers, descriptions of ancillary products to be offered, and customer benefits of receiving the service.)* Provide students with other examples of service businesses (for example, restaurants, dry cleaners, and copy shops) and have them give sample product descriptions of each.

The more product knowledge you can convey to your customers, the more credibility you will have. Why? *(Answers should indicate that if you convey a great deal of product knowledge, you portray yourself as the product expert. Thus, people will trust your product.)*

CAPTION ANSWER
Having the Required Skills The government seeks to ensure the health, safety, and welfare of residents, in addition to insuring that consumers receive the best possible services provided by educated and trained personnel.

Did You Know? How long should a business plan be? Depending on who is being approached, it can be anywhere from 10–40 pages. Banks are looking for tangible assets and evidence that the loan will be repaid. Investors, looking to predict growth, need to see more complex evidence of future success. For them, 40 pages may be necessary.

Cooperative Learning

Demographic and Economic Factors Divide students into four groups. Have each group research geographic, demographic, and economic data in your area. Define for students what geographical area you want them to research—for example, your town, your city, your county, etc. Also define the categories you wish them to research under demographic factors and economic factors.

Have each group compile its research into a written report, or charts/graphs showing analysis and comparison of the statistics, or both.

Have all groups present their information and tell where they got their statistics. Then have students make predictions about what businesses your area could and could not support.

REAL WORLD MARKETING

Legal Grounds

Would you like an "Equal Rights Espresso"? Sounds silly, but that is what you might hear David Musslewhite say when you enter his Legal Grounds Café. Knowing that meeting with an attorney can be stressful, Musslewhite opened the Legal Grounds Café, where customers can sip on capuccino while seeking legal counsel. They can order lunch and have their will or trusts prepared. After years of drinking bad coffee and conducting legal practice at a large Texas law firm, Musslewhite finds the overstuffed chairs at the café a perfect setting for consultations. You can find him on the café floor providing advice, cappuccino, and a smile.

Thinking Critically
What types of businesses could profit from an environment similar to that of Legal Grounds?

Information about the population in your trading area is available from your local chamber of commerce or state department of commerce. You can also consult the most recent local census data in your local library or on the Internet.

GEOGRAPHIC, DEMOGRAPHIC, AND ECONOMIC DATA *Geographic* data includes population distribution, or how many people live in a certain area. *Demographics* are identifiable and measurable population statistics such as age, gender, marital status, and race/ethnicity. Knowing the demographics of your trading area will help you identify market trends that may have a direct impact on your business. Your plans to open a travel agency might be adjusted if you learned that your trading area has an older population with high incomes.

Prevailing economic conditions are among the major factors affecting a business. *Economic factors* include economic growth projections, trends in employment, interest rates, business mergers, and governmental regulations. Tax increases or decreases levied by the local, state, or federal government will affect consumer buying power.

It is important to include how much *disposable income* the potential consumers in your trading area are likely to have. This is the personal income remaining from wages after all taxes are taken out. Disposable income is also referred to as *buying income.*

A special measurement called a *buying power index* has been developed to help new business owners determine the buying power for a given area. The index factors disposable income, population size, and retail sales figures to determine an overall indicator of an area's sales potential. These factors are then expressed as a percentage of total sales. You can find more information on buying power indexes in the *Survey of Buying Power,* which is published annually by *Sales and Marketing Management* magazine.

National and international economic conditions can have an effect locally, too. International trade agreements, like NAFTA, may affect your business by increasing or decreasing the demand for your product or service.

Will your business be affected by seasonal fluctuations? Could technological advancements that may occur now or in the future affect the demand or need for your product or service? You should know how to find the information you need to help you answer these questions.

A good source of information on local economic conditions is your local bank. Bank officials often have business projections for major geographical areas and for most types of businesses located in their immediate area. In addition, the U.S. Small Business Administration (SBA) has funded over 900 small business development centers (SBDCs) to provide management and technical assistance to small businesses and new entrepreneurs. Other good sources of information are related business publications available at schools, public libraries, colleges, universities, or on the Internet.

COMPETITION As a new business owner, you must analyze your competition. List all the competitors in your trading area, along with their types of products, prices, locations, general quality of products, and their strengths and weaknesses. Try to estimate your competitors' sales volume and identify how they promote and sell their products. You should be able to use these factors to demonstrate how your business will be superior to the competition.

REAL WORLD MARKETING

Legal Grounds
Answer Professional services from accountants to medical services might take a similar approach to conducting business.

■ **Knowing Your Customer**
New businesses need to
identify a target market for
their products and services.
*Why must businesses carefully
identify a target market?*

Independent Practice

1. **Research and Report** Have students research the current status of the North American Free Trade Agreement (NAFTA) and report on the economic implications and impact of this agreement for businesses in your community or region. (If the agreement will not directly impact businesses in your community, at least make sure that students understand NAFTA and its intent with respect to its impact on our national economy.)

2. **Analyze and Discuss** Have students list five different types of successful businesses in your community and analyze why each is located where it is. They should consider such things as accessibility to the public, to suppliers, and to transit routes; and each business's needs. *(For example, manufacturers and wholesalers, value low space costs and good access to transit routes over exposure to and accessibility by the public.)* Discuss students' findings in class.

Some good sources of information about your competitors can be found through annual reports, the local chamber of commerce, trade associations, the Yellow Pages, the Internet, business publications, and reports such as those published by as *Dun & Bradstreet*.

■ Market Segment Analysis

The next part of your business plan should contain a market segment analysis. A market segment analysis is a description of your target market and the buying behavior of your potential customers.

TARGET MARKET As you know, your target market represents the specific group of people you want to reach. You can identify your target market by common geographic characteristics such as region, county size, size of city, density of population, and climate of the area. You can also categorize it by demographic characteristics such as age, gender, marital status, family size, income, occupation, education, religion, and culture or ethnic background.

You must carefully identify your target market because the needs and wants of different markets must be addressed differently in the marketing of goods and services. Families can live in the same city and have similar education levels, occupations, and incomes, but have varying needs for entertainment, furniture, food, clothing, or personal services depending on their religious or ethnic background.

Your task as an entrepreneur is to decide which market to target and how to do it. The best way to make this decision is to be guided by the way the members of the target market perceive themselves and their own needs.

CUSTOMERS' BUYING BEHAVIOR After you have identified your target market, you will need to explain how the chosen market's *buying behavior* will be good for your business. Buying behavior is the process individuals use to decide what they will buy, from where they will buy it, and who they will buy it from. Imagine that you are planning to open a children's toy store. You have used demographic information to determine how many families with children are in your target market. You also know the approximate average family income. From your earlier analysis of the competition (other toy stores serving the same target market), you have an idea of how much disposable income these families have spent on children's toys and which toys they bought. You also know which stores in which locations did the most business. This is your target market's buying behavior.

Chapter 35 ■ *Developing A Business Plan* **643**

CAPTION ANSWER
Knowing Your Customer Individual needs and wants of various target markets must be addressed differently in the marketing of goods and services.

Reteaching

1. **Vocabulary** Assign and review the vocabulary terms for this section.
2. **Fact and Idea** Assign and review Fact and Idea Review questions 1–5 from the Chapter Assessment.

Electronic Frontiers

A Road Map to Success

Imagine that you wanted to drive from Gotham, New Jersey, to Metropolis, Illinois. Would you just start driving? Or, would you carefully map out your route? Now, imagine that you wanted to start a business. Would you just start your company or would you carefully map out your route? Business plans are the roadmap to success for businesses! A business plan is a good way to take a look at a business from a critical viewpoint. A company can use a business plan to target strengths and weaknesses, as well as address finances and marketing plans. Writing a business plan is usually a tremendous amount of work; however, individuals can get a head start on writing a business plan by using online resources, such as downloadable templates or programs. One such program, BizPlanBuilder, includes templates for every aspect of a successful business plan.

Thinking Critically

How might a template of a business plan assist in gaining financing?

You can then put this information together to make decisions about how your store might best serve these same customers. Do you want to try to take business away from other toy stores, or do you want to try to sell items not offered in the other stores? Do you want to entice your customers to buy a lot of low-priced items or a few high-priced ones?

■ Analysis of Potential Locations

You can select your location after you have analyzed your trading area and your market segment, including your target market and your competition. Location has a direct effect on your sales, making this a vital decision.

BUY, LEASE, OR BUILD Your analysis should include whether you want to buy, lease, or build your facility. The advantages of leasing outweigh the other options for most new businesses. When leasing, a large initial outlay of cash is avoided, risk is reduced because of a shorter commitment, and lease expenses are tax deductible. The process of buying or building is more complex and almost always requires applying for financing.

Regardless of whether you buy, lease, or build, you need to compare certain terms of each potential property. Those terms include monthly rent or payments and length of commitment. You will also need to find out who is responsible for insurance.

You should have an attorney review any lease or contract before you sign it. This will help you fully understand your obligations and negotiate the best possible terms before completing the deal.

■ **Location, Location, Location!** A location is very important to a business. *What are the advantages and disadvantages of locating along a heavily used thoroughfare?*

A Road Map to Success

Answer A good template can act as an industry standard form for professionals to more easily weigh the merits of one company against another.

CAPTION ANSWER
Location, Location, Location! The advantages are high visibility and good potential for sales. The disadvantages are traffic congestion and higher leases or purchase prices on building. The type of business will dictate the necessity of locating on a heavily traveled thoroughfare.

COMPETING AND COMPLEMENTARY BUSINESSES A major consideration in a business location should be the nearness to your competition. Consider the number and size of potential competitors in the area—if your business is similar in size and merchandise to its competitors, you may want to locate near them. This can encourage comparison shopping. That's why it's not uncommon to see an entire block of furniture stores or auto dealers. On the contrary, a larger business that offers more variety than the competition should be able to generate its own customers and therefore can be located away from the competition.

A complementary business is one that would help generate store traffic. A shoe or accessories store located next to a clothing store is one example of a complementary business.

HOURS OF OPERATION Whether you locate your business in a mall, neighborhood shopping center, freestanding location, or your own home depends upon the nature of your business. Your location will determine your hours of operation and the number of customers who will see and patronize your business.

A business located in a shopping mall will probably have regular hours that are set by the mall management. In such a situation, you can also usually depend on fairly constant customer traffic generated by the other businesses in the same location.

If you run your own small business, you can set your own hours based on when you have the most customers or clients. For example, if you own a nail salon and know that other nail salons in the area are closed on Sunday, you may consider having hours that day. If you run a coffee shop located in an office park or business complex, you may open very early and close in the early evening. Establishing your hours in this manner may give you an edge over your competition.

VISIBILITY Businesses that rely on high visibility, such as restaurants, may spend the extra money to locate in a highly visible location. A highly visible site may not be a priority for all businesses, but the money you save on the building can be used for advertising or promoting your business.

SAFETY Neighborhood safety should be a consideration when choosing a business location. Research the community's crime rate. You don't want to open your operation in an area where customers feel uncomfortable or are unlikely to visit in the evening or during off-peak hours.

Closeness to fire hydrants and the fire department is also important. Find out what type of fire department the community has, volunteer or municipal.

BRIGHT IDEAS

LEGO Maniac

The LEGO Empire was created brick by brick, literally! In 1932, Ole Kirk Christiansen established a carpentry firm in Denmark, which manufactured stepladders, ironing boards, and wooden toys. Formed from the Danish words "LegGOdt" ("play well"), the company adopted the name LEGO. The stepladders and ironing boards sold slowly, but the toy sales took off—mainly because of the beautiful varnish and attention to detail. In 1947, LEGO became the first company in Denmark to buy a plastic injection molding machine for making toys. Over the next decade, the LEGO company phased out production of their wooden toys and started to manufacture plastic building blocks, called LEGO Bricks. To make the product more interesting, Christiansen designed play sets modeled from everyday life, including cars, houses, and buildings. To keep models sturdy, LEGO patented the stud-and-tube coupling system, which allowed children's imagination to run wild, as the possible brick combinations are astronomical!

Thinking Creatively

How would you improve on LEGO?

Enrichment

1. **Review** Assign and review the appropriate Thinking Critically questions from the Chapter Assessment.
2. **Extend** Assign and review the corresponding activities from *BusinessWeek Case Studies* and *Internet Resources.* **ILP**
3. **Research and Write** Have students interview the owners or managers of two small businesses in your community that are in direct competition (for example, two dry cleaners).

   Have students determine: (1) what each business does to differentiate itself from the competition; (2) how each business "keeps tabs" on the competition's latest product offerings and on its level of success; and (3) what indirect competition each business faces. (Indirect competition is created by products that are the same as yours but offered through a different outlet, or through the use of new or newly applied technologies. For example, a moderately priced restaurant faces indirect competition from a take out food section in the supermarket.)

   Students should write their findings in 150 to 200 words. Have each student present his or her findings to the class.

BRIGHT IDEAS LEGO Maniac

Answer Answers will vary.

Evaluation

Assign and review the Section 35.1 Assessment.

Technology Resources

Assessment Resources
Go to the *Marketing Essentials* Web site (**www.marketing.glencoe. com**) for resources to teach and assess occupation-specific vocabulary.

VIRTUAL BUSINESS

The Business Plan
Introduce business plans to students using Knowledge Matters' Virtual Business visual simulation, "Office Applications—The Business Plan." Student teams observe competition, survey customers, and then write a business plan for a new venture. If needed, have students run the Virtual Business tutorial before beginning this activity. For additional instructions and teaching tips for this activity, go to the *Marketing Essentials* Web site (**www.marketing.glencoe.com**).

CLOSE

Section Wrap-Up

Have students complete this statement: The three key functions of a business plan are . . . *(obtain financing, guide opening of business, and manage business successfully.)*

Sealed with a Kiss
Answer A common greeting is a wave, handshake, or pat on the back.

CUSTOMER ACCESSIBILITY Identify the highways, streets, and transportation routes that lead to your business site. Customer accessibility should be a priority—if there is no convenient route to your business, customers can't reach you. Other important considerations include whether traffic congestion will be a problem and whether there is sufficient parking space. Also keep in mind that special considerations must be made to accommodate customers with special needs, including wheelchair accessible entrances and convenient parking spots.

PERSONAL ISSUES There are some personal issues regarding the location of your business. Do you want to be near family and friends? Do you want to locate in a neighborhood or city different from where you currently live? Intangible issues such as atmosphere, character, and personal preference will enter into a final decision.

ZONING AND OTHER REGULATIONS Now that you have answered these questions, you are ready to find a specific site. Your first step should be to learn about any local ordinances or laws that may affect your business. Research any restrictions that exist which might prevent you from locating in a particular commercial or residential area.

Plans to build or renovate will require the necessary building permits. Operating a regulated business, such as a childcare center or a service station, will call for the necessary local zoning approvals and state licenses. You may want to meet with your local or county officials to learn about local regulations.

Sealed with a Kiss

One of the most common non-verbal signals one can make is the "kiss." While kissing is reserved as a greeting for close friends or family in North America, it is not so in all countries. Don't be surprised if you see acquaintances greeting each other with a kiss. Latins, Europeans, and Russians, both men and women, are no strangers to this form of "hello." It is even more common for the kiss to land on the air next to the face rather than square on—but this "air kiss" symbolizes a proper greeting for some. A word of advice—don't try this with a stranger, as it may be returned with a slap across the face!

Thinking Critically
What are the more common forms of greeting in the United States?

35.1 ASSESSMENT

Reviewing Key Terms and Concepts

1. What is a business plan and why is it important?
2. What are three sections of a business plan?
3. What is a business philosophy? Why is it important?
4. Define buying behavior. Why is it important to understand customer buying behavior in your target market?
5. Identify at least three factors to consider when planning a location for a business.

Thinking Critically

6. What are some of the factors that a new business can control? What are some uncontrollable factors?

Integrating Academic Skills

7. **COMMUNICATION** Under the direction of your instructor, use a word processing program to develop a business letter inviting a local businessperson to speak to your marketing class on the importance of store location to the success of a business.

646 Unit 11 ■ *Entrepreneurship and Finance*

35.1 ASSESSMENT ANSWERS

Reviewing Key Terms and Concepts
1. It describes a new business to potential investors and financing agencies; provides a guide to owning, operating, and managing it.
2. description and analysis of business, organization and marketing plan, financial plan
3. It tells how you think the business should be run and your understanding of the business's role in the marketplace. It reveals your attitude toward customers, employees, and competitors.
4. process to decide what to buy and where
5. buy or lease; location; hours of operation; visibility; safety and accessibility; personal issues; and zoning

Thinking Critically
6. Business letters will vary.

Integrating Academic Skills
7. **COMMUNICATION** Letters will vary.

The Marketing Plan

Organizing the Plan

The second section of the business plan tells how you plan to organize the new business. It contains a description of your current and anticipated staffing needs. It also details how you plan to sell your product and how you intend to reach and satisfy customers with your product. The details of your proposed product are explained along with your potential suppliers, manufacturing or selling methods, and inventory policies.

Finally, it includes your marketing plan. Your marketing plan details your pricing strategies and promotional plans.

■ Proposed Organization

The organization part of your business plan is essentially a blueprint. It lays the foundation for the structure of your proposed business. It must be clearly laid out and solid, as the rest of your business will be built around it.

TYPES OF OWNERSHIP As you learned in Chapter 33, there are three main types of business ownership which include sole proprietorships, partnerships, and corporations. In this part of the business plan, you will need to identify the form of business ownership appropriate for your business and the rationale behind your choice. The rest of your plan will be affected by how you choose to establish ownership.

STEPS IN ESTABLISHING YOUR BUSINESS Once you have detailed what type of business ownership you have chosen, you need to show the steps you will take to establish your business. As you know from Chapter 33, the specific steps you will take will depend on how you organize your business.

PERSONNEL NEEDS Your personnel needs must be detailed in your business plan. Potential investors and lenders need to know that you can identify the jobs essential for your business to run properly. They also will want you to identify, as much as you can, the people who will do those jobs. If you are opening a small coffee shop, you need to consider what staffing needs you have to address. You will need various service staff, depending on your business's size, as well as people to manage the business and marketing for your shop. This information can all be worked out in the business plan.

Figure 35-2 on page 648 shows the typical functions in a business. Notice that some of the functions are repeated under more than one category. By identifying all the necessary functions, you will be able to begin planning an organizational structure for your business.

What You'll Learn

- How to develop a business's organization plan
- How to provide details related to goods or services to be offered
- How to develop a marketing plan

Why It's Important

The organization and marketing section of the business plan outlines how you plan to organize the business. It also explains how you will use advertising and promotional activities to help your business grow and prosper in the competitive marketplace.

Key Terms

- job descriptions
- organization chart

FOCUS

Bell Ringer Activity

Brainstorm Have each student pick a partner in the class. Each pair should brainstorm a list of the things that would be included in (1) the organization plan and (2) the marketing plan.

Introducing the Section

The Marketing Plan Review students' answers from the Bell Ringer Activity, creating a board list of their answers under column headings marked *organization plan* and *marketing plan*.

Tell students that this section explores the second part of a business plan, which tells how you would organize, manage, and develop your new business.

Concept Development

1. Read Section 35.2 with students.

Discussion Starter

Economic Environment Discuss with students the current economic environment locally and nationally. What correlation do students see between the local and national economic environment, and local prices? For example, have fast-food restaurants cut prices on their standard fare, or are they offering extremely low-priced specials? Are health clubs offering two-for-one membership deals? What predictions can students make about how long such price-cutting will last? *(Answers will vary.)*

FIGURE 35-2

Business Functions

Administration	Production	Marketing
Operations	Operations	Advertising
Personnel	Purchasing	Sales
Financial	Manufacturing	Public Relations
Legal	Distribution	Service
Public Relations	Service	

■ **Business Functions** This table shows the typical functions performed in most businesses in three general categories: administration (running the business), production (making the product), and marketing (selling the product). *What are two positions you would find in any one of the above functions?*

Many new businesses begin as one-person operations in which that person does most or all of the business functions. It is not unusual for an entrepreneur to handle everything from the management duties to the financial oversight functions to the advertising and promotional activities. As a business grows, these responsibilities need to be divided among additional partners or employees. Entrepreneurs must identify how everyone fits into the organizational structure.

You need to prepare job descriptions for your partners, employees, and yourself. Job descriptions are written statements listing the requirements of a particular job. Each job description includes the purpose of the job, qualifications needed, duties to be performed, equipment to be used, and expected working conditions.

Job descriptions set a standard against which all applicants for a job or employees in the same position can be rated. A sample of a solid job description is illustrated in Figure 35-3. Notice how it contains a long list of job functions, from the most basic to more specific. This leaves little room for confusion about what is expected on the job.

After job descriptions have been prepared, you are ready to develop an organization chart. An organization chart is a diagram of the various jobs and functions that are found in a company. It should be

648 Unit 11 ■ *Entrepreneurship and Finance*

FIGURE 35-3

Job Description

Position Purpose

Performs general warehouse duties including shipping/receiving, picking and packing orders, processing orders in the system, stocking and reshelving merchandise, and other warehouse related job tasks as assigned.

Essential Functions

- Conducts inventory audits on a regular basis to detect discrepancies.
- Marks materials with identifying information.
- Opens bales, crates, and other containers.
- Record amounts of materials or items received or distributed.
- Weighs or counts items for distribution within plant to ensure conformance to company standards.
- Responds in a professional, polite, and helpful manner when dealing with customers.
- Helps load and unload shipments into and out of transporting vehicles.
- Refers non-routine problems to supervisor.
- Learns, understands, and complies with all company and customer policies.
- Move material through facility with the use of material handling equipment (i.e., pallet, handcart) as required.
- Use the computer to dispense and receive information such as product codes, part numbers, quantities, locations, comments, etc.
- Must be able to lift up to 50 pounds, stoop, kneel, crouch, reach, stand, walk, push, pull, and grasp materials.
- Additional duties as assigned to meet department and company objectives.

Required Skills

Level of reading, writing, and math ability as demonstrated by a competent high school student or high school graduate. Personal computer literate. Ability to operate various types of material handling equipment, including a pallet jack, hand truck, and carton dolly.

Physical Requirements

Must be able to lift 50 pounds. Must be able to lift, carry, stoop, reach, pull, push, and bend repeatedly to transport materials from racks and bins for shipment. Must be able to climb stairs and ladders to stock and pull materials from shelves.

Scheduling Requirements

Must be available to work up to the required hours as scheduled in compliance with 1978 Public Act 90 (Youth Employment Standards Act).

■ **Job Description** Written statements of job requirements help employees recognize their responsibilities. *What items are typically found on a job description?*

FIGURE 35-2 ANSWER
Business Functions Answers will vary. For example, in the personnel department there could be a personnel director and a training administrator. In sales, there could be a sales associates and a sales manager.

FIGURE 35-3 ANSWER
Job Description Typical items found on a job description include: purpose of the job, qualifications needed, duties to be performed, equipment to be used, and expected working conditions.

■ **Knowing Your Competitors** Analyzing your competitors is important for determining your pricing strategy. *How can you determine a competitor's pricing policies?*

Cooperative Learning

New Businesses Organize the class into 3–5 member teams and have each student report to the group the results of the #1 Applying Marketing Concepts activity from the Chapter 35 Assessment that calls for a report on an article about a successful new business. Have each group discuss and record at least five things each successful business had in common. Spend time analyzing the results with the entire class by using each of the smaller groups' responses.

Independent Practice

Write Have students write a job description for the co-op job they may now hold. (Tell them not to look at their actual job description, if they were given one.) The description should include the purpose of the job, qualifications needed, duties performed, equipment used, and working conditions. For those students who do not have co-op jobs, ask them to write a description of a job they perform at home or in school.

drawn with the jobs and major duties identified and lines of authority clearly shown. Ideally, an organization chart outlines who each employee reports to and the chain of command in a company. This answers any questions regarding responsibility and how problems should be handled if they arise. It also makes clear what kind of work each department is responsible for. If you work for a large company in the public relations department and need to work with someone in the design department for a project, an organization chart should tell you to whom you would need to report.

Sometimes outside professional help is needed to keep a business going and growing. Entrepreneurs are often afraid to spend money on such professional services as accounting. This can be a fatal mistake. Trained professionals will help you avoid making serious mistakes that can result in business failure. If you decide to use outside professionals, identify them and their responsibilities on your organization chart. Professionals that can help you include accountants, attorneys, bankers, and insurance agents.

You can also use technical assistance to identify employment practices in your state or locality. New business owners must be familiar with laws regulating nondiscrimination laws, wages and hours regulations, occupational health and safety issues, unemployment compensation, and workers' disability insurance. State agencies—such as state

departments of civil rights, commerce, labor, licensing and regulation—publish many inexpensive or free publications and offer technical assistance to help new entrepreneurs understand various employment laws, rules, and regulations.

■ Proposed Good or Service

One part of your business plan should include information on the types of goods and services you will offer, as well as your potential suppliers, manufacturing plans, and inventory policies. Let's say you plan to introduce a new service, such as a pre-school center, to your trading area. Perhaps you are going to sell or produce an existing product in a new and creative way. In both cases, you would prepare a list of possible suppliers and develop a manufacturing plan that details all of the purchasing and manufacturing requirements.

Closely related to your manufacturing plan is your inventory policy. You need to show how you will manage the goods you purchase or manufacture. How much, for example, will you keep on hand? How will you keep track of what to order and what has been sold? Where will you store the goods that you have in stock?

Your inventory system depends on the size and scope of your proposed business. Trade associations and many suppliers can give you suggestions for the best inventory control system for your business.

Chapter 35 ■ *Developing A Business Plan* **649**

CAPTION ANSWER
Knowing Your Competitors
Depending on the type of business, a new entrepreneur could telephone for prices, visit in person, or read advertised prices, and observe the competitor over time.

THE *DECA* CONNECTION

COMPETITIVE EVENTS AND MARKETING ESSENTIALS

Business Plan for a New Business DECA's Entrepreneurship Participating Event will assist you with teaching this chapter. Entrepreneurship Participating offers the option for a student to develop a business plan for either a new independent business or a new franchise business. The student will develop a nine-page, three-part business prospectus including

a self-analysis, an analysis of the business situation, a description of the way the business will operate, and a detailed plan for financing the business through its first three years of operation. The student then explains his/her business plan outline to a businessperson/judge in a 20-minute presentation/interview. This event is for individual participants only.

ASSESS

Reteaching

1. **Vocabulary** Assign and review the vocabulary terms for this section.
2. **Fact and Idea** Assign and review Fact and Idea Review questions 6–7 from the Chapter Assessment.

Enrichment

1. **Review** Assign and review the appropriate Thinking Critically questions from the Chapter Assessment.
2. **Extend** Assign and review the corresponding activities from the *School-to-Work Activity Workbook.* **ILP**
3. **Research** Have students contact the owners or managers of three service businesses to discuss how each establishes his or her business's prices. Have them ask, for example: Why does one hair salon charge $55 for a haircut, while another charges $45? Discuss their findings in class.

Evaluation

Assign and review the Section 35.2 Assessment.

Technology Resources

 Assessment Resources
Go to the *Marketing Essentials* Web site (**www.marketing.glencoe.com**) for resources to teach and assess occupation-specific vocabulary.

CLOSE

Section Wrap-Up

Have students write a 50- to 100-word summary that tells the content of the organization and marketing section of a business plan.

Planning for a service business requires that you develop a plan that addresses how, when, and who will provide the service to your customers. State the services provided by your competitors, then describe the additional services you will provide, and estimate their costs.

■ Proposed Marketing Plan

At this point in your business plan, you have selected your business organization, identified your staffing needs, and detailed your goods and services policies. You are now ready to develop your marketing policies—that is, the way you will price and promote your product. These two aspects are vitally important because they can make or break your customer relations. The promotional activities get your business's name out there, and the appropriate price will ensure a profit for your business.

PRICING POLICIES As you learned in Unit 8, pricing is a vitally important aspect of running a successful business. You must be able to set a price high enough to cover your costs and make a profit, but competitive enough to attract customers. Your business plan must show your pricing policies.

The three main factors in reviewing pricing policies are cost, demand, and competition. Review Chapters 25, 26, and 27 about the important factors in pricing.

PROMOTIONAL ACTIVITIES Once pricing policies have been established, you need to describe your promotional activities. You must identify ways to reach the greatest number of potential customers in your target market. This must be done considering the most economical use of your time and money.

The simplest method of promoting your business is by providing top quality products and services to your customers. Satisfied customers generate word-of-mouth advertising when they pass the news on to their friends. This will attract additional customers, as people usually trust the opinions of friends.

As you may recall, a firm's promotional mix may comprise activities involving advertising, public relations, promotions, and personal selling. A business decides on the promotional mix that will be most effective in persuading potential customers (wholesalers, retailers, and consumers) to purchase and support their product.

A convincing business plan provides a rationale for your selection of activities and the costs involved. You need to present a yearlong budget for promotion, listing the types of promotional activities you intend to use and their costs in the budget. Make sure the dollar figures generated from this budget correspond to the promotional expenses noted on your income statement.

35.2 ASSESSMENT

Reviewing Key Terms and Concepts

1. What elements should be included in the proposed organization part of the business plan?
2. Why are job descriptions important?
3. What is the purpose of an organization chart?
4. What information should be included in your proposed good or service part of the business plan?
5. What items should be covered in the marketing plan for a new business?

Thinking Critically

6. How could a poorly written business plan hurt a new business venture?

Integrating Academic Skills

7. **MATH** An employee was paid $7.75 an hour and double time on Sunday. What was the total weekly wage, if the employee worked 4 hours on Sunday, 4 hours on Wednesday, $3\frac{1}{2}$ hours on Thursday, and 6 hours on Saturday?

35.2 ASSESSMENT ANSWERS

Reviewing Key Terms and Concepts
1. type of ownership, steps in establishing the business, and personnel needs
2. They determine job responsibilities by identifying requirements of job, purpose of job, qualifications, duties, equipment, and working conditions.
3. to show lines of authority and official reporting responsibilities
4. details related to a proposed product or service, manufacturing plans, inventory plans, and suppliers
5. the way you will produce and promote product

Thinking Critically
6. loss of financing for a new business

Integrating Academic Skills
7. **MATH** $166.63

Financial Aspects of the Business Plan

Financial Plan

The financial plan section shows lenders and investors what monies are needed to start and operate the business. It includes statements of personal and external sources of capital. It also shows statements of projected income and expenses expected for at least the first year of operation.

Sources of Capital

Capital means the funds needed to finance the operation of a business. The term *capital* also includes all goods used to produce other goods. In business, capital may also include owned property and cash resources. When we refer to capital in this chapter, we are talking about anything that can be converted into money.

Entrepreneurs usually need a substantial amount of capital to open a business. There are several ways to raise the capital for a new business. You can use money from personal savings or borrow money from banks, credit unions, relatives, friends, suppliers, and previous business owners.

The method you choose to raise money depends on the amount that you need. Money needed for operating expenses is usually repaid within a year. A large amount of money borrowed to build a new facility, to purchase equipment, or to start an inventory will be repaid over a longer period of time.

■ Equity Capital

Raising money from within your company or by selling part of the interest in the business is called using equity capital. The advantage of using equity capital is that you do not need to repay the money or pay interest. However, the investor becomes a co-owner in your business. The larger the amount of interest in your business you sell, the greater degree of control you lose to your investors.

Equity capital sources include personal savings, partners, and shareholders. The most common method of financing a business is using personal savings. Even though you might not want to do this, you probably cannot avoid investing all or part of your savings. As you know, starting any new business involves risk. Your prospective investors and lenders will expect you to share in that risk.

As you learned in Chapter 33, having partners is another way to raise money for your business. Partners may bring in their own money and have access to other sources. As with investors, forming

---

● What You'll Learn

- How to describe the elements found in the financial section of a business plan
- How to identify sources of equity capital
- How to identify sources of debt capital

● Why It's Important

It takes money to start and operate a business. Most entrepreneurs need to borrow money to begin business operations. Potential investors and lenders want to look at the financial estimates for a new business to ensure that their efforts will be profitable for them.

● Key Terms

- equity capital
- debt capital
- collateral
- credit union

Chapter 35 ■ *Developing A Business Plan* **651**

SECTION 35.3

FOCUS

Bell Ringer Activity

Brainstorm Have students brainstorm a list of the ways you can raise capital to start a business.

Introducing the Section

Financial Aspects of the Business Plan Review students' answers from the Bell Ringer Activity. It is often said that the financial section is the heart of a business plan. While a lender may only skim through the prior two sections, he or she will probably read every word of the financial section.

Explain to students that your financial data gives you and your lenders and investors the "big picture." It shows that the money put into the business will yield a profitable return. Thus, it's essential that your financial picture is in sharp focus.

TEACH

Technology Resources

PowerPoint The *Marketing Essentials* PowerPoint Presentation CD-ROM provides visual lecture aids for every chapter section.

Classroom Resources

For the Teacher
- Teacher Editions for all workbooks
- Assessment Package
- PowerPoint Presentation Software
- Interactive Lesson Planner
- ILP Block Scheduling, p. 11
- ILP Lesson Plans, p. 75
- ILP Internet Resources, p. 89

ILP *BusinessWeek* Case Studies, p. 219
ILP Marketing Career Portfolio, p. 41
- *Marketing Essentials* Web site (**www.marketing.glencoe.com**)

For the Student
- Student Activity Workbook, p. 307
- Marketing Math Workbook, p. 111

- Marketing Research Project Workbook
- ILP School-to-Work Activity Workbook, p. 143
- Virtual Business simulation
- *Marketing Essentials* Web site (**www.marketing.glencoe.com**)

ILP These resources are available in print and on the Interactive Lesson Planner (ILP)

651

Concept Development

1. Read Section 35.3 with students.
2. Have students read aloud the Case Study on page 653 and review the answers in class.
3. Have a loan officer from a local lending institution speak about obtaining financing for a business start-up. Ask this person to bring to class copies of loan applications so students can become familiar with the terminology and documentation necessary to begin the loan application process.

Discussion Starter

Business Planning Ask students: If you were an investor who was asked to put money into a business that had no business plan, what factors would determine whether or not you would do it? *(Possibilities include: whether the potential owner is starting a brand new business or buying an existing business; if the latter, whether or not the existing business is successful; the potential owner's experience with the type of business; and local market needs for the business.)*

Thinking Critically

Non-Bank Forms of Financing In a 1999 Levi Institute Survey of Small Business, 20 percent of the small companies surveyed relied on a variety of non-bank forms of financing. Ask students if they think state economic development agencies should use public dollars to create economic development loans for small business. What are the pros and cons? *(A pro is: New business expansions create jobs and help the economy; cons are: government is using public tax dollars and public employees to aid private businesses.)*

■ **Meeting with the Owners** Issuing stock can raise equity capital. *What is the principal disadvantage of selling stock to raise equity?*

a partnership will lessen your degree of ownership, and you may have to share control of the business.

You may sell stock to shareholders as a way of raising capital—this is known as forming a corporation. As you learned in Chapter 33, to operate as a corporation, you'll need to incorporate and obtain a charter. Each shareholder in a corporation has limited liability or responsibility for debt; therefore a corporation can raise large amounts of money from its shareholders. Shareholders influence general corporate policy decisions, but as long as you hold a majority of the shares, you control the corporation's daily activities.

■ Debt Capital

Raising funds by borrowing money that will be repaid later is called using debt capital. Debt capital can work to your advantage because borrowing money and repaying it builds your credit standing. Good credit standing makes it easier for you to borrow money in the future. While you must pay interest when you repay your loan, the interest you pay is a tax-deductible business expense. In addition, if you raise money by borrowing it, no ownership passes to the lender.

There is a major disadvantage to debt capital. If you cannot pay back your debt, you could be forced into bankruptcy. Investors or co-owners may not force bankruptcy; they might instead insist on telling you how to run the business. Some debt capital sources include banks, credit unions, the Small Business Administration, friends, relatives, suppliers, and previous business owners.

BANKS Commercial banks are the most numerous and widespread lending agencies in the United States. They are one of most common sources of business financing. They know their local area and local economy well and offer a number of different loans and services on competitive and government-regulated terms. A 1998 study of small owners and midsize businesses indicated that 45 percent of the businesses surveyed used commercial bank loans to finance their companies.

Banks evaluate potential borrowers on criteria called the six Cs of credit. The six Cs are made up of *capital, collateral, capability* and *character,* and *coverage* and *circumstances.*

How much of your own money, or *capital,* is to be invested in your new business? Banks, like other potential investors, will want to know how much capital you are willing to invest into your new venture.

What assets (things of monetary value) can be used as collateral for a loan? Collateral is something of value that a borrower pledges to a lender to ensure repayment of a loan. Some examples of collateral are jewelry, vehicles, bonds, stocks, machinery, the cash value of insurance policies, and real estate. Some businesses may use accounts receivable, which is the sum of money owed to a business by its customers, as collateral. Lenders will usually require the value of the collateral to be greater than the amount of the loan.

Some banks will require a guarantee of personal assets (in effect, a promise that you have the assets you claim to have) and a pledge that you will repay the loan. Banks want to know that your loan will be repaid, even if your business fails.

A résumé of your previous training and related work experience, including professional and personal references, will answer questions about your *capability* and *character.* Your personal credit history will also be reviewed to see if you regularly pay your bills on time.

CAPTION ANSWER
Meeting with the Owners The principal disadvantage is that there could be the potential loss of control in the management of the business.

Case Study

Seeing Red!

How do you get rid of red-eye? Here's a hint: You won't need eye drops! The answer is no riddle to the Private Label Products Company of New Jersey. The company creates unique and creative uses for existing products—pens and markers. Their first products were red-eye retouching pens used to "clean up" photographs. Specialty camera and photography shops originally sold the red-eye pens in stores for $12.95.

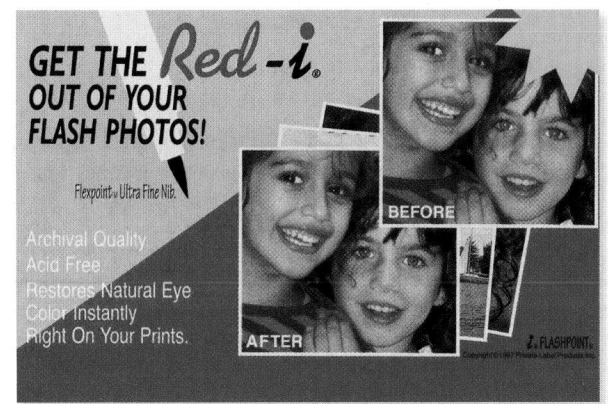

After realizing that distributors were making the profit, co-owners Jim Michael and David Naor decided to mass market the pens. The company began to produce and package the pens for the consumer market. The company targeted supermarkets and drugstores first because 60% of photo developing is done there. The company's first big order came from a Walgreen manager for 60,000 pens.

The pens are now available through the CVS and Walgreen chains and retail at about half of the original price. Increased volume allows the company to reduce the product price and make more money.

The company has expanded on the uses for its pens and markers, including surgical markers for marking skin during a surgery; invisible inks for security that are readable under ultraviolet light; fabric pens to permanently mark laundry; and food coloring markers for writing on cookies, pastries, and other edible products. The Private Label Products Company relies on creativity to market existing products for a new and ever-changing marketplace.

Case Study Review

1. Why is creativity an important ingredient for most new businesses?
2. What risks did the company's co-owners take to establish the business?

A MATTER OF ETHICS

3. Was it ethical for specialty photo stores to sell the red-eye pen for $12.95 when chain stores now sell it for approximately half of the original price? Why or why not?

SECTION 35.3

Independent Practice

Research and Report Use the Internet to obtain SBA copies of the *Business Plan for Retailers,* the *Business Plan for Small Manufacturers,* and the *Business Plan for Home-Based Businesses.* Give each student a copy of each business plan. Have each student compare and contrast these plans, and write a report on the information.

ASSESS

Reteaching

1. **Vocabulary** Assign and review the vocabulary terms for this section.
2. **Fact and Idea** Assign and review Fact and Idea Review questions 8–10 from the Chapter Assessment.

Banks will want to know the amount of insurance *coverage* that you carry and the general *circumstances* of your business. This is outlined in the description and analysis section of your business plan.

CREDIT UNIONS A **credit union** is a cooperative association formed by labor unions or groups of employees for the benefit of its members. Credit unions often charge lower interest rates on loans than banks do. To borrow money from a credit union, however, you must be a member. Check with your parents, guardians, and relatives to determine your eligibility, since credit unions often accept memberships for relatives. Credit unions also use the six Cs of credit to determine if they will accept your loan application.

Chapter 35 ■ *Developing A Business Plan* **653**

Case Study Review Answers

Seeing Red!

1. Many new businesses are really only selling existing products and services in new and unique ways that appeal to customers.
2. They negotiated for a loan that they may not have been able to repay. One co-owner sold his trucking business and gave up a secure job.

A MATTER OF ETHICS

3. Answers will vary, but it was probably ethical. The distribution costs and required profit margins are different for specialty stores versus chains.

Enrichment

1. **Review** Assign and review the Chapter 35 activities in the Student Activity Workbook.
2. **Review** Assign and review the appropriate Thinking Critically questions from the Chapter Assessment.
3. **Review** Assign and review the following Chapter Assessment activities: Building Workplace Skills, Applying Marketing Concepts, Linking School to Work, The DECA Connection Role Play, and Internet Connection.
4. **Research and Write** Have students contact a small business owner and review his or her business plan. Have students report on: difficulties creating the plan; how they were overcome; and how the plan helps to find investors.

Evaluation

Assign and review the Section 35.3 Assessment.

Technology Resources

Assessment Resources
Go to the *Marketing Essentials* Web site (**www.marketing.glencoe. com**) for resources to teach and assess occupation-specific vocabulary.

CLOSE

Section Wrap-Up

Have students write a 50-word summary of the financial section of a business plan.

CAPTION ANSWER
A Popular Funding Source
Bankers evaluate borrowers based on the six Cs of credit: capital, collateral, capability, character, coverage, and circumstances.

654

FRIENDS AND RELATIVES Many people begin their businesses with funds borrowed from relatives and friends. While this may seem like the most convenient option, you should be cautious about doing this. Remember the saying that two of the quickest ways to lose friends are to lend them money or to borrow money from them.

When borrowing money from family or friends, put all agreements in writing to avoid future problems and misunderstandings. Identify the period of the loan, any interest to be paid, and your payment schedule. It is essential to remember that even if you are borrowing money from a personal friend or family member, it is still a business situation.

SUPPLIERS AND PREVIOUS OWNERS Some suppliers may provide you with a low-interest loan to purchase inventory, furniture, fixtures, and equipment on a delayed payment basis. This method of raising capital can improve your credit rating and stretch available cash. Remember, the interest on loan payments is a tax-deductible business expense.

When purchasing an existing business, consider the previous owner as a potential source of capital. Many sole proprietors want to see their businesses continue after their retirement. They may be willing to provide you with a loan and a favorable repayment plan to get you started. The rates on a loan negotiated in this manner are often lower than those from a bank or credit union.

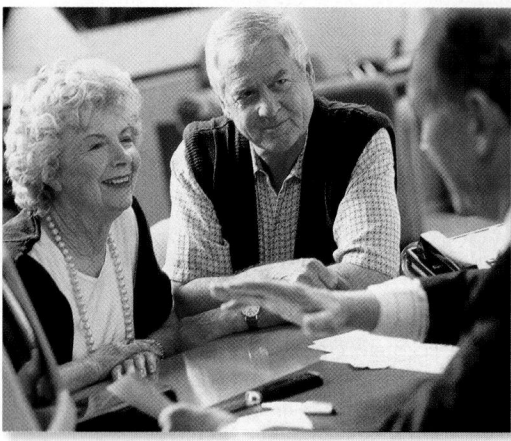

■ **A Popular Funding Source** Banks are a common source of business financing. *What criteria do banks use to evaluate borrowers?*

Financial Statements

After you have identified your source or sources of capital, the last part of your business plan is to develop your financial statements. Your financial statements display your business's projected income and expenses and help persuade investors to loan you money. These financial statements and the math needed to complete them will be discussed in Chapter 36.

35.3 ASSESSMENT

Reviewing Key Terms and Concepts

1. Name the two major parts in the financial section of a business plan.
2. Identify three main sources of equity capital.
3. How can a corporation raise capital?
4. What are the main sources of debt capital?
5. What are the six Cs of credit?

Thinking Critically

6. What factors would you consider in selecting a lender for a business?

Integrating Academic Skills

7. **TECHNOLOGY** Interview a small business owner about a new technological process or piece of equipment that is used in his or her business today, but was not available when the business was first started. Write a 100-word report on your findings.

35.3 ASSESSMENT ANSWERS

Reviewing Key Terms and Concepts

1. sources of capital and projected income and expenses
2. personal savings, partners, and shareholders
3. It can sell shares of stock in the company.
4. banks, credit unions, relatives and friends, suppliers, and previous owners
5. capital, collateral, capability, character, coverage, and circumstances

Thinking Critically

6. Factors to consider include: terms of the loan; reputation of the lender; ability to provide technical assistance; reputation for service; locations; and ability to provide related business services.

Integrating Academic Skills

7. **TECHNOLOGY** Reports will vary.

Careers in Marketing

FINANCIAL SERVICES

Trudy Brame
Bank Teller
ALL First Bank

What is your key to success?

"The key to success is ensuring that the customers stay happy and feel satisfied with the bank. We try to provide a friendly atmosphere—we want our customers to leave feeling satisfied with the services that we have provided. We must provide courteous, prompt, and efficient customer service."

What kind of training did you have?

"My company provides classroom training for customer service representatives. We aren't just tellers—we are expected to be more than that. The course lasts two weeks and teaches important skills for banking."

What kind of training would you suggest for students?

"On-the-job training in retail and cash handling are very important skills. Classes in marketing, business math, data processing, and accounting are recommended for high school or college course work."

What skills are most important?

"People skills are extremely important—it is very important to establish rapport with every customer. The technical skills of banking are also important—the teller must have not only an aptitude with the computer and math, but also a familiarity with our product. We are a service provider, offering banking products and packages to customers. I need to be able to answer questions about accounts, loan options, funds, investments, bonds, and money markets, as well as questions about overdraft, withdrawals, and deposits. After banking hours, we sort though the activity of the accounts that day."

Thinking Critically
How is technology affecting the banking industry?

Career Facts

Education and Training: A high school diploma, with classes in marketing, business math, data processing, and accounting, is usually required to become a bank teller. Similar course work at a community college provides good preparation. Jobs that require cash handling skills and customer service skills are excellent preparation for bank teller positions.

Aptitudes, Abilities, and Skills: Good arithmetic skills, organizational skills, basic clerical skills, ability to learn and apply the required banking standards, and good communication skills, both written and verbal, are essential.

Career Outlook: Growth is expected to be lower than average through the year 2006. Competition for bank teller positions is generally keen.

Career Path: A bank teller is often an entry-level position, which can lead to top positions in banking. Tellers may advance to supervisory positions such as bank operations officer and loan officer or to management training programs.

Careers in Marketing

Ask a student to read the Careers in Marketing feature aloud to the class. Discuss the skills and aptitudes required for a career in financial services. Ask students whether they think they would like or dislike a career in financial services. Discuss the pros and cons of such a career.

Thinking Critically Answer
The rise of online banking, direct deposit, and ATM machines may decrease the need for bank tellers.

 Guest Speakers
Invite a bank teller to class to discuss his/her job.

Exploring Careers

Entrepreneurial Planning
1. Explain to students that good planning is one of the most important factors in becoming a successful entrepreneur or small-business owner.
2. Read to students these basic questions entrepreneurs should answer and have them answer in discussion.
   1) What product will you sell, or what service will you provide?
   2) Where do you want to locate your business?
   3) Where will you get the money?
   4) What legal form of business organization will you use?
   5) How will you decide who your customer is?
   6) How will you sell your product or service?
   7) How many people will you need to hire?
   8) What kind of ratio of profit to cost will you need?
   9) How will you advertise?
   10) How will you keep records and calculate profits?

Lifelong Learning

Developing a Business Plan
Due to the importance of the business plan, students should do further study in this area of marketing. Business magazines and books devoted to the subject, including *Inc.* magazine's *How to Write a Successful Business Plan*, are good supplements. Taking courses on writing a business plan would be valuable.

Meeting Individual Needs

Students with Learning Disabilities
Students with learning disabilities may require additional assistance completing some of the activities in this chapter. Developing a business plan can be complex and requires analytical ability and methodical work. Divide the task into steps and provide additional assistance as needed. Peer assistance and adult mentors can offer support.

Chapter 35 ASSESSMENT

Vocabulary Review

Sentences will vary. See Glossary for definitions.

Fact and Idea Review

1. It identifies your personal education, strengths, weaknesses, and a plan for personal development.
2. It is the geographical area from which a business draws its customers. It is important to analyze your trading area because it will help you to identify the competition and any trends that will have an impact on your business.
3. It is personal income minus taxes. You need to know if the area has enough customers with enough buying income to support your proposed business.
4. Sources of research can include the Internet, *Yellow Pages*, annual reports, trade associations, local Chamber of Commerce, and business publications.
5. The needs and wants of different groups of potential buyers must be addressed differently.
6. Potential investors need to know that you can identify the essential jobs your business will need in order to run properly.
7. Provide quality goods and services that keep customers coming back and recommending your business to friends.
8. Debt capital is money raised from lenders while equity capital is money raised by selling part of the business.
9. use of personal savings
10. It is a cooperative association for the benefit of its members that often charges lower interest rates than other lending organizations.

VOCABULARY REVIEW

Use each of the following terms in a sentence.

- business plan
- business philosophy
- trading area
- buying behavior
- job descriptions
- organization chart
- equity capital
- debt capital
- collateral
- credit union

FACT AND IDEA REVIEW

1. Why is self-analysis critical in a business plan? (35.1)
2. What is a trading area? Why is an analysis of the trading area important in a business plan? (35.1)
3. What is disposable income? Why is it important to know the disposable income of potential customers? (35.1)
4. How can an entrepreneur research existing competition for a proposed product? (35.1)
5. Why is the identification of your target market essential to your business plan? (35.1)
6. Why is planning for personnel needs important for a new business? (35.2)
7. What is the simplest method to promote a business? (35.2)
8. What is the difference between debt capital and equity capital? (35.3)
9. What is the most common method of financing a business? (35.3)
10. Why is a credit union a good source of debt capital for a new business owner? (35.3)

THINKING CRITICALLY

1. "Employees are the most valued asset to a small business." Do you agree or disagree with this statement? Explain your answer.
2. How can you determine whether there is a need for a product or service?
3. How would you determine which job positions you need to fill in your new business?
4. Why would you have an accountant, attorney, or business advisor assist you in establishing your business?
5. "While debt capital can work to your advantage when establishing a business, there are many disadvantages if you cannot pay back your debt. Bankruptcy is one of these disadvantages, however it may not be the worst one." Explain what this statement means. Decide whether you agree or disagree with this idea.

BUILDING WORKPLACE SKILLS

1. **Political Science** Political and legal considerations affect all types of businesses. Prepare a 250-word paper on the reasons businesses establish and support political action committees (PACs).
2. **Technology** In 2000, over 123 million Americans had Internet access at home. Write a 250-word report on the impact of the Internet on small businesses.

Thinking Critically

1. Students should explain that the success of a business depends on employee performance.
2. Answers will vary. Point out that entrepreneurs determine a need for a good or service by thoroughly studying the market.
3. A thorough analysis should be done regarding the tasks that must be done and decisions made by the owner of how many of those tasks he or she can perform.
4. They can help to insure that the business will be in compliance with all local, state, and federal laws, rules and regulations.
5. While some investors or co-owners may not force bankruptcy, they may insist on telling the owner how to run the business.

Building Workplace Skills

1. Papers will vary.
2. Reports will vary.

APPLYING MARKETING CONCEPTS

1. **Researching New Business Ventures** Use business magazines to research a successful new business venture. Develop a 150-word report or an article on a word processing program.

2. **Finding SBA Resources** Find the U.S. Small Business Administration (SBA) Web site. Summarize at least five resources that are available through the SBA for new business start-ups in a 150-word report.

3. **Developing a Business Plan** Use word processing software to begin developing a business plan using instructor or DECA guidelines. Describe the type of business, the product/service involved, appealing factors about the business, and the factors you think will make it successful. Describe your aspirations and career objectives, educational experiences, and related work experiences. Finally, make a chart of your competitors' strengths and weaknesses.

4. **Establishing Pricing Strategies** Continue with the business plan that you created in the previous activity. Establish pricing policies and a one-year promotional plan for your business. The plan should contain a budget, selection of media, and a plan to evaluate its effectiveness. List special promotional events that would be conducted for each month of the year for your business.

LINKING SCHOOL TO WORK

Basic Writing and Information Skills Investigate a product line available at your place of employment or a local business. Compare the pricing policies used for selected items in the product line. Use word processing software to create a 100-word report on your findings.

THE **DECA** CONNECTION

Role Play: Restaurant Employee

Situation You are to assume the role of an employee at a restaurant. A co-worker (judge) plans to establish his own quick-serve restaurant. He believes that he will be successful because there is an available location and he is a good cook. He thinks he will have no trouble obtaining a loan because his proposed business has so much potential. He does not believe that it will be necessary to develop a business plan.

Activity Your task is to explain the importance of a business plan and convince your co-worker to develop one.

Evaluation You will be evaluated on how well you meet the following performance indicators:
• Explain the nature of business plans
• Develop a business plan
• Develop company objectives
• Develop strategies to achieve company goals
• Explain external planning considerations

*inter*NET CONNECTION

Learning From the Pros
The Senior Corps of Retired Executives (SCORE) is a voluntary group of counselors that helps America's small businesses. SCORE provides many resources to help individuals write business plans.

Connect
• Locate the SCORE Web site and find the address of the SCORE office nearest to your school.
• List at least three resources available from SCORE to help you develop a comprehensive business plan.

THE **DECA** CONNECTION

Students should be evaluated on the performance indicators noted in the Role Play.
• For another DECA Role Play go to the *Student Activity Workbook,* p. 307.
• For more in-depth Role Play practice, refer to DECA's *Essential Competitive Events Handbook.* To order, contact DECA at www.deca.org.

*inter*NET CONNECTION
Answers will vary.

Mini Quiz
Administer the Mini Quiz orally. For an expanded chapter quiz, go to page 207 of the *Reproducible Tests* book.

1. A proposal that describes every part of a new business to an investor is called a(n) business plan.
2. A business philosophy tells how an individual thinks a business should run and demonstrates an understanding of its role in the marketplace.
3. The geographical area from which a business draws its customers is known as its trading area.
4. Written statements about the requirements of a particular job are known as job descriptions.
5. A graphic representation of jobs and functions in a business is called a(n) organization chart.

Applying Marketing Concepts
1. Reports will vary.
2. Reports will vary.
3. Business plans will vary.
4. Pricing and promotion strategies will vary.

Linking School to Work
Reports will vary depending on the product line.

GO TO
1. **Assessment** Have students complete the Reproducible Test for Chapter 35 or construct your own tests using the ExamView software.
2. **Enrichment** Have students complete the corresponding activities in the following workbooks:
• *Marketing Math Workbook,* p. 111

657

Chapter Overview

This chapter tells how to identify and plan for the capital needs of a proposed business by developing a financial section to a business plan. It discusses estimating start-up costs and the importance of a personal financial statement. It explains the need for and preparation of an income statement, balance sheet, and cash flow statement.

 Springboard

Brainstorm Discuss the things for which a person is financially responsible when living on his or her own. Then have students list the costs involved in maintaining a business. *(Examples are rent, utilities, and buying supplies.)* Have students brainstorm some ways to achieve good financial planning. Meeting both personal and business financial needs takes good financial planning.

Prereading

List the section objectives to discuss with students. Have students skim the chapter, looking at the pictures, reading the captions, and noting the heads. Ask questions to ensure that the students have a minimal understanding of the chapter structure.

Preteaching Marketing Vocabulary

Have students write each bold-faced term in the chapter and, based on each definition, generate a personal symbol for the term. Review the vocabulary definitions before reading the chapter and have several students share their personal symbols for each term.

Marketing: What It Takes

Answer Having a working prototype is a good first step, but you need to convince a lender that your idea can make a profit. You must develop a business plan.

Chapter 36

Financing the Business

Marketing: What It Takes

Digging Up Some Cash

You and your friends in the manufacturing technology program have designed and built a prototype for a new and improved two-wheeled personal scooter. Your personal scooter is fun to use, and it can also transport an individual easily in crowded urban areas. You have determined that you will form a partnership with your friends and start a business. You currently have a facility to manufacture the units, but you need additional capital to purchase equipment, materials, supplies, and pay for operating expenses.

WHAT WILL YOU DO?
What will it take to convince a lender to provide the required capital for your new business?

THE DECA CONNECTION **ADVISOR CORNER**

Team Up for Charity Team up with a local charity and conduct a local fund-raising event. This activity will be motivational and fun for chapter members. You may want to bring in business people from your DECA Advisory Committee to discuss the different charities in your area. Students can form committees to work with adults in getting the job done. Building on their classroom lessons, the students can provide all the public relations functions. They will see all facets of public relations as they manage accounts, write copy, produce storyboards, and do the tasks of an ad agency.

(Jamie Brace, Northeast Vo-Tech, Claremore, OK)

Preparing Financial Documents

The Financial Part of a Business Plan

A major purpose of the business plan is to put together the financial information relating to your business. This information is presented on financial documents that describe your personal financial situation, as well as the financial needs of your business. Preparing financial statements helps you determine the amount of money you need to operate the business. The process also helps you estimate how much money you may need to borrow.

When you inquire about borrowing money, the lender will want to know that you will be able to repay a loan. A lender will look at your credit history, items you own that can be sold to pay off the loan (collateral), and your prospects for business success. Your financial documents give a potential lender a picture of you and your business.

Five important financial documents are the personal financial statement, the start-up cost estimate, the income statement, the balance sheet, and the cash flow statement. In this section you will look at the first two financial statements.

The Personal Financial Statement

The **personal financial statement** is a summary of your current personal financial condition. A personal financial statement is like a snapshot of your finances. It is an important part of any loan application for a new business. It measures your financial progress to date and shows how well you have met your personal expenses in the past. It compares your *assets* to your *liabilities* at a particular point in time. An **asset** is anything of monetary value that you own. A **liability** is a debt you owe.

To develop a personal financial statement, you first list your assets. You should be realistic about the current value of your assets. For example, if you have a van worth $9,000, do not round it up to $10,000. Be sure to list all your cash assets (checking and savings accounts) and any investments (stocks, bonds, mutual funds, and retirement funds) and personal assets (furniture, cars, clothes, and home). You will need to estimate the present value for each item. A lender will look for assets that you can sell to pay off the business loan if your business does not do as well as expected.

Next, list your debts, including your charge accounts, mortgage balance, and school and automobile loans. Add all your assets and all your debts to find a total for each. Then calculate your personal

What You'll Learn
- The purpose of preparing financial documents
- How to develop a personal financial statement
- How to determine start-up costs for a business

Why It's Important
The most common reason for writing a business plan is to obtain financing for a business. In order to get the money you will need to start your business, you will need to prepare financial statements.

Key Terms
- personal financial statement
- asset
- liability
- start-up costs

Technology Resources

PowerPoint The *Marketing Essentials* PowerPoint Presentation CD-ROM provides visual lecture aids for every chapter section.

Concept Development

1. Read Section 36.1 with students.
2. Invite a representative from a credit reporting or lending agency to discuss credit reports and the importance of maintaining good credit. Ask the speaker to bring sample credit reports to use as visual aids so students understand how to read them. Also have the speaker discuss how erroneous reporting on credit reports can be corrected.

Discussion Starter

Start-Up Costs Have students generate a list of the one-time start-up costs and the continuing costs of running your school store. *(Answers will vary. Possible one-time costs include renovation of and fixtures for an existing space in your school. Continuing costs include ongoing purchase of inventory and fixtures, purchase of supplies, repairs, etc.)*

If you do not have a school store, choose a local business with which all students are familiar and have them generate a list of what they think were its start-up costs and what are now its continuing costs.

FIGURE 36-1 ANSWER
Personal Financial Statement
$87,375 (Net worth is calculated by subtracting liabilities from your assets. $135,750 - $48,375 = $87,375)

---

net worth by subtracting your debts from your assets. Figure 36-1 shows an example of a personal financial statement.

Your personal financial statement will be one aspect used to determine whether you and your business are a good credit risk. In addition, a lender will require a copy of your personal tax returns. Your tax returns will show how you have earned money in the past. A credit report will also be requested to show how well you have paid off debts in the past. If you plan to continue working at another job, the lender will be interested in whether that income can support your personal expenses until your new business becomes profitable.

FIGURE 36-1

Personal Financial Statement

August, 20--

Assets		
Cash	$	500.00
Savings accounts		1,500.00
Stocks, bonds, other securities		750.00
Life insurance cash value		0.00
Auto (2000 van)		18,000.00
Real estate (residence)		75,000.00
Vested pension plan		25,000.00
Other assets (lakefront property)		15,000.00
TOTAL ASSETS	$	135,750.00
Liabilities		
Accounts payable (credit cards)		1,875.00
Contracts payable		0.00
Notes payable (mortgage)		28,500.00
Taxes payable		2,500.00
Real estate loans		0.00
Other liabilities (2000 van)		15,000.00
TOTAL LIABILITIES	$	47,875.00
TOTAL ASSETS	$	135,750.00
TOTAL LIABILITIES	$	47,875.00
NET WORTH	$	87,875.00

■ **Personal Financial Statement** A personal financial statement shows your financial condition to date. *Based upon the figures shown here, what is your total net worth? How is net worth calculated?*

GREAT IDEAS from the Marketing Classroom

Roger Cartee
North Country Career Center
Newport, VT

After determining some of the career paths that my senior students might take, I cluster students with related career paths into groups of three or four. Then, I invite local retailers and businesspeople into the class and match them up as guest presenters to each cluster of students. They meet with their individual groups for about 30 minutes and focus on topics related to those students' interests. After each group's discussions are completed, we meet as a large group for a panel discussion with our professional guests serving as the panelists. This allows students to ask questions that might relate to all the groups while allowing contact between all of our students and invited guests.

Estimating Start-up Costs

Before starting your business, you need to know how much it will cost you. Start-up costs are a projection of how much money you will need for your first year of operation. You also need an estimate of operating costs after the first year.

Assessing these start-up costs prior to getting involved in a project protects you as you start your business. You will need to spend money on goods and services ranging from furniture to advertising. Some examples of these costs are listed in Figure 36-2. As you can see, these costs vary depending on the type of business.

FIGURE 36-2

Start-Up Costs

Type of Costs	Type of Business			
	Manufacturing	Retail	Wholesale	Service
Deposits (rents, utilities, telephone)	$7,500–$20,300	$3,900–$35,300	$7,400–$17,700	$4,200–$14,000
Furniture and Equipment	$20,100–$42,000	$21,300–$42,300	$22,500–$54,900	$19,700–$54,100
Machinery and Equipment	$10,000–$60,000	$5,000–$32,500	$19,900–$33,900	———
Transportation Equipment	$32,000–$45,000	$32,000–$45,000	$32,000–$45,000	———
Building Improvements	$11,300–$42,000	$11,300–$52,500	$15,000–$30,000	$15,000–$60,000
Professional Fees	$1,500–$4,000	$1,500–$4,000	$1,500–$4,000	$1,500–$4,000
Advertising	$3,000–$10,000	$10,000–$15,000	$3,000–$10,000	$3,000–$10,000
Working Capital	$9,900–$45,000	$3,800–$93,700	$25,200–$75,000	$9,900–$35,100
Inventory	$13,000–$57,500	$35,000–$157,500	$23,000–$122,500	———
Totals	$108,300–$325,800	$123,800–$477,800	$149,500–$393,000	$53,300–$177,200

■ **Start-up Costs** Start-up costs vary depending on the type of business. *Why is less money generally needed to establish a service business than to establish a manufacturing, franchise, retail, or wholesale business?*

FIGURE 36-2 ANSWER
Start-Up Costs Service businesses often rely primarily on the managerial and technical skills of the business owner. The investment in raw materials, inventory, and merchandise for sale is less than for other businesses.

More About . . .

Start-up Costs
Many business consultants advise new businesses for a fee. Gaining practical advice and know-how from a consultant or from an accountant who works with similar businesses could actually save money. Many accountants will offer a free consultation to a new business owner to answer questions regarding start-up costs.

Thinking Critically

1. **Collateral** Ask students why banks require collateral to be worth more than the amount of the loan, and why lenders prefer to be repaid rather than cashing in on collateral. (*If the lender is forced to sell the collateral due to borrower default, the lender probably won't realize full value.*)
2. **Collateral** Ask students why a bank would require a borrower to insure property that the bank would hold as collateral. (*In case of the property's damage or loss, the insurance company will repay the lender.*)

Cooperative Learning

Financial Statements Divide the class into 3–5 member teams. Assign each group to do research on the types of software programs used to create financial statements. Have each group give a report on the capabilities of the financial software, such as Quicken. If possible, obtain demonstration disks to demonstrate on your classroom computer(s). Impress upon students that, even if they don't start a business, they should manage their personal finances.

Independent Practice

1. **Research and Write** Have students write a 200-word paper about a successful entrepreneur and use business publications in the marketing program or school media center. Ask them to focus on how the business got started and the financial resources that the entrepreneur used to begin the business.

2. **Research and Report** If you were not able to arrange for a guest speaker from a credit company or lending agency to visit the class, assign students the task of researching what type of information is contained in a credit report.

   Students may not realize that even delinquent payments on a gasoline credit card can show up on a credit report. Also, there is the possibility that information recorded on a credit report will belong to another person with a similar name. Consumers have varying rights in different states. Have students report on the rights in your state and on the way to go about verifying the information contained in a credit report.

Start-up costs vary for each type of business, but are based on factors such as:

- *The nature of your proposed business* Manufacturing, wholesale, or retail businesses all have different needs and requirements.
- *The size of your business* Small businesses usually do not require as much money to start as big businesses.
- *The amount and kind of inventory needed* For example, it is much more costly to purchase inventory for a large supermarket than for a neighborhood convenience store.
- *The estimated time between starting the business and earning income from the first sales*
- *The operating expenses that must be paid before cash is received from sales*

Business start-up costs may be one-time costs or continuing costs. *One-time costs* are expenses that will not be repeated after you begin operating the business. Examples of one-time costs include licenses and permits, deposits for telephone installation, and charges for installation of equipment, fixtures, and machinery.

Continuing costs are operating expenses you will pay throughout the life of the business. Examples of continuing costs include payroll, monthly rent, advertising, supplies, insurance, repairs, maintenance, and taxes. Most businesses are not profitable immediately, so estimate at least three months of

continuing costs when deciding the amount of cash you will need for start-up costs.

You can find information to help you plan your financial needs from several sources. The Small Business Administration (SBA) provides information to people who want to start a new business. The SBA offers a wide variety of loan programs. These programs help small businesses borrow money at reasonable interest rates from traditional lenders. The SBA has developed a worksheet for estimating start-up costs and operating expenses for new businesses (see Figure 36-4 on page 663).

You can also get estimates of start-up costs from people who are already in a similar business or from related trade associations. State and local government agencies, such as your state department of commerce and local chamber of commerce, are also valuable sources of cost information. Better Business Bureaus and local, regional, and state business development agencies are also sources of information. Figure 36-3 details sources of financing for a start-up business.

PRACTICE 2

You have one-time costs of $18,000 and average monthly costs of $3,200. What are your total costs for the first quarter of operation? Using the same average monthly costs, what are total costs for the year?

FIGURE 36-3

Financing Sources

Primary Sources		Secondary Sources	
Long-term financing	*Short-term financing*	*Long-term financing*	*Short-term financing*
• Personal financing • Family and friends • Private Investors • Equity financing • Leasing • Credit unions • SBA LowDoc	• Personal financing • Family and friends • Credit cards • Credit unions • Trade credit • Banks • SBA Microloans • SBA LowDoc	• Business alliances • SBA regular 7(a) program • Venture capital • SBICs • State and local public financing • Franchising • Asset-based financing	• SBA CAPlines • Consumer finance companies • Commercial finance companies • State and local public financing

■ **Financing Options** There are several funding sources used to start up a business. *Why are the sources divided into primary and secondary sources?*

FIGURE 36-3 ANSWER
Financing Options Primary sources are generally easier to obtain and less complicated to obtain for new entrepreneurs. However, secondary sources are also available to new businesses but are used less frequently.

More About . . .

The SBA
The SBA does not have a grant program and does not make loans, but it does guarantee loans up to $75,000 to qualified small businesses through banks and other financial institutions. There is no stated minimum loan, but most lenders are hesitant to process loans less than $25,000.

FIGURE 36-4

Start-Up Cost Worksheet

ESTIMATED MONTHLY EXPENSES	Your estimate of monthly espenses based on sales of $_____ per year	Your estimate of how much cash you need to start your business (See column 3)	What to put in column 2. (These figures are typical for one kind of business. You will have to decide how many months to allow for your business.)
Item	Column 1	Column 2	Column 3
Salary of owner	$	$	2 times column 1
All other salaries and wages			3 times column 1
Rent			3 times column 1
Advertising			3 times column 1
Delivery expense			3 times column 1
Supplies			3 times column 1
Telephone and telegraph			3 times column 1
Other utilities			3 times column 1
Insurance			Payment required by insurance company
Taxes, including Social Security			4 times column 1
Interest			3 times column 1
Maintenance			3 times column 1
Legal and other professional fees			3 times column 1
Miscellaneous			3 times column 1
STARTING COSTS YOU ONLY HAVE TO PAY ONCE			Leave column 2 blank
Fixtures and equipment			Fill in worksheet 3 on page 12 and put the total here
Decorating and remodeling			Talk it over with a contractor
Installation of fixtures and equipment			Talk to suppliers from whom you buy these
Starting inventory			Supplies will probably help you estimate this
Deposits with public utilities			Find out from utility companies
Legal and other professional fees			Lawyer, accountant, and so on
Licenses and permits			Find out from city offices what you have to have
Advertising and promotion			Estimate what you'll use for opening
Accounts receivable			What you need in order to buy more stock until credit customers pay
Cash			For unexpected expenses or losses, special purchases, etc.
Other			Make a separate list and enter total
TOTAL ESTIMATED CASH YOU NEED TO START WITH	$	$	Add up all the numbers in column 2

■ **Start-Up Cost Worksheet** The SBA provides worksheets to assist new business owners in estimating monthly expenses. *Why is a worksheet helpful to beginning businesses?*

FIGURE 36-4 ANSWER
Start-Up Cost Worksheet A worksheet is helpful because it provides a tabular representation of continuing and one-time costs and the approximate amount of expense for each, as well as the total estimated cash needed to start a business.

SECTION 36.1

Individualized Practice

Math Skills

L1 Give students the following scenario: You estimate that your business start-up costs will be $10,200. You have saved $8,400.

(a) What percentage of the total amount do you have? *(82%. $8,400 ÷ $10,200 = .82 = 82%)*

(b) What percentage of the total amount do you need? *(18%. $10,200 − $8,400 = $1,800. $1,800 ÷ $10,200 = 0.1766 or .18. Or, 1.00 − .82 = .18 = 18%)*

L2 Ask students to complete the following:

(a) Subtract the decimal numbers you calculated for the L1a and L1b activities above. What is your answer? *(.64. .82 − .18 5 = .64)*

(b) Multiply the decimal numbers you calculated for the L1a and L1b activities above. What is your answer? *(0.1476. .82 x .18 5 = 0.1476)*

(c) Divide your answer for the L1a activity by your answer for the L1b activity. Round your answer to the hundredth. *(4.56. .82 ÷ .18 = 4.55555 or 4.56)*

L3 Tell students the following: You refigured your business start-up costs and determined that you will need about 15 percent more than the amount you originally anticipated, which was $10,200. How much money will you need altogether to start your business? Write your answer in words. *(Eleven Thousand Seven Hundred Thirty Dollars. $10,200 x .15 = $1,530. $10,200 + $1,530 = $11,730)*

Reteaching

1. **Vocabulary** Assign and review the vocabulary terms for this section.
2. **Fact and Idea** Assign and review Fact and Idea Review questions 1–3 from the Chapter Assessment.

Enrichment

1. **Review** Assign and review the appropriate Thinking Critically questions from the Chapter Assessment.
2. **Extend** Assign and review the corresponding activities from *BusinessWeek Case Studies, Internet Resources,* and the *School-to-Work Activity Workbook.* **ILP**
3. **List and Calculate** Have students develop a personal financial statement, listing their assets and their liabilities. If they don't actually know the value of some of their personal belongings (for example, jewelry), have them make rough estimates. Students may use **Figure 36-1** on page 660 in the text as a model for their own statement. Be sure each student knows his or her own net worth, but they need not share this information.

    Remind students that the purpose of this exercise is to determine credit worthiness, and that students in general do not qualify for large loans because they do not own anything of value, such as real estate, stocks, bonds, and securities, nor do they typically have large savings accounts. They may need to work for a while to acquire the assets that would convince a bank to loan them money.

■ Personal Costs

Unless you are starting your new business while still working at another job, you will need money to live on during the start-up phase. Your *personal costs* are those expenses that are necessary for you to live. You will need to project your monthly living expenses and household cash needs for at least the first year of business. When starting a new business, you may be able to meet your personal expenses by working at another job or by relying on a spouse's income.

You may choose not to work outside your business or to have any other source of income, but you must plan to have enough cash on hand to pay your personal expenses. Some experts suggest that you have enough start-up capital available to pay for up to six months of living expenses.

Set aside the money for living expenses in a savings account. Do not use the money for any other purpose. This fund will help you get through the start-up period. The chart in Figure 36-5 on page 665 will help you estimate how much money you should have in this account. Figure 36-5 illustrates a cost-of-living budget for an average month. The table includes regular monthly payments, household operating expenses, food expenses, personal expenses, and tax expenses. Under each category is a breakdown of estimated and actual costs.

Virtual Banking

New breeds of Internet banking companies such as Wingspan have sprung up to meet the demands of businesses. Wingspan refers to themselves as more than a bank, but more as a "one-stop resource" for personal finance. It offers services such as checking and saving accounts, online bill payment, credit cards, ATM locations, mortgage loans, research resources, and financial tools. Without the traditional cost of increased payroll and rent associated with established brick-and-mortar banks, virtual banks offer greatly reduced rates for loans and higher rates for deposit interest.

Thinking Critically
What might an online bank not offer that a traditional brick-and-mortar bank does?

The bottom right hand corner of the chart shows a summary of each category and ends with a monthly total.

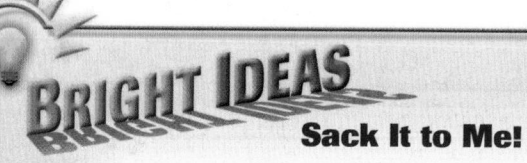

Sack It to Me!

Kicking around beans in a sack? The idea is not new, as team sports using bean sacks can be traced back to ancient times. Countries including China and Thailand have historical documentation showing the existence of recreational games very similar to soccer. In 1972, John Stalberger and Mike Marshall of Oregon City, Oregon, created a new version of an old game. Marshall designed a hand-made beanbag that he enjoyed kicking around. Stalberger, recovering from knee surgery, was looking for a way to exercise his knees. Together, they called the new game "Hackin' the Sack." They marketed the game under their new catchy trademark—Hacky Sack. Stalberger went on to form the National Hacky Sack Association and later sold the rights to Kransco, under the Wham-O label.

Thinking Creatively
You need financing to begin a business. Research typical means of financing today. What are the obstacles? What are some creative means of financing?

Virtual Banking
Answer Online banks are not able to offer personalized service and branch locations.

Answer Answers will vary depending on type of financing researched.

FIGURE 36-5

Estimating Personal Living Expenses

Cost-of-Living Budget for an Average Month
Based on an Average Income of $38,000

Regular Monthly Payments		Personal Expenses	
Rent or mortgage (including taxes)	$ 550.00	Clothing, cleaning, laundry	110.00
		Medications	10.00
Cars (including insurance)	350.00	Doctors and dentists	50.00
Appliances/TV	0.00	Education	0.00
Home improvement loan	200.00	Dues	10.00
Personal loan	55.00	Gifts and contributions	40.00
Health plan	50.00	Travel	50.00
Life insurance premiums	15.00	Newspapers, magazines, books	10.00
Other insurance premiums	20.00	Auto upkeep, gas, and parking	50.00
Miscellaneous (bank account service fees)	10.00	Spending money, allowances	20.00
		TOTAL	**$ 350.00**
TOTAL	**$ 1,250.00**	**Tax Expenses**	
Household Operating Expenses		Federal and state income taxes	175.00
Telephone	50.00	Personal property taxes	350.00
Gas and electricity	120.00	Other taxes	25.00
Water and garbage	30.00	**TOTAL**	**$ 550.00**
Other household expenses repairs, maintenance	20.00	**BUDGET SUMMARY**	
		Regulary Monthly Payments	1,250.00
TOTAL	**$ 220.00**	Household Operating Expenses	220.00
		Food Expenses	560.00
Food Expenses		Personal Expenses	350.00
Food—at home	500.00	Tax Expenses	550.00
Food—away from home	60.00		
TOTAL	**$ 560.00**	**MONTHLY TOTAL**	**$ _____**

■ **Estimating Personal Living Expenses** This form will help you to estimate how much you need for your living expenses when you start your business. *Based upon the figures shown here, what is your monthly total for cost-of-living expenses?*

36.1 ASSESSMENT

Reviewing Key Terms and Concepts

1. Why is financial information included as part of a business plan?

2. What items should be identified on a personal financial statement?

3. What is the difference between an asset and a liability?

4. What are start-up costs?

5. What is the difference between one-time costs and continuing costs?

Thinking Critically

6. Why are friends and family usually consulted first when looking for loans?

Integrating Academic Skills

7. **COMMUNICATION** Use a word processing program to write a business letter to your department of commerce requesting general information about the steps involved with starting a business in your state.

36.1 ASSESSMENT ANSWERS

Reviewing Key Terms and Concepts

1. It helps determine how the business will operate financially. Lenders want to see financial documents if you need a loan.

2. assets to liabilities at a particular time

3. An asset is anything of monetary value that you own; a liability is a debt that you owe.

4. They are a projection of how much money you will need for first year of operation.

5. One-time costs are expenses that will not be repeated after you begin operating business. Continuing costs are operating expenses you will pay throughout life of the business.

Thinking Critically

6. Those loans may carry a low or no interest rate.

Integrating Academic Skills

7. **COMMUNICATION** Letters will vary.

SECTION 36.2

Financial Aspects of a Business Plan

Bell Ringer Activity

Estimate Estimating expected earnings and expenses is a key part of writing the financial section of a business plan. Ask students to briefly write some of the ways that they would:

- estimate income and expenses for an existing business.
- estimate income and expenses for a new business.

Then ask students what factors would help them estimate (project) income, particularly for a new business.

Introducing the Section

Financial Aspect of a Business Plan
Review students' answers from the Bell Ringer Activity. Tell students that in estimating income and expenditures for an existing business, you can look at its prior operating results, figuring in your anticipated income and expenses if you plan to add additional products. You must consider why the owner is selling the business (strong businesses are rarely offered for sale) and how you will make the business more profitable, perhaps through better management or additional investment of cash for growth. You must also consider your overall goals and growth plans.

Have students practice estimating income and expenses by choosing a product students buy frequently, such as a music CD. Assume a royalty of 10 percent and a manufacturing cost of $1.80 per CD, including packaging. Ask students to estimate other expenses, such as advertising and distribution. Estimate income based on the price students typically pay, considering that the wholesale price will be less. Remind students that not all CDs will sell successfully.

What You'll Learn

- How to estimate business income and expenses
- How to prepare an income statement
- How to calculate payroll and other expenses itemized on an income statement
- How to prepare a balance sheet
- How to prepare a cash flow statement

Why It's Important

Financial institutions and investors in any new business will want to know why you need their money, how you are going to use it, and how you plan to repay them. The financial section of a business plan provides this information to prospective lenders.

Key Terms

- income statement
- gross sales
- net sales
- net income
- interest
- principal
- balance sheet
- net worth
- cash flow statement

Estimating Business Income and Expenses

After estimating your start-up costs and personal living expenses, the next step is to estimate the money you expect to earn and to spend in operating your business. Many small businesses fail because they do not bring in enough revenue to pay their costs and expenses. Estimating your business income and expenses is a key part of your business plan. Lenders will want to see your estimates before deciding to lend you money.

If you are buying an existing business, you will have previous operating results to use as a guide. You will need to estimate your potential revenue and the costs and expenses of operating the business if you are starting a new business.

The financial document that is used to calculate a business's revenue, costs, and expenses is the income statement. The **income statement** is a summary of your business's income and expenses during a specific period, such as a month, a quarter, or a year. This statement is often called a *profit and loss statement*.

The income statement for an existing business shows the previous year's income, costs, and expenses. The income statement for a new or planned business estimates earnings and expenses for the first few months (or the first year) of operation. Figure 36-6 on page 667 shows a sample projected quarterly income statement. Refer to this figure as you read about the different parts of the income statement.

Income statements have several major parts: total and net sales, cost of goods sold, gross profit, expenses of operating the business, net income from operations, net profit before income taxes, and net profit after income taxes. Each item on the income statement is added to or subtracted from total sales to find the amount of profit.

	Total Sales
2	Returns and Allowances
5	Net Sales
2	Cost of Goods Sold
5	Gross Profit
2	Expenses of Operating the Business
5	Net Income from Operations
2	Income Taxes
5	Net Profit

Let's look at how you calculate the amounts for each part of the income statement.

Classroom Resources

For the Teacher
- Teacher Editions for all workbooks
- Assessment Package
- PowerPoint Presentation Software
- Interactive Lesson Planner
- ILP Block Scheduling, p. 11
- ILP Lesson Plans, p. 77
- ILP Internet Resources, p. 91

- ILP Blackline Masters, p. 80
- ILP *BusinessWeek* Case Studies, p. 225
- ILP Marketing Career Portfolio, p. 41
- *Marketing Essentials* Web site (**www.marketing.glencoe.com**)

For the Student
- Student Activity Workbook, p. 317
- Marketing Math Workbook, p. 111

- Marketing Research Project Workbook
- ILP School-to-Work Activity Workbook, p. 147
- Virtual Business simulation
- *Marketing Essentials* Web site (**www.marketing.glencoe.com**)

ILP These resources are available in print and on the Interactive Lesson Planner (ILP)

FIGURE 36-6

Projected Quarterly Income Statement

	Month 1	Month 2	Month 3	TOTAL
Sales	30,900	34,000	36,400	101,300
Less Returns & Allowances	900	1,000	1,400	3,300
NET SALES	30,000	33,000	35,000	98,000
Cost of Goods Sold	19,500	21,000	22,750	63,250
GROSS PROFIT	10,500	12,000	12,250	34,750
Operating Expenses				
Variable Expenses				
Advertising	300	350	350	1,000
Automobile	450	400	525	1,375
Dues and Subscriptions	15	20	18	53
Legal and Accounting	300	400	350	1,050
Miscellaneous Expenses	360	480	420	1,260
Office Supplies	120	160	140	420
Security	300	400	350	1,050
Telephone	90	120	105	315
Utilities	90	120	105	315
Total Variable Expenses	2,025	2,450	2,363	6,838
Fixed Expenses				
Depreciation	180	180	180	540
Insurance	300	300	300	900
Rent	800	800	800	2,400
Salaries and Payroll Taxes	5,600	5,600	5,600	16,800
Total Fixed Expenses	6,880	6,880	6,880	20,640
TOTAL EXPENSES	8,905	9,330	9,243	27,478
NET INCOME FROM OPERATIONS	1,595	2,670	3,007	7,272
Other Income	0	0	0	0
Other Expenses (Interest)	300	300	300	900
NET PROFIT (LOSS) BEFORE TAXES	1,295	2,370	2,707	6,372
Taxes	325	590	680	1,595
NET PROFIT (LOSS) AFTER TAXES	970	1,780	2,027	4,777

Net Sales is determined by subtracting returns and allowances from total sales.

Gross Profit is the difference between net sales and the cost of goods sold.

Operating Expenses are the costs of operating a business. They are divided into variable and fixed expenses.

Total Expenses is determined by adding the total variable expenses to the total fixed expenses.

Net Income From Operations is found by subtracting total expenses from gross profit.

Net Profit Before Taxes is calculated by adding other income to net income from operations, then subtracting interest expense.

Net Profit After Taxes is found by subtracting taxes from net profit before taxes. This amount represents the actual profit after income taxes are paid from operating the business for a certain period of time.

■ **Projected Quarterly Income Statement** An income statement is a summary of your business's income and expenses during a specific period. *Based on the figures shown here, what are your total expenses and your net profit after taxes for the quarter?*

■ Estimating Total Sales

The income generated by a business depends on the yearly volume of sales. Most new businesses grow slowly in the beginning, so you should be conservative in estimating your first-year sales.

Most people who start a new business have some idea about where they will sell their products. You may already have discussed your new product with potential buyers. You may even have a contract to produce a certain number. Suppose you are starting a new tee shirt printing business. You have a contract for 2,000 tee shirts, which you will sell at $6 wholesale. Your estimated total sales will be $12,000. You would estimate your total sales at $120,000 if you think you can produce and sell ten times that amount during your first year.

It is important to calculate a reasonable estimated sales volume. You must verify your estimated sales volume by comparing it with projected industry

SECTION 36.2

TEACH

📊 Technology Resources

PowerPoint The *Marketing Essentials* PowerPoint Presentation CD-ROM provides visual lecture aids for every chapter section.

Concept Development

1. Read Section 36.2 with students.
2. Have students read aloud the Case Study on page 676 and review the answers in class.
3. Take students to your school and/or local library to make sure they understand how to use the available resources and industry publications on financial statistics that they can consult to create the financial section of a business plan.
4. Invite a local representative from the Small Business Administration or SCORE to your class to discuss how to create the financial section of a business plan. Ask this person to bring selections of business plans for various types of businesses (if you do not already have samples of these in your classroom), comparing and contrasting the financial sections of each plan.
5. Obtain the *Small Business Resource Guide 2000* (IRS Publication 3207) available from the Department of Treasury Internal Revenue Service on CD-ROM. The CD contains all business tax forms, instructions, and publications needed by business owners.

FIGURE 36-6 ANSWER
Projected Quarterly Income Statement Total Expense equals $27,478; Net Profit (Loss) after Taxes equals $4,777.

Did You Know?
Calculating sales volume for a service business involves establishing an hourly rate and multiplying that by the number of hours worked annually. Divide the result by 12 for a monthly income figure. Keep in mind industry averages and market trends. A service business cannot start out charging more than the industry average unless it offers something extra.

Discussion Starter

Estimating Earnings and Expenses
After you have reviewed the concepts presented in this section, choose existing and new manufacturing, retail or service businesses in your community. Have students discuss what factors the owners of each business would have considered when estimating earnings and expenses.

Keep a list of students' answers on the board. Compare this list to their findings in the Cooperative Learning activity that follows.

figures for your size of business and location. Trade associations, bankers, and industry publications can help you make sales and income estimates.

The accuracy of your sales estimates will also depend on the quality of your market analysis. Losses instead of profit are not uncommon during the first year in business. In your business plan, you will need to show how you will support any losses and your ability to invest more capital or reduce your operating expenses.

■ Calculating Net Sales

The total of all sales for any period of time is called gross sales. Your gross sales will simply be the total of all cash sales if your company sells only on a cash basis. When your company accepts credit and charge cards, sells gift certificates, and sells merchandise on account, then all of these different types of sales must be totaled to arrive at gross sales.

Most businesses have some customer returns and allowances (credit granted to customers for damaged or defective goods kept by the customer); therefore, the gross sales figure does not reflect the actual income from sales. The total of all sales returns and allowances is subtracted from gross sales to get net sales. Net sales, then, represents the amount left after gross sales have been adjusted for returns and allowances. Look at Figure 36-6 on page 667 to see the net sales line.

■ Cost of Goods Sold

The total amount spent to produce or to purchase the goods that are sold is called the *cost of goods sold*. To calculate cost of goods sold, add goods purchased during the year to the beginning inventory. Then subtract the amount of the ending inventory.

$$\begin{array}{r} \text{Beginning Inventory} \\ + \ \text{Net Purchases} \\ - \ \text{Ending Inventory} \\ \hline = \ \text{Cost of Goods Sold} \end{array}$$

As you learned in Chapter 24, beginning and ending inventory amounts are determined by figuring how much stock is on hand and calculating its value.

Service businesses do not provide goods to their customers. Therefore, they don't have to determine their cost of goods sold. Their gross profit is the same as net sales. Other businesses that produce or buy products to sell must calculate the cost of goods sold.

■ Determining Gross Profit

Gross profit on sales is the difference between the net sales and the cost of goods sold.

The formula for calculating gross profit is:

$$\begin{array}{r} \text{Net Sales} \\ - \ \text{Cost of Goods Sold} \\ \hline = \ \text{Gross Profit} \end{array}$$

Once you know the cost of goods sold, you can calculate your gross profit by subtracting the cost of goods sold from net sales. Suppose you are employed by Seaside Surfboards, a company that sold $96,785 worth of surfboards last year. The company books show a total of $1,470 in sales returns and allowances. When you subtract the sales returns and allowances from total (gross) sales, you get net sales of $95,315. The cost of goods sold for last year totals $53,769; therefore, your gross profit is: $95,315 − $53,769 = $41,546.

■ Projecting Business Expenses

The next major part of the income statement is the operating expenses. *Operating expenses* are the costs of operating the business, which include both variable and fixed expenses.

CALCULATING VARIABLE EXPENSES *Variable expenses* change from one month to the next. Variable costs can fluctuate up or down depending upon the needs of the business. Variable expenses include items such as advertising, office supplies, telephone, and utilities.

Variable expenses are often calculated as a percentage of some baseline amount. Advertising expenses may be planned to be 5 percent of total sales.

CALCULATING FIXED EXPENSES *Fixed expenses* are costs that remain the same for a period of time. Expenses that are fixed for a certain period of time include items such as depreciation, insurance, rent, and office salaries.

Depreciation is a complicated fixed expense. *Depreciation* essentially represents the amount by which the value of a business's assets has fallen in a given period of time. An accountant or financial advisor can assist you in determining the asset depreciation schedule for assets on your income statement.

More About . . .

Failure Rates
Some new businesses are riskier than others, and lenders will take this fact into consideration before granting a loan. Among the businesses with the highest failure rates are those providing recreation services and oil and gas extraction. Health services and private education services have one of the lowest failure rates.

Projecting other fixed expenses usually is easier because you simply add all your fixed costs, such as rent or insurance. Employee wages may be a significant part of your business expenses. Let's look at how to calculate payroll costs.

CALCULATING PAYROLL EXPENSES To calculate payroll expenses, you must estimate the number of employees you need to operate your business. Then research typical salaries in your area for the work you will have the employees perform. You can get help on salary information by consulting with your state employment security agency (SESA) office and by reviewing the help-wanted ads in the newspaper for similar jobs. You can also use the minimum wage as a starting point and decide how much more to pay for more skilled workers, recognizing that a skilled worker should have a higher salary than an unskilled worker.

When setting up your business, you need to pay particular attention to your payroll records. Payroll records are important to your employees and to your company. They are used to prepare income tax returns, so the federal and state governments are interested in their accuracy, too.

Your payroll records may be part of the cash disbursements journal where you keep records of all cash payments. You may prefer to keep your payroll records in a separate payroll journal. When using a separate journal for payroll records, you will want to use a separate record for each employee. Each record will show one employee's pay period, hours worked, earnings, deductions, and net pay. See Figure 36-7 for a payroll journal that is used to record payroll information for employees.

The amount earned by an employee is that person's *gross pay*. *Net pay* is what the employee receives after deductions for taxes, insurance, and voluntary deductions. Nancy Baker earns $11 an hour and worked 40 hours during the week; therefore, her gross pay is $440 ($11 times 40 hours).

Nancy's deductions total $125.66, so you would calculate her net pay by subtracting the deductions from her gross pay:

$$440 - \$125.66 = \$314.34 \text{ (net pay)}$$

Tax tables are available for calculating the amount to be deducted from each employee's pay for local, state, and federal income tax. The percentage of gross pay to be deducted for FICA (Social Security and Medicare taxes) changes almost every year. Get the latest information from your local social security office.

Example: Find the net pay for Carmen Lopez, who worked a total of 44 hours during a week at $12 per hour. Carmen is paid time and a half for overtime (hours worked beyond 40 hours in a week).

Thinking Critically

1. **Business Plan** Ask students the following: If you were a banker or investor reviewing a business plan in anticipation of lending or investing money for a business start-up, what questions would you ask the potential business owner regarding how he or she will use your money? *(Answers will vary but should include the following: How will the money make the business profitable? How will the money be repaid? How quickly will the money be repaid? Who will be making decisions regarding the use of the money? How qualified is this person to run a business? How knowledgeable about this particular business is this person? What experience does this person have in this area? How sound are the financial projections for this business? How do the projections compare to actual numbers of similar businesses?)*

2. **Financial Aspects of Different Businesses** Ask students: How would the financial aspects of financing a manufacturing, service, franchise, or retail business differ? *(Students' answers should be based on the type of business information found in Chapter 33.)*

FIGURE 36-7

Payroll Journal

Name _Nancy Baker_   Wage rate _____ $11.00/Hr _____

Date of Birth _11-19-64_   Date employed _____ 8-1-86 _____

Soc. Sec. No. _514-62-5254_   Employee No. _____ 9 _____

No. of Allowances _1_   Department _____ B _____

Address _317 Sycamore_

Pay Period Ending	Hours							Total Regular	Over-time	Earnings	Deductions					Net Pay
	S	M	T	W	T	F	S				Social Security	Medicare	Federal Income tax	State Income tax	Misc.	
8-14		8	8	8	8	8		40		440.00	27.28	6.38	53.00	22.00	17.00	314.34
8-21		7	8	8	8	8		39		429.00	26.60	6.22	50.00	21.45	17.00	

■ **Payroll Journal** A payroll journal summarizes each employee's pay period, hours worked, earnings, deductions, and net pay. *What is Nancy Baker's net pay for the period ending August 21?*

FIGURE 36-7 ANSWER
Payroll Journal Nancy Baker's net pay is $307.73.
($429 − [$26.60 + $6.22 + $50 + $21.45 + $17] = $307.73)

Cooperative Learning

Estimating Income and Expenses

Divide students into the same four groups they were in for the Bell Ringer Activity in Section 36.1: manufacturing, wholesale, retail or service businesses.

Help each group make an appointment with the owner and/or general manager of each type of business assigned. Each group should interview this person regarding how income and expenses were initially projected, and how ongoing projections are made. Each group should write a report of its findings and present it to the class.

STEP 1 Find the gross pay.

$480.00 ($12 × 40 hours)
+ 72.00 ($12 × 4 hours × 1.5)
$552.00

STEP 2 Subtract the total deductions.

$552.00 (gross pay)
+ 98.40 (total deductions)
$453.60 (net pay)

In estimating your total payroll expenses, you will need to use current tax rates for local, state, and federal income taxes. Remember that as the employer, you will also pay FICA and unemployment payroll taxes on your employees' earnings. You will need to include those amounts in your total payroll expense estimate.

CALCULATING TOTAL EXPENSES Once you have calculated all your operating (variable and fixed) expenses, you are ready to total your expenses. To calculate total expenses, add all the variable expenses to the fixed expenses.

Total Variable Expenses
+ Total Fixed Expenses
= Total Expenses

◼ Net Income from Operations

After calculating your total expenses, the next step is to calculate net income from operations. **Net income** is the amount left after the total expenses are subtracted from gross profit.

The formula for calculating net income from operations is:

Gross Profit on Sales
− Total Expenses
= Net Income from Operations

Suppose that you own Worldwide Travel Agency and had gross profit on sales of $145,540 during the year. Your total operating expenses for the year were $79,630, so your net income from operations was:

$145,540 − $79,630 = $65,910

During the first years of operation, a business may have a net loss from operations. A net loss results when total expenses are larger than the gross profit on sales. The financial plan should address how the business intends to pay its debts in the short term, especially if a loss is probable during the first months of operation.

CALCULATING OTHER INCOME In the "Net Income From Operations" section of the income statement, list money earned from sources other than sales. You may earn dividends on stocks or interest on money in the bank. **Interest** is the money paid for the use of money borrowed or invested.

To estimate your interest earnings, check with local banks and find the current interest rate paid on similar accounts. It is likely that you will use some of this money during the year, so you will need to calculate interest only on the amount actually on deposit. Unless the interest income you expect to earn is significant, you may want to list this amount as zero in your business plan.

CALCULATING OTHER EXPENSES You will pay interest on any money that you borrow to start your business. This is called the **principal**.

Interest is expressed as a percentage of the principal and is called the *rate* of interest. Imagine that you borrow $100 and the interest rate is 11 percent. The principal is $100 and the rate of interest is 11 percent. To find the amount of interest for one year, multiply the principal (p) times the rate of interest (r) times the length of time (t). This formula is stated as:

$$i = prt$$
($100 × 11% × 1 = $11).

You would pay $11 in interest for the example above.

The units in the rate of interest and time must agree. That is, if the rate of interest is expressed in years, then the time must be expressed in years as well. Both may be expressed in months. Check this before you do your math or your answers will be wrong. If the rate is given without reference to a time period, you can assume that it is for one year.

Suppose you are quoted a yearly rate and need to convert it to a monthly rate. There are 12 months in a year, so you would divide the yearly rate by 12, and you will get the monthly rate. When you are quoted a monthly rate and want to convert it to a yearly rate, multiply the monthly rate by 12.

Once you decide how much money you will need to borrow and how long it will take you to repay the loan, you can calculate your total annual (or monthly) interest. This amount is listed on the financial statement as "Other Expenses."

COMPETITIVE EVENTS AND MARKETING ESSENTIALS

Financing a Business Any of DECA's four entrepreneurship competitive events can reinforce the concept of financing a business. The Entrepreneurship Written Event requires the most in-depth study of business financing for the first year of operation. The Entrepreneurship Participating Event also requires an in-depth research of business financing, requiring a three-year financing plan. The International Marketing Event requires less in-depth research since basic financing is built into the event. This activity, however, does require Projected Income and Expenses and some business financing research. The Learn and Earn Project Event will only require the students prepare a budget and explain their earning outcomes.

▪ Net Profit or Loss Before Taxes

Net profit or *net loss before taxes* is calculated by adding other income to net income from operations. Then subtract other expenses from the total.

Net Income from Operations
+ Other Income
− Other Expenses
= Net profit (or loss) before taxes

▪ Net Profit or Loss After Taxes

Net profit (or loss) after taxes is the amount of money left over after federal, state, and local taxes are subtracted. This amount represents the actual profit from operating the business for a certain period of time.

The projected income statement should be done on a monthly basis for new businesses. After the first year, projected income statements can be prepared on a quarterly basis.

The steps that follow are a summary of how to prepare a monthly projected income statement.

STEP 1 Estimate total sales.

STEP 2 Subtract sales discounts, returns, and allowances from total sales to calculate net sales.

STEP 3 List the estimated cost of goods sold.

STEP 4 Subtract the cost of goods sold from net sales to find gross profit on sales.

STEP 5 List each monthly operating expense, categorizing each as a variable or fixed expense.

STEP 6 Total the monthly operating expenses.

STEP 7 Subtract total operating expenses from gross profit on sales to find net income from operations. Put parentheses around any projected losses; for example, a projected loss of $1,000 would be identified as ($1,000).

STEP 8 Add other income such as interest on bank deposits and subtract other expenses, such as interest expense, from net income from operations. The result is net profit (or loss) before income taxes.

STEP 9 Estimate total taxes on the net income and subtract that amount from net profit. The result is net profit (or loss) after taxes.

PRACTICE 3

Using the income statement shown below, answer the following questions:

1. How much did Mountain Air pay for the bikes it sold?

2. How much was the gross profit for the year?

3. How much were total operating expenses?

4. Which operating expense was the most costly?

5. How much net income was earned during the year?

Mountain Air Bikes
Income Statement for the Year Ended December 31, 20--

Net Sales	$ 212,015
Cost of Goods Sold	109,614
Gross Profit	$?
Operating Expenses:	
Salaries	$ 24,019
Rent	$ 11,211
Utilities	4,514
Advertising	2,422
Total Operating Expenses	$?
Net Income from Operations	$?

Bringing it Together

Cross your knees, but be sure not to show the bottom of your feet. Bow only after being acknowledged at a meeting. There are books filled with tips and hints for businesspeople doing business abroad. How can one person remember all of these facts? The folks at Globesmart, a global training and consulting company in San Francisco, wondered the same thing. Globesmart offers Web-based training for individuals who do business abroad. The program includes 30 different countries, and while it will not help you learn the language, it will fill you in on the most important dos and taboos of the culture.

Thinking Critically

Familiarizing yourself with foreign traditions is important. How is Globesmart helpful in this area?

Chapter 36 ▪ *Financing the Business*   **671**

Bringing It Together

Answer Globesmart picks out those facts that are most vital for business people to know, and is easily accessible on the Web which makes it convenient when traveling.

Independent Practice

1. **Research and Write** Have students research one of the following publications (or a publication of their choice) for an article on any aspect of small business financing discussed in this section: *American Journal of Small Business, Better Business Magazine, Black Enterprise, Cottage Connection, Entrepreneur Magazine, Executive Female, In Business, Inc.* magazine, *Journal of Entrepreneurship, Journal of Small Business Finance,* or *Journal of Small Business Management.* Students should read the article, write a 100- to 200-word abstract of it, and be prepared to discuss it in class. The article may apply to all businesses or to a specific business.

2. **Research, Summarize, and Chart** Have the students write to a major public company for a copy of its most recent annual report. Each student should develop a two-page paper summarizing the Chairman of the Board's letter to the stockholders, identifying any new goods and services planned for the future, the company's total sales, operating income and expenses, net income, and cash flow. Students should include any charts or graphs from the annual report that show these figures.

3. **Identify and Display** Using a large posterboard, identify and label separate columns for the five financial documents discussed in this chapter. Under each column, identify the reasons for including a document as part of the financial section of a business plan.

5. **Research** Use an Internet search engine to have students contact the U.S. Small Business Administration for information about starting a new business specifically targeted to women or minority business owners.

Individualized Practice

Math Skills

L1 Obtain tax tables for calculating the amount to be deducted from employees' pay for federal, state, and local taxes. Also obtain the gross pay to be deducted for FICA and unemployment.

Give students hourly or weekly salary amounts for imaginary employees at various skill levels (a non-skilled worker, a skilled worker, a supervisor, and an upper-level manager). Have them calculate each person's income for one month. Base an hourly employee's pay on a 40-hour week.

Depending on the level of your class, you may wish to have your students generate the salary amounts and work in pairs to solve the problems.

L2 Give each student a copy of a completed income statement that contains all of the elements in the income statement featured in the text. Ask each student to write a letter to a friend, describing the formula for how each of the following were achieved: net sales, gross profit, operating expenses, total expenses, net income from operations, net profit before taxes, and net profit after taxes.

L3 Have students research the current mortgage interest rate at three different financial institutions. Provide students with a loan amortization chart or table. Have them figure the fixed monthly payback amount for a five-year, ten-year, and fifteen-year $50,000 business loan, given the interest rate quoted at each financial institution.

FIGURE 36-8

Balance Sheet

August, 20- -	Year 1	Year 2
Current Assets		
Cash	$ 7,000	$ 10,000
Accounts receivable	10,000	10,000
Inventory	150,000	265,000
Fixed Assets		
Real Estate	$ 100,000	$ 100,000
Fixtures and equipment	50,000	45,000
Vehicles	25,000	24,000
Other Assets		
Licenses	$ 100	$ 100
TOTAL ASSETS	$ 342,100	$ 454,100
Current Liabilities		
Notes payable (due within one year)	$ 125,000	$ 250,000
Accounts payable	10,000	15,000
Accrued expenses	5,000	5,000
Taxes owed	7,000	7,500
Long-Term Liabilities		
Notes payable (due after one year)	$ 75,000	$ 80,000
Other	15,000	20,000
TOTAL LIABILITIES	$ 237,000	$ 377,500
NET WORTH (ASSETS minus LIABILITIES)	$	$
TOTAL LIABILITIES plus NET WORTH should equal ASSETS		

■ **Balance Sheet** A balance sheet is a dollar and cents description of your existing or projected business. *Based on the figures shown here, what is the net worth of your business for year 1 and year 2?*

The Balance Sheet

A balance sheet is a summary of a business' assets, liabilities, and owner's equity. Figure 36-8 shows a typical balance sheet.

Assets are anything of monetary value that you own. They are classified as either current or fixed. *Current assets* are expected to be converted into cash in the upcoming year. Examples of current assets include cash in the bank, accounts receivable (money owed to you by your customers), and inventory. *Fixed assets* are used over a period of years to operate your business. Examples of fixed assets include land, buildings, equipment, furniture, and fixtures. The assets of the business are important because they are needed to operate the business. When borrowing money to start a business, assets are also often used as collateral for the loan.

The next section of the balance sheet reports the liabilities of the business. Liabilities are amounts the business owes, including amounts owed for merchandise bought.

Liabilities are classified as current or long-term. *Current liabilities* are the debts the business expects to pay off during the upcoming business year. An example of current liabilities are accounts payable (money owed to suppliers), notes payable (money owed to a bank), taxes payable, and money owed to employees for salaries. *Long-term liabilities* are debts that are not due in the next 12 months. Some examples of long-term liabilities are mortgages and long-term loans.

The third section of the balance sheet is the equity, or net worth, section. When you start a new business, you will most likely invest some savings in the business. The amount of the savings is your equity, or ownership interest, in the business. The money invested will be used to buy assets and to operate the business. The assets owned by the business and the debts the business owes, then, affect your equity. Net worth is the difference between the assets of a business and its liabilities:

Assets − Liabilities = Net Worth (Equity)

FIGURE 36-8 ANSWER

Balance Sheet The net worth for year 1 is $105,100. ($342,100 - $237,000 = $105,100) The net worth for year 2 is $86,600. ($454,000 - $377,500 = $76,500)

Analysis of Financial Statements

Lenders use ratio analysis as a way of determining how a business is performing as compared to other businesses in the industry. Ratios tell whether a business has too much debt, is carrying too much inventory, or is not making enough gross profit. Information on the balance sheet and the income statement may be used to calculate these ratios. Lenders use ratio analysis to determine whether your business would be a good investment risk and whether it could repay a loan.

Figures on the balance sheet will show you the amount of your (stockholder's equity) ownership interest and the financial strength of a business on a given date. Figures on the income statement can give you an idea of how well the business is operating over a period of time. Sometimes you will need information from both statements to calculate the ratios. The following are some of the most basic operating ratios and how they may be used to analyze or interpret financial statements.

Liquidity Ratios are used to analyze the ability of a firm to meet its current debts. One Liquidity Ratio is *Current Ratio*. Its formula is current assets divided by current liabilities. In this case, the higher the ratio the better.

The *Acid Test Ratio* is used to see if the company can meet its short-term cash needs. Its formula is cash plus marketable securities plus net receivables divided by current liabilities.

Activity Ratios are used to determine how quickly assets can be turned into cash. One such ratio is *Accounts Receivable Turnover,* which tells you the number of days it takes to collect the money owed by customers. To calculate this ratio, divide net sales by average trade receivables. In this case, the lower the ratio, the better.

The *Stock Turnover Ratio* measures how many days it takes to turn the inventory. Excessive inventory ties up cash that a company can use to grow its business. The basic formula for this ratio is cost of goods sold divided by average inventory.

Profitability Ratios measure how well the company has operated the past year. One ratio is *Profit Margin on Sales*, which shows the rate of profit in percentages. This information is found on the income statement. Its formula is net income divided by net sales. Another Profitability Ratio is the *Rate of Return on Assets,* which shows how well you are doing when compared to other companies. The formula for this ratio is net income divided by average total assets.

A number of sources and directories exist to help you determine the common business ratios for your type of business. These include *Parameters of Small Businesses* published by the Accounting Corporation of America, *Costs of Doing Business* by Dun & Bradstreet, and *Annual Statement Studies* by Robert Morris Associates.

PRACTICE 4

Using the balance sheet shown below, answer the following questions:

1. How much are the total assets for Mountain Air Bikes?

2. How much are the total liabilities?

3. What is Mountain Air's net worth?

Mountain Air Bikes
Balance Sheet December 31, 20--

Current Assets

Cash	$ 10,000
Accounts Receivable	15,000
Inventory	68,000

Fixed Assets

Building	120,000
Equipment	80,000
Vehicles	30,000
Total Assets	$?

Current Liabilities

Notes Payable	$3,000
Accounts Payable	12,000
Salaries Payable	5,000
Taxes Payable	1,000

Long-Term Liabilities

Notes Payable	90,000
Total Liabilities	$?
Net Worth	$?

Did You Know?
Some companies have found that sharing financial statements with employees can be a significant tool for motivating employee performance. To help employees who lack a financial background, the financial statements are annotated to explain the meaning of each line of the statements.

Reteaching

1. **Vocabulary** Assign and review the vocabulary terms for this section.
2. **Fact and Idea** Assign and review Fact and Idea Review questions 4–10 from the Chapter Assessment.
3. **Terms and Concepts** Create 5" x 7" index cards with one of the following terms/concepts written on each card: *net sales, cost of goods sold, gross profit, operating expenses, total expenses, net income from operations, net profit before taxes, net profit after taxes, gross sales, operating expenses, variable expenses, fixed expenses, gross pay, net pay, balance sheet, current assets, fixed assets, current liabilities, long-term liabilities, cash flow* and *statement.* Choose any other terms/concepts from this section that you wish to have students review. Divide students into two teams. Flip a coin to determine which team goes first. Allow the first team to choose one index card from the stack. (Don't allow students to see the cards when they choose.) Allow the first team 30 seconds to give you a definition for the chosen term. If no team member can give a correct definition, allow the other team to try. Award ten points to the team that gives a correct definition for each term. Reward the winning team. Review the terms for which neither team could give a correct answer.
4. **Balance and Income Statements** Give students problems to complete on sample balance sheets and income statements. You may wish to use the financial statements from their annual reports that students obtained in the Independent Practice activity. Using these statements, eliminate several of the figures and then have students calculate the missing figures.

Cash Flow Statement

A **cash flow statement** is a monthly plan that shows when you anticipate cash coming into the business and when you expect to pay out cash. A cash flow statement helps you to see if you will have enough money when you need it to pay your bills.

Businesses need cash to pay bills, their employees, and unexpected expenses. The cash flow statement itemizes how much cash you started with, projected cash expenditures, and how and when you plan to receive cash. It also tells you when you will need to find additional funds and when you will have cash left over. Figure 36-9 on page 675 shows a typical cash flow statement for the first three months of operation. Most lenders will require you to estimate cash flow for the first year of operation.

When operating a retail business, one of your largest payments of cash will be for your merchandise. You will most likely have to pay for part of the merchandise in cash and part in credit. When estimating sales for the income statement, you include both cash and credit sales. In contrast, the cash flow statement shows only the amount you expect to receive in cash (for cash sales and payments for credit sales) during the month. You may receive payment for most of your credit sales 30 days after the sales.

You will also need to calculate your monthly costs for operating the business. Use the following steps to prepare a cash flow statement for your business.

STEP 1 Add the total cash on hand (in bank accounts) and money received from any loans to find your total start-up money.

STEP 2 Subtract the start-up costs to determine the amount of cash left for operation.

STEP 3 Enter the estimated cash you expect to receive from cash sales and credit sales for each month during the first year. Enter the amount of any income from business investments or additional loans.

STEP 4 Add all sources of cash receipts to find the total cash income for the month.

STEP 5 List the cost of goods that you will buy for your inventory. This cost should be separated into purchases for which you will pay cash and purchases on credit, which you will pay for the next month. For example, the cash flow statement shows goods

bought on credit in Month 1. This is a payment for items bought on credit prior to the opening of the business. Add the cash and credit purchases to find the total cost of inventory purchases.

STEP 6 List the expenses you expect to pay during the month. These amounts are the same as those listed on the income statement, except for depreciation expense. Depreciation is a means of spreading the cost of an asset over a period of years. The amount of depreciation is not an actual payment made by the business, so it is not listed on the cash flow statement.

STEP 7 Total all expenses for the month.

STEP 8 List amounts that will be paid out for capital expenditures. A capital expenditure is money paid for an asset used to operate the business. The purchase of a delivery truck would be a capital expenditure.

STEP 9 List any other payments that will be made, such as repayment of the principal and interest for the loan.

STEP 10 Add all the cash expenditures (cost of inventory purchased, expenses, capital expenditures, and other payments). Subtract the total cash payments from the total cash received during the month to determine net cash flow. The amount of any cash payments that are higher than cash receipts should be placed in parentheses.

STEP 11 Add the beginning cash balance from the start-up column to the net cash flow for the month. The result is the cash surplus for the month. When the costs of operating the business are higher than income added to the beginning of the cash balance, the business will have a deficit rather than a surplus. In that case, the business will need additional cash for its operations. The amount is listed on the "Cash Needs" line. Figure 36-9 shows cash flow projections with a need for additional cash of $175 by the end of month 2. If you compare month 2 on the income statement, you will see net profit for the month. What the income statement does not take into account is how long it may take a business to collect the cash from sales made on credit.

More About . . .

Cash Flow
The majority of new business start-ups fail within the first three years of operation. One of the most common reasons for business failure is inadequate cash flow. Being successful means not only selling the product, but also collecting the money for it within a reasonable time.

FIGURE 36-9

Projected Cash Flow Statement

Beginning of Month:	Start-Up	Month 1	Month 2	Month 3
Cash in Bank	$25,000			
Loans	$ 5,000			
	$30,000			
Less Start-up Costs	$20,000			
Total Beginning Cash	$10,000			
Income (during month):				
Cash Sales		$20,000	$20,000	$27,000
*Credit Sales			10,000	13,000
Investment Income		200	200	200
Loans		0	0	0
Other Cash Income		0	0	0
TOTAL CASH INCOME		$20,200	$30,200	$40,200
Inventory Purchases				
Purchases for Cash		$15,000	$16,000	$14,750
*Purchases for Credit		4,500	5,000	8,000
Total Inventory Purchases		$19,500	$21,000	$22,750
Expenses				
Variable Expenses				
Advertising		300	350	350
Automobile		450	400	525
Dues & Subscriptions		15	20	18
Legal & Accounting		300	400	350
Miscellaneous		360	480	420
Office Supplies		120	160	140
Security		300	400	350
Telephone		90	120	105
Utilities		90	120	105
Fixed Expenses				
Insurance		300	300	300
Rent		800	800	800
Salaries/Taxes (including owner's)		5,600	5,600	5,600
Total Expenses		$ 8,725	$ 9,150	$ 9,063
Capital Expenditures				
Purchases of Equipment				
and Other Assets		1,000		
Other Payments				
Loan Repayment		600	600	600
TOTAL CASH EXPENDITURES		$29,825	$30,750	$32,413
NET CASH FLOW				
(end of month)	$10,000	($ 9,625)	($ 550)	$ 7,787
CASH SURPLUS				
(monthly)	$10,000	$ 375	($ 175)	$ 7,612
CASH NEEDS	0	0	$ 175	0

* payment based on previous month

■ **Projected Cash Flow Statement** A cash flow statement is a helpful financial tool for a business. *What is the purpose behind completing a monthly cash flow statement?*

Enrichment

1. **Review** Assign and review the Chapter 36 activities in the *Student Activity Workbook*.
2. **Review** Assign and review the appropriate Thinking Critically questions from the Chapter Assessment.
3. **Review** Assign and review the following Chapter Assessment activities: Building Workplace Skills, Applying Marketing Concepts, Linking School to Work, The DECA Connection Role Play, and Internet Connection.
4. **Research and Estimate** Have the class review the sales from your school store during the last year. Given this information, have students project next year's income and expenses for the store.
5. **Analyze and Calculate** To discuss projecting business expenses, have students analyze several examples of income statements and balance sheets from existing businesses to determine the current and fixed assets and current and long-term liabilities.

FIGURE 36-9 ANSWER
Projected Cash Flow Statement A cash flow statement helps to avoid as well as plan for cash shortages or surpluses.

Technology Resources

Assessment Resources

Go to the *Marketing Essentials* Web site (**www.marketing.glencoe.com**) for resources to teach and assess occupation-specific vocabulary.

Case Study

Your Own Personal Franchise

Ever dreamed of owning your own fast food restaurant? That's right, as unlikely as it may seem, you can own your own McDonald's, Burger King, or Taco Bell. This is possible thanks to the franchise. A franchise is an agreement between a corporation and an independent individual or group who wishes to operate the business locally.

Quickserve restaurants first began in 1925 with A&W walk-up root beer stands. Baskin-Robbins, Dairy Queen, Kentucky Fried Chicken, McDonald's, and Taco Bell followed. The continued growth of both full and quickserve restaurants since the 1990s has been attributed to a booming economy.

Quickserve restaurants have become an international phenomena. From the original international franchises led by KFC and McDonald's in the 1960s, more and more companies are opening overseas stores. Because of the continuing growth in dining on the go, there will be a continuing need for entrepreneurs to start and investors to finance quickserve restaurants.

Franchisers make up a big part of the teams that lead these quickserve restaurants. Many entrepreneurs look to quickserve restaurants because of the tremendous growth in overall restaurant industry sales. The restaurant industry has nearly $400 billion in annual sales and employs 11 million people or 8 percent of the total number of workers in the United States.

Most quickserve restaurants require $10,000 to $20,000 for an initial franchise fee. The total investment, excluding real estate, usually runs between $100,000 to $250,000, according to the International Franchise Association. As more restaurants are popping up, one can only imagine that quickserve restaurants equal quick cash for investors!

Case Study Review

1. Why is the concept of quickserve restaurants so popular with today's consumers?
2. In your opinion do most quickserve restaurants build their marketing concept around adults, children, or teenagers? Provide your rationale.

A MATTER OF ETHICS

3. Do you think that it is ethical to take the U.S. quickserve restaurants to overseas markets? Why or why not?

Case Study Review Answers

Your Own Personal Franchise

1. More and more people are working, and consumers have less free time to prepare their own meals.
2. Answers will vary. Baby boomers are credited with fresher ingredients and healthier dishes. They make up the largest number of restaurant patrons. Teens and children are concerned about convenience; older consumers crave quality.

A MATTER OF ETHICS

3. KFC and McDonald's have led the way for many international quickserve restaurants. It is ethical as long as each international franchise respects the traditions, culture, rules, and laws of the country where it locates.

Loans

What can you do if you project that you will need additional money during the year? You should be able to borrow additional money if your business has potential and your balance sheet shows enough assets to serve as collateral. A loan can help you keep the business going during the start-up period and during slow sales months. When your cash flow projections indicate that you need to borrow money to meet monthly expenses, you will want to include monthly payments on the loan as a part of your cash needs for the rest of the year.

PRACTICE 5

1. You have total cash of $23,000 to start your business and start-up costs of $12,000. What amount of cash is available for operating the business?

2. Suppose cash income for the first three months is $100, $750, and $980. Total expenses for these same months are $4,800, $3,400, and $2,700. What is the cash flow for each month?

3. What is the cumulative amount of cash available at the end of each month?

Cyber Cash

The classic thwarted dream—an individual brainstorms an innovative and potentially successful business idea for a new business, but does not have the time to pursue it while making a living. This scenario is becoming a scene from the past, because the Internet has brought changes. The Web is becoming a vast source of capital for the entrepreneur who doesn't have the business connections or the time to find money the old-fashioned way. Web sites provide access to experts, free downloadable forms, and opportunities to chat with professionals who may be able to match new entrepreneurs with investors. A businessperson can post a proposal on a Web site where venture capitalists, banks, and others seeking investment opportunities get involved. In order to succeed, the entrepreneur can't show up unprepared. The standard principles of good business apply— a business plan and funding proposal are still necessary for consideration.

Thinking Critically

How would investors verify the legitimacy of an online start-up looking for capital?

VIRTUAL BUSINESS

GO TO

Forecasting
Introduce the concept of forecasting to students using Knowledge Matters' Virtual Business visual simulation, "Accounting and Finance—Forecasting." Students try to predict how much cash they will need to get their store off the ground. If needed, have students run the Virtual Business tutorial before beginning this activity. For additional instructions and teaching tips for this simulation, go to the *Marketing Essentials* Web site (**www. marketing.glencoe.com**).

CLOSE

Section Wrap-Up

Have each student write a 50-word summary that tells why the finance section of a business plan is so important.

Cyber Cash

Answer Once a deal is reviewed by a team of investment professionals, meetings might be set up to further verify assets, ideas, and management.

36.2 ASSESSMENT

Reviewing Key Terms and Concepts

1. What financial document can you use to calculate a business's earnings and expenses?

2. What are the major categories that are calculated on the income statement?

3. How are payroll expenses calculated?

4. What is the purpose of a balance sheet?

5. What is a cash flow statement? What is its purpose?

Thinking Critically

6. What steps could a business take to improve cash flow?

Integrating Academic Skills

7. **MATH** Total first-quarter sales for the Leon Company were $285,000. Goods returned by customers amounted to $4,100. The cost of goods sold to customers was $112,000. The company's total fixed and variable expenses were $84,500. Interest paid on a loan was $2,400. Taxes were estimated at a rate of 20 percent. Calculate the following amounts: net sales, gross profit, net income from operations, net profit before taxes, and net profit after taxes.

36.2 ASSESSMENT ANSWERS

Reviewing Key Terms and Concepts

1. income statement

2. net sales, cost of goods sold, gross profit, net income from operations, and net income before and after taxes

3. Determine total of employee wages and salaries and add government payments an employer must pay, e.g., unemployment insurance, workers' compensation insurance, and employers

share of FICA (social security). To calculate employee wages, multiply number of hours worked by hourly rate.

4. It shows the amount of ownership interest and financial strength of business on a given date.

5. It shows when you anticipate cash coming into the business and when you expect to pay out cash. It helps you see if you will have enough money to pay bills. *(continued on next page)*

Answers to Practice Problems

PRACTICE 1 (PAGE 660)

1. Total assets are $22,000 ($10,000 + $8,000 + $1,000 + $1,500 + $1,500 = $22,000).

2. Total liabilities are $10,000 ($7,000 + $2,500 + $500 = $10,000).

3. Net worth is $12,000 ($22,000 − $10,000 = $12,000).

PRACTICE 2 (PAGE 662)

Total costs for the first quarter are $27,600 [$18,000 + ($3,200 × 3) = $27,600]; Total costs for the year are $56,400 [$18,000 + ($3,200 × 12) = $56,400].

PRACTICE 3 (PAGE 671)

Mountain-Air Bikes
Income Statement For the Year Ended
December 31, 20--

Net Sales	$212,015
Cost of Goods Sold	109,614
Gross Profit	$102,401
Operating Expenses:	
Salaries	$ 24,019
Rent	11,211
Utilities	4,514
Advertising	2,422
Total Operating Expenses	$ 42,166
Net Income from Operations	$ 60,235

1. $109,614

2. $102,401 ($212,015 − $109,614 = $102,401)

3. $42,166 ($24,019 + $11,211 + $4,514 + $2,422 = $42,166)

4. Salaries

5. $60,235 ($102,401 − $42,166 = $60,235)

PRACTICE 4 (PAGE 673)

Mountain Air Bikes
Balance Sheet December 31, 20--

Current Assets	
Cash	$ 10,000
Accounts Receivable	15,000
Inventory	68,000
Fixed Assets	
Building	120,000
Equipment	80,000
Vehicles	30,000
Total Assets	$323,000
Current Liabilities	
Notes Payable	$ 3,000
Accounts Payable	12,000
Salaries Payable	5,000
Taxes Payable	1,000
Long-Term Liabilities	
Notes Payable	90,000
Total Liabilities	$ 111,000
Net Worth	$212,000

1. $323,000 ($10,000 + $15,000 + $68,000 + $120,000 + $80,000 + $30,000 = $323,000)

2. $111,000 ($3,000 + $12,000 + $5,000 + $1,000 + $90,000 = $111,000)

3. $212,000 ($323,000 − $111,000 = $212,000)

PRACTICE 5 (PAGE 677)

1. The amount of cash available for business operations is $11,000 ($23,000 − $12,000 = $11,000).

2. The cash flow is as follows: month 1; ($4,700) [$100 − $4,800 = ($4,700)]; month 2; ($2,650) [$750 − $3,400 = ($2,650)]; month 3; ($1,720) [$980 − $2,700 = ($1,720)].

3. The cumulative cash available at the end of each month is as follows: month 1; $6,300 ($11,000 − $4,700 = $6,300); month 2; $3,650 ($6,300 − $2,650 = $3,650); month 3; $1,930 ($3,650 − $1,720 = $1,930).

36.2 ASSESSMENT ANSWERS (CONT'D)

Thinking Critically

6. Answers will vary. Invoice promptly to customers with good credit; manage payables by making timely, accurate payments, and correcting overbilling; and control overhead costs.

Integrating Academic Skills

7. **MATH** (Total Sales) $285,000 − (Returns & Allowances) $4,100 = (Net Sales) $280,900. $280,900 − (Cost of Goods Sold) $112,000 = (Gross Profit) $168,900. $168,900 − (Total Expenses) $84,500 = (Net Income from Operations) $84,400. $84,400 − (Interest Expense) $2,400 = (Net Profit Before Taxes) $82,000. $82,000 − (Taxes at 20%) $16,400 = (Net Profit After Taxes) $65,600.

Total Operating Expenses: $42,166
Net Income from Operations: $60,235

Careers in Marketing

FINANCIAL SERVICES

Amanda Patterson
Financial Analyst Controller
UBS Warburg

What does your job entail?

"Financial analysts evaluate the cost and income effects of decisions that a company makes. Another job duty is forecasting the income from various investments and analyzing the costs of capital improvements. Financial analysts prepare and present budgets, income statements, and other financial reports. I am responsible for overseeing the process and accounting for trades that are booked by the Emerging Markets desk. My workload may be more intense during the end of the month when reports are issued. I have a routine of daily procedures that are required every day, and from there, specific projects may be assigned during the month."

What kind of training did you have?

"I have a background in accounting. I worked in public accounting in auditing and then moved away from auditing in this job. My training has included both formal classes and informal working with mentors."

What skills are most important?

"All jobs require you to be able to write effectively and properly. This specific job requires above-average math and computer skills as well. You must be accurate, detail-oriented, and familiar with laws and regulations related to investments and taxation."

What is your key to success?

"In my experience, the key to success is to be open to new opportunities. The hardest thing to accept when I started working was that I didn't know everything. There were times when I felt like I didn't know anything! It is necessary to be self-confident and willing to learn as you go along. The learning experience is challenging, but there are always people willing to help you."

Thinking Critically
How has technology increased efficiency in a career such as that of a financial analyst controller?

Career Facts

Education and Training: High school students desiring to work in financial services should take college preparatory courses. Additional classes in business law, math, and administration as well as classes in marketing, accounting economics, and computer science are recommended. Most employers require applicants to have an MBA degree. Preparation specific to the industry of employment may also be required.

Aptitudes, Abilities, and Skills: Above-average ability to work with numerical data and to understand financial concepts is required, in addition to good communication and computer skills.

Career Outlook: Average growth for the employment of financial analysts is projected through the year 2006. The growth in inter-state and international banking as well as international investing may create greater than average demand for financial analysts.

Career Path: An MBA from a desirable school and a strong background in computer science are increasingly important for candidates seeking jobs as financial analysts. Success as a financial analyst can lead to financial management positions such as treasurer, controller, or portfolio manager.

Chapter 36 ■ *Financing the Business* **679**

Vocabulary Review

See Glossary for definitions.

Fact and Idea Review

1. They help determine how much capital will be needed to start/operate the business and are also required to obtain financing.
2. Some factors include: nature of proposed business; size of business; amount of inventory needed; time between using start-up funds from personal assets or from potential lenders and first sales; and the timing of cash revenues and your expenses.
3. They are expenses that are necessary for you to live.
4. Project net sales and then determine the gross profit. The operating expenses are then subtracted from the gross profit, as well as the net income from operations, and then the net profit after any taxes have been taken out. The net profit after taxes is the figure that you can base your estimation on.
5. Fixed expenses do not change for a given period of time; variable expenses may change.
6. It shows the assets, liabilities, and net worth of a business.
7. Assets are anything of value owned by a business. Current assets are expected to be converted into cash in the upcoming year; fixed assets are used over a period of years to operate a business.
8. It is the difference between the assets of a business and its liabilities.
9. The income statement projects revenue, costs, and expenses. The balance sheet presents the assets, liabilities, and owner's equity in the business. The cash flow statement shows how cash will flow into and out of the business.

Thinking Critically

1. Up to 85 percent of bank loans are guaranteed by the federal or state government. Therefore, state or federal economic development loans lower the investment risk.
2. lending agencies, previous owners, industry publications, suppliers, manufacturers, trade associations, local, and state and federal economic development agencies

680

Chapter 36 ASSESSMENT

VOCABULARY REVIEW

Review the definitions for each of the following vocabulary terms with a classmate.

- personal financial statement
- asset
- liability
- start-up costs
- income statement
- gross sales
- net sales
- net income
- interest
- principal
- balance sheet
- net worth
- cash flow statement

FACT AND IDEA REVIEW

1. Why are financial documents important in a business plan? (36.1)
2. What factors determine start-up costs for a new business? (36.1)
3. What are personal costs? (36.1)
4. List the steps in projecting income for a new business. (36.2)
5. Compare fixed and variable expenses. (36.2)
6. What does a balance sheet show? (36.2)
7. Explain the difference between current and fixed assets. (36.2)
8. What is net worth? (36.2)
9. What different type of financial information does an income statement, a balance sheet, and a cash flow statement provide? (36.2)

THINKING CRITICALLY

1. Many states and the federal government have economic development programs devoted to the needs of small business. Why do a majority of economic development loans originate from banks rather than from the state or federal agencies?
2. What sources could you use to determine the total amount of cash needed to start a business?
3. What do you think are some of the legal issues that have impact on financial statements?
4. What do you think a lender looks for in considering a loan application for a new business?
5. What are some techniques that a small business owner can use to cultivate a good relationship with a local lending institution?

BUILDING WORKPLACE SKILLS

1. **Human Relations** A friend has decided to open an Internet consulting business. He believes that he will not need extra capital for personal living costs—the business will generate enough revenue when it gets started to cover this. What would you tell your friend about his lack of concern about personal living costs?
2. **Technology** Locate the *Inc.com* Web site on the Internet. Download the *Initial Cash Requirements Worksheet* and use the template and your estimate of expenses to calculate the total amount of cash needed to start a new business.

---

3. Answers will vary but might include money that is paid or made off the books, flaws on tax returns, or a misevaluation of the current worth of personal assets.
4. Lenders want to be assured that their loans will be repaid. They look at cash flow, personal credit cards, and individual retirement accounts, as well as the six Cs of granting credit, management experience, and customer contracts.
5. Establish rapport before needing a loan. Maintain balances in accounts, not overdrawing checking accounts, and not using uncollected funds.

Building Workplace Skills

1. Students should encourage the friend not to ignore personal living expenses to insure adequate capitalization to be successful.
2. Start-up costs will vary by type of business.

APPLYING MARKETING CONCEPTS

1. **Finding Franchise Opportunities** Find the International Franchise Association Web site on the Internet. Find an existing franchise opportunity to investigate. Use a word processing program to write a report describing the franchise opportunity, including the type of franchise, primary product or service, potential for growth and other pertinent facts about it.

2. **Calculating Projected Cash Flow** Use a spreadsheet program to calculate projected cash flow for a six-month period. Use the cash flow information to assist you in developing the financial section of a business plan.

3. **Preparing an Income Statement** Locate the American Express Small Business Exchange Web site on the Internet. Under "Financials" on the home page find the template for preparing an income statement. Place your projected income figures into the template to prepare an income statement for the financial section of your business plan.

4. **Developing a Personal Financial Statement** Develop a personal financial statement using a word processing program and a spreadsheet program. Create a one-year report based on the average month, including personal living expenses, projected monthly sales, fixed and variable expenses, estimated profits, and start-up costs. Include the cost of equipment, supplies, and inventory.

LINKING SCHOOL TO WORK

Information and Foundation Skills Interview your supervisor or training station sponsor regarding three business ratios that have proven to be most helpful to running the business. Identify the ratios and the reasons your supervisor has found them to be helpful.

THE DECA CONNECTION

Role Play: Bookkeeper

Situation You are to assume the role of recently hired part-time bookkeeper for a newly opened home repair service. The business owner (judge) has excellent technical skills but little experience with financial statements.

Activity The business owner (judge) has asked you to explain the difference between an income statement, a balance sheet, and a cash flow statement. He has also asked you to explain to him how to develop a cash flow statement for the business.

Evaluation You will be evaluated on how well you meet the following performance indicators:

- Explain the concept of accounting
- Explain the nature of balance sheets
- Describe the nature of cash-flow statements
- Prepare cash-flow statements
- Make oral presentations

*inter*NET CONNECTION

Investigate Funding Sources
Locate the Quicken Web site and find the *Quick Pick Chart for Financing Sources.* Investigate one primary source for long-term financing of a start-up business.

Connect
- Select one of the primary sources of long-term financing.
- Summarize the information presented in a 2-page report.

THE DECA CONNECTION

Students should be evaluated on the performance indicators noted in the Role Play.
- For another DECA Role Play go to the *Student Activity Workbook,* p. 317.
- For more in-depth Role Play practice, refer to DECA's *Essential Competitive Events Handbook.* To order, contact DECA at **www.deca.org**.

*inter*NET CONNECTION

Written reports will vary.

Mini Quiz

Administer the Mini Quiz orally. For an expanded chapter quiz, go to page 213 of the *Reproducible Tests* book.

1. Something of monetary value that you own is called a(n) <u>asset</u>.

2. A debt that you owe is called a(n) <u>liability</u>.

3. A summary of your business's income and expenses during a specific period, such as a month, a quarter, or a year is called a(n) <u>income statement or profit an loss statement</u>.

4. A summary of a business's assets, liabilities, and owner's equity is called a(n) <u>balance sheet</u>.

5. A monthly plan that shows when you anticipate cash coming into the business and when you expect to pay out cash is called a(n) <u>cash flow statement</u>.

Applying Marketing Concepts

1. Reports will vary.
2. Cash flow information and spreadsheets will vary by type of business.
3. Income statements will vary.
4. Personal financial statements and reports will vary but should include all requested information.

Linking School to Work

Answers will depend on the work situation.

1. **Assessment** Have students complete the Reproducible Tests for Chapter 36 and Unit 11 or construct your own tests using the ExamView software.

2. **Enrichment** Have students complete the corresponding activities in the following workbooks:
   - *Marketing Math Workbook*, p. 111

FOCUS

Unit Lab Overview

In this Zazz Lab, students will use their entrepreneurial knowledge of starting and managing a business, including creating a business plan and determining capital needs, for planning an amusement/water park.

Bell Ringer Activity

List and Analyze On a separate sheet of paper, ask students to list some theme amusement parks and water parks. Have them note if they have visited them, if they had fun, and if they would return.

Discussion Starter

Extending the Bell Ringer Activity, ask students to identify features that made certain amusement and water parks more fun than others. Write those features on the board and have students write them in their notebooks for future use. *(Possible answers might include short wait in lines, easy parking, and quality of rides.)*

TEACH

Thinking Critically

1. **Risk Management** Ask students: What safety precautions should be instituted in amusement and water parks? *(Possible answers might include: age, height, and weight restrictions for certain rides; requiring participants to be strapped in rides.)*
2. **Natural Risks** Ask students: How does weather affect this business? *(Cold and rainy weather has a negative effect.)* What might be done to reduce the unpredictable effects of weather? *(Possible answers may include design an indoor park.)*

The Zazz Lab

A Sports and Entertainment Marketing Simulation

WELCOME

Welcome to Zazz Sports and Entertainment Marketing Company. Zazz is devoted to serving the needs of its clients who include college, university, and professional sports teams, professional athletes, sporting events, and sports arenas plus major consumer product corporations, as well as television networks and movie studios. As an intern, you will have the opportunity to work on different clients' projects. All of your work will be assigned and reviewed by your department supervisor.

PREPARE A BUSINESS PROPOSAL FOR A NEW AMUSEMENT PARK

SITUATION

Zazz wants to tap the amusement and/or water park market. You need to research the amusement and water park industry to test the idea's feasibility.

ASSIGNMENT

Your supervisor wants you to prepare a business proposal for a new amusement and/or water park that Zazz would own and operate. You will need to study the market for this type of venture, as well as costs involved in a project of this magnitude. The organizational structure for operation and a comprehensive marketing plan are required. You have also been asked to design the theme and attractions to be included in this magnificent complex. Location and weather are important factors, as is park management. A "guest friendly" atmosphere needs to be established, from the park design to the training of employees. Practical considerations, such as the location of food services and infrastructure, are vital. Parking, the configuration of lines for rides, and customer hospitality services are also important details. The success of an amusement park is based on customer satisfaction with the experience—return rates and guest recommendations are very important.

Tools and Resources

To complete this assignment, you will need to conduct research at a library or on the Internet. You will also need a word processing program, a spreadsheet program, and presentation software. Trade publications and organizations that may be helpful are *Splash Magazine*, published by the World Waterpark Association, *Amusement Today*, and the Themed Entertainment Association.

Research

Research theme amusement parks and water parks. Identify the demographics and psychographics of typical attendees. Research locations and Web sites. Identify major competitors and their market shares. Identify strategies used by competitors with regard to product (theme and design of park), place (location), price (individual and group rates), and promotion (message and media used). Obtain samples of the competitors' park designs and promotional materials. Research the cost to build and operate a new amusement/water park. Consider the number of employees needed, employee training, and the park's mission statement.

AND THE WINNER IS . . .

Even amusement parks get nominated and receive awards. *Amusement Today* magazine conducts an annual survey to choose the best amusement parks, roller coasters, and water parks in the world. The winners receive the coveted "Golden Ticket Awards." For three consecutive years (1998–2000), Cedar Fair's Cedar Point Flagship Amusement Park in Sandusky, Ohio, has ranked number one in the amusement park category.

Report

Prepare a written report and a computer presentation for your supervisor. Use a word processing program to create a double-spaced report. Use a spreadsheet program to prepare pie charts to depict market share and other variables where parts of a whole are shown, as well as financial reports. Arrange your written report around the following headings:

- Analysis of the amusement/water park market
  - Market size and trends
  - Competitors
    - Location and market share
  - Customer profile
- Proposed amusement/water park
  - Theme and design
  - Suggested location
    - Weather
    - Trading area analysis
      - Population
      - Economic factors
    - Transportation—highways and roads
    - Other possible locations
  - Market segment analysis
    - Geographics, demographics, and psychographics
- Planned operation of amusement/water park
  - Proposed organization
    - Legal ownership
    - Mission statement
    - Personnel needs/training
  - Proposed products and services offered
    - Attractions
    - Food services
    - Merchandise (gift shops, souvenirs)
  - Proposed marketing plan
    - Pricing (individual/group)
    - Promotional plans
    - Selling
      - Major selling points—feature/benefit chart
      - Training sales office personnel
- Proposed financing
  - Project income statement
  - Projected balance sheet
  - Projected capital needs
  - Project cash flow statement
- Conclusion

Presentation and Evaluation

Present your ideas in a written report and an oral presentation. You will be evaluated on your oral presentation skills, including:

- Knowledge of the amusement/water park market
- Expertise in preparing a business proposal
- Comprehensiveness of business plan
- Creativity
- Continuity of presentation
- Voice quality
- Enthusiasm
- Eye contact

 Portfolio

Print a copy of your completed report and presentation for your Portfolio.

THE DECA CONNECTION

DECA Hospitality and Recreation Marketing Research Event
Conducting market research to determine who would attend an amusement/water park near your community and what they would want included in the design and operation of such a park could be a possible topic for this event.

DECA Entrepreneurship Participating Event
Developing and presenting your proposal for a new amusement/water park is a potential topic for this event.

DECA Entrepreneurship Written Event
Writing a comprehensive business proposal for a new amusement/water park, complete with details and financial plans, could be a topic for this event.

DECA Advertising Campaign Event
Creating an advertising campaign for an existing amusement/water park in your community is a potential resource for this event.

DECA Sports and Entertainment Marketing Management Team Decision-Making Event
Working on this project with a partner would make the experience similar to what is expected in a DECA Team Decision-Making Event.

COOPERATIVE LEARNING

Teamwork Have one or two groups plan a theme park, and one or two other groups plan a water park. Another way to approach this project is to assign different aspects of the project to different teams. Representatives from each team could meet periodically to make sure all teams are coordinated. This would be a cross-functional team responsible for making decisions and communicating them to their respective team members.

Independent Practice

Research and Analyze Ask students to research the concept of a mobile sports-related park, one that visits communities that are far from permanent theme parks. Ask why a water park would be more difficult to operate on a mobile basis than a permanent park. *(It would require about 100,000 gallons of water, motor controls, heating, steel beams and grids to support the system, a filtration system, etc.)*

ASSESS

Enrichment

Research Ask students to research the insurance Zazz would need for this venture. *(Personal and product liability insurance would be needed, as well as insurance related to a regular business.)*

Evaluation

The rubrics for evaluation of the written, oral, and computer presentation are included in the student text. (See the outline and guidelines for the written report, the computer presentation, and the skills' assessment for oral presentations.) It might be best to replicate those rubrics to evaluate the students' work. A separate rubric could be created to evaluate the work of a team.

CLOSE

Lab Wrap-Up

Have students name the parts of a business plan to prepare in order to apply for financing. *(Parts include: analysis of the business situation—location, trading area analysis, and market segment analysis; planned operation of the business—organization, proposed products and services, proposed marketing plan [pricing and promotion]; and proposed financing—income statement, balance sheet, cash flow statement, a plan to meet capital needs.)*

683

Career and Professional Development

Chapter 37
Identifying Career Opportunities

Chapter 38
Finding and Applying for a Job

Unit Objectives

After completing this unit, students will be able to:

- Assess personal values, goals, interests, and abilities for career decision making.
- Participate in career planning activities using various sources of career information.
- Develop a career plan based on career assessment and planning activities.
- Identify job search strategies.
- Write a letter of application, a résumé, and cover letter, and complete an application form.
- Prepare for and conduct themselves properly during a job interview.
- Follow up a job interview.

Enrichment Resources

Books
The Accelerated Job Search by Wayne D. Ford, Ph.D.
Occupational Outlook Handbook, U.S. Department of Labor
Résumés in Cyberspace: Your Complete Guide to a Computerized Job Search by Pat Criscito
Succeeding in the World of Work, Glencoe/McGraw-Hill

Magazines/Journals
Fast Company
Working Woman

Associations
American Marketing Association
311 S. Wacker Drive, Suite 5800
Chicago, IL 60606
(312) 648-0536
www.ama.com

DECA
Distributive Education Clubs of America
1908 Association Drive
Reston, VA 20191
(703) 860-5000
www.deca.org

Journal Writing Activity

1. Ask students to list in their journals ten strategies they could use to search for a job. Suggest that students work with a partner to share and evaluate their strategies. Then list some job hunting strategies on the board and discuss them with the class. Ask students which new strategies might work for them. They can revise or expand their lists to include these strategies.

2. Explain to students the meaning of a chronological résumé. Have students identify in their journals what they think are the main sections of a chronological résumé. Lead students in a discussion of the two other types of résumés—the functional résumé and skills résumé. Then have students list in their journals three advantages and three disadvantages for each type of résumé.

TEACHER CLASSROOM RESOURCES

Program Resources	Chapter 37	Chapter 38
Student Activity Workbook	p. 327	p. 337
Marketing Math Workbook	p. 135	p. 135
Marketing Research Project Workbook		
ILP School-to-Work Activity Workbook	p. 151	p. 155
ILP *BusinessWeek* Case Studies	p. 229	p. 235
ILP Marketing Career Portfolio	p. 42	p. 42
Reproducible Tests	p. 221	p. 225
ExamView User's Guide and Testbank	p. 37-1	p. 38-1
ILP Internet Resources	p. 93	p. 95
ILP Blackline Masters	p. 84	p. 85
ILP Lesson Plans	p. 78	p. 81
ILP Block Scheduling	p. 12	p. 12
Impact! Simulation		

ILP Each of these resources is available in print and on the Interactive Lesson Planner CD-ROM.

Technology Resources

- Interactive Lesson Planner (ILP) CD-ROM
- PowerPoint Presentation CD-ROM
- Marketing Essentials Web site
- ExamView! CD-ROM
- Impact! Simulation

Virtual Business

Virtual Business is a fully visual marketing and business simulation that introduces students to the principles of marketing by letting them start and run their own virtual businesses. In *Virtual Business*, students have the power to control all aspects of a retail convenience store. Students strategize marketing decisions using a powerful learning tool in the guise of a video game. They learn by experiencing how their decisions affect their virtual business.

Key to Individualized Academics Activities

L1 Level 1 activities are basic activities and should fall within the range of all students.

L2 Level 2 activities are average activities and should be within the range of average and above average students.

L3 Level 3 activities are challenging activities designed for the ability range of above average students.

National Marketing Education

CHAPTER	SECTION	PERFORMANCE INDICATOR
Chapter 37 **Identifying Career Opportunities**	**37.1**	Identify tentative occupational interest (PD)
		Assess personal interests and skills needed for success in business (PD)
	37.2	Analyze employer expectations in the business environment (PD)
		Identify desirable personality traits important to business (PD)
		Identify sources of career information (PD)
	37.3	Explain employment opportunities in business (PD)
		Identify skills needed to enhance career progression (PD)
Chapter 38 **Finding and Applying for a Job**	**38.1**	Utilize job-search strategies (PD)
		Identify sources of career information (PD)
	38.2	Complete a job application (PD)
		Write a letter of application (PD)
		Prepare a résumé (PD)
	38.3	Interview for a job (PD)
		Write a follow-up letter after job interviews (PD)

CIS Communication, Interpersonal Skills   **DIS** Distribution   **FIN** Financing   **PRI** Pricing   **SEL** Selling

Standards Assessment Correlation

SECTION ASSESSMENT			CHAPTER ASSESSMENT						UNIT LAB
Reviewing Key Terms and Concepts	Thinking Critically	Integrating Academic Skills	Fact and Idea Review	Thinking Critically	Building Workplace Skills	Applying Marketing Concepts	Linking School to Work	Internet Connection	Zazz Lab
3, 4	●	●	1, 2, 4	1, 2, 3	1, 2	2, 3, 4		●	●
1, 2, 3, 4	●	●	1, 2, 3, 4	1, 3, 4, 5	1, 2	1, 2, 3, 4	●		●
1, 2, 3	●	●	5		1	3, 4	●	●	
1	●	●		2, 3, 5	1	3			●
2, 3	●		6	1, 4	1, 2	1, 2, 4		●	●
2, 3		●	7, 8, 9	4	1	1, 2, 3, 4	●	●	
1, 2, 3	●	●	7, 9	1, 5	1	3, 4	●	●	●
1, 2, 3, 4	●			3	2	3		●	●
1, 2, 4	●			2, 3	2	2, 3		●	●
	●		1, 2, 3, 4	2					●
3, 5	●		2	2		4		●	
1, 4, 5	●		2, 4, 5			4		●	●
1, 2, 3	●		6, 7, 8, 9, 10			1	1, 2	●	●	●
4		●		4					

Unit Overview

This unit is the conclusion to *Marketing Essentials.* After studying the marketing field and the skills necessary to succeed in it, students are ready to get down to the practical aspects of planning their future careers. Chapter 37 introduces the means for identifying and researching career possibilities and suggests that a student prepare a plan of action when a career choice has been made. Finally, Chapter 38 includes proven methods for conducting a job search.

Introducing the Unit

Ask how many students have seriously considered what career they will pursue after graduation from high school. For those students who have not decided on a career direction, point out that current hobbies and interests, such as sports, computers, and drawing, could easily become the marketing jobs of tomorrow. Reinforce how important it is for students to begin career planning now, even if their direction is not clear.

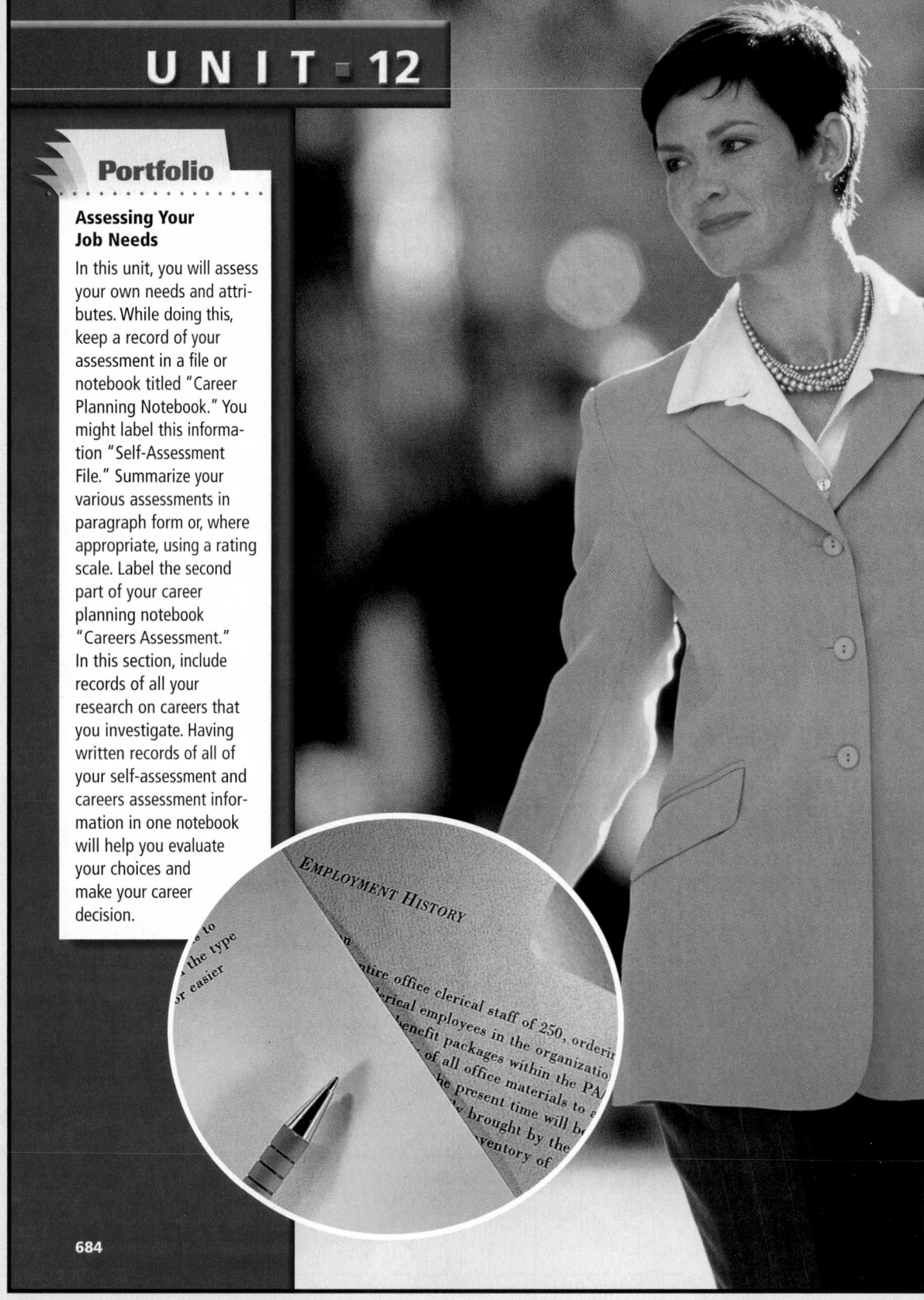

U N I T ■ 12

Portfolio

Assessing Your Job Needs

In this unit, you will assess your own needs and attributes. While doing this, keep a record of your assessment in a file or notebook titled "Career Planning Notebook." You might label this information "Self-Assessment File." Summarize your various assessments in paragraph form or, where appropriate, using a rating scale. Label the second part of your career planning notebook "Careers Assessment." In this section, include records of all your research on careers that you investigate. Having written records of all of your self-assessment and careers assessment information in one notebook will help you evaluate your choices and make your career decision.

684

Field Trip Suggestions

Plan a Trip to a Human Resources Office Arrange for your students to visit the human resources office of a large business. They should bring their résumés and be prepared to complete a job application and employment interview. Find out whether the business allows potential applicants to inquire about job openings by telephone or whether job openings are listed in a public place.

Career and Professional Development

Unit Overview

The work you do to earn a living will most likely become the central activity around which you plan your daily life. You'll spend close to half your waking hours working, and your career will span about 40 years. The focus of this unit—career planning—is the logical conclusion to *Marketing Essentials*.

Chapter 37 provides a six-step procedure to guide you in assessing your own needs and attributes along with the demands and opportunities of careers. It also shows you how to evaluate career choices, make a career decision, and develop a plan of action. Chapter 38 provides guidance in finding and applying for a job, including how to use the Internet for these purposes.

In this Unit:

Foundations of Marketing

○ Professional Development

○ Communication, Interpersonal Skills

DECA Unit Project

Have students prepare a file that includes their career profile, plan of action, sample job application, résumé, cover letter, list of references, and answers to common questions asked during an interview. Have them go through a simulated job interview with adults who will act as the interviewers. Ask school faculty and staff as well as other adults (parents or former students) to volunteer to be interviewers. Send a copy of the particular student's file to the adult evaluator (interviewer) prior to the scheduled interview day, along with a memo explaining the simulation. Provide sample questions and an eval-uation sheet for the interview. Some criteria to consider are: appearance, being on time, quality of application mater-ials, communication skills, poise, qualifications for the job for which the applicant is applying, and overall impression. Ask the interviewers to provide feedback on the evaluation sheet. Review evaluation sheets with students.

www Go to the *Marketing Essentials* Web site (**www.marketing.glencoe. com**) for resources to teach and assess occupation-specific vocabulary.

Unit Closure

Meet with students individually to make sure they finish this course with a career direction and an understanding of how to use career research resources. Also, ask each student to evaluate his or her job interview simulation experience.

Guest Speaker Suggestions

Employment Agency Representative Invite a representative of an employment agency to explain to your students how he or she does career counseling and employment aptitude testing.

School Guidance Counselor Ask your school guidance counselor to talk about career exploration opportunities and specialized career training opportunities available after graduation.

Chapter **37**

Identifying Career Opportunities

Chapter Overview

In this chapter, students look at the factors that will affect and influence their career decisions.

 Springboard

List and Describe Before beginning this chapter, have students list in writing their aptitudes, interests, hobbies, and courses taken in which they excelled as well as struggled. Then have them write five adjectives that describe their personality and three values that depict the way they feel about family, friends, and work. Have students save this work for future use.

Prereading

List the section objectives to discuss with students. Have students skim the chapter, looking at the pictures, reading the captions, and noting the heads. Ask questions to ensure that the students have a minimal understanding of chapter structure.

Preteaching Marketing Vocabulary

Write the vocabulary terms on the board. Have each student silently choose two terms from the list and look them up in the chapter. Have them close their texts and give the definition for each term to the person sitting next to them.

Marketing:
What It Takes
Answer Answers will vary.

Marketing: What It Takes

Marketing Yourself

Two very important elements of marketing any product are knowing your product well and researching the market in which you plan to sell the product. As you join the "race" to make a career choice, *you* are the product—and the world is your potential market.

WHAT WILL YOU DO?

What are some of the things you will want to learn about yourself and your potential market?

THE DECA CONNECTION — **ADVISOR CORNER**

DECA Career Day To help chapter members focus on career development, coordinate a Career Day with a local community group, such as the Rotary Club, Kiwanis Club, or a local chapter of Sales and Marketing Executives International. Ask the business volunteers to draw up a list of 4–6 jobs within their industry and provide a description of them. Students will develop their résumés and research a job and a company through the Internet, personal interviews, and publications. One class day can be spent learning interview techniques and role playing. On the DECA Career Day, business volunteers can give valuable feedback to students.

Important Career Decisions

Choosing a Career

Like many high school students, you may not have thought about what kind of career you would like to have. A career differs from a job in that it is a series of progressively more responsible jobs in one field or in related fields. Choosing a career requires careful thought and preparation. The following six-step procedure will help guide you in making important career choices:

1. Conduct a self-assessment.
2. Identify possible career choices.
3. Gather information on each choice.
4. Evaluate your choices.
5. Make your decision.
6. Plan how you will reach your goal.

■ Assessing Yourself

The first step in your career search is to conduct a self-assessment. You can begin by assessing your values, interest, and skills and aptitudes. Then you can assess your personality, learning style, lifestyle goals, and work environment and relationship preferences. As you make your assessment, record your findings in a notebook. Label the notebook "Self-Assessment File." Summarize your various assessments in paragraph form or, where appropriate, using a rating scale.

YOUR VALUES Values are beliefs that guide the way people live. Just as people have different abilities and personalities, they also have different values. Defining your system of values is essential in choosing a career. When you understand your values, you know what you want out of life. You can then choose a career that is suited to your values.

You can identify your values by identifying the kinds of actions that are important to you. If you are willing to work very hard to succeed, you value achievement. If you want your work to be acknowledged, you value recognition.

YOUR LIFESTYLE GOALS The word *lifestyle* refers to the way you spend your time, energy, and money. Your lifestyle goals reflect your vision of how you see yourself living in the future. Your career has a great effect on your lifestyle. The happiest, most satisfied people have the greatest control over their lifestyle. Most of these people are well educated, motivated to succeed, and have incomes well above the average.

● What You'll Learn

- How to assess your values, lifestyle goals, interests, skills and aptitudes
- How to appraise your personality
- How to visualize your work environment and relationship preferences

● Why It's Important

Understanding yourself is the first step in finding a career you'll enjoy. It is necessary to know your own attributes well when trying to select the most satisfying career for you. This section will help you begin to assess your attributes so you can match them with the right career.

● Key Terms

- values
- lifestyle goals
- aptitude

FOCUS

 Bell Ringer Activity

Brainstorm Everybody knows people who are happy and people who are unhappy in their jobs. Begin this section by having students generate some examples of each (but do not ask for actual names). Then have students help you generate a board list of probable reasons that could help explain why these people enjoy/ do not enjoy their work. Consider such things as personality type, aptitude for the type of work, whether or not the work agrees with each person's basic values, job stress, etc.

Write students' observations on the board, cautioning them that the purpose of this exercise is only to observe and not to make value judgments of others.

Introducing the Section

Important Career Decisions After you have finished the Bell Ringer Activity, have students consider the reasons why they might be happy or unhappy in their co-op jobs or with any other activity in their lives, such as participating in sports, school activities, or other extracurricular activities. Their reasons for being happy and/or unhappy will probably mirror with their observations generated in the Bell Ringer Activity. This section will help them explore such considerations as personal values, skills, and aptitudes when setting career goals.

Classroom Resources

For the Teacher
- Teacher Editions for all workbooks
- Assessment Package
- PowerPoint Presentation Software
- Interactive Lesson Planner
- **ILP** Block Scheduling, p. 12
- **ILP** Lesson Plans, p. 78
- **ILP** Internet Resources, p. 93

ILP *BusinessWeek* Case Studies, p. 229
ILP Marketing Career Portfolio, p. 42
- *Marketing Essentials* Web site (**www.marketing.glencoe.com**)

For the Student
- Student Activity Workbook, p. 327
- Marketing Math Workbook, p. 135

- Marketing Research Project Workbook
ILP School-to-Work Activity Workbook, p. 151
- Virtual Business simulation
- *Marketing Essentials* Web site (**www.marketing.glencoe.com**)

ILP These resources are available in print and on the Interactive Lesson Planner (ILP)

Concept Development

1. Read Section 37.1 with students.
2. Have students read aloud the Case Study on page 689 and review the answers in class.
3. This section recommends the use of the World of Work Career Interest Survey. You can also contact CTB/McGraw-Hill, (800) 538-9547, for information on its vocational preference record and vocational interest surveys.
4. Invite one of your school's guidance counselors to discuss the school's services and resources available to help students research careers. In addition, you may wish to invite representatives of local, state, and federal government offices, as well as military recruiters, to discuss how students can research marketing-related careers in government and/or military service.

CAPTION ANSWER
Work or Play? He may consider becoming a mechanic, car salesperson, or engineer.

As a child, your lifestyle was dependent almost entirely upon your family and your relationships with family members. As a student, your life revolves around your school, your studies, and your friends. As an adult, your lifestyle is made up of many things, but the following are major influences:

- where you live (city or rural area)
- the type of housing in which you live
- your choice of foods, clothing, and leisure activities
- your mode of transportation
- your relationships with your family and friends
- the work you do to earn a living

If attaining a certain lifestyle is important to you, then choosing a career that will allow you to reach your lifestyle goal is essential. Your career is the key because your earnings will pay for your lifestyle. The ideal career will be compatible with all of the other elements in life as well.

YOUR INTERESTS It is likely that you will spend 30 to 40 years working—so you will want to choose work that interests you. Your interests are the things you enjoy doing.

When you research careers, you will make judgments about how interesting each career would be. Your judgments will probably be more accurate if you first survey your own interests. To evaluate your interests, write down the things you like to do, including leisure activities, school activities, favorite classes, sports, and social activities. If you feel that your list is too short or unvaried, then you may want to try out some new activities to learn whether you enjoy them.

Another way to find out about your interests is to take a career interest survey. A career interest survey is similar to a test, but there are no right or wrong answers. You are given a long list of activities and you decide how much you would like doing each of them. Then you score your own survey to learn which career areas you would find most interesting. Your school counselor or marketing teacher can probably arrange for you to take one of these surveys.

YOUR SKILLS AND APTITUDES Values and interests are important in self-assessment because they help you picture what you want your life to become. They may even suggest certain careers. It takes

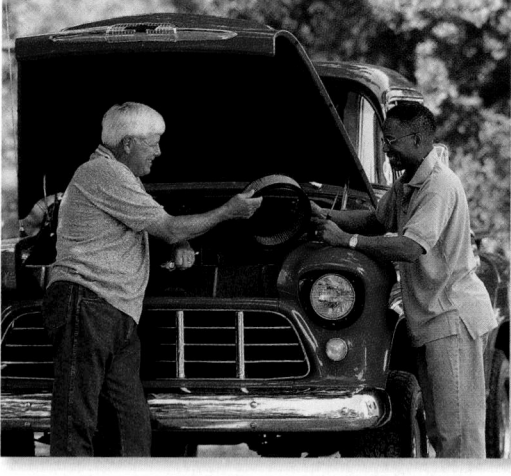

■ **Work or Play?** Your interests or hobbies can be a guide to help you narrow your career search. *What careers might be related to this young man's interest in cars?*

certain skills, and an aptitude for the work, to be successful in any career. An **aptitude** is an ability, or a potential, for learning a certain skill. Pursuing a career without having an aptitude for the required skills might prove to be a struggle instead of a pleasure—and real success would be harder to achieve. A person who can't describe the benefits of products won't have much success selling. You can see that it is important to identify your aptitudes before you choose a career.

Begin a new page in your self-assessment file, and list all the things you have done well. Do you find it easy to sell cookies, candy bars, or other items that your DECA chapter sells to raise funds? Are you good at organizing committees and getting everyone to do their jobs? Is math easy for you? Have you won any prizes for your creative ability?

The grades you earn in school may indicate some of your aptitudes. If most of your written reports earned A's and B's, you probably have an aptitude for writing. There are several tests that can help identify areas of strength.

Perhaps you have already developed certain skills that will be useful in a career that interests you. List them on a separate sheet of paper in your self-assessment file and update your list as you develop new skills. Your skills list will be very helpful when you apply for a job.

GREAT IDEAS from the Marketing Classroom

Kevin Reisenauer
Minot High School
Minot, ND

Teenagers Preparing for the Real World, by Chad Foster, helps students develop a formula for success. When we begin talking about individual success and their personal goals, we read this book. It inspires students to develop better plans for the future.

Then students research a career by interviewing someone in that area and using the Internet. They prepare a 20-minute presentation geared towards a fourth grade audience and present it in elementary schools to groups of young students. My students learn a great deal, including goal setting and planning for the future, as well as other skills. It is also a great effort to promote marketing to future high school students.

Case Study

Making Your Career Decision: From Doodles to Prime Time

While growing up, Matt Groening spent his time doodling when he was supposed to be working on his spelling. His unconventional personality made people think that he would not go far in life, but he proved them wrong.

After graduating from college, he went to Los Angeles to make a living as a writer. He worked at a sewage treatment plant, and then as a chauffeur. He kept up his doodling, and in 1977 he invented a comic strip that was syndicated to 250 newspapers. He quit his chauffeur job and began to make a living from his doodling.

In 1986, Groening was asked to create a 2½ minute animated feature for a television variety show and "The Simpsons" was born. In 1990, the half-hour "Simpsons" series began—the first animated prime time TV program in 20 years. It immediately became the most popular show on television. Ten years later the show was still among the ten most-watched TV programs in America every week, in addition to airing in many other countries. Simpsons merchandise is sold all over the world.

Matt Groening turned his love of doodling into a very profitable career. His interests and aptitude led him to the work that was right for him.

Case Study Review

1. What interests do you have that could lead to a career? What aptitudes?
2. What sort of personality do you think a television cartoonist needs?

A MATTER OF ETHICS

3. Sometimes the television network tries to control the content of the Simpsons. Do you think it is ethical for the network to overrule the creators of the show?

YOUR PERSONALITY Your personality is the combination of all of the unique qualities that make you who you are. Understanding your personality characteristics will help you to determine what types of work situations will best suit you. There are tests that you can take that will help you identify your personality type. It may not be necessary, however, to take a test to learn how your personality will fit with certain careers. To assess your personality traits, use a new page in your self-assessment file to list words that describe you. As you perform this exercise, remember that there is no right or wrong kind of personality. There are only different kinds of people.

Discussion Starter

Future Careers Ask students: If you were to pick the ideal job, what would it be? (This question will help students begin thinking about a future career.)

Cooperative Learning

Personality Traits Have students retrieve the Springboard activity they completed at the beginning of this chapter, specifically the five adjectives used to describe themselves. Have students who are friendly work on this exercise together. Ask each of them to list five adjectives that describe the other two without letting them see what that person wrote to describe him/herself. After five minutes or less, have the students compare lists to see if their self-perceptions match those of their friends. After the exercise, have each student write a short analysis of what they learned from the exercise. *(For example, others perceived them differently or the same as they perceived themselves.)*

Case Study Review Answers

Making Your Career Decision: From Doodles to Prime Time
1. Answers will vary for each student.
2. Some possible answers are outgoing, funny, and flexible.

A MATTER OF ETHICS
3. Students who think that it is ethical may say the network pays for the show to be made and is responsible for making a profit for stockholders. Students who disagree may say that it is a violation of freedom of speech.

Research and Write Ask students to research one marketing job that interests them. Based on their research, have them write a 50-word job description for the job. The description should include such things as job duties, salary range, work environment, educational requirements, and pathway for advancement. Students should list all of their resources and attach any ads that they used as source material. Review their source material and resources in class, but have students keep their job descriptions in their notebooks.

ASSESS

Reteaching

1. **Review** Assign and review the vocabulary terms for this section.
2. **Fact and Idea** Assign and review Fact and Idea Review questions 1–4 from the Chapter Assessment.
3. **Concepts** Review the following concepts to make sure students understand how they relate to their preferences in terms of a career: values, lifestyle, aptitude, and personality.

FIGURE 37-1

DATA, PEOPLE, THINGS

All jobs involve working with data, people, or things. Most jobs involve working with combinations of these.

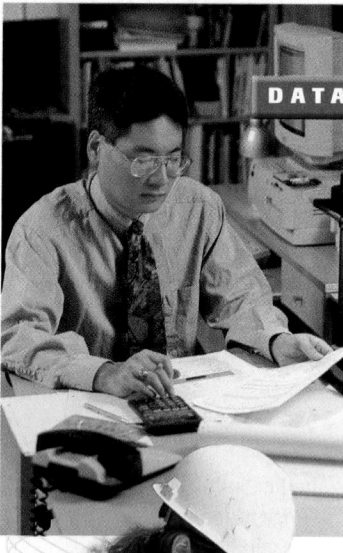

DATA

Accountants work mostly with data. Do you like doing involved math problems? Do the hours seem to pass quickly when you are working on a computer? If you answered yes, then you probably like working with data.

PEOPLE

Salespeople deal mostly with people. Think about your own preferences. Do you prefer working with large groups or with one person at a time? Do you get lonely working alone for hours on a project? A little reflection will probably tell you how much you like working with people.

THINGS

Carpenters spend most of their time working with things. Do you enjoy woodworking, building, working on your car, or fixing things around the house? If so, then you probably like working with things.

COMBINATIONS OF DATA, PEOPLE, THINGS

In most marketing careers, you will work with more than one of these three. A hotel registration clerk works mostly with people and data.

YOUR WORK ENVIRONMENT Your work environment refers to where you work—the place and the working conditions. Working conditions include sights, sounds, and smells.

Many factors affect working conditions, such as geographic location. If you are a carpenter who works outdoors, your working conditions would be quite different in California as opposed to Alaska.

Whether you work during the day or at night also affects your working conditions. If you prefer not to work nights, there are many careers you should rule out. For example, doctors and nurses as well as hotel and restaurant employees often work evening shifts and night shifts. While an event planner may book events during the day, he or she is often required to be on hand to see that things go smoothly during the event, regardless of what time of day or night it is held.

You don't have to know all your preferences about working conditions now, but start thinking about them. When you read about the working conditions of a certain career, you will have a better idea of your criteria for a positive work environment.

YOUR RELATIONSHIP PREFERENCES All jobs require working with data, people, or things—alone or in some combination (See Figure 37-1 on page 690). These categories can form the basis for describing different kinds of careers. Since any career you choose will likely involve an overlapping of these categories, think about which interests you most.

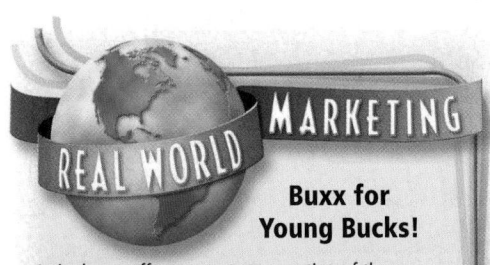

REAL WORLD MARKETING

Buxx for Young Bucks!

In its latest effort to capture a portion of the $153 billion teens spend annually, Visa USA has introduced VISA Buxx. Visa Buxx allows teens to spend money loaded onto cards by their parents. The card looks like a credit card and can be used to spend online or in stores to get cash at automated teller machines. Visa Buxx are not attached to any line of credit or bank accounts, but parents receive statements and can track their teen's spending. One added safety feature—parents must acknowledge they've given their teens a financial literacy test.

Thinking Critically
Why is Visa requiring that kids take financial literacy tests before using VISA Buxx?

37.1 ASSESSMENT

Reviewing Key Terms and Concepts

1. What should you consider when conducting a self-assessment?

2. What are values?

3. What are three influences on the lifestyle of an adult?

4. Why is it important to know what skills and aptitudes you have?

Thinking Critically

5. Why is it important to set goals? What can happen to someone who does not set goals?

Integrating Academic Skills

6. **COMMUNICATION** Select an area vocational school, technical institute, community college, college, or university in which you are interested. Write a letter requesting information about entrance requirements and courses of study. Conclude with a request for an admission application.

37.1 ASSESSMENT ANSWERS

Reviewing Key Terms and Concepts

1. Consider your values, lifestyle goals, interests, aptitudes, personality, and work environment and relationship preferences.
2. Values are things that are important to you.
3. where you live; the type of housing you live in; choice of foods, clothing, leisure activities; mode of transportation; relationships with family and friends; work you do for a living

4. You will be happier in your chosen work.

Thinking Critically

5. Goals provide people with career direction. Someone could end up in work he or she doesn't like and is less likely to succeed.

Integrating Academic Skills

6. **COMMUNICATION** Letters will vary.

Enrichment

1. **Review** Assign and review the appropriate Thinking Critically questions from the Chapter Assessment.

2. **Extend** Assign and review the corresponding activities from *BusinessWeek Case Studies* and *Internet Resources.* **ILP**

3. **Analyze** Suggest that students take a personality inventory to see if the results match their perception of themselves.

Evaluation

Assign and review the Section 37.1 Assessment.

Technology Resources

 Assessment Resources Go to the *Marketing Essentials* Web site (**www.marketing.glencoe.com**) for resources to teach and assess occupation-specific vocabulary.

CLOSE

Section Wrap-Up

Have students complete this statement: The most valuable thing I learned in this lesson regarding career planning is . . . *(Answers will vary.)*

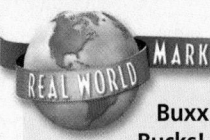

REAL WORLD MARKETING

Buxx for Young Bucks!

Answer Answers will vary but should concentrate on responsible spending and saving.

SECTION 37.2

Career Planning

Bell Ringer Activity

Research Ask students to answer these questions: (1) If you wanted to research one or several careers, what resources would you use? (2) In researching each career, what information would you want to know about the careers and how they relate to your perception of who you are and what you want?

Introducing the Section

Career Planning Make two lists of students' answers from the Bell Ringer Activity, based on (a) and (b) above. When discussing "b" encourage students to look beyond such things as duties and responsibilities, and include such things as values and lifestyle. Keep these lists on the board throughout this lesson, and add to them as you discuss additional research resources and information students might want to further explore.

What You'll Learn

- How to complete a career assessment
- Where to look for career research resources

Why It's Important

The more career information you have, the easier it will be to decide which one is right for you. Research can provide you with a wealth of information on subjects such as salaries, working conditions, and prospects in your field.

Key Terms

- career outlook
- *Dictionary of Occupational Titles (DOT)*
- *Occupational Outlook Handbook (OOH)*
- *Guide for Occupational Exploration (GOE)*
- career consultation
- internship

Career Assessment Planning

Once you identify careers that interest you, it's time to research if those careers are right for you. Even if you have already chosen a career goal, select two or three other careers to research and assess. You will save time by learning about several careers now if your first choice doesn't work out.

Now begin a new section in your career planning notebook and label it "Career Assessment File." Later, you will compare this information with that in your self-assessment section to help make your career decision.

■ Work Values

Certain values are important to success on the job. These include honesty, dependability, diligence, and team spirit. Each job and career field has its own special work values. Most retail marketing careers would place a high value on working long hours, getting along with others, coping with stress, and being willing initially to work for lower pay.

Study the work involved in potential jobs, but also look beyond the duties and responsibilities. Consider the values that are important for success in each field.

■ Lifestyle Fit

Some careers will fit your lifestyle goals better than others will. Try to determine how compatible each career will be with the other elements of your lifestyle goals.

You probably don't want a career that requires a lot of travel if spending time with your family is important to you. Similarly, you probably won't look for a job that requires working weekends if you cherish weekends for religious or leisure activities. Look for a career that enhances the other elements of your lifestyle, not one that conflicts with them.

■ Salaries and Benefits

Consider if each potential career will provide the financial support for your desired lifestyle. You must look at both salary and benefits such as paid vacations, life insurance, health insurance, and a pension (or retirement) plan.

Companies and businesses offer employees different kinds of benefit packages. Paid vacations will be a priority if you like to travel. Life insurance is especially important for families, and you can save

Classroom Resources

For the Teacher
- Teacher Editions for all workbooks
- Assessment Package
- PowerPoint Presentation Software
- Interactive Lesson Planner
- ILP Block Scheduling, p. 12
- ILP Lesson Plans, p. 79
- ILP Internet Resources, p. 93

- ILP *BusinessWeek* Case Studies, p. 229
- ILP Marketing Career Portfolio, p. 42
- *Marketing Essentials* Web site (**www.marketing.glencoe.com**)

For the Student
- Student Activity Workbook, p. 327
- Marketing Math Workbook, p. 135

- Marketing Research Project Workbook
- ILP School-to-Work Activity Workbook, p. 151
- Virtual Business simulation
- *Marketing Essentials* Web site (**www.marketing.glencoe.com**)

ILP These resources are available in print and on the Interactive Lesson Planner (ILP)

money if your employer pays for this or offers lower premiums through an employer-sponsored group plan. The high cost of health care today makes health insurance a necessity. Some employers pay the premiums for all their employees, while others have group plans that save you money. You may not think a retirement plan is important because retirement seems a long way off. Many older workers find themselves working into their seventies because they are not covered by such a plan. Others must rely on social security alone, which barely supports the most basic lifestyle.

Some careers provide more benefits than others do. Some, for example, regularly pay bonuses, give discounts on merchandise, or offer low interest loans on homes and autos. Others make recreational facilities available to their employees.

■ Career Outlook

Suppose you find a career that seems interesting, one in which you could do well and one that will satisfy your lifestyle goals. You now need to research the career outlook, or the availability of jobs in the field. A job with a good career outlook is one in an area that is growing and provides opportunities for advancement.

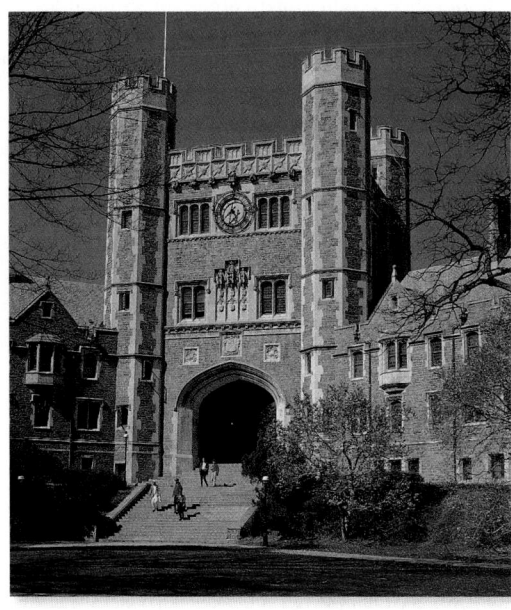

■ **Higher Education** Many careers require a college degree even for entry-level jobs. *What kinds of jobs do you know of that require only a high school diploma?*

■ Education and Training

Every job requires a certain level of education and training. Some require only graduation from high school or minimal post-high school education or training. Others will require four or more years of college.

Look at the education and training requirements of various careers. What if the career that fits your values, interests, aptitudes, and lifestyle goals requires more education and training than you are willing to pursue?

■ Duties and Responsibilities

Jobs are primarily distinguished by their duties and responsibilities. Job duties are the things you will be doing on the job. Responsibilities are the things for which you must be accountable. A duty may be to type business reports, while responsibilities include completing the work neatly, correctly, and on time. Learn all you can about the duties and responsibilities of each job you are considering. This offers certainty as you search for a career that you will find interesting and in which you can excel.

■ Skills and Aptitudes Required

You know that it takes more than just an interest in a job or career to succeed. Every job requires different types and levels of skills. First, you need to determine what skills are necessary to handle the required duties and responsibilities; then you can determine what aptitudes would be helpful in learning those skills. Suppose you are considering a career in advertising. When you look at the job description for an advertising copywriter, you learn that the skill used most is writing. In the event that you haven't done much writing, you must ask yourself what you can do to develop your writing skills.

Consider another example: when you look at the job description of an advertising layout artist, you learn that you would need good artistic skills. Perhaps you've done a lot of sketching and are developing your art skills further. You must determine if you have an aptitude for sketching and design work.

TEACH

▥ Technology Resources

PowerPoint The *Marketing Essentials* PowerPoint Presentation CD-ROM provides visual lecture aids for every chapter section.

Concept Development

1. Read Section 37.2 with students.
2. When discussing the DOT, the OOH, and the GOE, reproduce and distribute pages from each so students have a better idea of the content of each. Allow students to compare and contrast the similarities and differences between each resource.
3. There are numerous career texts available from trade publishers that give information on the current job market, specific careers, and trends for the future. Try to have some of these texts available in your classroom for independent student reading and/or for research. Many of them contain the latest projections from the Department of Labor and will help you provide an accurate picture of national employment trends.

Discussion Starter

Benefits Discuss with students what they consider to be the most important benefits in a job at this point in their lives. How might their preferences change when they (a) live on their own, (b) have a family, and (c) are not covered by their parents' or guardians' health insurance? *(Answers will vary. You may wish to give students other variables to consider.)*

CAPTION ANSWER
Higher Education Answers will vary, but may include many restaurant jobs and entry-level retail salesclerk jobs.

Thinking Critically

1. **Employment Trends** Have students relate their observations on employment trends locally, regionally, and nationally, and tell how such trends will affect their preparation for pursuing their anticipated careers. They should consider such things as employment outlook; ability to work in certain areas of the country; initial and continuing education needed to keep abreast of developments in the field; and how they can prepare now for the current and anticipated changes.

2. **Nonmaterial Benefits**
   Ask: Why are some people content to work in jobs where the salary is low when they have the skills and knowledge to be making more money elsewhere? *(Answers might include a discussion of the non-material benefits of working at any job, which include: enjoyment of the work; the joy of helping others; an alignment of one's personal values with the job and its requirements; an enjoyment of co-workers and/or the general atmosphere; and a good "fit" with one's lifestyle.)*

CAPTION ANSWER
Work Environment Students may mention that they would enjoy working with other people. Some negative aspects of the work environment in the photos may be heat in the kitchen, heavy lifting, being outdoors in building materials yard, or working alone in a phone- and computer-related job.

---

694   Unit 12 ■ *Career and Professional Development*

■ Helpful Personality Traits

You have probably noticed that people in certain careers have similar personality traits. Does the type of work you do affect your personality? Do people with certain personality traits tend to choose specific careers? Do people with similar personalities choose the same type of career? The answer to these questions is yes.

Your personality is affected by all your life experiences. Your job is likely to become the central activity in your life, therefore it will affect your personality. Your interpersonal relationships with other people at your workplace will also shape your personality.

A popular belief about salespeople is that they must have outgoing personalities. This is not completely true. You learned in the sales unit of this book that many successful salespeople do not have outgoing personalities; in some cases, they simply enjoy helping other people. Someone who is very quiet and uncomfortable with strangers however, will have a difficult time on most sales jobs.

■ Work Environment

Working conditions vary from one job to another. There are big differences in the work environments of an office, a department store, and a factory.

As you study the working conditions of the careers you have selected, try to learn these things about each job:

- Is the work done indoors or outdoors?
- Is the work done sitting down or standing up?
- Is the work environment dusty, smelly, or especially noisy?
- Is the work environment dangerous? What are the risks?
- Is the work physically tiring (does it involve a lot of lifting, stretching, or walking)?
- Is the work done on a 9–5 shift, at night, on weekends, or from home?

■ **Work Environment** Working conditions include the physical environment you will be working in, as well as the people you will be working with. *Which aspects of the working conditions of these three workplaces do you think you would like? Which would you rather avoid?*

THE **◆DECA** CONNECTION
COMPETITIVE EVENTS AND MARKETING ESSENTIALS

Exploring Marketing Careers You can use DECA's Individual Series Events to help your students with career exploration. The nine occupational areas allow students to sample a variety of fields, including Apparel and Accessories, Food Marketing, Retail Merchandising, Restaurant Marketing, Sports Marketing, and Vehicles and Petroleum Marketing. The Marketing Management event specifically deals with non-retailing marketing environments. The Business Services Marketing Event deals with the marketing of services regardless of the business. All these events require a 100-question comprehensive exam, two role-play situations, and role-playing before a businessperson/judge.

Work Relationships

As you research careers, note the data/people/things relationships in the specific jobs you have selected. Most jobs require working with other people to some extent. Some jobs, like those in retail sales, offer constant exposure to people. Other jobs require you to work almost constantly with data or things.

Research Resources

To research careers, you will need to gather information from a variety of sources. You'll find current information at libraries or on the Internet. You can also learn a great deal through career consultations and actual work experiences.

Libraries

You can find many good career information resources in your school or public library. Many school libraries have a special section devoted to career information. You will find books, magazines, pamphlets, films, videos, and special references with information about careers.

The U.S. Department of Labor publishes three reference books that are especially helpful in career research. They are the *Dictionary of Occupational Titles*, the *Occupational Outlook Handbook,* and the *Guide for Occupational Exploration.* Most school and public libraries have these reference books.

The *Dictionary of Occupational Titles (DOT)* describes about 20,000 jobs and their relationships with data, people, and things. Several hundred more jobs that have emerged since the publication of the dictionary are defined in the *DOT Supplement.* Following each job title you will find a nine-digit code number. Use this number to locate the job description you want in the front section of the *DOT.* The *DOT* number provides a sophisticated way of classifying jobs into career clusters and worker functions. Recall that every job requires a worker to function to some degree in relation to data, people, and things. The middle three digits of the *DOT* number indicate the nature of this relationship for the given job title. This is explained fully in the *DOT* introduction.

Write down the *DOT* numbers of the jobs you are researching. This will save you some time because other sources also use these numbers to organize their information.

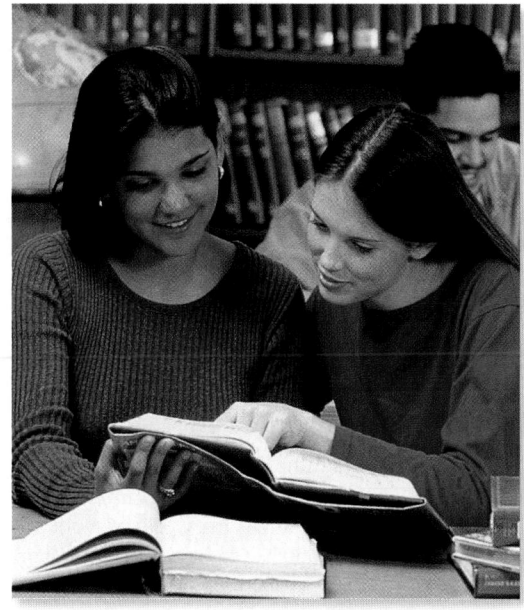

■ **Finding it at the Library** Public libraries often have sections devoted to career research. *What might you find at the library that could help you discover the right career?*

Job Listings...At Your Service

You may be aware of the popularity of Web sites that help you find a job. Some companies have taken it one step further, making the search process even easier for job seekers. Hotjobs.com is one Web site that offers job search agents. Job seekers submit a form listing their job criteria. Every day a search agent checks any new job listings to check for matching criteria; if the agent finds a match, it will send an e-mail informing the job seeker. Hotjobs.com adds hundreds of new jobs to their database every day. This service keeps seekers updated while cutting down on the work!

Thinking Critically

What other helpful services can job search Web sites offer?

Chapter 37 ■ *Identifying Career Opportunities* **695**

SECTION 37.2

Independent Practice

Research and Share Using the school library, the public library, and/or any other resources, have students list at least five additional career research resources. Have students share their resources in class. *(Resources may include student vocational organizations, magazines such as Inc. or Entrepreneur, national educational/vocational associations, college career research centers, military recruiters, United States Bureau of Labor Statistics, etc.)*

CAPTION ANSWER
Finding It at the Library Answers should include books, pamphlets, videos, Labor Department reference books (OOH, DOT, GOE), and other reference materials.

 Job Listings . . . At Your Service

Answer Job search Web sites may be able to offer services, such as a calendar for scheduling job interviews and a service that sends out reminders to send thank you notes.

Individualized Practice

Math Skills

Give students the following scenario: Julia pays for a group health insurance plan through her employer.

L1 Julia's company health insurance plan pays 80 percent of the first $1,000 worth of prescriptions and doctor's charges she incurs in a year. After this $1,000 limit is reached, the plan pays 95 percent. In 1999 her charges for prescriptions and doctor's visits were $1,765.60. How much did she pay out of pocket in 1999 for prescriptions and doctor's visits? *($238.28. $1,000 x .20 = $200. $765.50 x .05 = $38.28. $200 + $38.28 = $238.28)*

L2 From each paycheck, Julia has $7.65 deducted for health insurance, $2.50 deducted for life insurance, $1.75 deducted for dental insurance, and $5 deducted for a charitable contribution to United Way—totaling $405.60. Julia receives 24 paychecks a year. How much is deducted from her paycheck over the course of a year for insurance and charitable contributions? *($404.40. $7.65 + $2.50 + $1.75 + $5 = $16.90. $16.90 x 24 = $405.60)*

L3 Julia's monthly salary from January through June in 1999 was $2,765. After her raise in June, her monthly salary from July through December was $2,930. What percentage of her salary in 1999 went to deductions for health insurance, life insurance, dental insurance, and contributions to the United Way? *(One percent. January through June salary was $2,765 x 6 = $16,590. July through December salary was $2,930 x 6 = $17,580. Her total salary for the year was $34,170. Percentage of deductions for insurance and contributions was $34,170 ÷ $405.60 = .01 = 1%)*

The *Occupational Outlook Handbook (OOH)* provides information on more than two hundred occupations and is updated every two years. It is especially helpful and easy to use in locating such information as:

- Education and training requirements
- Usual hours of work
- Working conditions
- Salaries
- Job or career outlook
- Sources of additional information

Information on salaries and job outlook can change quickly. You should always use the latest edition of the *OOH*. Refer to the supplement to *OOH*, the *Occupational Outlook Quarterly*, for the most recent information.

The *Guide for Occupational Exploration (GOE)* is a reference that organizes the world of work into 12 interest areas that are subdivided into work groups and subgroups. The interest area Selling, for example, is divided into the three work groups: *Sales Technology, General Sales*, and *Vending*. Each work group is further divided into the subgroups *Wholesale, Retail, Demonstration, Sales*, and five others. The *GOE* includes the following types of career information:

- Kind of work done
- Skills and abilities needed
- Interests and aptitudes
- Required background or preparation

■ The Internet

The Internet is becoming a primary source for researching any topic. Career information is no exception. Information that was previously most easily accessible in a library is now available on the Internet, enabling you to do your research from home.

The Internet offers a multitude of career planning resources. You can find everything from accepted starting salaries to projected career paths. The Internet is not only a helpful tool while searching for a career, but for staying on top of developments in your career once you have chosen it.

In 1998, the U.S. Labor Department introduced the Occupational Information Network (O*NET). This online career information database was designed to eventually replace the DOT. O*NET online offers an interactive framework for exploring career information. You can enter key words relating to the career you wish to research, or you could search on Web sites that are devoted to career options.

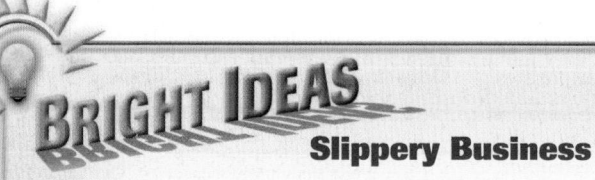

BRIGHT IDEAS
Slippery Business

Does the name Frank Zamboni sound familiar? If you are a hockey fan it might, because he is responsible for the invention that has simplified the process of maintaining the ice. Having been in the refrigeration and ice-block business for some years, Frank and some family members decided to build an open-air skating rink in 1940. It was one of the largest at the time. The intense Southern California sun and hot winds were one challenge that reduced ice quality. The Zamboni family covered the rink with a dome and came up against the next challenge—keeping the ice smooth. At the time, resurfacing meant pulling a scraper behind a trailer, scooping away the shavings, spraying water, using a squeegee to clean it, and finally allowing it to freeze. The process took more than an hour. It wasn't long before Frank began engineering a machine that would do all of that yet reduce time and effort—the Zamboni.

Thinking Creatively

What are some other inventions that could simplify a sports game?

BRIGHT IDEAS Slippery Business
Answer Answers will vary.

■ Career Consultations

A career consultation is an informational interview with a professional who works in a career that interests you. You can learn about the demands and opportunities of a career from someone with experience. You also get the opportunity to learn about the day-to-day realities on a job. Those who have met the challenges of a career are usually happy to talk about it.

Ask both your teacher and your counselor for suggestions about whom you should interview. They may have lists of people in the community who enjoy talking with young people about their work. Family members and friends of the family can also sometimes give you leads.

When you don't get some good suggestions from others, use the telephone directory to compile your own list of potential interviewees. You can then call each person from the list to find out whom you should interview. Suppose you are interested in becoming a retail buyer. Buyers are not listed under their own category in the Yellow Pages, so you will have to call the store that you are interested in first to get the name of someone you can contact.

It is always best to interview the person where he or she works. That's usually more convenient for the person. It will also give you a chance to see the workplace and form your own opinions. You may even get to see others actively engaged in the work you want to learn about.

You may also consider "shadowing" a person who works in a career field that interests you. This experience lets you follow a professional on the job for the day to see what the work is like—the daily duties, responsibilities, and challenges. Some schools set aside Groundhog Day for this purpose, while at others your guidance counselor can match you with a person in the career of your choice.

Before any career consultation, prepare a list of questions that you want to ask. Here are some suggestions.

- How do you spend most of your time on the job? Which work activities do you like most?
- What skills will I need to do this type of work? What skills will I need to advance?
- What education and training will I need? Can I complete some of the training after I begin working?
- How much time do you spend working with data? With people? With things?
- Will there be an increase in job opportunities in this field over the next several years? What impact will automation and new technology have on job opportunities in the next few years?

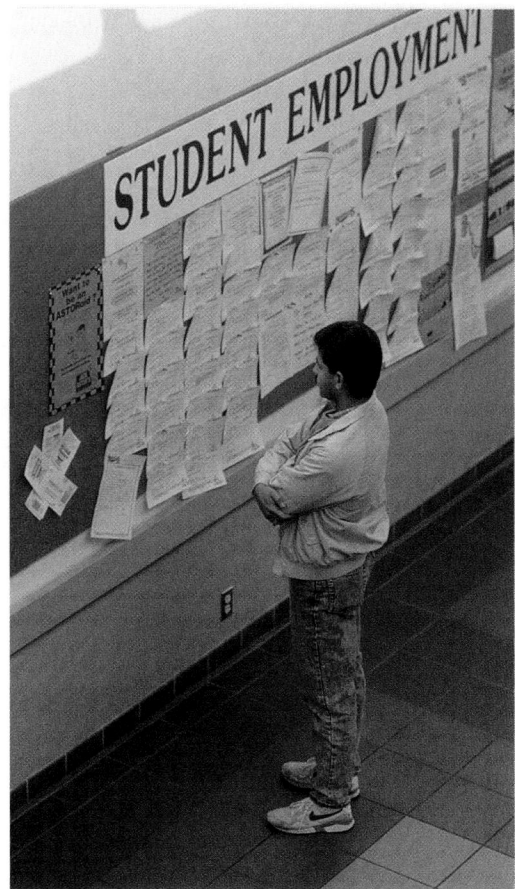

■ **Work to Learn** Work experience programs can give you valuable first-hand knowledge of what a job is like. *What can you learn from participating in such a program?*

CAPTION ANSWER
Work to Learn Answers will vary, but may include: the opportunity to see what environment and work duties are like; to develop work habits; get general information about world of work; and see how you like the work.

More About . . .

Career Counselors
Guidance counselors are employed by schools to help students make good decisions about courses and career choices. Outside of schools are specialists called career counselors who can help students make more complex decisions once they are on their career path.

SECTION 37.2

ASSESS

Reteaching

1. **Vocabulary** Assign and review the vocabulary terms for this section.
2. **Fact and Idea** Assign and review Fact and Idea Review questions 5–6 from the Chapter Assessment.
3. **Concepts** Review the following concepts to make sure students understand how they relate to their preferences in terms of a career: work values, lifestyle fit, career outlook, skills, aptitudes, personality traits, work environment, and work relationships.

Enrichment

1. **Review** Assign and review the appropriate Thinking Critically questions from the Chapter Assessment.
2. **Extend** Assign and review the corresponding activities from the *School-to-Work Activity Workbook.* **ILP**
3. **Research and Write** Have students locate a local business that could provide work experience in their career area of choice. Have them call to find out if that company offers internships, and if so, to whom they would address a letter requesting one. Have them write a letter to request an internship.
4. **Shadow** Contact local businesses to see if they would allow your students to "shadow" an employee of the company for a day or half a day. February 2nd (Ground Hog Day) is a good day to conduct this program. Your program and school as well as local businesses might get excellent publicity from such an endeavor.

CLOSE

Section Wrap-Up

Have students revisit the work they did in the Springboard exercise. Using a career of their choice, have them match up their characteristics to those of their intended career. Tell them to use pluses (+) and minuses (-) next to each item to indicate the correlation. Finally, ask them to decide if that career choice is a good. If not, what could they do to make it a better fit? This close will help introduce Section 37.3.

■ On-the-Job Experience

You can learn a great deal about a career by reading and by interviewing those who work in the field. There are many things, however, that you cannot learn about a job until you try it for yourself.

Many students work part-time after school, on weekends, or during the summer months. If you have an idea of what career you might be interested in pursuing, it is great experience to find an entry-level position in that field. Even if you are not sure exactly what you want to do, a part-time job can teach you valuable working skills. If you choose a job in a career field that interests you, you will benefit in the following ways:

- You can try out some of the work activities in your career field and decide how much you like doing them.
- You can experience the work environment of the career.
- You can develop work habits that will help you succeed in your career.
- You can broaden your understanding of the world of work and smooth the transition from school to work.
- You can make career contacts that can serve as mentors or assist you when you are searching for a job later.
- You can build up your résumé which will grow as you gain more working experience.

Does your school have a work-experience program? You may know it by another name, such as cooperative education, cooperative work-experience, work study, or diversified occupations. Many vocational work-experience programs include the word cooperative in their names because the programs represent a cooperative effort by schools and employers. In these programs, the teacher-coordinator teaches a class related to the job (such as marketing) and also supervises students on the job. This allows you not only to study an occupation but also to gain practical experience.

You may also look into an internship program at a company or organization that interests you. An **internship** offers a student direct work experience and exposure to various aspects of a career, either with or without pay. If you are considering a career in public relations, you might find an internship in a local public relations firm. While most of your duties will be basic, you will gain good exposure to the field through the professionals you work with.

The value of an internship is in the experience and the contacts that you make; often, students on internships are asked to stay on with a company after they have put in their time. Even if you choose not to stay at the company, your internship supervisor can be a great source of job contacts in addition to being a good reference. Employers seriously consider internship experience when reviewing candidates for new positions. It demonstrates high interest and a willingness to put in time to gain valuable experience.

37.2 ASSESSMENT

Reviewing Key Terms and Concepts

1. What are the major areas you should consider when you investigate possible careers?
2. Name three sources for information about careers.
3. What are the benefits of a career consultation?

Thinking Critically

4. You would love to work for a magazine but do not think that you have the necessary experience or talent as a writer. Is it possible for you to work for a magazine even if you don't have superior writing skills? Explain your answer.

Integrating Academic Skills

5. **MATH** Use the Occupational Outlook Handbook to find the current salaries for two marketing careers that interest you. What is the annual difference in those two salaries? Disregarding pay increases over the years, how much more would you make in the higher paying job over a ten-year period?

37.2 ASSESSMENT ANSWERS

Reviewing Key Terms and Concepts

1. Assess your work values, lifestyle fit, salaries and benefits, career outlook, education and training, duties and responsibilities, skills and aptitudes required, helpful personality traits, work environment, and work relationships.
2. Internet, libraries, career consultations, and work experience
3. It can give you a firsthand look at the duties and daily responsibilities associated with a job.

Thinking Critically

4. Answers will vary but may include working as an editorial assistant.

Integrating Academic Skills

5. **MATH** Answers will vary depending on the careers chosen.

Develop a Career Plan

Evaluating Your Choices

In the next step of the career planning process, you will match what you learned about yourself in your self-assessment with the career information you gathered. The best match that you find should be the most logical career choice.

You will be more efficient in evaluating your choices if you organize your task before you begin. Gather all of your self-assessment notes and research on different careers. It may be helpful to begin this matching process on paper. Create a personal career profile, or an evaluation format that allows you to compare your self-assessment side-by-side with a particular career assessment (see Figure 37-2 on page 700).

On the left side of the profile, write the information about yourself. Then make several photocopies of this form—one for each career that you researched and are interested in. Using these copies, fill in the career information on the right by referring to your notes. After you complete each profile, reread all the information carefully. Then ask yourself the following questions:

- Does this career match my personal values? Do the work values important in this career match my personal values?
- Does this career fit my lifestyle goals?
- Will this career provide an adequate income?
- Is the job outlook good for this career?
- Am I willing to continue my education and training as required for this career? Can I afford to do so? Will my employer possibly pay for it if I wait?
- Will the duties and responsibilities of this career interest me? Will I be able to perform them well?
- Will I have the skills required for this career? Do I have the aptitudes to learn the skills needed to advance in this career?
- How will my personality fit this career?
- Will I find the work environment and work relationships in this career satisfactory?

Using a personal career profile has a major advantage—you can refer to it again and again in the months and years ahead. Some people may doubt their decision after they have made their choice. It is not rare for an individual to choose one career path and later realize that it is not the best fit. The profile makes it easy to review your evaluation; then you can remind yourself of your priorities, change your decision based on your review, or change your profile based on what you have learned. It is helpful to constantly update your profiles as you develop new skills and find new possible career interests.

What You'll Learn

- How to match your own needs, wants, and potential qualifications with a realistic and satisfying career
- How to develop a plan to reach your career goals

Why It's Important

Once you have set a career goal, you must figure out the steps you must take to reach your goal. In this section, you will learn how to create a detailed plan of action that will show the steps leading to one of your career choices.

Key Terms

- planning goals
- specific goal
- realistic goal

FOCUS

Bell Ringer Activity

Explain Have students take a few minutes to answer these questions: What is a plan of action? Does a plan of action guarantee success?

Introducing the Section

Develop a Career Plan Review students' answers from the Bell Ringer Activity. A plan of action is a series of steps taken to achieve a particular goal. It does not necessarily guarantee success, but it gives you a sense of direction by helping you outline the steps you need to follow in order to reach a goal. In this lesson, students will develop their final plan of action for choosing a career by formulating goals.

TEACH

Technology Resources

PowerPoint The *Marketing Essentials* PowerPoint Presentation CD-ROM provides visual lecture aids for every chapter section.

Classroom Resources

For the Teacher
- Teacher Editions for all workbooks
- Assessment Package
- PowerPoint Presentation Software
- Interactive Lesson Planner
- ILP Block Scheduling, p. 12
- ILP Lesson Plans, p. 80
- ILP Internet Resources, p. 93

- ILP Blackline Masters, p. 84
- ILP *BusinessWeek* Case Studies, p. 229
- ILP Marketing Career Portfolio, p. 42
- *Marketing Essentials* Web site (**www.marketing.glencoe.com**)

For the Student
- Student Activity Workbook, p. 327
- Marketing Math Workbook, p. 135

- Marketing Research Project Workbook
- ILP School-to-Work Activity Workbook, p. 151
- Virtual Business simulation
- *Marketing Essentials* Web site (**www.marketing.glencoe.com**)

ILP These resources are available in print and on the Interactive Lesson Planner (ILP)

Concept Development

1. Read Section 37.3 with students.
2. Some students may have difficulty in setting career goals because they need more time for career exploration and self-assessment. Meet with those students individually to give them extra guidance and resources for research, or refer them to their counselors or to your school's career center.
3. Invite a panel of marketing education graduates to talk to students about where they are in their marketing careers, where they anticipate being in five to ten years, and how their goals have helped them chart a course for success. They should also talk about how they overcame potential obstacles (for example, obtaining funds for further education).

Discussion Starter

Changing Careers This section says that some people may discover, through first-hand experience, that a certain career is just not for them. Discuss with students the times that they tried such things as sports, school activities, or even their co-op jobs only to discover that they did not wish to pursue the activity further. Ask students the following questions:

- What have you learned about yourself after walking down a path and finding that it wasn't the best route to take after all?
- What skills and abilities did you learn you were able to apply to something you did enjoy?

FIGURE 37-2

Personal Career Profile

Name Joan Smith

Date September 4, 20--

Personal Information	Career Information	Match (1–5, with 5 being the best match)
Your Values: The value scales I took showed that I like to help other people (humanitarianism). I like to be a leader. Doing creative things is fun, too.	**Values:** As a teacher I would have a chance to help others—that's what it's all about. Teachers certainly have plenty of opportunities to be leaders, too. Teachers also need to be creative!	
Your Interests: My hobby interests have always been photography, reading, and theater. My career interest survey showed that I might like a career in leading/influencing, selling, the arts, or maybe a humanitarian career.	**Career Duties and Responsibilities:** As a teacher, I would present information, and direct student discussions and activities in class. I would help each student individually, too. (Maybe I could teach marketing or general business.) A teacher's working conditions would be good in most schools. (Summers off!)	
My Personality: I like people, and I have a good attitude toward learning. I have an open mind. I'm enthusiastic, too. However, I don't have the energy and drive that some people have. I don't know if I could work night after night.	**Type of Personality Needed:** A teacher must like kids, even when they aren't very likeable. I would have to prepare my lessons every day—couldn't just forget about them. Teachers need to be organized, too.	
Data-People-Things Preferences: I think I like working with people most of all. I wouldn't want to be stuck in an office all day with only "data" to talk to. I also wouldn't like working only with things. Some data would be all right, though.	**Data-People-Things Relationships:** Teachers work mostly with people—their students, the principal, parents. They work with data (information), too, though. I don't think they work much with things.	
Skills and Aptitudes: I may have some natural teaching skills—the kids at the YMCA always come to me for help. I helped several kids in Miss Moore's class. Business classes are easy for me.	**Skills and Aptitudes Needed:** Being able to present information so students can understand it is a very important skill. Of course, you must know your subject. An appetite for learning new approaches to teaching is important, too.	
Education/Training Acceptable: I sure never thought I would go to college—I never even liked doing the homework in high school. However, here I am a senior with no real prospects of a good job. Maybe college is the answer.	**Education/Training Required:** Four years of college (it sounds like forever, but I guess it does go fast) are required before you can begin teaching in most states. Some states require course work beyond that.	

■ **Personal Career Profile** A personal career profile helps you compare your self-assessment with a particular career assessment. *Based on this personal career profile, how does Joan Smith's personal information match the career information shown? Rank each category from 1–5.*

FIGURE 37-2 ANSWER
Personal Career Profile Rankings will vary. However, most students will likely agree that Joan's strongest matches for the career she has selected are the Values, Preferences, and Skills and Aptitudes sections. Her weakest match is Education/Training.

Making Your Decision

You are now ready to choose which career you would like to pursue. You may feel that you aren't ready to make such an important decision, or fear making a mistake that could affect you for years.

Your choice of a career is one of the most important decisions you will make. It is not necessary, however, to wait until you are absolutely certain about a career choice before you make your decision. You may wait for years if you do that. Make the best choice you can now, even if you think you may change it later. A flexible goal will give you something to aim for.

Making your first career decision now, even one you may change later, will be a positive influence on your life. It will give you a sense of direction. You can review your career planning process anytime. If you decide that another career is better for you, then it is no disgrace to change your goal. In fact, it's the right thing to do. You may find your career path taking many twists and turns before you establish yourself in the right job for you. Don't be afraid of making the wrong career decision—it is possible to learn from all of your experiences.

Developing a Plan of Action

Have you decided which of the marketing careers you researched is the best match with your self-assessment? If so, begin planning how you will achieve your career goal. A plan doesn't guarantee success, but it will outline the steps that you will need to follow to reach your ultimate goal.

▪ Formulating Planning Goals

The small steps you take to get from where you are now to where you want to be are **planning goals**. They give your life a sense of direction and move you steadily toward your ultimate career goal. Every time you reach a planning goal, you gain confidence to move on boldly toward the next one.

BE SPECIFIC You can make progress toward your ultimate goal by making your planning goals specific. A **specific goal** is stated in exact terms and includes some details. The goal statement "I want to become

a success," is not specific; however, "I want to complete my class in marketing this semester and earn at least a B," is specific. This is the type of planning goal that moves you toward your ultimate goal. The more specific you are about your career goals, the more likely it is that you will be able to formulate a plan to reach those goals. Each time you achieve a goal—no matter how small—it serves as motivation for you to keep working hard.

BE REALISTIC Planning goals must also be realistic. A **realistic goal** is one that you have a reasonable chance of achieving. Few people can reasonably expect to become the president of General Motors. If you have limited artistic talent, you can't realistically expect to become a commercial artist. Think about all of the different skills and aptitudes that you possess. They will guide you in both your ultimate career goal and your planning goals.

WORK BACKWARD When you set your planning goals, begin with your ultimate career goal. Then decide what goals you need to reach to achieve your ultimate goal. Work backward, starting with your most distant objective (long-term goals) and moving closer to your present position in time (medium- and short-term goals).

Suppose your career goal is be to become a chef. One short-term goal is to investigate what type of training you will need. Another short-term goal may be to work in a kitchen to gain practical experience. You may subscribe to a cooking magazine or keep up-to-date with new cookbooks. A medium-term goal may be to earn a degree from a culinary institute. Another medium-term goal is to get a job at a well-respected restaurant in your town or city. Finally, a long-term goal may be to study with a world-class chef.

Having a progressive series of goals allows you to test your ultimate career goal and make corrections along the way. While progressing toward your career goal, your experiences may reinforce your career decision or lead to your changing your career goal. You may discover another career that you find more interesting. On the basis of work experience in a kitchen, you may discover that you would rather own a restaurant than be a chef. At any point along the way you can adjust your path and your ultimate goal.

Cooperative Learning

Marketing Jobs Divide students into four to six groups. Give each group a list of three marketing jobs from various occupational interest areas. Have students brainstorm the following: the personality type(s) best suited to each job; the values a person might have if attracted to this job; the aptitudes, abilities, and/or skills needed; and the education needed. Review answers.

Thinking Critically

Coping with Change Ask students to generate some basic strategies for coping with change and for keeping abreast of innovations in their chosen careers. *(Strategies for coping with change may include developing new skills and flexibility in dealing with people and situations. Strategies for keeping abreast of innovations include reading news and trade journals; attending conferences, seminars; pursuing further education.)*

Independent Practice

Write and Review Have students write five of their planning goals. Since planning goals are so important, spend time with each student reviewing his or her goals. Help all students make their planning goals specific and realistic.

ASSESS

Reteaching

1. **Vocabulary** Assign and review the vocabulary terms for this section.
2. **Fact and Idea** Assign and review Fact and Idea Review questions 8–10 from the Chapter Assessment.
3. **Concepts** Review the following concepts to make sure students understand how they relate to their career preferences: ultimate career goal, short-range goals, medium-range goals, and long-range goals.

701

SECTION 37.3

Enrichment

1. **Review** Assign and review the Chapter 37 activities in the *Student Activity Workbook*.
2. **Review** Assign and review the appropriate Thinking Critically questions from the Chapter Assessment.
3. **Review** Assign and review the following Chapter Assessment activities: Building Workplace Skills, Applying Marketing Concepts, Linking School to Work, The DECA Connection Role Play, and Internet Connection.

Evaluation

Assign and review the Section 37.3 Assessment.

Technology Resources

 Assessment Resources
Go to the *Marketing Essentials* Web site (**www.marketing.glencoe. com**) for resources to teach and assess occupation-specific vocabulary.

CLOSE

Section Wrap-Up

Conclude with a discussion of personal responsibility. Students' success in their careers and personal lives depends on an ability to plan for and guide themselves, set new and more appropriate goals, and ask for help when they need it.

The Best Medicine
Answer Answers will vary.

702

■ Choosing the Best Education for You

Whatever your career choice, your plan of action to reach your goal will include some education and training. The amount can vary from a few days of on-the-job training to four or more years of college.

Choosing education is much like choosing a career. Follow the complete decision-making process to select the best program and the best school for you. Your school counselor is a good place to start when you want information on vocational schools and centers, technical institutes, community colleges, and colleges and universities. Your school and public libraries are also likely to have useful information. You can also search the Internet and visit the Web sites of those schools that you are interested in.

If you are planning education and training beyond high school, consider the following questions:

- What is my ultimate career goal?
- What course can I take now that will help me to reach that career goal?
- What education and training beyond high school is required to reach my career goal? Is there a specific college degree required?
- How much of this education and training must I complete before I enter this career?
- Where can I get this education and training?
- How much will this education and training cost, and how will I get the money? Are there scholarships or loans available to help me finance this education?
- How much education and training can I get on the job? What part-time jobs will help?

■ Outlining Your Plan

After you have answered these questions, begin writing your personal plan of action. Write down all of your goals, the date that you plan to begin working toward each one, and the date you expect to reach each goal. This will help keep you on track toward your ultimate career goal—the one that turns your dream lifestyle into reality!

The Best Medicine

When traveling in Singapore, you may notice that Singaporeans sometimes smile or laugh during situations that Westerners might deem laughing inappropriate. These behaviors may hide anxiety, shyness, bitterness, or loss of face. It is considered disrespectful and shameful to lose one's temper in public—and laughing is used as a way to hide negative feelings.

Thinking Critically

When might it be appropriate to hide feelings of anger in public?

37.3 ASSESSMENT

Reviewing Key Terms and Concepts

1. How does a career profile help in evaluating careers?
2. After evaluating career choices, what is the next step to take in choosing a career?
3. What steps should be involved in developing a plan of action?

Thinking Critically

4. Why is it important that your plan of action be written down?

Integrating Academic Skills

5. **COMMUNICATION** Your guidance counselor has requested that you write a personal plan of action for the summer. You are applying to colleges in the fall and would like to study fashion design at school. Considering these goals, develop an action plan following the suggestions discussed in this section.

37.3 ASSESSMENT ANSWERS

Reviewing Key Terms and Concepts

1. It helps to compare self-assessment side-by-side with a particular career assessment.
2. The next step is to make a career decision.
3. formulate planning goals, fulfill educational requirements, choose the best education for the chosen career, and outline the plan

Thinking Critically

4. It is possible to lose sight of your plan if it is not written down. Writing the plan helps you stay more organized, and you can revise it if any changes occur.

Integrating Academic Skills

5. **COMMUNICATION** Plans of action will vary.

Careers in Marketing

SPORTS MARKETING

E.J. Narcise
The SFX Sports Group
Senior Vice President

What does your job entail?

"I oversee our team, league, and venue services. My function is to develop and manage our goals and objectives. As part of SFX entertainment, the Sports Group merges entertainment and sports to maximize opportunities. Some of our clients are the Cleveland Browns, Denver Broncos, and San Francisco 49ers, as well as the University of Maryland, University of Connecticut, University of Miami, and Towson University. We work to develop incremental revenue streams—usually revolving around a new stadium or new project development. We also market sponsorships such as naming rights, for example the Baltimore Ravens' PSINet, and the Washington Redskins' FedEx Field."

What skills are important to you?

"People skills are most important in this career because you deal with an array of personalities, from owners of professional sports teams to project managers and contractors."

How did you get into sports management?

"I had a good friend who was the marketing director for the Baltimore Orioles. He introduced me to the owner of a minor league baseball team. At the time, I was a marketing manager for General Electric Company. I left GE to take a job running the AA affiliate of the Chicago Cubs. The rest is history . . . I've worked for several teams and went into the sports marketing business four years ago."

What training do you recommend for students?

"It is extremely important that students stay well rounded, especially through a liberal arts education. I think that specialization should be saved for graduate school. Maintaining an open mind and striving to broaden your academic horizons will open up many opportunities."

What is your key to success?

"Tenacity and passion for what I do. One breeds the other. I believe that your passion is your power."

Thinking Critically
Could you work in sports marketing if you were not a sports enthusiast?

Career Facts

Education and Training: Courses in marketing, accounting, communication, and business classes, and a strong interest in sports are necessary.

Aptitudes, Abilities, and Skills: Good communication and negotiation skills, administrative and supervisory ability, and financial aptitudes are necessary.

Career Path: Most sports and entertainment marketing managers come from college or professional sports programs. Many have previously worked in marketing or business prior to becoming a team manager.

Career Outlook: Average growth is projected in this field. Competition for the best positions is expected to be keen.

Careers in Marketing

Ask a student to read the Careers in Marketing feature aloud to the class. Discuss the skills and aptitudes required for a career in sports marketing. Ask students whether they think they would like or dislike a career in sports marketing. Discuss the pros and cons of such a career.

Thinking Critically Answer
Answers may vary. While it is certainly possible to pursue a career in sports even if you are not an avid fan, it is necessary to understand sports and the fans who make up the market.

 Guest Speakers
Invite a sports marketing executive to class to discuss his/her job.

Exploring Careers

Reading Job Ads
1. Ask each student to find a job ad in the classified ads of a newspaper or on a Web site. Have each student clip the ad or print it out, and attach it to a separate sheet of paper.
2. Read the following questions to students. Have them write and answer the questions about the ad on a separate sheet of paper.
- What is the title of the position?
- What is the type of work?
- What is the salary?
- What are the benefits of the job?
- Who is the employer?
- What are the qualifications for the job?
- What experience is needed?
- What training do you need?
- What is the work schedule?
- How or where do you apply?

3. In class discussion, ask students if they think they could apply for the advertised position. Ask them why or why not?

Lifelong Learning

Identifying Career Opportunities
Planning a career is a lifelong event, not something done once at age 18. It's helpful to focus on information sourcing and retrieval and to periodically reevaluate career choices. A conscious reexamination of educational choices is also necessary as the workforce takes on different characteristics. Being flexible is the key to a long, satisfying career.

Meeting Individual Needs

Students with Orthopaedic Impairments
Career choices for students with orthopaedic impairments need not be limited. In order to help all students overcome preconceived notions about career choices, invite a marketer, entrepreneur, or other successful person with physical impairments to class to speak about his or her career. Have him or her discuss any obstacles that were overcome.

Vocabulary Review

Paragraphs will vary. See Glossary for definitions.

Fact and Idea Review

1. Elements include: where you live; the type of housing you live in; your favorite foods, clothing, and leisure activities; your mode of transportation; your relationships with your family and friends; and the work you do to earn a living.
2. It can help you make judgments about how interesting the jobs you are researching would be.
3. Identifying your personality type can help you find a career that fits well with your own traits.
4. Assessing your preferences can help you choose a career that is compatible with those preferences.
5. Answers will vary but may include health insurance, pension benefits, paid vacation, life insurance, bonuses, discounts on merchandise, recreational facilities, and the use of a company car.
6. Resources include books, magazines, pamphlets, films, videocassettes, and special reference books.
7. evaluating your choices, making your decision, and planning to reach your goal
8. Three specific planning goals could be: "I want to earn a master's degree in business from Harvard." "I want to work in a large advertising company in New York City." "I want to own a retail store that sells sporting goods."
9. Answers will vary. A short-term goal might be to work as a sales clerk at a department store.

Thinking Critically

1. Answers will vary depending on hobby.
2. Answers will vary. Values usually formed in childhood and beyond by parents and experience with other people and situations, religious training, etc.
3. Answers will vary.
4. In many households both parents work, making child care necessary. Companies with good childcare might attract highly skilled employees.
5. Answers will vary but may suggest that planning a career increases the likelihood of success.

704

Chapter 37 ASSESSMENT

VOCABULARY REVIEW

Use these vocabulary terms in a paragraph on career research.

- values
- lifestyle
- aptitude
- career outlook
- *Dictionary of Occupational Titles (DOT)*
- *Occupational Outlook Handbook (OOH)*
- *Guide for Occupational Exploration (GOE)*
- career consultation
- internship
- planning goals
- specific goal
- realistic goal

FACT AND IDEA REVIEW

1. List six elements of lifestyle. (37.1)
2. How can making a list of your hobbies help you in the career planning process? (37.1)
3. How does personality type relate to career research? (37.1)
4. Why should you assess your preferences for working with data, people, or things? (37.1)
5. Name three benefits of a job or profession that could affect your career choice. (37.2)
6. List the career resources you might find in a school or public library. (37.2)
7. What are the three final steps in the career planning process outlined in the text? (37.3)
8. Name three specific planning goals. (37.3)
9. What is a short-term goal if you want to be a retail buyer? (37.3)

THINKING CRITICALLY

1. Think of your own hobbies or interests. Brainstorm ways that these could become professions.
2. How do you think your values were formed? What effect do you think your personal values will have on the career you choose?
3. Describe someone you know whose personality is a good match for the job he or she is in. Explain how their personality affects his or her work. Is the person happy in the job?
4. Childcare is a sought after benefit. Why do you think this is so? What are the advantages for the companies who provide childcare?
5. A successful friend tells you that she got to where she is because she is lucky, not because she set career goals. How would you respond to this?

BUILDING WORKPLACE SKILLS

1. **Human Relations** You love plants and flowers and have decided that your long-range goal is to own a retail garden shop. You have an opportunity to work in a local garden shop as soon as you graduate, get on-the-job training, work your way up, and eventually buy into the business. Your parents want you to go to college first. What should you do?
2. **Technology** A career in marketing sounds appealing to you, and you have always enjoyed looking for answers to problems. Some type of research in marketing seems like a possible career choice, but you're also interested in having a comfortable lifestyle. Use the Internet to find the salary ranges of some specific jobs in marketing research.

Building Workplace Skills

1. Answers will vary. One possibility is a part time job in the garden shop while attending college.
2. Salary ranges will vary.

Applying Marketing Concepts

1. Spreadsheets will vary, but students should discuss why certain areas are more important than others.
2. Summaries will vary.
3. Presentations will vary but should include the different job requirements covered in the text.
4. Summaries of articles will vary. Some suggested resources include *Forbes, BusinessWeek, Inc.,* and other professional journals.

APPLYING MARKETING CONCEPTS

1. **Researching Careers** Use a spreadsheet program to list the areas to consider when researching careers: work values, lifestyle goals, salary, benefits, career outlook, responsibilities, skills and aptitudes, education and training, personality traits, work environment, and involvement with data/people/things. Rank these items in importance when making a career choice. Compare your list with a classmate's and discuss differences.

2. **Considering Career Choices** Interview two people who work in the field of marketing. Ask them about the important considerations in choosing a career. Ask them if these considerations contribute to their like or dislike of their work. Ask them what was most important to them when they were job hunting. Use a word processing program to summarize your findings.

3. **Conducting a Career Consultation** Conduct a career consultation in one of the career areas you are researching. Use a presentation program to illustrate the importance of different job requirements. Present your findings to the class.

4. **Summarizing Career Concepts** Find a magazine article about someone who has made a mid-life career change. Summarize the article orally or in writing for your classmates. Be sure to explain why the career change was made and whether it turned out to be worthwhile.

LINKING SCHOOL TO WORK

Thinking Skills and Personal Qualities Ask your employer to describe how he or she chose his or her career, and the steps taken to achieve his or her short-, medium-, and long-range goals. Share this information with the class, comparing different paths taken by businesspeople.

THE DECA CONNECTION

Role Play: Interviewer

Situation You are to assume the role of interviewer for a local employment agency. You will be going into schools to talk to students about career planning.

Activity You must demonstrate to the agency manager (judge) that you are ready to begin your assigned task.

Evaluation You will be evaluated on how well you meet the following performance indicators:

- Identify tentative occupational interests
- Identify sources of career information
- Explain possible advancement patterns for jobs
- Describe techniques for obtaining work experience (e.g., volunteer activities, internships)
- Identify desirable personality traits important to business

interNET CONNECTION

Virtual College Visits

You have decided on a career in online marketing, and need to discover where you can get the skills and education you need.

Connect

- Use the Internet to identify colleges or technical schools with good programs in both computer science and business.
- Look at the different schools' Web sites and compare the programs and tuition costs.
- Choose the school that best fits your needs.

THE DECA CONNECTION

Students should be evaluated on the performance indicators noted in the Role Play.

- For another DECA Role Play go to the *Student Activity Workbook,* p. 327.
- For more in-depth Role Play practice, refer to DECA's *Essential Competitive Events Handbook.* To order, contact DECA at **www.deca.org**.

interNET CONNECTION

Web sites and choices will vary depending on student preferences.

Mini Quiz

Administer the Mini Quiz orally. For an expanded chapter quiz, go to page 221 of the *Reproducible Tests* book.

1. Self-assessment is the first step in a career search.
2. Values are beliefs that guide the way people live.
3. Lifestyle refers to the way you spend your time, energy, and money.
4. A(n) aptitude is an ability, or a potential for learning certain skill.
5. A(n) internship offers students direct work experience and exposure to various aspects of a career, either with or without pay.

Linking School to Work

Interviews and presentations will vary depending on the employer's career.

 GO TO

1. **Assessment** Have students complete the Reproducible Test for Chapter 37 or construct your own tests using the ExamView software.
2. **Enrichment** Have students complete the corresponding activities in the following workbooks:
   - *Marketing Math Workbook,* p. 135

Chapter **38**

Finding and Applying for a Job

Chapter Overview

In this chapter, students explore the job search process, including the process of applying and interviewing for a job.

 ## Springboard

Brainstorm Applying for a job is a process that begins with the job search and ends with the post-interview follow-up. Have students help you generate a board list of the things one must do to obtain and follow up on a job interview. *(Answers may include: get a work permit; search for and follow up on job openings and leads through referrals, newspaper ads, employment agencies, company personnel offices, direct calling, and letters of inquiry; apply for a job with letters of application, résumés, and application forms; prepare for the job interview; interview; and follow up with a phone call or note.)*

Prereading

List the section objectives to discuss with students. Have students skim the chapter, looking at the pictures, reading the captions, and noting the heads. Ask questions to ensure that the students have a minimal understanding of the chapter structure.

Preteaching Marketing Vocabulary

Students should be familiar with all of the vocabulary terms in this chapter. Review them orally with the class. Write on the board the terms that students may not know or fully understand, and reference them when you encounter them in discussing this chapter.

Marketing: What It Takes

The Marketing Plan for Your Career

Every marketing activity has a better chance of success with proper planning. Certainly, this is true when you are ready to market yourself. You will be looking for the best opportunity to enter your chosen career—the career around which your daily life will revolve as an adult. Take some time to reflect on what you've learned in this course, then consider how you will plan the most important marketing process of your life.

WHAT WILL YOU DO?
How will you organize your job finding program?

706

Marketing: What It Takes

Answer Answers will vary depending on students' interests, physical location, and desired career.

THE DECA CONNECTION

ADVISOR CORNER

Service for Job Seekers Employers often comment on the inability of some students to fill out job applications, to interview, and write good résumés. Have your DECA chapter take on a project that will serve the needs of all students in your school who are seeking employment. Put together a job seeking skills packet by copying appropriate materials from your teaching resources. Compose a cover letter to all sophomores and juniors from the DECA, and include a copy of the packet. The response to this public service will be excellent.

(Rhonda Cmerek, Taylor H.S., Taylor, TX)

Finding a Job

Finding Job Openings

When you are ready for a full-time job, you will want one that matches your needs, wants, and qualifications. Your main interest right now, however, is probably to find a job to gain work experience and earn some money. You should search for a job that you can enjoy and at which you can be successful.

How do you go about finding such a job? A productive first step is to contact all of the sources available to you that might produce a job lead. A **job lead** is information about a job opening. You may hear that a nearby department store is looking for part-time salespeople, but you don't know for which department or to whom you should apply. Sometimes you may have to act like a detective, following up skimpy leads and filling in the rest of the information yourself. Finding the right job requires getting as many leads as possible and following up on them.

■ Networking

One of your best sources of job leads is often family, friends, and acquaintances. The people that you know—family and friends, former employers, and professional people you know personally—form a network of individuals connected to you. Finding contacts among them is called **networking**.

Some young people are not comfortable asking people they know for job leads. They want to get a job on their own. There is nothing wrong with getting a job through networking, if you are qualified. While a friend may help you get your foot in the door, it is your hard work that will bring you success. Many jobs are never advertised because acquaintances of present employees fill them; therefore, it is important not to overlook this important source of job leads.

FAMILY AND FRIENDS Family members and friends often hear of job openings where they work. They may not immediately know of the perfect job for you, but they can ask their friends and coworkers about openings.

Do you have any friends who have started new jobs recently? Ask them if they have any leads. Make a list of family and personal friends who might help you find job leads. Do any of them own or manage their own business? They may need someone with your qualifications or have a business contact that is looking for a good worker like you.

List friends who work for companies where you would like to work to your list. Then add the names of school friends and neighbors who are somehow connected with a business that interests you. Perhaps

● What You'll Learn

- How to locate job leads from a variety of sources
- The best ways to contact your job leads
- How to expand your list of job leads

● Why It's Important

This section will help you understand how to use the best sources of job leads to find the job that will start you on your way to success in your chosen career.

● Key Terms

- job lead
- networking
- public employment agencies
- private employment agencies
- résumé
- direct contact

FOCUS

Bell Ringer Activity

Discuss Ask students: "Who is currently working?" Then ask: "How did you obtain the job in which you are now employed?" If no one in the class has a part-time job, ask, "If you wanted to get a job, where would you begin the job search process?" (Their answers will help you introduce the concept of networking, as well as all the other means of developing job leads, such as newspaper help wanted ads, signs in store windows, etc.)

Introducing the Section

Finding a Job On the board, make a list of students' answers from the Bell Ringer Activity. Once you have a substantial list of ways to get jobs, ask students what skills they think are needed to get job interviews. (*Answers will vary but could include perseverance and persistence, investigating the local job market, decision-making skills, deductive reasoning, memory skills, note-taking skills, and the ability to ask precise questions.*)

Students should begin to see that getting good job interviews is not a matter of luck but a matter of having good skills and using them well. In this section they will look at how to get good job leads.

Classroom Resources

For the Teacher
- Teacher Editions for all workbooks
- Assessment Package
- PowerPoint Presentation Software
- Interactive Lesson Planner
- ILP Block Scheduling, p. 12
- ILP Lesson Plans, p. 81
- ILP Internet Resources, p. 95

- ILP Blackline Masters, p. 85
- ILP *BusinessWeek* Case Studies, p. 235
- ILP Marketing Career Portfolio, p. 42
- *Marketing Essentials* Web site (**www.marketing.glencoe.com**)

For the Student
- Student Activity Workbook, p. 337
- Marketing Math Workbook, p. 135

- Marketing Research Project Workbook
- ILP School-to-Work Activity Workbook, p. 155
- Virtual Business simulation
- *Marketing Essentials* Web site (**www.marketing.glencoe.com**)

ILP These resources are available in print and on the Interactive Lesson Planner (ILP)

TEACH

📊 Technology Resources

PowerPoint The *Marketing Essentials* PowerPoint Presentation CD-ROM provides visual lecture aids for every chapter section.

Concept Development

1. Read Section 38.1 with students.
2. Have students read aloud the Case Study on page 712 and review the answers in class.
3. Some Glencoe resources appropriate for use with this chapter include *Succeeding in the World of Work* (along with the live-action career videos correlated to this text), *Independent Study for the World of Work, Job Finding Fast, The Work Book,* and *Dress Right for Business. Entering the World of Work* and *Advancing in the World of Work* are available for special needs students. Call (800) 334-7344 for more information and a Glencoe Career Education catalog.

CAPTION ANSWER
Getting Connected Answers will vary.

a classmate's mother or father works for a company that has an opening that's just what you are looking for. Most businesses welcome applications from friends of their employees because they trust their opinions. Valued company employees are good people to make referrals and recommendations because they understand the skills, values, and work ethic necessary to work for their company.

SCHOOL COUNSELOR Retail stores and other businesses often call school counselors for qualified students for part-time or temporary jobs. School counselors usually have contacts in the business community, therefore they sometimes hear about full-time jobs, too. Your counselor may know of a job that matches your interests and abilities and might be able to put in a good word for you.

PROFESSIONAL PEOPLE IN YOUR PERSONAL LIFE You probably have periodic contact with professional people in your personal life—doctors, businesspeople, dentists, or lawyers. If you have established a good rapport with these people, they will be happy to help you in your job search. Ask them for names of people that you can contact.

FORMER EMPLOYERS Have you ever held a job? Even if it was a temporary or part-time job, such as babysitting or mowing lawns, your former employers may be good sources of job leads. It is likely that they will want to help you find a job if they were pleased with your work. That is why it is always important to give every job your best effort.

■ Cooperative Education and Work Experience Programs

Many high schools have a cooperative education program in which students work part-time on a job related to one of their classes. You may already be working on a part-time job in marketing if the marketing class you are enrolled in is part of a cooperative education program. Cooperative education teachers have contacts in the business community because they place and supervise students on part-time jobs. Cooperative work experiences sometimes offer students both course credits and minimum wage payments.

Many schools also offer a work experience program that is not limited to just one career area,

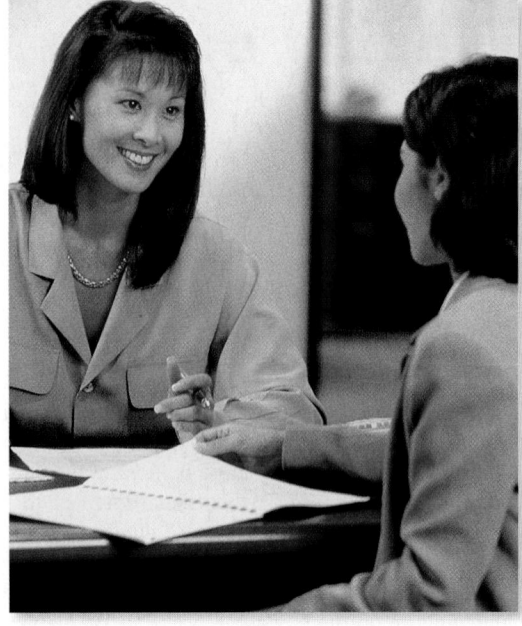

■ **Getting Connected** There may be professional people in your life who could be a source of job leads. *Who are some of the adults you know who could help you find a part-time job?*

such as marketing. The work experience coordinator has hundreds of contacts in the business community and may be a good source of job leads.

Schools have a good record of placing students in jobs that fit their interests and abilities. This is because teachers, counselors, and work experience coordinators know their students well. They also have the experience of seeing how former students fit into a particular career. Don't sit back and relax, however, thinking a teacher or someone else in your school will find the right job for you. There are almost always going to be more students looking for jobs than there are jobs to be filled. That means several well-qualified students will probably be referred for every job opening. It is possible to follow up several good leads and still not get a job because of the competition. You can't let this discourage you though—if you keep looking, the right job will eventually come through.

GREAT IDEAS from the Marketing Classroom

Barb Crum
Vidalia High School
Vidalia, LA

I demonstrate inappropriate dress for a job interview by coming to class dressed as "Prom Queen Pamela" or "Aerobic Amy." The students love this activity so much that, now, I select several students for a surprise day of inappropriate job interview

role plays. These students go all out—from odd clothing and bad hair to touching items on the interviewer's desk and answering cell phones during mock interviews. After each role play, we enthusiastically discuss what was wrong. The next day is "Dress for Success Day." Students come to school dressed as they would for an actual job interview, and we do interview role plays.

Newspaper Ads

Read the Help Wanted ads in your local newspaper, especially the Sunday edition. Most papers separate jobs by type. The Help Wanted ads are not only a good source of job leads, but they will also teach you about the local job market. You will learn the qualifications required for different types of jobs and the salaries offered.

Promptly follow up every ad that looks like it could lead to the job you want. The job will probably be filled quickly. Be aware, however, that not every ad represents a legitimate job offer. Ads that require you to make a deposit of money or enroll in a course are not usually genuine job offers but disguised attempts to sell you something. People who place ads like these will take your money, but they don't usually have any jobs to offer.

Employment Agencies

The main function of employment agencies is to match workers with jobs. Most larger cities have two types of employment agencies—public and private. Public employment agencies are supported by state or federal taxes and offer free services to both job applicants and employers. Private employment agencies, which are not supported by taxes, must earn a profit to stay in business. They charge a fee for their services, which is paid by either the job applicant or the employer.

Public employment agencies are identified by the names of the states in which they are located. The Texas Employment Commission and the California State Employment Development Department are examples. In some cities, the state employment service is the only one available.

When you fill out an application form at the public employment agency near you, you will be interviewed to determine your qualifications and interests. The agency will call you if they find a job that is a good match. You will be told about the company and the job duties, then referred for an interview if you are interested.

Private employment agencies often have job leads that are not listed with public agencies. Remember, however, that private agencies charge a fee if they place you on a job. Make sure you know who is expected to pay the fee—it might be you. This will be stated in a contract you must sign. The fee for matching workers with higher-level jobs is often paid

■ **Getting Acquainted** A company's personnel office can be a source of leads for the career you are interested in. *How can you show your interest to a personnel manager?*

by the employer. The employee usually pays the placement fee on entry-level jobs. The fee is usually a percentage of your salary for the first several months or even the first full year of employment.

Company Personnel Offices

Large companies have personnel offices to handle employment matters, including the hiring of new workers. You may check on job openings by telephoning that office or by scheduling a personal visit. Some personnel offices list openings on a public bulletin board. If this is the case, you can stop by at your convenience and see if any new jobs have been posted.

When you know that you would like to work for a certain company, make an effort to get to know the people who work in the human resources department. This way you will have a better chance of being hired.

Chapter 38 ■ *Finding and Applying for a Job* **709**

Discussion Starter

Job Leads One additional source of finding job leads is working for a temporary employment agency. How could working temporary assignments provide job leads? *(Answers will vary. With temporary assignments, you work daily, weekly, or monthly in a company or nonprofit organization for an hourly wage. You get the chance to demonstrate at least some of your skills, meet the key employees in one or a number of departments, ask questions about the company, and experience the work environment. Depending on the length of a temporary assignment, you may also have access to job listings on an employment board, and to personnel in the employment office.)*

CAPTION ANSWER
Getting Acquainted You can get to know the personnel manager and the people who work in the human resources department by telephoning the office or scheduling a personal visit.

More About . . .

Employment Agencies
Employment agencies are moving away from employee fee-based services. Encourage students to not sign any documentation regarding such fees without having the document reviewed by a trusted advisor. Some of these agencies are not endorsed by the Better Business Bureau.

Cooperative Learning

Job Leads Have students work in groups of 3-4 to share their results from the Independent Practice activities #2 and #3. Have them compile one list per group on a large sheet of paper. Post those sheets on the board. In order to condense all groups' lists down to one master list, use one group's list with which to compare all other groups' findings. Have a representative from each group complete that comparison by crossing off duplicate ideas. Note the most frequent responses and discuss the more unique methods.

■ Searching the Internet

You will certainly want to look into cyberspace for job openings. By searching the Internet using Web sites like Hotjobs.com or Monster.com, you can easily find out which companies have job openings.

Most large companies now list their job openings either on their own Web page or with an online employment service. There are tens of thousands of career-related Web sites, so the challenge will be locating the ones having jobs that interest you. Look for sites with up-to-date listings—nothing more than two months old.

Once you've narrowed your career decision to a specific job title, career, industry, or even location, begin your search with sites that specialize in those areas. Start with a Web directory like Yahoo! to get a listing of career-related Web sites from which to choose. Then, do a keyword search of the site, using words such as salesperson, research assistant, or marketing. You can also search by job location, selecting to view only jobs in the area where you live or want to move to.

Another way to begin your search is to look at the Web sites of companies that spark your interest. The Web site for *Fortune* magazine lists 100 companies that offer noteworthy education benefits, stock options, and childcare.

ELECTRONIC RÉSUMÉS When using the Internet for your job search, you may come across the option to apply for a particular position online. This can be done using an electronic résumé. A **résumé** is a brief summary of personal information, education, skills, work experience, activities, and interests. Applying for jobs over the Internet is different than submitting a traditional résumé and requires a different résumé writing technique. It is important to learn the different formats as applying for jobs online is increasingly popular. You will learn about traditional résumés later in this chapter.

You can write your electronic résumé using a word processing program. Upon completion, you can submit your résumé as part of an e-mail. It is best to "cut and paste" the résumé into the body of an e-mail rather than including it as an attached file. Attached files can be difficult to read if the file is created in a different word processing program, and some employers may be hesitant to open files because of the risk of computer viruses.

There are three main differences between electronic résumés and traditional résumés. These are format, phraseology, and confidentiality.

The format of your electronic résumé should be text only. Make sure to save your résumé as a text file; this is the easiest way to transmit and read electronic files. Avoid bold type, italics, and underlining, which does not transmit well and makes your résumé difficult to read. Stick to a commonly used traditional font, such as Times New Roman, and keep your font size between 12 and 14 point. Do not use tabs; use the space bar instead.

Many companies that accept résumés electronically will search for job qualifications by looking for key words. It is very likely that your résumé will not be read by a person, but will be scanned by a computer program instead. In the scanning process, key words and phrases are searched for and the résumé is summarized and ranked among other qualified candidates.

It is important to use key words to describe what you can do because of this. Key words consist primarily of nouns and are usually divided into three categories: job title, industry, and personal

■ **Help Wanted** Thingamajob.com is an online career service featuring résumé posting, job alerts, industry news and confidential career counseling. *How would you go about finding job listings, company research, and salary information on the Web?*

CAPTION ANSWER
Help Wanted Answers will vary.

traits. It is important to include industry specific jargon, as many employers will search by industry language. Be sure to spell out all acronyms—include your membership in the Distributive Education Clubs of America (DECA), not just DECA. You will not be considered for a job that you are qualified for if key words don't appear on your résumé.

Confidentiality is an issue when posting your résumé on the Internet. Remember that once posted on a career Web site, your résumé is a public document that is out of your control. You have the option of limiting your personal information by only including an e-mail address or post office box so that potential employers can contact you without the use of a phone number or address. Since most employers prefer to contact applicants by telephone, you could hire a voice mail account during your job search. This may become an issue for job seekers who already have a job. The concern is that the current employer will realize its workers are looking to change jobs.

Before e-mailing your résumé to employers, e-mail a copy to yourself so that you can review it. Be sure to include your cover letter in the body of the e-mail as well. Creating your résumé in a standardized, electronic, scannable format keeps you on top of the competition.

Contacting Your Job Leads

The more job leads you have, the better your chances of finding a job that is right for you. There are different ways to approach potential job contacts. You may choose to contact employers directly or to send a letter expressing your interest.

■ Direct Contact

The process of visiting potential employers in person or calling them on the telephone is known as **direct contact**. Do this when you think you would like to work for certain companies but are unsure whether they have any openings. Be sure to call ahead for an appointment. Showing up unannounced could be inconvenient to the potential employer and may start the relationship on the wrong foot.

You may get more consideration by calling in person than by inquiring about a job on the telephone with direct contact. Direct contact can be time consuming; however, if you contact enough employers you may find a job that interests you. It also shows your high level of interest in a company and your dedication and commitment to finding a job.

Independent Practice

1. **Brainstorm and List** Have students generate at least five job leads from various sources. They should write the leads on a sheet of paper and tell how they found them.
2. **Research and Write** Have students research the names and company addresses of three local personnel directors to whom they could write a letter of inquiry regarding an entry-level marketing job in the company or organization. Students should write a sentence or two telling how they found each person's name and address, and how they determined that this person was the appropriate contact.
3. **Research and Write** Ask students to use search engines to locate online sites where job openings are posted and to see if any listed jobs interest them. Have them record the sites and note their interest in certain jobs in a written memo addressed to you. *(Memos will vary. Web sites may include www.monster.com, www.careerweb.com, and www.careerpath.com.)*

The Launch of the MoonPie

In the early 1900s, Earl Mitchell, a salesman for the Chattanooga Bakery, was servicing his territory. He came across a company store for coal miners. While asking coal miners what they might enjoy as a snack, the need was identified for something solid and filling for their lunch pails. The salesman asked, "How big?" About that time the moon was rising, so a miner held out his hands to frame the moon and said, "About that big!" Earlier, the salesman had noticed some workers dipping graham crackers into marshmallow and laying them on the window to harden. He headed back to the bakery with an idea. The salesman asked a baker to experiment by adding another cookie to this graham cracker/marshmallow concoction, and then dip it in chocolate. They sent the product over to the workers to try. The experiment was a success and the MoonPie was launched!

Thinking Creatively
Design your own favorite snack food, determining your market, necessary ingredients, and selling price.

Chapter 38 ■ *Finding and Applying for a Job* **711**

BRIGHT IDEAS   The Launch of the MoonPie
Answer Answers will vary.

Reteaching

1. **Vocabulary** Assign and review the vocabulary terms for this section.
2. **Job Lead Sources** Review with students the sources of job leads. Add any additional sources that are not mentioned in this lesson, such as temporary job assignments, internships, Web sites, or sources that are specific to your area.

Enrichment

1. **Review** Assign and review the appropriate Thinking Critically questions from the Chapter Assessment.
2. **Extend** Assign and review the corresponding activities from *BusinessWeek Case Studies* and *Internet Resources.* **ILP**
3. **Write** Have students write a letter of inquiry to one of the personnel directors they discovered in doing the Independent Practice activity #2. They should keyboard and spell-check the letter. Have students work in pairs or in groups to share and critique their letters, or you may work with students individually.
4. **Research and Summarize** The text states that looking through the help wanted section of the newspaper will teach you a great deal about your local job market. Have students study the Sunday classified ads from your local newspaper, and write a 100-word summary of their observations about the local job market and the economic factors that are shaping it. You may wish to have students do this activity together as a class. (Many town and city newspapers will provide free copies of their papers for classroom use.)

Case Study

Do You Want to Be a Star?

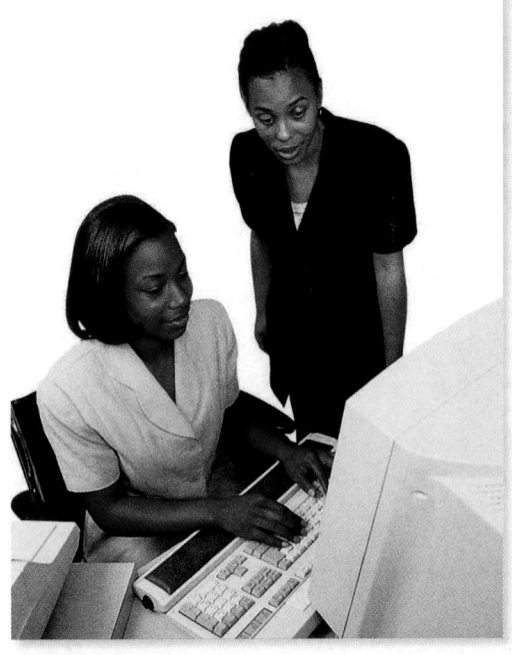

You've walked through the application process, sailed through the interview, and got your dream job. Are you ready for the next step? What kind of employee will you be?

Robert E. Kelley, a professor at Carnegie Mellon University, wants you to be a star. He has written a popular book called *How To Be a Star at Work: A Breakthrough Strategy You Need to Succeed* that outlines what sets star employees apart from the rest. He has studied successful workers to see what makes them different from their more average coworkers.

Surprisingly, it isn't brainpower or technical skill that is most important. What makes a star isn't what the employee does so much as how he or she does it. An employee can have the most advanced on-the-job skills and a college degree from a top school; however, if his or her people-skills are poor, it is unlikely that he or she will succeed.

Some of the tactics that Kelley focuses on include: initiative, networking, self-management, teamwork, leadership, perspective, and organizational skills. Star employees take the initiative to discover what might need doing that the manager hasn't thought of yet. Most employees make the effort to be on friendly terms with the boss. Kelley says that what sets stars apart is that they also make the effort to know the people who know how things work in the company, whether they are managers or coworkers. It is important to show respect for all people in the workplace—not just your own boss.

Star employees focus on the big picture—they make sure the way they do their job fits into the overall strategy of the company. They don't just go along with "business as usual." Instead, they offer their ideas to management even if they differ from the way the company usually does business. Showing initiative illustrates that you value your role in the company and are not just seeking personal success.

Companies work to keep and promote star employees. Won't you choose to be a star?

Case Study Review

1. How do you think helping others succeed could make you a star?
2. What qualities of a star employee do you already have?

A MATTER OF ETHICS

3. Do you think it is ethical to befriend someone at work because you think the friendship will help you improve your work?

Case Study Review Answers

Do You Want to Be a Star?
1. Answers will vary but might include that helping others can bring success to the whole company and create a support system for you.
2. Answers will vary but might include initiative, supportive of others, make friends easily, good teamwork skills, and creativity.

A MATTER OF ETHICS
3. Answers will vary. Some students may say that it is good to be friendly to all in your workplace as it makes the environment more pleasant and productive. Others might say that you should not befriend others with ulterior motives.

Letters of Inquiry

Writing a letter of inquiry is a variation of direct contact. You use the technique under the same circumstances and for the same reason—when you want to know whether a company has openings in the career area of your interest.

You must do some research to learn to whom you should address your correspondence. Call the company and ask for the name of the individual who hires new employees. At that point you will learn whether the company has a human resources department or whether department heads do their own hiring. Confirm the spelling of any names you are given and the position of the person to contact. Verify the company's address, particularly the zip code, postal box, floor, or suite numbers. Now you are ready to write a letter of inquiry. See Chapter 8 to review the elements of a business letter and Figure 38-1 for an example.

Expanding Your List of Job Leads

You should always be looking for new job leads even as you follow up on existing ones. Expand your list by getting referrals from people. Each time you follow up a lead that doesn't result in a job, ask your interviewer to suggest someone else to contact. Having other possibilities will keep you from getting discouraged if you don't get the job you want right away. If you have a long list of leads, you can simply follow up on the next one.

FIGURE 38-1
Letter of Inquiry

327 Hoyt Avenue
Berkeley, California 95212
April 27, 20—

Susan W. Peterson
Appleton Kitchen Products
5134 State Street
Berkeley, CA 95214

Dear Ms. Peterson:

On May 17, I shall graduate from Sam Houston High School with a major emphasis in sales and marketing. While in high school, I have worked in sales part-time, but I am most eager to begin my first full-time job in sales.

As I have always been impressed by the courteous, efficient salespeople in your store, I am very interested in a job at Appleton. If you anticipate a need for any full-time, permanent employees in the next several months, I would like to apply.

May I have an application form, or should I call for an interview at your convenience? My home telephone number is 924-7884.

Sincerely,

Charlene G. Graham

Charlene J. Graham

■ **Inquiry Letters** You will probably need to send letters of inquiry to many companies in order to come up with a few leads. *Why do you think that is true?*

38.1 ASSESSMENT

Reviewing Key Terms and Concepts

1. What are six possible sources of job leads?
2. What is networking?
3. What are two methods that you can use to contact job leads?
4. How can you expand your list of job leads?

Thinking Critically

5. How would you feel about getting a job through a family member or personal friend? Would you rather find a job on your own? Why or why not?

Integrating Academic Skills

6. **COMMUNICATION** Imagine that you would like to work for a local mail-order company that sells electronic gadgets, but you don't know if there are currently job openings. Write a letter of inquiry regarding summer employment.

Evaluation

Assign and review the Section 38.1 Assessment.

Technology Resources

 Assessment Resources
Go to the *Marketing Essentials* Web site (**www.marketing.glencoe.com**) for resources to teach and assess occupation-specific vocabulary.

CLOSE

Section Wrap-Up

Have students complete these statements:

1. A job lead is . . . *(information about a job opening.)*
2. The most common sources of job leads are . . . *(school counselors, cooperative education and work experience programs, family and friends, former employers, professional people in your personal life, employment agencies, company personnel offices, direct calling, letters of inquiry, newspaper ads, Web sites, and suggestions from interviewers.)*

FIGURE 38-1 ANSWER
Inquiry Letters You don't know if the company is hiring, and it may be difficult to make yourself seem like a desirable employee in just a letter.

38.1 ASSESSMENT ANSWERS

Reviewing Key Terms and Concepts

1. school counselor, cooperative education and work experience programs, family, friends, acquaintances, former employers, newspaper ads, agencies, personnel offices, Internet, and letters of inquiry
2. Networking is finding contacts among family, friends, former employees, and professionals you know, and then asking for job leads.

3. direct contact via phone call, scheduled visit to the office, or through a letter of inquiry
4. Get as many job leads from firsthand sources as possible, then get referrals from interviewers.

Thinking Critically

5. Answers will vary.

Integrating Academic Skills

6. **COMMUNICATION** Letters will vary.

Applying for a Job

What You'll Learn

- The legal document that you must have before you can begin working
- How to write a letter of application and complete an application form
- How to write a résumé and cover letter

Why It's Important

You've contacted the sources of job leads and found some jobs that interest you; your next step is to apply for them. This is done by completing application forms, writing letters of application, and preparing your own résumé.

Key Terms

- standard English
- references
- cover letter

Getting a Work Permit

Most states require that you have a work permit before you can legally begin working if you are under the age of 18. In some states, such as Michigan, a cooperative education training agreement can serve as a legal work permit.

State and federal labor laws designate certain jobs as too dangerous for young workers. Most of these jobs are performed in hazardous environments or involve the use of power-driven machinery. The laws also limit the number of hours that young people can work in one day or one week. More hours of work are allowed during summer vacations than during the school year.

A work permit establishes that it is legal for a young worker to do the type of work offered. In some states, work permits must specify the exact job duties and hours of work. In these cases, both the employer and the worker fill out sections of an application for the permit. The employer, worker, and the worker's parent must sign the application before a work permit is issued.

Ask your marketing teacher or counselor whether you will need a work permit and, if so, where you can get one. A designated school official usually issues work permits. Check on this now so you can avoid possible delays when you are ready to go to work.

Applying for a Job

Employers look for the most qualified person to fill a job. They will decide whether to hire you based in part on how you present yourself during an interview. More than anything else, they will want to know whether you have the ability to do the work.

Employers have several ways of getting this information. Many ask job seekers to fill out an application form. Some request additional documents—a separate letter of application or a résumé. Finally, some employers administer one or more employment tests to applicants.

How you present your qualifications is likely to be the determining factor in whether you are hired. Following the suggestions on the next few pages should increase your chances of success.

■ Using Standard English

Everything you write and say to a prospective employer should be in standard English. Standard English is the formal style of writing and speaking that you have learned in school. It is standard because it means the same thing to everyone.

Most people do not use standard English for all of their communications. When you write a letter to a close relative, for example, you simply write what is on your mind and don't usually worry about form. When you speak with a friend on the telephone, you may use slang or informal language. These practices make for comfortable and easy personal conversation, but they have no place in business. Most communication in business is formal, and that means standard English.

Standard English employs correct grammar, spelling, pronunciation, and usage. "Marilyn *has* a job interview" is standard English, while "Marilyn *have* a job interview" is not. The repeated use in conversation of the interjections *you know* or *like* is nonstandard English. Nonstandard pronunciations are another common lapse, although an accent, either regional or foreign, does not indicate nonstandard English.

Employers will have several opportunities to evaluate your English. When they read your application form, they will notice whether you use and spell words correctly. Your letter of application or résumé will indicate your ability (or inability) to write. Finally, when you are interviewed, the employer will listen to you speak and will evaluate your grammar and pronunciation.

■ Filling Out Application Forms

Most employment application forms are short (from one to four pages) and ask similar questions. Companies usually design their own application forms, so you may find differences between various applications. You can see an example of a completed application form in Figure 38-2 on page 716.

The application form provides information about your qualifications so company personnel can decide whether to interview you. The first rule of filling out an application form is to complete the form neatly. Spell all words correctly and use a dictionary to look up the spellings of any words you aren't sure about. When filling out the form at the place of employment, use words you know how to spell.

Take the application form home and fill it out on a typewriter if possible. Make a photocopy of the form if you are not a good typist, so you can practice first. When asked to complete the form at the place of employment, use a pen with blue or black ink;

REAL WORLD MARKETING

Spinning CDs

How about some listening enjoyment while you read that magazine? Riffage.com, an online music destination, and Spin Magazine, a leading music and youth culture magazine, broke new ground in marketing for the music industry. Five issues of Spin magazine were assembled with a special CD-ROM produced by Riffage.com. The deal marked the first time a music CD-ROM was distributed by a major national magazine to its entire newsstand circulation base of over 500,000 issues. The CD-ROM contained a collection of 150 MP3-formatted songs by artists whose music is available on Riffage.com.

Thinking Critically
Determine another innovative way to distribute CD-ROMs. What type of packaging would you use?

colored inks are considered to be not serious and inappropriate.

Answer every question that applies to you. Write "NA" (meaning "Not Applicable") or draw a short line in the space for those questions that are not applicable. This shows that you did not overlook the item.

Use your full name, not a nickname, on the form. On most applications, your first name, middle initial, and last name are requested. Provide your complete address, including your zip code.

List a specific job title if they ask for job preference; do not write "anything" as an answer. Employers expect you to know what type of work you can and want to do.

Most application forms include a section on education. Write the names of all the schools you have attended and the dates of attendance. There will also be a section on previous work experience. You may not have had much work experience, but

TEACH

📊 Technology Resources

PowerPoint The *Marketing Essentials* PowerPoint Presentation CD-ROM provides visual lecture aids for every chapter section.

Concept Development

1. Read Section 38.2 with students.
2. Provide good and poor examples of cover letters and résumés for overhead projection. Have students point out flaws in the poor examples, and tell why the good examples are better than the poor ones.
3. Provide students with copies of various résumé formats for their notebooks. Project each format overhead and review the benefits of each. Have students prepare their own résumé, using headings such as objective, education, work experience, activities, honors, community service, etc.
4. Many students may be given employment tests when applying for marketing jobs. Obtain copies of common employment tests to administer to students for practice in such areas as math, spelling, proofreading, and filing.

REAL WORLD MARKETING

Spinning CDs
Answer Answers will vary.

Discussion Starter

Submitting Résumés Ask students to give some alternative, high-tech ways of submitting résumés that, while not traditional, may become more commonplace in the near future. Ask them also to speculate on some "high-tech" recruitment and screening measures now used by employers. *(Answers will vary. Today businesses post jobs on the Internet at their own Web sites or on specific Web sites designed for that purpose. Job seekers may use high-tech methods to present themselves in a creative way through videotaping, burning portfolios onto CDs, and other technologically advanced audio and visual methods, such as creating a personal Web site to showcase expertise.)*

FIGURE 38-2

Job Application

Date April 6, 20 - -

SEARS, ROEBUCK AND CO.
APPLICATION FOR EMPLOYMENT

PLEASE PRINT INFORMATION REQUESTED IN INK

SEARS IS AN EQUAL OPPORTUNITY EMPLOYER and fully subscribes to the principles of Equal Opportunity unity. Sears has adopted an Affirmative Action Program to ensure that all applicants and employees are considered for hire, promotion and job status, without regard to race, color, religion, sex, national origin, age, handicap, or status as a disabled veteran or veteran of the Vietnam Era.

To protect the interests of all concerned, applicants for certain job assignments must pass a physical examination before they are hired.

NOTE: This application will be considered active for 90 days. If you have not been employed within this period and are still interested in employment at Sears, please contact the office where you applied and request that your application be reactivated.

Name Graham   Charlene   Joan
     Last   First   Middle

Social Security Number 541-62-6551
(Please present your Social Security Card for review.)

Address   753   North Fairfield Street   Dallas   Texas   75221
         Number   Street   City   State   Zip Code

County Dallas

Current phone or nearest phone (214) 924-7486

Previous Address _____ Number ___ Street ___ City ___ State ___ Zip Code

Best time of day to contact after 4 p.m.

(Answer only if position for which you are applying requires driving.)

If hired, can you furnish proof of age?   Yes ☒ No ☐
If hired, can you furnish proof that you are legally entitled to work in U.S.? Yes ☒ No ☐

Licensed to drive car?   YES ☐   NO ☐
Is license valid in this state? YES ☐   NO ☐

Have you ever been employed by Sears or a subsidiary of Sears? YES ☐ NO ☒
If so when and where last employed? _____   Position _____

Former employees of Sears and certain Subsidiaries may be entitled to service credit under the Pension Plan based on prior employment with Sears, Roebuck and Co., Homart Development Co., Sears Investment Management Co., Sears Roebuck Acceptance Corp., Sears, Roebuck de Puerto Rico, Inc., Sears Roebuck Overseas, Inc., Sears Securities Sales, Inc., Terminal Freight Handling Co., Allstate Insurance Company and their Subsidiaries, Lifetime Foam Products, Pacific Installers, and Sears, S.A. (Central America), Dean Witter Reynolds Organization, Inc. and their Subsidiaries, Coldwell Banker and their Subsidiaries and Sears World Trade.

Have you a relative in the employ of Sears in the store or unit to which you are applying? ___ No ___

A PHYSICAL OR MENTAL DISABILITY WILL NOT CAUSE REJECTION IF IN SEARS MEDICAL OPINION YOU ARE ABLE TO SATISFACTORILY PERFORM IN THE POSITION FOR WHICH YOU ARE BEING CONSIDERED. Alternative placement, if available, of an applicant who does not meet the physical standards of the job for which he/she was originally considered is permitted.

Do you have any physical or mental impairment which may limit your ability to perform the job for which you are applying? No

If yes, what can reasonably be done to accommodate your limitation? _____

EDUCATION	School Attended	No. of Years	Name of School	City/State	Graduate?	Course or College Major	Average Grades
	Grammar	7	Esperanza Elementary	Dallas, TX	Yes		B+
	Jr. High	3	Andrews Junior High	Dallas, TX	Yes		B
	Sr. High	3	Sam Houston High School	Dallas, TX	Yes	Marketing/Bus.	A–
	Other						
	College					Degree	

MILITARY SERVICE	BRANCH OF SERVICE	DATE ENTERED SERVICE*	DATE OF DISCHARGE*	HIGHEST RANK	SERVICE-RELATED SKILLS AND EXPERIENCE APPLICABLE TO CIVILIAN EMPLOYMENT

*Do not complete if applying in the state of California.
What experience or training have you had other than your work experience, military service and education? (Community activities, hobbies, etc.)

_____

I am interested in the type of work I have checked: ☒ Sales ☐ Office ☐ Mechanical ☐ Warehouse ☐ Other Specify _____

Or the following specific Job _____

I am seeking (check only one):
☐ Temporary employment (6 days or less)
☐ Seasonal employment (one season, e.g. Christmas)
☒ Regular employment (employment for indefinite period of time)
If temporary, indicate dates available _____

I am available for (check only one):
☐ Part Time
☒ Full-Time

If part-time, indicate maximum hours per week _____ and enter hours available in block to the right.

HOURS AVAILABLE FOR WORK	
Sun.	To
Mon.	8 a.m. To 6 p.m.
Tues.	8 a.m. To 6 p.m.
Wed.	8 a.m. To 6 p.m.
Thurs.	8 a.m. To 6 p.m.
Fri.	8 a.m. To 6 p.m.
Sat.	8 a.m. To 6 p.m.

Have you been convicted during the past seven years of a serious crime involving a person's life or property?
☒ NO ☐ YES   If yes explain _____

10534 Rev. 9/83   (SEE REVERSE SIDE)

More About . . .

Filling Out Application Forms
Besides having students ask permission of their reference, they should also let the reference know to whom they have given their name and the position for which they have applied. This courtesy gives the reference time to prepare comments or reflect on the type of question that may be asked should the company call.

REFERENCES

LIST BELOW YOUR FOUR MOST RECENT EMPLOYERS, BEGINNING WITH THE CURRENT OR MOST RECENT ONE. IF YOU HAD LESS THAN FOUR EMPLOYERS, USE THE REMAINING SPACES FOR PERSONAL REFERENCES. IF YOU WERE EMPLOYED UNDER A MAIDEN OR OTHER NAME, PLEASE ENTER THAT NAME IN THE RIGHT HAND MARGIN. IF APPLICABLE, ENTER SERVICE IN THE ARMED FORCES ON THE REVERSE SIDE.

NAMES AND ADDRESSES OF FORMER EMPLOYERS BEGINNING WITH THE CURRENT OR MOST RECENT	Nature of Employer's Business	Name of your Supervisor	What kind of work did you do?	Starting Date	Starting Pay	Date of Leaving	Pay at Leaving	Why did you leave? Give details
NOTE–State reason for and length of inactivity between present application date and last employer								
Name Merchandise Mart Address 2800 Tyler Avenue Tel No 925-9021 City Dallas, State Texas Zip Code 75221	Depart-ment Store	Mr. Travis	Sales	Month Nov. Year 95	Per Week	Month Per Week		Still employed part-time
NOTE–State reason for and length of inactivity between last employer and second last employer								
Name Chicken Annie's Address 1700 S. Vernon Avenue Tel No 924-6318 City Dallas, State Texas Zip Code 75221	Fast Food	Mrs. Riley	Sales	Month Jan. Year 95	$80 Per Week	Month Oct. Year 95	$95 Per Week	To accept a job with more hours
NOTE–State reason for and length of inactivity between second last employer and third last employer								
Name Mr. Paul Crawford (former teacher) Address 3614 Rayburn Avenue Tel No 925-1163 City Dallas, State Texas Zip Code 75221				Month Year Per Week		Month Year Per Week		
NOTE–State reason for and length of inactivity between third last employer and fourth last employer								
Name Miss Irene Jenkins Address 1222 Oakwood Street Tel No 925-7611 City Dallas, State Texas Zip Code 75221				Month Year Per Week		Month Year Per Week		

I certify that the information contained in this application is correct to the best of my knowledge and understand that any misstatement or omission of information is grounds for dismissal in accordance with Sears, Roebuck and Co. policy. I authorize the references listed above to give you any and all information concerning my previous employment and any pertinent information they may have, personal or otherwise, and release all parties from all liability for any damage that may result from furnishing same to you. In consideration of my employment, I agree to conform to the rules and regulations of Sears, Roebuck and Co., and my employment and compensation can be terminated with or without cause, and with or without notice, at any time, at the option of either the Company or myself. I understand that no unit manager or representative of Sears, Roebuck and Co. other than the President or Vice-President of the Company, has any authority to enter into any agreement for employment for any specified period of time, or to make any agreement contrary to the foregoing, in some states, the law requires that Sears have my written permission before obtaining reports on me, and I hereby authorize Sears to obtain such reports.

Applicant's Signature *Charlene J. Graham*

NOT TO BE FILLED OUT BY APPLICANT

INTERVIEWER'S COMMENTS	Date of Emp.		Tested	(Store will enter dates as required)	Mailed	Completed
	Dept. or Division	Regular ☐ Part-Time ☐	Physical examination scheduled for	References Requests		
	Job Title		Physical examination form completed	Consumer Report		
	Job Title Code	Job Grade		With. Tax (W-4)		
	Compensation Arrangement		Review Card prepared Minor's Work Permit	State With. Tax		
	Manager Approving		Time card prepared Proof of Birth			
Prospect for 1. 2.	Employee No.	Rack No.	Training Material Given to Employee			
			Unit Name and Number _____			

■ **Best Foot Forward** Filling out a job application carefully using a typewriter or printing in ink very neatly shows an employer that you are serious about the job. It is your introduction to the company, and will be used in deciding whether you will be interviewed. *Where do you list the names of people who the company could contact to learn more about your work habits and character?*

Chapter 38 ■ *Finding and Applying for a Job* **717**

Thinking Critically

1. **Application Essays** Some companies, such as The Body Shop, require job applicants to write an essay on a particular topic related to the business. Ask students: What would be the purpose of such a require-ment? (*Writing an essay is a way of screening out those who are not serious about applying for the position. Those appli-cants who do take the time to write the essay provide the potential employer with a way to evaluate their writing skills, their organizational skills, their knowledge of the business, and their sincerity in applying for the job.*)

2. **Researching Employers** Have students brainstorm some additional sources of informa-tion when researching a com-pany before an employment interview. (*Answers will vary but could include company Web sites, Web sites such as Yahoo Finance that provide related press releases on that company, annual reports, magazine and newspaper articles on the com-pany, information from the Chamber of Commerce, and local media advertising.*)

FIGURE 38-2 ANSWER
Best Foot Forward You list the names of people who can speak for your character and work ethics in the references section.

THE DECA CONNECTION — COMPETITIVE EVENTS AND MARKETING ESSENTIALS

Civic Consciousness Project As you teach this chapter, you can use DECA's Civic Consciousness Project event. This competitive event consists of an activity conducted by your chapter to benefit a community service or charitable project. This event produces many positive effects for your students. It allows them to participate in an activity that will give them a better understand-ing of the role civic activities have in society and a real sense of community spirit from their efforts on behalf of others. This event also provides an example of how community service and the resulting networking can lead to possible job opportunities and career exploration.

Independent Practice

Write Have students word process a cover letter for two entry-level jobs of their choice. Have them write the first letter and then copy and paste that letter into a new document so it can be revised to match the second job's requirements.

The jobs can be listings in the help-wanted section of your local newspaper, employment Web sites, postings from a local job board or employment service, or any other source—as long as the jobs are legitimate and students use the correct company names and contacts, etc.

Review students' letters, helping them to discover additional ways to adapt their cover letters to these specific positions. Have students keep these letters in their notebooks for reference.

you can include short-term or unpaid jobs. Fill out this section in reverse chronological order—begin with your current or most recent job and end with your first job.

Be prepared to list several references. **References** are people who know your work habits and personal traits well and who will recommend you for the job. Try to use professional references such as your teachers, friends established in business, or former employers. Make sure you ask permission of your references before listing them on an application form. Do not list classmates, relatives, or personal friends.

Sign your name using your first name, middle initial, and last name. Your signature should be written, never typed or printed.

■ Writing Letters of Application

Most employers prefer application forms because they provide just the information employers need to reach a decision on interviews. Some employers, however, request a letter of application.

Writing a letter of application is like writing a sales pitch about yourself. You must convince an employer that you are the best person to fill a specific job opening. Tell why you are interested in the position and what your special qualifications for it are. Don't write a sad story about needing the job. You want your enthusiasm to convince the employer that you are needed by the company.

Write a first draft to get down most of the main points, then revise your letter until you are pleased with the end result. Ask a teacher, parent or guardian, or friend in business to read and critique your letter; then, put the final touches on it and print out a copy.

Describe how you learned about the job opening in the first sentence. You might say, "At the suggestion of Mr. Charles Williams, I am writing about the job as mail-order clerk in your store" if a friend gave you a lead. When responding to a newspaper ad, you might say, "I am responding to your ad in the *Daily News* for an advertising assistant." State that you are applying for the job in the second sentence, for example, "I would like to be considered an applicant for this position."

The second paragraph should contain a description of how your education and experience qualify you for the job. Use a separate paragraph for each

if you have a lot to say about both your education and job experience. Don't worry if you don't have much experience—just write about your education in more detail. Mention classes you have taken that are related to the job. You may want to mention any class projects that you have excelled in, for example, developing a new advertising campaign for a local company.

List your references in the next paragraph. Finally, in your last paragraph, ask for an interview at the employer's convenience. State when you will be available and provide your telephone number.

Many businesses receive dozens of application letters every week. Businesses that advertise jobs in the newspaper may receive hundreds of letters. Businesses interview only a small portion of those who write—those people who have effectively presented their qualifications in a neatly written letter. Doing this gives you a big advantage over most applicants. Take the time to develop an effective letter of application that you are really proud of. You can use it as a model for other letters for other jobs, personalizing details of the letters to each job.

Life In The Diverse MARKETPLACE

Can You Repeat That in Spanish?

You have morning meetings with representatives from a large department store in Argentina. The only problem? Your translator is late and you don't speak Spanish! Knowledge of a foreign language is important for international business and advertising within the United States where there are large Hispanic and Asian-American populations. Learning Spanish or Japanese can give you an edge when applying for jobs. And now is the best time to start—the Modern Language Association estimates that 600 class hours are needed to establish fluency.

Thinking Critically
How can you illustrate your strong abilities in a foreign language when applying for a job?

Life In The Diverse MARKETPLACE

Can You Repeat That in Spanish?
Answer Highlight any language experience on your résumé. You also may include work in another language in your portfolio.

FIGURE 38-3

Letter of Application

Guadelupe Gomez-Pomeda
2517 Bath Street
Winfield, Colorado 36145
May 18, 2001

Mr. Harrison E. Frank
Sales Manager
Ferguson Aircraft Inc.
823 Dutton Avenue
Golden, Colorado 36053

Dear Mr. Frank:

Mr. Bernard Hubert, my marketing instructor at Winfield Community College, advised me this morning of the commercial artist position that you have open. I wish to apply for this position.

On May 17, I will graduate from Winfield Community College with a major in marketing and a special emphasis on advertising and commercial art. I have also taken commercial art courses during the past two summers at Colorado College. My overall grade average in college is B+.

For the past three years, I have assisted the advertising manager at Rubbermaid, here in Winfield, by preparing more than 30 ads that have run nationally. One of these ads, which I prepared myself, won an award at a recent advertising convention in Chicago.

My father taught me to fly while I was in high school, so a job in advertising with an aircraft manufacturing company would combine my two greatest interests. It would be a dream come true! May I have an interview at your convenience? You can reach me most weekdays after 3 P.M. at (316) 221-5288.

Yours truly,

Guadelupe Gomez-Pomeda

Guadelupe Gomez-Pomeda

■ **A Letter of Application** A good letter of application lets the prospective employer know why you have the best qualifications for the job offered. Guadelupe took several classes in fashion design at Colorado College. *Why doesn't she mention those in her letter to Mr. Frank?*

Individualized Practice

Human Relations Skills

Have students imagine they work in the Human Resources Department of a large company. One of their duties is to review all applications for part-time employment.

L1 One day a young man calls to follow up on his application, which was written very poorly and is barely legible. Ask students: What could be said to this man to help him fill out applications in the future? Have students write their answers on a sheet of paper. Then discuss their responses in class.

L2 Have students imagine that they receive a poorly written letter of application. (For example, it does not specify the job the person wants or give work history or education.) The letter is also written in slang. Ask students: What could be said to this applicant in response to the person's inquiry? Have students write their answers on a sheet of paper. Then discuss their responses in class.

L3 Have students imagine that they receive a student's résumé that has blatantly false information. (For example, the job listed calls for post-high school training, yet the student has not yet graduated from high school.) Ask students: What could be said to this person about the impression a falsified work history would give a potential employer? Have students write their answers on a sheet of paper. Then discuss their responses in class.

As with any sales pitch, a good first impression counts. Use the spell check function of your word processing program to eliminate any spelling errors. Before you send your letter, make sure you have read it over for accuracy.

The sample letter shown in Figure 38-3 will give you some idea of how your finished letter should look. Notice how this letter is not only neat and clear, but it follows the rules outlined in this section. The applicant focuses on special classes she has taken, as well as previous job experience. The letter conveys a personal interest, and uses standard English. Be sure to include all the elements of a business letter; in particular, duplicate the salutation and complimentary closing as shown.

Chapter 38 ■ *Finding and Applying for a Job* **719**

FIGURE 38-3 ANSWER
A Letter of Application She does not mention the fashion design classes because they are not related to the job she is applying for.

Reteaching

1. **Vocabulary** Assign and review the vocabulary terms for this section.
2. **Fact and Idea** Assign and review Fact and Idea Review questions 1–5 from the Chapter Assessment.
3. **Résumés** Have students review each others' résumés to provide constructive criticism. Allow all students the opportunity to revise the first draft of their résumé in order to improve it. Also, have students adjust their own résumés to match one of the cover letters they prepared in the Independent Practice activity. Tell them to save both of these documents in their notebooks for future use.

Enrichment

1. **Review** Assign and review the appropriate Thinking Critically questions from the Chapter Assessment.
2. **Extend** Assign and review the corresponding activities from the *School-to-Work Activity Workbook.* **ILP**
3. **Fill Out Forms and Critique** Provide a variety of application forms from local businesses. Allow students to fill out one or two forms from different businesses. Depending on the level of your class, have students work in pairs to review each other's forms for accuracy and completeness. Or you can meet with each student individually to review his or her forms.
4. **Research and Design** Have students search the Internet to find several types of résumés and suggestions for completing effective résumés. Have them use that research and a word processing program to redesign their résumés with different formats. Have them identify the résumé format they think showcases them best.

FIGURE 38-4
RÉSUMÉ

A résumé tells prospective employers what you are like and what you can do for them. A good résumé shows you at your best in a one or two page outline. It usually includes the following information.

1 **Identification** Include your name, address, telephone number, and e-mail address.

2 **Objective** Your objective statement should indicate the type of job you are looking for. Don't forget to change this item if you use the same résumé to apply for a different job.

3 **Experience** List experience related to the specific job for which you are applying, including volunteer work. It is a good idea to list any other work you have done if you have not worked in a related field.

4 **Education** List schools attended from high school on, the dates of attendance, and diplomas or degrees earned. It is fine to emphasize the courses that are related to the job you are applying for.

5 **Activities and Awards** This is the place to list school clubs or sports awards, any recognition you have received in work, school, or extracurricular settings.

6 **References** Include up to three references on a short résumé. Otherwise, indicate that they are available. Always ask people ahead of time if they are willing to be listed as references for you.

Frank Johnson
1235 East Tenth Avenue
Ventura, CA 93003
(805)964-6264
frankjohnson@yourname.com

Objective:
A marketing analyst position that would complement my academic and experiential skills.

Experience:
9/96-present Assistant Marketing Analyst
Ventura Volvo
6580 Leland Street
Ventura, CA 93003

Used computer to estimate sales by model and make recommendations for inventory. Accessed databases using computer terminal to study inventory in relation to buying estimates. Studied historical applications, including media ads, price and color changes, and impact of season.

9/95-9/96 Marketing Assistant
KVEN Radio
Ventura, CA 93003

Assisted Communications Manager in publishing articles and ads, sales presentations, vendor contracts, and trade shows. Contacted vendors for advertising needs (charts, overheads, banners).

Education:
1992-1996 Ventura College. AA in Marketing. Dean's Honor Roll four semesters.

Courses included:
Marketing I and II
Marketing Information Systems
Advertising
Economics I and II
Computer Science

1989-1992 Ventura High School, Graduated in upper 10 percent of class. Served as Vice President of DECA two years.

Personal:
Hobbies include writing computer programs, tennis, and photography.

References:
Available upon request.

Did You Know?

Choosing a way of producing a résumé is another important decision for students. Some may have the capability and equipment to produce a résumé, or the school may have the equipment. Other students will have to pay for the service. Prices can range from $10 for a word-processed, one-page résumé to hundreds of dollars for a résumé consultation.

FIGURE 38-5

Cover Letter

1235 East Tenth Avenue
Ventura, CA 93003
April 6, 2001

Ms. Linda Morrison
Metromedia-West Television
3200 Beverly Drive
Beverly Hills, CA 90123

Dear Ms. Morrison:

Your ad for a marketing analyst in Sunday's Los Angeles Times described exactly the position that I am seeking. As you will see from the résumé I have enclosed, my qualifications match up very well with the requirements listed in your ad.

My education, experiences, and DECA participation (for which our school won a national award) have prepared me to fulfill your needs in marketing analysis.

After you have read my résumé, I would appreciate an appointment for an interview. I will call you next week to arrange a time convenient to meet.

Sincerely,

Frank Johnson

■ **Cover Letter** A short cover letter accompanies your résumé. *Since your résumé includes the information about you that is relevant to the job, what is the purpose of sending a cover letter along with it?*

■ Preparing Résumés and Cover Letters

A good letter of application may convince an employer to grant you an interview; however, a résumé and cover letter sent together are even more impressive. You can see an example of a traditional print résumé in Figure 38-4 on page 720. A résumé organizes the facts about you related to the job, which saves the employer time before and during an interview.

A cover letter is similar to a letter of application but without the information on education and experience (see Figure 38-5). It simply introduces you and allows you to say why you can do a good job for the company. Your cover letter should reflect your understanding of the company and how you may be able to meet its needs. Emphasize facts that make you especially well qualified for the job.

Your résumé outlines your qualifications for a particular job; therefore, you won't need to accompany it with a complete letter of application. When you send an employer a résumé, include a brief cover letter. The résumé makes filling out job applications a simpler process because you have all of the information organized already. Many people prepare a résumé as the first step in the job application process.

Even if you are not hired, many employers will keep your résumé on file for a certain period of time. If they have an opening for which you qualify in the future, they may call you.

38.2 ASSESSMENT

Reviewing Key Terms and Concepts

1. What are four important components of standard English?
2. Why do most employers prefer application forms?
3. What is the purpose of a letter of application?
4. What are the basic types of information that are contained in a résumé?
5. What is the purpose of a cover letter?

Thinking Critically

6. If you were an employer, what qualities do you think you would look for in a job seeker's application, application letter, or résumé?

Integrating Academic Skills

7. **MATH** Your prospective employer tells you that you can have your choice of being paid two ways. Either you will be paid a straight salary of $400 per week or a base salary of $200 per week, plus commissions of 13 percent of your sales. In your last job, you sold $2,000 a week. Assuming you will continue to sell at least that amount, which salary option should you take? What is the difference between the two?

38.2 ASSESSMENT ANSWERS

Reviewing Key Terms and Concepts

1. correct grammar, spelling, pronunciation, and usage
2. They provide employers with the appropriate information to reach a decision on interviews.
3. It is used to convince an employer that you are the best person to fill a specific job opening.
4. A résumé contains a brief summary of personal information, education, skills, work experience, activities, and interests.
5. It introduces you and allows you to say how you can meet the company's needs.

Thinking Critically

6. Answers may include command of English, meeting qualifications, and willingness to work.

Integrating Academic Skills

7. **MATH** Base salary option. (2000 x 13% = 260. 260 + 200 = 460) $60.00 per week

FOCUS

Bell Ringer Activity

Analyze Tell each student to imagine he or she is the personnel director of a familiar local business who is interviewing candidates for a specific position (i.e., entry-level sales associate). Ask students what would impress them most about the candidates they are interviewing, and what would impress them the least.

Introducing the Section

The Job Interview Review students' answers from the Bell Ringer Activity. *(Qualities that impress most may include enthusiasm; good grooming; appropriate mode of dress; positive, open, and receptive body language during the interview; a knowledge of the company and its products; and thoughtful, appropriate answers to the interviewer's questions. Qualities that would impress the least include lack of enthusiasm; poor grooming and/or mode of dress; negative and/or inappropriate body language; lack of knowledge about the company and its products; and inability to answer questions during the interview.)*

Have students share some of their personal experiences in interviewing, both good and bad. Ask what they might do differently now. Tell students that this section will look at the "how to's" of good interviewing.

TEACH

Technology Resources

PowerPoint The *Marketing Essentials* PowerPoint Presentation CD-ROM provides visual lecture aids for every chapter section.

722

The Job Interview

What You'll Learn

- How to prepare for and conduct yourself properly during a job interview
- How to follow up a job interview

Why It's Important

Almost all decisions to hire are made during or following an interview of an applicant. The goal of your search is to secure a job interview in which you may present yourself as the best applicant for the job.

Interviewing for a Job

Preparing application forms, letters of application, and résumés and cover letters, and using the Internet are all important parts of the job application process. Their purpose is to make an employer want to interview you. It is what happens during the interview that causes most employers to choose one applicant over others.

You, of course, want the interviewer to choose you for the job, so you will need to plan for a successful interview. Your plan should include three steps—preparing for an interview, conducting yourself properly during an interview, and following up an interview.

■ Preparing for an Interview

The employer's first impression of you will greatly affect whether you are offered a job. Remember that you never have a second chance to make a first impression. Appropriate grooming and dress, body language that shows confidence, and use of standard English all combine to make a good first impression. These are all things that you can control with some preparation.

DRESS AND GROOMING Employees in sales and office jobs followed a strict dress code in the past. Men wore suits, white shirts, ties, and leather shoes with dark socks, while women wore business suits or very conservative dresses, medium heeled shoes, and nylons. Today, employees in many stores and offices have adopted a dress code known as corporate casual. This does not mean, however, that you should dress casually for an interview. It is better to make the extra effort to make a good impression.

Your clothes should always be neat, clean, and wrinkle-free for every interview. In some cases, appropriate interview dress depends on the job. In sales, for example, people dress formally to make a good impression on customers. You need to show in the interview that you are aware of that and can dress appropriately. Many employers feel that if you don't care enough to dress up for the interview, then you don't care enough about the job.

Regardless of its style, your hair should be clean and neat. While this may seem unfair, you will have to please your employer if you truly want the job.

Employers will notice whether your hands are clean and your nails are neatly trimmed. Wearing a great deal of jewelry, for both men and women, can be distracting in an interview; too much makeup on women can also distract the interviewer. Also beware of wearing too much perfume or cologne. Strong scents can be overwhelming and distracting.

THINGS TO KNOW Before you schedule an interview, do some research on the company. You will make a better impression if you can talk intelligently about the company's products. It will show that you are interested in the firm. You can read company brochures or catalogs, check out information on a company's Web site, search for related newspaper articles, or talk with family members or teachers.

Once you call for an interview appointment, write down the date and time and ask for the interviewer's name. Check the spelling and make sure you can pronounce it correctly.

Before your interview, carefully review your résumé. Be ready to answer any questions about your education, work experience, or other qualifications.

The following questions are often asked of job applicants during interviews. Practice answering these questions so that you feel more confident. Get a family member or friend to help you by asking the questions and giving you feedback on how you answer.

- Why do you want to work for this company?
- Do you want permanent or temporary work?
- Why do you think you can do this job?
- What jobs have you had? Why did you leave?
- What classes did you like best in school?
- In what school activities did you participate?
- What do you want to be doing five years from now?
- Do you prefer working alone or with others?
- What is your main strength?
- What salary do you expect?
- What grades have you received in school?

- How do you feel about working overtime?
- How many days were you absent from school last year?
- Why should I hire you?
- When can you begin work?

■ Conducting Yourself Properly During an Interview

Always go alone for a job interview. Some young people take a friend along for moral support, but this is a mistake. Employers seldom hire anyone who can't handle an interview alone.

Plan to arrive for your interview five to ten minutes early. Always allow some extra time in case you run into traffic. You will appear careless and make a bad impression if you are even a little late or rush in at the last minute. Don't be too early, though. Waiting outside the interviewer's door for half an hour is not comfortable for you or the employer.

Before you meet the interviewer, you may meet a receptionist, administrative assistant, or other employees. Be courteous and polite to anyone you meet—these people might be your future co-workers. The interviewer may ask these people for their opinion of you after you are gone.

You may be asked to complete an application form before you are interviewed if you have not already done this. Be prepared by having a good pen (or two) with you. Bring along two copies of your résumé to the interview—one to leave with your interviewer if he or she wants it and one to help you fill out an application form.

Concept Development

1. Read Section 38.3 with students.
2. Provide students with a list of questions that are commonly asked during a job interview. Have students write the key things they would include in response to those questions, as well as to the request, "Tell me a little bit about yourself."
3. Ask each student in your class the questions for which they have prepared responses. Have them orally respond as though they were being interviewed. This procedure will help others learn which responses sound better.

Discussion Starter

First Impressions Research indicates that most interviewers make up their minds about an applicant within the first five minutes of meeting him or her. Ask students what they might do to make a good first impression. (*Answers may include a firm handshake, good eye contact, smile, good posture, good grooming, conservative dress, enthusiastic introduction that shows interest.*)

■ **Dress Code** Although there is a trend to dress more casually in many jobs now, presenting yourself well at an interview includes being well dressed. *What can you tell about the man in this picture?*

Chapter 38 ■ *Finding and Applying for a Job* **723**

CAPTION ANSWER
Dress Code The way that this man is dressed implies that he is serious about the job and respectful of the prospective employer.

Thinking Critically

1. **Interview Role Plays** Have students write three situations that could be used as role-play questions for an interview in your area of interest. *(Answers will vary. The situation should be realistic and be worded in such a way that the applicant must respond fully. For example, "If you were a sales associate and your manager confronted you with the following problem, how would you handle it?")*

2. **Interview Questions** Ask students: What are the inappropriate and appropriate questions to ask when asked by an interviewer, "Do you have any questions for me?" *(Questions you should not ask until you are offered the job include those pertaining to salary, vacation, and benefits. Appropriate questions would be ones related to the responsibilities of your job, the organization's culture, current events that may affect the firm, and the potential career path for someone hired in a given position.)*

Cooperative Learning

Job Interviews Allow students to conduct simulated employment interviews in teams of two students. Have them alternate turns as interviewer and interviewee. Have them interview one another and then evaluate each other as an interviewer and as an interviewee. Select one group to demonstrate their interview in front of the class. For this simulation, give students the hypothetical position applied for and the company, as well as a list of 10 to 15 basic questions they should ask. Have students interview for a minimum of five minutes. Then have them describe how they plan to dress appropriately on the day they participate in this role play.

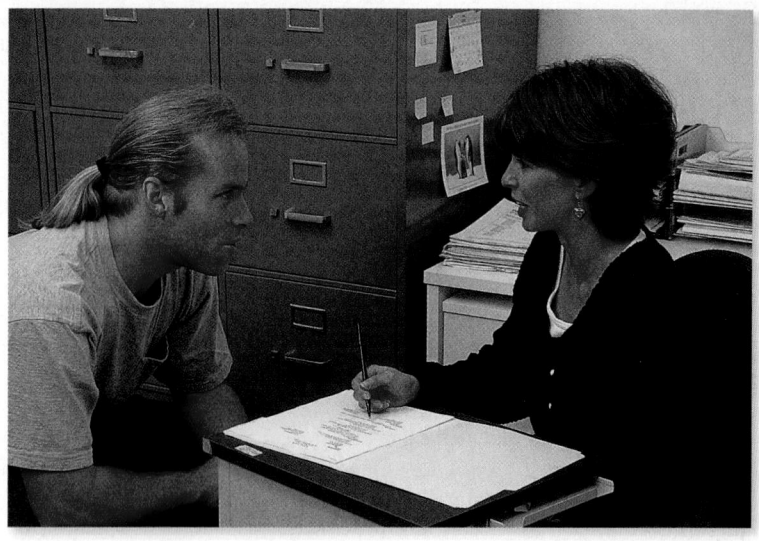

■ **Sending Signals** Your body language tells as much about you as your actual words. *What is this young man's body language telling his interviewer about him?*

The receptionist or assistant may introduce you to the interviewer, or you may have to introduce yourself. In the latter case, say something like, "Good afternoon, I'm Mario Spinello, and I'm here about the sales associate position." Speak clearly and audibly and remember to smile. You should never chew gum during an interview. Grasp the interviewer's hand firmly in a handshake.

Remain standing until you are asked to sit down. When you do sit down, lean forward slightly toward the interviewer to show your interest. Relax and focus on your purpose: to make the best possible impression.

Place your purse or briefcase on the floor by your chair. Never put anything on the interviewer's desk, even if there is room. This may appear disrespectful or too casual. Don't let your eyes wander over papers on the interviewer's desk—it may look as though you are trying to read company correspondence.

It is normal to feel a little nervous at the beginning of an interview. You will relax as the interview progresses. Keep your hands in your lap, and try to keep them still. Never place your hands on the interviewer's desk. Look the interviewer in the eye most of the time and listen to him or her carefully. Most importantly, act confident and be yourself. The employer has taken his or her time to interview you because he or she has confidence that you are a qualified candidate.

WHAT TO SAY IN AN INTERVIEW Most interviewers begin by asking specific questions. Answer each question honestly—if you don't know the answer to a particular question, say so. The interviewer will probably realize it if you try to fake knowing the answer. Keep your answers short as no interviewer wants to listen to long stories. It may be necessary to elaborate a little if many of the questions seem to call for a simple yes or no.

Two particular questions often cause problems for young job applicants. These questions are, "What type of work would you like to do?" and "What wage (or salary) do you expect?" You can answer the first question by giving the name of the specific job you want. The question about expected wage or salary is a little more difficult if you don't have a specific wage or salary in mind. The best answer is something like, "What do you usually pay for this type of work?" Try to turn the question back to the interviewer.

You might not be offered the job if you request too large a salary; however, you may find yourself making less than other employees in the same job if your request is too low. You could mention a rate you know others get for the same type of work if it seems acceptable to you. Prepare for this before the interview by finding out what the going rate is for the type of work you want.

Your interviewer may simply say something like, "Tell me about yourself." You will have to do most of the talking in this situation. You should anticipate

CAPTION ANSWER
Sending Signals His body language implies that he is not respectful and not very serious about the job.

what the interviewer would like to know and present the information clearly. This type of interview is often difficult for the job applicant. Be sure to cover all your qualifications for the job. You should also say why you would like to work for this particular company, which is where your company research will help you.

Your interviewer may not mention pay at all. In that case, wait until the interview is almost over, then ask how much the job pays. It may appear that you are only interested in the money if you ask too soon. You also may want to ask about benefits if you are applying for a full-time, permanent job. These may include a paid vacation and insurance coverage. Wages and benefits are usually discussed toward the end of an interview.

The interviewer will expect you to ask some questions. It may appear that you aren't interested in the job or the company if you don't ask anything. Your interviewer will probably pause after telling you about the job and asking about your qualifications when it is time for you to ask questions. This is your time to ask a question referring to an article that you read, a new product that you learned about, or new markets that the company might be entering. Specific questions show the interviewer that you have done your research and are interested in learning more. The questions listed below are often asked by young applicants:

- Why is the position vacant?
- What are the hours of work?
- Does the company allow flex time?
- Would I be expected to work on the weekend?
- Is overtime common on this job?
- What are the opportunities for advancement?
- What is the pay?
- When will I be notified if I am hired?
- Will I have regular evaluations or reviews?
- What are some of the issues the person hired will need to address immediately?
- Does the company have plans for national or international expansion?
- How are the departments structured?
- Would I report to you if I am offered this job?
- What is the typical career path of someone starting in this position?
- What kind of benefits do you offer?
- Would I work individually or with a team?
- What is the dress code?
- Does the position require any travel?

You may be asked to a second interview with someone else in the company, such as a department head. This usually means you've made a good impression in your first interview, and your chances of being offered the job are good.

CLOSING THE INTERVIEW At the close of the interview, one of several things can happen. You may be offered the job and accept, you may be offered the job but decline, or you may be told that you will not be hired. More likely, however, you will be told that a decision will be made later. Don't be discouraged if no definite offer is made or a specific salary is not discussed. The interviewer will probably want to communicate with others in the company first or interview more applicants before making a decision immediately. It is also possible that the interviewer may want for you to meet with another person in the company. This is always a good sign.

If you are interested in the position, let the interviewer know. You can ask for the job or ask for the next interview if another interview is required. Be a good salesperson and say something like: "Mr./Ms. Employer, I am very impressed with what I've seen and heard here today and am confident that I could do an excellent job in the position you've described to me. When might you be in a position to make an offer?" Your enthusiasm should make a favorable impression.

If an offer is extended, accept it only if you are ready. If you are sure that you want it, accept it on the spot. If you want some time to think it over, be courteous and tactful in asking for that time. It is not unreasonable to want to think about this decision before making a commitment. Set a definite date when you can provide an answer (usually no more than 24–48 hours).

You will be able to sense when the interview is almost over. The interviewer will say something like, "Well, Mario, thank you for coming in" or "We'll decide by the end of the week." This is your cue to ask any last-minute questions. Then you should stand, smile, and thank your interviewer for his or her time and consideration. If you have expressed why you are you interested in the company and what can you offer, you have done all that you can. Usually, the interviewer will extend a hand for a handshake. Shake hands and go. Be sure to thank the receptionist or administrative assistant on your way out.

Chapter 38 ■ *Finding and Applying for a Job* **725**

ASSESS

Reteaching

1. **Vocabulary** Assign and review the vocabulary terms for this section.
2. **Fact and Idea** Assign and review Fact and Idea Review questions 6–10 from the Chapter Assessment.
3. **Interview Techniques** Review with students the highlights of good interview techniques. Also, ask students to answer some of the most commonly asked interview questions. Have students connect those questions to specific jobs. *(For example, "Why do you think you would make a good sales associate?")*

1. **Review** Assign and review the Chapter 38 activities in the *Student Activity Workbook*.
2. **Review** Assign and review the appropriate Thinking Critically questions from the Chapter Assessment.
3. **Review** Assign and review the following Chapter Assessment activities: Building Workplace Skills, Applying Marketing Concepts, Linking School-to-Work, The DECA Connection Role Play, and Internet Connection.

Evaluation

Assign and review the Section 38.3 Assessment.

 Assessment Resources
Go to the *Marketing Essentials* Web site (**www.marketing.glencoe.com**) for resources to teach and assess occupation-specific vocabulary.

CLOSE

Section Wrap-Up

Have students complete this statement: Planning for a successful interview includes . . . (*preparing for interview, conducting yourself properly during interview, and following up interview.*)

Over the Counter Interviews

Answers Answers will vary. Some students may feel face-to-face interviews are important to solidify test results.

■ Following Up an Interview

Evaluate your performance after every interview whether you were offered the job or not. Which questions did you answer best? Which ones did you not answer very well? Were there any total disastrous questions? Did you use standard English? Each interview is a learning experience that will help prepare you for the next one.

It is unlikely you will be offered the job the same day as your interview if the employer is interviewing many people. The employer will want some time to consider all the applicants before making a decision. Many employers will check your references and call the school for a recommendation. This may take several days to a week or more. You can follow up your interview with a telephone call, a short thank-you letter sent a day or two after your interview, or a visit.

A thank-you letter is an appropriate way to follow up many interviews. Your letter should be brief and to the point. Simply thank the employer for the time given you and reaffirm your interest in the job. Include any information that you forgot to mention during the interview that will help qualify you for the position. Your letter may be either handwritten or typed, but it must be neat.

Unless you were told not to call, it is all right to telephone the employer five or six days after the interview. Ask to speak with the person who interviewed you. Then give your name and ask if he or she has made a decision on the job. This will let the employer know that you are still interested.

Over the Counter Interviews

Imagine having your big job interview with a computer. Dozens of big-name retailers, including Target and Macy's, are replacing paper applications and in-person interviews with in-store computer kiosks for screening applicants. The computer programs ask prospective employees about job history and work habits. They even serve up psychological tests that can help match an applicant's job skills and personalities with openings. Employers say that automated applications provide an edge in a tight labor market. They are able to sift through these new types of applications more quickly, weed out duds, identify talent, and attract candidates who might not have otherwise taken the time to apply. Some companies are beginning to offer computer applications over the Internet. Companies even foresee putting prospective employees into virtual video environments to see how they react in a stressful environment.

Thinking Critically

Do you think these applications can replace face-to-face interviews?

38.3 ASSESSMENT

Reviewing Key Terms and Concepts

1. What steps can you take to plan for a successful interview?
2. Why is it important to know something about the company before you interview?
3. How should you dress for a job interview?
4. How would you follow up a job interview?

Thinking Critically

5. What do you think about a situation in which a potential employer denies an applicant a job because he has long hair or a beard?

Integrating Academic Skills

6. **COMMUNICATION** Write a thank-you letter to follow-up an interview. The interview was for a job that you think you would enjoy doing and that you believe you could do very well. Remember to keep your letter brief and to the point.

38.3 ASSESSMENT ANSWERS

Reviewing Key Terms and Concepts

1. Prepare for the interview; conduct yourself properly during the interview; and follow up on the interview.
2. You can ask intelligent questions and emphasize skills you have that fit the company's needs.
3. Wear clean, pressed clothes, and keep your hair and nails neat and clean.
4. Send a short thank-you note and place a telephone call a few days later.

Thinking Critically

5. Answers will vary. Students should understand that some employers will demand that their appearance be businesslike.

Integrating Academic Skills

6. **COMMUNICATION** Letters will vary.

Careers in Marketing

FASHION MERCHANDISING

Renie Hanna
Fashion Illustrator

What does your job entail?

"As a fashion illustrator, I draw sketches of models, clothing, and fashion accessories for clients. I have to be both a business manager and an illustrator—I handle client billing, set up new contracts, and manage my own marketing through networking or my Web site. I always have new clients coming in which keeps my very busy. I have also been sent by my clients to various fashion shows worldwide to act as a consultant or to review my designs after they have been produced."

What kind of training did you have?

"I have been a fashion illustrator for 20 years. I am always perfecting and refining my talents. When I was younger, I had a very realistic style, but it has become more stylized—it's my signature style. I attended the Fashion Institute of Technology in New York, The Parsons School of Design, and the John Murray School of Art, and have studied with Antonio Lopez in the Dominican Republic."

How does your workload vary?

"I have to be my own business manager, and secretary, in addition to being an illustrator. On some days, I work on billing, updating my Web site, or answering e-mail, while other days I focus on my project designs in my studio or meet with clients. While I do get to set my own hours and be my own boss, I also always have to be available for the client at any time."

What is your key to success?

"The key to my success would have to be the level of professionalism I bring to my job. The development of my online portfolio was a great idea and brought many new clients. In the 20 years I have been working, I have NEVER missed a deadline. Every deadline is important—and everyone seems to need everything yesterday. I am prompt, enthusiastic, and professional. This industry is fueled by word of mouth, and I try to never disappoint my clients because that can come back to hurt you professionally."

Thinking Critically

Why is it essential to always meet deadlines?

Career Facts

Education and Training: A bachelor's or master's degree in graphic arts, or training from specialized art schools is recommended.

Aptitudes, Abilities, and Skills: Ability to visualize finished designs and to make detailed visual comparisons, as well as an accurate color sense, neatness, and precision are required to translate clients' ideas into two-dimensional representations.

Career Outlook: Employment is expected to grow through 2006 with keen competition, while the impact of computer-aided design programs may affect the need for trained artists.

Career Path: Internships, work as a paste-up artist, and freelancing help develop a reputation and clientele. Fashion artists may advance to art or design directors.

Chapter 38 ASSESSMENT

Vocabulary Review

Paragraphs will vary. See Glossary for definitions.

Fact and Idea Review

1. You usually need to be 18 years old.
2. It is the formal style of writing and speaking that you have learned in school. Business is conducted using standard English.
3. teachers, friends established in business, or former employers
4. List your jobs in reverse chronological order.
5. one page
6. Dress more formally for a job interview.
7. You should speak clearly and loudly enough to be heard, and say something like, "Good afternoon, I'm Mario Spinello. I'm here about the sales job."
8. Name the specific job that you want.
9. A good response might be: "What do you usually pay for this type of work?"
10. If the interviewer does not ask specific questions but says, "Tell me about yourself," you can recall of everything on your résumé.

Thinking Critically

1. Answers will vary but might suggest that the prospective employee should respond by saying he or she would prefer getting a work permit because it is legally required.
2. Answers will vary depending on the technique that the student chooses.
3. Advertising online may reach a wider range of applicants from different locations and backgrounds. Electronic résumés are easier to manage because they can be scanned for key words.
4. John might write a note thanking the manager for the interview and asking for a call. Or he might stop into the shop. He might decide to keep looking for a job.

VOCABULARY REVIEW

Use the following vocabulary terms in a paragraph describing an effective job search.

- job lead
- networking
- employment agencies
- private employment agencies
- direct contact
- standard English
- references
- résumé
- cover letter

FACT AND IDEA REVIEW

1. How old do you need to be to work without obtaining a work permit? (38.2)
2. What is standard English? Why should it be used when communicating with an employer? (38.2)
3. Who are good people to list as references on a job application? (38.2)
4. When listing your previous experience on a job application, what is the usual form? (38.2)
5. How long should your résumé be? (38.2)
6. How should you dress for a job interview? (38.3)
7. Describe how you would introduce yourself to an interviewer. (38.3)
8. What should you say if an interviewer asks what kind of work you would like to do? (38.3)
9. How should you respond if an interviewer asks you what salary you want? (38.3)
10. Why should you study your résumé before a job interview? (38.3)

THINKING CRITICALLY

1. How would you respond if you applied for a job at age 15 and the prospective employer told you it wasn't important for you to have a work permit, even though the law requires one?
2. If you were interested in working for a particular company, would you prefer to visit the personnel office in person, call on the phone, or write a letter of inquiry? Why?
3. What are some benefits to a company in advertising open positions online?
4. After the interview, John feels pretty confident he will get the job at Dal Pozzo Tires. When he doesn't hear anything in a week, John calls back a couple of times, but the manager doesn't return his calls. What further follow-up should John do?

BUILDING WORKPLACE SKILLS

1. **Human Relations** You are scheduled for a job interview. You arrive at the receptionist's desk terribly nervous and suddenly go completely blank. You can't remember the name of the person with whom you have the interview. What do you say to the receptionist? What might you have done to avoid this situation?
2. **Technology** Suppose that you are planning to attend a college in the Pacific Northwest—Washington or Oregon. You've previously spent some time in that area and think you would like to find a job there and make it your home after you graduate. Use the Internet to investigate the job market in that area. Use key words to focus on several specific market jobs in the Pacific Northwest, and list or print out your findings.

Building Workplace Skills

1. Be honest with the receptionist. Bringing along notes with the interviewer's name and other information would prevent this situation.
2. Findings will vary, but students may use Web sites such as **www.monster.com** or **www.careerpath.com**.

Applying Marketing Concepts

1. Skits will vary.
2. Research and interviews will vary, but classmates should offer constructive criticism to each other.
3. Databases will vary but should include a variety of contacts.
4. All elements discussed in the chapter should appear in the letter of application and résumé.

APPLYING MARKETING CONCEPTS

1. **Analyzing Body Language** With a classmate, use a word processing program to write a series of skits showing how body language and verbal communication can contribute to or detract from the success of a job interview. Present your skits to the class. Consider including the following characters:

   - the know-it-all applicant
   - the shy, nervous applicant who is unwilling (or unable) to provide information
   - the applicant who does not speak standard English

2. **Finding Jobs in Marketing** For one week, go through your newspaper's classified section and find jobs in the marketing field. Choose one company to research. Prepare for an imaginary interview at this firm by preparing the answers to the list of questions commonly asked by interviewers using a word processing program. Working in groups of four to five with one student acting as the interviewer, interview for the job. Have group members give you suggestions on ways to improve your performance.

3. **Creating a Networking System** Use a database program to create a file of all the professionals, friends, family members, and former employers who might be able to help you find work.

4. **Applying for a Job** Use your word processing program to prepare a letter of application and a résumé for a marketing job of your choice.

LINKING SCHOOL TO WORK

Interpersonal and Information Skills Ask an employer what the most important qualities are that he or she looks for during an interview. Write them down in order of importance. Compare your list with that of your classmates'.

THE DECA CONNECTION

Role Play: Interviewee

Situation You (participant) are going to be interviewed for a job at a financial services company.

Activity You have fifteen minutes to demonstrate to your career counselor (judge) that you are ready for the interview.

Evaluation You will be evaluated on how well you meet the following performance indicators:

- What clothing you should wear to the interview and why
- What 15 questions you are likely to be asked by the interviewer
- The attitude and body language you will use during the interview
- Familiarity with the elements of a typical résumé

*inter*NET CONNECTION

Jobs Online
You want a job in automotive retailing, and you are willing to move just about anywhere for the right position. You decide to make a search for openings nationwide.

Connect
- Find job search Web sites.
- Narrow your search to focus on auto sales.
- Compare job offerings in different parts of the United States.
- Write e-mail job queries in response to three of the most attractive offerings.

Chapter 38 ■ *Finding and Applying for a Job* **729**

THE DECA CONNECTION

Students should be evaluated on the performance indicators noted in the Role Play.
- For another DECA Role Play go to the *Student Activity Workbook,* p. 337.
- For more in-depth Role Play practice, refer to DECA's *Essential Competitive Events Handbook.* To order, contact DECA at **www.deca.org**.

*inter*NET CONNECTION
Web sites and job queries will vary depending on job.

Mini Quiz
Administer the Mini Quiz orally. For an expanded chapter quiz, go to page 225 of the *Reproducible Tests* book.

1. Sources of job leads are often family, friends, and acquaintances; finding contacts among them is called <u>networking</u>.
2. Many electronic résumés are not initially read by a person, but are <u>scanned</u> by a computer program, which looks for key words and phrases.
3. A(n) <u>work permit</u> establishes for the employer that it is legal for a young worker to do the type of work offered.
4. When applying for a job, it is a good idea to prepare a <u>cover letter</u> and <u>résumé</u>, which outline your qualifications for a particular job.
5. A(n) <u>thank-you letter</u> is an appropriate way to follow up many interviews.

Linking School to Work
Lists will vary depending on the work situation.

 GO TO

1. **Assessment** Have students complete the Reproducible Tests for Chapter 38 and Unit 12 or construct your own tests using the ExamView software.
2. **Reinforcement** Have students complete the corresponding activities in the following workbooks:
   - *Marketing Math Workbook,* p. 135

FOCUS

Unit Lab Overview

In this Zazz Lab, students will use their knowledge of planning for a future career, identifying career possibilities, and job searching to research and apply for a job or an internship program.

Bell Ringer Activity

Discuss Ask students if they have ever applied for a job or acceptance into a special program which required completing an application and/or going for an interview.

Discussion Starter

Ask the students who responded to the Bell Ringer Activity to share their experiences with the class. If needed, ask students the following questions: How did you learn of the job opening? (You may be able to introduce the concept of networking or other means of learning of job openings.) Were you required to complete an application? What information was requested on the application? What questions were asked during the interview?

TEACH

Thinking Critically

1. **Job Interviews** Ask students: How is a job interview similar to selling a product or service? *(In a job interview, you are selling yourself; you communicate your education, experience, and personality characteristics and present them as benefits to the employer.)*
2. **Networking** Ask students: How can networking help you in your search for a job? *(In many cases, you will learn of a job opening from an acquaintance, friend, or family member.)*

730

The Zazz Lab

A Sports and Entertainment Marketing Simulation

WELCOME

Welcome to Zazz Sports and Entertainment Marketing Company. Zazz is devoted to serving the needs of its clients who include college, university, and professional sports teams, professional athletes, sporting events, and sports arenas plus major consumer product corporations, as well as television networks and movie studios. As an intern, you will have the opportunity to work on different clients' projects. All of your work will be assigned and reviewed by your department supervisor.

RESEARCH AND APPLY FOR A JOB OR AN INTERNSHIP PROGRAM

SITUATION

Due to its tremendous success this past year, Zazz is expanding its operations. As a result, there are many permanent job opportunities available at Zazz for qualified applicants. Your internship at Zazz is now over and it is time for you to make career decisions and prepare for the job application process.

ASSIGNMENT

Before you can start your career search, conduct a self-assessment. Consider your values, interests, personality; preferences for data, people, or things; skills and aptitudes, and level of education. Analyze three career areas related to sports and/or entertainment marketing that interest you. Prepare a Personal Career Profile that shows the degree to which your personal assessment matches the career area you have researched. Select one area to pursue, and formulate goals (ultimate, short-, medium-, and long-range) and a plan for reaching those goals. Apply for a position that will help you satisfy your first job-related goal outlined in your plan. Prepare a cover letter, application, resume, list of references, and a sample thank-you note you would send to the person who interviewed you. Prepare responses to ten common job interview questions to use in an interview role play.

Tools and Resources

To complete this assignment you will need to conduct research at a library or on the Internet. You will also need a word processing program and possibly a typewriter to complete the job application. Other resources include *Dictionary of Occupational Titles, Occupational Outlook Handbook, Occupational Outlook Quarterly, Guide for Occupational Exploration,* and *General Aptitude Test Battery.*

Research

Research three career areas of your choice related to sports and/or entertainment marketing. Investigate career trends, career outlook, duties, responsibilities, salary range, benefits, necessary education or training, and required skills and aptitudes. Also consider the work environment, work relationships, and what a typical day would be like. Arrange an informational interview with someone in that occupation to get first-hand information about your career choice. Research the company where you are applying to gain insight into its current and future status in that industry.

LEISURE TIME + $ = FUN

Leisure time and discretionary income are increasing, which has had a positive effect on the amusement and recreation industry. Theme parks, fitness centers, and any activity that a person does during his or her free time (not including motion pictures and videotape rentals) are part of this growing industry, which is made up of about 99,000 establishments.

- Job-search documents
  - Résumé
  - Sample application
  - Cover letter
  - List of references
  - Sample thank-you note

Presentation and Evaluation

In addition to preparing your written report, your supervisor wants you to conduct a simulated job interview role play. You will be evaluated on the following:

- Knowledge of the career area and job for which you are applying
- Knowledge of the company with which you are seeking employment
- Knowledge of yourself
- Ability to sell yourself
- Personal appearance
- Enthusiasm
- Voice quality
- Eye contact

 Portfolio
....

Print a copy of your completed report and presentation for your Portfolio.

Report

Prepare a written report of your research findings, as well as written documents required for a job search (cover letter, résumé, and list of references). All written work is to be prepared using a word processing program. Arrange your written report around the following headings:

- Self Analysis
  - Values
  - Skills
  - Aptitudes
  - Interests
  - Preferences
  - Personality
  - Education
  - Other considerations
- Career research
  - Description of career area
    - Job responsibilities
    - Salary range and benefits
    - Education and/or special training
    - Experience required, if any
    - Employment trends and outlook
    - Skills and aptitudes required
    - Work environment
    - Work relationships
    - Interview with someone in the field
  - Personal career profile
  - Research on a prospective employer
  - Ten commonly asked interview questions and responses

THE ◀DECA CONNECTION

DECA Marketing Management Series
Reviewing job applicants and conducting job interviews with them could be a role play in this event.

DECA Sports and Entertainment Marketing Management Team Decision-Making Event
Establishing criteria for employment of new personnel in sports and entertainment industries, as well as deciding on an applicant's potential could be a topic for this event.

COOPERATIVE LEARNING

Teamwork Have students review each other's application materials, noting mistakes and tactfully explaining them. Create two-person teams for the purpose of reviewing résumés. Have students generate questions for a job interview simulation. Then have team members take turns interviewing each other, and provide constructive criticism.

Independent Practice

Research and Write Have students seek actual sports and/or entertainment job openings found in newspaper classified ads or on Internet sites. Ask them to prepare a memo addressed to you that lists similar qualities and requirements requested in all ads, as well as contact information. Request hard copies of the ads to check students' memos.

ASSESS

Enrichment

Read and Write Have students review the biography of an entertainment mogul or a sports star and write a synopsis of that person's characteristics. Have teams of four students each share their information with one other. Ask each team to compile the synopses to create one master list of characteristics of successful people. (Note: *Investor's Business Daily* runs a feature each day on "Leaders and Success.")

Evaluation

The rubrics for evaluation of the written, oral, and computer presentation are included in the student text. (See the outline and guidelines for the written report, the computer presentation, and the skills' assessment for oral presentations.) It might be best to replicate those rubrics to evaluate the students' work. A separate rubric could be created to evaluate the work of a team.

CLOSE

Lab Wrap-Up

Ask students: What three written documents are associated with the job application process. *(résumé, cover letter, and application)*

Glossary

A

absolute advantage A country has special natural resources or talents that allow it to produce an item at the lowest cost possible.

ad layout A rough draft that shows the general arrangement and appearance of a finished ad.

adjacent colors Colors located next to each other in the color wheel that contrast only slightly.

advertising Any paid form of nonpersonal presentation and promotion of ideas, goods, or services by an identified sponsor.

advertising agencies Companies that work jointly with business clients to develop advertising campaigns.

advertising campaign The creation and coordination of a series of advertisements (both broadcast and print) around a particular theme to promote a product.

advertising proof Prepared by a newspaper or magazine to show exactly how an ad will appear in print.

agents Intermediaries that bring buyers and sellers together.

agreement A specific commitment that each member makes with a group.

allowance A partial return of the sale price for merchandise that the customer has kept.

aptitude An ability or potential for learning a certain skill.

Articles of Incorporation Filed with the corporation and securities bureau in a state department of commerce; they identify the name and address of your business, its purpose, the names of the initial directors, and the amount of stock to be issued to each director.

assertive Standing up for your rights, beliefs, and ideas.

asset Anything of monetary value that you own.

attitude research Marketing research designed to obtain information on how people feel about certain products, ideas, or companies.

B

Baby Boom Generation The 76 million babies born in the United States between 1946 and 1964.

balance of trade The difference in value between exports and imports of a nation.

balance sheet A summary of a business's assets, liabilities, and owner's equity.

banner ad A wide shallow rectangle at the top or bottom of a Web page that takes the user to the advertiser's Web page when clicked with a mouse.

bar graph A drawing made up of parallel bars whose lengths are proportional to the qualities being measured.

basic stock list Inventory monitoring plan used for staple items that should always be in stock.

benefits Privileges, or monetary payments beyond salary or wages, that go with a job.

blind check method Way of checking inventory that requires the receiver to write the description of the merchandise, count the quantities received, and list them on a blank form or dummy invoice.

blocks Things that interfere with understanding the message, including distractions, emotional blocks, and planning a response.

body language The gestures, posture, mannerisms, and eye contact through which persons communicate their thoughts with others.

bonded warehouse Public or private warehouses that store products requiring the payment of a federal tax.

boomerang method Handling an objection by bringing it back to the customer as a selling point.

brand extension A branding strategy that uses an existing brand name for an improved or new product in the product line.

brand licensing The legal authorization by a trademarked brand owner to allow another company (the licensee) to use its brand, brand mark, or trade character for a fee.

brand mark The part of the brand that is a symbol or design.

brand name The word, group of words, letters, or numbers representing a brand that can be spoken.

brand A name, term, design, or symbol (or combination of them) that identifies a business or organization and its products.

break-even point The point at which sales revenue equals the costs and expenses of making and distributing a product.

brick and mortar retailers Traditional retailers that sell goods to the customer from their own physical stores.

broadcast media Advertising that uses radio and television.

browser The software program that allows you to view Web pages.

budget accounts Charge accounts that allow for the payment of a purchased item over a certain time period without a finance charge.

bundle pricing Psychological pricing technique that includes several complementary products in a package that is sold at a single price.

business cycle Recurring slow-down and growth of an economy.

business philosophy Describes how you think your business should be run and shows your understanding of your business's role in the marketplace.

business plan A proposal that describes a new business to potential investors and lenders.

business risks The possibility of business loss or failure.

business All of the activities involved in producing and marketing goods and services.

business-to-business selling Form of selling that takes place in a manufacturer's or whole-salers' showroom (inside sales) or a customer's place of business (outside sales).

buying behavior The process individuals use to decide what they will buy, from where they will buy it, and who they will buy it from.

buying signals The things customers do or say to indicate a readiness to buy.

C

capital The money needed to start and operate a business.

capitalism An economic system characterized by private owner-ship of businesses and market-place competition.

career consultation An informational interview with a professional who works in a career that interests you.

career outlook The availability of jobs in any field.

carload The minimum number of pounds of freight needed to fill a boxcar.

cash flow statement A monthly plan that shows when you anticipate cash coming into the business and when you expect to pay out cash.

cash on delivery (COD) sale A transaction that occurs when a customer pays for merchandise at the time of delivery.

cash sale A transaction in which the customer pays for the pur-chase with cash or a check.

category management A process that involves managing product categories as individual business units.

CD-ROM A type of optical storage device identical to audio music CDs.

centralized buying Buying for all branches in a central location, such as company headquarters.

channel of distribution The path a product takes from producer or manufacturer to final user.

channels The avenues by which a message is delivered.

circle graph A geometric repre-sentation of the relative sizes of the parts of a whole.

clip art Illustrations that take the form of images, stock drawings, and photographs.

closing the sale Obtaining posi-tive agreement from the customer to buy.

co-branding strategy A brand-ing strategy that combines one or more brands to increase customer loyalty and sales for each indi-vidual brand.

cold canvassing A salesperson tries to locate as many potential customers as possible without checking out leads beforehand.

collateral Something of value that a borrower pledges to a lender to ensure repayment of a loan.

command economy The government is responsible for answering the three basic eco-nomic questions.

common carrier A company that provides transportation services to any business in its operating area for a fee.

communication The process of exchanging information, ideas, and feelings.

communications programs Software applications used to establish communication between your computer and other computers.

communist Countries that have a totalitarian form of government which runs everything.

community relations The activities that a business uses to acquire or maintain the respect of the community.

comparative advantage The value that a nation gains by selling the goods that it produces most efficiently.

competition The struggle between companies for customers.

complementary colors Colors opposite each other on the color wheel that create the greatest contrasts.

consensus A decision that each team member agrees to.

consignment buying Goods are paid for only after they are purchased by the final customer.

consumer Person who uses the product.

consumer affairs specialists People who design programs to reflect customer needs for information.

Consumer Price Index (CPI) Measures the change in price over a time of some 400 specific retail goods and services used by the average urban household.

consumerism The societal effort to protect consumer rights by putting legal, moral, and economic pressure on business.

contract carrier A for-hire carrier that provides equipment and drivers for specific routes, accord-ing to agreements between the carrier and the shipper.

controlling The process of comparing what you planned with actual performance that involves setting standards, evaluating performance, and solving problems revealed.

cooperative advertising A cost-sharing arrangement whereby both a supplier and a local advertiser pay for advertising.

copy The selling message in a written advertisement.

corporation A business that is chartered by a state and legally operates apart from the owner or owners.

cost per thousand (CPM) The media cost of exposing 1,000 readers to an ad.

cost-plus pricing Pricing concept in which all costs and expenses are calculated, and then the desired profit is added to arrive at a price.

cover letter Letter that introduces you and allows you to say why you can do a good job for the company.

credit The opportunity to obtain money, goods, or services immediately in exchange for a promise to pay in the future.

credit union A cooperative association formed by labor unions or groups of employees for the benefit of its members.

customer Person who buys the product.

customer advisory boards Panels of consumers who make suggestions about products and businesses.

customer benefits The advantages or personal satisfaction a customer will get from a good or service.

customer profile Information about the target market with regard to the age, income level, ethnic background, occupation, attitudes, lifestyle, or geographic residence of the targeted customer.

customs brokers Specialists licensed by the U.S. Treasury Department.

D

data analysis The process of compiling, analyzing, and interpreting the results of primary and secondary data collection.

database programs Software applications used to collect related data, which can be sorted, searched through, and printed as needed.

database A collection or file of related information about a specific topic.

DBA "Doing Business As" designation for a sole proprietor or partnership.

debit card An ATM card used to make a purchase at a store.

debt capital Raising funds by borrowing money that will be repaid later.

decentralized buying Local store managers or their designated buyers are authorized to make special purchases for their individual stores.

decimal number A fraction or mixed number whose denominator is a multiple of 10.

demand The amount or quantity of goods and services that consumers are willing and able to buy at various prices.

demographics Statistics that describe a population in terms of personal characteristics.

denominator The bottom number in a fraction.

depression A period of prolonged recession.

derived demand The demand for industrial goods based on the demand for consumer goods and services.

desktop publishing programs Software applications used to design and produce professional printed materials.

Dictionary of Occupational Titles (DOT) U.S. Department of Labor publication that describes about 20,000 jobs and their relationships with data, people, and things.

digits The ten basic symbols: 0, 1, 2, 3, 4, 5, 6, 7, 8, 9.

direct check method Way of checking inventory in which the merchandise is checked directly against the actual invoice or purchase.

direct close The method of asking for the sale.

direct contact The process of visiting potential employers in person or calling them on the telephone.

direct distribution Goods or services are sold from the producer directly to the customer.

disclaimer A statement that contains exceptions to and exclusions from a warranty.

discount pricing Pricing technique that involves the seller's offering reductions from the usual price.

discretionary income The money left from a person's gross income after paying for basic living necessities such as food, shelter, and clothing.

disk drive Hardware used to read data from and write data to a disk.

display The visual and artistic aspects of presenting a product to a target group of customers.

disposable income The money left from a person's gross income after taking out taxes.

distractions Blocks to effective listening that include noises, environmental factors, interruptions, and competing thoughts.

distribution center A warehouse designed to speed delivery of goods and to minimize storage costs.

dollar control Method of stock control that represents the planning and monitoring of the total inventory investment that a business makes during a stated period of time.

drop shippers Wholesalers that own the goods they sell but do not physically handle the actual products.

DVD A high-density optical storage device capable of storing a full-length movie on a single disk the size of a CD.

E

e-commerce The buying and selling of goods through the use of electronic networks, usually the Internet.

economic risks Type of business risks that occur from changes in overall business conditions.

economy The way a nation makes economic choices.

elastic demand Situations in which a change in price creates a change in demand.

e-mail A system of exchanging written messages as well as voice and video messages.

e-marketplace An online shopping location.

embargo A total ban on specific goods coming into and out of a country.

emotional blocks Biases against the opinions expressed by the sender that prevent understanding.

emotional motive A feeling experienced by a customer through association with a product.

empathize To understand a person's situation or frame of mind.

employee discounts Discounts to encourage workers to buy the products their employer sells or manufactures.

empowerment Encouraging team members to contribute to and take responsibility for the management process.

endless chain method Salespeople ask previous customers for names of potential customers.

entrepreneurs People who organize, manage, and take the risk of owning and operating a business.

entrepreneurship The process of starting and managing your own business; the skills of people who are willing to risk their time and money to run a business.

equilibrium The point at which the amount of a product supplied equals the amount demanded.

equity capital Raising money from within your company or by selling part of the interest in the business.

e-tailing Retailers selling products over the Internet to the customer.

ethics Guidelines for good behavior.

euro The currency of the European Union.

European Union (EU) Europe's trading bloc.

everyday low prices (EDLP) Low prices are set on a consistent basis with no intention of raising them or offering discounts in the future.

exchange When something is sold in the marketplace; merchandise brought back to be replaced by other merchandise.

exclusive distribution Form of distribution that involves protected territories in a given geographic area.

excuses Insincere reasons for not buying or not seeing a salesperson.

exempt carrier Carrier of agricultural products, free from direct regulation of rates and operating procedures.

experimental method Research technique in which a researcher observes the results of changing one or more marketing variables while keeping certain other variables constant under controlled conditions.

exports Goods and services that are sold to other countries.

express warranty Warranty that is explicitly stated, in writing or spoken words, to encourage a customer to buy.

extended coverage Optional insurance coverage on a basic property coverage policy.

extension The result of multiplying the number of units by the cost per unit.

extensive decision making Used when there has been little or no previous experience with an item.

F

factors of production The technical term economists use for resources.

feature-benefit selling Matching the characteristics of a product to a customer's needs and wants.

feedback The receiver's response to the message.

fidelity bonds Protects a business from employee dishonesty.

finance Money or anything that can be sold very quickly to get money; borrowing money.

fixtures Permanent or movable store furnishings, such as display cases, counters, shelving, racks, and benches.

flexible-price policy Pricing policy that permits customers to bargain for merchandise.

floor limit The maximum amount a salesperson may allow a customer to charge without getting special authorization.

forced-choice questions Survey questions that ask respondents to choose answers from possibilities given on a questionnaire.

foreign corporation Corporation incorporated under the laws of a different state from the one in which it does business.

form utility Changing raw materials or putting parts together to make them more useful; dealing with making, or producing, things.

formal balance When a large item is placed on one side of a display, an equally large item should be placed on the other side.

fractions Numbers used to describe a part of some standard amount.

franchise A grant or right to sell a parent company's product or service within a given area or territory.

free enterprise system System in which individuals start and operate their own businesses without government involvement.

freight forwarders Private companies that combine less-than carload or less-than truckload shipments from several different businesses and deliver them to their destinations; in international business, companies licensed by the U.S. Maritime Commission to handle export details.

full warranty A warranty that guarantees that if a product is found to be defective within the warranty period, it will be repaired or replaced at no cost to the purchaser.

G

general partnership Each partner shares in the profits and losses of the business.

Generation X The more than 40 million Americans born between 1965 and 1976.

Generation Y The 77 million Americans born between 1977 and 1997.

generic brands Brands that represent a general product category and do not carry a company or brand name.

geographics Segmentation of the market based on where people live.

goods The kinds of things you can touch or hold in your hand.

graphics and design programs Software applications used to produce drawings and designs.

green marketing Companies make an effort to produce and promote environmentally safe products.

greeting approach method The salesperson welcomes the customer to the store.

gross domestic product (GDP) A measure of the goods and services produced using labor and property located in this country.

gross profit The difference between sales revenue and the cost of goods sold.

gross sales The total of all sales for any period of time.

Guide for Occupational Exploration (GOE) Reference that organizes the world of work into 12 interest areas that are subdivided into work groups and subgroups.

H

hardware The physical components of a computer system.

headline The saying that gets the readers' attention, arouses their interest by providing a benefit, and leads them to read the rest of the ad.

home page Web site page that has links to other pages throughout the site.

horizontal organization Self-managing teams that set their own goals and make their own decisions.

human risks Type of business risks caused by human mistakes, as well as the unpredictability of customers, employees, or the work environment.

hypertext markup language (HTML) Language in which Web pages are written.

hypertext transport protocol (http) links together documents on the World Wide Web.

I

illustration The photograph or drawing used in a print advertisement.

implied warranty A warranty that exists automatically by state law whenever a purchase takes place.

imports Goods and services purchased from other countries.

incentives Higher-priced products earned and given through contests, sweepstakes, and rebates.

income statement A summary of a business's income and expenses during a specific period, such as a month, a quarter, or a year; often called *profit and loss statement.*

indirect distribution Selling the goods or services involves one or more intermediaries between the producer and customer.

industrial market Based on, or derived from, the demand for consumer goods and services.

inelastic demand Situations in which a change in price has very little effect on demand for a product.

inflation A period of rising prices.

informal balance Balancing a large item with several small ones.

information utility Communication with the consumer.

infrastructure The physical development of a country, including its roads, ports, sanitation facilities, and utilities, especially telecommunications.

initiative Doing what needs to be done without being urged.

installment accounts Charge accounts that allow for payment over a period of time.

institutional advertising Advertising attempts to create a favorable impression and goodwill for a business or an organization.

institutional promotion Communication used by a business to create a favorable image for itself.

insurance policy A contract between a business and an insurance company to cover a certain business risk.

integrated distribution Form of exclusive distribution in which manufacturers own and run their own retail operations.

intensive distribution Form of distribution that involves the use of all suitable outlets to sell a product.

interest The money paid for the use of money borrowed or invested.

intermediaries Distribution channel that provides value to producers because they have expertise in areas that producers do not have.

international trade The exchange of goods and services between nations.

Internet The world's biggest computer network.

internship Student's direct work experience and exposure to various aspects of a career, either with or without pay.

inventory management The process of buying and storing products for sale while controlling costs for ordering, shipping, handling, and storage.

inventory An amount of goods stored, including raw materials, purchased components, manufactured subassemblies, works in process, packaging materials, and finished goods.

invoice Customer bill included with delivered merchandise when filling a PO-based order.

J

jargon Technical or specialized vocabulary used by members of a particular profession or industry.

job descriptions Written statements listing the requirements of a particular job.

job lead Information about a job opening.

joint ventures Partnerships that allow companies to participate in another country's economy.

just-in-time (JIT) inventory system An arrangement in which suppliers deliver parts and raw materials just before they are needed for production.

L

label An information tag, wrapper, seal, or imprinted message that is attached to a product or its package.

labor All of the people who work in the economy.

land Everything on the earth that is in its natural state.

laptop A small, portable personal computer.

law of diminishing marginal utility Law that states that consumers will buy only so much of a given product, even through the price is low.

layaway Merchandise removed from stock and kept in a separate storage area until the customer pays for it.

layman's terms Words the average customer can understand.

liability A debt that you owe.

lifestyle goals Reflect your vision of how you see yourself living in the future.

limited decision making Used when a person buys goods and services that he or she has purchased before but not regularly.

limited partnership Each limited partner is liable for any debts only up to the amount of his or her investment in the company.

limited warranty A warranty that may exclude certain parts of the product from coverage or require the customer to bear some of the expense for repairs resulting from defects.

line graph A graph that uses a line joining points representing changes in a variable quantity, usually over a specific period or time.

local radio advertising Advertising done by a local business for its target market.

loss leader An item priced at cost to draw customers into a store.

M

mainframe Large computers, sometimes filling a whole room.

maintained markup The difference between an item's final sale price and its cost.

management The business function used to plan, organize, and control all available resources to reach company goals.

manufacturer brand Brand owned and initiated by manufacturers; also called *producer brands*.

market All potential customers who share common needs and wants, and who have the ability and willingness to buy the product.

market economy Economy in which there is no government involvement in economic decisions.

Glossary

market position Marketers' relative standing in relation to their competitors.

market research The systematic gathering, recording, analyzing, and presentation of information related to marketing goods and services.

market segmentation A way of analyzing a market by specific characteristics in order to create a target market.

market share A firm's percentage of the total sales volume generated by all competitors in a given market.

marketing concept Businesses must satisfy customers' needs and wants in order to make a profit.

marketing information system A set of procedures and methods that regularly generates, stores, analyzes, and distributes marketing information for use in making marketing decisions.

marketing mix Four basic marketing strategies, collectively known as the four Ps—product, place, price, and promotion.

marketing research The marketing function that links the consumer, customer, and public to the market through information.

marketing The process of developing, promoting, and distributing products to satisfy customers' needs and wants.

marketplace Wherever two or more people agree to buy and sell a product.

markup pricing Pricing concept used by wholesalers and retailers involved in acquiring goods for resale; based on the difference between the price of an item and its cost.

marquee An architectural canopy that extends over store's entrance.

media research Marketing research that focuses on issues of media selection and frequency.

media The agencies, means, or instruments used to convey advertising messages to the public.

memorandum buying The supplier agrees to take back any unsold goods by a certain date.

merchandise approach method The salesperson makes a comment or asks questions about a product in which the customer shows interest.

microcomputer Personal computer (PC) used in most medium and smaller businesses.

middle management Implements the decisions of top management.

minicomputer Computers ideal for organizations and companies that cannot afford or do not need a mainframe system.

mini-nationals Midsize and smaller companies that have operations in foreign countries.

mission statement Describes the ultimate goals of a company.

mixed number A whole number and a fraction together.

mixed-brand strategy A branding strategy that involves simultaneously offering a combination of manufacturer, private distributor, and generic brands.

model stock list Inventory monitoring plan used for fashionable merchandise.

monopoly Exclusive control over a product or the means of producing it.

multinationals Large corporations that have operations in several countries.

multiple-unit pricing Setting prices to suggest a bargain and help to increase sales volume.

N

national spot radio advertising Used by national firms to advertise on a local station-by-station basis.

nationalize Government takes ownership of property and the owners get nothing in return.

natural risks Type of business risks that result from natural causes such as floods, tornadoes, hurricanes, fires, lightning, droughts, earthquakes, and unexpected changes in normal weather conditions.

net income The amount left after the total expenses are subtracted from gross profit.

net sales The amount left after gross sales have been adjusted for returns and allowances.

net worth The difference between the assets of a business and its liabilities.

network radio advertising A broadcast from a studio to all affiliated radio stations throughout the country.

networking Finding contacts among people you know, including family and friends, former employers, and professional people you know personally.

never-out list Inventory monitoring plan used for best-selling products that make up a large percentage of sales volume.

news release A prewritten story about a company that is sent to the various media.

nonprice competition Businesses choose to compete on the basis of factors not related to price.

nonprofit organizations Service organizations not operated for the purpose of making a profit.

nonverbal communication Expressing yourself through body language.

North American Free Trade Agreement (NAFTA) An international trade agreement among the United States, Canada, and Mexico.

numerator The top number in a fraction.

O

objection analysis sheet Lists common objections and possible responses to them.

objections Concerns, hesitations, doubts, or other honest reasons a customer has for not making a purchase.

observation method A research technique in which the actions of people are watched and recorded either by cameras or observers.

occupational area A category of jobs that involves similar skills and aptitudes.

Occupational Outlook Handbook (OOH) U.S. Department of Labor publication that provides information on more than two hundred occupations; updated every two years.

odd-even pricing Setting prices that all end in either odd or even numbers.

on-approval sale Customer permitted to take merchandise home for further consideration.

one-price policy Pricing policy in which all customers are charged the same price for goods and services.

online advertising Advertising messages on the Internet.

open-ended questions Questions that require more than a yes or no answer; survey questions that ask respondents to construct their own response.

opening cash fund The coins and currency designated for the register for a given day's business.

open-to-buy The amount of money left for buying goods after all other expenses have been considered.

organization chart A diagram of the various jobs and functions that are found in a company.

organizational buyers People who buy goods for business purposes, usually in much greater quantities than the average consumer.

organizing A coordinated effort to reach a company's planning goals.

P

package The physical container or wrapping for a product.

paraphrase Restating (objections) in a different way.

parcel post A type of standard surface package delivery offered by the U.S. Postal Service.

parliamentary procedure A structure for holding group meetings and making decisions.

partnership A legal agreement between two or more people to be jointly responsible for the success or failure of a business.

PDAs The smallest portable computers.

penetration pricing Pricing policy that sets the initial price for a new product very low.

percent Number expressed in parts per hundred.

performance bonds Insurance against losses that might occur when work or a contract is not finished on time or as agreed; also called *surety bonds*.

perpetual inventory system Tracks the number of items in inventory on a constant basis.

personal financial statement A summary of your current personal financial condition.

personal selling Any form of direct contact occurring between a salesperson and a customer.

physical distribution All the activities that help to ensure that the right amount of product is delivered to the right place at the right time.

physical inventory system Method of physical inventory control in which stock is inspected or actually counted to determine the quantity on hand.

pie chart A circle graph that looks like a pie cut into slices of different sizes.

place utility Having a product where customers can buy it.

planning goals Small steps you take to get from where you are now to where you want to be.

planning The first step in the management process that involves deciding what will be done and how it will be accomplished.

planogram Computer-developed diagrams that show retailers how and where products within a category should be displayed on a shelf at individual stores.

point-of-sale research A powerful form of research that combines natural observation with personal interviews to get people to explain buying behavior.

point-of-sale (POS) system Computers used in retailing that feed information directly from merchandise tags or product labels into a computer.

possession utility The exchange of a product for some monetary value.

preapproach Getting ready for the face-to-face encounter in a selling situation.

premiums Low-cost items given to consumers at a discount or for free.

preretailing marking method Pricing information is marked on merchandise in advance on the purchase order.

presentation software Software applications used to create slide shows or multimedia presentations all in one program.

press conference A meeting in which a business or organization invites media members to hear an announcement about a news-worthy event.

press kit A folder containing articles, news releases, feature stories, and photographs about a company, product, or person.

prestige pricing Setting higher-than-average prices to suggest status and prestige to the consumer.

price competition Competition that focuses on the sale price of a product.

price discrimination A firm charges different prices to similar customers in similar situations.

price fixing Competitors agree on certain price ranges within which they set their own prices.

price lining Pricing technique that requires a store to offer all merchandise in a given category at certain prices.

price The value of money (or its equivalent) placed on a good or service.

primary data Data obtained for the first time and used specifically for the particular problem or issue under study.

principal Amount of money that you borrow to start your business.

print media Written advertising that may be included in every-thing from newspapers and magazines to direct mail, signs, and billboards.

private carrier Carrier that trans-ports goods for an individual business.

private distributor brand Brand owned and initiated by whole-salers and retailers; also called *private brands, store brands,* or *dealer brands.*

private employment agencies Employment agencies not sup-ported by taxes, that must earn a profit to stay in business.

private sector Businesses not associated with government agencies.

private warehouse A facility designed to meet the specific needs of its owner.

privatization The process of selling government-owned busi-nesses to private individuals.

problem definition A business clearly identifies a problem or research issue and the informa-tion necessary to solve it.

Producer Price Index (PPI) Measures wholesale price levels in the economy.

product depth The number of product items offered within each product line.

product features Basic, physical, or extended attributes of the product or purchase.

product item A specific model, brand, or size of a product within a product line.

product life cycle The stages that a product goes through during its life, including introduction, growth, maturity, and decline.

product line A group of closely related products that are manu-factured or sold by a business.

product mix All of the different products that a company makes or sells.

product modification An altera-tion in a company's existing product.

product planning Making deci-sions about those features that are needed to sell a business's products, services, or ideas.

product positioning Focused on the image a product projects.

product promotion Commu-nication used by a business to convince potential customers to buy its products instead of buying from a competitor.

product research Marketing research that centers on evaluating product design, package design, product usage, and consumer acceptance of new and existing products.

product width The number of different product lines a business manufactures or sells.

production The process of cre-ating, growing, manufacturing, or improving on goods and services.

productivity Output per worker hour.

products Goods and services, both of which have monetary value and satisfy customers' needs and wants.

profit The money earned from conducting business after all costs and expenses have been paid.

promotion Any form of communi-cation a business or organization uses to inform, persuade, or remind.

promotional advertising Adver-tising designed to increase sales.

promotional mix A combination of the different types of promotion.

promotional pricing The psy-chological pricing technique generally used in conjunction with sales promotions when prices are lower than average.

promotional tie-ins Sales promotional arrangements between one or more retailers or manufacturers.

proportion The relationship between and among objects in a display.

prospect A potential customer; also called a *lead.*

prosperity Point in the business cycle when the economy flour-ishes; also called *expansion.*

psychographics Studies of consumers based on social and psychological characteristics.

Glossary

sychological pricing Pricing techniques that create an illusion for customers or that make shopping easier for them.

ublic employment agencies Employment agencies supported by state or federal taxes that offer free services to both job applicants and employers.

ublic relations Any activity designed to create a favorable image toward a business, its products, or its policies.

ublic sector Local, state, and federal government agencies and services, such as public schools and public libraries.

ublic warehouse A facility that offers storage and handling facilities to individuals or companies.

ublicity A specific kind of public relations that involves placing positive and newsworthy information about a business, its products, or its policies in the media.

ull policy Promotion policy designed to create consumer interest.

urchase order A legal contract between the buyer and the supplier.

ush policy Promotion policy used only with the next partner in the distribution channel.

Q

uality check method Checking inventory to inspect the workmanship and general characteristics of the received merchandise.

uorum A proportion of the membership needed to conduct official business.

uota Limits either the quantity or the monetary value of a product that may be imported.

R

rack jobbers Wholesalers that manage inventory and merchandising for retailers by counting stock, filling it in when needed, and maintaining store displays.

rational motive A conscious, logical reason for a purchase.

realistic goal Goal that you have a reasonable chance of achieving.

real-time inventory system System of inventory that lets a company constantly track every product it sells from when it's manufactured, or when it arrives in its warehouse, to when the customer orders it online, to when it arrives at the buyer's door.

receiving record A form that is used to describe the goods received by a business.

recession A period of economic slowdown that lasts for two quarters, or six months.

recovery The increase in the overall economic activity.

references People who know your work habits and personal traits well and who will recommend you for the job.

referrals The names of other people who might buy a product or use a service.

regular, or 30-day, charge accounts Charge accounts that allow customers to charge purchases during a month and pay the balance in full within 30 days after they are billed.

relationship marketing Strategies businesses use to stay close to their customers.

reliability A research technique that produces nearly identical results in repeated trials.

resident buying offices Retailers' representatives in a central market.

resources All the things used in producing goods and services.

résumé A brief summary of personal information, education, skills, work experience, activities, and interests.

retailers Channel of distribution that buys goods from wholesalers or directly from manufacturers and resells them to the final consumer.

return Merchandise brought back for a cash refund or credit.

return on investment A calculation used to determine the relative profitability of a product.

reverse auction Companies post what they want to buy and suppliers bid for the contract.

revolving accounts Charge accounts for which the retailer determines the credit limit and when payments are due.

risk management The systematic process of managing an organization's risk exposure to achieve objectives in a manner consistent with public interest, human safety, environmental factors, and the law.

risk The possibility of financial loss; the potential for loss or failure in relation to the potential for improved earnings.

routine decision making Used when a person needs little information about a product that he or she is buying.

S

sales incentives Awards given to managers and employees who successfully meet or exceed a sales quota.

sales promotion All marketing activities, other than personal selling, advertising, and public relations, that are used to stimulate consumer purchasing and sales effectiveness.

sales tax A fee placed on the sale of goods and services.

Glossary

sales transaction The process of recording a sale and presenting the customer with proof of payment.

sample A part of the target population that is assumed to represent the entire population.

scanner Hardware that reads documents and transforms images into digital data.

scarcity The difference between wants and needs and available resources.

seasonal discounts Offered to buyers willing to buy at a time outside the customary buying seasons.

secondary data Data that have already been collected for some purpose other than the current study.

selective distribution Form of distribution in which a limited number of outlets in a given geographic area are used to sell the product.

service approach method The salesperson asks the customer if he or she needs assistance.

service close Explains services that overcome obstacles or problems.

services The kinds of things you can't physically touch; tasks performed for a customer.

setting Where communication takes place.

shortages Market situation in which demand exceeds supply.

signature Logotype (logo) symbol used to distinctly identify a business.

six-month merchandise plan The budget that estimates planned purchases for a six-month period.

skimming pricing Pricing policy that sets a very high price for a new product.

slogan A catch phrase or small group of words that are combined in a special way to identify a product or company.

slotting allowance A cash premium paid by the manufacturer to a retail chain for the costs involved in placing a new product on its shelves.

socialist Countries that try to reduce the differences between rich and poor.

software A set of electronic instructions that directs the CPU to carry out a specific task.

sole proprietorship A business owned and operated by one person.

source marking Use of Universal Product Codes (UPCs) in which the seller or manufacturer marks the price before delivering the merchandise to the retailer.

specialty media Relatively inexpensive, useful items with an advertiser's name printed on them.

specific goal Goal stated in exact terms that includes some details.

spot check method Way of checking inventory in a random check of one carton in a shipment.

spreadsheet programs Software applications used to organize, calculate, and analyze numerical data.

standard English The formal style of writing and speaking that you have learned in school.

standing-room-only close Used when a product is in short supply or when the price will be going up in the near future.

start-up costs A projection of how much money you will need in your first year of operating a business.

stock turnover The number of times the average inventory has been sold and replaced in a given period of time.

stockholders The people who own the corporation with limited liability.

stockkeeping unit (sku) Each item or group of related items in a unit control inventory system.

storage The marketing function of holding goods until they are sold.

store layout The way store floor space is used to facilitate and promote sales and to best serve the customer.

storefront The store's sign, marquee, outdoor lighting, banners, planters, awnings, windows, and the building itself (its design and setting).

Subchapter S corporation A small business that is taxed like a partnership or proprietorship.

suggestion selling Selling additional goods or services to the customer.

supercomputer The largest and most powerful type of computer used for the most sophisticated work.

superior point method Salesperson acknowledges objections as valid yet still offset them with other features and benefits.

supervisory-level management Front-line managers that supervise the activities of employees who carry out the tasks determined by the plans of middle and top management.

supply The amount or quantity of goods and services that producers will provide at various prices.

surpluses Market situation in which supply exceeds demand.

survey method A research technique in which information is gathered from people through the use of surveys or questionnaires.

T

target marketing Focusing all marketing decisions on a very specific group of people who you want to reach.

ariff A tax on imports; also called *duty*.

elemarketing The process of selling over the telephone.

est marketing Type of marketing research that occurs when a new product is placed in one or more selected geographic areas.

hird party method Handling objections by using a previous customer or another neutral person who can give a testimonial about the product.

ickler control Method of physical inventory control in which a small portion of the inventory is physically counted each day so that the entire inventory is accounted for on a regular basis.

ill The cash drawer of a cash register.

ime utility Having a product available at a certain time of year or a convenient time of day.

on-mile The movement of one ton of freight one mile.

op management Those who make the planning decisions that affect the whole company.

trade character A brand mark with human form or characteristics.

trade discounts The way manufacturers quote prices to wholesalers and retailers.

trade name Identifies the company or a division of a particular corporation.

trademark A brand name, brand mark, trade name, trade character, or a combination of these, that is given legal protection by the federal government.

trading area The geographical area from which a business draws its customers.

transportation The marketing function of moving products from a seller to a buyer.

trial close An initial effort to close a sale.

U

unit control Method of stock control which measures quantities of merchandise that a business handles during a stated period of time.

unit pricing Method of pricing that allows consumers to compare prices in relation to a standard unit or measure, such as an ounce or a pound.

Universal Product Code (UPC) Bar code used for electronic entry.

Universal Vendor Marketing (UVM) Product code that appears as a series of numbers across the top of a price tag.

unlimited liability As a sole proprietor, your financial liability is not limited to the investment in the business, but extends to your total ability to make payments.

Uniform Resource Locator (URL) The code used to identify and locate Web pages on the Internet.

utility The attributes of a product or service that make it capable of satisfying consumers' wants and needs.

V

validity The questions asked in a questionnaire measure what was intended to be measured.

values Beliefs that guide the way people live.

vertical organization Up and down structure of an organization.

visual merchandising The coordination of all the physical elements in a place of business that are used to project the right image to its customers.

W

want slips Customer requests for items that are not carried in the store.

warranty A promise, or guarantee, given to a customer that a product will meet certain standards.

warranty of fitness for a particular purpose The seller advises a customer that a product is suitable for a particular use and the customer acts on that advice.

warranty of merchantability A promise from the seller that the product sold is fit for its intended purpose.

Web page Contains text, photos, graphics, and hyperlinks.

Web page editors Software applications used to create Web pages.

which close Customer is encouraged to make a decision between two items.

wholesale and retail buyers People who purchase goods for resale; they forecast customers' needs and buy the necessary products to meet those needs.

wholesalers Obtain goods from manufacturers and resell them to industrial users, other wholesalers, and retailers.

word processing programs Software applications used to create documents that are primarily text and some graphics

World Trade Organization (WTO) A global coalition of 135 governments that makes the rules governing international trade.

World Wide Web A collection of interlinked documents that resides on the Internet.

Index

Index

Index

Index

___

____

_____

_____

First USA, 594
Fishyback rail service, 397
Fixed assets, 672
Fixed expenses, 668–669
Fixed rate plans, 594
Fixtures, 322
Flexible-price policy, 470
Floor limit, 281
Focus group
  interview, 527
  technology for, 530
Food, Drug, and Cosmetic Act, 590
Food brokers, 380
Food and Drug Administration (FDA),
  49, 105, 518, 580, 590
Food labels, 578
Food Quality Act, 87
Food
  marketing, careers in, 291, 389
  for women, 180
Forbes magazine, 418, 525
Forced-choice questions, 533
Ford, Henry, 607, 617
Ford Motor Company
  Automobile Ownership Survey, 534
  co-branding strategy, 573
  cyberpirates and, 632
  pricing strategy, 468
  Spanish language catalog, 32
  truck pricing, 455
Forecasting software programs, 538
Foreign corporation, 615
Foreign direct investments (FDI), 106
Form utility, 7
Formal balance, 328
Formal speech, 144
Forrester Research Inc., 386
Fortune magazine, 641, 710
Fountain Pen Hospital, 164
Four Seasons Hotel, 17
Fractions, 120–121, 125
Franchise, 613, 676
Franchisee, 613
Franchisor, 613
Franscioni, Warren, 387
Free enterprise system, 40–57
  consumer's role in, 50, 52–54
  defined, 41
  government's role in, 48–50
  See also Capitalism
Free market economy, profits in, 83
Free standing inserts (FSIs), 477
Freelancers, 356
FreeMarkets.com, 421
Freight forwarders, 402
Freight forwarding companies, 105

Frequency discounts, 346
Frequent buyer programs, 309
Frequent flyer programs, 309
Fresh Fields, 291
Friedman, Carole, 203
Friendliness, 177–178
Frisbie Baking Company, 387
Frito-Lay, 568
Full warranty, 586
Full-service advertising agency, 355
Functional props, 324

G

Gap, the
  online promotions, 302
  product mix, 547
  Web kiosks, 166
Gas
  as pollutant, 89
  price of, 461
Gasoline credit cards, 594–595
Gates, Bill, 83
Gatorade, 568
GEICO, 635
Gender as demographic, 26
General Agreement on Tariffs and Trade
  (GATT), 102
General Electric
  manufacturer brands, 569
  Soft White light bulbs, 568
  Trading Process Network (TPN), 424
General Motors
  MasterCard, 595
  Saturn division, 548
  Web site, 260
General partnership, 614–615
Generalizations, 145
Generation gap, 26
Generation X, 25
Generation Y, 25
Generic brands, 570
Geographic data, in business plan, 642
Geographics, 31–32
Germany
  greetings in, 6
  Tekno Bubbles, 512
  vacation time in, 538
Gillespie, Beth, 315
Gillette, 549–550
Global economy, 58–75
Global marketplace, 99–104, 517
Global Positioning System, 171
Global recession, 71
Globesmart, 671
Goal setting, 180
Going-rate pricing, 468

Goods
  business plan analysis, 649–650
  defined, 3
  services vs., 83–84
  shortages of, 54
  storage of, 403–407
  surpluses of, 52
Government
  as business supporter, 48–49
  buyers for, 416
  as competitor, 50
  declining business profits and, 46
  regulation, 49–50, 459–463
  role in free enterprise system, 48–50
  as services provider, 48
  See also Laws; U.S. government
Government Units, 416
Goya foods, Inc., 579
Graco, 590
Grade label, 578
Graham, Bette, 607, 617
Grainger.com, 423
Graphics and design programs, 164–165
Graphs
  bar, 130–131
  circle, 132
  line, 131
Graves, Michael, 30
"Gray market," 459
Greener car, 47
Greenfield's Healthy Foods, 382
Green marketing, 89
Greeting approach method, 232
Greyhound Bus Company, 567
Groening, Matt, 689
Gross domestic product (GDP), 66, 611
Gross pay, 669
Gross profit, 485, 668
Gross sales, 668
Guarantee, 585. *See also* Warranties
Guerlain, 306
Guess jeans, 549
Guess-and-check method, 126–127
Guide for Occupational Exploration,
  695–696

H

Habbaz, Eddie, 407
Hacket, Frederick, 563
Hacky Sack game, 664
Hand Technologies, 244
Hanna, Renie, 727
Hardware, computer, 159
Harley-Davidson, 267, 568, 573
Harry Potter, 13
Hasbro, 303

Index

Index

Index

Index

Index

Index

Index

Competitive Event Correlation

Role Play

Technology Connections

• Internet Activities

A

Adobe Photoshop, 84
Advances in technology, 157–158
• Advertising online, 342
    rates, 348
    researching, 515
• Airline ticket sales online, 285, 386
Algorithms, 124
• Anticybersquatting Consumer
    Protection Act, 632
• ARPANET, 169
• Auctions
    for excess inventory, 430
    in Germany, 609
    See also Web sites, eBay.com
Automated dialers, 538
Automated job applications, 726

B

• B2B e-marketplace, 386
• B2C online sales, 171
Bar codes
    cell phone technology and, 424
    origin of, 435
    scanners, 509
• "Bots," 491
• Brand loyalty online, 572
• Browser, 170
• Business cards online, 10
Business plan programs, 644
• Business-to-business (B2B) sales
    marketing on, 170
    online ordering, 110
    purchasing, 423–424

C

• Career information online, 696
Cars
    computer-controlled, 172
    Global Positioning System in, 171
    • online sales, 260
    voice-activated technology in, 171
CD-ROM
    business cards, 10
    defined, 159
    Hasbro *Action Man,* 303
Cell phones
    bar codes and, 424
    e-mail and, 158
    for kids, 178
Central processing unit (CPU), 159
• Channel conflict, 399
Chinese households and technology,
    109
• Click-through ads, 342
• Competitive information online, 642
Computer, 157–158
    demonstrating, 244

direct sales of, 248
first Apple, 201
future of, 171
hardware, 159
interactive touch-screen, 168
interactive TV, 169
inventory systems, 432
Palm brands, 548
peripherals, 160
privacy and security, 94
software, 161–162. *See also*
    Computer applications
system components, 159–160
types of, 158–159
Computer applications
    business plan programs, 644
    communications programs, 167
    customer management software,
        220
    database programs, 163
    desktop publishing programs, 164
    graphics and design programs,
        164–165
    presentation software, 165
    spreadsheet programs, 163–164
    Web page editors, 165–166
    word processing programs, 162
    See also Software
Computer crime, 626
Computerized databases, 538
Computer hardware, 159
Computer peripherals, 160
Computer privacy and security, 94
Computer software, 161
Computer viruses, 634
• "Cookies," 54, 509
Customer management software, 220
• Customer service online, 233
Cyberpirates, 632

D

• Data spillage, 54
• Digital dossiers, 525
• Digital music distribution, 406
Digital surveys, 538
"Direct" computer systems, 248
• Direct Focus Web site, 384
Disk drives, 159
• Domain names, 570
DVD drive, 159
DVD textbooks, 589

E

E-billboards, 339
• E-commerce
    defined, 84, 170
    distribution via, 386
    sales techniques, 245
• E-commercials, 344

• E-GM, 441
Electronic data interchange (EDI), 442
• Electronic résumés, 710
• E-mail
    advantages of, 170
    airline e-savers, 285
    business, 151
    cell phones and, 158–159
    defined, 167
    disappearing sensitive, 631
    list services, 218
    résumé submission via, 710–711
    as sales tool, 267
    spam, 356
    viral marketing using, 215
    writing, 151
Employee monitoring, 94, 202
• E-tailers, 170
• E-tailing
    defined, 377
    extranets and pricing, 471
    physical distribution and, 401

F

• Federal Commission on Electronic
    Commerce, 285
• FedEx Home Delivery, 401
• Firewalls, 94
• Focus group technology, 530
• Free service providers, 343

H

Home shopping networks, 377
• Hotel rooms, wired, 90
• Hyperlinks, 170
• Hyper text markup language
    (HTML), 165–166
• Hypertext transport protocol (http),
    170

I

• Industrial distribution online, 385
• Information retrieval, 170
Interactive kiosks, 166
Interactive touch-screen computers,
    168
Interactive TV, 169
Interactive voice response, 538
• Internet, 169–171
    beginnings of, 169
    as business resource, 677
    cookies, 54
    data spillage, 54
    defined, 169
• Internet Connection
    Chapter 1: marketing degrees,
    Chapter 2: U.S. census, 29
    Chapter 3: ergonomics, 57
    Chapter 4: stock market, 75

School-to-Work Connections

School-to-Work Connections

School-to-Work Connections **769**

School-to-Work Connections

School-to-Work Connections

Photography Credits